Principles of Accounting, Volume 1: Financial Accounting

SENIOR CONTRIBUTING AUTHORS
MITCHELL FRANKLIN, LE MOYNE COLLEGE (FINANCIAL ACCOUNTING)
PATTY GRAYBEAL, UNIVERSITY OF MICHIGAN-DEARBORN (MANAGERIAL ACCOUNTING)
DIXON COOPER, OUACHITA BAPTIST UNIVERSITY

OpenStax
Rice University
6100 Main Street MS-375
Houston, Texas 77005

To learn more about OpenStax, visit https://openstax.org.
Individual print copies and bulk orders can be purchased through our website.

PRINT BOOK ISBN-10	**1-947172-68-9**
PRINT BOOK ISBN-13	**978-1-947172-68-5**
PDF VERSION ISBN-10	**1-947172-67-0**
PDF VERSION ISBN-13	**978-1-947172-67-8**

10 9 8 7 6 5 4 3 2 1

OpenStax

OpenStax provides free, peer-reviewed, openly licensed textbooks for introductory college and Advanced Placement® courses and low-cost, personalized courseware that helps students learn. A nonprofit ed tech initiative based at Rice University, we're committed to helping students access the tools they need to complete their courses and meet their educational goals.

Rice University

OpenStax, OpenStax CNX, and OpenStax Tutor are initiatives of Rice University. As a leading research university with a distinctive commitment to undergraduate education, Rice University aspires to path-breaking research, unsurpassed teaching, and contributions to the betterment of our world. It seeks to fulfill this mission by cultivating a diverse community of learning and discovery that produces leaders across the spectrum of human endeavor.

Philanthropic Support

OpenStax is grateful for our generous philanthropic partners, who support our vision to improve educational opportunities for all learners.

Laura and John Arnold Foundation

Arthur and Carlyse Ciocca Charitable Foundation

Ann and John Doerr

Bill & Melinda Gates Foundation

Girard Foundation

Google Inc.

The William and Flora Hewlett Foundation

Rusty and John Jaggers

The Calvin K. Kazanjian Economics Foundation

Charles Koch Foundation

Leon Lowenstein Foundation, Inc.

The Maxfield Foundation

Burt and Deedee McMurtry

Michelson 20MM Foundation

National Science Foundation

The Open Society Foundations

Jumee Yhu and David E. Park III

Brian D. Patterson USA-International Foundation

The Bill and Stephanie Sick Fund

Robin and Sandy Stuart Foundation

The Stuart Family Foundation

Tammy and Guillermo Treviño

TABLE OF CONTENTS

Preface

Welcome to *Principles of Accounting*, an OpenStax resource. This textbook was written to increase student access to high-quality learning materials, maintaining highest standards of academic rigor at little to no cost.

About OpenStax

OpenStax is a nonprofit based at Rice University, and it's our mission to improve student access to education. Our first openly licensed college textbook was published in 2012, and our library has since scaled to over 30 books for college and AP® courses used by hundreds of thousands of students. OpenStax Tutor, our low-cost personalized learning tool, is being used in college courses throughout the country. Through our partnerships with philanthropic foundations and our alliance with other educational resource organizations, OpenStax is breaking down the most common barriers to learning and empowering students and instructors to succeed.

About OpenStax resources

Customization

Principles of Accounting is licensed under a Creative Commons Attribution-NonCommercial-ShareAlike 4.0 International (CC BY-NC-SA) license, which means that you can distribute, remix, and build upon the content, as long as you provide attribution to OpenStax and its content contributors, do not use the content for commercial purposes, and distribute the content under the same CC BY-NC-SA license.

Because our books are openly licensed, you are free to use the entire book or pick and choose the sections that are most relevant to the needs of your course. Feel free to remix the content by assigning your students certain chapters and sections in your syllabus, in the order that you prefer. You can even provide a direct link in your syllabus to the sections in the web view of your book.

Instructors also have the option of creating a customized version of their OpenStax book. The custom version can be made available to students in low-cost print or digital form through their campus bookstore. Visit the Instructor Resources section of your book page on openstax.org for more information.

Art attribution in *Principles of Accounting*

In *Principles of Accounting*, most art contains attribution to its title, creator or rights holder, host platform, and license within the caption. Because the art is openly licensed, anyone may reuse the art as long as they provide the same attribution to its original source.

To maximize readability and content flow, some art does not include attribution in the text. If you reuse art from this text that does not have attribution provided, use the following attribution: Copyright Rice University, OpenStax, under CC BY-NC-SA 4.0 license.

Errata

All OpenStax textbooks undergo a rigorous review process. However, like any professional-grade textbook, errors sometimes occur. Since our books are web based, we can make updates periodically when deemed pedagogically necessary. If you have a correction to suggest, submit it through the link on your book page on openstax.org. Subject matter experts review all errata suggestions. OpenStax is committed to remaining transparent about all updates, so you will also find a list of past errata changes on your book page on openstax.org.

Format

You can access this textbook for free in web view or PDF through openstax.org, and for a low cost in print.

About *Principles of Accounting*

Principles of Accounting is designed to meet the scope and sequence requirements of a two-semester accounting course that covers the fundamentals of financial and managerial accounting. This book is specifically designed to appeal to both accounting and non-accounting majors, exposing students to the core concepts of accounting in familiar ways to build a strong foundation that can be applied across business fields. Each chapter opens with a relatable real-life scenario for today's college student. Thoughtfully designed examples are presented throughout each chapter, allowing students to build on emerging accounting knowledge. Concepts are further reinforced through applicable connections to more detailed business processes. Students are immersed in the "why" as well as the "how" aspects of accounting in order to reinforce concepts and promote comprehension over rote memorization.

Coverage and scope

Our *Principles of Accounting* textbook adheres to the scope and sequence requirements of accounting courses nationwide. We have endeavored to make the core concepts and practical applications of accounting engaging, relevant, and accessible to students.

Principles of Accounting, Volume 1: Financial Accounting

Chapter 1: The Role of Accounting in Society

Chapter 2: Introduction to Financial Statements

Chapter 3: Analyzing and Recording Transactions

Chapter 4: The Adjustment Process

Chapter 5: Completing the Accounting Cycle

Chapter 6: Merchandising Transactions

Chapter 7: Accounting Information Systems

Chapter 8: Fraud, Internal Controls, and Cash

Chapter 9: Accounting for Receivables

Chapter 10: Inventory

Chapter 11: Long-Term Assets

Chapter 12: Current Liabilities

Chapter 13: Long-Term Liabilities

Chapter 14: Corporation Accounting

Chapter 15: Partnership Accounting

Chapter 16: Statement of Cash Flows

Principles of Accounting, Volume 2: Managerial Accounting

Chapter 1: Accounting as a Tool for Managers

Chapter 2: Building Blocks of Managerial Accounting

Chapter 3: Cost-Volume-Profit Analysis

Chapter 4: Job Order Costing

Chapter 5: Process Costing

Chapter 6: Activity-Based, Variable, and Absorption Costing

Chapter 7: Budgeting

Chapter 8: Standard Costs and Variances

Chapter 9: Responsibility Accounting and Decentralization

Chapter 10: Short-Term Decision-Making

Chapter 11: Capital Budgeting Decisions

Chapter 12: Balanced Scorecard and Other Performance Measures

Chapter 13: Sustainability Reporting

Engaging feature boxes

Throughout *Principles of Accounting*, you will find features that engage students by taking selected topics a step further.

- **Your Turn.** This feature provides students an opportunity to apply covered concepts.
- **Concepts in Practice.** This feature takes students beyond mechanics and illustrates the utility of a given concept for accountants and non-accountants. We encourage instructors to reference these as part of their in-class lectures and assessments to provide easily relatable applications.
- **Think It Through.** This scenario-based feature puts students in the role of decision-maker. With topics ranging from ethical dilemmas to conflicting analytical results, the purpose of this feature is to teach students that in the real world not every question has just one answer.
- **Continuing Application at Work.** This feature follows an individual company or segment of an industry and examines how businesspeople conduct the decision-making process in different situations. It allows students to see how concepts build on each other.
- **Ethical Considerations.** This feature illustrates the ethical implication of decisions, how accounting concepts are applied to real-life examples, and how financial and managerial decisions can impact many stakeholders.
- **IFRS Connection.** This feature presents the differences and similarities between U.S. GAAP and IFRS, helping students understand how accounting concepts and rules between countries may vary and thus affect financial reporting and decision-making.
- **Link to Learning.** This feature provides a very brief introduction to online resources and videos that are pertinent to students' exploration of the topic at hand.

Pedagogical features that reinforce key concepts

- **Learning Objectives.** Each chapter is organized into sections based on clear and comprehensive learning objectives that help guide students on what they can expect to learn. After completing the modules and assessments, students should be able to demonstrate mastery of the learning objectives.
- **Summaries.** Designed to support both students and instructors, section summaries distill the information in each module down to key, concise points.
- **Key Terms.** Key terms are bolded the first time that they are used and are followed by a definition in context. Definitions of key terms are also listed in the glossary, which appears at the end of the chapter.

Assessments to test comprehension and practice skills

An assortment of assessment types are provided in this text to allow for practice and self-assessment throughout the course of study.

- **Multiple Choice**. are basic review questions that test comprehension.
- **Questions** include brief, open-response questions to test comprehension.
- **Exercises** (Sets A and B) are application Application questions that require a combination of quantitative and analytical skills.
- **Problems** (Sets A and B) are advanced Advanced activities that allow students to demonstrate learning and application of multiple learning objectives and skills concurrently in one set of facts. Problems are designed to assess higher levels of Bloom's taxonomy.
- **Thought Provokers** are open-ended questions, often with more than one acceptable response, designed to stretch students intellectually.

Effective art program

Our art program is designed to enhance students' understanding of concepts through clear and effective presentations of financial materials and diagrams.

JOURNAL			
Date	**Account**	**Debit**	**Credit**
	Cost of Goods Sold Finished Goods Inventory *To record the cost of products sold*	25,000	25,000

Figure 1 Journal Entry.

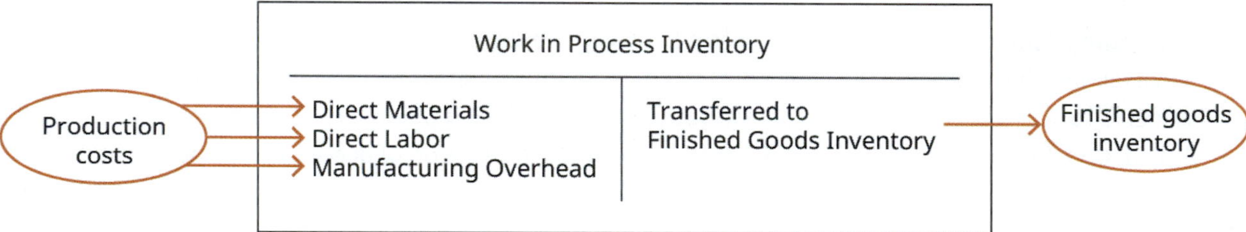

Figure 2 Work in Process Inventory T-Account.

WHICHARD & KLEIN, LLP Income Statement For the Year Ended December 31, 2019	
Service Revenue	$412,000
Operating Expenses	
Salaries	210,000
Office Expense	35,000
Office Equipment	9,000
Administrative Salaries	45,000
Utilities	11,000
Miscellaneous	7,500
Total Operating Expenses	317,500
Operating Income	$ 94,500

Figure 3 Income Statement.

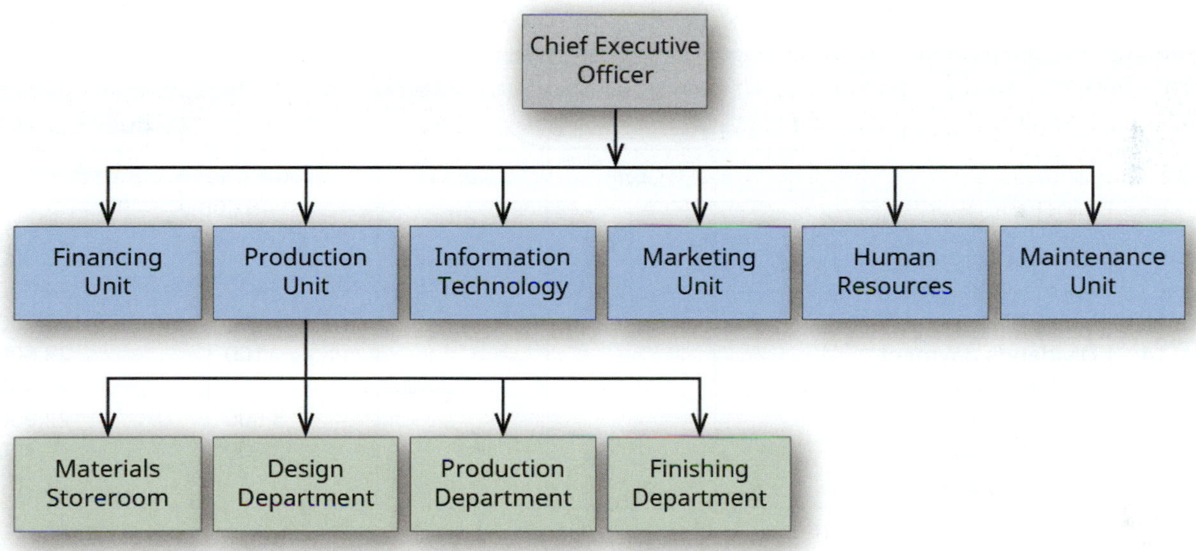

Figure 4 Organizational Chart.

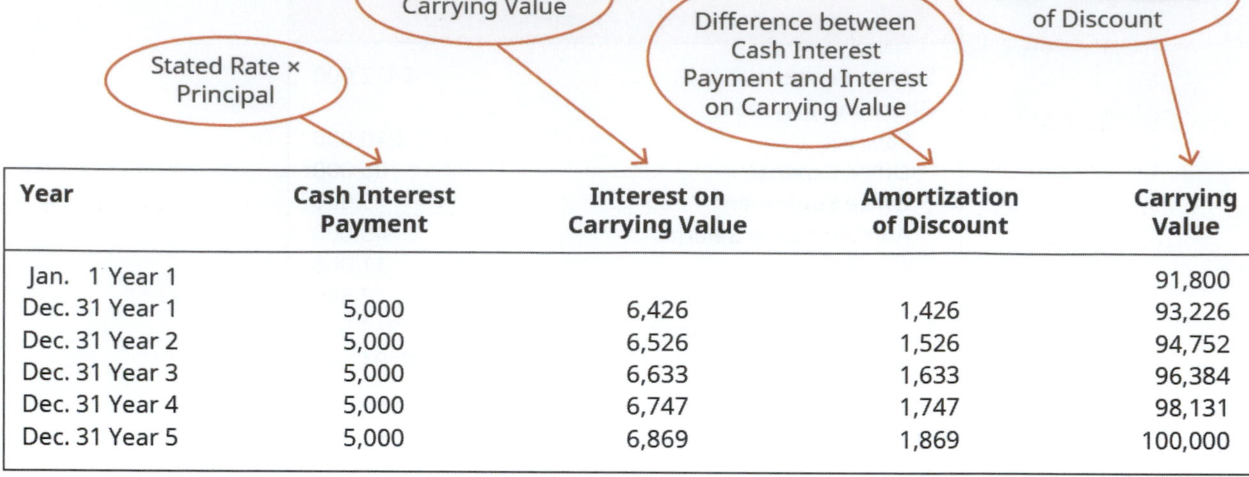

Year	Cash Interest Payment	Interest on Carrying Value	Amortization of Discount	Carrying Value
Jan. 1 Year 1				91,800
Dec. 31 Year 1	5,000	6,426	1,426	93,226
Dec. 31 Year 2	5,000	6,526	1,526	94,752
Dec. 31 Year 3	5,000	6,633	1,633	96,384
Dec. 31 Year 4	5,000	6,747	1,747	98,131
Dec. 31 Year 5	5,000	6,869	1,869	100,000

Figure 5 Cash Interest Payment.

GENERAL LEDGER					
Cash					Account No. 101
Date	Item	Ref.	Debit	Credit	Balance
2019					
Jan. 3	Cash for common stock		20,000		20,000
Jan. 9	Payment from client		4,000		24,000
Jan. 12	Utility bill			300	23,700
Jan. 14	Dividends payment			100	23,600
Jan. 17	Cash for services		2,800		26,400
Jan. 18	Paid cash for equipment			3,500	22,900
Jan. 20	Paid employee salaries			3,600	19,300
Jan. 23	Customer payment		5,500		24,800

Figure 6 General Ledger.

Additional resources

Student and instructor resources

We've compiled additional resources for both students and instructors, including Getting Started Guides, an instructor solution guide, and companion presentation slides. Instructor resources require a verified instructor account, which you can apply for when you log in or create your account on openstax.org. Instructor and student resources are typically available within a few months after the book's initial publication. Take advantage of these resources to supplement your OpenStax book.

Community Hubs

OpenStax partners with the Institute for the Study of Knowledge Management in Education (ISKME) to offer Community Hubs on OER Commons—a platform for instructors to share community-created resources that support OpenStax books, free of charge. Through our Community Hubs, instructors can upload their own materials or download resources to use in their own courses, including additional ancillaries, teaching material, multimedia, and relevant course content. We encourage instructors to join the hubs for the subjects most relevant to your teaching and research as an opportunity both to enrich your courses and to engage with other faculty.

To reach the Community Hubs, visit www.oercommons.org/hubs/OpenStax.

Technology partners

As allies in making high-quality learning materials accessible, our technology partners offer optional low-cost tools that are integrated with OpenStax books. To access the technology options for your text, visit your book page on openstax.org.

About the authors

Senior contributing authors

Mitchell Franklin, Le Moyne College (Financial Accounting)

Mitchell Franklin (PhD, CPA) is an Associate Professor and Director of Undergraduate and Graduate Accounting Programs at Le Moyne College's Madden School of Business. His research interests include the impact of tax law on policy, and innovative education in both financial accounting and taxation, with articles published in journals including *Issues in Accounting Education, Advances in Accounting Education, Tax Notes, Journal of Taxation*, and *The CPA Journal and Tax Adviser*. He teaches introductory and advanced courses in individual and corporate taxation as well as financial accounting. Prior to joining Le Moyne College, he served on the faculty at Syracuse University.

Patty Graybeal, University of Michigan-Dearborn (Managerial Accounting)

Patty Graybeal received her BBA from Radford University and her MACCT and PhD from Virginia Tech. She teaches undergraduate and graduate courses in financial, managerial, governmental, and international accounting. She has published scholarly articles on performance plans and compensation structures, as well as bankruptcy prediction, and she currently focuses on pedagogical issues related to instructional methods and resources that enhance student academic success. Prior to UM-Dearborn, she was on the faculty at Wake Forest University, George Mason University, and Virginia Tech. She brings significant real-world experience to the classroom from her prior work in healthcare administration and her current work with the auto industry.

Dixon Cooper, Ouachita Baptist University

Dixon Cooper received his BBA in Accounting and MS in Taxation from the University of North Texas. He has taught undergraduate and graduate courses in accounting, finance, and economics. In addition to his academic activities, he served for approximately fifteen years as an author/editor for the AICPA's continuing education program and maintained a tax compliance and financial services practice. He also has several years of experience in public accounting and consulting. Prior to teaching at Ouachita Baptist University, he was a faculty member at the University of North Texas, Texas Christian University Austin College, and the University of Arkansas.

Contributing authors

LuAnn Bean, Florida Institute of Technology

Ian Burt, Niagara University

Shana Carr, San Diego City College

David T. Collins, Bellarmine University

Shawna Coram, Florida State College at Jacksonville

Kenneth Creech, Briar Cliff University

Alan Czyzewski, Indiana State University

Michael Gauci, Florida Atlantic University

Cindy Greenman, Embry-Riddle Aeronautical University

Michael Haselkorn, Bentley University

Christine Irujo, Westfield State University

Cynthia Johnson, University of Arkansas at Little Rock

Cynthia Khanlarian, North Carolina Agricultural and Technical State University

Terri Lukshaitis, Ferris State University

Debra Luna, Southwest University

Bill Nantz, Houston Community College

Tatyana Pashnyak, Bainbridge State College

Brian Pusateri, University of Scranton

Ellen Rackas, Muhlenberg College

Marianne Rexer, Wilkes University

Roslyn Roberts, California State University, Sacramento

Rebecca Rosner, Long Island University

Jeffrey J. Sabolish, University of Michigan-Flint

Jason E. Swartzlander, Bluffton University

Diane Tanner, University of North Florida

Mark M. Ulrich, Queensborough Community College

Janis Weber, University of Louisiana Monroe

Linda Williams, Tidewater Community College

Darryl Woolley, University of Idaho

Reviewers

Janice Akao, Butler Community College

Chandra D. Arthur, Cuyahoga Community College

Kwadwo Asare, Bryant University

Dereck Barr-Pulliam, University of Wisconsin–Madison

John Bedient, Albion College

Debra Benson, Kennesaw State University

Amy Bourne, Oregon State University

Stacy Boyer-Davis, Northern Michigan University

Dena Breece, Methodist University

Lawrence Chui, University of St. Thomas, Minnesota

Sandra Cohen, Columbia College Chicago

Bryan Coleman, Assumption College

Sue Cooper, Salisbury University

Constance Crawford, Ramapo College of New Jersey

Cori O. Crews, Valdosta State University

Annette Davis, Glendale Community College

Ronald de Ramon, Rockland Community College

Julie Dilling, Moraine Park Technical College

Terry Elliott, Morehead State University

Jim Emig, Villanova University

Darius Fatemi, Northern Kentucky University

Rhonda Gilreath, Tiffin University

Alan Glazer, Franklin & Marshall College

Marina Grau, Houston Community College

Amber Gray, Adrian College

Jeffry Haber, Iona College

Michelle Hagadorn, Roanoke College

Regina Ivory Butts, Fort Valley State University

Simone Keize, Broward College

Christine Kloezeman, California State University, Los Angeles

Lauri L. Kremer, Lycoming College

W. Eric Lee, University of Northern Iowa

Julie G. Lindsey, University of Phoenix

Jennifer Mack, Lindenwood University

Suneel Maheshwari, Indiana University of Pennsylvania

Richard Mandau, Piedmont Technical College

Josephine Mathias, Mercer County Community College

Ermira Mazziotta, Muhlenberg College

Karen B. McCarron, Georgia Gwinnett College

Michelle A. McFeaters, Grove City College

Britton McKay, Georgia Southern University

Christopher McNamara, Finger Lakes Community College

Glenn McQueary, Houston Community College

Tammy Metzke, Milwaukee Area Technical College

Stacey Mirinaviciene, Keuka College

Eleonor Moore, Kirtland Community College

Hassan Niazi, Northern State University

Felicia Olagbemi, Colorado State University-Global Campus

Suzanne Owens, Colorado Mesa University

Jenice Prather-Kinsey, University of Alabama at Birmingham

Tom Prieto, College of the Canyons

Atul Rai, Wichita State University

Kevin Raiford, College of Southern Nevada

Dave Repp, Strayer University

Patrick Rogan, Cosumnes River College

John Rossi, Moravian College

Angela Seidel, Saint Francis University

Margaret Shackell, Cornell University

Debra Sinclair, University of South Florida St. Petersburg

Mohsen Souissi, Fayetteville State University

Zivia Sweeney, University of Southern California

Tim Swenson, Sullivan University

Hai Ta, Niagara University

Andress Walker, Ventura County Community College District

Teresa Walker, Greensboro College

Roland Warfield, Seton Hill University

Michael Wiggins, Georgia Southern University

Joseph Winter, Niagara University

David Ziebart, University of Kentucky

1

Role of Accounting in Society

Figure 1.1 Careers and Accounting. Promotional opportunities throughout a person's career may involve managerial responsibilities and often include responsibility for a portion of the organization's financial performance. Having an understanding of how accounting affects businesses can help the individual to be successful in meeting the organization's strategic and financial goals. (credit: modification of "Achievement" by unknown/Pixabay, CC0)

Chapter Outline

LO **1.1** Explain the Importance of Accounting and Distinguish between Financial and Managerial Accounting

LO **1.2** Identify Users of Accounting Information and How They Apply Information

LO **1.3** Describe Typical Accounting Activities and the Role Accountants Play in Identifying, Recording, and Reporting Financial Activities

LO **1.4** Explain Why Accounting Is Important to Business Stakeholders

LO **1.5** Describe the Varied Career Paths Open to Individuals with an Accounting Education

Why It Matters

Jennifer has been in the social work profession for over 25 years. After graduating college, she started working at an agency that provided services to homeless women and children. Part of her role was to work directly with the homeless women and children to help them acquire adequate shelter and other necessities. Jennifer currently serves as the director of an organization that provides mentoring services to local youth.

Looking back on her career in the social work field, Jennifer indicates that there are two things that surprised her. The first thing that surprised her was that as a trained social worker she would ultimately become a director of a social work agency and would be required to make financial decisions about programs and how the money is spent. As a college student, she thought social workers would spend their entire careers providing direct support to their clients. The second thing that surprised her was how valuable it is for directors to have an understanding of accounting. She notes, "The best advice I received in college was when my advisor suggested I take an accounting course. As a social work student, I was reluctant to do so because I did not see the relevance. I didn't realize so much of an administrator's role involves dealing with financial issues. I'm thankful that I took the advice and studied accounting. For example, I was surprised that I would be expected to routinely present to the board our agency's financial performance. The board includes several business professionals and leaders from other agencies. Knowing the accounting terms and having a good understanding of the information contained in the financial reports gives me a lot of confidence when answering their questions. In addition, understanding what influences the financial performance of our agency better prepares me to plan for the future."

1.1 Explain the Importance of Accounting and Distinguish between Financial and Managerial Accounting

Accounting is the process of organizing, analyzing, and communicating financial information that is used for decision-making. Financial information is typically prepared by accountants—those trained in the specific techniques and practices of the profession. This course explores many of the topics and techniques related to the accounting profession. While many students will directly apply the knowledge gained in this course to continue their education and become accountants and business professionals, others might pursue different career paths. However, a solid understanding of accounting can for many still serve as a useful resource. In fact, it is hard to think of a profession where a foundation in the principles of accounting would not be beneficial. Therefore, one of the goals of this course is to provide a solid understanding of how financial information is prepared and used in the workplace, regardless of your particular career path.

THINK IT THROUGH

Expertise

Every job or career requires a certain level of technical expertise and an understanding of the key aspects necessary to be successful. The time required to develop the expertise for a particular job or career varies from several months to much longer. For instance, doctors, in addition to the many years invested in the classroom, invest a significant amount of time providing care to patients under the supervision of more experienced doctors. This helps medical professionals develop the necessary skills to quickly and effectively diagnose and treat the various medical conditions they spent so many years learning about.

Figure 1.2 College Graduation. (credit: modification of "140501-A-XA877-046" by Fort Wainwright Public Affairs Office/Flickr, CC BY 2.0)

Accounting also typically takes specialized training. Top accounting managers often invest many years and have a significant amount of experience mastering complex financial transactions. Also, in addition to attending college, earning professional certifications and investing in continuing education are necessary to develop a skill set sufficient to becoming experts in an accounting professional field.

The level and type of training in accounting are often dependent on which of the myriad options of accounting fields the potential accountant chooses to enter. To familiarize you with some potential opportunities, Describe the Varied Career Paths Open to Individuals with an Accounting Education examines many of these career options. In addition to covering an assortment of possible career opportunities, we address some of the educational and experiential certifications that are available. Why do you think accountants (and doctors) need to be certified and secure continuing education? In your response, defend your position with examples.

In addition to doctors and accountants, what other professions can you think of that might require a significant investment of time and effort in order to develop an expertise?

A traditional adage states that "accounting is the language of business." While that is true, you can also say that "accounting is the language of life." At some point, most people will make a decision that relies on accounting information. For example, you may have to decide whether it is better to lease or buy a vehicle. Likewise, a college graduate may have to decide whether it is better to take a higher-paying job in a bigger city (where the cost of living is also higher) or a job in a smaller community where both the pay and cost of living may be lower.

In a professional setting, a theater manager may want to know if the most recent play was profitable. Similarly, the owner of the local plumbing business may want to know whether it is worthwhile to pay an employee to be "on call" for emergencies during off-hours and weekends. Whether personal or professional, accounting information plays a vital role in all of these decisions.

You may have noticed that the decisions in these scenarios would be based on factors that include both financial and nonfinancial information. For instance, when deciding whether to lease or buy a vehicle, you would consider not only the monthly payments but also such factors as vehicle maintenance and reliability. The college graduate considering two job offers might weigh factors such as working hours, ease of commuting, and options for shopping and entertainment. The theater manager would analyze the proceeds from ticket sales and sponsorships as well as the expenses for production of the play and operating the concessions. In addition, the theater manager should consider how the financial performance of the play might have been influenced by the marketing of the play, the weather during the performances, and other factors such as competing events during the time of the play. All of these factors, both financial and nonfinancial, are relevant to the financial performance of the play. In addition to the additional cost of having an employee "on call" during evenings and weekends, the owner of the local plumbing business would consider nonfinancial factors in the decision. For instance, if there are no other plumbing businesses that offer services during evenings and weekends, offering emergency service might give the business a strategic advantage that could increase overall sales by attracting new customers.

This course explores the role that accounting plays in society. You will learn about **financial accounting**, which measures the financial performance of an organization using standard conventions to prepare and distribute financial reports. Financial accounting is used to generate information for stakeholders *outside* of an organization, such as owners, stockholders, lenders, and governmental entities such as the Securities and Exchange Commission (SEC) and the Internal Revenue Service (IRS).

Financial accounting is also a foundation for understanding **managerial accounting**, which uses both financial and nonfinancial information as a basis for making decisions within an organization with the purpose of equipping decision makers to set and evaluate business goals by determining what information they need to make a particular decision and how to analyze and communicate this information. Managerial accounting information tends to be used internally, for such purposes as budgeting, pricing, and determining production costs. Since the information is generally used internally, you do not see the same need for financial oversight in an organization's managerial data.

You will also note in your financial accounting studies that there are governmental and organizational entities that oversee the accounting processes and systems that are used in financial accounting. These entities include organizations such as the Securities and Exchange Commission (SEC), the Financial Accounting Standards Board (FASB), the American Institute of Certified Public Accountants (AICPA), and the Public Company Accounting Oversight Board (PCAOB). The PCAOB was created after several major cases of corporate fraud, leading to the Sarbanes-Oxley Act of 2002, known as SOX. If you choose to pursue more advanced accounting courses, especially auditing courses, you will address the SOX in much greater detail.

For now, it is not necessary to go into greater detail about the mechanics of these organizations or other accounting and financial legislation. You just need to have a basic understanding that they function to provide a degree of protection for those outside of the organization who rely on the financial information.

Whether or not you aspire to become an accountant, understanding financial and managerial accounting is valuable and necessary for practically any career you will pursue. Management of a car manufacturer, for example, would use both financial and managerial accounting information to help improve the business. Financial accounting information is valuable as it measures whether or not the company was financially successful. Knowing this provides management with an opportunity to repeat activities that have proven effective and to make adjustments in areas in which the company has underperformed. Managerial accounting information is likewise valuable. Managers of the car manufacturer may want to know, for example, how much scrap is generated from a particular area in the manufacturing process. While identifying and improving the manufacturing process (i.e., reducing scrap) helps the company financially, it may also help other areas of the production process that are indirectly related, such as poor quality and shipping delays.

1.2 Identify Users of Accounting Information and How They Apply Information

The ultimate goal of accounting is to provide information that is useful for decision-making. Users of accounting information are generally divided into two categories: internal and external. Internal users are those within an organization who use financial information to make day-to-day decisions. Internal users include managers and other employees who use financial information to confirm past results and help make adjustments for future activities.

External users are those outside of the organization who use the financial information to make decisions or to evaluate an entity's performance. For example, investors, financial analysts, loan officers, governmental auditors, such as IRS agents, and an assortment of other stakeholders are classified as external users, while still having an interest in an organization's financial information. (Stakeholders are addressed in greater detail in Explain Why Accounting Is Important to Business Stakeholders.)

Characteristics, Users, and Sources of Financial Accounting Information

Organizations measure financial performance in monetary terms. In the United States, the dollar is used as the standard measurement basis. Measuring financial performance in monetary terms allows managers to compare the organization's performance to previous periods, to expectations, and to other organizations or industry standards.

Financial accounting is one of the broad categories in the study of accounting. While some industries and types of organizations have variations in how the financial information is prepared and communicated, accountants generally use the same methodologies—called accounting standards—to prepare the financial information. You learn in Introduction to Financial Statements that financial information is primarily communicated through financial statements, which include the Income Statement, Statement of Owner's Equity, Balance Sheet, and Statement of Cash Flows and Disclosures. These financial statements ensure the information is consistent from period to period and generally comparable between organizations. The conventions also ensure that the information provided is both reliable and relevant to the user.

Virtually every activity and event that occurs in a business has an associated cost or value and is known as a **transaction**. Part of an accountant's responsibility is to quantify these activities and events. In this course you will learn about the many types of transactions that occur within a business. You will also examine the effects of these transactions, including their impact on the financial position of the entity.

Accountants often use computerized accounting systems to record and summarize the financial reports, which offer many benefits. The primary benefit of a computerized accounting system is the efficiency by which transactions can be recorded and summarized, and financial reports prepared. In addition, computerized accounting systems store data, which allows organizations to easily extract historical financial information.

Common computerized accounting systems include QuickBooks, which is designed for small organizations, and SAP, which is designed for large and/or multinational organizations. QuickBooks is popular with smaller, less complex entities. It is less expensive than more sophisticated software packages, such as Oracle or SAP, and the QuickBooks skills that accountants developed at previous employers tend to be applicable to the needs of new employers, which can reduce both training time and costs spent on acclimating new employees to an employer's software system. Also, being familiar with a common software package such as QuickBooks helps provide employment mobility when workers wish to reenter the job market.

While QuickBooks has many advantages, once a company's operations reach a certain level of complexity, it will need a basic software package or platform, such as Oracle or SAP, which is then customized to meet the unique informational needs of the entity.

Financial accounting information is mostly historical in nature, although companies and other entities also incorporate estimates into their accounting processes. For example, you will learn how to use estimates to determine bad debt expenses or depreciation expenses for assets that will be used over a multiyear lifetime. That is, accountants prepare financial reports that summarize what has already occurred in an organization. This information provides what is called feedback value. The benefit of reporting what has already occurred is the reliability of the information. Accountants can, with a fair amount of confidence, accurately report the financial performance of the organization related to past activities. The feedback value offered by the accounting information is particularly useful to internal users. That is, reviewing how the organization performed in the past can help managers and other employees make better decisions about and adjustments to future activities.

Financial information has limitations, however, as a predictive tool. Business involves a large amount of uncertainty, and accountants cannot predict how the organization will perform in the future. However, by observing historical financial information, users of the information can detect patterns or trends that may be useful for estimating the company's future financial performance. Collecting and analyzing a series of historical financial data is useful to both internal and external users. For example, internal users can use financial information as a predictive tool to assess whether the long-term financial performance of the organization aligns with its long-term strategic goals.

External users also use the historical pattern of an organization's financial performance as a predictive tool. For example, when deciding whether to loan money to an organization, a bank may require a certain number of years of financial statements and other financial information from the organization. The bank will assess the historical performance in order to make an informed decision about the organization's ability to repay the loan and interest (the cost of borrowing money). Similarly, a potential investor may look at a business's past financial performance in order to assess whether or not to invest money in the company. In this scenario, the investor wants to know if the organization will provide a sufficient and consistent return on the investment. In these scenarios, the financial information provides value to the process of allocating scarce resources (money). If potential lenders and investors determine the organization is a worthwhile investment, money will be provided, and, if all goes well, those funds will be used by the organization to generate additional value at a rate greater than the alternate uses of the money.

Characteristics, Users, and Sources of Managerial Accounting Information

As you've learned, managerial accounting information is different from financial accounting information in several respects. Accountants use formal accounting standards in financial accounting. These accounting standards are referred to as **generally accepted accounting principles (GAAP)** and are the common set of rules, standards, and procedures that publicly traded companies must follow when composing their financial statements. The previously mentioned **Financial Accounting Standards Board (FASB)**, an independent, nonprofit organization that sets financial accounting and reporting standards for both public and private sector businesses in the United States, uses the GAAP guidelines as its foundation for its system of accepted accounting methods and practices, reports, and other documents.

Since most managerial accounting activities are conducted for internal uses and applications, managerial accounting is not prepared using a comprehensive, prescribed set of conventions similar to those required by financial accounting. This is because managerial accountants provide managerial accounting information that is intended to serve the needs of internal, rather than external, users. In fact, managerial accounting information is rarely shared with those outside of the organization. Since the information often includes strategic or competitive decisions, managerial accounting information is often closely protected. The business environment is constantly changing, and managers and decision makers within organizations need a variety of information in order to view or assess issues from multiple perspectives.

Accountants must be adaptable and flexible in their ability to generate the necessary information management decision-making. For example, information derived from a computerized accounting system is often the starting point for obtaining managerial accounting information. But accountants must also be able to extract information from other sources (internal and external) and analyze the data using mathematical, formula-driven software (such as Microsoft Excel).

Management accounting information as a term encompasses many activities within an organization. Preparing a budget, for example, allows an organization to estimate the financial performance for the upcoming year or years and plan for adjustments to scale operations according to the projections. Accountants often lead the budgeting process by gathering information from internal (estimates from the sales and engineering departments, for example) and external (trade groups and economic forecasts, for example) sources. These data are then compiled and presented to decision makers within the organization.

Examples of other decisions that require management accounting information include whether an organization should repair or replace equipment, make products internally or purchase the items from outside vendors, and hire additional workers or use automation.

As you have learned, management accounting information uses both financial and nonfinancial information. This is important because there are situations in which a purely financial analysis might lead to one decision, while considering nonfinancial information might lead to a different decision. For example, suppose a financial analysis indicates that a particular product is unprofitable and should no longer be offered by a company. If the company fails to consider that customers also purchase a complementary good (you might recall that term from your study of economics), the company may be making the wrong decision. For example, assume that you have a company that produces and sells both computer printers and the replacement ink cartridges. If the company decided to eliminate the printers, then it would also lose the cartridge sales. In the past, in some cases, the elimination of one component, such as printers, led to customers switching to a different producer for its computers and other peripheral hardware. In the end, an organization needs to consider both the financial and nonfinancial aspects of a decision, and sometimes the effects are not intuitively obvious at the time of the decision. Figure 1.3 offers an overview of some of the differences between financial and managerial accounting.

COMMUNICATION THROUGH REPORTING	FINANCIAL ACCOUNTING	MANAGERIAL ACCOUNTING
Users of reports	External users: stockholders, creditors, regulators	Internal users: managers, officers, and other employees
Types of reports	Financial statements: balance sheet, income statement, cash-flow statement, etc.	Internal reports: job cost sheet, cost of goods manufactured, production cost report, etc.
Frequency of reports	Quarterly; annually	As frequently as needed
Purpose of reports	Helps those external users make decisions: credit terms, investment, and other decisions	Assists the internal users in the planning and control decision-making process
Focus of reports	Pertains to company as a whole Uses GAAP structure Composed from a multitude or combination of other more individual data	Pertains to departments, sections of the business Very detailed reporting No GAAP constraints
Nature of reports	Monetary	Monetary and nonmonetary information
Verification of reports	Audited by CPA	No independent audits

Figure 1.3 Comparing Reports between Financial and Managerial Accounting. (attribution: Copyright Rice University, OpenStax, under CC BY-NC-SA 4.0 license)

1.3 Describe Typical Accounting Activities and the Role Accountants Play in Identifying, Recording, and Reporting Financial Activities

We can classify organizations into three categories: for profit, governmental, and not for profit. These organizations are similar in several aspects. For example, each of these organizations has inflows and outflows of cash and other resources, such as equipment, furniture, and land, that must be managed. In addition, all of these organizations are formed for a specific purpose or mission and want to use the available resources in an efficient manner—the organizations strive to be good stewards, with the underlying premise of being profitable. Finally, each of the organizations makes a unique and valuable contribution to society. Given the similarities, it is clear that all of these organizations have a need for accounting information and for accountants to provide that information.

There are also several differences. The main difference that distinguishes these organizations is the primary purpose or mission of the organization, discussed in the following sections.

For-Profit Businesses

As the name implies, the primary purpose or mission of a **for-profit business** is to earn a profit by selling goods and services. There are many reasons why a for-profit business seeks to earn a profit. The profits generated by these organizations might be used to create value for employees in the form of pay raises for existing employees as well as hiring additional workers. In addition, profits can be reinvested in the business to create value in the form of research and development, equipment upgrades, facilities expansions, and many other activities that make the business more competitive. Many companies also engage in charitable activities, such as donating money, donating products, or allowing employees to volunteer in the communities. Finally, profits can also be shared with employees in the form of either bonuses or commissions as well as with owners of the business as a reward for the owners' investment in the business. These issues, along with others, and the associated accounting conventions will be explored throughout this course.

In for-profit businesses, accounting information is used to measure the financial performance of the organization and to help ensure that resources are being used efficiently. Efficiently using existing resources allows the businesses to improve quality of the products and services offered, remain competitive in the marketplace, expand when appropriate, and ensure longevity of the business.

For-profit businesses can be further categorized by the types of products or services the business provides. Let's examine three types of for-profit businesses: manufacturing, retail (or merchandising), and service.

Manufacturing Businesses

A **manufacturing business** is a for-profit business that is designed to make a specific product or products. Manufacturers specialize in procuring components in the most basic form (often called direct or raw materials) and transforming the components into a finished product that is often drastically different from the original components.

As you think about the products you use every day, you are probably already familiar with products made by manufacturing firms. Examples of products made by manufacturing firms include automobiles, clothes, cell phones, computers, and many other products that are used every day by millions of consumers.

In Job Order Costing (http://cnx.org/content/m68122/latest/) , you will examine the process of job costing, learning how manufacturing firms transform basic components into finished, sellable products and the techniques accountants use to record the costs associated with these activities.

CONCEPTS IN PRACTICE

Manufacturing

Think about the items you have used today. Make a list of the products that were created by manufacturing firms. How many can you think of? Think of the many components that went into some of the items you use. Do you think the items were made by machines or by hand?

If you are in a classroom with other students, see who has used the greatest number of items today. Or, see who used the item that would be the most complex to manufacture.

If you are able, you might consider arranging a tour of a local manufacturer. Many manufacturers are happy to give tours of the facilities and describe the many complex processes that are involved in making the products. On your tour, take note of the many job functions that are required to make those items—from ordering the materials to delivering to the customer.

Retail Businesses

Manufacturing businesses and retail (or merchandising) businesses are similar in that both are for-profit businesses that sell products to consumers. In the case of manufacturing firms, by adding direct labor, manufacturing overhead (such as utilities, rent, and depreciation), and other direct materials, raw components are converted into a finished product that is sold to consumers. A **retail business** (or merchandising business), on the other hand, is a for-profit business that purchases products (called inventory) and then resells the products without altering them—that is, the products are sold directly to the consumer in the same condition (production state) as purchased.

Examples of retail firms are plentiful. Automobile dealerships, clothes, cell phones, and computers are all examples of everyday products that are purchased and sold by retail firms. What distinguishes a manufacturing firm from a retail firm is that in a retail firm, the products are sold in the same condition as when the products were purchased—no further alterations were made on the products.

Did you happen to notice that the product examples listed in the preceding paragraph (automobiles, clothes, cell phones, and computers) for manufacturing firms and retail firms are identical? If so, congratulations, because you are paying close attention to the details. These products are used as examples in two different contexts—that is, manufacturing firms *make* these products, and retail firms *sell* these products. These products are relevant to both manufacturing and retail because they are examples of goods that are both manufactured and sold directly to the consumer. While there are instances when a manufacturing firm also serves as the retail firm (Dell computers, for example), it is often the case that products will be manufactured and sold by separate firms.

CONCEPTS IN PRACTICE

NIKEiD

NIKEiD is a program that allows consumers to design and purchase customized equipment, clothes, and shoes. In 2007, Nike opened its first NIKEiD studio at Niketown in New York City.[1] Since its debut in 1999, the NIKEiD concept has flourished, and Nike has partnered with professional athletes to showcase their designs that, along with featured consumer designs, are available for purchase on the NIKEiD website.

1 Nike. "Nike Opens New NIKEiD Studio in New York." October 4, 2007. https://news.nike.com/news/nike-opens-new-nikeid-studio-in-new-york

Figure 1.4 NIKEiD Launch Store in Shanghai. (credit: "Nike-id-shanghai-launch" by "All.watson"/Wikimedia Commons, CC BY 2.0)

Assume you are the manager of a sporting goods store that sells Nike shoes. Think about the concept of NIKEiD, and consider the impact that this concept might have on your store sales. Would this positively or negatively impact the sale of Nike shoes in your store? What are steps you could take to leverage the NIKEiD concept to help increase your own store's sales?

Considerations like this are examples of what marketing professionals would address. Nike wants to ensure this concept does not negatively impact the existing relationships it has, and Nike works to ensure this program is also beneficial to its existing distribution partners.

In Merchandising Transactions you will learn about merchandising transactions, which include concepts and specific accounting practices for retail firms. You will learn, among other things, how to account for purchasing products from suppliers, selling the products to customers, and prepare the financial reports for retail firms.

Service Businesses

As the term implies, service businesses are businesses that provide services to customers. A major difference between manufacturing and retail firms and service firms is that service firms do not have a tangible product that is sold to customers. Instead, a **service business** does not sell tangible products to customers but rather provides intangible benefits (services) to customers. A service business can be either a for-profit or a not-for-profit business. Figure 1.5 illustrates the distinction between manufacturing, retail, and service businesses.

Examples of service-oriented businesses include hotels, cab services, entertainment, and tax preparers. Efficiency is one advantage service businesses offer to their customers. For example, while taxpayers can certainly read the tax code, read the instructions, and complete the forms necessary to file their annual tax returns, many choose to take their tax returns to a person who has specialized training and experience with preparing tax returns. Although it is more expensive to do so, many feel it is a worthwhile investment because the tax professional has invested the time and has the knowledge to prepare the forms properly and in a timely manner. Hiring a tax preparer is efficient for the taxpayer because it allows the taxpayer to file the required forms without having to invest numerous hours researching and preparing the forms.

The accounting conventions for service businesses are similar to the accounting conventions for manufacturing and retail businesses. In fact, the accounting for service businesses is easier in one respect. Because service businesses do not sell tangible products, there is no need to account for products that are being held for sale (inventory). Therefore, while we briefly discuss service businesses, we'll focus mostly on accounting for manufacturing and retail businesses.

Figure 1.5 Manufacturing, Retail, and Service. An auto manufacturing plant, a car sales lot, and a taxi represent three types of businesses: manufacturing, retail, and service. (credit left: modification of "Maquiladora" by "Guldhammer"/Wikimedia Commons, CC0; credit center: modification of "Mercedes Benz Parked" by unknown/Pixabay, CC0; credit right: modification of "Taxi Overtaking Bus" by "Kai Pilger"/Pixabay, CC0)

YOUR TURN

Categorizing Restaurants

So far, you've learned about three types of for-profit businesses: manufacturing, retail, and service. Previously, you saw how some firms such as Dell serve as both manufacturer and retailer.

Now, think of the last restaurant where you ate. Of the three business types (manufacturer, retailer, or service provider), how would you categorize the restaurant? Is it a manufacturer? A retailer? A service provider? Can you think of examples of how a restaurant has characteristics of all three types of businesses?

Solution

Answers will vary. Responses may initially consider a restaurant to be only a service provider. Students may also recognize that a restaurant possesses aspects of a manufacturer (by preparing the meals), retailer (by selling merchandise and/or gift cards), and service provider (by waiting on customers).

Governmental Entities

A **governmental entity** provides services to the general public (taxpayers). Governmental agencies exist at the federal, state, and local levels. These entities are funded through the issuance of taxes and other fees.

Accountants working in governmental entities perform the same function as accountants working at for-profit businesses. Accountants help to serve the public interest by providing to the public an accounting for the receipts and disbursements of taxpayer dollars. Governmental leaders are accountable to taxpayers, and accountants help assure the public that tax dollars are being utilized in an efficient manner.

Examples of governmental entities that require financial reporting include federal agencies such as the Social Security Administration, state agencies such as the Department of Transportation, and local agencies such as county engineers.

Students continuing their study of accounting may take a specific course or courses related to governmental accounting. While the specific accounting used in governmental entities differs from traditional accounting conventions, the goal of providing accurate and unbiased financial information useful for decision-making remains the same, regardless of the type of entity. Government accounting standards are governed by the **Governmental Accounting Standards Board (GASB)**. This organization creates standards that are specifically appropriate for state and local governments in the United States.

Not-for-Profit Entities

To be fair, the name "not-for-profit" can be somewhat confusing. As with "for-profit" entities, the name refers to the primary purpose or mission of the organization. In the case of for-profit organizations, the primary purpose is to generate a profit. The profits, then, can be used to sustain and improve the business through investments in employees, research, and development, and other measures intended to help ensure the long-term success of the business.

But in the case of a **nonprofit (not-for-profit) organization** the primary purpose or mission is to serve a particular interest or need in the community. A not-for-profit entity tends to depend on financial longevity based on donations, grants, and revenues generated. It may be helpful to think of not-for-profit entities as "mission-based" entities. It is important to note that not-for-profit entities, while having a primary purpose of serving a particular interest, also have a need for financial sustainability. An adage in the not-for-profit sector states that "being a not-for-profit organization does not mean it is for-loss." That is, not-for-profit entities must also ensure that resources are used efficiently, allowing for inflows of resources to be greater than (or, at a minimum, equal to) outflows of resources. This allows the organization to continue and perhaps expand its valuable mission.

Examples of not-for-profit entities are numerous. Food banks have as a primary purpose the collection, storage, and distribution of food to those in need. Charitable foundations have as a primary purpose the provision of funding to local agencies that support specific community needs, such as reading and after-school programs. Many colleges and universities are structured as not-for-profit entities because the primary purpose is to provide education and research opportunities.

Similar to accounting for governmental entities, students continuing their study of accounting may take a specific course or courses related to not-for-profit accounting. While the specific accounting used in not-for-profit entities differs slightly from traditional accounting conventions, the goal of providing reliable and unbiased financial information useful for decision-making is vitally important. Some of the governmental and regulatory entities involved in maintaining the rules and principles in accounting are discussed in Explain Why

Accounting Is Important to Business Stakeholders.

YOUR TURN

Types of Organizations

Think of the various organizations discussed so far. Now try to identify people in your personal and professional network who work for these types of agencies. Can you think of someone in a career at each of these types of organizations?

One way to explore career paths is to talk with professionals who work in the areas that interest you. You may consider reaching out to the individuals you identified and learning more about the work that they do. Find out about the positive and negative aspects of the work. Find out what advice they have relating to education. Try to gain as much information as you can to determine whether that is a career you can envision yourself pursuing. Also, ask about opportunities for job shadowing, co-ops, or internships

Solution

Answers will vary, but this should be an opportunity to learn about careers in a variety of organizations (for-profit including manufacturing, retail, and services; not-for-profit; and governmental agencies). You may have an assumption about a career that is based only on the positive aspects. Learning from experienced professionals may help you understand all aspects of the careers. In addition, this exercise may help you confirm or alter your potential career path, including the preparation required (based on advice given from those you talk with).

1.4 Explain Why Accounting Is Important to Business Stakeholders

The number of decisions we make in a single day is staggering. For example, think about what you had for breakfast this morning. What pieces of information factored into that decision? A short list might include the foods that were available in your home, the amount of time you had to prepare and eat the food, and what sounded good to eat this morning. Let's say you do not have much food in your home right now because you are overdue on a trip to the grocery store. Deciding to grab something at a local restaurant involves an entirely new set of choices. Can you think of some of the factors that might influence the decision to grab a meal at a local restaurant?

YOUR TURN

Daily Decisions

Many academic studies have been conducted on the topic of consumer behavior and decision-making. It is a fascinating topic of study that attempts to learn what type of advertising works best, the best place to locate a business, and many other business-related activities.

One such study, conducted by researchers at Cornell University, concluded that people make more than 200 food-related decisions per day.[2]

This is astonishing considering the number of decisions found in this particular study related only to decisions involving food. Imagine how many day-to-day decisions involve other issues that are important to us, such as what to wear and how to get from point A to point B. For this exercise, provide and discuss some of the food-related decisions that you recently made.

Solution

In consideration of food-related decisions, there are many options you can consider. For example, what types, in terms of ethnic groups or styles, do you prefer? Do you want a dining experience or just something inexpensive and quick? Do you have allergy-related food issues? These are just a few of the myriad potential decisions you might make.

It is no different when it comes to financial decisions. Decision makers rely on unbiased, relevant, and timely financial information in order to make sound decisions. In this context, the term **stakeholder** refers to a person or group who relies on financial information to make decisions, since they often have an interest in the economic viability of an organization or business. Stakeholders may be stockholders, creditors, governmental and regulatory agencies, customers, management and other employees, and various other parties and entities.

Stockholders

A **stockholder** is an owner of stock in a business. Owners are called stockholders because in exchange for cash, they are given an ownership interest in the business, called stock. Stock is sometimes referred to as "shares." Historically, stockholders received paper certificates reflecting the number of stocks owned in the business. Now, many stock transactions are recorded electronically. Introduction to Financial Statements discusses stock in more detail. Corporation Accounting offers a more extensive exploration of the types of stock as well as the accounting related to stock transactions.

Recall that organizations can be classified as for-profit, governmental, or not-for-profit entities. Stockholders are associated with for-profit businesses. While governmental and not-for-profit entities have constituents, there is no direct ownership associated with these entities.

For-profit businesses are organized into three categories: manufacturing, retail (or merchandising), and service. Another way to categorize for-profit businesses is based on the availability of the company stock (see Table 1.1). A **publicly traded company** is one whose stock is traded (bought and sold) on an organized stock exchange such as the New York Stock Exchange (NYSE) or the National Association of Securities Dealers Automated Quotation (NASDAQ) system. Most large, recognizable companies are publicly traded, meaning the stock is available for sale on these exchanges. A **privately held company**, in contrast, is one whose stock is not available to the general public. Privately held companies, while accounting for the largest number of businesses and employment in the United States, are often smaller (based on value) than publicly traded companies. Whereas financial information and company stock of publicly traded companies are available to those inside and outside of the organization, financial information and company stock of privately held companies are often limited exclusively to employees at a certain level within the organization as a part of compensation and incentive packages or selectively to individuals or groups (such as banks or other lenders) outside the organization.

2 B. Wansink and J. Sobal. "Mindless Eating: The 200 Daily Food Decisions We Overlook." 2007. *Environment & Behavior*, 39[1], 106–123.

Publicly Held versus Privately Held Companies

Publicly Held Company	Privately Held Company
• Stock available to general public • Financial information public • Typically larger in value	• Stock not available to general public • Financial information private • Typically smaller in value

Table 1.1

Whether the stock is owned by a publicly traded or privately held company, owners use financial information to make decisions. Owners use the financial information to assess the financial performance of the business and make decisions such as whether or not to purchase additional stock, sell existing stock, or maintain the current level of stock ownership.

Other decisions stockholders make may be influenced by the type of company. For example, stockholders of privately held companies often are also employees of the company, and the decisions they make may be related to day-to-day activities as well as longer-term strategic decisions. Owners of publicly traded companies, on the other hand, will usually only focus on strategic issues such as the company leadership, purchases of other businesses, and executive compensation arrangements. In essence, stockholders predominantly focus on profitability, expected increase in stock value, and corporate stability.

Creditors and Lenders

In order to provide goods and services to their customers, businesses make purchases from other businesses. These purchases come in the form of materials used to make finished goods or resell, office equipment such as copiers and telephones, utility services such as heating and cooling, and many other products and services that are vital to run the business efficiently and effectively.

It is rare that payment is required at the time of the purchase or when the service is provided. Instead, businesses usually extend "credit" to other businesses. Selling and purchasing on credit, which is explored further in Merchandising Transactions and Accounting for Receivables, means the payment is expected after a certain period of time following receipt of the goods or provision of the service. The term **creditor** refers to a business that grants extended payment terms to other businesses. The time frame for extended credit to other businesses for purchases of goods and services is usually very short, typically thirty-day to forty-five-day periods are common.

When businesses need to borrow larger amounts of money and/or for longer periods of time, they will often borrow money from a **lender**, a bank or other institution that has the primary purpose of lending money with a specified repayment period and stated interest rate. If you or your family own a home, you may already be familiar with lending institutions. The time frame for borrowing from lenders is typically measured in years rather than days, as was the case with creditors. While lending arrangements vary, typically the borrower is required to make periodic, scheduled payments with the full amount being repaid by a certain date. In addition, since the borrowing is for a long period of time, lending institutions require the borrower to pay a fee (called interest) for the use of borrowing. These concepts and the related accounting practices are covered in Long-Term Liabilities. Table 1.2 Summarizes the differences between creditors and lenders.

Creditor versus Lender

Creditor	Lender
• Business that grants extended payment terms to other businesses • Shorter time frame	• Bank or other institution that lends money • Longer time frame

Table 1.2

Both creditors and lenders use financial information to make decisions. The ultimate decision that both creditors and lenders have to make is whether or not the funds will be repaid by the borrower. The reason this is important is because lending money involves risk. The type of risk creditors and lenders assess is repayment risk—the risk the funds will not be repaid. As a rule, the longer the money is borrowed, the higher the risk involved.

Recall that accounting information is historical in nature. While historical performance is no guarantee of future performance (repayment of borrowed funds, in this case), an established pattern of financial performance using historical accounting information does help creditors and lenders to assess the likelihood the funds will be repaid, which, in turn, helps them to determine how much money to lend, how long to lend the money for, and how much interest (in the case of lenders) to charge the borrower.

Sources of Funding

Besides borrowing, there are other options for businesses to obtain or raise additional funding (also often labeled as capital). It is important for the business student to understand that businesses generally have three ways to raise capital: profitable operations is the first option; selling ownership—stock—which is also called equity financing, is the second option; and borrowing from lenders (called debt financing) is the final option.

In Introduction to Financial Statements, you'll learn more about the business concept called "profit." You are already aware of the concept of profit. In short, profit means the inflows of resources are greater than the outflow of resources, or stated in more business-like terms, the revenues that the company generates are larger or greater than the expenses. For example, if a retailer buys a printer for $150 and sells it for $320, then from the sale it would have revenue of $320 and expenses of $150, for a profit of $170. (Actually, the process is a little more complicated because there would typically be other expenses for the operation of the store. However, to keep the example simple, those were not included. You'll learn more about this later in the course.)

Developing and maintaining profitable operations (selling goods and services) typically provides businesses with resources to use for future projects such as hiring additional workers, maintaining equipment, or expanding a warehouse. While profitable operations are valuable to businesses, companies often want to engage in projects that are very expensive and/or are time sensitive. Businesses, then, have other options to raise funds quickly, such as selling stock and borrowing from lenders, as previously discussed.

An advantage of selling stock to raise capital is that the business is not committed to a specific payback schedule. A disadvantage of issuing new stock is that the administrative costs (legal and compliance) are high, which makes it an expensive way to raise capital.

There are two advantages to raising money by borrowing from lenders. One advantage is that the process, relative to profitable operations and selling ownership, is quicker. As you've learned, lenders (and creditors) review financial information provided by the business in order to make assessments on whether or not to lend money to the business, how much money to lend, and the acceptable length of time to lend. A second, and related, advantage of raising capital through borrowing is that it is fairly inexpensive. A disadvantage of borrowing money from lenders is the repayment commitments. Because lenders require the funds to be repaid within a specific time frame, the risk to the business (and, in turn, to the lender) increases.

These topics are covered extensively in the area of study called corporate finance. While finance and accounting are similar in many aspects, in practicality finance and accounting are separate disciplines that frequently work in coordination in a business setting. Students may be interested to learn more about the educational and career options in the field of corporate finance. Because there are many similarities in the study of finance and accounting, many college students double major in a combination of finance, accounting, economics, and information systems.

CONCEPTS IN PRACTICE

Profit

What is profit? In accounting, there is general consensus on the definition of profit. A typical definition of profit is, in effect, when inflows of cash or other resources are greater than outflows of resources.

Ken Blanchard provides another way to define profit. Blanchard is the author of *The One Minute Manager*, a popular leadership book published in 1982. He is often quoted as saying, "profit is the applause you get for taking care of your customers and creating a motivating environment for your people [employees]." Blanchard's definition recognizes the multidimensional aspect of profit, which requires successful businesses to focus on their customers, employees, and the community.

Check out this short video of Blanchard's definition of profit (https://openstax.org/l/50Blanchard) for more information. What are alternative approaches to defining profit?

Governmental and Regulatory Agencies

Publicly traded companies are required to file financial and other informational reports with the **Securities and Exchange Commission (SEC)**, a federal regulatory agency that regulates corporations with shares listed and traded on security exchanges through required periodic filings Figure 1.6. The SEC accomplishes this in two primary ways: issuing regulations and providing oversight of financial markets. The goal of these actions is to help ensure that businesses provide investors with access to transparent and unbiased financial information.

Figure 1.6 Securities and Exchange Commission. (credit: "Seal of the United States Securities and Exchange Commission" by U.S. Government/Wikimedia Commons, Public Domain)

As an example of its responsibility to issue regulations, you learn in Introduction to Financial Statements that the SEC is responsible for establishing guidelines for the accounting profession. These are called accounting standards or generally accepted accounting principles (GAAP). Although the SEC also had the responsibility of issuing standards for the auditing profession, they relinquished this responsibility to the Financial Accounting Standards Board (FASB).

In addition, you will learn in Describe the Varied Career Paths Open to Individuals with an Accounting Education that auditors are accountants charged with providing reasonable assurance to users that financial statements are prepared according to accounting standards. This oversight is administered through the Public Company Accounting Oversight Board (PCAOB), which was established in 2002.

The SEC also has responsibility for regulating firms that issue and trade (buy and sell) securities—stocks, bonds, and other investment instruments.

Enforcement by the SEC takes many forms. According to the SEC website, "Each year the SEC brings hundreds of civil enforcement actions against individuals and companies for violation of the securities laws. Typical infractions include insider trading, accounting fraud, and providing false or misleading information about securities and the companies that issue them."[3] Financial information is a valuable tool that is part of the investigatory and enforcement activities of the SEC.

CONCEPTS IN PRACTICE

Financial Professionals and Fraud

You may have heard the name Bernard "Bernie" Madoff. Madoff (Figure 1.7) was the founder of an investment firm, Bernard L. Madoff Investment Securities. The original mission of the firm was to provide financial advice and investment services to clients. This is a valuable service to many people because of the complexity of financial investments and retirement planning. Many people rely on financial professionals, like Bernie Madoff, to help them create wealth and be in a position to retire comfortably. Unfortunately, Madoff took advantage of the trust of his investors and was ultimately convicted of stealing (embezzling) over $50 billion (a low amount by some estimates). Madoff's embezzlement remains one of the biggest financial frauds in US history.

3 U.S. Securities and Exchange Commission. "What We Do." June 10, 2013. https://www.sec.gov/Article/whatwedo.html

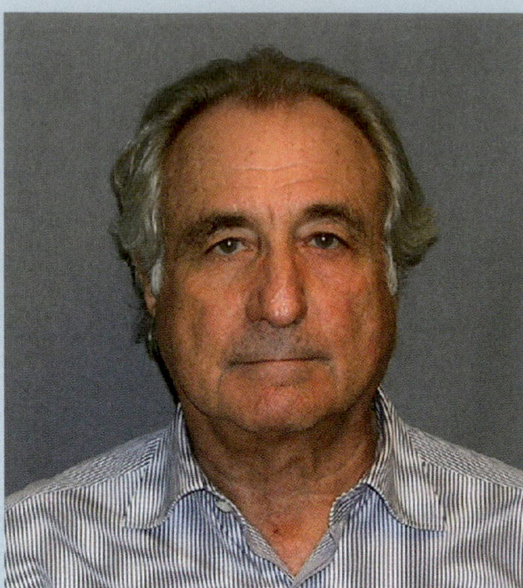

Figure 1.7 Bernie Madoff. Bernie Madoff's mug shot upon being arrested in March 2009. (credit: "BernardMadoff" by U.S. Department of Justice/Wikimedia Commons, Public Domain)

The fraud scheme was initially uncovered by a financial analyst named Harry Markopolos. Markopolos became suspicious because Madoff's firm purported to achieve for its investors abnormally high rates of return for an extended period of time. After analyzing the investment returns, Markopolos reported the suspicious activity to the Securities and Exchange Commission (SEC), which has enforcement responsibility for firms providing investment services. While Madoff was initially able to stay a few steps ahead of the SEC, he was charged in 2009 and will spend the rest of his life in prison.

There are many resources to explore the Madoff scandal. You might be interested in reading the book, *No One Would Listen: A True Financial Thriller*, written by Harry Markopolos. A movie and a TV series have also been made about the Madoff scandal.

In addition to governmental and regulatory agencies at the federal level, many state and local agencies use financial information to accomplish the mission of protecting the public interest. The primary goals are to ensure the financial information is prepared according to the relevant rules or practices as well as to ensure funds are being used in an efficient and transparent manner. For example, local school district administrators should ensure that financial information is available to the residents and is presented in an unbiased manner. The residents want to know their tax dollars are not being wasted. Likewise, the school district administrators want to demonstrate they are using the funding in an efficient and effective manner. This helps ensure a good relationship with the community that fosters trust and support for the school system.

Customers

Depending on the perspective, the term *customers* can have different meanings. Consider for a moment a retail store that sells electronics. That business has customers that purchase its electronics. These customers are considered the end users of the product. The customers, knowingly or unknowingly, have a stake in the financial performance of the business. The customers benefit when the business is financially successful. Profitable businesses will continue to sell the products the customers want, maintain and improve the business facilities, provide employment for community members, and undertake many other activities that contribute to a vibrant and thriving community.

Businesses are also customers. In the example of the electronics store, the business purchases its products from other businesses, including the manufacturers of the electronics. Just as end-user customers have a vested interest in the financial success of the business, business customers also benefit from suppliers that have financial success. A supplier that is financially successful will help ensure the electronics will continue to be available to purchase and resell to the end-use customer, investments in emerging technologies will be made, and improvements in delivery and customer service will result. This, in turn, helps the retail electronics store remain cost competitive while being able to offer its customers a wide variety of products.

Managers and Other Employees

Employees have a strong interest in the financial performance of the organizations for which they work. At the most basic level, employees want to know their jobs will be secure so they can continue to be paid for their work. In addition, employees increase their value to the organization through their years of service, improving knowledge and skills, and accepting positions of increased responsibility. An organization that is financially successful is able to reward employees for that commitment to the organization through bonuses and increased pay.

In addition to promotional and compensation considerations, managers and others in the organization have the responsibility to make day-to-day and long-term (strategic) decisions for the organization. Understanding financial information is vital to making good organizational decisions.

Not all decisions, however, are based on strictly financial information. Recall that managers and other decision makers often use nonfinancial, or managerial, information. These decisions take into account other relevant factors that may not have an immediate and direct link to the financial reports. It is important to understand that sound organizational decisions are often (and should be) based on both financial and nonfinancial information.

In addition to exploring managerial accounting concepts, you will also learn some of the common techniques that are used to analyze the financial reports of businesses. Appendix A further explores these techniques and how stakeholders can use these techniques for making financial decisions.

IFRS CONNECTION

Introduction to International Financial Reporting Standards (IFRS)

In the past fifty years, rapid advances in communications and technology have led the economy to become more global with companies buying, selling, and providing services to customers all over the world. This increase in globalization creates a greater need for users of financial information to be able to compare and evaluate global companies. Investors, creditors, and management may encounter a need to assess a company that operates outside of the United States.

For many years, the ability to compare financial statements and financial ratios of a company headquartered in the United States with a similar company headquartered in another country, such as Japan, was challenging, and only those educated in the accounting rules of both countries could easily handle the comparison. Discussions about creating a common set of international accounting standards that would apply to all publicly traded companies have been occurring since the 1950s and post–World War II economic growth, but only minimal progress was made. In 2002, the Financial Accounting Standards Board (FASB) and the International Accounting Standards Board (IASB) began working more closely together to create a common set of accounting rules. Since 2002, the two organizations have released many accounting standards that are identical or similar, and they continue to work toward unifying or aligning standards, thus improving financial statement comparability between countries.

Why create a common set of international standards? As previously mentioned, the global nature of business has increased the need for comparability across companies in different countries. Investors in the United States may want to choose between investing in a US-based company or one based in France. A US company may desire to buy out a company located in Brazil. A Mexican-based company may desire to borrow money from a bank in London. These types of activities require knowledge of financial statements. Prior to the creation of IFRS, most countries had their own form of generally accepted accounting principles (GAAP). This made it difficult for an investor in the United States to analyze or understand the financials of a France-based company or for a bank in London to know all of the nuances of financial statements from a Mexican company. Another reason common international rules are important is the need for similar reporting for similar business models. For example, Nestlé and the Hershey Company are in different countries yet have similar business models; the same applies to Daimler and Ford Motor Company. In these and other instances, despite the similar business models, for many years these companies reported their results differently because they were governed by different GAAP—Nestlé by French GAAP, Daimler by German GAAP, and both the Hershey Company and Ford Motor Company by US GAAP. Wouldn't it make sense that these companies should report the results of their operations in a similar manner since their business models are similar? The globalization of the economy and the need for similar reporting across business models are just two of the reasons why the push for unified standards took a leap forward in the early twenty-first century.

Today, more than 120 countries have adopted all or most of IFRS or permit the use of IFRS for financial reporting. The United States, however, has not adopted IFRS as an acceptable method of GAAP for financial statement preparation and presentation purposes but has worked closely with the IASB. Thus, many US standards are very comparable to the international standards. Interestingly, the Securities and Exchange Commission (SEC) allows foreign companies that are traded on US exchanges to present their statements under IFRS rules without restating to US GAAP. This occurred in 2009 and was an important move by the SEC to show solidarity toward creating financial statement comparability across countries.

Throughout this text, "IFRS Connection" feature boxes will discuss the important similarities and most significant differences between reporting using US GAAP as created by FASB and IFRS as created by IASB. For now, know that it is important for anyone in business, not just accountants, to be aware of some of the primary similarities and differences between IFRS and US GAAP, because these differences can impact analysis and decision-making.

1.5 Describe the Varied Career Paths Open to Individuals with an Accounting Education

There are often misunderstandings on what exactly accountants do or what attributes are necessary for a successful career in accounting. Often, people perceive accountants as "number-crunchers" or "bean counters" who sit behind a desk, working with numbers, and having little interaction with others. The fact is that this perception could not be further from the truth.

Personal Attributes

While it is true that accountants often work independently, much of the work that accountants undertake involves interactions with other people. In fact, accountants frequently need to gather information from others and explain complex financial concepts to others, making excellent written and verbal communication skills a must. In addition, accountants often deal with strict deadlines such as tax filings, making prioritizing work commitments and being goal oriented necessities. In addition to these skills, traditionally, an accountant can be described as someone who

- is goal oriented,
- is a problem solver,
- is organized and analytical,
- has good interpersonal skills,
- pays attention to detail,
- has good time-management skills, and
- is outgoing.

The Association of Chartered Certified Accountants (ACCA), the governing body of the global Chartered Certified Accountant (CCA) designation, and the Institute of Management Accountants (IMA), the governing body of the Certified Management Accountant (CMA) designation, conducted a study to research the skills accountants will need given a changing economic and technological context. The findings indicate that, in addition to the traditional personal attributes, accountants should possess "traits such as entrepreneurship, curiosity, creativity, and strategic thinking."[4]

Education

Entry-level positions in the accounting profession usually require a minimum of a bachelor's degree. For advanced positions, firms may consider factors such as years of experience, professional development, certifications, and advanced degrees, such as a master's or doctorate. The specific factors regarding educational requirements depend on the industry and the specific business.

After earning a bachelor's degree, many students decide to continue their education by earning a master's degree. A common question for students is when to begin a master's program, either entering a master's program immediately after earning a bachelor's degree or first entering the profession and pursuing a master's at a later point. On one hand, there are benefits of entering into a master's program immediately after earning a bachelor's degree, mainly that students are already into the rhythm of being a full-time student so an additional year or so in a master's program is appealing. On the other hand, entering the profession directly after earning a bachelor's degree allows the student to gain valuable professional experience that may enrich the graduate education experience. When to enter a graduate program is not an easy decision. There are pros and cons to either position. In essence, the final decision depends on the personal perspective and alternatives available to the individual student. For example, one student might not

4 The Association of Chartered Certified Accountants (ACCA) and The Association of Accountants and Financial Professionals in Business (IMA). "100 Drivers of Change for the Global Accountancy Profession." September 2012. https://www.imanet.org/insights-and-trends/the-future-of-management-accounting/100-drivers-of-change-for-the-global-accountancy-profession?ssopc=1

have the financial resources to continue immediately on to graduate school and will first need to work to fund additional education, while another student might have outside suppliers of resources or is considering taking on additional student loan debt. The best recommendation for these students is to consider all of the factors and realize that they must make the final decision as to their own best alternative. It is also important to note that if one makes the decision to enter public accounting, as all states require 150 hours of education to earn a Certified Public Accountant (CPA) license, it is customary for regional and national public accounting firms to require a master's degree or 150 hours earned by other means as a condition for employment; this may influence your decision to enter a master's degree program as soon as the bachelor's degree is complete.

Related Careers

An accounting degree is a valuable tool for other professions too. A thorough understanding of accounting provides the student with a comprehensive understanding of business activity and the importance of financial information to make informed decisions. While an accounting degree is a necessity to work in the accounting profession, it also provides a solid foundation for other careers, such as financial analysts, personal financial planners, and business executives. The number of career options may seem overwhelming at this point, and a career in the accounting profession is no exception. The purpose of this section is to simply highlight the vast number of options that an accounting degree offers. In the workforce, accounting professionals can find a career that best fits their interests.

Students may also be interested in learning more about professional certifications in the areas of financial analysis (Chartered Financial Analyst) and personal financial planning (Certified Financial Planner), which are discussed later in this section.

Major Categories of Accounting Functions

It is a common perception that an accounting career means preparing tax returns. While numerous accountants do prepare tax returns, many people are surprised to learn of the variety of career paths that are available within the accounting profession. An accounting degree is a valuable tool that gives accountants a high level of flexibility and many options. Often individual accountants apply skills in several of the following career paths simultaneously. Figure 1.8 illustrates some of the many career paths open to accounting students.

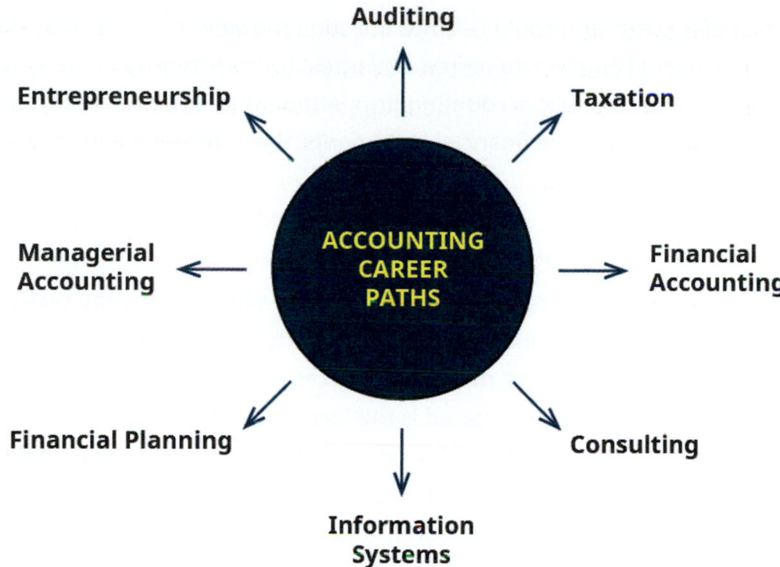

Figure 1.8 Career Paths. There are many career paths open to students of accounting. (attribution: Copyright Rice University, OpenStax, under CC BY-NC-SA 4.0 license)

Auditing

Auditing, which is performed by accountants with a specialized skill set, is the process of ensuring activities are carried out as intended or designed. There are many examples of the functions that auditors perform. For example, in a manufacturing company, auditors may sample products and assess whether or not the products conform to the customer specifications. As another example, county auditors may test pumps at gas stations to ensure the pumps are delivering the correct amount of gasoline and charging customers correctly.

Companies should develop policies and procedures to help ensure the company's goals are being met and the assets are protected. This is called the internal control system. To help maintain the effectiveness of the internal control system, companies often hire internal auditors, who evaluate internal controls through reviews and tests. For example, internal auditors may review the process of how cash is handled within a business. In this scenario, the goal of the company is to ensure that all cash payments are properly applied to customer accounts and that all funds are properly deposited into the company's bank account. As another example, internal auditors may review the shipping and receiving process to ensure that all products shipped or received have the proper paperwork and the product is handled and stored properly. While internal auditors also often work to ensure compliance with external regulations, the primary goal of internal auditors is to help ensure the company policies are followed, which helps the company attain its strategic goals and protect its assets. The professional certification most relevant to a career in internal audit is the Certified Internal Auditor (CIA). Financial fraud occurs when an individual or individuals act with intent to deceive for a financial gain. A Certified Fraud Examiner (CFE) is trained to prevent fraud from occurring and to detect when fraud has occurred. A thorough discussion of the internal control system and the role of accountants occurs in Fraud, Internal Controls, and Cash.

Companies also want to ensure the financial statements provided to outside parties such as banks, governmental agencies, and the investing public are reliable and consistent. That is, companies have a desire to provide financial statements that are free of errors or fraud. Since internal auditors are committed to providing unbiased financial information, it would be possible for the company to use internal auditors to attest to the integrity of the company's financial statements. With that said, doing so presents the appearance of a *possibility* of a conflict of interest and could call into question the validity of the financial statements. Therefore, companies hire external auditors to review and attest to the integrity of the financial statements. External auditors typically work for a public accounting firm. Although the public accounting firm is hired by the company to attest to the fairness of the financial statements, the external auditors are independent of the company and provide an unbiased opinion.

Taxation

There are many taxes that businesses are required to pay. Examples include income taxes, payroll and related taxes such as workers' compensation and unemployment, property and inventory taxes, and sales and use taxes. In addition to making the tax payments, many of the taxes require tax returns and other paperwork to be completed. Making things even more complicated is the fact that taxes are levied at the federal, state, and local levels. For larger worldwide companies, the work needed to meet their international tax compliance requirements can take literally thousands of hours of accountants' time. To sum up the process, the goal of tax accountants is to help ensure the taxes are paid properly and in a timely manner, from an individual level all the way to the company level (including at the level of such companies as Apple and Walmart).

Since accountants have an understanding of various tax laws and filing deadlines, they are also well-positioned to offer tax planning advice. Tax laws are complex and change frequently; therefore, it is helpful for businesses to include tax considerations in their short- and long-term planning. Accountants are a valuable resource in helping businesses minimize the tax liability.

Many businesses find it necessary to employ accountants to work on tax compliance and planning on a full-time basis. Other businesses need these services on a periodic (quarterly or annual) basis and hire external accountants accordingly.

Financial Accounting

Financial accounting measures, in dollars, the activities of an organization. Financial accounting is historical in nature and is prepared using standard conventions, called accounting standards or GAAP. Because nearly every activity in an organization has a financial implication, financial accounting might be thought of as a "monetary scorecard."

Financial accounting is used internally by managers and other decision makers to validate activities that were done well and to highlight areas that need adjusted in the future. Businesses often use discretion as to how much and with whom financial accounting information is shared.

Financial accounting is also provided to those outside the organization. For a publicly traded company, issuing financial statements is required by the SEC. Sharing financial information for a privately held company is usually reserved for those instances where the information is required, such as for audits or obtaining loans.

Consulting

Because nearly every activity within an organization has a financial implication, accountants have a unique opportunity to gain a comprehensive view of an organization. Accountants are able to see how one area of a business affects a different aspect of the business. As accountants gain experience in the profession, this unique perspective allows them to build a "knowledge database" that is valuable to businesses. In this capacity, accountants can provide **consulting** services, which means giving advice or guidance to managers and other decision makers on the impact (both financial and nonfinancial) of a potential course of action. This role allows the organization to gain knowledge from the accountants in a way that minimizes risk and/or financial investment.

As discussed previously, accountants may advise a business on tax-related issues. Other examples of consultative services that accountants perform include selection and installation of computer software applications and other technology considerations, review of internal controls, determination of compliance with relevant laws and regulations, review of compensation and incentive arrangements, and consideration of operational efficiencies within the production process.

Accounting Information Services

Computers are an integral part of business. Computers and related software programs allow companies to efficiently record, store, and process valuable data and information relevant to the business. Accountants are often an integral part of the selection and maintenance of the company's computerized accounting and information system. The goal of the accounting information system is to efficiently provide relevant information to internal decision makers, and it is important for businesses to stay abreast of advances in technology and invest in those technologies that help the business remain efficient and competitive.

Significant growth is expected in accounting information systems careers. According to the US Bureau of Labor Statistics, in 2010 there were over 130,000 jobs in the accounting informations systems sector, with over 49% growth expected through 2024. Median earnings in this field were over $73,000 in 2011.[5] For those interested in both accounting and computer information systems, there are tremendous career opportunities.

CONCEPTS IN PRACTICE

Enterprise Resource Planning

As companies grow in size and expand geographically, it is important to assess whether or not a current computerized system is *the right size and fit* for the organization. For example, a company with a single location can easily manage its business activities with a small, off-the-shelf software package such as QuickBooks and software applications such as Microsoft Excel. A company's computer system becomes more complex when additional locations are added.

5 Lauren Csorny. "Careers in the Growing Field of Information Technology Services." Bureau of Labor Statistics/U.S. Department of Labor. April 2013. https://www.bls.gov/opub/btn/volume-2/careers-in-growing-field-of-information-technology-services.htm

Figure 1.9 Growth. (credit: "Statistics Arrows Trends" by "geralt"/Pixabay, CC0)

As companies continue to grow, larger integrated computer systems, called enterprise resource planning (ERP) systems, may be implemented. Enterprise resource planning systems are designed to maintain the various aspects of the business within a single integrated computer system. For example, a leading ERP system is Microsoft Dynamics GP. Microsoft Dynamics GP is an integrated sytem with the capability to handle the human resource management, production, accounting, manufacturing, and many other aspects of a business. ERP systems, like Microsoft Dynamics GP, are also designed to accommodate companies that have international locations. The benefit of ERP systems is that information is efficiently stored and utilized across the entire business in real time.

Cost and Managerial Accounting

Cost accounting and managerial accounting are related, but different, types of accounting. In essence, a primary distinction between the two functions is that cost accounting takes a primarily quantitative approach, whereas managerial accounting takes both quantitative and qualitative approaches. The goal of cost accounting is to determine the costs involved with providing goods and services. In a manufacturing business, **cost accounting** is the recording and tracking of costs such as direct materials, employee wages, and supplies used in the manufacturing process.

Managerial accounting uses cost accounting and other financial accounting information, as well as nonfinancial information, to make short-term as well as strategic and other long-term decisions for a business.

Both cost and managerial accounting are intended to be used inside a business. Along with financial accounting information, managers and other decision makers within a business use the information to facilitate decision-making, develop long-term plans, and perform other functions necessary for the success of the business.

There are two major differences between cost and managerial accounting and financial accounting. Whereas financial accounting requires the use of standard accounting conventions (also called accounting standards or GAAP), there are no such requirements for cost and managerial accounting. In practice, management has different needs that require cost and managerial accounting information. In addition, financial information is prepared in specific intervals of time, usually monthly. The same is not true with cost and managerial accounting, which are prepared on an as-needed basis that is not reported as specific periods of time.

An example may be helpful in clarifying the difference between cost and managerial accounting. Manufacturing companies often face the decision of whether to make certain components or purchase the components from an outside supplier. Cost accounting would calculate the cost of each alternative. Managerial accounting would use that cost and supplement the cost with nonfinancial information to arrive at a decision. Let's say the cost accountants determine that a company would save $0.50 per component if the units were purchased from an outside supplier rather than being produced by the company. Managers would use the $0.50 per piece savings as well as nonfinancial considerations, such as the impact on the morale of current employees and the supplier's ability to produce a quality product, to make a decision whether or not to purchase the component from the outside supplier.

In summary, it may be helpful to think of cost accounting as a subset of managerial accounting. Another way to think about cost and managerial accounting is that the result of cost accounting is a number, whereas the result of managerial accounting is a decision.

Financial Planning

While accountants spend much of their time interacting with other people, a large component of their work involves numbers and finances. As mentioned previously, many people with an interest in data often go into the accounting profession and have a natural inclination toward solving problems. In addition, accountants also gain a comprehensive view of business. They understand how the diverse aspects of the business are connected and how those activities ultimately have a financial impact on the organization.

These attributes allow accountants to offer expertise in financial planning, which takes many forms. Within a business, making estimates and establishing a plan for the future—called a budget—are vital. These actions allow the business to determine the appropriate level of activity and make any adjustments accordingly. Training in accounting is also helpful for those who offer financial planning for individuals. When it comes to investing and saving for the future, there are many options available to individuals. Investing is complicated, and many people want help from someone who understands the complexities of the investment options, the tax implications, and ways to invest and build wealth. Accountants are well trained to offer financial planning services to the businesses they work with as well as individuals investing for their future.

Entrepreneurship

Many people have an idea for a product or service and decide to start their own business—they are often labeled as entrepreneurs. These individuals have a passion for their product or service and are experts at what they do. But that is not enough. In order for the business to be successful, the entrepreneur must understand all aspects of the business, including and especially the financial aspect. It is important for the entrepreneur to understand how to obtain the funding to start the business, measure the financial performance of the business, and know what adjustments to improve the performance of the business are necessary and when to make them. Understanding accounting, or hiring accountants who can perform these activities, is valuable to the entrepreneur. An entrepreneur works extremely hard and has often taken a great risk in starting his or her own business. Understanding the financial performance of the business helps ensure the business is successful.

CONCEPTS IN PRACTICE

Entrepreneurship

Entrepreneurs do not have to develop a brand new product or service in order to open their own business. Often entrepreneurs decide to purchase a store from a business that already exists. This is called a franchise arrangement. In these arrangements, the business owner (the franchisee) typically pays the franchisor (the business offering the franchise opportunity) a lump sum at the beginning of the arrangement. This lump sum payment allows the franchisee an opportunity to use the store logos and receive training, consulting, and other support from the franchisor. A series of scheduled payments is also common. The ongoing payments are often based on a percentage of the franchise store's sales.

The franchise arrangement is beneficial to both parties. For the franchisee, there is less risk involved because they often purchase a franchise from a business with an established track record of success. For the franchisor, it is an opportunity to build the brand without the responsbility of direct oversight for individual stores—each franchise is independently owned and operated (a phrase you might see on franchise stores).

The downside of the franchising arrangement is the amount of money that is paid to the franchisor through the initial lump sum as well as continued payments. These costs, however, are necessary for the ongoing support from the franchisor. In addition, franchisees often have restrictions relative to product pricing and offerings, geographic locations, and approved suppliers.

According to Entrepreneur.com, based on factors such as costs and fees, support, and brand strength, the number one–ranking franchise in 2017 was 7-Eleven, Inc. According to the website, 7-Eleven has been franchising since 1964 and has 61,086 franchise stores worldwide (7,025 are located in the United States). In addition, 7-Eleven has 1,019 company-owned stores.[6]

Major Categories of Employers

Now that you've learned about the various career paths that accountants can take, let's briefly look at the types of organizations that accountants can work for. Figure 1.10 illustrates some common types of employers that require accountants. While this is not an all-inclusive list, most accountants in the profession are employed by these types of organizations.

6 "7-Eleven." Entrepreneur.com. n.d. https://www.entrepreneur.com/franchises/7eleveninc/282052

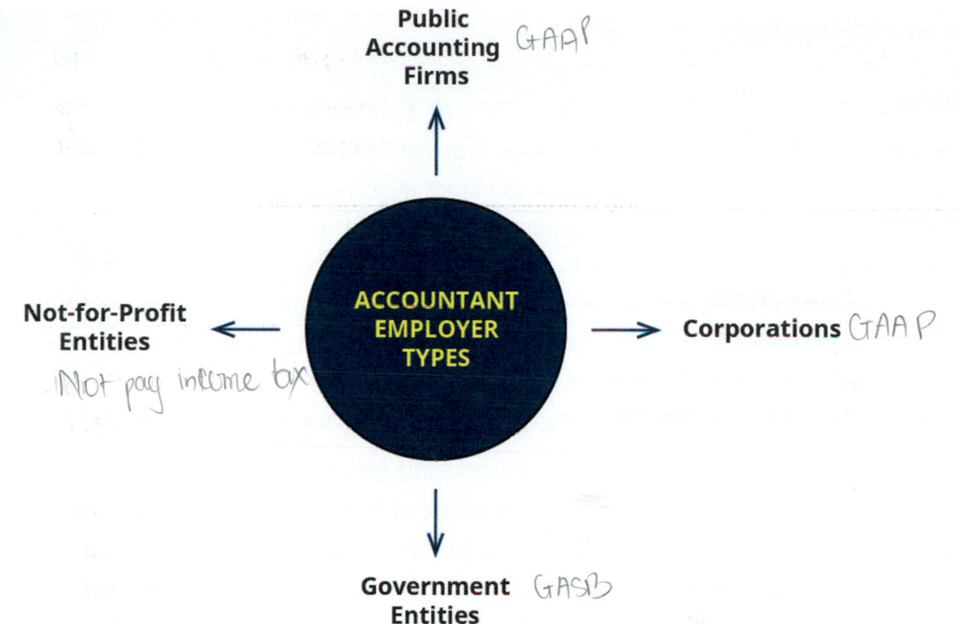

Figure 1.10 Accountant Employer Types. Accountants may find employment within a variety of types of entities. (attribution: Copyright Rice University, OpenStax, under CC BY-NC-SA 4.0 license)

Public Accounting Firms

Public accounting firms offer a wide range of accounting, auditing, consulting, and tax preparation services to their clients. A small business might use a public accounting firm to prepare the monthly or quarterly financial statements and/or the payroll. A business (of any size) might hire the public accounting firm to audit the company financial statements or verify that policies and procedures are being followed properly. Public accounting firms may also offer consulting services to their clients to advise them on implementing computerized systems or strengthening the internal control system. (Note that you will learn in your advanced study of accounting that accountants have legal limitations on what consulting services they can provide to their clients.) Public accounting firms also offer tax preparation services for their business and individual clients. Public accounting firms may also offer business valuation, forensic accounting (financial crimes), and other services.

Public accounting firms are often categorized based on the size (revenue). The biggest firms are referred to as the "Big Four" and include Deloitte Touche Tohmatsu Limited (DTTL), PricewaterhouseCoopers (PwC), Ernst & Young (EY), and KPMG. Following the Big Four in size are firms such as RSM US, Grant Thornton, BDO USA, Crowe, and CliftonLarsonAllen (CLA).[7] There are also many other regional and local public accounting firms.

Public accounting firms often expect the accountants they employ to have earned (or will earn) the Certified Public Accountant (CPA) designation. It is not uncommon for public accounting firms to specialize. For example, some public accounting firms may specialize in serving clients in the banking or aerospace industries. In addition to specializing in specific industries, public accounting firms may also specialize in areas of accounting such as tax compliance and planning.

Hiring public accounting firms to perform various services is an attractive option for many businesses. The primary benefit is that the business has access to experts in the profession without needing to hire accounting

7 "2017 Top 100 Firms." *Accounting Today*. 2017. https://lscpagepro.mydigitalpublication.com/publication/?i=390208#{%22issue_id%22:390208,%22page%22:0}

specialists on a full-time basis.

Corporations

Corporations hire accountants to perform various functions within the business. The primary responsibility of corporate accountants (which include cost and managerial accountants) is to provide information for internal users and decision makers, as well as implement and monitor internal controls. The information provided by corporate accountants takes many forms. For example, some of the common responsibilities of corporate accountants include calculating and tracking the costs of providing goods and services, analyzing the financial performance of the business in comparison to expectations, and developing budgets, which help the company plan for future operations and make any necessary adjustments. In addition, many corporate accountants have the responsibility for or help with the company's payroll and computer network.

In smaller corporations, an accountant may be responsible for or assist with several of these activities. In larger firms, however, accountants may specialize in one of the areas of responsibilities and may rotate responsibilities throughout their career. Many larger firms also use accountants as part of the internal audit function. In addition, many large companies are able to dedicate resources to making the organization more efficient. Programs such as Lean Manufacturing and Six Sigma focus on reducing waste and eliminating cost within the organization. Accountants trained in these techniques receive specialized training that focuses on the cost impact of the activities of the business.

As with many organizations, professional certifications are highly valued in corporations. The primary certification for corporate accounting is the Certified Management Accountant (CMA). Because corporations also undertake financial reporting and related activities, such as tax compliance, corporations often hire CPAs.

Governmental Entities

Accountants in governmental entities perform many of the same functions as accountants in public accounting firms and corporations. The primary goal of **governmental accounting** is to ensure proper tracking of the inflows and outflows of taxpayer funds using the proscribed standards. Some governmental accountants also prepare and may also audit the work of other governmental agencies to ensure the funds are properly accounted for. The major difference between accountants in governmental entities and accountants working in public accounting firms and corporations relates to the specific rules by which the financial reporting must be prepared. Whereas as accountants in public accounting firms and corporations use GAAP, governmental accounting is prepared under a different set of rules that are specific to governmental agencies, as previously referred to as the Governmental Accounting Standards Board (GASB). Students continuing their study of accounting may take specific courses related to governmental accounting.

Accountants in the governmental sector may also work in specialized areas. For example, many accountants work for tax agencies at the federal, state, and local levels to ensure the tax returns prepared by businesses and individuals comply with the tax code appropriate for the particular jurisdiction. As another example, accountants employed by the SEC may investigate instances where financial crimes occur, as in the case of Bernie Madoff, which was discussed in Concepts in Practice: Financial Professionals and Fraud.

CONCEPTS IN PRACTICE

Bringing Down Capone

Al Capone was one of the most notorious criminals in American history. Born in 1899 in Brooklyn, New York, Al Capone rose to fame as a gangster in Chicago during the era of Prohibition. By the late 1920s–1930s, Capone controlled a syndicate with a reported annual income of $100 million.

Al Capone was credited for many murders, including masterminding the famous 1929 St. Valentine's Day murder, which killed seven rival gang members. But law enforcement was unable to convict Capone for the murders he committed or orchestrated. Through bribes and extortion, Capone was able to evade severe punishment, being charged at one point with gun possession and serving a year in jail.

Capone's luck ran out in 1931 when he was convicted of federal tax evasion. In 1927, the United States Supreme Court ruled that earnings from illegal activities were taxable. Capone, however, did not claim the illegal earnings on his 1928 and 1929 income tax returns and was subsequently sentenced to eleven years in prison. Up to that point, it was the longest-ever sentence for tax evasion.

Al Capone was paroled from prison in November 1939 and died on January 25, 1947. His life has been the subject of many articles, books, movies including *Scarface* (1932), and the TV series *The Untouchables* (1993).

Those interested in stories like this might consider working for the Federal Bureau of Investigation (FBI). According to the FBI, as of 2012, approximately 15% of FBI agents are special agent accountants.

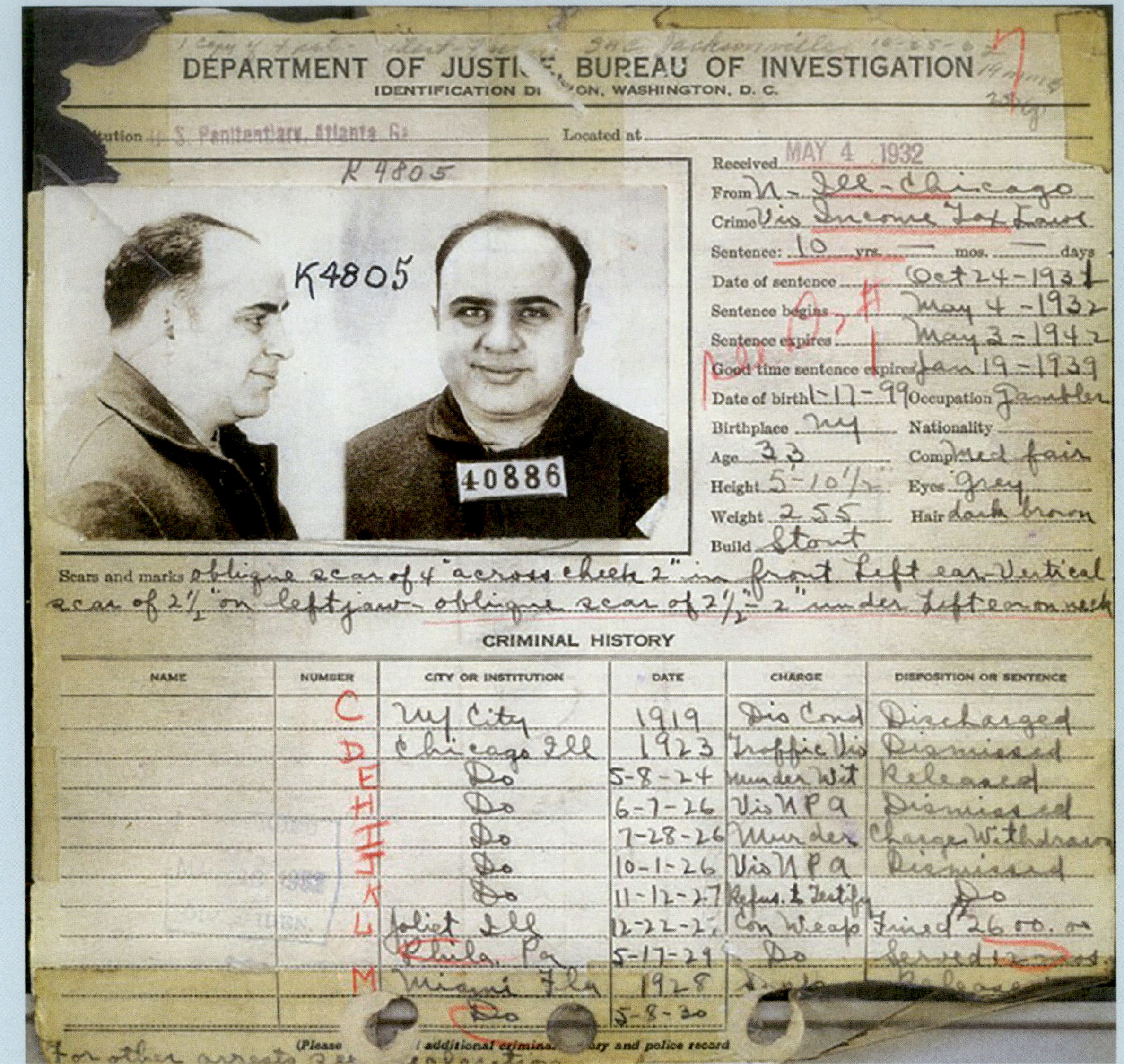

DEPARTMENT OF JUSTI[illegible]E, BUREAU OF INVESTIGATION
IDENTIFICATION DI[illegible]ON, WASHINGTON, D. C.

...tution U. S. Penitentiary, Atlanta Ga. Located at

K 4805

K4805

40886

Received MAY 4 1932
From N. Ill. Chicago
Crime Vio Income Tax Laws
Sentence: 10 yrs. — mos. — days
Date of sentence Oct 24-1931
Sentence begins May 4-1932
Sentence expires May 3-1942
Good time sentence expires Jan 19-1939
Date of birth 1-17-99 Occupation Gambler
Birthplace NY Nationality
Age 33 Comp Med fair
Height 5-10 1/2 Eyes grey
Weight 255 Hair dark brown
Build Stout

Scars and marks oblique scar of 4" across cheek 2" in front left ear. Vertical scar of 2 1/2" on left jaw. oblique scar of 2 1/2 - 2" under left ear on neck

CRIMINAL HISTORY

NAME	NUMBER	CITY OR INSTITUTION	DATE	CHARGE	DISPOSITION OR SENTENCE
	C	NY City	1919	Dis Cond	Discharged
	D	Chicago Ill	1923	Traffic Vio	Dismissed
	E	Do	5-8-24	Murder Wit	Released
	H	Do	6-7-26	Vio NPA	Dismissed
	I	Do	7-28-26	Murder	Charge Withdrawn
	J	Do	10-1-26	Vio NPA	Dismissed
	K	Do	11-12-27	Refus. to Testify	Do
	L	Joliet Ill	12-22-27	Con Weap	Fined 2600.00
		Phila. Pa	5-17-29	Do	Served 12 mos.
	M	Miami Fla	1928	[illegible]	Release[illegible]
		Do	5-8-30		

(Please [illegible] additional crimina[illegible] ory and police record

Figure 1.11 Al Capone. The FBI's 1932 criminal record on Al Capone shows the many charges against him, most of which were dismissed. (credit: modification of "Capone's criminal record in 1932" by FBI/ United States Bureau of Prisons/Wikimedia Commons, Public Domain)

Not-for-Profit Entities, Including Charities, Foundations, and Universities

Not-for-profit entities include charitable organizations, foundations, and universities. Unlike for-profit entities, not-for-profit organizations have a primary focus of a particular mission. Therefore, **not-for-profit (NFP) accounting** helps ensure that donor funds are used for the intended mission. Much like accountants in governmental entities, accountants in not-for-profit entities use a slightly different type of accounting than other types of businesses, with the primary difference being that not-for-profit entities typically do not pay income taxes.

However, even if a not-for-profit organization is not subjected to income taxes in a particular year, it generally must file informational returns, such as a Form 990, with the Internal Revenue Service (IRS). Information, such as sources and amounts of funding and major types and amounts of expenditures, is documented by the not-for-profit entities to provide information for potential and current donors. Once filed with the IRS, Form 990 is available for public view so that the public can monitor how the specific charity uses proceeds as well as its operational efficiency.

Potential Certifications for Accountants

As previously discussed, the study of accounting serves as a foundation for other careers that are similar to accounting, and the certifications described here reflect that relationship.

There are many benefits to attaining a professional certification (or multiple certifications) in addition to a college degree. Certifications often cover material at a deeper and more complex level than might typically be covered in a college program. Those earning a professional certification demonstrate their willingness to invest the additional time and energy into becoming experts in the particular field. Because of this, employees with professional certifications are often in higher demand and earn higher salaries than those without professional certifications. Companies also benefit by having employees with professional certifications. A well-trained staff with demonstrated expertise conveys a level of professionalism that gives the organization a competitive advantage. In addition, professional certifications often require a certain number of hours of ongoing training. This helps ensure that the certificate holder remains informed as to the current advances within the profession and benefits both the employee and the employer.

Certifications are developed and governed by the respective governing body. Each issuing body establishes areas of content and requirements for the specific certification. Links to the particular websites are provided so you can easily gain additional information.

It is also important to note that many of the certifications have review courses available. The review courses help students prepare for the exam by offering test-taking strategies, practice questions and exams, and other materials that help students efficiently and effectively prepare for the exams.

ETHICAL CONSIDERATIONS

Accounting Codes of Ethics

In the United States, accountants can obtain a number of different certifications and can be licensed by each state to practice as a Certified Public Accountant (CPA). Accountants can also belong to professional organizations that have their own codes of conduct. As the online Stanford Encyclopedia of Philosophy explains, "many people engaged in business activity, including accountants and lawyers, are professionals. As such, they are bound by codes of conduct promulgated by professional societies. Many firms also have detailed codes of conduct, developed and enforced by teams of ethics and compliance personnel."[8] CPAs can find a code of ethics in each state of practice and with the AICPA.[9] Certifications such as the CMA, CIA, CFE, CFA, and CFP each have their own codes of ethics.

To facilitate cross-border business activities and accounting, an attempt has been made to set international standards. To this end, accounting standards organizations in more than 100 countries use the International Federation of Accountants' (IFAC) Code of Ethics for Professional Accountants."[10]

When auditing a public company, CPAs may also have to follow a special code of ethics created by the Public Company Accounting Oversight Board (PCAOB), or when performing federal tax work, the US Treasury Department's Circular No. 230 code of ethics. These are just some examples of ethical codes that are covered in more detail in this course. Each area of accounting work has its own set of ethical rules, but they all require that a professional accountant perform his or her work with integrity.

Certified Public Accountant (CPA)

The Certified Public Accountant (CPA) designation is earned after passing a uniform exam issued by the American Institute of Certified Public Accountants (AICPA). While the exam is a uniform, nationally administered exam, each state issues and governs CPA licenses.

The CPA exam has four parts: Auditing and Attestation (AUD), Business Environment and Concepts (BEC), Financial Accounting and Reporting (FAR), and Regulation (REG). A score of at least 75% must be earned in order to earn the CPA designation.

Since each state determines the requirements for CPA licenses, students are encouraged to check the state board of accountancy for specific requirements. In Ohio, for example, candidates for the CPA exam must have 150 hours of college credit. Of those, thirty semester hours (or equivalent quarter hours) must be in accounting. Once the CPA designation is earned in Ohio, 120 hours of continuing education must be taken over a three-year period in order to maintain the certification. The requirements for the Ohio CPA exam are similar to the requirements for other states. Even though states issue CPA licenses, a CPA will not lose the designation should he or she move to another state. Each state has mobility or reciprocity requirements that allow CPAs to transfer licensure from one state to another. Reciprocity requirements can be obtained by contacting the respective state board of accountancy.

The majority of states require 150 hours of college credit. Students often graduate with a bachelor's degree with approximately 120–130 credit hours. In order to reach the 150-hour requirement that specific states have, students have a couple of options. The extra hours can be earned either by taking additional classes in their undergraduate program or by entering a graduate program, earning a master's degree. Master's degrees that would be most beneficial in an accounting or related field would be a master of accountancy, master in taxation, or a master in analytics, which is rapidly increasing in demand.

LINK TO LEARNING

Information about the Certified Public Accountant (CPA) exam is provided by the following:

- the American Institute of Certified Public Accountants (AICPA) (https://openstax.org/l/50AICPA_CPA)
- the National Association of State Boards of Accountancy (NASBA) (https://openstax.org/l/

8 Jeffrey Moriarty. "Business Ethics." Stanford Encyclopedia of Philosophy. November 17, 2016. https://plato.stanford.edu/entries/ethics-business/

9 American Institute of Certified Public Accountants (AICPA). "AICPA Code of Professional Conduct." n.d. https://www.aicpa.org/research/standards/codeofconduct.html

10 Catherine Allen and Robert Bunting. "A Global Standard for Professional Ethics: Cross-Border Business Concerns." May 2008. https://www.ifrs.com/overview/Accounting_Firms/Global_Standard.html

50NASBA_CPA)
- This Way to CPA (https://openstax.org/l/50ThisWayCPA)

Certified Management Accountant (CMA)

The Certified Management Accountant (CMA) exam is developed and administered by the Institute of Management Accountants (IMA). There are many benefits in earning the CMA designation, including career advancement and earnings potential. Management accountants, among other activities, prepare budgets, perform analysis of financial and operational variances, and determine the cost of providing goods and services. Earning a certification enables the management accountant to advance to management and executive positions within the organization.

The CMA exam has two parts: Financial Reporting, Planning, Performance, and Control (part 1) and Financial Decision-Making (part 2). A score of at least 72% must be earned in order to earn the CMA designation. A minimum of a bachelor's degree is required to take the CMA exam. An accounting degree or a specific number of credit hours in accounting is not required in order to take the CMA exam. Once the CMA designation is earned, thirty hours of continuing education with two of the hours focusing on ethics must be taken annually in order to maintain the certification.

LINK TO LEARNING

Visit the Institute of Management Accountants (IMA)'s page on the Certified Management Accountant (CMA) exam and certification (https://openstax.org/l/50CMAExamIMA) to learn more.

Certified Internal Auditor (CIA)

The Certified Internal Auditor (CIA) exam is developed and administered by the Institute of Internal Auditors (IIA). According to the IIA website, the four-part CIA exam tests "candidates' grasp of internal auditing's role in governance, risk, and control; conducting an audit engagement; business analysis and information technology; and business management skills."[11]

If a candidate does not have a bachelor's degree, eligibility to take the CIA is based on a combination of work experience and education experience. In order to earn the CIA designation, a passing score of 80% is required. After successful passage of the CIA exam, certificate holders are required to earn eighty hours of continuing education credit every two years.[12]

11 The Institute of Internal Auditors. "What Does It Take to Be a Professional?" n.d. https://na.theiia.org/about-ia/PublicDocuments/WDIT_Professional-WEB.pdf

12 The Institute of Internal Auditors. "What Does It Take to Be a Professional?" n.d. https://na.theiia.org/about-ia/PublicDocuments/WDIT_Professional-WEB.pdf

LINK TO LEARNING

Information about the Certified Internal Auditor (CIA) exam is provided by the following:

- the Institute of Internal Auditors (IIA), Global (https://openstax.org/l/50IIAGlobeCIA)
- the Institute of Internal Auditors (IIA), North America (https://openstax.org/l/50IIANorthAmCIA)

Certified Fraud Examiner (CFE)

The Certified Fraud Examiner (CFE) exam is developed and administered by the Association of Certified Fraud Examiners (ACFE). Eligibility to take the CFE is based on a points system based on education and work experience. Candidates with forty points may take the CFE exam, and official certification is earned with fifty points or more. A bachelor's degree, for example, is worth forty points toward eligibility of the fifty-point requirement for the CFE certification. The CFE offers an attractive supplement for students interested in pursuing a career in accounting fraud detection. Students might also consider studying forensic accounting in college. These courses are often offered at the graduate level.

The CFE exam has four parts: Fraud Prevention and Deterrence, Financial Transactions and Fraud Schemes, Investigation, and Law. Candidates must earn a minimum score of 75%. Once the CFE is earned, certificate holders must annually complete at least twenty hours of continuing education. The CFE certification is valued in many organizations, including governmental agencies at the local, state, and federal levels.

LINK TO LEARNING

Visit the Association of Certified Fraud Examiners (ACFE) page on the Certified Fraud Examiner (CFE) exam (https://openstax.org/l/50ACFE_CFEexam) to learn more.

Chartered Financial Analyst (CFA)

The Chartered Financial Analyst (CFA) certification is developed and administered by the CFA Institute. The CFA exam contains three levels (level I, level II, and level III), testing expertise in Investment Tools, Asset Classes, and Portfolio Management. Those with a bachelor's degree are eligible to take the CFA exam. In lieu of a bachelor's degree, work experience or a combination of work experience and education is considered satisfactory for eligibility to take the CFA exam. After taking the exam, candidates receive a "Pass" or "Did Not Pass" result. A passing score is determined by the CFA Institute once the examination has been administered. The passing score threshold is established after considering factors such as exam content and current best practices. After successful passage of all three levels of the CFA examination, chartered members must earn at least twenty hours annually of continuing education, of which two hours must be in Standards, Ethics, and Regulations (SER).

LINK TO LEARNING

Visit the the CFA Institute's page on the Chartered Financial Analyst (CFA) exam (https://openstax.org/l/50CFA_CFAexam) to learn more.

Certified Financial Planner (CFP)

The Certified Financial Planner (CFP) certification is developed and administered by the Certified Financial Planner (CFP) Board of Standards. The CFP exam consists of 170 multiple-choice questions that are taken over two, three-hour sessions. There are several ways in which the eligibility requirements can be met in order to take the CFP exam, which students can explore using the CFP Board of Standards website. As with the Chartered Financial Analyst (CFA) exam, the CFP Board of Standards does not predetermine a passing score but establishes the pass/fail threshold through a deliberative evaluation process. Upon successful completion of the exam, CFPs must obtain thirty hours of continuing education every two years, with two of the hours focused on ethics.

LINK TO LEARNING

Visit the Certified Financial Planners (CFP) Board of Standards page on the the Certified Financial Planner (CFP) exam (https://openstax.org/l/50CFP_CFPexam) to learn more.

Key Terms

accounting process of organizing, analyzing, and communicating financial information that is used for decision-making

auditing process of ensuring activities are carried out as intended or designed

consulting process of giving advice or guidance on financial and nonfinancial impact of a course of action

cost accounting recording and tracking of costs in the manufacturing process

creditor business that grants extended, but short-term, payment terms to other businesses

financial accounting measures the financial performance of an organization using standard conventions to prepare financial reports

Financial Accounting Standards Board (FASB) independent, nonprofit organization that sets financial accounting and reporting standards for both public and private sector businesses in the United States that use Generally Accepted Accounting Principles (GAAP)

for-profit business has the primary purpose of earning a profit by selling goods and services

generally accepted accounting principles (GAAP) common set of rules, standards, and procedures that publicly traded companies must follow when composing their financial statements

governmental accounting process of tracking the inflows and outflows of taxpayer funds using prescribed standards

Governmental Accounting Standards Board (GASB) source of generally accepted accounting principles (GAAP) used by state and local governments in the United States; is a private nongovernmental organization

governmental entity provides services to the general public (taxpayers)

lender bank or other institution that has the primary purpose of lending money

managerial accounting process that allows decision makers to set and evaluate business goals by determining what information they need to make a particular decision and how to analyze and communicate this information

manufacturing business for-profit business that is designed to make a specific product or products

nonprofit (not-for-profit) organization tax-exempt organization that serves its community in a variety of areas

not-for-profit (NFP) accounting including charities, universities, and foundations, helps ensure that donor funds are used for the intended mission of the not-for-profit entity

privately held company company whose stock is available only to employees or select individuals or groups

publicly traded company company whose stock is traded (bought and sold) on an organized stock exchange

retail business for-profit business that purchases products (called inventory) and resells the products without altering them

Securities and Exchange Commission (SEC) federal regulatory agency that regulates corporations with shares listed and traded on security exchanges through required periodic filings

service business business that does not sell tangible products to customers but rather sells intangible benefits (services) to customers; can be either a for-profit or a not-for-profit organization

stakeholder someone affected by decisions made by a company; may include an investor, creditor, employee, manager, regulator, customer, supplier, and layperson

stockholder owner of stock, or shares, in a business

transaction business activity or event that has an effect on financial information presented on financial statements

Summary

1.1 Explain the Importance of Accounting and Distinguish between Financial and Managerial Accounting

- Accounting is the process of organizing, analyzing, and communicating financial information that is used for decision-making.
- Accounting is often called the "language of business."
- Financial accounting measures performance using financial reports and communicates results to those outside of the organization who may have an interest in the company's performance, such as investors and creditors.
- Managerial accounting uses both financial and nonfinancial information to aid in decision-making.

1.2 Identify Users of Accounting Information and How They Apply Information

- The primary goal of accounting is to provide accurate, timely information to decision makers.
- Accountants provide information to internal and external users.
- Financial accounting measures an organization's performance in monetary terms.
- Accountants use common conventions to prepare and convey financial information.
- Financial accounting is historical in nature, but a series of historical events can be useful in establishing predictions.
- Financial accounting is intended for use by both internal and external users.
- Managerial accounting is primarily intended for internal users.

1.3 Describe Typical Accounting Activities and the Role Accountants Play in Identifying, Recording, and Reporting Financial Activities

- Accountants play a vital role in many types of organizations.
- Organizations can be placed into three categories: for profit, governmental, and not for profit.
- For-profit organizations have a primary purpose of earning a profit.
- Governmental entities provide services to the general public, both individuals and organizations.
- Governmental agencies exist at the federal, state, and local levels.
- Not-for-profit entities have the primary purpose of serving a particular interest or need in communities.
- For-profit businesses can be further categorized into manufacturing, retail (or merchandising), and service.
- Manufacturing businesses are for-profit businesses that are designed to make a specific product or products.
- Retail firms purchase products and resell the products without altering the products.
- Service-oriented businesses provide services to customers.

1.4 Explain Why Accounting Is Important to Business Stakeholders

- Stakeholders are persons or groups that rely on financial information to make decisions.
- Stakeholders include stockholders, creditors, governmental and regulatory agencies, customers, and managers and other employees.
- Stockholders are owners of a business.
- Publicly traded companies sell stock (ownership) to the general public.
- Privately held companies offer stock to employees or to select individuals or groups outside the organization.
- Creditors sometimes grant extended payment terms to other businesses, normally for short periods of time, such as thirty to forty-five days.

- Lenders are banks and other institutions that have a primary purpose of lending money for long periods of time.
- Businesses generally have three ways to raise capital (money): profitable operations, selling ownership (called equity financing), and borrowing from lenders (called debt financing).
- In business, profit means the inflows of resources are greater than the outflows of resources.
- Publicly traded companies are required to file with the Securities and Exchange Commission (SEC), a federal government agency charged with protecting the investing public.
- Guidelines for the accounting profession are called accounting standards or generally accepted accounting principles (GAAP).
- The Securities and Exchange Commission (SEC) is responsible for establishing accounting standards for companies whose stocks are traded publicly on a national or regional stock exchange, such as the New York Stock Exchange (NYSE).
- Governmental and regulatory agencies at the federal, state, and local levels use financial information to accomplish the mission of protecting the public interest.
- Customers, employees, and the local community benefit when businesses are financially successful.

1.5 Describe the Varied Career Paths Open to Individuals with an Accounting Education

- It is important for accountants to be well versed in written and verbal communication and possess other nonaccounting skill sets.
- A bachelor's degree is typically required for entry-level work in the accounting profession.
- Advanced degrees and/or professional certifications are beneficial for advancement within the accounting profession.
- Career paths within the accounting profession include auditing, taxation, financial accounting, consulting, accounting information systems, cost and managerial accounting, financial planning, and entrepreneurship.
- Internal control systems help ensure the company's goals are being met and company assets are protected.
- Internal auditors work inside business and evaluate the effectiveness of internal control systems.
- Accountants help ensure the taxes are paid properly and in a timely manner.
- Accountants prepare financial statements that are used by decision makers inside and outside of the organization.
- Accountants can advise managers and other decision makers.
- Accountants are often an integral part of managing a company's computerized accounting and information system.
- Cost accounting determines the costs involved with providing goods and services.
- Managerial accounting incorporates financial and nonfinancial information to make decisions for a business.
- Training in accounting is helpful for financial planning services for businesses and individuals.
- Accounting helps entrepreneurs understand the financial implications of their business.
- Accountants have opportunities to work for many types of organizations, including public accounting firms, corporations, governmental entities, and not-for-profit entities.
- Professional certifications offer many benefits to those in the accounting and related professions.
- Common professional certifications include Certified Public Accountant (CPA), Certified Management Accountant (CMA), Certified Internal Auditor (CIA), Certified Fraud Examiner (CFE), Chartered Financial Analyst (CFA), and Certified Financial Planner (CFP).

Multiple Choice

1. LO 1.2 Accounting is sometimes called the "language of ____."

A. Wall Street
B. business
C. Main Street
D. financial statements

2. LO 1.2 Financial accounting information _______.

A. should be incomplete in order to confuse competitors
B. should be prepared differently by each company
C. provides investors guarantees about the future
D. summarizes what has already occurred

3. LO 1.2 External users of financial accounting information include all of the following *except* _______.

A. lenders such as bankers
B. governmental agencies such as the IRS
C. employees of a business
D. potential investors

4. LO 1.2 Which of the following groups would have access to managerial accounting information?

A. bankers
B. investors
C. competitors of the business
D. managers

5. LO 1.2 All of the following are examples of managerial accounting activities *except* _______.

A. preparing external financial statements in compliance with GAAP
B. deciding whether or not to use automation
C. making equipment repair or replacement decisions
D. deciding whether or not to use automation

6. LO 1.3 Which of the following is *not* true?

A. Organizations share a common purpose or mission.
B. Organizations have inflows and outflows of resources.
C. Organizations add value to society.
D. Organizations need accounting information.

7. LO 1.3 The primary purpose of what type of business is to serve a particular need in the community?

A. for-profit
B. not-for-profit
C. manufacturing
D. retail

8. LO 1.3 Which of the following is *not* an example of a retailer?

A. electronics store
B. grocery store
C. car dealership
D. computer manufacturer
E. jewelry store

9. LO 1.3 A governmental agency can best be described by which of the following statements?

A. has a primary purpose of making a profit
B. has a primary purpose of using taxpayer funds to provide services
C. produces goods for sale to the public
D. has regular shareholder meetings

10. LO 1.3 Which of the following is likely *not* a type of not-for-profit entity?

A. public library
B. community foundation
C. university
D. local movie theater

11. LO 1.4 Which of the following is *not* considered a stakeholder of an organization?

A. creditors
B. lenders
C. employees
D. community residents
E. a business in another industry

12. LO 1.4 Stockholders can best be defined as which of the following?

A. investors who lend money to a business for a short period of time
B. investors who lend money to a business for a long period of time
C. investors who purchase an ownership in the business
D. analysts who rate the financial performance of the business

13. LO 1.4 Which of the following sell stock on an organized stock exchange such as the New York Stock Exchange?

A. publicly traded companies
B. not-for-profit businesses
C. governmental agencies
D. privately held companies
E. government-sponsored entities

14. LO 1.4 All of the following are sustainable methods businesses can use to raise capital (funding) *except* for ______.

A. borrowing from lenders
B. selling ownership shares
C. profitable operations
D. tax refunds

15. LO 1.4 The accounting information of a privately held company is generally available to all of the following *except for* _______.

A. governmental agencies
B. investors
C. creditors and lenders
D. competitors

16. LO 1.5 Which of the following skills/attributes is *not* a primary skill for accountants to possess?

A. written communication
B. verbal communication
C. ability to work independently
D. analytical thinking
E. extensive computer programing background

17. LO 1.5 Which of the following is typically required for entry-level positions in the accounting profession?

A. bachelor's degree
B. master's degree
C. Certified Public Accountant (CPA)
D. Certified Management Accountant (CMA)
E. only a high school diploma

18. LO 1.5 Typical accounting tasks include all of the following tasks *except* _______.

A. auditing
B. recording and tracking costs
C. tax compliance and planning
D. consulting
E. purchasing direct materials

19. LO 1.5 What type of organization primarily offers tax compliance, auditing, and consulting services?

A. corporations
B. public accounting firms
C. governmental entities
D. universities

20. LO 1.5 Most states require 150 semester hours of college credit for which professional certification?

A. Certified Management Accountant (CMA)
B. Certified Internal Auditor (CIA)
C. Certified Public Accountant (CPA)
D. Certified Financial Planner (CFP)

Questions

1. LO 1.2 Research your top five career choices. Identify financial factors that might influence your career choice. The following websites might be helpful in answering this question.

- Occupational Outlook Handbook: https://www.bls.gov/ooh/
- National Association of Colleges and Employers: http://www.naceweb.org/
- O*Net OnLine: https://www.onetonline.org/find/

2. LO 1.2 Using the same top five career choices, identify nonfinancial factors that might influence your career choice. The following websites might be helpful in answering this question.

- Occupational Outlook Handbook: https://www.bls.gov/ooh/
- National Association of Colleges and Employers: http://www.naceweb.org/
- O*Net OnLine: https://www.onetonline.org/find/

3. LO 1.2 Think about a recent purchase you made. Describe what financial and nonfinancial factors went into that purchase. Rank the factors, and explain how you made the final decision to purchase the item.

4. LO 1.2 Computerized accounting systems help businesses efficiently record and utilize financial information. QuickBooks is a popular software package for small businesses. Explore the QuickBooks website at https://quickbooks.intuit.com/. Select one of the QuickBooks plans, and discuss some of the capabilities of the software. Taking the perspective of a small business owner, explain how this software might help the business.

5. LO 1.2 The following information was taken from the Netflix financial statements.

NETFLIX, INC. **Consolidated Statement of Operations** **For the Years 2014, 2015, and 2016**			
	Dec. 31, 2014	**Dec. 31, 2015**	**Dec. 31, 2016**
Sales	$5,504,656*	$6,779,511	$8,830,669
**Dollar values are in thousands of US dollars.*			
Source: United States Security and Exchange Commission. “Netflix, Inc. Consolidated Statements of Operations.” www.sec.gov			

For Netflix, sales is the product of the number of subscribers and the price charged for each subscription. What observations can you make about the previous three years of Netflix’s sales? Given this data, provide any predictions you can make about the future financial performance of Netflix. What nonfinancial factors influenced that prediction?

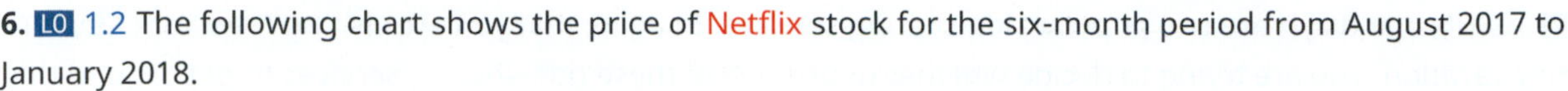

6. LO 1.2 The following chart shows the price of Netflix stock for the six-month period from August 2017 to January 2018.

Source: Nasdaq. "Netflix, Inc. Stock Chart." www.nasdaq.com

Assume you are considering purchasing Netflix stock. What considerations would influence your decision? Relative to Netflix's financial performance, what factors would influence the decision, and how would those factors rank in your decision? What about the nonfinancial factors?

7. LO 1.3 Use the internet to research one for-profit, one governmental, and one not-for-profit entity. For each entity, describe the following:

A. the primary purpose of the entity
B. the types of activities that accountants would record (hint: what is the source of the entity's funding, and what costs might the entity have?)
C. the types of decisions that might be made in this organization and how financial and nonfinancial information might help the decision-making process

8. LO 1.3 Use the Internet to research one manufacturing, one retail (or merchandising), and one service business. For each business, describe the following:

A. the primary purpose of the entity
B. the types of activities that accountants would record (hint: what is the source of the business' funding, and what costs might the business have?)
C. the types of decisions that might be made in this organization and how financial and nonfinancial information might help the decision-making process

9. LO 1.3 Assume you are considering opening a retail business. You are trying to decide whether to have a traditional "brick-and-mortar" store or to sell only online. Explain how the activities and costs differ between these two retail arrangements.

10. LO 1.3 Uber and Lyft are two popular ride-sharing services. Imagine that you are visiting New York City for a family vacation. You are trying to decide whether to use one of these ride-sharing services to get around the city or rent a car and drive yourself. Considering the perspectives of the passengers (your family), the drivers, and the company (Uber or Lyft), explain the following:

A. why ride-sharing services have gained in popularity
B. the financial considerations relevant to your decision
C. the nonfinancial considerations relevant to your decision

11. LO 1.3 How would you categorize or classify a company like Disney?

12. LO 1.3 Charity Navigator (https://www.charitynavigator.org) is a website dedicated to providing information regarding not-for-profit charitable organizations.

A. After reviewing the website, explain how not-for-profit organizations are rated.
B. Explain why there is a need for the type of information provided by Charity Navigator.
C. Choose one to two charities listed in the website. Explain the information provided about the charity (financial and nonfinancial), the rating of the charity, and any other relevant factors.

13. LO 1.4 Use the internet to visit the Securities and Exchange Commission (SEC) website (https://www.sec.gov/). Write a report discussing the following:

A. several of the services provided by the SEC
B. why the services are important to the investing public
C. why you think the SEC would require publicly traded companies to file financial information

14. LO 1.4 Imagine that you have just been elected president of your university's student senate. Assume the university is considering constructing a new student union—a place that offers a variety of stores, restaurants, and entertainment option for students—and has asked the student senate to develop a formal position in support or opposition of the new student union.

A. Identify the stakeholders involved in this decision. Discuss the relevant considerations that each stakeholder might have.
B. Discuss the financial information that might be helpful in formulating the student senate position.
C. Discuss the nonfinancial information that might be helpful in formulating the student senate position.

15. LO 1.4 According to a company press release, on January 5, 2012, Hansen Natural Corporation changed its name to Monster Beverage Corporation. According to Yahoo Finance, on that day the value of the company stock (symbol: MNST) was $15.64 per share. On January 5, 2018, the stock closed at $63.49 per share. This represents an increase of nearly 306%.

A. Discuss the factors that might influence the increase in share price.
B. Consider yourself as a potential shareholder. What factors would you consider when deciding whether or not to purchase shares in Monster Beverage Corporation today?

16. LO 1.4 The Dow Jones Industrial Average (DJIA) is often cited as a key metric for business activity. The average is a mathematical formula that uses the stock prices of thirty companies traded on the New York Stock Exchange (NYSE) and the National Association of Securities Dealers Automated Quotation (NASDAQ) system.

A. Identify several of the companies that are included in the DJIA.
B. Explain why this metric might be commonly used to measure business activity.
C. Research the history of the DJIA and note some interesting facts. When did the Dow begin? What was the first value? What was the lowest value? The following is an example of a website that may be helpful: http://www.dow-jones-djia.com/history-of-dow-jones-industrial-average-index/.
D. What is the current value of the DJIA? What factors might contribute to the difference between early and current values of the DJIA?

17. LO 1.5 Many professional certifications now have requirements for ethics training.

A. Define ethics.

B. Why does the accounting profession put so much emphasis on acting ethically?

18. LO 1.5 The Certified Public Accountant (CPA) exam is a uniform exam that is administered by a national organization. Licenses, however, are issued by individual states.

A. Explain why you think each state is responsible for issuing CPA licenses.

B. Choose two to three states, and compare and contrast the requirements to become a CPA. Are they fairly consistent or drastically different from each other? A helpful resource is https://www.thiswaytocpa.com/. You may also find it helpful to search the board of accountancy for each state.

C. Tax preparation is a large part of what many CPAs do. Students may be interested to know that a CPA (or any other licensing) is not required to prepare tax returns. Assume you know two friends who prepare tax returns for others, one is a CPA and one is not. Assume that both friends intend to move next year and will, therefore, prepare taxes in another state. Analyze this situation.

19. LO 1.5 Accounting is not the only profession to offer professional certifications. Many other professions have certifications that are either required or encouraged for entry or advancement in the profession. Think of two to three career paths that you have considered or are considering. After doing some research, complete the following:

A. Identify the name of the certification and the institute that administered the certification.

B. Explain the education and/or experience requirements for taking the exam and earning the license.

C. Discuss any of the benefits, financial or otherwise, of earning the certification.

20. LO 1.5 Assume you are considering earning a master's degree (or even doctorate) after earning your bachelor's degree. One option is to continue directly into a master's program and then enter the workforce. Another option is to gain some work experience and then return to graduate school and earn your master's degree.

A. Evaluate these options, and identify the advantages and disadvantages of each.

B. It may be helpful to do some research on earnings and advancement potential, available formats of graduate programs (full time, part time, online), and other factors that might influence your decision. You may want to research graduate programs and utilize sites such as the Occupational Outlook Handbook (https://www.bls.gov/ooh/).

2 Introduction to Financial Statements

Figure 2.1 Derek's Venture. Technology can be a great tool for those who are far away from friends and family. Tablets are one way for those unfamiliar with technology to become comfortable using technology to connect with others. (credit: modification of "Lady Elderly" by "MabelAmber"/Pixabay, CC0)

Chapter Outline

Why It Matters

As a teenager, Derek loves computers. He also enjoys giving back to the community by helping others. Derek understands that many senior citizens live far away from their families, resulting in infrequent visits and loneliness. This summer he is considering combining both things he enjoys by working with the local retirement center. His idea is to have workshops to show the senior citizens how to connect with their families through the use of technology. The director of the retirement center is enthused about Derek's idea and has agreed to pay him for the services. During his visits, he will set up tablets and then show the seniors how to use them. Since he lives nearby, he will also provide support on an as-needed basis.

While he is excited about this opportunity, he is also trying to save up money for college. Although the retirement center will pay him for the workshops, he knows the investment in providing tablets will be expensive, and he wants to ensure he can cover his costs. A neighbor who works in banking suggests that Derek get a small loan to cover the costs of the tablets and use the income he earns to repay the loan. Derek is excited by the idea but is anxious when his neighbor mentions he will have to provide the bank monthly financial information, such as checking account and other financial statements. While he enjoys technology and helping others, he is unfamiliar with financial statements. Derek decides to learn more about how financial statements will help both him and the bank make sound financial decisions.

2.1 Describe the Income Statement, Statement of Owner's Equity, Balance Sheet, and Statement of Cash Flows, and How They Interrelate

The study of accounting requires an understanding of precise and sometimes complicated terminology, purposes, principles, concepts, and organizational and legal structures. Typically, your introductory accounting courses will familiarize you with the overall accounting environment, and for those of you who want greater detail, there is an assortment of more advanced accounting courses available.

This chapter concentrates on the four major types of financial statements and their interactions, the major types of business structures, and some of the major terms and concepts used in this course. Coverage here is somewhat basic since these topics are accorded much greater detail in future chapters.

Types of Business Structure

As you learned in Role of Accounting in Society, virtually every activity that occurs in a business has an associated cost or value. Part of an accountant's role is to quantify these activities, or transactions.

Also, in business—and accounting in particular—it is necessary to distinguish the business entity from the individual owner(s). The personal transactions of the owners, employees, and other parties connected to the business should not be recorded in the organization's records; this accounting principle is called the *business entity concept*. Accountants should record only business transactions in business records.

This separation is also reflected in the legal structure of the business. There are several common types of legal business structures. While the accounting concepts for the various types of businesses are essentially the same regardless of the legal structure, the terminology will change slightly depending on the organization's legal structure, and it is important to understand the differences.

There are three broad categories for the legal structure of an organization: sole proprietorship, partnership, and corporation. A **sole proprietorship** is a legal business structure consisting of a single individual. Benefits of this type of structure include ease of formation, favorable tax treatment, and a high level of control over the business. The risks involved with sole proprietorships include unlimited personal liability and a limited life for the business. Unless the business is sold, the business ends when the owner retires or passes away. In addition, sole proprietorships have a fairly limited ability to raise capital (funding), and often sole proprietors have limited expertise—they are excellent at what they do but may have limited expertise in other important areas of business, such as accounting or marketing.

A **partnership** is a legal business structure consisting of an association of two or more people who contribute money, property, or services to operate as co-owners of a business. Benefits of this type of structure include favorable tax treatment, ease of formation of the business, and better access to capital and expertise. The downsides to a partnership include unlimited personal liability (although there are other legal structures—a limited liability partnership, for example—to help mitigate the risk); limited life of the partnership, similar to sole proprietorships; and increased complexity to form the venture (decision-making authority, profit-sharing arrangement, and other important issues need to be formally articulated in a written partnership agreement).

A **corporation** is a legal business structure involving one or more individuals (owners) who are legally distinct (separate) from the business. A primary benefit of a corporate legal structure is the owners of the organization have limited liability. That is, a corporation is "stand alone," conducting business as an entity separate from its owners. Under the corporate structure, owners delegate to others (called agents) the responsibility to make day-to-day decisions regarding the operations of the business. Other benefits of the corporate legal structure include relatively easy access to large amounts of capital by obtaining loans or selling ownership (stock), and since the stock is easily sold or transferred to others, the business operates beyond the life of the shareholders. A major disadvantage of a corporate legal structure is double taxation—the business pays income tax and the owners are taxed when distributions (also called dividends) are received.

Types of Business Structures

	Sole Proprietorship	Partnership	Corporation
Number of Owners	Single individual	Two or more individuals	One or more owners
Ease of Formation	Easier to form	Harder to form	Difficult to form
Ability to Raise Capital	Difficult to raise capital	Harder to raise capital	Easier to raise capital
Liability Risk	Unlimited liability	Unlimited liability	Limited liability
Taxation Consideration	Single taxation	Single taxation	Double taxation

Table 2.1

The Four Financial Statements

Are you a fan of books, movies, or sports? If so, chances are you have heard or said the phrase "spoiler alert." It is used to forewarn readers, viewers, or fans that the ending of a movie or book or outcome of a game is about to be revealed. Some people prefer knowing the end and skipping all of the details in the middle, while others prefer to fully immerse themselves and then discover the outcome. People often do not know or understand what accountants produce or provide. That is, they are not familiar with the "ending" of the accounting process, but that is the best place to begin the study of accounting.

Accountants create what are known as financial statements. Financial statements are reports that communicate the financial performance and financial position of the organization.

In essence, the overall purpose of financial statements is to evaluate the performance of a company, governmental entity, or not-for-profit entity. This chapter illustrates this through a company, which is considered to be in business to generate a profit. Each financial statement we examine has a unique function, and together they provide information to determine whether a company generated a profit or loss for a given period (such as a month, quarter, or year); the assets, which are resources of the company, and accompanying liabilities, which are obligations of the company, that are used to generate the profit or loss; owner interest in profits or losses; and the cash position of the company at the end of the period.

The four financial statements that perform these functions and the order in which we prepare them are:

1. Income Statement
2. Statement of Owner's Equity
3. Balance Sheet

4. Statement of Cash Flows.

The order of preparation is important as it relates to the concept of how financial statements are interrelated. Before explaining each in detail, let's explore the purpose of each financial statement and its main components.

CONTINUING APPLICATION AT WORK

Introduction to the Gearhead Outfitters Story

Gearhead Outfitters, founded by Ted Herget in 1997 in Jonesboro, Arkansas, is a retail chain that sells outdoor gear for men, women, and children. The company's inventory includes clothing, footwear for hiking and running, camping gear, backpacks, and accessories, by brands such as The North Face, Birkenstock, Wolverine, Yeti, Altra, Mizuno, and Patagonia. Herget fell in love with the outdoor lifestyle while working as a ski instructor in Colorado and wanted to bring that feeling back home to Arkansas. And so, Gearhead was born in a small downtown location in Jonesboro. The company has had great success over the years, expanding to numerous locations in Herget's home state, as well as Louisiana, Oklahoma, and Missouri.

While Herget knew his industry when starting Gearhead, like many entrepreneurs he faced regulatory and financial issues that were new to him. Several of these issues were related to accounting and the wealth of decision-making information that accounting systems provide.

For example, measuring revenue and expenses, providing information about cash flow to potential lenders, analyzing whether profit and positive cash flow is sustainable to allow for expansion, and managing inventory levels. Accounting, or the preparation of financial statements (balance sheet, income statement, and statement of cash flows), provides the mechanism for business owners such as Herget to make fundamentally sound business decisions.

Purpose of Financial Statements

Before exploring the specific financial statements, it is important to know why these are important documents. To understand this, you must first understand who the users of financial statements are. Users of the information found in financial statements are called stakeholders. A **stakeholder** is someone affected by decisions made by a company; this can include groups or individuals affected by the actions or policies of an organization, including include investors, creditors, employees, managers, regulators, customers, and suppliers. The stakeholder's interest sometimes is not directly related to the entity's financial performance. Examples of stakeholders include lenders, investors/owners, vendors, employees and management, governmental agencies, and the communities in which the businesses operate. Stakeholders are interested in the performance of an organization for various reasons, but the common goal of using the financial statements is to understand the information each contains that is useful for making financial decisions. For example, a banker may be interested in the financial statements to decide whether or not to lend the organization money.

Likewise, small business owners may make decisions based on their familiarity with the business—they know if the business is doing well or not based on their "gut feeling." By preparing the financial statements, accountants can help owners by providing clarity of the organization's financial performance. It is important to understand that, in the long term, every activity of the business has a financial impact, and financial statements are a way that accountants report the activities of the business. Stakeholders must make many decisions, and the financial statements provide information that is helpful in the decision-making process.

As described in Role of Accounting in Society, the complete set of financial statements acts as an X-ray of a company's financial health. By evaluating all of the financial statements together, someone with financial knowledge can determine the overall health of a company. The accountant can use this information to advise outside (and inside) stakeholders on decisions, and management can use this information as one tool to make strategic short- and long-term decisions.

ETHICAL CONSIDERATIONS

Utilitarian View of Accounting Decisions and Stakeholder Well-Being

Utilitarianism is a well-known and influential moral theory commonly used as a framework to evaluate business decisions. Utilitarianism suggests that an ethical action is one whose consequence achieves the greatest good for the greatest number of people. So, if we want to make an ethical decision, we should ask ourselves who is helped and who is harmed by it. Focusing on consequences in this way generally does not require us to take into account the means of achieving that particular end, however. Put simply, the utilitarian view is an ethical theory that the best action of a company is the one that maximizes utility of all stakeholders to the decision. This view assumes that all individuals with an interest in the business are considered within the decision.

Financial statements are used to understand the financial performance of companies and to make long- and short-term decisions. A utilitarian approach considers all stakeholders, and both the long- and short-term effects of a business decision. This allows corporate decision makers to choose business actions with the potential to produce the best outcomes for the majority of all stakeholders, not just shareholders, and therefore maximize stakeholder happiness.

Accounting decisions can change the approach a stakeholder has in relation to a business. If a company focuses on modifying operations and financial reporting to maximize short-term shareholder value, this could indicate the prioritization of certain stakeholder interests above others. When a company pursues only short-term profit for shareholders, it neglects the well-being of other stakeholders. Professional accountants should be aware of the interdependent relationship between all stakeholders and consider whether the results of their decisions are good for the majority of stakeholder interests.

YOUR TURN

Business Owners as Decision Makers

Think of a business owner in your family or community. Schedule some time to talk with the business owner, and find out how he or she uses financial information to make decisions.

Solution

Business owners will use financial information for many decisions, such as comparing sales from one period to another, determining trends in costs and other expenses, and identifying areas in which to reduce or reallocate expenses. This information will be used to determine, for example, staffing and inventory levels, streamlining of operations, and advertising or other investment decisions.

The Income Statement

The first financial statement prepared is the **income statement**, a statement that shows the organization's financial performance *for a given period of time*. Let's illustrate the purpose of an income statement using a real-life example. Assume your friend, Chris, who is a sole proprietor, started a summer landscaping business on August 1, 2020. It is categorized as a service entity. To keep this example simple, assume that she is using her family's tractor, and we are using the *cash basis* method of accounting to demonstrate Chris's initial operations for her business. The other available basis method that is commonly used in accounting is the *accrual basis* method. She is responsible for paying for fuel and any maintenance costs. She named the business Chris' Landscaping. On August 31, Chris checked the account balance and noticed there is only $250 in the checking account. This balance is lower than expected because she thought she had been paid by some customers. Chris decides to do some research to determine why the balance in the checking account is lower than expected. Her research shows that she earned a total of $1,400 from her customers but had to pay $100 to fix the brakes on her tractor, $50 for fuel, and also made a $1,000 payment to the insurance company for business insurance. The reason for the lower-than-expected balance was due to the fact that she spent ($1,150 for brakes, fuel, and insurance) only slightly less than she earned ($1,400)—a net increase of $250. While she would like the checking balance to grow each month, she realizes most of the August expenses were infrequent (brakes and insurance) and the insurance, in particular, was an unusually large expense. She is convinced the checking account balance will likely grow more in September because she will earn money from some new customers; she also anticipates having fewer expenses.

CHRIS' LANDSCAPING Income Statement For the Month Ended August 31, 2020		
Revenue	$1,400	
Total revenue		$1,400
Expenses		
Tractor brake repair	100	
Tractor fuel	50	
Business insurance	1,000	
Total expenses		1,150
Net income		$ 250

The Income Statement can also be visualized by the formula: Revenue – Expenses = Net Income/(Loss).

Let's change this example slightly and assume the $1,000 payment to the insurance company will be paid in September, rather than in August. In this case, the ending balance in Chris's checking account would be $1,250, a result of earning $1,400 and only spending $100 for the brakes on her car and $50 for fuel. This stream of cash flows is an example of cash basis accounting because it reflects when payments are received and made, not necessarily the time period that they affect. At the end of this section and in The Adjustment Process you will address accrual accounting, which does reflect the time period that they affect.

In accounting, this example illustrates an income statement, a financial statement that is used to measure the financial performance of an organization for a particular period of time. We use the simple landscaping account example to discuss the elements of the income statement, which are revenues, expenses, gains, and losses. Together, these determine whether the organization has net income (where revenues and gains are greater than expenses and losses) or net loss (where expenses and losses are greater than revenues and gains). Revenues, expenses, gains, and losses are further defined here.

Revenue

Revenue[1] is the value of goods and services the organization sold or provided to customers for a given period of time. In our current example, Chris's landscaping business, the "revenue" earned for the month of August would be $1,400. It is the value Chris received in exchange for the services provided to her clients. Likewise, when a business provides goods or services to customers for cash at the time of the service or in the future, the business classifies the amount(s) as revenue. Just as the $1,400 earned from a business made Chris's checking account balance increase, revenues increase the value of a business. In accounting, revenues are often also called sales or fees earned. Just as earning wages from a business or summer job reflects the number of hours worked for a given rate of pay or payments from clients for services rendered, revenues (and the other terms) are used to indicate the dollar value of goods and services provided to customers for a given period of time.

YOUR TURN

Coffee Shop Products

Think about the coffee shop in your area. Identify items the coffee shop sells that would be classified as revenues. Remember, revenues for the coffee shop are related to its primary purpose: selling coffee and related items. Or, better yet, make a trip to the local coffee shop and get a first-hand experience.

Solution

Many coffee shops earn revenue through multiple revenue streams, including coffee and other specialty drinks, food items, gift cards, and merchandise.

Expenses

An **expense**[2] is a cost associated with providing goods or services to customers. In our opening example, the expenses that Chris incurred totaled $1,150 (consisting of $100 for brakes, $50 for fuel, and $1,000 for

---

1 In a subsequent section of this chapter, you will learn that the accounting profession is governed by the Financial Accounting Standards Board (or FASB), a professional body that issues guidelines/pronouncements for the accounting profession. A set of theoretical pronouncements issued by FASB is called Statement of Financial Accounting Concepts (SFAC). In SFAC No. 6, FASB defines revenues as "inflows or other enhancements of assets of an entity or settlements of its liabilities (or a combination of both) from delivering or producing goods, rendering services, or other activities that constitute the entity's ongoing major or central operations" (SFAC No. 6, p. 23).

2 Expenses are formally defined by the FASB as "outflows or other using up of assets or incurrences of liabilities (or a combination of both) from delivering or producing goods, rendering services, or carrying out other activities that constitute the entity's ongoing major or central operations" (SFAC No. 6, p. 23).

insurance). You might think of expenses as the opposite of revenue in that expenses reduce Chris's checking account balance. Likewise, expenses decrease the value of the business and represent the dollar value of costs incurred to provide goods and services to customers for a given period of time.

YOUR TURN

Coffee Shop Expenses

While thinking about or visiting the coffee shop in your area, look around (or visualize) and identify items or activities that are the expenses of the coffee shop. Remember, expenses for the coffee shop are related to resources consumed while generating revenue from selling coffee and related items. Do not forget about any expenses that might not be so obvious—as a general rule, every activity in a business has an associated cost.

Solution

Costs of the coffee shop that might be readily observed would include rent; wages for the employees; and the cost of the coffee, pastries, and other items/merchandise that may be sold. In addition, costs such as utilities, equipment, and cleaning or other supplies might also be readily observable. More obscure costs of the coffee shop would include insurance, regulatory costs such as health department licensing, point-of-sale/credit card costs, advertising, donations, and payroll costs such as workers' compensation, unemployment, and so on.

Gains

A **gain**[3] can result from selling ancillary business items for more than the items are worth. (Ancillary business items are those that are used to support business operations.) To illustrate the concept of a gain, let's return to our example. However, this example and the accompanying *losses* example are not going to be part of our income statement, balance sheet, or owner's equity statement discussions. The gains and losses examples are only to be used in demonstrating the concepts of gains and losses. Assume that Chris paid $1,500 for a small piece of property to use for building a storage facility for her company. Further assume that Chris has an opportunity to sell the land for $2,000. She subsequently found a better storage option and decided to sell the property. After doing so, Chris will have a gain of $500 (a selling price of $2,000 and a cost of $1,500) and will also have $2,000 to deposit into her checking account, which would increase the balance.

Thinking back to the proceeds ($1,400) Chris received from her landscaping business, we might ask the question: how are gains similar to and different from revenues? The revenue of $1,400 that Chris earned from her business and the $2,000 she received from selling the land are similar in that both increase her checking account balance and make her business more valuable.

A difference, however, is evident if we consider how these funds were earned. Chris earned the $1,400 because she provided services (her labor) to her clients. Chris's primary objective is to earn revenue by working for her clients. In addition, earning money by selling her land was an infrequent event for Chris, since her primary job was serving as a landscaper. Her primary goal is to earn fees or revenue, not to earn money by selling land. In

3 FASB notes that gains represent an increase in organizational value from activities that are "*incidental* or *peripheral*" (SFAC No. 6, p. 24) to the primary purpose of the business.

fact, she cannot consider doing that again because she does not have additional land to sell.

The primary goal of a business is to earn revenue by providing goods and services to customers in exchange for cash at that time or in the future. While selling other items for more than the value of the item does occur in business, these transactions are classified as gains, because these sales are infrequent and not the primary purpose of the business.

Losses

A **loss**[4] results from selling ancillary business items for less than the items are worth. To illustrate, let's now assume that Chris sells her land that she purchased for $1,500 at a sales price of $1,200. In this case she would realize (incur) a loss of $300 on the sale of the property ($1,200 sales price minus the $1,500 cost of purchasing the property) and will also have $1,200 to deposit into her checking account, which would increase the balance.

You should not be confused by the fact that the checking account balance increased even though this transaction resulted in a financial loss. Chris received $1,200 that she can deposit into her checking account and use for future expenses. The $300 loss simply indicates that she received less for the land than she paid for it. These are two aspects of the same transaction that communicate different things, and it is important to understand the differences.

As we saw when comparing gains and revenues, losses are similar to expenses in that both losses and expenses decrease the value of the organization. In addition, just as Chris's primary goal is to earn money from her job rather than selling land, in business, losses refer to infrequent transactions involving ancillary items of the business.

Net Income (Net Loss)

Net income (net loss) is determined by comparing revenues and expenses. **Net income** is a result of revenues (inflows) being greater than expenses (outflows). A **net loss** occurs when expenses (outflows) are greater than revenues (inflows). In accounting it is common to present net income in the following format:

Net Income
Revenue (sometimes called Sales or Fees Earned)
– Expenses
Operating Profit (or Net Loss)

Recall that revenue is the value of goods and services a business provides to its customers and increase the value of the business. Expenses, on the other hand, are the costs of providing the goods and services and decrease the value of the business. When revenues exceed expenses, companies have net income. This means the business has been successful at earning revenues, containing expenses, or a combination of both. If, on the other hand, expenses exceed revenues, companies experience a net loss. This means the business was unsuccessful in earning adequate revenues, sufficiently containing expenses, or a combination of both. While businesses work hard to avoid net loss situations, it is not uncommon for a company to sustain a net loss from time-to-time. It is difficult, however, for businesses to remain viable while experiencing net losses over the long term.

Shown as a formula, the net income (loss) function is:

4 FASB notes losses represent a decrease in organizational value from activities that are "*incidental* or *peripheral*" (SFAC No. 6, p. 24) to the primary purpose of the business.

Revenues (R) – Expenses (E) = Net Income (when R > E)
Revenues (R) – Expenses (E) = Net Loss (when E > R)

To be complete, we must also consider the impact of gains and losses. While gains and losses are infrequent in a business, it is not uncommon that a business would present a gain and/or loss in its financial statements. Recall that gains are similar to revenue and losses are similar to expenses. Therefore, the traditional accounting format would be:

Gains and Losses
Revenue (sometimes called Sales or Fees Earned)
+ Gains
– Expenses
– Losses
Net Income (or Net Loss)

Shown as a formula, the net income (loss) function, including gains and losses, is:

Revenues (R) + Gains (G) – Expenses (E) – Losses (L) = Net Income [when (R + G) > (E + L)]
Revenues (R) + Gains (G) – Expenses (E) – Losses (L) = Net Loss [when (E + L) > (R + G)]

When assessing a company's net income, it is important to understand the source of the net income. Businesses strive to attain "high-quality" net income (earnings). High-quality earnings are based on sustainable earnings—also called permanent earnings—while relying less on infrequent earnings—also called temporary earnings. Recall that revenues represent the *ongoing* value of goods and services the business provides (sells) to its customers, while gains are *infrequent* and involve items ancillary to the primary purpose of the business. We should use caution if a business attains a significant portion of its net income as a result of gains, rather than revenues. Likewise, net losses derived as a result of losses should be put into the proper perspective due to the infrequent nature of losses. While net losses are undesirable for any reason, net losses that result from expenses related to ongoing operations, rather than losses that are infrequent, are more concerning for the business.

Statement of Owner's Equity

Equity is a term that is often confusing but is a concept with which you are probably already familiar. In short, equity is the value of an item that remains after considering what is owed for that item. The following example may help illustrate the concept of equity.

When thinking about the concept of equity, it is often helpful to think about an example many families are familiar with: purchasing a home. Suppose a family purchases a home worth $200,000. After making a down payment of $25,000, they secure a bank loan to pay the remaining $175,000. What is the value of the family's equity in the home? If you answered $25,000, you are correct. At the time of the purchase, the family owns a home worth $200,000 (an asset), but they owe $175,000 (a liability), so the equity or net worth in the home is $25,000.

The **statement of owner's equity**, which is the second financial statement created by accountants, is a statement that shows how the equity (or value) of the organization has changed over time. Similar to the income statement, the statement of owner's equity is *for a specific period of time, typically one year.* Recall that another way to think about equity is net worth, or value. So, the statement of owner's equity is a financial statement that shows how the net worth, or value, of the business has changed for a given period of time.

CHRIS' LANDSCAPING Statement of Owner's Equity For the Month Ended August 31, 2020	
Owner's equity, August 1	$ 0
+ Net income	250
	250
Owner's equity, August 31	$250

The elements of the financial statements shown on the statement of owner's equity include *investments by owners* as well as *distributions to owners*. Investments by owners and distributions to owners are two activities that impact the value of the organization (increase and decrease, respectively). In addition, net income or net loss affects the value of the organization (net income increases the value of the organization, and net loss decreases it). Net income (or net loss) is also shown on the statement of owner's equity; this is an example of how the statements are interrelated. Note that the word *owner's* (singular for a sole owner) changes to *owners'* (plural, for a group of owners) when preparing this statement for an entity with multiple owners versus a sole proprietorship.

In our example, to make it less complicated, we started with the first month of operations for Chris's Landscaping. In the first month of operations, the owner's equity total begins the month of August 2020, at $0, since there have been no transactions. During the month, the business received revenue of $1,400 and incurred expenses of $1,150, for net income of $250. Since Chris did not contribute any investment or make any withdrawals, other than the $1,150 for expenses, the ending balance in the owner's equity account on August 31, 2020, would be $250, the net income earned.

At this stage, it's important to point out that we are working with a sole proprietorship to help simplify the examples. We have addressed the owner's value in the firm as *capital* or *owner's equity*. However, later we switch the structure of the business to a corporation, and instead of owner's equity we begin using stockholder's equity, which includes account titles such as *common stock* and *retained earnings* to represent the owners' interests.

The corporate treatment is more complicated because corporations may have a few owners up to potentially thousands of owners (stockholders). More detail on this issue is provided in Define, Explain, and Provide Examples of Current and Noncurrent Assets, Current and Noncurrent Liabilities, Equity, Revenues, and Expenses.

Investments by Owners

Generally, there are two ways by which organizations become more valuable: profitable operations (when revenues exceed expenses) and investments by owners. Organizations often have long-term goals or projects that are very expensive (for example, building a new manufacturing facility or purchasing another company).

While having profitable operations is a viable way to "fund" these goals and projects, organizations often want to undertake these projects in a quicker time frame. Selling ownership is one way to quickly obtain the funding necessary for these goals. **Investments by owners** represent an exchange of cash or other assets for which the investor is given an ownership interest in the organization. This is a mutually beneficial arrangement: the organization gets the funding it needs on a timely basis, and the investor gets an ownership interest in the organization.

When organizations generate funding by selling ownership, the ownership interest usually takes the form of **common stock**, which is the corporation's primary class of stock issued, with each share representing a partial claim to ownership or a share of the company's business. When the organization issues common stock for the first time, it is called an **initial public offering (IPO)**. In Corporation Accounting, you learn more about the specifics of this type of accounting. Once a company issues (or sells) common stock after an IPO, we describe the company as a **publicly traded company**, which simply means the company's stock can be purchased by the general public on a public exchange like the New York Stock Exchange (NYSE). That is, investors can become owners of the particular company. Companies that issue publicly traded common shares in the United States are regulated by the **Securities and Exchange Commission (SEC)**, a federal regulatory agency that, among other responsibilities, is charged with oversight of financial investments such as common stock.

CONCEPTS IN PRACTICE

Roku Goes Public

On September 1, 2017, Roku, Inc. filed a Form S-1 with the Securities and Exchange Commission (SEC).[5] In this form, Roku disclosed its intention to become a publicly traded company, meaning its stock will trade (sell) on public stock exchanges, allowing individual and institutional investors an opportunity to own a portion (shares) of the company. The Form S-1 included detailed financial and nonfinancial information about the company. The information from Roku also included the purpose of the offering as well as the intended uses of the funds. Here is a portion of the disclosure: "The principal purposes of this offering are to increase our capitalization and financial flexibility and create a public market for our Class A common stock. We intend to use the net proceeds we receive from this offering primarily for general corporate purposes, including working capital . . . research and development, business development, sales and marketing activities and capital expenditures."[6]

On September 28, 2017, Roku "went public" and exceeded expectations. Prior to the IPO, Roku estimated it would sell between $12 and $14 per share, raising over $117 million for the company. The closing price per share on September 28 was $23.50, nearly doubling initial expectations for the share value.[7]

Distributions to Owners

There are basically two ways in which organizations become less valuable in terms of owners' equity: from unprofitable operations (when expenses or losses exceed revenues or gains) and by distributions to owners. Owners (investors) of an organization want to see their investment appreciate (gain) in value. Over time, owners of common stock can see the value of the stock increase in value—the share price increases—due to the success of the organization. Organizations may also make **distributions to owners**, which are periodic rewards issued to the owners in the form of cash or other assets. Distributions to owners represent some of the value (equity) of the organization.

5 Roku, Inc. "Form S-1 Filing with the Securities and Exchange Commission." September 1, 2017. https://www.sec.gov/Archives/edgar/data/1428439/000119312517275689/d403225ds1.htm

6 Roku, Inc. "Form S-1 Filing with the Securities and Exchange Commission." September 1, 2017. https://www.sec.gov/Archives/edgar/data/1428439/000119312517275689/d403225ds1.htm

7 Roku, Inc. Data. https://finance.yahoo.com/quote/ROKU/history?p=ROKU

For investors who hold common stock in the organization, these periodic payments or distributions to owners are called **dividends**. For sole proprietorships, distributions to owners are withdrawals or drawings. From the organization's perspective, dividends represent a portion of the net worth (equity) of the organization that is returned to owners as a reward for their investment. While issuing dividends does, in fact, reduce the organization's assets, some argue that paying dividends increases the organization's long-term value by making the stock more desirable. (Note that this topic falls under the category of "dividend policy" and there is a significant stream of research addressing this.)

Balance Sheet

Once the statement of owner's equity is completed, accountants typically complete the **balance sheet**, a statement that lists what the organization owns (*assets*), what it owes (*liabilities*), and what it is worth (*equity*) on a *specific date*. Notice the change in timing of the report. The income statement and statement of owner's equity report the financial performance and equity change for a period of time. The balance sheet, however, lists the financial position at the close of business on a specific date. (Refer to Figure 2.2 for the balance sheet as of August 31, 2020, for Chris' Landscaping.)

CHRIS' LANDSCAPING Balance Sheet August 31, 2020	
Assets	
Cash	$250
Liabilities	
None	0
Owner's Equity	
Owner's Equity	$250

Figure 2.2 "Balance Sheet for Chris' Landscaping." (attribution: Copyright, Rice University, OpenStax, under CC BY-NC-SA 4.0 license)

Assets

If you recall our previous example involving Chris and her newly established landscaping business, you are probably already familiar with the term **asset**[8]—these are resources used to generate revenue. In Chris's business, to keep the example relatively simple, the business ended the month with one asset, cash, assuming that the insurance was for one month's coverage.

However, as organizations become more complex, they often have dozens or more types of assets. An asset can be categorized as a **short-term asset** or current asset (which is typically used up, sold, or converted to cash in one year or less) or as a **long-term asset** or noncurrent asset (which is not expected to be converted into cash or used up within one year). Long-term assets are often used in the production of products and services.

Examples of short-term assets that businesses own include cash, accounts receivable, and inventory, while examples of long-term assets include land, machinery, office furniture, buildings, and vehicles. Several of the chapters that you will study are dedicated to an in-depth coverage of the special characteristics of selected

8 The FASB defines assets as "probable future economic benefits obtained or controlled by a particular entity as a result of past transactions or events" (SFAC No. 6, p. 12).

assets. Examples include Merchandising Transactions, which are typically short term, and Long-Term Assets, which are typically long term.

An asset can also be categorized as a tangible asset or an intangible asset. **Tangible assets** have a physical nature, such as trucks or many inventory items, while **intangible assets** have value but often lack a physical existence or corpus, such as insurance policies or trademarks.

Liabilities

You are also probably already familiar with the term **liability**[9]—these are amounts owed to others (called creditors). A liability can also be categorized as a **short-term liability** (or current liability) or a **long-term liability** (or noncurrent liability), similar to the treatment accorded assets. Short-term liabilities are typically expected to be paid within one year or less, while long-term liabilities are typically expected to be due for payment more than one year past the current balance sheet date.

Common short-term liabilities or amounts owed by businesses include amounts owed for items purchased on credit (also called *accounts payable*), taxes, wages, and other business costs that will be paid in the future. Long-term liabilities can include such liabilities as long-term notes payable, mortgages payable, or bonds payable.

Equity

In the Statement of Owner's Equity discussion, you learned that **equity** (or net assets) refers to book value or net worth. In our example, Chris's Landscaping, we determined that Chris had $250 worth of equity in her company at the end of the first month (see Figure 2.2).

At any point in time it is important for stakeholders to know the financial position of a business. Stated differently, it is important for employees, managers, and other interested parties to understand what a business owns, owes, and is worth at any given point. This provides stakeholders with valuable financial information to make decisions related to the business.

Statement of Cash Flows

The fourth and final financial statement prepared is the **statement of cash flows**, which is a statement that lists the cash inflows and cash outflows for the business *for a period of time*. At first glance, this may seem like a redundant financial statement. We know the income statement also reports the inflows and outflows for the business for a period of time. In addition, the statement of owner's equity and the balance sheet help to show the other activities, such as investments by and distributions to owners that are not included in the income statement. To understand why the statement of cash flows is necessary, we must first understand the two bases of accounting used to prepare the financial statements. The changes in cash within this statement are often referred to as sources and uses of cash. A source of cash lets one see where cash is coming from. For example, is cash being generated from sales to customers, or is the cash a result of an advance in a large loan. Use of cash looks at what cash is being used for. Is cash being used to make an interest payment on a loan, or is cash being used to purchase a large piece of machinery that will expand business capacity? The two bases of accounting are the cash basis and the accrual basis, briefly introduced in Describe the Income Statement, Statement of Owner's Equity, Balance Sheet, and Statement of Cash Flows, and How They Interrelate.

---

9 The FASB defines liabilities as "probable future sacrifices of economic benefits arising from present obligations of a particular entity to transfer assets or provide services to other entities in the future as a result of past transactions or events" (SFAC No. 6, p. 13).

Under **cash basis accounting**, transactions (i.e., a sale or a purchase) are not recorded in the financial statements until there is an exchange of cash. This type of accounting is permitted for nonprofit entities and small businesses that elect to use this type of accounting. Under **accrual basis accounting**, transactions are generally recorded in the financial statement when the transactions occur, and not when paid, although in some situations the two events could happen on the same day.

An example of the two methods (cash versus accrual accounting) would probably help clarify their differences. Assume that a mechanic performs a tune-up on a client's car on May 29, and the customer picks up her car and pays the mechanic $100 on June 2. If the mechanic were using the cash method, the revenue would be recognized on June 2, the date of payment, and any expenses would be recognized when paid.

If the accrual method were used, the mechanic would recognize the revenue and any related expenses on May 29, the day the work was completed. The accrual method will be the basis for your studies here (except for our coverage of the cash flow statement in Statement of Cash Flows). The accrual method is also discussed in greater detail in Explain the Steps within the Accounting Cycle through the Unadjusted Trial Balance.

While the cash basis of accounting is suited well and is more efficient for small businesses and certain types of businesses, such as farming, and those without inventory, like lawyers and doctors, the accrual basis of accounting is theoretically preferable to the cash basis of accounting. Accrual accounting is advantageous because it distinguishes between the timing of the transactions (when goods and services are provided) and when the cash involved in the transactions is exchanged (which can be a significant amount of time after the initial transaction). This allows accountants to provide, in a timely manner, relevant and complete information to stakeholders. The Adjustment Process explores several common techniques involved in accrual accounting.

Two brief examples may help illustrate the difference between cash accounting and accrual accounting. Assume that a business sells $200 worth of merchandise. In some businesses, there are two ways the customers pay: cash and credit (also referred to as "on account"). Cash sales include checks and credit cards and are paid at the time of the sale. Credit sales (not to be confused with credit card sales) allow the customer to take the merchandise but pay within a specified period of time, usually up to forty-five days.

A cash sale would be recorded in the financial statements under *both* the cash basis and accrual basis of accounting. It makes sense because the customer received the merchandise and paid the business at the same time. It is considered two events that occur simultaneously (exchange of merchandise for cash).

Similar to the previous example for the mechanic, a credit sale, however, would be treated differently under each of these types of accounting. Under the cash basis of accounting, a credit sale would not be recorded in the financial statements until the cash is received, under terms stipulated by the seller. For example, assume on April 1 a landscaping business provides $500 worth of services to one of its customers. The sale is made on account, with the payment due forty-five days later. Under the cash basis of accounting, the revenue would not be recorded until May 16, when the cash was received. Under the accrual basis of accounting, this sale would be recorded in the financial statements at the time the services were provided, April 1. The reason the sale would be recorded is, under accrual accounting, the business reports that it provided $500 worth of services to its customer. The fact the customers will pay later is viewed as a separate transaction under accrual accounting (Figure 2.3).

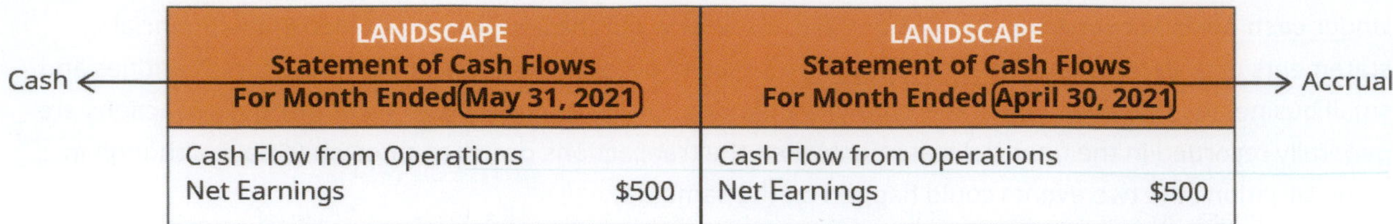

Figure 2.3 Credit versus Cash. On the left is a credit sale recorded under the cash basis of accounting. On the right the same credit sale is recorded under the accrual basis of accounting. (attribution: Copyright Rice University, OpenStax, under CC BY-NC-SA 4.0 license)

Let's now explore the difference between the cash basis and accrual basis of accounting using an expense. Assume a business purchases $160 worth of printing supplies from a supplier (vendor). Similar to a sale, a purchase of merchandise can be paid for at the time of sale using cash (also a check or credit card) or at a later date (on account). A purchase paid with cash at the time of the sale would be recorded in the financial statements under *both* cash basis and accrual basis of accounting. It makes sense because the business received the printing supplies from the supplier and paid the supplier at the same time. It is considered two events that occur simultaneously (exchange of merchandise for cash).

If the purchase was made on account (also called a *credit purchase*), however, the transaction would be recorded differently under each of these types of accounting. Under the cash basis of accounting, the $160 purchase on account would not be recorded in the financial statements until the cash is paid, as stipulated by the seller's terms. For example, if the printing supplies were received on July 17 and the payment terms were fifteen days, no transaction would be recorded until August 1, when the goods were paid for. Under the accrual basis of accounting, this purchase would be recorded in the financial statements at the time the business received the printing supplies from the supplier (July 17). The reason the purchase would be recorded is that the business reports that it bought $160 worth of printing supplies from its vendors. The fact the business will pay later is viewed as a separate issue under accrual accounting. Table 2.2 summarizes these examples under the different bases of accounting.

Transactions by Cash Basis versus Accrual Basis of Accounting

Transaction	Under Cash Basis Accounting	Under Accrual Basis Accounting
$200 sale for cash	Recorded in financial statements at time of sale	Recorded in financial statements at time of sale
$200 sale on account	*Not* recorded in financial statements until cash is received	Recorded in financial statements at time of sale
$160 purchase for cash	Recorded in financial statements at time of purchase	Recorded in financial statements at time of purchase

Table 2.2 Businesses often sell items for cash as well as on account, where payment terms are extended for a period of time (for example, thirty to forty-five days). Likewise, businesses often purchase items from suppliers (also called vendors) for cash or, more likely, on account. Under the cash basis of accounting, these transactions would not be recorded until the cash is exchanged. In contrast, under accrual accounting the transactions are recorded when the transaction occurs, regardless of when the cash is received or paid.

Transactions by Cash Basis versus Accrual Basis of Accounting

Transaction	Under Cash Basis Accounting	Under Accrual Basis Accounting
$160 purchase on account	*Not* recorded in financial statements until cash is paid	Recorded in financial statements at time of purchase

Table 2.2 Businesses often sell items for cash as well as on account, where payment terms are extended for a period of time (for example, thirty to forty-five days). Likewise, businesses often purchase items from suppliers (also called vendors) for cash or, more likely, on account. Under the cash basis of accounting, these transactions would not be recorded until the cash is exchanged. In contrast, under accrual accounting the transactions are recorded when the transaction occurs, regardless of when the cash is received or paid.

Knowing the difference between the cash basis and accrual basis of accounting is necessary to understand the need for the statement of cash flows. Stakeholders need to know the financial *performance* (as measured by the income statement—that is, net income or net loss) and financial *position* (as measured by the balance sheet—that is, assets, liabilities, and owners' equity) of the business. This information is provided in the income statement, statement of owner's equity, and balance sheet. However, since these financial statements are prepared using accrual accounting, stakeholders do not have a clear picture of the business's cash activities. The statement of cash flows solves this inadequacy by specifically focusing on the cash inflows and cash outflows.

2.2 Define, Explain, and Provide Examples of Current and Noncurrent Assets, Current and Noncurrent Liabilities, Equity, Revenues, and Expenses

In addition to what you've already learned about assets and liabilities, and their potential categories, there are a couple of other points to understand about assets. Plus, given the importance of these concepts, it helps to have an additional review of the material.

To help clarify these points, we return to our coffee shop example and now think of the coffee shop's assets—items the coffee shop owns or controls. Review the list of assets you created for the local coffee shop. Did you happen to notice many of the items on your list have one thing in common: the items will be used over a long period of time? In accounting, we classify assets based on whether or not the asset will be used or consumed within a certain period of time, generally one year. If the asset will be used or consumed in one year or less, we classify the asset as a **current asset**. If the asset will be used or consumed over more than one year, we classify the asset as a **noncurrent asset**.

Another thing you might have recognized when reviewing your list of coffee shop assets is that all of the items were something you could touch or move, each of which is known as a tangible asset. However, as you also learned in Describe the Income Statement, Statement of Owner's Equity, Balance Sheet, and Statement of Cash Flows, and How They Interrelate, not all assets are tangible. An asset could be an intangible asset, meaning the item lacks physical substance—it cannot be touched or moved. Take a moment to think about your favorite type of shoe or a popular type of farm tractor. Would you be able to recognize the maker of that shoe or the tractor by simply seeing the logo? Chances are you would. These are examples of intangible assets, trademarks to be precise. A trademark has value to the organization that created (or purchased) the trademark, and the trademark is something the organization controls—others cannot use the trademark without permission.

Similar to the accounting for assets, liabilities are classified based on the time frame in which the liabilities are expected to be settled. A liability that will be settled in one year or less (generally) is classified as a **current liability**, while a liability that is expected to be settled in more than one year is classified as a **noncurrent liability**.

Examples of current assets include **accounts receivable**, which is the outstanding customer debt on a credit sale; **inventory**, which is the value of products to be sold or items to be converted into sellable products; and sometimes a **notes receivable**, which is the value of amounts loaned that will be received in the future with interest, assuming that it will be paid within a year.

Examples of current liabilities include **accounts payable**, which is the value of goods or services purchased that will be paid for at a later date, and **notes payable**, which is the value of amounts borrowed (usually not inventory purchases) that will be paid in the future with interest.

Examples of noncurrent assets include notes receivable (notice notes receivable can be either current or noncurrent), land, buildings, equipment, and vehicles. An example of a noncurrent liability is notes payable (notice notes payable can be either current or noncurrent).

Why Does Current versus Noncurrent Matter?

At this point, let's take a break and explore why the distinction between current and noncurrent assets and liabilities matters. It is a good question because, on the surface, it does not seem to be important to make such a distinction. After all, assets are things owned or controlled by the organization, and liabilities are amounts owed by the organization; listing those amounts in the financial statements provides valuable information to stakeholders. But we have to dig a little deeper and remind ourselves that stakeholders are using this information to make decisions. Providing the amounts of the assets and liabilities answers the "what" question for stakeholders (that is, it tells stakeholders the value of assets), but it does not answer the "when" question for stakeholders. For example, knowing that an organization has $1,000,000 worth of assets is valuable information, but knowing that $250,000 of those assets are current and will be used or consumed within one year is more valuable to stakeholders. Likewise, it is helpful to know the company owes $750,000 worth of liabilities, but knowing that $125,000 of those liabilities will be paid within one year is even more valuable. In short, the *timing* of events is of particular interest to stakeholders.

THINK IT THROUGH

Borrowing

When money is borrowed by an individual or family from a bank or other lending institution, the loan is considered a personal or consumer loan. Typically, payments on these types of loans begin shortly after the funds are borrowed. Student loans are a special type of consumer borrowing that has a different structure for repayment of the debt. If you are not familiar with the special repayment arrangement for student loans, do a brief internet search to find out when student loan payments are expected to begin.

Now, assume a college student has two loans—one for a car and one for a student loan. Assume the person gets the flu, misses a week of work at his campus job, and does not get paid for the absence. Which loan would the person be most concerned about paying? Why?

Equity and Legal Structure

Recall that equity can also be referred to as net worth—the value of the organization. The concept of equity does not change depending on the legal structure of the business (sole proprietorship, partnership, and corporation). The terminology does, however, change slightly based on the type of entity. For example, investments by owners are considered "capital" transactions for sole proprietorships and partnerships but are considered "common stock" transactions for corporations. Likewise, distributions to owners are considered "drawing" transactions for sole proprietorships and partnerships but are considered "dividend" transactions for corporations.

As another example, in sole proprietorships and partnerships, the final amount of net income or net loss for the business becomes "Owner(s), Capital." In a corporation, net income or net loss for the business becomes **retained earnings**, which is the cumulative, undistributed net income or net loss, less dividends paid for the business since its inception.

The essence of these transactions remains the same: organizations become *more* valuable when owners make investments in the business and the businesses earn a profit (net income), and organizations become *less* valuable when owners receive distributions (dividends) from the organization and the businesses incur a loss (net loss). Because accountants are providing information to stakeholders, it is important for accountants to fully understand the specific terminology associated with the various legal structures of organizations.

The Accounting Equation

Recall the simple example of a home loan discussed in Describe the Income Statement, Statement of Owner's Equity, Balance Sheet, and Statement of Cash Flows, and How They Interrelate. In that example, we assumed a family purchased a home valued at $200,000 and made a down payment of $25,000 while financing the remaining balance with a $175,000 bank loan. This example demonstrates one of the most important concepts in the study of accounting: the **accounting equation**, which is:

Assets = Liabilities + Owner's Equity

In our example, the accounting equation would look like this:

$$\$200{,}000 = \$175{,}000 + \$25{,}000$$

As you continue your accounting studies and you consider the different major types of business entities available (sole proprietorships, partnerships, and corporations), there is another important concept for you to remember. This concept is that no matter which of the entity options that you choose, the accounting process for all of them will be predicated on the accounting equation.

It may be helpful to think of the accounting equation from a "sources and claims" perspective. Under this approach, the assets (items owned by the organization) were obtained by incurring liabilities or were provided by owners. Stated differently, every asset has a claim against it—by creditors and/or owners.

YOUR TURN

The Accounting Equation

On a sheet of paper, use three columns to create your own accounting equation. In the first column, list all of the things you own (assets). In the second column, list any amounts owed (liabilities). In the third column, using the accounting equation, calculate, you guessed it, the net amount of the asset (equity). When finished, total the columns to determine your net worth. Hint: do not forget to subtract the liability from the value of the asset.

Here is something else to consider: is it possible to have negative equity? It sure is . . . ask any college student who has taken out loans. At first glance there is no asset directly associated with the amount of the loan. But is that, in fact, the case? You might ask yourself why make an investment in a college education—what is the benefit (asset) to going to college? The answer lies in the difference in lifetime earnings with a college degree versus without a college degree. This is influenced by many things, including the supply and demand of jobs and employees. It is also influenced by the earnings for the type of college degree pursued. (Where do you think accounting ranks?)

Solution

Answers will vary but may include vehicles, clothing, electronics (include cell phones and computer/ gaming systems, and sports equipment). They may also include money owed on these assets, most likely vehicles and perhaps cell phones. In the case of a student loan, there may be a liability with no corresponding asset (yet). Responses should be able to evaluate the benefit of investing in college is the wage differential between earnings with and without a college degree.

Expanding the Accounting Equation

Let's continue our exploration of the accounting equation, focusing on the equity component, in particular. Recall that we defined equity as the net worth of an organization. It is helpful to also think of net worth as the *value* of the organization. Recall, too, that revenues (inflows as a result of providing goods and services) *increase* the value of the organization. So, every dollar of revenue an organization generates increases the overall value of the organization.

Likewise, expenses (outflows as a result of generating revenue) *decrease* the value of the organization. So, each dollar of expenses an organization incurs decreases the overall value of the organization. The same approach can be taken with the other elements of the financial statements:

- Gains *increase* the value (equity) of the organization.
- Losses *decrease* the value (equity) of the organization.
- Investments by owners *increase* the value (equity) of the organization.
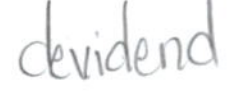
- Distributions to owners *decrease* the value (equity) of the organization.
- Changes in assets and liabilities can *either* increase or decrease the value (equity) of the organization depending on the net result of the transaction.

A graphical representation of this concept is shown in Figure 2.4.

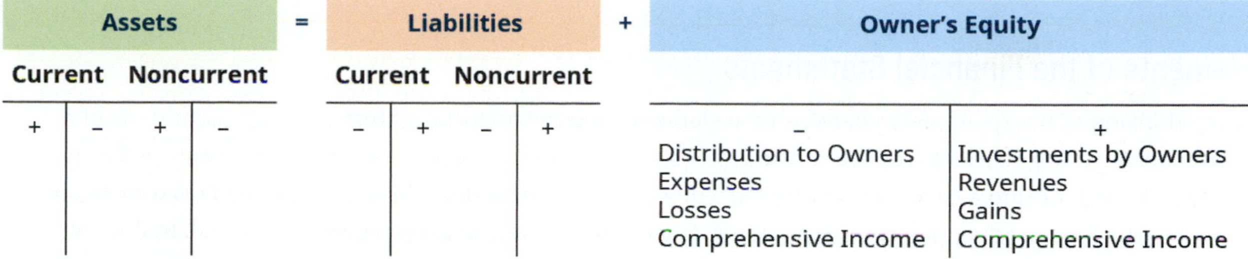

Figure 2.4 Graphical Representation of the Accounting Equation. Both assets and liabilities are categorized as current and noncurrent. Also highlighted are the various activities that affect the equity (or net worth) of the business. (attribution: Copyright Rice University, OpenStax, under CC BY-NC-SA 4.0 license)

The format of this illustration is also intended to introduce you to a concept you will learn more about in your study of accounting. Notice each account subcategory (Current Assets and Noncurrent Assets, for example) has an "increase" side and a "decrease" side. These are called T-accounts and will be used to analyze transactions, which is the beginning of the accounting process. See Analyzing and Recording Transactions for a more comprehensive discussion of analyzing transactions and T-Accounts.

Not All Transactions Affect Equity

As you continue to develop your understanding of accounting, you will encounter many types of transactions involving different elements of the financial statements. The previous examples highlighted elements that change the equity of an organization. Not all transactions, however, ultimately impact equity. For example, the following do not impact the equity or net worth of the organization:[10]

- Exchanges of assets for assets
- Exchanges of liabilities for liabilities
- Acquisitions of assets by incurring liabilities
- Settlements of liabilities by transferring assets

It is important to understand the inseparable connection between the elements of the financial statements and the possible impact on organizational equity (value). We explore this connection in greater detail as we return to the financial statements.

2.3 Prepare an Income Statement, Statement of Owner's Equity, and Balance Sheet

One of the key factors for success for those beginning the study of accounting is to understand how the elements of the financial statements relate to each of the financial statements. That is, once the transactions are categorized into the elements, knowing what to do next is vital. This is the beginning of the process to create the financial statements. It is important to note that financial statements are discussed in the order in which the statements are presented.

10 SFAC No. 6, p. 20.

Elements of the Financial Statements

When thinking of the relationship between the elements and the financial statements, we might think of a baking analogy: the elements represent the ingredients, and the financial statements represent the finished product. As with baking a cake (see Figure 2.5), knowing the ingredients (elements) and how each ingredient relates to the final product (financial statements) is vital to the study of accounting.

(a) (b)

Figure 2.5 Baking requires an understanding of the different ingredients, how the ingredients are used, and how the ingredients will impact the final product (a). If used correctly, the final product will be beautiful and, more importantly, delicious, like the cake shown in (b). In a similar manner, the study of accounting requires an understanding of how the accounting elements relate to the final product—the financial statements. (credit (a): modification of "U.S. Navy Culinary Specialist Seaman Robert Fritschie mixes cake batter aboard the amphibious command ship USS Blue Ridge (LCC 19) Aug. 7, 2013, while underway in the Solomon Sea 130807-N-NN332-044" by MC3 Jarred Harral/Wikimedia Commons, Public Domain; credit (b): modification of "Easter Cake with Colorful Topping" by Kaboompics .com/Pexels, CC0)

To help accountants prepare and users better understand financial statements, the profession has outlined what is referred to as **elements of the financial statements**, which are those categories or accounts that accountants use to record transactions and prepare financial statements. There are ten elements of the financial statements, and we have already discussed most of them.

- **Revenue**—value of goods and services the organization sold or provided.
- **Expenses**—costs of providing the goods or services for which the organization earns revenue.
- **Gains**—gains are similar to revenue but relate to "incidental or peripheral" activities of the organization.
- **Losses**—losses are similar to expenses but related to "incidental or peripheral" activities of the organization.
- **Assets**—items the organization owns, controls, or has a claim to.
- **Liabilities**—amounts the organization owes to others (also called creditors).
- **Equity**—the net worth (or net assets) of the organization.
- **Investment by owners**—cash or other assets provided to the organization in exchange for an ownership interest.

- **Distribution to owners**—cash, other assets, or ownership interest (equity) provided to owners.
- **Comprehensive income**—defined as the "change in equity of a business enterprise during a period from transactions and other events and circumstances from nonowner sources" (SFAC No. 6, p. 21). While further discussion of comprehensive income is reserved for intermediate and advanced studies in accounting, it is worth noting that comprehensive income has four components, focusing on activities related to foreign currency, derivatives, investments, and pensions.

Financial Statements for a Sample Company

Now it is time to bake the cake (i.e., prepare the financial statements). We have all of the ingredients (elements of the financial statements) ready, so let's now return to the financial statements themselves. Let's use as an example a fictitious company named Cheesy Chuck's Classic Corn. This company is a small retail store that makes and sells a variety of gourmet popcorn treats. It is an exciting time because the store opened in the current month, June.

Assume that as part of your summer job with Cheesy Chuck's, the owner—you guessed it, Chuck—has asked you to take over for a former employee who graduated college and will be taking an accounting job in New York City. In addition to your duties involving making and selling popcorn at Cheesy Chuck's, part of your responsibility will be doing the accounting for the business. The owner, Chuck, heard that you are studying accounting and could really use the help, because he spends most of his time developing new popcorn flavors.

The former employee has done a nice job of keeping track of the accounting records, so you can focus on your first task of creating the June financial statements, which Chuck is eager to see. Figure 2.6 shows the financial information (as of June 30) for Cheesy Chuck's.

CHEESY CHUCK'S CLASSIC CORN Trial Balance For the Month Ended June 30, 2018	
Revenues	**$85,000**
Expenses:	
Popcorn	22,800
Toppings and seasonings	17,300
Employee wages and benefits	10,700
Lease payments	24,000
Utilities	3,200
Advertising	900
Miscellaneous	300
Cash	**$ 6,200**
Equipment	**$12,500**
Accounts Payable	**$ 650**
Wages Payable	**$ 1,200**
Investment by Owner	**$12,500**
Drawings by Owner	**$ (1,450)**

Figure 2.6 Trial Balance for Cheesy Chuck's Classic Corn. Accountants record and summarize accounting information into accounts, which help to track, summarize, and prepare accounting information. This table is a variation of what accountants call a "trial balance." A trial balance is a summary of accounts and aids accountants in creating financial statements. (attribution: Copyright Rice University, OpenStax, under CC BY-NC-SA 4.0 license)

We should note that we are oversimplifying some of the things in this example. First, the amounts in the accounting records were given. We did not explain how the amounts would be derived. This process is explained starting in Analyzing and Recording Transactions. Second, we are ignoring the timing of certain cash flows such as hiring, purchases, and other startup costs. In reality, businesses must invest cash to prepare the store, train employees, and obtain the equipment and inventory necessary to open. These costs will precede the selling of goods and services. In the example to follow, for instance, we use Lease payments of $24,000, which represents lease payments for the building ($20,000) and equipment ($4,000). In practice, when companies lease items, the accountants must determine, based on accounting rules, whether or not the business "owns" the item. If it is determined the business "owns" the building or equipment, the item is listed on the balance sheet at the original cost. Accountants also take into account the building or equipment's value when the item is worn out. The difference in these two values (the original cost and the ending value) will be allocated over a relevant period of time. As an example, assume a business purchased equipment for $18,000 and the equipment will be worth $2,000 after four years, giving an estimated decline in value (due to usage) of $16,000 ($18,000 – $2,000). The business will allocate $4,000 of the equipment cost over each of the four years ($18,000 minus $2,000 over four years). This is called *depreciation* and is one of the topics that is covered in Long-Term Assets.

Also, the Equipment with a value of $12,500 in the financial information provided was purchased at the end of the first accounting period. It is an asset that will be depreciated in the future, but no depreciation expense is allocated in our example.

Income Statement

Let's prepare the income statement so we can inform how Cheesy Chuck's performed for the month of June (remember, an income statement is *for a period of time*). Our first step is to determine the value of goods and services that the organization sold or provided for a given period of time. These are the inflows to the business, and because the inflows relate to the primary purpose of the business (making and selling popcorn), we classify those items as Revenues, Sales, or Fees Earned. For this example, we use Revenue. The revenue for Cheesy Chuck's for the month of June is $85,000.

Next, we need to show the total expenses for Cheesy Chuck's. Because Cheesy Chuck's tracks different types of expenses, we need to add the amounts to calculate total expenses. If you added correctly, you get total expenses for the month of June of $79,200. The final step to create the income statement is to determine the amount of net income or net loss for Cheesy Chuck's. Since revenues ($85,000) are greater than expenses ($79,200), Cheesy Chuck's has a net income of $5,800 for the month of June.

Figure 2.7 displays the June income statement for Cheesy Chuck's Classic Corn.

CHEESY CHUCK'S CLASSIC CORN Income Statement For the Month Ended June 30, 2018		
Revenues		**$85,000**
Expenses:		
Popcorn	$22,800	
Toppings and seasonings	17,300	
Employee wages and benefits	10,700	
Lease payments	24,000	
Utilities	3,200	
Advertising	900	
Miscellaneous	300	
Total Expenses		**$79,200**
Net Income		**$ 5,800**

To be used in Statement of Owner's Equity

Figure 2.7 Income Statement for Cheesy Chuck's Classic Corn. The income statement for Cheesy Chuck's shows the business had Net Income of $5,800 for the month ended June 30. This amount will be used to prepare the next financial statement, the statement of owner's equity. (attribution: Copyright Rice University, OpenStax, under CC BY-NC-SA 4.0 license)

Financial statements are created using numerous standard conventions or practices. The standard conventions provide consistency and help assure financial statement users the information is presented in a similar manner, regardless of the organization issuing the financial statement. Let's look at the standard conventions shown in the Cheesy Chuck's income statement:

- The heading of the income statement includes three lines.
  - The first line lists the business name.
  - The middle line indicates the financial statement that is being presented.
  - The last line indicates the time frame of the financial statement. Do not forget the income statement is *for a period of time* (the month of June in our example).
- There are three columns.
  - Going from left to right, the first column is the category heading or account.
  - The second column is used when there are numerous accounts in a particular category (Expenses, in our example).
  - The third column is a total column. In this illustration, it is the column where subtotals are listed and net income is determined (subtracting Expenses from Revenues).
- Subtotals are indicated by a single underline, while totals are indicated by a double underline. Notice the amount of Miscellaneous Expense ($300) is formatted with a single underline to indicate that a subtotal will follow. Similarly, the amount of "Net Income" ($5,800) is formatted with a double underline to indicate that it is the final value/total of the financial statement.
- There are no gains or losses for Cheesy Chuck's. Gains and losses are not unusual transactions for businesses, but gains and losses may be infrequent for some, especially small, businesses.

CONCEPTS IN PRACTICE

McDonald's

For the year ended December 31, 2016, McDonald's had sales of $24.6 billion.[11] The amount of sales is often used by the business as the starting point for planning the next year. No doubt, there are a lot of people involved in the planning for a business the size of McDonald's. Two key people at McDonald's are the purchasing manager and the sales manager (although they might have different titles). Let's look at how McDonald's 2016 sales amount might be used by each of these individuals. In each case, do not forget that McDonald's is a global company.

A purchasing manager at McDonald's, for example, is responsible for finding suppliers, negotiating costs, arranging for delivery, and many other functions necessary to have the ingredients ready for the stores to prepare the food for their customers. Expecting that McDonald's will have over $24 billion of sales during 2017, how many eggs do you think the purchasing manager at McDonald's would need to purchase for the year? According to the McDonald's website, the company uses over two billion eggs a year.[12] Take a moment to list the details that would have to be coordinated in order to purchase and deliver over two billion eggs to the many McDonald's restaurants around the world.

A sales manager is responsible for establishing and attaining sales goals within the company. Assume that McDonald's 2017 sales are expected to exceed the amount of sales in 2016. What conclusions would you make based on this information? What do you think might be influencing these amounts? What factors do you think would be important to the sales manager in deciding what action, if any, to take? Now assume that McDonald's 2017 sales are expected to be below the 2016 sales level. What conclusions would you make based on this information? What do you think might be influencing these amounts? What factors do you think would be important to the sales manager in deciding what action, if any, to take?

Statement of Owner's Equity

Let's create the statement of owner's equity for Cheesy Chuck's for the month of June. Since Cheesy Chuck's is a brand-new business, there is no beginning balance of Owner's Equity. The first items to account for are the increases in value/equity, which are investments by owners and net income. As you look at the accounting information you were provided, you recognize the amount invested by the owner, Chuck, was $12,500. Next, we account for the increase in value as a result of net income, which was determined in the income statement to be $5,800. Next, we determine if there were any activities that decreased the value of the business. More specifically, we are accounting for the value of distributions to the owners and net loss, if any.

It is important to note that an organization will have either net income or net loss for the period, but not both. Also, small businesses in particular may have periods where there are no investments by, or distributions to, the owner(s). For the month of June, Chuck withdrew $1,450 from the business. This is a good time to recall the

11 McDonald's Corporation. U.S. Securities and Exchange Commission 10-K Filing. March 1, 2017. http://d18rn0p25nwr6d.cloudfront.net/CIK-0000063908/62200c2b-da82-4364-be92-79ed454e3b88.pdf

12 McDonald's. "Our Food. Your Questions. Breakfast." n.d. https://www.mcdonalds.com/us/en-us/about-our-food/our-food-your-questions/breakfast.html

terminology used by accountants based on the legal structure of the particular business. Since the account was titled "Drawings by Owner" and because Chuck is the only owner, we can assume this is a sole proprietorship. If the business was structured as a corporation, this activity would be called something like "Dividends Paid to Owners."

At this stage, remember that since we are working with a sole proprietorship to help simplify the examples, we have addressed the owner's value in the firm as *capital* or *owner's equity*. However, later we switch the structure of the business to a corporation, and instead of owner's equity, we begin using such account titles as *common stock* and *retained earnings* to represent the owner's interests. The corporate treatment is more complicated, because corporations may have a few owners up to potentially thousands of owners (stockholders). The details of accounting for the interests of corporations are covered in Corporation Accounting.

So how much did the value of Cheesy Chuck's change during the month of June? You are correct if you answered $16,850. Since this is a brand-new store, the beginning value of the business is zero. During the month, the owner invested $12,500 and the business had profitable operations (net income) of $5,800. Also, during the month the owner withdrew $1,450, resulting in a net change (and ending balance) to owner's equity of $16,850. Shown in a formula:

Beginning Balance + Investments by Owners ± Net Income (Net Loss) – Distributions, or

$$\$0 + \$12{,}500 + \$5{,}800 - \$1{,}450 = \$16{,}850$$

Figure 2.8 shows what the statement of owner's equity for Cheesy Chuck's Classic Corn would look like.

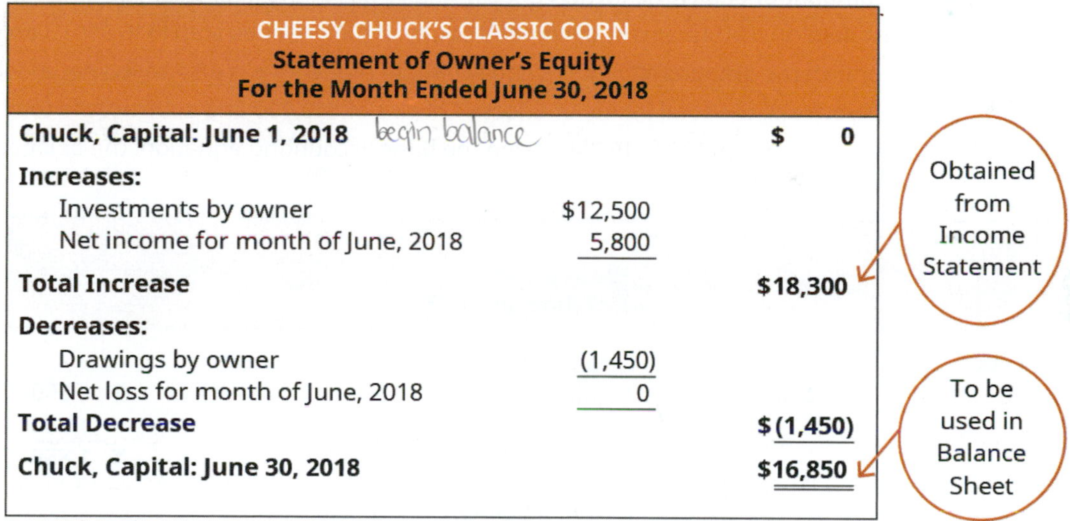

CHEESY CHUCK'S CLASSIC CORN Statement of Owner's Equity For the Month Ended June 30, 2018		
Chuck, Capital: June 1, 2018		**$ 0**
Increases:		
Investments by owner	$12,500	
Net income for month of June, 2018	5,800	
Total Increase		**$18,300**
Decreases:		
Drawings by owner	(1,450)	
Net loss for month of June, 2018	0	
Total Decrease		**$(1,450)**
Chuck, Capital: June 30, 2018		**$16,850**

Figure 2.8 Statement of Owner's Equity for Cheesy Chuck's Classic Corn. The statement of owner's equity demonstrates how the net worth (also called equity) of the business changed over the period of time (the month of June in this case). Notice the amount of net income (or net loss) is brought from the income statement. In a similar manner, the ending equity balance (Capital for Cheesy Chuck's because it is a sole proprietorship) is carried forward to the balance sheet. (attribution: Copyright Rice University, OpenStax, under CC BY-NC-SA 4.0 license)

Notice the following about the statement of owner's equity for Cheesy Chuck's:

- The format is similar to the format of the income statement (three lines for the heading, three columns).
- The statement follows a chronological order, starting with the first day of the month, accounting for the

changes that occurred throughout the month, and ending with the final day of the month.

The statement uses the final number from the financial statement previously completed. In this case, the statement of owner's equity uses the net income (or net loss) amount from the income statement (Net Income, $5,800).

Balance Sheet

Let's create a balance sheet for Cheesy Chuck's for June 30. To begin, we look at the accounting records and determine what assets the business owns and the value of each. Cheesy Chuck's has two assets: Cash ($6,200) and Equipment ($12,500). Adding the amount of assets gives a total asset value of $18,700. As discussed previously, the equipment that was recently purchased will be depreciated in the future, beginning with the next accounting period.

Next, we determine the amount of money that Cheesy Chuck's owes (liabilities). There are also two liabilities for Cheesy Chuck's. The first account listed in the records is Accounts Payable for $650. Accounts Payable is the amount that Cheesy Chuck's must pay *in the future* to vendors (also called suppliers) for the ingredients to make the gourmet popcorn. The other liability is Wages Payable for $1,200. This is the amount that Cheesy Chuck's must pay in the future to employees for work that has been performed. Adding the two amounts gives us total liabilities of $1,850. (Here's a hint as you develop your understanding of accounting: Liabilities often include the word "payable." So, when you see "payable" in the account title, know these are amounts owed in the future—liabilities.)

Finally, we determine the amount of equity the owner, Cheesy Chuck, has in the business. The amount of owner's equity was determined on the statement of owner's equity in the previous step ($16,850). Can you think of another way to confirm the amount of owner's equity? Recall that equity is also called net assets (assets minus liabilities). If you take the total assets of Cheesy Chuck's of $18,700 and subtract the total liabilities of $1,850, you get owner's equity of $16,850. Using the basic accounting equation, the balance sheet for Cheesy Chuck's as of June 30 is shown in Figure 2.9.

CHEESY CHUCK'S CLASSIC CORN Balance Sheet As of June 30, 2018			
Assets		**Liabilities**	
Cash	$ 6,200	Accounts Payable	$ 650
Equipment	12,500	Wages Payable	1,200
		Total Liabilities	**$ 1,850**
		Owner's Equity	
		Cheesy Chuck, Capital	16,850
		Total Owner's Equity	**$ 16,850**
Total Assets	**$18,700**	**Total Liabilities and Owner's Equity**	**$18,700**

Figure 2.9 Balance Sheet for Cheesy Chuck's Classic Corn. The balance sheet shows what the business owns (Assets), owes (Liabilities), and is worth (equity) on a given date. Notice the amount of Owner's Equity (Capital for Cheesy Chuck's) was brought forward from the statement of owner's equity. (attribution: Copyright Rice University, OpenStax, under CC BY-NC-SA 4.0 license)

Connecting the Income Statement and the Balance Sheet

Another way to think of the connection between the income statement and balance sheet (which is aided by the statement of owner's equity) is by using a sports analogy. The income statement summarizes the financial *performance* of the business for a given period of time. The income statement reports how the business performed financially each month—the firm earned either net income or net loss. This is similar to the outcome of a particular game—the team either won or lost.

The balance sheet summarizes the financial *position* of the business on a given date. Meaning, because of the financial *performance* over the past twelve months, for example, this is the financial *position* of the business as of December 31. Think of the balance sheet as being similar to a team's overall win/loss record—to a certain extent a team's strength can be perceived by its win/loss record.

However, because different companies have different sizes, you do not necessarily want to compare the balance sheets of two different companies. For example, you would not want to compare a local retail store with Walmart. In most cases you want to compare a company with its past balance sheet information.

Statement of Cash Flows

In Describe the Income Statement, Statement of Owner's Equity, Balance Sheet, and Statement of Cash Flows, and How They Interrelate, we discussed the function of and the basic characteristics of the statement of cash flows. This fourth and final financial statement lists the cash inflows and cash outflows for the business *for a period of time*. It was created to fill in some informational gaps that existed in the other three statements (income statement, owner's equity/retained earnings statement, and the balance sheet). A full demonstration of the creation of the statement of cash flows is presented in Statement of Cash Flows.

Creating Financial Statements: A Summary

In this example using a fictitious company, Cheesy Chuck's, we began with the account balances and demonstrated how to prepare the financial statements for the month of June, the first month of operations for the business. It will be helpful to revisit the process by summarizing the information we started with and how that information was used to create the four financial statements: income statement, statement of owner's equity, balance sheet, and statement of cash flows.

We started with the account balances shown in Figure 2.10.

CHEESY CHUCK'S CLASSIC CORN Account Balances For the Month Ended June 30, 2018	
Revenues	**$85,000**
Expenses:	
Popcorn	22,800
Toppings and seasonings	17,300
Employee wages and benefits	10,700
Lease payments	24,000
Utilities	3,200
Advertising	900
Miscellaneous	300
Cash	**$ 6,200**
Equipment	**$12,500**
Accounts Payable	**$ 650**
Wages Payable	**$ 1,200**
Investment by Owner	**$12,500**
Drawings by Owner	**$ (1,450)**

Figure 2.10 Account Balances for Cheesy Chuck's Classic Corn. Obtaining the account balances is the starting point for preparing financial statements. (attribution: Copyright Rice University, OpenStax, under CC BY-NC-SA 4.0 license)

The next step was to create the income statement, which shows the financial *performance* of the business. The income statement is shown in Figure 2.11.

CHEESY CHUCK'S CLASSIC CORN Income Statement For the Month Ended June 30, 2018		
Revenues		**$85,000**
Expenses:		
Popcorn	$22,800	
Toppings and seasonings	17,300	
Employee wages and benefits	10,700	
Lease payments	24,000	
Utilities	3,200	
Advertising	900	
Miscellaneous	300	
Total Expenses		**$79,200**
Net Income		**$ 5,800**

Figure 2.11 Income Statement for Cheesy Chuck's Classic Corn. The income statement uses information from the trial balance, which lists the accounts and account totals. The income statement shows the financial performance of a business for a period of time. The net income or net loss will be carried forward to the statement of owner's equity. (attribution: Copyright Rice University, OpenStax, under CC BY-NC-SA 4.0 license)

Next, we created the statement of owner's equity, shown in Figure 2.12. The statement of owner's equity demonstrates how the equity (or net worth) of the business changed for the month of June. Do not forget that the Net Income (or Net Loss) is carried forward to the statement of owner's equity.

CHEESY CHUCK'S CLASSIC CORN Statement of Owner's Equity For the Month Ended June 30, 2018		
Chuck, Capital: June 1, 2018		**$ 0**
Increases:		
Investments by owner	$12,500	
Net Income for month of June, 2018	5,800	
Total Increase		**$18,300**
Decreases:		
Drawings by owner	$(1,450)	
Total Decrease		**$(1,450)**
Chuck, Capital: June 30, 2018		**$16,850**

Figure 2.12 Statement of Owner's Equity for Cheesy Chuck's Classic Corn. The statement of owner's equity shows how the net worth/value (or equity) of business changed for the period of time. This statement includes Net Income (or Net Loss), which was brought forward from the income statement. The ending balance is carried forward to the balance sheet. (attribution: Copyright Rice University, OpenStax, under CC BY-NC-SA 4.0 license)

The third financial statement created is the balance sheet, which shows the company's financial *position* on a given date. Cheesy Chuck's balance sheet is shown in Figure 2.13.

CHEESY CHUCK'S CLASSIC CORN Balance Sheet As of June 30, 2018			
Assets		**Liabilities**	
Cash	$ 6,200	Accounts Payable	$ 650
Equipment	12,500	Wages Payable	1,200
		Total Liabilities	**$ 1,850**
		Owner's Equity	
		Cheesy Chuck, Capital	16,850
		Total Owner's Equity	**$16,850**
Total Assets	**$18,700**	**Total Liabilities and Owner's Equity**	**$18,700**

Figure 2.13 Balance Sheet for Cheesy Chuck's Classic Corn. The balance sheet shows the assets, liabilities, and owner's equity of a business on a given date. Notice the balance sheet is the accounting equation in financial statement form: Assets = Liabilities + Owner's Equity. (attribution: Copyright Rice University, OpenStax, under CC BY-NC-SA 4.0 license)

THINK IT THROUGH

Financial Statement Analysis

In Why It Matters, we pointed out that accounting information from the financial statements can be useful to business owners. The financial statements provide feedback to the owners regarding the financial performance and financial position of the business, helping the owners to make decisions about the business.

Using the June financial statements, analyze Cheesy Chuck's and prepare a brief presentation. Consider this from the perspective of the owner, Chuck. Describe the financial performance of and financial position of the business. What areas of the business would you want to analyze further to get additional information? What changes would you consider making to the business, if any, and why or why not?

ETHICAL CONSIDERATIONS

Financial Statement Manipulation at Waste Management Inc.

Accountants have an ethical duty to accurately report the financial results of their company and to ensure that the company's annual reports communicate relevant information to stakeholders. If accountants and company management fail to do so, they may incur heavy penalties.

For example, in 2002 the Securities and Exchange Commission (SEC) charged the top management of Waste Management, Inc. with inflating profits by $1.7 billion to meet earnings targets in the period 1992–1997. An SEC press release alleged "that defendants fraudulently manipulated the company's financial results to meet predetermined earnings targets. . . . They employed a multitude of improper accounting practices to achieve this objective."[13] The defendants in the case manipulated reports to defer or eliminate expenses, which fraudulently inflated their earnings. Because they failed to accurately report the financial results of their company, the top accountants and management of Waste Management, Inc. face charges.

Thomas C. Newkirk, the associate director of the SEC's Division of Enforcement, stated, "For years, these defendants cooked the books, enriched themselves, preserved their jobs, and duped unsuspecting shareholders"[14] The defendants, who included members of the company board and executives, benefited personally from their fraud in the millions of dollars through performance-based bonuses, charitable giving, and sale of company stock. The company's accounting form, Arthur Andersen, abetted the fraud by identifying the improper practices but doing little to stop them.

13 U.S. Securities and Exchange Commission. "Waste Management Founder, Five Other Former Top Officers Sued for Massive Fraud." March 26, 2002. https://www.sec.gov/news/headlines/wastemgmt6.htm

14 U.S. Securities and Exchange Commission. "Waste Management Founder, Five Other Former Top Officers Sued for Massive Fraud." March 26, 2002. https://www.sec.gov/news/headlines/wastemgmt6.htm

Liquidity Ratios

In addition to reviewing the financial statements in order to make decisions, owners and other stakeholders may also utilize financial ratios to assess the financial health of the organization. While a more in-depth discussion of financial ratios occurs in Appendix A: Financial Statement Analysis, here we introduce *liquidity ratios*, a common, easy, and useful way to analyze the financial statements.

Liquidity refers to the business's ability to convert assets into cash in order to meet short-term cash needs. Examples of the most liquid assets include accounts receivable and inventory for merchandising or manufacturing businesses). The reason these are among the most liquid assets is that these assets will be turned into cash more quickly than land or buildings, for example. Accounts receivable represents goods or services that have already been sold and will typically be paid/collected within thirty to forty-five days. Inventory is less liquid than accounts receivable because the product must first be sold before it generates cash (either through a cash sale or sale on account). Inventory is, however, more liquid than land or buildings because, under most circumstances, it is easier and quicker for a business to find someone to purchase its goods than it is to find a buyer for land or buildings.

Working Capital

The starting point for understanding liquidity ratios is to define **working capital**—current assets minus current liabilities. Recall that current assets and current liabilities are amounts generally settled in one year or less. Working capital (current assets minus current liabilities) is used to assess the dollar amount of assets a business has available to meet its short-term liabilities. A positive working capital amount is desirable and indicates the business has sufficient current assets to meet short-term obligations (liabilities) and still has financial flexibility. A negative amount is undesirable and indicates the business should pay particular attention to the composition of the current assets (that is, how liquid the current assets are) and to the timing of the current liabilities. It is unlikely that all of the current liabilities will be due at the same time, but the amount of working capital gives stakeholders of both small and large businesses an indication of the firm's ability to meet its short-term obligations.

One limitation of working capital is that it is a dollar amount, which can be misleading because business sizes vary. Recall from the discussion on materiality that $1,000, for example, is more material to a small business (like an independent local movie theater) than it is to a large business (like a movie theater chain). Using percentages or ratios allows financial statement users to more easily compare small and large businesses.

Current Ratio

The **current ratio** is closely related to working capital; it represents the current assets divided by current liabilities. The current ratio utilizes the same amounts as working capital (current assets and current liabilities) but presents the amount in ratio, rather than dollar, form. That is, the current ratio is defined as current assets/current liabilities. The interpretation of the current ratio is similar to working capital. A ratio of greater than one indicates that the firm has the ability to meet short-term obligations with a buffer, while a ratio of less than one indicates that the firm should pay close attention to the composition of its current assets as well as the timing of the current liabilities.

Sample Working Capital and Current Ratio Calculations

Assume that Chuck, the owner of Cheesy Chuck's, wants to assess the liquidity of the business. Figure 2.14 shows the June 30, 2018, balance sheet. Assume the Equipment listed on the balance sheet is a noncurrent asset. This is a reasonable assumption as this is the first month of operation and the equipment is expected to last several years. We also assume the Accounts Payable and Wages Payable will be paid within one year and are, therefore, classified as current liabilities.

CHEESY CHUCK'S CLASSIC CORN Balance Sheet As of June 30, 2018			
Assets		**Liabilities**	
Cash	$ 6,200	Accounts Payable	$ 650
Equipment	12,500	Wages Payable	1,200
		Total Liabilities	**$ 1,850**
		Owner's Equity	
		Cheesy Chuck, Capital	16,850
		Total Owner's Equity	**$16,850**
Total Assets	**$18,700**	**Total Liabilities and Owner's Equity**	**$18,700**

Figure 2.14 Balance Sheet for Cheesy Chuck's Classic Corn. The balance sheet provides a snapshot of the company's financial position. By showing the total assets, total liabilities, and total equity of the business, the balance sheet provides information that is useful for decision-making. In addition, using ratios can give stakeholders another view of the company, allowing for comparisons to prior periods and to other businesses. (attribution: Copyright Rice University, OpenStax, under CC BY-NC-SA 4.0 license)

Working capital is calculated as current assets minus current liabilities. Cheesy Chuck's has only two assets, and one of the assets, Equipment, is a noncurrent asset, so the value of current assets is the cash amount of $6,200. The working capital of Cheesy Chuck's is $6,200 – $1,850 or $4,350. Since this amount is over $0 (it is well over $0 in this case), Chuck is confident he has nothing to worry about regarding the liquidity of his business.

Let's further assume that Chuck, while attending a popcorn conference for store owners, has a conversation with the owner of a much larger popcorn store—Captain Caramel's. The owner of Captain Caramel's happens to share the working capital for his store is $52,500. At first Chuck feels his business is not doing so well. But then he realizes that Captain Caramel's is located in a much bigger city (with more customers) and has been around for many years, which has allowed them to build a solid business, which Chuck aspires to do. How would Chuck compare the liquidity of his new business, opened just one month, with the liquidity of a larger and more-established business in another market? The answer is by calculating the current ratio, which removes the size differences (materiality) of the two businesses.

The current ratio is calculated as current assets/current liabilities. We use the same amounts that we used in the working capital calculation, but this time we divide the amounts rather than subtract the amounts. So Cheesy Chuck's current ratio is $6,200 (current assets)/$1,850 (current liabilities), or 3.35. This means that for every dollar of current liabilities, Cheesy Chuck's has $3.35 of current assets. Chuck is pleased with the ratio but does not know how this compares to another popcorn store, so he asked his new friend from Captain Caramel's. The owner of Captain Caramel's shares that his store has a current ratio of 4.25. While it is still better than Cheesy Chuck's, Chuck is encouraged to learn that his store is performing at a more competitive level than he previously thought by comparing the dollar amounts of working capital.

IFRS CONNECTION

IFRS and US GAAP in Financial Statements

Understanding the elements that make up financial statements, the organization of those elements within the financial statements, and what information each statement relays is important, whether analyzing the financial statements of a US company or one from Honduras. Since most US companies apply generally accepted accounting principles (GAAP)[15] as prescribed by the Financial Accounting Standards Board (FASB), and most international companies apply some version of the International Financial Reporting Standards (IFRS),[16] knowing how these two sets of accounting standards are similar or different regarding the elements of the financial statements will facilitate analysis and decision-making.

Both IFRS and US GAAP have the same elements as components of financial statements: assets, liabilities, equity, income, and expenses. Equity, income, and expenses have similar subcategorization between the two types of GAAP (US GAAP and IFRS) as described. For example, income can be in the form of earned income (a lawyer providing legal services) or in the form of gains (interest earned on an investment account). The definition of each of these elements is similar between IFRS and US GAAP, but there are some differences that can influence the value of the account or the placement of the account on the financial statements. Many of these differences are discussed in detail later in this course when that element—for example, the nuances of accounting for liabilities—is discussed. Here is an example to illustrate how these minor differences in definition can impact placement within the financial statements when using US GAAP versus IFRS. ACME Car Rental Company typically rents its cars for a time of two years or 60,000 miles. At the end of whichever of these two measures occurs first, the cars are sold. Under both US GAAP and IFRS, the cars are noncurrent assets during the period when they are rented. Once the cars are being "held for sale," under IFRS rules, the cars become current assets. However, under US GAAP, there is no specific rule as to where to list those "held for sale" cars; thus, they could still list the cars as noncurrent assets. As you learn more about the analysis of companies and financial information, this difference in placement on the financial statements will become more meaningful. At this point, simply know that financial analysis can include ratios, which is the comparison of two numbers, and thus any time you change the denominator or the numerator, the ratio result will change.

There are many similarities and some differences in the actual presentation of the various financial statements, but these are discussed in The Adjustment Process at which point these similarities and differences will be more meaningful and easier to follow.

15 Publicly traded companies in the United States must file their financial statements with the SEC, and those statements must be compiled using US GAAP. However, in some states, private companies can apply IFRS for SMEs (small and medium entities).

16 The following site identifies which countries require IFRS, which use a modified version of IFRS, and which countries prohibit the use of IFRS. https://www.iasplus.com/en/resources/ifrs-topics/use-of-ifrs

Key Terms

accounting equation assets = liabilities + owner's equity

accounts payable value of goods or services purchased that will be paid for at a later date

accounts receivable outstanding customer debt on a credit sale, typically receivable within a short time period

accrual basis accounting accounting system in which revenue is recorded or recognized when earned yet not necessarily received, and in which expenses are recorded when legally incurred and not necessarily when paid

asset tangible or intangible resource owned or controlled by a company, individual, or other entity with the intent that it will provide economic value

balance sheet financial statement that lists what the organization owns (assets), owes (liabilities), and is worth (equity) on a specific date

cash basis accounting method of accounting in which transactions are not recorded in the financial statements until there is an exchange of cash

common stock corporation's primary class of stock issued, with each share representing a partial claim to ownership or a share of the company's business

comprehensive income change in equity of a business enterprise during a period from transactions and other events and circumstances from nonowner sources

corporation legal business structure involving one or more individuals (owners) who are legally distinct (separate) from the business

current asset asset that will be used or consumed in one year or less

current liability debt or obligation due within one year or, in rare cases, a company's standard operating cycle, whichever is greater

current ratio current assets divided by current liabilities; used to determine a company's liquidity (ability to meet short-term obligations)

distribution to owner periodic "reward" distributed to owner of cash or other assets

dividend portion of the net worth (equity) that is returned to owners of a corporation as a reward for their investment

elements of the financial statements categories or groupings used to record transactions and prepare financial statements

equity residual interest in the assets of an entity that remains after deducting its liabilities

expense cost associated with providing goods or services

gain increase in organizational value from activities that are "incidental or peripheral" to the primary purpose of the business

income statement financial statement that measures the organization's financial performance for a given period of time

initial public offering (IPO) when a company issues shares of its stock to the public for the first time

intangible asset asset with financial value but no physical presence; examples include copyrights, patents, goodwill, and trademarks

inventory value of products to be sold or items to be converted into sellable products

investment by owner exchange of cash or other assets in exchange for an ownership interest in the organization

liability probable future sacrifice of economic benefits arising from present obligations of a particular entity to transfer assets or provide services to other entities in the future as a result of past transactions or events

liquidity ability to convert assets into cash in order to meet primarily short-term cash needs or emergencies

long-term asset asset used ongoing in the normal course of business for more than one year that is not intended to be resold

long-term liability debt settled outside one year or one operating cycle, whichever is longer

loss decrease in organizational value from activities that are "incidental or peripheral" to the primary purpose of the business

net income when revenues and gains are greater than expenses and losses

net loss when expenses and losses are greater than revenues and gains

noncurrent asset asset that will be used or consumed over more than one year

noncurrent liability liability that is expected to be settled in more than one year

notes payable value of amounts borrowed that will be paid in the future with interest

notes receivable value of amounts loaned that will be received in the future with interest

partnership legal business structure consisting of an association of two or more people who contribute money, property, or services to operate as co-owners of a business

publicly traded company company whose stock is traded (bought and sold) on an organized stock exchange

retained earnings cumulative, undistributed net income or net loss for the business since its inception

revenue inflows or other enhancements of assets of an entity or settlements of its liabilities (or a combination of both) from delivering or producing goods, rendering services, or other activities that constitute the entity's ongoing major or central operations

Securities and Exchange Commission (SEC) federal regulatory agency that regulates corporations with shares listed and traded on security exchanges through required periodic filings

short-term asset asset typically used up, sold, or converted to cash in one year or less

short-term liability liability typically expected to be paid within one year or less

sole proprietorship legal business structure consisting of a single individual

stakeholder someone affected by decisions made by a company; may include an investor, creditor, employee, manager, regulator, customer, supplier, and layperson

statement of cash flows financial statement listing the cash inflows and cash outflows for the business for a period of time

statement of owner's equity financial statement showing how the equity of the organization changed for a period of time

tangible asset asset that has physical substance

working capital current assets less current liabilities; sometimes used as a measure of liquidity

Summary

2.1 Describe the Income Statement, Statement of Owner's Equity, Balance Sheet, and Statement of Cash Flows, and How They Interrelate

- Financial statements provide financial information to stakeholders to help them in making decisions.
- There are four financial statements: income statement, statement of owner's equity, balance sheet, and statement of cash flows.
- The income statement measures the financial *performance* of the organization for a period of time. The income statement lists revenues, expenses, gains, and losses, which make up net income (or net loss).
- The statement of owner's equity shows how the net worth of the organization changes for a period of time. In addition to showing net income or net loss, the statement of owner's equity shows the

investments by and distributions to owners.

- The balance sheet shows the organization's financial *position* on a given date. The balance sheet lists assets, liabilities, and owners' equity.
- The statement of cash flows shows the organization's cash inflows and cash outflows for a given period of time. The statement of cash flows is necessary because financial statements are usually prepared using *accrual* accounting, which records transactions when they occur rather than waiting until cash is exchanged.

2.2 Define, Explain, and Provide Examples of Current and Noncurrent Assets, Current and Noncurrent Liabilities, Equity, Revenues, and Expenses

- Assets and liabilities are categorized into current and noncurrent, based on when the item will be settled. Assets and liabilities that will be settled in one year or less are classified as current; otherwise, the items are classified as noncurrent.
- Assets are also categorized based on whether or not the asset has physical substance. Assets with physical substance are considered tangible assets, while intangible assets lack physical substance.
- The distinction between current and noncurrent assets and liabilities is important because it helps financial statement users assess the timing of the transactions.
- Three broad categories of legal business structures are sole proprietorship, partnership, and corporation, with each structure having advantages and disadvantages.
- The accounting equation is Assets = Liabilities + Owner's Equity. It is important to the study of accounting because it shows what the organization owns and the sources of (or claims against) those resources.
- Owners' equity can also be thought of as the net worth or value of the business. There are many factors that influence equity, including net income or net loss, investments by and distributions to owners, revenues, gains, losses, expenses, and comprehensive income.

2.3 Prepare an Income Statement, Statement of Owner's Equity, and Balance Sheet

- There are ten financial statement elements: revenues, expenses, gains, losses, assets, liabilities, equity, investments by owners, distributions to owners, and comprehensive income.
- There are standard conventions for the order of preparing financial statements (income statement, statement of owner's equity, balance sheet, and statement of cash flows) and for the format (three-line heading and columnar structure).
- Financial ratios, which are calculated using financial statement information, are often beneficial to aid in financial decision-making. Ratios allow for comparisons between businesses and determining trends between periods within the same business.
- Liquidity ratios assess the firm's ability to convert assets into cash.
- Working Capital (Current Assets – Current Liabilities) is a liquidity ratio that measures a firm's ability to meet current obligations.
- The Current Ratio (Current Assets/Current Liabilities) is similar to Working Capital but allows for comparisons between firms by determining the proportion of current assets to current liabilities.

Multiple Choice

1. LO 2.1 Which of these statements is *not* one of the financial statements?

A. income statement
B. balance sheet
C. statement of cash flows
D. statement of owner investments

2. LO 2.1 Stakeholders are less likely to include which of the following groups?

A. owners
B. employees
C. community leaders
D. competitors

3. LO 2.1 Identify the correct components of the income statement.

A. revenues, losses, expenses, and gains
B. assets, liabilities, and owner's equity
C. revenues, expenses, investments by owners, distributions to owners
D. assets, liabilities, and dividends

4. LO 2.1 The balance sheet lists which of the following?

A. assets, liabilities, and owners' equity
B. revenues, expenses, gains, and losses
C. assets, liabilities, and investments by owners
D. revenues, expenses, gains, and distributions to owners

5. LO 2.1 Assume a company has a $350 credit (not cash) sale. How would the transaction appear if the business uses *accrual* accounting?

A. $350 would show up on the balance sheet as a sale.
B. $350 would show up on the income statement as a sale.
C. $350 would show up on the statement of cash flows as a cash outflow.
D. The transaction would not be reported because the cash was not exchanged.

6. LO 2.2 Which of the following statements is true?

A. Tangible assets lack physical substance.
B. Tangible assets will be consumed in a year or less.
C. Tangible assets have physical substance.
D. Tangible assets will be consumed in over a year.

7. LO 2.2 Owners have no personal liability under which legal business structure?

A. a corporation
B. a partnership
C. a sole proprietorship
D. There is liability in every legal business structure.

8. LO 2.2 The accounting equation is expressed as ______.

A. Assets + Liabilities = Owner's Equity
B. Assets – Noncurrent Assets = Liabilities
C. Assets = Liabilities + Investments by Owners
D. Assets = Liabilities + Owner's Equity

9. LO 2.2 Which of the following decreases owner's equity?

A. investments by owners
B. losses
C. gains
D. short-term loans

10. LO 2.2 Exchanges of assets for assets have what effect on equity?

A. increase equity
B. may have no impact on equity
C. decrease equity
D. There is no relationship between assets and equity.

11. LO 2.2 All of the following increase owner's equity *except* for which one?

A. gains
B. investments by owners
C. revenues
D. acquisitions of assets by incurring liabilities

12. LO 2.3 Which of the following is not an element of the financial statements?

A. future potential sales price of inventory
B. assets
C. liabilities
D. equity

13. LO 2.3 Which of the following is the correct order of preparing the financial statements?

A. income statement, statement of cash flows, balance sheet, statement of owner's equity
B. income statement, statement of owner's equity, balance sheet, statement of cash flows
C. income statement, balance sheet, statement of owner's equity, statement of cash flows
D. income statement, balance sheet, statement of cash flows, statement of owner's equity

14. LO 2.3 The three heading lines of financial statements typically include which of the following?

A. company, statement title, time period of report
B. company headquarters, statement title, name of preparer
C. statement title, time period of report, name of preparer
D. name of auditor, statement title, fiscal year end

15. LO 2.3 Which financial statement shows the financial *performance* of the company on a cash basis?

A. balance sheet
B. statement of owner's equity
C. statement of cash flows
D. income statement

16. LO 2.3 Which financial statement shows the financial *position* of the company?

A. balance sheet
B. statement of owner's equity
C. statement of cash flows
D. income statement

17. LO 2.3 Working capital is an indication of the firm's ______.

A. asset utilization
B. amount of noncurrent liabilities
C. liquidity
D. amount of noncurrent assets

Questions

1. LO 2.1 Identify the four financial statements and describe the purpose of each.

2. LO 2.1 Define the term *stakeholders*. Identify two stakeholder groups, and explain how each group might use the information contained in the financial statements.

3. LO 2.1 Identify one similarity and one difference between revenues and gains. Why is this distinction important to stakeholders?

4. LO 2.1 Identify one similarity and one difference between expenses and losses. Why is this distinction important to stakeholders?

5. LO 2.1 Explain the concept of equity, and identify some activities that affect equity of a business.

6. LO 2.2 Explain the difference between current and noncurrent assets and liabilities. Why is this distinction important to stakeholders?

7. LO 2.2 Identify/discuss one similarity and one difference between tangible and intangible assets.

8. LO 2.2 Name the three types of legal business structure. Describe one advantage and one disadvantage of each.

9. LO 2.2 What is the "accounting equation"? List two examples of business transactions, and explain how the accounting equation would be impacted by these transactions.

10. LO 2.3 Identify the order in which the four financial statements are prepared, and explain how the first three statements are interrelated.

11. LO 2.3 Explain how the following items affect equity: revenue, expenses, investments by owners, and distributions to owners.

12. LO 2.3 Explain the purpose of the statement of cash flows and why this statement is needed.

Exercise Set A

EA1. LO 2.1 For each independent situation below, calculate the missing values.

Revenues	–	Expenses	+	Gains	–	Losses	=	Net Income/(Loss)
$ 1,250		$ 1,100		$ 125		$ 75		?
?		100,755		0		1,550		$ (485)
75,560		68,600		?		1,675		6,485
26,390		?		320		600		(990)
872,300		856,995		11,000		?		26,305

EA2. LO 2.1 For each independent situation below, calculate the missing values for owner's equity

Beginning Balance	+	Investments	–	Distributions	=	Ending Balance
$ 0		$ 22,750		$ 12,000		?
17,630		?		7,500		$ 66,330
?		75,300		163,200		138,900
0		175,300		?		159,530
85,800		62,750		43,900		?

EA3. LO 2.1 For each independent situation below, calculate the missing values.

Assets	–	Liabilities	=	Owner's Equity
$ 32,000		$ 17,000		?
168,700		?		$146,300
17,500		16,830		?
?		232,000		330,700
382,170		?		125,270

EA4. LO 2.1 For each independent situation below, place an (X) by the transactions that would be included in the statement of cash flows.

Transaction	Included
Sold items on account	
Wrote check to pay utilities	
Received cash investment by owner	
Recorded wages owed to employees	
Received bill for advertising	

Table 2.3

EA5. LO 2.2 For each of the following items, identify whether the item is considered current or noncurrent, and explain why.

Item	Current or Noncurrent?
Cash	
Inventory	
Machines	
Trademarks	
Accounts Payable	
Wages Payable	
Owner, Capital	
Accounts Receivable	

Table 2.4

EA6. LO 2.2 For the items listed below, indicate how the item affects equity (increase, decrease, or no impact.

Item	Increase? Decrease? or No Impact?
Expenses	
Assets	
Gains	
Liabilities	
Dividends	

Table 2.5

EA7. LO 2.2 Forest Company had the following transactions during the month of December. What is the December 31 cash balance?

Cash sales	$3,250
Payments for inventory	1,760
Investments by owners	3,000
Supplies used	175
Cash withdrawals	260
Inventory received	2,500
Wages paid	2,390
Cash balance Dec. 1	4,250

EA8. LO 2.2 Here are facts for the Hudson Roofing Company for December.

Hudson Alexander, Capital Dec. 1	$175,300
Dec. revenue	56,400
Dec. expenses	59,800

Assuming no investments or withdrawals, what is the ending balance in the owners' capital account?

EA9. LO 2.3 Prepare an income statement using the following information for DL Enterprises for the month of July 2018.

Sales revenue	$62,500
Rental revenue	15,300
Product expense	52,200
Wages expense	18,900
Owner investment	12,000
Equipment purchases	56,000
Utilities expense	1,800
Taxes expense	400

EA10. LO 2.3 Prepare a statement of owner's equity using the information provided for Pirate Landing for the month of October 2018.

Cash	$14,500
Pirate Pete, Capital Oct. 1	56,000
Net loss Oct. 2017	7,800
Owner investments	1,500
Wages payable	3,250
Supplies expense	750
Owner withdrawals	100

EA11. LO 2.3 Prepare a balance sheet using the following information for the Ginger Company as of March 31, 2019.

Accounts payable	$ 1,730
Cash	11,050
Ginger Ale, Capital Mar. 1	17,300
Inventory	8,230
Wages payable	2,150
Sales	13,600
Product expenses	8,200
Ginger Ale, Capital Mar. 31	22,700
Equipment	7,300

Exercise Set B

EB1. LO 2.1 For each independent situation below, calculate the missing values.

Revenues	–	Expenses	+	Gains	–	Losses	=	Net Income/(Loss)
$ 1,813		$ 1,595		$ 181		$ 109		?
?		146,095		$ 0		2,248		$ (703)
109,562		99,470		?		2,429		9,403
38,266		?		464		870		(1,436)
1,264,835		1,242,643		15,950		?		38,142

EB2. LO 2.1 For each independent situation below, calculate the missing values for Owner's Equity.

Beginning Balance	+	Investments	–	Distributions	=	Ending Balance
$ 0		$ 14,333		$ 7,560		?
11,107		?		4,725		$ 41,788
?		47,439		102,816		87,507
0		110,439		?		100,504
54,054		39,533		27,657		?

EB3. LO 2.1 For each independent situation below, calculate the missing values.

Assets	–	Liabilities	=	Owner's Equity
$ 81,600		$ 17,000		?
430,185		?		$373,065
44,625		42,917		?
?		591,600		843,285
974,534		?		319,439

EB4. LO 2.1 For each of the following independent situations, place an (X) by the transactions that would be included in the statement of cash flows.

Transaction	Included
Purchased supplies with check	
Received inventory (a bill was included)	
Paid cash to owner for withdrawal	
Gave cash donation to local charity	
Received bill for utilities	

Table 2.6

EB5. LO 2.2 For each of the following items, identify whether the item is considered current or noncurrent, and explain why.

Item	Current or Noncurrent?
Inventory	
Buildings	
Accounts Receivable	
Cash	
Trademarks	
Accounts Payable	
Wages Payable	
Common Stock	

Table 2.7

EB6. LO 2.2 For the items listed below, indicate how the item affects equity (increase, decrease, or no impact).

Item	Increase? Decrease? or No Impact?
Revenues	
Gains	
Losses	
Drawings	
Investments	

Table 2.8

EB7. LO 2.2 Gumbo Company had the following transactions during the month of December. What was the December 1 cash balance?

Dividends paid	$ 221
Credit sales	149
Payments for equipment	1,496
Taxes paid	2,032
Common stock sold	2,550
Inventory received	2,125
Cash sales	2,763
Cash balance Dec. 31	9,869

EB8. LO 2.2 Here are facts for Hailey's Collision Service for January.

Hailey Shusher, Capital Jan. 1	$61,355
Jan. revenue	23,240
Jan. expenses	20,930

Assuming no investments or withdrawals, what is the ending balance in the owners' capital account?

EB9. LO 2.3 Prepare an income statement using the following information for CK Company for the month of February 2019.

Sales revenue	$26,250
Rental revenue	6,426
Product expense	21,924
Wages expense	7,938
Owner investment	5,040
Equipment purchases	23,520
Utilities expense	756
Taxes expense	168

EB10. LO 2.3 Prepare a statement of owner's equity using the following information for the Can Due Shop for the month of September 2018.

Cash	$ 51,040
Steve due, Capital Sep.1	197,120
Net income Sep. 2018	27,456
Owner investments	5,280
Wages payable	11,440
Supplies expense	2,640
Owner withdraws	352

EB11. LO 2.3 Prepare a balance sheet using the following information for Mike's Consulting as of January 31, 2019.

Accounts payable	$ 570
Cash	3,646
Mike Michael, Capital Jan. 1	5,709
Inventory	2,716
Wages payable	710
Sales	4,488
Product expenses	2,706
Mike Michael, Capital Jan. 31	7,491
Equipment	2,409

Problem Set A

PA1. LO 2.1 The following information is taken from the records of Baklava Bakery for the year 2019.

Revenues: Jan.	$22,500
Gains: Feb.	1,200
Losses: Mar.	3,700
Expenses: Feb.	21,620
Gains: Jan.	0
Revenues: Mar.	42,800
Losses: Feb.	1,600
Expenses: Mar.	45,100
Losses: Jan.	0
Revenues: Feb.	37,550
Expenses: Jan.	20,760
Gains: Mar.	5,600

A. Calculate net income or net loss for January.

B. Calculate net income or net loss for February.

C. Calculate net income or net loss for March.

D. For each situation, comment on how a stakeholder might view the firm's performance. (Hint: Think about the source of the income or loss.)

PA2. LO 2.1 Each situation below relates to an independent company's owners' equity.

	Beginning Balance	+	Net Income	-	Net Loss	+	Investments	-	Distributions	=	Ending Balance
Co.1	?		$16,500		$ 0		$22,300		$ 1,750		$ 37,050
Co.2	$ 63,180		0		12,000		0		?		44,880
Co.3	275,300		?		0		0		24,100		299,400

A. Calculate the missing values.

B. Based on your calculations, make observations about each company.

PA3. LO 2.1 The following information is from a new business. Comment on the year-to-year changes in the accounts and possible sources and uses of funds (how were the funds obtained and used).

	Assets	-	Liabilities	=	Owner's Equity
End of Year 1	$245,000		$120,000		$125,000
End of Year 2	286,000		150,000		136,000
End of Year 3	212,000		80,000		132,000

PA4. LO 2.1 Each of the following situations relates to a different company.

		Company A	Company B	Company C	Company D
1	Revenues	$16,500	$167,320	?	$235,000
2	Expenses	12,400	?	$72,300	241,000
3	Gains	750	1,350	0	?
4	Losses	900	6,240	5,200	0
5	Net Income or (Loss)	?	(9,250)	5,100	6,300

A. For each of these independent situations, find the missing amounts.

B. How would stakeholders view the financial performance of each company? Explain.

PA5. LO 2.2 For each of the following independent transactions, indicate whether there was an increase, a decrease, or no impact for each financial statement element.

Transaction	Assets	Liabilities	Owners' Equity
Paid cash for expenses			
Sold common stock for cash			
Owe vendor for purchase of asset			
Paid owners for dividends			
Paid vendor for amount previously owed			

Table 2.9

PA6. LO 2.2 Olivia's Apple Orchard had the following transactions during the month of September, the first month in business.

Transaction	Amount	Asset	–	Liability	=	Owner's Equity
Amount owed for land purchase	$50,000	$50,000		$50,000		$0
Apple sales: cash	3,000	?		?		?
Apple sales: credit	6,000	?		?		?
Collections of credit sales	4,000	?		?		?
Cash purchase of equipment	10,000	?		?		?
Owner investments	25,000	?		?		?
Wages expenses paid	6,000	?		?		?
Fuel expenses paid	400	?		?		?
Amount owed for utility expense	1,000	?		?		?
Current totals		$50,000		$50,000		$0

Complete the chart to determine the ending balances. As an example, the first transaction has been completed. Note: Negative amounts should be indicated with minus signs (–) and unaffected should be noted as $0.

(Hints: 1. each transaction will involve two financial statement elements; 2. the net impact of the transaction may be $0.)

PA7. LO 2.2 Using the information in PA6, determine the amount of revenue and expenses for Olivia's Apple Orchard for the month of September.

PA8. LO 2.3 The following ten transactions occurred during the July grand opening of the Pancake Palace. Assume all Retained Earnings transactions relate to the primary purpose of the business.

	Assets			Liabilities		Owner's Equity	
	Cash	Inventory	Equipment	Accounts Payable	Wages Payable	Common Stock	Retained Earnings
1	$50,000					$50,000	
2	(6,000)	$6,000					
3			$22,000	$22,000			
4	1,250						$ 1,250
5	(750)						(750)
6				600			(600)
7					$3,000		(3,000)
8	3,200						3,200
9				175			(175)
10	(1,000)		1,000				
Ending Balance							

A. Calculate the ending balance for each account.

B. Create the income statement.

C. Create the statement of owner's equity.

D. Create the balance sheet.

Problem Set B

PB1. LO 2.1 The following information is taken from the records of Rosebloom Flowers for the year 2019.

Revenues: Jan.	$36,425
Gains: Feb.	2,820
Losses: Mar.	8,695
Expenses: Feb.	50,807
Gains: Jan.	0
Revenues: Mar.	53,580
Losses: Feb.	3,760
Expenses: Mar.	58,985
Losses: Jan.	0
Revenues: Feb.	88,243
Expenses: Jan.	48,786
Gains: Mar.	13,160

A. Calculate net income or net loss for January.

B. Calculate net income or net loss for February.

C. Calculate net income or net loss for March.

D. For each situation, comment on how a stakeholder might view the firm's performance. (Hint: think about the source of the income or loss.)

PB2. LO 2.1 Each situation below relates to an independent company's Owners' Equity.

	Beginning Balance	+	Net Income	-	Net Loss	+	Investments	-	Distributions	=	Ending Balance
Co.1	$163,800		$16,500		$ 0		?		$ 1,750		$254,150
Co.2	63,180		0		12,000		$ 0		51,180		?
Co.3	0		0		?		150,000		0		101,400

A. Calculate the missing values.

B. Based on your calculations, make observations about each company.

PB3. LO 2.1 The following information is from a new business. Comment on the year-to-year changes in the accounts and possible sources and uses funds (how were the funds obtained and used).

	Assets	-	Liabilities	=	Owner's Equity
End of Year 1	$137,000		$62,000		$75,000
End of Year 2	148,000		57,000		91,000
End of Year 3	168,000		80,000		88,000

PB4. LO 2.1 Each of the following situations relates to a different company.

		Company A	Company B	Company C	Company D
1	Revenues	?	$1,480,500	$103,950	$1,054,116
2	Expenses	$455,490	1,518,300	78,120	?
3	Gains	0	?	4,725	8,505
4	Losses	32,760	0	5,670	39,312
5	Net Income or (Loss)	32,130	39,690	?	(58,275)

A. For each of these independent situations, find the missing amounts.

B. How would stakeholders view the financial performance of each company? Explain.

PB5. LO 2.2 For each of the following independent transactions, indicate whether there was an increase, decrease, or no impact on each financial statement element.

Transaction	Assets	Liabilities	Owners' Equity
Received cash for sale of asset (no gain or loss)			
Cash distribution to owner			
Cash sales			
Investment by owners			
Owe vendor for inventory purchase			

Table 2.10

PB6. LO 2.2 Mateo's Maple Syrup had the following transactions during the month of February, its first month in business.

Transaction	Amount	Asset	-	Liability	=	Owner's Equity
Common stock sold	$ 3,000	$3,000		$0		$3,000
Amount owed for tax expense	1,950	?		?		?
Amount owed for insurance expense	750	?		?		?
Syrup sales: cash	13,000	?		?		?
Syrup sales: credit	6,000	?		?		?
Dividends paid	40	?		?		?
Collections of credit sales	1,700	?		?		?
Cash purchase for supplies expenses	250	?		?		?
Cash paid for amounts owed	1,600	?		?		?
Utility expenses paid	400	?		?		?
Taxes paid	600	?		?		?
		$3,000	-	$0		$3,000

Complete the chart to determine the ending balances. As an example, the first transaction has been completed. Note: negative amounts should be indicated with minus signs (–).

(Hints: 1. each transaction will involve two financial statement elements; 2. the net impact of the transaction may be $0.)

PB7. LO 2.2 Using the information in PB6, determine the amount of revenue and expenses for Mateo's Maple Syrup for the month of February.

Thought Provokers

TP1. LO 2.1 Choose three stakeholders (or stakeholder groups) for Walmart and prepare a written response for each stakeholder. In your written response, consider the factors about the business the particular stakeholder would be interested in. Consider the financial and any nonfinancial factors that would be relevant to the stakeholder (or stakeholder group). Explain why these factors are important. Do some research and see if you can find support for your points.

TP2. LO 2.1 Assume you purchased ten shares of Roku during the company's IPO. Comment on why this might be a good investment. Consider factors such as what you expect to get from your investment, why you think Roku would become a publicly traded company, and what you think is the landscape of the industry Roku is in. What other factors might be relevant to your decision to invest in Roku?

TP3. LO 2.2 A trademark is an intangible asset that has value to a business. Assume that you are an accountant with the responsibility of valuing the trademark of a well-known company such as Nike or McDonald's. What makes each of these companies unique and adds value? While the value of a trademark may not necessarily be recorded on the company's balance sheet, discuss what factors you think would affect (increase or decrease) the value of the company's trademark? Consider your answer through the perspective of various stakeholders.

TP4. LO 2.3 For each of the following ten independent transactions, provide a written description of what occurred in each transaction. Figure 2.4 might help you.

	Assets			Liabilities		Owner's Equity	
	Cash	Inventory	Equipment	Accounts Payable	Wages Payable	Common Stock	Retained Earnings
1	$57,500					$57,500	
2	(6,900)	$6,900					
3			$25,300	$25,300			
4	1,438						$ 1,438
5	(863)						(863)
6				460			(460)
7					$3,450		(3,450)
8	3,680						3,680
9				102			(102)
10	(1,150)		1,150				

TP5. LO 2.3 The following historical information is from Assisi Community Markets.

	Current Assets			Current Liabilities	
	Cash	Accounts Receivable	Inventory	Accounts Payable	Wages Payable
Year 1	$42,000	$12,500	$ 6,200	$12,500	$3,200
Year 2	37,500	16,800	7,600	14,600	3,700
Year 3	26,800	22,900	10,300	19,800	4,500
Year 4	22,100	28,000	15,400	20,600	6,000
Year 5	15,700	29,500	16,700	22,900	8,200

Calculate the working capital and current ratio for each year. What observations do you make, and what actions might the owner consider taking?

3 Analyzing and Recording Transactions

Figure 3.1 Dry-Cleaning Organization. Small businesses need an organized approach to recording daily business activities. (credit: modification of "Dry cleaned clothes Unsplash" by "m0851"/Wikimedia Commons, CC0)

Chapter Outline

LO **3.1** Describe Principles, Assumptions, and Concepts of Accounting and Their Relationship to Financial Statements

LO **3.2** Define and Describe the Expanded Accounting Equation and Its Relationship to Analyzing Transactions

LO **3.3** Define and Describe the Initial Steps in the Accounting Cycle

LO **3.4** Analyze Business Transactions Using the Accounting Equation and Show the Impact of Business Transactions on Financial Statements

LO **3.5** Use Journal Entries to Record Transactions and Post to T-Accounts

LO **3.6** Prepare a Trial Balance

Why It Matters

Mark Summers wants to start his own dry-cleaning business upon finishing college. He has chosen to name his business Supreme Cleaners. Before he embarks on this journey, Mark must establish what the new business will require. He needs to determine if he wants to have anyone invest in his company. He also needs to consider any loans that he might need to take out from his bank to fund the initial start-up. There are daily business activities that Mark will need to keep track of, such as sales, purchasing equipment, paying bills, collecting money from customers, and paying back investors, among other things. This process utilizes a standard accounting framework so that the financial operations are comparable to other company's financial operations.

He knows it is important for him to keep thorough documentation of these business activities to give his investors and creditors, and himself, a clear and accurate picture of operations. Without this, he may find it difficult to stay in business. He will maintain an organized record of all of Supreme Cleaners' financial activities from their inception, using an accounting process meant to result in accurate financial statement preparation.

3.1 Describe Principles, Assumptions, and Concepts of Accounting and Their Relationship to Financial Statements

If you want to start your own business, you need to maintain detailed and accurate records of business performance in order for you, your investors, and your lenders, to make informed decisions about the future of your company. Financial statements are created with this purpose in mind. A set of financial statements includes the income statement, statement of owner's equity, balance sheet, and statement of cash flows. These statements are discussed in detail in Introduction to Financial Statements. This chapter explains the relationship between financial statements and several steps in the accounting process. We go into much more detail in The Adjustment Process and Completing the Accounting Cycle.

Accounting Principles, Assumptions, and Concepts

In Introduction to Financial Statements, you learned that the Financial Accounting Standards Board (FASB) is an independent, nonprofit organization that sets the standards for financial accounting and reporting, including generally accepted accounting principles (GAAP), for both public- and private-sector businesses in the United States.

As you may also recall, GAAP are the concepts, standards, and rules that guide the preparation and presentation of financial statements. If US accounting rules are followed, the accounting rules are called US GAAP. International accounting rules are called International Financial Reporting Standards (IFRS). Publicly traded companies (those that offer their shares for sale on exchanges in the United States) have the reporting of their financial operations regulated by the Securities and Exchange Commission (SEC).

You also learned that the SEC is an independent federal agency that is charged with protecting the interests of investors, regulating stock markets, and ensuring companies adhere to GAAP requirements. By having proper accounting standards such as US GAAP or IFRS, information presented publicly is considered comparable and reliable. As a result, financial statement users are more informed when making decisions. The SEC not only enforces the accounting rules but also delegates the process of setting standards for US GAAP to the FASB.

Some companies that operate on a global scale may be able to report their financial statements using IFRS. The SEC regulates the financial reporting of companies selling their shares in the United States, whether US GAAP or IFRS are used. The basics of accounting discussed in this chapter are the same under either set of guidelines.

ETHICAL CONSIDERATIONS

Auditing of Publicly Traded Companies

When a publicly traded company in the United States issues its financial statements, the financial statements have been audited by a Public Company Accounting Oversight Board (PCAOB) approved auditor. The PCAOB is the organization that sets the auditing standards, after approval by the SEC. It is important to remember that auditing is not the same as accounting. The role of the Auditor is to examine and provide assurance that financial statements are reasonably stated under the rules of appropriate accounting principles. The auditor conducts the audit under a set of standards known as Generally Accepted Auditing Standards. The accounting department of a company and its auditors are employees of two different companies. The auditors of a company are required to be employed by a different company so that there is independence.

The nonprofit Center for Audit Quality explains auditor independence: "Auditors' independence from company management is essential for a successful audit because it enables them to approach the audit with the necessary professional skepticism."[1] The center goes on to identify a key practice to protect independence by which an external auditor reports not to a company's management, which could make it more difficult to maintain independence, but to a company's audit committee. The audit committee oversees the auditors' work and monitors disagreements between management and the auditor about financial reporting. Internal auditors of a company are not the auditors that provide an opinion on the financial statements of a company. According to the Center for Audit Quality, "By law, public companies' annual financial statements are audited each year by independent auditors—accountants who examine the data for conformity with U.S. Generally Accepted Accounting Principles (GAAP)."[2] The opinion from the independent auditors regarding a publicly traded company is filed for public inspection, along with the financial statements of the publicly traded company.

The Conceptual Framework

The FASB uses a **conceptual framework**, which is a set of concepts that guide financial reporting. These concepts can help ensure information is comparable and reliable to stakeholders. Guidance may be given on how to report transactions, measurement requirements, and application on financial statements, among other things.[3]

IFRS CONNECTION

GAAP, IFRS, and the Conceptual Framework

The procedural part of accounting—recording transactions right through to creating financial statements—is a universal process. Businesses all around the world carry out this process as part of their normal operations. In carrying out these steps, the timing and rate at which transactions are recorded and subsequently reported in the financial statements are determined by the accepted accounting principles used by the company.

1 Center for Audit Quality. *Guide to Public Company Auditing*. https://www.iasplus.com/en/binary/usa/aicpa/0905caqauditguide.pdf

2 Center for Audit Quality. *Guide to Public Company Auditing*. https://www.iasplus.com/en/binary/usa/aicpa/0905caqauditguide.pdf

3 Financial Accounting Standards Board. "The Conceptual Framework." http://www.fasb.org/jsp/FASB/Page/BridgePage&cid=1176168367774

As you learned in Role of Accounting in Society, US-based companies will apply US GAAP as created by the FASB, and most international companies will apply IFRS as created by the International Accounting Standards Board (IASB). As illustrated in this chapter, the starting point for either FASB or IASB in creating accounting standards, or principles, is the conceptual framework. Both FASB and IASB cover the same topics in their frameworks, and the two frameworks are similar. The conceptual framework helps in the standard-setting process by creating the foundation on which those standards should be based. It can also help companies figure out how to record transactions for which there may not currently be an applicable standard. Though there are many similarities between the conceptual framework under US GAAP and IFRS, these similar foundations result in different standards and/or different interpretations.

Once an accounting standard has been written for US GAAP, the FASB often offers clarification on how the standard should be applied. Businesses frequently ask for guidance for their particular industry. When the FASB creates accounting standards and any subsequent clarifications or guidance, it only has to consider the effects of those standards, clarifications, or guidance on US-based companies. This means that FASB has only one major legal system and government to consider. When offering interpretations or other guidance on application of standards, the FASB can utilize knowledge of the US-based legal and taxation systems to help guide their points of clarification and can even create interpretations for specific industries. This means that interpretation and guidance on US GAAP standards can often contain specific details and guidelines in order to help align the accounting process with legal matters and tax laws.

In applying their conceptual framework to create standards, the IASB must consider that their standards are being used in 120 or more different countries, each with its own legal and judicial systems. Therefore, it is much more difficult for the IASB to provide as much detailed guidance once the standard has been written, because what might work in one country from a taxation or legal standpoint might not be appropriate in a different country. This means that IFRS interpretations and guidance have fewer detailed components for specific industries as compared to US GAAP guidance.

The conceptual framework sets the basis for accounting standards set by rule-making bodies that govern how the financial statements are prepared. Here are a few of the principles, assumptions, and concepts that provide guidance in developing GAAP.

Revenue Recognition Principle

The **revenue recognition principle** directs a company to recognize revenue in the period in which it is earned; revenue is not considered earned until a product or service has been provided. This means the period of time in which you performed the service or gave the customer the product is the period in which revenue is recognized.

There also does not have to be a correlation between when cash is collected and when revenue is recognized. A customer may not pay for the service on the day it was provided. Even though the customer has not yet paid cash, there is a reasonable expectation that the customer will pay in the future. Since the company has provided the service, it would recognize the revenue as earned, even though cash has yet to be collected.

For example, Lynn Sanders owns a small printing company, Printing Plus. She completed a print job for a customer on August 10. The customer did not pay cash for the service at that time and was billed for the service, paying at a later date. When should Lynn recognize the revenue, on August 10 or at the later payment date? Lynn should record revenue as earned on August 10. She provided the service to the customer, and there is a reasonable expectation that the customer will pay at the later date.

Expense Recognition (Matching) Principle

The **expense recognition principle** (also referred to as the matching principle) states that we must match expenses with associated revenues in the period in which the revenues were earned. A mismatch in expenses and revenues could be an understated net income in one period with an overstated net income in another period. There would be no reliability in statements if expenses were recorded separately from the revenues generated.

For example, if Lynn earned printing revenue in April, then any associated expenses to the revenue generation (such as paying an employee) should be recorded on the same income statement. The employee worked for Lynn in April, helping her earn revenue in April, so Lynn must match the expense with the revenue by showing both on the April income statement.

Cost Principle

The **cost principle**, also known as the historical cost principle, states that virtually everything the company owns or controls (*assets*) must be recorded at its value at the date of acquisition. For most assets, this value is easy to determine as it is the price agreed to when buying the asset from the vendor. There are some exceptions to this rule, but always apply the cost principle unless FASB has specifically stated that a different valuation method should be used in a given circumstance.

The primary exceptions to this historical cost treatment, at this time, are financial instruments, such as stocks and bonds, which might be recorded at their fair market value. This is called mark-to-market accounting or fair value accounting and is more advanced than the general basic concepts underlying the introduction to basic accounting concepts; therefore, it is addressed in more advanced accounting courses.

Once an asset is recorded on the books, the value of that asset must remain at its historical cost, even if its value in the market changes. For example, Lynn Sanders purchases a piece of equipment for $40,000. She believes this is a bargain and perceives the value to be more at $60,000 in the current market. Even though Lynn feels the equipment is worth $60,000, she may only record the cost she paid for the equipment of $40,000.

Full Disclosure Principle

The **full disclosure principle** states that a business must report any business activities that could affect what is reported on the financial statements. These activities could be nonfinancial in nature or be supplemental details not readily available on the main financial statement. Some examples of this include any pending litigation, acquisition information, methods used to calculate certain figures, or stock options. These disclosures are usually recorded in footnotes on the statements, or in addenda to the statements.

Separate Entity Concept

The **separate entity concept** prescribes that a business may only report activities on financial statements that are specifically related to company operations, not those activities that affect the owner personally. This concept is called the separate entity concept because the business is considered an entity separate and apart from its owner(s).

For example, Lynn Sanders purchases two cars; one is used for personal use only, and the other is used for business use only. According to the separate entity concept, Lynn may record the purchase of the car used by the company in the company's accounting records, but not the car for personal use.

Conservatism

This concept is important when valuing a transaction for which the dollar value cannot be as clearly determined, as when using the cost principle. **Conservatism** states that if there is uncertainty in a potential financial estimate, a company should err on the side of caution and report the most conservative amount. This would mean that any uncertain or estimated expenses/losses should be recorded, but uncertain or estimated revenues/gains should not. This understates net income, therefore reducing profit. This gives stakeholders a more reliable view of the company's financial position and does not overstate income.

Monetary Measurement Concept

In order to record a transaction, we need a system of **monetary measurement**, or a *monetary unit* by which to value the transaction. In the United States, this monetary unit is the US dollar. Without a dollar amount, it would be impossible to record information in the financial records. It also would leave stakeholders unable to make financial decisions, because there is no comparability measurement between companies. This concept ignores any change in the purchasing power of the dollar due to inflation.

Going Concern Assumption

The **going concern assumption** assumes a business will continue to operate in the foreseeable future. A common time frame might be twelve months. However, one should presume the business is doing well enough to continue operations unless there is evidence to the contrary. For example, a business might have certain expenses that are paid off (or reduced) over several time periods. If the business will stay operational in the foreseeable future, the company can continue to recognize these long-term expenses over several time periods. Some red flags that a business may no longer be a going concern are defaults on loans or a sequence of losses.

Time Period Assumption

The **time period assumption** states that a company can present useful information in shorter time periods, such as years, quarters, or months. The information is broken into time frames to make comparisons and evaluations easier. The information will be timely and current and will give a meaningful picture of how the company is operating.

For example, a school year is broken down into semesters or quarters. After each semester or quarter, your grade point average (GPA) is updated with new information on your performance in classes you completed. This gives you timely grading information with which to make decisions about your schooling.

A potential or existing investor wants timely information by which to measure the performance of the company, and to help decide whether to invest. Because of the time period assumption, we need to be sure to recognize revenues and expenses in the proper period. This might mean allocating costs over more than one accounting or reporting period.

The use of the principles, assumptions, and concepts in relation to the preparation of financial statements is better understood when looking at the full accounting cycle and its relation to the detailed process required to record business activities (Figure 3.2).

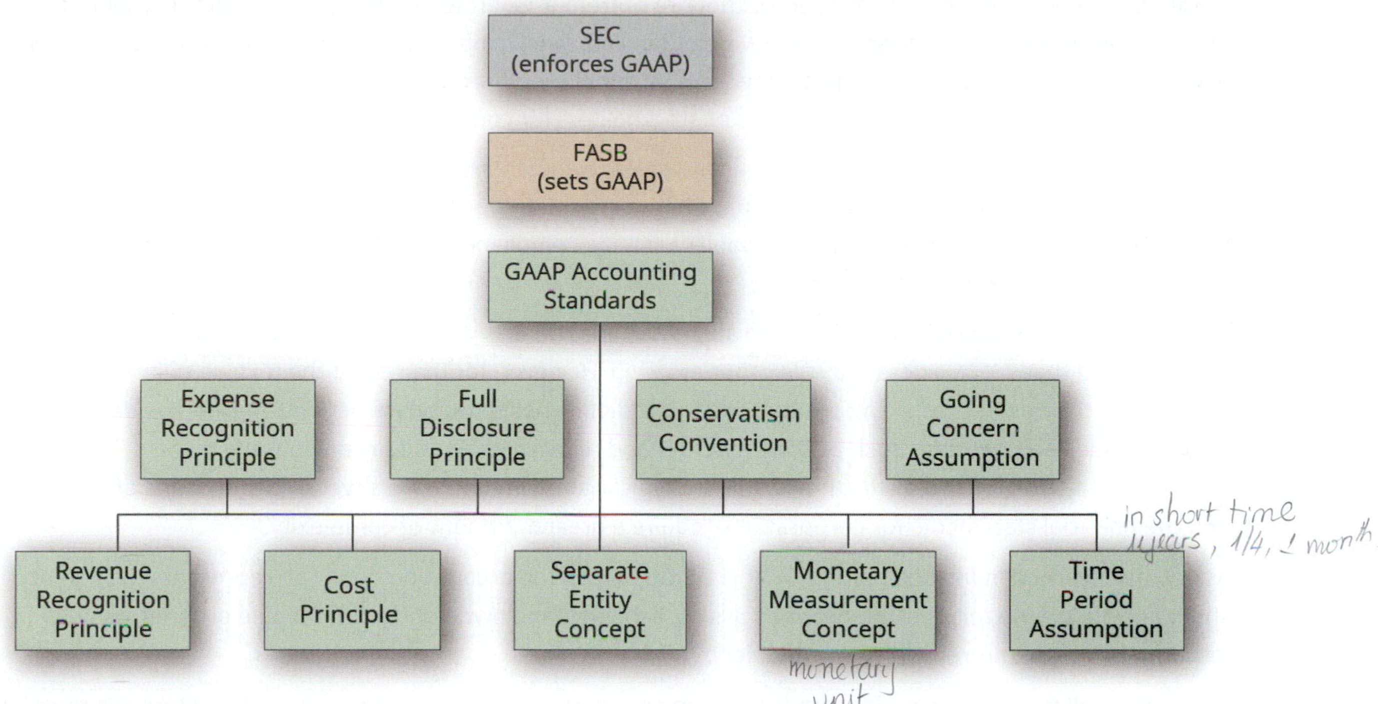

Figure 3.2 GAAP Accounting Standards Connection Tree. (attribution: Copyright Rice University, OpenStax, under CC BY-NC-SA 4.0 license)

CONCEPTS IN PRACTICE

Tax Cuts and Jobs Act

In 2017, the US government enacted the Tax Cuts and Jobs Act. As a result, financial stakeholders needed to resolve several issues surrounding the standards from GAAP principles and the FASB. The issues were as follows: "Current Generally Accepted Accounting Principles (GAAP) requires that deferred tax liabilities and assets be adjusted for the effect of a change in tax laws or rates," and "implementation issues related to the Tax Cuts and Jobs Act and income tax reporting."[4]

In response, the FASB issued updated guidance on both issues. You can explore these revised guidelines at the FASB website (https://www.fasb.org/taxcutsjobsact#section_1).

The Accounting Equation

Introduction to Financial Statements briefly discussed the accounting equation, which is important to the study of accounting because it shows what the organization owns and the sources of (or claims against) those resources. The accounting equation is expressed as follows:

Assets = Liabilities + Owner's Equity

4 Financial Accounting Standards Board (FASB). "Accounting for the Tax Cuts and Jobs Act." https://www.fasb.org/taxcutsjobsact#section_1

Recall that the accounting equation can be thought of from a "sources and claims" perspective; that is, the assets (items owned by the organization) were obtained by incurring liabilities or were provided by owners. Stated differently, everything a company owns must equal everything the company owes to creditors (lenders) and owners (individuals for sole proprietors or stockholders for companies or corporations).

In our example in Why It Matters, we used an individual owner, Mark Summers, for the Supreme Cleaners discussion to simplify our example. Individual owners are sole proprietors in legal terms. This distinction becomes significant in such areas as legal liability and tax compliance. For sole proprietors, the owner's interest is labeled "owner's equity."

In Introduction to Financial Statements, we addressed the owner's value in the firm as *capital* or *owner's equity*. This assumed that the business is a sole proprietorship. However, for the rest of the text we switch the structure of the business to a corporation, and instead of owner's equity, we begin using *stockholder's equity*, which includes account titles such as *common stock* and *retained earnings* to represent the owners' interests. The primary reason for this distinction is that the typical company can have several to thousands of owners, and the financial statements for corporations require a greater amount of complexity.

As you also learned in Introduction to Financial Statements, the accounting equation represents the balance sheet and shows the relationship between assets, liabilities, and owners' equity (for sole proprietorships/individuals) or common stock (for companies).

You may recall from mathematics courses that an equation must always be in balance. Therefore, we must ensure that the two sides of the accounting equation are always equal. We explore the components of the accounting equation in more detail shortly. First, we need to examine several underlying concepts that form the foundation for the accounting equation: the double-entry accounting system, debits and credits, and the "normal" balance for each account that is part of a formal accounting system.

Double-Entry Bookkeeping

The basic components of even the simplest accounting system are *accounts* and a *general ledger*. An **account** is a record showing increases and decreases to assets, liabilities, and equity—the basic components found in the accounting equation. As you know from Introduction to Financial Statements, each of these categories, in turn, includes many individual accounts, all of which a company maintains in its general ledger. A **general ledger** is a comprehensive listing of all of a company's accounts with their individual balances.

Accounting is based on what we call a **double-entry accounting system**, which requires the following:

- Each time we record a transaction, we must record a change in at least two different accounts. Having two or more accounts change will allow us to keep the accounting equation in balance.
- Not only will at least two accounts change, but there must also be at least one debit and one credit side impacted.
- The sum of the debits must equal the sum of the credits for each transaction.

In order for companies to record the myriad of transactions they have each year, there is a need for a simple but detailed system. Journals are useful tools to meet this need.

Debits and Credits

Each account can be represented visually by splitting the account into left and right sides as shown. This graphic representation of a general ledger account is known as a **T-account**. The concept of the T-account was briefly mentioned in Introduction to Financial Statements and will be used later in this chapter to analyze transactions. A T-account is called a "T-account" because it looks like a "T," as you can see with the T-account shown here.

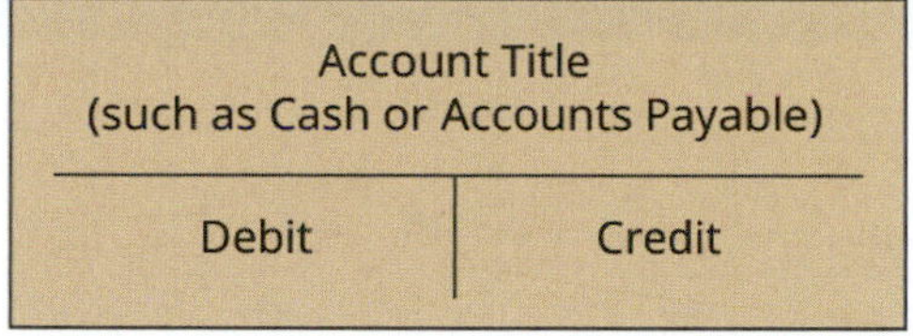

A **debit** records financial information on the left side of each account. A **credit** records financial information on the right side of an account. One side of each account will increase and the other side will decrease. The **ending account balance** is found by calculating the difference between debits and credits for each account. You will often see the terms *debit* and *credit* represented in shorthand, written as *DR* or *dr* and *CR* or *cr*, respectively. Depending on the account type, the sides that increase and decrease may vary. We can illustrate each account type and its corresponding debit and credit effects in the form of an *expanded accounting equation*. You will learn more about the expanded accounting equation and use it to analyze transactions in Define and Describe the Expanded Accounting Equation and Its Relationship to Analyzing Transactions.

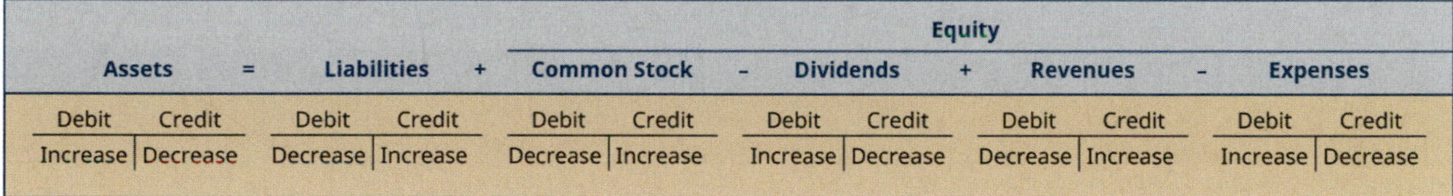

As we can see from this expanded accounting equation, Assets accounts increase on the debit side and decrease on the credit side. This is also true of Dividends and Expenses accounts. Liabilities increase on the credit side and decrease on the debit side. This is also true of Common Stock and Revenues accounts. This becomes easier to understand as you become familiar with the *normal balance* of an account.

Normal Balance of an Account

The **normal balance** is the expected balance each account type maintains, which is the side that increases. As assets and expenses increase on the debit side, their normal balance is a debit. Dividends paid to shareholders also have a normal balance that is a debit entry. Since liabilities, equity (such as common stock), and revenues increase with a credit, their "normal" balance is a credit. Table 3.1 shows the normal balances and increases for each account type.

Account Normal Balances and Increases

Type of account	Increases with	Normal balance
Asset	Debit	Debit
Liability	Credit	Credit
Common Stock	Credit	Credit
Dividends	Debit	Debit

Table 3.1

Account Normal Balances and Increases

Type of account	Increases with	Normal balance
Revenue	Credit	Credit
Expense	Debit	Debit

Table 3.1

When an account produces a balance that is contrary to what the expected normal balance of that account is, this account has an **abnormal balance**. Let's consider the following example to better understand abnormal balances.

Let's say there were a credit of $4,000 and a debit of $6,000 in the Accounts Payable account. Since Accounts Payable increases on the credit side, one would expect a normal balance on the credit side. However, the difference between the two figures in this case would be a debit balance of $2,000, which is an abnormal balance. This situation could possibly occur with an overpayment to a supplier or an error in recording.

CONCEPTS IN PRACTICE

Assets

We define an asset to be a resource that a company owns that has an economic value. We also know that the employment activities performed by an employee of a company are considered an expense, in this case a salary expense. In baseball, and other sports around the world, players' contracts are consistently categorized as assets that lose value over time (they are amortized).

For example, the Texas Rangers list "Player rights contracts and signing bonuses-net" as an asset on its balance sheet. They decrease this asset's value over time through a process called *amortization*. For tax purposes, players' contracts are treated akin to office equipment even though expenses for player salaries and bonuses have already been recorded. This can be a point of contention for some who argue that an owner does not assume the lost value of a player's contract, the player does.[5]

3.2 Define and Describe the Expanded Accounting Equation and Its Relationship to Analyzing Transactions

Before we explore how to analyze transactions, we first need to understand what governs the way transactions are recorded.

As you have learned, the accounting equation represents the idea that a company needs assets to operate, and there are two major sources that contribute to operations: liabilities and equity. The company borrows the funds, creating liabilities, or the company can take the funds provided by the profits generated in the current or past periods, creating retained earnings or some other form of stockholder's equity. Recall the accounting

5 Tommy Craggs. "MLB Confidential, Part 3: Texas Rangers." Deadspin. August 24, 2010. https://deadspin.com/5619951/mlb-confidential-part-3-texas-rangers

equation's basic form.

Assets = Liabilities + Equity

Expanded Accounting Equation

The **expanded accounting equation** breaks down the equity portion of the accounting equation into more detail. This expansion of the equity section allows a company to see the impact to equity from changes to revenues and expenses, and to owner investments and payouts. It is important to have more detail in this equity category to understand the effect on financial statements from period to period. For example, an increase to revenue can increase net income on the income statement, increase retained earnings on the statement of retained earnings, and change the distribution of stockholder's equity on the balance sheet. This may be difficult to understand where these changes have occurred without revenue recognized individually in this expanded equation.

The expanded accounting equation is shown here.

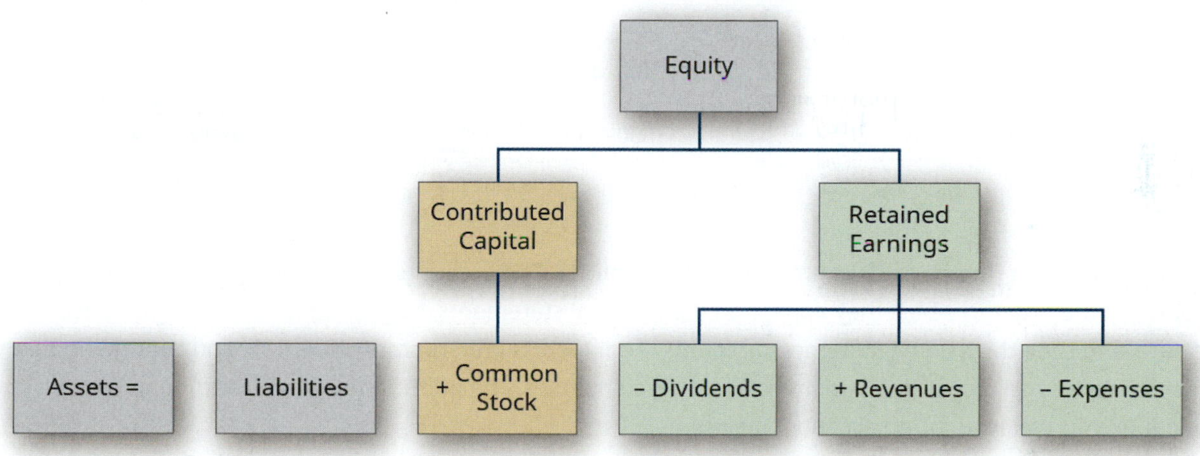

Figure 3.3 Expanded Accounting Equation. (attribution: Copyright Rice University, OpenStax, under CC BY-NC-SA 4.0 license)

Note that this expanded accounting equation breaks down Equity into four categories: common stock, dividends, revenues, and expenses. This considers each element of contributed capital and retained earnings individually to better illustrate each one's impact on changes in equity.

A business can now use this equation to analyze transactions in more detail. But first, it may help to examine the many accounts that can fall under each of the main categories of Assets, Liabilities, and Equity, in terms of their relationship to the expanded accounting equation. We can begin this discussion by looking at the *chart of accounts*.

Chart of Accounts

Recall that the basic components of even the simplest accounting system are accounts and a general ledger. Accounts shows all the changes made to assets, liabilities, and equity—the three main categories in the accounting equation. Each of these categories, in turn, includes many individual accounts, all of which a company maintains in its general ledger.

When a company first starts the analysis process, it will make a list of all the accounts used in day-to-day transactions. For example, a company may have accounts such as cash, accounts receivable, supplies, accounts payable, unearned revenues, common stock, dividends, revenues, and expenses. Each company will make a list that works for its business type, and the transactions it expects to engage in. The accounts may receive numbers using the system presented in Table 3.2.

Account Numbering System

Account category	Assigned account number will start with	Account numbers for a small company	Account numbers for a large company
Assets	1	100–199	1000–1999
Liabilities	2	200–299	2000–2999
Stockholders' equity	3	300–399	3000–3999
Revenues	4	400–499	4000–4999
Expenses	5	500–599	5000–5999

Table 3.2

We call this account numbering system a **chart of accounts**. The accounts are presented in the chart of accounts in the order in which they appear on the financial statements, beginning with the balance sheet accounts and then the income statement accounts. Additional numbers starting with six and continuing might be used in large merchandising and manufacturing companies. The information in the chart of accounts is the foundation of a well-organized accounting system.

Breaking Down the Expanded Accounting Equation

Refer to the expanded accounting equation (Figure 3.3). We begin with the left side of the equation, the assets, and work toward the right side of the equation to liabilities and equity.

Assets and the Expanded Accounting Equation

On the left side of the equation are assets. Assets are resources a company owns that have an economic value. Assets are represented on the balance sheet financial statement. Some common examples of assets are cash, accounts receivable, inventory, supplies, prepaid expenses, notes receivable, equipment, buildings, machinery, and land.

Cash includes paper currency as well as coins, checks, bank accounts, and money orders. Anything that can be quickly liquidated into cash is considered cash. Cash activities are a large part of any business, and the flow of cash in and out of the company is reported on the statement of cash flows.

Accounts receivable is money that is owed to the company, usually from a customer. The customer has not yet paid with cash for the provided good or service but will do so in the future. Common phrasing to describe this situation is that a customer purchased something "on account," meaning that the customer has asked to be billed and will pay at a later date: "Account" because a customer has not paid us yet but instead has asked to be billed; "Receivable" because we will receive the money in the future.

Inventory refers to the goods available for sale. Service companies do not have goods for sale and would thus not have inventory. Merchandising and manufacturing businesses do have inventory. You learn more about this topic in Inventory.

Examples of supplies (office supplies) include pens, paper, and pencils. Supplies are considered assets until an employee uses them. At the point they are used, they no longer have an economic value to the organization, and their cost is now an expense to the business.

Prepaid expenses are items paid for in advance of their use. They are considered assets until used. Some examples can include insurance and rent. Insurance, for example, is usually purchased for more than one month at a time (six months typically). The company does not use all six months of the insurance at once, it uses it one month at a time. However, the company prepays for all of it up front. As each month passes, the company will adjust its records to reflect the cost of one month of insurance usage.

Notes receivable is similar to accounts receivable in that it is money owed to the company by a customer or other entity. The difference here is that a note typically includes interest and specific contract terms, and the amount may be due in more than one accounting period.

Equipment examples include desks, chairs, and computers; anything that has a long-term value to the company that is used in the office. Equipment is considered a long-term asset, meaning you can use it for more than one accounting period (a year for example). Equipment will lose value over time, in a process called *depreciation*. You will learn more about this topic in The Adjustment Process.

Buildings, machinery, and land are all considered long-term assets. Machinery is usually specific to a manufacturing company that has a factory producing goods. Machinery and buildings also depreciate. Unlike other long-term assets such as machinery, buildings, and equipment, land is not depreciated. The process to calculate the loss on land value could be very cumbersome, speculative, and unreliable; therefore, the treatment in accounting is for land to *not* be depreciated over time.

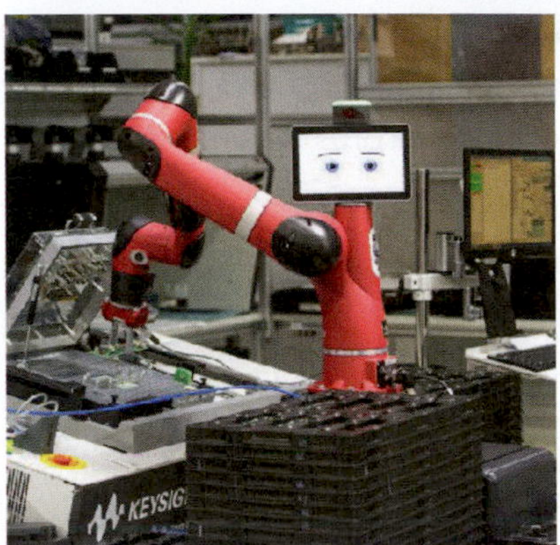

Figure 3.4 Assets. Cash, buildings, inventory, and equipment are all types of assets. (credit clockwise from top left: modification of "Cash money! 140606-A-CA521-021" by Sgt. Michael Selvage/Wikimedia Commons, Public Domain; modification of "41 Cherry Orchard Road" by "Pafcool2"/Wikimedia Commons, Public Domain; modification of "ASM-e1516805109201" by Jeff Green, Rethink Robotics/ Wikimedia Commons, CC BY 4.0; modification of "Gfp-inventory-space" by Yinan Chen/Wikimedia Commons, CC0)

Liabilities and the Expanded Accounting Equation

The accounting equation emphasizes a basic idea in business; that is, businesses need assets in order to operate. There are two ways a business can finance the purchase of assets. First, it can sell shares of its stock to the public to raise money to purchase the assets, or it can use profits earned by the business to finance its activities. Second, it can borrow the money from a lender such as a financial institution. You will learn about other assets as you progress through the book. Let's now take a look at the right side of the accounting equation.

Liabilities are obligations to pay an amount owed to a lender (creditor) based on a past transaction. Liabilities are reported on the balance sheet. It is important to understand that when we talk about liabilities, we are not just talking about loans. Money collected for gift cards, subscriptions, or as advance deposits from customers could also be liabilities. Essentially, anything a company owes and has yet to pay within a period is considered a liability, such as salaries, utilities, and taxes.

For example, a company uses $400 worth of utilities in May but is not billed for the usage, or asked to pay for the usage, until June. Even though the company does not have to pay the bill until June, the company owed money for the usage that occurred in May. Therefore, the company must record the usage of electricity, as well as the liability to pay the utility bill, in May.

Eventually that debt must be repaid by performing the service, fulfilling the subscription, or providing an asset such as merchandise or cash. Some common examples of liabilities include accounts payable, notes payable, and unearned revenue.

Accounts payable recognizes that the company owes money and has not paid. Remember, when a customer purchases something "on account" it means the customer has asked to be billed and will pay at a later date. In this case the purchasing company is the "customer." The company will have to pay the money due in the future, so we use the word "payable." The debt owed is usually paid off in less than one accounting period (less than a year typically) if it is classified as an account payable.

A notes payable is similar to accounts payable in that the company owes money and has not yet paid. Some key differences are that the contract terms are usually longer than one accounting period, interest is included, and there is typically a more formalized contract that dictates the terms of the transaction.

Unearned revenue represents a customer's advanced payment for a product or service that has yet to be provided by the company. Since the company has not yet provided the product or service, it cannot recognize the customer's payment as revenue, according to the revenue recognition principle. Thus, the account is called unearned revenue. The company owing the product or service creates the liability to the customer.

Equity and the Expanded Accounting Equation

Stockholder's equity refers to the owner's (stockholders) investments in the business and earnings. These two components are contributed capital and retained earnings.

The owner's investments in the business typically come in the form of common stock and are called **contributed capital**. There is a hybrid owner's investment labeled as preferred stock that is a combination of debt and equity (a concept covered in more advanced accounting courses). The company will issue shares of common stock to represent stockholder ownership. You will learn more about common stock in Corporation Accounting.

Another component of stockholder's equity is company earnings. These retained earnings are what the company holds onto at the end of a period to reinvest in the business, after any distributions to ownership occur. Stated more technically, retained earnings are a company's cumulative earnings since the creation of the company minus any dividends that it has declared or paid since its creation. One tricky point to remember is that retained earnings are not classified as assets. Instead, they are a component of the stockholder's equity account, placing it on the right side of the accounting equation.

Distribution of earnings to ownership is called a dividend. The dividend could be paid with cash or be a distribution of more company stock to current shareholders. Either way, dividends will decrease retained earnings.

Also affecting retained earnings are revenues and expenses, by way of net income or net loss. Revenues are earnings from the sale of goods and services. An increase in revenues will also contribute toward an increase in retained earnings. Expenses are the cost of resources associated with earning revenues. An increase to expenses will contribute toward a decrease in retained earnings. Recall that this concept of recognizing expenses associated with revenues is the expense recognition principle. Some examples of expenses include bill payments for utilities, employee salaries, and loan interest expense. A business does not have an expense until it is "incurred." Incurred means the resource is used or consumed. For example, you will not recognize utilities as an expense until you have used the utilities. The difference between revenues earned and expenses incurred is called net income (loss) and can be found on the income statement.

Net income reported on the income statement flows into the statement of retained earnings. If a business has net income (earnings) for the period, then this will increase its retained earnings for the period. This means that revenues exceeded expenses for the period, thus increasing retained earnings. If a business has net loss for the period, this decreases retained earnings for the period. This means that the expenses exceeded the revenues for the period, thus decreasing retained earnings.

You will notice that stockholder's equity increases with common stock issuance and revenues, and decreases from dividend payouts and expenses. Stockholder's equity is reported on the balance sheet in the form of contributed capital (common stock) and retained earnings. The statement of retained earnings computes the retained earnings balance at the beginning of the period, adds net income or subtracts net loss from the income statement, and subtracts dividends declared, to result in an ending retained earnings balance reported on the balance sheet.

Now that you have a basic understanding of the accounting equation, and examples of assets, liabilities, and stockholder's equity, you will be able to analyze the many transactions a business may encounter and determine how each transaction affects the accounting equation and corresponding financial statements. First, however, in Define and Examine the Initial Steps in the Accounting Cycle we look at how the role of identifying and analyzing transactions fits into the continuous process known as the *accounting cycle*.

LINK TO LEARNING

The Financial Accounting Standards Board had a policy that allowed companies to reduce their tax liability from share-based compensation deductions. This led companies to create what some call the "contentious debit," to defer tax liability and increase tax expense in a current period. See the article "The contentious debit—seriously" on continuous debt (https://openstax.org/l/50ContDebt) for further discussion of this practice.

3.3 Define and Describe the Initial Steps in the Accounting Cycle

This chapter on analyzing and recording transactions is the first of three consecutive chapters (including The Adjustment Process and Completing the Accounting Cycle) covering the steps in one continuous process known as the accounting cycle. The **accounting cycle** is a step-by-step process to record business activities and events to keep financial records up to date. The process occurs over one accounting period and will begin the cycle again in the following period. A **period** is one operating cycle of a business, which could be a month, quarter, or year. Review the accounting cycle in Figure 3.5.

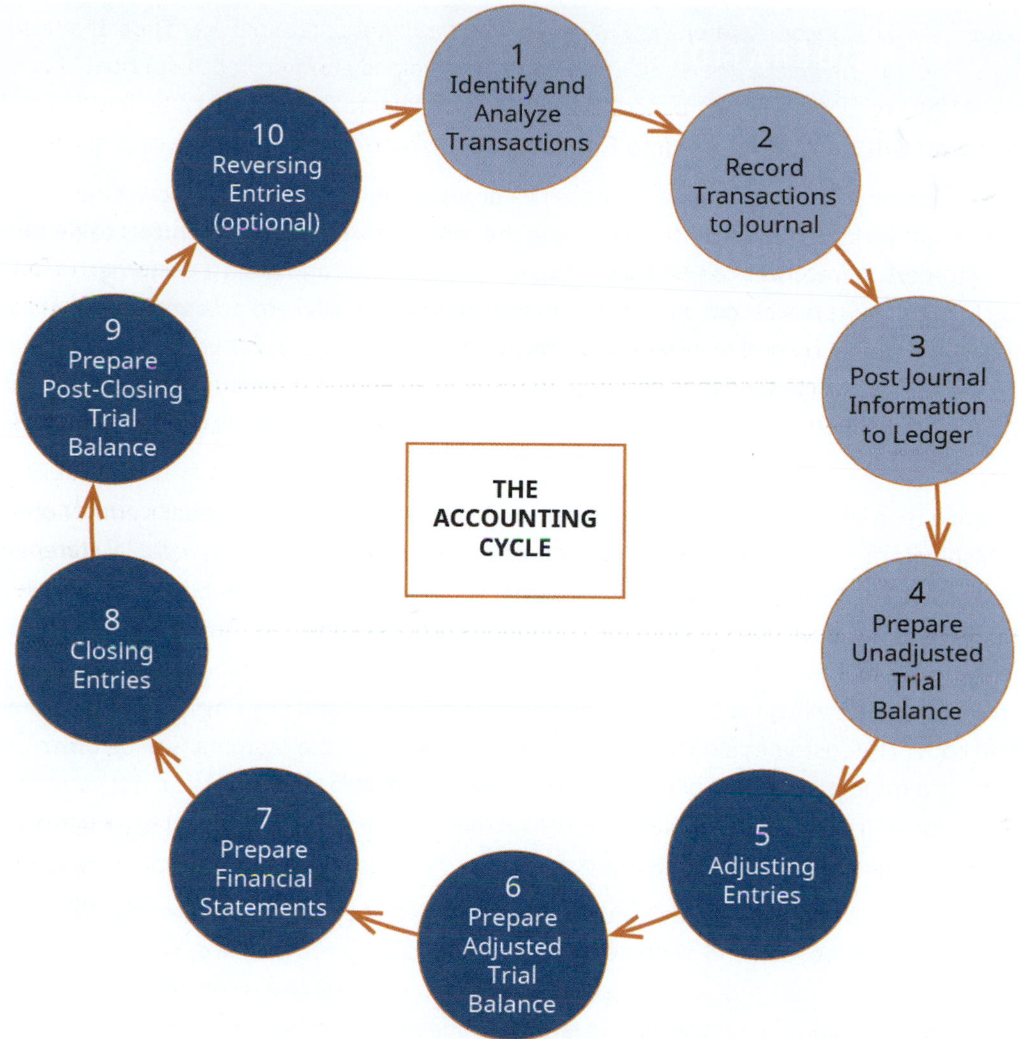

Figure 3.5 The Accounting Cycle. (attribution: Copyright Rice University, OpenStax, under CC BY-NC-SA 4.0 license)

As you can see, the cycle begins with identifying and analyzing transactions, and culminates in reversing entries (which we do not cover in this textbook). The entire cycle is meant to keep financial data organized and easily accessible to both internal and external users of information. In this chapter, we focus on the first four steps in the accounting cycle: identify and analyze transactions, record transactions to a journal, post journal information to a ledger, and prepare an unadjusted trial balance.

In The Adjustment Process we review steps 5, 6, and 7 in the accounting cycle: record adjusting entries, prepare an adjusted trial balance, and prepare financial statements. In Completing the Accounting Cycle, we review steps 8 and 9: closing entries and prepare a post-closing trial balance. As stated previously, we do not cover reversing entries.

ETHICAL CONSIDERATIONS

Turning Hacked Gift Card Accounts into Cash

Gift cards are a great way for a company to presell its products and to create cash flow. One of the problems with gift cards is that fraudsters are using the retailer's weak internal controls to defraud the retailer's customers. A fraudster can hack into autoloading gift cards and drain a customer's bank account by buying new, physical gift cards through the autoloading gift card account. This is a real problem, and an internal control to reduce this type of fraud is to use a double verification system for the transfer of money from a bank account to reloadable gift card account. Accountants can help their organization limit gift card fraud by reviewing their company's internal controls over the gift card process.

A simple explanation of this fraud is that a fraudster will gain access to an individual's email account through phishing or by other means, such as a fraudster putting a key logger on a public computer or in a corrupted public Wi-Fi. The individual uses the same password for the reloadable gift card as his or her email account, and the fraudster will see emails about the gift card. The fraudster contacts the retailor posing as the individual, and the retailor creates an in-store gift card redemption code, and the fraudster or his or her accomplice will go to the store posing as the individual and buy physical gift cards with the redemption code. The customer's bank account will be drained, and the customer will be upset. In another gift card fraud, the individual's credit card is stolen and used to buy physical gift cards from a retailor. This type of fraud causes problems for the retailer, for the retailer's reputation is damaged through the implementation of poor internal controls.

Does the fraudster use the fraudulently acquired gift cards? No, there is an entire market for selling gift cards on Craigslist, just go look and see how easy it is to buy discounted gift cards on Craigslist. Also, there are companies such as cardcash.com and cardhub.com that buy and resell gift cards. The fraudster just sells the gift cards, and the retailer has no idea it is redeeming fraudulently acquired gift cards. Through the implementation of proper internal controls, the accountant can help limit this fraud and protect his or her employer's reputation.

First Four Steps in the Accounting Cycle

The first four steps in the accounting cycle are (1) identify and analyze transactions, (2) record transactions to a journal, (3) post journal information to a ledger, and (4) prepare an unadjusted trial balance. We begin by introducing the steps and their related documentation.

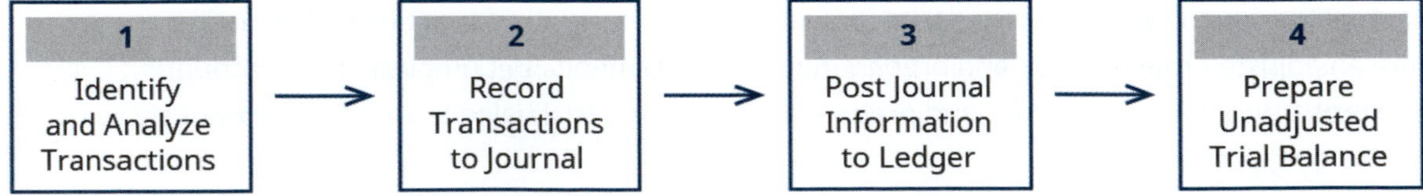

Figure 3.6 Accounting Cycle. The first four steps in the accounting cycle. (attribution: Copyright Rice University, OpenStax, under CC BY-NC-SA 4.0 license)

These first four steps set the foundation for the recording process.

Step 1. Identifying and analyzing transactions is the first step in the process. This takes information from original sources or activities and translates that information into usable financial data. An **original source** is a traceable record of information that contributes to the creation of a business transaction. For example, a sales invoice is considered an original source. Activities would include paying an employee, selling products, providing a service, collecting cash, borrowing money, and issuing stock to company owners. Once the original source has been identified, the company will analyze the information to see how it influences financial records.

Let's say that Mark Summers of Supreme Cleaners (from Why It Matters) provides cleaning services to a customer. He generates an invoice for $200, the amount the customer owes, so he can be paid for the service. This sales receipt contains information such as how much the customer owes, payment terms, and dates. This sales receipt is an original source containing financial information that creates a business transaction for the company.

Step 2. The second step in the process is recording transactions to a journal. This takes analyzed data from step 1 and organizes it into a comprehensive record of every company transaction. A **transaction** is a business activity or event that has an effect on financial information presented on financial statements. The information to record a transaction comes from an original source. A **journal** (also known as the book of original entry or general journal) is a record of all transactions.

For example, in the previous transaction, Supreme Cleaners had the invoice for $200. Mark Summers needs to record this $200 in his financial records. He needs to choose what accounts represent this transaction, whether or not this transaction will increase or decreases the accounts, and how that impacts the accounting equation before he can record the transaction in his journal. He needs to do this process for every transaction occurring during the period.

Figure 3.7 includes information such as the date of the transaction, the accounts required in the journal entry, and columns for debits and credits.

GENERAL JOURNAL			
Date	**Account Title**	**Debit**	**Credit**

Figure 3.7 General Journal. (attribution: Copyright Rice University, OpenStax, under CC BY-NC-SA 4.0 license)

Step 3. The third step in the process is posting journal information to a ledger. **Posting** takes all transactions from the journal during a period and moves the information to a general ledger, or ledger. As you've learned, account balances can be represented visually in the form of T-accounts.

Returning to Supreme Cleaners, Mark identified the accounts needed to represent the $200 sale and recorded them in his journal. He will then take the account information and move it to his general ledger. All of the accounts he used during the period will be shown on the general ledger, not only those accounts impacted by the $200 sale.

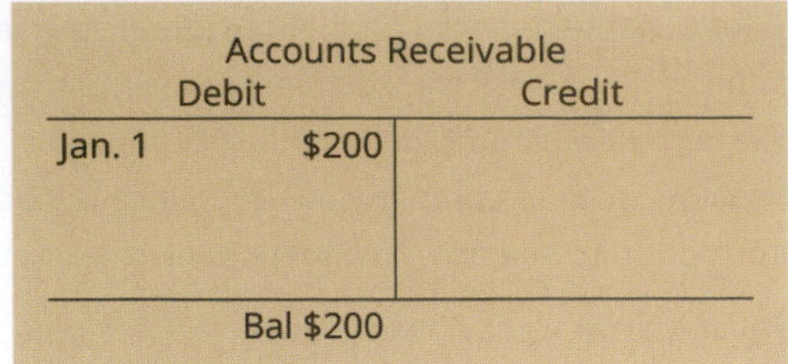

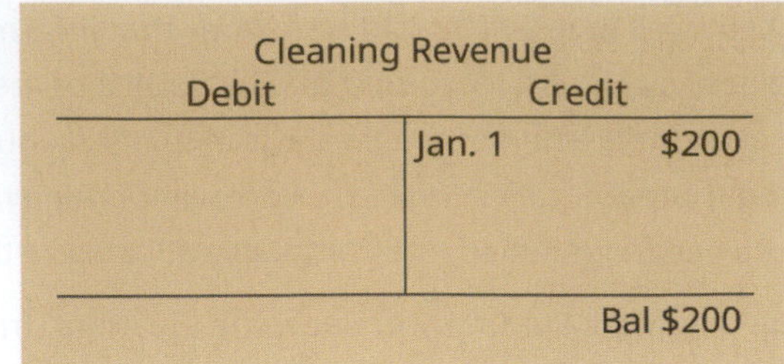

Figure 3.8 General Ledger in T-Account Form. (attribution: Copyright Rice University, OpenStax, under CC BY-NC-SA 4.0 license)

Step 4. The fourth step in the process is to prepare an unadjusted trial balance. This step takes information from the general ledger and transfers it onto a document showing all account balances, and ensuring that debits and credits for the period balance (debit and credit totals are equal).

Mark Summers from Supreme Cleaners needs to organize all of his accounts and their balances, including the $200 sale, onto a trial balance. He also needs to ensure his debits and credits are balanced at the culmination of this step.

SUPREME CLEAN Trial Balance April 30, 2018		
Account Title	**Debit**	**Credit**
Cash	XXX	
Accounts receivable	XXX	
Office supplies	XXX	
Prepaid insurance	XXX	
Equipment	XXX	
Accounts payable		XXX
Unearned cleaning revenue		XXX
Common stock		XXX
Dividends	XXX	
Cleaning revenue		XXX
Gas expense	XXX	
Advertising expense	XXX	
	XXX	XXX

Figure 3.9 Unadjusted Trial Balance. (attribution: Copyright Rice University, OpenStax, under CC BY-NC-SA 4.0 license)

It is important to note that recording the entire process requires a strong attention to detail. Any mistakes early on in the process can lead to incorrect reporting information on financial statements. If this occurs, accountants may have to go all the way back to the beginning of the process to find their error. Make sure that as you complete each step, you are careful and really take the time to understand how to record information and why you are recording it. In the next section, you will learn how the accounting equation is used to analyze transactions.

CONCEPTS IN PRACTICE

Forensic Accounting

Ever dream about working for the Federal Bureau of Investigation (FBI)? As a forensic accountant, that dream might just be possible. A forensic accountant investigates financial crimes, such as tax evasion, insider trading, and embezzlement, among other things. Forensic accountants review financial records looking for clues to bring about charges against potential criminals. They consider every part of the accounting cycle, including original source documents, looking through journal entries, general ledgers, and financial statements. They may even be asked to testify to their findings in a court of law.

To be a successful forensic accountant, one must be detailed, organized, and naturally inquisitive. This position will need to retrace the steps a suspect may have taken to cover up fraudulent financial activities. Understanding how a company operates can help identify fraudulent activities that veer from the company's position. Some of the best forensic accountants have put away major criminals such as Al Capone, Bernie Madoff, Ken Lay, and Ivan Boesky.

LINK TO LEARNING

A tool that can be helpful to businesses looking for an easier way to view their accounting processes is to have drillable financial statements. This feature can be found in several software systems, allowing companies to go through the accounting cycle from transaction entry to financial statement construction. Read this Journal of Accountancy column on drillable financial statements (https://openstax.org/l/50DrillFinState) to learn more.

3.4 Analyze Business Transactions Using the Accounting Equation and Show the Impact of Business Transactions on Financial Statements

You gained a basic understanding of both the basic and expanded accounting equations, and looked at examples of assets, liabilities, and stockholder's equity in Define and Examine the Expanded Accounting Equation and Its Relationship to Analyzing Transactions. Now, we can consider some of the transactions a business may encounter. We can review how each transaction would affect the basic accounting equation and the corresponding financial statements.

As discussed in Define and Examine the Initial Steps in the Accounting Cycle, the first step in the accounting cycle is to identify and analyze transactions. Each original source must be evaluated for financial implications. Meaning, will the information contained on this original source affect the financial statements? If the answer is yes, the company will then analyze the information for *how* it affects the financial statements. For example, if a company receives a cash payment from a customer, the company needs to know how to record the cash payment in a meaningful way to keep its financial statements up to date.

YOUR TURN

Monetary Value of Transactions

You are the accountant for a small computer programming company. You must record the following transactions. What values do you think you will use for each transaction?

A. The company purchased a secondhand van to be used to travel to customers. The sellers told you they believe it is worth $12,500 but agreed to sell it to your company for $11,000. You believe the company got a really good deal because the van has a $13,000 Blue Book value.
B. Your company purchased its office building five years ago for $175,000. Values of real estate have been rising quickly over the last five years, and a realtor told you the company could easily sell it for $250,000 today. Since the building is now worth $250,000, you are contemplating whether you should increase its value on the books to reflect this estimated current market value.
C. Your company has performed a task for a customer. The customer agreed to a minimum price of $2,350 for the work, but if the customer has absolutely no issues with the programming for the first month, the customer will pay you $2,500 (which includes a bonus for work well done). The owner of the company is almost 100% sure she will receive $2,500 for the job done. You have to record the revenue earned and need to decide how much should be recorded.
D. The owner of the company believes the most valuable asset for his company is the employees. The service the company provides depends on having intelligent, hardworking, dependable employees who believe they need to deliver exactly what the customer wants in a reasonable amount of time. Without the employees, the company would not be so successful. The owner wants to know if she can include the value of her employees on the balance sheet as an asset.

Solution

A. The van must be recorded on the books at $11,000 per the cost principle. That is the price that was agreed to between a willing buyer and seller.
B. The cost principle states that you must record an asset on the books for the price you bought it for and then leave it on the books at that value unless there is a specific rule to the contrary. The company purchased the building for $175,000. It must stay on the books at $175,000. Companies are not allowed to increase the value of an asset on their books just because they believe it is worth more.
C. You must record the revenue at $2,350 per the rules of conservatism. We do not want to record revenue at $2,500 when we are not absolutely 100% sure that is what we will earn. Recording it at $2,500 might mislead our statement users to think we have earned more revenue than we really have.
D. Even though the employees are a wonderful asset for the company, they cannot be included on the balance sheet as an asset. There is no way to assign a monetary value in US dollars to our employees. Therefore, we cannot include them in our assets.

Reviewing and Analyzing Transactions

Let us assume our business is a service-based company. We use Lynn Sanders' small printing company, Printing Plus, as our example. Please notice that since Printing Plus is a corporation, we are using the Common Stock account, instead of Owner's Equity. The following are several transactions from this business's current month:

1. Issues $20,000 shares of common stock for cash.
2. Purchases equipment on account for $3,500, payment due within the month.
3. Receives $4,000 cash in advance from a customer for services not yet rendered.
4. Provides $5,500 in services to a customer who asks to be billed for the services.
5. Pays a $300 utility bill with cash.
6. Distributed $100 cash in dividends to stockholders.

We now analyze each of these transactions, paying attention to how they impact the accounting equation and corresponding financial statements.

Transaction 1: Issues $20,000 shares of common stock for cash.

Assets	=	Liabilities	+	Equity
Cash +$20,000				Common Stock +$20,000

Analysis: Looking at the accounting equation, we know cash is an asset and common stock is stockholder's equity. When a company collects cash, this will increase assets because cash is coming into the business. When a company issues common stock, this will increase a stockholder's equity because he or she is receiving investments from owners.

Remember that the accounting equation must remain balanced, and assets need to equal liabilities plus equity. On the asset side of the equation, we show an increase of $20,000. On the liabilities and equity side of the equation, there is also an increase of $20,000, keeping the equation balanced. Changes to assets, specifically cash, will increase assets on the balance sheet and increase cash on the statement of cash flows. Changes to stockholder's equity, specifically common stock, will increase stockholder's equity on the balance sheet.

Transaction 2: Purchases equipment on account for $3,500, payment due within the month.

Assets	=	Liabilities	+	Equity
Equipment +$3,500		Accounts Payable +$3,500		

Analysis: We know that the company purchased equipment, which is an asset. We also know that the company purchased the equipment on account, meaning it did not pay for the equipment immediately and asked for payment to be billed instead and paid later. Since the company owes money and has not yet paid, this is a liability, specifically labeled as *accounts payable*. There is an increase to assets because the company has equipment it did not have before. There is also an increase to liabilities because the company now owes money. The more money the company owes, the more that liability will increase.

The accounting equation remains balanced because there is a $3,500 increase on the asset side, and a $3,500 increase on the liability and equity side. This change to assets will increase assets on the balance sheet. The change to liabilities will increase liabilities on the balance sheet.

Transaction 3: Receives $4,000 cash in advance from a customer for services not yet rendered.

Assets	=	Liabilities	+	Equity
Cash +$4,000		Unearned Revenue +$4,000		

Analysis: We know that the company collected cash, which is an asset. This collection of $4,000 increases assets because money is coming into the business.

The company has yet to provide the service. According to the revenue recognition principle, the company cannot recognize that revenue until it provides the service. Therefore, the company has a liability to the customer to provide the service and must record the liability as unearned revenue. The liability of $4,000 worth of services increases because the company has more unearned revenue than previously.

The equation remains balanced, as assets and liabilities increase. The balance sheet would experience an increase in assets and an increase in liabilities.

Transaction 4: Provides $5,500 in services to a customer who asks to be billed for the services.

Assets	=	Liabilities	+	Equity
Accounts Receivable +$5,500				Revenue +$5,500

Analysis: The customer asked to be billed for the service, meaning the customer did not pay with cash immediately. The customer owes money and has not yet paid, signaling an accounts receivable. Accounts receivable is an asset that is increasing in this case. This customer obligation of $5,500 adds to the balance in accounts receivable.

The company did provide the services. As a result, the revenue recognition principle requires recognition as revenue, which increases equity for $5,500. The increase to assets would be reflected on the balance sheet. The increase to equity would affect three statements. The income statement would see an increase to revenues, changing net income (loss). Net income (loss) is computed into retained earnings on the statement of retained earnings. This change to retained earnings is shown on the balance sheet under stockholder's equity.

Transaction 5: Pays a $300 utility bill with cash.

Assets	=	Liabilities	+	Equity
Cash –$300				Expense –$300

Analysis: The company paid with cash, an asset. Assets are decreasing by $300 since cash was used to pay for this utility bill. The company no longer has that money.

Utility payments are generated from bills for services that were used and paid for within the accounting period, thus recognized as an expense. The expense decreases equity by $300. The decrease to assets, specifically cash, affects the balance sheet and statement of cash flows. The decrease to equity as a result of the expense affects three statements. The income statement would see a change to expenses, changing net income (loss). Net income (loss) is computed into retained earnings on the statement of retained earnings. This change to retained earnings is shown on the balance sheet under stockholder's equity.

Transaction 6: Distributed $100 cash in dividends to stockholders.

Assets	=	Liabilities	+	Equity
Cash –$100				Dividends –$100

Analysis: The company paid the distribution with cash, an asset. Assets decrease by $100 as a result. Dividends affect equity and, in this case, decrease equity by $100. The decrease to assets, specifically cash, affects the balance sheet and statement of cash flows. The decrease to equity because of the dividend payout affects the statement of retained earnings by reducing ending retained earnings, and the balance sheet by reducing stockholder's equity.

Let's summarize the transactions and make sure the accounting equation has remained balanced. Shown are each of the transactions.

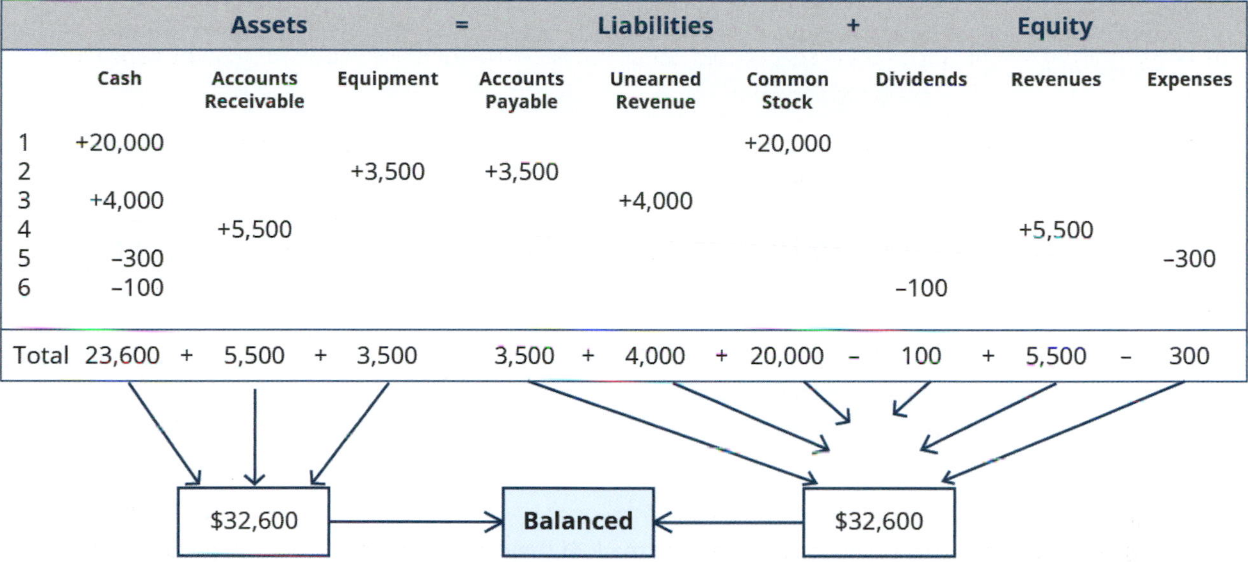

	Assets			= Liabilities		+ Equity			
	Cash	Accounts Receivable	Equipment	Accounts Payable	Unearned Revenue	Common Stock	Dividends	Revenues	Expenses
1	+20,000					+20,000			
2			+3,500	+3,500					
3	+4,000				+4,000				
4		+5,500						+5,500	
5	−300								−300
6	−100						−100		
Total	23,600 +	5,500 +	3,500	3,500 +	4,000 +	20,000 −	100 +	5,500 −	300

As you can see, assets total $32,600, while liabilities added to equity also equal $32,600. Our accounting equation remains balanced. In Use Journal Entries to Record Transactions and Post to T-Accounts, we add other elements to the accounting equation and expand the equation to include individual revenue and expense accounts.

YOUR TURN

Debbie's Dairy Farm

Debbie's Dairy Farm had the following transactions:

A. Debbie ordered shelving worth $750.
B. Debbie's selling price on a gallon of milk is $3.00. She finds out that most local stores are charging $3.50. Based on this information, she decides to increase her price to $3.25. She has an employee put a new price sticker on each gallon.
C. A customer buys a gallon of milk paying cash.
D. The shelving is delivered with an invoice for $750.

Which events will be recorded in the accounting system?

Solution

A. Debbie did not yet receive the shelving—it has only been ordered. As of now there is no new asset owned by the company. Since the shelving has not yet been delivered, Debbie does not owe any money to the other company. Debbie will not record the transaction.
B. Changing prices does not have an impact on the company at the time the price is changed. All that

happened was that a new price sticker was placed on the milk. Debbie still has all the milk and has not received any money. Debbie will not record the transaction.

C. Debbie now has a transaction to record. She has received cash and the customer has taken some of her inventory of milk. She has an increase in one asset (cash) and a decrease in another asset (inventory.) She also has earned revenue.

D. Debbie has taken possession of the shelving and is the legal owner. She also has an increase in her liabilities as she accepted delivery of the shelving but has not paid for it. Debbie will record this transaction.

3.5 Use Journal Entries to Record Transactions and Post to T-Accounts

When we introduced debits and credits, you learned about the usefulness of T-accounts as a graphic representation of any account in the general ledger. But before transactions are posted to the T-accounts, they are first recorded using special forms known as *journals*.

Journals

Accountants use special forms called *journals* to keep track of their business transactions. A journal is the first place information is entered into the accounting system. A journal is often referred to as the **book of original entry** because it is the place the information originally enters into the system. A journal keeps a historical account of all recordable transactions with which the company has engaged. In other words, a journal is similar to a diary for a business. When you enter information into a journal, we say you are **journalizing** the entry. Journaling the entry is the second step in the accounting cycle. Here is a picture of a journal.

JOURNAL			
Date	**Account**	**Debit**	**Credit**

You can see that a journal has columns labeled debit and credit. The debit is on the left side, and the credit is on the right. Let's look at how we use a journal.

When filling in a journal, there are some rules you need to follow to improve journal entry organization.

Formatting When Recording Journal Entries

- Include a date of when the transaction occurred.
- The debit account title(s) always come first and on the left.
- The credit account title(s) always come after all debit titles are entered, and on the right.
- The titles of the credit accounts will be indented below the debit accounts.
- You will have at least one debit (possibly more).
- You will always have at least one credit (possibly more).
- The dollar value of the debits must equal the dollar value of the credits or else the equation will go out of balance.
- You will write a short description after each journal entry.
- Skip a space after the description before starting the next journal entry.

An example journal entry format is as follows. It is not taken from previous examples but is intended to stand alone.

JOURNAL			
Date	**Description**	**Debit**	**Credit**
Apr. 1, 2018	Cash Common Stock *Received cash in exchange for common stock*	5,000	 5,000

Note that this example has only one debit account and one credit account, which is considered a **simple entry**. A **compound entry** is when there is more than one account listed under the debit and/or credit column of a journal entry (as seen in the following).

JOURNAL			
Date	**Account**	**Debit**	**Credit**
Apr. 1, 2018	Cash Supplies Common Stock *Received cash and supplies in exchange for common stock*	3,000 2,000	 5,000

Notice that for this entry, the rules for recording journal entries have been followed. There is a date of April 1, 2018, the debit account titles are listed first with Cash and Supplies, the credit account title of Common Stock is indented after the debit account titles, there are at least one debit and one credit, the debit amounts equal the credit amount, and there is a short description of the transaction.

Let's now look at a few transactions from Printing Plus and record their journal entries.

Recording Transactions

We now return to our company example of Printing Plus, Lynn Sanders' printing service company. We will analyze and record each of the transactions for her business and discuss how this impacts the financial statements. Some of the listed transactions have been ones we have seen throughout this chapter. More detail for each of these transactions is provided, along with a few new transactions.

1. On January 3, 2019, issues $20,000 shares of common stock for cash.
2. On January 5, 2019, purchases equipment on account for $3,500, payment due within the month.
3. On January 9, 2019, receives $4,000 cash in advance from a customer for services not yet rendered.
4. On January 10, 2019, provides $5,500 in services to a customer who asks to be billed for the services.
5. On January 12, 2019, pays a $300 utility bill with cash.
6. On January 14, 2019, distributed $100 cash in dividends to stockholders.
7. On January 17, 2019, receives $2,800 cash from a customer for services rendered.
8. On January 18, 2019, paid in full, with cash, for the equipment purchase on January 5.
9. On January 20, 2019, paid $3,600 cash in salaries expense to employees.
10. On January 23, 2019, received cash payment in full from the customer on the January 10 transaction.
11. On January 27, 2019, provides $1,200 in services to a customer who asks to be billed for the services.
12. On January 30, 2019, purchases supplies on account for $500, payment due within three months.

Transaction 1: On January 3, 2019, issues $20,000 shares of common stock for cash.

Analysis:

- This is a transaction that needs to be recorded, as Printing Plus has received money, and the stockholders have invested in the firm.
- Printing Plus now has more cash. Cash is an asset, which in this case is increasing. Cash increases on the debit side.
- When the company issues stock, stockholders purchase common stock, yielding a higher common stock figure than before issuance. The common stock account is increasing and affects equity. Looking at the expanded accounting equation, we see that Common Stock increases on the credit side.

JOURNAL			
Date	**Account**	**Debit**	**Credit**
Jan. 3, 2019	Cash	20,000	
	Common Stock		20,000
	To recognize issuance of common stock		

Impact on the financial statements: Both of these accounts are balance sheet accounts. You will see total assets increase and total stockholders' equity will also increase, both by $20,000. With both totals increasing by $20,000, the accounting equation, and therefore our balance sheet, will be in balance. There is no effect on the income statement from this transaction as there were no revenues or expenses recorded.

Assets	=	Liabilities	+	Stockholders' Equity
+$20,000	=	+$0	+	+$20,000
$20,000	=	$0	+	$20,000

Transaction 2: On January 5, 2019, purchases equipment on account for $3,500, payment due within the month.

Analysis:

- In this case, equipment is an asset that is increasing. It increases because Printing Plus now has more equipment than it did before. Assets increase on the debit side; therefore, the Equipment account would show a $3,500 debit.
- The company did not pay for the equipment immediately. Lynn asked to be sent a bill for payment at a future date. This creates a liability for Printing Plus, who owes the supplier money for the equipment. Accounts Payable is used to recognize this liability. This liability is increasing, as the company now owes money to the supplier. A liability account increases on the credit side; therefore, Accounts Payable will increase on the credit side in the amount of $3,500.

JOURNAL			
Date	**Account**	**Debit**	**Credit**
Jan. 5, 2019	Equipment	3,500	
	Accounts Payable		3,500
	To recognize purchase of equipment on account		

Impact on the financial statements: Since both accounts in the entry are balance sheet accounts, you will see no effect on the income statement.

Assets	=	Liabilities	+	Stockholders' Equity
+$3,500	=	+ $3,500	+	0
$3,500	=	$3,500	+	0

Transaction 3: On January 9, 2019, receives $4,000 cash in advance from a customer for services not yet rendered.

Analysis:

- Cash was received, thus increasing the Cash account. Cash is an asset that increases on the debit side.
- Printing Plus has not yet provided the service, meaning it cannot recognize the revenue as earned. The company has a liability to the customer until it provides the service. The Unearned Revenue account would be used to recognize this liability. This is a liability the company did not have before, thus increasing this account. Liabilities increase on the credit side; thus, Unearned Revenue will recognize the $4,000 on the credit side.

JOURNAL			
Date	**Account**	**Debit**	**Credit**
Jan. 9, 2019	Cash Unearned Revenue *To recognize receipt of customer advanced payment for services yet to be rendered*	4,000	 4,000

Impact on the financial statements: Since both accounts in the entry are balance sheet accounts, you will see no effect on the income statement.

Assets	=	Liabilities	+	Stockholders' Equity
+$4,000	=	+$4,000	+	0
$4,000	=	$4,000	+	0

Transaction 4: On January 10, 2019, provides $5,500 in services to a customer who asks to be billed for the services.

Analysis:

- The company provided service to the client; therefore, the company may recognize the revenue as earned (revenue recognition principle), which increases revenue. Service Revenue is a revenue account affecting equity. Revenue accounts increase on the credit side; thus, Service Revenue will show an increase of $5,500 on the credit side.
- The customer did not immediately pay for the services and owes Printing Plus payment. This money will be received in the future, increasing Accounts Receivable. Accounts Receivable is an asset account. Asset accounts increase on the debit side. Therefore, Accounts Receivable will increase for $5,500 on the debit side.

JOURNAL			
Date	**Account**	**Debit**	**Credit**
Jan. 10, 2019	Accounts Receivable Service Revenue *To recognize revenue earned, billed customer*	5,500	 5,500

Impact on the financial statements: You have revenue of $5,500. Revenue is reported on your income statement. The more revenue you have, the more net income (earnings) you will have. The more earnings you have, the more retained earnings you will keep. Retained earnings is a stockholders' equity account, so total equity will increase $5,500. Accounts receivable is going up so total assets will increase by $5,500. The accounting equation, and therefore the balance sheet, remain in balance.

Assets	=	Liabilities	+	Stockholders' Equity
+$5,500	=	0	+	+$5,500
$5,500	=	0	+	$5,500

Transaction 5: On January 12, 2019, pays a $300 utility bill with cash.

Analysis:

- Cash was used to pay the utility bill, which means cash is decreasing. Cash is an asset that decreases on the credit side.
- Paying a utility bill creates an expense for the company. Utility Expense increases, and does so on the debit side of the accounting equation.

JOURNAL			
Date	**Account**	**Debit**	**Credit**
Jan. 12, 2019	Utility Expense Cash *Paid utility bill with cash*	300	 300

Impact on the financial statements: You have an expense of $300. Expenses are reported on your income statement. More expenses lead to a decrease in net income (earnings). The fewer earnings you have, the fewer retained earnings you will end up with. Retained earnings is a stockholders' equity account, so total equity will decrease by $300. Cash is decreasing, so total assets will decrease by $300, impacting the balance sheet.

Assets	=	Liabilities	+	Stockholders' Equity
–$300	=	0	+	–$300
$300	=	0	+	$300

Transaction 6: On January 14, 2019, distributed $100 cash in dividends to stockholders.

Analysis:

- Cash was used to pay the dividends, which means cash is decreasing. Cash is an asset that decreases on the credit side.
- Dividends distribution occurred, which increases the Dividends account. Dividends is a part of stockholder's equity and is recorded on the debit side. This debit entry has the effect of reducing stockholder's equity.

JOURNAL			
Date	**Account**	**Debit**	**Credit**
Jan.14, 2019	Dividends Cash *Paid dividends with cash*	100	 100

Impact on the financial statements: You have dividends of $100. An increase in dividends leads to a decrease in stockholders' equity (retained earnings). Cash is decreasing, so total assets will decrease by $100, impacting the balance sheet.

Assets	=	Liabilities	+	Stockholders' Equity
–$100	=	0	+	–$100
$100	=	0	+	$100

Transaction 7: On January 17, 2019, receives $2,800 cash from a customer for services rendered.

Analysis:

- The customer used cash as the payment method, thus increasing the amount in the Cash account. Cash is an asset that is increasing, and it does so on the debit side.
- Printing Plus provided the services, which means the company can recognize revenue as earned in the Service Revenue account. Service Revenue increases equity; therefore, Service Revenue increases on the credit side.

JOURNAL			
Date	**Account**	**Debit**	**Credit**
Jan. 17, 2019	Cash Service Revenue *Collected cash for services rendered*	2,800	 2,800

Impact on the financial statements: Revenue is reported on the income statement. More revenue will increase net income (earnings), thus increasing retained earnings. Retained earnings is a stockholders' equity account, so total equity will increase $2,800. Cash is increasing, which increases total assets on the balance sheet.

Assets	=	Liabilities	+	Stockholders' Equity
+$2,800	=	0	+	+$2,800
$2,800	=	0	+	$2,800

Transaction 8: On January 18, 2019, paid in full, with cash, for the equipment purchase on January 5.

Analysis:

- Cash is decreasing because it was used to pay for the outstanding liability created on January 5. Cash is an asset and will decrease on the credit side.
- Accounts Payable recognized the liability the company had to the supplier to pay for the equipment. Since the company is now paying off the debt it owes, this will decrease Accounts Payable. Liabilities decrease on the debit side; therefore, Accounts Payable will decrease on the debit side by $3,500.

JOURNAL			
Date	**Account**	**Debit**	**Credit**
Jan. 18, 2019	Accounts Payable Cash *Paid liability for equipment in full*	3,500	3,500

Impact on the financial statements: Since both accounts in the entry are balance sheet accounts, you will see no effect on the income statement.

Assets	=	Liabilities	+	Stockholders' Equity
–$3,500	=	–$3,500	+	0
$3,500	=	$3,500	+	0

Transaction 9: On January 20, 2019, paid $3,600 cash in salaries expense to employees.

Analysis:

- Cash was used to pay for salaries, which decreases the Cash account. Cash is an asset that decreases on the credit side.
- Salaries are an expense to the business for employee work. This will increase Salaries Expense, affecting equity. Expenses increase on the debit side; thus, Salaries Expense will increase on the debit side.

JOURNAL			
Date	**Account**	**Debit**	**Credit**
Jan. 20, 2019	Salaries Expense Cash *Paid employee salaries*	3,600	3,600

Impact on the financial statements: You have an expense of $3,600. Expenses are reported on the income statement. More expenses lead to a decrease in net income (earnings). The fewer earnings you have, the fewer retained earnings you will end up with. Retained earnings is a stockholders' equity account, so total equity will decrease by $3,600. Cash is decreasing, so total assets will decrease by $3,600, impacting the balance sheet.

Assets	=	Liabilities	+	Stockholders' Equity
–$3,600	=	0	+	–$3,600
$3,600	=	0	+	$3,600

Transaction 10: On January 23, 2019, received cash payment in full from the customer on the January 10 transaction.

Analysis:

- Cash was received, thus increasing the Cash account. Cash is an asset, and assets increase on the debit side.
- Accounts Receivable was originally used to recognize the future customer payment; now that the customer has paid in full, Accounts Receivable will decrease. Accounts Receivable is an asset, and assets decrease on the credit side.

JOURNAL			
Date	**Account**	**Debit**	**Credit**
Jan. 23, 2019	Cash Accounts Receivable *Received customer payment from Jan. 10*	5,500	 5,500

Impact on the financial statements: In this transaction, there was an increase to one asset (Cash) and a decrease to another asset (Accounts Receivable). This means total assets change by $0, because the increase and decrease to assets in the same amount cancel each other out. There are no changes to liabilities or stockholders' equity, so the equation is still in balance. Since there are no revenues or expenses affected, there is no effect on the income statement.

Assets	=	Liabilities	+	Stockholders' Equity
+$5,500 –$5,500	=	0	+	0 0
$0	=	0	+	

Transaction 11: On January 27, 2019, provides $1,200 in services to a customer who asks to be billed for the services.

Analysis:

- The customer does not pay immediately for the services but is expected to pay at a future date. This creates an Accounts Receivable for Printing Plus. The customer owes the money, which increases Accounts Receivable. Accounts Receivable is an asset, and assets increase on the debit side.
- Printing Plus provided the service, thus earning revenue. Service Revenue would increase on the credit side.

JOURNAL			
Date	**Account**	**Debit**	**Credit**
Jan. 27, 2019	Accounts Receivable Service Revenue *Billed customer for services rendered*	1,200	 1,200

Impact on the financial statements: Revenue is reported on the income statement. More revenue will increase net income (earnings), thus increasing retained earnings. Retained earnings is a stockholders' equity account, so total equity will increase $1,200. Cash is increasing, which increases total assets on the balance sheet.

Assets	=	Liabilities	+	Stockholders' Equity
+$1,200	=	0	+	+$1,200
$1,200	=	0	+	$1,200

Transaction 12: On January 30, 2019, purchases supplies on account for $500, payment due within three months.

Analysis:

- The company purchased supplies, which are assets to the business until used. Supplies is increasing, because the company has more supplies than it did before. Supplies is an asset that is increasing on the debit side.

- Printing Plus did not pay immediately for the supplies and asked to be billed for the supplies, payable at a later date. This creates a liability for the company, Accounts Payable. This liability increases Accounts Payable; thus, Accounts Payable increases on the credit side.

JOURNAL			
Date	**Account**	**Debit**	**Credit**
Jan. 30, 2019	Supplies Accounts Payable *Billed customer for services rendered*	500	 500

Impact on the financial statements: There is an increase to a liability and an increase to assets. These accounts both impact the balance sheet but not the income statement.

Assets	=	Liabilities	+	Stockholders' Equity
+$500	=	+$500	+	0
$500	=	$500	+	0

The complete journal for these transactions is as follows:

JOURNAL			
Date	**Account**	**Debit**	**Credit**
Jan. 3, 2019	Cash Common Stock *Recognize issuance of common stock*	20,000	20,000
Jan. 5, 2019	Equipment Account Payable *Recognize purchase of equipment on account*	3,500	3,500
Jan. 9, 2019	Cash Unearned revenue *Received advanced payment for services yet to be rendered*	4,000	4,000
Jan. 10, 2019	Accounts receivable Service Revenue *Revenue earned, billed customer*	5,500	5,500
Jan. 12, 2019	Utility Expense Cash *Paid utility bill*	300	300
Jan. 14, 2019	Dividends Cash *Paid out dividends*	100	100
Jan. 17, 2019	Cash Service Revenue *Collected cash for services rendered*	2,800	2,800
Jan. 18, 2019	Accounts Payable Cash *Paid liability for equipment in full*	3,500	3,500
Jan. 20, 2019	Salaries Expense Cash *Paid employee salaries*	3,600	3,600
Jan. 23, 2019	Cash Accounts Receivable *Received customer payment from Jan. 10*	5,500	5,500
Jan. 27, 2019	Accounts Receivable Service Revenue *Billed customer for services rendered*	1,200	1,200
Jan. 30, 2019	Supplies Accounts Payable *Paid for supplies on account*	500	500

We now look at the next step in the accounting cycle, step 3: post journal information to the ledger.

CONTINUING APPLICATION AT WORK

Colfax Market

Colfax Market is a small corner grocery store that carries a variety of staple items such as meat, milk, eggs, bread, and so on. As a smaller grocery store, Colfax does not offer the variety of products found in a larger supermarket or chain. However, it records journal entries in a similar way.

Grocery stores of all sizes must purchase product and track inventory. While the number of entries might differ, the recording process does not. For example, Colfax might purchase food items in one large quantity at the beginning of each month, payable by the end of the month. Therefore, it might only have a few accounts payable and inventory journal entries each month. Larger grocery chains might have multiple deliveries a week, and multiple entries for purchases from a variety of vendors on their accounts payable weekly.

This similarity extends to other retailers, from clothing stores to sporting goods to hardware. No matter the size of a company and no matter the product a company sells, the fundamental accounting entries remain the same.

Posting to the General Ledger

Recall that the general ledger is a record of each account and its balance. Reviewing journal entries individually can be tedious and time consuming. The general ledger is helpful in that a company can easily extract account and balance information. Here is a small section of a general ledger.

GENERAL LEDGER					
Cash					Account No. 101
Date	**Description**	**Ref.**	**Debit**	**Credit**	**Balance**
2019					

You can see at the top is the name of the account "Cash," as well as the assigned account number "101." Remember, all asset accounts will start with the number 1. The date of each transaction related to this account is included, a possible description of the transaction, and a reference number if available. There are debit and credit columns, storing the financial figures for each transaction, and a balance column that keeps a running total of the balance in the account after every transaction.

Let's look at one of the journal entries from Printing Plus and fill in the corresponding ledgers.

JOURNAL			
Date	**Account**	**Debit**	**Credit**
Jan. 3, 2019	Cash Common stock *Received cash in exchange for common stock*	20,000	 20,000

GENERAL LEDGER					
Cash					**Account No. 101**
Date	**Description**	**Ref.**	**Debit**	**Credit**	**Balance**
2019 Jan. 3	Cash for common stock		20,000		20,000
Common Stock					**Account No. 301**
Date	**Description**	**Ref.**	**Debit**	**Credit**	**Balance**
2019 Jan. 3	Cash for common stock			20,000	20,000

As you can see, there is one ledger account for Cash and another for Common Stock. Cash is labeled account number 101 because it is an asset account type. The date of January 3, 2019, is in the far left column, and a description of the transaction follows in the next column. Cash had a debit of $20,000 in the journal entry, so $20,000 is transferred to the general ledger in the debit column. The balance in this account is currently $20,000, because no other transactions have affected this account yet.

Common Stock has the same date and description. Common Stock had a credit of $20,000 in the journal entry, and that information is transferred to the general ledger account in the credit column. The balance at that time in the Common Stock ledger account is $20,000.

Another key element to understanding the general ledger, and the third step in the accounting cycle, is how to calculate balances in ledger accounts.

LINK TO LEARNING

It is a good idea to familiarize yourself with the type of information companies report each year. Peruse Best Buy's 2017 annual report (https://openstax.org/l/50BestBuy2017) to learn more about Best Buy. Take note of the company's balance sheet on page 53 of the report and the income statement on page 54. These reports have much more information than the financial statements we have shown you; however, if you read through them you may notice some familiar items.

Calculating Account Balances

When calculating balances in ledger accounts, one must take into consideration which side of the account increases and which side decreases. To find the account balance, you must find the difference between the sum of all figures on the side that increases and the sum of all figures on the side that decreases.

For example, the Cash account is an asset. We know from the accounting equation that assets increase on the debit side and decrease on the credit side. If there was a debit of $5,000 and a credit of $3,000 in the Cash account, we would find the difference between the two, which is $2,000 (5,000 – 3,000). The debit is the larger of the two sides ($5,000 on the debit side as opposed to $3,000 on the credit side), so the Cash account has a debit balance of $2,000.

Another example is a liability account, such as Accounts Payable, which increases on the credit side and decreases on the debit side. If there were a $4,000 credit and a $2,500 debit, the difference between the two is $1,500. The credit is the larger of the two sides ($4,000 on the credit side as opposed to $2,500 on the debit side), so the Accounts Payable account has a credit balance of $1,500.

The following are selected journal entries from Printing Plus that affect the Cash account. We will use the Cash ledger account to calculate account balances.

JOURNAL			
Date	**Account**	**Debit**	**Credit**
Jan. 3, 2019	Cash	20,000	
	Common Stock		20,000
	Recognize issuance of common stock		
Jan. 9, 2019	Cash	4,000	
	Unearned Revenue		4,000
	Received advanced payment for services yet to be rendered		
Jan. 12, 2019	Utility Expense	300	
	Cash		300
	Paid utility bill		
Jan. 14, 2019	Dividends	100	
	Cash		100
	Paid out dividends		
Jan. 17, 2019	Cash	2,800	
	Service Revenue		2,800
	Collected cash for services rendered		
Jan. 18, 2019	Accounts Payable	3,500	
	Cash		3,500
	Paid liability for equipment in full		
Jan. 20, 2019	Salaries Expense	3,600	
	Cash		3,600
	Paid employee salaries		
Jan. 23, 2019	Cash	5,500	
	Accounts Receivable		5,500
	Received customer payment from Jan. 10		

The general ledger account for Cash would look like the following:

GENERAL LEDGER					
Cash					Account No. 101
Date	Item	Ref.	Debit	Credit	Balance
2019					
Jan. 3	Cash for common stock		20,000		20,000
Jan. 9	Payment from client		4,000		24,000
Jan. 12	Utility bill			300	23,700
Jan. 14	Dividends payment			100	23,600
Jan. 17	Cash for services		2,800		26,400
Jan. 18	Paid cash for equipment			3,500	22,900
Jan. 20	Paid employee salaries			3,600	19,300
Jan. 23	Customer payment		5,500		24,800

In the last column of the Cash ledger account is the running balance. This shows where the account stands after each transaction, as well as the final balance in the account. How do we know on which side, debit or credit, to input each of these balances? Let's consider the general ledger for Cash.

On January 3, there was a debit balance of $20,000 in the Cash account. On January 9, a debit of $4,000 was included. Since both are on the debit side, they will be added together to get a balance on $24,000 (as is seen in the balance column on the January 9 row). On January 12, there was a credit of $300 included in the Cash ledger account. Since this figure is on the credit side, this $300 is subtracted from the previous balance of $24,000 to get a new balance of $23,700. The same process occurs for the rest of the entries in the ledger and their balances. The final balance in the account is $24,800.

Checking to make sure the final balance figure is correct; one can review the figures in the debit and credit columns. In the debit column for this cash account, we see that the total is $32,300 (20,000 + 4,000 + 2,800 + 5,500). The credit column totals $7,500 (300 + 100 + 3,500 + 3,600). The difference between the debit and credit totals is $24,800 (32,300 – 7,500). The balance in this Cash account is a debit of $24,800. Having a debit balance in the Cash account is the normal balance for that account.

Posting to the T-Accounts

The third step in the accounting cycle is to post journal information to the ledger. To do this we can use a T-account format. A company will take information from its journal and post to this general ledger. Posting refers to the process of transferring data from the journal to the general ledger. It is important to understand that T-accounts are only used for illustrative purposes in a textbook, classroom, or business discussion. They are not official accounting forms. Companies will use ledgers for their official books, not T-accounts.

Let's look at the journal entries for Printing Plus and post each of those entries to their respective T-accounts.

The following are the journal entries recorded earlier for Printing Plus.

Transaction 1: On January 3, 2019, issues $20,000 shares of common stock for cash.

JOURNAL			
Date	**Account**	**Debit**	**Credit**
Jan. 3, 2019	Cash Common Stock *To recognize issuance of common stock*	20,000	 20,000

Cash	
Jan. 3 20,000	
Bal. 20,000	

Common Stock	
	20,000 Jan. 3
	Bal. 20,000

In the journal entry, Cash has a debit of $20,000. This is posted to the Cash T-account on the debit side (left side). Common Stock has a credit balance of $20,000. This is posted to the Common Stock T-account on the credit side (right side).

Transaction 2: On January 5, 2019, purchases equipment on account for $3,500, payment due within the month.

JOURNAL			
Date	**Account**	**Debit**	**Credit**
Jan. 5, 2019	Equipment Accounts Payable *To recognize purchase of equipment on account*	3,500	 3,500

Equipment	
Jan. 5 3,500	
Bal. 3,500	

Accounts Payable	
	3,500 Jan. 5
	Bal. 3,500

In the journal entry, Equipment has a debit of $3,500. This is posted to the Equipment T-account on the debit side. Accounts Payable has a credit balance of $3,500. This is posted to the Accounts Payable T-account on the credit side.

Transaction 3: On January 9, 2019, receives $4,000 cash in advance from a customer for services not yet rendered.

JOURNAL			
Date	**Account**	**Debit**	**Credit**
Jan. 9, 2019	Cash Unearned Revenue *To recognize receipt of customer advanced payment for services yet to be rendered*	4,000	 4,000

Cash	
Jan. 3 20,000 Jan. 9 4,000 **Bal. 24,000**	

Unearned Revenue	
	4,000 Jan. 9 **Bal. 4,000**

In the journal entry, Cash has a debit of $4,000. This is posted to the Cash T-account on the debit side. You will notice that the transaction from January 3 is listed already in this T-account. The next transaction figure of $4,000 is added directly below the $20,000 on the debit side. Unearned Revenue has a credit balance of $4,000. This is posted to the Unearned Revenue T-account on the credit side.

Transaction 4: On January 10, 2019, provides $5,500 in services to a customer who asks to be billed for the services.

JOURNAL			
Date	**Account**	**Debit**	**Credit**
Jan. 10, 2019	Accounts Receivable Service Revenue *To recognize revenue earned, billed customer*	5,500	 5,500

Accounts Receivable	
Jan. 10 5,500 **Bal. 5,500**	

Service Revenue	
	5,500 Jan. 10 **Bal. 5,500**

In the journal entry, Accounts Receivable has a debit of $5,500. This is posted to the Accounts Receivable T-account on the debit side. Service Revenue has a credit balance of $5,500. This is posted to the Service Revenue T-account on the credit side.

Transaction 5: On January 12, 2019, pays a $300 utility bill with cash.

JOURNAL			
Date	**Account**	**Debit**	**Credit**
Jan. 12, 2019	Utility Expense Cash *Paid utility bill with cash*	300	 300

Utility Expense	
Jan. 12 300	
Bal. 300	

Cash	
Jan. 3 20,000 Jan. 9 4,000	300 Jan. 12
Bal. 23,700	

In the journal entry, Utility Expense has a debit balance of $300. This is posted to the Utility Expense T-account on the debit side. Cash has a credit of $300. This is posted to the Cash T-account on the credit side. You will notice that the transactions from January 3 and January 9 are listed already in this T-account. The next transaction figure of $300 is added on the credit side.

Transaction 6: On January 14, 2019, distributed $100 cash in dividends to stockholders.

JOURNAL			
Date	**Account**	**Debit**	**Credit**
Jan. 14, 2019	Dividends Cash *Paid dividends with cash*	100	 100

Dividends	
Jan. 14 100	
Bal. 100	

Cash	
Jan. 3 20,000 Jan. 9 4,000	300 Jan. 12 100 Jan. 14
Bal. 23,600	

In the journal entry, Dividends has a debit balance of $100. This is posted to the Dividends T-account on the debit side. Cash has a credit of $100. This is posted to the Cash T-account on the credit side. You will notice that the transactions from January 3, January 9, and January 12 are listed already in this T-account. The next transaction figure of $100 is added directly below the January 12 record on the credit side.

Transaction 7: On January 17, 2019, receives $2,800 cash from a customer for services rendered.

JOURNAL			
Date	**Account**	**Debit**	**Credit**
Jan. 17, 2019	Cash Service Revenue *Collected cash for services rendered*	2,800	 2,800

Cash			
Jan. 3	20,000	300	Jan. 12
Jan. 9	4,000	100	Jan. 14
Jan. 17	2,800		
Bal.	**26,400**		

Service Revenue			
		5,500	Jan. 10
		2,800	Jan. 17
		Bal.	**8,300**

In the journal entry, Cash has a debit of $2,800. This is posted to the Cash T-account on the debit side. You will notice that the transactions from January 3, January 9, January 12, and January 14 are listed already in this T-account. The next transaction figure of $2,800 is added directly below the January 9 record on the debit side. Service Revenue has a credit balance of $2,800. This too has a balance already from January 10. The new entry is recorded under the Jan 10 record, posted to the Service Revenue T-account on the credit side.

Transaction 8: On January 18, 2019, paid in full, with cash, for the equipment purchase on January 5.

JOURNAL			
Date	**Account**	**Debit**	**Credit**
Jan. 18, 2019	Accounts Payable Cash *Paid liability for equipment in full*	3,500	 3,500

Cash			
Jan. 3	20,000	300	Jan. 12
Jan. 9	4,000	100	Jan. 14
Jan. 17	2,800	3,500	Jan. 18
Bal.	**22,900**		

Accounts Payable			
Jan. 18	3,500	3,500	Jan. 5
		Bal.	**0**

On this transaction, Cash has a credit of $3,500. This is posted to the Cash T-account on the credit side beneath the January 14 transaction. Accounts Payable has a debit of $3,500 (payment in full for the Jan. 5 purchase). You notice there is already a credit in Accounts Payable, and the new record is placed directly across from the January 5 record.

Transaction 9: On January 20, 2019, paid $3,600 cash in salaries expense to employees.

JOURNAL			
Date	**Account**	**Debit**	**Credit**
Jan. 20, 2019	Salaries Expense Cash *Paid employee salaries*	3,600	 3,600

Cash			
Jan. 3	20,000	300	Jan. 12
Jan. 9	4,000	100	Jan. 14
Jan. 17	2,800	3,500	Jan.18
		3,600	Jan.20
Bal.	**19,300**		

Salaries Expense			
Jan. 20	3,600		
Bal.	**3.600**		

On this transaction, Cash has a credit of $3,600. This is posted to the Cash T-account on the credit side beneath the January 18 transaction. Salaries Expense has a debit of $3,600. This is placed on the debit side of the Salaries Expense T-account.

Transaction 10: On January 23, 2019, received cash payment in full from the customer on the January 10 transaction.

JOURNAL			
Date	**Account**	**Debit**	**Credit**
Jan. 23, 2019	Cash Accounts Receivable *Received customer payment from Jan. 10*	5,500	 5,500

Cash			
Jan. 3	20,500	300	Jan. 12
Jan. 9	4,000	100	Jan. 14
Jan. 17	2,800	3,500	Jan. 18
Jan. 23	5,500	3,600	Jan. 20
Bal.	**24,800**		

Accounts Receivable			
Jan. 10	5,500	5,500	Jan. 23
Bal.	**0**		

On this transaction, Cash has a debit of $5,500. This is posted to the Cash T-account on the debit side beneath the January 17 transaction. Accounts Receivable has a credit of $5,500 (from the Jan. 10 transaction). The record is placed on the credit side of the Accounts Receivable T-account across from the January 10 record.

Transaction 11: On January 27, 2019, provides $1,200 in services to a customer who asks to be billed for the services.

JOURNAL			
Date	**Account**	**Debit**	**Credit**
Jan. 27, 2019	Accounts Receivable Service Revenue *Billed customer for services rendered*	1,200	 1,200

Accounts Receivable	
Jan. 10 5,500	5,500 Jan. 23
Jan. 27 1,200	
Bal. 1,200	

Service Revenue	
	5,500 Jan. 10
	2,800 Jan. 17
	1,200 Jan. 27
	Bal. 9,500

On this transaction, Accounts Receivable has a debit of $1,200. The record is placed on the debit side of the Accounts Receivable T-account underneath the January 10 record. Service Revenue has a credit of $1,200. The record is placed on the credit side of the Service Revenue T-account underneath the January 17 record.

Transaction 12: On January 30, 2019, purchases supplies on account for $500, payment due within three months.

JOURNAL			
Date	**Account**	**Debit**	**Credit**
Jan. 30, 2019	Supplies Accounts Payable *Purchased supplies on account*	500	 500

Supplies	
Jan. 30 500	
Bal. 500	

Accounts Payable	
Jan. 18 3,500	3,500 Jan. 9
	500 Jan. 30
	Bal. 500

On this transaction, Supplies has a debit of $500. This will go on the debit side of the Supplies T-account. Accounts Payable has a credit of $500. You notice there are already figures in Accounts Payable, and the new record is placed directly underneath the January 5 record.

T-Accounts Summary

Once all journal entries have been posted to T-accounts, we can check to make sure the accounting equation remains balanced. A summary showing the T-accounts for Printing Plus is presented in Figure 3.10.

Assets = **Liabilities** + **Equity**

Assets

Cash

Debit		Credit	
Jan. 3	20,000	300	Jan. 12
Jan. 9	4,000	100	Jan. 14
Jan. 17	2,800	3,500	Jan. 18
Jan. 23	5,500	3,600	Jan. 20
Bal.	**24,800**		

Accounts Receivable

Debit		Credit	
Jan. 10	5,500	5,500	Jan. 23
Jan. 27	1,200		
Bal.	**1,200**		

Supplies

Debit		Credit	
Jan. 30	500		
Bal.	**500**		

Equipment

Debit		Credit	
Jan. 5	3,500		
Bal.	**3,500**		

Liabilities

Accounts Payable

Debit		Credit	
Jan. 18	3,500	3,500	Jan. 5
		500	Jan. 30
		Bal. 500	

Unearned Revenue

Debit		Credit	
		4,000	Jan. 9
		Bal. 4,000	

Equity

Common Stock

Debit		Credit	
		20,000	Jan. 3
		Bal. 20,000	

Dividends

Debit		Credit	
Jan. 14	100		
Bal.	**100**		

Service Revenue

Debit		Credit	
		5,500	Jan. 10
		2,800	Jan. 17
		1,200	Jan. 27
		Bal. 9,500	

Salaries Expense

Debit		Credit	
Jan. 20	3,600		
Bal.	**3,600**		

Utility Expense

Debit		Credit	
Jan. 12	300		
Bal.	**300**		

Figure 3.10 Summary of T-Accounts for Printing Plus. (attribution: Copyright Rice University, OpenStax, under CC BY-NC-SA 4.0 license)

The sum on the assets side of the accounting equation equals $30,000, found by adding together the final balances in each asset account (24,800 + 1,200 + 500 + 3,500). To find the total on the liabilities and equity side of the equation, we need to find the difference between debits and credits. Credits on the liabilities and equity side of the equation total $34,000 (500 + 4,000 + 20,000 + 9,500). Debits on the liabilities and equity side of the equation total $4,000 (100 + 3,600 + 300). The difference $34,000 – $4,000 = $30,000. Thus, the equation remains balanced with $30,000 on the asset side and $30,000 on the liabilities and equity side. Now that we have the T-account information, and have confirmed the accounting equation remains balanced, we can create the unadjusted trial balance.

YOUR TURN

Journalizing Transactions

You have the following transactions the last few days of April.

Apr. 25	You stop by your uncle's gas station to refill both gas cans for your company, Watson's Landscaping. Your uncle adds the total of $28 to your account.
Apr. 26	You record another week's revenue for the lawns mowed over the past week. You earned $1,200. You received cash equal to 75% of your revenue.
Apr. 27	You pay your local newspaper $35 to run an advertisement in this week's paper.
Apr. 29	You make a $25 payment on account.

Table 3.3

A. Prepare the necessary journal entries for these four transactions.
B. Explain why you debited and credited the accounts you did.
C. What will be the new balance in each account used in these entries?

Solution

JOURNAL			
Date	**Account**	**Debit**	**Credit**
Apr. 25, 2018	Gas expense	28	
	Accounts payable		28
	Purchased gas on account		
Apr. 26, 2018	Cash	900	
	Accounts receivable	300	
	Lawnmowing revenue		1,200
	Earned $1,200 revenue: received 75% in cash		
Apr. 27, 2018	Advertising expense	35	
	Cash		35
	Paid cash to run an ad in the newspaper		
Apr. 29, 2018	Accounts payable	25	
	Cash		25
	Made a payment on account		

April 25

- You have incurred more gas expense. This means you have an increase in the total amount of gas expense for April. Expenses go up with debit entries. Therefore, you will debit gas expense.

- You purchased the gas on account. This will increase your liabilities. Liabilities increase with credit entries. Credit accounts payable to increase the total in the account.

April 26

- You have received more cash from customers, so you want the total cash to increase. Cash is an asset, and assets increase with debit entries, so debit cash.
- You also have more money owed to you by your customers. You have performed the services, your customers owe you the money, and you will receive the money in the future. Debit accounts receivable as asset accounts increase with debits.
- You have mowed lawns and earned more revenue. You want the total of your revenue account to increase to reflect this additional revenue. Revenue accounts increase with credit entries, so credit lawn-mowing revenue.

April 27

- Advertising is an expense of doing business. You have incurred more expenses, so you want to increase an expense account. Expense accounts increase with debit entries. Debit advertising expense.
- You paid cash for the advertising. You have less cash, so credit the cash account. Cash is an asset, and asset account totals decrease with credits.

April 29

- You paid "on account." Remember that "on account" means a service was performed or an item was received without being paid for. The customer asked to be billed. You were the customer in this case. You made a purchase of gas on account earlier in the month, and at that time you increased accounts payable to show you had a liability to pay this amount sometime in the future. You are now paying down some of the money you owe on that account. Since you paid this money, you now have less of a liability so you want to see the liability account, accounts payable, decrease by the amount paid. Liability accounts decrease with debit entries.
- You paid, which means you gave cash (or wrote a check or electronically transferred) so you have less cash. To decrease the total cash, credit the account because asset accounts are reduced by recording credit entries.

YOUR TURN

Normal Account Balances

Calculate the balances in each of the following accounts. Do they all have the normal balance they should have? If not, which one? How do you know this?

GENERAL LEDGER					
Cash					Account No. 101
Date	**Item**	**Ref.**	**Debit**	**Credit**	**Balance**
2019					
			9,500		
				3,500	
			1,750		
				5,800	
			500		
				1,500	

GENERAL LEDGER					
Accounts Receivable					Account No. 111
Date	**Item**	**Ref.**	**Debit**	**Credit**	**Balance**
2019					
			4,500		
			3,650		
				4,250	
				3,500	
			825		

GENERAL LEDGER					
Accounts Payable					Account No. 201
Date	**Item**	**Ref.**	**Debit**	**Credit**	**Balance**
2019					
				1,500	
				875	
			500		
				325	
			650		

Solution

GENERAL LEDGER					
Cash					Account No. 101
Date	**Item**	**Ref.**	**Debit**	**Credit**	**Balance**
2019					
			9,500		9,500
				3,500	6,000
			1,750		7,750
				5,800	1,950
			500		2,450
				1,500	950

GENERAL LEDGER					
Accounts Receivable					Account No. 111
Date	**Item**	**Ref.**	**Debit**	**Credit**	**Balance**
2019					
			4,500		4,500
			3,650		8,150
				4,250	3,900
				3,500	400
			825		1,225

GENERAL LEDGER					
Accounts Payable					Account No. 201
Date	**Item**	**Ref.**	**Debit**	**Credit**	**Balance**
201X					
				1,500	1,500
				875	2,375
			500		1,875
				325	2,200
			650		1,550

THINK IT THROUGH

Gift Cards

Gift cards have become an important topic for managers of any company. Understanding who buys gift cards, why, and when can be important in business planning. Also, knowing when and how to determine that a gift card will not likely be redeemed will affect both the company's balance sheet (in the liabilities section) and the income statement (in the revenues section).

According to a 2017 holiday shopping report from the National Retail Federation, gift cards are the most-requested presents for the eleventh year in a row, with 61% of people surveyed saying they are at the top of their wish lists, according to the National Retail Federation.[6] *CEB TowerGroup* projects that total gift card volume will reach $160 billion by 2018.[7]

How are all of these gift card sales affecting one of America's favorite specialty coffee companies, Starbucks?

In 2014 one in seven adults received a Starbucks gift card. On Christmas Eve alone $2.5 million gift cards were sold. This is a rate of 1,700 cards per minute.[8]

The following discussion about gift cards is taken from Starbucks's 2016 annual report:

> When an amount is loaded onto a stored value card we recognize a corresponding liability for the full amount loaded onto the card, which is recorded within stored value card liability on our consolidated balance sheets. When a stored value card is redeemed at a company-operated store or online, we recognize revenue by reducing the stored value card liability. When a stored value card is redeemed at a licensed store location, we reduce the corresponding stored value card liability and cash, which is reimbursed to the licensee. There are no expiration dates on our stored value cards, and in most markets, we do not charge service fees that cause a decrement to customer balances. While we will continue to honor all stored value cards presented for payment, management may determine the likelihood of redemption, based on historical experience, is deemed to be remote for certain cards due to long periods of inactivity. In these circumstances, unredeemed card balances may be recognized as breakage income. In fiscal 2016, 2015, and 2014, we recognized breakage income of $60.5 million, $39.3 million, and $38.3 million, respectively.[9]

As of October 1, 2017, Starbucks had a total of $1,288,500,000 in stored value card liability.

3.6 Prepare a Trial Balance

Once all the monthly transactions have been analyzed, journalized, and posted on a continuous day-to-day basis over the accounting period (a month in our example), we are ready to start working on preparing a trial balance (unadjusted). Preparing an unadjusted trial balance is the fourth step in the accounting cycle. A **trial balance** is a list of all accounts in the general ledger that have nonzero balances. A trial balance is an important step in the accounting process, because it helps identify any computational errors throughout the first three steps in the cycle.

Note that for this step, we are considering our trial balance to be unadjusted. The **unadjusted trial balance** in this section includes accounts before they have been adjusted. As you see in step 6 of the accounting cycle, we create another trial balance that is adjusted (see The Adjustment Process).

6 National Retail Federation (NRF). "NRF Consumer Survey Points to Busy Holiday Season, Backs Up Economic Forecast and Import Numbers." October 27, 2017. https://nrf.com/media-center/press-releases/nrf-consumer-survey-points-busy-holiday-season-backs-economic-forecast

7 CEB Tower Group. "2015 Gift Card Sales to Reach New Peak of $130 Billion." PR Newswire. December 8, 2015. https://www.prnewswire.com/news-releases/2015-gift-card-sales-to-reach-new-peak-of-130-billion-300189615.html

8 Sara Haralson. "Last-Minute Shoppers Rejoice! Starbucks Has You Covered." *Fortune*. December 22, 2015. http://fortune.com/video/2015/12/22/starbucks-gift-cards/

9 U.S. Securities and Exchange Commission. Communication from Starbucks Corporation regarding 2014 10-K Filing. November 14, 2014. https://www.sec.gov/Archives/edgar/data/829224/000082922415000020/filename1.htm

When constructing a trial balance, we must consider a few formatting rules, akin to those requirements for financial statements:

- The header must contain the name of the company, the label of a Trial Balance (Unadjusted), and the date.
- Accounts are listed in the accounting equation order with assets listed first followed by liabilities and finally equity.
- Amounts at the top of each debit and credit column should have a dollar sign.
- When amounts are added, the final figure in each column should be underscored.
- The totals at the end of the trial balance need to have dollar signs and be double-underscored.

Transferring information from T-accounts to the trial balance requires consideration of the final balance in each account. If the final balance in the ledger account (T-account) is a debit balance, you will record the total in the left column of the trial balance. If the final balance in the ledger account (T-account) is a credit balance, you will record the total in the right column.

Once all ledger accounts and their balances are recorded, the debit and credit columns on the trial balance are totaled to see if the figures in each column match each other. The final total in the debit column must be the same dollar amount that is determined in the final credit column. For example, if you determine that the final debit balance is $24,000 then the final credit balance in the trial balance must also be $24,000. If the two balances are not equal, there is a mistake in at least one of the columns.

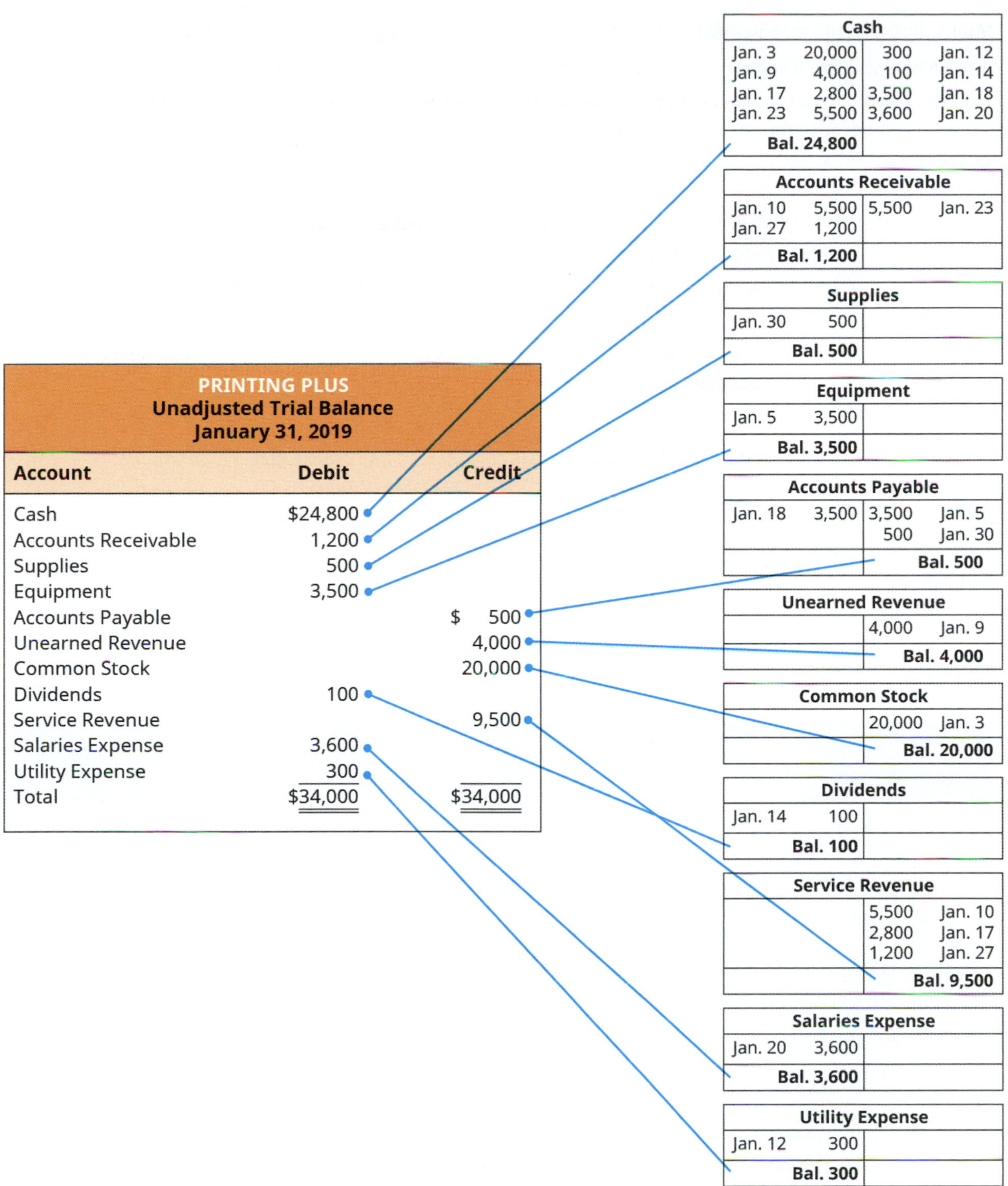

PRINTING PLUS
Unadjusted Trial Balance
January 31, 2019

Account	Debit	Credit
Cash	$24,800	
Accounts Receivable	1,200	
Supplies	500	
Equipment	3,500	
Accounts Payable		$ 500
Unearned Revenue		4,000
Common Stock		20,000
Dividends	100	
Service Revenue		9,500
Salaries Expense	3,600	
Utility Expense	300	
Total	$34,000	$34,000

Cash			
Jan. 3	20,000	300	Jan. 12
Jan. 9	4,000	100	Jan. 14
Jan. 17	2,800	3,500	Jan. 18
Jan. 23	5,500	3,600	Jan. 20
	Bal. 24,800		

Accounts Receivable			
Jan. 10	5,500	5,500	Jan. 23
Jan. 27	1,200		
	Bal. 1,200		

Supplies			
Jan. 30	500		
	Bal. 500		

Equipment			
Jan. 5	3,500		
	Bal. 3,500		

Accounts Payable			
Jan. 18	3,500	3,500	Jan. 5
		500	Jan. 30
		Bal. 500	

Unearned Revenue			
		4,000	Jan. 9
		Bal. 4,000	

Common Stock			
		20,000	Jan. 3
		Bal. 20,000	

Dividends			
Jan. 14	100		
	Bal. 100		

Service Revenue			
		5,500	Jan. 10
		2,800	Jan. 17
		1,200	Jan. 27
		Bal. 9,500	

Salaries Expense			
Jan. 20	3,600		
	Bal. 3,600		

Utility Expense			
Jan. 12	300		
	Bal. 300		

Let's now take a look at the T-accounts and unadjusted trial balance for Printing Plus to see how the information is transferred from the T-accounts to the unadjusted trial balance.

For example, Cash has a final balance of $24,800 on the debit side. This balance is transferred to the Cash account in the debit column on the unadjusted trial balance. Accounts Receivable ($1,200), Supplies ($500), Equipment ($3,500), Dividends ($100), Salaries Expense ($3,600), and Utility Expense ($300) also have debit final balances in their T-accounts, so this information will be transferred to the debit column on the unadjusted trial balance. Accounts Payable ($500), Unearned Revenue ($4,000), Common Stock ($20,000) and Service Revenue ($9,500) all have credit final balances in their T-accounts. These credit balances would transfer to the credit column on the unadjusted trial balance.

Once all balances are transferred to the unadjusted trial balance, we will sum each of the debit and credit columns. The debit and credit columns both total $34,000, which means they are equal and in balance. However, just because the column totals are equal and in balance, we are still not guaranteed that a mistake is not present.

PRINTING PLUS Unadjusted Trial Balance January 31, 2019		
Account	**Debit**	**Credit**
Cash	$24,800	
Accounts Receivable	1,200	
Supplies	500	
Equipment	3,500	
Accounts Payable		$ 500
Unearned Revenue		4,000
Common Stock		20,000
Dividends	100	
Service Revenue		9,500
Salaries Expense	3,600	
Utility Expense	300	
Total	$34,000	$34,000

What happens if the columns are not equal?

CONCEPTS IN PRACTICE

Enron and Arthur Andersen

One of the most well-known financial schemes is that involving the companies Enron Corporation and Arthur Andersen. Enron defrauded thousands by intentionally inflating revenues that did not exist. Arthur Andersen was the auditing firm in charge of independently verifying the accuracy of Enron's financial statements and disclosures. This meant they would review statements to make sure they aligned with GAAP principles, assumptions, and concepts, among other things.

It has been alleged that Arthur Andersen was negligent in its dealings with Enron and contributed to the collapse of the company. Arthur Andersen was brought up on a charge of obstruction of justice for shredding important documents related to criminal actions by Enron. They were found guilty but had that conviction overturned. However, the damage was done, and the company's reputation prevented it from operating as it had.[10]

Locating Errors

Sometimes errors may occur in the accounting process, and the trial balance can make those errors apparent when it does not balance.

10 James Titcomb. "Arthur Andersen Returns 12 Years after Enron Scandal." *The Telegraph.* September 2, 2014. https://www.telegraph.co.uk/finance/newsbysector/banksandfinance/11069713/Arthur-Andersen-returns-12-years-after-Enron-scandal.html

One way to find the error is to take the difference between the two totals and divide the difference by two. For example, let's assume the following is the trial balance for Printing Plus.

PRINTING PLUS Unadjusted Trial Balance January 31, 2019		
Account	**Debit**	**Credit**
Cash	$24,800	
Accounts Receivable	1,200	
Supplies	500	
Equipment	3,500	
Accounts Payable		$ 500
Unearned Revenue		4,000
Common Stock		20,000
Dividends		100
Service Revenue		9,500
Salaries Expense	3,600	
Utility Expense	300	
Total	$33,900	$34,100

You notice that the balances are not the same. Find the difference between the two totals: $34,100 – $33,900 = $200 difference. Now divide the difference by two: $200/2 = $100. Since the credit side has a higher total, look carefully at the numbers on the credit side to see if any of them are $100. The Dividends account has a $100 figure listed in the credit column. Dividends normally have a debit balance, but here it is a credit. Look back at the Dividends T-account to see if it was copied onto the trial balance incorrectly. If the answer is the same as the T-account, then trace it back to the journal entry to check for mistakes. You may discover in your investigation that you copied the number from the T-account incorrectly. Fix your error, and the debit total will go up $100 and the credit total down $100 so that they will both now be $34,000.

Another way to find an error is to take the difference between the two totals and divide by nine. If the outcome of the difference is a whole number, then you may have transposed a figure. For example, let's assume the following is the trial balance for Printing Plus.

PRINTING PLUS Unadjusted Trial Balance January 31, 2019		
Account	**Debit**	**Credit**
Cash	$24,800	
Accounts Receivable	1,200	
Supplies	500	
Equipment	5,300	
Accounts Payable		$ 500
Unearned Revenue		4,000
Common Stock		20,000
Dividends	100	
Service Revenue		9,500
Salaries Expense	3,600	
Utility Expense	300	
Total	$35,800	$34,000

Find the difference between the two totals: $35,800 – 34,000 = $1,800 difference. This difference divided by nine is $200 ($1,800/9 = $200). Looking at the debit column, which has the higher total, we determine that the Equipment account had transposed figures. The account should be $3,500 and not $5,300. We transposed the three and the five.

What do you do if you have tried both methods and neither has worked? Unfortunately, you will have to go back through one step at a time until you find the error.

If a trial balance is in balance, does this mean that all of the numbers are correct? Not necessarily. We can have errors and still be mathematically in balance. It is important to go through each step very carefully and recheck your work often to avoid mistakes early on in the process.

After the unadjusted trial balance is prepared and it appears error-free, a company might look at its financial statements to get an idea of the company's position before adjustments are made to certain accounts. A more complete picture of company position develops after adjustments occur, and an adjusted trial balance has been prepared. These next steps in the accounting cycle are covered in The Adjustment Process.

YOUR TURN

Completing a Trial Balance

Complete the trial balance for Magnificent Landscaping Service using the following T-account final balance information for April 30, 2018.

Cash	
10,000	6,000
Bal. 4,000	

Common Stock	
	2,050
	Bal. 2,050

Accounts Receivable	
400	
Bal. 400	

Service Revenue	
	2,000 400
	Bal. 2,400

Accounts Payable	
	50
	Bal. 50

Advertising Expense	
100	
Bal. 100	

Solution

MAGNIFICENT LANDSCAPING SERVICE Trial Balance April 30, 2018		
	Debit	**Credit**
Cash	$4,000	
Accounts receivable	400	
Accounts payable		50
Common stock		2,050
Service revenue		2,400
Advertising expense	100	
	$4,500	$4,500

THINK IT THROUGH

Correcting Errors in the Trial Balance

You own a small consulting business. Each month, you prepare a trial balance showing your company's position. After preparing your trial balance this month, you discover that it does not balance. The debit column shows $2,000 more dollars than the credit column. You decide to investigate this error.

What methods could you use to find the error? What are the ramifications if you do not find and fix this error? How can you minimize these types of errors in the future?

Key Terms

abnormal balance account balance that is contrary to the expected normal balance of that account

account record showing increases and decreases to assets, liabilities, and equity found in the accounting equation

accounting cycle step-by-step process to record business activities and events to keep financial records up to date

book of original entry journal is often referred to as this because it is the place the information originally enters into the system

chart of accounts account numbering system that lists all the accounts a business uses in its day-to-day transactions

compound entry more than one account is listed under the debit and/or credit column of a journal entry

conceptual framework interrelated objectives and fundamentals of accounting principles for financial reporting

conservatism concept that if there is uncertainty in a potential financial estimate, a company should err on the side of caution and report the most conservative amount

contributed capital owner's investment (cash and other assets) in the business which typically comes in the form of common stock

cost principle everything the company owns or controls (assets) must be recorded at its value at the date of acquisition

credit records financial information on the right side of an account

debit records financial information on the left side of each account

double-entry accounting system requires the sum of the debits to equal the sum of the credits for each transaction

ending account balance difference between debits and credits for an account

expanded accounting equation breaks down the equity portion of the accounting equation into more detail to see the impact to equity from changes to revenues and expenses, and to owner investments and payouts

expense recognition principle (also, matching principle) matches expenses with associated revenues in the period in which the revenues were generated

full disclosure principle business must report any business activities that could affect what is reported on the financial statements

general ledger comprehensive listing of all of a company's accounts with their individual balances

going concern assumption absent any evidence to the contrary, assumption that a business will continue to operate in the indefinite future

journal record of all transactions

journalizing entering information into a journal; second step in the accounting cycle

monetary measurement system of using a monetary unit by which to value the transaction, such as the US dollar

normal balance expected balance each account type maintains, which is the side that increases

original source traceable record of information that contributes to the creation of a business transaction

period one operating cycle of a business, which could be a month, quarter, or year

posting takes all transactions from the journal during a period and moves the information to a general ledger (ledger)

prepaid expenses items paid for in advance of their use

revenue recognition principle principle stating that a company must recognize revenue in the period in which it is earned; it is not considered earned until a product or service has been provided

separate entity concept business may only report activities on financial statements that are specifically related to company operations, not those activities that affect the owner personally

simple entry only one debit account and one credit account are listed under the debit and credit columns of a journal entry

stockholders' equity owner (stockholders') investments in the business and earnings

T-account graphic representation of a general ledger account in which each account is visually split into left and right sides

time period assumption companies can present useful information in shorter time periods such as years, quarters, or months

transaction business activity or event that has an effect on financial information presented on financial statements

trial balance list of all accounts in the general ledger that have nonzero balances

unadjusted trial balance trial balance that includes accounts before they have been adjusted

unearned revenue advance payment for a product or service that has yet to be provided by the company; the transaction is a liability until the product or service is provided

Summary

3.1 Describe Principles, Assumptions, and Concepts of Accounting and Their Relationship to Financial Statements

- The Financial Accounting Standards Board (FASB) is an independent, nonprofit organization that sets the standards for financial accounting and reporting standards for both public- and private-sector businesses in the United States, including generally accepted accounting principles (GAAP).
- GAAP are the concepts, standards, and rules that guide the preparation and presentation of financial statements.
- The Securities and Exchange Commission (SEC) is an independent federal agency that is charged with protecting the interests of investors, regulating stock markets, and ensuring companies adhere to GAAP requirements.
- The FASB uses a conceptual framework, which is a set of concepts that guide financial reporting.
- The revenue recognition principle requires companies to record revenue when it is earned. Revenue is earned when a product or service has been provided.
- The expense recognition principle requires that expenses incurred match with revenues earned in the same period. The expenses are associated with revenue generation.
- The cost principle records assets at their value at the date of acquisition. A company may not record what it estimates or thinks the value of the asset is, only what is verifiable. This verification is typically represented by an actual transaction.
- The full disclosure principle requires companies to relay any information to the public that may affect financials that are not readily available on the financial statements. This helps users of information make decisions that are more informed.
- The separate entity concept maintains that only business activities, and not the owner's personal financials, may be reported on company financial statements.
- Conservatism prescribes that a company should record expenses or losses when there is an expectation of their existence but only recognize gains or revenue when there is assurance that they will be realized.
- Monetary measurement requires a monetary unit be used to report financial information, such as the US

dollar. This makes information comparable.

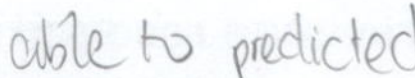

- The going concern assumption assumes that a business will continue to operate in the foreseeable future. If there is a concern the business will not continue operating, this needs to be disclosed to management and other users of information.
- Time period assumption presents financial information in equal and short time frames, such as a month, quarter, or year.
- The accounting equation shows that assets must equal the sum of liabilities and equity. Transactions are analyzed with this equation to prepare for the next step in the accounting cycle.

3.2 Define and Describe the Expanded Accounting Equation and Its Relationship to Analyzing Transactions

- The expanded accounting equation breaks down the equity portion of the accounting equation into more detail to show common stock, dividends, revenue, and expenses individually.
- The chart of accounts is a numbering system that lists all of a company's accounts in the order in which they appear on the financial statements, beginning with the balance sheet accounts and then the income statement accounts.

3.3 Define and Describe the Initial Steps in the Accounting Cycle

- Step 1 in the accounting cycle: Identifying and analyzing transactions requires a company to take information from an original source, identify its purpose as a financial transaction, and connect that information to an accounting equation.
- Step 2 in the accounting cycle: Recording transactions to a journal takes financial information identified in the transaction and copies that information, using the accounting equation, into a journal. The journal is a record of all transactions.
- Step 3 in the accounting cycle: Posting journal information to a ledger takes all information transferred to the journal and posts it to a general ledger. The general ledger in an accumulation of all accounts a company maintains and their balances.
- Step 4 in the accounting cycle: Preparing an unadjusted trial balance requires transfer of information from the general ledger (T-accounts) to an unadjusted trial balance showing all account balances.

3.4 Analyze Business Transactions Using the Accounting Equation and Show the Impact of Business Transactions on Financial Statements

- Both the basic and the expanded accounting equations are useful in analyzing how any transaction affects a company's financial statements.

3.5 Use Journal Entries to Record Transactions and Post to T-Accounts

- Journals are the first place where information is entered into the accounting system, which is why they are often referred to as books of original entry.
- Journalizing transactions transfers information from accounting equation analysis to a record of each transaction.
- There are several formatting rules for journalizing transactions that include where to put debits and credits, which account titles come first, the need for a date and inclusion of a brief description.
- Step 3 in the accounting cycle posts journal information to the general ledger (T-accounts). Final balances in each account must be calculated before transfer to the trial balance occurs.

3.6 Prepare a Trial Balance

- The trial balance contains a listing of all accounts in the general ledger with nonzero balances. Information is transferred from the T-accounts to the trial balance.
- Sometimes errors occur on the trial balance, and there are ways to find these errors. One may have to go

through each step of the accounting process to locate an error on the trial balance.

Multiple Choice

1. LO 3.1 That a business may only report activities on financial statements that are specifically related to company operations, not those activities that affect the owner personally, is known as which of the following?

A. separate entity concept
B. monetary measurement concept
C. going concern assumption
D. time period assumption

2. LO 3.1 That companies can present useful information in shorter time periods such as years, quarters, or months is known as which of the following?

A. separate entity concept
B. monetary measurement concept
C. going concern assumption
D. time period assumption

3. LO 3.1 The system of using a monetary unit, such as the US dollar, to value the transaction is known as which of the following?

A. separate entity concept
B. monetary measurement concept
C. going concern assumption
D. time period assumption

4. LO 3.1 Which of the following terms is used when assuming a business will continue to operate in the foreseeable future?

A. separate entity concept
B. monetary measurement concept
C. going concern assumption
D. time period assumption

5. LO 3.1 The independent, nonprofit organization that sets financial accounting and reporting standards for both public- and private-sector businesses that use generally accepted accounting principles (GAAP) in the United States is which of the following?

A. Financial Accounting Standards Board (FASB)
B. generally accepted accounting principles (GAAP)
C. Securities and Exchange Commission (SEC)
D. conceptual framework

6. LO 3.1 The standards, procedures, and principles companies must follow when preparing their financial statements are known as which of the following?

A. Financial Accounting Standards Board (FASB)
B. generally accepted accounting principles (GAAP)
C. Securities and Exchange Commission (SEC)
D. conceptual framework

7. LO 3.1 These are used by the FASB, and it is a set of concepts that guide financial reporting.

A. Financial Accounting Standards Board (FASB)
B. generally accepted accounting principles (GAAP)
C. Securities and Exchange Commission (SEC)
D. conceptual framework

8. LO 3.1 This is the independent federal agency protecting the interests of investors, regulating stock markets, and ensuring companies adhere to GAAP requirements.

A. Financial Accounting Standards Board (FASB)
B. generally accepted accounting principles (GAAP)
C. Securities and Exchange Commission (SEC)
D. conceptual framework

9. LO 3.1 Which of the following is the principle that a company must recognize revenue in the period in which it is earned; it is not considered earned until a product or service has been provided?

A. revenue recognition principle
B. expense recognition (matching) principle
C. cost principle
D. full disclosure principle

10. LO 3.1 Which of the following is the principle that a business must report any business activities that could affect what is reported on the financial statements?

A. revenue recognition principle
B. expense recognition (matching) principle
C. cost principle
D. full disclosure principle

11. LO 3.1 Also known as the historical cost principle, _______ states that everything the company owns or controls (assets) must be recorded at their value at the date of acquisition.

A. revenue recognition principle
B. expense recognition (matching) principle
C. cost principle
D. full disclosure principle

12. LO 3.1 Which of the following principles matches expenses with associated revenues in the period in which the revenues were generated?

A. revenue recognition principle
B. expense recognition (matching) principle
C. cost principle
D. full disclosure principle

13. LO 3.2 Which of the following does *not* accurately represent the accounting equation?

A. Assets – Liabilities = Stockholders' Equity
B. Assets – Stockholders' Equity = Liabilities
C. Assets = Liabilities + Stockholders' Equity
D. Assets + Liabilities = Stockholders' Equity

14. LO 3.2 Which of these statements is *false*?

A. Assets = Liabilities + Equity
B. Assets – Liabilities = Equity
C. Liabilities – Equity = Assets
D. Liabilities = Assets – Equity

15. LO 3.2 Which of these accounts is an asset?

A. Common Stock
B. Supplies
C. Accounts Payable
D. Fees Earned

16. LO 3.2 Which of these accounts is a liability?

A. Accounts Receivable
B. Supplies
C. Salaries Expense
D. Accounts Payable

17. LO 3.2 If equity equals $100,000, which of the following is true?

A. Assets exceed liabilities by $100,000.
B. Liabilities exceed equity by $100,000.
C. Assets + liabilities equal $100,000.
D. None of the above is true.

18. LO 3.3 Which process of the accounting cycle often requires the most analytical thought?

A. making a journal entry
B. posting transactions to accounts
C. summarizing the trial balance
D. preparing the financial statements

19. LO 3.3 The step-by-step process to record business activities and events to keep financial records up to date is _______.

A. day-to-day cycle
B. accounting cycle
C. general ledger
D. journal

20. LO 3.3 One operating cycle of a business, which could be a month, quarter, or year, is commonly referred to as which of the following?

A. period
B. round
C. tally
D. mark

21. LO 3.3 _______ takes all transactions from the journal during a period and moves the information to a general ledger (ledger).

A. Hitching
B. Posting
C. Vetting
D. Laxing

22. LO 3.4 Which of these events will *not* be recognized?

A. A service is performed, but the payment is not collected on the same day.
B. Supplies are purchased. They are not paid for; the company will be billed.
C. A copy machine is ordered. It will be delivered in two weeks.
D. Electricity has been used but has not been paid for.

23. LO 3.4 A company purchased a building twenty years ago for $150,000. The building currently has an appraised market value of $235,000. The company reports the building on its balance sheet at $235,000. What concept or principle has been violated?

A. separate entity concept
B. recognition principle
C. monetary measurement concept
D. cost principle

24. LO 3.4 What is the impact on the accounting equation when a current month's utility expense is paid?

A. both sides increase
B. both sides decrease
C. only the Asset side changes
D. neither side changes

25. LO 3.4 What is the impact on the accounting equation when a payment of account payable is made?

A. both sides increase
B. both sides decrease
C. only the Asset side changes
D. neither side changes

26. LO 3.4 What is the impact on the accounting equation when an accounts receivable is collected?

A. both sides increase
B. both sides decrease
C. only the Asset side changes
D. the total of neither side changes

27. LO 3.4 What is the impact on the accounting equation when a sale occurs?

A. both sides increase
B. both sides decrease
C. only the Asset side changes
D. neither side changes

28. LO 3.4 What is the impact on the accounting equation when stock is issued, in exchange for assets?

A. both sides increase
B. both sides decrease
C. only the Asset side changes
D. neither side changes

29. LO 3.5 Which of the following accounts is increased by a debit?

A. Common Stock
B. Accounts Payable
C. Supplies
D. Service Revenue

30. LO 3.5 Which of the following accounts does not increase with a debit entry?
A. Retained Earnings
B. Buildings
C. Prepaid Rent
D. Electricity Expense

31. LO 3.5 Which of the following pairs increase with credit entries?
A. supplies and retained earnings
B. rent expense and unearned revenue
C. prepaid rent and common stock
D. unearned service revenue and accounts payable

32. LO 3.5 Which of the following pairs of accounts are impacted the same with debits and credits?
A. Cash and Unearned Service Revenue
B. Electricity Expense and Office Supplies
C. Accounts Receivable and Accounts Payable
D. Buildings and Common Stock

33. LO 3.5 Which of the following accounts will normally have a debit balance?
A. Common Stock
B. Fees Earned
C. Supplies
D. Accounts Payable

34. LO 3.5 What type of account is prepaid insurance?
A. Stockholders' Equity
B. Expense
C. Liability
D. Asset

35. LO 3.5 Unearned service revenue occurs when which of the following occurs?
A. company receives cash from a customer before performing the service
B. company pays cash before receiving a service from a supplier
C. company pays cash after receiving a service from a supplier
D. company receives cash from a customer after performing a service

36. LO 3.5 Which set of accounts has the same type of normal balance?
A. Cash, accounts payable
B. Prepaid rent, unearned service revenue
C. Dividends, common stock
D. Accounts payable, retained earnings

37. LO 3.5 Which of these transactions requires a debit entry to Cash?
A. paid balance due to suppliers
B. sold merchandise on account
C. collected balance due from customers
D. purchased supplies for cash

38. LO 3.5 Which of these transactions requires a credit entry to Revenue?

A. received cash from services performed this month
B. collected balance due from customers
C. received cash from bank loan
D. refunded a customer for a defective product

39. LO 3.5 Which of these accounts commonly requires both debit and credit entries?

A. Sales Revenue
B. Utilities Expense
C. Accounts Receivable
D. Common Stock

40. LO 3.5 Which of the following accounting records is the main source of information used to prepare the financial statements?

A. journal entries
B. T-accounts
C. trial balance
D. chart of accounts

41. LO 3.5 Which of the following financial statements should be prepared first?

A. Balance Sheet
B. Income Statement
C. Retained Earnings Statement
D. Statement of Cash Flows

Questions

1. LO 3.1 Explain what conservatism means, and give an example in your own words.

2. LO 3.2 State the accounting equation, and explain what each part represents.

3. LO 3.2 How do revenues and expenses affect the accounting equation?

4. LO 3.2 Does every transaction affect both sides of the accounting equation? Explain your answer.

5. LO 3.3 Which is the "book of original entry"?

6. LO 3.4 What is the effect on the accounting equation when a business purchases supplies on account?

7. LO 3.4 What is the effect on the accounting equation when a business pays the balance due on accounts payable?

8. LO 3.4 Is it still necessary to record a transaction if it has no net effect on the accounting equation? Explain your answer.

9. LO 3.4 Why does the combined total of the company's liabilities and equity always equal the total of the company's assets?

10. LO 3.5 What do the terms "debit" and "credit" mean?

11. LO 3.5 Will an accounts receivable balance increase with a debit or a credit entry? How do you know?

12. LO 3.5 What types of accounts will increase with a credit?

13. LO 3.5 What is a journal?

14. LO 3.5 Why is a journal referred to as the "book of original entry"?

15. LO 3.5 What does the term *recognize* mean?

16. LO 3.5 What are the rules you should follow when recording journal entries?

17. LO 3.5 What is the general ledger?

18. LO 3.5 Explain the steps in posting.

19. LO 3.5 What is a T-account? When would we use T-accounts?

20. LO 3.5 Explain normal balances. Give three examples of accounts that will normally have a debit balance and three accounts that will normally have a credit balance.

21. LO 3.5 What is a prepaid account? What type of account is it?

22. LO 3.5 What is an unearned account? What type of account is it?

23. LO 3.5 Explain what a T-account is and what purpose it serves.

24. LO 3.5 Can a credit entry be described as a generally positive or negative transaction? Explain.

25. LO 3.5 What types of accounts are increased with a debit?

26. LO 3.5 What types of accounts are increased with a credit?

27. LO 3.5 What does an account's "normal balance" indicate?

28. LO 3.5 Does the order in which financial statements are prepared matter?

29. LO 3.5 Answer the following questions about the trial balance: What is the purpose of it? What is the primary usefulness of it?

Exercise Set A

EA1. LO 3.1 Match the correct term with its definition.

A. cost principle	i. if uncertainty in a potential financial estimate, a company should err on the side of caution and report the most conservative amount
B. full disclosure principle	ii. also known as the historical cost principle, states that everything the company owns or controls (assets) must be recorded at their value at the date of acquisition
C. separate entity concept	iii. (also referred to as the matching principle) matches expenses with associated revenues in the period in which the revenues were generated
D. monetary measurement concept	iv. business must report any business activities that could affect what is reported on the financial statements
E. conservatism	v. system of using a monetary unit by which to value the transaction, such as the US dollar
F. revenue recognition principle	vi. period of time in which you performed the service or gave the customer the product is the period in which revenue is recognized
G. expense recognition principle	vii. business may only report activities on financial statements that are specifically related to company operations, not those activities that affect the owner personally

EA2. LO 3.2 Consider the following accounts, and determine if the account is an asset (A), a liability (L), or equity (E).

A. Accounts Payable
B. Cash
C. Dividends
D. Notes Payable

EA3. LO 3.2 Provide the missing amounts of the accounting equation for each of the following companies.

	Gianni	**Forest**
Assets	$222,000	$387,000
Liabilities	?	7,000
Equity	147,000	?

EA4. LO 3.2 Identify the financial statement on which each of the following accounts would appear: the income statement (IS), the retained earnings statement (RE), or the Balance Sheet (BS).

A. Insurance Expense
B. Accounts Receivable
C. Office Supplies
D. Sales Revenue
E. Common Stock
F. Notes Payable

EA5. LO 3.2 Cromwell Company has the following trial balance account balances, given in no certain order, as of December 31, 2018. Using the information provided, prepare Cromwell's annual financial statements (omit the Statement of Cash Flows).

Supplies	$ 865
Fees earned	22,850
Accounts receivable	2,580
Accounts payable	1,945
Office furniture	12,685
Rent expense	12,240
Retained earnings	3,600
Cash	4,695
Electricity expense	1,380
Common stock	10,000
Miscellaneous expenses	1,450
Dividends	2,500

EA6. LO 3.3 From the following list, identify which items are considered original sources:

A. prepaid insurance
B. bank statement
C. sales ticket
D. general journal
E. trial balance
F. balance sheet
G. telephone bill
H. invoice from supplier
I. company sales account
J. income statement

EA7. LO 3.4 Indicate what impact the following transactions would have on the accounting equation, Assets = Liabilities + Equity.

		Impact 1	Impact 2
A.	Received cash from issuance of common stock		
B.	Sold goods to customers on account		
C.	Collected cash from customer sales made in previous month		
D.	Paid cash to vendors for supplies delivered last month		
E.	Purchased inventory on account		

Table 3.4

EA8. LO 3.4 For the following accounts please indicate whether the normal balance is a debit or a credit.

A. Sales
B. Dividends
C. Office Supplies
D. Retained Earnings
E. Accounts Receivable
F. Prepaid Rent
G. Prepaid Insurance
H. Wages Payable
I. Building
J. Wages Expense

EA9. LO 3.4 Indicate what impact the following transactions would have on the accounting equation, Assets = Liabilities + Equity.

		Impact 1	Impact 2
A.	Paid monthly note payment to bank		
B.	Sold inventory on account		
C.	Bought supplies, to be paid for next month		
D.	Received cash from sales this month		
E.	Paid for inventory purchased on account last month		

Table 3.5

EA10. LO 3.4 Identify the normal balance for each of the following accounts. Choose Dr for Debit; Cr for Credit.

		Normal balance
A.	Utilities Expense	
B.	Cash	
C.	Equipment	
D.	Rent Revenue	
E.	Preferred Stock	
F.	Interest Payable	

Table 3.6

EA11. LO 3.4 Identify whether each of the following transactions would be recorded with a debit (Dr) or credit (Cr) entry.

		Debit or credit?
A.	Cash increase	
B.	Supplies decrease	
C.	Accounts Payable increase	
D.	Common Stock decrease	
E.	Interest Payable decrease	
F.	Notes Payable decrease	

Table 3.7

EA12. LO 3.4 Identify whether each of the following transactions would be recorded with a debit (Dr) or credit (Cr) entry.

		Debit or credit?
A.	Equipment decrease	
B.	Common Stock Sold increase	
C.	Gas and Oil Expense increase	
D.	Service revenue decrease	
E.	Miscellaneous Expense decrease	
F.	Bonds Payable decrease	

Table 3.8

EA13. LO 3.4 Identify whether ongoing transactions posted to the following accounts would normally have *only* debit entries (Dr), *only* credit entries (Cr), or *both* debit and credit entries (both).

		Type of entry
A.	Accounts Payable	
B.	Cash	
C.	Gas and Oil Expense	
D.	Rent Revenue	
E.	Supplies Expense	
F.	Common Stock	

Table 3.9

EA14. LO 3.5 Determine whether the balance in each of the following accounts increases with a debit or a credit.

A. Cash
B. Common Stock
C. Equipment
D. Accounts Payable
E. Fees Earned
F. Electricity Expense

EA15. LO 3.5 Journalize for Harper and Co. each of the following transactions or state no entry required and explain why. Be sure to follow proper journal writing rules.

A. A corporation is started with an investment of $50,000 in exchange for stock.
B. Equipment worth $4,800 is ordered.
C. Office supplies worth $750 are purchased on account.
D. A part-time worker is hired. The employee will work 15–20 hours per week starting next Monday at a rate of $18 per hour.
E. The equipment is received along with the invoice. Payment is due in three equal monthly installments, with the first payment due in sixty days.

EA16. LO 3.5 Discuss how each of the following transactions for Watson, International, will affect assets, liabilities, and stockholders' equity, and prove the company's accounts will still be in balance.

A. An investor invests an additional $25,000 into a company receiving stock in exchange.
B. Services are performed for customers for a total of $4,500. Sixty percent was paid in cash, and the remaining customers asked to be billed.
C. An electric bill was received for $35. Payment is due in thirty days.
D. Part-time workers earned $750 and were paid.
E. The electric bill in "C" is paid.

EA17. LO 3.5 For each item that follows, indicate whether a debit or a credit applies.

A. increase in prepaid insurance
B. increase in utilities expense
C. increase in commissions earned
D. increase in supplies
E. decrease in retained earnings
F. decrease in income taxes payable
G. increase in unearned revenue
H. increase in salaries expense
I. decrease in notes receivable
J. increase in common stock

EA18. LO 3.5 Indicate whether each account that follows has a normal debit or credit balance.

A. Unearned Revenue
B. Office Machines
C. Prepaid Rent
D. Cash
E. Legal Fees Earned
F. Salaries Payable
G. Dividends
H. Accounts Receivable
I. Advertising Expense
J. Retained Earnings

EA19. LO 3.5 A business has the following transactions:

- The business is started by receiving cash from an investor in exchange for common stock $20,000
- The business purchases supplies on account $500
- The business purchases furniture on account $2,000
- The business renders services to various clients on account totaling $9,000
- The business pays salaries $2,000
- The business pays this month's rent $3,000
- The business pays for the supplies purchased on account.
- The business collects from one of its clients for services rendered earlier in the month $1,500.

What is total income for the month?

EA20. LO 3.5 Prepare journal entries to record the following transactions.

A. January 22, purchased, an asset, merchandise inventory
B. on account for $2,800.
C. February 10, paid creditor for part of January 22 purchase, $1,600

EA21. LO 3.5 Prepare journal entries to record the following transactions.

A. July 1, issued common stock for cash, $15,000
B. July 15, purchased supplies, on account, $1,800
C. July 25, billed customer for accounting services provided, $950

EA22. LO 3.5 Prepare journal entries to record the following transactions.

A. March 1, purchased land for cash, $20,000
B. March 11, purchased merchandise inventory, on account, $18,500
C. March 15, Sold merchandise to customer for cash, $555

EA23. LO 3.5 Post the following February transactions to T-accounts for Accounts Receivable and Cash, indicating the ending balance (assume no beginning balances in these accounts).

A. provided legal services to customers for cash, $5,600
B. provided legal services to customers on account, $4,700
C. collected cash from customer accounts, $3,500

EA24. LO 3.5 Post the following November transactions to T-accounts for Accounts Payable and Inventory, indicating the ending balance (assume no beginning balances in these accounts).

A. purchased merchandise inventory on account, $22,000
B. paid vendors for part of inventory purchased earlier in month, $14,000
C. purchased merchandise inventory for cash, $6,500

EA25. LO 3.6 Prepare an unadjusted trial balance, in correct format, from the alphabetized account information as follows. Assume all accounts have normal balances.

Accounts payable	$11,100
Accounts receivable	16,500
Administrative expense	54,712
Cash	64,888
Common stock	50,000
Service revenue	75,000

Exercise Set B

EB1. LO 3.1 Match the correct term with its definition.

A. Financial Accounting Standards Board (FASB)	i. used by the FASB, which is a set of concepts that guide financial reporting
B. generally accepted accounting principles (GAAP)	ii. independent, nonprofit organization that sets financial accounting and reporting standards for both public- and private-sector businesses that use generally accepted accounting principles (GAAP) here in the United States
C. Securities and Exchange Commission (SEC)	iii. standards, procedures, and principles companies must follow when preparing their financial statements
D. conceptual framework	iv. assumes a business will continue to operate in the foreseeable future
E. going concern assumption	v. independent federal agency protecting the interests of investors, regulating stock markets, and ensuring companies adhere to GAAP requirements
F. time period assumption	vi. companies can present useful information in shorter time periods such as years, quarters, or months

EB2. LO 3.2 Consider the following accounts and determine if the account is an asset (A), a liability (L), or equity (E).

A. Accounts Receivable
B. Sales Revenue
C. Land
D. Unearned Revenue

EB3. LO 3.2 Provide the missing amounts of the accounting equation for each of the following companies.

	Elias	Patel
Assets	?	$125,000
Liabilities	$ 33,000	?
Equity	186,000	63,000

EB4. LO 3.3 From the following list, identify which items are considered original sources:

A. accounts receivable
B. receipt from post office for post office box
C. purchase order
D. general ledger
E. adjusted trial balance
F. statement of retained earnings
G. electric bill
H. packing slip
I. company expense account
J. statement of cash flows

EB5. LO 3.4 Indicate what impact the following transactions would have on the accounting equation, Assets = Liabilities + Equity.

		Impact 1	Impact 2
A.	Paid this month's utility bill		
B.	Purchased supplies for cash		
C.	Received cash for services performed		
D.	Collected cash from customer accounts receivable		
E.	Paid creditors on account		

Table 3.10

EB6. LO 3.4 For the following accounts indicate whether the normal balance is a debit or a credit.

A. Unearned Revenue
B. Interest Expense
C. Rent Expense
D. Rent Revenue
E. Accounts Payable
F. Cash
G. Supplies
H. Accounts Payable
I. Equipment
J. Utilities Expense

EB7. LO 3.4 Which two accounts are affected by each of the following transactions?

		Account 1	Account 2
A.	Received cash from issuance of common stock		
B.	Purchased land by issuing a note payable		
C.	Paid balance on account for last month's inventory purchases		
D.	Received cash from customers for this month's sales		
E.	Sold merchandise to customers on account		

Table 3.11

EB8. LO 3.4 Identify the normal balance for each of the following accounts. Choose Dr for Debit; Cr for Credit.

		Normal balance
A.	Insurance Expense	
B.	Accounts Receivable	
C.	Office Supplies	
D.	Sales Revenue	
E.	Common Stock	
F.	Notes Payable	

Table 3.12

EB9. LO 3.4 Identify whether each of the following transactions would be recorded with a debit (Dr) or credit (Cr) entry.

		Debit or credit?
A.	Cash decrease	
B.	Supplies increase	
C.	Accounts Payable decrease	
D.	Common Stock increase	
E.	Accounts Payable increase	
F.	Notes Payable increase	

Table 3.13

EB10. LO 3.4 Identify whether each of the following transactions would be recorded with a debit (Dr) or credit (Cr) entry.

		Debit or credit?
A.	Equipment increase	
B.	Dividends Paid increase	
C.	Repairs Expense increase	
D.	Service revenue increase	
E.	Miscellaneous Expense increase	
F.	Bonds Payable increase	

Table 3.14

EB11. LO 3.4 Identify whether ongoing transactions posted to the following accounts would normally have *only* debit entries (Dr), *only* credit entries (Cr), or *both* debit and credit entries (both).

		Type of entry
A.	Notes Payable	
B.	Accounts Receivable	
C.	Utilities Expense	
D.	Sales Revenue	
E.	Insurance Expense	
F.	Dividends	

Table 3.15

EB12. LO 3.2 LO 3.4 West End Inc., an auto mechanic shop, has the following account balances, given in no certain order, for the quarter ended March 31, 2019. Based on the information provided, prepare West End's annual financial statements (omit the Statement of Cash Flows).

Electricity expense	$ 2,365
Accounts payable	4,835
Dividends	1,200
Garage machines	145,000
Office supplies	235
Repair revenue	68,245
Mortgage interest expense	12,240
Accounts receivable	2,580
Retained earnings	23,600
Miscellaneous expenses	725
Cash	10,745
Common stock	150,000
Garage supplies	1,565
Real estate tax expense	5,200
Waiting room furniture	3,450
Machine maintenance expense	1,375
Mechanic shop	185,000
Mortgage payable	125,000

Prepare West End's annual financial statements. (Omit the Statement of Cash Flows.)

EB13. LO 3.5 State whether the balance in each of the following accounts increases with a debit or a credit.

A. Office Supplies
B. Retained Earnings
C. Salaries Expense
D. Accounts Receivable
E. Service Revenue

EB14. LO 3.5 Journalize each of the following transactions or state no entry required and explain why. Be sure to follow proper journal writing rules.

A. A company is started with an investment of a machine worth $40,000. Common stock is received in exchange.
B. Office furniture is ordered. The furniture worth $7,850 will be delivered in one week. The payment will be due forty-five days after delivery.
C. An advertisement was run in the newspaper at a total cost of $250. Cash was paid when the order was placed.
D. The office furniture is delivered.
E. Services are performed for a client. The client was billed for $535.

EB15. LO 3.5 Discuss how each of the following transactions will affect assets, liabilities, and stockholders' equity, and prove the company's accounts will still be in balance.

A. A company purchased $450 worth of office supplies on credit.
B. The company parking lot was plowed after a blizzard. A check for $75 was given to the plow truck operator.
C. $250 was paid on account.
D. A customer paid $350 on account.
E. Provided services for a customer, $500. The customer asked to be billed.

EB16. LO 3.5 For each of the following items, indicate whether a debit or a credit applies.

A. increase in retained earnings
B. decrease in prepaid rent
C. increase in dividends
D. decrease in salaries payable
E. increase in accounts receivable
F. decrease in common stock
G. decrease in prepaid insurance
H. decrease in advertising expense
I. decrease in unearned service fees
J. increase in office equipment

EB17. LO 3.5 Indicate whether each of the following accounts has a normal debit or credit balance.

A. prepaid landscaping expense
B. common stock
C. delivery vans
D. maintenance expense
E. retained earnings
F. office supplies
G. revenue earned
H. accounts payable
I. unearned painting revenue
J. interest payable

EB18. LO 3.5 Krespy Corp. has a cash balance of $7,500 before the following transactions occur:

A. received customer payments of $965
B. supplies purchased on account $435
C. services worth $850 performed, 25% is paid in cash the rest will be billed
D. corporation pays $275 for an ad in the newspaper
E. bill is received for electricity used $235.
F. dividends of $2,500 are distributed

What is the balance in cash after these transactions are journalized and posted?

EB19. LO 3.5 A business has the following transactions:

A. The business is started by receiving cash from an investor in exchange for common stock $10,000.
B. Rent of $1,250 is paid for the first month.
C. Office supplies are purchased for $375.
D. Services worth $3,450 are performed. Cash is received for half.
E. Customers pay $1,250 for services to be performed next month.
F. $6,000 is paid for a one year insurance policy.
G. We receive 25% of the money owed by customers in "D".
H. A customer has placed an order for $475 of services to be done this coming week.

How much total revenue does the company have?

EB20. LO 3.5 Prepare journal entries to record the following transactions.

A. November 19, purchased merchandise inventory, on account, $12,000
B. November 29, paid creditor for part of November 19 purchase, $10,000

EB21. LO 3.5 Prepare journal entries to record the following transactions:

A. December 1, collected balance due from customer account, $5,500
B. December 12, paid creditors for supplies purchased last month, $4,200
C. December 31, paid cash dividend to stockholders, $1,000

EB22. LO 3.5 Prepare journal entries to record the following transactions:

A. October 9, issued common stock in exchange for building, $40,000
B. October 12, purchased supplies on account, $3,600
C. October 24, paid cash dividend to stockholders, $2,500

EB23. LO 3.5 Post the following August transactions to T-accounts for Accounts Payable and Supplies, indicating the ending balance (assume no beginning balances in these accounts):

A. purchased supplies on account, $600
B. paid vendors for supplies delivered earlier in month, $500
C. purchased supplies for cash, $450

EB24. LO 3.5 Post the following July transactions to T-accounts for Accounts Receivable and Cash, indicating the ending balance (assume no beginning balances in these accounts):

A. sold products to customers for cash, $8,500
B. sold products to customers on account, $2,900
C. collected cash from customer accounts, $1,600

EB25. LO 3.6 Prepare an unadjusted trial balance, in correct format, from the alphabetized account information as follows. Assume all accounts have normal balances.

Accounts payable	$ 8,005
Accounts receivable	12,500
Cash	56,015
Common stock	28,000
Fees earned revenue	75,510
Operating expense	43,000

Problem Set A

PA1. LO 3.1 For each of the following situations write the principle, assumption, or concept that justifies or explains what occurred.

A. A landscaper received a customer's order and cash prepayment to install sod at a house that would not be ready for installation until March of next year. The owner should record the revenue from the customer order in March of next year, not in December of this year.

B. A company divides its income statements into four quarters for the year.

C. Land is purchased for $205,000 cash; the land is reported on the balance sheet of the purchaser at $205,000.

D. Brandy's Flower Shop is forecasting its balance sheet for the next five years.

E. When preparing financials for a company, the owner makes sure that the expense transactions are kept separate from expenses of the other company that he owns.

F. A company records the expenses incurred to generate the revenues reported.

PA2. LO 3.2 Assuming the following account balances, what is the missing value?

Assets	$865,430
Liabilities	?
Equity	759,121

PA3. LO 3.2 LO 3.4 Assuming the following account balance changes for the period, what is the missing value?

Assets	$246,300
Liabilities	?
Common stock	160,000
Dividends	30,000
Revenue	245,800
Expenses	175,000

PA4. LO 3.2 LO 3.4 Assuming the following account balance changes for the period, what is the missing value?

Assets	$450,600
Liabilities	250,000
Common stock	120,000
Dividends	?
Revenue	433,600
Expenses	323,000

PA5. LO 3.2 LO 3.4 Identify the financial statement on which each of the following account categories would appear: the balance sheet (BS), the income statement (IS), or the retained earnings statement (RE). Indicate the normal balance (Dr for debit; Cr for credit) for each account category.

	Financial statement	Normal balance
Assets		
Common stock		
Dividends		
Expenses		
Liabilities		
Revenue		

Table 3.16

PA6. LO 3.4 Indicate what impact (+ for increase; – for decrease) the following transactions would have on the accounting equation, Assets = Liabilities + Equity.

		Impact 1	Impact 2
A.	Issued stock for cash		
B.	Purchased supplies on account		
C.	Paid employee salaries		
D.	Paid note payment to bank		
E.	Collected balance on accounts receivable		

Table 3.17

PA7. LO 3.4 Indicate how changes in the following types of accounts would be recorded (Dr for debit; Cr for credit).

		Increase	Decrease
A.	Asset accounts		
B.	Liability accounts		
C.	Common stock		
D.	Revenue		
E.	Expense		

Table 3.18

PA8. LO 3.4 Identify the normal balance (Dr for Debit; Cr for Credit) and type of account (A for asset, L for liability, E for equity, E-rev for revenue, E-exp for expense, and E-eq for equity) for each of the following items.

		Normal balance	Account type
A.	Accounts Payable		
B.	Supplies		
C.	Inventory		
D.	Common Stock		
E.	Dividends		
F.	Salaries Expense		

Table 3.19

PA9. LO 3.4 Indicate the net effect (+ for increase; – for decrease; 0 for no effect) of each of the following transactions on each part of the accounting equation, Assets = Liabilities + Equity. For example, for payment of an accounts payable balance, A (–) = L (–) + E (0).

A. sale of merchandise to customer on account
B. payment on note payable
C. purchase of equipment for cash
D. collection of accounts receivable
E. purchase of supplies on account

PA10. LO 3.4 Identify whether the following transactions would be recorded with a debit (Dr) or credit (Cr) entry. Indicate the normal balance of the account.

	Transaction	Debit or credit?	Normal balance
A.	Equipment increase		
B.	Dividends Paid increase		
C.	Repairs Expense increase		
D.	Service revenue decrease		
E.	Miscellaneous Expense increase		
F.	Bonds Payable decrease		

Table 3.20

PA11. LO 3.5 The following information is provided for the first month of operations for Legal Services Inc.:

A. The business was started by selling $100,000 worth of common stock.
B. Six months' rent was paid in advance, $4,500.
C. Provided services in the amount of $1,000. The customer will pay at a later date.
D. An office worker was hired. The worker will be paid $275 per week.
E. Received $500 in payment from the customer in "C".
F. Purchased $250 worth of supplies on credit.
G. Received the electricity bill. We will pay the $110 in thirty days.
H. Paid the worker hired in "D" for one week's work.
I. Received $100 from a customer for services we will provide next week.
J. Dividends in the amount of $1,500 were distributed.

Prepare the necessary journal entries to record these transactions. If an entry is not required for any of these transactions, state this and explain why.

PA12. LO 3.5 Sewn for You had the following transactions in its first week of business.

A. Jessica Johansen started Sewn for You, a seamstress business, by contributing $20,000 and receiving stock in exchange.
B. Paid $2,250 to cover the first three months' rent.
C. Purchased $500 of sewing supplies. She paid cash for the purchase.
D. Purchased a sewing machine for $1,500 paying $200 cash and signing a note for the balance.
E. Finished a job for a customer earning $180. The customer paid cash.
F. Received a $500 down payment to make a wedding dress.
G. Received an electric bill for $125 which is due to be paid in three weeks.
H. Completed an altering job for $45. The customer asked to be billed.

Prepare the necessary journal entries to record these transactions. If an entry is not required for any of these transactions, state this and explain why.

PA13. LO 3.5 George Hoskin started his own business, Hoskin Hauling. The following transactions occurred in the first two weeks:

A. George Hoskin contributed cash of $12,000 and a truck worth $10,000 to start the business. He received Common Stock in return.
B. Paid two months' rent in advance, $800.
C. Agreed to do a hauling job for a price of $1,200.
D. Performed the hauling job discussed in "C." We will get paid later.
E. Received payment of $600 on the hauling job done in "D."
F. Purchased gasoline on credit, $50.
G. Performed another hauling job. Earned $750, was paid cash.

Record the following transactions in T-accounts. Label each entry with the appropriate letter. Total the T-accounts when you are done.

PA14. LO 3.5 Prepare journal entries to record the following transactions. Create a T-account for Cash, post any entries that affect the account, and calculate the ending balance for the account. Assume a Cash beginning balance of $16,333.

A. February 2, issued stock to shareholders, for cash, $25,000
B. March 10, paid cash to purchase equipment, $16,000

PA15. LO 3.5 Prepare journal entries to record the following transactions. Create a T-account for Accounts Payable, post any entries that affect the account, and tally ending balance for the account. Assume an Accounts Payable beginning balance of $5,000.

A. February 2, purchased an asset, merchandise inventory, on account, $30,000
B. March 10, paid creditor for part of February purchase, $12,000

PA16. LO 3.5 Prepare journal entries to record the following transactions for the month of July:

A. on first day of the month, paid rent for current month, $2,000
B. on tenth day of month, paid prior month balance due on accounts, $3,100
C. on twelfth day of month, collected cash for services provided, $5,500
D. on twenty-first day of month, paid salaries to employees, $3,600
E. on thirty-first day of month, paid for dividends to shareholders, $800

PA17. LO 3.5 Prepare journal entries to record the following transactions for the month of November:

A. on first day of the month, issued common stock for cash, $20,000
B. on third day of month, purchased equipment for cash, $10,500
C. on tenth day of month, received cash for accounting services, $14,250
D. on fifteenth day of month, paid miscellaneous expenses, $3,200
E. on last day of month, paid employee salaries, $8,600

PA18. LO 3.5 Post the following July transactions to T-accounts for Accounts Receivable, Sales Revenue, and Cash, indicating the ending balance. Assume no beginning balances in these accounts.

A. on first day of the month, sold products to customers for cash, $13,660
B. on fifth day of month, sold products to customers on account, $22,100
C. on tenth day of month, collected cash from customer accounts, $18,500

PA19. LO 3.5 Post the following November transactions to T-accounts for Accounts Payable, Inventory, and Cash, indicating the ending balance. Assume no beginning balances in Accounts Payable and Inventory, and a beginning Cash balance of $36,500.

A. purchased merchandise inventory on account, $16,000
B. paid vendors for part of inventory purchased earlier in month, $12,000
C. purchased merchandise inventory for cash, $10,500

PA20. LO 3.6 Prepare an unadjusted trial balance, in correct format, from the following alphabetized account information. Assume accounts have normal balances.

Accounts payable	$ 9,500
Accounts receivable	14,260
Cash	22,222
Common stock	30,000
Dividends	5,000
Equipment	12,000
Investments (short term)	25,444
Land	20,000
Notes payable	26,000
Retained earnings	12,815
Salaries expense	53,500
Service revenue	89,550
Supplies	2,750
Utility expense	12,689

PA21. LO 3.6 Prepare an unadjusted trial balance, in correct format, from the following alphabetized account information. Assume all the accounts have normal balances.

Accounts payable	$26,000
Accounts receivable	8,000
Cash	29,000
Common stock	33,000
Dividends	9,000
Equipment	68,000
Notes payable (due next month)	29,000
Salaries expense	42,000
Salaries payable	2,000
Service revenue	75,000
Supplies	5,000
Transportation expense	4,000

Problem Set B

PB1. LO 3.2 Assuming the following account balances, what is the missing value?

Assets	$1,150,000
Liabilities	588,000
Equity	?

PB2. LO 3.2 LO 3.4 Assuming the following account balance changes for the period, what is the missing value?

Assets	$ 73,000
Liabilities	33,000
Common stock	10,000
Dividends	5,000
Revenue	120,000
Expenses	?

PB3. LO 3.2 LO 3.4 Assuming the following account balance changes for the period, what is the missing value?

Assets	?
Liabilities	$110,500
Common stock	60,000
Dividends	15,000
Revenue	785,000
Expenses	234,750

PB4. LO 3.2 LO 3.4 Identify the financial statement on which each of the following account categories would appear: the balance sheet (BS), the income statement (IS), or the retained earnings statement (RE).

	Financial statement	Normal balance
Accounts Receivable		
Automobile Expense		
Cash		
Equipment		
Notes Payable		
Service Revenue		

Table 3.21

PB5. LO 3.4 Indicate what impact (+ for increase; – for decrease) the following transactions would have on the accounting equation, Assets = Liabilities + Equity.

	Transaction	Impact 1	Impact 2
A.	Paid balance due for accounts payable		
B.	Charged clients for legal services provided		
C.	Purchased supplies on account		
D.	Collected legal service fees from clients for current month		
E.	Issued stock in exchange for a note receivable		

Table 3.22

PB6. LO 3.4 Indicate how changes in these types of accounts would be recorded (Dr for debit; Cr for credit).

		Debit or credit?
A.	Asset accounts	
B.	Liability accounts	
C.	Common Stock	
D.	Revenue	
E.	Expense	

Table 3.23

PB7. LO 3.4 Identify the normal balance (Dr for Debit; Cr for Credit) and type of account (A for asset, L for liability, E for equity, E-rev for revenue, E-exp for expense, and E-eq for equity) for each of the following accounts.

		Normal balance	Account type
A.	Utility Expense		
B.	Accounts Receivable		
C.	Interest Revenue		
D.	Retained Earnings		
E.	Land		
F.	Sales Revenue		

Table 3.24

PB8. LO 3.4 Indicate the net effect (+ for increase; – for decrease; 0 for no effect) of each of the following transactions on each part of the accounting equation, Assets = Liabilities + Equity. For example, for payment of an accounts payable balance, A (–) = L (–) + E (0).

A. Payment of principal balance of note payable
B. Purchase of supplies for cash
C. Payment of dividends to stockholders
D. Issuance of stock for cash
E. Billing customer for physician services provided

PB9. LO 3.5 Prepare journal entries to record the following transactions. Create a T-account for Cash, post any entries that affect the account, and calculate the ending balance for the account. Assume a Cash beginning balance of $37,400.

A. May 12, collected balance due from customers on account, $16,000
B. June 10, purchased supplies for cash, $4,444

PB10. LO 3.5 Prepare journal entries to record the following transactions. Create a T-account for Accounts Payable, post any entries that affect the account, and calculate the ending balance for the account. Assume an Accounts Payable beginning balance of $7,500.

A. May 12, purchased merchandise inventory on account. $9,200
B. June 10, paid creditor for part of previous month's purchase, $11,350

PB11. LO 3.5 Prepare journal entries to record the following transactions that occurred in April:

A. on first day of the month, issued common stock for cash, $15,000
B. on eighth day of month, purchased supplies, on account, $1,800
C. on twentieth day of month, billed customer for services provided, $950
D. on twenty-fifth day of month, paid salaries to employees, $2,000
E. on thirtieth day of month, paid for dividends to shareholders, $500

PB12. LO 3.5 Prepare journal entries to record the following transactions that occurred in March:

A. on first day of the month, purchased building for cash, $75,000
B. on fourth day of month, purchased inventory, on account, $6,875
C. on eleventh day of month, billed customer for services provided, $8,390
D. on nineteenth day of month, paid current month utility bill, $2,000
E. on last day of month, paid suppliers for previous purchases, $2,850

PB13. LO 3.5 Post the following November transactions to T-accounts for Accounts Payable, Inventory, and Cash, indicating the ending balance. Assume no beginning balances in Accounts Payable and Inventory, and a beginning Cash balance of $21,220.

A. purchased merchandise inventory on account, $9,900
B. paid vendors for part of inventory purchased earlier in month, $6,500
C. purchased merchandise inventory for cash, $4,750

PB14. LO 3.5 Post the following July transactions to T-accounts for Accounts Receivable, Sales Revenue, and Cash, indicating the ending balance. Assume no beginning balances in these accounts.

A. sold products to customers for cash, $7,500
B. sold products to customers on account, $12,650
C. collected cash from customer accounts, $9,500

PB15. LO 3.6 Prepare an unadjusted trial balance, in correct format, from the following alphabetized account information. Assume all accounts have normal balances.

Accounts payable	$ 3,600
Accounts receivable	45,333
Building	156,000
Cash	50,480
Common stock	110,000
Dividends	18,000
Equipment	33,500
Fees earned revenue	225,430
Land	18,000
Miscellaneous expense	5,123
Notes payable	85,500
Retained earnings	60,606
Salaries expense	151,900
Supplies	6,800

PB16. LO 3.6 Prepare an unadjusted trial balance, in correct format, from the following alphabetized account information. Assume all accounts have normal balances.

Accounts payable	$ 18,000
Accounts receivable	4,000
Automobile	28,000
Cash	19,000
Common stock	30,000
Dividends	16,000
Equipment	80,000
Insurance expense	8,000
Land	26,000
Notes payable (long term)	55,000
Salaries expense	37,000
Sales revenue	115,000

PB17. LO 3.6 Prepare an unadjusted trial balance, in correct format, from the following alphabetized account information. Assume all accounts have normal balances.

Accounts payable	$ 3,600
Accounts receivable	45,333
Building	156,000
Cash	50,480
Common stock	110,000
Dividends	18,000
Equipment	33,500
Fees earned revenue	225,430
Land	18,000
Miscellaneous expense	5,123
Notes payable	85,500
Retained earnings	60,606
Salaries expense	151,900
Supplies	6,800

PB18. LO 3.6 Prepare an unadjusted trial balance, in correct format, from the following alphabetized account information. Assume all accounts have normal balances.

Accounts payable	$ 18,000
Accounts receivable	4,000
Automobile	28,000
Cash	19,000
Common stock	30,000
Dividends	16,000
Equipment	80,000
Insurance expense	8,000
Land	26,000
Notes payable (long term)	55,000
Salaries expense	37,000
Sales revenue	115,000

Thought Provokers

TP1. LO 3.1 Is it possible to be too conservative? Explain your answer.

TP2. LO 3.1 Why is it important to learn all of this terminology when accounting is a quantitative subject?

TP3. LO 3.2 Assume that you are the controller of a business that provides legal services to clients. Suppose that the company has had a tough year, so the revenues have been lagging behind, based on previous years' standards. What would you do if your boss (the chief executive officer [CEO] of the company) asked to reclassify a transaction to report loan proceeds of $150,000 as if the cash came from service fee revenue from clients instead. Would following the CEO's advice impact the company's accounting equation? How would reclassifying this one transaction change the outcome of the balance sheet, the income statement, and the statement of retained earnings? Would making this reclassification change the perception that users of the financial statements would have of the company's current year success and future year potential?

Write a memo, detailing your willingness (or not) to embrace this suggestion, giving reasons behind your decision. Remember to exercise diplomacy, even if you must dissent from the opinion of a supervisor. Note that the challenge of the assignment is to keep your integrity intact, while also keeping your job, if possible.

TP4. LO 3.2 Visit the website of the US Securities and Exchange Commission (SEC) (https://www.sec.gov/edgar/searchedgar/companysearch.html). Search for the latest Form 10-K for a company you would like to analyze. Submit a short memo that

A. Includes the name and ticker symbol of the company you have chosen.
B. Reviews the company's end-of-period Balance Sheet to determine the following:
   i. total assets
   ii. total liabilities
   iii. total equity
C. Presents the company's accounting equation at the end of the period, from the information you collected in (A), (B), and (C):
   i. provide the web link to the company's Form 10-K to allow accurate verification of your answers

TP5. LO 3.3 Is the order in which we place information in the journal and ledger important?

TP6. LO 3.4 Visit the website of the SEC (https://www.sec.gov/edgar/searchedgar/companysearch.html). Search for the latest Form 10-K for a company you would like to analyze. Submit a short memo that

A. Includes the name and ticker symbol of the company you have chosen
B. Reviews the company's comparative Balance Sheet to gather the following information:
   i. Compare beginning and ending Assets totals, noting amount of change for the most recent period
   ii. Compare beginning and ending Liabilities totals, noting amount of change for the most recent period
   iii. Compare beginning and ending Equity totals, noting amount of change for the most recent period
C. State the changes identified in (A), (B), and (C) in accounting equation format. If the "change" equation does not balance, explain why not. Hint: Double-check your calculations, and if the accounting equation change still does not balance, search for notes in the company's files about prior period adjustments, which will often explain why balances may differ.
   i. Provide the web link to the company's Form 10-K to allow accurate verification of your answers.

TP7. LO 3.5 Visit the website of the US Securities and Exchange Commission (SEC) (https://www.sec.gov/edgar/searchedgar/companysearch.html). Search for the latest Form 10-K for a company you would like to. When you are choosing, make sure the company sells a product (has inventory on the Balance Sheet, and Cost of Goods Sold on the Income Statement). Submit a short memo:

A. Include the name and ticker symbol of the company you have chosen.
B. Follow the financial statement progression from the Income Statement to the Retained Earnings Statement to the Balance Sheet. Find the net income amount from the Income Statement and identify where it appears on the Statement of Retained Earnings (or the Statement of Stockholders' Equity).
C. On the statement found for instruction (A), find the ending retained earnings balance, and identify where it appears on the Balance Sheet for year-end.
D. Provide the web link to the company's Form 10-K to allow accurate verification of your answers.

TP8. LO 3.6 Analyze Trusty Company's trial balance and the additional information provided to determine the following:

A. what is causing the trial balance to be out of balance
B. any other errors that require corrections that are identified during your analysis
C. the effect (if any) that correcting the errors will have on the accounting equation

TRUSTY COMPANY Trial Balance For the Month Ended December 31, 2018		
	Debit	**Credit**
Cash	$ 77,500	
Accounts receivable	5,600	
Supplies	2,450	
Equipment	11,200	
Accounts payable		$ 17,000
Notes payable		27,400
Common stock		20,000
Retained earnings		7,900
Dividends	6,000	
Service revenue		99,300
Advertising expense	4,350	
Salaries expense	46,500	
	$153,600	$171,600

A review of transactions revealed the following facts:

- A service fee of $18,000 was earned (but not yet collected) by the end of the period but was accidentally not recorded as revenue at that time.
- A transposition error occurred when transferring the account balances from the ledger to the trial balance. Salaries expense should have been listed on the trial balance as $64,500 but was inadvertently recorded as $46,500.
- Two machines that cost $9,000 each were purchased on account but were not recorded in company accounting records.

4 The Adjustment Process

Figure 4.1 Mark's Dry-Cleaning Business. (credit: modification of "Dry Cleaning" by Donald West/Flickr, CC BY 2.0)

Chapter Outline

- LO 4.1 Explain the Concepts and Guidelines Affecting Adjusting Entries
- LO 4.2 Discuss the Adjustment Process and Illustrate Common Types of Adjusting Entries
- LO 4.3 Record and Post the Common Types of Adjusting Entries
- LO 4.4 Use the Ledger Balances to Prepare an Adjusted Trial Balance
- LO 4.5 Prepare Financial Statements Using the Adjusted Trial Balance

Why It Matters

As we learned in Analyzing and Recording Transactions, upon finishing college Mark Summers wanted to start his own dry-cleaning business called Supreme Cleaners. After four years, Mark finished college and opened Supreme Cleaners. During his first month of operations, Mark purchased dry-cleaning equipment and supplies. He also hired an employee, opened a savings account, and provided services to his first customers, among other things.

Mark kept thorough records of all of the daily business transactions for the month. At the end of the month, Mark reviewed his trial balance and realized that some of the information was not up to date. His equipment and supplies had been used, making them less valuable. He had not yet paid his employee for work completed. His business savings account earned interest. Some of his customers had paid in advance for their dry cleaning, with Mark's business providing the service during the month.

What should Mark do with all of these events? Does he have a responsibility to record these transactions? If so, how would he go about recording this information? How does it affect his financial statements? Mark will have to explore his accounting process to determine if these end-of-period transactions require recording and adjust his financial statements accordingly. This exploration is performed by taking the next few steps in the *accounting cycle*.

4.1 Explain the Concepts and Guidelines Affecting Adjusting Entries

Analyzing and Recording Transactions was the first of three consecutive chapters covering the steps in the accounting cycle (Figure 4.2).

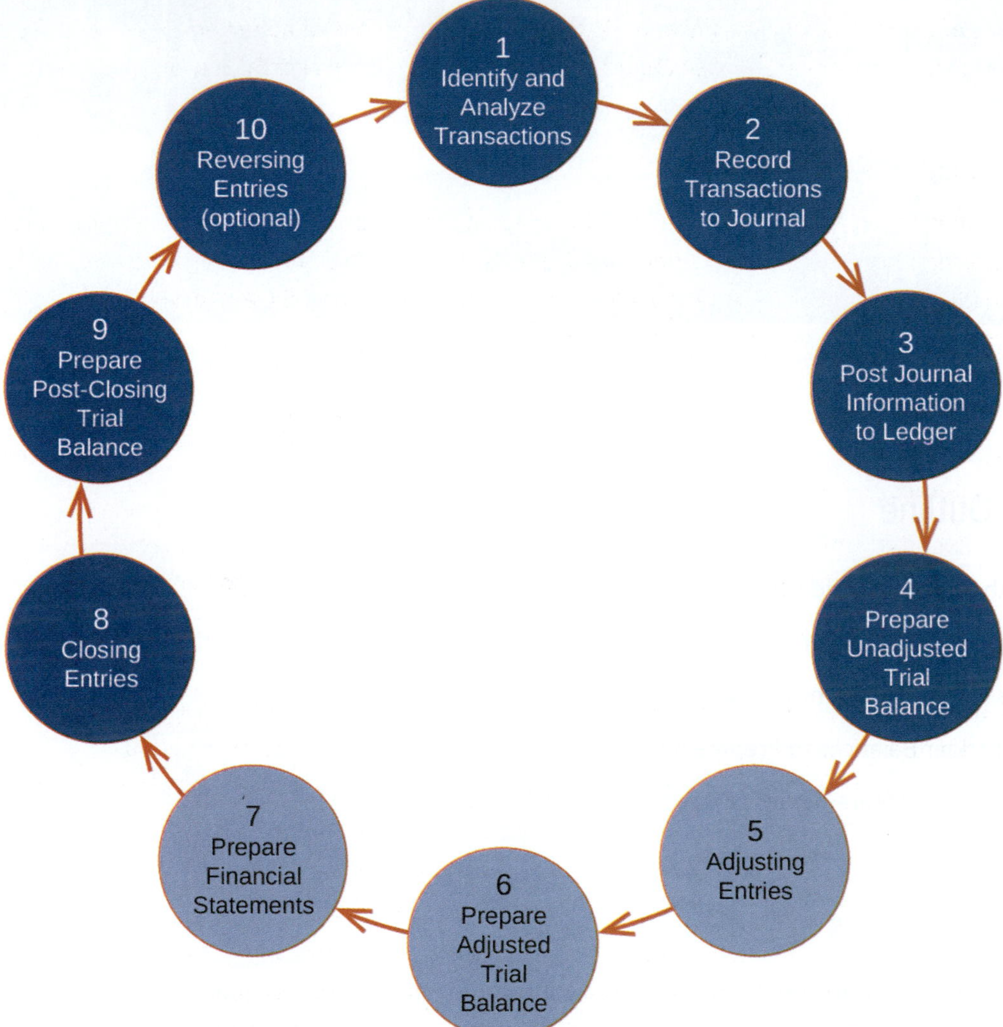

Figure 4.2 The Basic Accounting Cycle. In this chapter, we examine the next three steps in the accounting cycle—5, 6, and 7—which cover adjusting entries (journalize and post), preparing an adjusted trial balance, and preparing the financial statements. (attribution: Copyright Rice University, OpenStax, under CC BY-NC-SA 4.0 license)

In Analyzing and Recording Transactions, we discussed the first four steps in the accounting cycle: identify and analyze transactions, record transactions to a journal, post journal information to the general ledger, and prepare an (unadjusted) trial balance. This chapter examines the next three steps in the cycle: record adjusting entries (journalizing and posting), prepare an adjusted trial balance, and prepare the financial statements (Figure 4.3).

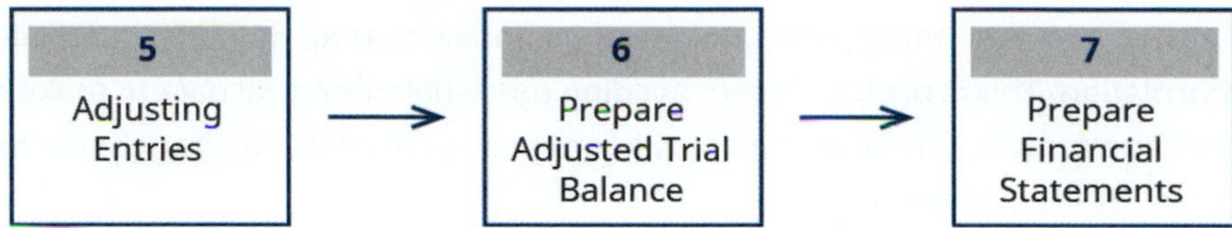

Figure 4.3 Steps 5, 6, and 7 in the Accounting Cycle. (attribution: Copyright Rice University, OpenStax, under CC BY-NC-SA 4.0 license)

As we progress through these steps, you learn why the trial balance in this phase of the accounting cycle is referred to as an "adjusted" trial balance. We also discuss the purpose of adjusting entries and the accounting concepts supporting their need. One of the first concepts we discuss is accrual accounting.

Accrual Accounting

Public companies reporting their financial positions use either US generally accepted accounting principles (GAAP) or International Financial Reporting Standards (IFRS), as allowed under the Securities and Exchange Commission (SEC) regulations. Also, companies, public or private, using US GAAP or IFRS prepare their financial statements using the rules of accrual accounting. Recall from Introduction to Financial Statements that accrual basis accounting prescribes that revenues and expenses must be recorded in the accounting period in which they were earned or incurred, no matter when cash receipts or payments occur. It is because of accrual accounting that we have the *revenue recognition principle* and the *expense recognition principle* (also known as the *matching principle*).

The accrual method is considered to better match revenues and expenses and standardizes reporting information for comparability purposes. Having comparable information is important to external users of information trying to make investment or lending decisions, and to internal users trying to make decisions about company performance, budgeting, and growth strategies.

Some nonpublic companies may choose to use cash basis accounting rather than accrual basis accounting to report financial information. Recall from Introduction to Financial Statements that cash basis accounting is a method of accounting in which transactions are not recorded in the financial statements until there is an exchange of cash. Cash basis accounting sometimes delays or accelerates revenue and expense reporting until cash receipts or outlays occur. With this method, cash flows are used to measure business performance in a given period and can be simpler to track than accrual basis accounting.

There are several other accounting methods or concepts that accountants will sometimes apply. The first is **modified accrual accounting**, which is commonly used in governmental accounting and merges accrual basis and cash basis accounting. The second is **tax basis accounting** that is used in establishing the tax effects of transactions in determining the tax liability of an organization.

One fundamental concept to consider related to the accounting cycle—and to accrual accounting in particular—is the idea of the accounting period.

The Accounting Period

As we discussed, accrual accounting requires companies to report revenues and expenses in the accounting period in which they were earned or incurred. An **accounting period** breaks down company financial information into specific time spans, and can cover a month, a quarter, a half-year, or a full year. Public companies governed by GAAP are required to present quarterly (three-month) accounting period financial statements called 10-Qs. However, most public and private companies keep monthly, quarterly, and yearly (annual) period information. This is useful to users needing up-to-date financial data to make decisions about company investment and growth. When the company keeps yearly information, the year could be based on a fiscal or calendar year. This is explained shortly.

CONTINUING APPLICATION AT WORK

Adjustment Process for Grocery Stores

In every industry, adjustment entries are made at the end of the period to ensure revenue matches expenses. Companies with an online presence need to account for items sold that have not yet been shipped or are in the process of reaching the end user. But what about the grocery industry? At first glance, it might seem that no such adjustment entries are necessary. However, grocery stores have adapted to the current retail environment. For example, your local grocery store might provide catering services for a graduation party. If the contract requires the customer to put down a 50% deposit, and occurs near the end of a period, the grocery store will have unearned revenue until it provides the catering service. Once the party occurs, the grocery store needs to make an adjusting entry to reflect that revenue has been earned.

The Fiscal Year and the Calendar Year

A company may choose its yearly reporting period to be based on a calendar or fiscal year. If a company uses a **calendar year**, it is reporting financial data from January 1 to December 31 of a specific year. This may be useful for businesses needing to coincide with a traditional yearly tax schedule. It can also be easier to track for some businesses without formal reconciliation practices, and for small businesses.

A **fiscal year** is a twelve-month reporting cycle that can begin in any month and records financial data for that consecutive twelve-month period. For example, a business may choose its fiscal year to begin on April 1, 2019, and end on March 31, 2020. This can be common practice for corporations and may best reflect the operational flow of revenues and expenses for a particular business. In addition to annual reporting, companies often need or choose to report financial statement information in interim periods.

Interim Periods

An **interim period** is any reporting period shorter than a full year (fiscal or calendar). This can encompass monthly, quarterly, or half-year statements. The information contained on these statements is timelier than waiting for a yearly accounting period to end. The most common interim period is three months, or a quarter. For companies whose common stock is traded on a major stock exchange, meaning these are *publicly traded* companies, quarterly statements must be filed with the SEC on a Form 10-Q. The companies must file a Form 10-K for their annual statements. As you've learned, the SEC is an independent agency of the federal government that provides oversight of public companies to maintain fair representation of company financial activities for investors to make informed decisions.

In order for information to be useful to the user, it must be timely—that is, the user has to get it quickly enough so it is relevant to decision-making. You may recall from Analyzing and Recording Transactions that this is the basis of the time period assumption in accounting. For example, a potential or existing investor wants timely information by which to measure the performance of the company, and to help decide whether to invest, to stay invested, or to sell their stockholdings and invest elsewhere. This requires companies to organize their information and break it down into shorter periods. Internal and external users can then rely on the information that is both timely and relevant to decision-making.

The accounting period a company chooses to use for financial reporting will impact the types of adjustments they may have to make to certain accounts.

ETHICAL CONSIDERATIONS

Illegal Cookie Jar Accounting Used to Manage Earnings

From 2000 through the end of 2001, Bristol-Myers Squibb engaged in "Cookie Jar Accounting," resulting in $150 million in SEC fines. The company manipulated its accounting to create a false indication of income and growth to create the appearance that it was meeting its own targets and Wall Street analysts' earnings estimates during the years 2000 and 2001. The SEC describes some of what occurred:

> Bristol-Myers inflated its results primarily by (1) stuffing its distribution channels with excess inventory near the end of every quarter in amounts sufficient to meet its targets by making pharmaceutical sales to its wholesalers ahead of demand; and (2) improperly recognizing $1.5 billion in revenue from such pharmaceutical sales to its two biggest wholesalers. In connection with the $1.5 billion in revenue, Bristol-Myers covered these wholesalers' carrying costs and guaranteed them a return on investment until they sold the products. When Bristol-Myers recognized the $1.5 billion in revenue upon shipment, it did so contrary to generally accepted accounting principles.[1]

In addition to the improper distribution of product to manipulate earnings numbers, which was not enough to meet earnings targets, the company improperly used divestiture reserve funds (a "cookie jar" fund that is funded by the sale of assets such as product lines or divisions) to meet those targets. In this circumstance, earnings management was considered illegal, costing the company millions of dollars in fines.

4.2 Discuss the Adjustment Process and Illustrate Common Types of Adjusting Entries

When a company reaches the end of a period, it must update certain accounts that have either been left unattended throughout the period or have not yet been recognized. **Adjusting entries** update accounting records at the end of a period for any transactions that have not yet been recorded. One important accounting principle to remember is that just as the accounting equation (Assets = Liabilities + Owner's equity/or common stock/or capital) must be equal, it must remain equal after you make adjusting entries. Also note that in this equation, owner's equity represents an individual owner (sole proprietorship), common stock represents a corporation's owners' interests, and capital represents a partnership's owners' interests. We discuss the effects of adjusting entries in greater detail throughout this chapter.

1 U.S. Securities and Exchange Commission. "Bristol-Myers Squibb Company Agrees to Pay $150 Million to Settle Fraud Charges." August 4, 2004. https://www.sec.gov/news/press/2004-105.htm

There are several steps in the accounting cycle that require the preparation of a trial balance: step 4, preparing an unadjusted trial balance; step 6, preparing an adjusted trial balance; and step 9, preparing a post-closing trial balance. You might question the purpose of more than one trial balance. For example, why can we not go from the unadjusted trial balance straight into preparing financial statements for public consumption? What is the purpose of the adjusted trial balance? Does preparing more than one trial balance mean the company made a mistake earlier in the accounting cycle? To answer these questions, let's first explore the (unadjusted) trial balance, and why some accounts have incorrect balances.

Why Some Accounts Have Incorrect Balances on the Trial Balance

The unadjusted trial balance may have incorrect balances in some accounts. Recall the trial balance from Analyzing and Recording Transactions for the example company, Printing Plus.

PRINTING PLUS Unadjusted Trial Balance January 31, 2019		
Account	**Debit**	**Credit**
Cash	$24,800	
Accounts Receivable	1,200	
Supplies	500	
Equipment	3,500	
Accounts Payable		$ 500
Unearned Revenue		4,000
Common Stock		20,000
Dividends	100	
Service Revenue		9,500
Salaries Expense	3,600	
Utility Expense	300	
Total	$34,000	$34,000

Figure 4.4 Unadjusted Trial Balance for Printing Plus. (attribution: Copyright Rice University, OpenStax, under CC BY-NC-SA 4.0 license)

The trial balance for Printing Plus shows Supplies of $500, which were purchased on January 30. Since this is a new company, Printing Plus would more than likely use some of their supplies right away, before the end of the month on January 31. Supplies are only an asset when they are unused. If Printing Plus used some of its supplies immediately on January 30, then why is the full $500 still in the supply account on January 31? How do we fix this incorrect balance?

Similarly, what about Unearned Revenue? On January 9, the company received $4,000 from a customer for printing services to be performed. The company recorded this as a liability because it received payment without providing the service. To clear this liability, the company must perform the service. Assume that as of January 31 some of the printing services have been provided. Is the full $4,000 still a liability? Since a portion of the service was provided, a change to unearned revenue should occur. The company needs to correct this balance in the Unearned Revenue account.

Having incorrect balances in Supplies and in Unearned Revenue on the company's January 31 trial balance is not due to any error on the company's part. The company followed all of the correct steps of the accounting cycle up to this point. So why are the balances still incorrect?

Journal entries are recorded when an activity or event occurs that triggers the entry. Usually the trigger is from an original source. Recall that an original source can be a formal document substantiating a transaction, such as an invoice, purchase order, cancelled check, or employee time sheet. Not every transaction produces an original source document that will alert the bookkeeper that it is time to make an entry.

When a company purchases supplies, the original order, receipt of the supplies, and receipt of the invoice from the vendor will all trigger journal entries. This trigger does not occur when using supplies from the supply closet. Similarly, for unearned revenue, when the company receives an advance payment from the customer for services yet provided, the cash received will trigger a journal entry. When the company provides the printing services for the customer, the customer will not send the company a reminder that revenue has now been earned. Situations such as these are why businesses need to make adjusting entries.

THINK IT THROUGH

Keep Calm and Adjust . . .

Elliot Simmons owns a small law firm. He does the accounting himself and uses an accrual basis for accounting. At the end of his first month, he reviews his records and realizes there are a few inaccuracies on this unadjusted trial balance.

One difference is the supplies account; the figure on paper does not match the value of the supplies inventory still available. Another difference was interest earned from his bank account. He did not have anything recognizing these earnings.

Why did his unadjusted trial balance have these errors? What can be attributed to the differences in supply figures? What can be attributed to the differences in interest earned?

The Need for Adjusting Entries

Adjusting entries update accounting records at the end of a period for any transactions that have not yet been recorded. These entries are necessary to ensure the income statement and balance sheet present the correct, up-to-date numbers. Adjusting entries are also necessary because the initial trial balance may not contain complete and current data due to several factors:

- The inefficiency of recording every single day-to-day event, such as the use of supplies.
- Some costs are not recorded during the period but must be recognized at the end of the period, such as depreciation, rent, and insurance.
- Some items are forthcoming for which original source documents have not yet been received, such as a utility bill.

There are a few other guidelines that support the need for adjusting entries.

Guidelines Supporting Adjusting Entries

Several guidelines support the need for adjusting entries:

- Revenue recognition principle: Adjusting entries are necessary because the revenue recognition principle requires revenue recognition when earned, thus the need for an update to unearned revenues.

- Expense recognition (matching) principle: This requires matching expenses incurred to generate the revenues earned, which affects accounts such as insurance expense and supplies expense.
- Time period assumption: This requires useful information be presented in shorter time periods such as years, quarters, or months. This means a company must recognize revenues and expenses in the proper period, requiring adjustment to certain accounts to meet these criteria.

The required adjusting entries depend on what types of transactions the company has, but there are some common types of adjusting entries. Before we look at recording and posting the most common types of adjusting entries, we briefly discuss the various types of adjusting entries.

Types of Adjusting Entries

Adjusting entries requires updates to specific account types at the end of the period. Not all accounts require updates, only those not naturally triggered by an original source document. There are two main types of adjusting entries that we explore further, deferrals and accruals.

Deferrals

Deferrals are prepaid expense and revenue accounts that have delayed recognition until they have been used or earned. This recognition may not occur until the end of a period or future periods. When deferred expenses and revenues have yet to be recognized, their information is stored on the balance sheet. As soon as the expense is incurred and the revenue is earned, the information is transferred from the balance sheet to the income statement. Two main types of deferrals are prepaid expenses and unearned revenues.

Prepaid Expenses

Recall from Analyzing and Recording Transactions that *prepaid expenses* (prepayments) are assets for which advanced payment has occurred, before the company can benefit from use. As soon as the asset has provided benefit to the company, the value of the asset used is transferred from the balance sheet to the income statement as an expense. Some common examples of prepaid expenses are supplies, depreciation, insurance, and rent.

When a company purchases supplies, it may not use all supplies immediately, but chances are the company has used some of the supplies by the end of the period. It is not worth it to record every time someone uses a pencil or piece of paper during the period, so at the end of the period, this account needs to be updated for the value of what has been used.

Let’s say a company paid for supplies with cash in the amount of $400. At the end of the month, the company took an inventory of supplies used and determined the value of those supplies used during the period to be $150. The following entry occurs for the initial payment.

JOURNAL			
Date	Account	Debit	Credit
	Supplies Cash *To recognize purchase of supplies*	400	 400

Supplies increases (debit) for $400, and Cash decreases (credit) for $400. When the company recognizes the supplies usage, the following adjusting entry occurs.

JOURNAL			
Date	**Account**	**Debit**	**Credit**
	Supplies Expense Supplies *To recognize supplies used during the period*	150	 150

Supplies Expense is an expense account, increasing (debit) for $150, and Supplies is an asset account, decreasing (credit) for $150. This means $150 is transferred from the balance sheet (asset) to the income statement (expense). Notice that not all of the supplies are used. There is still a balance of $250 (400 – 150) in the Supplies account. This amount will carry over to future periods until used. The balances in the Supplies and Supplies Expense accounts show as follows.

Supplies	
400	150
Bal. 250	

Salaries Expense	
150	
Bal. 150	

Depreciation may also require an adjustment at the end of the period. Recall that *depreciation* is the systematic method to record the allocation of cost over a given period of certain assets. This allocation of cost is recorded over the **useful life** of the asset, or the time period over which an asset cost is allocated. The allocated cost up to that point is recorded in Accumulated Depreciation, a contra asset account. A **contra account** is an account paired with another account type, has an opposite normal balance to the paired account, and reduces the balance in the paired account at the end of a period.

Accumulated Depreciation is contrary to an asset account, such as Equipment. This means that the normal balance for Accumulated Depreciation is on the credit side. It houses all depreciation expensed in current and prior periods. Accumulated Depreciation will reduce the asset account for depreciation incurred up to that point. The difference between the asset's value (cost) and accumulated depreciation is called the **book value** of the asset. When depreciation is recorded in an adjusting entry, Accumulated Depreciation is credited and Depreciation Expense is debited.

For example, let's say a company pays $2,000 for equipment that is supposed to last four years. The company wants to depreciate the asset over those four years equally. This means the asset will lose $500 in value each year ($2,000/four years). In the first year, the company would record the following adjusting entry to show depreciation of the equipment.

JOURNAL			
Date	**Account**	**Debit**	**Credit**
	Depreciation Expense Accumulated Depreciation: Equipment *To recognize depreciation for the year*	500	 500

Depreciation Expense increases (debit) and Accumulated Depreciation, Equipment, increases (credit). If the company wanted to compute the book value, it would take the original cost of the equipment and subtract accumulated depreciation.

$$\text{Book value of equipment} = \$2{,}000 - \$500 = \$1{,}500$$

This means that the current book value of the equipment is $1,500, and depreciation will be subtracted from this figure the next year. The following account balances after adjustment are as follows:

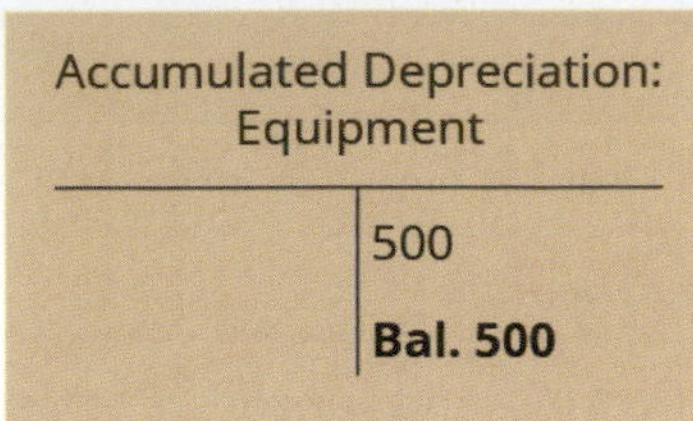

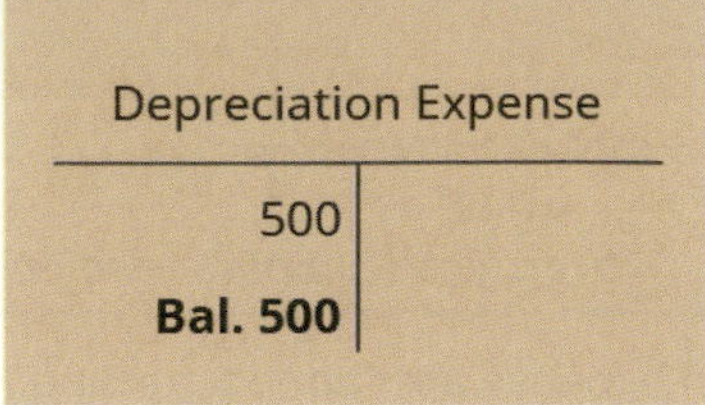

You will learn more about depreciation and its computation in Long-Term Assets. However, one important fact that we need to address now is that the book value of an asset is not necessarily the price at which the asset would sell. For example, you might have a building for which you paid $1,000,000 that currently has been depreciated to a book value of $800,000. However, today it could sell for more than, less than, or the same as its book value. The same is true about just about any asset you can name, except, perhaps, cash itself.

Insurance policies can require advanced payment of fees for several months at a time, six months, for example. The company does not use all six months of insurance immediately but over the course of the six months. At the end of each month, the company needs to record the amount of insurance expired during that month.

For example, a company pays $4,500 for an insurance policy covering six months. It is the end of the first month and the company needs to record an adjusting entry to recognize the insurance used during the month. The following entries show the initial payment for the policy and the subsequent adjusting entry for one month of insurance usage.

JOURNAL			
Date	**Account**	**Debit**	**Credit**
	Prepaid Insurance	4,500	
	Cash		4,500
	To recognize payment for insurance policy covering six months		
	Insurance Expense	750	
	Prepaid Insurance		750
	To recognize insurance used during one month		

In the first entry, Cash decreases (credit) and Prepaid Insurance increases (debit) for $4,500. In the second entry, Prepaid Insurance decreases (credit) and Insurance Expense increases (debit) for one month's insurance usage found by taking the total $4,500 and dividing by six months (4,500/6 = 750). The account balances after adjustment are as follows:

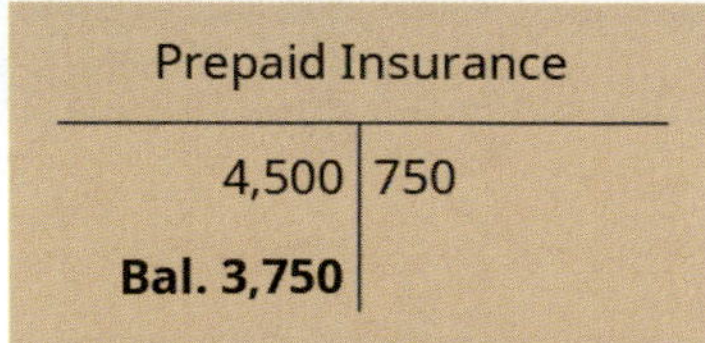

Insurance Expense	
750	
Bal. 750	

Similar to prepaid insurance, rent also requires advanced payment. Usually to rent a space, a company will need to pay rent at the beginning of the month. The company may also enter into a lease agreement that requires several months, or years, of rent in advance. Each month that passes, the company needs to record rent used for the month.

Let's say a company pays $8,000 in advance for four months of rent. After the first month, the company records an adjusting entry for the rent used. The following entries show initial payment for four months of rent and the adjusting entry for one month's usage.

JOURNAL			
Date	**Account**	**Debit**	**Credit**
	Prepaid Rent	8,000	
	Cash		8,000
	To recognize payment for rent covering four months		
	Rent Expense	2,000	
	Prepaid Rent		2,000
	To recognize rent used during one month		

In the first entry, Cash decreases (credit) and Prepaid Rent increases (debit) for $8,000. In the second entry, Prepaid Rent decreases (credit) and Rent Expense increases (debit) for one month's rent usage found by taking the total $8,000 and dividing by four months (8,000/4 = 2,000). The account balances after adjustment are as follows:

Prepaid Rent	
8,000	2,000
Bal. 6,000	

Rent Expense	
2,000	
Bal. 2,000	

Another type of deferral requiring adjustment is unearned revenue.

Unearned Revenues

Recall that unearned revenue represents a customer's advanced payment for a product or service that has yet to be provided by the company. Since the company has not yet provided the product or service, it cannot recognize the customer's payment as revenue. At the end of a period, the company will review the account to see if any of the unearned revenue has been earned. If so, this amount will be recorded as revenue in the current period.

For example, let's say the company is a law firm. During the year, it collected retainer fees totaling $48,000 from clients. Retainer fees are money lawyers collect in advance of starting work on a case. When the company collects this money from its clients, it will debit cash and credit unearned fees. Even though not all of the $48,000 was probably collected on the same day, we record it as if it was for simplicity's sake.

JOURNAL			
Date	**Account**	**Debit**	**Credit**
	Cash	48,000	
	Unearned Fee Revenue		48,000
	To recognize collection of retainer fees		

In this case, Unearned Fee Revenue increases (credit) and Cash increases (debit) for $48,000.

At the end of the year after analyzing the unearned fees account, 40% of the unearned fees have been earned.

This 40% can now be recorded as revenue. Total revenue recorded is $19,200 ($48,000 × 40%).

JOURNAL			
Date	**Account**	**Debit**	**Credit**
	Unearned Fee Revenue Fee Revenue *To recognize fees earned*	19,200	 19,200

For this entry, Unearned Fee Revenue decreases (debit) and Fee Revenue increases (credit) for $19,200, which is the 40% earned during the year. The company will have the following balances in the two accounts:

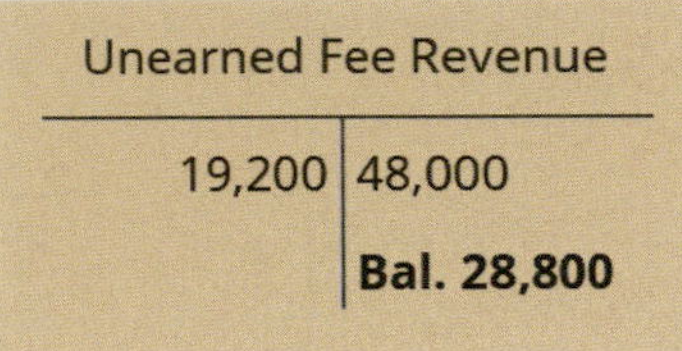

Fee Revenue	
	19,200
	Bal. 19,200

Besides deferrals, other types of adjusting entries include accruals.

Accruals

Accruals are types of adjusting entries that accumulate during a period, where amounts were previously unrecorded. The two specific types of adjustments are accrued revenues and accrued expenses.

Accrued Revenues

Accrued revenues are revenues earned in a period but have yet to be recorded, and no money has been collected. Some examples include interest, and services completed but a bill has yet to be sent to the customer.

Interest can be earned from bank account holdings, notes receivable, and some accounts receivables (depending on the contract). Interest had been accumulating during the period and needs to be adjusted to reflect interest earned at the end of the period. Note that this interest has not been paid at the end of the period, only earned. This aligns with the revenue recognition principle to recognize revenue when earned, even if cash has yet to be collected.

For example, assume that a company has one outstanding note receivable in the amount of $100,000. Interest on this note is 5% per year. Three months have passed, and the company needs to record interest earned on this outstanding loan. The calculation for the interest revenue earned is $100,000 × 5% × 3/12 = $1,250. The following adjusting entry occurs.

JOURNAL			
Date	**Account**	**Debit**	**Credit**
	Interest Receivable Interest Revenue *To recognize interest revenue earned and due*	1,250	 1,250

Interest Receivable increases (debit) for $1,250 because interest has not yet been paid. Interest Revenue increases (credit) for $1,250 because interest was earned in the three-month period but had been previously unrecorded.

Interest Receivable	
1,250	
Bal. 1,250	

Interest Revenue	
	1,250
	Bal. 1,250

Previously unrecorded service revenue can arise when a company provides a service but did not yet bill the client for the work. This means the customer has also not yet paid for services. Since there was no bill to trigger a transaction, an adjustment is required to recognize revenue earned at the end of the period.

For example, a company performs landscaping services in the amount of $1,500. However, they have not yet received payment. At the period end, the company would record the following adjusting entry.

JOURNAL			
Date	**Account**	**Debit**	**Credit**
	Accounts Receivable	1,500	
	Service Revenue		1,500
	To recognize service revenue earned and due		

Accounts Receivable increases (debit) for $1,500 because the customer has not yet paid for services completed. Service Revenue increases (credit) for $1,500 because service revenue was earned but had been previously unrecorded.

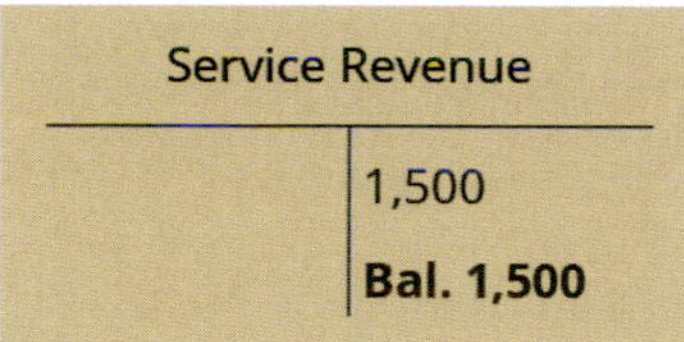

Service Revenue	
	1,500
	Bal. 1,500

Accounts Receivable	
1,500	
Bal. 1,500	

Accrued Expenses

Accrued expenses are expenses incurred in a period but have yet to be recorded, and no money has been paid. Some examples include interest, tax, and salary expenses.

Interest expense arises from notes payable and other loan agreements. The company has accumulated interest during the period but has not recorded or paid the amount. This creates a liability that the company must pay at a future date. You cover more details about computing interest in Current Liabilities, so for now amounts are given.

For example, a company accrued $300 of interest during the period. The following entry occurs at the end of the period.

JOURNAL			
Date	**Account**	**Debit**	**Credit**
	Interest Expense	300	
	Interest Payable		300
	To recognize interest expense incurred but not paid		

Interest Expense increases (debit) and Interest Payable increases (credit) for $300. The following are the updated ledger balances after posting the adjusting entry.

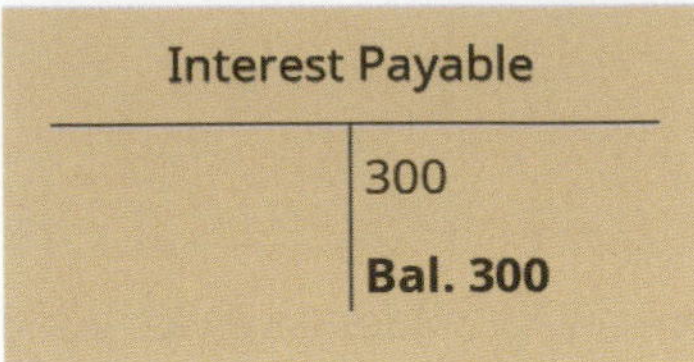

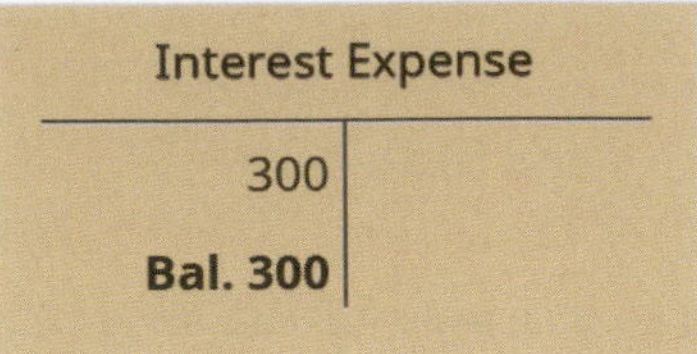

Taxes are only paid at certain times during the year, not necessarily every month. Taxes the company owes during a period that are unpaid require adjustment at the end of a period. This creates a liability for the company. Some tax expense examples are income and sales taxes.

For example, a company has accrued income taxes for the month for $9,000. The company would record the following adjusting entry.

JOURNAL			
Date	**Account**	**Debit**	**Credit**
	Income Tax Expense Income Tax Payable *To recognize income tax expense incurred but not paid*	9,000	9,000

Income Tax Expense increases (debit) and Income Tax Payable increases (credit) for $9,000. The following are the updated ledger balances after posting the adjusting entry.

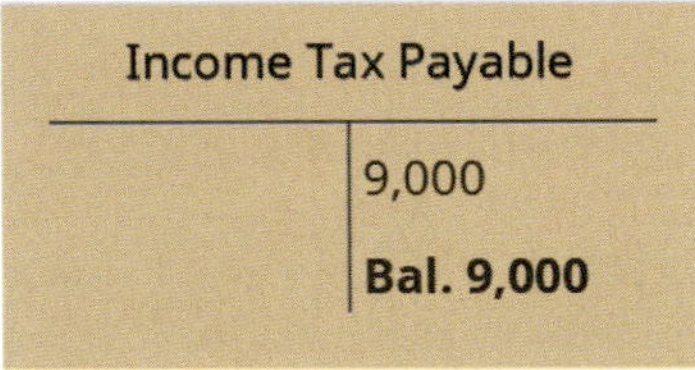

Income Tax Expense
9,000
Bal. 9,000

Many salaried employees are paid once a month. The salary the employee earned during the month might not be paid until the following month. For example, the employee is paid for the prior month's work on the first of the next month. The financial statements must remain up to date, so an adjusting entry is needed during the month to show salaries previously unrecorded and unpaid at the end of the month.

Let's say a company has five salaried employees, each earning $2,500 per month. In our example, assume that they do not get paid for this work until the first of the next month. The following is the adjusting journal entry for salaries.

JOURNAL			
Date	**Account**	**Debit**	**Credit**
	Salaries Expense Salaries Payable *To recognize salaries expense incurred but not paid*	12,500	12,500

Salaries Expense increases (debit) and Salaries Payable increases (credit) for $12,500 ($2,500 per employee × five employees). The following are the updated ledger balances after posting the adjusting entry.

Salaries Payable	
	12,500
	Bal. 12,500

Salaries Expense	
12,500	
Bal. 12,500	

In Record and Post the Common Types of Adjusting Entries, we explore some of these adjustments specifically for our company Printing Plus, and show how these entries affect our general ledger (T-accounts).

YOUR TURN

Adjusting Entries

Example	Income Statement Account	Balance Sheet Account	Cash in Entry?

Table 4.1

Review the three adjusting entries that follow. Using the table provided, for each entry write down the income statement account and balance sheet account used in the adjusting entry in the appropriate column. Then in the last column answer yes or no.

	Supplies Expense Supplies	500	500
	Unearned Revenue Service Revenue	2,000	2,000
	Rent Expense Prepaid Machine Rent	1,200	1,200

Solution

Example	Income Statement Account	Balance Sheet Account	Cash in Entry?
1	Supplies expense	Supplies	no
2	Service Revenue	Unearned Revenue	no

Table 4.2

Example	Income Statement Account	Balance Sheet Account	Cash in Entry?
3	Rent Expense	Prepaid machine rent	no

Table 4.2

YOUR TURN

Adjusting Entries Take Two

Did we continue to follow the rules of adjusting entries in these two examples? Explain.

	Electricity Expense Accounts Payable	100	 100
	Salaries Expense Salaries Payable	4,000	 4,000

Example	Income Statement Account	Balance Sheet Account	Cash in Entry?

Table 4.3

Solution

Yes, we did. Each entry has one income statement account and one balance sheet account, and cash does not appear in either of the adjusting entries.

Example	Income Statement Account	Balance Sheet Account	Cash in Entry?
1	Electricity Expense	Accounts Payable	no
2	Salaries Expense	Salaries Payable	no

Table 4.4

4.3 Record and Post the Common Types of Adjusting Entries

Before beginning adjusting entry examples for Printing Plus, let's consider some rules governing adjusting entries:

- Every adjusting entry will have at least one income statement account and one balance sheet account.
- Cash will never be in an adjusting entry.
- The adjusting entry records the change in amount that occurred during the period.

What are "income statement" and "balance sheet" accounts? Income statement accounts include revenues and expenses. Balance sheet accounts are assets, liabilities, and stockholders' equity accounts, since they appear on a balance sheet. The second rule tells us that cash can never be in an adjusting entry. This is true because paying or receiving cash triggers a journal entry. This means that every transaction with cash will be recorded at the time of the exchange. We will not get to the adjusting entries and have cash paid or received which has not already been recorded. If accountants find themselves in a situation where the cash account must be adjusted, the necessary adjustment to cash will be a *correcting entry* and not an adjusting entry.

With an adjusting entry, the amount of change occurring during the period is recorded. For example, if the supplies account had a $300 balance at the beginning of the month and $100 is still available in the supplies account at the end of the month, the company would record an adjusting entry for the $200 used during the month (300 – 100). Similarly for unearned revenues, the company would record how much of the revenue was earned during the period.

Let's now consider new transaction information for Printing Plus.

CONCEPTS IN PRACTICE

Earnings Management

Recording adjusting entries seems so cut and dry. It looks like you just follow the rules and all of the numbers come out 100 percent correct on all financial statements. But in reality this is not always the case. Just the fact that you have to make estimates in some cases, such as depreciation estimating residual value and useful life, tells you that numbers will not be 100 percent correct unless the accountant has ESP. Some companies engage in something called earnings management, where they follow the rules of accounting mostly but they stretch the truth a little to make it look like they are more profitable. Some companies do this by recording revenue before they should. Others leave assets on the books instead of expensing them when they should to decrease total expenses and increase profit.

Take Mexico-based home-building company Desarrolladora Homex S.A.B. de C.V. This company reported revenue earned on more than 100,000 homes they had not even build yet. The SEC's complaint states that Homex reported revenues from a project site where every planned home was said to have been "built and sold by Dec. 31, 2011. Satellite images of the project site on March 12, 2012, show it was still largely undeveloped and the vast majority of supposedly sold homes remained unbuilt."[2]

Is managing your earnings illegal? In some situations it is just an unethical stretch of the truth easy enough to do because of the estimates made in adjusting entries. You can simply change your estimate and insist the new estimate is really better when maybe it is your way to improve the bottom line, for example, changing your annual depreciation expense calculated on expensive plant assets from assuming a ten-year useful life, a reasonable estimated expectation, to a twenty-year useful life, not so reasonable but you insist your company will be able to use these assets twenty years while knowing that is a slim possibility. Doubling the useful life will cause 50% of the depreciation expense you would have had. This will make a positive impact on net income. This method of earnings management would probably not be considered illegal but is definitely a breach of ethics. In other situations, companies manage their earnings in a way that the SEC believes is actual fraud and charges the company with the illegal activity.

Recording Common Types of Adjusting Entries

Recall the transactions for Printing Plus discussed in Analyzing and Recording Transactions.

Jan. 3, 2019	issues $20,000 shares of common stock for cash
Jan. 5, 2019	purchases equipment on account for $3,500, payment due within the month
Jan. 9, 2019	receives $4,000 cash in advance from a customer for services not yet rendered
Jan. 10, 2019	provides $5,500 in services to a customer who asks to be billed for the services
Jan. 12, 2019	pays a $300 utility bill with cash
Jan. 14, 2019	distributed $100 cash in dividends to stockholders
Jan. 17, 2019	receives $2,800 cash from a customer for services rendered
Jan. 18, 2019	paid in full, with cash, for the equipment purchase on January 5
Jan. 20, 2019	paid $3,600 cash in salaries expense to employees
Jan. 23, 2019	received cash payment in full from the customer on the January 10 transaction
Jan. 27, 2019	provides $1,200 in services to a customer who asks to be billed for the services
Jan. 30, 2019	purchases supplies on account for $500, payment due within three months

On January 31, 2019, Printing Plus makes adjusting entries for the following transactions.

1. On January 31, Printing Plus took an inventory of its supplies and discovered that $100 of supplies had been used during the month.
2. The equipment purchased on January 5 depreciated $75 during the month of January.
3. Printing Plus performed $600 of services during January for the customer from the January 9 transaction.
4. Reviewing the company bank statement, Printing Plus discovers $140 of interest earned during the month of January that was previously uncollected and unrecorded.
5. Employees earned $1,500 in salaries for the period of January 21–January 31 that had been previously unpaid and unrecorded.

We now record the adjusting entries from January 31, 2019, for Printing Plus.

Transaction 13: On January 31, Printing Plus took an inventory of its supplies and discovered that $100 of supplies had been used during the month.

2 U.S. Securities and Exchange Commission. “SEC Charges Mexico-Based Homebuilder in $3.3 Billion Accounting Fraud. Press Release.” March 3, 2017. https://www.sec.gov/news/pressrelease/2017-60.html

Analysis:

- $100 of supplies were used during January. Supplies is an asset that is decreasing (credit).
- Supplies is a type of prepaid expense that, when used, becomes an expense. Supplies Expense would increase (debit) for the $100 of supplies used during January.

JOURNAL			
Date	**Account**	**Debit**	**Credit**
Jan. 31, 2019	Supplies Expense Supplies *To recognize supply usage for January*	100	 100

Impact on the financial statements: Supplies is a balance sheet account, and Supplies Expense is an income statement account. This satisfies the rule that each adjusting entry will contain an income statement and balance sheet account. We see total assets decrease by $100 on the balance sheet. Supplies Expense increases overall expenses on the income statement, which reduces net income.

Assets	=	Liabilities	+	Stockholders' Equity
–$100	=	+$0	+	–$100
–$100	=	$0	+	–$100

Transaction 14: The equipment purchased on January 5 depreciated $75 during the month of January.

Analysis:

- Equipment lost value in the amount of $75 during January. This depreciation will impact the Accumulated Depreciation–Equipment account and the Depreciation Expense–Equipment account. While we are not doing depreciation calculations here, you will come across more complex calculations in the future.
- Accumulated Depreciation–Equipment is a contra asset account (contrary to Equipment) and increases (credit) for $75.
- Depreciation Expense–Equipment is an expense account that is increasing (debit) for $75.

JOURNAL			
Date	**Account**	**Debit**	**Credit**
Jan. 31, 2019	Depreciation Expense: Equipment Accumulated Depreciation: Equipment *To recognize equipment depreciation for January*	75	 75

Impact on the financial statements: Accumulated Depreciation–Equipment is a contra account to Equipment. When calculating the book value of Equipment, Accumulated Depreciation–Equipment will be deducted from the original cost of the equipment. Therefore, total assets will decrease by $75 on the balance sheet. Depreciation Expense will increase overall expenses on the income statement, which reduces net income.

Assets	=	Liabilities	+	Stockholders' Equity
–$75	=	+$0	+	–$75
–$75	=	$0	+	–$75

Transaction 15: Printing Plus performed $600 of services during January for the customer from the January 9 transaction.

Analysis:

- The customer from the January 9 transaction gave the company $4,000 in advanced payment for services. By the end of January the company had earned $600 of the advanced payment. This means that the company still has yet to provide $3,400 in services to that customer.
- Since some of the unearned revenue is now earned, Unearned Revenue would decrease. Unearned Revenue is a liability account and decreases on the debit side.
- The company can now recognize the $600 as earned revenue. Service Revenue increases (credit) for $600.

JOURNAL			
Date	**Account**	**Debit**	**Credit**
Jan. 31, 2019	Unearned Revenue Service Revenue *To recognize revenue earned from January 9 transaction*	600	 600

Impact on the financial statements: Unearned revenue is a liability account and will decrease total liabilities and equity by $600 on the balance sheet. Service Revenue will increase overall revenue on the income statement, which increases net income.

Assets	=	Liabilities	+	Stockholders' Equity
$0	=	–$600	+	+$600
$0	=	–$600	+	$600

Transaction 16: Reviewing the company bank statement, Printing Plus discovers $140 of interest earned during the month of January that was previously uncollected and unrecorded.

Analysis:

- Interest is revenue for the company on money kept in a savings account at the bank. The company only sees the bank statement at the end of the month and needs to record interest revenue that has not yet been collected or recorded.
- Interest Revenue is a revenue account that increases (credit) for $140.
- Since Printing Plus has yet to collect this interest revenue, it is considered a receivable. Interest Receivable increases (debit) for $140.

JOURNAL			
Date	**Account**	**Debit**	**Credit**
Jan. 31, 2019	Interest Receivable Interest Revenue *To recognize interest revenue earned but not yet collected*	140	 140

Impact on the financial statements: Interest Receivable is an asset account and will increase total assets by $140 on the balance sheet. Interest Revenue will increase overall revenue on the income statement, which increases net income.

Assets	=	Liabilities	+	Stockholder's Equity
+$140	=	$0	+	+$140
+$140	=	$0	+	+$140

Transaction 17: Employees earned $1,500 in salaries for the period of January 21–January 31 that had been previously unpaid and unrecorded.

Analysis:

- Salaries have accumulated since January 21 and will not be paid in the current period. Since the salaries expense occurred in January, the expense recognition principle requires recognition in January.
- Salaries Expense is an expense account that is increasing (debit) for $1,500.
- Since the company has not yet paid salaries for this time period, Printing Plus owes the employees this money. This creates a liability for Printing Plus. Salaries Payable increases (credit) for $1,500.

JOURNAL			
Date	Account	Debit	Credit
Jan. 31, 2019	Salaries Expense Salaries Payable *To recognize salaries expense but not yet paid*	1,500	 1,500

Impact on the financial statements: Salaries Payable is a liability account and will increase total liabilities and equity by $1,500 on the balance sheet. Salaries expense will increase overall expenses on the income statement, which decreases net income.

Assets	=	Liabilities	+	Stockholder's Equity
$0	=	+$1,500	+	–$1,500
$0	=	+$1,500	+	–$1,500

We now explore how these adjusting entries impact the general ledger (T-accounts).

YOUR TURN

Deferrals versus Accruals

Label each of the following as a deferral or an accrual, and explain your answer.

1. The company recorded supplies usage for the month.
2. A customer paid in advance for services, and the company recorded revenue earned after providing service to that customer.
3. The company recorded salaries that had been earned by employees but were previously unrecorded and have not yet been paid.

Solution

1. The company is recording a deferred expense. The company was deferring the recognition of supplies from supplies expense until it had used the supplies.

2. The company has deferred revenue. It deferred the recognition of the revenue until it was actually earned. The customer already paid the cash and is currently on the balance sheet as a liability.
3. The company has an accrued expense. The company is bringing the salaries that have been incurred, added up since the last paycheck, onto the books for the first time during the adjusting entry. Cash will be given to the employees at a later time.

LINK TO LEARNING

Several internet sites can provide additional information for you on adjusting entries. One very good site where you can find many tools to help you study this topic is Accounting Coach (https://openstax.org/l/50AcctCoach) which provides a tool that is available to you free of charge. Visit the website and take a quiz on accounting basics (https://openstax.org/l/50AcctQuiz) to test your knowledge.

Posting Adjusting Entries

Once you have journalized all of your adjusting entries, the next step is posting the entries to your ledger. Posting adjusting entries is no different than posting the regular daily journal entries. T-accounts will be the visual representation for the Printing Plus general ledger.

Transaction 13: On January 31, Printing Plus took an inventory of its supplies and discovered that $100 of supplies had been used during the month.

Journal entry and T-accounts:

JOURNAL			
Date	**Account**	**Debit**	**Credit**
Jan. 31, 2019	Supplies Expense Supplies *To recognize supply usage for January*	100	 100

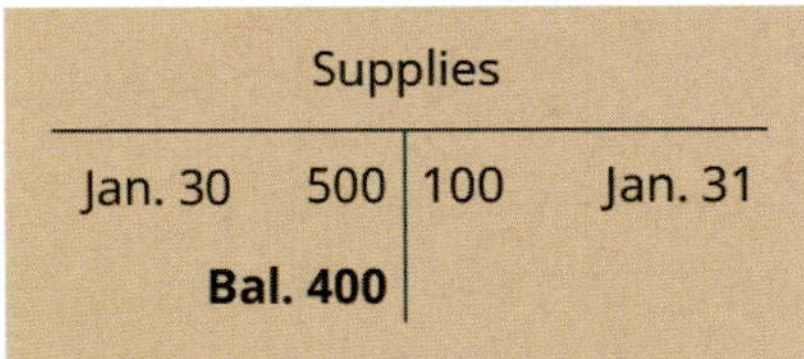

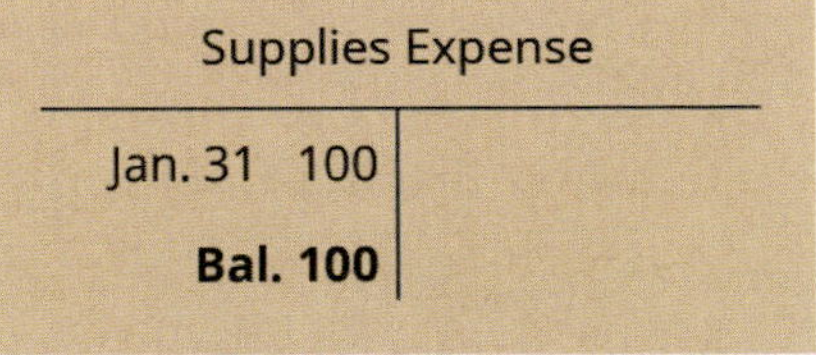

In the journal entry, Supplies Expense has a debit of $100. This is posted to the Supplies Expense T-account on the debit side (left side). Supplies has a credit balance of $100. This is posted to the Supplies T-account on the credit side (right side). You will notice there is already a debit balance in this account from the purchase of supplies on January 30. The $100 is deducted from $500 to get a final debit balance of $400.

Transaction 14: The equipment purchased on January 5 depreciated $75 during the month of January.

Journal entry and T-accounts:

JOURNAL			
Date	**Account**	**Debit**	**Credit**
Jan. 31, 2019	Depreciation Expense: Equipment Accumulated Depreciation: Equipment *To recognize equipment depreciation for January*	75	 75

Depreciation Expense: Equipment			
Jan. 31	75		
	Bal. 75		

Accumulated Depreciation: Equipment			
		75	Jan. 31
		Bal. 75	

In the journal entry, Depreciation Expense–Equipment has a debit of $75. This is posted to the Depreciation Expense–Equipment T-account on the debit side (left side). Accumulated Depreciation–Equipment has a credit balance of $75. This is posted to the Accumulated Depreciation–Equipment T-account on the credit side (right side).

Transaction 15: Printing Plus performed $600 of services during January for the customer from the January 9 transaction.

Journal entry and T-accounts:

JOURNAL			
Date	**Account**	**Debit**	**Credit**
Jan. 31, 2019	Unearned Revenue Service Revenue *To recognize revenue earned from January 9 transaction*	600	 600

Unearned Revenue			
		4,000	Jan. 9
Jan. 31	600		
		Bal. 3,400	

Service Revenue			
		5,500	Jan. 10
		2,800	Jan. 17
		1,200	Jan. 27
		600	Jan. 31
		Bal. 10,100	

In the journal entry, Unearned Revenue has a debit of $600. This is posted to the Unearned Revenue T-account on the debit side (left side). You will notice there is already a credit balance in this account from the January 9 customer payment. The $600 debit is subtracted from the $4,000 credit to get a final balance of $3,400 (credit). Service Revenue has a credit balance of $600. This is posted to the Service Revenue T-account on the credit side (right side). You will notice there is already a credit balance in this account from other revenue transactions in January. The $600 is added to the previous $9,500 balance in the account to get a new final credit balance of $10,100.

Transaction 16: Reviewing the company bank statement, Printing Plus discovers $140 of interest earned during the month of January that was previously uncollected and unrecorded.

Journal entry and T-accounts:

JOURNAL			
Date	**Account**	**Debit**	**Credit**
Jan. 31, 2019	Interest Receivable Interest Revenue *To recognize interest revenue earned but not yet collected*	140	 140

Interest Receivable	
Jan. 31 140	
Bal. 140	

Interest Revenue	
	140 Jan. 31
	Bal. 140

In the journal entry, Interest Receivable has a debit of $140. This is posted to the Interest Receivable T-account on the debit side (left side). Interest Revenue has a credit balance of $140. This is posted to the Interest Revenue T-account on the credit side (right side).

Transaction 17: Employees earned $1,500 in salaries for the period of January 21–January 31 that had been previously unpaid and unrecorded.

Journal entry and T-accounts:

JOURNAL			
Date	**Account**	**Debit**	**Credit**
Jan. 31, 2019	Interest Receivable Interest Revenue *To recognize interest revenue earned but not yet collected*	140	 140

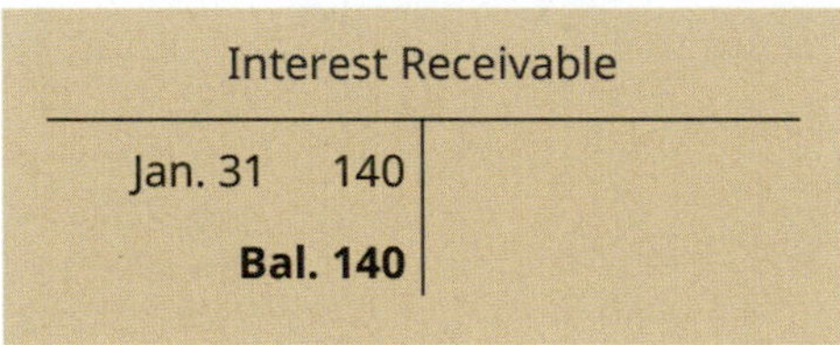

Interest Revenue	
	140 Jan. 31
	Bal. 140

In the journal entry, Salaries Expense has a debit of $1,500. This is posted to the Salaries Expense T-account on the debit side (left side). You will notice there is already a debit balance in this account from the January 20 employee salary expense. The $1,500 debit is added to the $3,600 debit to get a final balance of $5,100 (debit). Salaries Payable has a credit balance of $1,500. This is posted to the Salaries Payable T-account on the credit side (right side).

T-accounts Summary

Once all adjusting journal entries have been posted to T-accounts, we can check to make sure the accounting equation remains balanced. Following is a summary showing the T-accounts for Printing Plus including adjusting entries.

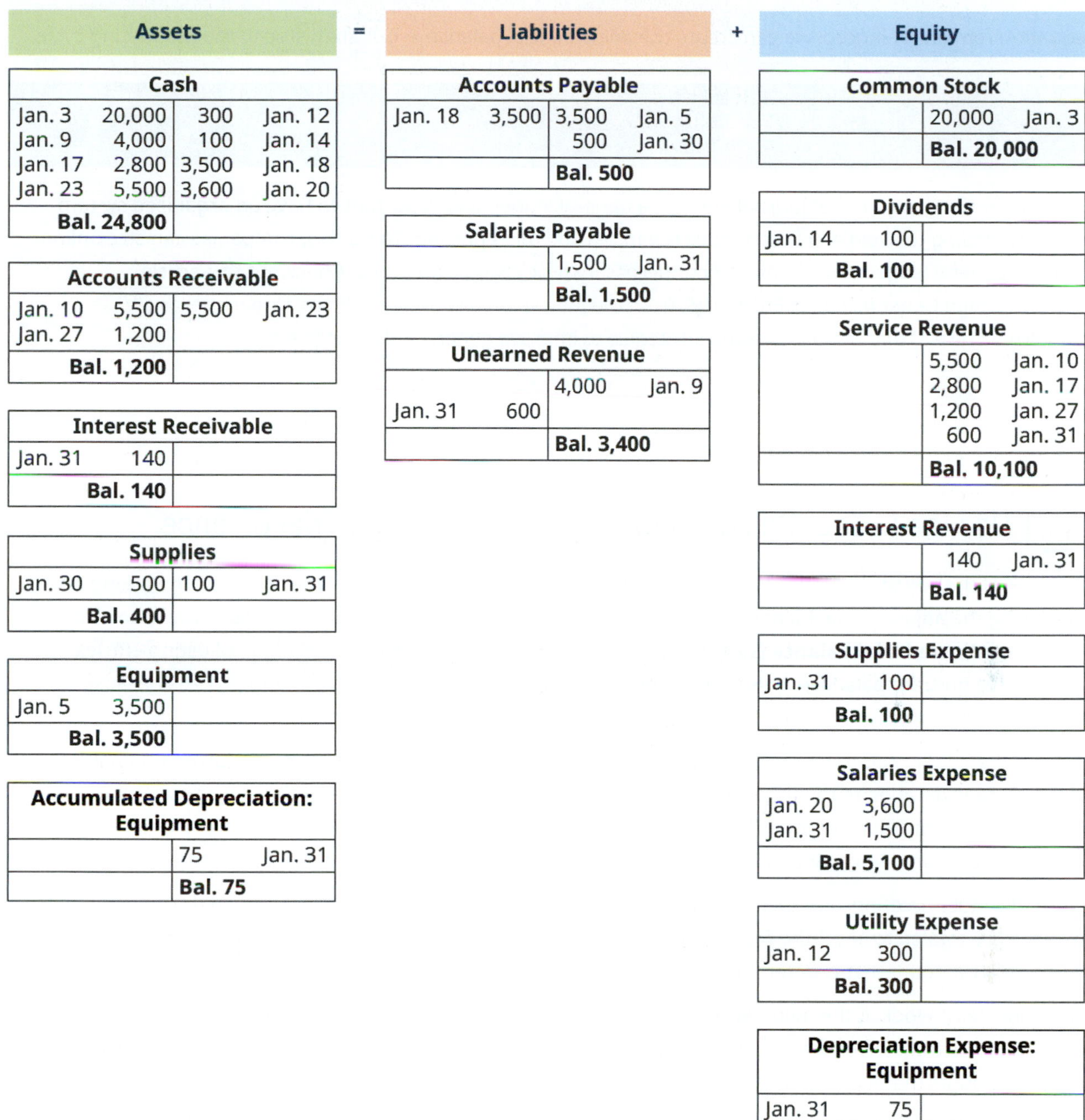

Figure 4.5 Printing Plus summary of T-accounts with Adjusting Entries. (attribution: Copyright Rice University, OpenStax, under CC BY-NC-SA 4.0 license)

The sum on the assets side of the accounting equation equals $29,965, found by adding together the final balances in each asset account (24,800 + 1,200 + 140 + 400 + 3,500 – 75). To find the total on the liabilities and equity side of the equation, we need to find the difference between debits and credits. Credits on the liabilities and equity side of the equation total $35,640 (500 + 1,500 + 3,400 + 20,000 + 10,100 + 140). Debits on the liabilities and equity side of the equation total $5,675 (100 + 100 + 5,100 + 300 + 75). The difference between $35,640 – $5,675 = $29,965. Thus, the equation remains balanced with $29,965 on the asset side and $29,965 on the liabilities and equity side. Now that we have the T-account information, and have confirmed the accounting equation remains balanced, we can create the adjusted trial balance in our sixth step in the accounting cycle.

LINK TO LEARNING

When posting any kind of journal entry to a general ledger, it is important to have an organized system for recording to avoid any account discrepancies and misreporting. To do this, companies can streamline their general ledger and remove any unnecessary processes or accounts. Check out this article "Encourage General Ledger Efficiency" from the Journal of Accountancy (https://openstax.org/l/50JrnAcctArticl) that discusses some strategies to improve general ledger efficiency.

4.4 Use the Ledger Balances to Prepare an Adjusted Trial Balance

Once all of the adjusting entries have been posted to the general ledger, we are ready to start working on preparing the adjusted trial balance. Preparing an adjusted trial balance is the sixth step in the accounting cycle. An **adjusted trial balance** is a list of all accounts in the general ledger, including adjusting entries, which have nonzero balances. This trial balance is an important step in the accounting process because it helps identify any computational errors throughout the first five steps in the cycle.

As with the unadjusted trial balance, transferring information from T-accounts to the adjusted trial balance requires consideration of the final balance in each account. If the final balance in the ledger account (T-account) is a debit balance, you will record the total in the left column of the trial balance. If the final balance in the ledger account (T-account) is a credit balance, you will record the total in the right column.

Once all ledger accounts and their balances are recorded, the debit and credit columns on the adjusted trial balance are totaled to see if the figures in each column match. The final total in the debit column must be the same dollar amount that is determined in the final credit column.

Let's now take a look at the adjusted T-accounts and adjusted trial balance for Printing Plus to see how the information is transferred from these T-accounts to the adjusted trial balance. We only focus on those general ledger accounts that had balance adjustments.

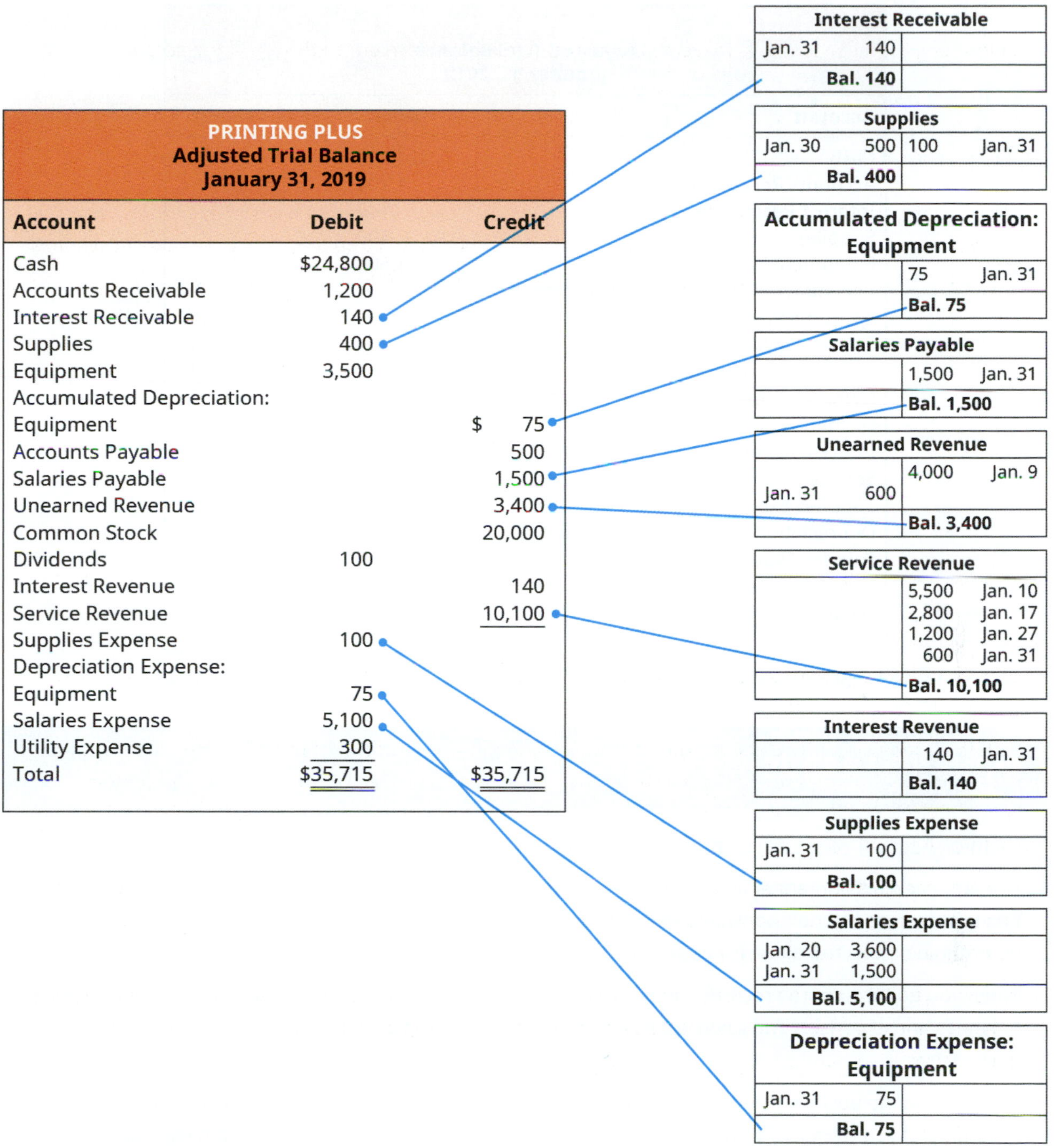

PRINTING PLUS Adjusted Trial Balance January 31, 2019		
Account	**Debit**	**Credit**
Cash	$24,800	
Accounts Receivable	1,200	
Interest Receivable	140	
Supplies	400	
Equipment	3,500	
Accumulated Depreciation: Equipment		$ 75
Accounts Payable		500
Salaries Payable		1,500
Unearned Revenue		3,400
Common Stock		20,000
Dividends	100	
Interest Revenue		140
Service Revenue		10,100
Supplies Expense	100	
Depreciation Expense: Equipment	75	
Salaries Expense	5,100	
Utility Expense	300	
Total	$35,715	$35,715

For example, Interest Receivable is an adjusted account that has a final balance of $140 on the debit side. This balance is transferred to the Interest Receivable account in the debit column on the adjusted trial balance. Supplies ($400), Supplies Expense ($100), Salaries Expense ($5,100), and Depreciation Expense–Equipment ($75) also have debit final balances in their adjusted T-accounts, so this information will be transferred to the debit column on the adjusted trial balance. Accumulated Depreciation–Equipment ($75), Salaries Payable ($1,500), Unearned Revenue ($3,400), Service Revenue ($10,100), and Interest Revenue ($140) all have credit final balances in their T-accounts. These credit balances would transfer to the credit column on the adjusted trial balance.

Once all balances are transferred to the adjusted trial balance, we sum each of the debit and credit columns. The debit and credit columns both total $35,715, which means they are equal and in balance.

PRINTING PLUS Adjusted Trial Balance January 31, 2019		
Account	**Debit**	**Credit**
Cash	$24,800	
Accounts Receivable	1,200	
Interest Receivable	140	
Supplies	400	
Equipment	3,500	
Accumulated Depreciation: Equipment		$ 75
Accounts Payable		500
Salaries Payable		1,500
Unearned Revenue		3,400
Common Stock		20,000
Dividends	100	
Interest Revenue		140
Service Revenue		10,100
Supplies Expense	100	
Depreciation Expense: Equipment	75	
Salaries Expense	5,100	
Utility Expense	300	
Total	$35,715	$35,715

After the adjusted trial balance is complete, we next prepare the company’s financial statements.

THINK IT THROUGH

Cash or Accrual Basis Accounting?

You are a new accountant at a salon. The salon had previously used cash basis accounting to prepare its financial records but now considers switching to an accrual basis method. You have been tasked with determining if this transition is appropriate.

When you go through the records you notice that this transition will greatly impact how the salon reports revenues and expenses. The salon will now report some revenues and expenses before it receives or pays cash.

How will change positively impact its business reporting? How will it negatively impact its business reporting? If you were the accountant, would you recommend the salon transition from cash basis to accrual basis?

CONCEPTS IN PRACTICE

Why Is the Adjusted Trial Balance So Important?

As you have learned, the adjusted trial balance is an important step in the accounting process. But outside of the accounting department, why is the adjusted trial balance important to the rest of the organization? An employee or customer may not immediately see the impact of the adjusted trial balance on his or her involvement with the company.

The adjusted trial balance is the key point to ensure all debits and credits are in the general ledger accounts balance before information is transferred to financial statements. Financial statements drive decision-making for a business. Budgeting for employee salaries, revenue expectations, sales prices, expense reductions, and long-term growth strategies are all impacted by what is provided on the financial statements.

So if the company skips over creating an adjusted trial balance to make sure all accounts are balanced or adjusted, it runs the risk of creating incorrect financial statements and making important decisions based on inaccurate financial information.

4.5 Prepare Financial Statements Using the Adjusted Trial Balance

Once you have prepared the adjusted trial balance, you are ready to prepare the financial statements. Preparing financial statements is the seventh step in the accounting cycle. Remember that we have four financial statements to prepare: an income statement, a statement of retained earnings, a balance sheet, and the statement of cash flows. These financial statements were introduced in Introduction to Financial Statements and Statement of Cash Flows dedicates in-depth discussion to that statement.

To prepare the financial statements, a company will look at the adjusted trial balance for account information. From this information, the company will begin constructing each of the statements, beginning with the income statement. Income statements will include all revenue and expense accounts. The statement of retained earnings will include beginning retained earnings, any net income (loss) (found on the income statement), and dividends. The balance sheet is going to include assets, contra assets, liabilities, and stockholder equity accounts, including ending retained earnings and common stock.

YOUR TURN

Magnificent Adjusted Trial Balance

MAGNIFICENT LANDSCAPING SERVICE Adjusted Trial Balance April 30, 2018		
Account Title	**Debit**	**Credit**
Cash	$2,950	
Accounts Receivable	575	
Office Supplies	40	
Prepaid Insurance	240	
Equipment	2,500	
Accumulated Depreciation: Equipment		$ 35
Accounts Payable		28
Salaries Payable		420
Unearned Lawn Mowing Revenue		100
Common Stock		5,000
Dividends	1,000	
Lawn Mowing Revenue		2,350
Gas Expense	53	
Advertising Expense	35	
Depreciation Expense: Equipment	35	
Supplies Expense	85	
Salaries Expense	420	
	$7,933	$7,933

Go over the adjusted trial balance for Magnificent Landscaping Service. Identify which income statement each account will go on: Balance Sheet, Statement of Retained Earnings, or Income Statement.

Solution

Balance Sheet: Cash, accounts receivable, office supplied, prepaid insurance, equipment, accumulated depreciation (equipment), accounts payable, salaries payable, unearned lawn mowing revenue, and common stock. Statement of Retained Earnings: Dividends. Income Statement: Lawn mowing revenue, gas expense, advertising expense, depreciation expense (equipment), supplies expense, and salaries expense.

Income Statement

An income statement shows the organization's financial performance for a given period of time. When preparing an income statement, revenues will always come before expenses in the presentation. For Printing Plus, the following is its January 2019 Income Statement.

PRINTING PLUS Income Statement For the Month Ended January 31, 2019		
Revenues		
Interest Revenue	$ 140	
Service Revenue	10,100	
Total Revenues		$10,240
Expenses		
Supplies Expense	100	
Depreciation Expense		
Equipment	75	
Salaries Expense	5,100	
Utility Expense	300	
Total Expenses		5,575
Net Income		$ 4,665

Revenue and expense information is taken from the adjusted trial balance as follows:

PRINTING PLUS Income Statement For the Month Ended January 31, 2019		
Revenues		
Interest Revenue	$ 140	
Service Revenue	10,100	
Total Revenues		$10,240
Expenses		
Supplies Expense	100	
Depreciation Expense:		
Equipment	75	
Salaries Expense	5,100	
Utility Expense	300	
Total Expenses		5,575
Net Income		$ 4,665

PRINTING PLUS
Adjusted Trial Balance
January 31, 2019

Account	Debit	Credit
Cash	$24,800	
Accounts Receivable	1,200	
Interest Receivable	140	
Supplies	400	
Equipment	3,500	
Acc. Dep: Equipment		$ 75
Accounts Payable		500
Salaries Payable		1,500
Unearned Revenue		3,400
Common Stock		20,000
Dividends	100	
Interest Revenue		140
Service Revenue		10,100
Supplies Expense	100	
Depreciation Expense:		
Equipment	75	
Salaries Expense	5,100	
Utility Expense	300	
Total	$35,715	$35,715

Total revenues are $10,240, while total expenses are $5,575. Total expenses are subtracted from total revenues to get a net income of $4,665. If total expenses were more than total revenues, Printing Plus would have a net loss rather than a net income. This net income figure is used to prepare the statement of retained earnings.

CONCEPTS IN PRACTICE

The Importance of Accurate Financial Statements

Financial statements give a glimpse into the operations of a company, and investors, lenders, owners, and others rely on the accuracy of this information when making future investing, lending, and growth decisions. When one of these statements is inaccurate, the financial implications are great.

For example, Celadon Group misreported revenues over the span of three years and elevated earnings during those years. The total overreported income was approximately $200–$250 million. This gross misreporting misled investors and led to the removal of Celadon Group from the New York Stock Exchange. Not only did this negatively impact Celadon Group's stock price and lead to criminal investigations, but investors and lenders were left to wonder what might happen to their investment.

That is why it is so important to go through the detailed accounting process to reduce errors early on and hopefully prevent misinformation from reaching financial statements. The business must have strong internal controls and best practices to ensure the information is presented fairly.[3]

Statement of Retained Earnings

The statement of retained earnings (which is often a component of the statement of stockholders' equity) shows how the equity (or value) of the organization has changed over a period of time. The statement of retained earnings is prepared second to determine the ending retained earnings balance for the period. The statement of retained earnings is prepared before the balance sheet because the ending retained earnings amount is a required element of the balance sheet. The following is the Statement of Retained Earnings for Printing Plus.

PRINTING PLUS Statement of Retained Earnings For Month Ended January 31, 2019	
Beginning Retained Earnings (Jan 1)	$
Net Income	4,665
	4,665
– Dividends	100
Ending Retained Earnings (Jan 31)	$4,565

Net income information is taken from the income statement, and dividends information is taken from the adjusted trial balance as follows.

3 James Jaillet. "Celadon under Criminal Investigation over Financial Statements." *Commercial Carrier Journal*. July 25, 2018. https://www.ccjdigital.com/200520-2/

PRINTING PLUS Income Statement For Month Ended January 31, 2019		
Revenues		
Interest Revenue	$ 140	
Service Revenue	10,100	
Total Revenues		$10,240
Expenses		
Supplies Expense	100	
Depreciation Expense Equipment	75	
Salaries Expense	5,100	
Utility Expense	300	
Total Expenses		5,575
Net Income		$ 4,665

PRINTING PLUS Statement of Retained Earnings For Month Ended January 31, 2019	
Beginning Retained Earnings (Jan 1)	$
Net Income	4,665
	4,665
– Dividends	100
Ending Retained Earnings (Jan 31)	$4,565

PRINTING PLUS
Adjusted Trial Balance
January 31, 2019

Account	Debit	Credit
Cash	$24,800	
Accounts Receivable	1,200	
Interest Receivable	140	
Supplies	400	
Equipment	3,500	
Accumulated Depreciation Equipment		$ 75
Accounts Payable		500
Salaries Payable		1,500
Unearned Revenue		3,400
Common Stock		20,000
Dividends	100	
Interest Revenue		140
Service Revenue		10,100
Supplies Expense	100	
Depreciation Expense Equipment	75	
Salaries Expense	5,100	
Utility Expense	300	
Total	$35,715	$35,715

The statement of retained earnings always leads with beginning retained earnings. Beginning retained earnings carry over from the previous period's ending retained earnings balance. Since this is the first month of business for Printing Plus, there is no beginning retained earnings balance. Notice the net income of $4,665 from the income statement is carried over to the statement of retained earnings. Dividends are taken away from the sum of beginning retained earnings and net income to get the ending retained earnings balance of

$4,565 for January. This ending retained earnings balance is transferred to the balance sheet.

LINK TO LEARNING

Concepts Statements give the Financial Accounting Standards Board (FASB) a guide to creating accounting principles and consider the limitations of financial statement reporting. See the FASB's "Concepts Statements" page (https://openstax.org/l/50FASBConState) to learn more.

Balance Sheet

The balance sheet is the third statement prepared after the statement of retained earnings and lists what the organization owns (*assets*), what it owes (*liabilities*), and what the shareholders control (*equity*) on a specific date. Remember that the balance sheet represents the accounting equation, where assets equal liabilities plus stockholders' equity. The following is the Balance Sheet for Printing Plus.

PRINTING PLUS Balance Sheet January 31, 2019		
Assets		
Cash		$24,800
Accounts Receivable		1,200
Interest Receivable		140
Supplies		400
Equipment	$3,500	
Accumulated Depreciation: Equipment	(75)	3,425
Total Assets		**$29,965**
Liabilities		
Accounts Payable		$ 500
Salaries Payable		1,500
Unearned Revenue		3,400
Total Liabilities		5,400
Stockholders' Equity		
Common Stock		20,000
Ending Retained Earnings		4,565
Total Stockholders' Equity		24,565
Total Liabilities and Stockholders' Equity		**$29,965**

Ending retained earnings information is taken from the statement of retained earnings, and asset, liability, and common stock information is taken from the adjusted trial balance as follows.

PRINTING PLUS Balance Sheet January 31, 2019		
Assets		
Cash		$24,800
Accounts Receivable		1,200
Interest Receivable		140
Supplies		400
Equipment	$3,500	
Accumulated Depreciation Equipment	75	3,425
Total Assets		$29,965
Liabilities		
Accounts Payable		$ 500
Salaries Payable		1,500
Unearned Revenue		3,400
Total Liabilities		5,400
Stockholders' Equity		
Common Stock		20,000
Ending Retained Earnings		4,565
Total Stockholders' Equity		24,565
Total Liabilities and Stockholders' Equity		$29,965

PRINTING PLUS Adjusted Trial Balance January 31, 2019		
Account	**Debit**	**Credit**
Cash	$24,800	
Accounts Receivable	1,200	
Interest Receivable	140	
Supplies	400	
Equipment	3,500	
Acc. Dep: Equip.		$ 75
Accounts Payable		500
Salaries Payable		1,500
Unearned Revenue		3,400
Common Stock		20,000
Dividends	100	
Interest Revenue		140
Service Revenue		10,100
Supplies Expense	100	
Dep. Expense: Equip.	75	
Salaries Expense	5,100	
Utility Expense	300	
Total	$35,715	$35,715

PRINTING PLUS Statement of Retained Earnings For the Month Ended January 31, 2019	
Beginning Retained Earnings (Jan. 1)	$ 0
Net Income	4,665
Dividends	(100)
Ending Retained Earnings (Jan. 31)	$4,565

Looking at the asset section of the balance sheet, Accumulated Depreciation–Equipment is included as a contra asset account to equipment. The accumulated depreciation ($75) is taken away from the original cost of the equipment ($3,500) to show the book value of equipment ($3,425). The accounting equation is balanced, as shown on the balance sheet, because total assets equal $29,965 as do the total liabilities and stockholders' equity.

There is a worksheet approach a company may use to make sure end-of-period adjustments translate to the correct financial statements.

IFRS CONNECTION

Financial Statements

Both US-based companies and those headquartered in other countries produce the same primary financial statements—Income Statement, Balance Sheet, and Statement of Cash Flows. The presentation of these three primary financial statements is largely similar with respect to what should be reported under US GAAP and IFRS, but some interesting differences can arise, especially when presenting the Balance Sheet.

While both US GAAP and IFRS require the same minimum elements that must be reported on the Income Statement, such as revenues, expenses, taxes, and net income, to name a few, publicly traded companies in the United States have further requirements placed by the SEC on the reporting of financial statements. For example, IFRS-based financial statements are only required to report the current period of information and the information for the prior period. US GAAP has no requirement for reporting prior periods, but the SEC requires that companies present one prior period for the Balance Sheet and three prior periods for the Income Statement. Under both IFRS and US GAAP, companies can report more than the minimum requirements.

Presentation differences are most noticeable between the two forms of GAAP in the Balance Sheet. Under US GAAP there is no specific requirement on how accounts should be presented. However, the SEC requires that companies present their Balance Sheet information in liquidity order, which means current assets listed first with cash being the first account presented, as it is a company's most liquid account. Liquidity refers to how easily an item can be converted to cash. IFRS requires that accounts be classified into current and noncurrent categories for both assets and liabilities, but no specific presentation format is required. Thus, for US companies, the first category always seen on a Balance Sheet is Current Assets, and the first account balance reported is cash. This is not always the case under IFRS. While many Balance Sheets of international companies will be presented in the same manner as those of a US company, the lack of a required format means that a company can present noncurrent assets first, followed by current assets. The accounts of a Balance Sheet using IFRS might appear as shown here.

INTERNATIONAL COMPANY Balance Sheet December 31, 2020		
Assets		
Noncurrent Assets		
Buildings	$1,500,000	
Equipment	800,000	
Total Noncurrent Assets		$2,300,000
Current Assets		
Investments	$ 100,000	
Inventory	500,000	
Accounts Receivable	400,000	
Cash	200,000	
Total Current Assets		1,200,000
Total Assets		$3,500,000
Share Equity and Liabilities		
Share Equity		
Share Capital	$ 550,000	
Retained Earnings	750,000	
Total Share Equity		$1,300,000
Long-term Liabilities		
Pensions	$ 875,000	
Note Payable	$ 225,000	
Total Long-term Liabilities		1,200,000
Current Liabilities		
Short-term Note Payable	$ 650,000	
Accounts Payable	$ 350,000	
Total Current Liabilities		1,000,000
Total Share Equity and Liabilities		$3,500,000

Review the annual report of Stora Enso (https://openstax.org/l/50StoraEnso2017) which is an international company that utilizes the illustrated format in presenting its Balance Sheet, also called the Statement of Financial Position. The Balance Sheet is found on page 31 of the report.

Some of the biggest differences that occur on financial statements prepared under US GAAP versus IFRS relate primarily to measurement or timing issues: in other words, how a transaction is valued and when it is recorded.

Ten-Column Worksheets

The **10-column worksheet** is an all-in-one spreadsheet showing the transition of account information from the trial balance through the financial statements. Accountants use the 10-column worksheet to help calculate end-of-period adjustments. Using a 10-column worksheet is an optional step companies may use in their accounting process.

Here is a picture of a 10-column worksheet for Printing Plus.

PRINTING PLUS										
10-Column Worksheet										
For the Month Ended January, 2019										
Account Name	Trial Balance		Adjustments		Adjusted Trial Balance		Income Statement		Balance Sheet	
	Debit	Credit	Debit	Credit	Debit	Credit	Debit	Credit	Debit	Credit
Cash	24,800				24,800				24,800	
Accounts Receivable	1,200				1,200				1,200	
Interest Receivable			140		140				140	
Supplies	500			100	400				400	
Equipment	3,500				3,500				3,500	
Accumulated Depreciation: Equipment				75		75				75
Accounts Payable		500				500				500
Salaries Payable				1,500		1,500				1,500
Unearned Revenue		4,000	600			3,400				3,400
Common Stock		20,000				20,000				20,000
Dividends	100				100				100	
Interest Revenue				140		140		140		
Service Revenue		9,500		600		10,100		10,100		
Supplies Expense			100		100		100			
Depreciation Expense: Equipment			75		75		75			
Salaries Expense	3,600		1,500		5,100		5,100			
Utility Expense	300				300		300			
Totals	34,000	34,000	2,415	2,415	35,715	35,715	5,575	10,240	30,140	25,475
Net Income							4,665			4,665
							10,240	10,240	30,140	30,140

There are five sets of columns, each set having a column for debit and credit, for a total of 10 columns. The five column sets are the trial balance, adjustments, adjusted trial balance, income statement, and the balance sheet. After a company posts its day-to-day journal entries, it can begin transferring that information to the trial balance columns of the 10-column worksheet.

PRINTING PLUS		
10-Column Worksheet		
For the Month Ended January, 2019		
Account Name	**Trial Balance**	
	Debit	**Credit**
Cash	24,800	
Accounts Receivable	1,200	
Interest Receivable		
Supplies	500	
Equipment	3,500	
Accumulated Depreciation: Equipment		
Accounts Payable		500
Salaries Payable		
Unearned Revenue		4,000
Common Stock		20,000
Dividends	100	
Interest Revenue		
Service Revenue		9,500
Supplies Expense		
Depreciation Expense: Equipment		
Salaries Expense	3,600	
Utility Expense	300	
Totals	34,000	34,000
Net Income		

The trial balance information for Printing Plus is shown previously. Notice that the debit and credit columns both equal $34,000. If we go back and look at the trial balance for Printing Plus, we see that the trial balance shows debits and credits equal to $34,000.

PRINTING PLUS Unadjusted Trial Balance January 31, 2019		
Account	**Debit**	**Credit**
Cash	$24,800	
Accounts Receivable	1,200	
Supplies	500	
Equipment	3,500	
Accounts Payable		$ 500
Unearned Revenue		4,000
Common Stock		20,000
Dividends	100	
Service Revenue		9,500
Salaries Expense	3,600	
Utility Expense	300	
Total	$34,000	$34,000

Once the trial balance information is on the worksheet, the next step is to fill in the adjusting information from the posted adjusted journal entries.

PRINTING PLUS				
10-Column Worksheet				
For the Month Ended January, 2019				
Account Name	Trial Balance		Adjustments	
	Debit	Credit	Debit	Credit
Cash	24,800			
Accounts Receivable	1,200			
Interest Receivable			140	
Supplies	500			100
Equipment	3,500			
Accumulated Depreciation: Equipment				75
Accounts Payable		500		
Salaries Payable				1,500
Unearned Revenue		4,000	600	
Common Stock		20,000		
Dividends	100			
Interest Revenue				140
Service Revenue		9,500		600
Supplies Expense			100	
Depreciation Expense: Equipment			75	
Salaries Expense	3,600		1,500	
Utility Expense	300			
Totals	34,000	34,000	2,415	2,415
Net Income				

The adjustments total of $2,415 balances in the debit and credit columns.

The next step is to record information in the adjusted trial balance columns.

PRINTING PLUS						
10-Column Worksheet						
For the Month Ended January, 2019						
Account Name	Trial Balance		Adjustments		Adjusted Trial Balance	
	Debit	Credit	Debit	Credit	Debit	Credit
Cash	24,800				24,800	
Accounts Receivable	1,200				1,200	
Interest Receivable			140		140	
Supplies	500			100	400	
Equipment	3,500				3,500	
Accumulated Depreciation: Equipment				75		75
Accounts Payable		500				500
Salaries Payable				1,500		1,500
Unearned Revenue		4,000	600			3,400
Common Stock		20,000				20,000
Dividends	100				100	
Interest Revenue				140		140
Service Revenue		9,500		600		10,100
Supplies Expense			100		100	
Depreciation Expense: Equipment			75		75	
Salaries Expense	3,600		1,500		5,100	
Utility Expense	300				300	
Totals	34,000	34,000	2,415	2,415	35,715	35,715
Net Income						

To get the numbers in these columns, you take the number in the trial balance column and add or subtract any number found in the adjustment column. For example, Cash shows an unadjusted balance of $24,800. There is no adjustment in the adjustment columns, so the Cash balance from the unadjusted balance column is transferred over to the adjusted trial balance columns at $24,800. Interest Receivable did not exist in the trial balance information, so the balance in the adjustment column of $140 is transferred over to the adjusted trial balance column.

Unearned revenue had a credit balance of $4,000 in the trial balance column, and a debit adjustment of $600 in the adjustment column. Remember that adding debits and credits is like adding positive and negative numbers. This means the $600 debit is subtracted from the $4,000 credit to get a credit balance of $3,400 that is translated to the adjusted trial balance column.

Service Revenue had a $9,500 credit balance in the trial balance column, and a $600 credit balance in the Adjustments column. To get the $10,100 credit balance in the adjusted trial balance column requires adding together both credits in the trial balance and adjustment columns (9,500 + 600). You will do the same process for all accounts. Once all accounts have balances in the adjusted trial balance columns, add the debits and credits to make sure they are equal. In the case of Printing Plus, the balances equal $35,715. If you check the adjusted trial balance for Printing Plus, you will see the same equal balance is present.

PRINTING PLUS Adjusted Trial Balance January 31, 2019		
Account	**Debit**	**Credit**
Cash	$24,800	
Accounts Receivable	1,200	
Interest Receivable	140	
Supplies	400	
Equipment	3,500	
Accumulated Depreciation: Equipment		$ 75
Accounts Payable		500
Salaries Payable		1,500
Unearned Revenue		3,400
Common Stock		20,000
Dividends	100	
Interest Revenue		140
Service Revenue		10,100
Supplies Expense	100	
Depreciation Expense: Equipment	75	
Salaries Expense	5,100	
Utility Expense	300	
Total	$35,715	$35,715

Next you will take all of the figures in the adjusted trial balance columns and carry them over to *either* the income statement columns or the balance sheet columns.

YOUR TURN

Income Statement and Balance Sheet

MAGNIFICENT LANDSCAPING SERVICE										
Worksheet										
April 30, 2018										
Account Name	Trial Balance		Adjustments		Adjusted Trial		Income Statement		Balance Sheet	
	Debit	Credit	Debit	Credit	Debit	Credit	Debit	Credit	Debit	Credit
Cash	2,950				2,950					
Accounts Receivable	575				575					
Office Supplies	85			(c) 45	40					
Prepaid Insurance	240				240					
Equipment	2,540			(b) 40	2,500					
Accounts Payable		28				28				
Unearned Lawn Mowing Revenue		200	(d) 100			100				
Common Stock		5,000				5,000				
Dividends	1,000				1,000					
Lawn Mowing Revenue		2,250		(d) 100		2,350				
Gas Expense	53				53					
Advertising Expense	35				35					
	7,478	7,478								
Depreciation Expense: Equipment			(a) 35		35					
Accumulated Depreciating: Equipment				(a) 35		35				
Supplies Expense			(b) 40 (c) 45		85					
Salaries Expense			(e) 420		420					
Salaries Payable				(e) 420		420				
			640	640	7,933	7,933				

Take a couple of minutes and fill in the income statement and balance sheet columns. Total them when you are done. Do not panic when they do not balance. They will not balance at this time.

Solution

MAGNIFICENT LANDSCAPING SERVICE										
Worksheet										
April 30, 2018										
Account Name	**Trial Balance**		**Adjustments**		**Adjusted Trial**		**Income Statement**		**Balance Sheet**	
	Debit	**Credit**	**Debit**	**Credit**	**Debit**	**Credit**	**Debit**	**Credit**	**Debit**	**Credit**
Cash	2,950				2,950				2,950	
Accounts Receivable	575				575				575	
Office Supplies	85			(c) 45	40				40	
Prepaid Insurance	240				240				240	
Equipment	2,540			(b) 40	2,500				2,500	
Accounts Payable		28				28				28
Unearned Lawn Mowing Revenue		200	(d) 100			100				100
Common Stock		5,000				5,000				5,000
Dividends	1,000				1,000				1,000	
Lawn Mowing Revenue		2,250		(d) 100		2,350		2,350		
Gas Expense	53				53		53			
Advertising Expense	35				35		35			
	7,478	7,478								
Depreciation Expense: Equipment			(a) 35		35		35			
Accumulated Depreciation: Equipment				(a) 35		35				35
Supplies Expense			(b) 40 (c) 45		85		85			
Salaries Expense			(e) 420		420		420			
Salaries Payable				(e) 420		420				420
			640	640	7,933	7,933	628	2,350	7,305	5,583

Every other account title has been highlighted to help your eyes focus better while checking your work.

Looking at the income statement columns, we see that all revenue and expense accounts are listed in either the debit or credit column. This is a reminder that the income statement itself does not organize information into debits and credits, but we do use this presentation on a 10-column worksheet.

PRINTING PLUS								
10-column Worksheet								
For the Month Ended January, 2019								
Account Name	**Trial Balance**		**Adjustments**		**Adjusted Trial Balance**		**Income Statement**	
	Debit	**Credit**	**Debit**	**Credit**	**Debit**	**Credit**	**Debit**	**Credit**
Cash	24,800				24,800			
Accounts Receivable	1,200				1,200			
Interest Receivable			140		140			
Supplies	500			100	400			
Equipment	3,500				3,500			
Accumulated Depreciation: Equipment				75		75		
Accounts Payable		500				500		
Salaries Payable				1,500		1,500		
Unearned Revenue		4,000	600			3,400		
Common Stock		20,000				20,000		
Dividends	100				100			
Interest Revenue				140		140		140
Service Revenue		9,500		600		10,100		10,100
Supplies Expense			100		100		100	
Depreciation Expense: Equipment			75		75		75	
Salaries Expense	3,600		1,500		5,100		5,100	
Utility Expense	300				300		300	
Totals	34,000	34,000	2,415	2,415	35,715	35,715	5,575	10,240
Net Income							4,665	
							10,240	10,240

You will notice that when debit and credit income statement columns are totaled, the balances are not the same. The debit balance equals $5,575, and the credit balance equals $10,240. Why do they not balance?

If the debit and credit columns equal each other, it means the expenses equal the revenues. This would happen if a company broke even, meaning the company did not make or lose any money. If there is a difference between the two numbers, that difference is the amount of net income, or net loss, the company has earned.

In the Printing Plus case, the credit side is the higher figure at $10,240. The credit side represents revenues. This means revenues exceed expenses, thus giving the company a net income. If the debit column were larger, this would mean the expenses were larger than revenues, leading to a net loss. You want to calculate the net income and enter it onto the worksheet. The $4,665 net income is found by taking the credit of $10,240 and subtracting the debit of $5,575. When entering net income, it should be written in the column with the lower total. In this instance, that would be the debit side. You then add together the $5,575 and $4,665 to get a total of $10,240. This balances the two columns for the income statement. If you review the income statement, you see that net income is in fact $4,665.

PRINTING PLUS Income Statement For the Month Ended January 31, 2019		
Revenues		
Interest Revenue	$ 140	
Service Revenue	10,100	
Total Revenues		$10,240
Expenses		
Supplies Expense	100	
Depreciation Expense: Equip.	75	
Salaries Expense	5,100	
Utility Expense	300	
Total Expenses		5,575
Net Income		$ 4,665

PRINTING PLUS										
10-Column Worksheet										
For the Month Ended January, 2019										
Account Name	**Trial Balance**		**Adjustments**		**Adjusted Trial Balance**		**Income Statement**		**Balance Sheet**	
	Debit	**Credit**	**Debit**	**Credit**	**Debit**	**Credit**	**Debit**	**Credit**	**Debit**	**Credit**
Cash	24,800				24,800				24,800	
Accounts Receivable	1,200				1,200				1,200	
Interest Receivable			140		140				140	
Supplies	500			100	400				400	
Equipment	3,500				3,500				3,500	
Acc. Dep: Equip.				75		75				75
Accounts Payable		500				500				500
Salaries Payable				1,500		1,500				1,500
Unearned Revenue		4,000	600			3,400				3,400
Common Stock		20,000				20,000				20,000
Dividends	100				100				100	
Interest Revenue				140		140		140		
Service Revenue		9,500		600		10,100		10,100		
Supplies Expense			100		100		100			
Dep. Exp: Equip.			75		75		75			
Salaries Expense	3,600		1,500		5,100		5,100			
Utility Expense	300				300		300			
Totals	34,000	34,000	2,415	2,415	35,715	35,715	5,575	10,240	30,140	25,475
Net Income							4,665			4,665
							10,240	10,240	30,140	30,140

We now consider the last two columns for the balance sheet. In these columns we record all asset, liability, and equity accounts.

When adding the total debits and credits, you notice they do not balance. The debit column equals $30,140, and the credit column equals $25,475. How do we get the columns to balance?

Treat the income statement and balance sheet columns like a double-entry accounting system, where if you have a debit on the income statement side, you must have a credit equaling the same amount on the credit side. In this case we added a debit of $4,665 to the income statement column. This means we must add a credit of $4,665 to the balance sheet column. Once we add the $4,665 to the credit side of the balance sheet column, the two columns equal $30,140.

You may notice that dividends are included in our 10-column worksheet balance sheet columns even though this account is not included on a balance sheet. So why is it included here? There is actually a very good reason we put dividends in the balance sheet columns.

When you prepare a balance sheet, you must first have the most updated retained earnings balance. To get that balance, you take the beginning retained earnings balance + net income – dividends. If you look at the worksheet for Printing Plus, you will notice there is no retained earnings account. That is because they just started business this month and have no beginning retained earnings balance.

If you look in the balance sheet columns, we do have the new, up-to-date retained earnings, but it is spread out through two numbers. You have the dividends balance of $100 and net income of $4,665. If you combine these two individual numbers ($4,665 – $100), you will have your updated retained earnings balance of $4,565, as seen on the statement of retained earnings.

PRINTING PLUS Statement of Retained Earnings For the Month Ended January 31, 2019	
Beginning Retained Earnings (Jan. 1)	$ 0
Net Income	4,665
Dividends	(100)
Ending Retained Earnings (Jan. 31)	$4,565

You will not see a similarity between the 10-column worksheet and the balance sheet, because the 10-column worksheet is categorizing all accounts by the type of balance they have, debit or credit. This leads to a final balance of $30,140.

The balance sheet is classifying the accounts by type of accounts, assets and contra assets, liabilities, and equity. This leads to a final balance of $29,965. Even though they are the same numbers in the accounts, the totals on the worksheet and the totals on the balance sheet will be different because of the different presentation methods.

LINK TO LEARNING

Publicly traded companies release their financial statements quarterly for open viewing by the general public, which can usually be viewed on their websites. One such company is Alphabet, Inc. (trade name Google). Take a look at Alphabet's quarter ended March 31, 2018, financial statements (https://openstax.org/l/50AlphaMar2018) from the SEC Form 10-Q.

YOUR TURN

Frank's Net Income and Loss

What amount of net income/loss does Frank have?

FRANK INVESTMENT ADVISERS

Work Sheet

For the Month Ended December 31, 2016

Account Name	Trial Balance		Adjustments		Adjusted Trial		Income Statement		Balance Sheet	
	Debit	Credit	Debit	Credit	Debit	Credit	Debit	Credit	Debit	Credit
Cash	28,000				28,000				28,000	
Accounts Receivable	46,000				46,000				46,000	
Office Supplies	5,000			(b) 1,000	4,000				4,000	
Equipment	28,000				28,000				28,000	
Accumulated Depreciation-Equipment		14,000		(c) 2,800		16,800				16,800
Accounts Payable		16,000				16,000				16,000
Salaries Payable				(d) 2,000		2,000				2,000
Uneamed Revenue		2,000	(a) 100			1,900				1,900
Notes Payable (Long Term)		23,000				23,000				23,000
Common Stock		15,000				15,000				15,000
Retained Earnings		52,000				52,000				52,000
Dividends	20,000				20,000				20,000	
Service Revenue		55,000		(a) 100		55,100		55,100		
Insurance Expense	3,000				3,000		3,000			
Salaries Expense	35,000		(d) 2,000		37,000		37,000			
Supplies Expense			(b) 1,000		1,000		1,000			
Interest Expense	4,000				4,000		4,000			
Rent Expense	8,000				8,000		8,000			
Deprecation Expense-Equipment			(c) 2,800		2,800		2,800			
	177,000	177,000	5,900	5,900	181,800	181,800	55,800	55,100	126,000	126,700

Solution

FRANK INVESTMENT ADVISERS										
Worksheet										
For the Month Ended December 31, 2016										
Account Name	**Trial Balance**		**Adjustments**		**Adjusted Trial Balance**		**Income Statement**		**Balance Sheet**	
	Debit	**Credit**	**Debit**	**Credit**	**Debit**	**Credit**	**Debit**	**Credit**	**Debit**	**Credit**
Cash	24,800				28,000				24,800	
Accounts Receivable	46,000				46,000				46,000	
Office Supplies	5,000			1,000 b	4,000				4,000	
Equipment	28,000				28,000				28,000	
Accumulated Depreciation: Equipment		14,000		2,800 c		16,800				16,800
Accounts Payable		16,000				16,000				16,000
Salaries Payable				2,000 d		2,000				2,000
Unearned Revenue		2,000	a 100			1,900				1,900
Notes Payable (long term)		23,000				23,000				23,000
Common Stock		15,000				15,000				15,000
Retained Earnings		52,000				52,000				52,000
Dividends	20,000				20,000				20,000	
Service Revenue		55,000		100 a		55,100		55,100		
Insurance Expense	3,000				3,000		3,000			
Salaries Expense	35,000		d 2,000		37,000		37,000			
Supplies Expense			b 1,000		1,000		1,000			
Interest Expense	4,000				4,000		4,000			
Rent Expense	8,000				8,000		8,000			
Depreciation Expense: Equipment			c 2,800		2,800		2,800			
	177,000	177,000	5,900	5,900	181,800	181,800	55,800	55,100	126,000	126,700
Net Loss								**700**		
							55,800	55,800		

In Completing the Accounting Cycle, we continue our discussion of the accounting cycle, completing the last steps of journalizing and posting closing entries and preparing a post-closing trial balance.

Key Terms

10-column worksheet all-in-one spreadsheet showing the transition of account information from the trial balance through the financial statements

accounting period breaks down company financial information into specific time spans and can cover a month, quarter, half-year, or full year

accrual type of adjusting entry that accumulates during a period, where an amount was previously unrecorded

accrued expense expense incurred in a period but not yet recorded, and no money has been paid

accrued revenue revenue earned in a period but not yet recorded, and no money has been collected

adjusted trial balance list of all accounts in the general ledger, including adjusting entries, which have nonzero balances

adjusting entries update accounting records at the end of a period for any transactions that have not yet been recorded

book value difference between the asset's value (cost) and accumulated depreciation; also, value at which assets or liabilities are recorded in a company's financial statements

calendar year reports financial data from January 1 to December 31 of a specific year

contra account account paired with another account type that has an opposite normal balance to the paired account; reduces or increases the balance in the paired account at the end of a period

deferral prepaid expense and revenue accounts that have delayed recognition until they have been used or earned

fiscal year twelve-month reporting cycle that can begin in any month, and records financial data for that twelve-month consecutive period

interim period any reporting period shorter than a full year (fiscal or calendar)

modified accrual accounting commonly used in governmental accounting and combines accrual basis and cash basis accounting

tax basis accounting establishes the tax effects of transactions in determining the tax liability of an organization

useful life time period over which an asset cost is allocated

Summary

4.1 Explain the Concepts and Guidelines Affecting Adjusting Entries

- The next three steps in the accounting cycle are adjusting entries (journalizing and posting), preparing an adjusted trial balance, and preparing the financial statements. These steps consider end-of-period transactions and their impact on financial statements.
- Accrual basis accounting is used by US GAAP or IFRS-governed companies, and it requires revenues and expenses to be recorded in the accounting period in which they occur, not necessarily where an associated cash event happened. This is unlike cash basis accounting that will delay reporting revenues and expenses until a cash event occurs.
- Companies need timely and consistent financial information presented for users to consider in their decision-making. Accounting periods help companies do this by breaking down information into months, quarters, half-years, and full years.
- A calendar year considers financial information for a company for the time period of January 1 to December 31 on a specific year. A fiscal year is any twelve-month reporting cycle not beginning on

January 1 and ending on December 31.

- An interim period is any reporting period that does not cover a full year. This can be useful when needing timely information for users making financial decisions.

4.2 Discuss the Adjustment Process and Illustrate Common Types of Adjusting Entries

- Incorrect balances: Incorrect balances on the unadjusted trial balance occur because not every transaction produces an original source document that will alert the bookkeeper it is time to make an entry. It is not that the accountant made an error, it means an adjustment is required to correct the balance.
- Need for adjustments: Some account adjustments are needed to update records that may not have original source documents or those that do not reflect change on a daily basis. The revenue recognition principle, expense recognition principle, and time period assumption all further the need for adjusting entries because they require revenue and expense reporting occur when earned and incurred in a current period.
- Prepaid expenses: Prepaid expenses are assets paid for before their use. When they are used, this asset's value is reduced and an expense is recognized. Some examples include supplies, insurance, and depreciation.
- Unearned revenues: These are customer advanced payments for product or services yet to be provided. When the company provides the product or service, revenue is then recognized.
- Accrued revenues: Accrued revenues are revenues earned in a period but have yet to be recorded and no money has been collected. Accrued revenues are updated at the end of the period to recognize revenue and money owed to the company.
- Accrued expenses: Accrued expenses are incurred in a period but have yet to be recorded and no money has been paid. Accrued expenses are updated to reflect the expense and the company's liability.

4.3 Record and Post the Common Types of Adjusting Entries

- Rules for adjusting entries: The rules for recording adjusting entries are as follows: every adjusting entry will have one income statement account and one balance sheet account, cash will never be in an adjusting entry, and the adjusting entry records the change in amount that occurred during the period.
- Posting adjusting entries: Posting adjusting entries is the same process as posting general journal entries. The additional adjustments may add accounts to the end of the period or may change account balances from the earlier journal entry step in the accounting cycle.

4.4 Use the Ledger Balances to Prepare an Adjusted Trial Balance

- Adjusted trial balance: The adjusted trial balance lists all accounts in the general ledger, including adjusting entries, which have nonzero balances. This trial balance is an important step in the accounting process because it helps identify any computational errors throughout the first five steps in the cycle.

4.5 Prepare Financial Statements Using the Adjusted Trial Balance

- Income Statement: The income statement shows the net income or loss as a result of revenue and expense activities occurring in a period.
- Statement of Retained Earnings: The statement of retained earnings shows the effects of net income (loss) and dividends on the earnings the company maintains.
- Balance Sheet: The balance sheet visually represents the accounting equation, showing that assets balance with liabilities and equity.
- 10-column worksheet: The 10-column worksheet organizes data from the trial balance all the way through the financial statements.

Multiple Choice

1. LO 4.1 Which of the following is any reporting period shorter than a full year (fiscal or calendar) and can encompass monthly, quarterly, or half-year statements?
   A. fiscal year
   B. interim period
   C. calendar year
   D. fixed year

2. LO 4.1 Which of the following is the federal, independent agency that provides oversight of public companies to maintain fair representation of company financial activities for investors to make informed decisions?
   A. IRS (Internal Revenue Service)
   B. SEC (Securities and Exchange Commission)
   C. FASB (Financial Accounting Standards Board)
   D. FDIC (Federal Deposit Insurance Corporation)

3. LO 4.1 Revenues and expenses must be recorded in the accounting period in which they were earned or incurred, no matter when cash receipts or outlays occur under which of the following accounting methods?
   A. accrual basis accounting
   B. cash basis accounting
   C. tax basis accounting
   D. revenue basis accounting

4. LO 4.1 Which of the following breaks down company financial information into specific time spans, and can cover a month, quarter, half-year, or full year?
   A. accounting period
   B. yearly period
   C. monthly period
   D. fiscal period

5. LO 4.1 Which of the following is a twelve-month reporting cycle that can begin in any month, except January 1, and records financial data for that twelve-month consecutive period?
   A. fixed year
   B. interim period
   C. calendar year
   D. fiscal year

6. LO 4.2 Which type of adjustment occurs when cash is either collected or paid, but the related income or expense is *not* reportable in the current period?
   A. accrual
   B. deferral
   C. estimate
   D. cull

7. LO 4.2 Which type of adjustment occurs when cash *is not* collected or paid, but the related income or expense *is* reportable in the current period?
   A. accrual
   B. deferral
   C. estimate
   D. cull

8. LO 4.2 If an adjustment includes an entry to a payable or receivable account, which type of adjustment is it?
   A. accrual
   B. deferral
   C. estimate
   D. cull

9. LO 4.2 If an adjustment includes an entry to Accumulated Depreciation, which type of adjustment is it?
   A. accrual
   B. deferral
   C. estimate
   D. cull

10. LO 4.2 Rent collected in advance is an example of which of the following?
   A. accrued expense
   B. accrued revenue
   C. deferred expense (prepaid expense)
   D. deferred revenue (unearned revenue)

11. LO 4.2 Rent paid in advance is an example of which of the following?
   A. accrued expense
   B. accrued revenue
   C. deferred expense (prepaid expense)
   D. deferred revenue (unearned revenue)

12. LO 4.2 Salaries owed but *not* yet paid is an example of which of the following?
   A. accrued expense
   B. accrued revenue
   C. deferred expense (prepaid expense)
   D. deferred revenue (unearned revenue)

13. LO 4.2 Revenue earned but *not* yet collected is an example of which of the following?
   A. accrued expense
   B. accrued revenue
   C. deferred expense (prepaid expense)
   D. deferred revenue (unearned revenue)

14. LO 4.3 What adjusting journal entry is needed to record depreciation expense for the period?
   A. a debit to Depreciation Expense; a credit to Cash
   B. a debit to Accumulated Depreciation; a credit to Depreciation Expense
   C. a debit to Depreciation Expense; a credit to Accumulated Depreciation
   D. a debit to Accumulated Depreciation; a credit to Cash

15. LO 4.3 Which of these transactions requires an adjusting entry (debit) to Unearned Revenue?

A. revenue earned but not yet collected
B. revenue collected but not yet earned
C. revenue earned before being collected, when it is later collected
D. revenue collected before being earned, when it is later earned

16. LO 4.4 What critical purpose does the adjusted trial balance serve?

A. It proves that transactions have been posted correctly
B. It is the source document from which to prepare the financial statements
C. It shows the beginning balances of every account, to be used to start the new year's records
D. It proves that all journal entries have been made correctly.

17. LO 4.4 Which of the following accounts' balance would be a different number on the Balance Sheet than it is on the adjusted trial balance?

A. accumulated depreciation
B. unearned service revenue
C. retained earnings
D. dividends

18. LO 4.5 On which financial statement would the Supplies account appear?

A. Balance Sheet
B. Income Statement
C. Retained Earnings Statement
D. Statement of Cash Flows

19. LO 4.5 On which financial statement would the Dividends account appear?

A. Balance Sheet
B. Income Statement
C. Retained Earnings Statement
D. Statement of Cash Flows

20. LO 4.5 On which financial statement would the Accumulated Depreciation account appear?

A. Balance Sheet
B. Income Statement
C. Retained Earnings Statement
D. Statement of Cash Flows

21. LO 4.5 On which two financial statements would the Retained Earnings account appear?

A. Balance Sheet
B. Income Statement
C. Retained Earnings Statement
D. Statement of Cash Flows

Questions

1. LO 4.1 Describe the revenue recognition principle. Give specifics.

2. LO 4.1 Describe the expense recognition principle (matching principle). Give specifics.

3. LO 4.2 What parts of the accounting cycle require analytical processes, rather than methodical processes? Explain.

4. LO 4.2 Why is the adjusting process needed?

5. LO 4.2 Name two types of adjusting journal entries that are commonly made before preparing financial statements? Explain, with examples.

6. LO 4.2 Are there any accounts that would never have an adjusting entry? Explain.

7. LO 4.2 Why do adjusting entries always include both balance sheet and income statement accounts?

8. LO 4.2 Why are adjusting journal entries needed?

9. LO 4.3 If the Supplies account had an ending balance of $1,200 and the actual count for the remaining supplies was $400 at the end of the period, what adjustment would be needed?

10. LO 4.3 When a company collects cash from customers before performing the contracted service, what is the impact, and how should it be recorded?

11. LO 4.3 If the Prepaid Insurance account had a balance of $12,000, representing one year's policy premium, which was paid on July 1, what entry would be needed to adjust the Prepaid Insurance account at the end of December, before preparing the financial statements?

12. LO 4.3 If adjusting entries include these listed accounts, what other account must be in that entry as well? (A) Depreciation expense; (B) Unearned Service Revenue; (C) Prepaid Insurance; (D) Interest Payable.

13. LO 4.4 What is the difference between the trial balance and the adjusted trial balance?

14. LO 4.4 Why is the adjusted trial balance trusted as a reliable source for building the financial statements?

15. LO 4.5 Indicate on which financial statement the following accounts (from the adjusted trial balance) would appear: (A) Sales Revenue; (B) Unearned Rent Revenue; (C) Prepaid Advertising; (D) Advertising Expense; (E) Dividends; (F) Cash.

Exercise Set A

EA1. LO 4.2 Identify whether each of the following transactions, which are related to revenue recognition, are accrual, deferral, or neither.

A. sold goods to customers on credit
B. collected cash from customer accounts
C. sold goods to customers for cash
D. collected cash in advance for goods to be delivered later

EA2. LO 4.2 Identify whether each of the following transactions, which are related to expense recognition, are accrual, deferral, or neither.

A. paid an expense for the current month
B. prepaid an expense for future months
C. made a payment to reduce accounts payable
D. incurred a current-month expense, to be paid next month

EA3. LO 4.2 Identify which type of adjustment is indicated by these transactions. Choose accrued revenue, accrued expense, deferred revenue, or deferred expense.

A. rent paid in advance for use of property
B. cash received in advance for future services
C. supplies inventory purchased
D. fees earned but not yet collected

EA4. LO 4.2 The following accounts were used to make year-end adjustments. Identify the related account that is associated with this account (the other account in the adjusting entry).

A. Salaries Payable
B. Depreciation Expense
C. Supplies
D. Unearned Rent

EA5. LO 4.2 Reviewing insurance policies revealed that a single policy was purchased on August 1, for one year's coverage, in the amount of $6,000. There was no previous balance in the Prepaid Insurance account at that time. Based on the information provided:

A. Make the December 31 adjusting journal entry to bring the balances to correct.
B. Show the impact that these transactions had.

EA6. LO 4.3 On July 1, a client paid an advance payment (retainer) of $5,000 to cover future legal services. During the period, the company completed $3,500 of the agreed-on services for the client. There was no beginning balance in the Unearned Revenue account for the period. Based on the information provided,

A. Make the December 31 adjusting journal entry to bring the balances to correct.
B. Show the impact that these transactions had.

EA7. LO 4.3 Reviewing payroll records indicates that employee salaries that are due to be paid on January 3 include $3,575 in wages for the last week of December. There was no previous balance in the Salaries Payable account at that time. Based on the information provided, make the December 31 adjusting journal entry to bring the balances to correct.

EA8. LO 4.3 Supplies were purchased on January 1, to be used throughout the year, in the amount of $8,500. On December 31, a physical count revealed that the remaining supplies totaled $1,200. There was no beginning of the year balance in the Supplies account. Based on the information provided:

A. Create journal entries for the original transaction
B. Create journal entries for the December 31 adjustment needed to bring the balances to correct
C. Show the activity, with ending balance

EA9. LO 4.3 Prepare journal entries to record the following business transaction and related adjusting entry.

A. January 12, purchased supplies for cash, to be used all year, $3,850
B. December 31, physical count of remaining supplies, $800

EA10. LO 4.3 Prepare journal entries to record the following adjustments.

A. Insurance that expired this period, $18,000
B. Depreciation on assets, $4,800
C. Salaries earned by employees but unpaid, $1,200

EA11. LO 4.3 Prepare adjusting journal entries, as needed, considering the account balances excerpted from the unadjusted trial balance and the adjustment data.

Unadjusted Trial Balance		
Account Title	**Debit**	**Credit**
Fixed assets	120,000	
Accumulated depreciation		24,000
Prepaid rent	18,000	
Unearned revenue		3,500

A. depreciation on fixed assets, $ 8,500
B. unexpired prepaid rent, $12,500
C. remaining balance of unearned revenue, $555

EA12. LO 4.4 Prepare an adjusted trial balance from the following adjusted account balances (assume accounts have normal balances).

Accounts payable	$ 6,600
Accounts receivable	12,750
Administrative expense	49,150
Cash	28,900
Common stock	15,000
Prepaid insurance	8,800
Service revenue	78,000

EA13. LO 4.4 Prepare an adjusted trial balance from the following account information, considering the adjustment data provided (assume accounts have normal balances).

Accounts payable	$11,700
Accounts receivable	17,100
Administrative expense	54,800
Cash	44,800
Common stock	30,000
Prepaid insurance	16,000
Service revenue	91,000

Adjustments needed:

Salaries due to administrative employees, but unpaid at period end, $2,000

Insurance still unexpired at end of the period, $12,000

EA14. LO 4.5 From the following Company A adjusted trial balance, prepare simple financial statements, as follows:

A. Income Statement
B. Retained Earnings Statement
C. Balance Sheet

Adjusted Trial Balance		
	Debit	**Credit**
Cash	$ 42,000	
Accounts receivable	11,300	
Prepaid insurance	14,800	
Accounts payable		$ 10,900
Salaries payable		14,000
Common stock		25,000
Service revenue		61,000
Administrative expenses	42,800	
	110,900	110,900

Exercise Set B

EB1. LO 4.1 Identify whether each of the following transactions, which are related to revenue recognition, are accrual, deferral, or neither.

A. provided legal services to client, who paid at the time of service
B. received cash for legal services performed last month
C. received cash from clients for future services to be provided
D. provided legal services to client, to be collected next month

EB2. LO 4.1 Identify whether each of the following transactions, which are related to expense recognition, are accrual, deferral, or neither.

A. recorded employee salaries earned, to be paid in future month
B. paid employees for current month salaries
C. paid employee salaries for work performed in a prior month
D. gave an employee an advance on future wages

EB3. LO 4.2 Indicate what impact the following adjustments have on the accounting equation, Assets = Liabilities + Equity (assume normal balances).

		Impact 1	Impact 2
A.	Prepaid Insurance adjusted from $5,000 to $3,600		
B.	Interest Payable adjusted from $5,300 to $6,800		
C.	Prepaid Insurance adjusted from $18,500 to $6,300		
D.	Supplies account balance $500, actual count $220		

Table 4.5

EB4. LO 4.2 What two accounts are affected by the needed adjusting entries?

A. supplies actual counts are lower than account balance
B. employee salaries are due but not paid at year end
C. insurance premiums that were paid in advance have expired

EB5. LO 4.3 Reviewing insurance policies revealed that a single policy was purchased on March 1, for one year's coverage, in the amount of $9,000. There was no previous balance in the Prepaid Insurance account at that time. Based on the information provided,

A. Make the December 31 adjusting journal entry to bring the balances to correct.
B. Show the impact that these transactions had.

EB6. LO 4.3 On September 1, a company received an advance rental payment of $12,000, to cover six months' rent on an office building. There was no beginning balance in the Unearned Rent account for the period. Based on the information provided,

A. Make the December 31 adjusting journal entry to bring the balances to correct.
B. Show the impact that these transactions had.

EB7. LO 4.3 Reviewing payroll records indicates that one-fifth of employee salaries that are due to be paid on the first payday in January, totaling $15,000, are actually for hours worked in December. There was no previous balance in the Salaries Payable account at that time. Based on the information provided, make the December 31 adjusting journal entry to bring the balances to correct.

EB8. LO 4.3 On July 1, a client paid an advance payment (retainer) of $10,000, to cover future legal services. During the period, the company completed $6,200 of the agreed-on services for the client. There was no beginning balance in the Unearned Revenue account for the period. Based on the information provided, make the journal entries needed to bring the balances to correct for:

A. original transaction
B. December 31 adjustment

EB9. LO 4.3 Prepare journal entries to record the business transaction and related adjusting entry for the following:

A. March 1, paid cash for one year premium on insurance contract, $18,000
B. December 31, remaining unexpired balance of insurance, $3,000

EB10. LO 4.3 Prepare journal entries to record the following adjustments:

A. revenue earned but not collected, nor recorded, $14,000
B. revenue earned that had originally been collected in advance, $8,500
C. taxes due but not yet paid, $ 2,750

EB11. LO 4.3 Prepare adjusting journal entries, as needed, considering the account balances excerpted from the unadjusted trial balance and the adjustment data.

Unadjusted Trial Balance		
Account Title	**Debit**	**Credit**
Equipment	66,000	
Accumulated depreciation		22,000
Supplies	6,000	
Salaries payable		3,500

A. amount due for employee salaries, $4,800
B. actual count of supplies inventory, $ 2,300
C. depreciation on equipment, $3,000

EB12. LO 4.4 Prepare an adjusted trial balance from the following adjusted account balances (assume accounts have normal balances).

Accounts payable	$ 22,400
Accounts receivable	45,750
Administrative expense	57,700
Cash	56,500
Common stock	40,000
Prepaid rent	8,750
Revenue	106,300

EB13. LO 4.4 Prepare an adjusted trial balance from the following account information, considering the adjustment data provided (assume accounts have normal balances).

Accounts payable	$10,075
Accounts receivable	15,500
Cash	64,575
Common stock	31,000
Fees earned revenue	82,000
Operating expense	38,000
Supplies	5,000

Adjustments needed:

- Physical count of supplies inventory remaining at end of period, $2,150
- Taxes payable at end of period, $3,850

EB14. LO 4.5 From the following Company B adjusted trial balance, prepare simple financial statements, as follows:

A. Income Statement
B. Retained Earnings Statement
C. Balance Sheet

Adjusted Trial Balance		
	Debit	**Credit**
Cash	$ 77,800	
Accounts receivable	19,500	
Supplies	7,650	
Accounts payable		$ 8,500
Taxes payable		5,350
Common stock		35,000
Fees earned revenue		95,300
Operating expense	39,200	
	144,150	144,150

Problem Set A

PA1. LO 4.1 Identify whether each of the following transactions, which are related to revenue recognition, are accrual, deferral, or neither.

A. earn now, collect now
B. earn now, collect later
C. earn later, collect now

PA2. LO 4.1 To demonstrate the difference between cash account activity and accrual basis profits (net income), note the amount each transaction affects cash *and* the amount each transaction affects net income.

A. paid balance due for accounts payable $6,900
B. charged clients for legal services provided $5,200
C. purchased supplies on account $1,750
D. collected legal service fees from clients for current month $3,700
E. issued stock in exchange for a note payable $10,000

PA3. LO 4.2 Identify which type of adjustment is indicated by these transactions. Choose accrued revenue, accrued expense, deferred revenue, deferred expense, or estimate.

A. utilities owed but not paid
B. cash received in advance for future services
C. supplies inventory purchased
D. fees earned but not yet collected
E. depreciation expense recorded
F. insurance paid for future periods

PA4. LO 4.2 Identify which type of adjustment is associated with this account, and what is the other account in the adjustment? Choose accrued revenue, accrued expense, deferred revenue, or deferred expense.

A. accounts receivable
B. interest payable
C. prepaid insurance
D. unearned rent

PA5. LO 4.2 Indicate what impact the following adjustments have on the accounting equation, Assets = Liabilities + Equity (assume normal balances).

		Impact 1	Impact 2
A.	Unearned Fees adjusted from $7,000 to $5,000		
B.	Recorded depreciation expense of $12,000		
C.	Prepaid Insurance adjusted from $18,500 to $6,300		
D.	Supplies account balance $500, actual count $220		

Table 4.6

PA6. LO 4.2 What two accounts are affected by each of these adjustments?

A. billed customers for services provided
B. adjusted prepaid insurance to correct
C. recorded depreciation expense
D. recorded unpaid utility bill
E. adjusted supplies inventory to correct

PA7. LO 4.3 Using the following information:

A. make the December 31 adjusting journal entry for depreciation
B. determine the net book value (NBV) of the asset on December 31

- Cost of asset, $250,000
- Accumulated depreciation, beginning of year, $80,000
- Current year depreciation, $25,000

PA8. LO 4.3 Use the following account T-balances (assume normal balances) and correct balance information to make the December 31 adjusting journal entries.

	T-Account Balance	Correct Balance
Prepaid insurance	$26,000	$14,500
Salaries payable	$5,500	$6,200
Unearned rental revenue	$8,000	$1,600

PA9. LO 4.3 Use the following account T-balances (assume normal balances) and correct balance information to make the December 31 adjusting journal entries.

	T-Account Balance	Correct Balance
Unearned service revenue	24,000	10,500
Supplies	8,500	2,600
Interest payable	2,400	2,000

PA10. LO 4.3 Prepare journal entries to record the following transactions. Create a T-account for Interest Payable, post any entries that affect the account, and tally the ending balance for the account (assume Interest Payable beginning balance of $2,500).

A. March 1, paid interest due on note, $2,500

B. December 31, interest accrued on note payable, $4,250

PA11. LO 4.3 Prepare journal entries to record the following transactions. Create a T-account for Prepaid Insurance, post any entries that affect the account, and tally the ending balance for the account (assume Prepaid Insurance beginning balance of $9,000).

A. April 1, paid cash for one-year policy, $18,000

B. December 31, unexpired premiums, $4,500

PA12. LO 4.3 Determine the amount of cash expended for Salaries during the month, based on the entries in the following accounts (assume 0 beginning balances).

Account	Debit	Credit
Salaries Expense		
	55,000	
Balance	55,000	
Salaries Payable		
		6,000
Balance		6,000

PA13. LO 4.3 Prepare adjusting journal entries, as needed, considering the account balances excerpted from the unadjusted trial balance and the adjustment data.

Unadjusted Trial Balance		
	Debit	**Credit**
Property plant and equipment	320,000	
Accumulated depreciation		89,500
Prepaid insurance	24,000	
Supplies	7,500	
Unearned service revenue		3,000

A. supplies actual count at year end, $6,500

B. remaining unexpired insurance, $6,000

C. remaining unearned service revenue, $1,200

D. salaries owed to employees, $2,400

E. depreciation on property plant and equipment, $18,000

PA14. LO 4.4 Prepare an adjusted trial balance from the adjusted account balances; solve for the one missing account balance: Cash (assume accounts have normal balances).

Accounts payable	$19,000
Accounts receivable	23,760
Cash	?
Common stock	38,000
Dividends	9,000
Equipment	20,000
Prepaid insurance	21,466
Land	45,000
Notes payable	61,000
Retained earnings	18,815
Insurance expense	19,689
Service revenue	90,550
Supplies	5,250
Salaries expense	51,000

PA15. LO 4.4 Prepare an adjusted trial balance from the following account information, considering the adjustment data provided (assume accounts have normal balances). Equipment was recently purchased, so there is neither depreciation expense nor accumulated depreciation.

Accounts payable	$ 9,500
Accounts receivable	14,260
Cash	22,222
Common stock	30,000
Dividends	5,000
Equipment	12,000
Prepaid insurance	25,444
Land	20,000
Notes payable	26,000
Retained earnings	12,815
Insurance expense	12,689
Service revenue	89,550
Supplies	2,750
Salaries expense	53,500

Adjustments needed:

- Salaries due to employees, but unpaid at the end of the period, $2,000
- Insurance still unexpired at end of the period, $12,000

PA16. LO 4.4 Prepare an adjusted trial balance from the following account information, and also considering the adjustment data provided (assume accounts have normal balances). Equipment was recently purchased, so there is neither depreciation expense nor accumulated depreciation.

Accounts payable	$26,000
Accounts receivable	8,000
Cash	29,000
Common stock	33,000
Dividends	9,000
Equipment	68,000
Notes payable (due next month)	29,000
Salaries expense	42,000
Salaries payable	2,000
Service revenue	75,000
Supplies	5,000
Transportation expense	4,000

Adjustments needed:

- Remaining unpaid Salaries due to employees at the end of the period, $0
- Accrued Interest Payable at the end of the period, $7,700

PA17. LO 4.5 Using the following Company W information, prepare a Retained Earnings Statement.

- Retained earnings balance January 1, 2019, $43,500
- Net income for year 2019, $55,289
- Dividends declared and paid for year 2019, $18,000

PA18. LO 4.5 From the following Company Y adjusted trial balance, prepare simple financial statements, as follows:

A. Income Statement
B. Retained Earnings Statement
C. Balance Sheet

Adjusted Trial Balance		
	Debit	**Credit**
Cash	$ 32,000	
Accounts receivable	17,300	
Prepaid insurance	6,400	
Land	10,000	
Accounts payable		$ 10,900
Salaries payable		6,000
Common stock		31,000
Retained earnings		4,200
Dividends	8,000	
Service revenue		74,000
Insurance expense	5,600	
Salaries expense	24,000	
Miscellaneous expense	22,800	
	126,100	126,100

Problem Set B

PB1. LO 4.1 Identify whether each of the following transactions, which are related to revenue recognition, are accrual, deferral, or neither.

A. expense now, pay now
B. expense later, pay now
C. expense now, pay later

PB2. LO 4.1 To demonstrate the difference between cash account activity and accrual basis profits (net income), note the amount each transaction affects cash *and* the amount each transaction affects net income.

A. issued stock for cash $20,000
B. purchased supplies inventory on account $1,800
C. paid employee salaries; assume it was current day's expenses $950
D. paid note payment to bank (principal only) $1,200
E. collected balance on accounts receivable $4,750

PB3. LO 4.2 Identify which type of adjustment is indicated by these transactions. Choose accrued revenue, accrued expense, deferred revenue, or deferred expense.

A. fees earned and billed, but not collected
B. recorded depreciation expense
C. fees collected in advance of services
D. salaries owed but not yet paid
E. property rentals costs, prepaid for future months
F. inventory purchased for cash

PB4. LO 4.2 Identify which type of adjustment is associated with this account, and what the other account is in the adjustment. Choose accrued revenue, accrued expense, deferred revenue, or deferred expense.

A. Salaries Payable
B. Interest Receivable
C. Unearned Fee Revenue
D. Prepaid Rent

PB5. LO 4.2 Indicate what impact the following adjustments have on the accounting equation: Assets = Liabilities + Equity (assume normal balances).

		Impact 1	Impact 2
A.	Unearned Rent adjusted from $15,000 to $9,500		
B.	Recorded salaries payable of $3,750		
C.	Prepaid Rent adjusted from $6,000 to $4,000		
D.	Recorded depreciation expense of $5,500		

Table 4.7

PB6. LO 4.2 What two accounts are affected by each of these adjustments?

A. recorded accrued interest on note payable
B. adjusted unearned rent to correct
C. recorded depreciation for the year
D. adjusted salaries payable to correct
E. sold merchandise to customers on account

PB7. LO 4.3 Using the following information,

A. Make the December 31 adjusting journal entry for depreciation.
B. Determine the net book value (NBV) of the asset on December 31.

- Cost of asset, $195,000
- Accumulated depreciation, beginning of year, $26,000
- Current year depreciation, $13,000

PB8. LO 4.3 Use the following account T-balances (assume normal balances) and correct balance information to make the December 31 adjusting journal entries.

	T-Account Balance	Correct Balance
Unearned fee revenue	$12,000	$9,000
Supplies	3,200	1,050
Interest payable	1,850	1,975

PB9. LO 4.3 Use the following account T-balances (assume normal balances) and correct balance information to make the December 31 adjusting journal entries.

	T-Account Balance	Correct Balance
Prepaid insurance	$12,000	$5,000
Taxes payable	8,850	9,900
Unearned rental revenue	6,000	2,000

PB10. LO 4.3 Prepare journal entries to record the following transactions. Create a T-account for Supplies, post any entries that affect the account, and tally ending balance for the account (assume Supplies beginning balance of $6,550).

A. January 26, purchased additional supplies for cash, $9,500
B. December 31, actual count of supplies, $8,500

PB11. LO 4.3 Prepare journal entries to record the following transactions. Create a T-account for Unearned Revenue, post any entries that affect the account, tally ending balance for the account (assume Unearned Revenue beginning balance of $12,500).

A. May 1, collected an advance payment from client, $15,000
B. December 31, remaining unearned advances, $7,500

PB12. LO 4.3 Determine the amount of cash expended for Insurance Premiums during the month, based on the entries in the following accounts (assume 0 beginning balances).

Account	Debit	Credit
Insurance Expense		
	31,000	
Balance	31,000	
Prepaid Insurance		
	9,000	
Balance	9,000	

PB13. LO 4.3 Prepare adjusting journal entries, as needed, considering the account balances excerpted from the unadjusted trial balance and the adjustment data.

Unadjusted Trial Balance		
	Debit	**Credit**
Buildings and equipment	250,000	
Accumulated depreciation		56,000
Prepaid advertising	6,400	
Unearned rental revenue		8,900
Interest payable		3,500

A. depreciation on buildings and equipment, $17,500
B. advertising still prepaid at year end, $2,200
C. interest due on notes payable, $4,300
D. unearned rental revenue, $6,900
E. interest receivable on notes receivable, $1,200

PB14. LO 4.4 Prepare an adjusted trial balance from the adjusted account balances; solve for the one missing account balance: Dividends (assume accounts have normal balances). Equipment was recently purchased, so there is neither depreciation expense nor accumulated depreciation.

Accounts payable	$ 9,000
Accounts receivable	16,032
Cash	20,450
Common stock	24,000
Dividends	?
Equipment	29,000
Prepaid insurance	9,444
Land	34,000
Notes payable	48,000
Retained earnings	31,315
Insurance expense	12,689
Service revenue	82,500
Supplies	9,700
Salaries expense	51,500

PB15. LO 4.4 Prepare an adjusted trial balance from the following account information, considering the adjustment data provided (assume accounts have normal balances). Building and Equipment were recently purchased, so there is neither depreciation expense nor accumulated depreciation.

Accounts payable	$ 3,600
Accounts receivable	45,333
Building	156,000
Cash	50,480
Common stock	110,000
Dividends	18,000
Equipment	33,500
Fees earned revenue	225,430
Land	18,000
Supplies expense	5,123
Notes payable	85,500
Retained earnings	60,606
Salaries expense	151,900
Supplies	6,800

Adjustments needed:

- Physical count of supplies inventory remaining at end of period, $3,300
- Customer fees collected in advance (payments were recorded as Fees Earned), $18,500

PB16. LO 4.4 Prepare an adjusted trial balance from the following account information, and also considering the adjustment data provided (assume accounts have normal balances).

Accounts payable	$ 18,000
Accounts receivable	4,000
Investments	88,000
Cash	19,000
Common stock	30,000
Dividends	16,000
Prepaid insurance	20,000
Insurance expense	8,000
Land	26,000
Notes payable (long term)	55,000
Salaries expense	37,000
Sales revenue	115,000

Adjustments needed:

- Accrued interest revenue on investments at period end, $2,200
- Insurance still unexpired at end of the period, $12,000

PB17. LO 4.5 Using the following Company X information, prepare a Retained Earnings Statement:

- Retained earnings balance January 1, 2019, $121,500
- Net income for year 2019, $145,800
- Dividends declared and paid for year 2019, $53,000

PB18. LO 4.5 From the following Company Z adjusted trial balance, prepare simple financial statements, as follows:

A. Income Statement
B. Retained Earnings Statement
C. Balance Sheet

Adjusted Trial Balance		
	Debit	**Credit**
Cash	$ 54,650	
Accounts receivable	28,750	
Prepaid insurance	8,000	
Land	22,000	
Accounts payable		$ 14,300
Salaries payable		4,250
Common stock		50,000
Retained earnings		38,900
Dividends	36,000	
Service revenue		257,350
Insurance expense	32,000	
Salaries expense	126,500	
Miscellaneous expense	56,900	
	364,800	364,800

Thought Provokers

TP1. LO 4.1 Assume you are the controller of a large corporation, and the chief executive officer (CEO) has requested that you explain to them why the net income that you are reporting for the year is so low, when the CEO knows for a fact that the cash accounts are much higher at the end of the year than they were at the beginning of the year. Write a memo to the CEO to offer some possible explanations for the disparity between financial statement net income and the change in cash during the year.

TP2. LO 4.2 Search the US Securities and Exchange Commission website (https://www.sec.gov/edgar/searchedgar/companysearch.html), and locate the latest Form 10-K for a company you would like to analyze. Submit a short memo:

- State the name and ticker symbol of the company you have chosen.
- Review the company's end-of-period Balance Sheet for the most recent annual report, in search of accruals and deferrals.
- List the name and account balance of at least four accounts that represent accruals or deferrals—these could be accrued revenues, accrued expenses, deferred (unearned) revenues, or deferred (prepaid) expenses.
- Provide the web link to the company's Form 10-K, to allow accurate verification of your answers.

TP3. LO 4.3 Search the web for instances of possible impropriety relating to earnings management. This could be news reports, Securities and Exchange Commission violation reports, fraud charges, or any other source of alleged financial statement judgement lapse.

- Write down the name and industry type of the company you are discussing.
- Describe the purported indiscretion, and how it relates to mis-reporting earnings or shady accounting.
- Estimate the impact of the potential misrepresented amount.
- Note: You do not have to have proof that a compromise occurred, but you do need to have a source of your reporting of the potential trouble.
- Provide the web link to the information you found, to allow accurate verification of your answers.

TP4. LO 4.4 Assume you are employed as the chief financial officer of a corporation and are responsible for preparation of the financial statements, including the adjusting process and preparation of the adjusted trial balance. The company is facing a slow year, and after your adjusting entries, the financial statements are accurately reflecting that fact. However, as you are discussing the matter with your boss, the chief executive officer (CEO), he suggests that you have the power to make further adjustments to the statements, and that you should use that power to "adjust" the profits and equity into a stronger position, so that investor confidence in the company's prospects will be restored.

Write a short memo to the CEO, stating your intentions about what you can and/or will do to make the financial statements more appealing. Be specific about any planned adjustments that could be made, assuming that normal period-end adjustments have already been reflected accurately in the financial statements that you prepared.

TP5. LO 4.5 Search the SEC website (https://www.sec.gov/edgar/searchedgar/companysearch.html) and locate the latest Form 10-K for a company you would like to analyze. Submit a short memo:

- State the name and ticker symbol of the company you have chosen.
- Review the company's end-of-period Balance Sheet, Income Statement, and Statement of Retained Earnings.
- Reconstruct an adjusted trial balance for the company, from the information presented in the three specified financial statements.
- Provide the web link to the company's Form 10-K, to allow accurate verification of your answers.

5 Completing the Accounting Cycle

Figure 5.1 Mark reviews the financial data from Supreme Cleaners. (credit left: modification of "Numbers and Finance" by "reynermedia"/Flickr, CC BY 2.0; credit right: modification of "Dry cleaned clothes (Unsplash)" by "m0851"/Wikimedia Commons, CC0)

Chapter Outline

LO 5.1 Describe and Prepare Closing Entries for a Business

LO 5.2 Prepare a Post-Closing Trial Balance

LO 5.3 Apply the Results from the Adjusted Trial Balance to Compute Current Ratio and Working Capital Balance, and Explain How These Measures Represent Liquidity

LO 5.4 Appendix: Complete a Comprehensive Accounting Cycle for a Business

Why It Matters

As we learned in Analyzing and Recording Transactions and The Adjustment Process, Mark Summers has started his own dry-cleaning business called Supreme Cleaners. Mark had a busy first month of operations, including purchasing equipment and supplies, paying his employees, and providing dry-cleaning services to customers. Because Mark had established a sound accounting system to keep track of his daily transactions, he was able to prepare complete and accurate financial statements showing his company's progress and financial position.

In order to move forward, Mark needs to review how financial data from his first month of operations transitions into his second month of operations. It is important for Mark to make a smooth transition so he can compare the financials from month to month, and continue on the right path toward growth. It will also assure his investors and lenders that the company is operating as expected. So what does he need to do to prepare for next month?

5.1 Describe and Prepare Closing Entries for a Business

In this chapter, we complete the final steps (steps 8 and 9) of the accounting cycle, the closing process. You will notice that we do not cover step 10, reversing entries. This is an optional step in the accounting cycle that you will learn about in future courses. Steps 1 through 4 were covered in Analyzing and Recording Transactions and Steps 5 through 7 were covered in The Adjustment Process.

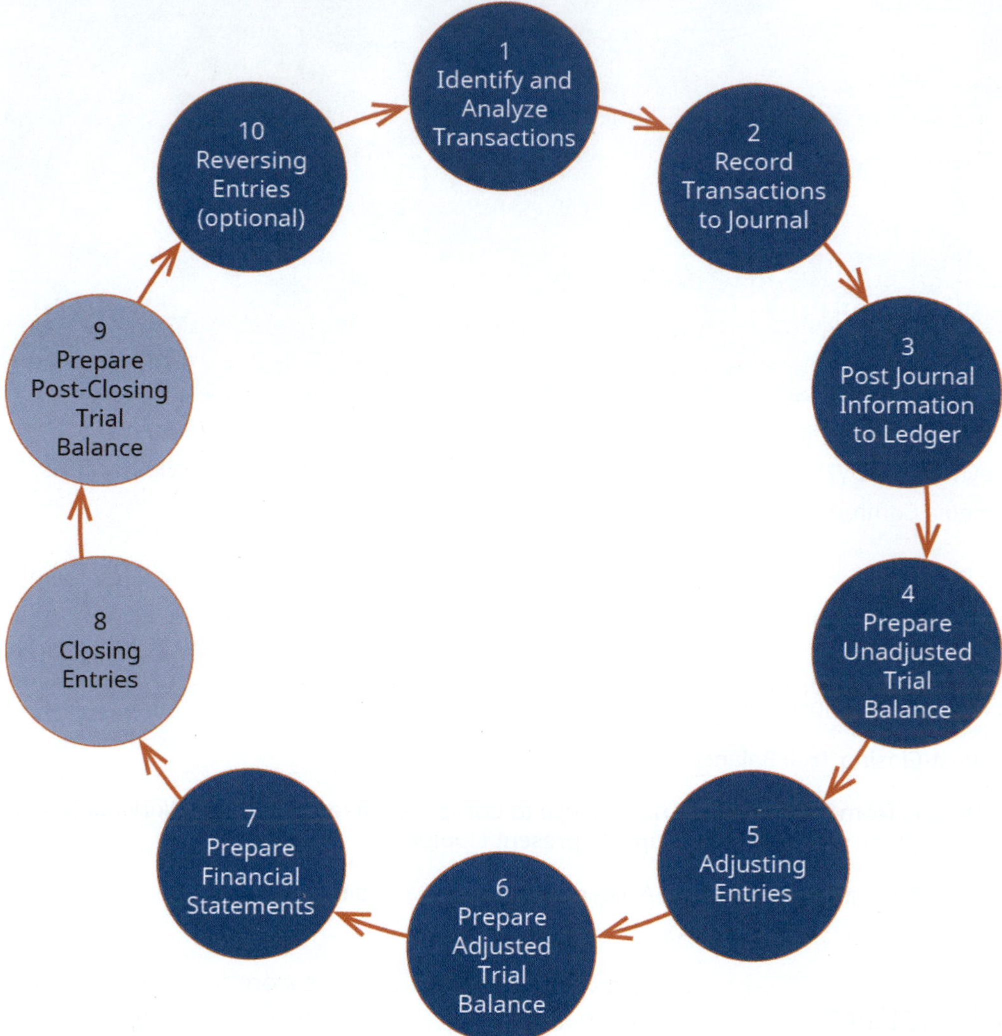

Our discussion here begins with journalizing and posting the closing entries (Figure 5.2). These posted entries will then translate into a **post-closing trial balance**, which is a trial balance that is prepared after all of the closing entries have been recorded.

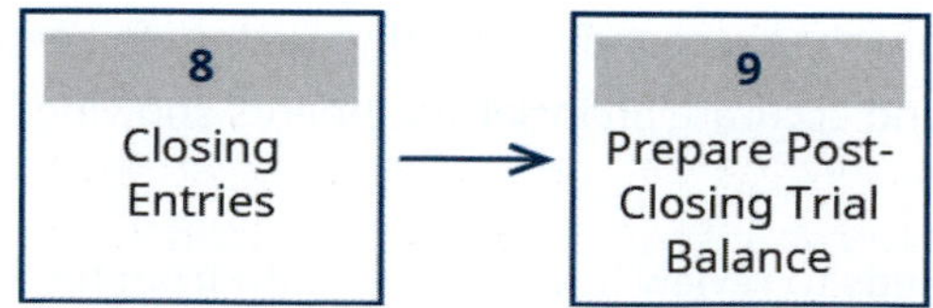

Figure 5.2 Final steps in the accounting cycle. (attribution: Copyright Rice University, OpenStax, under CC BY-NC-SA 4.0 license)

THINK IT THROUGH

Should You Compromise to Please Your Supervisor?

You are an accountant for a small event-planning business. The business has been operating for several years but does not have the resources for accounting software. This means you are preparing all steps in the accounting cycle by hand.

It is the end of the month, and you have completed the post-closing trial balance. You notice that there is still a service revenue account balance listed on this trial balance. Why is it considered an error to have a revenue account on the post-closing trial balance? How do you fix this error?

Introduction to the Closing Entries

Companies are required to close their books at the end of each fiscal year so that they can prepare their annual financial statements and tax returns. However, most companies prepare monthly financial statements and close their books annually, so they have a clear picture of company performance during the year, and give users timely information to make decisions.

Closing entries prepare a company for the next accounting period by clearing any outstanding balances in certain accounts that should not transfer over to the next period. **Closing**, or clearing the balances, means returning the account to a zero balance. Having a zero balance in these accounts is important so a company can compare performance across periods, particularly with income. It also helps the company keep thorough records of account balances affecting retained earnings. Revenue, expense, and dividend accounts affect retained earnings and are closed so they can accumulate new balances in the next period, which is an application of the time period assumption.

To further clarify this concept, balances are closed to assure all revenues and expenses are recorded in the proper period and then start over the following period. The revenue and expense accounts should start at zero each period, because we are measuring how much revenue is earned and expenses incurred during the period. However, the cash balances, as well as the other balance sheet accounts, are carried over from the end of a current period to the beginning of the next period.

For example, a store has an inventory account balance of $100,000. If the store closed at 11:59 p.m. on January 31, 2019, then the inventory balance when it reopened at 12:01 a.m. on February 1, 2019, would still be $100,000. The balance sheet accounts, such as inventory, would carry over into the next period, in this case February 2019.

The accounts that need to start with a clean or $0 balance going into the next accounting period are revenue, income, and any dividends from January 2019. To determine the income (profit or loss) from the month of January, the store needs to close the income statement information from January 2019. Zeroing January 2019 would then enable the store to calculate the income (profit or loss) for the next month (February 2019), instead of merging it into January's income and thus providing invalid information solely for the month of February.

However, if the company also wanted to keep year-to-date information from month to month, a separate set of records could be kept as the company progresses through the remaining months in the year. For our purposes, assume that we are closing the books at the end of each month unless otherwise noted.

Let's look at another example to illustrate the point. Assume you own a small landscaping business. It is the end of the year, December 31, 2018, and you are reviewing your financials for the entire year. You see that you earned $120,000 this year in revenue and had expenses for rent, electricity, cable, internet, gas, and food that totaled $70,000.

You also review the following information:

	Value December 31
Bank account balance	$ 7,500
Electronics	3,250
Car	26,545
Furniture	7,200
Credit card balances	9,270
Bank loans	48,350

The next day, January 1, 2019, you get ready for work, but before you go to the office, you decide to review your financials for 2019. What are your year-to-date earnings? So far, you have not worked at all in the current year. What are your total expenses for rent, electricity, cable and internet, gas, and food for the current year? You have also not incurred any expenses yet for rent, electricity, cable, internet, gas or food. This means that the current balance of these accounts is zero, because they were closed on December 31, 2018, to complete the annual accounting period.

Next, you review your assets and liabilities. What is your current bank account balance? What is the current book value of your electronics, car, and furniture? What about your credit card balances and bank loans? Are the value of your assets and liabilities now zero because of the start of a new year? Your car, electronics, and furniture did not suddenly lose all their value, and unfortunately, you still have outstanding debt. Therefore, these accounts still have a balance in the new year, because they are not closed, and the balances are carried forward from December 31 to January 1 to start the new annual accounting period.

This is no different from what will happen to a company at the end of an accounting period. A company will see its revenue and expense accounts set back to zero, but its assets and liabilities will maintain a balance. Stockholders' equity accounts will also maintain their balances. In summary, the accountant resets the temporary accounts to zero by transferring the balances to permanent accounts.

LINK TO LEARNING

Understanding the accounting cycle and preparing trial balances is a practice valued internationally. The Philippines Center for Entrepreneurship and the government of the Philippines hold regular seminars going over this cycle with small business owners. They are also transparent with their internal trial balances in several key government offices. Check out this article talking about the seminars on the accounting cycle (https://openstax.org/l/50PhilAcctSem) and this public pre-closing trial balance (https://openstax.org/l/50PhilTrialBal) presented by the Philippines Department of Health.

Temporary and Permanent Accounts

All accounts can be classified as either permanent (real) or temporary (nominal) (Figure 5.3).

Permanent (real) accounts are accounts that transfer balances to the next period and include balance sheet accounts, such as assets, liabilities, and stockholders' equity. These accounts will not be set back to zero at the beginning of the next period; they will keep their balances. Permanent accounts are not part of the closing process.

Temporary (nominal) accounts are accounts that are closed at the end of each accounting period, and include income statement, dividends, and income summary accounts. The new account, Income Summary, will be discussed shortly. These accounts are temporary because they keep their balances during the current accounting period and are set back to zero when the period ends. Revenue and expense accounts are closed to Income Summary, and Income Summary and Dividends are closed to the permanent account, Retained Earnings.

	Financial Statement Presented On			Account	
Type of Account	**Income Statement**	**Statement of Retained Earnings**	**Balance Sheet**	**Temporary**	**Permanent**
Asset			X		X
Contra Asset			X		X
Liability			X		X
Stockholders' Equity			X		X
Dividends*		X		X	
Revenues	X			X	
Expenses	X			X	

*Contra Stockholders' Equity

Figure 5.3 Location Chart for Financial Statement Accounts. (attribution: Copyright Rice University, OpenStax, under CC BY-NC-SA 4.0 license)

The **income summary** account is an intermediary between revenues and expenses, and the Retained Earnings account. It stores all of the closing information for revenues and expenses, resulting in a "summary" of income or loss for the period. The balance in the Income Summary account equals the net income or loss for the period. This balance is then transferred to the Retained Earnings account.

Income summary is a nondefined account category. This means that it is not an asset, liability, stockholders' equity, revenue, or expense account. The account has a zero balance throughout the entire accounting period until the closing entries are prepared. Therefore, it will not appear on any trial balances, including the adjusted trial balance, and will not appear on any of the financial statements.

You might be asking yourself, "is the Income Summary account even necessary?" Could we just close out revenues and expenses directly into retained earnings and not have this extra temporary account? We could do this, but by having the Income Summary account, you get a balance for net income a second time. This gives you the balance to compare to the income statement, and allows you to double check that all income statement accounts are closed and have correct amounts. If you put the revenues and expenses directly into retained earnings, you will not see that check figure. No matter which way you choose to close, the same final balance is in retained earnings.

YOUR TURN

Permanent versus Temporary Accounts

Following is a list of accounts. State whether each account is a permanent or temporary account.

A. rent expense
B. unearned revenue
C. accumulated depreciation, vehicle
D. common stock
E. fees revenue
F. dividends
G. prepaid insurance
H. accounts payable

Solution

A, E, and F are temporary; B, C, D, G, and H are permanent.

Let's now look at how to prepare closing entries.

Journalizing and Posting Closing Entries

The eighth step in the accounting cycle is preparing closing entries, which includes journalizing and posting the entries to the ledger.

Four entries occur during the closing process. The first entry closes revenue accounts to the Income Summary account. The second entry closes expense accounts to the Income Summary account. The third entry closes the Income Summary account to Retained Earnings. The fourth entry closes the Dividends account to Retained Earnings. The information needed to prepare closing entries comes from the adjusted trial balance.

Let's explore each entry in more detail using Printing Plus's information from Analyzing and Recording Transactions and The Adjustment Process as our example. The Printing Plus adjusted trial balance for January 31, 2019, is presented in Figure 5.4.

PRINTING PLUS Adjusted Trial Balance For the Month Ended January 31, 2019		
Account Title	**Debit**	**Credit**
Cash	$24,800	
Accounts Receivable	1,200	
Interest Receivable	140	
Supplies	400	
Equipment	3,500	
Accumulated Depreciation: Equipment		$ 75
Accounts Payable		500
Salaries Payable		1,500
Unearned Revenue		3,400
Common Stock		20,000
Dividends	100	
Interest Revenue		140
Service Revenue		10,100
Supplies Expense	100	
Depreciation Expense: Equipment	75	
Salaries Expense	5,100	
Utility Expense	300	
Total	$35,715	$35,715

Figure 5.4 Adjusted Trial Balance for Printing Plus. (attribution: Copyright Rice University, OpenStax, under CC BY-NC-SA 4.0 license)

The first entry requires revenue accounts close to the Income Summary account. To get a zero balance in a revenue account, the entry will show a debit to revenues and a credit to Income Summary. Printing Plus has $140 of interest revenue and $10,100 of service revenue, each with a credit balance on the adjusted trial balance. The closing entry will debit both interest revenue and service revenue, and credit Income Summary.

JOURNAL			
Date	**Account**	**Debit**	**Credit**
Jan. 31, 2019	Interest Revenue	140	
	Service Revenue	10,100	
	Income Summary		10,240
	To close revenue accounts to Income Summary		

The T-accounts after this closing entry would look like the following.

Service Revenue			
		5,500	Jan. 10
		2,800	Jan. 17
		1,200	Jan. 27
		600	Jan. 31
Jan. 31 Cls.	10,100	10,100	
		0	

Interest Revenue			
		140	Jan. 31
Jan. 31 Cls.	140	140	
		0	

Income Summary			
		10,240	Jan. 31 Cls. #1
		Bal. 10,240	

Notice that the balances in interest revenue and service revenue are now zero and are ready to accumulate revenues in the next period. The Income Summary account has a credit balance of $10,240 (the revenue sum).

The second entry requires expense accounts close to the Income Summary account. To get a zero balance in an expense account, the entry will show a credit to expenses and a debit to Income Summary. Printing Plus has $100 of supplies expense, $75 of depreciation expense–equipment, $5,100 of salaries expense, and $300 of utility expense, each with a debit balance on the adjusted trial balance. The closing entry will credit Supplies Expense, Depreciation Expense–Equipment, Salaries Expense, and Utility Expense, and debit Income Summary.

JOURNAL			
Date	**Account**	**Debit**	**Credit**
Jan. 31, 2019	Income Summary	5,575	
	Supplies Expense		100
	Depreciation Expense: Equipment		75
	Salaries Expense		5,100
	Utility Expense		300
	To close expense accounts to Income Summary		

The T-accounts after this closing entry would look like the following.

Supplies Expense			
Jan. 31	100		
	100	100	Jan. 31 Cls.
	0		

Salaries Expense			
Jan. 20	3,600		
Jan. 31	1,500		
	5,100	5,100	Jan. 31 Cls.
	0		

Depreciation Expense: Equipment			
Jan. 31	75		
	75	75	Jan. 31 Cls.
	0		

Utility Expense			
Jan. 12	300		
	300	300	Jan. 31 Cls.
	0		

Income Summary				
Jan. 31	Cls. #2	5,575	10,240	Jan. 31 Cls. #1
			Bal. 4,665	

Notice that the balances in the expense accounts are now zero and are ready to accumulate expenses in the next period. The Income Summary account has a new credit balance of $4,665, which is the difference between revenues and expenses (Figure 5.5). The balance in Income Summary is the same figure as what is reported on Printing Plus's Income Statement.

PRINTING PLUS Income Statement For the Month Ended January 31, 2019		
Revenues		
Interest Revenue	$ 140	
Service Revenue	10,100	
Total Revenues		$10,240
Expenses		
Supplies Expense	100	
Depreciation Expense: Equipment	75	
Salaries Expense	5,100	
Utility Expense	300	
Total Expenses		5,575
Net Income		$ 4,665

Figure 5.5 Income Statement for Printing Plus. (attribution: Copyright Rice University, OpenStax, under CC BY-NC-SA 4.0 license)

Why are these two figures the same? The income statement summarizes your income, as does income summary. If both summarize your income in the same period, then they must be equal. If they do not match, then you have an error.

The third entry requires Income Summary to close to the Retained Earnings account. To get a zero balance in the Income Summary account, there are guidelines to consider.

- If the balance in Income Summary before closing is a credit balance, you will debit Income Summary and credit Retained Earnings in the closing entry. This situation occurs when a company has a net income.
- If the balance in Income Summary before closing is a debit balance, you will credit Income Summary and debit Retained Earnings in the closing entry. This situation occurs when a company has a net loss.

Remember that net income will increase retained earnings, and a net loss will decrease retained earnings. The Retained Earnings account increases on the credit side and decreases on the debit side.

Printing Plus has a $4,665 credit balance in its Income Summary account before closing, so it will debit Income Summary and credit Retained Earnings.

JOURNAL			
Date	**Account**	**Debit**	**Credit**
Jan. 31, 2019	Income Summary	4,665	
	Retained Earnings		4,665
	To close Income Summary to Retained Earnings		

The T-accounts after this closing entry would look like the following.

Retained Earnings			
		4,665	Jan. 31 Cls. #3
		Bal. 4,665	

Income Summary			
Jan. 31 Cls. #2	5,575	10,240	Jan. 31 Cls. #1
Jan. 31 Cls.	4,665	4,665	
		0	

Notice that the Income Summary account is now zero and is ready for use in the next period. The Retained Earnings account balance is currently a credit of $4,665.

The fourth entry requires Dividends to close to the Retained Earnings account. Remember from your past studies that dividends are not expenses, such as salaries paid to your employees or staff. Instead, declaring and paying dividends is a method utilized by corporations to return part of the profits generated by the company to the owners of the company—in this case, its shareholders.

If dividends were not declared, closing entries would cease at this point. If dividends are declared, to get a zero balance in the Dividends account, the entry will show a credit to Dividends and a debit to Retained Earnings. As you will learn in Corporation Accounting, there are three components to the declaration and payment of dividends. The first part is the date of declaration, which creates the obligation or liability to pay the dividend. The second part is the date of record that determines who receives the dividends, and the third part is the date of payment, which is the date that payments are made. Printing Plus has $100 of dividends with a debit balance on the adjusted trial balance. The closing entry will credit Dividends and debit Retained Earnings.

JOURNAL			
Date	Account	Debit	Credit
Jan. 31, 2019	Retained Earnings Dividends *To close dividends account to Retained Earnings*	100	 100

The T-accounts after this closing entry would look like the following.

Retained Earnings	
Jan. 31 Cls. #4 100	4,665 Jan. 31 Cls. #3
	Bal. 4,565

Dividends	
Jan. 14 100	
100	100 Jan. 31 Cls.
0	

Why was income summary not used in the dividends closing entry? Dividends are not an income statement account. Only income statement accounts help us summarize income, so only income statement accounts should go into income summary.

Remember, dividends are a contra stockholders' equity account. It is contra to retained earnings. If we pay out dividends, it means retained earnings decreases. Retained earnings decreases on the debit side. The remaining balance in Retained Earnings is $4,565 (Figure 5.6). This is the same figure found on the statement of retained earnings.

PRINTING PLUS Statement of Retained Earnings For the Month Ended January 31, 2019	
Beginning Retained Earnings (Jan. 1)	$ 0
Net Income	4,665
Dividends	(100)
Ending Retained Earnings (Jan. 31)	$4,565

Figure 5.6 Statement of Retained Earnings for Printing Plus. (attribution: Copyright Rice University, OpenStax, under CC BY-NC-SA 4.0 license)

The statement of retained earnings shows the period-ending retained earnings after the closing entries have been posted. When you compare the retained earnings ledger (T-account) to the statement of retained earnings, the figures must match. It is important to understand retained earnings is *not* closed out, it is only updated. Retained Earnings is the only account that appears in the closing entries that does not close. You should recall from your previous material that retained earnings are the earnings retained by the company over time—not cash flow but earnings. Now that we have closed the temporary accounts, let's review what the post-closing ledger (T-accounts) looks like for Printing Plus.

T-Account Summary

The T-account summary for Printing Plus after closing entries are journalized is presented in Figure 5.7.

Cash

Date	Debit	Credit	Date
Jan. 3	20,000	300	Jan. 12
Jan. 9	4,000	100	Jan. 14
Jan. 17	2,800	3,500	Jan. 18
Jan. 23	5,500	3,600	Jan. 20
	Bal. 24,800		

Accounts Receivable

Date	Debit	Credit	Date
Jan. 10	5,500	5,500	Jan. 23
Jan. 27	1,200		
	Bal. 1,200		

Interest Receivable

Date	Debit	Credit	Date
Jan. 31	140		
	Bal. 140		

Supplies

Date	Debit	Credit	Date
Jan. 30	500	100	Jan. 31
	Bal. 400		

Equipment

Date	Debit	Credit	Date
Jan. 5	3,500		
	Bal. 3,500		

Accumulated Depreciation - Equipment

Date	Debit	Credit	Date
		75	Jan. 31
		Bal. 75	

Accounts Payable

Date	Debit	Credit	Date
Jan. 18	3,500	3,500	Jan. 5
		500	Jan. 30
		Bal. 500	

Salaries Payable

Date	Debit	Credit	Date
		1,500	Jan. 31
		Bal. 1,500	

Unearned Revenue

Date	Debit	Credit	Date
		4,000	Jan. 9
Jan. 31	600		
		Bal. 3,400	

Common Stock

Date	Debit	Credit	Date
		20,000	Jan. 3
		Bal. 20,000	

Dividends

Date	Debit	Credit	Date
Jan. 14	100		
	100	100	Jan. 31 Cls.
	0		

Service Revenue

Date	Debit	Credit	Date
		5,500	Jan. 10
		2,800	Jan. 17
		1,200	Jan. 27
		600	Jan. 31
Jan. 31 Cls.	10,100	10,100	
		0	

Interest Revenue

Date	Debit	Credit	Date
		140	Jan. 31
Jan. 31 Cls.	140	140	
		0	

Supplies Expense

Date	Debit	Credit	Date
Jan. 31	100		
	100	100	Jan. 31 Cls.
	0		

Salaries Expense

Date	Debit	Credit	Date
Jan. 20	3,600		
Jan. 31	1,500		
	5,100	5,100	Jan. 31 Cls.
	0		

Depreciation Expense - Equipment

Date	Debit	Credit	Date
Jan. 31	75		
	75	75	Jan. 31 Cls.
	0		

Utility Expense

Date	Debit	Credit	Date
Jan. 12	300		
	300	300	Jan. 31 Cls.
	0		

Income Summary

Date	Debit	Credit	Date
Jan. 31 Cls. #2	5,575	10,240	Jan. 31 Cls. #1
Jan. 31 Cls.	4,665	4,665	
		0	

Retained Earnings

Date	Debit	Credit	Date
Jan. 31 Cls. #4	100	4,665	Jan. 31 Cls. #3
		Bal. 4,565	

Figure 5.7 T-Account Summary. (attribution: Copyright Rice University, OpenStax, under CC BY-NC-SA 4.0 license)

Notice that revenues, expenses, dividends, and income summary all have zero balances. Retained earnings maintains a $4,565 credit balance. The post-closing T-accounts will be transferred to the post-closing trial balance, which is step 9 in the accounting cycle.

THINK IT THROUGH

Closing Entries

A company has revenue of $48,000 and total expenses of $52,000. What would the third closing entry be? Why?

YOUR TURN

Frasker Corp. Closing Entries

Prepare the closing entries for Frasker Corp. using the adjusted trial balance provided.

FRASKER CORPORATION Adjusted Trial Balance For the Month Ended June 30, 2018		
Cash	$ 5,840	
Accounts Receivable	6,575	
Prepaid Machine Rental	6,000	
Office Supplies	435	
Accounts Payable		$ 2,840
Common Stock		10,000
Retained Earnings		4,350
Dividends	15,000	
Fees Earned		22,350
Salaries Expense	2,970	
Advertising Expense	325	
Machine Rental Expense	1,000	
Office Rent Expense	1,250	
Utility Expense	145	
	$39,540	$39,540

Solution

June 30	Fee Earned	$22,350	
	Income Summary		$22,350
	To close all income statement accounts with credit balances		
June 30	Income Summary	5,690	
	Salaries Expense		2,970
	Advertising Expense		325
	Machine Rental Expense		1,000
	Office Rent Expense		1,250
	Utilities Expense		145
	To close out all income statement accounts with debit balances		
June 30	Retained Earnings	16,660	
	Income Summary		16,660
	To close out income summary and update retained earnings		
June 30	Retained Earnings	15,000	
	Dividends		15,000
	To close out dividends and update retained earnings		

5.2 Prepare a Post-Closing Trial Balance

The ninth, and typically final, step of the process is to prepare a post-closing trial balance. The word "post" in this instance means "after." You are preparing a trial balance *after* the closing entries are complete.

Like all trial balances, the post-closing trial balance has the job of verifying that the debit and credit totals are equal. The post-closing trial balance has one additional job that the other trial balances do not have. The post-closing trial balance is also used to double-check that the only accounts with balances after the closing entries are permanent accounts. If there are any temporary accounts on this trial balance, you would know that there was an error in the closing process. This error must be fixed before starting the new period.

The process of preparing the post-closing trial balance is the same as you have done when preparing the unadjusted trial balance and adjusted trial balance. Only permanent account balances should appear on the post-closing trial balance. These balances in post-closing T-accounts are transferred over to either the debit or credit column on the post-closing trial balance. When all accounts have been recorded, total each column and verify the columns equal each other.

The post-closing trial balance for Printing Plus is shown in Figure 5.8.

PRINTING PLUS Post-Closing Trial Balance For the Month Ended January 31, 2019		
Account	**Debit**	**Credit**
Cash	$24,800	
Accounts Receivable	1,200	
Interest Receivable	140	
Supplies	400	
Equipment	3,500	
Accumulated Depreciation: Equipment		$ 75
Accounts Payable		500
Salaries Payable		1,500
Unearned Revenue		3,400
Common Stock		20,000
Retained Earnings		4,565
Total	$30,040	$30,040

Figure 5.8 Printing Plus's Post-Closing Trial Balance. (attribution: Copyright Rice University, OpenStax, under CC BY-NC-SA 4.0 license)

Notice that only permanent accounts are included. All temporary accounts with zero balances were left out of this statement. Unlike previous trial balances, the retained earnings figure is included, which was obtained through the closing process.

At this point, the accounting cycle is complete, and the company can begin a new cycle in the next period. In essence, the company's business is always in operation, while the accounting cycle utilizes the cutoff of month-end to provide financial information to assist and review the operations.

It is worth mentioning that there is one step in the process that a company may or may not include, step 10, reversing entries. Reversing entries reverse an adjusting entry made in a prior period at the start of a new period. We do not cover reversing entries in this chapter, but you might approach the subject in future accounting courses.

Now that we have completed the accounting cycle, let's take a look at another way the adjusted trial balance assists users of information with financial decision-making.

LINK TO LEARNING

If you like quizzes, crossword puzzles, fill-in-the-blank, matching exercise, and word scrambles to help you learn the material in this course, go to My Accounting Course (https://openstax.org/l/50MyAcctCourse) for more. This website covers a variety of accounting topics including financial accounting basics, accounting principles, the accounting cycle, and financial statements, all topics introduced in the early part of this course.

CONCEPTS IN PRACTICE

The Importance of Understanding How to Complete the Accounting Cycle

Many students who enroll in an introductory accounting course do not plan to become accountants. They will work in a variety of jobs in the business field, including managers, sales, and finance. In a real company, most of the mundane work is done by computers. Accounting software can perform such tasks as posting the journal entries recorded, preparing trial balances, and preparing financial statements. Students often ask why they need to do all of these steps by hand in their introductory class, particularly if they are never going to be an accountant. It is very important to understand that no matter what your position, if you work in business you need to be able to read financial statements, interpret them, and know how to use that information to better your business. If you have never followed the full process from beginning to end, you will never understand how one of your decisions can impact the final numbers that appear on your financial statements. You will not understand how your decisions can affect the outcome of your company.

As mentioned previously, once you understand the effect your decisions will have on the bottom line on your income statement and the balances in your balance sheet, you can use accounting software to do all of the mundane, repetitive steps and use your time to evaluate the company based on what the financial statements show. Your stockholders, creditors, and other outside professionals will use your financial statements to evaluate your performance. If you evaluate your numbers as often as monthly, you will be able to identify your strengths and weaknesses before any outsiders see them and make any necessary changes to your plan in the following month.

5.3 Apply the Results from the Adjusted Trial Balance to Compute Current Ratio and Working Capital Balance, and Explain How These Measures Represent Liquidity

In The Adjustment Process, we were introduced to the idea of accrual-basis accounting, where revenues and expenses must be recorded in the accounting period in which they were earned or incurred, no matter when cash receipts or outlays occur. We also discussed cash-basis accounting, where income and expenses are recognized when receipts and disbursements occur. In this chapter, we go into more depth about why a company may choose accrual-basis accounting as opposed to cash-basis accounting.

LINK TO LEARNING

Go to the Internal Revenue Service's website, and look at the most recently updated Pub 334 Tax Guide for Small Business (https://openstax.org/l/50IRSPub334) to learn more about the rules for income tax preparation for a small business.

Cash Basis versus Accrual Basis Accounting

There are several reasons accrual-basis accounting is preferred to cash-basis accounting. Accrual-basis accounting is required by US generally accepted accounting principles (GAAP), as it typically provides a better sense of the financial well-being of a company. Accrual-based accounting information allows management to analyze a company's progress, and management can use that information to improve their business. Accrual accounting is also used to assist companies in securing financing, because banks will typically require a company to provide accrual-basis financial income statements. The Internal Revenue Service might also require businesses to report using accrual basis information when preparing tax returns. In addition, companies with inventory must use accrual-based accounting for income tax purposes, though there are exceptions to the general rule.

So why might a company use cash-basis accounting? Companies that do not sell stock publicly can use cash-basis instead of accrual-basis accounting for internal-management purposes and externally, as long as the Internal Revenue Service does not prevent them from doing so, and they have no other reasons such as agreements per a bank loan. Cash-basis accounting is a simpler accounting system to use than an accrual-basis accounting system when tracking real-time revenues and expenses.

Let's take a look at one example illustrating why accrual-basis accounting might be preferred to cash-basis accounting.

In the current year, a company had the following transactions:

January to March Transactions

Date	Transaction
Jan. 1	Annual insurance policy purchased for $6,000 cash
Jan. 8	Sent payment for December's electricity bill, $135
Jan. 15	Performed services worth $2,500; customer asked to be billed
Jan. 31	Electricity used during January is estimated at $110
Feb. 16	Realized you forgot to pay January's rent, so sent two months' rent, $2,000
Feb. 20	Performed services worth $2,400; customer asked to be billed
Feb. 28	Electricity used during February is estimated at $150
Mar. 2	Paid March rent, $1,000
Mar. 10	Received all money owed from services performed in January and February
Mar. 14	Performed services worth $2,450. Received $1,800 cash
Mar. 30	Electricity used during March is estimated at $145

Table 5.1

IFRS CONNECTION

Issues in Comparing Closing Procedures

Regardless of whether a company uses US GAAP or International Financial Reporting Standards (IFRS), the closing and post-closing processes are the same. However, the results generated by these processes are not the same. These differences can be seen most easily in the ratios formulated from the financial statement information and used to assess various financial qualities of a company.

You have learned about the current ratio, which is used to assess a company's ability to pay debts as they come due. How could the use of IFRS versus US GAAP affect this ratio? US GAAP and IFRS most frequently differ on how certain transactions are measured, or on the timing of measuring and reporting that transaction. You will later learn about this in more detail, but for now we use a difference in inventory measurement to illustrate the effect of the two different sets of standards on the current ratio.

US GAAP allows for three different ways to measure ending inventory balances: first-in, first-out (FIFO); last-in, first-out (LIFO); and weighted average. IFRS only allows for FIFO and weighted average. If the prices of inventory being purchased are rising, the FIFO method will result in a higher value of ending inventory on the Balance Sheet than would the LIFO method.

Think about this in the context of the current ratio. Inventory is one component of current assets: the numerator of the ratio. The higher the current assets (numerator), the higher is the current ratio. Therefore, if you calculated the current ratio for a company that applied US GAAP, and then recalculated the ratio assuming the company used IFRS, you would get not only different numbers for inventory (and other accounts) in the financial statements, but also different numbers for the ratios.

This idea illustrates the impact the application of an accounting standard can have on the results of a company's financial statements and related ratios. Different standards produce different results. Throughout the remainder of this course, you will learn more details about the similarities and differences between US GAAP and IFRS, and how these differences impact financial reporting.

Remember, in a cash-basis system you will record the revenue when the money is received no matter when the service is performed. There was no money received from customers in January or February, so the company, under a cash-basis system, would not show any revenue in those months. In March they received the $2,500 customers owed from January sales, $2,400 from customers for February sales, and $1,800 from cash sales in March. This is a total of $6,700 cash received from customers in March. Since the cash was received in March, the cash-basis system would record revenue in March.

In accrual accounting, we record the revenue as it is earned. There was $2,500 worth of service performed in January, so that will show as revenue in January. The $2,400 earned in February is recorded in February, and the $2,450 earned in March is recorded as revenue in March. Remember, it does not matter whether or not the cash came in.

For expenses, the cash-basis system is going to record an expense the day the payment leaves company hands. In January, the company purchased an insurance policy. The insurance policy is for the entire year, but since the cash went to the insurance company in January, the company will record the entire amount as an expense in January. The company paid the December electric bill in January. Even though the electricity was used to earn revenue in December, the company will record it as an expense in January. Electricity used in

January, February, and March to help earn revenue in those months will show no expense because the bill has not been paid. The company forgot to pay January's rent in January, so no rent expense is recorded in January. However, in February there is $2,000 worth of rent expense because the company paid for the two months in February.

Under accrual accounting, expenses are recorded when they are incurred and not when paid. Electricity used in a month to help earn revenue is recorded as an expense in that month whether the bill is paid or not. The same is true for rent expense. Insurance expense is spread out over 12 months, and each month 1/12 of the total insurance cost is expensed. The comparison of cash-basis and accrual-basis income statements is presented in Figure 5.9.

Cash Basis Accounting	Jan.	Feb.	Mar.
Revenue	$ -	$ -	$6,700
Expenses			
Electricity	135	-	-
Rent		2,000	1,000
Insurance	6,000		
Net income	$(6,135)	$(2,000)	$5,700

Accrual Basis Accounting	Jan.	Feb.	Mar.
Revenue	$2,500	$2,400	$2,450
Expenses			
Electricity	110	150	145
Rent	1,000	1,000	1,000
Insurance	500	500	500
Net income	$ 890	$ 750	$ 805

Figure 5.9 Cash Basis versus Accrual Basis Accounting. (attribution: Copyright Rice University, OpenStax, under CC BY-NC-SA 4.0 license)

CONCEPTS IN PRACTICE

Fundamentals of Financial Ratios

One method used by everyone who evaluates financial statements is to calculate financial ratios. Financial ratios take numbers from your income statements and/or your balance sheet to evaluate important financial outcomes that will impact user decisions.

There are ratios to evaluate your liquidity, solvency, profitability, and efficiency. Liquidity ratios look at your ability to pay the debts that you owe in the near future. Solvency will show if you can pay your bills not only in the short term but also in the long term. Profitability ratios are calculated to see how much profit is being generated from a company's sales. Efficiency ratios will be calculated to see how efficient a company is using its assets in running its business. You will be introduced to these ratios and how to interpret them throughout this course.

Compare the two sets of income statements. The cash-basis system looks as though no revenue was earned in the first two months, and expenses were excessive. Then in March it looks like the company earned a lot of revenue. How realistic is this picture? Now look at the accrual basis figures. Here you see a better picture of what really happened over the three months. Revenues and expenses stayed relatively even across periods.

This comparison can show the dangers of reporting in a cash-basis system. In a cash-basis system, the timing of cash flows can make the business look very profitable one month and not profitable the next. If your company was having a bad year and you do not want to report a loss, just do not pay the bills for the last month of the year and you can suddenly show a profit in a cash-basis system. In an accrual-basis system, it does not matter if you do not pay the bills, you still need to record the expenses and present an income statement that accurately portrays what is happening in your company. The accrual-basis system lends itself to more transparency and detail in reporting. This detail is carried over into what is known as a classified balance sheet.

The Classified Balance Sheet

A **classified balance sheet** presents information on your balance sheet in a more informative structure, where asset and liability categories are divided into smaller, more detailed sections. Classified balance sheets show more about the makeup of our assets and liabilities, allowing us to better analyze the current health of our company and make future strategic plans.

Assets can be categorized as current; property, plant, and equipment; long-term investments; intangibles; and, if necessary, other assets. As you learned in Introduction to Financial Statements, a *current asset* (also known as a *short-term asset*) is any asset that will be converted to cash, sold, or used up within one year, or one operating cycle, whichever is longer. An **operating cycle** is the amount of time it takes a company to use its cash to provide a product or service and collect payment from the customer (Figure 5.10). For a merchandising firm that sells inventory, an operating cycle is the time it takes for the firm to use its cash to purchase inventory, sell the inventory, and get its cash back from its customers.

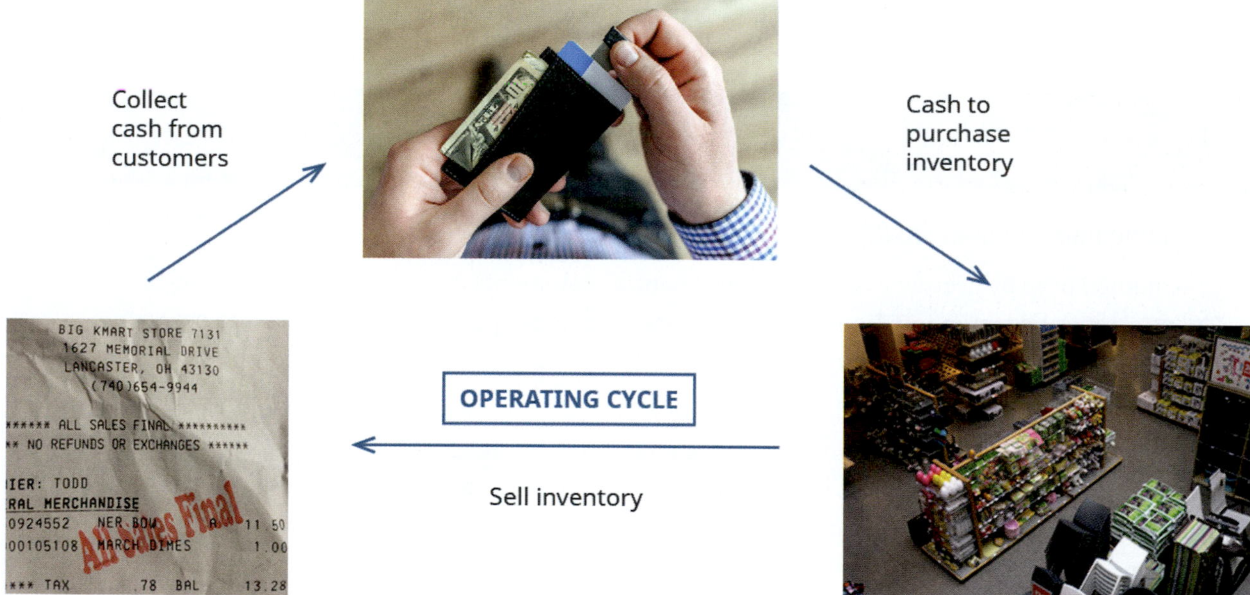

Figure 5.10 Operating Cycle. (credit left: modification of "All Sales Final" by Dan Keck/Flickr, Public Domain; credit center: modification of "Money Wallet Finance" by "Goumbik"/Pixabay, CC0; credit right: modification of "Inventory for Seasonal Decoration" by Mirko Tobias Schäfer/Flickr, CC BY 2.0)

LINK TO LEARNING

Newport News Shipbuilding is an American shipbuilder located in Newport News, Virginia. According to information provided by the company, the company has designed and built 30 aircraft carriers in the past 75 years. That is 30 carriers in 75 years. Newport News constructed the USS *Gerald R. Ford*. It took the company eight years to build the carrier, christening it in 2013. The ship then underwent rigorous testing until it was finally delivered to its home port, Naval Station Norfolk in 2017. That is 12 years after work commenced on the project.

With large shipbuilding projects that take many years to complete, the operating cycle for this type of company could expand beyond a year mark, and Newport News would use this longer operating cycle when dividing current and long-term assets and liabilities.

Learn more about Newport News and its parent company Huntington Ingalls Industries (https://openstax.org/l/50IngallsShip) and see a time-lapse video of the construction of the carrier (https://openstax.org/l/50ShipBuilding) . You can easily tell the passage of time if you watch the snow come and go in the video.

If an asset does not meet the requirements of a current asset, then it is classified as a long-term asset. It can be further defined as property, plant, and equipment; a long-term investment; or an intangible asset (Figure 5.11). **Property, plant, and equipment** are tangible assets (those that have a physical presence) held for more than one operating cycle or one year, whichever is longer. A **long-term investment** is stocks, bonds, or other types of investments that management intends to hold for more than one operating cycle or one year, whichever is longer. **Intangible assets** do not have a physical presence but give the company a long-term future benefit. Some examples include patents, copyrights, and trademarks.

Liabilities are classified as either current liabilities or long-term liabilities. Liabilities also use the one year, or one operating cycle, for the cut-off between current and noncurrent. As we first discussed in Introduction to Financial Statements, if the debt is due within one year or one operating cycle, whichever is longer, the liability is a current liability. If the debt is settled outside one year or one operating cycle, whichever is longer, the liability is a **long-term liability**.

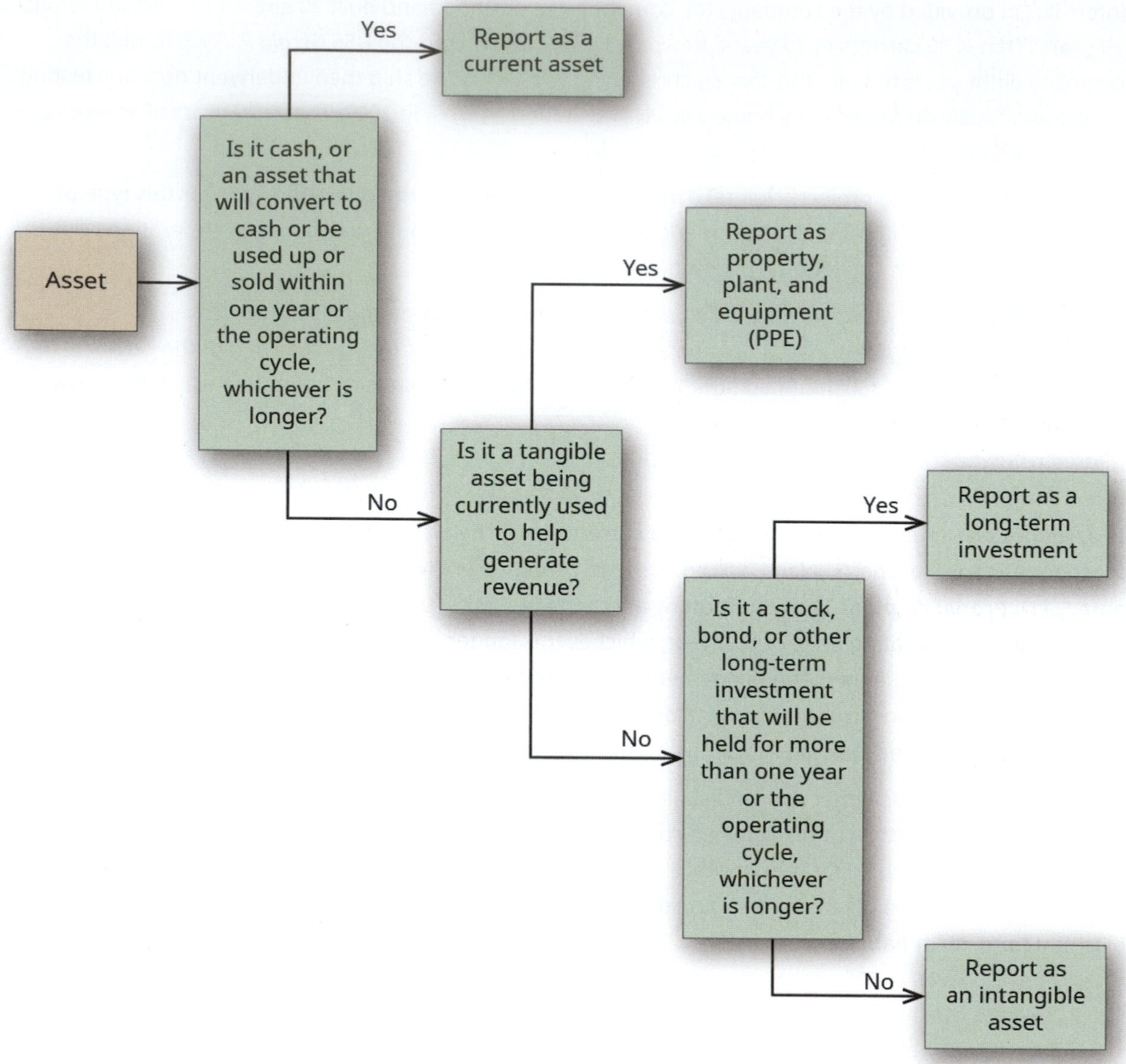

Figure 5.11 Asset Classification Flowchart. A flowchart for asset classification can assist with financial reporting. (attribution: Copyright Rice University, OpenStax, under CC BY-NC-SA 4.0 license)

YOUR TURN

How to Classify Assets

Classify each of the following assets as current asset; property, plant, and equipment; long-term investment; or intangible asset.

A. machine
B. patent
C. supplies

D. building
E. investment in bonds with intent to hold until maturity in 10 years
F. copyright
G. land being held for future office
H. prepaid insurance
I. accounts receivable
J. investment in stock that will be held for six months

Solution

A. property, plant, and equipment. B. intangible asset. C. current asset. D. property, plant, and equipment. E. long-term investment. F. intangible asset. G. long-term investment. H. current asset. I. current asset. J. current asset.

The land is considered a long-term investment, because it is not land being used currently by the company to earn revenue. Buying real estate is an investment. If the company decided in the future that it was not going to build the new office, it could sell the land and would probably be able to sell the land for more than it was purchased for, because the value of real estate tends to go up over time. But like any investment, there is the risk that the land might actually go down in value.

The investment in stock that we only plan to hold for six months will be called a marketable security in the current asset section of the balance sheet.

As an example, the balance sheet in Figure 5.12 is classified.

MAGNIFICENT LANDSCAPING SERVICE Balance Sheet For the Month Ended April 30, 2018		
Assets		
Current Assets		
Cash		$2,950
Accounts Receivable		575
Office Supplies		40
Prepaid Insurance		240
Total Current Assets		$3,805
Property, Plant, and Equipment		
Equipment	$2,500	
Accumulated Depreciation: Equipment	35	2,465
Total Assets		$6,270
Liabilities		
Current Liabilities		
Accounts Payable		$ 28
Salaries Payable		420
Unearned Lawn Mowing Revenue		100
Total Current Liabilities		$ 548
Stockholders' Equity		
Common Stock	$5,000	
Retained Earnings	722	
Total Stockholders' Equity		5,722
Total Liabilities and Stockholders' Equity		$6,270

Figure 5.12 Classified Balance Sheet for Magnificent Landscaping Service. (attribution: Copyright Rice University, OpenStax, under CC BY-NC-SA 4.0 license)

CONTINUING APPLICATION AT WORK

Interim Reporting in the Grocery Industry

Interim reporting helps determine how well a company is performing at a given time during the year. Some companies revise their earnings estimates depending on how profitable the company has been up until a certain point in time. The grocery industry, which includes both private and publicly traded companies, performs the same exercise.

However, grocery companies use such information to inform other important business decisions. Consider the last time you walked through the grocery store and purchased your favorite brand but found another item out of stock. What if the next time you shop, the product you loved is no longer carried, but the out-of-stock item is available?

Grocery store profitably is based on small margins of revenue on a multitude of products. The bar codes scanned at checkout not only provide the price of a product but also track how much inventory has been sold. The grocery store analyzes such information to determine how quickly the product turns over, which drives profit on small margins. If a product sells well, the store might stock it all of the time, but if a product does not sell quickly enough, it could be discontinued.

Using Classified Balance Sheets to Evaluate Liquidity

Categorizing assets and liabilities on a balance sheet helps a company evaluate its business. One way a company can evaluate its business is with financial statement ratios. We consider two measures of liquidity, working capital, and the current ratio. Let's first explore this idea of liquidity.

We first described liquidity in Introduction to Financial Statements as the ability to convert assets into cash. **Liquidity** is a company's ability to convert assets into cash in order to meet short-term cash needs, so it is very important for a company to remain liquid. A critical piece of information to remember at this point is that most companies use the accrual accounting method to determine and maintain their accounting records. This fact means that even with a positive income position, as reflected by its income statement, a company can go bankrupt due to poor cash flow. It is also important to note that even if a company has a lot of cash, it may still be in bankruptcy trouble if all or much of that cash is borrowed. According to an article published in *Money* magazine, one in four small businesses fail because of cash flow issues.[1] They are making a profit and seem financially healthy but do not have cash when needed.

Companies should analyze liquidity constantly to avoid cash shortages that may result in a need for a short-term loan. Intermittently taking out a short-term loan is often expected, but a company cannot keep coming up short on cash every year if it is going to remain liquid. A seasonal business, such as a specialized holiday retailer, may require a short-term loan to continue its operations during slower revenue-generating periods. Companies will use numbers from their classified balance sheet to test for liquidity. They want to make sure they have enough current assets to pay their current liabilities. Only cash is used to directly pay liabilities, but other current assets, such as accounts receivable or short-term investments, might be sold for cash, converted to cash, or used to bring in cash to pay liabilities.

ETHICAL CONSIDERATIONS

Liquidity Is as Important as Net Worth

How does a company like Lehman Brothers Holdings, with over $639 billion in assets and $613 billion in liabilities, go bankrupt? That question still confuses many, but it comes down to the fact that having assets recorded on the books at their purchase price is not the same as the immediate value of the assets. Lehman Brothers had a liquidity crisis that led to a solvency crisis, because Lehman Brothers could not sell the assets on its books at book value to cover its short-term cash demands. Matt Johnston, in an article for the online publication *Coinmonks*, puts it simply: "Liquidity is all about being able to access cash when it's needed. If you can settle your current obligations with ease, you've got liquidity. If you've got debts coming due and you don't have the cash to settle them, then you've got a liquidity crisis."[2] Continuing this *Coinmonks* discussion, the inability to timely pay debts leads to a business entity

1 Elaine Pofeldt. "5 Ways to Tackle the Problem That Kills One of Every Four Small Businesses." *Money*. May 19, 2015. http://time.com/money/3888448/cash-flow-small-business-startups/

becoming insolvent because bills cannot be paid on time and assets need to be written down. When Lehman Brothers could not timely pay their bills in 2008, it went bankrupt, sending a shock throughout the entire banking system. Accountants need to understand the differences between net worth, equity, liquidity, and solvency, and be able to inform stakeholders of their organization's actual financial position, not just the recorded numbers on the balance sheet.

Two calculations a company might use to test for liquidity are working capital and the current ratio. **Working capital**, which was first described in Introduction to Financial Statements, is found by taking the difference between current assets and current liabilities.

Working Capital = Current Assets – Current Liabilities

A positive outcome means the company has enough current assets available to pay its current liabilities or current debts. A negative outcome means the company does not have enough current assets to cover its current liabilities and may have to arrange short-term financing. Though a positive working capital is preferred, a company needs to make sure that there is not too much of a difference between current assets and current liabilities. A company that has a high working capital might have too much money in current assets that could be used for other company investments. Things such as industry and size of a company will dictate what type of margin is best.

Let's consider Printing Plus and its working capital (Figure 5.13).

2 Matt Johnson. "Revisiting the Lehman Brothers Collapse, the Business of Banking and Its Inherent Crises." *Coinmonks*. February 1, 2018. https://medium.com/coinmonks/revisiting-the-lehman-brothers-collapse-fb18769d6cf8

PRINTING PLUS Balance Sheet For the Month Ended January 31, 2019		
Assets		
Cash		$24,800
Accounts Receivable		1,200
Interest Receivable		140
Supplies		400
Equipment	$3,500	
Accumulated Depreciation: Equipment	75	3,425
Total Assets		**$29,965**
Liabilities		
Accounts Payable		$ 500
Salaries Payable		1,500
Unearned Revenue		3,400
Total Liabilities		5,400
Stockholders' Equity		
Common Stock		20,000
Ending Retained Earnings		4,565
Total Stockholders' Equity		24,565
Total Liabilities and Stockholders' Equity		**$29,965**

Figure 5.13 Balance Sheet for Printing Plus. (attribution: Copyright Rice University, OpenStax, under CC BY-NC-SA 4.0 license)

Printing Plus's current assets include cash, accounts receivable, interest receivable, and supplies. Their current liabilities include accounts payable, salaries payable, and unearned revenue. The following is the computation of working capital:

$$\text{Working capital} = \$26{,}540 - \$5{,}400 = \$21{,}140$$

This means that you have more than enough working capital to pay the current liabilities your company has recorded. This figure may seem high, but remember that this is the company's first month of operations and this much cash may need to be available for larger, long-term asset purchases. However, there is also the possibility that the company might choose to identify long-term financing options for the acquisition of expensive, long-term assets, assuming that it can qualify for the increased debt.

Notice that part of the current liability calculation is unearned revenue. If a company has a surplus of unearned revenue, it can sometimes get away with less working capital, as it will need less cash to pay its bills. However, the company must be careful, since the cash was recorded before providing the services or products associated with the unearned revenue. This relationship is why the unearned revenue was initially created, and there often will be necessary cash outflows associated with meeting the terms of the unearned revenue creation.

Companies with inventory will usually need a higher working capital than a service company, as inventory can tie up a large amount of a company's cash with less cash available to pay its bills. Also, small companies will normally need a higher working capital than larger companies, because it is harder for smaller companies to get loans, and they usually pay a higher interest rate.

LINK TO LEARNING

PricewaterhouseCoopers (PwC) released its 2015 Annual Global Working Capital Survey (https://openstax.org/l/50PwC2015WorCap) which is a detailed study on working capital. Though the report does not show the working capital calculation you just learned, there is very interesting information about working capital in different industries, business sizes, and locations. Take a few minutes and peruse this document.

The **current ratio** (also known as the working capital ratio), which was first described in Introduction to Financial Statements, tells a company how many times over company current assets can cover current liabilities. It is found by dividing current assets by current liabilities and is calculated as follows:

$$\textbf{Current Ratio} = \frac{\textbf{Current Assets}}{\textbf{Current Liabilities}}$$

For example, if a company has current assets of $20,000 and current liabilities of $10,000, its current ratio is $20,000/$10,000 = two times. This means the company has enough current assets to cover its current liabilities twice. Ideally, many companies would like to maintain a 1.5:2 times current assets over current liabilities ratio. However, depending on the company's function or purpose, an optimal ratio could be lower or higher than the previous recommendation. For example, many utilities do not have large fluctuations in anticipated seasonal current ratios, so they might decide to maintain a current ratio of 1.25:1.5 times current assets over current liabilities ratio, while a high-tech startup might want to maintain a ratio of 2.5:3 times current assets over current liabilities ratio.

The current ratio for Printing Plus is $26,540/$5,400 = 4.91 times. That is a very high current ratio, but since the business was just started, having more cash might allow the company to make larger purchases while still paying its liabilities. However, this ratio might be a result of short-term conditions, so the company is advised to still plan on maintaining a ratio that is considered both rational and not too risky.

Using ratios for a single year does not provide a broad picture. A company will get much better information if it compares the working capital and current ratio numbers for several years so it can see increases, decreases, and where numbers remain fairly consistent. Companies can also benefit from comparing this financial data to that of other companies in the industry.

ETHICAL CONSIDERATIONS

Computers Still Use Debits and Credits: Check behind the Dashboard for Fraud

Newly hired accountants are often sat at a computer to work off of a dashboard, which is a computer screen where entries are made into the accounting system. New accountants working with modern accounting software may not be aware that their software uses the debit and credit system you learned about, and that the system may automatically close the books without the accountant's review of closing entries. Manually closing the books gives accountants a chance to review the balances of different accounts; if accountants do not review the entries, they will not know what is occurring in the accounting system or in their organization's financial statements.

Many accounting systems automatically close the books if the command is made in the system. While debits and credits are being entered and may not have been reviewed, the system can be instructed to close out the revenue and expense accounts and create an Income Statement.

A knowledgeable accountant can review entries within the software's audit function. The accountant will be able to look at every entry, its description, both sides of the entry (debit and credit), and any changes made in the entry. This review is important in determining if any incorrect entry was either a mistake or fraud. The accountant can see who made the entry and how the entry occurred in the accounting system.

To ensure the integrity of the system, each person working in the system must have a unique user identification, and no users may know others' passwords. If there is an entry or updated entry, the accountant will be able to see the entry in the audit function of the software. If an employee has changed expense items to pay his or her personal bills, the accountant can see the change. Similarly, changes in transaction dates can be reviewed to determine whether they are fraudulent. Professional accountants know what goes on in their organization's accounting system.

5.4 Appendix: Complete a Comprehensive Accounting Cycle for a Business

We have gone through the entire accounting cycle for Printing Plus with the steps spread over three chapters. Let's go through the complete accounting cycle for another company here. The full accounting cycle diagram is presented in Figure 5.14.

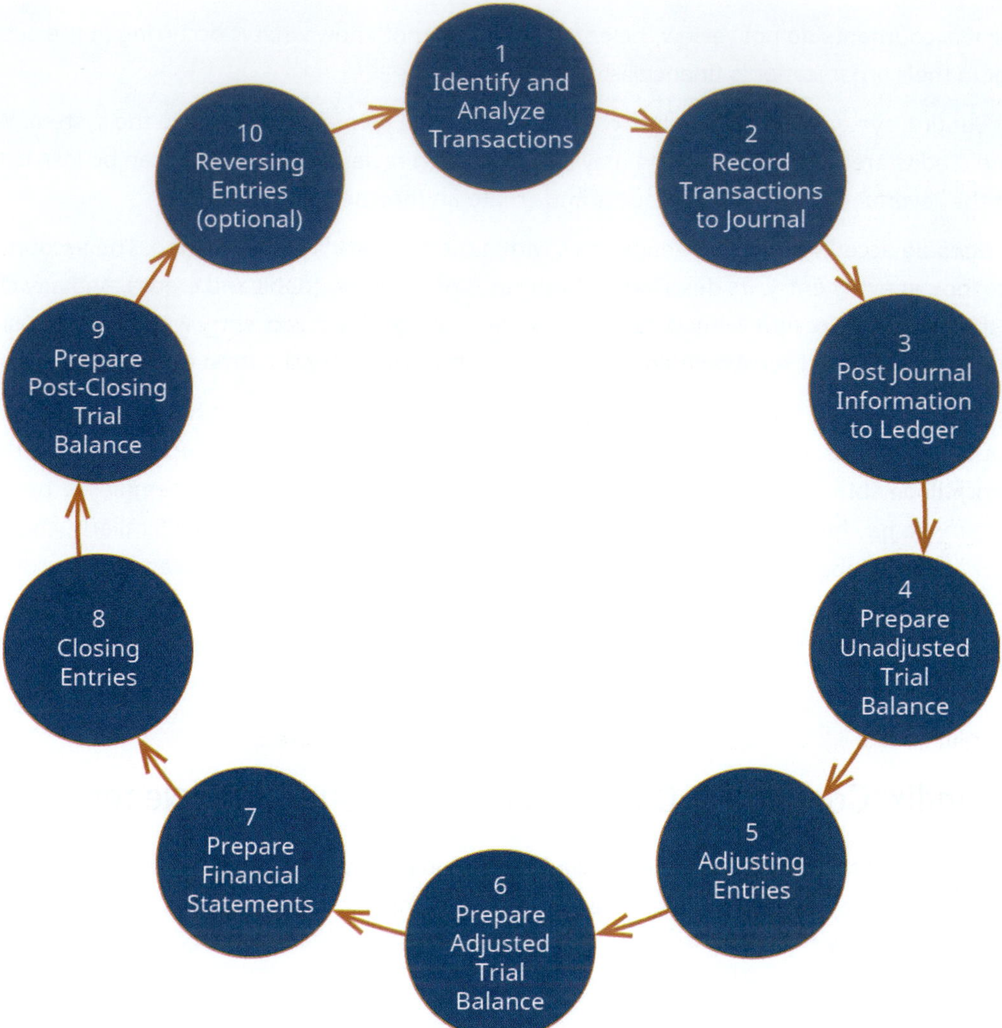

Figure 5.14 The Accounting Cycle. (attribution: Copyright Rice University, OpenStax, under CC BY-NC-SA 4.0 license)

We next take a look at a comprehensive example that works through the entire accounting cycle for Clip'em Cliff. Clifford Girard retired from the US Marine Corps after 20 years of active duty. Cliff decides it would be fun to become a barber and open his own shop called "Clip'em Cliff." He will run the barber shop out of his home for the first couple of months while he identifies a new location for his shop.

Since his Marines career included several years of logistics, he is also going to operate a consulting practice where he will help budding barbers create a barbering practice. He will charge a flat fee or a per hour charge. His consulting practice will be recognized as service revenue and will provide additional revenue while he develops his barbering practice.

He obtains a barber's license after the required training and is ready to open his shop on August 1. Table 5.2 shows his transactions from the first month of business.

Transactions for August

Date	Transaction
Aug. 1	Cliff issues $70,000 shares of common stock for cash.
Aug. 3	Cliff purchases barbering equipment for $45,000; $37,500 was paid immediately with cash, and the remaining $7,500 was billed to Cliff with payment due in 30 days. He decided to buy used equipment, because he was not sure if he truly wanted to run a barber shop. He assumed that he will replace the used equipment with new equipment within a couple of years.
Aug. 6	Cliff purchases supplies for $300 cash.
Aug. 10	Cliff provides $4,000 in services to a customer who asks to be billed for the services.
Aug. 13	Cliff pays a $75 utility bill with cash.
Aug. 14	Cliff receives $3,200 cash in advance from a customer for services not yet rendered.
Aug. 16	Cliff distributed $150 cash in dividends to stockholders.
Aug. 17	Cliff receives $5,200 cash from a customer for services rendered.
Aug. 19	Cliff paid $2,000 toward the outstanding liability from the August 3 transaction.
Aug. 22	Cliff paid $4,600 cash in salaries expense to employees.
Aug. 28	The customer from the August 10 transaction pays $1,500 cash toward Cliff's account.

Table 5.2

Transaction 1: On August 1, 2019, Cliff issues $70,000 shares of common stock for cash.

Analysis:

- Clip'em Cliff now has more cash. Cash is an asset, which is increasing on the debit side.
- When the company issues stock, this yields a higher common stock figure than before issuance. The common stock account is increasing on the credit side.

JOURNAL			
Date	**Account**	**Debit**	**Credit**
Aug. 1, 2019	Cash Common Stock *To recognize issuance of common stock*	70,000	 70,000

Assets	=	Liabilities	+	Stockholders' Equity
+$70,000	=	+$0	+	+$70,000
$70,000	=	$0	+	$70,000

Transaction 2: On August 3, 2019, Cliff purchases barbering equipment for $45,000; $37,500 was paid immediately with cash, and the remaining $7,500 was billed to Cliff with payment due in 30 days.

Analysis:

- Clip'em Cliff now has more equipment than before. Equipment is an asset, which is increasing on the debit side for $45,000.
- Cash is used to pay for $37,500. Cash is an asset, decreasing on the credit side.
- Cliff asked to be billed, which means he did not pay cash immediately for $7,500 of the equipment. Accounts Payable is used to signal this short-term liability. Accounts payable is increasing on the credit side.

JOURNAL			
Date	**Account**	**Debit**	**Credit**
Aug. 3, 2019	Equipment Cash Accounts Payable *To recognize purchase of equipment*	45,000	 37,500 7,500

Assets	=	Liabilities	+	Stockholders' Equity
+$45,000 –$37,500	=	+$7,500	+	+$0
$ 7,500	=	$7,500	+	$0

Transaction 3: On August 6, 2019, Cliff purchases supplies for $300 cash.

Analysis:

- Clip'em Cliff now has less cash. Cash is an asset, which is decreasing on the credit side.
- Supplies, an asset account, is increasing on the debit side.

JOURNAL			
Date	**Account**	**Debit**	**Credit**
Aug. 6, 2019	Supplies Cash *To recognize supplies purchase*	300	 300

Assets	=	Liabilities	+	Stockholders' Equity
+$300 –$300	=	+$0	+	+$0
$0	=	$0	+	$0

Transaction 4: On August 10, 2019, provides $4,000 in services to a customer who asks to be billed for the services.

Analysis:

- Clip'em Cliff provided service, thus earning revenue. Revenue impacts equity, and increases on the credit side.
- The customer did not pay immediately for the service and owes Cliff payment. This is an Accounts Receivable for Cliff. Accounts Receivable is an asset that is increasing on the debit side.

JOURNAL			
Date	**Account**	**Debit**	**Credit**
Aug. 10, 2019	Accounts Receivable Service Revenue *To recognize revenue earned, customer purchased on account*	4,000	4,000

Assets	=	Liabilities	+	Stockholders' Equity
+$4,000	=	+$0	+	+$4,000
$4,000	=	$0	+	$4,000

Transaction 5: On August 13, 2019, Cliff pays a $75 utility bill with cash.

Analysis:

- Clip'em Cliff now has less cash than before. Cash is an asset that is decreasing on the credit side.
- Utility payments are billed expenses. Utility Expense negatively impacts equity, and increases on the debit side.

JOURNAL			
Date	**Account**	**Debit**	**Credit**
Aug. 13, 2019	Utility Expense Cash *To recognize payment of utility bill*	75	75

Assets	=	Liabilities	+	Stockholder's Equity
–$75	=	+$0	+	–$75
–$75	=	$0	+	–$75

Transaction 6: On August 14, 2019, Cliff receives $3,200 cash in advance from a customer for services to be rendered.

Analysis:

- Clip'em Cliff now has more cash. Cash is an asset, which is increasing on the debit side.
- The customer has not yet received services but already paid the company. This means the company owes the customer the service. This creates a liability to the customer, and revenue cannot yet be recognized. Unearned Revenue is the liability account, which is increasing on the credit side.

JOURNAL			
Date	**Account**	**Debit**	**Credit**
Aug. 14, 2019	Cash Unearned Revenue *To recognize customer's advanced payment*	3,200	 3,200

Assets	=	Liabilities	+	Stockholders' Equity
+$3,200	=	+$3,200	+	+$0
$3,200	=	$3,200	+	$0

Transaction 7: On August 16, 2019, Cliff distributed $150 cash in dividends to stockholders.

Analysis:

- Clip'em Cliff now has less cash. Cash is an asset, which is decreasing on the credit side.
- When the company pays out dividends, this decreases equity and increases the dividends account. Dividends increases on the debit side.

JOURNAL			
Date	**Account**	**Debit**	**Credit**
Aug. 16, 2019	Dividends Cash *To recognize distribution of dividends*	150	 150

Assets	=	Liabilities	+	Stockholders' Equity
–$150	=	+$0	+	–$150
–$150	=	$0	+	–$150

Transaction 8: On August 17, 2019, Cliff receives $5,200 cash from a customer for services rendered.

Analysis:

- Clip'em Cliff now has more cash than before. Cash is an asset, which is increasing on the debit side.
- Service was provided, which means revenue can be recognized. Service Revenue increases equity. Service Revenue is increasing on the credit side.

JOURNAL			
Date	**Account**	**Debit**	**Credit**
Aug. 17, 2019	Cash Service Revenue *To recognize revenue earned*	5,200	 5,200

Assets	=	Liabilities	+	Stockholders' Equity
+$5,200	=	+$0	+	+$5,200
$5,200	=	$0	+	$5,200

Transaction 9: On August 19, 2019, Cliff paid $2,000 toward the outstanding liability from the August 3 transaction.

Analysis:

- Clip'em Cliff now has less cash. Cash is an asset, which is decreasing on the credit side.
- Accounts Payable is a liability account, decreasing on the debit side.

JOURNAL			
Date	**Account**	**Debit**	**Credit**
Aug. 19, 2019	Accounts Payable Cash *To recognize partial payment of liability*	2,000	 2,000

Assets	=	Liabilities	+	Stockholders' Equity
–$2,000	=	–$2,000	+	+$0
–$2,000	=	–$2,000	+	$0

Transaction 10: On August 22, 2019, Cliff paid $4,600 cash in salaries expense to employees.

Analysis:

- Clip'em Cliff now has less cash. Cash is an asset, which is decreasing on the credit side.
- When the company pays salaries, this is an expense to the business. Salaries Expense reduces equity by increasing on the debit side.

JOURNAL			
Date	**Account**	**Debit**	**Credit**
Aug. 22, 2019	Salaries Expense Cash *To recognize employee salary payment*	4,600	 4,600

Assets	=	Liabilities	+	Stockholders' Equity
–$4,600	=	+$0	+	–$4,600
–$4,600	=	$0	+	–$4,600

Transaction 11: On August 28, 2019, the customer from the August 10 transaction pays $1,500 cash toward Cliff's account.

Analysis:

- The customer made a partial payment on their outstanding account. This reduces Accounts Receivable. Accounts Receivable is an asset account decreasing on the credit side.
- Cash is an asset, increasing on the debit side.

JOURNAL			
Date	**Account**	**Debit**	**Credit**
Aug. 28, 2019	Cash Accounts Receivable *To recognize customer partial payment*	1,500	 1,500

Assets	=	Liabilities	+	Stockholders' Equity
+$1,500 –$1,500	=	+$0	+	+$0
$0	=	$0	+	$0

The complete journal for August is presented in Figure 5.15.

JOURNAL			
Date	**Account**	**Debit**	**Credit**
Aug. 1, 2019	Cash	70,000	
	Common Stock		70,000
Aug. 3, 2019	Equipment	45,000	
	Cash		37,500
	Account Payable		7,500
Aug. 6, 2019	Supplies	300	
	Cash		300
Aug. 10, 2019	Accounts Receivable	4,000	
	Service Revenue		4,000
Aug. 13, 2019	Utility Expense	75	
	Cash		75
Aug. 14, 2019	Cash	3,200	
	Unearned Revenue		3,200
Aug. 16, 2019	Dividends	150	
	Cash		150
Aug. 17, 2019	Cash	5,200	
	Service Revenue		5,200
Aug. 19, 2019	Accounts Payable	2,000	
	Cash		2,000
Aug. 22, 2019	Salaries Expense	4,600	
	Cash		4,600
Aug. 28, 2019	Cash	1,500	
	Accounts Receivable		1,500

Figure 5.15 Journal Entries for August. (attribution: Copyright Rice University, OpenStax, under CC BY-NC-SA 4.0 license)

Once all journal entries have been created, the next step in the accounting cycle is to post journal information to the ledger. The ledger is visually represented by T-accounts. Cliff will go through each transaction and transfer the account information into the debit or credit side of that ledger account. Any account that has more than one transaction needs to have a final balance calculated. This happens by taking the difference between the debits and credits in an account.

Clip'em Cliff's ledger represented by T-accounts is presented in Figure 5.16.

Cash	
Aug. 1 70,000	37,500 Aug. 3
Aug. 14 3,200	300 Aug. 6
Aug. 17 5,200	75 Aug. 13
Aug. 28 1,500	150 Aug. 16
	2,000 Aug. 19
	4,600 Aug. 22
Bal. 35,275	

Accounts Payable	
Aug. 19 2,000	7,500 Aug. 3
	Bal. 5,500

Common Stock	
	70,000 Aug. 1
	Bal. 70,000

Accounts Receivable	
Aug. 10 4,000	1,500 Aug. 28
Bal. 2,500	

Unearned Revenue	
	3,200 Aug. 14
	Bal. 3,200

Dividends	
Aug. 16 150	
Bal. 150	

Supplies	
Aug. 6 300	
Bal. 300	

Service Revenue	
	4,000 Aug. 10
	5,200 Aug. 17
	Bal. 9,200

Equipment	
Aug. 3 45,000	
Bal. 45,000	

Salaries Expense	
Aug. 22 4,600	
Bal. 4,600	

Utility Expense	
Aug. 13 75	
Bal. 75	

Figure 5.16 T-Accounts for August. (attribution: Copyright Rice University, OpenStax, under CC BY-NC-SA 4.0 license)

You will notice that the sum of the asset account balances in Cliff's ledger equals the sum of the liability and equity account balances at $83,075. The final debit or credit balance in each account is transferred to the unadjusted trial balance in the corresponding debit or credit column as illustrated in Figure 5.17.

CLIP'EM CLIFF Unadjusted Trial Balance For the Month Ended August 31, 2019		
Account	**Debit**	**Credit**
Cash	$35,275	
Accounts Receivable	2,500	
Supplies	300	
Equipment	45,000	
Accounts Payable		$ 5,500
Unearned Revenue		3,200
Common Stock		70,000
Dividends	150	
Service Revenue		9,200
Salaries Expense	4,600	
Utility Expense	75	
Total	$87,900	$87,900

Service Revenue	
	4,000 Aug. 10 5,200 Aug. 17
	Bal. 9,200

Salaries Expense	
Aug. 22 4,600	
Bal. 4,600	

Figure 5.17 Unadjusted Trial Balance for Clip'em Cliff. (attribution: Copyright Rice University, OpenStax, under CC BY-NC-SA 4.0 license)

Once all of the account balances are transferred to the correct columns, each column is totaled. The total in the debit column must match the total in the credit column to remain balanced. The unadjusted trial balance for Clip'em Cliff appears in Figure 5.18.

CLIP'EM CLIFF Unadjusted Trial Balance For the Month Ended August 31, 2019		
Account	**Debit**	**Credit**
Cash	$35,275	
Accounts Receivable	2,500	
Supplies	300	
Equipment	45,000	
Accounts Payable		$ 5,500
Unearned Revenue		3,200
Common Stock		70,000
Dividends	150	
Service Revenue		9,200
Salaries Expense	4,600	
Utility Expense	75	
Total	$87,900	$87,900

Figure 5.18 Unadjusted Trial Balance for Clip'em Cliff. (attribution: Copyright Rice University, OpenStax, under CC BY-NC-SA 4.0 license)

The unadjusted trial balance shows a debit and credit balance of $87,900. Remember, the unadjusted trial balance is prepared before any period-end adjustments are made.

On August 31, Cliff has the transactions shown in Table 5.3 requiring adjustment.

August 31 Transactions

Date	Transaction
Aug. 31	Cliff took an inventory of supplies and discovered that $250 of supplies remain unused at the end of the month.
Aug. 31	The equipment purchased on August 3 depreciated $2,500 during the month of August.
Aug. 31	Clip'em Cliff performed $1,100 of services during August for the customer from the August 14 transaction.
Aug. 31	Reviewing the company bank statement, Clip'em Cliff discovers $350 of interest earned during the month of August that was previously uncollected and unrecorded. As a new customer for the bank, the interest was paid by a bank that offered an above-market-average interest rate.
Aug. 31	Unpaid and previously unrecorded income taxes for the month are $3,400. The tax payment was to cover his federal quarterly estimated income taxes. He lives in a state that does not have an individual income tax

Table 5.3

Adjusting Transaction 1: Cliff took an inventory of supplies and discovered that $250 of supplies remain unused at the end of the month.

Analysis:

- $250 of supplies remain at the end of August. The company began the month with $300 worth of supplies. Therefore, $50 of supplies were used during the month and must be recorded (300 – 250). Supplies is an asset that is decreasing (credit).
- Supplies is a type of prepaid expense, that when used, becomes an expense. Supplies Expense would increase (debit) for the $50 of supplies used during August.

JOURNAL			
Date	Account	Debit	Credit
Aug. 31, 2019	Supplies Expense Supplies *To recognize supply usage for August*	50	 50

Assets	=	Liabilities	+	Stockholders' Equity
–$50	=	+$0	+	–$50
–$50	=	$0	+	–$50

Adjusting Transaction 2: The equipment purchased on August 3 depreciated $2,500 during the month of August.

Analysis:

- Equipment cost of $2,500 was allocated during August. This depreciation will affect the Accumulated Depreciation–Equipment account and the Depreciation Expense–Equipment account. While we are not doing depreciation calculations here, you will come across more complex calculations, such as depreciation in Long-Term Assets.

- Accumulated Depreciation–Equipment is a contra asset account (contrary to Equipment) and increases (credit) for $2,500.
- Depreciation Expense–Equipment is an expense account that is increasing (debit) for $2,500.

JOURNAL			
Date	**Account**	**Debit**	**Credit**
Aug. 31, 2019	Depreciation Expense - Equipment Accumulated Depreciation - Equipment *To recognize equipment depreciation for August*	2,500	2,500

Assets	=	Liabilities	+	Stockholders' Equity
–$2,500	=	+$0	+	–$2,500
–$2,500	=	$0	+	–$2,500

Adjusting Transaction 3: Clip'em Cliff performed $1,100 of services during August for the customer from the August 14 transaction.

Analysis:

- The customer from the August 14 transaction gave the company $3,200 in advanced payment for services. By the end of August the company had earned $1,100 of the advanced payment. This means that the company still has yet to provide $2,100 in services to that customer.
- Since some of the unearned revenue is now earned, Unearned Revenue would decrease. Unearned Revenue is a liability account and decreases on the debit side.
- The company can now recognize the $1,100 as earned revenue. Service Revenue increases (credit) for $1,100.

JOURNAL			
Date	**Account**	**Debit**	**Credit**
Aug. 31, 2019	Unearned Revenue Service Revenue *To recognize revenue earned from Aug. 14 transaction*	1,100	1,100

Assets	=	Liabilities	+	Stockholders' Equity
$0	=	–$1,100	+	+$1,100
$0	=	–$1,100	+	$1,100

Adjusting Transaction 4: Reviewing the company bank statement, Clip'em Cliff identifies $350 of interest earned during the month of August that was previously unrecorded.

Analysis:

- Interest is revenue for the company on money kept in a money market account at the bank. The company only sees the bank statement at the end of the month and needs to record as received interest revenue reflected on the bank statement.

- Interest Revenue is a revenue account that increases (credit) for $350.
- Since Clip'em Cliff has yet to collect this interest revenue, it is considered a receivable. Interest Receivable increases (debit) for $350.

JOURNAL			
Date	**Account**	**Debit**	**Credit**
Aug. 31, 2019	Interest Receivable Interest Revenue *To recognize interest revenue earned but not yet collected*	350	 350

Assets	=	Liabilities	+	Stockholders' Equity
+$350	=	$0	+	+$350
+$350	=	$0	+	+$350

Adjusting Transaction 5: Unpaid and previously unrecorded income taxes for the month are $3,400.

Analysis:

- Income taxes are an expense to the business that accumulate during the period but are only paid at predetermined times throughout the year. This period did not require payment but did accumulate income tax.
- Income Tax Expense is an expense account that negatively affects equity. Income Tax Expense increases on the debit side.
- The company owes the tax money but has not yet paid, signaling a liability. Income Tax Payable is a liability that is increasing on the credit side.

JOURNAL			
Date	**Account**	**Debit**	**Credit**
Aug. 31, 2019	Income Tax Expense Income Tax Payable *To recognize taxes incurred but not yet paid*	3,400	 3,400

Assets	=	Liabilities	+	Stockholders' Equity
$0	=	+$3,400	+	–$3,400
$0	=	$3,400	+	–$3,400

The summary of adjusting journal entries for Clip'em Cliff is presented in Figure 5.19.

JOURNAL			
Date	**Account**	**Debit**	**Credit**
Aug. 31, 2019	Supplies Expense	50	
	Supplies		50
Aug. 31, 2019	Depreciation Expense: Equipment	2,500	
	Accumulated Depreciation: Equipment		2,500
Aug. 31, 2019	Unearned Revenue	1,100	
	Service Revenue		1,100
Aug. 31, 2019	Interest Receivable	350	
	Interest Revenue		350
Aug. 31, 2019	Income Tax Expense	3,400	
	Income Tax Payable		3,400

Figure 5.19 Adjusting Journal Entries for Clip'em Cliff. (attribution: Copyright Rice University, OpenStax, under CC BY-NC-SA 4.0 license)

Now that all of the adjusting entries are journalized, they must be posted to the ledger. Posting adjusting entries is the same process as posting the general journal entries. Each journalized account figure will transfer to the corresponding ledger account on either the debit or credit side as illustrated in Figure 5.20.

JOURNAL			
Date	**Account**	**Debit**	**Credit**
Aug. 31, 2019	Supplies Expense	50	
	Supplies		50

Supplies			
Aug. 6	300	50	Aug. 31
Bal. 250			

Supplies Expense		
Aug. 31	50	
Bal.	**50**	

Figure 5.20 Posting Ledger Entries for Clip'em Cliff. (attribution: Copyright Rice University, OpenStax, under CC BY-NC-SA 4.0 license)

We would normally use a general ledger, but for illustrative purposes, we are using T-accounts to represent the ledgers. The T-accounts after the adjusting entries are posted are presented in Figure 5.21.

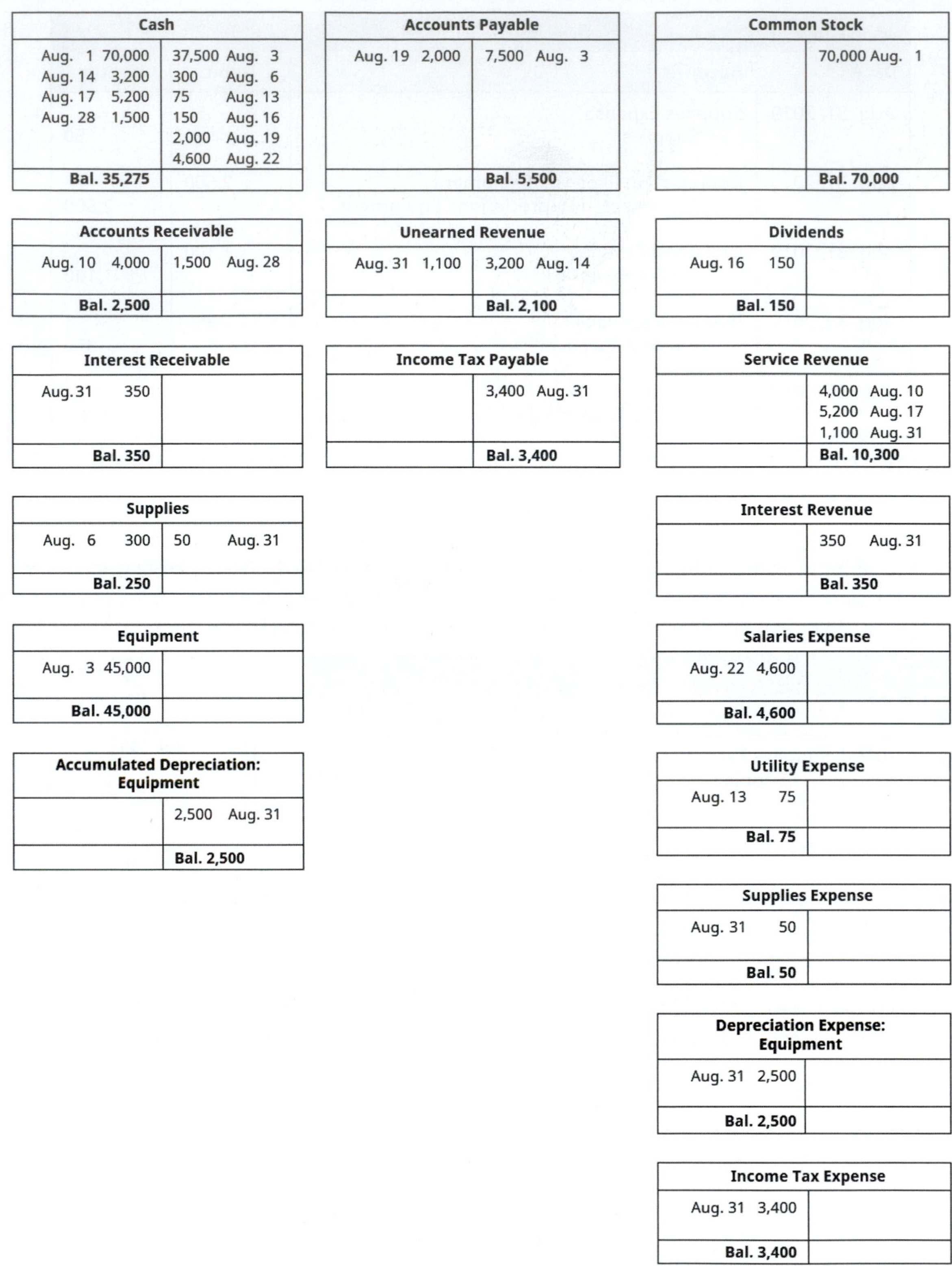

Figure 5.21 Ledger Entries (in T-Accounts) for Clip’em Cliff. (attribution: Copyright Rice University, OpenStax, under CC BY-NC-SA 4.0 license)

You will notice that the sum of the asset account balances equals the sum of the liability and equity account balances at $80,875. The final debit or credit balance in each account is transferred to the adjusted trial balance, the same way the general ledger transferred to the unadjusted trial balance.

The next step in the cycle is to prepare the adjusted trial balance. Clip'em Cliff's adjusted trial balance is shown in Figure 5.22.

CLIP'EM CLIFF Adjusted Trial Balance For the Month Ended August 31, 2019		
Account	**Debit**	**Credit**
Cash	$35,275	
Accounts Receivable	2,500	
Interest Receivable	350	
Supplies	250	
Equipment	45,000	
Accumulated Depreciation: Equipment		$ 2,500
Accounts Payable		5,500
Unearned Revenue		2,100
Income Tax Payable		3,400
Common Stock		70,000
Dividends	150	
Interest Revenue		350
Service Revenue		10,300
Supplies Expense	50	
Depreciation Expense: Equipment	2,500	
Income Tax Expense	3,400	
Salaries Expense	4,600	
Utility Expense	75	
Total	$94,150	$94,150

Figure 5.22 Adjusted Trial Balance for Clip'em Cliff. (attribution: Copyright Rice University, OpenStax, under CC BY-NC-SA 4.0 license)

The adjusted trial balance shows a debit and credit balance of $94,150. Once the adjusted trial balance is prepared, Cliff can prepare his financial statements (step 7 in the cycle). We only prepare the income statement, statement of retained earnings, and the balance sheet. The statement of cash flows is discussed in detail in Statement of Cash Flows.

To prepare your financial statements, you want to work with your adjusted trial balance.

Remember, revenues and expenses go on an income statement. Dividends, net income (loss), and retained earnings balances go on the statement of retained earnings. On a balance sheet you find assets, contra assets, liabilities, and stockholders' equity accounts.

The income statement for Clip'em Cliff is shown in Figure 5.23.

CLIP'EM CLIFF Income Statement For the Month Ended August 31, 2019		
Revenues		
Interest Revenue	$ 350	
Service Revenue	10,300	
Total Revenues		$10,650
Expenses		
Supplies Expense	50	
Depreciation Expense: Equipment	2,500	
Salaries Expense	4,600	
Utility Expense	75	
Income Tax Expense	3,400	
Total Expenses		10,625
Net Income		$ 25

Figure 5.23 Income Statement for Clip'em Cliff. (attribution: Copyright Rice University, OpenStax, under CC BY-NC-SA 4.0 license)

Note that expenses were only $25 less than revenues. For the first month of operations, Cliff welcomes any income. Cliff will want to increase income in the next period to show growth for investors and lenders.

Next, Cliff prepares the following statement of retained earnings (Figure 5.24).

CLIP'EM CLIFF Statement of Retained Earnings For the Month Ended August 31, 2019	
Beginning Retained Earnings (Aug. 1)	$ 0
Net Income	25
Dividends	(150)
Ending Retained Earnings (Aug. 31)	$(125)

Figure 5.24 Statement of Retained Earnings for Clip'em Cliff. (attribution: Copyright Rice University, OpenStax, under CC BY-NC-SA 4.0 license)

The beginning retained earnings balance is zero because Cliff just began operations and does not have a balance to carry over to a future period. The ending retained earnings balance is –$125. You probably never want to have a negative value on your retained earnings statement, but this situation is not totally unusual for an organization in its initial operations. Cliff will want to improve this outcome going forward. It might make sense for Cliff to not pay dividends until he increases his net income.

Cliff then prepares the balance sheet for Clip'em Cliff as shown in Figure 5.25.

CLIP'EM CLIFF Balance Sheet For the Month Ended August 31, 2019		
Assets		
Cash		$35,275
Accounts Receivable		2,500
Interest Receivable		350
Supplies		250
Equipment	$45,000	
Accumulated Depreciation: Equipment	2,500	42,500
Total Assets		**$80,875**
Liabilities		
Accounts Payable		$ 5,500
Income Tax Payable		3,400
Unearned Revenue		2,100
Total Liabilities		11,000
Stockholders' Equity		
Common Stock		70,000
Ending Retained Earnings		(125)
Total Stockholders' Equity		69,875
Total Liabilities and Stockholders' Equity		**$80,875**

Figure 5.25 Balance Sheet for Clip'em Cliff. (attribution: Copyright Rice University, OpenStax, under CC BY-NC-SA 4.0 license)

The balance sheet shows total assets of $80,875, which equals total liabilities and equity. Now that the financial statements are complete, Cliff will go to the next step in the accounting cycle, preparing and posting closing entries. To do this, Cliff needs his adjusted trial balance information.

Cliff will only close temporary accounts, which include revenues, expenses, income summary, and dividends. The first entry closes revenue accounts to income summary. To close revenues, Cliff will debit revenue accounts and credit income summary.

JOURNAL			
Date	**Account**	**Debit**	**Credit**
Aug. 31, 2019	Service Revenue	10,300	
	Interest Revenue	350	
	Income Summary		10,650
	To close revenue accounts to Income Summary		

The second entry closes expense accounts to income summary. To close expenses, Cliff will credit expense accounts and debit income summary.

JOURNAL			
Date	**Account**	**Debit**	**Credit**
Aug. 31, 2019	Income Summary	10,625	
	Supplies Expense		50
	Depreciation Expense: Equipment		2,500
	Income Tax Expense		3,400
	Salaries Expense		4,600
	Utility Expense		75
	To close expense accounts to Income Summary		

The third entry closes income summary to retained earnings. To find the balance, take the difference between the income summary amount in the first and second entries (10,650 – 10,625). To close income summary, Cliff would debit Income Summary and credit Retained Earnings.

JOURNAL			
Date	**Account**	**Debit**	**Credit**
Aug. 31, 2019	Income Summary	25	
	Retained Earnings		25
	To close Income Summary to Retained Earnings		

The fourth closing entry closes dividends to retained earnings. To close dividends, Cliff will credit Dividends, and debit Retained Earnings.

JOURNAL			
Date	**Account**	**Debit**	**Credit**
Aug. 31, 2019	Retained Earnings	150	
	Dividends		150
	To close Dividends to Retained Earnings		

Once all of the closing entries are journalized, Cliff will post this information to the ledger. The closed accounts with their final balances, as well as Retained Earnings, are presented in Figure 5.26.

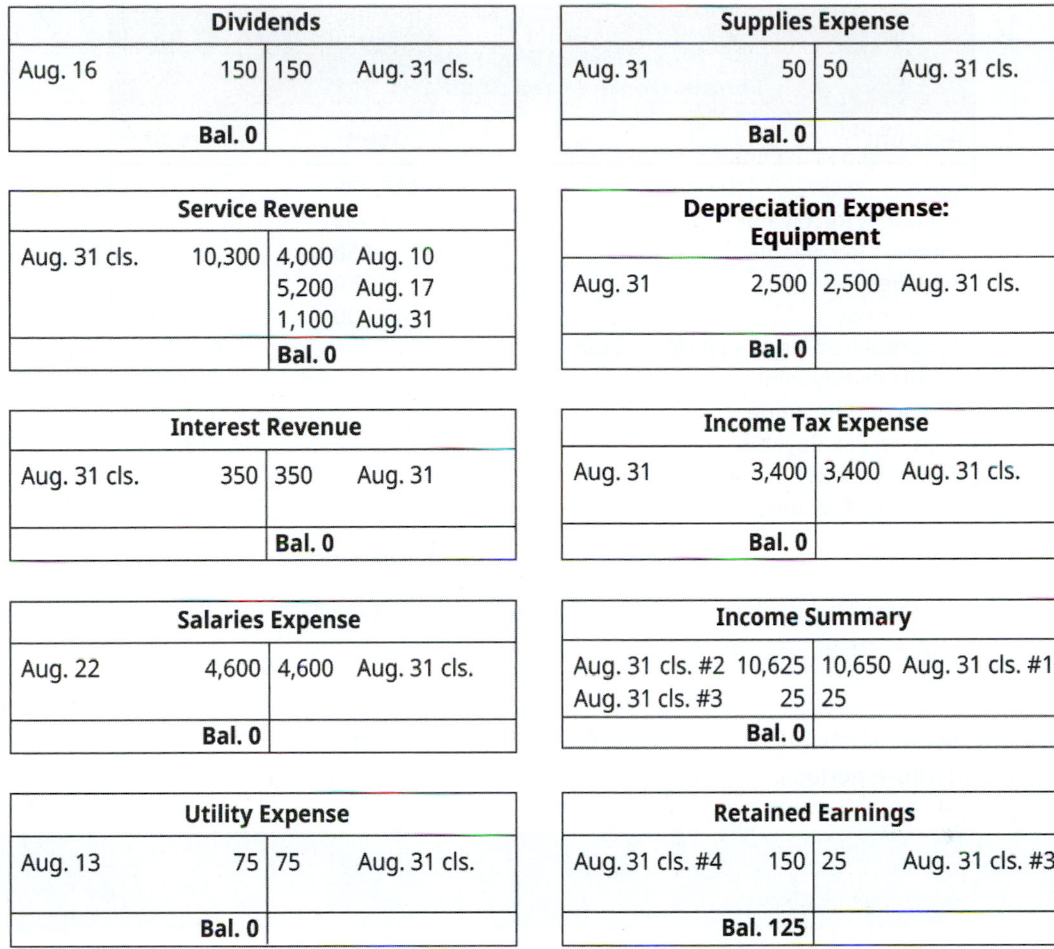

Figure 5.26 Closed Accounts with Final Balances for Clip'em Cliff. (attribution: Copyright Rice University, OpenStax, under CC BY-NC-SA 4.0 license)

Now that the temporary accounts are closed, they are ready for accumulation in the next period.

The last step for the month of August is step 9, preparing the post-closing trial balance. The post-closing trial balance should only contain permanent account information. No temporary accounts should appear on this trial balance. Clip'em Cliff's post-closing trial balance is presented in Figure 5.27.

CLIP'EM CLIFF Post-closing Trial Balance For the Month Ended August 31, 2019		
Account	**Debit**	**Credit**
Cash	$35,275	
Accounts Receivable	2,500	
Interest Receivable	350	
Supplies	250	
Equipment	45,000	
Accumulated Depreciation: Equipment		$ 2,500
Accounts Payable		5,500
Unearned Revenue		2,100
Income Tax Payable		3,400
Common Stock		70,000
Retained Earnings	125	
Total	$83,500	$83,500

Figure 5.27 Post-Closing Trial Balance for Clip'em Cliff. (attribution: Copyright Rice University, OpenStax, under CC BY-NC-SA 4.0 license)

At this point, Cliff has completed the accounting cycle for August. He is now ready to begin the process again for September, and future periods.

CONCEPTS IN PRACTICE

Reversing Entries

One step in the accounting cycle that we did not cover is reversing entries. Reversing entries can be made at the beginning of a new period to certain accruals. The company will reverse adjusting entries made in the prior period to the revenue and expense accruals.

It can be difficult to keep track of accruals from prior periods, as support documentation may not be readily available in current or future periods. This requires an accountant to remember when these accruals came from. By reversing these accruals, there is a reduced risk for counting revenues and expenses twice. The support documentation received in the current or future period for an accrual will be easier to match to prior revenues and expenses with the reversal.

LINK TO LEARNING

As we have learned, the current ratio shows how well a company can cover short-term debt with short-term assets. Look through the balance sheet in the 2017 Annual Report for Target (https://openstax.org/l/50Target2017Bal) and calculate the current ratio. What does the outcome mean for Target?

THINK IT THROUGH

Using Liquidity Ratios to Evaluate Financial Performance

You own a landscaping business that has just begun operations. You made several expensive equipment purchases in your first month to get your business started. These purchases very much reduced your cash-on-hand, and in turn your liquidity suffered in the following months with a low working capital and current ratio.

Your business is now in its eighth month of operation, and while you are starting to see a growth in sales, you are not seeing a significant change in your working capital or current ratio from the low numbers in your early months. What could you attribute to this stagnancy in liquidity? Is there anything you can do as a business owner to better these liquidity measurements? What will happen if you cannot change your liquidity or it gets worse?

Key Terms

classified balance sheet presents information on your balance sheet in a more informative structure, where asset and liability categories are divided into smaller, more detailed sections

closing returning the account to a zero balance

closing entry prepares a company for the next accounting period by clearing any outstanding balances in certain accounts that should not transfer over to the next period

current ratio current assets divided by current liabilities; used to determine a company's liquidity (ability to meet short-term obligations)

income summary intermediary between revenues and expenses, and the Retained Earnings account, storing all the closing information for revenues and expenses, resulting in a "summary" of income or loss for the period

intangible asset asset with financial value but no physical presence; examples include copyrights, patents, goodwill, and trademarks

liquidity ability to convert assets into cash in order to meet primarily short-term cash needs or emergencies

long-term investment stocks, bonds, or other types of investments held for more than one operating cycle or one year, whichever is longer

long-term liability debt settled outside one year or one operating cycle, whichever is longer

operating cycle amount of time it takes a company to use its cash to provide a product or service and collect payment from the customer

permanent (real) account account that transfers balances to the next period, and includes balance sheet accounts, such as assets, liabilities, and stockholder's equity

post-closing trial balance trial balance that is prepared after all the closing entries have been recorded

property, plant, and equipment tangible assets (those that have a physical presence) held for more than one operating cycle or one year, whichever is longer

temporary (nominal) account account that is closed at the end of each accounting period, and includes income statement, dividends, and income summary accounts

working capital current assets less current liabilities; sometimes used as a measure of liquidity

Summary

5.1 Describe and Prepare Closing Entries for a Business

- Closing entries: Closing entries prepare a company for the next period and zero out balance in temporary accounts.
- Purpose of closing entries: Closing entries are necessary because they help a company review income accumulation during a period, and verify data figures found on the adjusted trial balance.
- Permanent accounts: Permanent accounts do not close and are accounts that transfer balances to the next period. They include balance sheet accounts, such as assets, liabilities, and stockholder's equity
- Temporary accounts: Temporary accounts are closed at the end of each accounting period and include income statement, dividends, and income summary accounts.
- Income Summary: The Income Summary account is an intermediary between revenues and expenses, and the Retained Earnings account. It stores all the closing information for revenues and expenses, resulting in a "summary" of income or loss for the period.
- Recording closing entries: There are four closing entries; closing revenues to income summary, closing expenses to income summary, closing income summary to retained earnings, and close dividends to

retained earnings.

- Posting closing entries: Once all closing entries are complete, the information is transferred to the general ledger T-accounts. Balances in temporary accounts will show a zero balance.

5.2 Prepare a Post-Closing Trial Balance

- Post-closing trial balance: The post-closing trial balance is prepared after closing entries have been posted to the ledger. This trial balance only includes permanent accounts.

5.3 Apply the Results from the Adjusted Trial Balance to Compute Current Ratio and Working Capital Balance, and Explain How These Measures Represent Liquidity

- Cash-basis versus accrual-basis system: The cash-basis system delays revenue and expense recognition until cash is collected, which can mislead investors about the daily operations of a business. The accrual-basis system recognizes revenues and expenses in the period in which they were earned or incurred, allowing for an even distribution of income and a more accurate business of daily operations.
- Classified balance sheet: The classified balance sheet breaks down assets and liabilities into subcategories focusing on current and long-term classifications. This allows investors to see company position in both the short term and long term.
- Liquidity: Liquidity means a business has enough cash available to pay bills as they come due. Being too liquid can mean that a company is not using its assets efficiently.
- Working capital: Working capital shows how efficiently a company operates. The formula is current assets minus current liabilities.
- Current ratio: The current ratio shows how many times over a company can cover its liabilities. It is found by dividing current assets by current liabilities.

5.4 Appendix: Complete a Comprehensive Accounting Cycle for a Business

- The comprehensive accounting cycle is the process in which transactions are recorded in the accounting records and are ultimately reflected in the ending period balances on the financial statements.
- Comprehensive accounting cycle for a business: A service business is taken through the comprehensive accounting cycle, starting with the formation of the entity, recording all necessary journal entries for its transactions, making all required adjusting and closing journal entries, and culminating in the preparation of all requisite financial statements

Multiple Choice

1. LO 5.1 Which of the following accounts is considered a temporary or nominal account?

A. Fees Earned Revenue
B. Prepaid Advertising
C. Unearned Service Revenue
D. Prepaid Insurance

2. LO 5.1 Which of the following accounts is considered a permanent or real account?

A. Interest Revenue
B. Prepaid Insurance
C. Insurance Expense
D. Supplies Expense

3. LO 5.1 If a journal entry includes a debit or credit to the Cash account, it is most likely which of the following?

A. a closing entry
B. an adjusting entry
C. an ordinary transaction entry
D. outside of the accounting cycle

4. LO 5.1 If a journal entry includes a debit or credit to the Retained Earnings account, it is most likely which of the following?

A. a closing entry
B. an adjusting entry
C. an ordinary transaction entry
D. outside of the accounting cycle

5. LO 5.1 Which of these accounts would be present in the closing entries?

A. Dividends
B. Accounts Receivable
C. Unearned Service Revenue
D. Sales Tax Payable

6. LO 5.1 Which of these accounts would *not* be present in the closing entries?

A. Utilities Expense
B. Fees Earned Revenue
C. Insurance Expense
D. Dividends Payable

7. LO 5.1 Which of these accounts is *never* closed?

A. Dividends
B. Retained Earnings
C. Service Fee Revenue
D. Income Summary

8. LO 5.1 Which of these accounts is *never* closed?

A. Prepaid Rent
B. Income Summary
C. Rent Revenue
D. Rent Expense

9. LO 5.1 Which account would be credited when closing the account for fees earned for the year?

A. Accounts Receivable
B. Fees Earned Revenue
C. Unearned Fee Revenue
D. Income Summary

10. LO 5.1 Which account would be credited when closing the account for rent expense for the year?

A. Prepaid Rent
B. Rent Expense
C. Rent Revenue
D. Unearned Rent Revenue

11. LO 5.2 Which of these accounts is included in the post-closing trial balance?

A. Sales Revenue
B. Salaries Expense
C. Retained Earnings
D. Dividends

12. LO 5.2 Which of these accounts is *not* included in the post-closing trial balance?

A. Land
B. Notes Payable
C. Retained Earnings
D. Dividends

13. LO 5.2 On which of the following would the year-end Retained Earnings balance be stated correctly?

A. Unadjusted Trial Balance
B. Adjusted Trial Balance
C. Post-Closing Trial Balance
D. The Worksheet

14. LO 5.2 Which of these accounts is included in the post-closing trial balance?

A. Supplies Expense
B. Accounts Payable
C. Sales Revenue
D. Insurance Expense

15. LO 5.3 If current assets are $112,000 and current liabilities are $56,000, what is the current ratio?

A. 200 percent
B. 50 percent
C. 2.0
D. $50,000

16. LO 5.3 If current assets are $100,000 and current liabilities are $42,000, what is the working capital?

A. 200 percent
B. 50 percent
C. 2.0
D. $58,000

Questions

1. LO 5.1 Explain what is meant by the term *real accounts* (also known as permanent accounts).

2. LO 5.1 Explain what is meant by the term *nominal accounts* (also known as temporary accounts).

3. LO 5.1 What is the purpose of the closing entries?

4. LO 5.1 What would happen if the company failed to make closing entries at the end of the year?

5. LO 5.1 Which of these account types (Assets, Liabilities, Equity, Revenue, Expense, Dividend) are credited in the closing entries? Why?

6. LO 5.1 Which of these account types (Assets, Liabilities, Equity, Revenue, Expense, Dividend) are debited in the closing entries? Why?

7. LO 5.1 The account called Income Summary is often used in the closing entries. Explain this account's purpose and how it is used.

8. LO 5.1 What are the four entries required for closing, assuming that the Income Summary account is used?

9. LO 5.1 After the first two closing entries are made, Income Summary has a credit balance of $125,500. What does this indicate about the company's net income or loss?

10. LO 5.1 After the first two closing entries are made, Income Summary has a debit balance of $22,750. What does this indicate about the company's net income or loss?

11. LO 5.2 What account types are included in a post-closing trial balance?

12. LO 5.2 Which of the basic financial statements can be directly tied to the post-closing trial balance? Why is this so?

13. LO 5.3 Describe the calculation required to compute working capital. Explain the significance.

14. LO 5.3 Describe the calculation required to compute the current ratio. Explain the significance.

15. LO 5.4 Describe the progression of the three trial balances that a company would have during the period, and explain the difference between the three.

Exercise Set A

EA1. LO 5.1 Identify whether each of the following accounts is nominal/temporary or real/permanent.

A. Accounts Receivable
B. Fees Earned Revenue
C. Utility Expense
D. Prepaid Rent

EA2. LO 5.1 For each of the following accounts, identify whether it is nominal/temporary or real/permanent, and whether it is reported on the Balance Sheet or the Income Statement.

A. Interest Expense
B. Buildings
C. Interest Payable
D. Unearned Rent Revenue

EA3. LO 5.1 For each of the following accounts, identify whether it would be closed at year-end (yes or no) and on which financial statement the account would be reported (Balance Sheet, Income Statement, or Retained Earnings Statement).

A. Accounts Payable
B. Accounts Receivable
C. Cash
D. Dividends
E. Fees Earned Revenue
F. Insurance Expense
G. Prepaid Insurance
H. Supplies

EA4. LO 5.1 The following accounts and normal balances existed at year-end. Make the four journal entries required to close the books:

Advertising expense	$ 5,600
Dividends	4,000
Rent expense	6,000
Salaries expense	48,000
Service revenue	85,000
Utilities expense	7,500

EA5. LO 5.1 The following accounts and normal balances existed at year-end. Make the four journal entries required to close the books:

Retained earnings	$22,000
Dividends	6,000
Fees earned revenue	90,000
Selling expenses	45,000
Administrative expenses	16,000
Miscellaneous expense	2,300

EA6. LO 5.1 Use the following excerpts from the year-end Adjusted Trial Balance to prepare the four journal entries required to close the books:

Adjusted Trial Balance		
	Debit	**Credit**
Dividends	$24,000	
Sales Revenue		$194,000
Automobile Expense	15,500	
Insurance Expense	30,000	
Salaries Expense	96,000	
Supplies Expense	6,500	

EA7. LO 5.1 Use the following T-accounts to prepare the four journal entries required to close the books:

Debit	Credit
Cash	
Bal. 75,000	
Service Revenue	
	Bal. 220,000
Advertising Expense	
Bal. 12,000	
Rent Expense	
Bal. 18,000	
Salaries Expense	
Bal. 120,000	
Dividends	
Bal. 25,000	
Retained Earnings	
	Bal. 30,000

EA8. LO 5.1 Use the following T-accounts to prepare the four journal entries required to close the books:

Debit	Credit
Cash	
Bal. 23,300	
Revenue Earned	
	Bal. 43,000
Commission Expense	
Bal. 6,000	
Supplies Expense	
Bal. 3,200	
Wages Expense	
Bal. 28,000	
Dividends	
Bal. 4,000	
Retained Earnings	
	Bal. 21,500

EA9. LO 5.2 Identify whether each of the following accounts would be listed in the company's Post-Closing Trial Balance.

A. Accounts Payable
B. Advertising Expense
C. Dividends
D. Fees Earned Revenue
E. Prepaid Advertising
F. Supplies
G. Supplies Expense
H. Unearned Fee Revenue

EA10. LO 5.2 Identify which of the following accounts would *not* be listed on the company's Post-Closing Trial Balance.

Prepaid insurance	$ 9,444
Land	34,000
Notes payable	48,000
Retained earnings	31,315
Insurance expense	12,689
Service revenue	82,500
Supplies	9,700
Salaries expense	51,500

EA11. LO 5.3 For each of the following accounts, identify in which section of the classified balance sheet it would be presented: current assets, property, intangibles, other assets, current liabilities, long-term liabilities, or stockholder's equity.

A. Accounts Payable
B. Accounts Receivable
C. Cash
D. Equipment
E. Land
F. Notes Payable (due two years later)
G. Prepaid Insurance
H. Supplies

EA12. LO 5.3 Using the following Balance Sheet summary information, calculate for the two years presented:

A. working capital
B. current ratio

	12/31/2018	12/31/2019
Current assets	$76,000	$295,000
Current liabilities	48,000	163,500

EA13. LO 5.3 Using the following account balances, calculate for the two years presented:

A. working capital

B. current ratio

	12/31/2018	12/31/2019
Accounts payable	$2,000	$ 6,120
Accounts receivable	3,000	8,450
Cash	4,500	18,600
Prepaid advertising	1,200	4,000
Utilities payable	950	6,500
Wages payable	1,675	8,600

EA14. LO 5.3 Using the following Balance Sheet summary information, calculate for the two companies presented:

A. working capital

B. current ratio

Then:

A. evaluate which company's liquidity position appears stronger, and why.

	Company J	Company K
Current assets	$158,500	$122,000
Current liabilities	141,000	104,000

EA15. LO 5.3 Using the following account balances, calculate:

A. working capital

B. current ratio

	Debit	Credit
Cash	$ 27,000	
Accounts Receivable	7,300	
Prepaid Insurance	17,000	
Accounts Payable		$ 14,900
Salaries Payable		16,200
Common Stock		12,000
Service Revenue		66,000
Administrative Expenses	57,800	
	$109,100	$109,100

Exercise Set B

EB1. LO 5.1 Identify whether each of the following accounts are nominal/temporary or real/permanent.

A. Rent Expense

B. Unearned Service Fee Revenue

C. Interest Revenue

D. Accounts Payable

EB2. LO 5.1 For each of the following accounts, identify whether it is nominal/temporary or real/permanent, and whether it is reported on the Balance Sheet or the Income Statement.

A. Salaries Payable
B. Sales Revenue
C. Salaries Expense
D. Prepaid Insurance

EB3. LO 5.1 For each of the following accounts, identify whether it would be closed at year-end (yes or no) and on which financial statement the account would be reported (Balance Sheet, Income Statement, or Retained Earnings Statement).

A. Retained Earnings
B. Prepaid Rent
C. Rent Expense
D. Rent Revenue
E. Salaries Expense
F. Salaries Payable
G. Supplies Expense
H. Unearned Rent Revenue

EB4. LO 5.1 The following accounts and normal balances existed at year-end. Make the four journal entries required to close the books:

Automobile expense	$ 9,000
Dividends	6,000
Insurance expense	7,500
Office expense	14,000
Sales revenue	120,000
Wage expenses	60,000

EB5. LO 5.1 The following accounts and normal balances existed at year-end. Make the four journal entries required to close the books:

Retained earnings	$ 78,500
Dividends	12,500
Fees earned revenue	195,000
Selling expenses	101,000
Administrative expenses	46,500
Miscellaneous expense	3,600

EB6. LO 5.1 Use the following excerpts from the year-end Adjusted Trial Balance to prepare the four journal entries required to close the books:

Adjusted Trial Balance		
	Debit	**Credit**
Dividends	$ 20,000	
Service Revenue		$225,000
Advertising Expense	18,000	
Rent Expense	30,000	
Utilities Expense	6,600	
Wages Expense	148,000	

EB7. LO 5.1 Use the following T-accounts to prepare the four journal entries required to close the books:

Debit	Credit
Cash	
Bal. 35,580	
Sales Revenue	
	Bal. 146,000
Advertising Expense	
Bal. 24,000	
Insurance Expense	
Bal. 18,000	
Salaries Expense	
Bal. 90,000	
Dividends	
Bal. 5,000	
Retained Earnings	
	Bal. 26,580

EB8. LO 5.1 Use the following T-accounts to prepare the four journal entries required to close the books:

Debit	Credit
Cash	
Bal. 25,222	
Rent Revenue	
	Bal. 112,000
Advertising Expense	
Bal. 6,000	
Insurance Expense	
Bal. 12,000	
Salaries Expense	
Bal. 75,000	
Dividends	
Bal. 16,000	
Retained Earnings	
	Bal. 22,222

EB9. LO 5.2 Identify which of the following accounts would be listed on the company's Post-Closing Trial Balance.

A. Accounts Receivable
B. Accumulated Depreciation
C. Cash
D. Office Expense
E. Note Payable
F. Rent Revenue
G. Retained Earnings
H. Unearned Rent Revenue

EB10. LO 5.2 Identify which of the following accounts would *not* be listed on the company's Post-Closing Trial Balance.

Accounts payable	$19,000
Advertising expense	23,760
Cash	55,332
Common stock	38,000
Dividends	9,000
Fee revenue	60,000
Prepaid insurance	21,466
Land	45,000

EB11. LO 5.3 For each of the following accounts, identify in which section of the classified balance sheet it would be presented: current assets, property, intangibles, other assets, current liabilities, long-term liabilities, or stockholder's equity.

A. Building
B. Cash
C. Common Stock
D. Copyright
E. Prepaid Advertising
F. Notes Payable (due six months later)
G. Taxes Payable
H. Unearned Rent Revenue

EB12. LO 5.3 Using the following Balance Sheet summary information, calculate for the two years presented:

A. working capital
B. current ratio

	12/31/2018	12/31/2019
Current assets	$366,500	$132,000
Current liabilities	120,000	141,500

EB13. LO 5.3 Using the following account balances, calculate for the two years presented:

A. working capital

B. current ratio

	12/31/2018	12/31/2019
Accounts payable	$45,000	$12,600
Accounts receivable	52,000	15,200
Cash	11,500	19,780
Prepaid insurance	1,060	2,400
Salaries payable	9,400	12,800
Utilities payable	3,500	2,550

EB14. LO 5.3 Using the following Balance Sheet summary information, calculate for the two companies presented:

A. working capital

B. current ratio

Then:

A. evaluate which company's liquidity position appears stronger, and why.

	Company L	Company M
Current assets	$425,000	$215,500
Current liabilities	335,000	132,700

EB15. LO 5.3 From the following Company B adjusted trial balance, prepare simple financial statements, as follows:

Adjusted Trial Balance		
	Debit	Credit
Cash	$ 35,300	
Accounts Receivable	16,750	
Supplies	12,650	
Accounts Payable		$ 20,850
Tax Payable		3,000
Common Stock		30,000
Fee Earned Revenue		92,550
Operating Expense	81,700	
	$146,400	$146,400

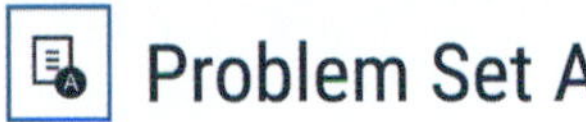

Problem Set A

PA1. LO 5.1 Identify whether each of the following accounts would be considered a permanent account (yes/no) and which financial statement it would be reported on (Balance Sheet, Income Statement, or Retained Earnings Statement).

A. Accumulated Depreciation
B. Buildings
C. Depreciation Expense
D. Equipment
E. Fees Earned Revenue
F. Insurance Expense
G. Prepaid Insurance
H. Supplies Expense
I. Dividends

PA2. LO 5.1 The following selected accounts and normal balances existed at year-end. Make the four journal entries required to close the books:

Accounts receivable	$45,000
Prepaid insurance	4,500
Land	50,000
Accounts payable	39,000
Notes payable	55,000
Retained earnings	12,000
Dividends	2,000
Fees earned revenue	65,000
Selling expenses	34,500
Administrative expenses	12,750
Miscellaneous expense	1,250

PA3. LO 5.1 The following selected accounts and normal balances existed at year-end. Notice that *expenses exceed revenue* in this period. Make the four journal entries required to close the books:

Accounts receivable	$46,200
Prepaid insurance	5,800
Land	12,000
Accounts payable	29,900
Notes payable	32,500
Retained earnings	55,400
Dividends	8,000
Fees earned revenue	89,200
Selling expenses	62,000
Administrative expenses	29,500
Miscellaneous expense	4,140

PA4. LO 5.1 Use the following Adjusted Trial Balance to prepare the four journal entries required to close the books:

Adjusted Trial Balance		
	Debit	**Credit**
Cash	$ 38,750	
Prepaid Insurance	4,500	
Equipment	35,000	
Notes Payable		$ 32,000
Common Stock		10,000
Retained Earnings		17,325
Dividends	22,000	
Sales Revenue		200,000
Automobile Expense	24,575	
Insurance Expense	18,000	
Salaries Expense	110,000	
Supplies Expense	6,500	
	$259,325	$259,325

PA5. LO 5.1 Use the following Adjusted Trial Balance to prepare the four journal entries required to close the books:

Adjusted Trial Balance		
	Debit	**Credit**
Cash	$ 22,900	
Prepaid Insurance	4,000	
Fixed Assets	44,000	
Notes Payable		$ 40,000
Common Stock		25,000
Retained Earnings		48,350
Dividends	22,000	
Sales Revenue		150,000
Automobile Expense	26,500	
Insurance Expense	20,000	
Salaries Expense	122,500	
Supplies Expense	1,450	
	$263,350	$263,350

PA6. LO 5.1 Use the following T-accounts to prepare the four journal entries required to close the books:

Debit	Credit
Accounts Receivable	
Bal. 45,500	
Fees Earned Revenue	
	Bal. 60,000
Commission Expense	
Bal. 7,200	
Supplies Expense	
Bal. 5,500	
Wages Expense	
Bal. 42,000	
Dividends	
Bal. 3,500	
Retained Earnings	
	Bal. 51,000

PA7. LO 5.1 Assume that the first two closing entries have been made and posted. Use the T-accounts provided as follows to:

A. complete the closing entries

B. determine the ending balance in the Retained Earnings account

Debit	Credit
Income Summary	
212,000	277,500
Retained Earnings	
	Bal. 45,900
Dividends	
Bal. 7,500	

PA8. LO 5.1 Correct any obvious errors in the following closing entries by providing the four corrected closing entries. Assume all accounts held normal account balances in the Adjusted Trial Balance.

A.

Income Summary	$280,000	
Service Revenue		$280,000

B.

Automobile Expense	$ 16,500	
Insurance Expense	24,000	
Salaries Expense	190,000	
Supplies Expense	18,500	
Income Summary		$249,000

C.

Retained Earnings	$263,500	
Income Summary		$263,500

D.

Dividends	$10,000	
Retained Earnings		$10,000

PA9. LO 5.2 Assuming the following Adjusted Trial Balance, create the Post-Closing Trial Balance that would result, after all closing journal entries were made and posted:

Adjusted Trial Balance		
	Debit	**Credit**
Cash	$ 22,900	
Prepaid Insurance	4,000	
Fixed Assets	44,000	
Notes Payable		$ 40,000
Common Stock		25,000
Retained Earnings		48,350
Dividends	22,000	
Sales Revenue		150,000
Automobile Expense	26,500	
Insurance Expense	20,000	
Salaries Expense	122,500	
Supplies Expense	1,450	
	$263,350	$263,350

PA10. LO 5.2 The following Post-Closing Trial Balance contains errors. Prepare a corrected Post-Closing Trial Balance:

Post-Closing Trial Balance		
	Debit	**Credit**
Cash	$29,900	
Prepaid Insurance	5,500	
Fixed Assets		$ 50,000
Notes Payable		46,000
Common Stock	32,000	
Retained Earnings		7,400
	$67,400	$103,400

PA11. LO 5.2 Assuming the following Adjusted Trial Balance, recreate the Post-Closing Trial Balance that would result after all closing journal entries were made and posted:

Adjusted Trial Balance		
	Debit	**Credit**
Cash	$17,900	
Accounts Receivable	9,900	
Supplies	1,600	
Prepaid Insurance	2,500	
Salaries Payable		$ 8,600
Common Stock		10,000
Retained Earnings		2,800
Dividends	4,000	
Service Fee Revenue		37,050
Salaries Expense	16,900	
Supplies Expense	4,200	
Insurance Expense	1,450	
	$58,450	$58,450

PA12. LO 5.3 Use the following Adjusted Trial Balance to prepare a classified Balance Sheet:

Adjusted Trial Balance		
	Debit	**Credit**
Cash	$16,500	
Accounts Receivable	17,200	
Supplies	2,200	
Prepaid Insurance	2,100	
Equipment	14,000	
Accounts Payable		$14,200
Unearned Fee Revenue		4,300
Common Stock		30,000
Service Fee Revenue		21,500
Salaries Expense	12,000	
Rent Expense	6,000	
	$70,000	$70,000

PA13. LO 5.3 Using the following Balance Sheet summary information, for the two years presented calculate:

A. working capital
B. current ratio

	12/31/2018	12/31/2019
Current assets	$101,600	$97,350
Current liabilities	33,650	32,800

PA14. LO 5.3 Using the following Balance Sheet summary information, calculate for the two companies presented:

A. working capital
B. current ratio

	Company N	Company O
Current assets	$124,680	$180,550
Current liabilities	63,250	153,250

PA15. LO 5.3 Using the following account balances, calculate for the two years presented:

A. working capital
B. current ratio

	12/31/2018	12/31/2019
Unearned revenue	$12,600	$ 6,000
Cash	33,200	12,750
Prepaid rent	9,000	6,000
Supplies	5,600	2,500
Taxes payable	4,800	5,500
Wages payable	8,500	9,250

PA16. LO 5.4 From the following Company R adjusted trial balance, prepare the following:

A. Income Statement
B. Retained Earnings Statement
C. Balance Sheet (simple—unclassified)
D. Closing journal entries
E. Post-Closing Trial Balance

Adjusted Trial Balance		
	Debit	**Credit**
Cash	$ 44,000	
Accounts Receivable	13,800	
Prepaid Insurance	6,400	
Land	16,000	
Accounts Payable		$ 14,900
Salaries Payable		4,500
Common Stock		31,000
Retained Earnings		10,200
Dividends	12,000	
Service Revenue		86,000
Insurance Expense	7,600	
Salaries Expense	32,000	
Miscellaneous Expense	14,800	
	$146,600	$146,600

PA17. LO 5.4 From the following Company T adjusted trial balance, prepare the following:

A. Income Statement
B. Retained Earnings Statement
C. Balance Sheet (simple—unclassified)
D. Closing journal entries
E. Post-Closing Trial Balance

Adjusted Trial Balance		
	Debit	**Credit**
Cash	$ 24,000	
Accounts Receivable	14,900	
Prepaid Insurance	5,300	
Land	13,500	
Accounts Payable		$ 12,400
Salaries Payable		1,500
Common Stock		34,000
Retained Earnings		10,200
Dividends	5,000	
Service Revenue		56,300
Insurance Expense	7,900	
Salaries Expense	39,000	
Miscellaneous Expense	4,800	
	$114,400	$114,400

Problem Set B

PB1. LO 5.1 Identify whether each of the following accounts would be considered a permanent account (yes/no) and which financial statement it would be reported on (Balance Sheet, Income Statement, or Retained Earnings Statement).

A. Common Stock
B. Dividends
C. Dividends Payable
D. Equipment
E. Income Tax Expense
F. Income Tax Payable
G. Service Revenue
H. Unearned Service Revenue
I. Net Income

PB2. LO 5.1 The following selected accounts and normal balances existed at year-end. Make the four journal entries required to close the books:

Accounts receivable	$33,200
Prepaid insurance	6,000
Land	48,000
Accounts payable	27,050
Notes payable	65,800
Retained earnings	9,350
Dividends	2,200
Fees earned revenue	70,500
Selling expenses	41,770
Administrative expenses	22,400
Miscellaneous expense	1,835

PB3. LO 5.1 The following selected accounts and normal balances existed at year-end. Notice that *expenses exceed revenue* in this period. Make the four journal entries required to close the books:

Accounts receivable	$ 85,500
Prepaid insurance	18,000
Land	15,000
Accounts payable	82,350
Notes payable	35,000
Retained earnings	129,650
Dividends	15,000
Fees earned revenue	311,000
Selling expenses	210,000
Administrative expenses	105,000
Miscellaneous expense	8,500

PB4. LO 5.1 Use the following Adjusted Trial Balance to prepare the four journal entries required to close the books:

Adjusted Trial Balance		
	Debit	**Credit**
Cash	$ 75,500	
Accounts Receivable	15,500	
Accounts Payable		$ 4,000
Unearned Revenue		6,000
Common Stock		20,000
Retained Earnings		12,500
Dividends	30,000	
Service Revenue		355,000
Advertising Expense	30,000	
Rent Expense	36,000	
Utilities Expense	9,500	
Wages Expense	201,000	
	$397,500	$397,500

PB5. LO 5.1 Use the following Adjusted Trial Balance to prepare the four journal entries required to close the books:

Adjusted Trial Balance		
	Debit	**Credit**
Cash	$ 8,625	
Accounts Receivable	11,600	
Accounts Payable		$ 8,450
Unearned Revenue		1,500
Common Stock		10,000
Retained Earnings		12,275
Dividends	2,000	
Service Revenue		97,500
Advertising Expense	2,500	
Rent Expense	18,000	
Utilities Expense	12,000	
Wages Expense	75,000	
	$129,725	$129,725

PB6. LO 5.1 Use the following T-accounts to prepare the four journal entries required to close the books:

Debit	Credit
Cash	
Bal. 17,340	
Rent Revenue	
	Bal. 240,000
Advertising Expense	
Bal. 12,000	
Insurance Expense	
Bal. 34,500	
Salaries Expense	
Bal. 128,000	
Dividends	
Bal. 22,000	
Retained Earnings	
	Bal. 59,500

PB7. LO 5.1 Assume that the first two closing entries have been made and posted. Use the T-accounts provided below to:

A. complete the closing entries
B. determine the ending balance in the Retained Earnings account

Debit	Credit
Income Summary	
148,500	162,200
Retained Earnings	
	Bal. 11,500
Dividends	
Bal. 4,000	

PB8. LO 5.1 Correct any obvious errors in the following closing entries by providing the four corrected closing entries. Assume all accounts held normal account balances in the Adjusted Trial Balance.

A.

Income Summary	$75,000	
Service Revenue		$75,000

B.

Automobile Expense	$ 8,800	
Insurance Expense	4,800	
Salaries Expense	45,000	
Supplies Expense	3,500	
Income Summary		$62,100

C.

Retained Earnings	$45,222	
Income Summary		$45,222

D.

Dividends	$6,000	
Retained Earnings		$6,000

PB9. LO 5.2 Assuming the following Adjusted Trial Balance, create the Post-Closing Trial Balance that would result after all closing journal entries were made and posted:

Adjusted Trial Balance		
	Debit	**Credit**
Cash	$ 8,625	
Accounts Receivable	11,600	
Accounts Payable		$ 8,450
Unearned Revenue		1,500
Common Stock		10,000
Retained Earnings		12,275
Dividends	2,000	
Service Revenue		97,500
Advertising Expense	2,500	
Rent Expense	18,000	
Utilities Expense	12,000	
Wages Expense	75,000	
	$129,725	$129,725

PB10. LO 5.2 The following Post-Closing Trial Balance contains errors. Prepare a corrected Post-Closing Trial Balance:

Post-Closing Trial Balance		
	Debit	**Credit**
Cash		$32,660
Supplies	$ 7,200	
Land		25,000
Notes Payable	47,700	
Common Stock		7,000
Retained Earnings		10,160
	$54,900	$74,820

PB11. LO 5.2 Assuming the following Adjusted Trial Balance, re-create the Post-Closing Trial Balance that would result after all closing journal entries were made and posted:

Adjusted Trial Balance		
	Debit	**Credit**
Cash	$ 5,450	
Accounts Receivable	4,700	
Supplies	250	
Prepaid Insurance	1,250	
Salaries Payable		$ 650
Common Stock		5,000
Retained Earnings		750
Dividends	1,400	
Service Fee Revenue		17,300
Salaries Expense	9,050	
Supplies Expense	1,000	
Insurance Expense	600	
	$23,700	$23,700

PB12. LO 5.3 Use the following Adjusted Trial Balance to prepare a classified Balance Sheet:

Adjusted Trial Balance		
	Debit	**Credit**
Cash	$17,000	
Accounts Receivable	8,500	
Supplies	1,500	
Prepaid Insurance	5,000	
Equipment	12,000	
Accounts Payable		$ 5,000
Unearned Fee Revenue		4,000
Common Stock		15,000
Service Fee Revenue		32,500
Salaries Expense	9,500	
Rent Expense	3,000	
	$56,500	$56,500

PB13. LO 5.3 Using the following Balance Sheet summary information, calculate for the two years presented:

A. working capital
B. current ratio

	Company P	Company Q
Current assets	$88,500	$39,000
Current liabilities	67,430	18,800

PB14. LO 5.3 Using the following Balance Sheet summary information, calculate for the two years presented:

A. working capital
B. current ratio

	12/31/2018	12/31/2019
Current assets	$10,500	$12,050
Current liabilities	7,500	10,800

PB15. LO 5.3 Using the following account balances, calculate for the two years presented:

A. working capital
B. current ratio

	12/31/2018	12/31/2019
Accounts payable	$12,790	$1,530
Accounts receivable	16,330	2,200
Cash	21,040	5,550
Prepaid insurance	4,500	1,200
Salaries payable	6,500	4,000
Utilities payable	1,200	550

PB16. LO 5.4 From the following Company S adjusted trial balance, prepare the following:

A. Income Statement
B. Retained Earnings Statement
C. Balance Sheet (simple—unclassified)
D. Closing journal entries
E. Post-Closing Trial Balance

Adjusted Trial Balance		
	Debit	Credit
Cash	$ 55,200	
Accounts Receivable	30,200	
Prepaid Insurance	6,000	
Land	30,000	
Accounts Payable		$ 14,300
Salaries Payable		6,100
Common Stock		26,000
Retained Earnings		38,900
Dividends	16,500	
Service Revenue		211,850
Insurance Expense	24,000	
Salaries Expense	128,350	
Miscellaneous Expense	6,900	
	$297,150	$297,150

Thought Provokers

TP1. LO 5.1 Assume you are the controller of a large corporation, and the chief executive officer (CEO) has requested that you refrain from posting closing entries at 20X1 year-end, with the intention of combining the two years' profits in year 20X2, in an effort to make that year's profits appear stronger.

Write a memo to the CEO, to offer your response to the request to skip the closing entries for year 20X1.

TP2. LO 5.1 Search the Securities and Exchange Commission website (https://www.sec.gov/edgar/searchedgar/companysearch.html) and locate the latest Form 10-K for a company you would like to analyze. Submit a short memo:

- State the name and ticker symbol of the company you have chosen.
- Review the company's end-of-period Balance Sheet, Income Statement, and Statement of Retained Earnings.
- Use the information in these financial statements to answer these questions:
    A. If the company had used the income summary account for its closing entries, how much would the company have credited the Income Summary account in the first closing entry?
    B. How much would the company have debited the Income Summary account in the second closing entry?

Provide the web link to the company's Form 10-K, to allow accurate verification of your answers.

TP3. LO 5.1 Assume you are a senior accountant and have been assigned the responsibility for making the entries to close the books for the year. You have prepared the following four entries and presented them to your boss, the chief financial officer of the company, along with the company CEO, in the weekly staff meeting:

Service revenue	$522,000	
Income summary		$522,000
Income summary	463,520	
Promotional expenses		48,520
Salaries expense		375,500
Travel expenses		39,500
Income summary	58,480	
Retained earnings		58,480
Retained earnings	28,000	
Dividends		28,000

As the CEO was reviewing your work, he asked the question, "What do these entries mean? Can we learn anything about the company from reviewing them?"

Provide an explanation to give to the CEO about what the entries reveal about the company's operations this year.

TP4. LO 5.2 Search the US Securities and Exchange Commission website (https://www.sec.gov/edgar/searchedgar/companysearch.html) and locate the latest Form 10-K for a company you would like to analyze. Submit a short memo:

- State the name and ticker symbol of the company you have chosen.
- Review the company's Balance Sheets.
- Reconstruct a Post-Closing Trial Balance for the company from the information presented in the financial statements.

Provide the web link to the company's Form 10-K, to allow accurate verification of your answers.

TP5. LO 5.3 Search the Securities and Exchange Commission website (https://www.sec.gov/edgar/searchedgar/companysearch.html) and locate the latest Form 10-K for a company you would like to analyze. Submit a short memo:

- State the name and ticker symbol of the company you have chosen.
- Review the company's end-of-period Balance Sheet for the most recent annual report.
- List the amount of Current Assets and Current Liabilities for the currently reported year, and for the previous year. Use these amounts to calculate the company's (A) working capital and (B) current ratio.

Provide the web link to the company's Form 10-K, to allow accurate verification of your answers.

6 Merchandising Transactions

Figure 6.1 J&J Games. Proper recognition of merchandising transactions gives management a clear inventory picture to make informed business decisions. (credit: modification of "Video game retail store, consumerism at its finest" by Bas de Reuver/Flickr, CC BY 2.0)

Chapter Outline

- LO **6.1** Compare and Contrast Merchandising versus Service Activities and Transactions
- LO **6.2** Compare and Contrast Perpetual versus Periodic Inventory Systems
- LO **6.3** Analyze and Record Transactions for Merchandise Purchases Using the Perpetual Inventory System
- LO **6.4** Analyze and Record Transactions for the Sale of Merchandise Using the Perpetual Inventory System
- LO **6.5** Discuss and Record Transactions Applying the Two Commonly Used Freight-In Methods
- LO **6.6** Describe and Prepare Multi-Step and Simple Income Statements for Merchandising Companies
- LO **6.7** Appendix: Analyze and Record Transactions for Merchandise Purchases and Sales Using the Periodic Inventory System

Why It Matters

Jason and his brother James own a small business called J&J Games, specializing in the sale of video games and accessories. They purchase their merchandise from a Marcus Electronics manufacturer and sell directly to consumers.

When J&J Games (J&J) purchases merchandise from Marcus, they establish a contract detailing purchase costs, payment terms, and shipping charges. It is important to establish this contract so that J&J and Marcus understand the inventory responsibilities of each party. J&J Games typically does not pay with cash immediately and is given an option for delayed payment with the possibility of a discount for early payment. The delayed payment helps continue the strong relationship between the two parties, but the option for early payment gives J&J a monetary incentive to pay early and allow Marcus to use the funds for other business purposes. Until J&J pays on their account, this outstanding balance remains a liability for J&J.

J&J Games successfully sells merchandise on a regular basis to customers. As the business grows, the company later considers selling gaming accessories in bulk orders to other businesses. While these bulk sales will provide a new growth opportunity for J&J, the company understands that these clients may need time to pay for their orders. This can create a dilemma; J&J Games needs to offer competitive incentives for these clients while also maintaining the ability to pay their own obligations. They will carefully consider sales discounts, returns, and allowance policies that do not overextend their company's financial position while giving them an opportunity to create lasting relationships with a new customer base.

6.1 Compare and Contrast Merchandising versus Service Activities and Transactions

Every week, you run errands for your household. These errands may include buying products and services from local retailers, such as gas, groceries, and clothing. As a consumer, you are focused solely on purchasing your items and getting home to your family. You are probably not thinking about how your purchases impact the businesses you frequent. Whether the business is a service or a merchandising company, it tracks sales from customers, purchases from manufacturers or other suppliers, and costs that affect their everyday operations. There are some key differences between these business types in the manner and detail required for transaction recognition.

Comparison of Merchandising Transactions versus Service Transactions

Some of the biggest differences between a service company and a merchandising company are what they sell, their typical financial transactions, their operating cycles, and how these translate to financial statements.

A **service company** provides intangible services to customers and does not have inventory. Some examples of service companies include lawyers, doctors, consultants, and accountants. Service companies often have simple financial transactions that involve taking customer deposits, billing clients after services have been provided, providing the service, and processing payments. These activities may occur frequently within a company's accounting cycle and make up a portion of the service company's operating cycle.

An **operating cycle** is the amount of time it takes a company to use its cash to provide a product or service and collect payment from the customer. Completing this cycle faster puts the company in a more stable financial position. A typical operating cycle for a service company begins with having cash available, providing service to a customer, and then receiving cash from the customer for the service (Figure 6.2).

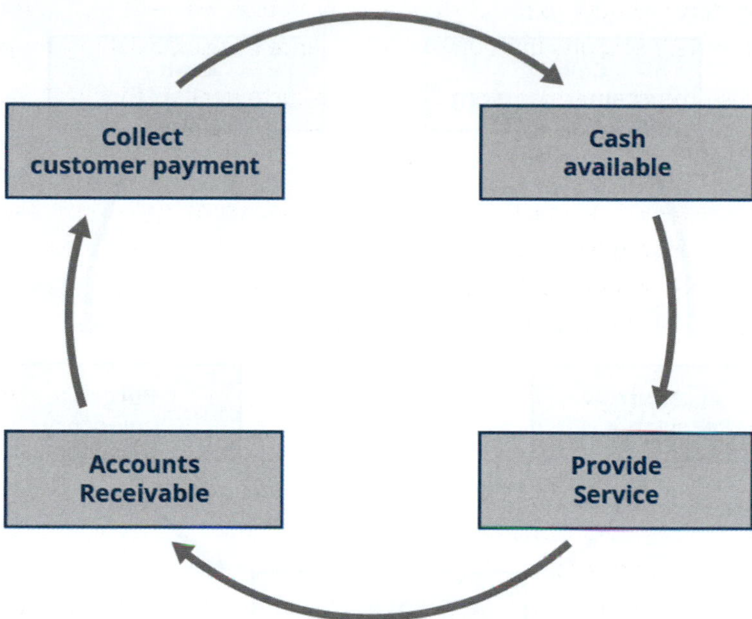

Figure 6.2 Typical Operating Cycle for a Service Firm. (attribution: Copyright Rice University, OpenStax, under CC BY-NC-SA 4.0 license)

The income statement format is fairly simple as well (see Figure 6.3). Revenues (sales) are reported first, followed by any period operating expenses. The outcome of sales less expenses, which is net income (loss), is calculated from these accounts.

APPLE GOODS Income Statement Year Ended December 31, 2018	
Sales	$300,000
Expenses	175,000
Net Income (Loss)	125,000

Figure 6.3 Service Company Income Statement. Expenses are subtracted directly from Sales to produce net income (loss). (attribution: Copyright Rice University, OpenStax, under CC BY-NC-SA 4.0 license)

A **merchandising company** resells finished goods (inventory) produced by a manufacturer (supplier) to customers. Some examples of merchandising companies include Walmart, Macy's, and Home Depot. Merchandising companies have financial transactions that include: purchasing merchandise, paying for merchandise, storing inventory, selling merchandise, and collecting customer payments. A typical operating cycle for a merchandising company starts with having cash available, purchasing inventory, selling the merchandise to customers, and finally collecting payment from customers (Figure 6.4).

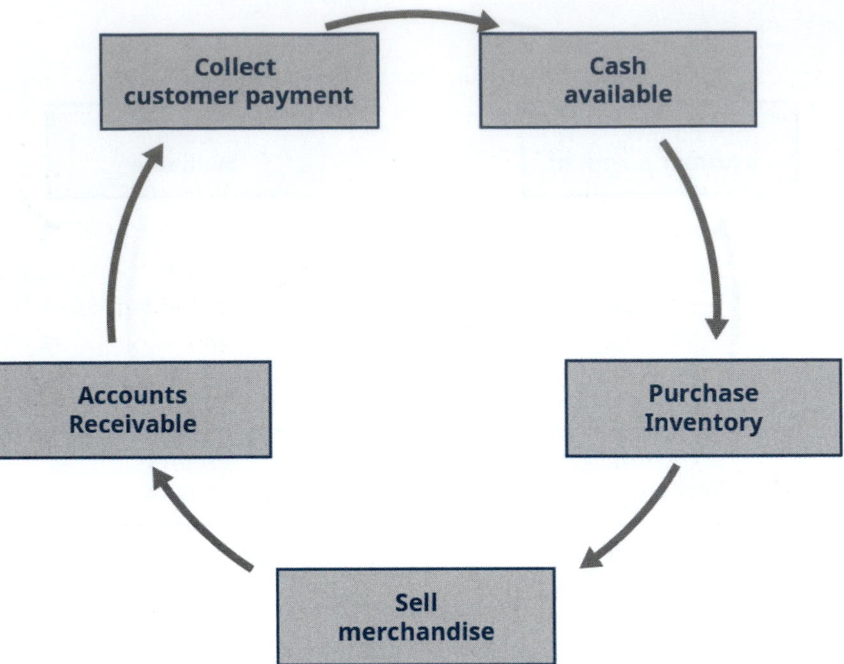

Figure 6.4 Typical Operating Cycle for a Merchandising Company. (attribution: Copyright Rice University, OpenStax, under CC BY-NC-SA 4.0 license)

Their income statement format is a bit more complicated than for a service company and is discussed in greater detail in Describe and Prepare Multi-Step and Simple Income Statements for Merchandising Companies. Note that unlike a service company, the merchandiser, also sometimes labeled as a retailer, must first resolve any sale reductions and merchandise costs, known as Cost of Goods Sold, before determining other expenses and net income (loss). A simple retailer income statement is shown in Figure 6.5 for comparison.

AIR SUPPLY PLUS Income Statement Year Ended December 31, 2018	
Net Sales	$350,000
Cost of Goods Sold	50,000
Gross Margin	300,000
Expenses	100,000
Net Income (Loss)	$200,000

Figure 6.5 Merchandise Company Income Statement. Cost of Goods Sold is deducted from net sales to calculate gross margin. (attribution: Copyright Rice University, OpenStax, under CC BY-NC-SA 4.0 license)

Characteristics of Merchandising Transactions

Merchandising transactions are separated into two categories: purchases and sales. In general, a purchase transaction occurs between a manufacturer and the merchandiser, also called a retailer. A sales transaction occurs between a customer and the merchandiser or retailer. We will now discuss the characteristics that create purchase and sales transactions for a retailer. A merchandiser will need to purchase merchandise for its business to continue operations and can use several purchase situations to accomplish this.

Purchases with Cash or on Credit

A retailer typically conducts business with a manufacturer or with a supplier who buys from a manufacturer. The retailer will purchase their finished goods for resale. When the purchase occurs, the retailer may pay for the merchandise with cash or on credit. If the retailer pays for the merchandise with cash, they would be trading one current asset, Cash, for another current asset, Merchandise Inventory or just Inventory, depending upon the company's account titles. In this example, they would record a debit entry to Merchandise Inventory and a credit entry to Cash. If they decide to pay on credit, a liability would be created, and Accounts Payable would be credited rather than Cash. For example, a clothing store may pay a jeans manufacturer cash for 50 pairs of jeans, costing $25 each. The following entry would occur.

JOURNAL			
Date	Account	Debit	Credit
	Merchandise Inventory Cash *To recognize purchase with cash*	1,250	1,250

If this same company decides to purchase merchandise on credit, Accounts Payable is credited instead of Cash.

JOURNAL			
Date	Account	Debit	Credit
	Merchandise Inventory Accounts Payable *To recognize purchase on credit*	1,250	1,250

Merchandise Inventory is a current asset account that houses all purchase costs associated with the transaction. This includes the cost of the merchandise, shipping charges, insurance fees, taxes, and any other costs that gets the products ready for sale. **Gross purchases** are defined as the original amount of the purchase without considering reductions for purchase discounts, returns, or allowances. Once the purchase reductions are adjusted at the end of a period, net purchases are calculated. **Net purchases** (see Figure 6.6) equals gross purchases less purchase discounts, purchase returns, and purchase allowances.

Income Statement
Gross Purchases
– Purchase Discounts
– Purchase Returns
– Purchase Allowances
= Net Purchases

Figure 6.6 Purchase Transactions' Effects on Gross Purchases. Deducting purchase discounts, returns, and allowances from gross purchases will result in net purchases. (attribution: Copyright Rice University, OpenStax, under CC BY-NC-SA 4.0 license)

Purchase Discounts

If a retailer, pays on credit, they will work out payment terms with the manufacturer. These payment terms establish the purchase cost, an invoice date, any discounts, shipping charges, and the final payment due date.

Purchase discounts provide an incentive for the retailer to pay early on their accounts by offering a reduced rate on the final purchase cost. Receiving payment in a timely manner allows the manufacturer to free up cash for other business opportunities and decreases the risk of nonpayment.

To describe the discount terms, the manufacturer can write descriptions such as 2/10, n/30 on the invoice. The "2" represents a discount rate of 2%, the "10" represents the discount period in days, and the "n/30" means "net of 30" days, representing the entire payment period without a discount application. So, "2/10, n/30" reads as, "The company will receive a 2% discount on their purchase if they pay in 10 days. Otherwise, they have 30 days from the date of the sale to pay in full, no discount received." In some cases, if the retailer exceeds the full payment period (30 days in this example), the manufacturer may charge interest as a penalty for late payment. The number of days allowed for both the discount period and the full payment period begins counting from the invoice date.

If a merchandiser pays an invoice within the discount period, they receive a discount, which affects the cost of the inventory. Let's say a retailer pays within the discount window. They would need to show a credit to the Merchandise Inventory account, recognizing the decreased final cost of the merchandise. This aligns with the cost principle, which requires a company to record an asset's value at the cost of acquisition. In addition, since cash is used to pay the manufacturer, Cash is credited. The debit to Accounts Payable does not reflect the discount taken: it reflects fulfillment of the liability in full, and the credits to Merchandise Inventory and Cash reflect the discount taken, as demonstrated in the following example.

If the retailer does not pay within the discount window, they do not receive a discount but are still required to pay the full invoice price at the end of the term. In this case, Accounts Payable is debited and Cash is credited, but no reductions are made to Merchandise Inventory.

For example, suppose a kitchen appliances retailer purchases merchandise for their store from a manufacturer on September 1 in the amount of $1,600. Credit terms are 2/10, n/30 from the invoice date of September 1. The retailer makes payment on September 5 and receives the discount. The following entry occurs.

JOURNAL			
Date	**Account**	**Debit**	**Credit**
Sept. 5	Accounts Payable	1,600	
	Cash		1,568
	Merchandise Inventory		32
	To recognize purchase payment with discount taken		

Let's consider the same situation except the retailer did not make the discount window and paid in full on September 30. The entry would recognize the following instead.

JOURNAL			
Date	**Account**	**Debit**	**Credit**
	Accounts Payable	1,600	
	Cash		1,600
	To recognize purchase payment without discount applied		

There are two kinds of purchase discounts, cash discounts and trade discounts. **Cash discount** provides a discount on the final price after purchase if a retailer pays within a discount window. On the other hand, a **trade discount** is a reduction to the advertised manufacturer's price that occurs during negotiations of a final purchase price before the inventory is purchased. The trade discount may become larger if the retailer purchases more in one transaction. While the cash discount is recognized in journal entries, a trade discount is not, since it is negotiated before purchase.

For example, assume that a retailer is considering an order for $4,000 in inventory on September 1. The manufacturer offers the retailer a 15% discount on the price if they place the order by September 5. Assume that the retailer places the $4,000 order on September 3. The purchase price would be $4,000 less the 15% discount of $600, or $3,400. Since the trade discount is based on when the order was placed and not on any potential payment discounts, the initial journal entry to record the purchase would reflect the discounted amount of $3,400. Even if the retailer receives a trade discount, they may still be eligible for an additional purchase discount if they pay within the discount window of the invoice.

JOURNAL			
Date	Account	Debit	Credit
	Merchandise Inventory	3,400	
	Accounts Payable		3,400
	To record purchase on credit		

Purchase Returns and Allowances

If a retailer is unhappy with their purchase—for example, if the order is incorrect or if the products are damaged—they may receive a partial or full refund from the manufacturer in a **purchase returns and allowances** transaction. A purchase return occurs when merchandise is returned and a full refund is issued. A purchase allowance occurs when merchandise is kept and a partial refund is issued. In either case, a manufacturer will issue a debit memo to acknowledge the change in contract terms and the reduction in the amount owed.

To recognize a return or allowance, the retailer will reduce Accounts Payable (or increase Cash) and reduce Merchandise Inventory. Accounts Payable decreases if the retailer has yet to pay on their account, and Cash increases if they had already paid and received a subsequent refund. Merchandise Inventory decreases to show the reduction of inventory cost from the retailer's inventory stock. Note that if a retailer receives a refund before they make a payment, any discount taken must be from the new cost of the merchandise less the refund.

To illustrate, assume that Carter Candle Company received a shipment from a manufacturer that had 150 candles that cost $150. Assume that they have not yet paid for these candles and 100 of the candles are badly damaged and must be returned. The other 50 candles are marketable, but are not the right style. The candle company returned the 100 defective candles for a full refund and requested and received an allowance of $20 for the 50 improper candles they kept. The first entry shows the return and the second entry shows the allowance.

JOURNAL			
Date	Account	Debit	Credit
	Accounts Payable	100	
	Merchandise Inventory		100
	To recognize purchase return for full refund		
	Accounts Payable	20	
	Merchandise Inventory		20
	To recognize purchase allowance with partial refund		

It is possible to show these entries as one, since they affect the same accounts and were requested at the same time. From a manager's standpoint, though, it may be better to record these as separate transactions to better understand the specific reasons for the reduction to inventory (either return or allowance) and restocking needs.

ETHICAL CONSIDERATIONS

Internal Controls over Merchandise Returns[1]

Returning merchandise requires more than an accountant making journal entries or a clerk restocking items in a warehouse or store. An ethical accountant understands that there must be internal controls governing the return of items. As used in accounting, the term "internal control" describes the methodology of implementing accounting and operational checkpoints in a system to ensure compliance with sound business and operational practices while permitting the proper recording of accounting information. All transactions require both operational and accounting actions to ensure that the amounts have been recorded in the accounting records and that operational requirements have been met.

Merchandise return controls require that there be a separation of duties between the employee approving the return and the person recording the return of merchandise in the accounting records. Basically, the person performing the return should not be the person recording the event in the accounting records. This is called *separation of duties* and is just one example of an internal control that should be used when merchandise is returned.

Every company faces different challenges with returns, but one of the most common challenges includes fake or fictitious returns. The use of internal controls is a protective action the company undertakes, with the assistance of professional accountants, to ensure that fictitious returns do not occur. The internal controls may include prescribed actions of employees, special tags on merchandise, specific store layouts that ensure customers pass checkout points before leaving the store, cameras to record activity in the facility, and other activities and internal controls that go beyond accounting and journal entries to ensure that assets of a company are protected.

Characteristics of Sales Transactions

Business owners may encounter several sales situations that can help meet customer needs and control inventory operations. For example, some customers will expect the opportunity to buy using short-term credit and often will assume that they will receive a discount for paying within a brief period. The mechanics of sales discounts are demonstrated later in this section.

Sales with Cash or on Credit

As previously mentioned, a sale is usually considered a transaction between a merchandiser or retailer and a customer. When a sale occurs, a customer has the option to pay with cash or credit. For our purposes, let's consider "credit" as credit extended from the business directly to the customer.

Whether or not a customer pays with cash or credit, a business must record two accounting entries. One entry recognizes the sale and the other recognizes the cost of the sale. The sales entry consists of a debit to either

---

1 Committee of Sponsoring Organizations of the Treadway Commission (COSO). *Internal Control—Integrated Framework*. May 2013. https://na.theiia.org/standards-guidance/topics/Documents/Executive_Summary.pdf

Cash or Accounts Receivable (if paying on credit), and a credit to the revenue account, Sales.

The amount recorded in the Sales account is the gross amount. **Gross sales** is the original amount of the sale without factoring in any possible reductions for discounts, returns, or allowances. Once those reductions are recorded at the end of a period, net sales are calculated. **Net sales** (see Figure 6.7) equals gross sales less sales discounts, sales returns, and sales allowances. Recording the sale as it occurs allows the company to align with the revenue recognition principle. The revenue recognition principle requires companies to record revenue when it is earned, and revenue is earned when a product or service has been provided.

Income Statement
Gross Sales
– Sales Discounts
– Sales Returns
– Sales Allowances
= Net Sales

Figure 6.7 Sales Transactions' Effect on Gross Sales. Deducting sales discounts, returns, and allowances from gross sales, will result in net sales. (attribution: Copyright Rice University, OpenStax, under CC BY-NC-SA 4.0 license)

The second accounting entry that is made during a sale describes the cost of sales. The cost of sales entry includes decreasing Merchandise Inventory and increasing Cost of Goods Sold (COGS). The decrease to Merchandise Inventory reflects the reduction in the inventory account value due to the sold merchandise. The increase to COGS represents the expense associated with the sale. The **cost of goods sold (COGS)** is an expense account that houses all costs associated with getting the product ready for sale. This could include purchase costs, shipping, taxes, insurance, stocking fees, and overhead related to preparing the product for sale. By recording the cost of sale when the sale occurs, the company aligns with the matching principle. The matching principle requires companies to match revenues generated with related expenses in the period in which they are incurred.

For example, when a shoe store sells 150 pairs of athletic cleats to a local baseball league for $1,500 (cost of $900), the league may pay with cash or credit. If the baseball league elects to pay with cash, the shoe store would debit Cash as part of the sales entry. If the baseball league decides to use a line of credit extended by the shoe store, the shoe store would debit Accounts Receivable as part of the sales entry instead of Cash. With the sales entry, the shoe store must also recognize the $900 cost of the shoes sold and the $900 reduction in Merchandise Inventory.

JOURNAL			
Date	Account	Debit	Credit
	Cash	1,500	
	Sales		1,500
	To recognize cash sale		
	Cost of Goods Sold	900	
	Merchandise Inventory		900
	To recognize the cost of sale		

You may have noticed that sales tax has not been discussed as part of the sales entry. Sales taxes are liabilities that require a portion of every sales dollar be remitted to a government entity. This would reduce the amount of cash the company keeps after the sale. Sales tax is relevant to consumer sales and is discussed in detail in Current Liabilities.

There are a few transactional situations that may occur after a sale is made that have an effect on reported sales at the end of a period.

Sales Discounts

Sales discounts are incentives given to customers to entice them to pay off their accounts early. Why would a retailer offer this? Wouldn't they rather receive the entire amount owed? The discount serves several purposes that are similar to the rationale manufacturers consider when offering discounts to retailers. It can help solidify a long-term relationship with the customer, encourage the customer to purchase more, and decreases the time it takes for the company to see a liquid asset (cash). Cash can be used for other purposes immediately such as reinvesting in the business, paying down loans quicker, and distributing dividends to shareholders. This can help grow the business at a more rapid rate.

Similar to credit terms between a retailer and a manufacturer, a customer could see credit terms offered by the retailer in the form of 2/10, n/30. This particular example shows that if a customer pays their account within 10 days, they will receive a 2% discount. Otherwise, they have 30 days to pay in full but do not receive a discount. If the customer does not pay within the discount window, but pays within 30 days, the retailing company records a credit to Accounts Receivable, and a debit to Cash for the full amount stated on the invoice. If the customer is able to pay the account within the discount window, the company records a credit to Accounts Receivable, a debit to Cash, and a debit to Sales Discounts.

The **sales discounts** account is a contra revenue account that is deducted from gross sales at the end of a period in the calculation of net sales. Sales Discounts has a normal debit balance, which offsets Sales that has a normal credit balance.

Let's assume that a customer purchased 10 emergency kits from a retailer at $100 per kit on credit. The retailer offered the customer 2/10, n/30 terms, and the customer paid within the discount window. The retailer recorded the following entry for the initial sale.

JOURNAL			
Date	**Account**	**Debit**	**Credit**
	Accounts Receivable	1,000	
	Sales		1,000
	To reflect the sale on credit		

Since the retail doesn't know at the point of sale whether or not the customer will qualify for the sales discount, the entire account receivable of $1,000 is recorded on the retailer's journal.

Also assume that the retail's costs of goods sold in this example were $560 and we are using the perpetual inventory method. The journal entry to record the sale of the inventory follows the entry for the sale to the customer.

JOURNAL			
Date	**Account**	**Debit**	**Credit**
	Cost of Goods Sold Merchandise inventory *To reflect the sale of inventory*	560	560

Since the customer paid the account in full within the discount qualification period of ten days, the following journal entry on the retailer's books reflects the payment.

JOURNAL			
Date	**Account**	**Debit**	**Credit**
	Cash Sales Discounts Accounts Receivable *To recognize a sales discount and collection of receivable ($1,000 × 2%)*	980 20	1,000

Now, assume that the customer paid the retailer within the 30-day period but did not qualify for the discount. The following entry reflects the payment without the discount.

JOURNAL			
Date	**Account**	**Debit**	**Credit**
	Cash Accounts Receivable *To reflect the collection of accounts receivable*	1,000	1,000

Please note that the entire $1,000 account receivable created is eliminated under both payment options. When the discount is missed, the retail received the entire $1,000. However, when the discount was received by the customer, the retailer received $980, and the remaining $20 is recorded in the sales discount account.

ETHICAL CONSIDERATIONS

Ethical Discounts

Should employees or companies provide discounts to employees of other organizations? An accountant's employing organization usually has a code of ethics or conduct that addresses policies for employee discounts. While many companies offer their employees discounts as a benefit, some companies also offer discounts or free products to non-employees who work for governmental organizations. Accountants may need to work in situations where other entities' codes of ethics/conduct do not permit employees to accept discounts or free merchandise. What should the accountant's company do when an outside organization's code of ethics and conduct does not permit its employees to accept discounts or free merchandise?

The long-term benefits of discounts are contrasted with organizational codes of ethics and conduct that limit others from accepting discounts from your organization. The International Association of Chiefs of Police's Law Enforcement Code of Ethics limits the ability of police officers to accept discounts.[2] These discounts may be as simple as a free cup of coffee, other gifts, rewards points, and hospitality points or discounts for employees or family members of the governmental organization's employees. Providing discounts may create ethical dilemmas. The ethical dilemma may not arise from the accountant's employer, but from the employer of the person outside the organization receiving the discount.

The World Customs Organization's *Model Code of Ethics and Conduct* states that "customs employees are called upon to use their best judgment to avoid situations of real or perceived conflict. In doing so, they should consider the following criteria on gifts, hospitality and other benefits, bearing in mind the full context of this Code. Public servants shall not accept or solicit any gifts, hospitality or other benefits that may have a real or apparent influence on their objectivity in carrying out their official duties or that may place them under obligation to the donor."[3]

At issue is that the employee of the outside organization is placed in a conflict between their personal interests and the interest of their employer. The accountant's employer's discount has created this conflict. In these situations, it is best for the accountant's employer to respect the other organization's code of conduct. As well, it might be illegal for the accountant's employer to provide discounts to a governmental organization's employees. The professional accountant should always be aware of the discount policy of any outside company prior to providing discounts to the employees of other companies or organizations.

Sales Returns and Allowances

If a customer purchases merchandise and is dissatisfied with their purchase, they may receive a refund or a partial refund, depending on the situation. When the customer returns merchandise and receives a full refund, it is considered a sales return. When the customer keeps the defective merchandise and is given a partial refund, it is considered a sales allowance. The biggest difference is that a customer returns merchandise in a sales return and keeps the merchandise in a sales allowance.

When a customer returns the merchandise, a retailer issues a credit memo to acknowledge the change in contract and reduction to Accounts Receivable, if applicable. The retailer records an entry acknowledging the return by reducing either Cash or Accounts Receivable and increasing Sales Returns and Allowances. Cash would decrease if the customer had already paid for the merchandise and cash was thus refunded to the customer. Accounts Receivable would decrease if the customer had not yet paid on their account. Like Sales Discounts, the **sales returns and allowances** account is a contra revenue account with a normal debit balance that reduces the gross sales figure at the end of the period.

Beyond recording the return, the retailer must also determine if the returned merchandise is in "sellable condition." An item is in sellable condition if the merchandise is good enough to warrant a sale to another customer in the future. If so, the company would record a decrease to Cost of Goods Sold (COGS) and an increase to Merchandise Inventory to return the merchandise back to the inventory for resale. This is recorded at the merchandise's costs of goods sold value. If the merchandise is in sellable condition but will not realize the original cost of the good, the company must estimate the loss at this time.

2 International Association of Chiefs of Police (IACP). Law Enforcement Code of Ethics. October, 1957. https://www.theiacp.org/resources/law-enforcement-code-of-ethics

3 World Customs Organization. *Model Code of Ethics and Conduct*. n.d. http://www.wcoomd.org/~/media/wco/public/global/pdf/topics/integrity/instruments-and-tools/model-code-of-ethics-and-conduct.pdf?la=en

On the other hand, when the merchandise is returned and is not in sellable condition, the retailer must estimate the value of the merchandise in its current condition and record a loss. This would increase Merchandise Inventory for the assessed value of the merchandise in its current state, decrease COGS for the original expense amount associated with the sale, and increase Loss on Defective Merchandise for the unsellable merchandise lost value.

JOURNAL			
Date	**Account**	**Debit**	**Credit**
	Merchandise Inventory Loss on Defective Merchandise Cost of Goods Sold *To account for merchandise in unsellable condition*	$$$ $$$	 $$$

Let's say a customer purchases 300 plants on credit from a nursery for $3,000 (with a cost of $1,200). The first entry reflects the initial sale by the nursery. The second entry reflects the cost of goods sold.

JOURNAL			
Date	**Account**	**Debit**	**Credit**
	Accounts receivable Sales *To recognize the sale of 300 plants*	3,000	 3,000
	Cost of goods sold Merchandise inventory *To reflect the cost of goods sold for sale of 300 plants*	1,200	 1,200

Upon receipt, the customer discovers the plants have been infested with bugs and they send all the plants back. Assuming that the customer had not yet paid the nursery any of the $3,000 accounts receivable and assuming that the nursery determines the condition of the returned plants to be sellable, the retailer would record the following entries.

JOURNAL			
Date	**Account**	**Debit**	**Credit**
	Sales Returns and Allowances Accounts Receivable *To recognize a sales return*	3,000	 3,000
	Merchandise Inventory Cost of Goods Sold *To return inventory to stock for resale*	1,200	 1,200

For another example, let's say the plant customer was only dissatisfied with 100 of the plants. After speaking with the nursery, the customer decides to keep 200 of the plants for a partial refund of $1,000. The nursery would record the following entry for sales allowance associated with 100 plants.

JOURNAL			
Date	**Account**	**Debit**	**Credit**
	Sales Returns and Allowances Accounts Receivable *To record a sales allowance for 100 plants*	1,000	 1,000

The nursery would also record a corresponding entry for the inventory and the cost of goods sold for the 100 returned plants.

JOURNAL			
Date	Account	Debit	Credit
	Merchandise Inventory Cost of Goods Sold *To reflect the return of 100 plants*	400	 400

For both the return and the allowance, if the customer had already paid their account in full, Cash would be affected rather than Accounts Receivable.

There are differing opinions as to whether sales returns and allowances should be in separate accounts. Separating the accounts would help a retailer distinguish between items that are returned and those that the customer kept. This can better identify quality control issues, track whether a customer was satisfied with their purchase, and report how many resources are spent on processing returns. Most companies choose to combine returns and allowances into one account, but from a manager's perspective, it may be easier to have the accounts separated to make current determinations about inventory.

You may have noticed our discussion of credit sales did not include third-party credit card transactions. This is when a customer pays with a credit or debit card from a third-party, such as Visa, MasterCard, Discover, or American Express. These entries and discussion are covered in more advanced accounting courses. A more comprehensive example of merchandising purchase and sale transactions occurs in Calculate Activity-Based Product Costs (http://cnx.org/content/m68137/latest/) and Compare and Contrast Traditional and Activity-Based Costing Systems (http://cnx.org/content/m68138/latest/) , applying the perpetual inventory method.

LINK TO LEARNING

Major retailers must find new ways to manage inventory and reduce operating cycles to stay competitive. Companies such as Amazon.com Inc., have been able to reduce their operating cycles and increase their receivable collection rates to a level better than many of their nearest competitors. Check out Stock Analysis on Net (https://openstax.org/l/50StockAnalyNet) to find out how they do this and to see a comparison of operating cycles for top retail brands.

6.2 Compare and Contrast Perpetual versus Periodic Inventory Systems

There are two ways in which a company may account for their inventory. They can use a perpetual or periodic inventory system. Let's look at the characteristics of these two systems.

Characteristics of the Perpetual and Periodic Inventory Systems

A **perpetual inventory system** automatically updates and records the inventory account every time a sale, or purchase of inventory occurs. You can consider this "recording as you go." The recognition of each sale or purchase happens immediately upon sale or purchase.

A **periodic inventory system** updates and records the inventory account at certain, scheduled times at the end of an operating cycle. The update and recognition could occur at the end of the month, quarter, and year. There is a gap between the sale or purchase of inventory and when the inventory activity is recognized.

Generally Accepted Accounting Principles (GAAP) do not state a required inventory system, but the periodic inventory system uses a Purchases account to meet the requirements for recognition under GAAP. IFRS requirements are very similar. The main difference is that assets are valued at net realizable value and can be increased or decreased as values change. Under GAAP, once values are reduced they cannot be increased again.

Figure 6.8 Inventory Systems. (credit: "Untitled" by Marcin Wichary/Flickr, CC BY 2.0)

CONTINUING APPLICATION AT WORK

Merchandising Transactions

Gearhead Outfitters is a retailer of outdoor-related gear such as clothing, footwear, backpacks, and camping equipment. Therefore, one of the biggest assets on Gearhead's balance sheet is inventory. The proper presentation of inventory in a company's books leads to a number of accounting challenges, such as:

- What method of accounting for inventory is appropriate?
- How often should inventory be counted?
- How will inventory in the books be valued?
- Is any of the inventory obsolete and, if so, how will it be accounted for?
- Is all inventory included in the books?
- Are items included as inventory in the books that should not be?

Proper application of accounting principles is vital to keep accurate books and records. In accounting for inventory, matching principle, valuation, cutoff, completeness, and cost flow assumptions are all important. Did Gearhead match the cost of sale with the sale itself? Was only inventory that belonged to the company as of the period end date included? Did Gearhead count all the inventory? Perhaps some goods were in transit (on a delivery truck for a sale just made, or en route to Gearhead). What is the correct cost flow assumption for Gearhead to accurately account for inventory? Should it use a first-in, first-out method, or last-in, first-out?

These are all accounting challenges Gearhead faces with respect to inventory. As inventory will represent one of the largest items on the balance sheet, it is vital that Gearhead management take due care with decisions related to inventory accounting. Keeping in mind considerations such as gross profit, inventory turnover, meeting demand, point-of-sale systems, and timeliness of accounting information, what other accounting challenges might arise regarding the company's inventory accounting processes?

Inventory Systems Comparison

There are some key differences between perpetual and periodic inventory systems. When a company uses the perpetual inventory system and makes a purchase, they will automatically update the Merchandise Inventory account. Under a periodic inventory system, Purchases will be updated, while Merchandise Inventory will remain unchanged until the company counts and verifies its inventory balance. This count and verification typically occur at the end of the annual accounting period, which is often on December 31 of the year. The Merchandise Inventory account balance is reported on the balance sheet while the Purchases account is reported on the Income Statement when using the periodic inventory method. The Cost of Goods Sold is reported on the Income Statement under the perpetual inventory method.

JOURNAL			
Date	**Account**	**Debit**	**Credit**
Perpetual			
	Merchandise Inventory	$$$	
	Accounts Payable		$$$
Periodic			
	Purchases	$$$	
	Accounts Payable		$$$

A purchase return or allowance under perpetual inventory systems updates Merchandise Inventory for any decreased cost. Under periodic inventory systems, a temporary account, Purchase Returns and Allowances, is updated. Purchase Returns and Allowances is a contra account and is used to reduce Purchases.

JOURNAL			
Date	**Account**	**Debit**	**Credit**
Perpetual			
	Accounts Payable	$$$	
	Merchandise Inventory		$$$
Periodic			
	Accounts Payable	$$$	
	Purchase Returns and Allowances		$$$

When a purchase discount is applied under a perpetual inventory system, Merchandise Inventory decreases for the discount amount. Under a periodic inventory system, Purchase Discounts (a temporary, contra account), increases for the discount amount and Merchandise Inventory remains unchanged.

JOURNAL			
Date	**Account**	**Debit**	**Credit**
Perpetual			
	Accounts Payable	$$$	
	Cash		$$$
	Merchandise Inventory		$$$
Periodic			
	Accounts Payable	$$$	
	Cash		$$$
	Purchase Discounts		$$$

When a sale occurs under perpetual inventory systems, two entries are required: one to recognize the sale, and the other to recognize the cost of sale. For the cost of sale, Merchandise Inventory and Cost of Goods Sold are updated. Under periodic inventory systems, this cost of sale entry does not exist. The recognition of merchandise cost only occurs at the end of the period when adjustments are made and temporary accounts are closed.

JOURNAL			
Date	**Account**	**Debit**	**Credit**
Perpetual			
	Accounts Receivable	$$$	
	Sales		$$$
	Cost of Goods Sold	$$$	
	Merchandise Inventory		$$$
Periodic			
	Accounts Receivable	$$$	
	Sales		$$$

When a sales return occurs, perpetual inventory systems require recognition of the inventory's condition. This means a decrease to COGS and an increase to Merchandise Inventory. Under periodic inventory systems, only the sales return is recognized, but not the inventory condition entry.

JOURNAL			
Date	Account	Debit	Credit
Perpetual			
	Sales Returns and Allowances	$$$	
	Accounts Receivable		$$$
	Merchandise Inventory	$$$	
	Cost of Goods Sold		$$$
Periodic			
	Sales Returns and Allowances	$$$	
	Accounts Receivable		$$$

A sales allowance and sales discount follow the same recording formats for either perpetual or periodic inventory systems.

JOURNAL			
Date	Account	Debit	Credit
Perpetual and Periodic			
	Sales Returns and Allowances	$$$	
	Accounts Receivable		$$$
	Cash	$$$	
	Sales Discount	$$$	
	Accounts Receivable		$$$

Adjusting and Closing Entries for a Perpetual Inventory System

You have already explored adjusting entries and the closing process in prior discussions, but merchandising activities require additional adjusting and closing entries to inventory, sales discounts, returns, and allowances. Here, we'll briefly discuss these additional closing entries and adjustments as they relate to the perpetual inventory system.

At the end of the period, a perpetual inventory system will have the Merchandise Inventory account up-to-date; the only thing left to do is to compare a physical count of inventory to what is on the books. A **physical inventory count** requires companies to do a manual "stock-check" of inventory to make sure what they have recorded on the books matches what they physically have in stock. Differences could occur due to mismanagement, shrinkage, damage, or outdated merchandise. Shrinkage is a term used when inventory or other assets disappear without an identifiable reason, such as theft. For a perpetual inventory system, the adjusting entry to show this difference follows. This example assumes that the merchandise inventory is overstated in the accounting records and needs to be adjusted downward to reflect the actual value on hand.

JOURNAL			
Date	Account	Debit	Credit
	Cost of Goods Sold	$$$	
	Merchandise Inventory		$$$
	To adjust merchandise inventory of books		

If a physical count determines that merchandise inventory is understated in the accounting records, Merchandise Inventory would need to be increased with a debit entry and the COGS would be reduced with a credit entry. The adjusting entry is:

JOURNAL			
Date	Account	Debit	Credit
	Merchandise Inventory Cost of Goods Sold *To adjust merchandise inventory of books*	$$$	 $$$

To sum up the potential adjustment process, after the merchandise inventory has been verified with a physical count, its book value is adjusted upward or downward to reflect the actual inventory on hand, with an accompanying adjustment to the COGS.

Not only must an adjustment to Merchandise Inventory occur at the end of a period, but closure of temporary merchandising accounts to prepare them for the next period is required. Temporary accounts requiring closure are Sales, Sales Discounts, Sales Returns and Allowances, and Cost of Goods Sold. Sales will close with the temporary credit balance accounts to Income Summary.

JOURNAL			
Date	Account	Debit	Credit
	Sales Income Summary	$$$	 $$$

Sales Discounts, Sales Returns and Allowances, and Cost of Goods Sold will close with the temporary debit balance accounts to Income Summary.

JOURNAL			
Date	Account	Debit	Credit
	Income Summary Sales Discounts Sales Returns and Allowances Cost of Goods Sold	$$$	 $$$ $$$ $$$

Note that for a periodic inventory system, the end of the period adjustments require an update to COGS. To determine the value of Cost of Goods Sold, the business will have to look at the beginning inventory balance, purchases, purchase returns and allowances, discounts, and the ending inventory balance.

The formula to compute COGS is:

Cost of Goods Sold = Beginning Inventory + Net Purchases – Ending inventory

where:

Net Purchases = (Gross) Purchases – Purchase Discounts – Purchase Returns and Allowances

Once the COGS balance has been established, an adjustment is made to Merchandise Inventory and COGS, and COGS is closed to prepare for the next period.

Table 6.1 summarizes the differences between the perpetual and periodic inventory systems.

Perpetual and Periodic Transaction Comparison

Transaction	Perpetual Inventory System	Periodic Inventory System
Purchase of Inventory	Record cost to Inventory account	Record cost to Purchases account
Purchase Return or Allowance	Record to update Inventory	Record to Purchase Returns and Allowances
Purchase Discount	Record to update Inventory	Record to Purchase Discounts
Sale of Merchandise	Record two entries: one for sale and one for cost of sale	Record one entry for the sale
Sales Return	Record two entries: one for sales return, one for cost of inventory returned	Record one entry: sales return, cost not recognized
Sales Allowance	Same under both systems	Same under both systems
Sales Discount	Same under both systems	Same under both systems

Table 6.1 There are several differences in account recognition between the perpetual and periodic inventory systems.

There are advantages and disadvantages to both the perpetual and periodic inventory systems.

CONCEPTS IN PRACTICE

Point-of-Sale Systems

Advancements in point-of-sale (POS) systems have simplified the once tedious task of inventory management. POS systems connect with inventory management programs to make real-time data available to help streamline business operations. The cost of inventory management decreases with this connection tool, allowing all businesses to stay current with technology without "breaking the bank."

One such POS system is Square. Square accepts many payment types and updates accounting records every time a sale occurs through a cloud-based application. Square, Inc. has expanded their product offerings to include Square for Retail POS. This enhanced product allows businesses to connect sales and inventory costs immediately. A business can easily create purchase orders, develop reports for cost of goods sold, manage inventory stock, and update discounts, returns, and allowances. With this application, customers have payment flexibility, and businesses can make present decisions to positively affect growth.

Advantages and Disadvantages of the Perpetual Inventory System

The perpetual inventory system gives real-time updates and keeps a constant flow of inventory information available for decision-makers. With advancements in point-of-sale technologies, inventory is updated automatically and transferred into the company's accounting system. This allows managers to make decisions as it relates to inventory purchases, stocking, and sales. The information can be more robust, with exact purchase costs, sales prices, and dates known. Although a periodic physical count of inventory is still required, a perpetual inventory system may reduce the number of times physical counts are needed.

The biggest disadvantages of using the perpetual inventory systems arise from the resource constraints for cost and time. It is costly to keep an automatic inventory system up-to-date. This may prohibit smaller or less established companies from investing in the required technologies. The time commitment to train and retrain staff to update inventory is considerable. In addition, since there are fewer physical counts of inventory, the figures recorded in the system may be drastically different from inventory levels in the actual warehouse. A company may not have correct inventory stock and could make financial decisions based on incorrect data.

Advantages and Disadvantages of the Periodic Inventory System

The periodic inventory system is often less expensive and time consuming than perpetual inventory systems. This is because there is no constant maintenance of inventory records or training and retraining of employees to upkeep the system. The complexity of the system makes it difficult to identify the cost justification associated with the inventory function.

While both the periodic and perpetual inventory systems require a physical count of inventory, periodic inventorying requires more physical counts to be conducted. This updates the inventory account more frequently to record exact costs. Knowing the exact costs earlier in an accounting cycle can help a company stay on budget and control costs.

However, the need for frequent physical counts of inventory can suspend business operations each time this is done. There are more chances for shrinkage, damaged, or obsolete merchandise because inventory is not constantly monitored. Since there is no constant monitoring, it may be more difficult to make in-the-moment business decisions about inventory needs.

While each inventory system has its own advantages and disadvantages, the more popular system is the perpetual inventory system. The ability to have real-time data to make decisions, the constant update to inventory, and the integration to point-of-sale systems, outweigh the cost and time investments needed to maintain the system. (While our main coverage focuses on recognition under the perpetual inventory system, Appendix: Analyze and Record Transactions for Merchandise Purchases and Sales Using the Periodic Inventory System discusses recognition under the periodic inventory system.)

THINK IT THROUGH

Comparing Inventory Systems

Your company uses a perpetual inventory system to control its operations. They only check inventory once every six months. At the 6-month physical count, an employee notices several inventory items missing and many damaged units. In the company records, it shows an inventory balance of $300,000.

The actual physical count values inventory at $200,000. This is a significant difference in valuation and has jeopardized the future of the company. As a manager, how might you avoid this large discrepancy in the future? Would a change in inventory systems benefit the company? Are you constrained by any resources?

6.3 Analyze and Record Transactions for Merchandise Purchases Using the Perpetual Inventory System

The following example transactions and subsequent journal entries for merchandise purchases are recognized using a perpetual inventory system. The periodic inventory system recognition of these example transactions and corresponding journal entries are shown in Appendix: Analyze and Record Transactions for Merchandise Purchases and Sales Using the Periodic Inventory System.

Basic Analysis of Purchase Transaction Journal Entries

To better illustrate merchandising activities, let's follow California Business Solutions (CBS), a retailer providing electronic hardware packages to meet small business needs. Each electronics hardware package (see Figure 6.9) contains a desktop computer, tablet computer, landline telephone, and a 4-in-1 desktop printer with a printer, copier, scanner, and fax machine.

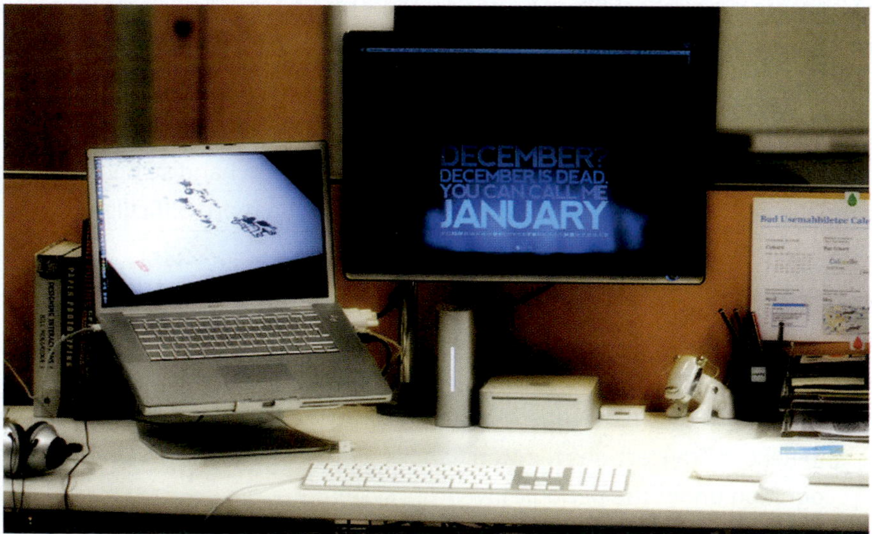

Figure 6.9 California Business Solutions. Providing businesses electronic hardware solutions. (credit: modification of "Professionnal desk" by "reynermedia"/Flickr, CC BY 2.0)

CBS purchases each electronic product from a manufacturer. The following are the per-item purchase prices from the manufacturer.

Product	Price per Unit
Desktop computer	$400
Tablet computer	60
Landline telephone	60
4-in-1 desktop printer	100

Cash and Credit Purchase Transaction Journal Entries

On April 1, CBS purchases 10 electronic hardware packages at a cost of $620 each. CBS has enough cash-on-hand to pay immediately with cash. The following entry occurs.

JOURNAL			
Date	**Account**	**Debit**	**Credit**
Apr. 1	Merchandise Inventory: Packages Cash *To recognize purchase of 10 packages*	6,200	 6,200

Merchandise Inventory-Packages increases (debit) for 6,200 ($620 × 10), and Cash decreases (credit) because the company paid with cash. It is important to distinguish each inventory item type to better track inventory needs.

On April 7, CBS purchases 30 desktop computers on credit at a cost of $400 each. The credit terms are n/15 with an invoice date of April 7. The following entry occurs.

JOURNAL			
Date	**Account**	**Debit**	**Credit**
Apr. 7	Merchandise Inventory: Desktop Computers Accounts Payable *To recognize purchase of 30 computers on credit, n/15*	12,000	 12,000

Merchandise Inventory is specific to desktop computers and is increased (debited) for the value of the computers by $12,000 ($400 × 30). Since the computers were purchased on credit by CBS, Accounts Payable increases (credit).

On April 17, CBS makes full payment on the amount due from the April 7 purchase. The following entry occurs.

JOURNAL			
Date	**Account**	**Debit**	**Credit**
Apr. 17	Accounts Payable Cash *To recognize payment in full*	12,000	 12,000

Accounts Payable decreases (debit), and Cash decreases (credit) for the full amount owed. The credit terms were n/15, which is net due in 15 days. No discount was offered with this transaction. Thus the full payment of $12,000 occurs.

Purchase Discount Transaction Journal Entries

On May 1, CBS purchases 67 tablet computers at a cost of $60 each on credit. The payment terms are 5/10, n/

30, and the invoice is dated May 1. The following entry occurs.

JOURNAL			
Date	**Account**	**Debit**	**Credit**
May 1	Merchandise Inventory: Tablet Computers Accounts Payable *To recognize purchase of 67 tablets, 5/10, n/30*	4,020	 4,020

Merchandise Inventory-Tablet Computers increases (debit) in the amount of $4,020 (67 × $60). Accounts Payable also increases (credit) but the credit terms are a little different than the previous example. These credit terms include a discount opportunity (5/10), meaning, CBS has 10 days from the invoice date to pay on their account to receive a 5% discount on their purchase.

On May 10, CBS pays their account in full. The following entry occurs.

JOURNAL			
Date	**Account**	**Debit**	**Credit**
May 10	Accounts Payable Merchandise Inventory: Tablet Computers Cash *To recognize payment, less purchase discount*	4,020	 201 3,819

Accounts Payable decreases (debit) for the original amount owed of $4,020 before any discounts are taken. Since CBS paid on May 10, they made the 10-day window and thus received a discount of 5%. Cash decreases (credit) for the amount owed, less the discount. Merchandise Inventory-Tablet Computers decreases (credit) for the amount of the discount ($4,020 × 5%). Merchandise Inventory decreases to align with the Cost Principle, reporting the value of the merchandise at the reduced cost.

Let's take the same example purchase with the same credit terms, but now CBS paid their account on May 25. The following entry would occur instead.

JOURNAL			
Date	**Account**	**Debit**	**Credit**
May 25	Accounts Payable Cash *To recognize payment for tablets, no discount*	4,020	 4,020

Accounts Payable decreases (debit) and Cash decreases (credit) for $4,020. The company paid on their account outside of the discount window but within the total allotted timeframe for payment. CBS does not receive a discount in this case but does pay in full and on time.

Purchase Returns and Allowances Transaction Journal Entries

On June 1, CBS purchased 300 landline telephones with cash at a cost of $60 each. On June 3, CBS discovers that 25 of the phones are the wrong color and returns the phones to the manufacturer for a full refund. The following entries occur with the purchase and subsequent return.

JOURNAL			
Date	**Account**	**Debit**	**Credit**
Jun. 1	Merchandise Inventory: Phones Cash *To recognize phone purchase with cash*	18,000	18,000

Both Merchandise Inventory-Phones increases (debit) and Cash decreases (credit) by $18,000 ($60 × 300).

JOURNAL			
Date	**Account**	**Debit**	**Credit**
Jun. 3	Cash Merchandise Inventory: Phones *To recognize return of 25 phones, cash refund*	1,500	1,500

Since CBS already paid in full for their purchase, a full cash refund is issued. This increases Cash (debit) and decreases (credit) Merchandise Inventory-Phones because the merchandise has been returned to the manufacturer or supplier.

On June 8, CBS discovers that 60 more phones from the June 1 purchase are slightly damaged. CBS decides to keep the phones but receives a purchase allowance from the manufacturer of $8 per phone. The following entry occurs for the allowance.

JOURNAL			
Date	**Account**	**Debit**	**Credit**
Jun. 8	Cash Merchandise Inventory: Phones *To recognize allowance for 60 phones*	480	480

Since CBS already paid in full for their purchase, a cash refund of the allowance is issued in the amount of $480 (60 × $8). This increases Cash (debit) and decreases (credit) Merchandise Inventory-Phones because the merchandise is less valuable than before the damage discovery.

CBS purchases 80 units of the 4-in-1 desktop printers at a cost of $100 each on July 1 on credit. Terms of the purchase are 5/15, n/40, with an invoice date of July 1. On July 6, CBS discovers 15 of the printers are damaged and returns them to the manufacturer for a full refund. The following entries show the purchase and subsequent return.

JOURNAL			
Date	**Account**	**Debit**	**Credit**
July 1	Merchandise Inventory: Printers Accounts Payable *To recognize printer purchase on credit, 5/15, n/40*	8,000	8,000

Both Merchandise Inventory-Printers increases (debit) and Accounts Payable increases (credit) by $8,000 ($100 × 80).

JOURNAL			
Date	**Account**	**Debit**	**Credit**
July 6	Accounts Payable Merchandise Inventory: Printers *To recognize return of 15 printers, AP reduction*	1,500	1,500

Both Accounts Payable decreases (debit) and Merchandise Inventory-Printers decreases (credit) by $1,500 (15 × $100). The purchase was on credit and the return occurred before payment, thus decreasing Accounts Payable. Merchandise Inventory decreases due to the return of the merchandise back to the manufacturer.

On July 10, CBS discovers that 4 more printers from the July 1 purchase are slightly damaged but decides to keep them, with the manufacturer issuing an allowance of $30 per printer. The following entry recognizes the allowance.

JOURNAL			
Date	**Account**	**Debit**	**Credit**
July 10	Accounts Payable Merchandise Inventory: Printers *To recognize allowance for 4 printers, AP reduction*	120	 120

Both Accounts Payable decreases (debit) and Merchandise Inventory-Printers decreases (credit) by $120 (4 × $30). The purchase was on credit and the allowance occurred before payment, thus decreasing Accounts Payable. Merchandise Inventory decreases due to the loss in value of the merchandise.

On July 15, CBS pays their account in full, less purchase returns and allowances. The following payment entry occurs.

JOURNAL			
Date	**Account**	**Debit**	**Credit**
July 15	Accounts Payable Merchandise Inventory: Printers Cash *To recognize payment, less discount, return and allowance*	6,380	 319 6,061

Accounts Payable decreases (debit) for the amount owed, less the return of $1,500 and the allowance of $120 ($8,000 – $1,500 – $120). Since CBS paid on July 15, they made the 15-day window, thus receiving a discount of 5%. Cash decreases (credit) for the amount owed, less the discount. Merchandise Inventory-Printers decreases (credit) for the amount of the discount ($6,380 × 5%). Merchandise Inventory decreases to align with the Cost Principle, reporting the value of the merchandise at the reduced cost.

Summary of Purchase Transaction Journal Entries

The chart in Figure 6.10 represents the journal entry requirements based on various merchandising purchase transactions using the perpetual inventory system.

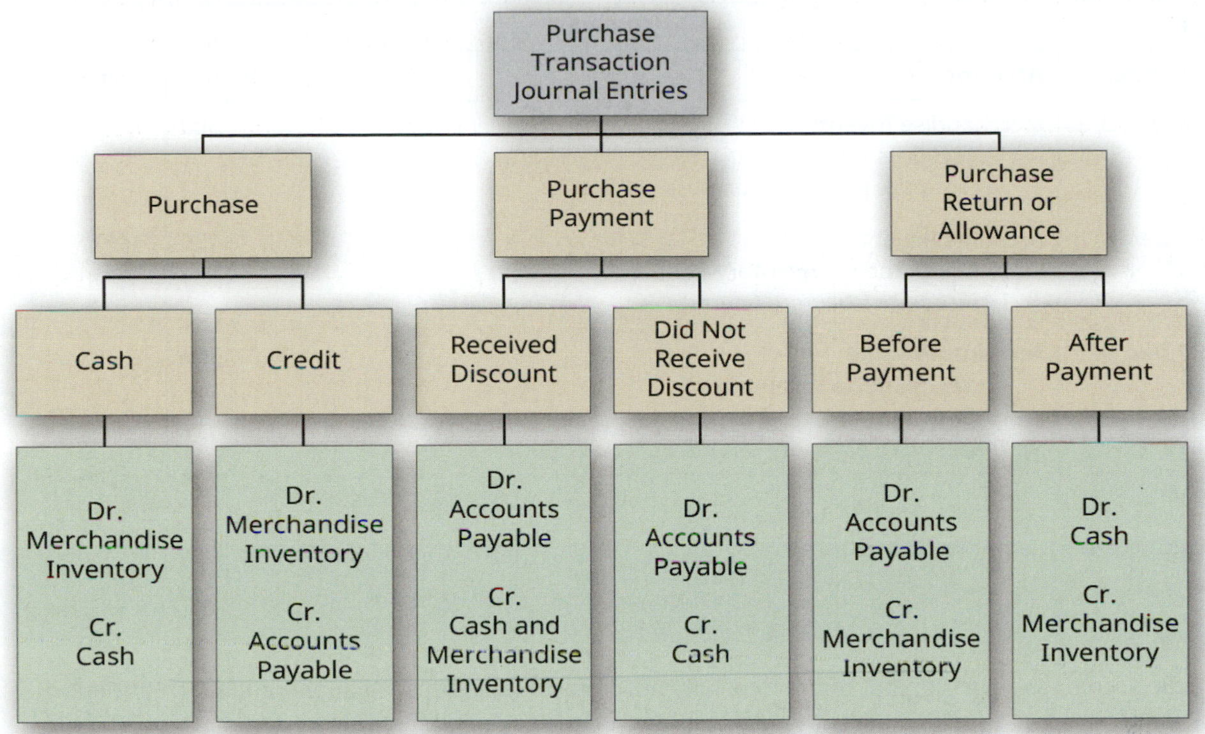

Figure 6.10 Purchase Transaction Journal Entries Using a Perpetual Inventory System. (attribution: Copyright Rice University, OpenStax, under CC BY-NC-SA 4.0 license)

Note that Figure 6.10 considers an environment in which inventory physical counts and matching books records align. This is not always the case given concerns with shrinkage (theft), damages, or obsolete merchandise. In this circumstance, an adjustment is recorded to inventory to account for the differences between the physical count and the amount represented on the books.

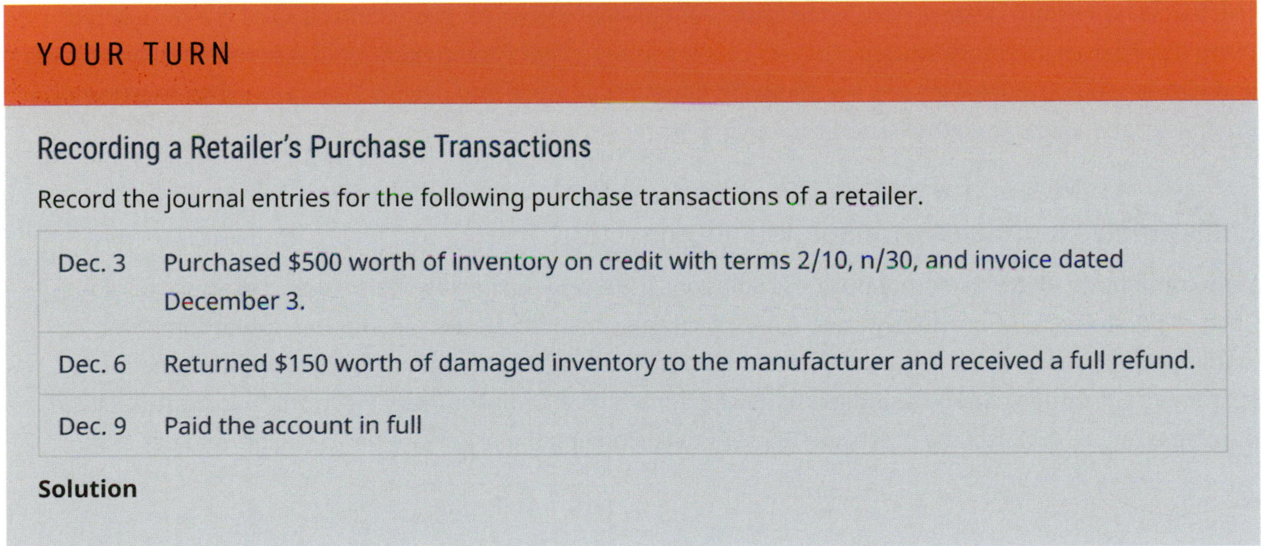

YOUR TURN

Recording a Retailer's Purchase Transactions

Record the journal entries for the following purchase transactions of a retailer.

Dec. 3	Purchased $500 worth of inventory on credit with terms 2/10, n/30, and invoice dated December 3.
Dec. 6	Returned $150 worth of damaged inventory to the manufacturer and received a full refund.
Dec. 9	Paid the account in full

Solution

JOURNAL			
Date	**Account**	**Debit**	**Credit**
Dec. 3	Merchandise Inventory	500	
	Accounts Payable		500
	To recognize inventory purchase, 2/10, n/30		
Dec. 6	Accounts Payable	150	
	Merchandise Inventory		150
	To recognize inventory return		
Dec. 9	Accounts Payable	350	
	Merchandise Inventory		7
	Cash		343
	To recognize payment, less discount and return		

LINK TO LEARNING

Bean Counter is a website that offers free, fun and interactive games, simulations, and quizzes about accounting. You can “Fling the Teacher,” “Walk the Plank,” and play “Basketball” while learning the fundamentals of accounting topics. Check out Bean Counter (https://openstax.org/l/50BeanCounter) to see what you can learn.

6.4 Analyze and Record Transactions for the Sale of Merchandise Using the Perpetual Inventory System

The following example transactions and subsequent journal entries for merchandise sales are recognized using a perpetual inventory system. The periodic inventory system recognition of these example transactions and corresponding journal entries are shown in Appendix: Analyze and Record Transactions for Merchandise Purchases and Sales Using the Periodic Inventory System.

Basic Analysis of Sales Transaction Journal Entries

Let’s continue to follow California Business Solutions (CBS) and their sales of electronic hardware packages to business customers. As previously stated, each package contains a desktop computer, tablet computer, landline telephone, and a 4-in-1 printer. CBS sells each hardware package for $1,200. They offer their customers the option of purchasing extra individual hardware items for every electronic hardware package purchase. Figure 6.11 lists the products CBS sells to customers; the prices are per-package, and per unit.

Product	Sales Price per-package, per unit	Cost to CBS per-package, per unit
Electronic hardware package	$1,200	$620
Desktop computer	750	400
Tablet computer	300	60
Landline telephone	150	60
4-in-1 printer	350	100

Figure 6.11 CBS's Product Line. (attribution: Copyright Rice University, OpenStax, under CC BY-NC-SA 4.0 license)

Cash and Credit Sales Transaction Journal Entries

On July 1, CBS sells 10 electronic hardware packages to a customer at a sales price of $1,200 each. The customer pays immediately with cash. The following entries occur.

JOURNAL			
Date	**Account**	**Debit**	**Credit**
July 1	Cash	12,000	
	Sales		12,000
	To recognize sale of 10 packages		
July 1	Cost of Goods Sold	6,200	
	Merchandise Inventory: Packages		6,200
	To recognize cost of sale, 10 packages		

In the first entry, Cash increases (debit) and Sales increases (credit) for the selling price of the packages, $12,000 ($1,200 × 10). In the second entry, the cost of the sale is recognized. COGS increases (debit) and Merchandise Inventory-Packages decreases (credit) for the cost of the packages, $6,200 ($620 × 10).

On July 7, CBS sells 20 desktop computers to a customer on credit. The credit terms are n/15 with an invoice date of July 7. The following entries occur.

JOURNAL			
Date	**Account**	**Debit**	**Credit**
July 7	Accounts Receivable	15,000	
	Sales		15,000
	To recognize sale of 20 desktop computers, n/15		
July 7	Cost of Goods Sold	8,000	
	Merchandise Inventory: Desktop Computers		8,000
	To recognize cost of sale, 20 desktop computers		

Since the computers were purchased on credit by the customer, Accounts Receivable increases (debit) and Sales increases (credit) for the selling price of the computers, $15,000 ($750 × 20). In the second entry, Merchandise Inventory-Desktop Computers decreases (credit), and COGS increases (debit) for the cost of the computers, $8,000 ($400 × 20).

On July 17, the customer makes full payment on the amount due from the July 7 sale. The following entry occurs.

JOURNAL			
Date	**Account**	**Debit**	**Credit**
July 17	Cash Accounts Receivable *To recognize payment in full*	15,000	 15,000

Accounts Receivable decreases (credit) and Cash increases (debit) for the full amount owed. The credit terms were n/15, which is net due in 15 days. No discount was offered with this transaction; thus the full payment of $15,000 occurs.

Sales Discount Transaction Journal Entries

On August 1, a customer purchases 56 tablet computers on credit. The payment terms are 2/10, n/30, and the invoice is dated August 1. The following entries occur.

JOURNAL			
Date	**Account**	**Debit**	**Credit**
Aug. 1	Accounts Receivable Sales *To recognize sale of 56 tablet computers, 2/10, n/30*	16,800	 16,800
Aug. 1	Cost of Goods Sold Merchandise Inventory: Tablet Computers *To recognize cost of sale, 56 tablet computers*	3,360	 3,360

In the first entry, both Accounts Receivable (debit) and Sales (credit) increase by $16,800 ($300 × 56). These credit terms are a little different than the earlier example. These credit terms include a discount opportunity (2/10), meaning the customer has 10 days from the invoice date to pay on their account to receive a 2% discount on their purchase. In the second entry, COGS increases (debit) and Merchandise Inventory–Tablet Computers decreases (credit) in the amount of $3,360 (56 × $60).

On August 10, the customer pays their account in full. The following entry occurs.

JOURNAL			
Date	**Account**	**Debit**	**Credit**
Aug. 10	Cash Sales Discounts Accounts Receivable *To recognize payment, less sales discount*	16,464 336	 16,800

Since the customer paid on August 10, they made the 10-day window and received a discount of 2%. Cash increases (debit) for the amount paid to CBS, less the discount. Sales Discounts increases (debit) for the amount of the discount ($16,800 × 2%), and Accounts Receivable decreases (credit) for the original amount owed, before discount. Sales Discounts will reduce Sales at the end of the period to produce net sales.

Let's take the same example sale with the same credit terms, but now assume the customer paid their account on August 25. The following entry occurs.

JOURNAL			
Date	**Account**	**Debit**	**Credit**
Aug. 25	Cash Accounts Receivable *To recognize payment for tablets, no discount*	16,800	 16,800

Cash increases (debit) and Accounts Receivable decreases (credit) by $16,800. The customer paid on their account outside of the discount window but within the total allotted timeframe for payment. The customer does not receive a discount in this case but does pay in full and on time.

YOUR TURN

Recording a Retailer's Sales Transactions

Record the journal entries for the following sales transactions by a retailer.

Jan. 5	Sold $2,450 of merchandise on credit (cost of $1,000), with terms 2/10, n/30, and invoice dated January 5.
Jan. 9	The customer returned $500 worth of slightly damaged merchandise to the retailer and received a full refund. The retailer returned the merchandise to its inventory at a cost of $130.
Jan. 14	Account paid in full.

Solution

JOURNAL			
Date	**Account**	**Debit**	**Credit**
Jan. 5	Accounts Receivable Sales *To recognize sale on credit, 2/10, n/30*	2,450	 2,450
Jan. 5	Cost of Goods Sold Merchandise Inventory *To recognize cost of sale*	1,000	 1,000
Jan. 9	Sales Returns and Allowances Accounts Receivable *To recognize customer return*	500	 500
Jan. 9	Merchandise Inventory Cost of Goods Sold *To recognize merchandise return to inventory*	130	 130
Jan. 14	Cash Sales Discounts Accounts Receivable *To recognize payment, less discount and return*	1,911 39	 1,950

Sales Returns and Allowances Transaction Journal Entries

On September 1, CBS sold 250 landline telephones to a customer who paid with cash. On September 3, the customer discovers that 40 of the phones are the wrong color and returns the phones to CBS in exchange for a full refund. CBS determines that the returned merchandise can be resold and returns the merchandise to inventory at its original cost. The following entries occur for the sale and subsequent return.

JOURNAL			
Date	**Account**	**Debit**	**Credit**
Sept. 1	Cash	37,500	
	Sales		37,500
	To recognize sale of 250 phones with cash		
Sept. 1	Cost of Goods Sold	15,000	
	Merchandise Inventory: Phones		15,000
	To recognize cost of sale, 250 phones		

In the first entry on September 1, Cash increases (debit) and Sales increases (credit) by $37,500 (250 × $150), the sales price of the phones. In the second entry, COGS increases (debit), and Merchandise Inventory-Phones decreases (credit) by $15,000 (250 × $60), the cost of the sale.

JOURNAL			
Date	**Account**	**Debit**	**Credit**
Sept. 3	Sales Returns and Allowances	6,000	
	Cash		6,000
	To recognize return of 40 phones, cash refund		
Sept. 3	Merchandise Inventory: Phones	2,400	
	Cost of Goods Sold		2,400
	To return merchandise to inventory, sellable condition		

Since the customer already paid in full for their purchase, a full cash refund is issued on September 3. This increases Sales Returns and Allowances (debit) and decreases Cash (credit) by $6,000 (40 × $150). The second entry on September 3 returns the phones back to inventory for CBS because they have determined the merchandise is in sellable condition at its original cost. Merchandise Inventory–Phones increases (debit) and COGS decreases (credit) by $2,400 (40 × $60).

On September 8, the customer discovers that 20 more phones from the September 1 purchase are slightly damaged. The customer decides to keep the phones but receives a sales allowance from CBS of $10 per phone. The following entry occurs for the allowance.

JOURNAL			
Date	**Account**	**Debit**	**Credit**
Sept. 8	Sales Returns and Allowances	200	
	Cash		200
	To recognize allowance for 20 phones		

Since the customer already paid in full for their purchase, a cash refund of the allowance is issued in the amount of $200 (20 × $10). This increases (debit) Sales Returns and Allowances and decreases (credit) Cash. CBS does not have to consider the condition of the merchandise or return it to their inventory because the customer keeps the merchandise.

A customer purchases 55 units of the 4-in-1 desktop printers on October 1 on credit. Terms of the sale are 10/

15, n/40, with an invoice date of October 1. On October 6, the customer returned 10 of the printers to CBS for a full refund. CBS returns the printers to their inventory at the original cost. The following entries show the sale and subsequent return.

JOURNAL			
Date	**Account**	**Debit**	**Credit**
Oct. 1	Accounts Receivable	19,250	
	Sales		19,250
	To recognize sale of 55 printers on credit, 10/15, n/40		
Oct. 1	Cost of Goods Sold	5,500	
	Merchandise Inventory: Printers		5,500
	To recognize cost of sale, 55 printers		

In the first entry on October 1, Accounts Receivable increases (debit) and Sales increases (credit) by $19,250 (55 × $350), the sales price of the printers. Accounts Receivable is used instead of Cash because the customer purchased on credit. In the second entry, COGS increases (debit) and Merchandise Inventory–Printers decreases (credit) by $5,500 (55 × $100), the cost of the sale.

JOURNAL			
Date	**Account**	**Debit**	**Credit**
Oct. 6	Sales Returns and Allowances	3,500	
	Accounts Receivable		3,500
	To recognize return of 10 printers		
Oct. 6	Merchandise Inventory: Printers	1,000	
	Cost of Goods Sold		1,000
	To return merchandise to inventory, sellable condition		

The customer has not yet paid for their purchase as of October 6. Therefore, the return increases Sales Returns and Allowances (debit) and decreases Accounts Receivable (credit) by $3,500 (10 × $350). The second entry on October 6 returns the printers back to inventory for CBS because they have determined the merchandise is in sellable condition at its original cost. Merchandise Inventory–Printers increases (debit) and COGS decreases (credit) by $1,000 (10 × $100).

On October 10, the customer discovers that 5 printers from the October 1 purchase are slightly damaged, but decides to keep them, and CBS issues an allowance of $60 per printer. The following entry recognizes the allowance.

JOURNAL			
Date	**Account**	**Debit**	**Credit**
Oct. 10	Sales Returns and Allowances	300	
	Accounts Receivable		300
	To recognize allowance for 5 printers		

Sales Returns and Allowances increases (debit) and Accounts Receivable decreases (credit) by $300 (5 × $60). A reduction to Accounts Receivable occurs because the customer has yet to pay their account on October 10. CBS does not have to consider the condition of the merchandise or return it to their inventory because the customer keeps the merchandise.

On October 15, the customer pays their account in full, less sales returns and allowances. The following payment entry occurs.

JOURNAL			
Date	**Account**	**Debit**	**Credit**
Oct. 15	Cash Sales Discounts Accounts Receivable *To recognize payment, less sales discount, return and allowance*	13,905 1,545	 15,450

Accounts Receivable decreases (credit) for the original amount owed, less the return of $3,500 and the allowance of $300 ($19,250 – $3,500 – $300). Since the customer paid on October 15, they made the 15-day window, thus receiving a discount of 10%. Sales Discounts increases (debit) for the discount amount ($15,450 × 10%). Cash increases (debit) for the amount owed to CBS, less the discount.

Summary of Sales Transaction Journal Entries

The chart in Figure 6.12 represents the journal entry requirements based on various merchandising sales transactions.

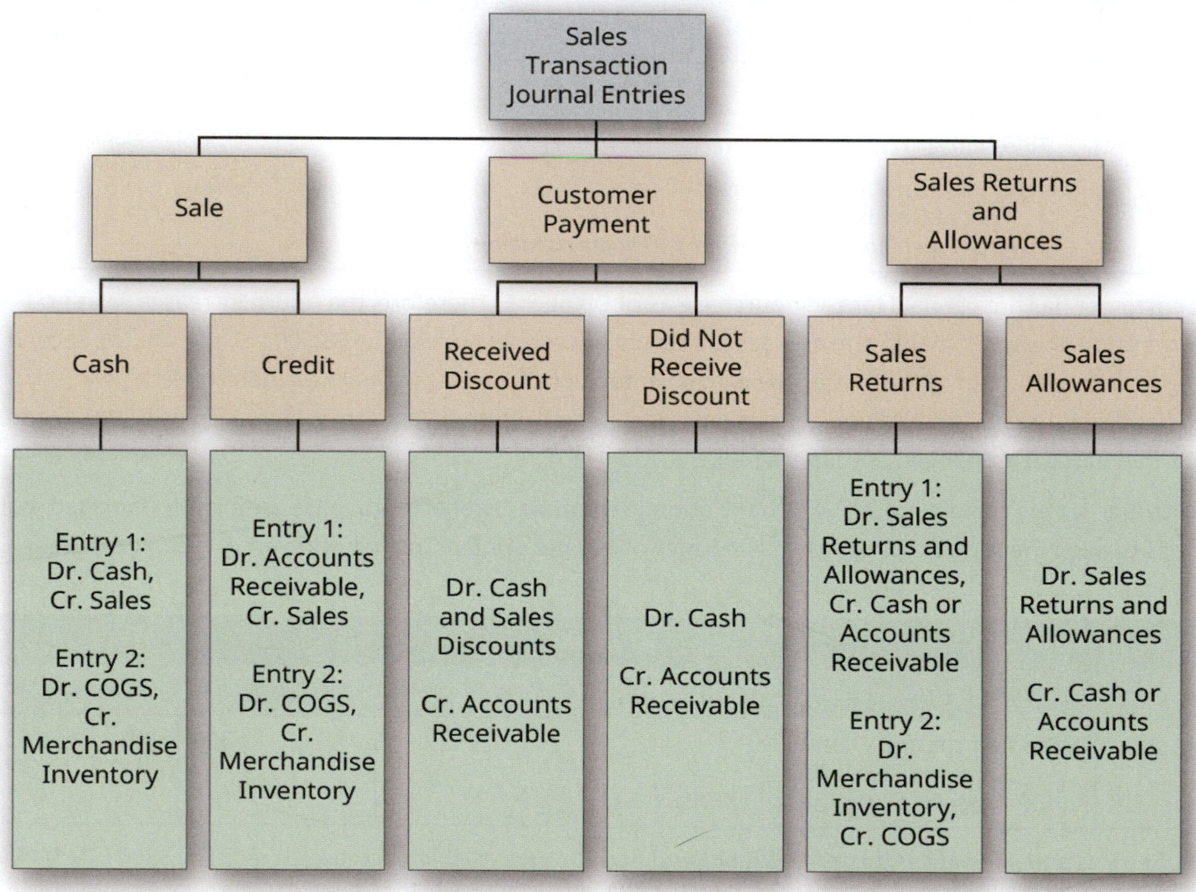

Figure 6.12 Journal Entry Requirements for Merchandise Sales Transaction. (attribution: Copyright Rice University, OpenStax, under CC BY-NC-SA 4.0 license)

YOUR TURN

Recording a Retailer's Sales Transactions

Record the journal entries for the following sales transactions of a retailer.

May 10	Sold $8,600 of merchandise on credit (cost of $2,650), with terms 5/10, n/30, and invoice dated May 10.
May 13	The customer returned $1,250 worth of slightly damaged merchandise to the retailer and received a full refund. The retailer returned the merchandise to its inventory at a cost of $380.
May 15	The customer discovered some merchandise were the wrong color and received an allowance from the retailer of $230.
May 20	The customer paid the account in full, less the return and allowance.

Solution

JOURNAL			
Date	**Account**	**Debit**	**Credit**
May 10	Accounts Receivable	8,600	
	Sales		8,600
	To recognize sale on credit, 5/10, n/30		
May 10	Cost of Goods Sold	2,650	
	Merchandise Inventory		2,650
	To recognize cost of sale		
May 13	Sales Returns and Allowances	1,250	
	Accounts Receivable		1,250
	To recognize customer return		
May 13	Merchandise Inventory	380	
	Cost of Goods Sold		380
	To recognize merchandise return to inventory		
May 15	Sales Returns and Allowances	230	
	Accounts Receivable		230
	To recognize customer allowance		
May 20	Cash	6,764	
	Sales Discounts	356	
	Accounts Receivable		7,120
	To recognize payment, less discount, allowance and return		

6.5 Discuss and Record Transactions Applying the Two Commonly Used Freight-In Methods

When you buy merchandise online, shipping charges are usually one of the negotiated terms of the sale. As a consumer, anytime the business pays for shipping, it is welcomed. For businesses, shipping charges bring both benefits and challenges, and the terms negotiated can have a significant impact on inventory operations.

Figure 6.13 Shipping Merchandise. (credit: "Guida Siebert Dairy Milk Delivery Truck tractor trailer!" by Mike Mozart/Flickr, CC BY 2.0)

IFRS CONNECTION

Shipping Term Effects

Companies applying US GAAP as well as those applying IFRS can choose either a perpetual or periodic inventory system to track purchases and sales of inventory. While the tracking systems do not differ between the two methods, they have differences in when sales transactions are reported. If goods are shipped FOB shipping point, under IFRS, the total selling price of the item would be allocated between the item sold (as sales revenue) and the shipping (as shipping revenue). Under US GAAP, the seller can elect whether the shipping costs will be an additional component of revenue (separate performance obligation) or whether they will be considered fulfillment costs (expensed at the time shipping as shipping expense). In an FOB destination scenario, the shipping costs would be considered a fulfillment activity and expensed as incurred rather than be treated as a part of revenue under both IFRS and US GAAP.

Example

Wally's Wagons sells and ships 20 deluxe model wagons to Sam's Emporium for $5,000. Assume $400 of the total costs represents the costs of shipping the wagons and consider these two scenarios: (1) the wagons are shipped FOB shipping point or (2) the wagons are shipped FOB destination. If Wally's is applying IFRS, the $400 shipping is considered a separate performance obligation, or shipping revenue, and the other $4,600 is considered sales revenue. Both revenues are recorded at the time of shipping and the $400 shipping revenue is offset by a shipping expense. If Wally's used US GAAP instead, they would choose between using the same treatment as described under IFRS or considering the costs of shipping to be costs of fulfilling the order and expense those costs at the time they are incurred. In this latter case, Wally's would record Sales Revenue of $5,000 at the time the wagons are shipped and $400 as shipping expense at the time of shipping. Notice that in both cases, the total net revenues are the same $4,600, but the distribution of those revenues is different, which impacts analyses of sales revenue versus total revenues. What happens if the wagons are shipped FOB destination instead? Under both IFRS and US GAAP, the $400 shipping would be treated as an order fulfillment cost and recorded as an expense at the time the goods are shipped. Revenue of $5,000 would be recorded at the time the goods are received by Sam's emporium.

Financial Statement Presentation of Cost of Goods Sold

IFRS allows greater flexibility in the presentation of financial statements, including the income statement. Under IFRS, expenses can be reported in the income statement either by nature (for example, rent, salaries, depreciation) or by function (such as COGS or Selling and Administrative). US GAAP has no specific requirements regarding the presentation of expenses, but the SEC requires that expenses be reported by function. Therefore, it may be more challenging to compare merchandising costs (cost of goods sold) across companies if one company's income statement shows expenses by function and another company shows them by nature.

The Basics of Freight-in Versus Freight-out Costs

Shipping is determined by contract terms between a buyer and seller. There are several key factors to consider when determining who pays for shipping, and how it is recognized in merchandising transactions. The establishment of a transfer point and ownership indicates who pays the shipping charges, who is responsible for the merchandise, on whose balance sheet the assets would be recorded, and how to record the transaction for the buyer and seller.

Ownership of inventory refers to which party owns the inventory at a particular point in time—the buyer or the seller. One particularly important point in time is the **point of transfer**, when the responsibility for the inventory transfers from the seller to the buyer. Establishing ownership of inventory is important to determine who pays the shipping charges when the goods are in transit as well as the responsibility of each party when the goods are in their possession. **Goods in transit** refers to the time in which the merchandise is transported from the seller to the buyer (by way of delivery truck, for example). One party is responsible for the goods in transit and the costs associated with transportation. Determining whether this responsibility lies with the buyer or seller is critical to determining the reporting requirements of the retailer or merchandiser.

Freight-in refers to the shipping costs for which the buyer is responsible when receiving shipment from a seller, such as delivery and insurance expenses. When the buyer is responsible for shipping costs, they recognize this as part of the purchase cost. This means that the shipping costs stay with the inventory until it is sold. The cost principle requires this expense to stay with the merchandise as it is part of getting the item ready for sale from the buyer's perspective. The shipping expenses are held in inventory until sold, which means these costs are reported on the balance sheet in Merchandise Inventory. When the merchandise is sold, the shipping charges are transferred with all other inventory costs to Cost of Goods Sold on the income statement.

For example, California Business Solutions (CBS) may purchase computers from a manufacturer and part of the agreement is that CBS (the buyer) pays the shipping costs of $1,000. CBS would record the following entry to recognize freight-in.

JOURNAL			
Date	Account	Debit	Credit
	Accounts Receivable	4,500	
	Sales		4,500
	To recognize sale, FOB Destination, 30 × $150		
	Cost of Goods Sold	1,800	
	Merchandise Inventory		1,800
	To recognize cost of sale, 30 × $60		
	Delivery Expense	120	
	Cash		120
	To recognize freight-out shipping costs		

Merchandise Inventory increases (debit), and Cash decreases (credit), for the entire cost of the purchase, including shipping, insurance, and taxes. On the balance sheet, the shipping charges would remain a part of inventory.

Freight-out refers to the costs for which the seller is responsible when shipping to a buyer, such as delivery and insurance expenses. When the seller is responsible for shipping costs, they recognize this as a delivery expense. The delivery expense is specifically associated with selling and not daily operations; thus, delivery expenses are typically recorded as a selling and administrative expense on the income statement in the current period.

For example, CBS may sell electronics packages to a customer and agree to cover the $100 cost associated with shipping and insurance. CBS would record the following entry to recognize freight-out.

JOURNAL			
Date	Account	Debit	Credit
	Delivery Expense	100	
	Cash		100
	To recognize freight-out shipping costs		

Delivery Expense increases (debit) and Cash decreases (credit) for the shipping cost amount of $100. On the income statement, this $100 delivery expense will be grouped with Selling and Administrative expenses.

LINK TO LEARNING

Shipping term agreements provide clarity for buyers and sellers with regards to inventory responsibilities. Use the animation on FOB Shipping Point and FOB Destination (https://openstax.org/l/50ShippingTerms) to learn more.

Discussion and Application of FOB Destination

As you've learned, the seller and buyer will establish terms of purchase that include the purchase price, taxes, insurance, and shipping charges. So, who pays for shipping? On the purchase contract, shipping terms establish who owns inventory in transit, the point of transfer, and who pays for shipping. The shipping terms are known as "free on board," or simply FOB. Some refer to FOB as the point of transfer, but really, it incorporates more than simply the point at which responsibility transfers. There are two FOB considerations: FOB Destination and FOB Shipping Point.

If **FOB destination point** is listed on the purchase contract, this means the seller pays the shipping charges (freight-out). This also means goods in transit belong to, and are the responsibility of, the seller. The point of transfer is when the goods reach the buyer's place of business.

To illustrate, suppose CBS sells 30 landline telephones at $150 each on credit at a cost of $60 per phone. On the sales contract, FOB Destination is listed as the shipping terms, and shipping charges amount to $120, paid as cash directly to the delivery service. The following entries occur.

JOURNAL			
Date	**Account**	**Debit**	**Credit**
	Accounts Receivable	4,500	
	Sales		4,500
	To recognize sale, FOB Destination, 30 × $150		
	COGS	1,800	
	Merchandise Inventory		1,800
	To recognize cost of sale, 30 × $60		
	Delivery Expense	120	
	Cash		120
	To recognize freight-out shipping costs		

Accounts Receivable (debit) and Sales (credit) increases for the amount of the sale (30 × $150). Cost of Goods Sold increases (debit) and Merchandise Inventory decreases (credit) for the cost of sale (30 × $60). Delivery Expense increases (debit) and Cash decreases (credit) for the delivery charge of $120.

Discussion and Application of FOB Shipping Point

If **FOB shipping point** is listed on the purchase contract, this means the buyer pays the shipping charges (freight-in). This also means goods in transit belong to, and are the responsibility of, the buyer. The point of transfer is when the goods leave the seller's place of business.

Suppose CBS buys 40 tablet computers at $60 each on credit. The purchase contract shipping terms list FOB Shipping Point. The shipping charges amount to an extra $5 per tablet computer. All other taxes, fees, and insurance are included in the purchase price of $60. The following entry occurs to recognize the purchase.

JOURNAL			
Date	**Account**	**Debit**	**Credit**
	Merchandise Inventory	2,600	
	Accounts Payable		2,600
	To recognize purchase on credit, FOB Shipping Point, 40 × $65		

Merchandise Inventory increases (debit) and Accounts Payable increases (credit) by the amount of the purchase, including all shipping, insurance, taxes, and fees [(40 × $60) + (40 × $5)].

Figure 6.14 shows a comparison of shipping terms.

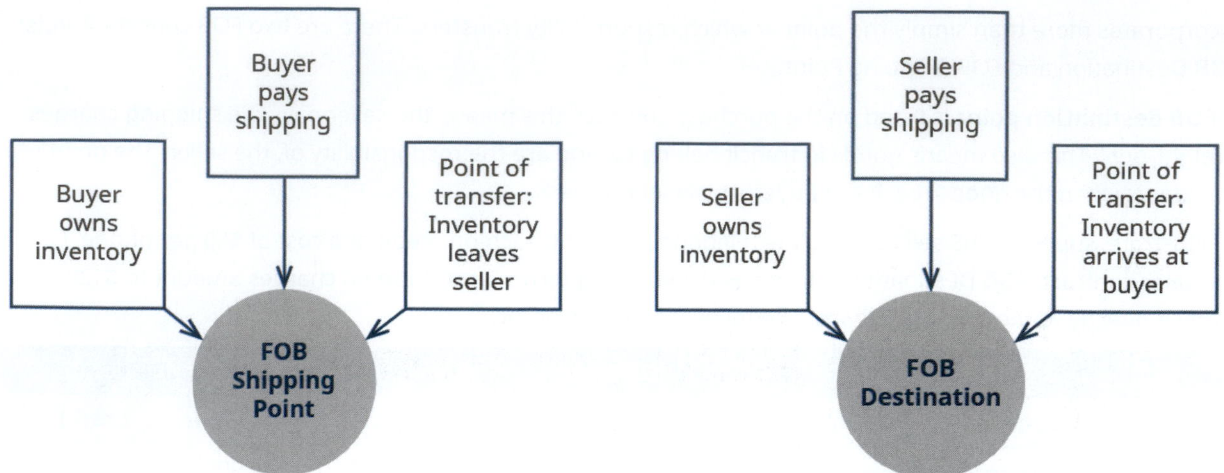

Figure 6.14 FOB Shipping Point versus FOB Destination. A comparison of shipping terms. (attribution: Copyright Rice University, OpenStax, under CC BY-NC-SA 4.0 license)

THINK IT THROUGH

Choosing Suitable Shipping Terms

You are a seller and conduct business with several customers who purchase your goods on credit. Your standard contract requires an FOB Shipping Point term, leaving the buyer with the responsibility for goods in transit and shipping charges. One of your long-term customers asks if you can change the terms to FOB Destination to help them save money.

Do you change the terms, why or why not? What positive and negative implications could this have for your business, and your customer? What, if any, restrictions might you consider if you did change the terms?

6.6 Describe and Prepare Multi-Step and Simple Income Statements for Merchandising Companies

Merchandising companies prepare financial statements at the end of a period that include the income statement, balance sheet, statement of cash flows, and statement of retained earnings. The presentation format for many of these statements is left up to the business. For the income statement, this means a company could prepare the statement using a multi-step format or a simple format (also known as a single-step format). Companies must decide the format that best fits their needs.

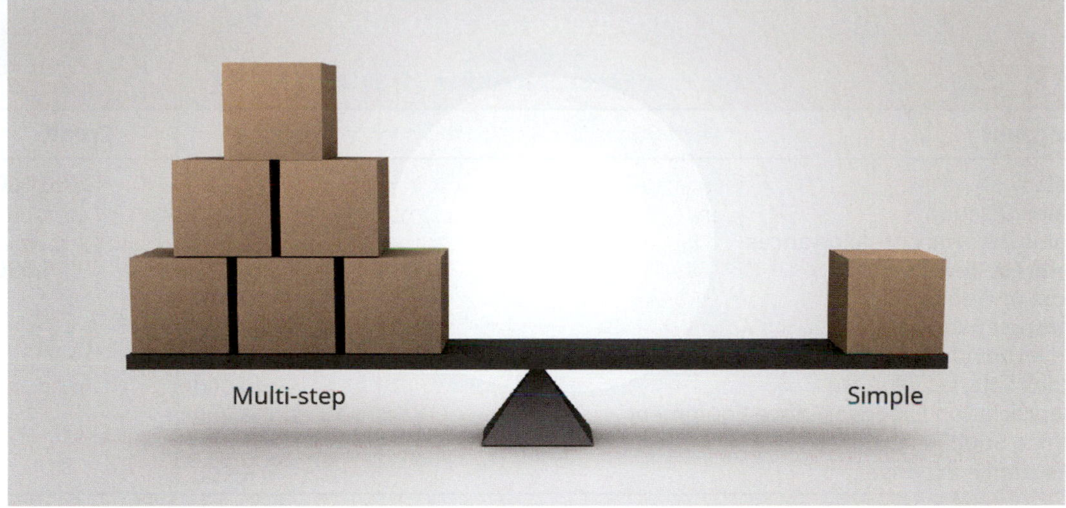

Figure 6.15 Multi-Step versus Single-Step Formats. (credit: modification of "Balance Swing Equality" by "Mediamodifier"/Pixabay, CC0)

Similarities and Differences between the Multi-Step and Simple Income Statement Format

A multi-step income statement is more detailed than a simple income statement. Because of the additional detail, it is the option selected by many companies whose operations are more complex. Each revenue and expense account is listed individually under the appropriate category on the statement. The multi-step statement separates cost of goods sold from operating expenses and deducts cost of goods sold from net sales to obtain a **gross margin**.

Operating expenses are daily operational costs not associated with the direct selling of products or services. Operating expenses are broken down into selling expenses (such as advertising and marketing expenses) and general and administrative expenses (such as office supplies expense, and depreciation of office equipment). Deducting the operating expenses from gross margin produces **income from operations**.

Following income from operations are **other revenue and expenses** not obtained from selling goods or services or other daily operations. Other revenue and expenses examples include interest revenue, gains or losses on sales of assets (buildings, equipment, and machinery), and interest expense. Other revenue and expenses added to (or deducted from) income from operations produces **net income** (loss).

A simple income statement is less detailed than the multi-step format. A simple income statement combines all revenues into one category, followed by all expenses, to produce net income. There are very few individual accounts and the statement does not consider cost of sales separate from operating expenses.

Demonstration of the Multi-Step Income Statement Format

To demonstrate the use of the multi-step income statement format, let's continue to discuss California Business Solutions (CBS). The following is select account data from the adjusted trial balance for the year ended, December 31, 2018. We will use this information to create a multi-step income statement. Note that the statements prepared are using a perpetual inventory system.

CALIFORNIA BUSINESS SOLUTIONS Trial Balance For Year Ended December 31, 2018		
Account	**Debit**	**Credit**
Sales		$300,000
Sales Discounts	$ 2,000	
Sales Returns and Allowances	4,500	
Interest Revenue		5,650
Cost of Goods Sold	180,000	
Interest Expense	8,400	
Advertising Expense	6,250	
Sales Salaries Expense	40,000	
Depreciation Expense: Office Equipment	4,700	
Office Supplies Expense	1,200	
Insurance Expense	6,900	

The following is the multi-step income statement for CBS.

CALIFORNIA BUSINESS SOLUTIONS Multi-step Income Statement For Year Ended December 31, 2018		
Sales		$300,000
Less:		
Sales Discounts	$ 2,000	
Sales Returns and Allowances	4,500	6,500
Net sales		293,500
Cost of Goods Sold		180,000
Gross Margin		113,500
Operating Expenses		
Selling Expenses		
Advertising Expense	6,250	
Sales Salaries Expense	40,000	
Total Selling Expenses	46,250	
General and Administrative Expenses		
Depreciation Expense: Office Equipment	4,700	
Office Supplies Expense	1,200	
Insurance Expense	6,900	
Total General and Administrative Expenses	12,800	
Total Operating Expenses		59,050
Income from Operations		54,450
Other Revenue and Expenses		
Interest Revenue	5,650	
Interest Expense	(8,400)	
Total other revenue and expenses		(2,750)
Net Income		$ 51,700

Demonstration of the Simple Income Statement Format

We will use the same adjusted trial balance information for CBS but will now create a simple income statement.

The following is the simple income statement for CBS.

CALIFORNIA BUSINESS SOLUTIONS Simple Income Statement For Year Ended December 31, 2018		
Revenues		
Net sales		$293,500
Interest Revenue		5,650
Total Revenues		299,150
Expenses		
Cost of Goods Sold	$180,000	
Total Selling Expenses	46,250	
Total General and Administrative Expenses	12,800	
Interest Expense	8,400	
Total Expenses		247,450
Net Income		$ 51,700

Final Analysis of the Two Income Statement Options

While companies may choose the format that best suits their needs, some might choose a combination of both the multi-step and simple income statement formats. The multi-step income statement may be more beneficial for internal use and management decision-making because of the detail in account information. The simple income statement might be more appropriate for external use, as a summary for investors and lenders.

From the information obtained on the income statement, a company can make decisions related to growth strategies. One ratio that can help them in this process is the Gross Profit Margin Ratio. The **gross profit margin ratio** shows the margin of revenue above the cost of goods sold that can be used to cover operating expenses and profit. The larger the margin, the more availability the company has to reinvest in their business, pay down debt, and return dividends to shareholders.

$$\textbf{Gross Profit Margin Ratio} = \frac{\textbf{(Net sales – COGS)}}{\textbf{Net sales}}$$

Taking our example from CBS, net sales equaled $293,500 and cost of goods sold equaled $180,000. Therefore, the Gross Profit Margin Ratio is computed as 0.39 (rounded to the nearest hundredth). This means that CBS has a margin of 39% to cover operating expenses and profit.

$$\text{Gross profit margin ratio} = \frac{(\$293{,}500 - \$180{,}000)}{\$293{,}500} = 0.39, \text{ or } 39\%$$

THINK IT THROUGH

Which Income Statement Format Do I Choose?

You are an accountant for a small retail store and are tasked with determining the best presentation for your income statement. You may choose to present it in a multi-step format or a simple income statement format. The information on the statement will be used by investors, lenders, and management to make financial decisions related to your company. It is important to the store owners that you give enough information to assist management with decision-making, but not too much information to possibly deter investors or lenders. Which statement format do you choose? Why did you choose this format? What are the benefits and challenges of your statement choice for each stakeholder group?

LINK TO LEARNING

Target Brands, Inc. is an international retailer providing a variety of resale products to consumers. Target uses a multi-step income statement format found at Target Brands, Inc. annual report (https://openstax.org/l/50TargetAnnual) to present information to external stakeholders.

6.7 Appendix: Analyze and Record Transactions for Merchandise Purchases and Sales Using the Periodic Inventory System

Some organizations choose to report merchandising transactions using a periodic inventory system rather than a perpetual inventory system. This requires different account usage, transaction recognition, adjustments, and closing procedures. We will not explore the entries for adjustment or closing procedures but will look at some of the common situations that occur with merchandising companies and how these transactions are reported using the periodic inventory system.

Merchandise Purchases

The following example transactions and subsequent journal entries for merchandise purchases are recognized using a periodic inventory system.

Basic Analysis of Purchase Transaction Journal Entries

To better illustrate merchandising activities under the periodic system, let's return to the example of California Business Solutions (CBS). CBS is a retailer providing electronic hardware packages to meet small business needs. Each electronics hardware package contains a desktop computer, tablet computer, landline telephone, and a 4-in-1 desktop printer with a printer, copier, scanner, and fax machine.

CBS purchases each electronic product from a manufacturer. The per-item purchase prices from the manufacturer are shown.

Product	Price per unit
Desktop computer	$400
Tablet computer	60
Landline telephone	60
4-in-1 desktop printer	100

Cash and Credit Purchase Transaction Journal Entries

On April 1, CBS purchases 10 electronic hardware packages at a cost of $620 each. CBS has enough cash-on-hand to pay immediately with cash. The following entry occurs.

JOURNAL			
Date	**Account**	**Debit**	**Credit**
Apr. 1	Purchases: Packages Cash *To recognize purchase of 10 packages*	6,200	6,200

Purchases-Packages increases (debit) by $6,200 ($620 × 10), and Cash decreases (credit) by the same amount because the company paid with cash. Under a periodic system, Purchases is used instead of Merchandise Inventory.

On April 7, CBS purchases 30 desktop computers on credit at a cost of $400 each. The credit terms are n/15 with an invoice date of April 7. The following entry occurs.

JOURNAL			
Date	**Account**	**Debit**	**Credit**
Apr. 7	Purchases: Desktop Computers Accounts Payable *To recognize purchase of 30 computers on credit, n/15*	12,000	12,000

Purchases-Desktop Computers increases (debit) for the value of the computers, $12,000 ($400 × 30). Since the computers were purchased on credit by CBS, Accounts Payable increases (credit) instead of cash.

On April 17, CBS makes full payment on the amount due from the April 7 purchase. The following entry occurs.

JOURNAL			
Date	**Account**	**Debit**	**Credit**
Apr. 17	Accounts Payable Cash *To recognize payment in full*	12,000	12,000

Accounts Payable decreases (debit) and Cash decreases (credit) for the full amount owed. The credit terms were n/15, which is net due in 15 days. No discount was offered with this transaction. Thus the full payment of $12,000 occurs.

Purchase Discount Transaction Journal Entries

On May 1, CBS purchases 67 tablet computers at a cost of $60 each on credit. Terms are 5/10, n/30, and invoice dated May 1. The following entry occurs.

JOURNAL			
Date	**Account**	**Debit**	**Credit**
May 1	Purchases: Tablet Computers Accounts Payable *To recognize purchase of 67 tablets, 5/10, n/30*	4,020	4,020

Purchases–Tablet Computers increases (debit) in the amount of $4,020 (67 × $60). Accounts Payable also increases (credit), but the credit terms are a little different than the earlier example. These credit terms include a discount opportunity (5/10). This means that CBS has 10 days from the invoice date to pay on their account to receive a 5% discount on their purchase.

On May 10, CBS pays their account in full. The following entry occurs.

JOURNAL			
Date	**Account**	**Debit**	**Credit**
May 10	Accounts Payable Purchase Discounts Cash *To recognize payment, less purchase discount*	4,020	 201 3,819

Accounts Payable decreases (debit) for the original amount owed of $4,020 before any discounts are taken. Since CBS paid on May 10, they made the 10-day window, thus receiving a discount of 5%. Cash decreases (credit) for the amount owed, less the discount. Purchase Discounts increases (credit) for the amount of the discount ($4,020 × 5%). Purchase Discounts is considered a contra account and will reduce Purchases at the end of the period.

Let's take the same example purchase with the same credit terms, but now assume that CBS paid their account on May 25. The following entry occurs.

JOURNAL			
Date	**Account**	**Debit**	**Credit**
May 25	Accounts Payable Cash *To recognize payment for tablets, no discount*	4,020	 4,020

Accounts Payable decreases (debit) and Cash decreases (credit) for $4,020. The company paid on their account outside of the discount window but within the total allotted timeframe for payment. CBS does not receive a discount in this case but does pay in full and on time.

Purchase Returns and Allowances Transaction Journal Entries

On June 1, CBS purchased 300 landline telephones with cash at a cost of $60 each. On June 3, CBS discovers that 25 of the phones are the wrong color and returns the phones to the manufacturer for a full refund. The following entries occur with the purchase and subsequent return.

JOURNAL			
Date	**Account**	**Debit**	**Credit**
Jun. 1	Purchases: Phones Cash *To recognize phone purchase with cash*	18,000	 18,000

Purchases-Phones increases (debit) and Cash decreases (credit) by $18,000 ($60 × 300).

JOURNAL			
Date	**Account**	**Debit**	**Credit**
Jun. 3	Cash Purchase Returns and Allowances *To recognize return of 25 phones, cash refund*	1,500	 1,500

Since CBS already paid in full for their purchase, a full cash refund is issued. This increases Cash (debit) and increases (credit) Purchase Returns and Allowances. Purchase Returns and Allowances is a contra account and decreases Purchases at the end of a period.

On June 8, CBS discovers that 60 more phones from the June 1 purchase are slightly damaged. CBS decides to keep the phones but receives a purchase allowance from the manufacturer of $8 per phone. The following entry occurs for the allowance.

JOURNAL			
Date	**Account**	**Debit**	**Credit**
Jun. 8	Cash Purchase Returns and Allowances *To recognize allowance for 60 phones*	480	 480

Since CBS already paid in full for their purchase, a cash refund of the allowance is issued in the amount of $480 (60 × $8). This increases Cash (debit) and increases Purchase Returns and Allowances.

CBS purchases 80 units of the 4-in-1 desktop printers at a cost of $100 each on July 1 on credit. Terms of the purchase are 5/15, n/40, with an invoice date of July 1. On July 6, CBS discovers 15 of the printers are damaged and returns them to the manufacturer for a full refund. The following entries show the purchase and subsequent return.

JOURNAL			
Date	**Account**	**Debit**	**Credit**
July 1	Purchases: Printers Accounts Payable *To recognize printer purchase on credit, 5/15, n/40*	8,000	 8,000

Purchases-Printers increases (debit) and Accounts Payable increases (credit) by $8,000 ($100 × 80).

JOURNAL			
Date	**Account**	**Debit**	**Credit**
July 6	Accounts Payable Purchase Returns and Allowances *To recognize return of 15 printers, AP reduction*	1,500	 1,500

Accounts Payable decreases (debit) and Purchase Returns and Allowances increases (credit) by $1,500 (15 × $100). The purchase was on credit and the return occurred before payment. Thus Accounts Payable is debited.

On July 10, CBS discovers that 4 more printers from the July 1 purchase are slightly damaged but decides to keep them because the manufacturer issues an allowance of $30 per printer. The following entry recognizes the allowance.

JOURNAL			
Date	**Account**	**Debit**	**Credit**
July 10	Accounts Payable Purchase Returns and Allowances *To recognize allowance for 4 printers, AP reduction*	120	 120

Accounts Payable decreases (debit) and Purchase Returns and Allowances increases (credit) by $120 (4 × $30). The purchase was on credit and the allowance occurred before payment. Thus, Accounts Payable is debited.

On July 15, CBS pays their account in full, less purchase returns and allowances. The following payment entry occurs.

JOURNAL			
Date	**Account**	**Debit**	**Credit**
July 15	Accounts Payable Purchase Discount Cash *To recognize payment, less discount, return and allowance*	6,380	 319 6,061

Accounts Payable decreases (debit) for the amount owed, less the return of $1,500 and the allowance of $120 ($8,000 – $1,500 – $120). Since CBS paid on July 15, they made the 15-day window and received a discount of 5%. Cash decreases (credit) for the amount owed, less the discount. Purchase Discounts increases (credit) for the amount of the discount ($6,380 × 5%).

Summary of Purchase Transaction Journal Entries

The chart in Figure 6.16 represents the journal entry requirements based on various merchandising purchase transactions using the periodic inventory system.

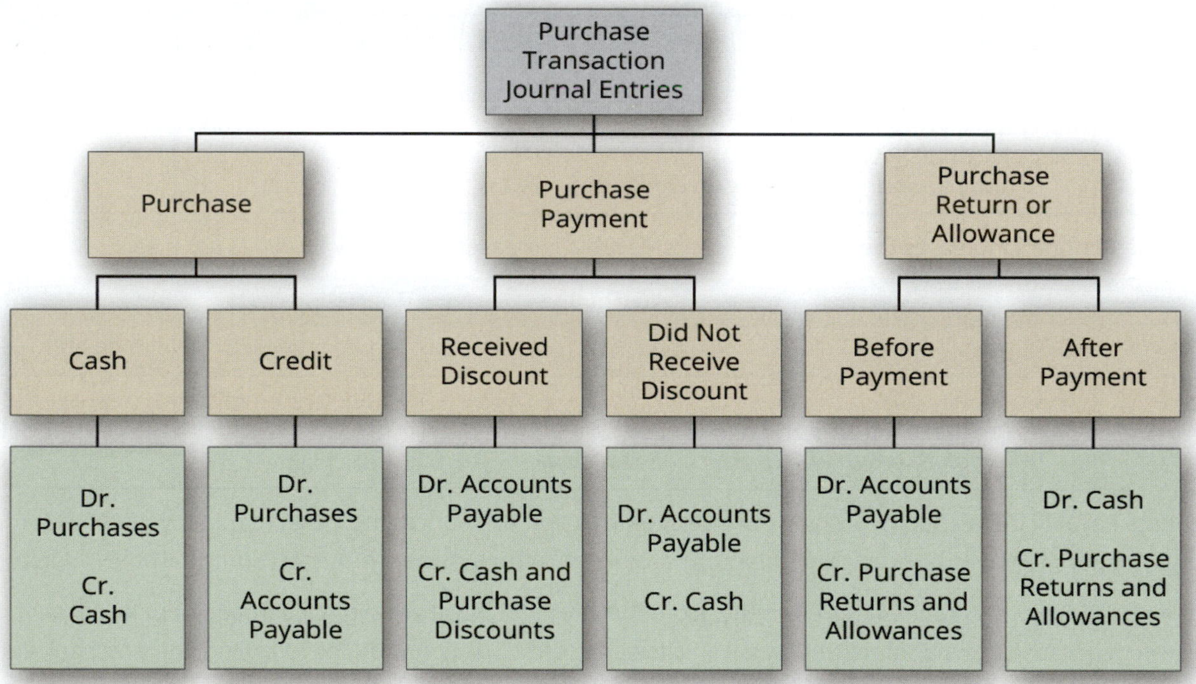

Figure 6.16 Purchase Transaction Journal Entries Flow Chart. (attribution: Copyright Rice University, OpenStax, under CC BY-NC-SA 4.0 license)

YOUR TURN

Recording a Retailer's Purchase Transactions using a Periodic Inventory System

Record the journal entries for the following purchase transactions of a retailer, using the periodic inventory system.

Dec. 3	Purchased $500 worth of inventory on credit with terms 2/10, n/30, and invoice dated December 3.
Dec. 6	Returned $150 worth of damaged inventory to the manufacturer and received a full refund.
Dec. 9	Customer paid the account in full, less the return.

Solution

JOURNAL			
Date	**Account**	**Debit**	**Credit**
Dec. 3	Purchases	500	
	Accounts Payable		500
	To recognize inventory purchase, 2/10, n/30		
Dec. 6	Accounts Payable	150	
	Purchase Returns and Allowances		150
	To recognize inventory return		
Dec. 9	Accounts Payable	350	
	Purchase Discounts		7
	Cash		343
	To recognize payment, less discount and return		

Merchandise Sales

The following example transactions and subsequent journal entries for merchandise sales are recognized using a periodic inventory system.

Basic Analysis of Sales Transaction Journal Entries

Let's continue to follow California Business Solutions (CBS) and the sale of electronic hardware packages to business customers. As previously stated, each package contains a desktop computer, tablet computer, landline telephone, and 4-in-1 printer. CBS sells each hardware package for $1,200. They offer their customers the option of purchasing extra individual hardware items for every electronic hardware package purchase. The following is the list of products CBS sells to customers; the prices are per-package, and per unit.

Product	Sales Price per-package, per unit	Cost to CBS per-package, per unit
Electronic hardware package	$1,200	$620
Desktop computer	750	400
Tablet computer	300	60
Landline telephone	150	60
4-in-1 printer	350	100

Cash and Credit Sales Transaction Journal Entries

On July 1, CBS sells 10 electronic packages to a customer at a sales price of $1,200 each. The customer pays immediately with cash. The following entries occur.

JOURNAL			
Date	**Account**	**Debit**	**Credit**
July 1	Cash	12,000	
	Sales		12,000
	To recognize sale of 10 packages		

Cash increases (debit) and Sales increases (credit) by the selling price of the packages, $12,000 ($1,200 × 10). Unlike the perpetual inventory system, there is no entry for the cost of the sale. This recognition occurs at the end of the period with an adjustment to Cost of Goods Sold.

On July 7, CBS sells 20 desktop computers to a customer on credit. The credit terms are n/15 with an invoice date of July 7. The following entries occur.

JOURNAL			
Date	**Account**	**Debit**	**Credit**
July 7	Accounts Receivable	15,000	
	Sales		15,000
	To recognize sale of 20 desktop computers, n/15		

Since the computers were purchased on credit by the customer, Accounts Receivable increases (debit) and Sales increases (credit) by the selling price of the computers, $15,000 ($750 × 20).

On July 17, the customer makes full payment on the amount due from the July 7 sale. The following entry occurs.

JOURNAL			
Date	**Account**	**Debit**	**Credit**
July 17	Cash	15,000	
	Accounts Receivable		15,000
	To recognize payment in full		

Accounts Receivable decreases (credit) and Cash increases (debit) by the full amount owed. The credit terms were n/15, which is net due in 15 days. No discount was offered with this transaction, thus the full payment of $15,000 occurs.

Sales Discount Transaction Journal Entries

On August 1, a customer purchases 56 tablet computers on credit. Terms are 2/10, n/30, and invoice dated August 1. The following entries occur.

JOURNAL			
Date	**Account**	**Debit**	**Credit**
Aug. 1	Accounts Receivable Sales *To recognize sale of 56 tablet computers, 2/10, n/30*	16,800	 16,800

Accounts Receivable increases (debit) and Sales increases (credit) by $16,800 ($300 × 56). These credit terms are a little different than the earlier example. These credit terms include a discount opportunity (2/10). This means that the customer has 10 days from the invoice date to pay on their account to receive a 2% discount on their purchase.

On August 10, the customer pays their account in full. The following entry occurs.

JOURNAL			
Date	**Account**	**Debit**	**Credit**
Aug. 10	Cash Sales Discounts Accounts Receivable *To recognize payment, less sales discount*	16,464 336	 16,800

Since the customer paid on August 10, they made the 10-day window, thus receiving a discount of 2%. Cash increases (debit) for the amount paid to CBS, less the discount. Sales Discounts increases (debit) by the amount of the discount ($16,800 × 2%), and Accounts Receivable decreases (credit) by the original amount owed, before discount. Sales Discounts will reduce Sales at the end of the period to produce net sales.

Let’s take the same example sale with the same credit terms, but now assume that the customer paid their account on August 25. The following entry occurs.

JOURNAL			
Date	**Account**	**Debit**	**Credit**
Aug. 25	Cash Accounts Receivable *To recognize payment for tablets, no discount*	16,800	 16,800

Cash increases (debit) and Accounts Receivable decreases (credit) by $16,800. The customer paid on their account outside of the discount window but within the total allotted timeframe for payment. The customer does not receive a discount in this case but does pay in full and on time.

Sales Returns and Allowances Transaction Journal Entries

On September 1, CBS sold 250 landline telephones to a customer who paid with cash. On September 3, the customer discovers that 40 of the phones are the wrong color and returns the phones to CBS in exchange for a full refund. The following entries occur for the sale and subsequent return.

JOURNAL			
Date	**Account**	**Debit**	**Credit**
Sept. 1	Cash Sales *To recognize sale of 250 phones with cash*	37,500	37,500

Cash increases (debit) and Sales increases (credit) by $37,500 (250 × $150), the sales price of the phones.

JOURNAL			
Date	**Account**	**Debit**	**Credit**
Sept. 3	Sales Returns and Allowances Cash *To recognize return of 40 phones, cash refund*	6,000	6,000

Since the customer already paid in full for their purchase, a full cash refund is issued on September 3. This increases Sales Returns and Allowances (debit) and decreases Cash (credit) by $6,000 (40 × $150). Unlike in the perpetual inventory system, CBS does not recognize the return of merchandise to inventory. Instead, CBS will make an adjustment to Merchandise Inventory at the end of the period.

On September 8, the customer discovers that 20 more phones from the September 1 purchase are slightly damaged. The customer decides to keep the phones but receives a sales allowance from CBS of $10 per phone. The following entry occurs for the allowance.

JOURNAL			
Date	**Account**	**Debit**	**Credit**
Sept. 8	Sales Returns and Allowances Cash *To recognize allowance for 20 phones*	200	200

Since the customer already paid in full for their purchase, a cash refund of the allowance is issued in the amount of $200 (20 × $10). This increases (debit) Sales Returns and Allowances and decreases (credit) Cash.

A customer purchases 55 units of the 4-in-1 desktop printers on October 1 on credit. Terms of the sale are 10/15, n/40, with an invoice date of October 1. On October 6, the customer discovers 10 of the printers are damaged and returns them to CBS for a full refund. The following entries show the sale and subsequent return.

JOURNAL			
Date	**Account**	**Debit**	**Credit**
Oct. 1	Accounts Receivable Sales *To recognize sale of 55 printers on credit, 10/15, n/40*	19,250	19,250

Accounts Receivable increases (debit) and Sales increases (credit) by $19,250 (55 × $350), the sales price of the printers. Accounts Receivable is used instead of Cash because the customer purchased on credit.

JOURNAL			
Date	**Account**	**Debit**	**Credit**
Oct. 6	Sales Returns and Allowances Accounts Receivable *To recognize return of 10 printers*	3,500	 3,500

The customer has not yet paid for their purchase as of October 6. This increases Sales Returns and Allowances (debit) and decreases Accounts Receivable (credit) by $3,500 (10 × $350).

On October 10, the customer discovers that 5 more printers from the October 1 purchase are slightly damaged, but decides to keep them because CBS issues an allowance of $60 per printer. The following entry recognizes the allowance.

JOURNAL			
Date	**Account**	**Debit**	**Credit**
Oct. 10	Sales Returns and Allowances Accounts Receivable *To recognize allowance for 5 printers*	300	 300

Sales Returns and Allowances increases (debit) and Accounts Receivable decreases (credit) by $300 (5 × $60). A reduction to Accounts Receivable occurs because the customer has yet to pay their account on October 10.

On October 15, the customer pays their account in full, less sales returns and allowances. The following payment entry occurs.

JOURNAL			
Date	**Account**	**Debit**	**Credit**
Oct. 15	Cash Sales Discounts Accounts Receivable *To recognize payment, less sales discount, return and allowance*	13,905 1,545	 15,450

Accounts Receivable decreases (credit) for the original amount owed, less the return of $3,500 and the allowance of $300 ($19,250 – $3,500 – $300). Since the customer paid on October 15, they made the 15-day window and receiving a discount of 10%. Sales Discounts increases (debit) for the discount amount ($15,450 × 10%). Cash increases (debit) for the amount owed to CBS, less the discount.

Summary of Sales Transaction Journal Entries

The chart in Figure 6.17 represents the journal entry requirements based on various merchandising sales transactions using a periodic inventory system.

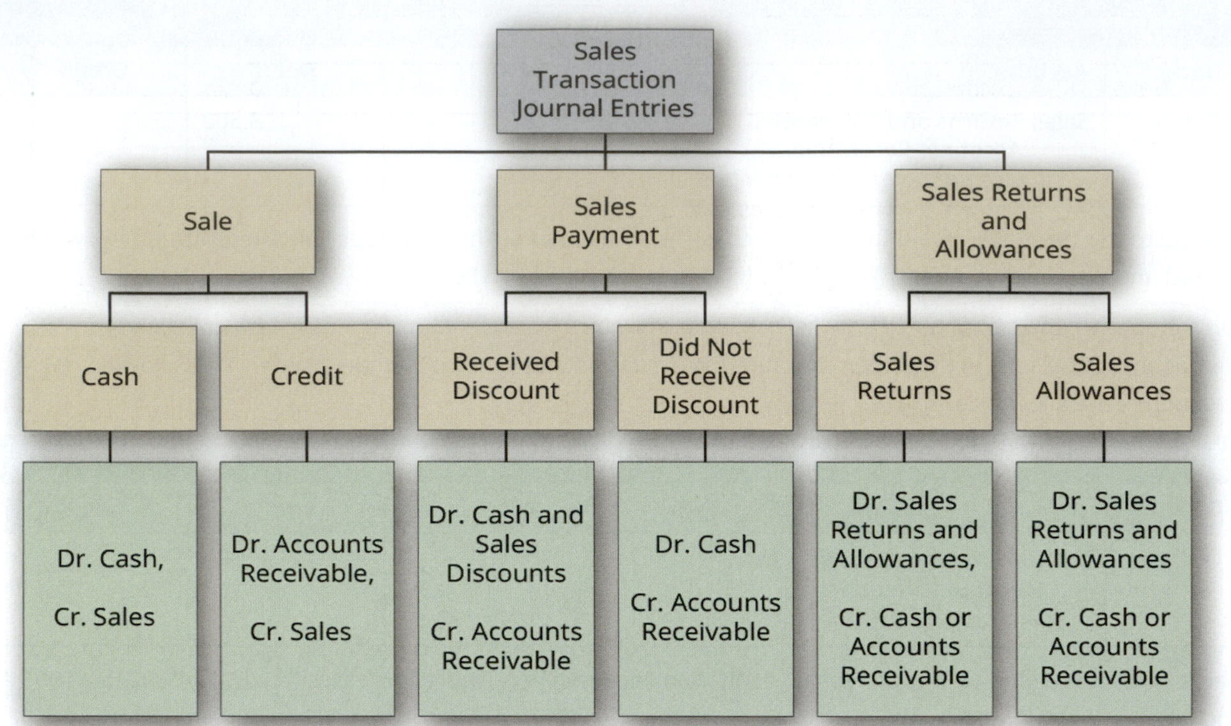

Figure 6.17 Journal Entry Requirements for Merchandise Sales Transaction Using a Periodic Inventory System. (attribution: Copyright Rice University, OpenStax, under CC BY-NC-SA 4.0 license)

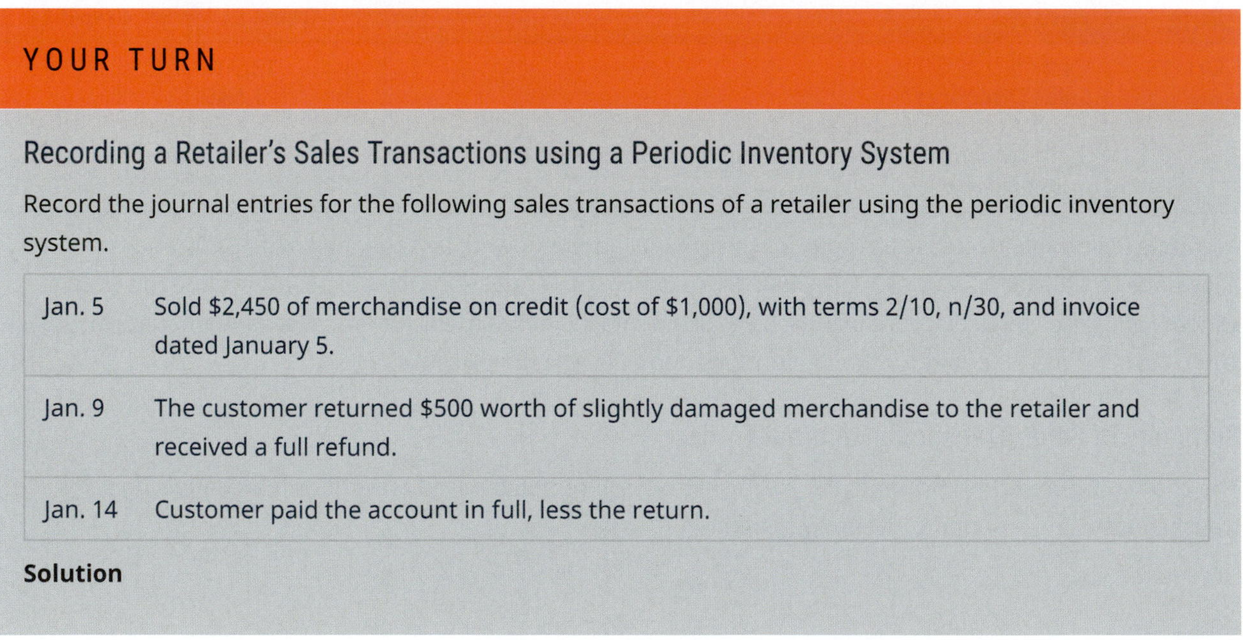

YOUR TURN

Recording a Retailer's Sales Transactions using a Periodic Inventory System

Record the journal entries for the following sales transactions of a retailer using the periodic inventory system.

Jan. 5	Sold $2,450 of merchandise on credit (cost of $1,000), with terms 2/10, n/30, and invoice dated January 5.
Jan. 9	The customer returned $500 worth of slightly damaged merchandise to the retailer and received a full refund.
Jan. 14	Customer paid the account in full, less the return.

Solution

JOURNAL			
Date	**Account**	**Debit**	**Credit**
Jan. 5	Accounts Receivable	2,450	
	Sales		2,450
	To recognize sale on credit, 2/10, n/30		
Jan. 9	Sales Returns and Allowances	500	
	Accounts Receivable		500
	To recognize customer return		
Jan. 14	Cash	1,911	
	Sales Discounts	39	
	Accounts Receivable		1,950
	To recognize payment, less discount and return		

Key Terms

cash discount provides a discount on the final price after purchase, if a retailer pays within a discount window, typically stated in days

cost of goods sold (COGS) expense account that houses all costs associated with getting a product ready for sale

FOB destination point transportation terms whereby the seller transfers ownership and financial responsibility at the time of delivery

FOB shipping point transportation terms whereby the seller transfers ownership and financial responsibility at the time of shipment

freight-in buyer is responsible for when receiving shipment from a seller

freight-out seller is responsible for when shipping to a buyer

goods in transit time in which the merchandise is being transported from the seller to the buyer

gross margin amount available after deducting cost of goods sold from net sales, to cover operating expenses and profit

gross profit margin ratio proportion of margin a company attains, above their cost of goods sold to cover operating expenses and profit, calculated by subtracting cost of goods sold from total net revenue to arrive at gross profit and then taking gross profit divided by total net revenues

gross purchases original amount of the purchase without factoring in reductions for purchase discounts, returns, or allowances

gross sales original amount of the sale without factoring in reductions for sales discounts, returns, or allowances

income from operations gross margin less deductions for operating expenses

merchandising company resells finished goods produced by a manufacturer (supplier) to customers

net income when revenues and gains are greater than expenses and losses

net purchases outcome of purchase discounts, returns, and allowances deducted from gross purchases

net sales outcome of sales discounts, returns, and allowances deducted from gross sales

operating cycle amount of time it takes a company to use its cash to provide a product or service and collect payment from the customer

operating expenses daily operational costs not associated with the direct selling of products or services

other revenue and expenses revenues and expenses not associated with daily operations, or the sale of goods and services

ownership of inventory which party owns the inventory at a particular point in time, the buyer or the seller

periodic inventory system updates and records the inventory account at certain, scheduled times at the end of an operating cycle

perpetual inventory system system that automatically updates and records the inventory account every time a sale or purchase of inventory occurs

physical inventory count manual stock check of inventory to make sure what is recorded on the books matches what is actually in the warehouse and on the sales floor

point of transfer when the responsibility for the inventory transfers from the seller to the buyer

purchase discounts provide an incentive for the retailer to pay early on their accounts, by issuing a reduced rate on their final purchase cost; the discount reduces the value of merchandise inventory

purchase returns and allowances retailer receives a partial or full refund from the manufacturer for defective merchandise

sales discounts reduction in the selling price offered to customers who pay their account within the discount period; the actual account is a contra revenue account that reduces sales

sales returns and allowances contra revenue account with a normal debit balance that reduces the gross sales figure at the end of the period; the customer returns merchandise with a sales return, and keeps the merchandise with a sales allowance

service company provides intangible services to customers, and does not have inventory

trade discount reduction to the advertised manufacturer's price during negotiation of a final purchase price

Summary

6.1 Compare and Contrast Merchandising versus Service Activities and Transactions

- Service companies sell intangible services and do not have inventory. Their operating cycle begins with cash-on-hand, providing service to customers, and collecting customer payments.
- Merchandising companies resell goods to consumers. Their operating cycle begins with cash-on-hand, purchasing inventory, selling merchandise, and collecting customer payments.
- A purchase discount is an incentive for a retailer to pay their account early. Credit terms establish the percentage discount, and Merchandise Inventory decreases if the discount is taken.
- A retailer receives a full or partial refund for returning or keeping defective merchandise. This can reduce the value of the Merchandise Inventory account.
- A customer receives an incentive for paying on their account early. Sales Discounts is a contra revenue account that will reduce Sales at the end of a period.
- A customer receives a refund for returning or keeping defective merchandise. Sales returns and allowances is a contra revenue account that will reduce Sales at the end of a period.

6.2 Compare and Contrast Perpetual versus Periodic Inventory Systems

- A perpetual inventory system inventory updates purchase and sales records constantly, particularly impacting Merchandise Inventory and Cost of Goods Sold.
- A periodic inventory system only records updates to inventory and costs of sales at scheduled times throughout the year, not constantly. Merchandise Inventory and Cost of Goods Sold are updated at the end of a period.
- Cost of goods sold (COGS) includes all elements of cost related to the sale of merchandise. The formula to determine COGS if one is using the periodic inventory system, is Beginning Inventory + Net Purchases – Ending Inventory.
- The perpetual inventory system keeps real-time data and the information is more robust. However, it is costly and time consuming, and physical counts of inventory are scarce.
- With the periodic inventory system, there are more frequent inventory counts and reduced chances for shrinkage and damaged merchandise. However, the periodic system makes it difficult for businesses to keep track of inventory costs and to make present decisions about their business.

6.3 Analyze and Record Transactions for Merchandise Purchases Using the Perpetual Inventory System

- A retailer can pay with cash or on credit. If paying with cash, Cash decreases. If paying on credit instead of cash, Accounts Payable increases.
- If a company pays for merchandise within the discount window, they debit Accounts Payable, credit Merchandise Inventory, and credit Cash. If they pay outside the discount window, the company debits Accounts Payable and credits Cash.
- If a company returns merchandise before remitting payment, they would debit Accounts Payable and credit Merchandise Inventory. If the company returns merchandise after remitting payment, they would debit Cash and credit Merchandise Inventory.

- If a company obtains an allowance for damaged merchandise before remitting payment, they would debit Accounts Payable and credit Merchandise Inventory. If the company obtains an allowance for damaged merchandise after remitting payment, they would debit Cash and credit Merchandise Inventory.

6.4 Analyze and Record Transactions for the Sale of Merchandise Using the Perpetual Inventory System

- A customer can pay with cash or on credit. If paying on credit instead of cash, Accounts Receivable increases rather than Cash; Sales increases in both instances. A company must also record the cost of sale entry, where Merchandise Inventory decreases and COGS increases.
- If a customer pays for merchandise within the discount window, the company would debit Cash and Sales Discounts while crediting Accounts Receivable. If the customer pays outside the discount window, the company debits Cash and credits Accounts Receivable only.
- If a customer returns merchandise before remitting payment, the company would debit Sales Returns and Allowances and credit Accounts Receivable or Cash. The company may return the merchandise to their inventory by debiting Merchandise Inventory and crediting COGS.
- If a customer obtains an allowance for damaged merchandise before remitting payment, the company would debit Sales Returns and Allowances and credit Accounts Receivable or Cash. The company does not have to consider the merchandise condition because the customer keeps the merchandise in this instance.

6.5 Discuss and Record Transactions Applying the Two Commonly Used Freight-In Methods

- Establishing ownership of inventory is important because it helps determine who is responsible for shipping charges, goods in transit, and transfer points. Ownership also determines reporting requirements for the buyer and seller. The buyer is responsible for the merchandise, and the cost of shipping, insurance, purchase price, taxes, and fees are held in inventory in its Merchandise Inventory account. The buyer would record an increase (debit) to Merchandise Inventory and either a decrease to Cash or an increase to Accounts Payable (credit) depending on payment method.
- FOB Shipping Point means the buyer should record the merchandise as inventory when it leaves the seller's location. FOB destination means the seller should continue to carry the merchandise in inventory until it reaches the buyer's location. This becomes really important at year-end when each party is trying to determine their actual balance sheet inventory accounts.
- FOB Destination means the seller is responsible for the merchandise, and the cost of shipping is expensed immediately in the period as a delivery expense. The seller would record an increase (debit) to Delivery Expense, and a decrease to Cash (credit).
- In FOB Destination, the seller is responsible for the shipping charges and like expenses. The point of transfer is when the merchandise reaches the buyer's place of business, and the seller owns the inventory in transit.
- In FOB Shipping Point, the buyer is responsible for the shipping charges and like expenses. The point of transfer is when the merchandise leaves the seller's place of business, and the buyer owns the inventory in transit.

6.6 Describe and Prepare Multi-Step and Simple Income Statements for Merchandising Companies

- Multi-step income statements provide greater detail than simple income statements. The format differentiates sales costs from operating expenses and separates other revenue and expenses from operational activities. This statement is best used internally by managers to make pricing and cost reduction decisions.
- Simple income statements are not as detailed as multi-step income statements and combine all revenues and all expenses into general categories. There is no differentiation between operational and non-

operational activities. Therefore, this statement is sometimes used as a summary for external users to view general company information.

- The gross profit margin ratio can show a company if they have a significant enough margin after sales revenue and cost data are computed to cover operational costs and profit goals. If a company is not meeting their target for this ratio, they may consider increasing prices or decreasing costs.

6.7 Appendix: Analyze and Record Transactions for Merchandise Purchases and Sales Using the Periodic Inventory System

- A retailer can pay with cash or credit. Unlike in the perpetual inventory system, purchases of inventory in the periodic inventory system will debit Purchases rather than Merchandise Inventory.
- If a company pays for merchandise within the discount window, it debits Accounts Payable, credits Purchase Discounts, and credits Cash. If they pay outside the discount window, the company debits Accounts Payable and credits Cash.
- If a company returns merchandise before remitting payment, they would debit Accounts Payable and credit Purchase Returns and Allowances. If the company returns merchandise after remitting payment, they would debit Cash and credit Purchase Returns and Allowances.
- If a company obtains an allowance for damaged merchandise before remitting payment, they would debit Accounts Payable and credit Purchase Returns and Allowances. If the company obtains an allowance for damaged merchandise after remitting payment, they would debit Cash and credit Purchase Returns and Allowances.
- A customer can pay with cash or on credit. Unlike a perpetual inventory system, when recording a sale under a periodic system, there is no cost entry.
- If a customer pays for merchandise within the discount window, the company would debit Cash and Sales Discounts and credit Accounts Receivable. If the customer pays outside the discount window, the company debits Cash and credits Accounts Receivable only.
- If a customer returns merchandise before remitting payment, the company would debit Sales Returns and Allowances and credit Accounts Receivable or Cash.
- If a customer obtains an allowance for damaged merchandise before remitting payment, the company would debit Sales Returns and Allowances and credit Accounts Receivable or Cash.

Note: All of the following assessments assume a periodic inventory system unless otherwise noted.

Multiple Choice

1. LO 6.1 Which of the following is an example of a contra revenue account?

A. sales
B. merchandise inventory
C. sales discounts /sale return/allowance
D. accounts payable

2. LO 6.1 What accounts are used to recognize a retailer's purchase from a manufacturer on credit?

A. accounts receivable, merchandise inventory
B. accounts payable, merchandise inventory
C. accounts payable, cash
D. sales, accounts receivable

3. LO 6.1 Which of the following numbers represents the discount percentage applied if a customer pays within a discount window and credit terms are 3/15, n/60?

A. 3
B. 15
C. 60
D. 3 and 15

4. LO 6.1 If a customer purchases merchandise on credit and returns the defective merchandise before payment, what accounts would recognize this transaction?

A. sales discount, cash
B. sales returns and allowances, cash
C. accounts receivable, sales discount
D. accounts receivable, sales returns and allowances

5. LO 6.2 Which of the following is a disadvantage of the perpetual inventory system?

A. Inventory information is in real-time.
B. Inventory is automatically updated.
C. It allows managers to make current decisions about purchases, stock, and sales.
D. It is cost-prohibitive.

6. LO 6.2 Which of the following is an advantage of the periodic inventory system?

A. frequent physical inventory counts
B. cost prohibitive
C. time consuming
D. real-time information for managers

7. LO 6.2 Which of the following is *not* a reason for the physical inventory count to differ from what is recognized on the company's books?

A. mismanagement
B. shrinkage
C. damage
D. sale of services to customers

8. LO 6.2 Which of the following is not included when computing Net Purchases?

A. purchase discounts
B. beginning inventory
C. purchase returns
D. purchase allowances

9. LO 6.3 Which of the following accounts are used when recording a purchase?

A. cash, merchandise inventory
B. accounts payable, merchandise inventory
C. A or B
D. cash, accounts payable

10. LO 6.3 A retailer pays on credit for $650 worth of inventory, terms 3/10, n/40. If the merchandiser pays within the discount window, how much will the retailer remit in cash to the manufacturer?

A. $19.50
B. $630.50
C. $650
D. $195

11. LO 6.3 A retailer returns $400 worth of inventory to a manufacturer and receives a full refund. What accounts recognize this return before the retailer remits payment to the manufacturer?

A. accounts payable, merchandise inventory
B. accounts payable, cash
C. cash, merchandise inventory
D. merchandise inventory, cost of goods sold

12. LO 6.3 A retailer obtains a purchase allowance from the manufacturer in the amount of $600 for faulty inventory parts. Which of the following represents the journal entry for this transaction if the retailer has already remitted payment?

A.

Accounts Payable Merchandise Inventory	600	 600

B.

Cash Merchandise Inventory	600	 600

C.

Accounts Payable Merchandise Inventory Cash	600	 10 590

13. LO 6.4 Which of the following accounts are used when recording the sales entry of a sale on credit?

A. merchandise inventory, cash
B. accounts receivable, merchandise inventory
C. accounts receivable, sales
D. sales, cost of goods sold

14. LO 6.4 A customer pays on credit for $1,250 worth of merchandise, terms 4/15, n/30. If the customer pays within the discount window, how much will they remit in cash to the retailer?

A. $1,250
B. $1,200
C. $50
D. $500

15. LO 6.4 A customer returns $870 worth of merchandise and receives a full refund. What accounts recognize this sales return (disregarding the merchandise condition entry) if the return occurs before the customer remits payment to the retailer?

A. accounts receivable, sales returns and allowances
B. accounts receivable, cash
C. sales returns and allowances, merchandise inventory
D. accounts receivable, cost of goods sold

16. LO 6.4 A customer obtains a purchase allowance from the retailer in the amount of $220 for damaged merchandise. Which of the following represents the journal entry for this transaction if the customer has not yet remitted payment?

A.

Sales Returns and Allowances Cash	220	 220

B.

Sales Returns and Allowances Accounts Receivable	220	 220

C.

Cash Sales Returns and Allowances Accounts Receivable	200 20	 220

17. LO 6.5 Which of the following is *not* a characteristic of FOB Destination?

A. The seller pays for shipping.
B. The seller owns goods in transit.
C. The point of transfer is when the goods leave the seller's place of business.
D. The point of transfer is when the goods arrive at the buyer's place of business.

18. LO 6.5 Which two accounts are used to recognize shipping charges for a buyer, assuming the buyer purchases with cash and the terms are FOB Shipping Point?

A. delivery expense, cash
B. merchandise inventory, cash
C. merchandise inventory, accounts payable
D. The buyer does not record anything for shipping since it is FOB Shipping Point.

19. LO 6.5 Which of the following is *not* a characteristic of FOB Shipping Point?

A. The buyer pays for shipping.
B. The buyer owns goods in transit.
C. The point of transfer is when the goods leave the seller's place of business.
D. The point of transfer is when the goods arrive at the buyer's place of business.

20. LO 6.6 A multi-step income statement ________.

A. separates cost of goods sold from operating expenses
B. considers interest revenue an operating activity
C. is another name for a simple income statement
D. combines cost of goods sold and operating expenses

21. LO 6.6 Which of the following accounts would be reported under operating expenses on a multi-step income statement?

A. sales
B. advertising expense
C. sales returns and allowances
D. interest expense

22. LO 6.6 A simple income statement ________.

A. combines all revenues into one category
B. does not combine all expenses into one category
C. separates cost of goods sold from operating expenses
D. separates revenues into several categories

23. LO 6.6 Which of the following accounts would *not* be reported under revenue on a simple income statement?

A. interest revenue
B. net sales
C. rent revenue
D. operating expenses

24. LO 6.7 Which of the following accounts are used when recording a purchase using a periodic inventory system?

A. cash, purchases
B. accounts payable, sales
C. accounts payable, accounts receivable
D. cash, merchandise inventory

25. LO 6.7 A retailer obtains a purchase allowance from the manufacturer in the amount of $600 for faulty inventory parts. Which of the following represents the journal entry for this transaction, assuming the retailer has already remitted payment?

A.

Accounts Payable Merchandise Inventory	600	 600

B.

Cash Purchase Returns and Allowances	600	 600

C.

Accounts Payable Purchase Discounts Cash	600	 10 590

26. LO 6.7 A customer returns $690 worth of merchandise and receives a full refund. What accounts recognize this sales return, assuming the customer has not yet remitted payment to the retailer?

A. accounts receivable, sales returns and allowances
B. accounts receivable, cash
C. sales returns and allowances, purchases
D. sales discounts, cost of goods sold

27. LO 6.7 A customer obtains an allowance from the retailer in the amount of $450 for damaged merchandise. Which of the following represents the journal entry for this transaction, assuming the customer has not remitted payment?

A.

Sales Returns and Allowances Cash	450	 450

B.

Sales Returns and Allowances Accounts Receivable	450	 450

C.

Cash Sales Returns and Allowances Accounts Receivable	400 50	 450

Questions

1. LO 6.1 What are some benefits to a retailer for offering a discount to a customer?

2. LO 6.1 What do credit terms of 4/10, n/30 mean in regard to a purchase?

3. LO 6.1 What is the difference between a sales return and a sales allowance?

4. LO 6.1 If a retailer made a purchase in the amount of $350 with credit terms of 2/15, n/60. What would the retailer pay in cash if they received the discount?

5. LO 6.2 What are two advantages and disadvantages of the perpetual inventory system?

6. LO 6.2 What are two advantages and disadvantages of the periodic inventory system?

7. LO 6.2 Sunrise Flowers sells flowers to a customer on credit for $130 on October 18, with a cost of sale to Sunrise of $50. What entry to recognize this sale is required if Sunrise Flowers uses a *periodic* inventory system?

8. LO 6.2 Sunrise Flowers sells flowers to a customer on credit for $130 on October 18, with a cost of sale to Sunrise of $50. What entry to recognize this sale is required if Sunrise Flowers uses a *perpetual* inventory system?

9. LO 6.3 Name two situations where cash would be remitted to a retailer from a manufacturer after purchase.

10. LO 6.3 If a retailer purchased inventory in the amount of $750, terms 2/10, n/60, returned $30 of the inventory for a full refund, and received an allowance for $95, how much would the discount be if the retailer remitted payment within the discount window?

11. LO 6.3 A retailer discovers that 50% of the total inventory items delivered from the manufacturer are damaged. The original purchase for all inventory was $1,100. The retailer decides to return 20% of the damaged inventory for a full refund and keep the remaining 80% of damaged inventory. What is the value of the merchandise returned?

12. LO 6.4 Name two situations where cash would be remitted to a customer from a retailer after purchase.

13. LO 6.4 If a customer purchased merchandise in the amount of $340, terms 3/10, n/30, returned $70 of the inventory for a full refund, and received an allowance for $65, how much discount would be applied if the customer remitted payment within the discount window?

14. LO 6.4 A customer discovers 60% of the total merchandise delivered from a retailer is damaged. The original purchase for all merchandise was $3,600. The customer decides to return 35% of the damaged merchandise for a full refund and keep the remaining 65%. What is the value of the merchandise returned?

15. LO 6.5 What are the main differences between FOB Destination and FOB Shipping Point?

16. LO 6.5 A buyer purchases $250 worth of goods on credit from a seller. Shipping charges are $50. The terms of the purchase are 2/10, n/30, FOB Destination. What, if any, journal entry or entries will the buyer record for these transactions?

17. LO 6.5 A seller sells $800 worth of goods on credit to a customer, with a cost to the seller of $300. Shipping charges are $100. The terms of the sale are 2/10, n/30, FOB Destination. What, if any, journal entry or entries will the seller record for these transactions?

18. LO 6.5 Which statement and where on the statement is freight-out recorded? Why is it recorded there?

19. LO 6.6 The following is select account information for Sunrise Motors. Sales: $256,400; Sales Returns and Allowances: $34,890; COGS: $120,470; Sales Discounts: $44,760. Given this information, what is the Gross Profit Margin Ratio for Sunrise Motors? (Round to the nearest whole percentage.)

20. LO 6.6 What is the difference between a multi-step and simple income statement?

21. LO 6.6 How can an investor or lender use the Gross Profit Margin Ratio to make financial contribution decisions?

22. LO 6.6 The following is select account information for August Sundries. Sales: $850,360; Sales Returns and Allowances: $148,550; COGS: $300,840; Operating Expenses: $45,770; Sales Discounts: $231,820. If August Sundries uses a multi-step income statement format, what is their gross margin?

23. LO 6.7 If a retailer purchased inventory in the amount of $680, terms 3/10, n/60, returned $120 of the inventory for a full refund, and received an allowance for $70, how much would the discount be if the retailer remitted payment within the discount window?

24. LO 6.7 A customer discovers 50% of the total merchandise delivered from the retailer is damaged. The original purchase for all merchandise was $5,950. The customer decides to return 40% of the damaged merchandise for a full refund and keep the remaining 60%. What is the value of the merchandise returned?

25. LO 6.7 What is the difference in reporting requirements for customer-returned merchandise in sellable condition under a perpetual inventory system versus a periodic inventory system?

Exercise Set A

EA1. LO 6.1 On March 1, Bates Board Shop sells 300 surfboards to a local lifeguard station at a sales price of $400 per board. The cost to Bates is $140 per board. The terms of the sale are 3/15, n/30, with an invoice date of March 1. Create the journal entries for Bates to recognize the following transactions.

A. the initial sale
B. the subsequent customer payment on March 10

EA2. LO 6.1 Marx Corp. purchases 135 fax machines on credit from a manufacturer on April 7 at a price of $250 per machine. Terms of the purchase are 4/10, n/20 with an invoice date of April 7. Marx Corp pays in full for the fax machines on April 17. Create the journal entries for Marx Corp. to record:

A. the initial purchase
B. the subsequent payment on April 17

EA3. LO 6.1 Match each of the following terms with the best corresponding definition.

A. Sales allowance	i. A customer returns merchandise for a full refund
B. Purchase return	ii. A retailer receives a partial refund but keeps the defective merchandise
C. Sales discount	iii. A customer receives a partial refund but keeps the defective merchandise
D. Purchase discount	iv. A customer pays their account in full within the discount window
E. Sales return	v. A type of purchase discount negotiated between a manufacturer and a retailer before settlement on a final price
F. Trade discount	vi. A retailer returns merchandise for a full refund
G. Purchase allowance	vii. A retailer pays their account in full within the discount window

EA4. LO 6.2 The following is selected information from Mars Corp. Compute net purchases, and cost of goods sold for the month of March.

Inventory, February 28, 2018	$450,000
Inventory, March 31, 2018	330,500
Purchase discounts	12,450
Purchase returns and allowances	23,870
Sales	276,900
Sales discounts	34,660
Gross purchases	120,400

EA5. LO 6.2 On April 5, a customer returns 20 bicycles with a sales price of $250 per bike to Barrio Bikes. Each bike cost Barrio Bikes $100. The customer had yet to pay on their account. The bikes are in sellable condition. Prepare the journal entry or entries to recognize this return if the company uses

A. the perpetual inventory system
B. the periodic inventory system

EA6. LO 6.3 Record journal entries for the following purchase transactions of Flower Company.

Oct. 13	Purchased 85 bushels of flowers with cash for $1,300.
Oct. 20	Purchased 240 bushels of flowers for $20 per bushel on credit. Terms of the purchase are 5/10, n/30, invoice dated October 20.
Oct. 30	Paid account in full from the October 20 purchase.

EA7. LO 6.3 Record journal entries for the following purchase transactions of Apex Industries.

Nov. 6	Purchased 24 computers on credit for $560 per computer. Terms of the purchase are 4/10, n/60, invoice dated November 6.
Nov. 10	Returned 5 defective computers for a full refund from the manufacturer.
Nov. 22	Paid account in full from the November 6 purchase.

EA8. LO 6.3 Record the journal entry for each of the following transactions. Glow Industries purchases 750 strobe lights at $23 per light from a manufacturer on April 20. The terms of purchase are 10/15, n/40, invoice dated April 20. On April 22, Glow discovers 100 of the lights are the wrong model and is granted an allowance of $8 per light for the error. On April 30, Glow pays for the lights, less the allowance.

EA9. LO 6.4 Record journal entries for the following sales transactions of Flower Company.

Oct. 12	Sold 25 bushels of flowers to a customer for $1,000 cash; cost of sale $700.
Oct. 21	Sold 40 bushels of flowers for $30 per bushel on credit. Terms of the sale are 4/10, n/30, invoice dated October 21. Cost per bushel is $20 to Flower Company.
Oct. 31	Received payment in full from the October 21 sale.

EA10. LO 6.4 Record the journal entries for the following sales transactions of Apache Industries.

Nov. 7	Sold 10 computers on credit for $870 per computer. Terms of the sale are 5/10, n/60, invoice dated November 7. The cost per computer to Apache is $560.
Nov. 14	The customer returned 2 computers for a full refund from Apache. Apache returns the computers to their inventory at full cost of $560 per computer.
Nov. 21	The customer paid their account in full from the November 7 sale.

EA11. LO 6.4 Record the journal entry or entries for each of the following sales transactions. Glow Industries sells 240 strobe lights at $40 per light to a customer on May 9. The cost to Glow is $23 per light. The terms of the sale are 5/15, n/40, invoice dated May 9. On May 13, the customer discovers 50 of the lights are the wrong color and are granted an allowance of $10 per light for the error. On May 21, the customer pays for the lights, less the allowance.

EA12. LO 6.5 Review the following situations and record any necessary journal entries for Mequon's Boutique.

May 10	Mequon's Boutique purchases $2,400 worth of merchandise with cash from a manufacturer. Shipping charges are an extra $130 cash. Terms of the purchase are FOB Shipping Point.
May 14	Mequon's Boutique sells $3,000 worth of merchandise to a customer who pays with cash. The merchandise has a cost to Mequon's of $1,750. Shipping charges are an extra $150 cash. Terms of the sale are FOB Shipping Point.

EA13. LO 6.5 Review the following situations and record any necessary journal entries for Letter Depot.

Mar. 9	Letter Depot purchases $11,420 worth of merchandise on credit from a manufacturer. Shipping charges are an extra $480 cash. Terms of the purchase are 2/10, n/40, FOB Destination, invoice dated March 9.
Mar. 20	Letter Depot sells $7,530 worth of merchandise to a customer who pays on credit. The merchandise has a cost to Letter Depot of $2,860. Shipping charges are an extra $440 cash. Terms of the sale are 3/15, n/50, FOB Destination, invoice dated March 20.

EA14. LO 6.5 Review the following situations and record any necessary journal entries for Nine Lives Inc.

Jan. 15	Nine Lives Inc. purchases $8,770 worth of merchandise with cash from a manufacturer. Shipping charges are an extra $345 cash. Terms of the purchase are FOB Shipping Point.
Jan. 23	Nine Lives Inc. sells $4,520 worth of merchandise to a customer who pays with cash. The merchandise has a cost to Nine Lives of $3,600. Shipping charges are an extra $190 cash. Terms of the sale are FOB Destination.

EA15. LO 6.6 The following select account data is taken from the records of Reese Industries for 2019.

Sales	$640,363
Merchandise inventory	582,620
Sales discounts	58,040
Interest expense	3,677
Sales returns and allowances	90,232
Interest revenue	10,268
Cost of goods sold	224,598
Rent expense	15,080
Depreciation expense: office equipment	3,200
Insurance expense	2,450
Advertising expense	12,906
Accounts receivable	100,440
Office supplies expense	1,600
Rent revenue	23,622
Sales salaries expense	30,410
Accounts payable	135,404
Common stock	59,419
Marketing expense	31,000

A. Use the data provided to compute net sales for 2019.
B. Prepare a simple income statement for the year ended December 31, 2019.
C. Compute the gross margin for 2019.
D. Prepare a multi-step income statement for the year ended December 31, 2019.

EA16. LO 6.7 Record journal entries for the following purchase transactions of Flower Company.

A. On October 13, Flower Company purchased 85 bushels of flowers with cash for $1,300.
B. On October 20, Flower Company purchased 240 bushels of flowers for $20 per bushel on credit. Terms of the purchase were 5/10, n/30, invoice dated October 20.
C. On October 30, Flower Company paid its account in full for the October 20 purchase.

EA17. LO 6.7 Record journal entries for the following purchase transactions of Apex Industries.

Nov. 6	Purchased 24 computers on credit for $560 per computer. Terms of the purchase are 4/10, n/60, invoice dated November 6.
Nov. 10	Returned 5 defective computers for a full refund from the manufacturer.
Nov. 22	Paid account in full from the November 6 purchase.

EA18. LO 6.7 Record the journal entries for the following sales transactions of Julian Sundries.

Nov. 7	Sold 10 tables on credit for $870 per table. Terms of the sale are 5/10, n/60, invoice dated November 7. The cost per table to Julian is $560.
Nov. 14	The customer returned 2 slightly damaged tables for a full refund from Julian.
Nov. 21	The customer paid their account in full from the November 7 sale.

EA19. LO 6.7 Record the journal entry or entries for each of the following sales transactions. Glow Industries sells 240 strobe lights at $40 per light to a customer on May 9. The cost to Glow is $23 per light. The terms of the sale are 5/15, n/40, invoice dated May 9. On May 13, the customer discovers 50 of the lights are the wrong color and are granted an allowance of $10 per light for the error. On May 21, the customer pays for the lights, less the allowance.

Exercise Set B

EB1. LO 6.1 On June 1, Lupita Candy Supplies sells 1,250 candy buckets to a local school at a sales price of $10 per bucket. The cost to Lolita is $2 per bucket. The terms of the sale are 2/10, n/60, with an invoice date of June 1. Create the journal entries for Lupita to recognize the following transactions.

A. the initial sale
B. the subsequent customer payment on July 12

EB2. LO 6.1 Ariel Enterprises purchases 32 cellular telephones on credit from a manufacturer on November 3 at a price of $400 per phone. Terms of the purchase are 3/5, n/30 with an invoice date of November 3. Ariel Enterprises pays in full for the phones on November 6. Create the journal entries for Ariel Enterprises for the following transactions.

A. the initial purchase
B. the subsequent payment on November 6

EB3. LO 6.1 For each of the following statements, fill in the blanks with the correct account names.

A. A retailer purchases merchandise on credit. The retailer would recognize this transaction by debiting ____ and crediting ______.

B. A retailer pays for purchased merchandise within the discount window. The retailer would recognize this transaction by debiting _______ and crediting ________ and _______.

C. A customer returns merchandise to the retailer and receives a full refund. The retailer would recognize this transaction by debiting ________ and crediting ________ if the customer had not yet paid on their account.

D. A customer pays for purchased merchandise within the discount window. The retailer would recognize this transaction by debiting _______ and ______, and crediting ________.

EB4. LO 6.2 The following is selected information from Orange Industries. Compute net purchases, and cost of goods sold for the month of June.

Sales	$870,000
Gross purchases	435,080
Sales discounts	82,650
Purchase returns and allowances	50,932
Beginning inventory	321,908
Purchase discounts	14,664
Ending inventory	254,075

EB5. LO 6.2 On April 20, Barrio Bikes purchased 30 bicycles at a cost of $100 per bike. Credit terms were 4/10, n/30, with an invoice date of April 20. On April 26, Barrio Bikes pays in full for the purchase. Prepare the journal entry or entries to recognize the purchase and subsequent payment if Barrio Bikes uses:

A. the perpetual inventory system

B. the periodic inventory system

EB6. LO 6.3 Blue Barns purchased 888 gallons of paint at $19 per gallon from a supplier on June 3. Terms of the purchase are 2/15, n/45, invoice dated June 3. Blue Barns pays their account in full on June 20. On June 22, Blue Barns discovers 20 gallons are the wrong color and returns the gallons for a full cash refund. Record the journal entries to recognize these transactions for Blue Barns.

EB7. LO 6.3 Canary Lawnmowers purchased 300 lawnmower parts at $3.50 per part from a supplier on December 4. Terms of the purchase are 4/10, n/25, invoice dated December 4. Canary Lawnmowers pays their account in full on December 16. On December 21, Canary discovers 34 of the parts are the wrong size but decides to keep them after the supplier gives Canary an allowance of $1.00 per part. Record the journal entries to recognize these transactions for Canary Lawnmowers.

EB8. LO 6.3 Record journal entries for the following purchase transactions of Balloon Depot.

Feb. 8	Purchased 3,000 balloon bundles on credit for $25 per bundle. Terms of the purchase are 10/10, n/30, invoice dated February 8.
Feb. 11	Returned 450 defective bundles for a full refund from the manufacturer.
Feb. 18	Paid account in full from the February 8 purchase.

EB9. LO 6.4 Blue Barns sold 136 gallons of paint at $31 per gallon on July 6 to a customer with a cost of $19 per gallon to Blue Barns. Terms of the sale are 2/15, n/45, invoice dated July 6. The customer pays their account in full on July 24. On July 28, the customer discovers 17 gallons are the wrong color and returns the paint for a full cash refund. Blue Barns returns the gallons to their inventory at the original cost per gallon. Record the journal entries to recognize these transactions for Blue Barns.

EB10. LO 6.4 Canary Lawnmowers sold 70 lawnmower parts at $5.00 per part to a customer on December 4 with a cost to Canary of $3.00 per part. Terms of the sale are 5/10, n/25, invoice dated December 4. The customer pays their account in full on December 16. On December 21, the customer discovers 22 of the parts are the wrong size but decides to keep them after Canary gives them an allowance of $1.00 per part. Record the journal entries to recognize these transactions for Canary Lawnmowers.

EB11. LO 6.4 Record journal entries for the following sales transactions of Balloon Depot.

Mar. 8	Sold 570 balloon bundles to a customer on credit for $38 per bundle. The cost to Balloon Depot was $25 per bundle. Terms of the sale are 3/10, n/30, invoice dated March 8.
Mar. 11	The customer returned 70 bundles for a full refund from Balloon Depot. Balloon Depot returns the balloons to their inventory at the original cost of $25 per bundle.
Mar. 18	The customer paid their account in full from the March 8 purchase.

EB12. LO 6.5 Review the following situations and record any necessary journal entries for Lumber Farm.

Feb. 13	Lumber Farm purchases $9,650 worth of merchandise with cash from a manufacturer. Shipping charges are an extra $210 cash. Terms of the purchase are FOB Destination.
Feb. 19	Lumber Farm sells $5,670 worth of merchandise to a customer who pays with cash. The merchandise has a cost to Lumber Farm of $2,200. Shipping charges are an extra $230 cash. Terms of the sale are FOB Destination.

EB13. LO 6.5 Review the following situations and record any necessary journal entries for Clubs Unlimited.

Jun. 12	Clubs Unlimited purchases $3,540 worth of merchandise on credit from a manufacturer. Shipping charges are an extra $150 cash. Terms of the purchase are 2/10, n/45, FOB Shipping Point, invoice dated June 12.
Jun. 18	Clubs Unlimited sells $8,200 worth of merchandise to a customer who pays on credit. The merchandise has a cost to Clubs Unlimited of $3,280. Shipping charges are an extra $150 cash. Terms of the sale are 3/15, n/30, FOB Shipping Point, invoice dated June 18.

EB14. LO 6.5 Review the following situations and record any necessary journal entries for Wall World.

Dec. 6	Wall World purchases $5,510 worth of merchandise on credit from a manufacturer. Shipping charges are an extra $146 cash. Terms of the purchase are 2/15, n/40, FOB Shipping Point, invoice dated December 6.
Dec. 10	Wall World sells $3,590 worth of merchandise to a customer, who pays on credit. The merchandise has a cost to Wall World of $1,400. Shipping charges are an extra $115 cash. Terms of the sale are 4/10, n/30, FOB Destination, invoice dated December 10.

EB15. LO 6.6 The following select account data is taken from the records of Carnival Express for 2019.

Sales	$790,866
Merchandise inventory	465,000
Accounts receivable	115,509
Office supplies expense	2,312
Rent revenue	42,900
Sales salaries expense	65,300
Accounts payable	158,234
Common stock	80,963
Marketing expense	25,450
Sales discounts	62,750
Interest expense	5,444
Sales returns and allowances	100,043
Interest revenue	12,321
Cost of goods sold	295,840
Rent expense	12,678
Depreciation expense: office equipment	4,210
Insurance expense	2,000
Advertising expense	14,650

A. Use the data provided to compute net sales for 2019.
B. Prepare a simple income statement for the year ended December 31, 2019.
C. Compute the gross margin for 2019.
D. Prepare a multi-step income statement for the year ended December 31, 2019.

EB16. LO 6.7 Canary Lawnmowers purchased 300 lawnmower parts at $3.50 per part from a supplier on December 4. Terms of the purchase are 4/10, n/25, invoice dated December 4. Canary Lawnmowers pays their account in full on December 16. On December 21, Canary discovers 34 of the parts are the wrong size, but decides to keep them after the supplier gives Canary an allowance of $1.00 per part. Record the journal entries to recognize these transactions for Canary Lawnmowers.

EB17. LO 6.7 Record journal entries for the following purchase transactions of Balloon Depot.

Feb. 8	Purchased 3,000 balloon bundles on credit for $25 per bundle. Terms of the purchase are 2/10, n/30, invoice dated February 8.
Feb. 11	Returned 450 defective bundles for a full refund from the manufacturer.
Feb. 18	Paid account in full from the February 8 purchase.

EB18. LO 6.7 Canary Lawnmowers sold 75 lawnmower parts at $5.00 per part to a customer on December 4. The cost to Canary is $3.00 per part. Terms of the sale are 4/10, n/25, invoice dated December 4. The customer pays their account in full on December 16. On December 21, the customer discovers 22 of the parts are the wrong size, but decides to keep them after Canary gives them an allowance of $1.00 per part. Record the journal entries to recognize these transactions for Canary Lawnmowers.

EB19. LO 6.7 Record journal entries for the following sales transactions of Balloon Depot.

Mar. 8	Sold 570 balloon bundles to a customer on credit for $38 per bundle. The cost to Balloon Depot is $25 per bundle. Terms of the sale are 3/10, n/30, invoice dated March 8.
Mar. 11	The customer returned 70 bundles for a full refund from Balloon Depot.
Mar. 18	The customer paid their account in full from the March 8 purchase.

Problem Set A

PA1. LO 6.1 Record journal entries for the following transactions of Furniture Warehouse.

A. Aug. 3: Sold 15 couches at $500 each to a customer, credit terms 2/15, n/30, invoice date August 3; the couches cost Furniture Warehouse $150 each.
B. Aug. 8: Customer returned 2 couches for a full refund. The merchandise was in sellable condition at the original cost.
C. Aug. 15: Customer found 4 defective couches but kept the merchandise for an allowance of $1,000.
D. Aug. 18: Customer paid their account in full with cash.

PA2. LO 6.1 Record journal entries for the following transactions of Barrera Suppliers.

A. May 12: Sold 32 deluxe hammers at $195 each to a customer, credit terms 10/10, n/45, invoice date May 12; the deluxe hammers cost Barrera Suppliers $88 each.
B. May 15: Customer returned 6 hammers for a full refund. The merchandise was in sellable condition at the original cost.
C. May 20: Customer found 2 defective hammers but kept the merchandise for an allowance of $200.
D. May 22: Customer paid their account in full with cash.

PA3. LO 6.2 Costume Warehouse sells costumes and accessories. Review the following transactions and prepare the journal entry or entries if Costume Warehouse uses:

A. the perpetual inventory system
B. the periodic inventory system

May 3	A customer purchases 45 costumes at a sales price of $35 per costume. The cost to Costume Warehouse per costume is $15. The terms of the sale are 3/15, n/60, with an invoice date of May 3.
May 10	The customer who made the May 3 purchase returns 5 of the costumes to the store for a full refund, claiming they were the wrong size. The costumes were returned to Costume Warehouse's inventory at $15 per costume.
May 16	The customer pays in full for the remaining costumes, less the return.

PA4. LO 6.2 Pharmaceutical Supplies sells medical supplies to customers. Review the following transactions and prepare the journal entry or entries if Pharmaceutical Supplies uses:

A. the perpetual inventory system
B. the periodic inventory system

Jul. 9	A customer purchases 50 pairs of crutches at a sales price of $20 per pair. The cost to Pharmaceutical Supplies per pair is $8.00. The terms of the sale are 5/10, n/30, with an invoice date of July 9.
Jul. 12	The customer who made the July 9 purchase returns 9 of the pairs to the store for a full refund, claiming they were the wrong size. The crutch pairs were returned to the store's inventory at $8.00 per pair.
Jul. 18	The customer pays in full for the remaining crutches, less the return.

PA5. LO 6.3 Review the following transactions for Birdy Birdhouses and record any required journal entries.

Sep. 6	Birdy Birdhouses purchases 55 birdhouses at $40 each with cash.
Sep. 8	Birdy Birdhouses purchases 80 birdhouses at $45 each on credit. Terms of the purchase are 2/10, n/30, invoice date September 8.
Sep. 10	Birdy discovers 10 of the birdhouses are damaged from the Sept 6 purchase and returns them to the supplier for a full refund. Birdy also discovers that 10 of the birdhouses from the Sept 8 purchase are painted the wrong color but keeps them since the supplier granted an allowance of $20 per birdhouse.
Sep. 18	Birdy pays their account in full from the September 8 purchase, less any returns, allowances, and/or discounts.

PA6. LO 6.3 Review the following transactions for Dish Mart and record any required journal entries. Note that all purchase transactions are with the same supplier.

Nov. 5	Dish Mart purchases 26 sets of dishes for $460 per set with cash.
Nov. 9	Dish Mart purchases 30 sets of dishes for $430 per set on credit. Terms of the purchase are 10/15, n/60, invoice date November 9.
Nov. 13	Dish Mart discovers 5 of the dish sets are damaged from the November 9 purchase and returns them to the supplier for a full refund.
Nov. 14	Dish Mart purchases 10 sets of dishes for $450 per set, on credit. Terms of the purchase are 10/10, n/60, invoice date November 14.
Nov. 15	Dish Mart discovers that 2 of the dish sets from the November 14 purchase and 4 of the dish sets from the November 5 purchase are missing a few dishes but keeps them since the supplier granted an allowance of $50 per set for the November 14 dish sets and $75 per set for the November 5 dish sets. Dish Mart and the supplier have agreed to reduce the amount Dish Mart has outstanding debt, instead of sending a separate check for the November 5 allowance in cash.
Nov. 24	Dish Mart pays their account in full for all outstanding purchases, less any returns, allowances, and/or discounts.

PA7. LO 6.4 Review the following sales transactions for Birdy Birdhouses and record any required journal entries.

Aug. 10	Birdy Birdhouses sells 20 birdhouses to customer Julia Brand at a price of $70 each in exchange for cash. The cost to Birdy is $46 per birdhouse.
Aug. 12	Birdy Birdhouses sells 30 birdhouses to customer Julia Brand at a price of $68 each on credit. The cost of sale for Birdy is $44 per birdhouse. Terms of the sale are 2/10, n/30, invoice date August 12.
Aug. 14	Julia discovers 6 of the birdhouses are slightly damaged from the August 10 purchase and returns them to Birdy for a full refund. Birdy is able to return the birdhouses to their inventory at the original cost of $46 each. Julia also discovers that 10 of the birdhouses from the August 12 purchase are painted the wrong color but keeps them since Birdy granted an allowance of $24 per birdhouse.
Aug. 20	Julia pays her account in full from the August 12 purchase, less any returns, allowances, and/or discounts.

PA8. LO 6.4 Review the following sales transactions for Dish Mart and record any required journal entries. Note that all sales transactions are with the same customer, Emma Purcell.

Mar. 5	Dish Mart made a cash sale of 13 sets of dishes at a price of $700 per set to customer Emma Purcell. The cost per set is $460 to Dish Mart.
Mar. 9	Dish Mart sold 23 sets of dishes to Emma for $650 per set on credit, at a cost to Dish Mart of $435 per set. Terms of the sale are 5/15, n/60, invoice date March 9.
Mar. 13	Emma returns eight of the dish sets from the March 9 sale to Dish Mart for a full refund. Dish Mart returns the dish sets to inventory at their original cost of $435 per set.
Mar. 14	Dish Mart sells 6 sets of dishes to Emma for $670 per set on credit, at a cost to Dish Mart of $450 per set. Terms of the sale are 5/10, n/60, invoice date March 14.
Mar. 15	Emma discovers that 3 of the dish sets from the March 14 purchase, and 7 of the dish sets from the March 5 sale are missing a few dishes, but keeps them since Dish Mart granted an allowance of $2,670 for all 10 dish sets. Dish Mart and Emma have agreed to reduce the amount Dish Mart has outstanding instead of sending a separate check for the March 5 allowance in cash.
Mar. 24	Emma Purcell pays her account in full for all outstanding purchases, less any returns, allowances, and/or discounts.

PA9. LO 6.5 Record the following purchase transactions of Money Office Supplies.

Aug. 3	Purchased 45 chairs on credit, at a cost of $55 per chair. Shipping charges are an extra $3 cash per chair and are not subject to discount. Terms of the purchase are 4/10, n/60, FOB Shipping Point, invoice dated August 3.
Aug. 7	Purchased 30 chairs with cash, at a cost of $50 per chair. Shipping charges are an extra $4.50 cash per chair and are not subject to discount. Terms of the purchase are FOB Destination.
Aug. 12	Money Office Supplies pays in full for their purchase on August 3.

PA10. LO 6.6 The following is the adjusted trial balance data for Nino's Pizzeria as of December 31, 2019.

NINO'S PIZZERIA Adjusted Trial Balance Year Ended December 31, 2019		
	Debit	**Credit**
Cash	$ 775,984	
Accounts Receivable	45,688	
Buildings	200,460	
Merchandise Inventory	135,624	
Accounts Payable		$437,880
Common Stock		410,542
Sales		555,696
Interest Revenue		84,652
Rent Revenue		86,900
Sales Salaries Expense	24,500	
Office Supplies Expense	6,270	
Sales Discounts	102,890	
Interest Expense	4,577	
Sales Returns and Allowances	105,854	
Cost of goods sold	122,853	
Rent Expense	20,000	
Depreciation Expense: Office Equipment	10,555	
Insurance Expense	2,780	
Advertising Expense	17,635	
Totals	**$1,575,670**	**$1,575,670**

A. Use the data provided to compute net sales for 2019.
B. Compute the gross margin for 2019.
C. Compute the gross profit margin ratio (rounded to nearest hundredth).
D. Prepare a simple income statement for the year ended December 31, 2019.
E. Prepare a multi-step income statement for the year ended December 31, 2019.

PA11. LO 6.6 The following is the adjusted trial balance data for Emma's Alterations as of December 31, 2019.

EMMA'S ALTERATIONS Adjusted Trial Balance Year Ended December 31, 2019		
	Debit	**Credit**
Cash	$ 600,538	
Accounts Receivable	50,689	
Equipment	199,430	
Merchandise Inventory	169,744	
Accounts Payable		$ 234,893
Common Stock		502,200
Sales		393,426
Interest Revenue		100,976
Rent Revenue		65,500
Sales Salaries Expense	26,750	
Office Supplies Expense	4,903	
Sales Discounts	61,347	
Interest Expense	3,570	
Sales Returns and Allowances	55,432	
Cost of Goods Sold	90,333	
Rent Expense	10,400	
Depreciation Expense: Office Equipment	8,560	
Insurance Expense	3,421	
Advertising Expense	11,878	
Totals	**$1,296,995**	**$1,296,995**

A. Use the data provided to compute net sales for 2019.
B. Compute the gross margin for 2019.
C. Compute the gross profit margin ratio (rounded to nearest hundredth).
D. Prepare a simple income statement for the year ended December 31, 2019.
E. Prepare a multi-step income statement for the year ended December 31, 2019.

PA12. LO 6.7 Review the following transactions for Birdy Birdhouses and record any required journal entries.

Sep. 6	Birdy Birdhouses purchases 57 birdhouses at $46 each with cash.
Sep. 8	Birdy Birdhouses purchases 94 birdhouses at $44 each on credit. Terms of the purchase are 2/10, n/30, invoice date September 8.
Sep. 10	Birdy discovers 12 of the birdhouses are damaged from the Sept 6 purchase and returns them to the supplier for a full refund. Birdy also discovers that 11 of the birdhouses from the Sept 8 purchase are painted the wrong color but keeps them since the supplier granted an allowance of $136.
Sep. 18	Birdy pays their account in full from the September 8 purchase, less any returns, allowances, and/or discounts.

PA13. LO 6.7 Review the following sales transactions for Dish Mart and record any required journal entries. Note that all sales transactions are with the same customer, Emma Purcell.

Mar. 5	Dish Mart made a cash sale of 13 sets of dishes at a price of $700 per set to customer Emma Purcell. The cost per set is $460 to Dish Mart.
Mar. 9	Dish Mart sold 23 sets of dishes to Emma for $650 per set on credit, at a cost to Dish Mart of $435 per set. Terms of the sale are 10/15, n/60, invoice date March 9.
Mar. 13	Emma discovers 8 of the dish sets are damaged from the March 9 sale and returns them to Dish Mart for a full refund.
Mar. 14	Dish Mart sells 6 sets of dishes to Emma for $670 per set on credit, at a cost to Dish Mart of $450 per set. Terms of the sale are 10/10, n/60, invoice date March 14.
Mar. 15	Emma discovers that 3 of the dish sets from the March 14 purchase and 7 of the dish sets from the March 5 sale are missing a few dishes but keeps them since Dish Mart granted an allowance of $200 per set for all 10 dish sets. Dish Mart and Emma have agreed to reduce the amount Dish Mart has outstanding instead of sending a separate check for the March 5 allowance in cash.
Mar. 24	Emma Purcell pays her account in full for all outstanding purchases, less any returns, allowances, and/or discounts.

Problem Set B

PB1. LO 6.1 Record journal entries for the following transactions of Furniture Warehouse.

A. July 5: Purchased 30 couches at a cost of $150 each from a manufacturer. Credit terms are 2/15, n/30, invoice date July 5.
B. July 10: Furniture Warehouse returned 5 couches for a full refund.
C. July 15: Furniture Warehouse found 6 defective couches, but kept the merchandise for an allowance of $500.
D. July 20: Furniture Warehouse paid their account in full with cash.

PB2. LO 6.1 Record journal entries for the following transactions of Mason Suppliers.

A. Sep. 8: Purchased 50 deluxe hammers at a cost of $95 each from a manufacturer. Credit terms are 5/20, n/60, invoice date September 8.
B. Sep. 12: Mason Suppliers returned 8 hammers for a full refund.
C. Sep. 16: Mason Suppliers found 4 defective hammers, but kept the merchandise for an allowance of $250.
D. Sep. 28: Mason Suppliers paid their account in full with cash.

PB3. LO 6.2 Costume Warehouse sells costumes and accessories and purchases their merchandise from a manufacturer. Review the following transactions and prepare the journal entry or entries if Costume Warehouse uses

A. the perpetual inventory system
B. the periodic inventory system

Jun. 4	Costume Warehouse purchases 88 costumes on credit at a purchase price of $15 per costume. The terms of the purchase are 5/15, n/30, with an invoice date of June 4.
Jun. 12	Costume Warehouse returns 20 costumes to the manufacturer for a full refund.
Jun. 19	Costume Warehouse pays in full for the remaining costumes, less the return.

PB4. LO 6.2 Pharmaceutical Supplies sells medical supplies and purchases their merchandise from a manufacturer. Review the following transactions and prepare the journal entry or entries if Pharmaceutical Supplies uses

A. the perpetual inventory system
B. the periodic inventory system

Apr. 7	Pharmaceutical Supplies purchases 50 medical stands on credit at a purchase price of $15 per stand. The terms of the purchase are 5/10, n/45, with an invoice date of April 7.
Apr. 11	Pharmaceutical Supplies returns 18 stands to the manufacturer for a full refund.
Apr. 17	Pharmaceutical Supplies pays in full for the remaining stands, less the return.

PB5. LO 6.3 Review the following transactions for April Anglers and record any required journal entries.

Oct. 4	April Anglers purchases 82 fishing poles at $33 each with cash.
Oct. 5	April Anglers purchases 116 fishing poles at $30 each on credit. Terms of the purchase are 3/15, n/30, invoice date October 5.
Oct. 12	April discovers 18 of the fishing poles are damaged from the October 4 purchase and returns them to the supplier for a full refund. April also discovers that 32 of the fishing poles from the October 5 purchase are the wrong length but keeps them since the supplier granted an allowance of $15 per fishing pole.
Oct. 24	April pays their account in full from the October 5 purchase, less any returns, allowances, and/or discounts.

PB6. LO 6.3 Review the following transactions for Dish Mart and record any required journal entries. Note that all purchase transactions are with the same supplier.

Nov. 5	Dish Mart purchases 45 sets of cutlery for $100 per set with cash.
Nov. 9	Dish Mart purchases 50 sets of cutlery for $120 per set on credit. Terms of the purchase are 5/15, n/60, invoice date November 9.
Nov. 13	Dish Mart discovers 15 of the cutlery sets are damaged from the November 9 purchase and returns them to the supplier for a full refund.
Nov. 14	Dish Mart purchases 30 sets of cutlery for $130 per set on credit. Terms of the purchase are 5/10, n/60, invoice date November 14.
Nov. 15	Dish Mart discovers that 10 of the cutlery sets from the November 14 purchase and 20 of the cutlery sets from the November 5 purchase are missing a few spoons but keeps them since the supplier granted an allowance of $30 per set for the November 14 cutlery sets and $35 per set for the November 5 cutlery sets. Dish Mart and the supplier have agreed to reduce the amount of debt Dish Mart has outstanding instead of sending a separate check for the November 5 allowance in cash.
Nov. 24	Dish Mart pays their account in full for all outstanding purchases, less any returns, allowances, and/or discounts.

PB7. LO 6.4 Review the following sales transactions for April Anglers and record any required journal entries.

Oct. 4	April Anglers made a cash sale of 40 fishing poles to customer Billie Dyer at a price of $55 per pole. The cost to April is $33 per pole.
Oct. 5	April Anglers sells 24 fishing poles to customer Billie Dyer at a price of $52 per pole on credit. The cost to April is $30 per pole. Terms of the sale are 2/10, n/30, invoice date October 5.
Oct. 12	Billie returns seven of the fishing poles from the October 4 purchase to April Anglers for a full refund. April returns these poles to their inventory at the original cost per pole. Billie also discovers that 6 of the fishing poles from the October 5 purchase are the wrong color but keeps them since April granted an allowance of $18 per fishing pole.
Oct. 24	April pays their account in full from the October 5 purchase, less any returns, allowances, and/or discounts.

PB8. LO 6.4 Review the following sales transactions for Dish Mart and record any required journal entries. Note that all sales transactions are with the same customer, Bella Davies.

Apr. 5	Dish Mart made a cash sale of 22 sets of cutlery to Bella Davies for $330 per set. The cost per set to Dish Mart is $125 per set.
Apr. 9	Dish Mart sells 14 sets of cutlery to Bella Davies on credit for $345 per set. The cost per set to Dish Mart is $120 per set. Terms of the sale are 2/15, n/60, invoice date April 9.
Apr. 13	Bella returns nine of the cutlery sets from the April 9 sale to Dish Mart for a full refund. Dish Mart restores the cutlery to its inventory at the original cost of $120 per set.
Apr. 14	Bella purchases 18 sets of cutlery for $275 per set on credit, at a cost to Dish Mart of $124 per set. Terms of the sale are 2/10, n/60, invoice date April 14.
Apr. 15	Bella discovers that 5 of the cutlery sets from the April 14 purchase and 10 of the cutlery sets from the April 5 purchase are missing a few spoons but keeps them since Dish Mart granted an allowance of $175 per set for all dish sets. Dish Mart and Bella have agreed to reduce the amount Bella has outstanding instead of sending a separate check for the April 5 allowance in cash.
Apr. 28	Bella Davies pays her account in full for all outstanding purchases, less any returns, allowances, and/or discounts.

PB9. LO 6.5 Record the following purchase transactions of Custom Kitchens Inc.

Oct. 6	Purchased 230 cabinet doors on credit at a cost of $46 per door. Shipping charges are an extra $2 cash per door and are not subject to discount. Terms of the purchase are 5/15, n/35, FOB Shipping Point, invoice dated October 6.
Oct. 9	Purchased 100 cabinet doors with cash at cost of $40 per door. Shipping charges are an extra $3.25 cash per door and are not subject to discount. Terms of the purchase are FOB Destination.
Oct. 20	Custom Kitchens Inc. pays in full for their purchase from October 6.

PB10. LO 6.5 Record the following sales transactions of Money Office Supplies.

Apr. 4	Made a cash sale to a customer for 15 chairs at a sales price of $80 per chair. The cost to Money Office Supplies is $55 per chair. Shipping charges are an extra $4 cash per chair and are not subject to discount. Terms of the sale are FOB Shipping Point.
Apr. 9	Sold 20 chairs on credit for $85 per chair to a customer. The cost per chair to Money Office Supplies is $50 per chair. Shipping charges are an extra $4.50 cash per chair and are not subject to discount. Terms of the sale are 3/10, n/30, FOB Destination, invoice dated April 9.
Apr. 19	The customer pays in full for their purchase on April 9.

PB11. LO 6.5 Record the following sales transactions of Custom Kitchens Inc.

Nov. 12	Made a cash sale to a customer for 34 cabinet doors at a sales price of $72 per door. The cost to Custom Kitchens Inc. is $46 per door. Shipping charges are an extra $3.15 cash per door and are not subject to discount. Terms of the sale are FOB Shipping Point.
Nov. 16	Sold 22 doors on credit for $80 per door to a customer. The cost per door to Custom Kitchens Inc. is $40 per door. Shipping charges are an extra $4.00 cash per door and are not subject to discount. Terms of the sale are 5/15, n/40, FOB Destination, invoice dated November 12.
Nov. 24	The customer pays in full for their purchase on November 16.

PB12. LO 6.6 The following is the adjusted trial balance data for Elm Connections as of December 31, 2019.

ELM CONNECTIONS
Adjusted Trial Balance
Year Ended December 31, 2019

	Debit	Credit
Cash	$ 596,823	
Accounts Receivable	34,672	
Buildings	350,000	
Merchandise Inventory	263,909	
Accounts Payable		$ 502,690
Common Stock		432,975
Sales		603,427
Interest Revenue		94,568
Rent Revenue		90,000
Sales Salaries Expense	25,180	
Office Supplies Expense	5,942	
Sales Discounts	99,651	
Interest Expense	3,566	
Sales Returns and Allowances	110,285	
Cost of Goods Sold	180,630	
Rent Expense	15,485	
Depreciation Expense: Office Equipment	9,000	
Insurance Expense	9,324	
Advertising Expense	19,193	
Totals	**$1,723,660**	**$1,723,660**

A. Use the data provided to compute net sales for 2019.
B. Compute the gross margin for 2019.
C. Compute the gross profit margin ratio (rounded to nearest hundredth)
D. Prepare a simple income statement for the year ended December 31, 2019.
E. Prepare a multi-step income statement for the year ended December 31, 2019.

PB13. LO 6.6 Following is the adjusted trial balance data for Garage Parts Unlimited as of December 31, 2019.

GARAGE PARTS UNLIMITED Adjusted Trial Balance Year Ended December 31, 2019		
	Debit	**Credit**
Cash	$ 624,500	
Accounts Receivable	100,233	
Equipment	465,099	
Merchandise Inventory	277,340	
Accounts Payable		$ 287,693
Common Stock		564,500
Sales		885,244
Interest Revenue		216,745
Rent Revenue		101,600
Sales Salaries Expense	29,878	
Office Supplies Expense	5,942	
Sales Discounts	112,431	
Interest Expense	9,560	
Sales Returns and Allowances	162,312	
Cost of Goods Sold	208,016	
Rent Expense	19,191	
Depreciation Expense: Office Equipment	8,657	
Insurance Expense	10,234	
Advertising Expense	22,389	
Totals	**$2,055,782**	**$2,055,782**

A. Use the data provided to compute net sales for 2019.
B. Compute the gross margin or 2019.
C. Compute the gross profit margin ratio (rounded to nearest hundredth)
D. Prepare a simple income statement for the year ended December 31, 2019.
E. Prepare a multi-step income statement for the year ended December 31, 2019.

PB14. LO 6.7 Review the following transactions for April Anglers and record any required journal entries.

Oct. 4	April Anglers purchases 82 fishing poles at $33 each with cash.
Oct. 5	April Anglers purchases 116 fishing poles at $30 each on credit. Terms of the purchase are 3/15, n/30, invoice date October 5.
Oct. 12	April discovers 18 of the fishing poles are damaged from the October 4 purchase and returns them to the supplier for a full refund. April also discovers that 32 of the fishing poles from the October 5 purchase are the wrong length but keeps them since the supplier granted an allowance of $15 per fishing pole.
Oct. 24	April pays their account in full from the October 5 purchase, less any returns, allowances, and/or discounts.

PB15. LO 6.7 Review the following sales transactions for Dish Mart and record any required journal entries. Note that all sales transactions are with the same customer, Bella Davies.

Apr. 5	Dish Mart made a cash sale of 22 sets of cutlery to Bella Davies for $330 per set. The cost per set to Dish Mart is $125 per set.
Apr. 9	Dish Mart sells 14 sets of cutlery to Bella Davies on credit for $345 per set, with a cost to Dish Mart of $120 per set. Terms of the sale are 2/15, n/60, invoice date April 9.
Apr. 13	Bella discovers 9 of the cutlery sets are damaged from the April 9 sale and returns them to Dish Mart for a full refund.
Apr. 14	Bella purchases 18 sets of cutlery for $275 per set on credit, at a cost to Dish Mart of $124 per set. Terms of the sale are 2/10, n/60, invoice date April 14.
Apr. 15	Bella discovers that 5 of the cutlery sets from the April 14 purchase and 10 of the cutlery sets from the April 5 purchase are missing a few spoons but keeps them since Dish Mart granted an allowance of $175 per set for all dish sets. Dish Mart and Bella have agreed to reduce the amount Bella has outstanding instead of sending a separate check for the April 5 allowance in cash.
Apr. 28	Bella Davies pays her account in full for all outstanding purchases, less any returns, allowances, and/or discounts.

Thought Provokers

TP1. LO 6.1 Conduct research on a real-world retailer's trade discounts and policies, and discuss the following questions.

- Which company did you choose? What do they sell?
- What is a trade discount?
- What products are subject to a trade discount?
- Describe the discount terms/program in detail. Give examples.
- Are there any restrictions?
- What incentive does this company have to give a trade discount?
- How does this discount benefit the buyer?
- If the buyer had to choose between receiving a trade discount or regular cash purchase discount, which would benefit them more? Why?

TP2. LO 6.2 You have decided to open up a small convenience store in your hometown. As part of the initial set-up process, you need to determine whether to use a perpetual inventory system or a periodic inventory system. Write an evaluation paper comparing the perpetual and periodic inventory systems. Describe the benefits and challenges of each system as it relates to your industry and to your business size. Compare at least one example transaction using the perpetual and periodic inventory systems (a purchase transaction, for example). Research and describe the impact each system has on your financial statements. Decide which system would be the best fit for your business, and support your decision with research.

TP3. LO 6.5 You own your own outdoor recreation supply store. You are in the process of drafting a standard invoice agreement for customer sales conducted on credit. Create a sample sales invoice with the following minimum information listed:

- Your company information
- Date of sale
- Your customer's information
- An example product you sell with name, description, price per unit, and number of units sold
- Terms of sale including credit terms and shipping charges, with numerical figures for shipping charges
- Any contract language necessary to further establish the terms of sale (for example, warranties, limitations on shipping, and returns)

Write a reflection about your invoice choice, as it relates to format, terms, contract language, and pricing strategies. Conduct a comparison study to others in your industry (such as REI) to evaluate your choices. Make sure to support your decisions with concrete examples and research.

TP4. LO 6.6 Review the most recent yearly (or quarterly) income statement for a publicly-traded company and answer the following questions.

- What company did you choose, and which income statement format do they use (multi-step, simple, or combination)?
- What information is included on the statement?
- Do you agree with the format presentation? Why or why not?
- What are the benefits and limitations with the income statement format choice?
- Compute the Gross Profit Margin Ratio. Discuss the results.

TP5. LO 6.7 You own a clothing store and use a periodic inventory system. Research like companies in the clothing industry and answer the following questions.

- Which inventory system is most used in clothing stores, periodic or perpetual?
- Why can periodic inventory reporting be a better approach to use than perpetual inventory reporting for this type of industry?
- What are some of the advantages and disadvantages to the periodic inventory method?
- What other types of businesses may use the periodic inventory method rather than the perpetual method?

7 Accounting Information Systems

Figure 7.1 Accounting Information Systems. Is this the best way to keep up with your business transactions? No. (credit: modification of “4 months of paperwork to sort” by Joel Bez/Flickr, CC BY 2.0)

Chapter Outline

LO **7.1** Define and Describe the Components of an Accounting Information System

LO **7.2** Describe and Explain the Purpose of Special Journals and Their Importance to Stakeholders

LO **7.3** Analyze and Journalize Transactions Using Special Journals

LO **7.4** Prepare a Subsidiary Ledger

LO **7.5** Describe Career Paths Open to Individuals with a Joint Education in Accounting and Information Systems

Why It Matters

Shane was a talented tennis player at his university. He had a hard time finding a job in his field upon graduation. While he worked toward finding employment, he spent time on a tennis court playing, and parents began asking if he would give lessons to their kids. Excited for the opportunity and income, he started giving lessons and kept track of sessions and payments by printing out notes and piling them on his desk. When it came time to file a tax return, though, he realized that he should have been keeping up with his bookkeeping all along, either manually in some sort of ledger or electronically on his computer.

Rather quickly, his student pool grew. Some clients paid up front for lessons, others paid after a few lessons were complete, and still others were not sure if they had paid yet. These various payment methods created a record-keeping challenge for Shane. With winter coming, Shane was exploring the idea of securing court time at an indoor facility to continue teaching and knew he would need to consider court time rental costs in his lesson expenses. Additionally, Shane planned to offer group lessons as well as camps and would need to hire another coach. As Shane’s impromptu business blossomed, it came with additional sources and types of revenues as well as new expenses. He needed a better system to keep track of the financial aspects of his business.

A friend told him he needed an accounting information system to organize the financial aspects of his business and to allow him to measure the financial performance of his growing business. But what did Shane's friend mean? What is an accounting information system? In this chapter, we explain accounting information systems, their evolution from paper-based to digital formats, and how a company—whether small like Shane's tennis lesson venture or large like a major corporation—uses these systems to stay on top of its finances and to inform important business decisions.

7.1 Define and Describe the Components of an Accounting Information System

Today, when we refer to an **accounting information system (AIS)**, we usually mean a computerized accounting system, because computers and computer software that help us process accounting transactions have become relatively inexpensive. The benefits of using a computerized accounting system outweigh the costs of purchasing one, and almost all companies, even very small ones, can afford to and do use a computerized accounting system. That is not to say that paper-based or manual accounting systems and processes have disappeared. Most businesses have some form of both noncomputerized and computerized systems. QuickBooks is an example of a relatively inexpensive accounting software application that is popular with small and medium-sized businesses.

Manual and Computerized Accounting Information Systems

Interestingly, the term *accounting information system* predates computers. Technically, an AIS is a system or set of processes for collecting data about accounting transactions; recording, organizing, and summarizing the data; and culminating with the preparation of financial statements and other reports for internal and external users. These systems or processes can exist as a series of paper ledgers, computer databases, or some combination of the two. Examples of external users include banks that might lend the company money, investors, and the Securities and Exchange Commission (SEC), which requires that publicly traded companies submit audited financial statements. Since business enterprises needed to produce financial statements long before computers existed, they used manual accounting systems to gather the data needed. **Data** is the term for parts of accounting transactions that constitute the input to an AIS. You have examined many forms of data in this course, for example, the cash received upon the sale of an item is one data point, the reduction of the inventory account related to that specific sold item is another data point, and both the revenue and the cost of goods sold would be additional data points associated with that single transaction of a sale. These data points are summarized and aggregated (in other words "processed") into more meaningful and useful numbers that appear in the financial statements, and all this data is typically referred to as financial information. A company that may have used a manual AIS years ago likely uses a computerized AIS today. It is important to remember that a computerized accounting system does not change *what* we do with accounting transactions, it only changes *how* we do it, and how we can present the information to different users.

Let's consider the example of a company that came into existence before we had computers, the department store Macy's, which currently operates stores in nearly all fifty US states. Macy's began as a small, fancy dry goods store that opened in New York City in 1858, became a department store, R.H. Macy & Co., in 1877 using the same red star logo it still uses today. We can assume that even one hundred years ago, Macy's needed to perform the same tasks it does today:

- purchase merchandise inventory to sell to customers;
- record returns of some of the inventory;
- record sales made to customers at the sales price;
- record the cost of the goods sold at the amount Macy's paid to purchase them;
- record payments from customers;
- record returns from customers;
- purchase other kinds of items needed for operations, like office supplies and fixed assets;
- pay for prior purchases;
- pay for rent, utilities, and other services;
- pay employees;
- enter all of these transactions;
- post all transactions;
- record adjusting journal entries;
- record closing journal entries;
- keep track of its receivables, payables, and inventory; and
- produce financial statements for internal and external users as well as other reports useful to managers in assessing various performance measures needed to evaluate the success of the company.

As you might imagine, doing all this without computers is quite different than performing these tasks with the aid of computers. In a manual system, each business transaction is recorded, in the form of a journal entry in the general journal or one of the four common other special journals described in Describe and Explain the Purpose of Special Journals and Their Importance to Stakeholders, using pen and paper. Journal entries are then posted to a general ledger; balances would be computed by hand or with an adding machine/calculator for each general ledger account; a trial balance is prepared; adjusting journal entries are prepared; and finally financial statements prepared, all manually.

CONCEPTS IN PRACTICE

Modernization of Accounting Systems

In 1955, in one of the earliest uses of a true computer to facilitate accounting tasks, General Electric Company used a UNIVAC computer to process its payroll. Initially it took the computer forty hours just to process payroll for one pay period. The first modern era spreadsheet software for personal computers, VisiCalc, became available in 1978. Thus, between these time periods there were minor improvements to the use of computerized accounting tools, but it was not until the mid-1980s that comprehensive computerized accounting programs became widely used. Thus, prior to the mid-1980s, much accounting was done manually or using a variety of less-advanced computer systems in conjunction with manual systems. Imagine the number of bookkeepers it would take to record the transactions of many companies. For example, on the first day of business at Macy's in 1858, the store had revenues of $11.06.[1] The actual accounting ledger used to record those sales is shown in Figure 7.2, which seems quite simple. Today Macy's has over $24 billion in sales revenue—can you imagine accounting for all of those transactions (along with all expenses) by hand?

1 Fraser Sherman. "The History of Computerized Accounting." Career Trend. January 14, 2019. https://careertrend.com/about-6328213-history-computerized-accounting.html

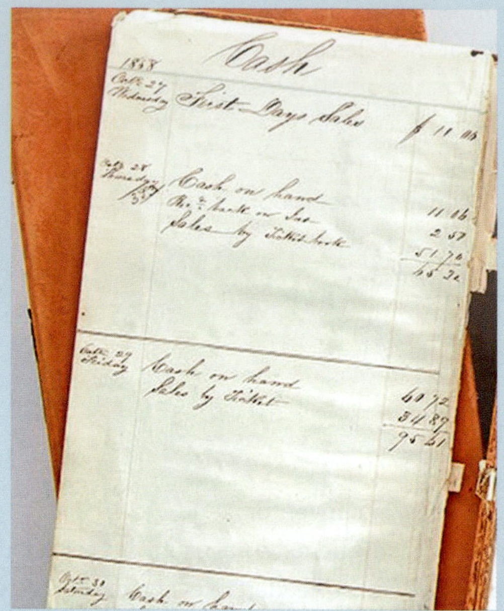

Figure 7.2 Macy's Accounting Ledger. Accounting ledger showing the transactions for Macy's first day. Total revenues were $11.06 or a little over $340 in today's dollars. (credit: used with permission of Macy's Corporation)

Today, Macy's and other large and small companies perform the same accounting tasks using computer hardware (computers, printers, and keyboards), and software. For example, cashiers can enter transactions into a computer using a keyboard, scanner, or touch screen. The screen displays the data entered or fields available for data entry. As an example, most retail stores have a **point-of-sale system (POS)** that enters the sale by scanning the item at the **point of sale**, meaning at the time the transaction is made. This system records the sale and at the same time updates inventory by reducing it based on the number of items purchased.

Later in the section on how to Prepare a Subsidiary Ledger, you will be provided with a series of transactions for a small business and you will be asked to first enter the transactions manually into the appropriate journal, post the information from the journals to the general ledger, prepare trial balances, adjusting and closing entries, and manually produce financial statements just as Macy's or any other business would have done prior to the use of various computer technologies. You will then perform the same tasks using QuickBooks, a popular accounting software program used by many small and medium-sized businesses. A company as large as Macy's has stores in locations all over the country and a large volume of transactions, so it is more likely to use a software package designed to meet the needs of a very large business. This is often referred to as an enterprise resource planning (ERP) system which stands for enterprise resource planning (ERP) system. An ERP system integrates all of the company's computerized systems including accounting systems and nonaccounting systems. That is, large companies have various accounting subsystems such as the revenue system (sales/accounts receivable/cash receipts), the expenditure system (purchasing/accounts payable/cash disbursements), the production system, the payroll system, and the general ledger system. Nonaccounting systems might include research and development, marketing, and human resources, which, while not an integral part of the accounting system, in a large companywide ERP system are integrated with the accounting modules. Examples of popular ERP software systems are PeopleSoft and SAP.

Like many businesses today, Macy's also maintains a company website and engages in e-commerce by offering the sale of many company products online. Accounting software companies like QuickBooks and larger software vendors have upgraded the ways in which they can provide AIS software to meet these needs. For example, a small local retail shoe store can purchase QuickBooks software provided on an electronic storage device such as a CD and upload it to be stored on the hard drive of the company's computers, or the store can purchase a "cloud" version. The cloud version provides the shoe store purchasing the software with access to the QuickBooks software online via a user ID and password with no need to load the software on the store's computers. QuickBooks updates the software when new versions are released and stores the company's accounting data in the cloud. **Cloud computing** refers to using the internet to access software and information storage facilities provided by companies rather than, or in addition to, storing this data on the company's computer hard drive or in paper form. An advantage of cloud computing is that company employees can access the software and enter transactions from any device with an internet connection at any location. The company pays a monthly fee for access to updated software, which can be less costly than buying software stored on individual computers. Potential disadvantages include security concerns because an outside company is storing company programs and data, and if the hosting company experiences technical difficulties, companies paying for these services may temporarily be unable to access their own data or conduct business. Nevertheless, cloud services are increasingly popular.

Here, we illustrate the concepts and practices of an AIS using Intuit QuickBooks, a popular and widely used AIS.

While a company typically selects an AIS to suit its specific needs, all systems should have components capable of:

- inputting/entering data (e.g., entering a sale to a customer);
- storing data;
- processing data and computing additional amounts related to transactions (e.g., computing sales tax on the sale, as well as shipping costs and insurance fees; computing an employee's pay by multiplying hours worked by hourly pay rate; processing inventory changes from both inventory purchases and inventory sales and data from any other transaction that occurs in the business);
- aggregating/summarizing data (e.g., computing total sales for the year);
- presenting data (e.g., producing a balance sheet and other financial statements and reports for the year); and
- storing data (such as the customer's name, address, shipping address, and credit limit).

AISs, whether computerized or manual, generally involve three stages: input, processing, and output. We enter raw data into our system at the input stage and try to correct any errors prior to going on to the next stage of processing the data. We ultimately produce "output," which is in the form of useful information.

Inputting/Entering Data

A **source document** is the original document that provides evidence that a transaction occurred. If you hire a company to paint your house, it will most likely provide a document showing how much you owe. That is the company's sales document and your invoice. When you pay, your check or digital transaction record is also a source document for the company that provided the service, in this case, the home painter.

Assume you go into the university bookstore to purchase a school sweatshirt, and it is sold out. You then fill out a document ordering a size medium sweatshirt in blue. The form you fill out is a purchase order to you, and it is a sales order to the university bookstore. It is also a source document that provides evidence that you have ordered the sweatshirt. Assume the bookstore does not ask you to pay in advance because it is not sure it will be able to obtain the sweatshirt for you. At that point, no sale has been made, and you owe no money to the bookstore. A few days later, the bookstore manages to acquire the sweatshirt you ordered and sends you an email notifying you of this. When you return to the bookstore, you are presented with the sweatshirt and an invoice (also known as a bill) that you must pay in order to take your sweatshirt home. This invoice/bill is also a source document. It provides evidence of the sale and your obligation to pay that amount. Let's look at an example.

Figure 7.3 is a source document—an invoice (bill) from Symmetry Mold Design for mold design services. Note the terms (agreements about payments) are listed at the top and how the company calculates those outcomes at the bottom.

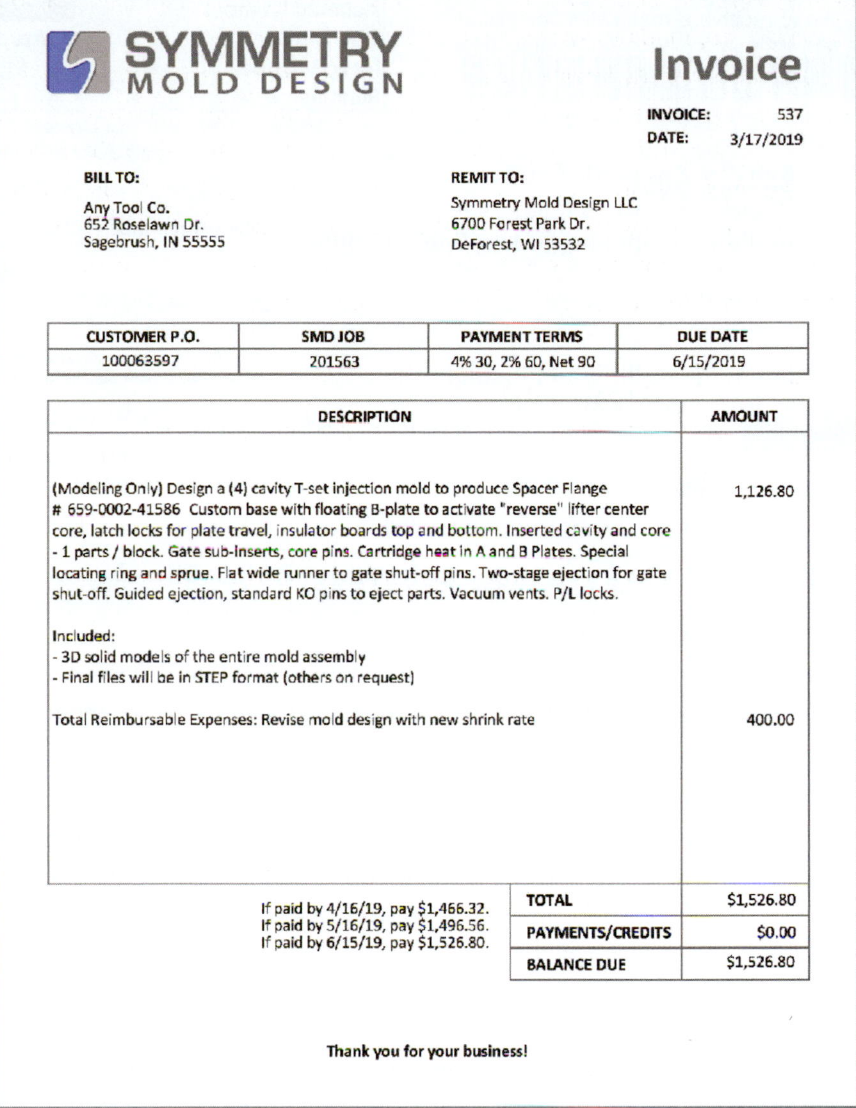

SYMMETRY MOLD DESIGN

Invoice

INVOICE: 537
DATE: 3/17/2019

BILL TO:

Any Tool Co.
652 Roselawn Dr.
Sagebrush, IN 55555

REMIT TO:

Symmetry Mold Design LLC
6700 Forest Park Dr.
DeForest, WI 53532

CUSTOMER P.O.	SMD JOB	PAYMENT TERMS	DUE DATE
100063597	201563	4% 30, 2% 60, Net 90	6/15/2019

DESCRIPTION	AMOUNT
(Modeling Only) Design a (4) cavity T-set injection mold to produce Spacer Flange # 659-0002-41586 Custom base with floating B-plate to activate "reverse" lifter center core, latch locks for plate travel, insulator boards top and bottom. Inserted cavity and core - 1 parts / block. Gate sub-Inserts, core pins. Cartridge heat in A and B Plates. Special locating ring and sprue. Flat wide runner to gate shut-off pins. Two-stage ejection for gate shut-off. Guided ejection, standard KO pins to eject parts. Vacuum vents. P/L locks.	1,126.80
Included: - 3D solid models of the entire mold assembly - Final files will be in STEP format (others on request)	
Total Reimbursable Expenses: Revise mold design with new shrink rate	400.00

If paid by 4/16/19, pay $1,466.32.
If paid by 5/16/19, pay $1,496.56.
If paid by 6/15/19, pay $1,526.80.

TOTAL	$1,526.80
PAYMENTS/CREDITS	$0.00
BALANCE DUE	$1,526.80

Thank you for your business!

Figure 7.3 Invoice from Symmetry Mold Design showing payment terms. (credit: modification of "Invoice" by James Ceszyk/Flickr, CC B 4.0)

Some companies send paper bills in the mail, often asking the recipient to tear off part of the bill and return it with the payment. This tear-off portion is a **turn-around document** and helps ensure that the payment is applied to the correct customer account and invoice. Generally, this document began as printed output, an invoice, from the billing part of the AIS. When the customer tears off a part of it and returns it in the envelope with a check to the company, it has now been “turned around” and will be used as an input source document, called a remittance advice. A remittance advice is a document that customers send along with checks and informs the recipient as to which invoice the customer is paying for. Figure 7.4 is an example of a turn-around document.

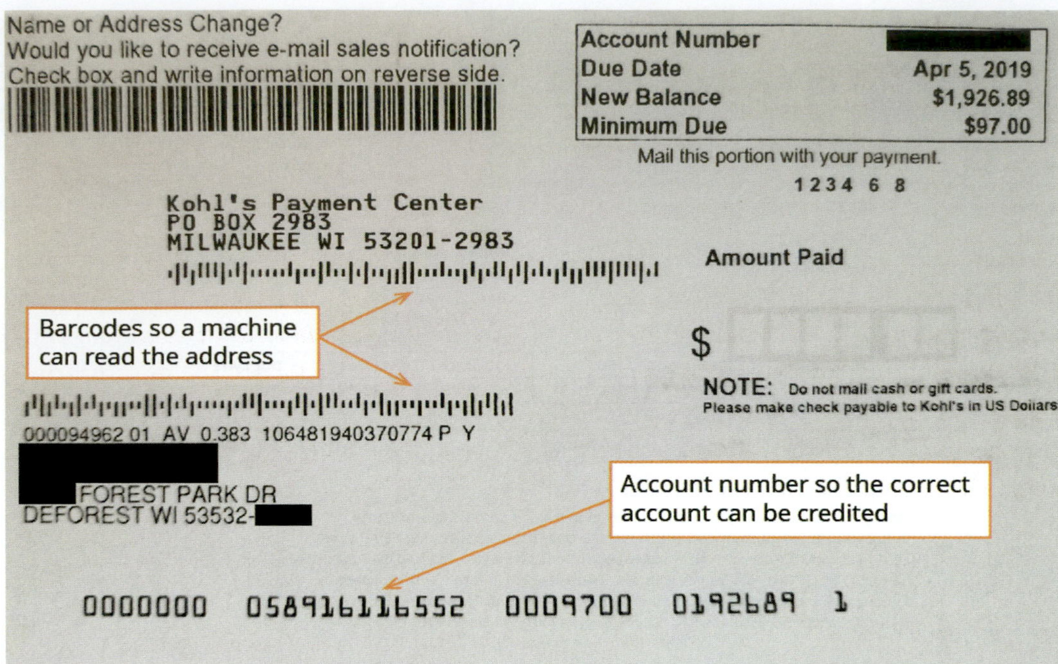
Name or Address Change?
Would you like to receive e-mail sales notification?
Check box and write information on reverse side.

Account Number	
Due Date	Apr 5, 2019
New Balance	$1,926.89
Minimum Due	$97.00

Mail this portion with your payment.
1234 6 8

Kohl's Payment Center
PO BOX 2983
MILWAUKEE WI 53201-2983

Amount Paid

Barcodes so a machine can read the address

$

NOTE: Do not mail cash or gift cards.
Please make check payable to Kohl's in US Dollars

000094962 01 AV 0.383 106481940370774 P Y

FOREST PARK DR
DEFOREST WI 53532-

Account number so the correct account can be credited

0000000 058916116552 0009700 0192689 1

Figure 7.4 Turn-Around Document from Kohl's. The use of automation (bar codes) saves time and ensures accuracy since a machine can read the address, the account number, and even the amount on the check. (credit: modification of "Bill" by Kerry Ceszyk/Flickr, CC BY 4.0)

Both manual and computerized accounting systems utilized source documents. E-commerce systems have some additional source documents related to online transactions. Source documents help to establish an **audit trail**, which is a trail of evidence documenting the history of a specific transaction starting from its inception/source document and showing all the steps it went through until its final disposition. The trail of source documents and other records (the audit trail) makes it easier to investigate errors or questions by customers, vendors, employees, and others. For example, when a customer places an order by phone, by mail, or online, the sales order becomes the source document. If the customer does not receive the product ordered, the company can locate the original order, see if a picking ticket was generated (a picking ticket tells warehouse employees what inventory items the customer ordered, that now need to be picked off the shelf), locate the shipping documents, which provide evidence that the product was given to the shipper, and check for customer signature confirming receipt of goods. The trail of documents and entries in journals and ledgers and their electronic equivalent generated by this transaction provides evidence of all the steps that took place along the way. This makes it easy for anyone to verify or investigate, and perhaps find the weak links, where the process may have broken down. It allows the company to identify the reason why the customer never received the goods ordered. Maybe the order was never shipped because the company was out of stock of this specific product, maybe it was shipped and left at the customer's doorstep with no signature requested, or maybe the order was shipped to the wrong customer or to an incorrect address. An audit trail will help company personnel investigate any of these common issues. It should also help them identify weaknesses in their processes and precipitate improvements.

Businesses need a way to input data from the source document such as a sales invoice or purchase order. This was previously done with pen and paper and is currently done by keying it in on a computer keyboard; scanning, with a scanner such as one that reads MICR (magnetic ink character recognition) symbols (found on bank checks) or POS system scanners at cash registers that scan product bar codes/UPC symbols; or receiving it by e-transmission (or electronic funds transfer [EFT]). Input often involves the use of hardware such as scanners, keypads, keyboards, touch screens, or fingerprint readers called biometric devices. Once data has been input, it must be processed in order to be useful.

Processing Data

Companies need the accounting system to process the data that has been entered and transform it into useful information. In manual accounting systems, employees process all transaction data by journalizing, posting, and creating financial reports using paper. However, as technology has advanced, it became easier to keep records by using computers with software programs specifically developed for accounting transactions. Computers are good at repetition and calculations, both of which are involved in accounting, and computers can perform these calculations and analyses more quickly, and with fewer errors, thus making them a very effective tool for accounting from both an input and an output standpoint.

LINK TO LEARNING

See a list of popular bookkeeping software (https://openstax.org/l/50AcctSW) packages. With this information, potential options for sample accounting software options can be evaluated.

Output: Presenting Information

An AIS should provide a way to present system output (printed page, screen image, e-transmission). Any accounting software application such as that used by large companies (an ERP system) or one used by smaller businesses (QuickBooks) can easily print financial statements and other documents as well as display them on the screen.

Some financial information must be provided to other sources such as banks or government agencies, and though in past decades everything was presented and submitted on paper, today, most of this information is submitted electronically, and AISs help facilitate having the information in the necessary electronic format. Many banks require electronic data, and the Internal Revenue System (IRS) accepts your information as a digital transmission instead of a paper form. In 2017, 92 percent of all taxpayers who filed their own taxes did so electronically.[2] Most corporations choose to file their taxes electronically, and those with assets over $10 million are required to file electronically with the IRS.[3] Since May 5, 1996, all publicly traded companies are required to submit their filings, such as financial statements and stock offerings, to the SEC electronically.[4] The SEC places all the data into an electronic database known as the Electronic Data Gathering, Analysis, and Retrieval System (EDGAR). This database allows anyone to search the database for financial and other information about any publicly traded company. Thus, AISs facilitate not only internal access to financial information, but the sharing of that information externally as needed or required. Just as the EDGAR system used by the SEC stores data for retrieval, an AIS must provide a way to store and retrieve data.

2 Income Tax Return Statistics. eFile. May 2018. https://www.efile.com/efile-tax-return-direct-deposit-statistics/
3 Income Tax Return Statistics. eFile. May 2018. https://www.efile.com/efile-tax-return-direct-deposit-statistics/
4 There is a hardship exemption for companies that cannot file their documents electronically. See U.S. Securities and Exchange Commission. Important Information about EDGAR. February 16, 2010. https://www.sec.gov/edgar/aboutedgar.htm

Storing Data

Data can be stored by an AIS in paper, digital, or cloud formats. Before computers were widely used, financial data was stored on paper, like the journal and ledger shown in Figure 7.5.

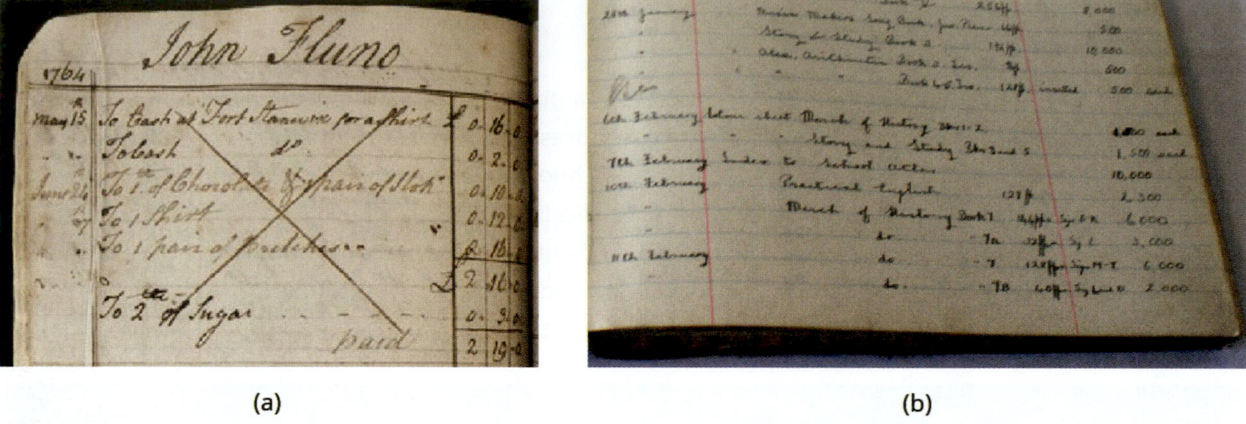

Figure 7.5 Data Storage. (a) General journal and (b) general ledger. (credit a: modification of "Entry in Barent Roseboom's ledger detailing transactions with John Fluno in 1764" by National Park Service, Public Domain; credit b: modification of "Print Order Book, Holmes McDougall" by Edinburgh City of Print/Flickr, CC BY 2.0)

As technology has evolved, so have storage systems—from floppy disks to CDs, thumb drives, and the cloud. The hard drive on your computer is a data storage device, as is an external hard drive you can purchase. Data that is stored must have the ability to be retrieved when needed. As you can see from Figure 7.6, stored data comes from and/or flows through the three main functions of an AIS (input, processes, and output) with the end result being the use of the data in forms needed for decision-making, such as financial statements. Access to the ability to input data, manage processes, or retrieve data requires adequate controls to prevent fraud or unauthorized access and requires the implementation of data security measures. Figure 7.6 illustrates the key functions performed by an AIS.

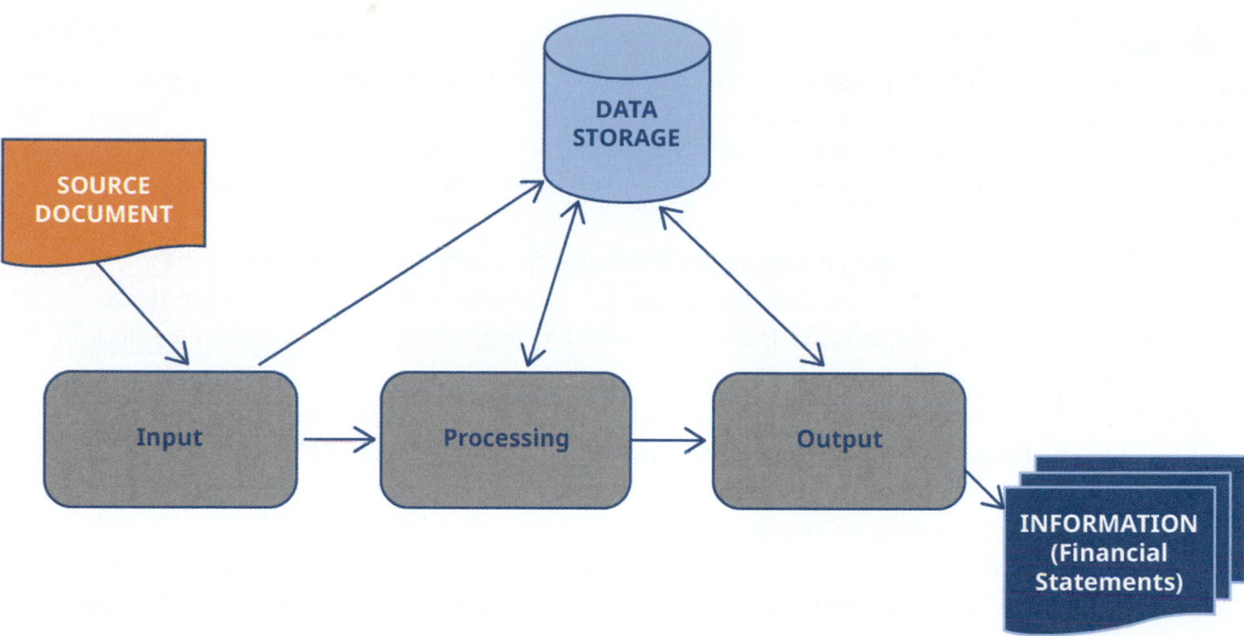

Figure 7.6 Accounting Information System. The four key functions performed by an accounting information system. (attribution: Copyright Rice University, OpenStax, under CC BY-NC-SA 4.0 license)

YOUR TURN

The Steps in an Accounting Information System

The three steps of an accounting information system are input, processing, and output. Data is the raw ingredient used in these processes. Some of the data may be obtained from a source document, and other data is obtained from the database where it had previously been stored. When the data has been processed, the final result is usually information. Information is more useful than data. Take, for example, another process that a bakery might use to bake chocolate chip cookies. While computers might not necessarily need to be involved, we begin the process by assembling a bunch of raw ingredients such as eggs, sugar, flour, chocolate chips, and oil, in a large bowl. Taking a spoonful of what is in the bowl at the time is not very pleasing to the taste buds or "useful" to someone craving a chocolate chip cookie. We process the raw ingredients by mixing them well and turning them into dough, cutting them into shapes, baking them, and glazing them. Similarly, raw data about a single sale contained on the sales invoice, such as customer name, date of sale, and amount of sale, is individually not very useful to a financial statement user such as an investor. However, by processing the data related to the sale, making sure it is correct by checking that the number of items ordered were in stock and actually shipped, aggregating it with other sales for the period, and producing an income statement containing the sales for the period is substantially more useful than the individual pieces of data relating to a single sale.

Can you give an example of each of the three steps, as well as a source document that might be used in the input stage and stored data that might be used in the input and processing stages, first for a grocery store, and then a medical office?

Solution

Grocery store:

- Source Document: This would include a check to be deposited; totals from each cash register, including total cash; an invoice for produce; an application for employment by a potential new employee; time card information; a W-4 form (employment information); and so on.
- Input: This includes entering the data from the source document on the computer keyboard, electronically scanning the bar code of each product purchased at the grocery store (at checkout counter and to receive goods from vendor off the truck), maybe fingerprinting at the time clock, or keying in a price on the register.
- Processing: A cash register processes (accumulates and totals) different categories of items (coupons, checks, and charges) by the user; inventory can be tracked by RFID (radio-frequency identification); and software programs can process information gathered by individual cash registers as well as employee information.
- Output: Data that has been processed can be viewed on a computer screen, printed as a hard copy (paper output), or sent as electronic output from the cash register to the computer (can be done wirelessly or with a cable).
- Storage: Data can be stored in the company database on its computer hard drive or as cloud storage. Hopefully the store is also paying for safe backup storage offsite (in case of fire at the store or hackers attempting to obtain information), generally accessed through the internet and stored in "the cloud." Otherwise, storage can be on paper printouts, the computer hard drive, disks, or external drives. The data that is stored may be retrieved and used at the input, processing, and output stages.

Doctor's office:

- Source Document: This includes a check to be deposited from the patient; the patient's insurance information on file; a doctor's record of the diagnosis and procedures performed on the patient, to be submitted to the insurance company; and an invoice for medical supplies.
- Input: Data from the source document, for example, containing the diagnosis and a treatment plan, would be entered on the computer keyboard.
- Processing: The system might retrieve the treatment codes corresponding to every procedure the doctor performed, so it contains the appropriate information for the insurance company.
- Output: The treatment form is printed and then mailed to the insurance company for payment.
- Storage: The diagnosis and treatment plan are stored on the computer database for retrieval on the next visit for this patient. The form to be sent to the insurance company is also stored electronically so there can be follow-up until the payment from the insurance company is received. Also note that during processing, the system had to retrieve the treatment codes from a file of all of the codes that was stored in the database.

YOUR TURN

The Accounting Information System (AIS)

What are some of the types of information the accounting information system should be able to provide to the owners, managers, and employees of business, at the end of the day, or week, or month, which they in turn may need to provide to other external users?

Solution

- Information for internal purposes will include total sales and how much it cost to generate the sales. Also considered is how much inventory is on hand so a decision can be made as to whether or not to order more inventory.
- The company will need to record all of the economic events of the business in order to find total sales, cost of goods sold, expenses, and net income, as well as the number of hours employees worked, the employee's social security number, and how much the company promised to pay the employee per hour.
- Information for external users, such as the IRS or state and local government agencies, would include income tax returns and sales and payroll tax forms. The business owners and managers will need all sales and expenses, sales tax collected, and employees' earnings.
- In other words, the company needs an AIS.

While an AIS has the primary functions of input, processing, output, and storage, each company or system will decide on the exact steps and processes under each of these broad functions. We know that data is used to create the types of information needed by users to make decisions. One way in which a retail organization may obtain, input, process, and store data related to a sales transaction is through a point-of-sale system (POS). When a customer is ready to buy an item, the cashier scans the product being purchased, the price is retrieved from the price file, the sale is recorded, and inventory is updated. Most POS systems include a scanner, a computer screen, or a tablet with a touch screen. Customer payments are stored in the cash drawer. For noncash sales, credit card readers allow customers to insert, swipe, or tap their cards to pay (which also helps prevent keyboard input errors and keeps the information safer).

ETHICAL CONSIDERATIONS

Ethical Standards in Retail Stores

Professional sales employees operate the POS systems. There is an ethical code for sales professionals created by the Association of Professional Sales to help sales professionals maintain good judgment.[5] The organization sets forth standards such as the following:

- Maintain the highest standards of integrity in all business relationships.
- Provide our customers with a buying experience in which we "do the right thing and thereby help get the right results."
- Promote and protect good sales practices.

- Always act in line with my organization's codes and within the law.

Accountants can assist sales professionals in creating an ethical environment. The ethical environment will permit the users of accounting data to make solid business decisions and to better operate a company.

However, the POS is just part of the AIS. As each sale is entered into the register, other data is collected, recorded, and processed by the AIS and becomes information. Data about each sale is recorded in the information system: what was sold, how much it cost, the sales price, and any sales tax. It also records the time of day, the clerk, and anything else the company programmed the cash register to record. When all the sales for the day are totaled, it provides information in the form of organized and processed data with meaning to the company. A business might want to see which hour of the day resulted in the most sales, or to know which product was the best seller. An AIS can provide this information.

A system is created when processes work together to generate information for the business. The sales process accesses customers, accounts receivable, and inventory data and updates the appropriate files. The purchases process also accesses inventory and accounts payable and updates them, because most companies buy goods on credit. Since no two companies operate exactly the same way, you would expect each company to have a slightly different AIS. Some businesses do not have a cash register, but they will still have a Sales account. Some companies only have cash sales, so they would not have an Accounts Receivable account. Regardless of the type of business—retail, manufacturing, or service—an AIS is an important component of the business as it is this system that provides the information needed by internal and external decision-makers.

CONCEPTS IN PRACTICE

Is This an Accounting Information System?

Do you think your average food truck proprietor has an accounting information system?

Figure 7.7 Food Truck. (credit: modification of "Food Trucks" by Daniel Lobo/Flickr, Public Domain)

5 Association of Professional Sales. "APS Sales Code of Conduct." n.d. https://www.associationofprofessionalsales.com/professional-development/sales-code-conduct-aps-ethical-professional/aps-sales-code-conduct/

Food trucks will have some type of accounting information system whether paper based or electronic. One common method of creating an accounting information system in this type of business environment is to use an app, such as Square Point of Sale (Square Inc.). The Square Point of Sale (POS) software system keeps track of the sales. With this type of system, a food truck will likely have a Square Stand (a tablet-based POS), a cash drawer, and printers. The information input into the Square Stand is stored on Square servers using the cloud (online storage space offered by different companies and products) and is accessible by the company via an online dashboard. This system allows the handling of both cash sales and credit card sales. These components—the Square Point of Sale software, the Square Stand, cash drawer, and the printers—make up part of the accounting information system for a food truck.

IFRS CONNECTION

Accounting Information Systems in an International Business Environment

All companies, regardless of whether they are domestic or international, will have an accounting information system with the features described in this chapter. It would be easy to assume that the accounting information systems created by public companies in the United States are created based on US generally accepted accounting principles (GAAP). This implies that these companies design their processes and controls so that in addition to meeting the reporting and monitoring goals of the company, the system also collects, measures, and reports the information that is required under US GAAP. But is this true? What about companies that have subsidiaries or a portion of their operations in another country? Do purely international companies use accounting information systems similar to their US counterparts?

As previously indicated, all companies will create some sort of accounting information system. General Electric (GE), as a US-based manufacturer, uses an accounting information system that allows it to record, collect, produce, and analyze the operations of its various businesses. Since GE is a US corporation, headquartered in Boston, Massachusetts, its accounting information system is designed around the rules set out by US GAAP. Fiat Chrysler Automobiles (FCA) is headquartered in the United Kingdom, and it designs its accounting information system to produce financials under International Financial Reporting Standards (IFRS). On the surface, it looks as though each company will create an information system based on the accounting rules in its own home country. However, it is not quite that simple. Today, companies take advantage of the ability to borrow money across borders. The lenders often require the financial statements of the borrower to be presented using the accounting rules required by the lender's country. For example, if GE wanted to borrow money from the Royal Bank of Scotland, it would likely have to present its financial statements based on IFRS rules. Similarly, if FCA wanted to borrow from Citibank, it would need its financial statements in US GAAP form.

Borrowing is not the only reason a company may need to present financial statements based on a different set of accounting principles. As of 2017, GE had over 130 subsidiaries, and these businesses were located across 130 countries. A subsidiary is a business over which the parent company has decision-making control, usually indicated by an ownership interest of more than 50 percent. Many of these GE subsidiaries established their accounting information systems based on the accepted accounting principles in the countries in which they were located, as required in order to be in compliance with local regulations such as for local taxes. Thus, GE must convert the financial information obtained from the subsidiary's accounting information system, often based on IFRS, to US GAAP in order to consolidate the transactions and operations of all of the subsidiaries with those of the parent company to create one set of financial statements.

We have basically become a two GAAP world—IFRS and US GAAP—and many companies will find it necessary to have accounting information systems that can handle both sets of rules due to the global nature of business and the global nature of raising money through borrowing and issuing stock. This may seem crazy, to have two systems, but a little over ten years ago there were more than seventy different GAAP. Today, since many countries now use IFRS, the quality and consistency of financial reporting have improved. As a result, the cost associated with having accounting information systems that can combine many different sets of accounting rules has decreased.

7.2 Describe and Explain the Purpose of Special Journals and Their Importance to Stakeholders

The larger the business, the greater the likelihood that that business will have a large volume of transactions that need to be recorded in and processed by the company's accounting information system. You've learned that each transaction is recorded in the general journal, which is a chronological listing of transactions. In other words, transactions are recorded into the general journal as they occur. While this is correct accounting methodology, it also can create a cumbersome general journal with which to work and may make finding specific pieces of information very challenging. For example, assume customer John Smith charged an item for $100 on June 1. In the general journal, the company would record the following.

JOURNAL			
Date	**Account**	**Debit**	**Credit**
Jun. 1	Accounts Receivable: John Smith	100	
	Sales		100
	To record sale on account to customer		

This journal entry would be followed by a journal entry for every other transaction the company had for the remainder of the period. Suppose, on June 27, Mr. Smith asked, "How much do I owe?" To answer this question, the company would need to review all of the pages of the general journal for nearly an entire month to find all of the sales transactions relating to Mr. Smith. And if Mr. Smith said, "I thought I paid part of that two weeks ago," the company would have to go through the general journal to find all payment entries for Mr. Smith. Imagine if there were 1,000 similar credit sales transactions for the month, each one would be written in the general journal in a similar fashion, and all other transactions, such as the paying of bills, or the buying of inventory, would also be recorded, in chronological order, in the general journal. Thus, recording all transactions to the general journal makes it difficult to find the particular tidbits of information that are needed for one of our customers, Mr. Smith. The use of special journal and subsidiary ledgers can make the accounting information system more effective and allow for certain types of information to be obtained more easily.

YOUR TURN

Using General Ledger (Control) Accounts

Here is the information from the accounts payable subsidiary ledger:

ACCOUNTS PAYABLE SUBSIDIARY LEDGER					
Account: E. Presley Ltd		**AP No. 34**			
					Balance
Date	**Item**	**Ref.**	**Debit**	**Credit**	**Credit**
Dec. 1	Beginning Balance				3,512
Dec. 31	Cash Disbursements	144	2,150		1,362

Account: M. Jackson Inc.		**AP No. 71**			
					Balance
Date	**Item**	**Ref.**	**Debit**	**Credit**	**Credit**
Dec. 1	Beginning Balance				1,879
Dec. 31	Purchases Journal			2,589	4,468

Account: Madonna Inc.		**AP No. 171**			
					Balance
Date	**Item**	**Ref.**	**Debit**	**Credit**	**Credit**
Dec. 1	Beginning Balance				3,467
Dec. 31	Purchases Journal			3,450	6,917
Dec. 31	Purchases Journal			1,500	8,417
Dec. 31	General Journal: Return	119	250		8,167

What should the total be in the Accounts Payable Control Total?

Here is the information from the accounts receivable subsidiary ledger.

ACCOUNTS RECEIVABLE SUBSIDIARY LEDGER					
Account: M. Jordan Inc.		No. 102045			
					Balance
Date	Item	Ref.	Debit	Credit	Debit
Dec. 1	Beginning Balance				2,500
Dec. 4	Sales Journal	27	2,750		5,250
Dec. 10	Cash Receipts	24		3,000	2,250

Account: R. Federer Ltd		No. 460708			
					Balance
Date	Item	Ref.	Debit	Credit	Debit
Dec. 1	Beginning Balance				2,670
Dec. 1	Cash Receipts	24		2,670	0

Account: T. Woods Inc.		No. 564300			
					Balance
Date	Item	Ref.	Debit	Credit	Debit
Dec. 1	Beginning Balance				2,140
Dec. 17	Sales Journal	27	600		2,740
Dec. 15	Cash Receipts	24		1,240	1,500

Account: S. Williams Inc.		No. 42005			
					Balance
Date	Item	Ref.	Debit	Credit	Debit
Dec. 1	Beginning Balance				7,160
Dec. 3	Sales Journal	27	1,800		8,960
Dec. 8	General Journal	119		800	8,160

What should the total be in the Accounts Receivable Control Total?

Solution

Accounts Payable Control Total is: 1,362 + 4,468 + 8,167 = 13,997

Accounts Receivable Control Total is: 2,250 + 0 + 1,500 + 8,160 = 11,910

Special Journals

Instead of having just one general journal, companies group transactions of the same kind together and record them in **special journals** rather than in the general journal. This makes it easier and more efficient to find a specific type of transaction and speeds up the process of posting these transactions. In each special journal, all transactions are totaled at the end of the month, and these totals are posted to the general ledger. In addition, instead of one person entering all of the transactions in all of the journals, companies often assign a given special journal's entries to one person. The relationship between the special journals, the general journal, and the general ledger can be seen in Figure 7.8.

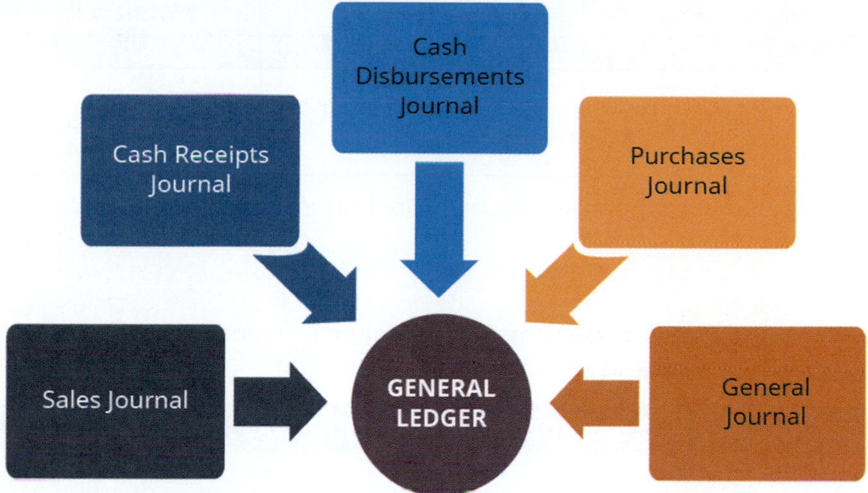

Figure 7.8 Special and General. Transaction summaries form the special journals, and all transactions in the general journal are posted to the general ledger. (attribution: Copyright Rice University, OpenStax, under CC BY-NC-SA 4.0 license)

Most companies have four special journals, but there can be more depending on the business needs. The four main special journals are the **sales journal**, **purchases journal**, **cash disbursements journal**, and **cash receipts journal**. These special journals were designed because some journal entries occur repeatedly. For example, selling goods for cash is always a debit to Cash and a credit to Sales recorded in the cash receipts journal. Likewise, we would record a sale of goods on credit in the sales journal, as a debit to accounts receivable and a credit to sales. Companies using a perpetual inventory system also record a second entry for a sale with a debit to cost of goods sold and a credit to inventory. You can see sample entries in Figure 7.9.

SALES JOURNAL					Page 10
Date	**Account**	**Invoice No.**	**Ref.**	**DR Accts. Receivable CR Sales**	**DR COGS CR Merchandise Inventory**
2019					
Feb. 21	Jack Customer	715		$ 5,200	$3,800
Feb. 23	Susan Carol	716		$10,600	$8,400

Figure 7.9 Sales Journal. (attribution: Copyright Rice University, OpenStax, under CC BY-NC-SA 4.0 license)

Note there is a column to enter the date the transaction took place; a column to indicate the customer to whom the transaction pertains; an invoice number that should match the number on the invoice given (in paper or electronically) to the customer; a reference box that indicates the transaction has been posted to the customer's account and can include something as simple as a check mark or a code that links the transaction to other journals and ledgers; and the last two columns that indicate the accounts and amounts debited and credited.

Purchases of inventory on credit would be recorded in the purchases journal (Figure 7.10) with a debit to Merchandise Inventory and a credit to Accounts Payable.

PURCHASES JOURNAL					Page 36
Date	Account	Invoice No.	Ref.	Merchandise Inventory DR	Accounts Payable CR
2019					
Feb. 14	Irving's Inventory	1542		$35,000	$35,000
Feb. 27	Greta's Goods	612		$14,700	$14,700

Figure 7.10 Purchases Journal. (attribution: Copyright Rice University, OpenStax, under CC BY-NC-SA 4.0 license)

Paying bills is recorded in the cash disbursements journal (Figure 7.11) and is always a debit to Accounts Payable (or another payable or expense) and a credit to Cash.

CASH DISBURSEMENTS JOURNAL					Page 100
Date	Account	Invoice No.	Ref.	Accounts Payable (or other account) DR	Cash CR
2019					
Feb. 7	Mumford, Inc.	1,100		$15,000	$15,000
Feb. 18	Ballyho, Co.	716		$21,200	$21,200

Figure 7.11 Cash Disbursements Journal. (attribution: Copyright Rice University, OpenStax, under CC BY-NC-SA 4.0 license)

The receipt of cash from the sale of goods, as payment on accounts receivable or from other transactions, is recorded in a cash receipts journal (Figure 7.12) with a debit to cash and a credit to the source of the cash, whether that is from sales revenue, payment on an account receivable, or some other account.

CASH RECEIPTS JOURNAL					
Date	Account	Invoice No.	Ref.	Cash DR	Accounts Receivable, Sales, or other accounts CR
2019					
Feb. 8	Connie Customer	450		$ 300	$ 300
Feb. 27	Billy May	602		$1,000	$1,000

Figure 7.12 Cash Receipts Journal. (attribution: Copyright Rice University, OpenStax, under CC BY-NC-SA 4.0 license)

Table 7.1 summarizes the typical transactions in the special journals previously illustrated.

Types and Purposes of Special Journals

Journal Name	Journal Purpose	Account(s) Debited	Account(s) Credited
Sales Journal	Sales on credit	Accounts Receivable, Cost of Goods Sold	Sales, Inventory
Purchases Journal	Purchases on credit	Inventory	Accounts Payable
Cash Disbursements Journal	Paying cash	*Could be:* Accounts Payable, or other accounts	Cash
Cash Receipts Journal	Receiving cash	Cash	*Could be:* Sales, Accounts Receivable, or other accounts
General Journal	Any transaction not covered previously; adjusting and closing entries	*Could be:* Depreciation Expense	*Could be:* Accumulated Depreciation

Table 7.1

How will you remember all of this? Remember, "Cash Is King," so we consider cash transactions first. If you receive cash, regardless of the source of the transaction, and even if it is only a part of the transaction, it goes in the cash receipts journal. For example, if the company made a sale for $1,000 and the customer gave $300 in cash and promised to pay the remaining balance in the future, the entire transaction would go into the cash receipts journal, because some cash was received, even if it was only part of a transaction. You could not split this journal entry between two journals, because each transaction's debits must equal the credits or else your journal totals will not balance at the end of the month. You might consider splitting this transaction into two separate transactions and considering it a cash sale for $300 and a sale on account for $700, but that would also be inappropriate. Although the balances in the general ledger accounts would technically be correct if you did that, this is not the right approach. Good internal control dictates that this is a single transaction, associated with one invoice number on a given date, and should be recorded in its entirety in a single journal, which in this case is the cash receipts journal. If any cash is received, even if it is only a part of the transaction, the entire transaction is entered in the cash receipts journal. For this example, the transaction entered in the cash receipts journal would have a debit to cash for $300, a debit to Accounts Receivable for $700, and a credit to Sales for $1,000.

If you pay cash (usually by writing a check), for any reason, even if it is only a part of the transaction, the entire transaction is recorded in the cash disbursements journal. For example, if the company purchased a building for $500,000 and gave a check for $100,000 as a down payment, the entire transaction would be recorded in the cash disbursements journal as a credit to cash for $100,000, a credit to mortgage payable for $400,000, and a debit to buildings for $500,000.

If the transaction does not involve cash, it will be recorded in one of the other special journals. If it is a credit sale (also known as a sale on account), it is recorded in the sales journal. If it is a credit purchase (also known as a purchase on account), it is recorded in the purchases journal. If it is none of the above, it is recorded in the general journal.

CONTINUING APPLICATION AT WORK

Accounting Information Systems

Let's consider what Gearhead Outfitters' accounting information system might look like. What information will company management find important? Likewise, what information might external users of Gearhead's financial reports need? Do regulatory requirements dictate what Gearhead needs to track in its accounting system?

Gearhead will want to know its financial position, results of operations, and cash flows. Such data will help management make decisions about the company. Likewise, external users want this data (balance sheet, income statement, and statement of cash flows) to make decisions such as whether or not to extend credit to Gearhead.

To keep accurate records, company operations must be considered. For example, inventory is purchased, sales are made, customers are billed, cash is collected, employees work and need to be paid, and other expenses are incurred. All of these operations involve different recording processes. Inventory will require a purchases journal. Sales will require a sales journal, cash receipts journal, and accounts receivable subsidiary ledger (discussed later) journal. Payroll and other disbursements will require their own journals to accurately track transactions.

Such journals allow a company to record accounting information and generate financial statements. The data also provides management with the information needed to make sound business decisions. For example, subsidiary ledgers, such as the accounts receivable ledger, provide data about the aging and collectability of receivables. Thus, the proper design, implementation, and maintenance of the accounting information system are vital to a company's sustainability.

What other questions can be answered through the analysis of information gathered by the accounting information system? Think in terms of the timing of inventory orders and cash flow needs. Is there nonfinancial information to extract from the accounting system? An accounting information system should provide the information needed for a business to meet its goals.

Subsidiary Ledgers

In addition to the four special journals, there are two special ledgers, the accounts receivable subsidiary ledger and the accounts payable subsidiary ledger. The **accounts receivable subsidiary ledger** gives details about each person who owes the company money, as shown in Figure 7.13. Each colored block represents an individual's account and shows only the amount that person owes the company. Notice that the subsidiary ledger provides the date of the transaction and a reference column to link the transaction to the same information posted in one of the special journals (or general journal if special journals are not used)—this reference is usually a code that references the special journal such as SJ for the sales special journal, as well as the amounts owed in the debit column and the payments made in the credit column. The amounts owed by all of the individuals, as indicated in the subsidiary ledger, are added together to form the **accounts receivable**

control total, and this should equal the Accounts Receivable balance reported in the general ledger as shown in Figure 7.14. Key points about the accounts receivable subsidiary ledger are:

- Accounts Receivable in the general ledger is the total of all of the individual account totals that are listed in the accounts receivable subsidiary ledger.
- All of the amounts owed to the company in the accounts receivable subsidiary ledger must equal the amounts in the accounts receivable general ledger account.

SUBSIDIARY LEDGER					SUBSIDIARY LEDGER					SUBSIDIARY LEDGER				
Smith					Jones					Lee				
Date	Ref.	DR	CR	Balance	Date	Ref.	DR	CR	Balance	Date	Ref.	DR	CR	Balance
Feb. 1		$100		$100	Feb. 2		$200	$100	$200	Feb. 1		$300		$300
Feb. 9		$300		$400	Feb. 8		$300	$300	$500	Feb. 4			$200	$100

Figure 7.13 Accounts Receivable Subsidiary Ledger. (attribution: Copyright Rice University, OpenStax, under CC BY-NC-SA 4.0 license)

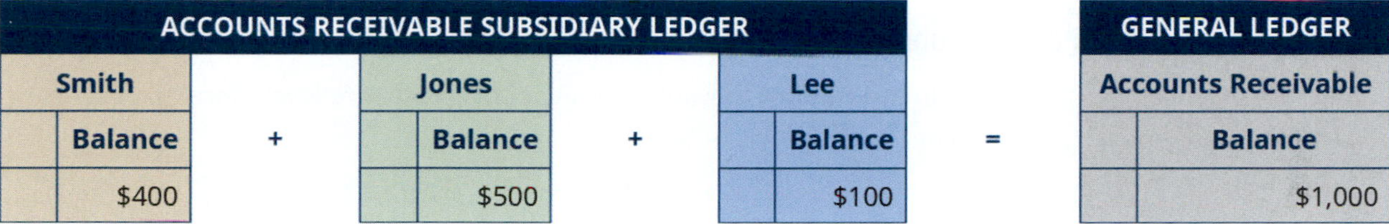

Figure 7.14 Accounts Receivable. (attribution: Copyright Rice University, OpenStax, under CC BY-NC-SA 4.0 license)

ETHICAL CONSIDERATIONS

Subsidiary Ledger Fraud[6]

Subsidiary ledgers have to balance and agree with the general ledger. Accountants using QuickBooks and other accounting systems may not have to perform this step, because in these systems the subsidiary ledger updates the general ledger automatically. However, a dishonest person might manipulate accounting records by recording a smaller amount of cash receipts in the control account than is recorded on the subsidiary ledger cards. The ethical accountant must be vigilant to ensure that the ledgers remain balanced and that proper internal controls are in place to ensure the soundness of the accounting system.

The **accounts payable subsidiary ledger** holds the details about all of the amounts a company owes to people and/or companies. In the accounts payable subsidiary ledger, each vendor (the person or company from whom you purchased inventory or other items) has an account that shows the details of all transactions. Similar to the accounts receivable subsidiary ledger, the purchases subsidiary journal indicates the date on which a transaction took place; a reference column used in the same manner as previously described for

6 Joseph R. Dervaes. "Accounts Receivable Fraud, Part Five: Other Accounting Manipulations." *Fraud Magazine*. July/August, 2004. http://www.fraud-magazine.com/article.aspx?id=4294967822

accounts receivable subsidiary ledgers; and finally, the subsidiary ledger shows the amount charged or the amount paid. Following are the transactions for ABC Inc. and XYZ Inc. The final balance indicated on each subsidiary purchases journal shows the amount the company owes ABC and XYZ.

SUBSIDIARY LEDGER						SUBSIDIARY LEDGER					
ABC Inc.						XYZ Inc.					
Date	**Ref.**	**Item**	**DR**	**CR**	**Balance**	**Date**	**Ref.**	**Item**	**DR**	**CR**	**Balance**
Jan. 1		Purchase		$200	$200	Jan. 3		Purchase		$100	$100
Jan. 15		Payment	$75		125	Jan. 15		Payment	$20		80
Jan. 20		Purchase		$ 50	$175	Jan. 20		Purchase		$ 50	$130

If the two amounts are added together, the company owes $305 in total to the two companies. The $305 is the amount that will show in the Accounts Payable general ledger account.

YOUR TURN

Using the Accounts Payable Subsidiary Ledger

Find the balance in each account in the accounts payable subsidiary ledger that follows. Note that each vendor account has a unique account number or AP No.

ACCOUNTS PAYABLE SUBSIDIARY LEDGER					
Account: Elizabeth I Inc.		**AP No. 734**			
					Balance
Date	**Item**	**Ref.**	**Debit**	**Credit**	**Credit**
2019					
Dec. 1	Beginning Balance				3,134
Dec. 15	Cash Disbursements	124	2,150		?
Dec. 16	Purchases Journal	76		3,112	?
Dec. 29	Cash Disbursements	125	1,250		?

Account: F. Nightingale Inc.		**AP No. 731**			
					Balance
Date	**Item**	**Ref.**	**Debit**	**Credit**	**Credit**
Dec. 1	Beginning Balance				3,446
Dec. 9	Purchases Journal	76		2,589	?
Dec. 15	Purchases Journal	77		1,234	?

Account: L.M. Alcott Inc.		**AP No. 671**			
					Balance
Date	**Item**	**Ref.**	**Debit**	**Credit**	**Credit**
Dec. 1	Beginning Balance				3,467
Dec. 15	Purchases Journal	77		3,450	?
Dec. 28	Purchases Journal	77		1,500	?
Dec. 31	General Journal: Return	127	250		?

Solution

ACCOUNTS PAYABLE SUBSIDIARY LEDGER					
Account: Elizabeth I Inc.		AP No. 734			
Date	Item	Ref.	Debit	Credit	Balance Credit
2019					
Dec. 1	Beginning Balance				3,134
Dec. 15	Cash Disbursements	124	2,150		984
Dec. 16	Purchases Journal	76		3,112	4,096
Dec. 29	Cash Disbursements	125	1,250		2,846

Account: F. Nightingale Inc.		AP No. 731			
Date	Item	Ref.	Debit	Credit	Balance Credit
Dec. 1	Beginning Balance				3,446
Dec. 9	Purchases Journal	76		2,589	6,035
Dec. 15	Purchases Journal	77		1,234	7,269

Account: L.M. Alcott Inc.		AP No. 671			
Date	Item	Ref.	Debit	Credit	Balance Credit
Dec. 1	Beginning Balance				3,467
Dec. 15	Purchases Journal	77		3,450	6,917
Dec. 28	Purchases Journal	77		1,500	8,417
Dec. 31	General Journal: Return	127	250		8,167

7.3 Analyze and Journalize Transactions Using Special Journals

Accounting information systems were paper based until the introduction of the computer, so special journals were widely used. When accountants used a paper system, they had to write the same number in multiple places and thus could make a mistake. Now that most businesses use digital technology, the step of posting to journals is performed by the accounting software. The transactions themselves end up on transaction files rather than in paper journals, but companies still print or make available on the screen something that closely resembles the journals. Years ago, all accounting record keeping was manual. If a company had many transactions, that meant many journal entries to be recorded in the general journal. People soon realized that certain types of transactions occurred more frequently than any other types of transaction, so to save time, they designed a special journal for each type that occurs frequently (e.g., credit sales, credit purchases, receipts of cash, and disbursements of cash). We would enter these four types of transactions into their own journals, respectively, rather than in the general journal. Thus, in addition to the general journal, we also have the sales journal, cash receipts journal, purchases journal, and cash disbursements journals.

The main difference between special journals using the perpetual inventory method and the periodic inventory method is that the sales journal in the perpetual method, as you have seen in the prior examples in the chapter, will have a column to record a debit to Cost of Goods Sold and a credit to Inventory. In the purchases journal, using the perpetual method will require we debit Inventory instead of Purchases. Another difference is that the perpetual method will include freight charges in the Inventory account, while the periodic method will have a special Freight-in account that will be added when Cost of Goods Sold will be computed. For a refresher on perpetual versus periodic and related accounts such as freight-in, please refer to Merchandising Transactions.

THINK IT THROUGH

Which Journal?

If you received a check from Mr. Jones for $500 for work you performed last week, which journal would you use to record receipt of the amount they owed you? What would be recorded?

The Sales Journal

The sales journal is used to record sales on account (meaning sales on credit or credit sale). Selling on credit always requires a debit to Accounts Receivable and a credit to Sales. Because every credit sales transaction is recorded in the same way, recording all of those transactions in one place simplifies the accounting process. Figure 7.15 shows an example of a sales journal. Note there is a single column for both the debit to Accounts Receivable and the credit to Sales, although we need to post to both Accounts Receivable and Sales at the end of each month. There is also a single column for the debit to Cost of Goods Sold and the credit to Merchandise Inventory, though again, we need to post to both of those. In addition, for companies using the perpetual inventory method, there is another column representing a debit to Cost of Goods Sold and a credit to Merchandise Inventory, since two entries are made to record a sale on account under the perpetual inventory method.

SALES JOURNAL							Page 26
Date	Account	Address	Acct. No.	Terms	Sales Invoice No.	Ref.	DR A/R CR Sales
2019							
Jan. 3	Baker Co.	PO Box 12	1231	n/30	45321		850
Jan. 3	Alpha Co.	Rt 2	2134	2/10, n/30	45322		625
Jan. 5	Tau Inc.	29 Main St.	1257	n/30	45323		700
Jan. 6	Baker Co.	PO Box 12	1231	n/30	45324		600

Figure 7.15

The information in the sales journal was taken from a copy of the sales invoice, which is the source document representing the sale. The sales invoice number is entered so the bookkeeper could look up the sales invoice and assist the customer. One benefit of using special journals is that one person can work with this journal while someone else works with a different special journal.

At the end of the month, the bookkeeper, or computer program, would total the A/R Dr and Sales Cr column and post the amount to the Accounts Receivable control account in the general ledger and the Sales account in the general ledger. The Accounts Receivable control account in the general ledger is the total of all of the amounts customers owed the company. Also at the end of the month, the total debit in the cost of goods sold column and the total credit to the merchandise inventory column would be posted to their respective general ledger accounts.

The company could have made these entries in the general journal instead of the special journal, but if it had, this would have likely caused the sales transactions to be separated from each other and spread throughout the journal, making it harder to find and keep track of them. When a sales journal is used, if the company is one where sales tax is collected from the customer, then the journal entry would be a debit to Accounts Receivable and a credit to Sales and Sales Tax Payable, and this would require an additional column in the sales journal to record the sales tax. For example, a $100 sale with $10 additional sales tax collected would be recorded as a debit to Accounts Receivable for $110, a credit to Sales for $100 and a credit to Sales Tax Payable for $10.

The use of a reference code in any of the special journals is very important. Remember, after a sale is recorded in the sales journal, it is posted to the accounts receivable subsidiary ledger, and the use of a reference code helps link the transactions between the journals and ledgers. Recall that the accounts receivable subsidiary ledger is a record of each customer's account. It looked like Figure 7.16 for Baker Co.

ACCOUNTS RECEIVABLE SUBSIDIARY LEDGER					
	Account: Baker Co.				Account No. 1231
Date	**Item**	**Ref.**	**Debit**	**Credit**	**Balance**
2019	Beginning Balance				0
Jan. 3	45321	SJ 26	850		850
Jan. 6	45324	SJ 26	600		1,450

Figure 7.16 Accounts Receivable Subsidiary Ledger. (attribution: Copyright Rice University, OpenStax, under CC BY-NC-SA 4.0 license)

Using the reference information, if anyone had a question about this entry, he or she would go to the sales journal, page 26, transactions #45321 and #45324. This helps to create an audit trail, or a way to go back and find the original documents supporting a transaction.

YOUR TURN

Which Journal Do You Use?

Match each of the transactions in the right column with the appropriate journal from the left column.

A. Purchases journal	i. Sales on account
B. Cash receipts journal	ii. Adjusting entries
C. Cash disbursements journal	iii. Receiving cash from a charge customer
D. Sales journal	iv. Buying inventory on credit
E. General journal	v. Paying the electric bill

Solution

A. iv; B. iii; C. v; D. i; E. ii.

Comprehensive Example

Let us return to the sales journal, shown in Figure 7.17 that includes information about Baker Co. as well as other companies with whom the company does business.

SALES JOURNAL							Page 26
Date	**Account**	**Address**	**Acct. No.**	**Terms**	**Sales Invoice No.**	**Ref.**	**DR A/R CR Sales**
2019							
Jan. 3	Baker Co.	PO Box 12	1231	n/30	45321		850
Jan. 3	Alpha Co.	Rt 2	2134	2/10, n/30	45322		625
Jan. 5	Tau Inc.	29 Main St.	1257	n/30	45323		700
Jan. 6	Baker Co.	PO Box 12	1231	n/30	45324		600
	Total						$2,775

Figure 7.17 Partial Sales Journal. (attribution: Copyright Rice University, OpenStax, under CC BY-NC-SA 4.0 license)

At the end of the month, the total Sales on credit were $2,775. The transactions would be posted in chronological order in the sales journal. As you can see, the first transaction is posted to Baker Co., the second one to Alpha Co., then Tau Inc., and then another to Baker Co. On the date each transaction is posted in the sales journal, the appropriate information would be posted in the subsidiary ledger for each of the customers. As an example, on January 3, amounts related to invoices 45321 and 45322 are posted to Baker's and Alpha's accounts, respectively, in the appropriate subsidiary ledger. At the end of the month, the total of $2,775 would be posted to the Accounts Receivable control account in the general ledger. Baker Co.'s account in the subsidiary ledger would show that they owe $1,450; Alpha Co. owes $625; and Tau Inc. owes $700 (Figure 7.18).

ACCOUNTS RECEIVABLE SUBSIDIARY LEDGER					
	Account: Baker Co.				Account No. 1231
Date	Item	Ref.	Debit	Credit	Balance
2019	Beginning Balance				0
Jan. 3	45321	SJ 26	850		850
Jan. 6	45324	SJ 26	600		1,450

	Account: Alpha Co.				Account No. 2134
Date	Item	Ref.	Debit	Credit	Balance
2019	Beginning Balance				0
Jan. 3	45322	SJ 26	625		625

	Account: Tau Inc.				Account No. 1257
Date	Item	Ref.	Debit	Credit	Balance
2019	Beginning Balance				0
Jan. 3	45323	SJ 26	700		700

Figure 7.18 Accounts Receivable Subsidiary Ledger. Individual accounts in the accounts receivable subsidiary ledger. (attribution: Copyright Rice University, OpenStax, under CC BY-NC-SA 4.0 license)

At the end of the month, we would post the totals from the sales journal to the general ledger (Figure 7.19).

ACCOUNTS RECEIVABLE GENERAL LEDGER (CONTROL TOTAL)						
Date	Item	Ref.			Balance	
			Debit	Credit	Debit	Credit
2019	Beginning Balance				00	
Jan. 31	January	SJ 26	2,775		2,775	

Figure 7.19 Accounts Receivable General Ledger. End-of-month posting to the Accounts Receivable Control Total account in the general ledger. (attribution: Copyright Rice University, OpenStax, under CC BY-NC-SA 4.0 license)

Altogether, the three individual accounts owe the company $2,775, which is the amount shown in the Accounts Receivable control account. It is called a *control total* because it helps keep accurate records, and the total in the accounts receivable must equal the balance in Accounts Receivable in the general ledger. If the amount of all the individual accounts receivable accounts did not add up to the total in the Accounts Receivable general ledger/control account, it would indicate that we made a mistake. Figure 7.20 shows how the accounts and amounts are posted.

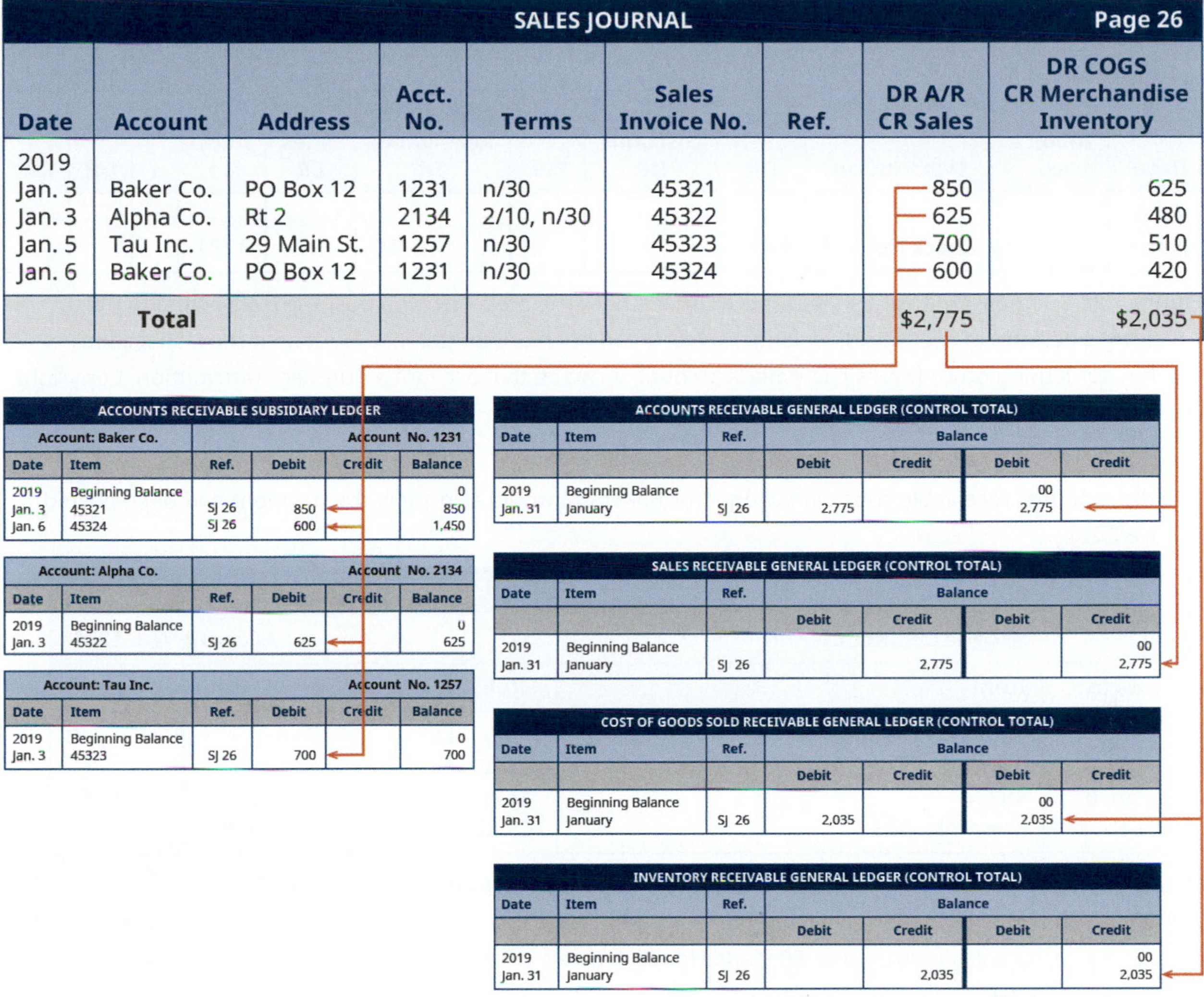

SALES JOURNAL — Page 26

Date	Account	Address	Acct. No.	Terms	Sales Invoice No.	Ref.	DR A/R CR Sales	DR COGS CR Merchandise Inventory
2019								
Jan. 3	Baker Co.	PO Box 12	1231	n/30	45321		850	625
Jan. 3	Alpha Co.	Rt 2	2134	2/10, n/30	45322		625	480
Jan. 5	Tau Inc.	29 Main St.	1257	n/30	45323		700	510
Jan. 6	Baker Co.	PO Box 12	1231	n/30	45324		600	420
	Total						$2,775	$2,035

ACCOUNTS RECEIVABLE SUBSIDIARY LEDGER

Account: Baker Co. — Account No. 1231

Date	Item	Ref.	Debit	Credit	Balance
2019	Beginning Balance				0
Jan. 3	45321	SJ 26	850		850
Jan. 6	45324	SJ 26	600		1,450

Account: Alpha Co. — Account No. 2134

Date	Item	Ref.	Debit	Credit	Balance
2019	Beginning Balance				0
Jan. 3	45322	SJ 26	625		625

Account: Tau Inc. — Account No. 1257

Date	Item	Ref.	Debit	Credit	Balance
2019	Beginning Balance				0
Jan. 3	45323	SJ 26	700		700

ACCOUNTS RECEIVABLE GENERAL LEDGER (CONTROL TOTAL)

Date	Item	Ref.	Debit	Credit	Balance Debit	Balance Credit
2019	Beginning Balance				00	
Jan. 31	January	SJ 26	2,775		2,775	

SALES RECEIVABLE GENERAL LEDGER (CONTROL TOTAL)

Date	Item	Ref.	Debit	Credit	Balance Debit	Balance Credit
2019	Beginning Balance					00
Jan. 31	January	SJ 26		2,775		2,775

COST OF GOODS SOLD RECEIVABLE GENERAL LEDGER (CONTROL TOTAL)

Date	Item	Ref.	Debit	Credit	Balance Debit	Balance Credit
2019	Beginning Balance				00	
Jan. 31	January	SJ 26	2,035		2,035	

INVENTORY RECEIVABLE GENERAL LEDGER (CONTROL TOTAL)

Date	Item	Ref.	Debit	Credit	Balance Debit	Balance Credit
2019	Beginning Balance					00
Jan. 31	January	SJ 26		2,035		2,035

Figure 7.20 Sales Journal. Sales journal transactions are posted individually to the accounts receivable subsidiary ledger and in total to the general ledger. (attribution: Copyright Rice University, OpenStax, under CC BY-NC-SA 4.0 license)

The Cash Receipts Journal

When the customer pays the amount owed, (generally using a check), bookkeepers use another shortcut to record its receipt. They use a second special journal, the cash receipts journal. The cash receipts journal is used to record all receipts of cash (recorded by a debit to Cash). In the preceding example, if Baker Co. paid the $1,450 owed, there would be a debit to Cash for $1,450 and a credit to Accounts Receivable. A notation would be made in the reference column to indicate the payment had been posted to Baker Co.'s accounts receivable subsidiary ledger. After Baker Co.'s payment, the cash receipts journal would appear as in Figure 7.21.

CASH RECEIPTS JOURNAL											Page 87
								Other Accounts			
Date	Invoice No.	Description	Cash DR	Sales Discount DR	Ref.	Accounts Receivable CR	Sales CR	Acct. No.	√	DR	CR
2019 Feb. 3		Check No. 123	1,450			1,450		1231			

Figure 7.21 Page from the Cash Receipts Journal. Check the box when you post the transaction to the customer's account in the subsidiary ledger. (Acct # can be the customer's account or, if the transaction touches something other than a customer's account, it can be that account's number.) (attribution: Copyright Rice University, OpenStax, under CC BY-NC-SA 4.0 license)

And the accounts receivable subsidiary ledger for Baker Co. would also show the payment had been posted (Figure 7.22).

ACCOUNTS RECEIVABLE SUBSIDIARY LEDGER					
	Account: Baker Co.				Account No. 1231
Date	Item	Ref.	Debit	Credit	Balance
	Beginning Balance				0
Jan. 3	45321	SJ 26			850
Jan. 6	45324	SJ 26	850		1,450
Feb. 3	Check No. 123	CR 87	600	1,450	0

Figure 7.22 Accounts Receivable Subsidiary Ledger. This is Baker Co.'s account in the accounts receivable subsidiary ledger. Note that we always know how much Baker owes us and how long it has been since Baker paid. SJ stands for sales journal, and CR stands for cash receipts journal. (attribution: Copyright Rice University, OpenStax, under CC BY-NC-SA 4.0 license)

In the cash receipts journal, the credit can be to Accounts Receivable when a customer pays on an account, or Sales, in the case of a cash sale, or to some other account when cash is received for other reasons. For example, if we overpaid our electric bill, we could get a refund check in the mail. We would use the cash receipts journal because we are receiving cash, but the credit would be to our Utility Expense account. If you look at the example in Figure 7.23, you see that there is no column for Utility Expense, so how would it be recorded? We would use some generic column title such as "other" to represent those cash transactions in the subsidiary ledger though the specific accounts would actually be identified by account number in the special journal. We would look up the account number for Utility Expense and credit the account for the amount of the check. If we received a refund from the electric company on June 10 in the amount of $100, we would find the account number for utility expense (say it is 615) and record it.

CASH RECEIPTS JOURNAL											Page 87
								Other Accounts			
Date	Invoice No.	Description	Cash DR	Sales Discount DR	Ref.	Accounts Receivable CR	Sales CR	Acct. No.	√	DR	CR
Jun. 10		Refund	100					615			100

Figure 7.23 Cash Receipts Journal. The "Ref" column stands for reference and can be anything that helps us remember. For example, in the problem, the Ref could be the number of the check the company sent us. Or it could be the account number we use for that company. It is part of the audit trail. *Other* means "various," so we would use the account number for utility expense and credit it. When it is posted to the general ledger, we will "check" the box next to 615 to remind ourselves that it has been posted. (attribution: Copyright Rice University, OpenStax, under CC BY-NC-SA 4.0 license)

At the end of the month, we total the Cash column in the cash receipts journal and debit the Cash account in the general ledger for the total. In this case there were two entries in the cash receipts journal, the cash received from Baker and the refund check for an overpayment on utilities for a total cash received and recorded in the cash receipts journal of $1,550, as shown in Figure 7.24.

GENERAL LEDGER: CASH						
Date	Item	Ref.			Balance	
			Debit	Credit	Debit	Credit
2019	Beginning Balance				20,000	
Jan. 31	January	CRJ	1,550		21,550	

Figure 7.24 General Ledger: Cash. Cash receipts journal ending balance for January is posted to the cash account in the general ledger. (attribution: Copyright Rice University, OpenStax, under CC BY-NC-SA 4.0 license)

Any accounts used in the Other Accounts column must be entered separately in the general ledger to the appropriate account. Figure 7.25 shows how the refund would be posted to the utilities expense account in the general ledger.

GENERAL LEDGER: UTILITIES EXPENSE							
Date	Item	Ref.	Acct No.		Balance		
				Debit	Credit	Debit	Credit
2019	Beginning Balance					6,000	
Jan. 31	Refund		615		100		100

Figure 7.25 General Ledger: Utilities Expense. Any postings to Other accounts in the cash receipts journal are posted to the appropriate account in the general ledger. (attribution: Copyright Rice University, OpenStax, under CC BY-NC-SA 4.0 license)

The Cash Disbursements Journal

Many transactions involve cash. We enter all cash received into the cash receipts journal, and we enter all cash payments into the cash disbursements journal, sometimes also known as the cash payments journal. Good internal control dictates the best rule is that all cash received by a business should be deposited, and all cash paid out for monies owed by the business should be made by check. Money paid out is recorded in the cash disbursements journal, which is generally kept in numerical order by check number and includes all of the checks recorded in the checkbook register. If we paid this month's phone bill of $135 with check #4011, we would enter it as shown in Figure 7.26 in the cash disbursements journal.

CASH DISBURSEMENTS JOURNAL										Page 18
						Other Accounts				
Date	Check No.	Payee	Cash DR	Accounts Payable DR	Purchases DR	Acct. No.	√	DR	CR	
Jan. 31	401	Phone Co.	134	134						

Figure 7.26 Using the Cash Disbursements Journal. (attribution: Copyright Rice University, OpenStax, under CC BY-NC-SA 4.0 license)

The total of all of the cash disbursements for the month would be recorded in the general ledger Cash account (Figure 7.27) as follows. Note that the information for both the cash receipts journal and the cash disbursements journal are recorded in the general ledger Cash account.

GENERAL LEDGER: CASH						
Date	Item	Ref.			Balance	
			Debit	Credit	Debit	Credit
2019	Beginning Balance				20,000	
Jan. 31	January	CRJ	1,550		21,550	
Jan. 31	January	CPJ		135	21,415	

Figure 7.27 General Ledger: Cash. (attribution: Copyright Rice University, OpenStax, under CC BY-NC-SA 4.0 license)

The Purchases Journal

Many companies enter only purchases of inventory on account in the purchases journal. Some companies also use it to record purchases of other supplies on account. However, in this chapter we use the purchases journal for purchases of inventory on account, only. It will always have a debit to Merchandise Inventory if you are using the perpetual inventory method and a credit to Accounts Payable, or a debit to Purchases and a credit to Accounts Payable if using the periodic inventory method. It is similar to the sales journal because it has a corresponding subsidiary ledger, the accounts payable subsidiary ledger. Since the purchases journal is only for purchases of inventory on account, it means the company owes money. To keep track of whom the company owes money to and when payment is due, the entries are posted daily to the accounts payable subsidiary ledger. Accounts Payable in the general ledger becomes a control account just like Accounts Receivable. If we ordered inventory from Jones Mfg. (account number 789) using purchase order #123 and received the bill for $250, this would be recorded in the purchases journal as shown in Figure 7.28.

PURCHASES JOURNAL					
Date	Purchase Order No.	Account Credited	Acct. No.	Posting Reference	Inventory DR Acct. Payable CR
XX	123	Jones Mfg.	789	√	250

Figure 7.28 Purchases Journal. Recording the purchase of merchandise on account in the purchases journal. (attribution: Copyright Rice University, OpenStax, under CC BY-NC-SA 4.0 license)

The posting reference would be to indicate that we had entered the amount in the accounts payable subsidiary ledger (Figure 7.29).

ACCOUNTS PAYABLE SUBSIDIARY LEDGER					
Account: Jones Mfg.					Account No. 789
Date	Item	Ref.	Debit	Credit	Balance
Jan. 12	Inventory			250	250

Figure 7.29 Accounts Payable Subsidiary Ledger. (attribution: Copyright Rice University, OpenStax, under CC BY-NC-SA 4.0 license)

The total of all accounts payable subsidiary ledgers would be posted at the end of the month to the general ledger Accounts Payable control account. The sum of all the subsidiary ledgers must equal the amount reported in the general ledger.

General Journal

Why use a general journal if we have all the special journals? The reason is that some transactions do not fit in any special journal. In addition to the four special journals presented previously (sales, cash receipts, cash disbursements, and purchases), some companies also use a special journal for Sales returns and allowances and another special journal for Purchase returns and allowances if they have many sales returns and purchase returns transactions. However, most firms enter those transactions in the general journal, along with other transactions that do not fit the description of the specific types of transactions contained in the four special journals. The general journal is also necessary for adjusting entries (such as to recognize depreciation, prepaid rent, and supplies that we have consumed) and closing entries.

YOUR TURN

Using the Sales and Cash Receipts Journals

You own and operate a business that sells goods to other businesses. You allow established customers to buy goods from you on account, meaning you let them charge purchases and offer terms of 2/10, n/30. Record the following transactions in the sales journal and cash receipts journal:

Jan. 3	Sales on credit to VJ Armitraj, Ltd., amount of $7,200, Invoice # 317745
Jan. 9	Sales on credit to M. Baghdatis Inc., amount of $5,200, Invoice # 317746
Jan. 16	Receive $7,200 from VJ Armitraj, Ltd. (did not receive during the discount period)
Jan. 17	Sales on credit to A. Ashe Inc., amount of $3,780, Invoice #317747
Jan. 18	Receive the full amount owed from M. Baghdatis Inc. within the discount period

Solution

SALES JOURNAL					Page 27
Date	Invoice No.	Account Debited	Acct. No.	Acct. Rec. DR Sales CR	
2019					
Jan. 3	317745	VJ Armitraj, Ltd.	AR 354	7	200
Jan. 9	317746	M. Baghdatis Inc.	AR 471	5	200
Jan. 17	317747	A. Ashe Inc.	AR 371	3	780
				16	180

CASH RECEIPTS JOURNAL								OTHER ACCOUNTS			
Date	Invoice No.	Description	Cash DR	Sales Discounts DR	Ref.	Accounts Receivable CR	Sales CR	Acct. No.	√	DR	CR
2019											
Jan. 8	317740	VJ Armitraj	7,200			7,200		AR354			
Jan. 12	317746	M. Baghdatis	5,096	104		5,200		AR471			
		Total debits = 12,400	12,296	104		12,400					
		Total credits = 12,400									

Accounts Receivable Subsidiary Ledger					
Account: VJ Armitraj Ltd		**AR No. 354**			
					Balance
Date	**Item**	**Ref.**	**Debit**	**Credit**	**Debit**
Jan. 3	Sales Journal	27	7,200		7,200
Jan. 16	Cash Receipts	24		7,200	0

Account: A. Ashe Inc.		**AR No. 371**			
					Balance
Date	**Item**	**Ref.**	**Debit**	**Credit**	**Debit**
Jan. 17	Sales Journal	27	3,780		3,780

Account: M. Baghdatis Inc.		**AR No. 471**			
					Balance
Date	**Item**	**Ref.**	**Debit**	**Credit**	**Debit**
Jan. 9	Sales Journal	27	5,200		5,200
Jan. 18	Cash Receipts	24		5,200	0

Ensure that the total of all individual accounts receivable equals the total of accounts receivable, or:

0 + $3,780 + 0 = $3,780.

Accounts Receivable	
16,180	7,200 5,200
3,780	

7.4 Prepare a Subsidiary Ledger

Now that you have seen four special journals and two special ledgers, it is time to put all the pieces together.

Record the following transactions for Store Inc. in the special journals and post to the general ledger provided. Also post to the subsidiary ledgers provided. Beginning account balances are shown below. Use the perpetual inventory method and the gross method of dealing with sales terms.

First, enter these transactions manually by creating the relevant journals and subsidiary ledgers. Then enter them using QuickBooks.

BEGINNING BALANCES			
Cash	$3,116		
Accounts Receivable	3,576	Accounts Payable	$6,382
Prepaid Insurance	130	Stock	5,000
Inventory	8,917	Retained Earnings	4,357

Transactions for Store Inc.

Jan. 2	Issued check #629 for January store rent: $350.00
Jan. 3	Received check from PB&J in payment for December sale on credit, $915.00
Jan. 4	Issued check #630 to D & D in payment for December purchase on credit of $736.00
Jan. 5	Sold goods for $328.00 to Jones Co. on credit, Invoice # 234 (Note: COGS is $164)
Jan. 6	Bought goods from BSA for $4,300.00, Purchase Order # 71, terms: 2/10, net/30
Jan. 8	Sold goods on credit to Black & White Inc. for $2,100, Invoice # 235, terms: 1/10, net/30 (Note: COGS is $1,050)
Jan. 9	Issued check #63 for telephone bill received today, $72.00
Jan. 10	Issued check #632 to pay BSA in full, PO #71.
Jan. 15	Received full payment from Black & White, Inc., Invoice # 235
Jan. 20	Bought merchandise from Dow John, $525.00 payable in 30 days, Purchase Order # 72
Jan. 26	Returned $100 of merchandise to Dow John, relating to Purchase Order #72
Jan. 31	Recorded cash sales for the month of $3,408 (Note: COGS is $1,704)
Jan. 31	Recognized that half of the Prepaid Insurance has been consumed

Table 7.2

Record all transactions using the sales journal, purchases journal, cash receipts journal, cash disbursements journal, and the general journal and post to the accounts receivable and accounts payable subsidiary ledgers. Then prepare a schedule of accounts receivable and a schedule of accounts payable.

CASH RECEIPTS JOURNAL SOLUTION											Page 65
								Other Accounts			
Date	Invoice No.	Description	Cash DR	Discounts DR	Ref.	Receivable CR	Sales CR	Acct. No.	√	DR	CR
2019											
Jan. 3	234	PB&J	915			915					
Jan. 15		Black & White	2,079	21		2,100					
Jan. 31		Jan. Cash Sales	3,408				3,408	501		1,204	
								106			1,204
		Total	6,402	21		3,015	3,408			1,204	1,204

Explanation:

Jan. 3	The company received payment from PB&J; thus, a cash receipt is recorded.
Jan. 15	The company received payment on goods that were sold on Jan. 8 with credit terms if paid within the discount period. The payment was received within the discount period.

Jan. 31	Cash sales are recorded.

GENERAL JOURNAL SOLUTION				119
Date	**Description**	**Ref.**	**Debit**	**Credit**
2019				
Jan. 26	Accounts Payable: Dow John	200	100	
	Merchandise Inventory	106		100
	To record return of defective merchandise (Dow John AP No. 115)			
Jan. 31	Insurance Expense	504	65	
	Prepaid Insurance	105		65
	To record expiration of Prepaid Insurance			

Explanation:

Jan. 26	The company returns merchandise (inventory) previously purchased. Since the company is using the perpetual method, a credit is made to Inventory.
Jan. 31	An adjusting entry is made to recognize insurance expense for the current month that had previously been prepaid.

SALES JOURNAL					Page 143
Date	**Invoice No.**	**Account Debited**	**Acct. No.**	**A/R DR Sales CR**	**COGS DR Inventory CR**
Jan. 5	234	Jones Co.	JC1	328	164
Jan. 8	235	Black & White Inc.	BW1	2,100	1,050
				2,428	1,214

Explanation:

Jan. 8	Sales on credit are recorded

CASH DISBURSEMENTS JOURNAL										Page 102
							Other Accounts			
Date	**Check No.**	**Payee**	**Cash CR**	**Ref.**	**Accounts Payable DR**	**Purchases Discounts CR**	**Acct. No.**	**√**	**DR**	**CR**
2019										
Jan. 1	629	Rent	350				535		350	
Jan. 4	630	D&D	736	D1218	736					
Jan. 9	631	Phone	72				545		72	
Jan. 10	632	BSA	4,214		4,300	86				
			5,372		5,036	86			422	
		Debits = 5,458								
		Credits = 5,458								

Explanation:

Jan. 2	Rent for the month is paid.
Jan. 4	Payment is made for inventory purchased on account in a prior month.

Jan. 9	Paid the telephone bill.
Jan. 10	Paid for inventory purchased earlier on account. The payment arrangement had credit terms; the invoice was paid within the time allowed, and the discount was taken.

PURCHASES JOURNAL				Page 54
Date	Purchase Order No.	Account Credited	Acct. No.	Debit Inventory Credit AP
2019				
Jan. 6	71	BSA	110	4,300
Jan. 20	72	Dow John	115	525
				4,825

Explanation:

Jan. 6	Inventory is purchased on account.
Jan. 20	Inventory is purchased on account.

At the end of the month, each of the previous journal totals are posted to the appropriate account in the general ledger, and any individual account postings, such as to Rent Expense (Jan. 2 transaction) would also be posted to the general ledger. Note that each account used by the company has its own account section in the general ledger.

GENERAL LEDGER SOLUTION						
	Account: Cash					**No. 101**
					Balance	
Date	**Item**	**Ref.**	**Debit**	**Credit**	**Debit**	**Credit**
2019						
Jan. 1	Beginning Balance				3,116	
Jan. 31	Cash Receipts	CR 65	6,402		9,518	
Jan. 31	Cash Disbursements	CD 18		5,372	4,146	

	Account: Accounts Receivable					**No. 102**
					Balance	
Date	**Item**	**Ref.**	**Debit**	**Credit**	**Debit**	**Credit**
Jan. 1	Beginning Balance				3,576	
Jan. 31	Sales Journal	SJ 143	2,248		6,004	
Jan. 31	Cash Receipts	CR 122		3,015	2,989	

	Account: Prepaid Insurance					**No. 106**
					Balance	
Date	**Item**	**Ref.**	**Debit**	**Credit**	**Debit**	**Credit**
Jan. 1	Beginning Balance				130	
Jan. 31	Adjusting Entry	GJ 119	65		65	

	Account: Inventory					**No. 106**
					Balance	
Date	**Item**	**Ref.**	**Debit**	**Credit**	**Debit**	**Credit**
Jan. 1	Beginning Balance				8,917	
Jan. 14	Purchases Journal	PJ 54	4,825		13,742	
Jan. 31	Purchase Return	GJ 119		100	13,642	
Jan. 31	Cash Receipts Journal	CR 65		1,704	11,938	
Jan. 31	Cash Disbursements	CD 18		86	11,852	
Jan. 31	Sales Journal	SJ 24		1,214	10,638	

	Account: Accounts Payable					**No. 200**
					Balance	
Date	**Item**	**Ref.**	**Debit**	**Credit**	**Debit**	**Credit**
Jan. 1	Beginning Balance					6,382
Jan. 31	Purchases Journal	PJ 54		4,825		11,207
Jan. 31	Cash Disbursements	CD 18	5,036			6,171
Jan. 31	General Journal	GJ	100			6,071

GENERAL LEDGER SOLUTION

Account: Common Stock						No. 301
					Balance	
Date	Item	Ref.	Debit	Credit	Debit	Credit
2019 Jan. 1	Beginning Balance					5,000

Account: Retained Earnings						No. 350
					Balance	
Date	Item	Ref.	Debit	Credit	Debit	Credit
Jan. 1	Beginning Balance					4,357

Account: Sales						No. 401
					Balance	
Date	Item	Ref.	Debit	Credit	Debit	Credit
Jan. 1	Beginning Balance					
Jan. 13	Sales Journal	SJ 24		2,428		2,428
Jan. 31	Cash Receipts	CR		3,408		5,836

Account: Sales Discounts						No. 410
					Balance	
Date	Item	Ref.	Debit	Credit	Debit	Credit
Jan. 1	Beginning Balance					
Jan. 15	General Journal	GJ 119	65		65	

Account: Cost of Goods Sold						No. 501
					Balance	
Date	Item	Ref.	Debit	Credit	Debit	Credit
Jan. 31	Sales Journal	SJ 24	1,214		1,214	
Jan. 31	Cash Receipts	CR 65	1,704		2,918	

Account: Insurance Expense						No. 521
					Balance	
Date	Item	Ref.	Debit	Credit	Debit	Credit
Jan. 1	Beginning Balance					
Jan. 15	General Journal	GJ 119	65		65	

Account: Rent Expense						No. 535
					Balance	
Date	Item	Ref.	Debit	Credit	Debit	Credit
Jan. 1	Beginning Balance					
Jan. 31	Cash Disbursements	CD 18	350		350	

Account: Utilities Expense						No. 545
					Balance	
Date	Item	Ref.	Debit	Credit	Debit	Credit
Jan. 1	Beginning Balance					
Jan. 31	Cash Disbursements	CD 18	72		72	

ACCOUNTS RECEIVABLE SUBSIDIARY LEDGER SOLUTION

PB&J

Date	Item	Ref.	Debit	Credit	Balance Debit
2019					
Dec. 20	Sales Journal	SJ 23	915		915
Jan. 3	Cash Receipts	CR		915	

Jones Co.

Date	Item	Ref.	Debit	Credit	Balance Debit
Jan. 5	Sales Journal	SJ 24	328		328

Black & White Inc.

Date	Item	Ref.	Debit	Credit	Balance Debit
Jan. 8	Sales Journal	SJ 24	2,100		2,100
Jan. 15	Cash Receipts	CR		2,100	

Tiny Tim's Inc.

Date	Item	Ref.	Debit	Credit	Balance Debit
Dec. 15	Sales Journal	23	2,661		2,661

ACCOUNTS PAYABLE SUBSIDIARY LEDGER					
Account: D & D Inc.					**AP No. 34**
					Balance
Date	**Item**	**Ref.**	**Debit**	**Credit**	**Credit**
2019					
Dec. 1	Purchases Journal	PJ 44		736	736
Dec. 10	Purchases Journal	PJ 44		5,646	6,382
Jan. 4	Cash Disbursements	CD	736		5,646
Account: BSA					**AP No. 71**
					Balance
Date	**Item**	**Ref.**	**Debit**	**Credit**	**Credit**
Jan. 6	Purchases Journal	PJ 45		4,300	4,300
Jan. 10	Cash Disbursements	CD	4,300		0

Account: Dow John					**AP No. 171**
					Balance
Date	**Item**	**Ref.**	**Debit**	**Credit**	**Credit**
Jan. 20	Purchases	PJ 45		525	525
Jan. 26	General Journal	GJ 119	100		425

Store Inc.	
Schedule of Accounts Receivable	
Jan. 31	
PB&J	$ 0
Jones Co.	328
Black & White Inc.	0
Tiny Tim's Inc.	2,661
	$2,989

Store Inc.	
Schedule of Accounts Payable	
Jan. 31	
D & D Inc.	$5,646
BSA	0
Dow John	425
	$6,071

If you check Accounts Receivable in the general ledger, you see the balance is $2,989, and the balance in Accounts Payable is $6,071. If the numbers did not match, we would have to find out where the error was and then fix it.

The purpose of keeping subsidiary ledgers is for accuracy and efficiency. They aid us in keeping accurate records. Since the total of the accounts receivable subsidiary ledger must agree with the balance shown in the accounts receivable general ledger account, the system helps us find mistakes. Since bookkeeping using ledgers is older than the United States, it was an ingenious way to double-check without having to actually do everything twice. It provided an internal control over record keeping. Today, computerized accounting information systems use the same method to store and total amounts, but it takes a lot less time.

7.5 Describe Career Paths Open to Individuals with a Joint Education in Accounting and Information Systems

We use accounting information to make decisions about the business. Computer applications now provide so much data that **data analytics** is one of the newest career areas in business. Universities are beginning to offer degrees in data analysis. Software companies have created different applications to analyze data including SAS, Apache Hadoop, Apache Spark, SPSS, RapidMiner, Power BI, ACL, IDEA, and many more to help companies discover useful information from the transactions that occur. **Big data** refers to the availability of large amounts of data from various sources, including the internet. For example, social media sites contain tremendous amounts of data that marketing companies analyze to determine how popular a product is, and how best to market it. There is so much data to analyze that new ways of mining it for predictive value have evolved.

Another emerging area involves **cryptocurrency**, or the use of a digital currency that uses encryption technologies that make these cryptocurrencies impossible to counterfeit. The use of cryptocurrency does not require a bank to transfer or clear funds as is the case with other currencies. Bitcoin is the most well-known cryptocurrency. **Blockchain** is the platform on which Bitcoin is built. Blockchain serves as a shared ledger for Bitcoin but is also the foundation of many other applications. Simply put, blockchain offers different parties to a transaction (e.g., a buyer and a seller) the opportunity to use a shared ledger rather than each having their own separate ledgers as is the case with traditional systems. Bitcoin is currently accepted by some large, well-known companies including PwC and EY (the two largest of the "big 4" accounting firms), and Overstock.com.

Enterprise resource planning (ERP) software is a collection of integrated programs that track all operations in a company, from payroll to accounts payable, manufacturing, and maintaining electronic connections with suppliers. For example, companies that sell goods to Walmart, have access to Walmart's electronic inventory records so the vendors can make sure Walmart has the right amount of goods on hand. Having such a close relationship brings rewards. They will probably receive payment sooner, using EFT (electronic funds transfer).

The use of accounting information systems (AISs) has drastically changed the way we prepare tax returns. Software is now written to walk anyone through preparing his or her own tax return using an **expert system**. An expert system asks questions like: are you married? If the answer is yes, the software knows to use the married tax tables, and if the answer is no, it uses the single tables. Based on this answer, it will know what kind of question to ask next. Accountants who understand expert systems and tax will be writing and auditing tax software programs.

Firms are also developing and using **artificial intelligence** (AI) systems to perform tasks previously performed by accounting professionals, but now are freeing up the professionals to perform higher-level tasks requiring analysis and judgment. Finally, security of all of this available data is a very important issue, and there are a number of career paths and certifications that information technology professionals can attain. The Information Systems Audit and Control Association (ISACA) offers several certifications including Certified Information Systems Auditor (CISA), Certified in Risk and Information System Controls (CRISC), Certified Information Security Manager (CISM), and others. There is so much technology that we are inundated with more information than we can use. Because the information is being generated by a machine, we generally trust the computation (although there are cases where a bug in the program can even cause problems with simple math), but we also know the old saying, "garbage in, garbage out." The computer does not always know that your typo is garbage. If you enter the wrong number, the system processes it as if it were the right number. That means we have to build some way into the program to control what is input into the system. For example, if you fill out a form online and it asks for your zip code, does it let you enter just four digits? No—the computer knows that it should only go to the next step if you enter five digits. However, you can enter the wrong digits and it might not catch it. It is critical that we build as many internal controls into our computerized systems as possible so that we can find errors at the input stage before they get into our system. In other words, by using these "preventive" controls, we do not allow "garbage" data to get into our system.

Computerized AISs have also brought changes to the audit trail. In the past, accountants had a set of books that were paper based. You could see where a transaction was recorded and posted (and see if it had been erased). Once you enter it into a computer, it becomes part of an electronic audit trail, but the trail is only as good as the program that runs it. The screen could show you one number, but the system could be working with a different number all together. In fact, there have been criminal cases in which people wrote programs to cover up fraud. One such program functioned so that when an item was scanned, the correct amount displayed to the customer, but it was recorded in the books as a smaller amount, so the company paid less in sales tax and much less in income tax.

AISs have become more important because information and technology are more important.

CONCEPTS IN PRACTICE

Is Technology *Always* Better?

Technology allows one person to do a job that once took a dozen people to do. However, that can also lead to problems. For example, years ago, one person working in the accounts receivable department at Burlington Industries would have been in charge of a few customers. If those customers were not paying their bills on time, a person would be aware of it. Today, one person might be in charge of all accounts receivable. That person may not have time to call individual customers, so everything is preprogrammed. If the customer wanted to place a large order that caused them to go over their limit, the software would deny it instead of having a person weigh the risk of extending more credit.

A risk inherent in an AIS is that one person has access to a lot of information, and sometimes the information crosses department lines. Companies have to figure out ways to mitigate the risk, because AISs are truly essential to businesses today, especially with the growth of e-business and e-commerce. Think of the different business processes when a purchase is made through Amazon.com. Their AIS must be able to access inventory records, access customer information and records, process credit cards, calculate delivery dates, handle coupons or discounts, and remember where to ship the goods. Amazon would not be what it is today without all of its systems working together. Seeing what Amazon has accomplished opens the door for other companies to follow, and they will need people who understand the system.

Forensic accounting involves the use of accounting skills to inspect the accounting records in order to determine if fraud or embezzlement have occurred. Many universities are offering forensic accounting degrees to prepare students who can testify to criminal activity present in the accounting records.

CONCEPTS IN PRACTICE

The Founding of the Securities and Exchange Commission

In 1933 and 1934, the US Congress passed two acts that established the Securities and Exchange Commission (SEC), giving it the right to regulate and enforce the regulations concerning commerce in the United States. The website of the SEC (https://www.SEC.gov/) allows you to view all public company financial reporting and provides a link to all current litigation against individuals and companies that have been accused of breaking an SEC regulation. If you go to the site and look for the Litigation Releases section, you can click on individual cases and find that some cases of fraud involve the use of an accounting information system.

The Patriot Act also came out of the 9/11 attacks (signed October 26, 2001). The letters in Patriot stand for the following: providing appropriate tools required to intercept and obstruct terrorism. The goal of the act was to prevent any other attacks on the United States by allowing enhanced surveillance procedures.

The act gave law enforcement officials the right to access computers to track IP addresses, websites visited, credit card information provided electronically, and so on, in an effort to uncover terrorism before an attack was made. Several parts of the act call for banks to report suspected money laundering activities. Money laundering is an attempt to hide the facts of the original transaction and would involve an accountant. If you were selling drugs for cash and then tried to deposit that much cash in a bank, the bank would report it, so you would try to cover up where the cash came from and run it through a legitimate company. That is money laundering.

The Patriot Act also includes a section requiring auditors to verify that a company has controls in place to prevent an attack on its accounting information system and that the company has a disaster plan including backup records in case of a disaster.

The AIS enables a company to record all of its business transactions. Systems are different depending on the company's needs. The AIS holds a lot of the information used to run a business. One system can provide everything needed for external reporting to government agencies involving payroll and income taxation. The same system can provide the data needed for managerial analysis used for pricing, budgeting, decision-making, and efficiency studies. Every company is required to keep records of their financial activity, and this means job security for people who are knowledgeable about AISs.

Key Terms

accounting information system (AIS) set of business processes that record transactions using journals and ledgers (for paper systems) and computer files (for computerized systems) to keep track of a company's transactions, process the data associated with these transactions, and produce output useful for internal and external decision-making and analysis

accounts payable subsidiary ledger special ledger that contains information about all vendors and the amounts we owe them; the total of all accounts in the accounts payable subsidiary ledger *must* equal the total of accounts payable control account in the general ledger

accounts receivable control accounts receivable account in the general ledger

accounts receivable subsidiary ledger special ledger that contains information about all customers and the amounts they owe; the total of all accounts in the accounts receivable subsidiary ledger *must* equal the total of accounts receivable control account in the general ledger

artificial intelligence computerized systems that are taught to use reasoning and other aspects of human intelligence to mimic some of the tasks humans perform

audit trail step-by-step trail of evidence documenting the history of a transaction from its inception and all the steps it went through until its completion

big data data sets from online transactions and other sources that are so large that new software and methods have been created to analyze and mine them so they can provide insight into trends and patterns of the business

blockchain underlying technology Bitcoin is built on; provides a single shared ledger used by all of the parties to a transaction resulting in cheaper, more secure, and more private transactions

cash disbursements journal special journal that is used to record outflows of cash; every time cash leaves the business, usually when we issue a check, we record in this journal

cash receipts journal special journal that is used to record inflows of cash; every time we receive checks and currency from customers and others, we record these cash receipts in this journal

cloud computing using the internet to access software and information storage facilities provided by companies (there is usually a charge) rather than, or in addition to, storing this data on the company's computer hard drive or in paper form

cryptocurrency digital currency that uses encryption techniques to verify transfer of the funds but operates independently of a bank

data parts of accounting transactions that constitute the input to an accounting information system

data analytics analyzing the huge amount of data generated by all the electronic transactions occurring in a business

data/information storage way to save data and information; can be on paper, computer hard drive, or through the internet to save in the cloud

enterprise resource planning (ERP) system that helps a company streamline its operations and helps management respond quickly to change

expert system software program that is built on a database; software asks question and uses the response to ask the next question or offer advice

forensic accounting using accounting and computer skills to look for fraud and to analyze financial records in hard copy and electronic formats

point of sale point of time when a sales transaction occurs

point-of-sale system (POS) computerized system to record and process a sale immediately when it occurs, usually by scanning the product bar code

purchases journal special journal that is used to record purchases of merchandise inventory on credit; it always debits the merchandise inventory account (if using the perpetual inventory method) or the Purchases account (if using the periodic method)

sales journal special journal that is used to record all sales on credit; it always debits accounts receivable and credits sales, and if the company uses the perpetual inventory method it also debits cost of goods sold and credits merchandise inventory

schedule of accounts payable table showing each amount owed and to whom it must be paid; total of the schedule should equal the total of accounts payable in the general ledger

schedule of accounts receivable table showing each customer and the amount owed; total of the schedule should equal the total of accounts receivable in the general ledger

source document paper document or electronic record that provides evidence that a transaction has occurred and includes details about the transaction

special journal book of original entry that is used to record transactions of a similar type in addition to the general journal

turn-around document paper document that starts off as an output document from one part of the accounting information system (billing sends bill to customer), that becomes input to another part of the accounting information system upon completion of the next phase of the process (accounts receivable receives payment made on bill)

Summary

7.1 Define and Describe the Components of an Accounting Information System

- An accounting information system is a set of business processes that record transactions using journals and ledgers (a paper-based system) or computer files (using a computerized system) to keep track of a company's money and other assets.
- The key steps in an accounting information system are input, processing, and output.
    - Input: This is any way to record the transaction.
    - Processing: This is a method of combining similar kinds of information (like adding all cash sales together to get a total that is separate from all credit sales; and then adding everything to find total sales).
    - Output: Any way used to display the results of the processing is output.
    - Source document: This is a record that a transaction has taken place; it is often used at the input stage.
    - Storage: This is any method used to save the results generated by the system. Data that is stored is retrieved and used in the input, processing, or output stage. Additional data and information are also stored during these processes.

7.2 Describe and Explain the Purpose of Special Journals and Their Importance to Stakeholders

- We use special journals to keep track of similar types of transactions.
- We use special journals to save time because the same types of transactions occur over and over.
- To decide which special journal to use, first ask, "Is cash involved?" If the answer is "Yes," then use either the cash receipts or cash disbursements journal.
- The cash receipts journal always debits cash but can credit almost anything (primarily sales, Accounts Receivable, or a new loan from the bank).
- The cash disbursements journal always credits cash but can debit almost anything (Accounts Payable, Notes Payable, sales returns and allowances, telephone expense, etc.).

- The sales journal always debits Accounts Receivable and always credits Sales. If the company uses a perpetual inventory method, it also debits cost of goods sold and credits inventory.
- The purchases journal always debits Purchases (if using the periodic inventory method) or Inventory (if using the perpetual inventory method) and credits Accounts Payable.
- We post the monthly balance from each of the special journals to the general ledger at the end of the month.
- We post from all journals to the subsidiary ledgers daily.
- We use the general journal for transactions that do not fit anywhere else—generally, for adjusting and closing entries, and can be for sales returns and/or purchase returns.
- The accounts receivable subsidiary ledger contains all of the details about individual accounts.
- The total of the accounts receivable subsidiary ledger must equal the total in the Accounts Receivable general ledger account.
- The accounts payable subsidiary ledger contains all of the details about individual accounts payable accounts.
- The total of the accounts payable subsidiary ledger must equal the total in the Accounts Payable general ledger account.

7.3 Analyze and Journalize Transactions Using Special Journals

- Rules of cash receipts journals: Use any time you receive cash. Always debit Cash and credit Accounts Receivable or some other account.
- Rules of cash disbursements journals: Any time a check is issued, there should be a credit to cash and a debit to AP or typically an expense. Always credit Cash and debit Accounts Payable or some other account.
- Rules of sales journals: Use only for sales of goods on credit (when customers charge the amount). Always debit Accounts Receivable and credit Sales and debit Cost of Goods Sold and credit Merchandise Inventory when using a perpetual inventory system.
- Rules of purchases journals: Use only for purchase of goods (inventory) on credit (when you charge the amount). Always debit Merchandise Inventory when using a perpetual inventory system (or Purchases when using a periodic inventory system) and credit Accounts Payable.
- Post daily to the subsidiary ledgers.
- Monthly, at the end of each month, after totaling all of the columns in each journal, post to the general ledger accounts which include the Accounts Receivable and Accounts Payable (general ledger) controlling accounts. Note that the only column that you do not post the total to the general ledger account is the Other Accounts column. There is no general ledger account called Other accounts. As mentioned, each entry in that column is posted individually to its respective account.

7.4 Prepare a Subsidiary Ledger

- A schedule of accounts receivable is a list of all individual accounts and balances that make up accounts receivable.
- A schedule of accounts payable is a list of all individual accounts and balances that make up accounts payable.

7.5 Describe Career Paths Open to Individuals with a Joint Education in Accounting and Information Systems

- Data analytics, artificial intelligence systems, data security credentials, blockchain applications, and forensic accounting are some of the areas that provide newer career avenues for accounting professionals.
- Taxes will continue to be prepared using software that pulls information from the accounting information system.

- Integrating accounting software with inventory management and electronic payment as used by Walmart and Amazon will set new standards of business process automation.
- Forensic accounting, data security, artificial intelligence, and data analytics, are all areas for which companies and government agencies will be seeking accounting graduates who are also knowledgeable about information systems.

Multiple Choice

1. LO 7.1 So far, computer systems cannot yet _______.

A. receive data and instructions from input devices such as a scanner.
B. decide how to record a business transaction.
C. communicate with other computers electronically.
D. recognize that you made a mistake entering $100 when you meant to enter $101.

2. LO 7.1 Any device used to provide the results of processing data is a(n) _______ device.

A. sources
B. input
C. output
D. storage

3. LO 7.1 Source documents _______.

A. are input devices
B. are output devices
C. do not have to be on paper
D. cannot be electronic files

4. LO 7.1 All of the following can provide source data *except* _______.

A. a scanning device at the grocery store
B. a utility bill received in the mail
C. a bar code reader
D. software to process the source data

5. LO 7.1 A document that asks you to return an identifying part of it with your payment is a(n) _______.

A. source document
B. cloud document
C. point-of-sale document
D. turn-around document

6. LO 7.1 Which of the following is *false* about accounting information systems?

A. They provide reports that people analyze.
B. They prevent errors and stop employees from stealing inventory.
C. They are designed to gather data about the company's transactions.
D. They consist of processes that involve input of data from source documents, processing, output, and storage.

7. LO 7.2 An unhappy customer just returned $50 of the items he purchased yesterday when he charged the goods to the company's store credit card. Which special journal would the company use to record this transaction?

A. sales journal
B. purchases journal
C. cash receipts journal
D. cash disbursements journal
E. general journal

8. LO 7.2 A customer just charged $150 of merchandise on the company's own charge card. Which special journal would the company use to record this transaction?

A. sales journal
B. purchases journal
C. cash receipts journal
D. cash disbursements journal
E. general journal

9. LO 7.2 A customer just charged $150 of merchandise using MasterCard. Which special journal would the company use to record this transaction?

A. sales journal
B. purchases journal
C. cash receipts journal
D. cash disbursements journal
E. general journal

10. LO 7.2 The company just took a physical count of inventory and found $75 worth of inventory was unaccounted for. It was either stolen or damaged. Which journal would the company use to record the correction of the error in inventory?

A. sales journal
B. purchases journal
C. cash receipts journal
D. cash disbursements journal
E. general journal

11. LO 7.2 Your company paid rent of $1,000 for the month with check number 1245. Which journal would the company use to record this?

A. sales journal
B. purchases journal
C. cash receipts journal
D. cash disbursements journal
E. general journal

12. LO 7.2 On January 1, Incredible Infants sold goods to Babies Inc. for $1,540, terms 30 days, and received payment on January 18. Which journal would the company use to record this transaction on the 18th?

A. sales journal
B. purchases journal
C. cash receipts journal
D. cash disbursements journal
E. general journal

13. LO 7.2 Received a check for $72 from a customer, Mr. White. Mr. White owed you $124. Which journal would the company use to record this transaction?

A. sales journal
B. purchases journal
C. cash receipts journal
D. cash disbursements journal
E. general journal

14. LO 7.2 You returned damaged goods you had previously purchased from C.C. Rogers Inc. and received a credit memo for $250. Which journal would your company use to record this transaction?

A. sales journal
B. purchases journal
C. cash receipts journal
D. cash disbursements journal
E. general journal

15. LO 7.2 Sold goods for $650 cash. Which journal would the company use to record this transaction?

A. sales journal
B. purchases journal
C. cash receipts journal
D. cash disbursements journal
E. general journal

16. LO 7.2 Sandren & Co. purchased inventory on credit from Acto Supply Co. for $4,000. Sandren & Co. would record this transaction in the ______.

A. general journal
B. cash receipts journal
C. cash disbursements journal
D. purchases journal
E. sales journal

17. LO 7.3 Sold goods for $650, credit terms net 30 days. Which journal would the company use to record this transaction?

A. sales journal
B. purchases journal
C. cash receipts journal
D. cash disbursements journal
E. general journal

18. LO 7.3 You returned damaged goods to C.C. Rogers Inc. and received a credit memo for $250. Which journal(s) would the company use to record this transaction?

A. sales journal only
B. purchases journal and the accounts payable subsidiary ledger
C. cash receipts journal and the accounts receivable subsidiary ledger
D. cash disbursements journal and the accounts payable subsidiary ledger
E. general journal and the accounts payable subsidiary ledger

19. LO 7.3 The sum of all the accounts in the accounts receivable subsidiary ledger should ______.

A. equal the accounts receivable account balance in the general ledger before posting any amounts
B. equal the accounts payable account balance in the general ledger before posting any amounts
C. equal the accounts receivable account balance in the general ledger after posting all amounts
D. equal the cash account balance in the general ledger after posting all amounts

20. LO 7.3 AB Inc. purchased inventory on account from YZ Inc. The amount was $500. AB Inc. uses an accounting information system with special journals. Which special journal would the company use to record this transaction?

A. sales journal
B. purchases journal
C. cash receipts journal
D. cash disbursements journal
E. general journal

21. LO 7.3 You just posted a debit to ABC Co. in the accounts receivable subsidiary ledger. Which special journal did it come from?

A. sales journal
B. cash receipts journal
C. purchases journal
D. cash disbursements journal
E. general journal

22. LO 7.3 You just posted a credit to Stars Inc. in the accounts receivable subsidiary ledger. Which special journal did it come from?

A. sales journal
B. cash receipts journal
C. purchases journal
D. cash disbursements journal
E. general journal

23. LO 7.3 You just posted a debit to Cash in the general ledger. Which special journal did it come from?

A. sales journal
B. cash receipts journal
C. purchases journal
D. cash disbursements journal
E. general journal

24. LO 7.3 You just posted a credit to Accounts Receivable. Which special journal did it come from?

A. sales journal
B. cash receipts journal
C. purchases journal
D. cash disbursements journal
E. general journal

25. LO 7.3 You just posted a credit to Sales and a debit to Cash. Which special journal did it come from?

A. sales journal
B. cash receipts journal
C. purchases journal
D. cash disbursements journal
E. general journal

26. LO 7.5 An enterprise resource planning (ERP) system ______.

A. is software to help you prepare your tax return
B. requires that you pay ransom before you can operate it
C. is a large, company-wide integrated accounting information system that connects all of a company's applications
D. is part of the darknet

27. LO 7.5 Which of the following is not a way to prevent your computer from being attacked by ransomware?

A. making sure your antivirus security programs are up to date
B. opening all attachments from emails from unknown senders
C. using secure (password protected) networks and backing up your files regularly
D. not using open Wi-Fi (nonpassword, nonencrypted) in public locations

28. LO 7.5 Big data is mined ______.

A. to find business trends
B. to record transactions
C. as an alternative to creating an accounting information system
D. as an alternative to the darknet

29. LO 7.5 Artificial intelligence refers to ______.

A. tutorials that can make humans smarter than they naturally are
B. programming computers to mimic human reasoning and perform tasks previously performed by humans
C. humans that do not possess reasonably high IQs
D. a concept that exists only in science fiction but has not yet been achieved today

30. LO 7.5 Blockchain is a technology that ______.

A. is in the early stages of being developed
B. was a failed attempt to change the way we do business
C. refers to an application developed strictly for the real estate business
D. involves the use of a single shared ledger between the many parties that may be involved in a transaction.

31. LO 7.5 Which of the following is not true about cybercurrency?

A. Bitcoin is one of several cybercurrencies.
B. It is an alternate currency that does not go through the banking system.
C. It does not involve the actual exchange of physical currency.
D. It is not accepted by any legitimate businesses.

Questions

1. LO 7.1 Why does a student need to understand how to use a manual, paper-based accounting information system since everyone uses computerized systems?

2. LO 7.1 Provide an example of how paper-based accounting information systems are different from computerized systems.

3. LO 7.1 Why are scanners better than keyboards?

4. LO 7.1 Why are there so many different accounting information system software packages?

5. LO 7.1 Which area of accounting needs a computerized accounting information system the most—payroll, tax, or preparing financial statements?

6. LO 7.1 The American Institute of Certified Public Accountants (AICPA) has stated that accountants will need to have an even better understanding of computer systems in the future. Why do you think computer skills will be more important?

7. LO 7.4 Which special journals also require an entry to a subsidiary ledger?

8. LO 7.4 What is a schedule of accounts receivable?

9. LO 7.4 How often do we post the cash column in the cash receipts journal to the subsidiary ledger?

10. LO 7.4 The schedule of accounts payable should equal what?

11. LO 7.4 Which amounts do we post daily and which do we post monthly?

12. LO 7.4 Why are special journals used?

13. LO 7.4 Name the four main special journals.

14. LO 7.4 A journal entry that requires a debit to Accounts Receivable and a credit to Sales goes in which special journal?

15. LO 7.4 The purchase of equipment for cash would be recorded in which special journal?

16. LO 7.4 Can a sales journal be used to record sales on account and a cash sale? Why or why not?

17. LO 7.4 When should entries from the sales journal be posted?

18. LO 7.4 We record a sale on account that involves sales tax in which journal?

19. LO 7.4 We record purchases of inventory for cash in which journal(s)?

20. LO 7.4 Should the purchases journal have a column that is a debit to Accounts Payable?

21. LO 7.5 Forensic means "suitable for use in a court of law." How does that have anything to do with accounting?

Exercise Set A

EA1. LO 7.1 For each of the following, indicate if the statement reflects an input component, output component, or storage component of an accounting information system.

A. A credit card scanner at a grocery store.
B. A purchase order for 1,000 bottles of windshield washing fluid to be used as inventory by an auto parts store.
C. A report of patients who missed appointments at a doctor's office.
D. A list of the day's cash and credit sales.
E. Electronic files containing a list of current customers.

EA2. LO 7.1 All of the following information pertains to Green's Grocery. Match each of the following parts of Green's accounting information system in the left-hand column with the appropriate item(s) from the right-hand column. You may use items in the right-hand column more than once or not at all. There may be several answers for each item in the left-hand column.

A. Source document	i. Check written for office supplies
B. Output device	ii. Invoice from a supplier of inventory
C. Input device	iii. Payroll check
D. Data and information storage	iv. Time card
E. Information processing	v. Computer software
	vi. Keyboard
	vii. Grocery store bar code scanner
	viii. Printer
	ix. Flash drive
	x. Hard drive
	xi. The cloud
	xii. Computer screen

EA3. LO 7.2 Match the special journal you would use to record the following transactions. Select from the following:

A. cash receipts journal	i. Sold inventory for cash
B. cash disbursements journal	ii. Sold inventory on account
C. sales journal	iii. Received cash a week after selling items on credit
D. purchases journal	iv. Paid cash to purchase inventory
E. general journal	v. Paid a cash dividend to shareholders
	vi. Sold shares of stock for cash
	vii. Bought equipment for cash
	viii. Recorded an adjusting entry for supplies
	ix. Paid for a purchase of inventory on account within the discount period
	x. Paid for a purchase of inventory on account after the discount period has passed

EA4. LO 7.2 For each of the transactions, state which special journal (sales journal, cash receipts journal, cash disbursements journal, purchases journal, or general journal) and which subsidiary ledger (Accounts Receivable, Accounts Payable, or neither) would be used in recording the transaction.

A. Paid utility bill
B. Sold inventory on account
C. Received but did not pay phone bill
D. Bought inventory on account
E. Borrowed money from a bank
F. Sold old office furniture for cash
G. Recorded depreciation
H. Accrued payroll at the end of the accounting period
I. Sold inventory for cash
J. Paid interest on bank loan

EA5. LO 7.3 Catherine's Cookies has a beginning balance in the Accounts Payable control total account of $8,200. In the cash disbursements journal, the Accounts Payable column has total debits of $6,800 for November. The Accounts Payable credit column in the purchases journal reveals a total of $10,500 for the current month. Based on this information, what is the ending balance in the Accounts Payable account in the general ledger?

EA6. LO 7.3 Record the following transactions in the sales journal:

Jan. 15	Invoice # 325, sold goods on credit for $2,400, to Maroon 4, account # 4501
Jan. 22	Invoice #326, sold goods on credit for $3,500 to BTS, account # 5032
Jan. 27	Invoice #327, sold goods on credit for $1,250 to Imagine Fireflies, account # 3896

EA7. LO 7.3 Record the following transactions in the cash receipts journal.

Jun. 12	Your company received payment in full from Jolie Inc. in the amount of $1,225 for merchandise purchased on June 4 for $1,250, invoice number #1032. Jolie Inc. was offered terms of 2/10, n/30. Record the payment.
Jun. 15	Portman Inc. mailed you a check for $2500. The company paid for invoice #1027, dated June 1, in the amount of $2,500, terms offered 3/10, n/30.
Jun. 17	Your company received a refund check (its check #12440) from the State Power Company because you overpaid your electric bill. The check was in the amount of $72. The Utility Expense account number is #450. Record receipt of the refund.

EA8. LO 7.4 Maddie Inc. has the following transactions for its first month of business.

May 1	Credit sale to Green Lantern Inc. for $1,999
May 2	Credit sale to Wonder Woman Inc. for $2,000
May 3	Credit sale to Flash Inc. for $3,050
May 4	Received $1,000 on account from Green Lantern Inc.
May 5	Credit sale to Black Panther Inc. for $1,875
May 6	Received the full amount from Flash Inc.

A. What are the individual account balances, and the total balance, in the accounts receivable subsidiary ledger?
B. What is the balance in the accounts receivable general ledger (control) account?

Exercise Set B

EB1. LO 7.1 For each of the following, indicate if the statement reflects an input component, output component, or storage component of the accounting information system for a bank.

A. Online customer check ordering system.
B. Approved loan applications.
C. Report of customers with savings accounts over $5,000.
D. Desktop hard drive on computer used by bank president's administrative assistant.
E. List of the amount of money withdrawn from all of the bank's ATMs on a given day.

EB2. LO 7.1 The following information pertains to Crossroads Consulting, Inc. Match each of the following parts of Crossroad's accounting information system in the left-hand column with the appropriate item(s) from the right-hand column. You may use items in the right-hand column more than once or not at all. There may be several answers for each item in the left-hand column. You may choose items in the right-hand column more than once.

A. Source document	i. Sales invoice from cleaning company
B. Output device	ii. Printed check to be mailed to phone company
C. Input device	iii. Dropbox (online storage)
D. Data and information storage	iv. Voice-to-text software
E. Information processing	v. QuickBooks Accounting Software
	vi. Keyboard
	vii. Printer
	viii. Bar code scanner
	ix. Computer screen
	x. Flash drive
	xi. Text scanner
	xii. Computing interest on a loan

EB3. LO 7.2 Match the special journal you would use to record the following transactions.

A. Cash Receipts Journal	i. Took out a loan from the bank
B. Cash Disbursements Journal	ii. Paid employee wages
C. Sales Journal	iii. Paid income taxes
D. Purchases Journal	iv. Sold goods with credit terms 1/10, 2/30, n/60
E. General Journal	v. Purchased inventory with credit terms n/90
	vi. Sold inventory for cash
	vii. Paid the phone bill
	viii. Purchased stock for cash
	ix. Recorded depreciation on the factory equipment
	x. Returned defective goods purchased on credit to the supplier. The company had not yet paid for them.

EB4. LO 7.2 For each of the following transactions, state which special journal (Sales Journal, Cash Receipts Journal, Cash Disbursements Journal, Purchases Journal, or General Journal) and which subsidiary ledger (Accounts Receivable, Accounts Payable, neither) would be used in recording the transaction.

A. Sold inventory for cash
B. Issued common stock for cash
C. Received and paid utility bill
D. Bought office equipment on account
E. Accrued interest on a loan at the end of the accounting period
F. Paid a loan payment
G. Bought inventory on account
H. Paid employees
I. Sold inventory on account
J. Paid monthly insurance bill

EB5. LO 7.3 Catherine's Cookies has a beginning balance in the Accounts Receivable control total account of $8,200. $15,700 was credited to Accounts Receivable during the month. In the sales journal, the Accounts Receivable debit column shows a total of $12,000. What is the ending balance of the Accounts Receivable account in the general ledger?

EB6. LO 7.3 Record the following transactions in the purchases journal:

Feb. 2	Purchased inventory on account from Pinetop Inc. (vendor account number 3765), Purchase Order (PO) # 12345 in the amount of $3,456.
Feb. 8	Purchased inventory on account from Sherwood Company (vendor account number 5461), PO# 12346, in the amount of $2,951.
Feb. 12	Purchased inventory on account from Green Valley Inc. (vendor #4653), PO# 12347, in the amount of $4,631.

EB7. LO 7.3 Record the following transactions in the cash disbursements journal:

Mar. 1	Paid Duke Mfg (account number D101) $980 for inventory purchased on Feb. 27 for $1,000. Duke Mfg offered terms of 2/10, n/30, and you paid within the discount period using check #4012.
Mar. 3	Paid Emergency Plumbing $450. They just came to fix the leak in the coffee room. Give them account number E143. Use check #4013 and debit the Repairs and Maintenance account, #655.
Mar. 5	Used check #4014 to pay Wake Mfg (account number W210) $1,684 for inventory purchased on Feb. 25, no terms offered.

EB8. LO 7.4 Piedmont Inc. has the following transactions for its first month of business:

Jun. 1	Purchased inventory from Montana Inc. on credit for $4,500
Jun. 2	Purchased inventory from Payton Inc. on credit for $2,400
Jun. 3	Purchased inventory from Montana Inc. on credit for $1,800
Jun. 4	Paid $2,000 on account to Montana Inc.
Jun. 8	Purchased inventory on credit from Taylor Inc. for $2,000
Jun. 9	Paid Payton

A. What are the individual account balances, and the total balance, in the accounts payable subsidiary ledger?

B. What is the balance in the Accounts Payable general ledger account?

Problem Set A

PA1. LO 7.2 On June 30, Oscar Inc.'s bookkeeper is preparing to close the books for the month. The accounts receivable control total shows a balance of $2,820.76, but the accounts receivable subsidiary ledger shows total account balances of $2,220.76. The accounts receivable subsidiary ledger is shown here. Can you help find the mistake?

ACCOUNTS RECEIVABLE SUBSIDIARY LEDGER

Account: Amazoon		**AR No. 246**			
					Balance
Date	**Item**	**Ref.**	**Debit**	**Credit**	**Debit**
	Beginning Balance				1,200.50
Apr. 5	Payment	CR 175		1200.50	0.00

Account: Cadberry		**AR No. 357**			
					Balance
Date	**Item**	**Ref.**	**Debit**	**Credit**	**Debit**
	Beginning Balance				877.30
Apr. 8	Invoice 210	SJ 123	300		1,177.30

Account: Hewlit Pickard		**AR No. 468**			
					Balance
Date	**Item**	**Ref.**	**Debit**	**Credit**	**Debit**
	Beginning Balance				172.99
Apr. 28	Invoice 211	SJ 123	100		272.99

Account: Neatflicks inc.		**AR No. 579**			
					Balance
Date	**Item**	**Ref.**	**Debit**	**Credit**	**Debit**
	Beginning Balance				1,570.47
Apr. 6	Payment	CR 175		500	1,070.47
Apr. 22	Invoice 212	CJ 123		300	770.47

PA2. LO 7.4 Evie Inc. has the following transactions during its first month of business. Journalize the transactions that go in the sales journal.

Jun. 1	Credit sale (invoice #1) to Green Lantern Inc. (acc #101) for $1,999
Jun. 2	Credit sale (invoice #2) to Wonder Woman Inc. (acc #102) for $2,000
Jun. 3	Credit sale to Flash Inc. (invoice #3) (acc #103) for $3,050
Jun. 4	Received $1,000 on account from Green Lantern Inc.
Jun. 5	Credit sale (invoice #4) to Black Panther Inc. (acc #104) for $1,875
Jun. 6	Received the full amount from Flash Inc.

PA3. LO 7.4 The following transactions occurred for Donaldson Inc. during the month of July.

Jul. 1	Sold 50 items to Palm Springs Inc. and offered terms of 2/10, n/30, $4,000 on July 1, and issued invoice #12 on account number #312
Jul. 5	Sold 20 thing-a-jigs to Miami Inc. for $2,150 cash on July 5, and issued invoice #13
Jul. 8	Sold 30 what-is to Smith Mfg. for $5,000 and offered terms of 2/10, n/30; issued invoice #14 on account number #178
Jul. 9	Received payment from Palm Springs Inc.
Jul. 22	Received payment from Smith Mfg. after expiration of the discount period

A. Record the transactions for Donaldson Inc. in the proper special journal and subsidiary ledger.

B. Record the same transactions using QuickBooks, and print the journals and subsidiary ledger. They should match.

PA4. LO 7.4 Use the journals and ledgers that follow. Total the journals. Post the transactions to the subsidiary ledger and (using T-accounts) to the general ledger accounts. Then prepare a schedule of accounts receivable.

SALES JOURNAL					Page 79
Date	**Account**	**Invoice No.**	**Ref.**	**DR Accts. Receivable CR Sales**	**DR COGS CR Merchandise Inventory**
2019					
Feb. 4	Evert Company (E123)	17433		1,000.00	
Feb. 8	King Inc. (K331)	17434		775.30	
Feb. 14	Martina Inc. (M132)	17435		2,301.99	
Feb. 16	Shriver Company (S101)	17436		500.00	

SALES JOURNAL						Page 102
Date	**Account**	**Invoice No.**	**Ref.**	**Cash DR**	**Sales Discounts DR**	**Accounts Receivable, Sales, or Other Accounts CR**
2019						
Feb. 1	Cash Sales			465		465
Feb. 5	Payment from Evert	1723		980	20	1,000
Feb. 15	Bank loan (230)			2,000		2,000
Feb. 21	Payment from Shriver Co.	1719		500		500

PA5. LO 7.4 Brown Inc. records purchases in a purchases journal and purchase returns in the general journal. Record the following transactions using a purchases journal, a general journal, and an accounts payable subsidiary ledger. The company uses the periodic method of accounting for inventory.

Oct. 1	Purchased inventory on account from Price Inc. for $2,000
Oct. 1	Purchased inventory on account from Cabrera Inc. for $3,000
Oct. 8	Returned half of the inventory to Price Inc.
Oct. 9	Purchased inventory on account from Price Inc. for $4,200

Problem Set B

PB1. LO 7.2 On June 30, Isner Inc.'s bookkeeper is preparing to close the books for the month. The accounts receivable control total shows a balance of $550, but the accounts receivable subsidiary ledger shows total account balances of $850. The accounts receivable subsidiary ledger is shown here. Can you help find the mistake?

ACCOUNTS RECEIVABLE SUBSIDIARY LEDGER

Account: Apple			No. 1103		
					Balance
Date	Item	Ref.	Debit	Credit	Debit
Jun. 1	Beginning Balance		150		150
Jun. 12	Check received	CR 122	150		300

Account: Orange			No. 1107		
					Balance
Date	Item	Ref.	Debit	Credit	Debit
Jun. 15	Invoice 234	SJ 24	200		200

Account: Pear			No. 1110		
					Balance
Date	Item	Ref.	Debit	Credit	Debit
Jun. 20	Invoice 235	SJ 24	350		350

Account: Banana			No. 1115		
					Balance
Date	Item	Ref.	Debit	Credit	Debit
	Beginning Balance		2,661		2,661
Jun. 18	Check received	CR 122		2,661	0

PB2. LO 7.4 Piedmont Inc. has the following transactions for the month of July.

Jul. 1	Sold merchandise for $4,000 to Pinetop Inc. (account number PT152) and offered terms of 1/10, n/30, on July 1, invoice # 1101
Jul. 5	Sold merchandise to Sherwood Inc. (account number SH 224), Invoice # 1102 for $2,450 cash on July 5
Jul. 9	Sold merchandise, invoice #1103, to Cardinal Inc. (account number CA 118) for $5,000, and offered terms of 3/10, n/30
Jul. 9	Received payment from Pinetop Inc.
Jul. 22	Received payment from Cardinal Inc. after expiration of the discount period
Jul. 30	Received a refund check in the amount of $120 from the insurance company (credit Insurance Expense, account number 504)

A. Record the transactions for Piedmont Inc. in the proper special journal, and post them to the subsidiary ledger and general ledger account.

B. Record the same transactions using QuickBooks, and print the special journals and subsidiary and general ledger. Your solution done manually should match your solution using QuickBooks.

PB3. LO 7.4 Use the journals and ledgers that follows. Total and rule (draw a line under the column of numbers) the journals. Post the transactions to the subsidiary ledger and (using T-accounts) to the general ledger accounts. Then prepare a schedule of Accounts Payable.

PURCHASES JOURNAL					
Date	**Purchase Order No.**	**Account Credited**	**Acct. No.**	**Debit Merchandise Inventory Credit AP**	
2019					
Apr. 4	57346	Murphy Corp.	AP146	1,235	50
Apr. 7	57347	Jensen Company	AP234	678	25
Apr. 15	57348	Murphy Corp.	AP146	715	19

CASH DISBURSEMENTS JOURNAL										Page 102
							Other Accounts			
Date	**Check No.**	**Payee**	**Cash CR**	**Ref.**	**Accounts Payable DR**	**Purchases Discounts CR**	**Acct. No.**	**√**	**DR**	**CR**
Apr. 1	1251	Rent	800				526		800	
Apr. 7	1252	Murphy Corp.	1,210.79	AP 155	1,235.50	24.71				
Apr. 15	1253	Country Bank (loan)	3090				222		3,000	
		Interest					563		90	
Apr. 16	1254	Jensen Company	657.90	AP 234	678.25	20.35				

PB4. LO 7.4 Comprehensive Problem: Manual Accounting Information System versus QuickBooks

The following problem is a comprehensive problem requiring you to compete all of the steps in the accounting cycle, first manually and then by entering the same transactions and performing the same steps using QuickBooks. This will demonstrate the important point that a manual accounting information system (AIS) and a computerized AIS both allow the user to perform the same steps in the accounting cycle, but they are done differently.

In a manual system, every step must be performed by the user. In contrast to this, in a computerized system, for each transaction, the user determines the type of transaction it is and enters it in the appropriate data entry screen. The computer then automatically places the transactions in transaction files (the equivalent of journals in a manual system). The user then instructs the system to post the transaction to the subsidiary ledger and at the end of the month to the general ledger. The computer can do the posting automatically.

Other steps done automatically by the computer are preparing a trial balance, closing entries, and generating financial statements. The user would have to provide the computer with information about adjusting entries at the end of the period. Some adjusting entries can be set up to be done automatically every month, but not all. When we say the computer can do a specific step "automatically," this presumes that a programmer wrote the programs (i.e., detailed step-by-step instructions in a computer language) that tell the computer how to do the task. The computer can then follow those instructions and do it "automatically" without human intervention.

Problem

Assume there is a small shoe store in your neighborhood with a single owner. The owner started the business on December 1, 2018, and sells two types of shoes: a comfortable sneaker that is something athletes would purchase, and a comfortable dress shoe that looks dressy but has the comfort of a sneaker. The name of the business is *The Shoe Horn*. Complete tasks A and B that follow, using the detailed instructions for each. Following is a list of all transactions that occurred during December 2018.

a.	Dec. 1	Jack Simmons, the owner contributed a $500,000 check from his personal account, which he deposited into an account opened in the name of the business, to start the business.
b.	Dec. 1	He rented space that had previously been used by a shoe store and wrote check no. 100 for $9,000 for the first six month's rent.
c.	Dec. 2	He paid for installation and phone usage $300 (check no. 101)
d.	Dec. 2	He paid for advertising in the local paper $150 (check no. 102). The ads will all run in December.
e.	Dec. 2	He purchased $500 of office supplies (check no. 103)
f.	Dec. 3	He paid $300 for insurance for three months (December 2018, January and February 2019 using check no, 104).
g.	Dec. 4	He purchased 800 pairs of sneakers at $40 a pair– on account from Nike (using purchase order no. 301). Payment terms were 2/10, net 30. Assume the shoe store uses the perpetual inventory system.
h.	Dec. 5	He purchased 500 pairs of dress shoes from Footwear Corp. on account for $20 a pair (using purchase order no. 302). Payment terms were 2/10, net 30

i.	Dec. 10	He made a sale on account of 20 pairs of sneakers at $100 a pair, to a local University – Highland University (sales invoice number 2000) for their basketball team. Payment terms were 2/10 net 30.
j.	Dec. 11	He made a sale on account of 2 pairs of dress shoes at $50 a pair (sales invoice no. 2001) to a local charity, U.S. Veterans, that intended to raffle them off at one of their events.
k.	Dec. 12	He made a sale on account to The Jenson Group of 300 pairs of dress shoes at $50 a pair, to use as part of an employee uniform. Payment terms were 2/10 net 30.
l.	Dec. 14	He made a cash sale for 2 sneakers at $120 each and 1 pair of shoes for $60.
m.	Dec. 14	He paid the amount owed to Footwear Corp (check no 105)
n.	Dec. 17	Highland University returned 2 pairs of sneakers they had previously purchased on account.
o.	Dec. 18	He received a check from Highland University in full payment of their balance.
p.	Dec. 20	He made a cash sale to Charles Wilson of three pairs of sneakers at $120 each and 1 pair of dress shoes at $60.
q.	Dec. 20	He made a partial payment to Nike for $20,000 (check number 106)
r.	Dec. 23	Received a $400 utility bill which will be paid in January.
s.	Dec. 27	Received a check from The Jenson Group in the amount of $9,000.
t.	Dec. 28	He paid $2,000 of his balance to Nike (check number 107)

A. Enter all of the transactions and complete all of the steps in the accounting cycle assuming a manual system. Follow the *steps to be performed using a manual system*.

B. Enter the transactions into QuickBooks, complete all of the steps in the accounting cycle, and generate the same reports (journals trial balances, ledgers, financial statements). Follow the steps to be performed using a manual system. Follow the *steps to be performed using QuickBooks*.

Steps to be performed using a manual system

1. For each of the transactions listed for the month of December 2018, identify the journal to which the entry should be recorded. Your possible choices are as follows: general journal (GJ), cash receipts journal (CR), cash disbursements journal (CD), sales journal (SJ), or purchases journal (PJ). Templates for the journals and ledgers have been provided.

2. Enter each transaction in the appropriate journal using the format provided.

SALES JOURNAL						Page 10
Date	Account	Terms	Ref.	Invoice No.	Accounts Receivable DR Sales CR	Cost of Goods Sold DR Inventory CR

PURCHASES JOURNAL					Page 15
Date	Account	Terms	Ref.	Invoice No.	Inventory DR Accounts Payable CR

CASH DISBURSEMENTS JOURNAL											Page 25
								Other			
Date	Description	Check No.	Ref.	Cash CR	Acct. Payable DR	Inventory DR	Purchases Discount CR	Acct. No.	Ref.	Debit	Credit
Debits = Credits =											

CASH RECEIPTS JOURNAL										Page 30
							Other			
Date	Description	Ref.	Cash DR	Acct. Receivable CR	Sales Cr	Sales Discount DR	Acct. No.	Ref.	Debit	Credit
Debits = Credits =										

3. Open up Accounts Receivable subsidiary ledger accounts for customers and Accounts Payable subsidiary ledger accounts for vendors using the format provided. Post each entry to the appropriate subsidiary ledger on the date the transaction occurred.

ACCOUNTS RECEIVABLE SUBSIDIARY LEDGER

Highland University (HU)

Date	Item	Ref.	Debit	Credit	Balance	
					Debit	Credit

U.S. VETERANS (USV)

Date	Item	Ref.	Debit	Credit	Balance	
					Debit	Credit

JENSEN GROUP (JG)

Date	Item	Ref.	Debit	Credit	Balance	
					Debit	Credit

ACCOUNTS PAYABLE SUBSIDIARY LEDGER

Nike

Date	Item	Ref.	Debit	Credit	Balance	
					Debit	Credit

FOOTWEAR CORP. (FC)

Date	Item	Ref.	Debit	Credit	Balance	
					Debit	Credit

4. Total the four special journals, and post from all of them to the general ledger on the last day of December. You should open ledger accounts for the following accounts:
    - Cash
    - Accounts Receivable
    - Merchandise Inventory
    - Prepaid Insurance
    - Prepaid Rent
    - Office Supplies
    - Accounts Payable
    - Purchases Discounts
    - Utilities Expense Payable
    - Jack Simmons, Capital
    - Sales
    - Sales Returns and Allowances
    - Sales Discounts
    - Cost of Goods Sold
    - Rent Expense
    - Advertising Expense
    - Telephone Expense
    - Utilities Expense
    - Office Supplies Expense
    - Insurance Expense

GENERAL LEDGER						
ACCOUNT: CASH					No. 100	
					Balance	
Date	Item	Ref.	Debit	Credit	Debit	Credit

ACCOUNT: ACCOUNTS RECEIVABLE					No. 102	
					Balance	
Date	Item	Ref.	Debit	Credit	Debit	Credit

ACCOUNT: MERCHANDISE INVENTORY					No. 110	
					Balance	
Date	Item	Ref.	Debit	Credit	Debit	Credit

ACCOUNT: PREPAID INSURANCE						No. 118
					Balance	
Date	Item	Ref.	Debit	Credit	Debit	Credit

ACCOUNT: PREPAID RENT						No. 119
					Balance	
Date	Item	Ref.	Debit	Credit	Debit	Credit

ACCOUNT: OFFICE SUPPLIES						No. 125
					Balance	
Date	Item	Ref.	Debit	Credit	Debit	Credit

ACCOUNT: ACCOUNTS PAYABLE						No. 200
					Balance	
Date	Item	Ref.	Debit	Credit	Debit	Credit

ACCOUNT: PURCHASES DISCOUNT						No. 111
					Balance	
Date	Item	Ref.	Debit	Credit	Debit	Credit

ACCOUNT: UTILITIES EXPENSE PAYABLE						No. 210
					Balance	
Date	Item	Ref.	Debit	Credit	Debit	Credit

ACCOUNT: JACK SIMMONS, CAPITAL						No. 500
					Balance	
Date	Item	Ref.	Debit	Credit	Debit	Credit

ACCOUNT: SALES						No. 300
					Balance	
Date	Item	Ref.	Debit	Credit	Debit	Credit

ACCOUNT: SALES RETURNS AND ALLOWANCES						No. 301
					Balance	
Date	Item	Ref.	Debit	Credit	Debit	Credit

ACCOUNT: SALES DISCOUNTS						No. 302
					Balance	
Date	Item	Ref.	Debit	Credit	Debit	Credit

ACCOUNT: COST OF GOODS SOLD						No. 400
					Balance	
Date	Item	Ref.	Debit	Credit	Debit	Credit

ACCOUNT: ADVERTISING EXPENSE						No. 420
					Balance	
Date	Item	Ref.	Debit	Credit	Debit	Credit

ACCOUNT: RENT EXPENSE						No. 403
					Balance	
Date	Item	Ref.	Debit	Credit	Debit	Credit

ACCOUNT: TELEPHONE EXPENSE						No. 410
					Balance	
Date	Item	Ref.	Debit	Credit	Debit	Credit

ACCOUNT: UTILITIES EXPENSE						No. 405
					Balance	
Date	Item	Ref.	Debit	Credit	Debit	Credit

ACCOUNT: OFFICE SUPPLIES EXPENSE						No. 418
					Balance	
Date	Item	Ref.	Debit	Credit	Debit	Credit

ACCOUNT: INSURANCE EXPENSE						No. 408
					Balance	
Date	Item	Ref.	Debit	Credit	Debit	Credit

5. Compute balances for each general ledger account and for each Accounts Receivable and Accounts Payable subsidiary ledger account.
6. Prepare a trial balance.
7. Prepare an accounts receivable schedule and an accounts payable schedule.
8. Prepare adjusting journal entries based on the following information given, record the entries in the appropriate journal, and post the entries.
    - There were $100 worth of office supplies remaining at the end of December.
    - Make an adjusting entry relative to insurance.
    - There was an additional bill received in the mail for utilities expense for the month of December in the amount of $100 that is due by January 10, 2019. Jack Simmons intends to pay it in January.

GENERAL JOURNAL				Page 1
Date	Description	Ref.	Debit	Credit

9. Prepare an adjusted trial balance
10. Prepare closing journal entries, record them in the general journal, and post them.

GENERAL JOURNAL				Page 1
Date	Description	Ref.	Debit	Credit

11. Prepare an Income statement, Statement of Owner's Equity, and Balance Sheet.

Steps to be performed using QuickBooks. You can access a **trial version of QuickBooks** (https://quickbooks.intuit.com/pricing/) to work through this problem.

1. Set up a new company called *The Shoe Horn* using easy step interview.
2. You will be adding a bank account, customizing preferences, adding customers, adding vendors, adding products, and customizing the chart of accounts. You will *not* need to enter opening adjustments since you are entering transactions for a new company, so there are no opening balances. QuickBooks should automatically create a chart of accounts, but you can customize it, and you will need to enter information for a customer list, vendor list, and (inventory) items list.
3. Use “QB transactions” to enter each of the following transactions for the month of December 2018. You can use Onscreen Journal to enter transactions into the general journal, and Onscreen Forms to enter transactions that will end up in the special journals. Identify the type of transaction it is: a sale, a purchase, a receipt of cash, or a payment by check. The categories QuickBooks uses are banking and credit card, customers and sales, vendors and expenses, employees and payroll (not needed in this problem), and other. Note: there is no need to identify the journal as in a manual system or to enter a journal entry, because in an AIS like QuickBooks, you enter the transaction information, and behind the scenes, QuickBooks creates a journal entry that gets added to a transaction file (the equivalent of a journal). After the transactions for the month have been entered, you can print out each of the five journals.

4. Enter the following transactions using the appropriate data entry screens based on the type of transaction it is, as identified in step 3.

a.	Dec. 1	Jack Simmons, the owner contributed a $500,000 check from his personal account, which he deposited into an account opened in the name of the business, to start the business.
b.	Dec. 1	He rented space that had previously been used by a shoe store and wrote check no. 100 for $9,000 for the first six month's rent.
c.	Dec. 2	He paid for installation and phone usage $300 (check no. 101)
d.	Dec. 2	He paid for advertising in the local paper $150 (check no. 102). The ads will all run in December.
e.	Dec. 2	He purchased $500 of office supplies (check no. 103)
f.	Dec. 3	He paid $300 for insurance for three months (December 2018, January and February 2019 using check no, 104).
g.	Dec. 4	He purchased 800 pairs of sneakers at $40 a pair– on account from Nike (using purchase order no. 301). Payment terms were 2/10, net 30. Assume the shoe store uses the perpetual inventory system.
h.	Dec. 5	He purchased 500 pairs of dress shoes from Footwear Corp. on account for $20 a pair (using purchase order no. 302). Payment terms were 2/10, net 30
i.	Dec. 10	He made a sale on account of 20 pairs of sneakers at $100 a pair, to a local University – Highland University (sales invoice number 2000) for their basketball team. Payment terms were 2/10 net 30.
j.	Dec. 11	He made a sale on account of 2 pairs of dress shoes at $50 a pair (sales invoice no. 2001) to a local charity, U.S. Veterans, that intended to raffle them off at one of their events.
k.	Dec. 12	He made a sale on account to The Jenson Group of 300 pairs of dress shoes at $50 a pair, to use as part of an employee uniform. Payment terms were 2/10 net 30.
l.	Dec. 14	He made a cash sale for 2 sneakers at $120 each and 1 pair of shoes for $60.
m.	Dec. 14	He paid the amount owed to Footwear Corp (check no 105)
n.	Dec. 17	Highland University returned 2 pairs of sneakers they had previously purchased on account.
o.	Dec. 18	He received a check from Highland University in full payment of their balance.
p.	Dec. 20	He made a cash sale to Charles Wilson of three pairs of sneakers at $120 each and 1 pair of dress shoes at $60.
q.	Dec. 20	He made a partial payment to Nike for $20,000 (check number 106)
r.	Dec. 23	Received a $400 utility bill which will be paid in January.

s.	Dec. 27	Received a check from The Jenson Group in the amount of $9,000.
t.	Dec. 28	He paid $2,000 of his balance to Nike (check number 107)

5. Generate and print a trial balance. Use QB reports to print this and other reports.
6. Prepare and enter adjusting entries based on the following information given, and print them.
    - There were $100 worth of office supplies remaining at the end of December.
    - Make an adjusting entry relative to insurance
    - There was an additional bill received in the mail for utilities expense for the month of December in the amount of $100 that is due by January 10, 2019. Jack Simmons intends to pay it in January.
7. Generate and print an adjusted trial balance.
8. QuickBooks will automatically prepare closing journal entries.
9. Print the financial statements: the Income Statement (same as Profit and Loss Statement) and the Balance Sheet.
10. Print all of the five journals. After the transactions for the month have been entered, you can print out each of the five journals (general journal, cash receipts journal, cash disbursements journal, sales journal, purchases journal).
11. Print the general ledger and the accounts receivable and accounts payable subsidiary ledgers.
12. Compare the items you printed from QuickBooks to what you have manually prepared. The content should be identical, although the format may be slightly different. Note: while the results are the same, the QuickBooks software did many of the steps for you automatically.

Thought Provokers

TP1. LO 7.2 Why must the Accounts Receivable account in the general ledger match the totals of all the subsidiary Accounts Receivable accounts?

TP2. LO 7.2 Why would a company use a subsidiary ledger for its Accounts Receivable?

TP3. LO 7.2 If a customer owed your company $100 on the first day of the month, then purchased $200 of goods on credit on the fifth and paid you $50 on fifteenth, the customer's ending balance for the month would show a (debit or credit) of how much?

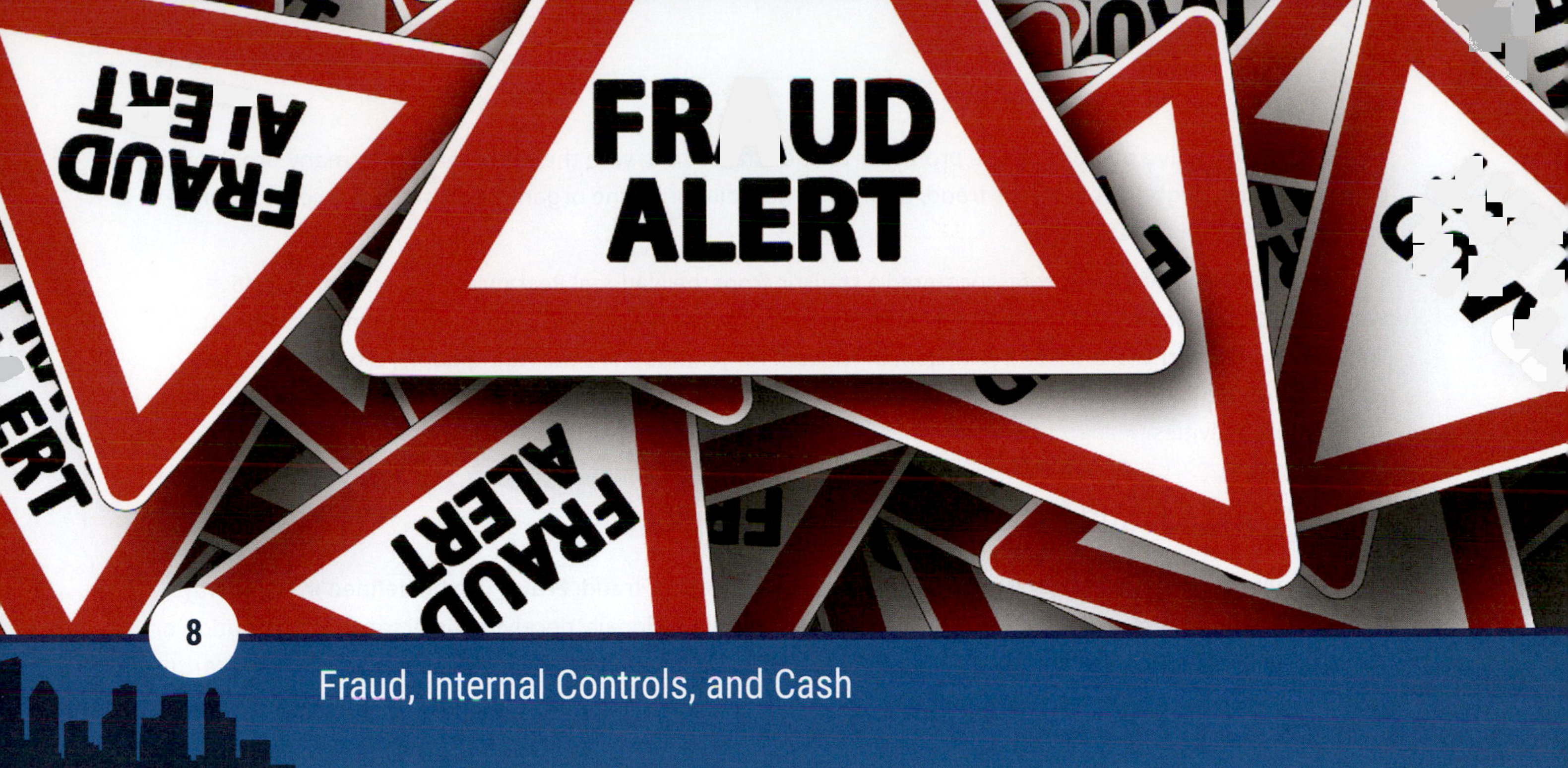

8 Fraud, Internal Controls, and Cash

Figure 8.1 Fraud. Fraud and theft can be very dangerous to the health and survival of a company. This is an issue that companies of all sizes face. (credit: modification of "Road Sign Attention" by "geralt"/Pixabay, CC0)

Chapter Outline

Why It Matters

One of Jennifer's fondest memories was visiting her grandparents' small country store when she was a child. She was impressed by how happy the customers seemed to be in the welcoming environment. While attending college, she decided that the college community needed a coffee/pastry shop where students and the local citizens could congregate, spend time together, and enjoy a coffee or other beverage, along with a pastry that Jennifer would buy from a local bakery. In a sense, she wanted to replicate the environment that people found in her grandparents' store.

After graduation, while she was in the planning stage, she asked her former accounting professor for advice on planning and operating a business since she had heard that the attrition rate for new businesses is quite high. The professor told her that one of the most important factors was the selection, hiring, and treatment of happy and productive personnel. The professor further stated that, with the right personnel, many problems that companies might face, such as fraud, theft, and the violation of the organization's internal control policies and principles, can be lessened.

To emphasize her point, the professor stated a statistic from the National Restaurant Association's *2016 Restaurant Operations Report* that restaurant staff were responsible for an estimated 75% of inventory theft.[1] This statistic led to the professor's final gem of wisdom for Jennifer: hire the right people, create a pleasant work environment, and also create an environment that does not tempt your personnel to consider fraudulent or felonious activities.

8.1 Analyze Fraud in the Accounting Workplace

In this chapter, one of the major issues examined is the concept of fraud. **Fraud** can be defined in many ways, but for the purposes of this course we define it as the act of intentionally deceiving a person or organization or misrepresenting a relationship in order to secure some type of benefit, either financial or nonfinancial. We initially discuss it in a broader sense and then concentrate on the issue of fraud as it relates to the accounting environment and profession.

Workplace fraud is typically detected by anonymous tips or by accident, so many companies use the fraud triangle to help in the analysis of workplace fraud. Donald Cressey, an American criminologist and sociologist, developed the **fraud triangle** to help explain why law-abiding citizens sometimes commit serious workplace-related crimes. He determined that people who embezzled money from banks were typically otherwise law-abiding citizens who came into a "non-sharable financial problem." A non-sharable financial problem is when a trusted individual has a financial issue or problem that he or she feels can't be shared. However, it is felt that the problem can be alleviated by surreptitiously violating the position of trust through some type of illegal response, such as embezzlement or other forms of misappropriation. The guilty party is typically able to rationalize the illegal action. Although they committed serious financial crimes, for many of them, it was their first offense.

The fraud triangle consists of three elements: incentive, opportunity, and rationalization (Figure 8.2). When an employee commits fraud, the elements of the fraud triangle provide assistance in understanding the employee's methods and rationale. Each of the elements needs to be present for workplace fraud to occur.

1 National Restaurant Association. "2016 Restaurant Operations Report." 2016. https://www.restaurant.org/research/reports/restaurant-operations-report

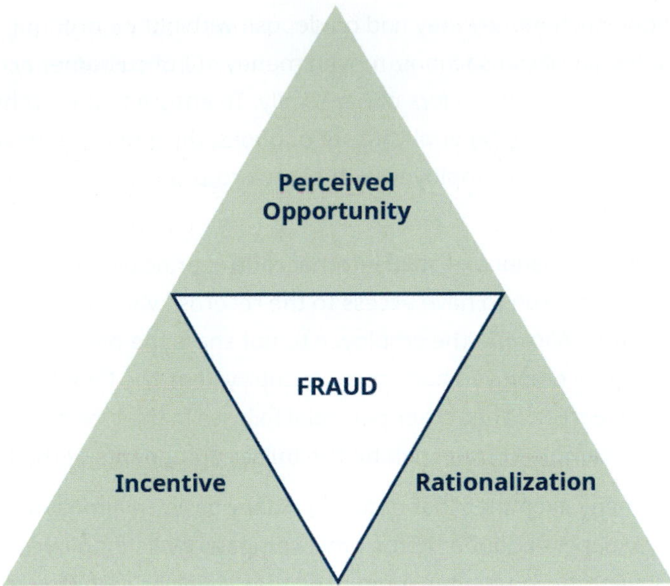

Figure 8.2 Fraud Triangle. The three components identified in the fraud triangle are perceived opportunity, incentive, and rationalization. (attribution: Copyright Rice University, OpenStax, under CC BY-NC-SA 4.0 license)

Perceived opportunity is when a potential fraudster thinks that the internal controls are weak or sees a way to override them. This is the area in which an accountant has the greatest ability to mitigate fraud, as the accountant can review and test internal controls to locate weaknesses. After identifying a weak, circumvented, or nonexistent internal control, management, along with the accountant, can implement stronger internal controls.

Rationalization is a way for the potential fraudster to internalize the concept that the fraudulent actions are acceptable. A typical fraudster finds ways to personally justify his or her illegal and unethical behavior. Using rationalization as a tool to locate or combat fraud is difficult, because the outward signs may be difficult to recognize.

Incentive (or pressure) is another element necessary for a person to commit fraud. The different types of pressure are typically found in (1) vices, such as gambling or drug use; (2) financial pressures, such as greed or living beyond their means; (3) work pressure, such as being unhappy with a job; and (4) other pressures, such as the desire to appear successful. Pressure may be more recognizable than rationalization, for instance, when coworkers seem to be living beyond their means or complain that they want to get even with their employer because of low pay or other perceived slights.

Typically, all three elements of the triangle must be in place for an employee to commit fraud, but companies usually focus on the opportunity aspect of mitigating fraud because, they can develop internal controls to manage the risk. The rationalization and pressure to commit fraud are harder to understand and identify. Many organizations may recognize that an employee may be under pressure, but many times the signs of pressure are missed.

Virtually all types of businesses can fall victim to fraudulent behavior. For example, there have been scams involving grain silos in Texas inflating their inventory, the sale of mixed oils labeled as olive oil across the globe, and the tens of billions of dollars that Bernie Madoff swindled out of investors and not-for-profits.

To demonstrate how a fraud can occur, let's examine a sample case in a little more detail. In 2015, a long-term employee of the SCICAP Federal Credit Union in Iowa was convicted of stealing over $2.7 million in cash over a 37-year period. The employee maintained two sets of financial records: one that provided customers with correct information as to how much money they had on deposit within their account, and a second set of books that, through a complex set of transactions, moved money out of customer accounts and into the employee's account as well as those of members of her family. To ensure that no other employee within the small credit union would have access to the duplicate set of books, the employee never took a vacation over the 37-year period, and she was the only employee with password-protected access to the system where the electronic records were stored.

There were, at least, two obvious violations of solid internal control principles in this case. The first was the failure to require more than one person to have access to the records, which the employee was able to maintain by not taking a vacation. Allowing the employee to not share the password-protected access was a second violation. If more than one employee had access to the system, the felonious employee probably would have been caught much earlier. What other potential failures in the internal control system might have been present? How does this example of fraud exhibit the three components of the fraud triangle?

Unfortunately, this is one of many examples that occur on a daily basis. In almost any city on almost any day, there are articles in local newspapers about a theft from a company by its employees. Although these thefts can involve assets such as inventory, most often, employee theft involves cash that the employee has access to as part of his or her day-to-day job.

LINK TO LEARNING

Small businesses have few employees, but often they have certain employees who are trusted with responsibilities that may not have complete internal control systems. This situation makes small businesses especially vulnerable to fraud. The article "Small Business Fraud and the Trusted Employee" from the Association of Certified Fraud Examiners (https://openstax.org/l/50ACFEFraud) describes how a trusted employee may come to commit fraud, and how a small business can prevent it from happening.

Accountants, and other members of the management team, are in a good position to control the perceived opportunity side of the fraud triangle through good internal controls, which are policies and procedures used by management and accountants of a company to protect assets and maintain proper and efficient operations within a company with the intent to minimize fraud. An **internal auditor** is an employee of an organization whose job is to provide an independent and objective evaluation of the company's accounting and operational activities. Management typically reviews the recommendations and implements stronger internal controls.

Another important role is that of an **external auditor**, who generally works for an outside certified public accountant (CPA) firm or his or her own private practice and conducts audits and other assignments, such as reviews. Importantly, the external auditor is not an employee of the client. The external auditor prepares reports and then provides opinions as to whether or not the financial statements accurately reflect the financial conditions of the company, subject to generally accepted accounting principles (GAAP). External auditors can maintain their own practice, or they might be employed by national or regional firms.

ETHICAL CONSIDERATIONS

Internal Auditors and Their Code of Ethics

Internal auditors are employees of an organization who evaluate internal controls and other operational metrics, and then ethically report their findings to management. An internal auditor may be a Certified Internal Auditor (CIA), an accreditation granted by the Institute of Internal Auditors (IIA). The IIA defines internal auditing as "an independent, objective assurance and consulting activity designed to add value and improve an organization's operations. It helps an organization accomplish its objectives by bringing a systematic, disciplined approach to evaluate and improve the effectiveness of risk management, control, and governance processes."[2]

Internal auditors have their own organizational code of ethics. According to the IIA, "the purpose of The Institute's Code of Ethics is to promote an ethical culture in the profession of internal auditing."[3] Company management relies on a disciplined and truthful approach to reporting. The internal auditor is expected to keep confidential any received information, while reporting results in an objective fashion. Management trusts internal auditors to perform their work in a competent manner and with integrity, so that the company can make the best decisions moving forward.

One of the issues faced by any organization is that internal control systems can be overridden and can be ineffective if not followed by management or employees. The use of internal controls in both accounting and operations can reduce the risk of fraud. In the unfortunate event that an organization is a victim of fraud, the internal controls should provide tools that can be used to identify who is responsible for the fraud and provide evidence that can be used to prosecute the individual responsible for the fraud. This chapter discusses internal controls in the context of accounting and controlling for cash in a typical business setting. These examples are applicable to the other ways in which an organization may protect its assets and protect itself against fraud.

8.2 Define and Explain Internal Controls and Their Purpose within an Organization

Internal controls are the systems used by an organization to manage risk and diminish the occurrence of fraud. The internal control structure is made up of the control environment, the accounting system, and procedures called *control activities*. Several years ago, the **Committee of Sponsoring Organizations (COSO)**, which is an independent, private-sector group whose five sponsoring organizations periodically identify and address specific accounting issues or projects, convened to address the issue of internal control deficiencies in the operations and accounting systems of organizations. They subsequently published a report that is known as COSO's *Internal Control-Integrated Framework*. The five components that they determined were necessary in an effective internal control system make up the components in the internal controls triangle shown in Figure 8.3.

2 The Institute of Internal Auditors (IIA). "Code of Ethics." n.d. https://na.theiia.org/standards-guidance/mandatory-guidance/Pages/Code-of-Ethics.aspx

3 The Institute of Internal Auditors (IIA). "Code of Ethics." n.d. https://na.theiia.org/standards-guidance/mandatory-guidance/Pages/Code-of-Ethics.aspx

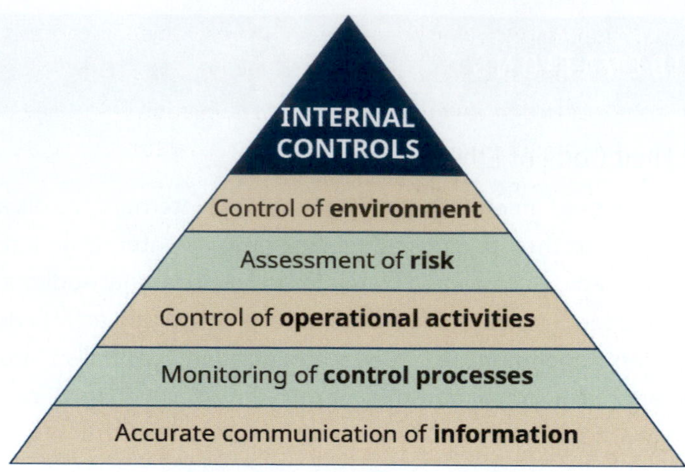

Figure 8.3 The Internal Control Environment. (attribution: Copyright Rice University, OpenStax, under CC BY-NC-SA 4.0 license)

Here we address some of the practical aspects of internal control systems. The internal control system consists of the formal policies and procedures that do the following:

- ensure assets are properly used
- ensure that the accounting system is functioning properly
- monitor operations of the organization to ensure maximum efficiency
- ensure that assets are kept secure
- ensure that employees are in compliance with corporate policies

A properly designed and functioning internal control system will not eliminate the risk of loss, but it will reduce the risk.

Different organizations face different types of risk, but when internal control systems are lacking, the opportunity arises for fraud, misuse of the organization's assets, and employee or workplace corruption. Part of an accountant's function is to understand and assist in maintaining the internal control in the organization.

LINK TO LEARNING

See the Institute of Internal Auditors website (https://openstax.org/l/50IIA) to learn more about many of the professional functions of the internal auditor.

Internal control keeps the assets of a company safe and keeps the company from violating any laws, while fairly recording the financial activity of the company in the accounting records. Proper accounting records are used to create the financial statements that the owners use to evaluate the operations of a company, including all company and employee activities. Internal controls are more than just reviews of how items are recorded in the company's accounting records; they also include comparing the accounting records to the actual operations of the company.

For example, a movie theater earns most of its profits from the sale of popcorn and soda at the concession stand. The prices of the items sold at the concession stand are typically high, even though the costs of popcorn and soda are low. Internal controls allow the owners to ensure that their employees do not give away the profits by giving away sodas and popcorn.

If you were to go to the concession stand and ask for a cup of water, typically, the employee would give you a clear, small plastic cup called a courtesy cup. This internal control, the small plastic cup for nonpaying customers, helps align the accounting system and the theater's operations. A movie theater does not use a system to directly account for the sale of popcorn, soda, or ice used. Instead, it accounts for the containers. A point-of-sale system compares the number of soda cups used in a shift to the number of sales recorded in the system to ensure that those numbers match. The same process accounts for popcorn buckets and other containers. Providing a courtesy cup ensures that customers drinking free water do not use the soda cups that would require a corresponding sale to appear in the point-of-sale system. The cost of the popcorn, soda, and ice will be recorded in the accounting system as an inventory item, but the internal control is the comparison of the recorded sales to the number of containers used. This is just one type of internal control. As we discuss the internal controls, we see that the internal controls are used both in accounting, to provide information for management to properly evaluate the operations of the company, and in business operations, to reduce fraud.

It should be clear how important internal control is to all businesses, regardless of size. An effective internal control system allows a business to monitor its employees, but it also helps a company protect sensitive customer data. Consider the 2017 massive data breach at Equifax that compromised data of over 143 million people. With proper internal controls functioning as intended, there would have been protective measures to ensure that no unauthorized parties had access to the data. Not only would internal controls prevent outside access to the data, but proper internal controls would protect the data from corruption, damage, or misuse.

YOUR TURN

Bank Fraud in Enid, Oklahoma

The retired mayor of Enid, Oklahoma, Ernst Currier, had a job as a loan officer and then as a senior vice president at Security National Bank. In his bank job, he allegedly opened 61 fraudulent loans. He used the identities of at least nine real people as well as eight fictitious people and stole about $6.2 million.[4] He was sentenced to 13 years in prison on 33 felony counts.

Currier was able to circumvent one of the most important internal controls: segregation of duties. The American Institute of Certified Public Accountants (AICPA) states that segregation of duties "is based on shared responsibilities of a key process that disperses the critical functions of that process to more than one person or department. Without this separation in key processes, fraud and error risks are far less manageable."[5] Currier used local residents' identities and created false documents to open loans for millions of dollars and then collect the funds himself, without any oversight by any other employee. Creating these loans allowed him to walk up to the bank vault and take cash out of the bank without anyone questioning him. There was no segregation of duties for opening loans, or if there was, he was able to easily override those internal controls.

How could internal controls have helped prevent Currier's bank fraud in Enid, Oklahoma?

Solution

Simply having someone else confirm the existence of the borrower and make the payment for the loan directly to the borrower would have saved this small bank millions of dollars.

4 Jack Money. "Fraudulent Loans Lead to Enid Banker's Arrest on Numerous Felony Complaints." *The Oklahoman*. November 15, 2017. https://newsok.com/article/5572195/fraudulent-loans-lead-to-enid-bankers-arrest-on-numerous-felony-complaints

5 American Institute of Certified Public Accountants (AICPA). "Segregation of Duties." n.d. https://www.aicpa.org/interestareas/informationtechnology/resources/value-strategy-through-segregation-of-duties.html

Consider a bank that has to track deposits for thousands of customers. If a fire destroys the building housing the bank's servers, how can the bank find the balances of each customer? Typically, organizations such as banks mirror their servers at several locations around the world as an internal control. The bank might have a main server in Tennessee but also mirror all data in real time to identical servers in Arizona, Montana, and even offshore in Iceland. With multiple copies of a server at multiple locations across the country, or even the world, in the event of disaster to one server, a backup server can take control of operations, protecting customer data and avoiding any service interruptions.

Internal controls are the basic components of an **internal control system**, the sum of all internal controls and policies within an organization that protect assets and data. A properly designed system of internal controls aims to ensure the integrity of assets, allows for reliable accounting information and financial reporting, enhances efficiency within an organization, and provides guidelines and possible consequences for dealing with breaches. Internal controls drive many decisions and overall operational procedures within an organization. A properly designed internal control system will not prevent all loss from occurring, but it will significantly reduce the risk of loss and increase the chance of identifying the responsible party.

CONTINUING APPLICATION AT WORK

Fraud Controls for Grocery Stores

All businesses are concerned with internal controls over reporting and assets. For the grocery industry this concern is even greater, because profit margins on items are so small that any lost opportunity hurts profitability. How can an individual grocery store develop effective controls?

Consider the two biggest items that a grocery store needs to control: food (inventory) and cash. Inventory controls are set up to stop shrinkage (theft). While it is not profitable for each aisle to be patrolled by a security guard, cameras throughout the store linked to a central location allow security staff to observe customers. More controls are placed on cash registers to prevent employees from stealing cash. Cameras at each register, cash counts at each shift change, and/or a supervisor who observes cashiers are some potential internal control methods. Grocery stores invest more resources in controlling cash because they have determined it to be the greatest opportunity for fraudulent activity.

The Role of Internal Controls

The accounting system is the backbone of any business entity, whether it is profit based or not. It is the responsibility of management to link the accounting system with other functional areas of the business and ensure that there is communication among employees, managers, customers, suppliers, and all other internal and external users of financial information. With a proper understanding of internal controls, management can design an internal control system that promotes a positive business environment that can most effectively serve its customers.

For example, a customer enters a retail store to purchase a pair of jeans. As the cashier enters the jeans into the point-of-sale system, the following events occur internally:

1. A sale is recorded in the company's journal, which increases revenue on the income statement. If the transaction occurred by credit card, the bank typically transfers the funds into the store's bank account in a timely manner.
2. The pair of jeans is removed from the inventory of the store where the purchase was made.

3. A new pair of jeans is ordered from the distribution center to replace what was purchased from the store's inventory.
4. The distribution center orders a new pair of jeans from the factory to replace its inventory.
5. Marketing professionals can monitor over time the trend and volume of jeans sold in a specific size. If an increase or decrease in sales volume of a specific size is noted, store inventory levels can be adjusted.
6. The company can see in real time the exact inventory levels of all products in all stores at all times, and this can ensure the best customer access to products.

Because many systems are linked through technology that drives decisions made by many stakeholders inside and outside of the organization, internal controls are needed to protect the integrity and ensure the flow of information. An internal control system also assists all stakeholders of an organization to develop an understanding of the organization and provide assurance that all assets are being used efficiently and accurately.

Environment Leading to the Sarbanes-Oxley Act

Internal controls have grown in their importance as a component of most business decisions. This importance has grown as many company structures have grown in complexity. Despite their importance, not all companies have given maintenance of controls top priority. Additionally, many small businesses do not have adequate understanding of internal controls and therefore use inferior internal control systems. Many large companies have nonformalized processes, which can lead to systems that are not as efficient as they could be. The failure of the SCICAP Credit Union discussed earlier is a direct result of a small financial institution having a substandard internal control system leading to employee theft. One of the largest corporate failures of all time was Enron, and the failure can be directly attributed to poor internal controls.

Enron was one of the largest energy companies in the world in the late twentieth century. However, a corrupt management attempted to hide weak financial performance by manipulating revenue recognition, valuation of assets on the balance sheet, and other financial reporting disclosures so that the company appeared to have significant growth. When this practice was uncovered, the owners of Enron stock lost $40 billion as the stock price dropped from $91 per share to less than $1 per share, as shown in Figure 8.4.[6] This failure could have been prevented had proper internal controls been in place.

For example, Enron and its accounting firm, Arthur Andersen, did not maintain an adequate degree of independence. Arthur Andersen provided a significant amount of services in both auditing and consulting, which prevented them from approaching the audit of Enron with a proper degree of independence. Also, among many other violations, Enron avoided the proper use of several acceptable reporting requirements.

6 Douglas O. Linder, ed. "Enron Historical Stock Price." Famous Trials. n.d. https://www.famous-trials.com/images/ftrials/Enron/documents/enronstockchart.pdf

Figure 8.4 Change in Enron Stock Price. The Enron scandal was one of the largest frauds in the history of modern business. It was the main fraud that was responsible for creation of the Sarbanes-Oxley Act as well as the Public Company Accounting Oversight Board (PCAOB). (attribution: Copyright Rice University, OpenStax, under CC BY-NC-SA 4.0 license)

As a result of the Enron failure and others that occurred during the same time frame, Congress passed the **Sarbanes-Oxley Act (SOX)** to regulate practice to manage conflicts of analysts, maintain governance, and impose guidelines for criminal conduct as well as sanctions for violations of conduct. It ensures that internal controls are properly documented, tested, and used consistently. The intent of the act was to ensure that corporate financial statements and disclosures are accurate and reliable. It is important to note that SOX only applies to public companies. A **publicly traded company** is one whose stock is traded (bought and sold) on an organized stock exchange. Smaller companies still struggle with internal control development and compliance due to a variety of reasons, such as cost and lack of resources.

Major Accounting Components of the Sarbanes-Oxley Act

As it pertains to internal controls, the SOX requires the certification and documentation of internal controls. Specifically, the act requires that the auditor do the following:

1. Issue an internal control report following the evaluation of internal controls.
2. Limit nonaudit services, such as consulting, that are provided to a client.
3. Rotate who can lead the audit. The person in charge of the audit can serve for a period of no longer than seven years without a break of two years.

Additionally, the work conducted by the auditor is to be overseen by the **Public Company Accounting Oversight Board (PCAOB)**. The PCAOB is a congressionally established, nonprofit corporation. Its creation was included in the Sarbanes-Oxley Act of 2002 to regulate conflict, control disclosures, and set sanction guidelines for any violation of regulations. The PCAOB was assigned the responsibilities of ensuring independent, accurate, and informative audit reports, monitoring the audits of securities brokers and dealers, and maintaining oversight of the accountants and accounting firms that audit publicly traded companies.

LINK TO LEARNING

Visit the Public Company Accounting Oversight Board (PCAOB) website (https://openstax.org/l/50PCAOB) to learn more about what it does.

Any employee found to violate SOX standards can be subject to very harsh penalties, including $5 million in fines and up to 20 to 25 years in prison. The penalty is more severe for securities fraud (25 years) than for mail or wire fraud (20 years).

The SOX is relatively long and detailed, with Section 404 having the most application to internal controls. Under Section 404, management of a company must perform annual audits to assess and document the effectiveness of all internal controls that have an impact on the financial reporting of the organization. Also, selected executives of the firm under audit must sign the audit report and state that they attest that the audit fairly represents the financial records and conditions of the company.

The financial reports and internal control system must be audited annually. The cost to comply with this act is very high, and there is debate as to how effective this regulation is. Two primary arguments that have been made against the SOX requirements is that complying with their requirements is expensive, both in terms of cost and workforce, and the results tend not to be conclusive. Proponents of the SOX requirements do not accept these arguments.

One available potential response to mandatory SOX compliance is for a company to decertify (remove) its stock for trade on the available stock exchanges. Since SOX affects publicly traded companies, decertifying its stock would eliminate the SOX compliance requirement. However, this has not proven to be a viable option, primarily because investors enjoy the protection SOX provides, especially the requirement that the companies in which they invest undergo a certified audit prepared by CPAs employed by national or regional accounting firms. Also, if a company takes its stock off of an organized stock exchange, many investors assume that a company is in trouble financially and that it wants to avoid an audit that might detect its problems.

YOUR TURN

The Growing Importance of the Report on Internal Controls

Internal controls have become an important aspect of financial reporting. As part of the financial statements, the auditor has to issue a report with an opinion on the financial statements, as well as internal controls. Use the internet and locate the annual report of a company, specifically the report on internal controls. What does this report tell the user of financial information?

Solution

The annual report informs the user about the financial results of the company, both in discussion by management as well as the financial statements. Part of the financial statements involves an independent auditor's report on the integrity of the financial statements as well as the internal controls.

LINK TO LEARNING

Many companies have their own internal auditors on staff. The role of the internal auditor is to test and ensure that a company has proper internal controls in place, and that they are functioning. Read about how the internal audit works from I.S. Partners (https://openstax.org/l/50ISPartAudit) to learn more.

8.3 Describe Internal Controls within an Organization

The use of internal controls differs significantly across organizations of different sizes. In the case of small businesses, implementation of internal controls can be a challenge, due to cost constraints, or because a small staff may mean that one manager or owner will have full control over the organization and its operations. An owner in charge of all functions has enough knowledge to keep a close eye on all aspects of the organization and can track all assets appropriately. In smaller organizations in which responsibilities are delegated, procedures need to be developed in order to ensure that assets are tracked and used properly.

When an owner cannot have full oversight and control over an organization, internal control systems need to be developed. When an appropriate internal control system is in place, it is interlinked to all aspects of the entity's operations. An appropriate internal control system links the accounting, finance, operations, human resources, marketing, and sales departments within an organization. It is important that the management team, as well as employees, recognize the importance of internal controls and their role in preventing losses, monitoring performance, and planning for the future.

Elements of Internal Control

A strong internal control system is based on the same consistent elements:

- establishment of clear responsibilities
- proper documentation
- adequate insurance
- separation of assets from custody
- separation of duties
- use of technology

Establishment of Clear Responsibilities

A properly designed system of internal control clearly dictates responsibility for certain roles within an organization. When there is a clear statement of responsibility, issues that are uncovered can be easily traced and responsibility placed where it belongs.

As an example, imagine that you are the manager of the Galaxy's Best Yogurt. On any shift, you have three employees working in the store. One employee is designated as the shift supervisor who oversees the operations of the other two employees on the shift and ensures that the store is presented and functioning properly. Of the other two employees, one may be solely responsible for management of the cash register, while the others serve the customers. When only one employee has access to an individual cash register, if there is an overage or shortage of cash, it can be traced to the one employee who is in charge of the cash register.

Proper Documentation

An effective internal control system maintains proper documentation, including backups, to trace all transactions. The documentation can be paper copies, or documents that are computer generated and stored, on flash drives or in the cloud, for example. Given the possibility of some type of natural (tornado or flood) or man-made (arson) disasters, even the most basic of businesses should create backup copies of documentation that are stored off-site.

In addition, any documentation generated by daily operations should be managed according to internal controls. For example, when the Galaxy's Best Yogurt closes each day, one employee should close out and reconcile the cash drawer using prenumbered forms in pen to ensure that no forms can be altered or changed by another employee who may have access to the cash. In case of an error, the employee responsible for making the change should initial any changes on the form. If there are special orders for cakes or other products, the order forms should be prenumbered. The use of prenumbered documents provides assurance that all sales are recorded. If a form is not prenumbered, an order can be prepared, and the employee can then take the money without ringing the order into the cash register, leaving no record of the sale.

Adequate Insurance

Insurance may be a significant cost to an organization (especially liability coverage), but it is necessary. With adequate insurance on an asset, if it is lost or destroyed, an outside party will recoup the company for the loss. If assets are lost to fraud or theft, an insurance company will investigate the loss and will press criminal charges against any employee found to be involved. Very often, the employer will be hesitant to pursue criminal charges against an employee due to the risk of lawsuit or bad publicity. For example, an employee might assume that the termination was age related and is going to sue the company. Also, there might be a situation where the company experienced a loss, such as theft, and it does not want to let the general public know that there are potential deficiencies in its security system.

If the insurance company presses charges on behalf of the company, this protects the organization and also acts as a deterrent if employees know that the insurance company will always prosecute theft. For example, suppose the manager of the Galaxy's Best Yogurt stole $10,000 cash over a period of two years. The owner of the yogurt store will most likely file an insurance claim to recover the $10,000 that was stolen. With proper insurance, the insurance company will reimburse the yogurt store for the money but then has the right to press charges and recover its losses from the employee who was caught stealing. The store owner will have no control over the insurance company's efforts to recover the $10,000 and will likely be forced to fire the employee in order to keep the insurance policy.

Separation of Assets from Custody

Separation of assets from custody ensures that the person who controls an asset cannot also keep the accounting records. This action prevents one employee from taking income from the business and entering a transaction on the accounting records to cover it up. For example, one person within an organization may open an envelope that contains a check, but a different person would enter the check into the organization's accounting system. In the case of the Galaxy's Best Yogurt, one employee may count the money in the cash register drawer at the end of the night and reconcile it with the sales, but a different employee would recount the money, prepare the bank deposit, and ensure that the deposit is made at the bank.

Separation of Duties

A properly designed internal control system assures that at least two (if not more) people are involved with most transactions. The purpose of separating duties is to ensure that there is a check and balance in place. One common internal control is to have one employee place an inventory order and a different employee receive the order as it is delivered. For example, assume that an employee at the Galaxy's Best Yogurt places an inventory order. In addition to the needed inventory, the employee orders an extra box of piecrusts. If that employee also receives the order, he or she can take the piecrusts home, and the store will still pay for them. Check signing is another important aspect of separation of duties. Typically, the person who writes a check should not also sign the check. Additionally, the person who places supply orders should not write checks to pay the bills for these supplies.

Use of Technology

Technology has made the process of internal control simpler and more approachable to all businesses. There are two reasons that the use of technology has become more prevalent. The first is the development of more user-friendly equipment, and the second is the reduction in costs of security resources. In the past, if a company wanted a security system, it often had to go to an outside security firm, and the costs of providing and monitoring the system were prohibitive for many small businesses. Currently, security systems have become relatively inexpensive, and not only do many small businesses now have them, they are now commonly used by residential homeowners.

In terms of the application of security resources, some businesses use surveillance cameras focused on key areas of the organization, such as the cash register and areas where a majority of work is performed. Technology also allows businesses to use password protection on their data or systems so that employees cannot access systems and change data without authorization. Businesses may also track all employee activities within an information technology system.

Even if a business uses all of the elements of a strong internal control system, the system is only as good as the oversight. As responsibilities, staffing, and even technology change, internal control systems need to be constantly reviewed and refined. Internal control reviews are typically not conducted by inside management but by internal auditors who provide an impartial perspective of where controls are working and where they can be improved.

Purposes of Internal Controls within a Governmental Entity

Internal controls apply not only to public and private corporations but also to governmental entities. Often, a government controls one of the most important assets of modern times: data. Unprotected financial information, including tax data, social security, and governmental identifications, could lead to identity theft and could even provide rogue nations access to data that could compromise the security of our country. Governmental entities require their contractors to have proper internal controls and to maintain proper codes of ethics.

ETHICAL CONSIDERATIONS

Ethics in Governmental Contractors

Government entities are not the only organizations required to implement proper internal controls and codes of ethics. As part of the business relationship between different organizations, governmental agencies also require contractors and their subcontractors to implement internal controls to ensure compliance with proper ethical conduct. The Federal Acquisition Regulation (FAR) Council outlines regulations under FAR 3.10,[7] which require governmental contractors and their subcontractors to implement a written "Contractor Code of Business Ethics and Conduct," and the proper internal controls to ensure that the code of ethics is followed. An employee training program, posting of agency inspector general hotline posters, and an internal control system to promote compliance with the established ethics code are also required. Contractors must disclose violations of federal criminal law involving fraud, conflicts of interest, bribery, or gratuity violations; violations of the civil False Claims Act; and significant overpayments on a contract not resulting from contract financing payments.[8] Such internal controls help ensure that an organization and its business relationships are properly managed.

To recognize the significant need for internal controls within the government, and to ensure and enforce compliance, the US Government Accountability Office (GAO) has its own standards for internal control within the federal government. All government agencies are subject to governance under these standards, and one of the objectives of the GAO is to provide audits on agencies to ensure that proper controls are in place and within compliance. Standards for internal control within the federal government are located within a publication referred to as the "Green Book," or *Standards for Internal Control in the Federal Government.*

LINK TO LEARNING

Government organizations have their own needs for internal controls. Read the GAO "Green Book" (https://openstax.org/l/50GAOGreenBook) to learn more about these internal control procedures.

Purposes of Internal Controls within a Not-for-Profit

Not-for-profit (NFP) organizations have the same needs for internal control as many traditional for-profit entities. At the same time, there are unique challenges that these entities face. Based on the objectives and charters of NFP organizations, in many cases, those who run the organizations are volunteers. As volunteers, leaders of NFPs may not have the same training background and qualifications as those in a similar for-profit position. Additionally, a volunteer leader often splits time between the organization and a full-time career. For these reasons, internal controls in an NFP often are not properly implemented, and there may be a greater risk of control lapse. A **control lapse** occurs when there is a deviation from standard control protocol that leads to

7 Federal Acquisition Regulation. "Subpart 3.10: Contractor Code of Business Ethics and Conduct." January 22, 2019. https://www.acquisition.gov/content/subpart-310-contractor-code-business-ethics-and-conduct

8 National Contract Management Association. https://www.ncmahq.org/

a failure in the internal control and/or fraud prevention processes or systems. A failure occurs in a situation when results did not achieve predetermined goals or meet expectations.

Not-for-profit organizations have an extra category of finances that need protection, in addition to their assets. They need to ensure that incoming donations are used as intended. For example, many colleges and universities are classified as NFP organizations, and donations are a significant source of revenue. However, donations are often directed to a specific source. For example, suppose an alumnus of Alpha University wants to make a $1,000,000 donation to the business school for undergraduate student scholarships. Internal controls would track that donation to ensure it paid for scholarships for undergraduate students in the business school and was not used for any other purpose at the school, in order to avoid potential legal issues.

Identify and Apply Principles of Internal Controls to the Receipt and Disbursement of Cash

Cash can be a major part of many business operations. Imagine a Las Vegas casino, or a large grocery store, such as Publix Super Markets, Wegmans Food Markets, or ShopRite; in any of these settings, millions of dollars in cash can change hands within a matter of minutes, and it can pass through the hands of thousands of employees. Internal controls ensure that all of this cash reaches the bank account of the business entity. The first control is monitoring. Not only are cameras strategically placed throughout the store to prevent shoplifting and crime by customers, but cameras are also located over all areas where cash changes hands, such as over every cash register, or in a casino over every gaming table. These cameras are constantly monitored, often offsite at a central location by personnel who have no relationship with the employees who handle the cash, and all footage is recorded. This close monitoring makes it more difficult for misuse of cash to occur.

Additionally, access to cash is tightly controlled. Within a grocery store, each employee has his or her own cash drawer with a set amount of cash. At any time, any employee can reconcile the sales recorded within the system to the cash balance that should be in the drawer. If access to the drawer is restricted to one employee, that employee is responsible when cash is missing. If one specific employee is consistently short on cash, the company can investigate and monitor the employee closely to determine if the shortages are due to theft or if they are accidental, such as if they resulted from errors in counting change. Within a casino, each time a transaction occurs and when there is a shift change for the dealers, cash is counted in real time. Casino employees dispersed on the gaming floor are constantly monitoring play, in addition to those monitoring cameras behind the scenes.

Technology plays a major role in the maintenance of internal controls, but other principles are also important. If an employee makes a mistake involving cash, such as making an error in a transaction on a cash register, the employee who made the mistake typically cannot correct the mistake. In most cases, a manager must review the mistake and clear it before any adjustments are made. These changes are logged to ensure that managers are not clearing mistakes for specific employees in a pattern that could signify **collusion**, which is considered to be a private cooperation or agreement primarily for a deceitful, illegal, or immoral cause or purpose. Duties are also separated to count cash on hand and ensure records are accurate. Often, at the end of the shift, a manager or employee other than the person responsible for the cash is responsible for counting cash on hand within the cash drawer. For example, at a grocery store, it is common for an employee who has been checking out customers for a shift to then count the money in the register and prepare a document providing the counts for the shift. This employee then submits the counted tray to a supervisor, such as a head cashier, who then repeats the counting and documentation process. The two counts should be equal. If there is a discrepancy, it should immediately be investigated. If the store accepts checks and credit/debit card payments, these methods of payments are also incorporated into the verification process.

In many cases, the sales have also been documented either by a paper tape or by a computerized system. The ultimate goal is to determine if the cash, checks, and credit/debit card transactions equal the amount of sales for the shift. For example, if the shift's register had sales of $800, then the documentation of counted cash and checks, plus the credit/debit card documentation should also add up to $800.

Despite increased use of credit cards by consumers, our economy is still driven by cash. As cash plays a very important role in society, efforts must be taken to control it and ensure that it makes it to the proper areas within an organization. The cost of developing, maintaining, and monitoring internal controls is significant but important. Considering the millions of dollars of cash that can pass through the hands of employees on any given day, the high cost can be well worth it to protect the flow of cash within an organization.

LINK TO LEARNING

Internal controls are as important for not-for-profit businesses as they are within the for-profit sector. See this guide for not-for-profit businesses to set up and maintain proper internal control systems (https://openstax.org/l/50IntConNonProf) provided by the National Council of Nonprofits.

THINK IT THROUGH

Hiring Approved Vendors

One internal control that companies often have is an official "approved vendor" list for purchases. Why is it important to have an approved vendor list?

8.4 Define the Purpose and Use of a Petty Cash Fund, and Prepare Petty Cash Journal Entries

As we have discussed, one of the hardest assets to control within any organization is cash. One way to control cash is for an organization to require that all payments be made by check. However, there are situations in which it is not practical to use a check. For example, imagine that the Galaxy's Best Yogurt runs out of milk one evening. It is not possible to operate without milk, and the normal shipment does not come from the supplier for another 48 hours. To maintain operations, it becomes necessary to go to the grocery store across the street and purchase three gallons of milk. It is not efficient for time and cost to write a check for this small purchase, so companies set up a **petty cash fund**, which is a predetermined amount of cash held on hand to be used to make payments for small day-to-day purchases. A petty cash fund is a type of **imprest account**, which means that it contains a fixed amount of cash that is replaced as it is spent in order to maintain a set balance.

To maintain internal controls, managers can use a petty cash receipt (Figure 8.5), which tracks the use of the cash and requires a signature from the manager.

PETTY CASH RECEIPT	
Date: ______	Approved by: ______
Receipt number: ______	Received by: ______

Description	Amount

Figure 8.5 Petty Cash Voucher. A petty cash voucher is an important internal control document to trace the use of cash within a petty cash fund. This voucher allows management to track the use of cash, the balance that should be within the account, and the person responsible for the approval of a payment from the account. (attribution: Copyright Rice University, OpenStax, under CC BY-NC-SA 4.0 license)

As cash is spent from a petty cash fund, it is replaced with a receipt of the purchase. At all times, the balance in the petty cash box should be equal to the cash in the box plus the receipts showing purchases.

For example, the Galaxy's Best Yogurt maintains a petty cash box with a stated balance of $75 at all times. Upon review of the box, the balance is counted in the following way.

Cash in box	$50
Receipt showing purchase of stamps from Postal Service	15
Receipt from Quick Market for the purchase of milk and bananas	10
Total balance in petty cash box	75

Because there may not always be a manager with check signing privileges available to sign a check for unexpected expenses, a petty cash account allows employees to make small and necessary purchases to support the function of a business when it is not practical to go through the formal expense process. In all cases, the amount of the purchase using petty cash would be considered to not be material in nature. Recall that materiality means that the dollar amount in question would have a significant impact in financial results or influence investor decisions.

Demonstration of Typical Petty Cash Journal Entries

Petty cash accounts are managed through a series of journal entries. Entries are needed to (1) establish the fund, (2) increase or decrease the balance of the fund (replenish the fund as cash is used), and (3) adjust for overages and shortages of cash. Consider the following example.

The Galaxy's Best Yogurt establishes a petty cash fund on July 1 by cashing a check for $75 from its checking account and placing cash in the petty cash box. At this point, the petty cash box has $75 to be used for small expenses with the authorization of the responsible manager. The journal entry to establish the petty cash fund would be as follows.

JOURNAL			
Date	**Account**	**Debit**	**Credit**
July 1	Petty cash Cash *To record establishment of petty cash fund*	75	 75

As this petty cash fund is established, the account titled "Petty Cash" is created; this is an asset on the balance sheet of many small businesses. In this case, the cash account, which includes checking accounts, is decreased, while the funds are moved to the petty cash account. One asset is increasing, while another asset is decreasing by the same account. Since the petty cash account is an imprest account, this balance will never change and will remain on the balance sheet at $75, unless management elects to change the petty cash balance.

Throughout the month, several payments are made from the petty cash account of the Galaxy's Best Yogurt. Assume the following activities.

Date	Transaction	Amount
Jul. 10	Postage stamps are purchased	$30
Jul. 15	Milk purchased	10
Jul. 25	Window cleaner purchased from Dollar Store	5

At the end of July, in the petty cash box there should be a receipt for the postage stamp purchase, a receipt for the milk, a receipt for the window cleaner, and the remaining cash. The employee in charge of the petty cash box should sign each receipt when the purchase is made. The total amount of purchases from the receipts ($45), plus the remaining cash in the box should total $75. As the receipts are reviewed, the box must be replenished for what was spent during the month. The journal entry to replenish the petty cash account will be as follows.

JOURNAL			
Date	**Account**	**Debit**	**Credit**
Jul. 31	Postage Expense Inventory Miscellaneous Expense Cash *To record replenishment of petty cash fund*	30 10 5	 45

Typically, petty cash accounts are reimbursed at a fixed time period. Many small businesses will do this monthly, which ensures that the expenses are recognized within the proper accounting period. In the event that all of the cash in the account is used before the end of the established time period, it can be replenished in the same way at any time more cash is needed. If the petty cash account often needs to be replenished before the end of the accounting period, management may decide to increase the cash balance in the account. If, for example, management of the Galaxy's Best Yogurt decides to increase the petty cash balance to $100 from the current balance of $75, the journal entry to do this on August 1 would be as follows.

JOURNAL			
Date	**Account**	**Debit**	**Credit**
Aug. 1	Petty Cash Cash *To increase balance of petty cash fund to $100*	25	 25

If the management at a later date decides to decrease the balance in the petty cash account, the previous entry would be reversed, with cash being debited and petty cash being credited.

Occasionally, errors may occur that affect the balance of the petty cash account. This may be the result of an employee not getting a receipt or getting back incorrect change from the store where the purchase was made. In this case, an expense is created that creates a *cash overage or shortage*.

Consider Galaxy's expenses for July. During the month, $45 was spent on expenses. If the balance in the petty cash account is supposed to be $75, then the petty cash box should contain $45 in signed receipts and $30 in cash. Assume that when the box is counted, there are $45 in receipts and $25 in cash. In this case, the petty cash balance is $70, when it should be $75. This creates a $5 shortage that needs to be replaced from the checking account. The entry to record a cash shortage is as follows.

JOURNAL			
Date	**Account**	**Debit**	**Credit**
Jul. 30	Cash Over and Short Cash *To replenish petty cash balance for cash shortage during period*	5	 5

When there is a shortage of cash, we record the shortage as a "debit" and this has the same effect as an expense. If we have an overage of cash, we record the overage as a credit, and this has the same impact as if we are recording revenue. If there were cash overage, the petty cash account would be debited and the cash over and short account would be credited. In this case, the expense balance decreases, and the year-end balance is the net balance from all overages and shortages during the year.

If a petty cash account is consistently short, this may be a warning sign that there is not a proper control of the account, and management may want to consider additional controls to better monitor petty cash.

THINK IT THROUGH

Cash versus Debit Card

A petty cash system in some businesses may be replaced by use of a prepaid credit card (or debit card) on site. What would be the pros and cons of actually maintaining cash on premises for the petty cash system, versus a rechargeable debit card that employees may use for petty cash purposes? Which option would you select for your petty cash account if you were the owner of a small business?

LINK TO LEARNING

See this article on tips for companies to establish and manage petty cash systems (https://openstax.org/l/50IntConPetCash) to learn more.

8.5 Discuss Management Responsibilities for Maintaining Internal Controls within an Organization

Because internal controls do protect the integrity of financial statements, large companies have become highly regulated in their implementation. In addition to Section 404 of the SOX, which addresses reporting and testing requirements for internal controls, there are other sections of the act that govern management responsibility for internal controls. Although the auditor reviews internal controls and advises on the improvement of controls, ultimate responsibility for the controls is on the management of the company. Under SOX Section 302, in order to provide additional assurance to the financial markets, the **chief executive officer (CEO)**, who is the executive within a company with the highest-ranking title and the overall responsibility for management of the company, and the **chief financial officer (CFO)**, who is the corporation officer who reports to the CEO and oversees all of the accounting and finance concerns of a company, must personally certify that (1) they have reviewed the internal control report provided by the auditor; (2) the report does not contain any inaccurate information; and (3) they believe that all financial information fairly states the financial conditions, income, and cash flows of the entity. The sign-off under Section 302 makes the CEO and CFO personally responsible for financial reporting as well as internal control structure.

While the executive sign-offs seem like they would be just a formality, they actually have a great deal of power in court cases. Prior to SOX, when an executive swore in court that he or she was not aware of the occurrence of some type of malfeasance, either committed by his or her firm or against his or her firm, the executive would claim a lack of knowledge of specific circumstances. The typical response was, "I can't be expected to know everything." In fact, in virtually all of the trials involving potential malfeasance, this claim was made and often was successful in a not-guilty verdict.

The initial response to the new SOX requirements by many people was that there was already sufficient affirmation by the CEO and CFO and other executives to the accuracy and fairness of the financial statements and that the SOX requirements were unnecessary. However, it was determined that the SOX requirements provided a degree of legal responsibility that previously might have been assumed but not actually stated.

Even if a company is not public and not governed by the SOX, it is important to note that the tone is set at the managerial level, called the *tone at the top*. If management respects the internal control system and emphasizes the importance of maintaining proper internal controls, the rest of the staff will follow and create a cohesive environment. A proper tone at the top demonstrates management's commitment toward openness, honesty, integrity, and ethical behavior.

YOUR TURN

Defending the Sarbanes-Oxley Act

You are having a conversation with the CFO of a public company. Imagine that the CFO complains that there is no benefit to Sections 302 and 404 of the Sarbanes-Oxley Act relative to the cost, as "our company has always valued internal controls before this regulation and never had an issue." He believes that this regulation is an unnecessary overstep. How would you respond and defend the need for Sections 302 and 404 of the Sarbanes-Oxley Act?

Solution

I would tell the CFO the following:

1. Everyone says that they have always valued internal controls, even those who did not.
2. Better security for the public is worth the cost.
3. The cost of compliance is more than recovered in the company's market price for its stock.

THINK IT THROUGH

Personal Internal Controls

Technology plays a very important role in internal controls. One recent significant security breach through technology was the Equifax breach. What is an internal control that you can personally implement to protect your personal data as a result of this breach, or any other future breach?

8.6 Define the Purpose of a Bank Reconciliation, and Prepare a Bank Reconciliation and Its Associated Journal Entries

The bank is a very important partner to all businesses. Not only does the bank provide basic checking services, but they process credit card transactions, keep cash safe, and may finance loans when needed.

Bank accounts for businesses can involve thousands of transactions per month. Due to the number of ongoing transactions, an organization's book balance for its checking account rarely is the same as the balance that the bank records reflect for the entity at any given point. These timing differences are typically caused by the fact that there will be some transactions that the organization is aware of before the bank, or transactions the bank is aware of before the company.

For example, if a company writes a check that has not cleared yet, the company would be aware of the transaction before the bank is. Similarly, the bank might have received funds on the company's behalf and recorded them in the bank's records for the company before the organization is aware of the deposit.

With the large volume of transactions that impact a bank account, it becomes necessary to have an internal control system in place to assure that all cash transactions are properly recorded within the bank account, as well as on the ledger of the business. The **bank reconciliation** is the internal financial report that explains and documents any differences that may exist between the balance of a checking account as reflected by the bank's records (bank balance) for a company and the company's accounting records (company balance).

The bank reconciliation is an internal document prepared by the company that owns the checking account. The transactions with timing differences are used to adjust and reconcile both the bank and company balances; after the bank reconciliation is prepared accurately, both the bank balance and the company balance will be the same amount.

Note that the transactions the company is aware of have already been recorded (journalized) in its records. However, the transactions that the bank is aware of but the company is not must be journalized in the entity's records.

Fundamentals of the Bank Reconciliation Procedure

The balance on a bank statement can differ from company's financial records due to one or more of the following circumstances:

- An **outstanding check**: a check that was written and deducted from the financial records of the company but has not been cashed by the recipient, so the amount has not been removed from the bank account.
- A **deposit in transit**: a deposit that was made by the business and recorded on its books but has not yet been recorded by the bank.
- Deductions for a **bank service fee**: fees often charged by banks each month for management of the bank account. These may be fixed maintenance fees, per-check fees, or a fee for a check that was written for an amount greater than the balance in the checking account, called an **nonsufficient funds (NSF) check**. These fees are deducted by the bank from the account but would not appear on the financial records.
- Errors initiated by either the client or the bank: for example, the client might record a check incorrectly in its records, for either a greater or lesser amount than was written. Also, the bank might report a check either with an incorrect balance or in the wrong client's checking account.
- Additions such as interest or funds collected by the bank for the client: interest is added to the bank account as earned but is not reported on the financial records. These additions might also include funds collected by the bank for the client.

Demonstration of a Bank Reconciliation

A bank reconciliation is structured to include the information shown in Figure 8.6.

COMPANY NAME **Bank Reconciliation** **December 31, 2018**			
Bank Statement Balance at 12/31/18	$ XXX	Book Balance at 12/31/18	$ XXX
Deposits in transit	XXX	Income not recorded on books	XXX
Outstanding checks	(XXX)	Bank interest income	XXX
		Expenses not recorded on books	(XXX)
		Bank account charges	(XXX)
Adjusted Bank Balance	$ XXX	Adjusted Book Balance	$ XXX

Figure 8.6 Bank Reconciliation. A bank reconciliation includes categories for adjustments to both the bank balance and the book balance. (attribution: Copyright Rice University, OpenStax, under CC BY-NC-SA 4.0 license)

Assume the following circumstances for Feeter Plumbing Company, a small business located in Northern Ohio.

1. After all posting is up to date, at the end of July 31, the book balance shows $32,760, and the bank statement balance shows $77,040.
2. Check 5523 for $9,620 and 6547 for $10,000 are outstanding.
3. Check 5386 for $2,000 is removed from the bank account correctly but is recorded on the accounting records for $1,760. This was in payment of dues. The effects of this transaction resulted in an error of $320 that must be deducted from the company's book balance.
4. The July 31 night deposit of $34,300 was delivered to the bank after hours. As a result, the deposit is not on the bank statement, but it is on the financial records.
5. Upon review of the bank statement, an error is uncovered. A check is removed from the account from Feeter for $240 that should have been removed from the account of another customer of the bank.

6. In the bank statement is a note stating that the bank collected $60,000 in charges (payments) from the credit card company as well as $1,800 in interest. This transaction is on the bank statement but not in the company's financial records.
7. The bank notified Feeter that a $2,200 check was returned unpaid from customer Berson due to insufficient funds in Berson's account. This check return is reflected on the bank statement but not in the records of Feeter.
8. Bank service charges for the month are $80. They have not been recorded on Feeter's records.

Each item would be recorded on the bank reconciliation as follows:

FEETER PLUMBING
Bank Reconciliation
July 31, 2018

Bank Statement Balance		$ 77,040	Book Balance		$32,760
Deposit	$ 34,300		Collection of account	$60,000	
Bank error	320	34,620	Interest earned	1,800	61,800
		$111,600			$94,560
Outstanding checks			NSF check	(2,200)	
5523	(9,620)		Recording error	(240)	
6547	(10,000)	(19,620)	Service charge	(80)	(2,520)
Adjusted Bank Balance		$ 92,040			$92,040

One important trait of the bank reconciliation is that it identifies transactions that have not been recorded by the company that are supposed to be recorded. Journal entries are required to adjust the book balance to the correct balance.

In the case of Feeter, the first entry will record the collection of the note, as well as the interest collected.

JOURNAL

Date	Account	Debit	Credit
	Cash	31,800	
	Notes Receivable		30,000
	Interest Receivable		1,800
	To recognize the note that was collected and charged interest expense		

The second entry required is to adjust the books for the check that was returned from Berson.

JOURNAL

Date	Account	Debit	Credit
	Accounts Receivable	2,200	
	Cash		2,200
	To adjust the account for the returned check for insufficient funds		

The third entry is to adjust the recording error for check 5386.

JOURNAL

Date	Account	Debit	Credit
	Dues Expense	240	
	Cash		240
	To adjust for check that was not recorded properly		

The final entry is to record the bank service charges that are deducted by the bank but have not been recorded on the records.

JOURNAL			
Date	Account	Debit	Credit
	Bank Service Charges Cash *To record monthly bank service charges*	80	 80

The previous entries are standard to ensure that the bank records are matching to the financial records. These entries are necessary to update Feeter's general ledger cash account to reflect the adjustments made by the bank.

LINK TO LEARNING

This practical article illustrates the key points of why a bank reconciliation is important (https://openstax.org/l/50BankReconcil) for both business and personal reasons.

8.7 Describe Fraud in Financial Statements and Sarbanes-Oxley Act Requirements

Financial statements are the end result of an accountant's work and are the responsibility of management. Proper internal controls help the accountant determine that the financial statements fairly present the financial position and performance of a company. **Financial statement fraud** occurs when the financial statements are used to conceal the actual financial condition of a company or to hide specific transactions that may be illegal. Financial statement fraud may take on many different methods, but it is generally called **cooking the books**. This issue may occur for many purposes.

A common reason to cook the books is to create a false set of a company's books used to convince investors or lenders to provide money to the company. Investors and lenders rely on a properly prepared set of financial statements in making their decision to provide the company with money. Another reason to misstate a set of financial statements is to hide corporate looting such as excessive retirement perks of top executives, unpaid loans to top executives, improper stock options, and any other wrongful financial action. Yet another reason to misreport a company's financial data is to drive the stock price higher. Internal controls assist the accountant in locating and identifying when management of a company wants to mislead the inventors or lenders.

The financial accountant or members of management who set out to cook the books are intentionally attempting to deceive the user of the financial statements. The actions of upper management are being concealed, and in most cases, the entire financial position of the company is being purposely misreported. Regardless of the reason for misstating the true condition of a company's financial position, doing so misleads any person using the financial statements of a company to evaluate the company and its operations.

How Companies Cook the Books to Misrepresent Their Financial Condition

One of the most common ways companies cook the books is by manipulating revenue accounts or accounts receivables. Proper **revenue recognition** involves accounting for revenue when the company has met its obligation on a contract. Financial statement fraud involves early revenue recognition, or recognizing revue that does not exist, and receivable accountings, used in tandem with false revenue reporting. HealthSouth used a combination of false revenue accounts and misstated accounts receivable in a direct manipulation of the revenue accounts to commit a multibillion-dollar fraud between 1996 and 2002. Several chief financial officers and other company officials went to prison as a result.[9]

CONCEPTS IN PRACTICE

Internal Controls at HealthSouth

The fraud at HealthSouth was possible because some of the internal controls were ignored. The company failed to maintain standard segregation of duties and allowed management override of internal controls. The fraud required the collusion of the entire accounting department, concealing hundreds of thousands of fraudulent transactions through the use of falsified documents and fraudulent accounting schemes that included revenue recognition irregularities (such as recognizing accounts receivables to be recorded as revenue before collection), misclassification of expenses and asset acquisitions, and fraudulent merger and acquisition accounting. The result was billions of dollars of fraud. Simply implementing and following proper internal control procedures would have stopped this massive fraud.[10]

Many companies may go to great lengths to perpetuate financial statement fraud. Besides the direct manipulation of revenue accounts, there are many other ways fraudulent companies manipulate their financial statements. Companies with large inventory balances can misrepresent their inventory account balances and use this misrepresentation to overstate the amount of their assets to get larger loans or use the increased balance to entice investors through claims of exaggerated revenues. The inventory accounts can also be used to overstate income. Such inventory manipulations can include the following:

- Channel stuffing: encouraging customers to buy products under favorable terms. These terms include allowing the customer to return or even not pick up goods sold, without a corresponding reserve to account for the returns.
- Sham sales: sales that have not occurred and for which there are no customers.
- Bill-and-hold sales: recognition of income before the title transfers to the buyer, and holding the inventory in the seller's warehouse.
- Improper cutoff: recording sales of inventory in the wrong period and before the inventory is sold; this is a type of early revenue recognition.
- Round-tripping: selling items with the promise to buy the items back, usually on credit, so there is no economic benefit.

9 Melinda Dickinson. "Former HealthSouth Boss Found Liable for $2.9 Billion." *Reuters*. June 18, 2009. https://www.reuters.com/article/us-healthsouth-scrushy/former-healthsouth-boss-found-liable-for-2-9-billion-idUSTRE55H4IP20090618

10 David McCann. "Two CFOs Tell a Tale of Fraud at HealthSouth." CFO.com. March 27, 2017. .http://ww2.cfo.com/fraud/2017/03/two-cfos-tell-tale-fraud-healthsouth/

These are just a few examples of the way an organization might manipulate inventory or sales to create false revenue.

One of the most famous financial statement frauds involved Enron, as discussed previously. Enron started as an interstate pipeline company, but then branched out into many different ventures. In addition to the internal control deficiencies discussed earlier, the financial statement fraud started when the company began to attempt to hide its losses.

The fraudulent financial reporting schemes included building assets and immediately taking as income any projected profits on construction and hiding the losses from operating assets in an off-the-balance sheet transaction called **special purpose entities**, which are separate, often complicated legal entities that are often used to absorb risk for a corporation. Enron moved assets that were losing money off of its books and onto the books of the Special Purpose Entity. This way, Enron could hide its bad business decisions and continue to report a profit, even though its assets were losing money. Enron's financial statement fraud created false revenues with the misstatement of assets and liability balances. This was further supported by inadequate balance sheet footnotes and the related disclosures. For example, required disclosures were ramped up as a result of these special purpose entities.

Sarbanes-Oxley Act Compliance Today

The Enron scandal and related financial statement frauds led to investors requiring that public companies maintain better internal controls and develop stronger governance systems, while auditors perform a better job at auditing public companies. These requirements, in turn, led to the regulations developed under SOX that were intended to protect the investing public.

Since SOX was first passed, it has adapted to changing technology and now requires public companies to protect their accounting and financial data from hackers and other outside or internal forces through stronger internal controls designed to protect the data. The *Journal of Accountancy* supported these new requirements and reported that the results of SOX have been positive for both companies and investors.

As discussed in the *Journal of Accountancy* article,[11] there are three conditions that are increasingly affecting compliance with SOX requirements:

- **PCAOB requirements.** The PCAOB has increased the requirements for inspection reports, with a greater emphasis on deficiency evaluation.
- **Revenue recognition**. The Financial Accounting Standards Board has introduced a new standard for revenue recognition. This requirement has led to the need for companies to update control documentation.
- **Cybersecurity**. **Cybersecurity** is the practice of protecting software, hardware, and data from digital attacks. As would be expected in today's environment, the number of recent cybersecurity disclosures has significantly grown.

Under current guidelines, instead of the SOX requiring compliance with just the financial component of reporting and internal control, the guidelines now allow application to information technology (IT) activities as well. A major change under the SOX guidelines involves the method of storage of a company's electronic records. While the act did not specifically require a particular storage method, it did provide guidance on which records were to be stored and for how long they should be stored.

---

11 Ken Tysiac. "Companies Spending More Time on SOX Compliance." *Journal of Accountancy*. June 12, 2017. https://www.journalofaccountancy.com/news/2017/jun/companies-spending-more-time-on-sox-compliance-201716857.html

The SOX now requires that all business records, electronic records, and electronic messages must be stored for at least five years. The penalties for noncompliance include either imprisonment or fines, or a combination of the two options.

Key Terms

bank reconciliation internal financial report that explains and documents any differences that may exist between a balance within a checking account and the company's records

bank service fee fee often charged by a bank each month for management of the bank account

chief executive officer (CEO) executive within a company with the highest ranking title who has the overall responsibility for the management of a company; reports to the board of directors

chief financial officer (CFO) corporation officer who reports to the CEO and oversees all of the accounting and finance concerns of a company

collusion private cooperation or agreement, between more than one person, primarily for a deceitful, illegal, or immoral cause or purpose

Committee of Sponsoring Organizations (COSO) independent, private-sector group whose five sponsoring organizations periodically identify and address specific accounting issues or projects related to internal controls

control lapse when there is a deviation from standard control protocol that leads to a failure in the internal control and/or fraud prevention processes or systems

cooking the books (also, financial statement fraud) financial statements are used to conceal the actual financial condition of a company or to hide specific transactions that may be illegal

cybersecurity practice of protecting software, hardware, and data from digital attacks

deposit in transit deposit that was made by the business and recorded on its books but has not yet been recorded by the bank

external auditor generally works for an outside CPA firm or his or her own private practice and conducts audits and other assignments, such as reviews

financial statement fraud using financial statements to conceal the actual financial condition of a company or to hide specific transactions that may be illegal

fraud act of intentionally deceiving a person or organization or misrepresenting a relationship in order to secure some type of benefit, either financial or nonfinancial

fraud triangle concept explaining the reasoning behind a person's decision to commit fraud; the three elements are perceived opportunity, rationalization, and incentive

imprest account account that is only debited when the account is established or the total ending balance is increased

internal auditor employee of an organization whose job is to provide an independent and objective evaluation of the company's accounting and operational activities

internal control system sum of all internal controls and policies within an organization that protect assets and data

internal controls systems used by an organization to manage risk and diminish the occurrence of fraud, consisting of the control environment, the accounting system, and control activities

nonsufficient funds (NSF) check check written for an amount that is greater than the balance in the checking account

outstanding check check that was written and deducted from the financial records of the company but has not been cashed by the recipient, so the amount has not been removed from the bank account

petty cash fund amount of cash held on hand to be used to make payments for small day-to-day purchases

Public Company Accounting Oversight Board (PCAOB) organization created under the Sarbanes-Oxley Act to regulate conflict, control disclosures, and set sanction guidelines for any violation of regulation

publicly traded company company whose stock is traded (bought and sold) on an organized stock exchange

revenue recognition accounting for revenue when the company has met its obligation on a contract

Sarbanes-Oxley Act (SOX) federal law that regulates business practices; intended to protect investors by enhancing the accuracy and reliability of corporate financial statements and disclosures through governance guidelines including sanctions for criminal conduct

special purpose entities separate, often complicated legal entities that are often used to absorb risk for a corporation

Summary

8.1 Analyze Fraud in the Accounting Workplace

- The fraud triangle helps explain the mechanics of fraud by examining the common contributing factors of perceived opportunity, incentive, and rationalization.
- Due to the nature of their functions, internal and external auditors, through the implementation of effective internal controls, are in excellent positions to prevent opportunity-based fraud.

8.2 Define and Explain Internal Controls and Their Purpose within an Organization

- A system of internal control is the policies combined with procedures created by management to protect the integrity of assets and ensure efficiency of operations.
- The system prevents losses and helps management maintain an effective means of performance.

8.3 Describe Internal Controls within an Organization

- Principles of an effective internal control system include having clear responsibilities, documenting operations, having adequate insurance, separating duties, and setting clear responsibilities for action.
- Internal controls are applicable to all types of organizations: for profit, not-for-profit, and governmental organizations.

8.4 Define the Purpose and Use of a Petty Cash Fund, and Prepare Petty Cash Journal Entries

- The purpose of a petty cash fund is to make payments for small amounts that are immaterial, such as postage, minor repairs, or day-to-day supplies.
- A petty cash account is an imprest account, so it is only debited when the fund is initially established or increased in amount. Transactions to replenish the account involve a debit to the expenses and a credit to the cash account (e.g., bank account).

8.5 Discuss Management Responsibilities for Maintaining Internal Controls within an Organization

- It is the responsibility of management to assure that internal controls of a company are effective and in place.
- Though management has always had responsibility over internal controls, the Sarbanes-Oxley Act has added additional assurances that management takes this responsibility seriously, and placed sanctions against corporate officers and boards of directors who do not take appropriate responsibility.
- Sarbanes-Oxley only applies to public companies. Even though the rules of this act only apply to public companies, proper internal controls are an important aspect of all businesses of any size. Tone at the top is a key component of a proper internal control system.

8.6 Define the Purpose of a Bank Reconciliation, and Prepare a Bank Reconciliation and Its Associated Journal Entries

- The bank reconciliation is an internal document that verifies the accuracy of records maintained by the depositor and the financial institution. The balance on the bank statement is adjusted for outstanding checks and uncleared deposits. The record balance is adjusted for service charges and interest earned.

- The bank reconciliation is an internal control document that ensures transactions to the bank account are properly recorded, and allows for verification of transactions.

8.7 Describe Fraud in Financial Statements and Sarbanes-Oxley Act Requirements

- Financial statement fraud has occurred when financial statements intentionally hide illegal transactions or fail to accurately reflect the true financial condition of an entity.
- Cooking the books can be used to create false records to present to lenders or investors. It also is used to hide corporate looting of funds and other resources, or to increase stock prices. Cooking the books is an intentional action and is often achieved through the manipulation of the entity's revenues or accounts receivable.
- Health South and Enron were used as examples of past corporate financial fraud.
- The section takes a brief look at the current state of SOX compliance.

Multiple Choice

1. LO 8.1 Which of the following would a fraudster perceive as a pressure?

A. lack of management oversight
B. everyone does it
C. living beyond one's means
D. lack of an internal audit function

2. LO 8.2 Internal control is said to be the backbone of all businesses. Which of the following is the best description of internal controls?

A. Internal controls ensure that the financial statements published are correct.
B. The only role of internal controls is to protect customer data.
C. Internal controls and company policies are important to protect and safeguard assets and to protect all company data and are designed to protect the company from fraud.
D. Internal controls are designed to keep employees from committing fraud against the company.

3. LO 8.3 What is the best way for owners of small businesses to maintain proper internal controls?

A. The owner must have enough knowledge of all aspects of the company and have controls in place to track all assets.
B. Small businesses do not need to worry about internal controls.
C. Small businesses should make one of their employees in charge of all aspects of the company, giving the owner the ability to run the company and generate sales.
D. Only managers need to be concerned about internal controls.

4. LO 8.3 Which of the following is *not* considered to be part of the internal control structure of a company?

A. Ensure that assets are kept secure.
B. Monitor operations of the organization to ensure maximum efficiency.
C. Publish accurate financial statements on a regular basis.
D. Ensure assets are properly used.

5. LO 8.3 There are several elements to internal controls. Which of the following would not address the issue of having cash transactions reported in the accounting records?

A. One employee would have access to the cash register.
B. The cash drawer should be closed out, and cash and the sales register should be reconciled on a prenumbered form.
C. Ask customers to report to a manager if they do not receive a sales receipt or invoice.
D. The person behind the cash register should also be responsible for making price adjustments.

6. LO 8.3 A company is trying to set up proper internal controls for their accounts payable/inventory purchasing system. Currently the purchase order is generated by the same person who receives the inventory. Together the purchase order and the receiving ticket are sent to accounts payable for payment. What changes would you make to improve the internal control structure?

A. No changes would be made since the person paying the bills is different from the person ordering the inventory.
B. The person in accounts payable should generate the purchase order.
C. The person in accounts payable should generate the receiving ticket once the invoice from the supplier is received.
D. The responsibilities of generating the purchase order and receiving the inventory should be separated among two different people.

7. LO 8.3 There are three employees in the accounting department: payroll clerk, accounts payable clerk, and accounts receivable clerk. Which one of these employees should *not* make the daily deposit?

A. payroll clerk
B. account payable clerk
C. accounts receivable clerk
D. none of them

8. LO 8.3 Which one of the following documents is *not* needed to process a payment to a vendor?

A. vendor invoice
B. packing slip
C. check request
D. purchase order

9. LO 8.3 What is the advantage of using technology in the internal control system?

A. Passwords can be used to allow access by employees.
B. Any cash received does not need to be reconciled because the computer tracks all transactions.
C. Transactions are easily changed.
D. Employees cannot steal because all cash transactions are recorded by the computer/cash register.

10. LO 8.3 Which of the following assets require the strongest of internal controls?

A. inventory
B. credit cards
C. computer equipment
D. cash

11. LO 8.4 Which of the following is true about the Sarbanes-Oxley Act?

A. It was passed to ensure that internal controls are properly documented and tested by public companies.
B. It applies to both public and smaller companies.
C. It requires all companies to report their internal control policies to the US Securities and Exchange Commission.
D. It does not require additional costs or resources to have adequate controls.

12. LO 8.4 The external auditor of a company has certain requirements due to Sarbanes-Oxley. Which of the following best describes these requirements?

A. The auditor is required to only report weaknesses in the internal control design of the company he or she is auditing.
B. The auditor must issue an internal control report on the evaluation of internal controls overseen by the Public Company Accounting Oversight Board
C. The auditor in charge can serve for a period of only two years.
D. The Public Company Accounting Oversight Board reviews reports submitted by the auditors when no evaluations have been performed.

13. LO 8.4 Petty cash is used to _______.

A. avoid having to use checks frequently
B. make small payments
C. avoid having to retain receipts because the amounts are very small
D. avoid having to get approvals due to the small amount of cash being paid

14. LO 8.4 A company has decided to start a petty cash fund for $150. Which of the following is the correct journal entry?

A.

Petty Cash	150	
Cash		150

B.

Cash	150	
Petty Cash		150

C. No entry is required.

D.

Expenses	150	
Petty Cash		150

15. LO 8.6 Which of the following items are found on a book side of the bank reconciliation?

A. beginning bank balance
B. outstanding checks
C. interest income
D. error made by bank

16. LO 8.6 Which of the following are found on the bank side of the bank reconciliation?

A. NSF check
B. interest income
C. wire transfer into client's account
D. deposit in transit

17. LO 8.7 What would be a reason a company would want to understate income?

A. to help nudge its stock price higher
B. to lower its tax bill
C. to show an increase in overall profits
D. to increase investor confidence

18. LO 8.7 What would be a reason a company would want to overstate income?

A. to help nudge its stock price higher
B. to lower its tax bill
C. to show a decrease in overall profits
D. none of the above

19. LO 8.7 At what point does revenue recognition occur?

A. When the purchase order is received
B. When the seller receives the money for the job
C. When the seller has met "performance"
D. When the purchaser makes payment

Questions

1. LO 8.1 What is an example of *perceived opportunity* as one of the three elements causing a person to commit fraud?

2. LO 8.1 What is an example of *rationalization* as one of the three elements causing a person to commit fraud?

3. LO 8.1 What is an example of *incentive* as one of the three elements causing a person to commit fraud?

4. LO 8.2 Why is it important to have a very sound and well-developed internal control structure?

5. LO 8.2 The information technology departments of all companies have significant and important roles in the internal control systems. Discuss them and their importance.

6. LO 8.2 What are the functions of the internal control?

7. LO 8.3 Discuss the importance of a company having proper insurance and bonding its employees.

8. LO 8.4 What is the role of the Sarbanes-Oxley Act and the Public Company Accounting Oversight Board?

9. LO 8.4 Why is it important to have a petty cash fund available in a company?

10. LO 8.3 LO 8.4 Is it required to have only one petty cashier or should the company appoint more than one person to administer the fund? Why?

11. LO 8.5 Technology can be used to support a strong internal control system. Discuss how technology has improved the point-of-sale transactions.

12. LO 8.6 What is the purpose of the bank reconciliation?

13. LO 8.6 What should be done if differences are found between the bank statement and the book account?

Exercise Set A

EA1. LO 8.4 Record the following transactions:

A. Started a petty cash fund in the amount of $300.
B. Replenished petty cash fund using the following expenses: Auto $18, Office Expenses $35, Postage Expense $56, Miscellaneous Expenses $67. Cash on hand is $124.
C. Increased petty cash by $50.

EA2. LO 8.4 Record the following transactions:

A. Started a petty cash fund in the amount of $200.
B. Replenished petty cash fund using the following expenses: Auto $15, Office Expenses $20, Postage Expense $81, Miscellaneous Expenses $66. Cash on hand is $10.
C. Increased petty cash by $75.

EA3. LO 8.4 Record the following transactions:

A. Started a petty cash fund in the amount of $300.
B. Replenished petty cash fund using the following expenses: Auto $69, Office Expenses $77, Postage Expense $56, Miscellaneous Expenses $98. Cash on hand is $6.
C. Increased petty cash by $60.

EA4. LO 8.4 Record the following transactions:

A. Started a petty cash fund in the amount of $500.
B. Replenished petty cash fund using the following expenses: Auto $24, Office Expenses $43, Postage Expense $19, Miscellaneous Expenses $25. Cash on hand is $389.
C. The company has decided to reduce the petty cash fund to $300.

EA5. LO 8.6 The bank reconciliation shows the following adjustments:

- Deposits in transit: $1,234
- Outstanding checks: $558
- Bank service charges: $50
- NSF checks: $250

Prepare the correcting journal entry.

EA6. LO 8.6 The bank reconciliation shows the following adjustments:

- Deposits in transit: $852
- Notes receivable collected by bank: $1,000; interest: $20
- Outstanding checks: $569
- Error by bank: $300
- Bank charges: $30

Prepare the correcting journal entry.

EA7. LO 8.6 Using the following information, prepare a bank reconciliation.

- Bank balance: $3,678
- Book balance: $2,547
- Deposits in transit: $321
- Outstanding checks: $108 and $334
- Bank charges: $25
- Notes receivable: $1,000; interest: $35

EA8. LO 8.6 Prepare the journal entry to reconcile the bank statement in EA7.

EA9. LO 8.6 Using the following information, prepare a bank reconciliation.

- Bank balance: $4,587
- Book balance: $5,577
- Deposits in transit: $1,546
- Outstanding checks: $956
- Interest income: $56
- NSF check: $456

EA10. LO 8.6 Prepare the journal entry to reconcile the bank statement in EA9.

EA11. LO 8.6 Using the following information, prepare a bank reconciliation.

- Bank balance: $6,988
- Book balance: $6,626
- Deposits in transit: $1,600
- Outstanding checks: $599 and $1,423
- Bank charges: $75
- Bank incorrectly charged the account $75. The bank will correct the error next month.
- Check number 2456 correctly cleared the bank in the amount of $234 but posted in the accounting records as $324. This check was expensed to Utilities Expense.

EA12. LO 8.6 Prepare the journal entry to reconcile the bank statement in EA11.

 Exercise Set B

EB1. LO 8.4 Record the following transactions:

A. Started a petty cash fund in the amount of $575
B. Replenished petty cash fund using the following expenses: Auto $18, Office Expenses $35, Postage Expense $56, Miscellaneous Expenses $67. Cash on hand is $399.
C. Increased petty cash by $25.

EB2. LO 8.4 Record the following transactions:

A. Started a petty cash fund in the amount of $260.
B. Replenished petty cash fund using the following expenses: Auto $15, Office Expenses $20, Postage Expense $81, Miscellaneous Expenses $104. Cash on hand is $37.
C. Increased petty cash by $80.

EB3. LO 8.4 Record the following transactions:

A. Started a petty cash fund in the amount of $340.
B. Replenished petty cash fund using the following expenses: Auto $69, Office Expenses $77, Postage Expense $56, Miscellaneous Expenses $98. Cash on hand is $45.
C. Increased petty cash by $65.

EB4. LO 8.4 Record the following transactions:

A. Started a petty cash fund in the amount of $1,000.
B. Replenished petty cash fund using the following expenses: Auto $61, Office Expenses $23, Postage Expense $57, Miscellaneous Expenses $30.
C. The company has decided to reduce the petty cash fund to $600.

EB5. LO 8.6 The bank reconciliation shows the following adjustments.

- Deposits in transit: $526
- Outstanding checks: $328
- Bank charges: $55
- NSF checks: $69

Prepare the correcting journal entry.

EB6. LO 8.6 The bank reconciliation shows the following adjustments.

- Deposits in transit: $1,698
- Notes receivable collected by bank: $2,500; interest: $145
- Outstanding checks: $987
- Error by bank: $436
- Bank charges: $70

Prepare the correcting journal entry.

EB7. LO 8.6 Using the following information, prepare a bank reconciliation.

- Bank balance: $4,021
- Book balance: $2,928
- Deposits in transit: $1,111
- Outstanding checks: $679
- Bank charges: $35
- Notes receivable: $1,325; interest: $235

EB8. LO 8.6 Prepare the journal entry to reconcile the bank statement in EB7.

EB9. LO 8.6 Using the following information, prepare a bank reconciliation.

- Bank balance: $7,651
- Book balance: $10,595
- Deposits in transit: $2,588
- Outstanding checks: $489
- Interest income: $121
- NSF check: $966

EB10. LO 8.6 Prepare the journal entry to reconcile the bank statement in EB9.

EB11. LO 8.6 Using the following information, prepare a bank reconciliation.

- Bank balance: $12,565.
- Book balance: $13,744.
- Deposits in transit: $2,509.
- Outstanding checks: $1,777.
- Bank charges: $125.
- Bank incorrectly charged the account for $412. The bank will correct the error next month.
- Check number 1879 correctly cleared the bank in the amount of $562 but posted in the accounting records as $652. This check was expensed to Utilities Expense.

EB12. LO 8.6 Prepare the journal entry to reconcile the bank statement in EB11.

Problem Set A

PA1. LO 8.4 On September 1, French company has decided to initiate a petty cash fund in the amount of $800. Prepare journal entries for the following transactions:

A. On September 5, the petty cash fund needed replenishment, and the following are the receipts: Auto Expense $37, Supplies $124, Postage Expense $270, Repairs and Maintenance Expense $168, Miscellaneous Expense $149. The cash on hand at this time was $48.
B. On September 14, the petty cash fund needed replenishment and the following are the receipts: Auto Expense $18, Supplies $175, Postage Expense $50, Repairs and Maintenance Expense $269, Miscellaneous Expense $59. The cash on hand at this time was $210.
C. On September 23, the petty cash fund needed replenishment and the following are the receipts: Auto Expense $251, Supplies $88, Postage Expense $63, Repairs and Maintenance Expense $182, Miscellaneous Expense $203. The cash on hand at this time was $20.
D. On September 29, the company determined that the petty cash fund needed to be increased to $1,000.
E. On September 30, the petty cash fund needed replenishment as it was month end. The following are the receipts: Auto Expense $18, Supplies $15, Postage Expense $57, Repairs and Maintenance Expense $49, Miscellaneous Expense $29. The cash on hand at this time was $837.

PA2. LO 8.4 On May 2 Kellie Company has decided to initiate a petty cash fund in the amount of $1,200. Prepare journal entries for the following transactions:

A. On July 5, the petty cash fund needed replenishment, and the following are the receipts: Auto Expense $125, Supplies $368, Postage Expense $325, Repairs and Maintenance Expense $99, Miscellaneous Expense $259. The cash on hand at this time was $38.
B. On June 14, the petty cash fund needed replenishment, and the following are the receipts: Auto Expense $425, Supplies $95, Postage Expense $240, Repairs and Maintenance Expense $299, Miscellaneous Expense $77. The cash on hand at this time was $80.
C. On June 23, the petty cash fund needed replenishment, and the following are the receipts: Auto Expense $251, Supplies $188, Postage Expense $263, Repairs and Maintenance Expense $182, Miscellaneous Expense $203. The cash on hand at this time was $93.
D. On June 29, the company determined that the petty cash fund needed to be decreased to $1,000.
E. On June 30, the petty cash fund needed replenishment as it was month-end. The following are the receipts: Auto Expense $114, Supplies $75, Postage Expense $50, Repairs and Maintenance Expense $121, Miscellaneous Expense $39. The cash on hand at this time was $603.

PA3. LO 8.4 Domingo Company started its business on January 1, 2019. The following transactions occurred during the month of May. Prepare the journal entries in the journal on Page 1.

A. The owners invested $10,000 from their personal account to the business account.
B. Paid rent $500 with check #101.
C. Initiated a petty cash fund $500 with check #102.
D. Received $1,000 cash for services rendered.
E. Purchased office supplies for $158 with check #103.
F. Purchased computer equipment $2,500, paid $1,350 with check #104, and will pay the remainder in 30 days.
G. Received $800 cash for services rendered.
H. Paid wages $600, check #105.
I. Petty cash reimbursement: office supplies $256, maintenance expense $108, postage expense $77, miscellaneous expense $55. Cash on hand $11. Check #106.
J. Increased petty cash by $30, check #107.

PA4. LO 8.4 Prepare a trial balance using the journal entries in PA3.

PA5. LO 8.4 Inner Resources Company started its business on April 1, 2019. The following transactions occurred during the month of April. Prepare the journal entries in the journal on Page 1.

A. The owners invested $8,500 from their personal account to the business account.
B. Paid rent $650 with check #101.
C. Initiated a petty cash fund $550 check #102.
D. Received $750 cash for services rendered.
E. Purchased office supplies for $180 with check #103.
F. Purchased computer equipment $8,500, paid $1,600 with check #104 and will pay the remainder in 30 days.
G. Received $1,200 cash for services rendered.
H. Paid wages $560, check #105.
I. Petty cash reimbursement office supplies $200, Maintenance Expense $140, Miscellaneous Expense $65. Cash on Hand $93. Check #106.
J. Increased Petty Cash by $100, check #107.

PA6. LO 8.4 Prepare a trial balance using the journal entries in PA5.

PA7. LO 8.6 Identify where each of the following transactions would be found on the bank reconciliation.

Transaction	Increase to Bank Side	Decrease to Bank Side	Increase to Book Side	Decrease to Book Side
Outstanding check				
Interest income				
NFS check				
Wire transfer by customer				
Deposit in transit				
Bank charges				

Table 8.1

PA8. LO 8.6 Which of the following transactions will require a journal entry? Indicate if it will be a debit or a credit and to what account the entry will be recorded.

Transaction	No Journal Entry Needed	Journal Entry Needed	Debit	Credit
Outstanding check				
Interest income				
NFS check				
Wire transfer by customer				
Deposit in transit				
Bank charges				

Table 8.2

PA9. LO 8.6 Domingo Company received the following bank statement. Using PA9, prepare the bank reconciliation.

Bank Statement				
Beginning Balance				$0
	Deposits	**Checks**		
A.	$10,000	101	$ 500	
D.	1,000	102	500	
		103	158	
		106	489	
		Bank service charges	100	
Total	11,000		1,747	
Ending Balance				$9,253

PA10. LO 8.6 Prepare the journal entry required to reconcile the book balance to the bank balance.

PA11. LO 8.6 Inner Resources Company received the following bank statement. Using the information from PA11 and PA12, prepare the bank reconciliation.

Bank Statement				
Beginning Balance				$0
	Deposits	**Checks**		
A.	$8,500	101	$ 650	
D.	1,200	102	550	
		103	180	
		106	457	
		Bank service charges	100	
Total	9,700		1,937	
Ending Balance				$7,763

PA12. LO 8.6 Prepare the journal entry required to reconcile the book balance to the bank balance.

Problem Set B

PB1. LO 8.4 On June 1 French company has decided to initiate a petty cash fund in the amount of $800. Prepare journal entries for the following transactions:

A. On June 5, the petty cash fund needed replenishment, and the following are the receipts: Auto Expense $37, Supplies $124, Postage Expense $270, Repairs and Maintenance Expense $168, Miscellaneous Expense $149. The cash on hand at this time was $48.
B. On June 14, the petty cash fund needed replenishment, and the following are the receipts: Auto Expense $18, Supplies $175, Postage Expense $50, Repairs and Maintenance Expense $269, Miscellaneous Expense $59. The cash on hand at this time was $220.
C. On June 23, the petty cash fund needed replenishment, and the following are the receipts: Auto Expense $251, Supplies $88, Postage Expense $63, Repairs and Maintenance Expense $182, Miscellaneous Expense $203. The cash on hand at this time was $20.
D. On June 29, the company determined that the petty cash fund needed to be increased to $1,000.
E. On June 30, the petty cash fund needed replenishment, as it was month end. The following are the receipts: Auto Expense $18, Supplies $175, Postage Expense $50, Repairs and Maintenance Expense $269, Miscellaneous Expense $59. The cash on hand at this time was $437.

PB2. LO 8.4 On July 2 Kellie Company has decided to initiate a petty cash fund in the amount of $1,200. Prepare journal entries for the following transactions:

A. On July 5, the petty cash fund needed replenishment, and the following are the receipts: Auto Expense $125, Supplies $368, Postage Expense $325, Repairs and Maintenance Expense $99, Miscellaneous Expense $259. The cash on hand at this time was $38.
B. On June 14, the petty cash fund needed replenishment, and the following are the receipts: Auto Expense $425, Supplies $95, Postage Expense $240, Repairs and Maintenance Expense $299, Miscellaneous Expense $77. The cash on hand at this time was $110.
C. On June 23, the petty cash fund needed replenishment and the following are the receipts: Auto Expense $251, Supplies $188, Postage Expense $263, Repairs and Maintenance Expense $182, Miscellaneous Expense $203. The cash on hand at this time was $93.
D. On June 29, the company determined that the petty cash fund needed to be decreased to $1,000.
E. On June 30, the petty cash fund needed replenishment, as it was month end. The following are the receipts: Auto Expense $14, Supplies $75, Postage Expense $150, Repairs and Maintenance Expense $121, Miscellaneous Expense $39. The cash on hand at this time was $603.

PB3. LO 8.4 Hajun Company started its business on May 1, 2019. The following transactions occurred during the month of May. Prepare the journal entries in the journal on Page 1.

A. The owners invested $5,000 from their personal account to the business account.
B. Paid rent $400 with check #101.
C. Initiated a petty cash fund $200 check #102.
D. Received $400 cash for services rendered
E. Purchased office supplies for $90 with check #103.
F. Purchased computer equipment $1,000 , paid $350 with check #104 and will pay the remainder in 30 days.
G. Received $500 cash for services rendered.
H. Paid wages $250, check #105.
I. Petty cash reimbursement office supplies $25, Maintenance Expense $125, Miscellaneous Expense $35. Cash on hand $18. Check #106.
J. Increased Petty Cash by $50, check #107.

PB4. LO 8.4 Prepare a trial balance using the journal entries in PB3.

PB5. LO 8.4 Lavender Company started its business on April 1, 2019. The following are the transactions that happened during the month of April. Prepare the journal entries in the journal on Page 1.

A. The owners invested $7,500 from their personal account to the business account.
B. Paid rent $600 with check #101.
C. Initiated a petty cash fund $250 check #102.
D. Received $350 cash for services rendered.
E. Purchased office supplies for $125 with check #103.
F. Purchased computer equipment $1,500, paid $500 with check #104, and will pay the remainder in 30 days.
G. Received $750 cash for services rendered.
H. Paid wages $375, check #105.
I. Petty cash reimbursement Office Supplies $50, Maintenance Expense $80, Miscellaneous Expense $60. Cash on hand $8. Check #106.
J. Increased Petty Cash by $70, check #107.

PB6. LO 8.4 Prepare a trial balance for Lavender Company using the journal entries in PB5.

PB7. LO 8.6 Identify where each of the following transactions would be found on the bank reconciliation.

Transaction	Increase to Bank Side	Decrease to Bank Side	Increase to Book Side	Decrease to Book Side
Overcharge by Bank (Error)				
Interest Income				
Automatic Loan Payment				
Wire Transfer by Customer				
Deposit in Transit				
Outstanding Check				

Table 8.3

PB8. LO 8.6 Which of the following transactions will require a journal entry? Indicate if it will be a debit or a credit, and to which account the entry will be recorded.

Transaction	No Journal Entry	Journal Entry Needed	Debit	Credit
Overcharge by Bank (Error)				
Interest Income				
Automatic Loan Payment				
Wire Transfer by Customer				
Deposit in Transit				
Outstanding Check				

Table 8.4

PB9. LO 8.6 Hajun Company received the following bank statement. Using the information from PB9 and PB10, prepare the bank reconciliation.

Bank Statement				
Beginning Balance				$0
	Deposits	**Checks**		
A.	$5,000	101	$400	
D.	400	102	200	
		103	90	
		106	182	
		Bank service charges	75	
Total	5,400		947	
Ending Balance				$4,453

PB10. LO 8.6 Prepare the journal entry required to reconcile the book balance to the bank balance.

PB11. LO 8.6 Leann Company received the following bank statement. Using the information from PB11 and PB12, prepare the bank reconciliation.

Bank Statement				
Beginning Balance				$0
	Deposits	**Checks**		
A.	$7,500	101	$ 600	
D.	350	102	250	
		103	125	
		106	242	
		Bank service charges	90	
Total	7,850		1,307	
Ending Balance				$6,543

PB12. LO 8.6 Prepare the journal entry required to reconcile the book balance to the bank balance.

Thought Provokers

TP1. LO 8.2 A retail store normally has three people working in the evening. All of the employees have access to the same cash register. For the last month, the cash count at the end of the evening has been recording losses. The losses range from $5 to $300. So the manager has decided to be the only one to count the cash at the end of the evening to keep the losses from happening. Discuss if the change made by the manager is a good one. Will the losses keep happening, or will this change prevent losses due to theft? What other recommendations and changes should be considered by this manager?

TP2. LO 8.2 LO 8.3 Visit a favorite eatery. Describe some of the internal controls that are implemented in the workplace. Discuss the good and effective internal controls and also discuss areas that need to be addressed where the eatery is vulnerable to losses.

TP3. LO 8.3 A manufacturing plant was finding a huge increase in the scrapping of raw materials. Its internal controls were reviewed, and the plant appeared to be strong; segregation of duties was in place. As the accountant was reconciling some inventory accounts, she found more than a normal amount of scrap tickets. The tickets were for scrapping the same inventory part, signed by the same person, and the scrap was sold to only one company. The inventory item was still being ordered, and only one supplier was used to purchase the parts. After further investigation by the accountant, the company buying the inventory and the company selling the inventory to the company had different names but shared the same address. Comment on what went wrong. What happened to the internal controls the company had in place?

TP4. LO 8.3 The vice president of finance asks the accounts payable (AP) clerk to write a check in the name of the president for $10,000. He and the president will sign the check (two signatures needed on a check of this size). He further instructs the AP clerk not to disclose this check to her immediate supervisor. What should the AP clerk do? Should she prepare the check? Should she inform her immediate supervisor? Discuss with internal controls in mind.

TP5. LO 8.3 Even though technology has improved the internal control structure of a company, a supervisor cannot depend totally on technology. Discuss other internal controls a supervisor needs to implement to ensure a strong structure.

TP6. LO 8.6 A bank reconciliation takes time and must balance. An employee was struggling in balancing the bank reconciliation. Her supervisor told her to "plug" (make an unsupported entry for) the difference, record to Miscellaneous Expense, and simply move on. Discuss the internal controls problem with this directive.

TP7. LO 8.6 The bank reconciliation revealed that one deposit had cleared the bank two weeks after the date of the deposit. Should this be of concern? Why, or why not?

9 Accounting for Receivables

Figure 9.1 Skateboards Unlimited. Business success is realized with effective receivable management. (credit: modification of "2013 Street Arts Festival" by Eli Christman/Flickr, CC BY 2.0)

Chapter Outline

LO 9.1 Explain the Revenue Recognition Principle and How It Relates to Current and Future Sales and Purchase Transactions

LO 9.2 Account for Uncollectible Accounts Using the Balance Sheet and Income Statement Approaches

LO 9.3 Determine the Efficiency of Receivables Management Using Financial Ratios

LO 9.4 Discuss the Role of Accounting for Receivables in Earnings Management

LO 9.5 Apply Revenue Recognition Principles to Long-Term Projects

LO 9.6 Explain How Notes Receivable and Accounts Receivable Differ

LO 9.7 Appendix: Comprehensive Example of Bad Debt Estimation

Why It Matters

Marie owns Skateboards Unlimited, a skateboard lifestyle shop offering a variety of skate-specific clothing, equipment, and accessories. Marie prides herself on her ability to accommodate customer needs. One way she accomplishes this goal is by extending to the customer a line of credit, which would create an account receivable for Skateboards Unlimited. Even though she has yet to collect cash from her credit customers, she recognizes the revenue as earned when the sale occurs. This is important, as it allows her to match her sales correctly with sales-associated expenses in the proper period, based on the matching principle and revenue recognition guidelines.

By offering credit terms, Skateboards Unlimited operates in good faith that customers will pay their accounts in full. Sometimes this does not occur, and the bad debt from the receivable has to be written off. Marie typically estimates this write-off amount, to show potential investors and lenders a consistent financial position. When writing off bad debt, Marie is guided by specific accounting principles that dictate the estimation and bad debt processes. Skateboards Unlimited will need to carefully manage its receivables and bad debt to reach budget projections and grow the business. This chapter explains and demonstrates demonstrate the two major methods of estimating and recording bad debt expenses that Skateboards Unlimited can apply under generally accepted accounting principles (GAAP).

9.1 Explain the Revenue Recognition Principle and How It Relates to Current and Future Sales and Purchase Transactions

You own a small clothing store and offer your customers cash, credit card, or in-house credit payment options. Many of your customers choose to pay with a credit card or charge the purchase to their in-house credit accounts. This means that your store is owed money in the future from either the customer or the credit card company, depending on payment method. Regardless of credit payment method, your company must decide when to recognize revenue. Do you recognize revenue when the sale occurs or when cash payment is received? When do you recognize the expenses associated with the sale? How are these transactions recognized?

Accounting Principles and Assumptions Regulating Revenue Recognition

Revenue and expense recognition timing is critical to transparent financial presentation. **GAAP** governs recognition for publicly traded companies. Even though GAAP is required only for public companies, to display their financial position most accurately, private companies should manage their financial accounting using its rules. Two principles governed by GAAP are the revenue recognition principle and the matching principle. Both the revenue recognition principle and the matching principle give specific direction on revenue and expense reporting.

The **revenue recognition principle**, which states that companies must recognize revenue in the period in which it is earned, instructs companies to recognize revenue when a four-step process is completed. This may not necessarily be when cash is collected. Revenue can be recognized when all of the following criteria have been met:

- There is credible evidence that an arrangement exists.
- Goods have been delivered or services have been performed.
- The selling price or fee to the buyer is fixed or can be reasonably determined.
- There is reasonable assurance that the amount owed to the seller is collectible.

The **accrual accounting** method aligns with this principle, and it records transactions related to revenue earnings as they occur, not when cash is collected. The revenue recognition principle may be updated periodically to reflect more current rules for reporting.

For example, a landscaping company signs a $600 contract with a customer to provide landscaping services for the next six months (assume the landscaping workload is distributed evenly throughout the six months). The customer sets up an in-house credit line with the company, to be paid in full at the end of the six months. The landscaping company records revenue earnings each month and provides service as planned. To align with the revenue recognition principle, the landscaping company will record one month of revenue ($100) each month as earned; they provided service for that month, even though the customer has not yet paid cash for the service.

Let's say that the landscaping company also sells gardening equipment. It sells a package of gardening equipment to a customer who pays on credit. The landscaping company will recognize revenue immediately, given that they provided the customer with the gardening equipment (product), even though the customer has not yet paid cash for the product.

Accrual accounting also incorporates the **matching principle** (otherwise known as the expense recognition principle), which instructs companies to record expenses related to revenue generation in the period in which they are incurred. The principle also requires that any expense not directly related to revenues be reported in an appropriate manner. For example, assume that a company paid $6,000 in annual real estate taxes. The principle has determined that costs cannot effectively be allocated based on an individual month's sales; instead, it treats the expense as a period cost. In this case, it is going to record 1/12 of the annual expense as a monthly period cost. Overall, the "matching" of expenses to revenues projects a more accurate representation of company financials. When this matching is not possible, then the expenses will be treated as period costs.

For example, when the landscaping company sells the gardening equipment, there are costs associated with that sale, such as the costs of materials purchased or shipping charges. The cost is reported in the same period as revenue associated with the sale. There cannot be a mismatch in reporting expenses and revenues; otherwise, financial statements are presented unfairly to stakeholders. Misreporting has a significant impact on company stakeholders. If the company delayed reporting revenues until a future period, net income would be understated in the current period. If expenses were delayed until a future period, net income would be overstated.

Let's turn to the basic elements of accounts receivable, as well as the corresponding transaction journal entries.

ETHICAL CONSIDERATIONS

Ethics in Revenue Recognition

Because each industry typically has a different method for recognizing income, revenue recognition is one of the most difficult tasks for accountants, as it involves a number of ethical dilemmas related to income reporting. To provide an industry-wide approach, Accounting Standards Update No. 2014-09 and other related updates were implemented to clarify revenue recognition rules. The American Institute of Certified Public Accountants (AICPA) announced that these updates would replace U.S. GAAP's current industry-specific revenue recognition practices with a principle-based approach, potentially affecting both day-to-day business accounting and the execution of business contracts with customers.[1] The AICPA and the International Federation of Accountants (IFAC) require professional accountants to act with due care and to remain abreast of new accounting rules and methods of accounting for different transactions, including revenue recognition.

The IFAC emphasizes the role of professional accountants working within a business in ensuring the quality of financial reporting: "Management is responsible for the financial information produced by the company. As such, professional accountants in businesses therefore have the task of defending the quality of financial reporting right at the source where the numbers and figures are produced!"[2] In accordance with proper revenue recognition, accountants do not recognize revenue before it is earned.

CONCEPTS IN PRACTICE

Gift Card Revenue Recognition

Gift cards have become an essential part of revenue generation and growth for many businesses. Although they are practical for consumers and low cost to businesses, navigating revenue recognition guidelines can be difficult. Gift cards with expiration dates require that revenue recognition be delayed until customer use or expiration. However, most gift cards now have no expiration date. So, when do you recognize revenue?

Companies may need to provide an estimation of projected gift card revenue and usage during a period based on past experience or industry standards. There are a few rules governing reporting. If the company determines that a portion of all of the issued gift cards will never be used, they may write this off to income. In some states, if a gift card remains unused, in part or in full, the unused portion of the card is transferred to the state government. It is considered unclaimed property for the customer, meaning that the company cannot keep these funds as revenue because, in this case, they have reverted to the state government.

Short-Term Revenue Recognition Examples

As mentioned, the revenue recognition principle requires that, in some instances, revenue is recognized before receiving a cash payment. In these situations, the customer still owes the company money. This money owed to the company is a type of receivable for the company and a payable for the company's customer.

A **receivable** is an outstanding amount owed from a customer. One specific receivable type is called accounts receivable. **Accounts receivable** is an outstanding customer debt on a credit sale. The company expects to receive payment on accounts receivable within the company's operating period (less than a year). Accounts receivable is considered an asset, and it typically does not include an interest payment from the customer. Some view this account as extending a line of credit to a customer. The customer would then be sent an invoice with credit payment terms. If the company has provided the product or service at the time of credit extension, revenue would also be recognized.

For example, Billie's Watercraft Warehouse (BWW) sells various watercraft vehicles. They extend a credit line to customers purchasing vehicles in bulk. A customer bought 10 Jet Skis on credit at a sales price of $100,000. The cost of the sale to BWW is $70,000. The following journal entries occur.

---

1 American Institute of Certified Public Accountants (AICPA). "Revenue from Contracts with Customers." *Revenue Recognition*. n.d. https://www.aicpa.org/interestareas/frc/accountingfinancialreporting/revenuerecognition.html

2 International Federation of Accountants (IFAC). "Roles and Importance of Professional Accountants in Business." n.d. https://www.ifac.org/news-events/2013-10/roles-and-importance-professional-accountants-business

JOURNAL			
Date	**Account**	**Debit**	**Credit**
	Accounts Receivable Sales Revenue *To record the sale of 10 jet skis*	100,000	 100,000
	Cost of Goods Sold Merchandise Inventory *To record the cost of sale*	70,000	 70,000

Accounts Receivable increases (debit) and Sales Revenue increases (credit) for $100,000. Accounts Receivable recognizes the amount owed from the customer, but not yet paid. Revenue recognition occurs because BWW provided the Jet Skis and completed the earnings process. Cost of Goods Sold increases (debit) and Merchandise Inventory decreases (credit) for $70,000, the expense associated with the sale. By recording both a sale and its related cost entry, the matching principle requirement is met.

When the customer pays the amount owed, the following journal entry occurs.

JOURNAL			
Date	**Account**	**Debit**	**Credit**
	Cash Accounts Receivable *To record payment in full*	100,000	 100,000

Cash increases (debit) and Accounts Receivable decreases (credit) for the full amount owed. If the customer made only a partial payment, the entry would reflect the amount of the payment. For example, if the customer paid only $75,000 of the $100,000 owed, the following entry would occur. The remaining $25,000 owed would remain outstanding, reflected in Accounts Receivable.

JOURNAL			
Date	**Account**	**Debit**	**Credit**
	Cash Accounts Receivable *To record partial payment*	75,000	 75,000

Another credit transaction that requires recognition is when a customer pays with a credit card (Visa and MasterCard, for example). This is different from credit extended directly to the customer from the company. In this case, the third-party credit card company accepts the payment responsibility. This reduces the risk of nonpayment, increases opportunities for sales, and expedites payment on accounts receivable. The tradeoff for the company receiving these benefits from the credit card company is that a fee is charged to use this service. The fee can be a flat figure per transaction, or it can be a percentage of the sales price. Using BWW as the example, let's say one of its customers purchased a canoe for $300, using his or her Visa credit card. The cost to BWW for the canoe is $150. Visa charges BWW a service fee equal to 5% of the sales price. At the time of sale, the following journal entries are recorded.

JOURNAL			
Date	**Account**	**Debit**	**Credit**
	Accounts Receivable: Visa Credit Card Expense Sales Revenue *To record the sale of one canoe, Visa credit fee 5%*	285 15	 300
	Cost of Goods Sold Merchandise Inventory *To record the cost of sale*	150	 150

Accounts Receivable: Visa increases (debit) for the sale amount ($300) less the credit card fee ($15), for a $285 Accounts Receivable balance due from Visa. BWW's Credit Card Expense increases (debit) for the amount of the credit card fee ($15; 300 × 5%), and Sales Revenue increases (credit) for the original sales amount ($300). BWW recognizes revenue as earned for this transaction because it provided the canoe and completed the earnings process. Cost of Goods Sold increases (debit) and Merchandise Inventory decreases (credit) for $150, the expense associated with the sale. As with the previous example, by recording both a sale and cost entry, the matching principle requirement is met. When Visa pays the amount owed to BWW, the following entry occurs in BMW's records.

JOURNAL			
Date	**Account**	**Debit**	**Credit**
	Cash Accounts Receivable: Visa *To record payment in full, less credit card fee*	285	 285

Cash increases (debit) and Accounts Receivable: Visa decreases (credit) for the full amount owed, less the credit card fee. Once BWW receives the cash payment from Visa, it may use those funds in other business activities.

An alternative to the journal entries shown is that the credit card company, in this case Visa, gives the merchant immediate credit in its cash account for the $285 due the merchant, without creating an account receivable. If that policy were in effect for this transaction, the following single journal entry would replace the prior two journal entry transactions. In the immediate cash payment method, an account receivable would not need to be recorded and then collected. The separate journal entry—to record the costs of goods sold and to reduce the canoe inventory that reflects the $150 cost of the sale—would still be the same.

JOURNAL			
Date	**Account**	**Debit**	**Credit**
	Cash Credit Card Expense Sales Revenue *To record the sale of one canoe and Visa credit card fee of 5%*	285 15	 300

Here's a final credit transaction to consider. A company allows a sales discount on a purchase if a customer charges a purchase but makes the payment within a stated period of time, such as 10 or 15 days from the point of sale. In such a situation, a customer would see credit terms in the following form: 2/10, n/30. This particular example shows that a customer who pays his or her account within 10 days will receive a 2% discount. Otherwise, the customer will have 30 days from the date of the purchase to pay in full, but will not receive a discount. Both sales discounts and purchase discounts were addressed in detail in Merchandising

Transactions.

YOUR TURN

Maine Lobster Market

Maine Lobster Market (MLM) provides fresh seafood products to customers. It allows customers to pay with cash, an in-house credit account, or a credit card. The credit card company charges Maine Lobster Market a 4% fee, based on credit sales using its card. From the following transactions, prepare journal entries for Maine Lobster Market.

Aug. 5	Pat paid $800 cash for lobster. The cost to MLM was $480.
Aug. 10	Pat purchased 30 pounds of shrimp at a sales price per pound of $25. The cost to MLM was $18.50 per pound and is charged to Pat's in-store account.
Aug. 19	Pat purchased $1,200 of fish with a credit card. The cost to MLM is $865.

Solution

JOURNAL			
Date	**Account**	**Debit**	**Credit**
Aug. 5	Cash	800	
	Sales Revenue		800
	To record cash sale		
Aug. 5	Cost of Goods Sold	480	
	Merchandise Inventory: Lobster		480
	To record cost of sale		
Aug. 10	Accounts Receivable	750	
	Sales Revenue		750
	To record credit sale, 30 × $25		
Aug. 10	Cost of Goods Sold	555	
	Merchandise Inventory: Shrimp		555
	To record cost of sale; 30 × $18.50		
Aug. 19	Accounts Receivable	1,152	
	Credit Card Expense	48	
	Sales Revenue		1,200
	To record credit card sale, 4% fee, 1200 × 4%		
Aug. 19	Cost of Goods Sold	865	
	Merchandise Inventory: Fish		865
	To record cost of sale		

YOUR TURN

Jamal's Music Supply

Jamal's Music Supply allows customers to pay with cash or a credit card. The credit card company charges Jamal's Music Supply a 3% fee, based on credit sales using its card. From the following transactions, prepare journal entries for Jamal's Music Supply.

May 10	Kerry paid $1,790 for music supplies with a credit card. The cost to Jamal's Music Supply was $1,100.
May 19	Kerry purchased 80 drumstick pairs at a sales price per pair of $14 with a credit card. The cost to Jamal's Music Supply was $7.30 per pair.
May 28	Kerry purchased $345 of music supplies with cash. The cost to Jamal's Music Supply was $122.

Solution

JOURNAL			
Date	**Account**	**Debit**	**Credit**
May 10	Accounts Receivable Credit Card Expense Sales Revenue *To record credit card sale, 3% fee, 1790 × 3%*	1,736.30 53.70	 1,790
May 10	Cost of Goods Sold Merchandise Inventory *To record cost of sale*	1,100	 1,100
May 19	Accounts Receivable Credit Card Expense Sales Revenue *To record credit card sale, 3% fee, (80 × $14) x 3%*	1,086.40 33.60	 1,120
May 19	Cost of Goods Sold Merchandise Inventory *To record cost of sale; 80 × $7.30*	584	 584
May 28	Cash Sales Revenue *To record cash sale*	345	 345
May 28	Cost of Goods Sold Merchandise Inventory *To record cost of sale*	122	 122

9.2 Account for Uncollectible Accounts Using the Balance Sheet and Income Statement Approaches

You lend a friend $500 with the agreement that you will be repaid in two months. At the end of two months, your friend has not repaid the money. You continue to request the money each month, but the friend has yet to repay the debt. How does this affect your finances?

Think of this on a larger scale. A bank lends money to a couple purchasing a home (mortgage). The understanding is that the couple will make payments each month toward the principal borrowed, plus interest. As time passes, the loan goes unpaid. What happens when a loan that was supposed to be paid is not paid? How does this affect the financial statements for the bank? The bank may need to consider ways to recognize this bad debt.

Fundamentals of Bad Debt Expenses and Allowances for Doubtful Accounts

Bad debts are uncollectible amounts from customer accounts. Bad debt negatively affects accounts receivable (see Figure 9.2). When future collection of receivables cannot be reasonably assumed, recognizing this potential nonpayment is required. There are two methods a company may use to recognize bad debt: the direct write-off method and the allowance method.

Figure 9.2 Bad Debt Expenses. Uncollectible customer accounts produce bad debt. (credit: modification of "Past Due Bills" by "Maggiebug 21"/Wikimedia Commons, CC0)

The **direct write-off method** delays recognition of bad debt until the specific customer accounts receivable is identified. Once this account is identified as uncollectible, the company will record a reduction to the customer's accounts receivable and an increase to bad debt expense for the exact amount uncollectible.

Under generally accepted accounting principles (GAAP), the direct write-off method is not an acceptable method of recording bad debts, because it violates the matching principle. For example, assume that a credit transaction occurs in September 2018 and is determined to be uncollectible in February 2019. The direct write-off method would record the bad debt expense in 2019, while the matching principle requires that it be associated with a 2018 transaction, which will better reflect the relationship between revenues and the accompanying expenses. This matching issue is the reason accountants will typically use one of the two accrual-based accounting methods introduced to account for bad debt expenses.

It is important to consider other issues in the treatment of bad debts. For example, when companies account for bad debt expenses in their financial statements, they will use an accrual-based method; however, they are required to use the direct write-off method on their income tax returns. This variance in treatment addresses taxpayers' potential to manipulate when a bad debt is recognized. Because of this potential manipulation, the Internal Revenue Service (IRS) requires that the direct write-off method must be used when the debt is determined to be uncollectible, while GAAP still requires that an accrual-based method be used for financial accounting statements.

For the taxpayer, this means that if a company sells an item on credit in October 2018 and determines that it is uncollectible in June 2019, it must show the effects of the bad debt when it files its 2019 tax return. This application probably violates the matching principle, but if the IRS did not have this policy, there would typically be a significant amount of manipulation on company tax returns. For example, if the company wanted the deduction for the write-off in 2018, it might claim that it was actually uncollectible in 2018, instead of in 2019.

The final point relates to companies with very little exposure to the possibility of bad debts, typically, entities that rarely offer credit to its customers. Assuming that credit is not a significant component of its sales, these sellers can also use the direct write-off method. The companies that qualify for this exemption, however, are typically small and not major participants in the credit market. Thus, virtually all of the remaining bad debt expense material discussed here will be based on an allowance method that uses accrual accounting, the matching principle, and the revenue recognition rules under GAAP.

For example, a customer takes out a $15,000 car loan on August 1, 2018 and is expected to pay the amount in full before December 1, 2018. For the sake of this example, assume that there was no interest charged to the buyer because of the short-term nature or life of the loan. When the account defaults for nonpayment on December 1, the company would record the following journal entry to recognize bad debt.

JOURNAL			
Date	**Account**	**Debit**	**Credit**
Dec. 1	Bad Debt Expense Accounts Receivable *To record bad debts*	15,000	 15,000

Bad Debt Expense increases (debit), and Accounts Receivable decreases (credit) for $15,000. If, in the future, any part of the debt is recovered, a reversal of the previously written-off bad debt, and the collection recognition is required. Let's say this customer unexpectedly pays in full on May 1, 2019, the company would record the following journal entries (note that the company's fiscal year ends on June 30)

JOURNAL			
Date	**Account**	**Debit**	**Credit**
May 1, 2019	Accounts Receivable Bad Debt Expense *To reverse previous bad debt write-off*	15,000	 15,000
May 1, 2019	Cash Accounts Receivable *To record payment on account*	15,000	 15,000

The first entry reverses the bad debt write-off by increasing Accounts Receivable (debit) and decreasing Bad Debt Expense (credit) for the amount recovered. The second entry records the payment in full with Cash increasing (debit) and Accounts Receivable decreasing (credit) for the amount received of $15,000.

As you've learned, the delayed recognition of bad debt violates GAAP, specifically the matching principle. Therefore, the direct write-off method is not used for publicly traded company reporting; the allowance method is used instead.

The allowance method is the more widely used method because it satisfies the matching principle. The

allowance method estimates bad debt during a period, based on certain computational approaches. The calculation matches bad debt with related sales during the period. The estimation is made from past experience and industry standards. When the estimation is recorded at the end of a period, the following entry occurs.

JOURNAL			
Date	Account	Debit	Credit
	Bad Debt Expense Allowance for Doubtful Accounts *To record estimated bad debt*	$$$	 $$$

The journal entry for the Bad Debt Expense increases (debit) the expense's balance, and the Allowance for Doubtful Accounts increases (credit) the balance in the Allowance. The **allowance for doubtful accounts** is a contra asset account and is subtracted from Accounts Receivable to determine the **Net Realizable Value** of the Accounts Receivable account on the balance sheet. A **contra account** has an opposite normal balance to its paired account, thereby reducing or increasing the balance in the paired account at the end of a period; the adjustment can be an addition or a subtraction from a controlling account. In the case of the allowance for doubtful accounts, it is a contra account that is used to reduce the Controlling account, Accounts Receivable.

At the end of an accounting period, the Allowance for Doubtful Accounts reduces the Accounts Receivable to produce Net Accounts Receivable. Note that allowance for doubtful accounts reduces the overall accounts receivable account, not a specific accounts receivable assigned to a customer. Because it is an estimation, it means the exact account that is (or will become) uncollectible is not yet known.

To demonstrate the treatment of the allowance for doubtful accounts on the balance sheet, assume that a company has reported an Accounts Receivable balance of $90,000 and a Balance in the Allowance of Doubtful Accounts of $4,800. The following table reflects how the relationship would be reflected in the current (short-term) section of the company's Balance Sheet.

Accounts Receivable	$90,000	
– Allowance for Doubtful Accounts	($4,800)	$85,200

There is one more point about the use of the contra account, Allowance for Doubtful Accounts. In this example, the $85,200 total is the net realizable value, or the amount of accounts anticipated to be collected. However, the company is owed $90,000 and will still try to collect the entire $90,000 and not just the $85,200.

Under the balance sheet method of calculating bad debt expenses, if there is already a balance in Allowance for Doubtful Accounts from a previous period and accounts written off in the current year, this must be considered before the adjusting entry is made. For example, if a company already had a credit balance from the prior period of $1,000, plus any accounts that have been written off this year, and a current period estimated balance of $2,500, the company would need to subtract the prior period's credit balance from the current period's estimated credit balance in order to calculate the amount to be added to the Allowance for Doubtful Accounts.

Current period	= $2,500 credit
Prior period	= $1,000 credit
Allowance for Doubtful Accounts	= $1,500 credit

Therefore, the adjusting journal entry would be as follows.

JOURNAL			
Date	**Account**	**Debit**	**Credit**
	Bad Debt Expense Allowance for Doubtful Accounts *To record estimated bad debt*	1,500	 1,500

If a company already had a debit balance from the prior period of $1,000, and a current period estimated balance of $2,500, the company would need to add the prior period's debit balance to the current period's estimated credit balance.

Current period	= $2,500 credit
Prior period	= $1,000 debit
Allowance for Doubtful Accounts	= $3,500 credit

Therefore, the adjusting journal entry would be as follows.

JOURNAL			
Date	**Account**	**Debit**	**Credit**
	Bad Debt Expense Allowance for Doubtful Accounts *To record estimated bad debt*	3,500	 3,500

When a specific customer has been identified as an uncollectible account, the following journal entry would occur.

JOURNAL			
Date	**Account**	**Debit**	**Credit**
	Allowance for Doubtful Accounts Accounts Receivable: Customer *To record bad debt for specific customer*	$$$	 $$$

Allowance for Doubtful Accounts decreases (debit) and Accounts Receivable for the specific customer also decreases (credit). Allowance for doubtful accounts decreases because the bad debt amount is no longer unclear. Accounts receivable decreases because there is an assumption that no debt will be collected on the identified customer's account.

Let's say that the customer unexpectedly pays on the account in the future. The following journal entries would occur.

JOURNAL			
Date	**Account**	**Debit**	**Credit**
	Accounts Receivable: Customer Allowance for Doubtful Accounts *To reinstate previously written-off bad debt*	$$$	 $$$
	Cash Accounts Receivable: Customer *To record bad debt for specific customer*	$$$	 $$$

The first entry reverses the previous entry where bad debt was written off. This reinstatement requires Accounts Receivable: Customer to increase (debit), and Allowance for Doubtful Accounts to increase (credit). The second entry records the payment on the account. Cash increases (debit) and Accounts Receivable: Customer decreases (credit) for the amount received.

To compute the most accurate estimation possible, a company may use one of three methods for bad debt expense recognition: the income statement method, balance sheet method, or balance sheet aging of receivables method.

THINK IT THROUGH

Bad Debt Estimation

As the accountant for a large publicly traded food company, you are considering whether or not you need to change your bad debt estimation method. You currently use the income statement method to estimate bad debt at 4.5% of credit sales. You are considering switching to the balance sheet aging of receivables method. This would split accounts receivable into three past- due categories and assign a percentage to each group.

While you know that the balance sheet aging of receivables method is more accurate, it does require more company resources (e.g., time and money) that are currently applied elsewhere in the business. Using the income statement method is acceptable under generally accepted accounting principles (GAAP), but should you switch to the more accurate method even if your resources are constrained? Do you have a responsibility to the public to change methods if you know one is a better estimation?

Income Statement Method for Calculating Bad Debt Expenses

The **income statement method** (also known as the percentage of sales method) estimates bad debt expenses based on the assumption that at the end of the period, a certain percentage of sales during the period will not be collected. The estimation is typically based on credit sales only, not total sales (which include cash sales). In this example, assume that any credit card sales that are uncollectible are the responsibility of the credit card company. It may be obvious intuitively, but, by definition, a cash sale cannot become a bad debt, assuming that the cash payment did not entail counterfeit currency. The income statement method is a simple method for calculating bad debt, but it may be more imprecise than other measures because it does not consider how long a debt has been outstanding and the role that plays in debt recovery.

To illustrate, let’s continue to use Billie’s Watercraft Warehouse (BWW) as the example. Billie’s end-of-year credit sales totaled $458,230. BWW estimates that 5% of its overall credit sales will result in bad debt. The following adjusting journal entry for bad debt occurs.

JOURNAL			
Date	**Account**	**Debit**	**Credit**
Dec. 31	Bad Debt Expense Allowance for Doubtful Accounts *To record estimated bad debts, income statement method*	22,911.50	22,911.50

Bad Debt Expense increases (debit), and Allowance for Doubtful Accounts increases (credit) for $22,911.50 ($458,230 × 5%). This means that BWW believes $22,911.50 will be uncollectible debt. Let's say that on April 8, it was determined that Customer Robert Craft's account was uncollectible in the amount of $5,000. The following entry occurs.

JOURNAL			
Date	**Account**	**Debit**	**Credit**
Apr. 8	Allowance for Doubtful Accounts	5,000	
	Accounts Receivable: Craft		5,000
	To record known bad debt		

In this case, Allowance for Doubtful Accounts decreases (debit) and Accounts Receivable: Craft decreases (credit) for the known uncollectible amount of $5,000. On June 5, Craft unexpectedly makes a partial payment on his account in the amount of $3,000. The following journal entries show the reinstatement of bad debt and the subsequent payment.

JOURNAL			
Date	**Account**	**Debit**	**Credit**
Jun. 5	Accounts Receivable: Craft	3,000	
	Allowance for Doubtful Accounts		3,000
	To reinstate previously written-off bad debt		
Jun. 5	Cash	3,000	
	Accounts Receivable: Craft		3,000
	To record bad debt for specific customer		

The outstanding balance of $2,000 that Craft did not repay will remain as bad debt.

YOUR TURN

Heating and Air Company

You run a successful heating and air conditioning company. Your net credit sales, accounts receivable, and allowance for doubtful accounts figures for year-end 2018, follow.

Net credit sales	$831,400
Accounts receivable	222,850
Allowance for doubtful accounts	0

A. Compute bad debt estimation using the income statement method, where the percentage uncollectible is 5%.
B. Prepare the journal entry for the income statement method of bad debt estimation.
C. Compute bad debt estimation using the balance sheet method of percentage of receivables, where the percentage uncollectible is 9%.
D. Prepare the journal entry for the balance sheet method bad debt estimation.

Solution

A. $41,570; $831,400 × 5%

B.

JOURNAL			
Date	**Account**	**Debit**	**Credit**
Dec. 31	Bad Debt Expense Allowance for Doubtful Accounts *To record estimated bad debts, income statement method*	41,570	 41,570

C. $20,056.50; $222,850 × 9%

D.

Date	Account	Debit	Credit
Dec. 31	Bad Debt Expense Allowance for Doubtful Accounts *To record estimated bad debts, balance sheet method*	20,056.50	 20,056.50

Balance Sheet Method for Calculating Bad Debt Expenses

The **balance sheet method** (also known as the percentage of accounts receivable method) estimates bad debt expenses based on the balance in accounts receivable. The method looks at the balance of accounts receivable at the end of the period and assumes that a certain amount will not be collected. Accounts receivable is reported on the balance sheet; thus, it is called the balance sheet method. The balance sheet method is another simple method for calculating bad debt, but it too does not consider how long a debt has been outstanding and the role that plays in debt recovery. There is a variation on the balance sheet method, however, called the aging method that does consider how long accounts receivable have been owed, and it assigns a greater potential for default to those debts that have been owed for the longest period of time.

Continuing our examination of the balance sheet method, assume that BWW's end-of-year accounts receivable balance totaled $324,850. This entry assumes a zero balance in Allowance for Doubtful Accounts from the prior period. BWW estimates 15% of its overall accounts receivable will result in bad debt. The following adjusting journal entry for bad debt occurs.

JOURNAL			
Date	**Account**	**Debit**	**Credit**
Dec. 31	Bad Debt Expense Allowance for Doubtful Accounts *To record estimated bad debts, balance sheet method*	48,727.50	 48,727.50

Bad Debt Expense increases (debit), and Allowance for Doubtful Accounts increases (credit) for $48,727.50 ($324,850 × 15%). This means that BWW believes $48,727.50 will be uncollectible debt. Let's consider that BWW had a $23,000 credit balance from the previous period. The adjusting journal entry would recognize the following.

JOURNAL			
Date	**Account**	**Debit**	**Credit**
Dec. 31	Bad Debt Expense Allowance for Doubtful Accounts *To record estimated bad debts, balance sheet method*	25,727.50	 25,727.50

This is different from the last journal entry, where bad debt was estimated at $48,727.50. That journal entry assumed a zero balance in Allowance for Doubtful Accounts from the prior period. This journal entry takes into account a credit balance of $23,000 and subtracts the prior period's balance from the estimated balance in the current period of $48,727.50.

Current period	= $48,727.50 credit
Prior period	= $23,000.00 credit
Allowance for Doubtful Accounts	= $25,727.50 credit

Balance Sheet Aging of Receivables Method for Calculating Bad Debt Expenses

The **balance sheet aging of receivables method** estimates bad debt expenses based on the balance in accounts receivable, but it also considers the uncollectible time period for each account. The longer the time passes with a receivable unpaid, the lower the probability that it will get collected. An account that is 90 days overdue is more likely to be unpaid than an account that is 30 days past due.

With this method, accounts receivable is organized into categories by length of time outstanding, and an uncollectible percentage is assigned to each category. The length of uncollectible time increases the percentage assigned. For example, a category might consist of accounts receivable that is 0–30 days past due and is assigned an uncollectible percentage of 6%. Another category might be 31–60 days past due and is assigned an uncollectible percentage of 15%. All categories of estimated uncollectible amounts are summed to get a total estimated uncollectible balance. That total is reported in Bad Debt Expense and Allowance for Doubtful Accounts, if there is no carryover balance from a prior period. If there is a carryover balance, that must be considered before recording Bad Debt Expense. The balance sheet aging of receivables method is more complicated than the other two methods, but it tends to produce more accurate results. This is because it considers the amount of time that accounts receivable has been owed, and it assumes that the longer the time owed, the greater the possibility that individual accounts receivable will prove to be uncollectible.

Looking at BWW, it has an accounts receivable balance of $324,850 at the end of the year. The company splits its past-due accounts into three categories: 0–30 days past due, 31–90 days past due, and over 90 days past due. The uncollectible percentages and the accounts receivable breakdown are shown here.

Past-Due Category	Accounts Receivable Total	Uncollectible Percentage	Total
0–30 days	$145,740	10%	$14,574
31–90 days	102,100	20%	20,420
Over 90 days	77,010	30%	23,103
		Total Estimated Uncollectible:	**$58,097**

For each of the individual categories, the accountant multiplies the uncollectible percentage by the accounts receivable total for that category to get the total balance of estimated accounts that will prove to be uncollectible for that category. Then all of the category estimates are added together to get one total estimated uncollectible balance for the period. The entry for bad debt would be as follows, if there was no carryover balance from the prior period.

JOURNAL			
Date	**Account**	**Debit**	**Credit**
Dec. 31	Bad Debt Expense Allowance for Doubtful Accounts *To record estimated bad debts, balance sheet aging method*	58,097	 58,097

Bad Debt Expense increases (debit) as does Allowance for Doubtful Accounts (credit) for $58,097. BWW believes that $58,097 will be uncollectible debt.

Let's consider a situation where BWW had a $20,000 debit balance from the previous period. The adjusting journal entry would recognize the following.

JOURNAL			
Date	**Account**	**Debit**	**Credit**
Dec. 31	Bad Debt Expense Allowance for Doubtful Accounts *To record estimated bad debts, balance sheet aging method*	78,097	 78,097

This is different from the last journal entry, where bad debt was estimated at $58,097. That journal entry assumed a zero balance in Allowance for Doubtful Accounts from the prior period. This journal entry takes into account a debit balance of $20,000 and adds the prior period's balance to the estimated balance of $58,097 in the current period.

Current period	= $58,097 credit
Prior period	= $20,000 debit
Allowance for Doubtful Accounts	= $78,097 credit

You may notice that all three methods use the same accounts for the adjusting entry; only the method changes the financial outcome. Also note that it is a requirement that the estimation method be disclosed in the notes of financial statements so stakeholders can make informed decisions.

CONCEPTS IN PRACTICE

Generally Accepted Accounting Principles

As of January 1, 2018, GAAP requires a change in how health-care entities record bad debt expense. Before this change, these entities would record revenues for billed services, even if they did not expect to collect any payment from the patient. This uncollectible amount would then be reported in Bad Debt Expense. Under the new guidance, the bad debt amount may only be recorded if there is an unexpected circumstance that prevented the patient from paying the bill, and it may only be calculated from the amount that the providing entity anticipated collecting.

For example, a patient receives medical services at a local hospital that cost $1,000. The hospital knows in advance that the patient will pay only $100 of the amount owed. The previous GAAP rules would allow the company to write off $900 to bad debt. Under the current rule, the company may only consider revenue to be the expected amount of $100. For example, if the patient ran into an unexpected job loss and is able to pay only $20 of the $100 expected, the hospital would record the $20 to revenue and the $80 ($100 - $20) as a write-off to bad debt. This is a significant change in revenue reporting and bad debt expense. Health-care entities will more than likely see a decrease in bad debt expense and revenues as a result of this change.[3]

9.3 Determine the Efficiency of Receivables Management Using Financial Ratios

You received an unexpected tax refund this year and want to invest the money in a profitable and growing company. After conducting research, you determine that it is important for a company to collect on outstanding debt quickly, while showing a willingness to offer customers credit options to increase sales opportunities, among other things. You are new to investing, so where do you begin?

Stakeholders, such as investors, lenders, and management, look to financial statement data to make informed decisions about a company's financial position. They will look at each statement—as well as ratio analysis—for trends, industry comparisons, and past performance to help make financing determinations. Because you are reviewing companies for quick debt collection, as well as credit extension to boost sales, you would consider receivables ratios to guide your decision. Discuss the Role of Accounting for Receivables in Earnings Management will explain and demonstrate two popular ratios—the accounts receivable turnover ratio and the number of days' sales in receivables ratio—used to evaluate a company's receivables experiences.

It is important to remember, however, that for a comprehensive evaluation of a company's true potential as an investment, you need to consider other types of ratios, in addition to the receivables ratios. For example, you might want to look at the company's profitability, solvency, and liquidity performances using ratios. (See Appendix A for more information on ratios.)

3 Tara Bannow. "New Bad Debt Accounting Standards Likely to Remake Community Benefit Reporting." *Modern Healthcare*. March 17, 2018. http://www.modernhealthcare.com/article/20180317/NEWS/180319904

Figure 9.3 Which Company Is the Best Investment? Receivables ratios can help make this determination. (credit: "Black Laptop Computer Showing Stock Graph" by "Negative Space"/Pexels, CC0)

Basic Functions of the Receivables Ratios

Receivables ratios show company performance in relation to current debt collection, as well as credit policy effect on sales growth. One receivables ratio is called the **accounts receivable turnover ratio**. This ratio determines how many times (i.e., how often) accounts receivable are collected during an operating period and converted to cash (see Figure 9.3). A higher number of times indicates that receivables are collected quickly. This quick cash collection may be viewed as a positive occurrence, because liquidity improves, and the company may reinvest in its business sooner when the value of the dollar has more buying power (time value of money). The higher number of times may also be a negative occurrence, signaling that credit extension terms are too tight, and it may exclude qualified consumers from purchasing. Excluding these customers means that they may take their business to a competitor, thus reducing potential sales.

In contrast, a lower number of times indicates that receivables are collected at a slower rate. A slower collection rate could signal that lending terms are too lenient; management might consider tightening lending opportunities and more aggressively pursuing outstanding debt. The lower turnover also shows that the company has cash tied up in receivable longer, thus hindering its ability to reinvest this cash in other current projects. The lower turnover rate may signal a high level of bad debt accounts. The determination of a high or low turnover rate really depends on the standards of the company's industry.

Another receivables ratio one must consider is the **number of days' sales in receivables ratio**. This ratio is similar to accounts receivable turnover in that it shows the expected days it will take to convert accounts receivable into cash. The reflected outcome is in number of days, rather than in number of times.

Companies often have outstanding debt that requires scheduled payments. If it takes longer for a company to collect on outstanding receivables, this means it may not be able to meet its current obligations. It helps to know the number of days it takes to go through the accounts receivable collection cycle so a company can plan its debt repayments; this receivables ratio also signals how efficient its collection procedures are. As with the accounts receivable turnover ratio, there are positive and negative elements with a smaller and larger amount of days; in general, the fewer number of collection days on accounts receivable, the better.

To illustrate the use of these ratios to make financial decisions, let's use Billie's Watercraft Warehouse (BWW) as the example. Included are the comparative income statement (Figure 9.4) and the comparative balance sheet (Figure 9.5) for BWW, followed by competitor ratio information, for the years 2016, 2017, and 2018 as shown in Table 9.1.

BILLIE'S WATERCRAFT WAREHOUSE Comparative Income Statement Year Ended December 31, 2016, 2017, and 2018			
	2018	2017	2016
Net Credit Sales	$450,000	$400,000	$375,000
Cost of Goods Sold	70,000	65,000	62,000
Gross Margin	380,000	335,000	313,000
Expenses	$100,000	$110,000	$ 95,000
Net Income (Loss)	$280,000	$225,000	$218,000

Figure 9.4 Comparative Income Statements for Billie's Watercraft Warehouse for the Years 2016, 2017, and 2018. (attribution: Copyright Rice University, OpenStax, under CC BY-NC-SA 4.0 license)

BILLIE'S WATERCRAFT WAREHOUSE Comparative Balance Sheet December 31, 2016, 2017, and 2018			
	2018	2017	2016
Assets:			
Cash	$120,000	$100,000	$ 85,000
Accounts Receivable	85,000	90,000	70,000
Notes Receivable	20,500	15,200	18,450
Inventory	60,400	55,000	47,600
Equipment	31,000	35,000	28,000
Total Assets:	**$316,900**	**$295,200**	**$249,050**
Liabilities:			
Unearned Revenue	$ 5,000	$ 14,500	$ 4,200
Accounts Payable	10,000	15,600	9,500
Notes Payable	9,500	13,700	7,250
Equity:			
Common Stock	$ 12,400	$ 26,400	$ 10,100
Retained Earnings	280,000	225,000	218,000
Total Liabilities and Equity:	**$316,900**	**$295,200**	**$249,050**

Figure 9.5 Comparative Income Statements for Billie's Watercraft Warehouse for the Years 2016, 2017, and 2018. (attribution: Copyright Rice University, OpenStax, under CC BY-NC-SA 4.0 license)

Comparison of Ratios: Industry Competitor to BWW

Year	Accounts Receivable Turnover Ratio	Number of Days' Sales in Receivables Ratio
2016	4.89 times	80 days
2017	4.92 times	79.23 days
2018	5.25 times	76.44 days

Table 9.1 Industry Competitor Ratios for the years 2016, 2017, and 2018.

YOUR TURN

The Investor

You are an investor looking to contribute financially to either Company A or Company B. The following select financial information follows.

	Company A	Company B
Beginning accounts receivable	$ 50,000	$ 60,000
Ending accounts receivable	80,000	90,000
Net credit sales	550,000	460,000

Based on the information provided:

- Compute the accounts receivable turnover ratio
- Compute the number of days' sales in receivables ratio for both Company A and Company B (round all answers to two decimal places)
- Interpret the outcomes, stating which company you would invest in and why

Solution

Company A: ART = 8.46 times, Days' Sales = 43.14 days, Company B: ART = 6.13 times, Days' Sales = 59.54 days. Upon initial review of this limited information, Company A seems to be the better choice, since their turnover ratio is higher and the collection time is lower with 43.14 days. One might want more information on trends for each company with these ratios and a comparison to others in the same industry. More information is needed before making an informed decision.

Accounts Receivable Turnover Ratio

The ratio to determine accounts receivable turnover is as follows.

$$\frac{\textbf{Net Credit Sales}}{\textbf{Average Accounts Receivable}}$$

$$\textbf{Average Accounts Receivable} = \frac{\textbf{(Beginning Accounts Receivable + Ending Accounts Receivable)}}{\textbf{2}}$$

Net credit sales are sales made on credit only; cash sales are not included because they do not produce receivables. However, many companies do not report credit sales separate from cash sales, so "net sales" may be substituted for "net credit sales" in this case. Beginning and ending accounts receivable refer to the beginning and ending balances in accounts receivable for the period. The beginning accounts receivable balance is the same figure as the ending accounts receivable balance from the prior period.

Use this formula to compute BWW's accounts receivable turnover for 2017 and 2018.

The accounts receivable turnover ratio for 2017 is 5 × ($400,000/$80,000). Net credit sales for 2017 are $400,000, so

$$\text{Average accounts receivable} = \frac{(\$70{,}000 + \$90{,}000)}{2} = \$80{,}000$$

The accounts receivable turnover ratio for 2018 is 5.14 times (rounded to two decimal places). Net credit sales for 2018 are $450,000, so

$$\text{Average accounts receivable} = \frac{(\$90{,}000 + \$85{,}000)}{2} = \$87{,}500$$

The outcome for 2017 means that the company turns over receivables (converts receivables into cash) 5 times during the year. The outcome for 2018 shows that BWW converts cash at a quicker rate of 5.14 times. There is a trend increase from 2017 to 2018. BWW sells various watercraft. These products tend to have a higher sales price, making a customer more likely to pay with credit. This can also increase the length of debt repayment. Comparing to another company in the industry, BWW's turnover rate is standard. To increase the turnover rate, BWW can consider extending credit to more customers who the company has determined will pay on a quicker basis or schedule, or BWW can more aggressively pursue the outstanding debt from current customers.

Number of Days' Sales in Receivables Ratio

The ratio to determine number of days' sales in receivables is as follows.

$$\frac{\textbf{365}}{\textbf{Accounts Receivable Turnover Ratio}}$$

The numerator is 365, the number of days in the year. Because the accounts receivable turnover ratio determines an average accounts receivable figure, the outcome for the days' sales in receivables is also an average number. Using this formula, compute BWW's number of days' sales in receivables ratio for 2017 and 2018.

The ratio for 2017 is 73 days (365/5), and for 2018 is 71.01 days (365/5.14), rounded. This means it takes 73 days in 2017 and 71.01 days in 2018 to complete the collection cycle, which is a decrease from 2017 to 2018. A downward trend is a positive for the company, and BWW outperforms the competition slightly. This is good because BWW can use the cash toward other business expenditures, or the downward trend could signal that the company needs to loosen credit terms or more aggressively collect outstanding accounts.

Looking at both ratios, BWW seems well positioned within the industry, and a potential investor or lender may be more apt to contribute financially to the organization with this continued positive trend.

LINK TO LEARNING

American Superconductor Corporation specializes in the production and service of energy-efficient wind turbine systems, as well as energy grid construction solutions. On the company's 2018–2019 financial statements, the accounts receivable turnover ratio is approximately 6.32 times, and the number of day's sales in receivables ratio is approximately 58 days. This site providing American Superconductor Corporation's current financial statements (https://openstax.org/l/50AMSCfinan2017) is available for review.

9.4 Discuss the Role of Accounting for Receivables in Earnings Management

Assume that you are an accountant at a large public corporation and are on a team responsible for preparing financial statements. In one team discussion, a dilemma arises: What is the best way to report earnings to create the most favorable possible financial position for your company, while still complying in an ethical manner and also complying fully with generally accepted accounting procedures (GAAP)? Your company is required to follow GAAP rules, but is there a way to comply with these rules while showing the company in its best light? How does receivables accounting factor into this quandary?

Before examining potential ways to improve the company's financial image, let's consider some important conditions. To begin, if the company is publicly traded on a national or regional stock exchange, it is subject to the accounting and financial regulations set by the Securities and Exchange Commission (SEC). Included in these rules is the requirement that each publicly traded company must prepare and make public each year its annual report, including the results of an extensive audit procedure performed by a major public accounting firm.

In the process of auditing the company, the auditing firm will conduct tests to determine whether, in the auditor's opinion, the financial statements accurately reflect the financial position of the company. If the auditor feels that transactions, financial schedules, or other records do not accurately reflect the company's performance for the past year, then the auditor can issue a negative audit report, which could have major negative effects on the company's image in the financial community.

To sum up this issue, any attempts by companies to make their financial position look better must be based on assumptions by the company that can be verified by an outside, independent party, such as a major public accounting firm. As you learn about this topic, assume that any recommendations suggested must be legitimate changes in assumptions by the company and that the recommendations will pass public examination and scrutiny.

Earnings management works within GAAP constraints to improve stakeholders' views of the company's financial position. **Earnings manipulation** is noticeably different in that it typically ignores GAAP rules to alter earnings significantly. Carried to an extreme, manipulation can lead to fraudulent behavior by a company. The major problem in income manipulation is not in manipulating the numbers that constitute the financial reports. Instead, the bigger issue is the engineering of the short-term financial operating decisions. Some of the techniques used include applying universal standards, loose interpretations of revenue recognition, unofficial earnings measures, fair value accounting, and cooking the decision and not the books.[4]

A company may be enticed to manipulate earnings for several reasons. It may want to show a healthier income level, meet or exceed market expectations, and receive management bonuses. This can produce more investment interest from potential investors. An increase to receivables and inventory can help a business to secure more borrowed funds.

4 H. David Sherman and S. David Young. "Where Financial Reporting Still Falls Short." *Harvard Business Review*. July-August 2016. https://hbr.org/2016/07/where-financial-reporting-still-falls-short

ETHICAL CONSIDERATIONS

Improper Revenue Recognition Leads to New Accounting Laws and Regulations

The complete financial collapse of the Enron Corporation was a catalyst for major changes in the accounting profession. Fraudulent revenue recognition and financial statement manipulation at Enron—an energy, commodities, and services company—helped provide support for the implementation of the Sarbanes-Oxley Act of 2002 (SOX). A federal law, SOX included the creation of the Public Company Accounting Oversight Board (PCAOB), a regulatory agency to oversee auditors and ensure compliance with SOX requirements.

The PCAOB is charged by the Sarbanes-Oxley Act of 2002 with establishing auditing and professional practice standards for registered public accounting firms to follow in the preparation and issuing of audit reports.[5] The PCAOB regulates how publicly traded companies are audited and provides requirements and ethical standards that direct professional accountants in their work with publicly traded companies. Visit their website at www.pcaobus.org to learn more.

Accounts receivable may also be manipulated to delay revenue recognition. These deferred earnings allow for a reduced tax obligation in the current year. A company involved in the sale or acquisition of a business may show a higher income level to increase the value of the business. Whatever the reason, a company often has the flexibility to manage their earnings slightly, given the amount of estimations and potential bad debt write-offs required to meet the revenue recognition and matching principles.

One area of estimation involves bad debt in relation to accounts receivable. As you've learned, the income statement method, balance sheet method, and the balance sheet aging method all require estimations of bad debt with receivables. The percentage uncollectible is supposed to be presented as an educated estimation based on past performance, industry standards, and other economic factors. However, this estimation is just that—an estimation—and it can be slightly manipulated or managed to overstate or understate bad debt, as well as accounts receivable. For example, a company does not usually benefit from bad debt write-off. It might legitimately—if past experience justifies the change—alter past-due dates to current accounts to avoid having to write off bad debt. This overstates accounts receivable and understates bad debt. The company could also change the percentage uncollectible to a lower or higher figure, if its financial information and the present economic environment justify the change. The company could change the percentage from 2% uncollectible to 1% uncollectible. This increases accounts receivable and potential earnings and reduces bad debt expenses in the current period.

LINK TO LEARNING

The Beneish M-Score is an earnings manipulation measurement system that incorporates eight financial ratios to identify potentially compromised companies. In 2000, a group of students from Cornell University used this measurement to sell all the "Cayuga Fund" stock holdings in Enron, one year before the total collapse of company. Read this article on the Cornell University Enron Case Study (https://openstax.org/l/50CornellEnron) to learn more.

5 Public Company Accounting Oversight Board (PCAOB). "Standards." n.d. https://pcaobus.org/Standards

Let's take Billie's Watercraft Warehouse (BWW), for example. BWW had the following net credit sales and accounts receivable from 2016–2018.

	2018	2017	2016
Net Credit Sales	$450,000	$400,000	$375,000
Accounts Receivable	85,000	90,000	70,000

It also used the following percentage calculations for doubtful accounts under each bad debt estimation method.

Income Statement Method	Balance Sheet Method	Balance Sheet Aging Method
5% of credit sales	15% of accounts receivable	0–30 days past due = 10% 31–90 days past due = 20% Over 90 days past due = 30%

Legitimate current economic conditions could allow BWW to alter its estimation percentages, aging categories, and method used. Altering estimation percentages could mean an increase or decrease in percentages. If BWW decreases its income statement method percentage from 5% of credit sales to 4% of credit sales, the bad debt estimation would go from $22,500 (5% × $450,000) in 2018 to $18,000 (4% × $450,000). The bad debt expense would decrease for the period, and net income would increase. If BWW decreases its balance sheet method percentage from 15% of accounts receivable to 12% of accounts receivable, the bad debt estimation would go from $12,750 (15% × $85,000) in 2018 to $10,200 (12% × $85,000). The bad debt expense would decrease for the period and net income would increase. Accounts receivable would also increase, and allowances for doubtful accounts would decrease. As mentioned, this increase to earnings and asset increase is attractive to investors and lenders.

Another earnings management opportunity may occur with the balance sheet aging method. Past-due categories could expand to encompass greater (or fewer) time periods, accounts receivable balances could be placed in different categories, or estimation percentages could change for each category. However, please remember that such changes would need to be considered acceptable by the company's outside auditors during the annual independent audit.

To demonstrate the recommendation, assume that BWW has three categories: 0–30 days past due, 31–90 days past due, and over 90 days past due. These categories could change to 0–60 days, 61–120 days, and over 120 days. This could move accounts that previously had a higher bad debt percentage assigned to them into a lower percentage category. This category shift could produce an increase to accounts receivable, and a decrease to bad debt expense; thus, increasing net income estimation percentages can change within each category. The following is the original uncollectible distribution for BWW in 2018.

	0–30 days past due	31–90 days past due	Over 90 days past due
Accounts receivable amount	$40,000	$20,000	$25,000
Percent uncollectible	10%	20%	30%
Total per category	$ 4,000	$ 4,000	$ 7,500
Total uncollectible $15,500			

The following is the uncollectible percentage distribution change.

	0–30 days past due	31–90 days past due	Over 90 days past due
Accounts receivable amount	$40,000	$20,000	$25,000
Percent uncollectible	8%	15%	25%
Total per category	$ 3,200	$ 3,000	$ 6,250
Total uncollectible $12,450			

Comparing the two outcomes, the original uncollectible figure was $15,500 and the changed uncollectible figure is $12,450. This reduction produces a higher accounts receivable balance, a lower bad debt expense, and a higher net income.

A company may also change the estimation method to produce a different net income outcome. For example, BWW may go from the income statement method to the balance sheet method. However, as mentioned, the change would have to be considered to reflect the company's actual bad debt experiences accurately, and not just made for the sake of manipulating the income and expenses reported on their financial statements. A change in the estimation method that provides a comparison of the 2018 income statement follows.

BILLIE'S WATERCRAFT WAREHOUSE Income Statement (Method Comparison) Year Ended December 31, 2018		
	Income Statement Method	**Balance Sheet Method**
Net Credit Sales	$450,000	$450,000
Cost of Goods Sold	70,000	70,000
Gross Margin	$380,000	$380,000
Expenses:		
General and Administrative Expense	77,500	77,500
Bad Debt Expense	22,500	12,750
Total Expenses	$100,000	$ 90,250
Net Income (Loss)	$280,000	$289,750

In this example, net income appears higher under the balance sheet method than the income statement method: $280,000 compared to $289,750, respectively. BWW could change to the balance sheet method for estimating bad debt to give the appearance that income is greater. An investor or lender looking at BWW may consider providing funds given the earnings performance, unaware that the estimation method alone may result in an inflated income. So, what can an investor or lender do to recognize earnings management (or manipulation)?

An investor or lender can compare ratio analysis to others in the industry, and year-to-year trend analysis can be helpful. The number of days' sales in receivables ratio is a usually a good indicator of manipulation activity. A quicker collection period found in the first two years of operation can signal negative earnings behavior (as compared to industry standards). Earnings management can be a bit more difficult, given its acceptability under GAAP. As with uncovering earnings manipulation, due diligence with ratio and trend analysis is paramount. These topics will be covered in more depth in Appendix A: Financial Statement Analysis.

CONCEPTS IN PRACTICE

Competitor Acquisitions

As companies become large players in industry, they may consider acquiring competitors. When acquisition discussions occur, financial information, future growth channels, and business organizational structure play heavy roles in the decision process. A level of financial transparency is expected with an acquisition candidate, but during buying negotiations, each business will present the best financial position possible. The seller's goal is to yield a high sales price; the desire to present a rosy picture could lead to earnings manipulation. An acquirer needs to be mindful of this and review trend analysis and ratio comparisons before making a purchase decision.

Consider General Electric Company (GE). GE's growth model in recent years was based on acquiring additional businesses within the industry. The company did not do its due diligence on several acquisitions, including Baker Hughes, and it was misled to believe the acquired businesses were in a stable financial earnings position. The acquisitions led to a declining financial position and reduced stock price. In order for GE to restructure and return to a positive growth model, it had to sell its interests in Baker Hughes and other acquisitions that were underperforming based on expectations.

9.5 Apply Revenue Recognition Principles to Long-Term Projects

While most receivable reporting is straightforward when recognizing revenue and matching expenses in the same period, a few unique situations require special revenue distribution for long-term projects. Long-term construction-company projects, real estate installment sales, multi-year magazine subscriptions, and a combined equipment sale with an accompanying service contract have special reporting requirements to meet revenue recognition and matching principles.

Long-term construction projects, such as construction of a major sports stadium, can take several years to complete. Typically, revenue is recognized when the earnings process is complete; however, if the construction project did not begin work immediately, this could delay recognition of revenue, and expenses accumulated during the period would be unmatched. These unmatched expenses can misstate financial statements (particularly the income statement) and mislead stakeholders. There are also tax implications, where a company may benefit from tax breaks with reduced earnings.

Two methods can be applied to long-term construction projects that are consistent with the revenue recognition criteria you've learned about. The methods commonly utilized by construction contractors are the percentage of completion and completed contract (see Figure 9.6). The **percentage of completion method** takes the percentage of work completed for the period and divides that by the total revenues from the contract. The percentage of work completed for the period distributes the estimated total project costs over the contract term based on the actual completion amount, up to that point. The percentage can be based on such factors as percentage of anticipated final costs incurred at a given point or an engineering report that estimates the percentage of completion of the project at a stage of production.

Figure 9.6 Long-Term Construction Project. Revenue recognition requires use of the percentage of completion or completion contract method. (credit: modification of "Construction of Millennium Stadium, Cardiff" by Seth Whales/Wikimedia Commons, CC BY 2.0)

The **completed contract method** delays reporting of both revenues and expenses until the entire contract is complete. This can create reporting issues and is typically used only where cost and earnings cannot be reasonably estimated throughout the contract term.

Unlike most residential home loan transactions (usually labeled as mortgage loans), which tend to require monthly payments, commercial real estate sales are often structured as an **installment sale** (see Figure 9.7) and usually involve periodic installment payments from buyers. These payments can be structured with annual payments, interest-only payments, or any other payment format to which the parties agree.

Figure 9.7 Real Estate Installment Sales. Revenue recognition requires use of the installment method to account for long-term risk. (credit: modification of "Boost-the-Market-Value-of-Your-Home_L" by Dan Moyle/ Flickr, CC BY 2.0)

However, a seller/lender has no guarantee that the buyer will pay the debt in its entirety. In this event, the property serves as security for the seller/lender if legal action is taken. The longer the debt remains outstanding, the higher the risk the buyer will not complete payment. With traditional accrual accounting, risk is not considered and revenue is reported immediately. The installment method accounts for risk and defers revenue using a gross profit percentage. As installment payments are made, this percentage is applied to the current period.

Multi-year magazine subscriptions are long-term service contracts with payment usually occurring in advance of any provided service. The company may not recognize this revenue until the subscription has been provided, but there is also no guarantee that the contract will be honored in its entirety at the conditions expected. Financial Accounting Standards Board, Topic 606, *Revenue from Contracts with Customers*, requires businesses to report revenue "in an amount that reflects the consideration to which the entity expects to be entitled in exchange for the goods or services."[6] Thus, once a change occurs to the expected revenue distribution, this new amount is recorded going forward.

A combined equipment purchase with an accompanying service contract requires separate reporting of the sale and service contract. An example of this is a cell phone purchase that has a service contract (warranty) for any damage to the unit. There is no guarantee that damage will occur or that service will be provided, but the customer has purchased this policy as insurance. Thus, the company must reasonably estimate this revenue each period and distribute this estimation over the life of the service contract. Or, the company may wait until the contract expires before reporting any revenue or expenses associated with the service contract.

CONCEPTS IN PRACTICE

U.S. Bank Stadium Construction

HKS, Inc. received a construction contract from the Minnesota Sports Facilities Authority to build the new U.S. Bank Stadium. The construction contract services began in 2012, but the stadium was not complete until 2016. The total construction cost was approximately $1.129 billion.

The portion of construction revenues earned by HKS, Inc. could not be reported upon initial receipt of funds but were instead distributed using the percentage of completion method. Much of the costs and completion associated with building the stadium occurred in the later years of the project (specifically 2015); thus, the company experienced a sharp increase in percentage of completion in the 2015 period. This showed a substantial increase to revenues during this period.

IFRS CONNECTION

Revenue and Receivables

When Financial Accounting Standards Board (FASB) and International Accounting Standards Board (IASB) began their joint work to create converged standards, a primary goal was to develop a single, comprehensive revenue recognition standard. At the time work began, International Financial Reporting Stands (IFRS) had one general standard that was applied to all companies with little guidance for various

6 Financial Accounting Standards Board (FASB). "Revenue from Contracts with Customers (Topic 606)." *FASB Accounting Standards Update, Financial Accounting Series*. April 2016. https://asc.fasb.org/imageRoot/32/79982032.pdf

industries or different revenue scenarios. On the other hand, U.S. generally accepted accounting principles (GAAP) had more than 100 standards that applied to revenue recognition. Because of the global nature of business, including investing and borrowing, it was important to increase the comparability of revenue measurement and reporting. After years of work, a new standard was agreed upon; both FASB and IASB released a revenue recognition standard that is essentially the same, with only a few differences. In the United States, the new revenue recognition standards became effective for reporting in 2018 for publicly traded companies.

A few differences remain in the reporting of revenue. In accounting for long-term projects, IFRS does not allow the completed contract method. If estimating the percentage of completion of the project is not possible, IFRS allows revenues equal to costs to be recognized. This results in no profit recognized in the current period, but rather all profit being deferred until the completion of the project.

Receivables represent amounts owed to the business from sales or service activities that have been charged or loans that have been made to customers or others. Proper reporting of receivables is important because it affects ratios used in the analysis of a company's solvency and liquidity, and also because reporting of receivables should reflect future cash receipts.

Under both U.S. GAAP and IFRS, receivables are reported as either current or noncurrent assets depending on when they are due. Also, receivables that do not have an interest component are carried at net realizable value or the amount the company expects to receive for the receivable. This requires estimation and reporting of an allowance for uncollectible accounts (sometimes referred to as "provisions" under IFRS). However, receivables that do have a significant financing component are reported at amortized cost adjusted for an estimate of uncollectible accounts.

GAAP and IFRS can differ in the financial statement presentation of receivables. GAAP requires a liquidity presentation on the balance sheet, meaning assets are listed in order of liquidity (those assets most easily converted into cash to those assets least easily converted to cash). Thus, receivables—particularly accounts receivable, which are highly liquid—are presented right after cash. However, IFRS allows reverse liquidity presentation. Therefore, receivables may appear as one of the last items in the asset section of the balance sheet under IFRS. This requires careful observance of the presentation being used when comparing a company reporting under U.S. GAAP to one using IFRS when assessing receivables.

In the case of notes receivable, the method for estimating uncollectible accounts differs between U.S. GAAP and IFRS. IFRS estimates uncollectible accounts on notes receivable in a three-level process, depending upon whether the note receivable has maintained its original credit risk, increased slightly in credit risk, or increased significantly in riskiness. For companies using U.S. GAAP, estimated uncollectible accounts are based on the overall lifetime riskiness.

9.6 Explain How Notes Receivable and Accounts Receivable Differ

So far, our discussion of receivables has focused solely on accounts receivable. Companies, however, can expand their business models to include more than one type of receivable. This receivable expansion allows a company to attract a more diverse clientele and increase asset potential to further grow the business.

As you've learned, accounts receivable is typically a more informal arrangement between a company and customer that is resolved within a year and does not include interest payments. In contrast, **notes receivable** (an asset) is a more formal legal contract between the buyer and the company, which requires a specific payment amount at a predetermined future date. The length of contract is typically over a year, or beyond one operating cycle. There is also generally an interest requirement because the financial loan amount may be larger than accounts receivable, and the length of contract is possibly longer. A note can be requested or extended in exchange for products and services or in exchange for cash (usually in the case of a financial lender). Several characteristics of notes receivable further define the contract elements and scope of use.

Key Feature Comparison of Accounts Receivable and Notes Receivable

Accounts Receivable	Notes Receivable
• An informal agreement between customer and company • Receivable in less than one year or within a company's operating cycle • Does not include interest	• A legal contract with established payment terms • Receivable beyond one year and outside of a company's operating cycle • Includes interest

Table 9.2

THINK IT THROUGH

Dishonored Note

You are the owner of a retail health food store and have several large companies with whom you do business. Many competitors in your industry are vying for your customers' business. For each sale, you issue a notes receivable to the company, with an interest rate of 10% and a maturity date 18 months after the issue date. Each note has a minimum principal amount of $500,000.

Let's say one of these companies is unable to pay in the established timeframe and dishonors the note. What would you do? How does this dishonored note affect your company both financially and nonfinancially? If your customer wanted to renegotiate the terms of the agreement, would you agree? If so, what would be the terms?

Characteristics of Notes Receivable

Notes receivable have several defining characteristics that include principal, length of contract terms, and interest. The **principal** of a note is the initial loan amount, not including interest, requested by the customer. If a customer approaches a lender, requesting $2,000, this amount is the principal. The date on which the security agreement is initially established is the **issue date**. A note's **maturity date** is the date at which the principal and interest become due and payable. The maturity date is established in the initial note contract. For example, when the previously mentioned customer requested the $2,000 loan on January 1, 2018, terms of repayment included a maturity date of 24 months. This means that the loan will mature in two years, and the principal and interest are due at that time. The following journal entries occur at the note's established start date. The first entry shows a note receivable in exchange for a product or service, and the second entry illustrates the note from the point of view that a $2,000 loan was issued by a financial institution to a customer (borrower).

JOURNAL			
Date	**Account**	**Debit**	**Credit**
Jan. 1, 2018	Notes Receivable Sales Revenue *To record sale in exchange for notes receivable*	2,000	 2,000

JOURNAL			
Date	**Account**	**Debit**	**Credit**
Jan. 1, 2018	Notes Receivable Cash *To record notes receivable in exchange for a cash loan*	2,000	 2,000

Before realization of the maturity date, the note is accumulating interest revenue for the lender. **Interest** is a monetary incentive to the lender that justifies loan risk. An annual interest rate is established with the loan terms. The **interest rate** is the part of a loan charged to the borrower, expressed as an annual percentage of the outstanding loan amount. Interest is accrued daily, and this accumulation must be recorded periodically (each month for example). The Revenue Recognition Principle requires that the interest revenue accrued is recorded in the period when earned. Periodic interest accrued is recorded in Interest Revenue and Interest Receivable. To calculate interest, the company can use the following formulas. The following example uses months but the calculation could also be based on a 365-day year.

$$\text{Interest} = \text{Annual Interest Rate} \times \text{Loan Principle} \times \text{Part of Year}$$

$$\text{where}$$

$$\text{Part of Year} = \frac{\text{Number of Accrued Interest Months}}{\text{12 Months}}$$

Another common way to state the interest formula is Interest = Principal × Rate × Time. From the previous example, the company offered a $2,000 note with a maturity date of 24 months. The annual interest rate on the loan is 10%. Each period the company needs to record an entry for accumulated interest during the period. In this example, the first year's interest revenue accumulation is computed as 10% × $2,000 × (12/12) = $200. The $200 is recognized in Interest Revenue and Interest Receivable.

JOURNAL			
Date	**Account**	**Debit**	**Credit**
Dec. 31, 2018	Interest Receivable Interest Revenue *To record interest accumulated after first 12 months*	200	 200

When interest is due at the end of the note (24 months), the company may record the collection of the loan principal and the accumulated interest. These transactions can be recorded as one entry or two. The first set of entries show collection of principal, followed by collection of the interest.

JOURNAL			
Date	**Account**	**Debit**	**Credit**
Dec. 31, 2019	Cash	2,000	
	Notes Receivable		2,000
	To record collection of note principal		
Dec. 31, 2019	Cash	400	
	Interest Receivable		200
	Interest Revenue		200
	To record interest collection after 24-month term		

Interest revenue from year one had already been recorded in 2018, but the interest revenue from 2019 is not recorded until the end of the note term. Thus, Interest Revenue is increasing (credit) by $200, the remaining revenue earned but not yet recognized. Interest Receivable decreasing (credit) reflects the 2018 interest owed from the customer that is paid to the company at the end of 2019. The second possibility is one entry recognizing principal and interest collection.

JOURNAL			
Date	**Account**	**Debit**	**Credit**
Dec. 31, 2019	Cash	2,400	
	Notes Receivable		2,000
	Interest Receivable		200
	Interest Revenue		200
	To record collection of principal and accumulated interest		

If the note term does not exceed one accounting period, the entry showing note collection may not reflect interest receivable. For example, let's say the company's note maturity date was 12 months instead of 24 (payment in full occurs December 31, 2018). The entry to record collection of the principal and interest follows.

JOURNAL			
Date	**Account**	**Debit**	**Credit**
Dec. 31, 2018	Cash	2,200	
	Notes Receivable		2,000
	Interest Revenue		200
	To record collection of principle and interest		

The examples provided account for collection of the note in full on the maturity date, which is considered an honored note. But what if the customer does not pay within the specified contract length? This situation is considered a dishonored note. A lender will still pursue collection of the note but will not maintain a long-term receivable on its books. Instead, the lender will convert the notes receivable and interest due into an account receivable. Sometimes a company will classify and label the uncollected account as a Dishonored Note Receivable. Using our example, if the company was unable to collect the $2,000 from the customer at the 12-month maturity date, the following entry would occur.

JOURNAL			
Date	**Account**	**Debit**	**Credit**
Dec. 31, 2018	Accounts Receivable	2,200	
	Notes Receivable		2,000
	Interest Revenue		200
	To record conversion of note to Accounts Receivable		

If it is still unable to collect, the company may consider selling the receivable to a collection agency. When this occurs, the collection agency pays the company a fraction of the note's value, and the company would write off any difference as a factoring (third-party debt collection) expense. Let's say that our example company turned over the $2,200 accounts receivable to a collection agency on March 5, 2019 and received only $500 for its value. The difference between $2,200 and $500 of $1,700 is the factoring expense.

JOURNAL			
Date	**Account**	**Debit**	**Credit**
Mar. 5, 2019	Cash Factoring Expense Accounts Receivable *To record sale of Accounts Receivable to third-party factor*	500 1,700	 2,200

Notes receivable can convert to accounts receivable, as illustrated, but accounts receivable can also convert to notes receivable. The transition from accounts receivable to notes receivable can occur when a customer misses a payment on a short-term credit line for products or services. In this case, the company could extend the payment period and require interest.

For example, a company may have an outstanding account receivable in the amount of $1,000. The customer negotiates with the company on June 1 for a six-month note maturity date, 12% annual interest rate, and $250 cash up front. The company records the following entry at contract establishment.

JOURNAL			
Date	**Account**	**Debit**	**Credit**
Jun. 1	Cash Notes Receivable Accounts Receivable *To record conversion of Accounts Receivable to Notes Receivable*	250 750	 1,000

This examines a note from the lender's perspective; see Current Liabilities for an in-depth discussion on the customer's liability with a note (payable).

Illustrated Examples of Notes Receivable

To illustrate notes receivable scenarios, let's return to Billie's Watercraft Warehouse (BWW) as the example. BWW has a customer, Waterways Corporation, that tends to have larger purchases that require an extended payment period. On January 1, 2018, Waterways purchased merchandise in the amount of $250,000. BWW agreed to lend the $250,000 purchase cost (sales price) to Waterways under the following conditions. First, BWW agrees to accept a note payable issued by Waterways. The conditions of the note are that the principal amount is $250,000, the maturity date on the note is 24 months, and the annual interest rate is 12%. On January 1, 2018, BWW records the following entry.

JOURNAL			
Date	**Account**	**Debit**	**Credit**
Jan. 1, 2018	Notes Receivable: Waterways Sales Revenue *To record sale in exchange for notes receivable, 24-month maturity, 12% interest rate*	250,000	 250,000

Notes Receivable: Waterways increases (debit), and Sales Revenue increases (credit) for the principal amount of $250,000. On December 31, 2018, BWW records interest accumulated on the note for 12 months.

JOURNAL			
Date	**Account**	**Debit**	**Credit**
Dec. 31, 2018	Interest Receivable: Waterways	30,000	
	Interest Revenue		30,000
	To record interest accumulated after first 12 months		

Interest Receivable: Waterways increases (debit) as does Interest Revenue (credit) for 12 months of interest computed as $250,000 × 12% × (12/12). On December 31, 2019, Waterways Corporation honors the note; BWW records this collection as a single entry.

JOURNAL			
Date	**Account**	**Debit**	**Credit**
Dec. 31, 2019	Cash	310,000	
	Notes Receivable: Waterways		250,000
	Interest Receivable: Waterways		30,000
	Interest Revenue		30,000
	To record collection of principal and accumulated interest		

Cash increases (debit) for the principal and interest total of $310,000, Notes Receivable: Waterways decreases (credit) for the principal amount of $250,000, Interest Receivable: Waterways decreases (credit) for the 2018 accumulated interest amount of $30,000, and Interest Revenue increases (credit) for the 2019 interest collection amount of $30,000.

BWW does business with Sea Ferries Inc. BWW issued Sea Ferries a note in the amount of $100,000 on January 1, 2018, with a maturity date of six months, at a 10% annual interest rate. On July 2, BWW determined that Sea Ferries dishonored its note and recorded the following entry to convert this debt into accounts receivable.

JOURNAL			
Date	**Account**	**Debit**	**Credit**
Jun. 2, 2018	Accounts Receivable: Sea Ferries	105,000	
	Notes Receivable: Sea Ferries		100,000
	Interest Revenue		5,000
	To record conversion of note to Accounts Receivable, dishonored note		

Accounts Receivable: Sea Ferries increases (debit) for the principal note amount plus interest, Notes Receivable: Sea Ferries decreases (credit) for the principal amount due, and Interest Revenue increases (credit) for interest earned at maturity. Interest is computed as $100,000 × 10% × (6/12). On September 1, 2018, BWW determines that Sea Ferries's account will be uncollectible and sells the balance to a collection agency for a total of $35,000.

JOURNAL			
Date	**Account**	**Debit**	**Credit**
Sept. 1, 2018	Cash	35,000	
	Factoring Expense	70,000	
	Accounts Receivable: Sea Ferries		105,000
	To record sale of Accounts Receivable to third-party factor		

Cash increases (debit) for the agreed-upon discounted value of $35,000, Factoring Expense increases (debit) for the outstanding amount and the discounted sales price, and Accounts Receivable: Sea Ferries decreases (credit) for the original amount owed.

Alliance Cruises is a customer of BWW with an outstanding accounts receivable balance of $50,000. Alliance is unable to pay in full on schedule, so it negotiates with BWW on March 1 to convert its accounts receivable into a notes receivable. BWW agrees to the following terms: six-month note maturity date, 18% annual interest rate, and $10,000 cash up front. BWW records the following entry at contract establishment.

JOURNAL			
Date	**Account**	**Debit**	**Credit**
Mar. 1	Cash Notes Receivable: Alliance Accounts Receivable: Alliance *To record conversion of Accounts Receivable to Notes Receivable*	10,000 40,000	 50,000

Cash increases (debit) for the up-front collection of $10,000, Notes Receivable: Alliance increases (debit) for the principal amount on the note of $40,000, and Accounts Receivable: Alliance decreases (credit) for the original amount Alliance owed of $50,000.

LINK TO LEARNING

Another opportunity for a company to issue a notes receivable is when one business tries to acquire another. As part of an acquisition sale between MMA Capital Management LLC and Hunt Companies Inc., MMA "provided financing for the purchase price in the form of a seven-year, note receivable from Hunt" with an interest rate of 5%, payable in quarterly installments. Read this article on the terms of sale and the role of the notes receivable in the MMA/Hunt Acquisition (https://openstax.org/l/50MMAHuntAcq) to learn more.

9.7 Appendix: Comprehensive Example of Bad Debt Estimation

The following comprehensive example will illustrate the bad debt estimation process from the sales transaction to adjusting entry reporting for all three bad debt estimation methods: income statement, balance sheet, and balance sheet aging of receivables.

Furniture Direct sells office furniture to large scale businesses. Because the purchases are typically large, Furniture Direct allows customers to pay on credit using an in-house account. At the end of the year, Furniture Direct must estimate bad debt using one of the three estimation methods. It is currently using the income statement method and estimates bad debt at 5% of credit sales. If it were to switch to the balance sheet method, it would estimate bad debt at 8% of accounts receivable. If it were to use the balance sheet aging of receivables method, it would split its receivables into three categories: 0–30 days past due at 5%, 31–90 days past due at 10%, and over 90 days past due at 20%. There is currently a zero balance, transferred from the prior year's Allowance for Doubtful Accounts. The following information is available from the year-end income statement and balance sheet.

2018 Year-end Totals for Furniture Direct	
Credit sales	$1,350,000
Accounts receivable	745,000

There is also additional information regarding the distribution of accounts receivable by age.

Past-Due Category	Accounts Receivable Total
0–30 days	$485,000
31–90 days	180,000
Over 90 days	80,000

If the company were to maintain the income statement method, the total bad debt estimation would be $67,500 ($1,350,000 × 5%), and the following adjusting entry would occur.

JOURNAL			
Date	**Account**	**Debit**	**Credit**
Dec. 31	Bad Debt Expense	67,500	
	Allowance for Doubtful Accounts		67,500
	To record estimated bad debts, income statement method		

If the company were to use the balance sheet method, the total bad debt estimation would be $59,600 ($745,000 × 8%), and the following adjusting entry would occur.

JOURNAL			
Date	**Account**	**Debit**	**Credit**
Dec. 31	Bad Debt Expense	59,600	
	Allowance for Doubtful Accounts		59,600
	To record estimated bad debts, balance sheet method		

If the company were to use the balance sheet aging of receivables method, the total bad debt estimation would be $58,250, calculated as shown:

Past Due Category	Accounts Receivable Total	Uncollectible Percentage	Total
0–30 days	$485,000	5%	$24,250
31–90 days	180,000	10%	18,000
Over 90 days	80,000	20%	16,000
		Total Estimated Uncollectible:	**$58,250**

The adjusting entry recorded using the aging method is as follows.

JOURNAL			
Date	**Account**	**Debit**	**Credit**
Dec. 31	Bad Debt Expense	58,250	
	Allowance for Doubtful Accounts		58,250
	To record estimated bad debts, balance sheet aging method		

As you can see, the methods provide different financial figures.

Bad Debt Estimation Method Comparison for Furniture Direct	
	Total Bad Debt Estimation
Income Statement Method	$67,500
Balance Sheet Method	59,600
Balance Sheet Aging of Receivables Method	58,250

While it is up to the company to determine which method best describes its financial position, as you see in Account for Uncollectible Accounts Using the Balance Sheet and Income Statement Approaches, a company may manage these methods and figures to present the best financial position possible.

CONTINUING APPLICATION AT WORK

Grocery Store Offerings

Every week, millions of shoppers visit grocery stores. Consider the various transactions that are occurring at any given time. Most of the items found within a grocery store are perishable and have a finite shelf life. The majority of purchases are paid with cash, check, or credit card. Therefore, you might assume that a grocery store would not have a balance in accounts receivable.

However, grocery stores have evolved to become a one-stop shop for many items. You can now purchase gas, seasonal decorations, cooking utensils, and even fill your prescriptions at many stores.

Key Terms

accounts receivable outstanding customer debt on a credit sale, typically receivable within a short time period

accounts receivable turnover ratio how many times accounts receivable is collected during an operating period and converted to cash

accrual accounting records transactions related to revenue earnings as they occur, not when cash is collected

allowance for doubtful accounts contra asset account that is specifically contrary to accounts receivable; it is used to estimate bad debt when the specific customer is unknown

allowance method estimates bad debt during a period based on certain computational approaches, and it matches this to sales

bad debts uncollectible amounts from customer accounts

balance sheet aging of receivables method allowance method approach that estimates bad debt expenses based on the balance in accounts receivable, but it also considers the uncollectible time period for each account

balance sheet method (also, percentage of accounts receivable method) allowance method approach that estimates bad debt expenses based on the balance in accounts receivable

completed contract method delays reporting of both revenues and expenses until the entire contract is complete

contra account account paired with another account type that has an opposite normal balance to the paired account; reduces or increases the balance in the paired account at the end of a period

direct write-off method delays recognition of bad debt until the specific customer accounts receivable is identified

earnings management works within GAAP constraints to improve stakeholders' views of the company's financial position

earnings manipulation ignores GAAP rules to alter earnings significantly to improve stakeholder's views of the company's financial position

income statement method allowance method approach that estimates bad debt expenses based on the assumption that at the end of the period, a certain percentage of sales during the period will not be collected

installment sale periodic installment payments from buyers

interest monetary incentive to the lender, which justifies loan risk; interest is paid to the lender by the borrower

interest rate part of a loan charged to the borrower, expressed as an annual percentage of the outstanding loan amount

issue date point at which the security agreement is initially established

matching principle (also, expense recognition principle) records expenses related to revenue generation in the period in which they are incurred

maturity date date a bond or note becomes due and payable

net realizable value amount of an account balance that is expected to be collected; for example, if a company has a balance of $10,000 in accounts receivable and a $300 balance in the allowance for doubtful accounts, the net realizable value is $9,700

note receivable formal legal contract between the buyer and the company, which requires a specific payment amount at a predetermined future date, usually includes interest, and is payable beyond a company's operating cycle

number of days' sales in receivables expected days it will take to convert accounts receivable into cash

percentage of completion method percentage of work completed for the period divided by the total revenues from the contract

principal initial borrowed amount of a loan, not including interest; also, face value or maturity value of a bond (the amount to be paid at maturity)

receivable outstanding amount owed from a customer

revenue recognition principle principle stating that company must recognize revenue in the period in which it is earned; it is not considered earned until a product or service has been provided

Summary

9.1 Explain the Revenue Recognition Principle and How It Relates to Current and Future Sales and Purchase Transactions

- According to the revenue recognition principle, a company will recognize revenue when a product or service is provided to a client. The revenue must be reported in the period when the earnings process completes.
- According to the matching principle, expenses must be matched with revenues in the period in which they are incurred. A mismatch in revenues and expenses can lead to financial statement misreporting.
- When a customer pays for a product or service on a line of credit, the Accounts Receivable account is used. Accounts receivable must satisfy the following criteria: the customer owes money and has yet to pay, the amount is due in less than a company's operating cycle, and the account usually does not incur interest.
- When a customer purchases a product or service on credit, using an in-house account, Accounts Receivable increases and Sales Revenue increases. When the customer pays the amount due, Accounts Receivable decreases and Cash increases.
- When a customer purchases a product or service with a third-party credit card, such as Visa, Accounts Receivable increases, Credit Card Expense increases, and Sales Revenue increases. When the credit card company pays the amount due, Accounts Receivable decreases and Cash increases for the original sales price less the credit card usage fee.

9.2 Account for Uncollectible Accounts Using the Balance Sheet and Income Statement Approaches

- Bad debt is a result of unpaid and uncollectible customer accounts. Companies are required to record bad debt on financial statements as expenses.
- The direct write-off method records bad debt only when the due date has passed for a known amount. Bad Debt Expense increases (debit) and Accounts Receivable decreases (credit) for the amount uncollectible.
- The allowance method estimates uncollectible bad debt and matches the expense in the current period to revenues generated. There are three ways to calculate this estimation: the income statement method, balance sheet method/percentage of receivables, and balance sheet aging of receivables method.
- The income statement method estimates bad debt based on a percentage of credit sales. Bad Debt Expense increases (debit) and Allowance for Doubtful Accounts increases (credit) for the amount estimated as uncollectible.
- The balance sheet method estimates bad debt based on a percentage of outstanding accounts receivable. Bad Debt Expense increases (debit) and Allowance for Doubtful Accounts increases (credit) for the amount estimated as uncollectible.
- The balance sheet aging of receivables method estimates bad debt based on outstanding accounts

receivable, but it considers the time period that an account is past due. Bad Debt Expense increases (debit) and Allowance for Doubtful Accounts increases (credit) for the amount estimated as uncollectible.

9.3 Determine the Efficiency of Receivables Management Using Financial Ratios

- Receivable ratios are best used to determine quick debt collection and lending practices. An investor, lender, or management may use these ratios—in conjunction with financial statement review, past performance, industry standards, and trends—to make an informed financial decision.
- The accounts receivable turnover ratio shows how many times receivables are collected during a period and converted to cash. The ratio is found by taking net credit sales and dividing by average accounts receivable for the period.
- The number of days' sales in receivables ratio shows the expected number of days it will take to convert accounts receivable into cash. The ratio is found by taking 365 days and dividing by the accounts receivable turnover ratio.

9.4 Discuss the Role of Accounting for Receivables in Earnings Management

- Companies may look to report earnings differently to improve stakeholder's views of financial position. Earnings management works within GAAP to accomplish this, while earnings manipulation ignores GAAP.
- Companies may choose to manage earnings to improve income level, increase borrowing opportunities, decrease tax liabilities, and improve company valuation for sales transactions. Accounts receivable is often prey to earnings manipulations.
- Earnings management can occur in several ways, including changes to bad debt estimation methods, percentage uncollectible figures, and category distribution within the balance sheet aging method.
- To understand company performance and unveil any management or manipulation to earnings, ratio analysis is paramount. Number of days' sales in receivables ratio, and trend analysis, are most commonly used.

9.5 Apply Revenue Recognition Principles to Long-Term Projects

- Long-term construction projects may recognize revenue under the percentage of completion method or the completed contract method. The percentage of completion method distributes cost and revenues based on the amount of estimated contract completion during the period.
- Real estate installment sales require periodic payment from buyers. The installment method takes into account risk and distributes revenue based on a percentage of gross profit realized each period.
- With multi-year magazine subscriptions, customers pay in advance for subscription services, and the amount reported for revenue each period is reasonably estimated, until any disruption to the contract occurs. At that time, a new estimation will be distributed over the life of the subscription.
- In a combined equipment purchase with accompanying service contract, the customer pays for the contract up front, but there is no guarantee that service will be provided. Thus, a company may distribute estimated service revenues over the life of the contract or defer recognition and associated expenses until the contract period is complete.

9.6 Explain How Notes Receivable and Accounts Receivable Differ

- Accounts receivable is an informal agreement between customer and company, with collection occurring in less than a year, and no interest requirement. In contrast, notes receivable is a legal contract, with collection occurring typically over a year, and interest requirements.
- The terms of a note contract establish the principal collection amount, maturity date, and annual interest rate.
- Interest is computed as the principal amount multiplied by the part of the year, multiplied by the annual interest rate. The entry to record accumulated interest increases interest receivable and interest revenue.

- An honored note means collection occurred on time and in full. Recording an honored note includes an increase to cash and interest revenue, and a decrease to interest receivable and notes receivable.
- A dishonored note means collection did not occur on time or in full. In this case, a note and the accumulated interest would be converted to accounts receivable.
- When a company cannot collect on account, the company may consider selling the receivable to a collection agency. They will sell the receivable at a fraction of the value in order to apply resources elsewhere.
- If a customer cannot pay its accounts receivable on time, it may renegotiate terms that include a note and interest, thereby converting the accounts receivable to notes receivable. in this case, accounts receivable decreases, and notes receivable and cash increase.

Multiple Choice

1. LO 9.1 Which of the following is *not* a criterion to recognize revenue under GAAP?

A. The earnings process must be completed.
B. A product or service must be provided.
C. Cash must be collected.
D. GAAP requires that the accrual basis accounting principle be used in the revenue recognition process.

2. LO 9.1 Which of the following best represents the matching principle criteria?

A. Expenses are reported in the period in which they were incurred.
B. Expenses may be reported in a different period than the matching revenues.
C. Revenue and expenses are matched based on when expenses are paid.
D. Revenue is recognized when an order occurs and not when the actual sale is initiated.

3. LO 9.1 If a customer pays with a credit card and the service has been provided, which of the following accounts will be used to record the sales entry for this transaction?

A. Cost of Goods Sold, Merchandise Inventory, Sales Revenue
B. Sales Revenue, Credit Card Expense, Accounts Receivable
C. Accounts Receivable, Merchandise Inventory, Credit Card Expense
D. Cost of Goods Sold, Credit Card Expense, Sales Revenue

4. LO 9.1 A car dealership sells a car to a customer for $35,000. The customer makes a 10% down payment, and the dealership finances the remaining 90% in-house. How much will the car dealership record in Accounts Receivable for this customer?

A. $31,500
B. $19,250
C. $8,750
D. $7,000

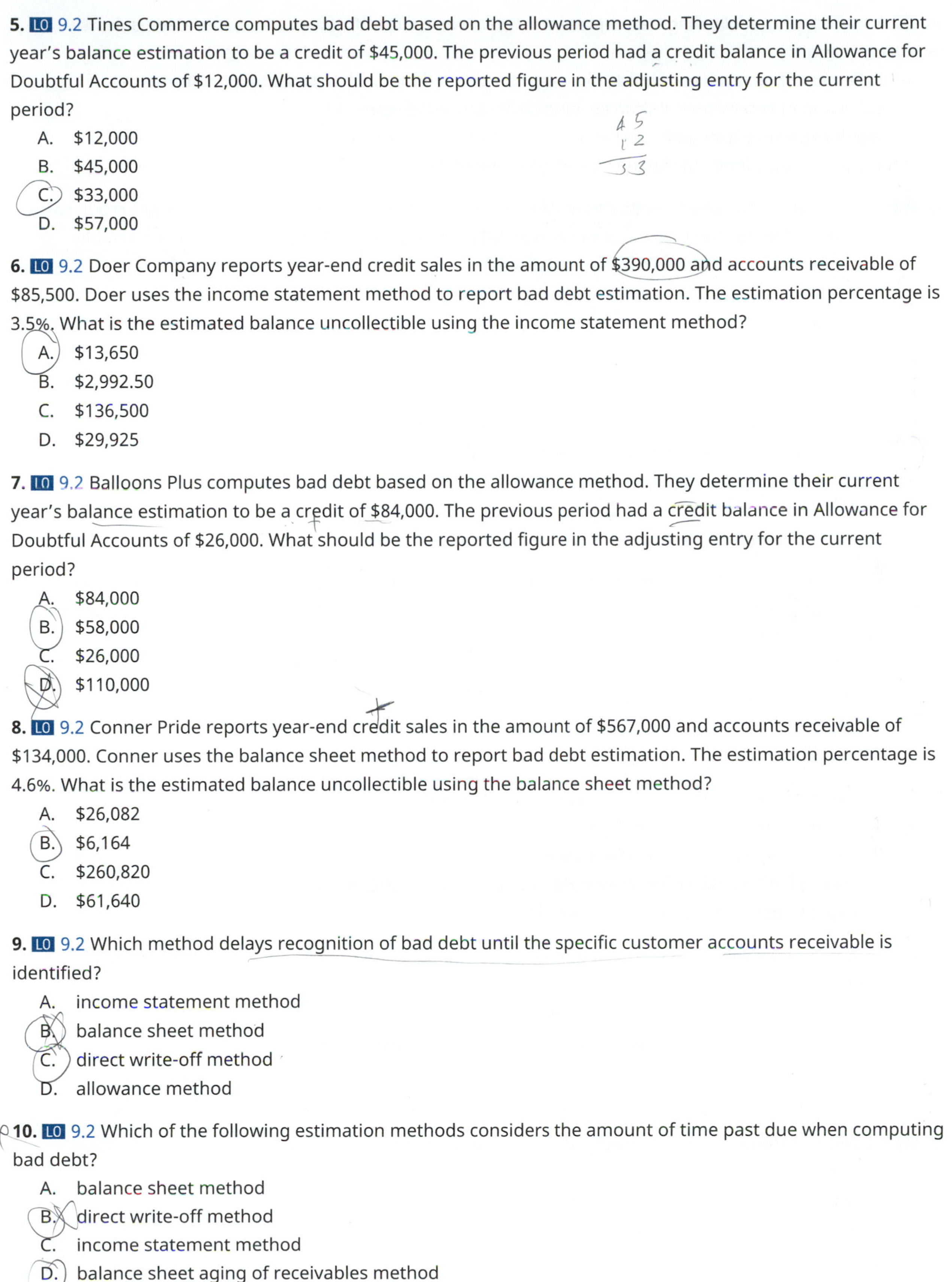

5. LO 9.2 Tines Commerce computes bad debt based on the allowance method. They determine their current year's balance estimation to be a credit of $45,000. The previous period had a credit balance in Allowance for Doubtful Accounts of $12,000. What should be the reported figure in the adjusting entry for the current period?

A. $12,000
B. $45,000
C. $33,000
D. $57,000

6. LO 9.2 Doer Company reports year-end credit sales in the amount of $390,000 and accounts receivable of $85,500. Doer uses the income statement method to report bad debt estimation. The estimation percentage is 3.5%. What is the estimated balance uncollectible using the income statement method?

A. $13,650
B. $2,992.50
C. $136,500
D. $29,925

7. LO 9.2 Balloons Plus computes bad debt based on the allowance method. They determine their current year's balance estimation to be a credit of $84,000. The previous period had a credit balance in Allowance for Doubtful Accounts of $26,000. What should be the reported figure in the adjusting entry for the current period?

A. $84,000
B. $58,000
C. $26,000
D. $110,000

8. LO 9.2 Conner Pride reports year-end credit sales in the amount of $567,000 and accounts receivable of $134,000. Conner uses the balance sheet method to report bad debt estimation. The estimation percentage is 4.6%. What is the estimated balance uncollectible using the balance sheet method?

A. $26,082
B. $6,164
C. $260,820
D. $61,640

9. LO 9.2 Which method delays recognition of bad debt until the specific customer accounts receivable is identified?

A. income statement method
B. balance sheet method
C. direct write-off method
D. allowance method

10. LO 9.2 Which of the following estimation methods considers the amount of time past due when computing bad debt?

A. balance sheet method
B. direct write-off method
C. income statement method
D. balance sheet aging of receivables method

11. LO 9.3 Which of the following best represents a positive product of a lower number of days' sales in receivables ratio?

A. collection of receivables is quick, and cash can be used for other business expenditures
B. collection of receivables is slow, keeping cash secured to receivables
C. credit extension is lenient
D. the lender only lends to the top 10% of potential creditors

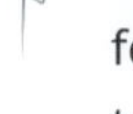

12. LO 9.3 South Rims has an accounts receivable balance at the end of 2018 of $357,470. The net credit sales for the year are $769,346. The balance at the end of 2017 was $325,300. What is the accounts receivable turnover rate for 2018 (rounded to two decimal places)?

A. 2.02 times
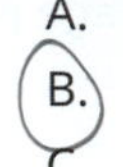
B. 2.25 times

C. 2.15 times

D. 1.13 times
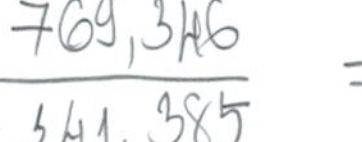

13. LO 9.3 What information can best be elicited from a receivable ratio?

A. company performance with current debt collection
B. credit extension effect on cash sales
C. likelihood of future customer bankruptcy filings
D. an increase in future credit sales to current customers

14. LO 9.3 Ancient Grains Unlimited has an accounts receivable turnover ratio of 3.34 times. The net credit sales for the year are $567,920. What is the days' sales in receivables ratio for 2018 (rounded to the nearest whole number)?

A. 190 days
B. 109 days
C. 110 days
D. 101 days

15. LO 9.4 Which of the following is *not* a way to manage earnings?

A. Change the method for bad debt estimation.
B. Change the figure for the uncollectible percentage.
C. Under the balance sheet aging method, change the past-due categories.
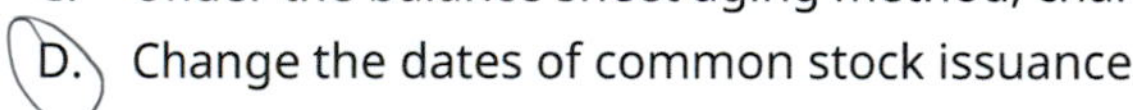
D. Change the dates of common stock issuance.

16. LO 9.4 Which of the following is true about earnings management?

A. It works within the constraints of GAAP.
B. It works outside the constraints of GAAP.
C. It tries to improve stakeholder's views of the company's financial position.
D. Both B and C
E. Both A and C

17. LO 9.4 Which statement is most directly affected by a change to net income?

A. balance sheet
B. income statement
C. statement of retained earnings
D. statement of cash flows

18. LO 9.4 Michelle Company reports $345,000 in credit sales and $267,500 in accounts receivable at the end of 2019. Michelle currently uses the income statement method to record bad debt estimation at 4%. To manage earnings more efficiently, Michelle changes bed debt estimation to the balance sheet method at 4%. How much is the difference in net income between the income statement and balance sheet methods?

A. $3,100
B. $13,800
C. $10,700
D. $77,500

19. LO 9.6 Which of the following is true of a maturity date?

A. It must be calculated in days, not in months or years.
B. It is the date when principal and interest on a note are to be repaid to the lender.
C. It is the date of establishment of note terms between a lender and customer.
D. It is not a characteristic of a note receivable.

20. LO 9.6 Mark Industries issues a note in the amount of $45,000 on August 1, 2018 in exchange for the sale of merchandise. Which of the following is the correct journal entry for this sale?

A.

Cash Sales Revenue	45,000	 45,000

B.

Cash Notes Receivable: Mark	45,000	 45,000

C.

Accounts Receivable: Mark Sales Revenue	45,000	 45,000

D.

Notes Receivable: Mark Sales Revenue	45,000	 45,000

21. LO 9.6 A customer takes out a loan of $130,000 on January 1, with a maturity date of 36 months, and an annual interest rate of 11%. If 6 months have passed since note establishment, what would be the recorded interest figure at that time?

A. $7,150
B. $65,000
C. $14,300
D. $2,383

22. LO 9.6 A company collects an honored note with a maturity date of 24 months from establishment, a 10% interest rate, and an initial loan amount of $30,000. Which accounts are used to record collection of the honored note at maturity date?

A. Interest Revenue, Interest Expense, Cash
B. Interest Receivable, Cash, Notes Receivable
C. Interest Revenue, Interest Receivable, Cash, Notes Receivable
D. Notes Receivable, Interest Revenue, Cash, Interest Expense

23. LO 9.6 Orion Rentals is unable to collect on a note worth $25,000 and has accumulated interest of $250. It convert this note and interest to accounts receivable. After some time, Orion is still unable to collect the debt and it decides to sell the converted note to a collection agency. The collection agency will pay only 20% of the value of accounts receivable to Orion. What is the amount of cash paid to Orion from the collection agency?

A. $5,000
B. $5,050
C. $20,000
D. $19,950

Questions

1. LO 9.1 What is the matching principle?

2. LO 9.1 A beverage wholesale outlet sells beverages by the case. On April 13, a customer purchased 18 cases of wine at $42 per case, 20 cases of soda at $29 per case, and 45 cases of water at $17 per case. The customer pays with a Merill credit card. Merill charges a usage fee to the company of 5% of the total sale. What is the sales entry for this purchase?

3. LO 9.1 On January 1, a flower shop contracts with customers to provide flowers for their wedding on June 2. The total contract price is $3,000, payable in equal installments for the next six months on the first of each month (with the first payment due January 1). How much will be recorded as revenue during the month of April?

4. LO 9.1 American Signs allows customers to pay with their Jones credit card and cash. Jones charges American Signs a 3.5% service fee for each credit sale using its card. Credit sales for the month of June total $328,430, where 40% of those sales were made using the Jones credit card. Based on this information, what will be the total in Credit Card Expense at the end of June?

5. LO 9.2 Which account type is used to record bad debt estimation and is a contra account to Accounts Receivable?

6. LO 9.2 Earrings Depot records bad debt using the allowance, balance sheet method. They recorded $97,440 in accounts receivable for the year and $288,550 in credit sales. The uncollectible percentage is 5.5%. What is the bad debt estimation for the year using the balance sheet method?

7. LO 9.2 Racing Adventures records bad debt using the allowance, income statement method. They recorded $134,560 in accounts receivable for the year and $323,660 in credit sales. The uncollectible percentage is 6.8%. What is the bad debt estimation for the year using the income statement method?

8. LO 9.2 Aron Larson is a customer of Bank Enterprises. Mr. Larson took out a loan in the amount of $120,000 on August 1. On December 31, Bank Enterprises determines the loan to be uncollectible. Larson had not paid anything toward the balance due on account. What is the journal entry recording the bad debt write-off?

9. LO 9.2 The following accounts receivable information pertains to Growth Markets LLC.

Past-Due Category	Accounts Receivable Total	Percentage Uncollectible
0–30 days	$22,480	6%
31–90 days	36,540	17%
Over 90 days	15,330	25%

What is the total uncollectible estimated bad debt for Growth Markets LLC?

10. LO 9.2 What are bad debts?

11. LO 9.3 What are some possible negative signals when the product of the accounts receivable turnover ratio is lower (i.e., fewer times)?

12. LO 9.3 Berry Farms has an accounts receivable balance at the end of 2018 of $425,650. The net credit sales for the year are $924,123. The balance at the end of 2017 was $378,550. What is the number of days' sales in receivables ratio for 2018 (round all answers to two decimal places)?

13. LO 9.3 What are the two most common receivables ratios, and what do these ratios tell a stakeholder about the company?

14. LO 9.4 What is the difference between earnings management and earnings manipulation?

15. LO 9.4 What is an earnings management benefit from showing a reduced figure for bad debt expense?

16. LO 9.4 Angelo's Outlet used to report bad debt using the balance sheet method and is now switching to the income statement method. The percentage uncollectible will remain constant at 5%. Credit sales figures for 2019 were $866,000, and accounts receivable was $732,000. How much will Angelo's Outlet report for 2019 bad debt estimation under the income statement method?

17. LO 9.4 What is an earnings management benefit from showing an increased figure for bad debt expense?

18. LO 9.5 What are the two methods of revenue recognition for long-term construction projects?

19. LO 9.5 What is the installment method?

20. LO 9.5 What is a possible ramification of deferred revenue reporting?

21. LO 9.5 What is the completed contract method?

22. LO 9.5 What is the percentage of completion method?

23. LO 9.6 British Imports is unable to collect on a note worth $215,000 that has accumulated interest of $465. What is the journal entry to record the conversion of the note to accounts receivable?

24. LO 9.6 Chemical Enterprises issues a note in the amount of $156,000 to a customer on January 1, 2018. Terms of the note show a maturity date of 36 months, and an annual interest rate of 8%. What is the accumulated interest entry if 9 months have passed since note establishment?

25. LO 9.6 What is the principal of a note?

26. LO 9.6 A customer was unable to pay the accounts receivable on time in the amount of $34,000. The customer was able to negotiate with the company and transferred the accounts receivable into a note that includes interest, along with an up-front cash payment of $6,000. The note maturity date is 24 months with a 15% annual interest rate. What is the entry to recognize this transfer?

27. LO 9.6 What are three differences between accounts receivable and notes receivable?

Exercise Set A

EA1. LO 9.1 Prepare journal entries for the following transactions from Restaurant Depot.

Nov. 8	Customer Miles Shandy purchased 200 pans at $35 per pan, costing Restaurant Depot $21 per pan. Terms of the sale are 2/10, n/30, invoice dated November 8.
Nov. 17	Miles Shandy pays in full with cash for his purchase of November 8.

EA2. LO 9.1 Prepare journal entries for the following transactions from Cars Plus.

Oct. 18	Customer Angela Sosa purchased $132,980 worth of car parts with her Standard credit card. The cost to Cars Plus for the sale is $86,250. Standard credit card charges Cars Plus a fee of 4% of the sale.
Oct. 24	Standard remits payment to Cars Plus, less any fees.

EA3. LO 9.1 Consider the following transaction: On March 6, Fun Cards sells 540 card decks with a sales price of $7 per deck to Padma Singh. The cost to Fun Cards is $4 per deck. Prepare a journal entry under each of the following conditions. Assume MoneyPlus charges a 2% fee for each sales transaction using its card.

A. Payment is made using a credit, in-house account.
B. Payment is made using a MoneyPlus credit card.

EA4. LO 9.2 Window World extended credit to customer Nile Jenkins in the amount of $130,900 for his purchase of window treatments on April 2. Terms of the sale are 2/60, n/150. The cost of the purchase to Window World is $56,200. On September 4, Window World determined that Nile Jenkins's account was uncollectible and wrote off the debt. On December 3, Mr. Jenkins unexpectedly paid in full on his account. Record each Window World transaction with Nile Jenkins. In order to demonstrate the write-off and then subsequent collection of an account receivable, assume in this example that Window World rarely extends credit directly, so this transaction is permitted to use the direct write-off method. Remember, however, that in most cases the direct write-off method is not allowed.

EA5. LO 9.2 Millennium Associates records bad debt using the allowance, income statement method. They recorded $299,420 in accounts receivable for the year, and $773,270 in credit sales. The uncollectible percentage is 3.2%. On February 5, Millennium Associates identifies one uncollectible account from Molar Corp in the amount of $1,330. On April 15, Molar Corp unexpectedly pays its account in full. Record journal entries for the following.

A. Year-end adjusting entry for 2017 bad debt
B. February 5, 2018 identification entry
C. Entry for payment on April 15, 2018

EA6. LO 9.2 Millennium Associates records bad debt using the allowance, balance sheet method. They recorded $299,420 in accounts receivable for the year, and $773,270 in credit sales. The uncollectible percentage is 3.2%. On November 22, Millennium Associates identifies one uncollectible account from Angel's Hardware in the amount of $3,650. On December 18, Angel's Hardware unexpectedly pays its account in full. Record journal entries for the following.

A. Year-end adjusting entry for 2017 bad debt
B. November 22, 2018 identification entry
C. Entry for payment on December 18, 2018

EA7. LO 9.2 The following accounts receivable information pertains to Marshall Inc.

Past-Due Category	Accounts Receivable Total	Percentage Uncollectible
0–30 days	$84,550	8%
31–90 days	32,230	16%
Over 90 days	22,170	37%

Determine the estimated uncollectible bad debt from Marshall Inc. using the balance sheet aging of receivables method, and record the year-end adjusting journal entry for bad debt.

EA8. LO 9.3 Using the following select financial statement information from Black Water Industries, compute the accounts receivable turnover ratios for 2018 and 2019 (round answers to two decimal places). What do the outcomes tell a potential investor about Black Water Industries?

BLACK WATER INDUSTRIES		
Year	**Net Credit Sales**	**Ending Accounts Receivable**
2017	$685,430	$330,250
2018	700,290	360,450
2019	768,500	401,650

EA9. LO 9.3 Using the following select financial statement information from Black Water Industries, compute the number of days' sales in receivables ratios for 2018 and 2019 (round answers to two decimal places). What do the outcomes tell a potential investor about Black Water Industries?

BLACK WATER INDUSTRIES		
Year	**Net Credit Sales**	**Ending Accounts Receivable**
2017	$685,430	$330,250
2018	700,290	360,450
2019	768,500	401,650

EA10. LO 9.3 Millennial Manufacturing has net credit sales for 2018 in the amount of $1,433,630, beginning accounts receivable balance of $585,900, and an ending accounts receivable balance of $621,450. Compute the accounts receivable turnover ratio and the number of days' sales in receivables ratio for 2018 (round answers to two decimal places). What do the outcomes tell a potential investor about Millennial Manufacturing if industry average is 2.6 times and number of day's sales ratio is 180 days?

EA11. LO 9.4 Mirror Mart uses the balance sheet aging method to account for uncollectible debt on receivables. The following is the past-due category information for outstanding receivable debt for 2019.

	0–30 days past due	**31–90 days past due**	**Over 90 days past due**
Accounts receivable amount	$50,000	$30,000	$15,000
Percent uncollectible	8%	15%	30%
Total per category	?	?	?
Total uncollectible?			

To manage earnings more efficiently, Mirror Mart decided to change past-due categories as follows.

	0–60 days past due	**61–120 days past due**	**Over 120 days past due**
Accounts receivable amount	$80,000	$10,000	$5,000
Percent uncollectible	8%	15%	30%
Total per category?			
Total uncollectible?			

Complete the following.

A. Complete each table by filling in the blanks.
B. Determine the difference between total uncollectible.
C. Explain how the new total uncollectible amount affects net income and accounts receivable.

EA12. LO 9.4 Aerospace Electronics reports $567,000 in credit sales for 2018 and $632,500 in 2019. They have a $499,000 accounts receivable balance at the end of 2018, and $600,000 at the end of 2019. Aerospace uses the income statement method to record bad debt estimation at 5% during 2018. To manage earnings more favorably, Aerospace changes bad debt estimation to the balance sheet method at 7% during 2019.

A. Determine the bad debt estimation for 2018.
B. Determine the bad debt estimation for 2019.
C. Describe a benefit to Aerospace Electronics in 2019 as a result of its earnings management.

EA13. LO 9.4 Dortmund Stockyard reports $896,000 in credit sales for 2018 and $802,670 in 2019. It has a $675,000 accounts receivable balance at the end of 2018, and $682,000 at the end of 2019. Dortmund uses the balance sheet method to record bad debt estimation at 8% during 2018. To manage earnings more favorably, Dortmund changes bad debt estimation to the income statement method at 6% during 2019.

A. Determine the bad debt estimation for 2018.
B. Determine the bad debt estimation for 2019.
C. Describe a benefit to Dortmund Stockyard in 2019 as a result of its earnings management.

EA14. LO 9.6 Arvan Patel is a customer of Bank's Hardware Store. For Mr. Patel's latest purchase on January 1, 2018, Bank's Hardware issues a note with a principal amount of $480,000, 13% annual interest rate, and a 24-month maturity date on December 31, 2019. Record the journal entries for Bank's Hardware Store for the following transactions.

A. Note issuance
B. Subsequent interest entry on December 31, 2018
C. Honored note entry at maturity on December 31, 2019.

EA15. LO 9.6 Resin Milling issued a $390,500 note on January 1, 2018 to a customer in exchange for merchandise. The merchandise had a cost to Resin Milling of $170,000. The terms of the note are 24-month maturity date on December 31, 2019 at a 5% annual interest rate. The customer does not pay on its account and dishonors the note. Record the journal entries for Resin Milling for the following transactions.

A. Initial sale on January 1, 2018
B. Dishonored note entry on January 1, 2020, assuming interest has not been recognized before note maturity

EA16. LO 9.6 Mystic Magic issued a $120,250 note on January 1, 2018 to a customer, Amy Arnold, in exchange for merchandise. Terms of the note are 9-month maturity date on October 1, 2018 at a 9.6% annual interest rate. Amy Arnold does not pay on her account and dishonors the note. On November 10, 2018, Mystic Magic decides to sell the dishonored note to a collection agency for 25% of its value. Record the journal entries for Mystic Magic for the following transactions.

A. Initial sale on January 1, 2018
B. Dishonored note entry on October 1, 2018
C. Receivable sale on November 10, 2018

Exercise Set B

EB1. LO 9.1 Prepare journal entries for the following transactions from Movie Mart.

Sept. 10	Customer Ellie Monk purchased $43,820 worth of merchandise from Movie Mart, costing Movie Mart $28,745. Terms of the sale are 3/10, n/60, invoice dated September 10.
Sept. 22	Ellie Monk pays in full with cash for her purchase on September 22.

EB2. LO 9.1 Prepare journal entries for the following transactions from Angled Pictures.

June 21	Customer LeShaun Rogers purchased 167 picture frames at a sales price of $28 per frame with her American credit card. The cost to Angled Pictures for the sale is $19 per frame. American credit card charges Angled Pictures a fee of 3% of the sale.
June 30	American remits payment to Angled Pictures, less any fees.

EB3. LO 9.1 Consider the following transaction: On February 15, Darling Dolls sells 110 dolls with a sales price of $15 per doll to Rosemary Cummings The cost to Darling Dolls is $5 per doll. Prepare a journal entry under each of the following conditions. Assume Gentry charges a 3.5% fee for each sales transaction using its card.

A. Payment is made using a credit, in-house account.
B. Payment is made using a Gentry credit card.

EB4. LO 9.2 Laminate Express extended credit to customer Amal Sunderland in the amount of $244,650 for his January 4 purchase of flooring. Terms of the sale are 2/30, n/120. The cost of the purchase to Laminate Express is $88,440. On April 5, Laminate Express determined that Amal Sunderland's account was uncollectible and wrote off the debt. On June 22, Amal Sunderland unexpectedly paid 30% of the total amount due in cash on his account. Record each Laminate Express transaction with Amal Sunderland. In order to demonstrate the write-off and then subsequent collection of an account receivable, assume in this example that Laminate Express rarely extends credit directly, so this transaction is permitted to use the direct write-off method. Remember, though, that in most cases the direct write-off method is not allowed.

EB5. LO 9.2 Olena Mirrors records bad debt using the allowance, income statement method. They recorded $343,160 in accounts receivable for the year and $577,930 in credit sales. The uncollectible percentage is 4.4%. On May 10, Olena Mirrors identifies one uncollectible account from Elsa Sweeney in the amount of $2,870. On August 12, Elsa Sweeney unexpectedly pays $1,441 toward her account. Record journal entries for the following.

A. Year-end adjusting entry for 2017 bad debt
B. May 10, 2018 identification entry
C. Entry for payment on August 12, 2018

EB6. LO 9.2 Olena Mirrors records bad debt using the allowance, balance sheet method. They recorded $343,160 in accounts receivable for the year and $577,930 in credit sales. The uncollectible percentage is 4.4%. On June 11, Olena Mirrors identifies one uncollectible account from Nadia White in the amount of $4,265. On September 14, Nadia Chernoff unexpectedly pays $1,732 toward her account. Record journal entries for the following.

A. Year-end adjusting entry for 2017 bad debt
B. June 11, 2018 identification entry
C. Entry for payment on September 14, 2018

EB7. LO 9.2 The following accounts receivable information pertains to Envelope Experts.

Past-Due Category	Accounts Receivable Total	Percentage Uncollectible
0–30 days	$39,540	10%
31–90 days	23,280	26%
Over 90 days	14,630	42%

Determine the estimated uncollectible bad debt from Envelope Experts using the balance sheet aging of receivables method, and record the year-end adjusting journal entry for bad debt.

EB8. LO 9.3 Using the following select financial statement information from Mover Supply Depot, compute the accounts receivable turnover ratios for 2018 and 2019 (round answers to two decimal places). What do the outcomes tell a potential investor about Mover Supply Depot if the industry average is 4 times?

MOVER SUPPLY DEPOT		
Year	**Net Credit Sales**	**Ending Accounts Receivable**
2017	$1,230,680	$321,500
2018	1,477,440	345,700
2019	1,724,400	326,600

EB9. LO 9.3 Using the following select financial statement information from Mover Supply Depot, compute the number of days' sales in receivables ratios for 2018 and 2019 (round answers to two decimal places). What do the outcomes tell a potential investor about Mover Supply Depot if the competition collects in approximately 65 days?

MOVER SUPPLY DEPOT		
Year	**Net Credit Sales**	**Ending Accounts Receivable**
2017	$1,230,680	$321,500
2018	1,477,440	345,700
2019	1,724,400	326,600

EB10. LO 9.3 Starlight Enterprises has net credit sales for 2019 in the amount of $2,600,325, beginning accounts receivable balance of $844,260, and an ending accounts receivable balance of $604,930. Compute the accounts receivable turnover ratio and the number of days' sales in receivables ratio for 2019 (round answers to two decimal places). What do the outcomes tell a potential investor about Starlight Enterprises if the industry average is 1.5 times and the number of days' sales ratio is 175 days?

EB11. LO 9.4 Outpost Designs uses the balance sheet aging method to account for uncollectible debt on receivables. The following is the past due category information for outstanding receivable debt for 2019.

	0–30 days past due	**31–90 days past due**	**Over 90 days past due**
Accounts receivable amount	$35,000	$40,000	$25,000
Percent uncollectible	10%	22%	35%
Total per category?			
Total uncollectible?			

To manage earnings more favorably, Outpost Designs decided to change past-due categories as follows.

	0–60 days past due	**61–120 days past due**	**Over 120 days past due**
Accounts receivable amount	$50,000	$35,000	$15,000
Percent uncollectible	10%	22%	35%
Total per category?			
Total uncollectible?			

Complete the following.

A. Complete each table by filling in the blanks.
B. Determine the difference between total uncollectible.
C. Explain how the new total uncollectible amount affects net income and accounts receivable.

EB12. LO 9.4 Clovis Enterprises reports $845,500 in credit sales for 2018 and $933,000 in 2019. It has a $758,000 accounts receivable balance at the end of 2018 and $841,000 at the end of 2019. Clovis uses the income statement method to record bad debt estimation at 4% during 2018. To manage earnings more favorably, Clovis changes bad debt estimation to the balance sheet method at 5% during 2019.

A. Determine the bad debt estimation for 2018.
B. Determine the bad debt estimation for 2019.
C. Describe a benefit to Clovis Enterprises in 2019 as a result of its earnings management.

EB13. LO 9.4 Fortune Accounting reports $1,455,000 in credit sales for 2018 and $1,678,430 in 2019. It has an $825,000 accounts receivable balance at the end of 2018 and $756,000 at the end of 2019. Fortune uses the balance sheet method to record bad debt estimation at 7.5% during 2018. To manage earnings more favorably, Fortune changes bad debt estimation to the income statement method at 5.5% during 2019.

A. Determine the bad debt estimation for 2018.
B. Determine the bad debt estimation for 2019.
C. Describe a benefit to Fortune in 2019 as a result of its earnings management.

EB14. LO 9.6 Anderson Air is a customer of Handler Cleaning Operations. For Anderson Air's latest purchase on January 1, 2018, Handler Cleaning Operations issues a note with a principal amount of $1,255,000, 6% annual interest rate, and a 24-month maturity date on December 31, 2019. Record the journal entries for Handler Cleaning Operations for the following transactions.

A. Entry for note issuance
B. Subsequent interest entry on December 31, 2018
C. Honored note entry at maturity on December 31, 2019

EB15. LO 9.6 Rain T-Shirts issued a $440,600 note on January 1, 2018 to a customer, Larry Potts, in exchange for merchandise. The merchandise had a cost to Rain T-Shirts of $220,300. The terms of the note are 24-month maturity date on December 31, 2019 at a 4.5% annual interest rate. Larry Potts does not pay on his account and dishonors the note. Record journal entries for Rain T-Shirts for the following transactions.

A. Initial sale on January 1, 2018
B. Dishonored note entry on January 1, 2020, assuming interest has not been recognized before note maturity

EB16. LO 9.6 Element Surfboards issued a $210,800 note on January 1, 2018 to a customer, Leona Marland, in exchange for merchandise. Terms of the note are 9-month maturity date on October 1, 2018 at a 10.2% annual interest rate. Leona Marland does not pay on her account and dishonors the note. On December 2, 2018, Element Surfboards decides to sell the dishonored note to a collection agency for 30% of its value. Record the journal entries for Element Surfboards for the following transactions.

A. Initial sale on January 1, 2018
B. Dishonored note entry on October 1, 2018
C. Receivable sale on December 2, 2018

Problem Set A

PA1. LO 9.1 Prepare journal entries for the following transactions from Barrels Warehouse.

Jul. 1	Sold 2,000 barrels with a sales price of $30 per barrel to customer Luck's Vineyards. Luck's Vineyards paid with cash. The cost for this sale is $18 per barrel.
Jul. 3	Sold 1,200 barrels with a sales price of $32 per barrel to customer Paramount Apparel. Paramount paid using its in-house credit account. Terms of the sale are 3/10, n/30. The cost for this sale is $17 per barrel.
Jul. 5	Sold 1,400 barrels with a sales price of $31 per barrel to customer Melody Sharehouse. Melody paid using her MoneyPlus credit card. The cost for this sale is $18 per barrel. MoneyPlus Credit Card Company charges Barrels Warehouse a 2% usage fee based on the total sale per transaction.
Jul. 8	MoneyPlus Credit Card Company made a cash payment in full to Barrels Warehouse for the transaction from July 5, less any usage fees.
Jul. 13	Paramount Apparel paid its account in full with a cash payment, less any discounts.

PA2. LO 9.1 Prepare journal entries for the following transactions of Dulce Delights.

Apr. 10	Sold 320 ice cream buckets with a sales price of $12 per bucket to customer Livia Diaz. Livia paid using her in-house credit account; terms 2/10, n/30. The cost for this sale to Dulce Delights is $4.50 per bucket.
Apr. 13	Sold 290 ice cream buckets with a sales price of $12.50 per bucket to customer Selene Arnold. Selene paid using her Max credit card. The cost for this sale to Dulce Delights is $4.50 per bucket. Max Credit Card Company charges Dulce Delights a 5% usage fee based on the total sale per transaction.
Apr. 20	Livia Diaz paid her account in full with a cash payment, less any discounts.
Apr. 25	Max Credit Card Company made a cash payment in full to Dulce Delights for the transaction from April 13, less any usage fees.

PA3. LO 9.1 Prepare journal entries for the following transactions from Forest Furniture.

Oct. 3	Sold 2 couches with a sales price of $2,450 per couch to customer Norman Guzman. Norman Guzman paid with his Draw Plus credit card. The Draw Plus credit card charges Forest Furniture a 3.5% usage fee based on the total sale per transaction. The cost for this sale is $1,700 per couch.
Oct. 6	Sold 4 end chairs for a total sales price of $1,250 to April Orozco. April paid in full with cash. The cost of the sale is $800.
Oct. 9	Sold 18 can lights with a sales price of $50 per light to customer James Montgomery. James Montgomery paid using his Fund Max credit card. Fund Max charges Forest Furniture a 2.4% usage fee based on the total sale per transaction. The cost for this sale is $29 per light.
Oct. 12	Draw Plus made a cash payment in full to Forest Furniture for the transaction from Oct 3, less any usage fees.
Oct. 15	Fund Max made a cash payment of 25% of the total due to Forest Furniture for the transaction from October 9th, less any usage fees.
Oct. 25	Fund Max made a cash payment of the remainder due to Forest Furniture for the transaction from October 9, less any usage fees.

PA4. LO 9.2 Jars Plus recorded $861,430 in credit sales for the year and $488,000 in accounts receivable. The uncollectible percentage is 2.3% for the income statement method, and 3.6% for the balance sheet method.

A. Record the year-end adjusting entry for 2018 bad debt using the income statement method.
B. Record the year-end adjusting entry for 2018 bad debt using the balance sheet method.
C. Assume there was a previous debit balance in Allowance for Doubtful Accounts of $10,220, record the year-end entry for bad debt using the income statement method, and then the entry using the balance sheet method.
D. Assume there was a previous credit balance in Allowance for Doubtful Accounts of $5,470, record the year-end entry for bad debt using the income statement method, and then the entry using the balance sheet method.

PA5. LO 9.2 The following accounts receivable information pertains to Luxury Cruises.

Past-Due Category	Accounts Receivable Total	Percentage Uncollectible
0–30 days	$1,166,350	15%
31–90 days	577,870	33%
Over 90 days	324,450	48%

A. Determine the estimated uncollectible bad debt for Luxury Cruises in 2018 using the balance sheet aging of receivables method.
B. Record the year-end 2018 adjusting journal entry for bad debt.
C. Assume there was a previous debit balance in Allowance for Doubtful Accounts of $187,450; record the year-end entry for bad debt, taking this into consideration.
D. Assume there was a previous credit balance in Allowance for Doubtful Accounts of $206,770; record the year-end entry for bad debt, taking this into consideration.
E. On January 24, 2019, Luxury Cruises identifies Landon Walker's account as uncollectible in the amount of $4,650. Record the entry for identification.

PA6. LO 9.2 Funnel Direct recorded $1,345,780 in credit sales for the year and $695,455 in accounts receivable. The uncollectible percentage is 4.4% for the income statement method and 4% for the balance sheet method.

A. Record the year-end adjusting entry for 2018 bad debt using the income statement method.
B. Record the year-end adjusting entry for 2018 bad debt using the balance sheet method.
C. Assume there was a previous credit balance in Allowance for Doubtful Accounts of $13,888; record the year-end entry for bad debt using the income statement method, and then the entry using the balance sheet method.

PA7. LO 9.3 Review the select information for Bean Superstore and Legumes Plus (industry competitors), and then complete the following.

A. Compute the accounts receivable turnover ratios for each company for 2018 and 2019.
B. Compute the number of days' sales in receivables ratios for each company for 2018 and 2019.
C. Determine which company is the better investment and why. Round answers to two decimal places.

	BEAN SUPERSTORE Comparative Balance Sheet December 31, 2017, 2018, and 2019			LEGUMES PLUS Comparative Balance Sheet December 31, 2017, 2018, and 2019		
	2019	2018	2017	2019	2018	2017
Assets						
Cash	$345,600	$330,460	$300,000	$407,000	$386,450	$356,367
Accounts Receivable	67,000	62,000	59,000	85,430	82,670	79,230
Inventory	145,830	178,011	155,205	128,080	40,036	52,142
Equipment	100,465	101,202	103,085	182,006	23,400	111,701
Total Assets	**$658,895**	**$671,673**	**$617,290**	**$802,516**	**$532,556**	**$599,440**
Liabilities						
Salaries Payable	$ 90,200	$ 88,563	$ 84,209	$ 95,100	$ 91,455	$ 89,467
Accounts Payable	70,000	71,670	69,331	62,430	86,331	87,197
Notes Payable	41,000	50,650	58,250	63,222	67,880	68,312
Equity						
Common Stock	$ 22,695	$ 20,990	$ 19,100	$ 25,464	$ 22,090	$ 22,188
Retained Earnings	435,000	439,800	386,400	556,300	264,800	332,276
Total Liabilities and Equity	**$658,895**	**$671,673**	**$617,290**	**$802,516**	**$532,556**	**$599,440**

	BEAN SUPERSTORE Comparative Income Statement Year Ended December 31, 2017, 2018, and 2019			LEGUMES PLUS Comparative Income Statement Year Ended December 31, 2017, 2018, and 2019		
	2019	2018	2017	2019	2018	2017
Net Credit Sales	$1,000,000	$984,400	$875,350	$1,256,300	$1,020,570	$967,478
Cost of Goods Sold	450,000	419,600	388,950	500,000	580,320	465,780
Gross Margin	550,000	564,800	486,400	756,300	440,250	501,698
Expenses	115,000	125,000	100,000	200,000	175,450	169,422
Net Income (Loss)	435,000	439,800	386,400	556,300	264,800	332,276

PA8. LO 9.3 The following select financial statement information from Candid Photography.

CANDID PHOTOGRAPHY		
Year	**Net Credit Sales**	**Ending Accounts Receivable**
2017	$2,988,000	$1,290,450
2018	3,750,860	1,345,600
2019	4,000,350	1,546,550

Compute the accounts receivable turnover ratios and the number of days' sales in receivables ratios for 2018 and 2019 (round answers to two decimal places). What do the outcomes tell a potential investor about Candid Photography if industry average for accounts receivable turnover ratio is 3 times and days' sales in receivables ratio is 150 days?

PA9. LO 9.4 Noren Company uses the balance sheet aging method to account for uncollectible debt on receivables. The following is the past-due category information for outstanding receivable debt for 2019.

	0–30 Days Past Due	**31–90 Days Past Due**	**Over 90 Days Past Due**
Accounts receivable amount	$120,000	$80,000	$65,500
Percent uncollectible	7%	20%	40%
Total per category?			
Total uncollectible?			

To manage earnings more favorably, Noren Company considers changing the past-due categories as follows.

	0–60 Days Past Due	**61–120 Days Past Due**	**Over 120 Days Past Due**
Accounts receivable amount	$160,000	$50,500	$55,000
Percent uncollectible	7%	20%	40%
Total per category	?	?	?
Total uncollectible?			

A. Complete each table by filling in the blanks.
B. Determine the difference between totals uncollectible.
C. Complete the following 2019 comparative income statements for 2019, showing net income changes as a result of the changes to the balance sheet aging method categories.
D. Describe the categories change effect on net income and accounts receivable.

NOREN COMPANY Comparative Income Statements Year Ended December 31, 2019		
	Original Categories	**Categories Change**
Net Credit Sales	$1,240,000	$1,240,000
Cost of Goods Sold	60,000	60,000
Gross Margin	1,180,000	1,180,000
Expenses:		
General and Administrative Expense	300,500	300,500
Bad Debt Expense	?	?
Total Expenses	?	?
Net Income (Loss)	?	?

PA10. LO 9.4 Elegant Universal uses the balance sheet aging method to account for uncollectible debt on receivables. The following is the past-due category information for outstanding receivable debt for 2019.

	0–30 Days Past Due	31–90 Days Past Due	Over 90 Days Past Due
Accounts receivable amount	$1,330,000	$321,000	$200,650
Percent uncollectible	8%	24%	35%
Total per category	?	?	?
Total uncollectible?			

To manage earnings more favorably, Elegant Universal considers changing the past-due categories as follows.

	0–60 Days Past Due	61–120 Days Past Due	Over 120 Days Past Due
Accounts receivable amount	$1,532,000	$289,550	$30,100
Percent uncollectible	8%	24%	35%
Total per category	?	?	?
Total uncollectible?			

A. Complete each table by filling in the blanks.
B. Determine the difference between totals uncollectible.
C. Describe the categories change effect on net income and accounts receivable.

PA11. LO 9.6 Record journal entries for the following transactions of Telesco Enterprises.

Jan. 1, 2018	Issued a $330,700 note to customer Abe Willis as terms of a merchandise sale. The merchandise's cost to Telesco is $120,900. Note contract terms included a 36-month maturity date, and a 4% annual interest rate.
Dec. 31, 2018	Telesco records interest accumulated for 2018.
Dec. 31, 2019	Telesco records interest accumulated for 2019.
Dec. 31, 2020	Abe Willis honors the note and pays in full with cash.

PA12. LO 9.6 Record journal entries for the following transactions of Wind Solutions.

Jan. 1, 2018	Issued a $2,350,100 note to customer Solar Plex as terms of a merchandise sale. The merchandise's cost to Wind Solutions is $1,002,650. Note contract terms included a 24-month maturity date, and a 2.1% annual interest rate.
Dec. 31, 2018	Wind Solutions records interest accumulated for 2018.
Dec. 31, 2019	Wind Solutions converts Solar Plex's dishonored note into account receivable. This includes accumulated interest for the 24-month period.
Mar. 8, 2020	Wind Solutions sells the outstanding debt from Solar Plex to a collection agency at 25% of the accounts receivable value.

PA13. LO 9.6 Record journal entries for the following transactions of Commissary Productions.

Jan. 1, 2018	Issued a $425,530 note to customer June Solkowski as terms of a merchandise sale. The merchandise's cost to Commissary is $231,700. Note contract terms included a 36-month maturity date, and a 5% annual interest rate.
Dec. 31, 2018	Commissary records interest accumulated for 2018.
Dec. 31, 2019	Commissary records interest accumulated for 2019.
Dec. 31, 2020	June Stevens honors the note and pays in full with cash.

PA14. LO 9.6 Record journal entries for the following transactions of Piano Wholesalers.

Jan. 1, 2018	Issued a $1,235,650 note to customer Arrowstar as terms of a merchandise sale. The merchandise's cost to Piano Wholesalers is $602,000. Note contract terms included a 24-month maturity date and a 3.4% annual interest rate.
Dec. 31, 2018	Piano Wholesalers records interest accumulated for 2018.
Dec. 31, 2019	Piano Wholesalers converts Arrowstar's dishonored note into account receivable. This includes accumulated interest for the 24-month period.
Apr. 12, 2020	Piano Wholesalers sells the outstanding debt from Arrowstar to a collection agency at 32% of the accounts receivable value.

PA15. LO 9.7 Organics Plus is considering which bad debt estimation method works best for its company. It is deciding between the income statement method, balance sheet method of receivables, and balance sheet aging of receivables method. If it uses the income statement method, bad debt would be estimated at 4% of credit sales. If it were to use the balance sheet method, it would estimate bad debt at 12% of accounts receivable. If it were to use the balance sheet aging of receivables method, it would split its receivables into three categories: 0–30 days past due at 6%, 31–90 days past due at 19%, and over 90 days past due at 26%. There is currently a zero balance, transferred from the prior year's Allowance for Doubtful Accounts. The following information is available from the year-end income statement and balance sheet.

2018 Year-End Totals for Organics Plus	
Credit sales	$1,850,000
Accounts receivable	600,000

There is also additional information regarding the distribution of accounts receivable by age.

Past-Due Category	**Accounts Receivable Total**
0–30 days	$350,000
31–90 days	100,000
Over 90 days	150,000

Prepare the year-end adjusting entry for bad debt, using

A. Income statement method
B. Balance sheet method of receivables
C. Balance sheet aging of receivables method.
D. Which method should the company choose, and why?

Problem Set B

PB1. LO 9.1 Prepare journal entries for the following transactions from Lumber Wholesale.

Aug. 9	Sold 48,320 pounds of lumber with a sales price of $5.50 per pound to customer Homes Unlimited. Homes Unlimited paid with cash. The cost for this sale is $1.35 per pound.
Aug. 10	Sold 34,700 pounds of lumber with a sales price of $6.75 per pound to customer Barry Njegren. Njegren paid using his in-house credit account. Terms of the sale are 4/15, n/35. The cost for this sale is $1.20 per pound.
Aug. 11	Sold 50,330 pounds of lumber with a sales price of $4.60 per pound to customer Goodson Houses. Goodson paid using its American credit card. The cost for this sale is $1.40 per pound. American Credit Card Company charged Lumber Wholesale a 2.5% usage fee based on the total sale per transaction.
Aug. 14	American Credit Card Company made a cash payment in full to Lumber Wholesale for the transaction from August 11, less any usage fees.
Aug. 25	Barry Njegren paid his account in full with a cash payment, less any discounts.

PB2. LO 9.1 Prepare journal entries for the following transactions of Maritime Memories.

May 2	Sold $864,920 worth of maritime products to customer Jordan Scott. Jordan paid using his in-house credit account; terms 3/15, n/60. The cost to Maritime Memories for this sale is $532,187.
May 6	Sold $567,120 worth of maritime products to customer Joe Hsu. Joe paid using his Longstand credit card. The cost to Maritime Memories is $321,864. Longstand Credit Card Company charged Maritime Memories a 1.5% usage fee based on the total sale per transaction.
May 16	Jordan Scott paid his account in full with a cash payment, less any discounts.
May 23	Longstand Credit Card Company made a cash payment in full to Maritime Memories for the transaction from May 6, less any usage fees.

PB3. LO 9.1 Prepare journal entries for the following transactions from School Mart.

Mar. 6	Sold 1,000 pencil packages with a sales price of $5.72 per package to customer Sonia Norris. Sonia Norris paid with her American credit card. The American credit card charges School Mart a 4.6% usage fee based on the total sale per transaction. The cost for this sale is $1.27 per package.
Mar. 8	Sold 76 dry erase boards for a total sales price of $6,535 to Henry Malta. Henry paid in full with cash. The cost of the sale is $4,308.
Mar. 11	Sold 55 reams of paper with a sales price of $3.25 per ream to customer Alex Forsun. Alex Forsun paid using his Union credit card. Union charges School Mart a 2% usage fee based on the total sale per transaction. The cost for this sale is $1.99 per ream.
Mar. 14	American made a cash payment in full to School Mart for the transaction from March 6, less any usage fees.
Mar. 21	Union made a cash payment of 40% of the total due to School Mart for the transaction from March 11, less any usage fees.
Mar. 29	Union made a cash payment of the remainder due to School Mart for the transaction from March 11, less any usage fees.

PB4. LO 9.2 Bristax Corporation recorded $1,385,660 in credit sales for the year, and $732,410 in accounts receivable. The uncollectible percentage is 3.1% for the income statement method and 4.5% for the balance sheet method.

A. Record the year-end adjusting entry for 2018 bad debt using the income statement method.
B. Record the year-end adjusting entry for 2018 bad debt using the balance sheet method.
C. Assume there was a previous debit balance in Allowance for Doubtful Accounts of $20,550; record the year-end entry for bad debt using the income statement method, and then the entry using the balance sheet method.
D. Assume there was a previous credit balance in Allowance for Doubtful Accounts of $17,430; record the year-end entry for bad debt using the income statement method, and then the entry using the balance sheet method.

PB5. LO 9.2 The following accounts receivable information pertains to Select Distributors.

Past-Due Category	Accounts Receivable Total	Percentage Uncollectible
0–30 days	$945,620	19%
31–90 days	499,110	35%
Over 90 days	211,960	52%

A. Determine the estimated uncollectible bad debt for Select Distributors in 2018 using the balance sheet aging of receivables method.

B. Record the year-end 2018 adjusting journal entry for bad debt.

C. Assume there was a previous debit balance in Allowance for Doubtful Accounts of $233,180; record the year-end entry for bad debt, taking this into consideration.

D. Assume there was a previous credit balance in Allowance for Doubtful Accounts of $199,440; record the year-end entry for bad debt, taking this into consideration.

E. On March 21, 2019, Select Distributors identifies Aida Norman's account as uncollectible in the amount of $10,890. Record the entry for identification.

PB6. LO 9.2 Ink Records recorded $2,333,898 in credit sales for the year and $1,466,990 in accounts receivable. The uncollectible percentage is 3% for the income statement method and 5% for the balance sheet method.

A. Record the year-end adjusting entry for 2018 bad debt using the income statement method.

B. Record the year-end adjusting entry for 2018 bad debt using the balance sheet method.

C. Assume there was a previous credit balance in Allowance for Doubtful Accounts of $20,254; record the year-end entry for bad debt using the income statement method, and then the entry using the balance sheet method.

PB7. LO 9.3 Review the select information for Liquor Plaza and Beer Buddies (industry competitors) and complete the following.

A. Compute the accounts receivable turnover ratios for each company for 2018 and 2019.
B. Compute the number of day's sales in receivables ratios for each company for 2018 and 2019.
C. Determine which company is the better investment and why. Round answers to two decimal places.

	LIQUOR PLAZA Comparative Balance Sheet December 31, 2017, 2018, and 2019			BEER BUDDIES Comparative Balance Sheet December 31, 2017, 2018, and 2019		
	2019	**2018**	**2017**	**2019**	**2018**	**2017**
Assets:						
Cash	$ 552,932	$ 544,307	$520,000	$384,140	$322,620	$ 300,466
Accounts Receivable	300,050	298,450	287,650	365,500	356,000	324,400
Inventory	190,704	209,726	60,301	96,440	72,555	284,428
Equipment	201,101	230,334	84,281	106,412	55,891	302,780
Total Assets:	**$1,244,787**	**$1,282,817**	**$952,232**	**$952,492**	**$807,066**	**$1,212,074**
Liabilities:						
Salaries Payable	$ 200,801	$ 188,632	$184,210	$232,100	$212,120	$ 202,655
Accounts Payable	107,657	113,828	115,222	99,464	101,360	111,111
Notes Payable	95,464	98,272	100,460	88,521	92,208	94,885
Equity:						
Common Stock	$ 67,435	$ 64,955	$ 62,800	$ 50,000	$ 50,000	$ 50,000
Retained Earnings	773,430	817,130	489,540	482,407	351,378	753,423
Total Liabilities and Equity:	**$1,244,787**	**$1,282,817**	**$952,232**	**$952,492**	**$807,066**	**$1,212,074**

	LIQUOR PLAZA Comparative Income Statement Year Ended December 31, 2017, 2018, and 2019			BEER BUDDIES Comparative Income Statement Year Ended December 31, 2017, 2018, and 2019		
	2019	**2018**	**2017**	**2019**	**2018**	**2017**
Net Credit Sales	$2,675,430	$2,310,000	$1,967,820	$2,200,770	$2,020,570	$2,154,480
Cost of Goods Sold	1,400,000	999,870	989,950	1,268,000	1,243,530	1,000,650
Gross Margin	1,275,430	1,310,130	977,870	932,770	777,040	1,153,830
Expenses	502,000	493,000	488,330	450,363	425,662	400,407
Net Income (Loss)	**773,430**	**817,130**	**489,540**	**482,407**	**351,378**	**753,423**

PB8. LO 9.3 The following select financial statement information from Vortex Computing.

VORTEX COMPUTING		
Year	**Net Credit Sales**	**Ending Accounts Receivable**
2017	$1,557,200	$398,000
2018	1,755,310	444,400
2019	1,965,170	500,780

Compute the accounts receivable turnover ratios and the number of days' sales in receivables ratios for 2018 and 2019 (round answers to two decimal places). What do the outcomes tell a potential investor about Vortex Computing if industry average for accounts receivable turnover ratio is 4 times and days' sales in receivables ratio is 85 days?

PB9. LO 9.4 Elegant Linens uses the balance sheet aging method to account for uncollectible debt on receivables. The following is the past-due category information for outstanding receivable debt for 2019.

	0–30 Days Past Due	31–90 Days Past Due	Over 90 Days Past Due
Accounts receivable amount	$232,000	$129,000	$100,400
Percent uncollectible	8%	17%	31%
Total per category	?	?	?
Total uncollectible?			

To manage earnings more favorably, Elegant Linens considers changing the past-due categories as follows.

	0–60 Days Past Due	61–120 Days Past Due	Over 120 Days Past Due
Accounts receivable amount	$263,000	$134,200	$64,200
Percent uncollectible	8%	17%	31%
Total per category	?	?	?
Total uncollectible?			

A. Complete each table by filling in the blanks.
B. Determine the difference between total uncollectible.
C. Complete the following 2019 comparative income statements for 2019, showing net income changes as a result of the changes to the balance sheet aging method categories.
D. Describe the categories change effect on net income and accounts receivable.

ELEGANT LINENS Comparative Income Statements Year Ended December 31, 2019		
	Original Categories	**Categories Change**
Net Credit Sales	$1,454,500	$1,454,500
Cost of goods sold	85,250	85,250
Gross Margin	1,369,250	1,369,250
Expenses:		
General and Administrative Expense	425,000	425,000
Bad Debt Expense	?	?
Total Expenses	?	?
Net Income (Loss)	?	?

PB10. LO 9.4 Goods for Less uses the balance sheet aging method to account for uncollectible debt on receivables. The following is the past-due category information for outstanding receivable debt for 2019.

	0–30 Days Past Due	31–90 Days Past Due	Over 90 Days Past Due
Accounts receivable amount	$1,000,000	$422,000	$210,800
Percent uncollectible	9%	31%	52%
Total per category	?	?	?
Total uncollectible?			

To manage earnings more favorably, Goods for Less considers changing the past-due categories as follows.

	0–60 Days Past Due	61–120 Days Past Due	Over 120 Days Past Due
Accounts receivable amount	$1,245,400	$200,500	$186,900
Percent uncollectible	9%	31%	52%
Total per category	?	?	?
Total uncollectible?			

A. Complete each table by filling in the blanks.
B. Determine the difference between totals uncollectible.
C. Describe the categories change effect on net income and accounts receivable.

PB11. LO 9.6 Record journal entries for the following transactions of Noreen Turbines.

Jan. 1, 2018	Issued a $1,800,500 note to customer Axel Premium Metal as terms of a merchandise sale. The merchandise's cost to Noreen is $760,430. Note contract terms included a 36-month maturity date, and a 3.8% annual interest rate.
Dec. 31, 2018	Noreen Turbines records interest accumulated for 2018.
Dec. 31, 2019	Noreen Turbines records interest accumulated for 2019.
Dec. 31, 2020	Axel Premium Metal honors the note and pays in full with cash.

PB12. LO 9.6 Record journal entries for the following transactions of Mesa Construction.

Jan. 1, 2018	Issued a $1,460,200 note to customer Miramar Industries as terms of a merchandise sale. The merchandise's cost to Mesa Construction is $812,110. Note contract terms included a 24-month maturity date, and a 3.3% annual interest rate.
Dec. 31, 2018	Mesa Construction records interest accumulated for 2018.
Dec. 31, 2019	Mesa Construction converts Miramar Industries' dishonored note into account receivable. This includes accumulated interest for the 24-month period.
Apr. 4, 2020	Mesa Construction sells the outstanding debt from Miramar Industries to a collection agency at 40% of the accounts receivable value.

PB13. LO 9.6 Record journal entries for the following transactions of Graphics & Signs.

Jan. 1, 2018	Issued a $248,400 note to customer Elliott Thompson as terms of a merchandise sale. The merchandise's cost to Graphics & Signs is $99,500. Note contract terms included a 36-month maturity date, and a 4.3% annual interest rate.
Dec. 31, 2018	Graphics & Signs records interest accumulated for 2018.
Dec. 31, 2019	Graphics & Signs records interest accumulated for 2019.
Dec. 31, 2020	Elliott Thompson honors the note and pays in full with cash.

PB14. LO 9.6 Record journal entries for the following transactions of Trout Masters.

Jan. 1, 2018	Issued a $390,820 note to customer Fishing Warehouse as terms of a merchandise sale. The merchandise's cost to Trout Masters is $155,770. Note contract terms included a 24-month maturity date, and a 3% annual interest rate.
Dec. 31, 2018	Trout Masters records interest accumulated for 2018.
Dec. 31, 2019	Trout Masters converts Fishing Warehouse's dishonored note into account receivable. This includes accumulated interest for the 24-month period.
May 6, 2020	Trout Masters sells the outstanding debt from Fishing Warehouse to a collection agency at 40% of the accounts receivable value.

PB15. LO 9.7 Shimmer Products is considering which bad debt estimation method works best for its company. It is deciding between the income statement method, balance sheet method of receivables, and balance sheet aging of receivables method. If it uses the income statement method, bad debt would be estimated at 5.6% of credit sales. If it were to use the balance sheet method, it would estimate bad debt at 13.7% percent of accounts receivable. If it were to use the balance sheet aging of receivables method, it would split its receivables into three categories: 0–30 days past due at 5%, 31–90 days past due at 21%, and over 90 days past due at 30%. There is currently a zero balance, transferred from the prior year's Allowance for Doubtful Accounts. The following information is available from the year-end income statement and balance sheet.

2018 Year-End Totals for Shimmer Products	
Credit sales	$2,410,000
Accounts receivable	950,000

There is also additional information regarding the distribution of accounts receivable by age.

Past-Due Category	Accounts Receivable Total
0–30 days	$475,000
31–90 days	240,000
Over 90 days	235,000

Prepare the year-end adjusting entry for bad debt, using

A. Income statement method
B. Balance sheet method of receivables
C. Balance sheet aging of receivables method
D. Which method should the company choose, and why?

 Thought Provokers

TP1. LO 9.1 Review the new revenue recognition guidance issued by the Financial Accounting Standards Board http://www.fasb.org/jsp/FASB/Page/ImageBridgePage&cid=1176169257359 and answer the following questions.

- What is the new standard as of ASC 606? What does that mean to you?
- What are the recommended steps companies should follow to achieve the core principle?
- How does this change current GAAP standards?
- Who is required to adhere to this new standard?

TP2. LO 9.2 You run an office supplies chain. You must determine the most appropriate bad debt estimation method to use for financial statement reporting. Your choices are the income statement, balance sheet, and balance sheet aging of receivables methods.

- Research a real competitor in your industry and determine which method the competitor selected. Give a detailed description of the method used and any supporting calculations.
- Create a hypothetical credit sale, an accounts receivable figure for your business, and compute the bad debt estimation using the competitor's method.
- Create the journal entry to record bad debt.
- Compute bad debt using the other two methods and show the journal entry for each.
- What are the benefits and challenges for all of these methods?
- Which method would you choose for your business? Explain why.

TP3. LO 9.3 You are considering a $100,000 investment in one of two publicly traded companies in the same industry. Review the last three annual financial statements (same fiscal year) for two publicly traded companies in the same industry. Based on the information obtained, complete the following.

A. Compute the accounts receivable turnover ratio (round all answers to two decimal places).
B. Compute the number of days' sales in receivables ratio for both companies for the two most current years (round all answers to two decimal places).
C. Describe and interpret the outcomes, stating which company you would invest in and why.
D. What information is missing that could help you make a more informed decision?

TP4. LO 9.4 You are considering two possible companies for investment purposes. The following data is available for each company.

	Company A	Company B
Net credit sales, Dec. 31, 2019	$540,000	$620,000
Net accounts receivable, Dec. 31, 2018	$120,000	$145,000
Net accounts receivable, Dec. 31, 2019	$180,000	$175,000
Number of days' sales in receivables ratio, 2018	103 days	110 days
Net income, Dec. 31, 2018	$250,000	$350,000

Additional Information: Company A: Bad debt estimation percentage using the income statement method is 6%, and the balance sheet method is 10%. The $230,000 in Other Expenses includes all company expenses except Bad Debt Expense. Company B: Bad debt estimation percentage using the income statement method is 6.5%, and the balance sheet method is 8%. The $140,000 in Other Expenses includes all company expenses except Bad Debt Expense.

A. Compute the number of days' sales in receivables ratio for each company for 2019 and interpret the results (round answers to nearest whole number).
B. If Company A changed from the income statement method to the balance sheet method for recognizing bad debt estimation, how would that change net income in 2019? Explain (show calculations).
C. If Company B changed from the balance sheet method to the income statement method for recognizing bad debt estimation, how would that change net income in 2019? Explain (show calculations).
D. What benefits do each company gain by changing their method of bad debt estimation?
E. Which company would you invest in and why? Provide supporting details.

TP5. LO 9.5 You own a construction company and have recently received a contract with the local school district to refurbish one of its elementary schools. You are given an up-front payment from the school district in the amount of $5 million. The contract terms extend from years 2018 to 2020.

- When would you recognize revenue for this payment?
- What method of accounting would you use for this construction project and why?
- What would be the benefits and challenges with your method selection?
- Give an example of your distribution selection and associated costs of the project (you may estimate based on other industry competitors).
- What might be some benefits and challenges associated with the other method of construction revenue recognition?

TP6. LO 9.6 When a customer is delinquent on paying a notes receivable, your company has the option to continue to attempt collection or sell the debt to a collection agency. Research the benefits and challenges with each of these options and in a short essay, answer the following questions.

A. What are the benefits and challenges of continuing to attempt collection yourself?
B. What are the benefits and challenges of selling debt to a collection agency?
C. If you had a dishonored notes receivable, which option would you select and why?
D. Would you weight certain benefits or challenges differently when making your selection? How?

10 Inventory

Figure 10.1 Inventory. (credit: modification of "warehouse pallet food" by "jaymethunt"/Pixabay, CC0)

Chapter Outline

LO **10.1** Describe and Demonstrate the Basic Inventory Valuation Methods and Their Cost Flow Assumptions

LO **10.2** Calculate the Cost of Goods Sold and Ending Inventory Using the Periodic Method

LO **10.3** Calculate the Cost of Goods Sold and Ending Inventory Using the Perpetual Method

LO **10.4** Explain and Demonstrate the Impact of Inventory Valuation Errors on the Income Statement and Balance Sheet

LO **10.5** Examine the Efficiency of Inventory Management Using Financial Ratios

Why It Matters

Did you ever decide to start a healthy eating plan and meticulously planned your shopping list, including foods for meals, drinks, and snacks? Maybe you stocked your cabinets and fridge with the best healthy foods you could find, including lots of luscious-looking fruit and vegetables, to make sure that you could make tasty and healthy smoothies when you got hungry. Then, at the end of the week, if everything didn't go as you had planned, you may have discovered that a lot of your produce was still uneaten but not very fresh anymore. Stocking up on goods, so that you will have them when you need them, is only a good idea if the goods are used before they become worthless.

Just like with someone whose preparation for healthy eating can backfire in wasted produce, businesses have to balance a fine line between being prepared for any volume of inventory demand that customers request and being careful not to overstock those goods so the company will not be left holding excess inventory they cannot sell. Not having the goods that a customer wants available is bad, of course, but extra inventory is wasteful. That is one reason why inventory accounting is important.

10.1 Describe and Demonstrate the Basic Inventory Valuation Methods and Their Cost Flow Assumptions

Accounting for inventory is a critical function of management. Inventory accounting is significantly complicated by the fact that it is an ongoing process of constant change, in part because (1) most companies offer a large variety of products for sale, (2) product purchases occur at irregular times, (3) products are acquired for differing prices, and (4) inventory acquisitions are based on sales projections, which are always uncertain and often sporadic. Merchandising companies must meticulously account for every individual product that they sell, equipping them with essential information, for decisions such as these:

- What is the quantity of each product that is available to customers?
- When should inventory of each product item be replenished and at what quantity?
- How much should the company charge customers for each product to cover all costs plus profit margin?
- How much of the inventory cost should be allocated toward the units sold (cost of goods sold) during the period?
- How much of the inventory cost should be allocated toward the remaining units (ending inventory) at the end of the period?
- Is each product moving robustly or have some individual inventory items' activity decreased?
- Are some inventory items obsolete?

The company's financial statements report the combined cost of all items sold as an offset to the proceeds from those sales, producing the net number referred to as **gross margin** (or gross profit). This is presented in the first part of the results of operations for the period on the multi-step income statement. The unsold inventory at period end is an asset to the company and is therefore included in the company's financial statements, on the balance sheet, as shown in Figure 10.2. The total cost of all the inventory that remains at period end, reported as **merchandise inventory** on the balance sheet, plus the total cost of the inventory that was sold or otherwise removed (through shrinkage, theft, or other loss), reported as cost of goods sold on the income statement (see Figure 10.2), represent the entirety of the inventory that the company had to work with during the period, or goods available for sale.

SIERRA SPORTS Balance Sheet (partial) December 31, 2017	
Assets	
Current Assets	
Cash	$21,580
Accounts Receivable	2,000
Inventory	60,000

SIERRA SPORTS Income Statement (partial) For Year Ended December 31, 2017	
Revenues	
Total Revenues	$19,500
Cost of Goods Sold	9,000
Gross Profit	10,500

Figure 10.2 Financial Statement Effects of Inventory Transactions. (attribution: Copyright Rice University, OpenStax, under CC BY-NC-SA 4.0 license)

Fundamentals of Inventory

Although our discussion will consider inventory issues from the perspective of a retail company, using a resale or merchandising operation, inventory accounting also encompasses recording and reporting of manufacturing operations. In the manufacturing environment, there would be separate inventory calculations for the various process levels of inventory, such as raw materials, work in process, and finished goods. The manufacturer's finished goods inventory is equivalent to the merchandiser's inventory account in that it includes finished goods that are available for sale.

In merchandising companies, inventory is a company asset that includes beginning inventory plus **purchases**, which include all additions to inventory during the period. Every time the company sells products to customers, they dispose of a portion of the company's inventory asset. **Goods available for sale** refers to the total cost of all inventory that the company had on hand at any time during the period, including beginning inventory and all inventory purchases. These goods were normally either sold to customers during the period (occasionally lost due to spoilage, theft, damage, or other types of shrinkages) and thus reported as cost of goods sold, an expense account on the income statement, or these goods are still in inventory at the end of the period and reported as ending merchandise inventory, an asset account on the balance sheet. As an example, assume that Harry's Auto Parts Store sells oil filters. Suppose that at the end of January 31, 2018, they had 50 oil filters on hand at a cost of $7 per unit. This means that at the beginning of February, they had 50 units in inventory at a total cost of $350 (50 × $7). During the month, they purchased 20 filters at a cost of $7, for a total cost of $140 (20 × $7). At the end of the month, there were 18 units left in inventory. Therefore, during the month of February, they sold 52 units. Figure 10.3 illustrates how to calculate the goods available for sale and the cost of goods sold.

	Number of Units	Cost per Unit	Total Cost
Beginning Inventory, January 31, 2018	50	$7	$350
+ purchases during February 2018	20	$7	140
Total Goods Available for Sale	**70**		**$490**
– Ending Inventory, February 28, 2018	18	$7	126
Cost of Goods Sold for February 2018	**52**		**$364**

Figure 10.3 Fundamentals of Inventory Accounting. (attribution: Copyright Rice University, OpenStax, under CC BY-NC-SA 4.0 license)

Inventory costing is accomplished by one of four specific costing methods: (1) specific identification, (2) first-in, first-out, (3) last-in, first-out, and (4) weighted-average cost methods. All four methods are techniques that allow management to distribute the costs of inventory in a logical and consistent manner, to facilitate matching of costs to offset the related revenue item that is recognized during the period, in accordance with GAAP expense recognition and matching concepts. Note that a company's cost allocation process represents management's chosen method for expensing product costs, based strictly on estimates of the flow of inventory costs, which is unrelated to the actual flow of the physical inventory. Use of a cost allocation strategy eliminates the need for often cost-prohibitive individual tracking of costs of each specific inventory item, for which purchase prices may vary greatly. In this chapter, you will be provided with some background concepts and explanations of terms associated with inventory as well as a basic demonstration of each of the four allocation methods, and then further delineation of the application and nuances of the costing methods.

A critical issue for inventory accounting is the frequency for which inventory values are updated. There are two primary methods used to account for inventory balance timing changes: the periodic inventory method and the perpetual inventory method. These two methods were addressed in depth in Merchandising Transactions).

Periodic Inventory Method

A **periodic inventory system** updates the inventory balances at the end of the reporting period, typically the end of a month, quarter, or year. At that point, a journal entry is made to adjust the merchandise inventory asset balance to agree with the physical count of inventory, with the corresponding adjustment to the expense account, cost of goods sold. This adjustment shifts the costs of all inventory items that are no longer held by the company to the income statement, where the costs offset the revenue from inventory sales, as reflected by the gross margin. As sales transactions occur throughout the period, the periodic system requires that only the sales entry be recorded because costs will only be updated during end-of-period adjustments when financial statements are prepared. However, any additional goods for sale acquired during the month are recorded as purchases. Following are examples of typical journal entries for periodic transactions. The first is an example entry for an inventory sales transaction when using periodic inventory, and the second records the purchase of additional inventory when using the periodic method. Note: Periodic requires no corresponding cost entry at the time of sale, since the inventory is adjusted only at period end.

JOURNAL			
Date	Account	Debit	Credit
	Accounts Receivable	XXX	
	Sales Revenue		XXX

A purchase of inventory for sale by a company under the periodic inventory method would necessitate the following journal entry. (This is discussed in more depth in Merchandising Transactions.)

JOURNAL			
Date	Account	Debit	Credit
	Purchases	XXX	
	Cash (or Accounts Payable)		XXX

Perpetual Inventory Method

A **perpetual inventory system** updates the inventory account balance on an ongoing basis, at the time of each individual sale. This is normally accomplished by use of auto-ID technology, such as optical-scan barcode or radio frequency identification (RFIF) labels. As transactions occur, the perpetual system requires that every sale is recorded with two entries, first recording the sales transaction as an increase to Accounts Receivable and a decrease to Sales Revenue, and then recording the cost associated with the sale as an increase to Cost of Goods Sold and a decrease to Merchandise Inventory. The journal entries made at the time of sale immediately shift the costs relating to the goods being sold from the merchandise inventory account on the balance sheet to the cost of goods sold account on the income statement. Little or no adjustment is needed to inventory at period end because changes in the inventory balances are recorded as both the sales and purchase transactions occur. Any necessary adjustments to the ending inventory account balances would typically be caused by one of the types of shrinkage you've learned about. These are example entries for an inventory sales transaction when using perpetual inventory updating:

JOURNAL			
Date	Account	Debit	Credit
	Accounts Receivable	XXX	
	Sales Revenue		XXX
	Cost of Goods Sold	XXX	
	Merchandise Inventory		XXX

A purchase of inventory for sale by a company under the perpetual inventory method would necessitate the following journal entry. (Greater detail is provided in Merchandising Transactions.)

JOURNAL			
Date	Account	Debit	Credit
	Inventory Cash (or Accounts Payable)	XXX	 XXX

CONTINUING APPLICATION AT WORK

Inventory

As previously discussed, Gearhead Outfitters is a retail chain selling outdoor gear and accessories. As such, the company is faced with many possible questions related to inventory. How much inventory should be carried? What products are the most profitable? Which products have the most sales? Which products are obsolete? What timeframe should the company allow for inventory to be replenished? Which products are the most in demand at each location?

In addition to questions related to type, volume, obsolescence, and lead time, there are many issues related to accounting for inventory and the flow of goods. As one of the biggest assets of the company, the way inventory is tracked can have an effect on profit. Which method of accounting—first-in first-out, last-in first out, specific identification, weighted average— provides the most accurate reflection of inventory and cost of goods sold is important in determining gross profit and net income. The method selected affects profits, taxes, and can even change the opinion of potential lenders concerning the financial strength of the company. In choosing a method of accounting for inventory, management should consider many factors, including the accurate reflection of costs, taxes on profits, decision-making about purchases, and what effect a point-of-sale (POS) system may have on tracking inventory.

Gearhead exists to provide a positive shopping experience for its customers. Offering a clear picture of its goods, and maintaining an appealing, timely supply at competitive prices is one way to keep the shopping experience positive. Thus, accounting for inventory plays an instrumental role in management's ability to successfully run a company and deliver the company's promise to customers.

Data for Demonstration of the Four Basic Inventory Valuation Methods

The following dataset will be used to demonstrate the application and analysis of the four methods of inventory accounting.

Company: Spy Who Loves You Corporation

Product: Global Positioning System (GPS) Tracking Device

Description: This product is an economical real-time GPS tracking device, designed for individuals who wish to monitor others' whereabouts. It is marketed to parents of middle school and high school students as a safety measure. Parents benefit by being apprised of the child's location, and the student benefits by not having to constantly check in with parents. Demand for the product has spiked during the current fiscal period, while supply is limited, causing the selling price to escalate rapidly.

SPY WHO LOVES YOU TRACKER			
	Number of Units	Unit Cost	Sales Price
Beginning Inventory Jul. 1	150	$21	
Sold Jul. 5	120		$36
Purchased Jul. 10	225	27	
Sold Jul. 15	180		39
Purchased Jul. 25	210	33	
Ending Inventory Jul. 31	285		

Specific Identification Method

The **specific identification method** refers to tracking the actual cost of the item being sold and is generally used only on expensive items that are highly customized (such as tracking detailed costs for each individual car in automobiles sales) or inherently distinctive (such as tracking origin and cost for each unique stone in diamond sales). This method is too cumbersome for goods of large quantity, especially if there are not significant feature differences in the various inventory items of each product type. However, for purposes of this demonstration, assume that the company sold one specific identifiable unit, which was purchased in the second lot of products, at a cost of $27.

Three separate lots of goods are purchased:

	Number of Units	Unit Cost
Lot 1	150	$21
Lot 2*	225	27
Lot 3	210	33

Sales revenue	$36
- Cost, assuming SI, unit assumed sold from Lot 2*	27
= Gross margin for one unit	9

Note: one unit sold for $36, using the specific identification (SI) costing method

First-in, First-out (FIFO) Method

The **first-in, first-out method (FIFO)** records costs relating to a sale as if the earliest purchased item would be sold first. However, the physical flow of the units sold under both the periodic and perpetual methods would be the same. Due to the mechanics of the determination of costs of goods sold under the perpetual method, based on the timing of additional purchases of inventory during the accounting period, it is possible that the costs of goods sold might be slightly different for an accounting period. Since FIFO assumes that the first items purchased are sold first, the latest acquisitions would be the items that remain in inventory at the end of the period and would constitute ending inventory.

Three separate lots of goods are purchased:

	Number of Units	Unit Cost
Lot 1*	150	$21
Lot 2	225	27
Lot 3	210	33

Sales revenue	$36
- Cost, assuming FIFO, unit assumed sold from Lot 1*	21
= Gross margin for one unit	15

Note: one unit sold for $36, using the FIFO costing method

Last-in, First-out (LIFO) Method

The **last-in, first out method (LIFO)** records costs relating to a sale as if the latest purchased item would be sold first. As a result, the earliest acquisitions would be the items that remain in inventory at the end of the period.

Three separate lots of goods are purchased:

	Number of Units	Unit Cost
Lot 1	150	$21
Lot 2	225	27
Lot 3*	210	33

Sales revenue	$36
– Cost, assuming LIFO, unit assumed sold from Lot 3*	33
= Gross margin for one unit	3

Note: one unit sold for $36, using the LIFO costing method

IFRS CONNECTION

Inventory

For many companies, inventory is a significant portion of the company's assets. In 2018, the inventory of Walmart, the world's largest international retailer, was 70% of current assets and 21% of total assets. Because inventory also affects income as it is sold through the cost of goods sold account, inventory plays a significant role in the analysis and evaluation of many companies. Ending inventory affects both the balance sheet and the income statement. As you've learned, the ending inventory balance is reflected as a current asset on the balance sheet and the ending inventory balance is used in the calculation of costs of goods sold. Understanding how companies report inventory under US GAAP versus under IFRS is important when comparing companies reporting under the two methods, particularly because of a significant difference between the two methods.

Similarities

- When inventory is purchased, it is accounted for at historical cost and then evaluated at each balance sheet date to adjust to the lower of cost or net realizable value.
- Both IFRS and US GAAP allow FIFO and weighted-average cost flow assumptions as well as specific identification where appropriate and applicable.

Differences

- IFRS does not permit the use of LIFO. This is a major difference between US GAAP and IFRS. The AICPA estimates that roughly 35–40% of all US companies use LIFO, and in some industries, such as oil and gas, the use of LIFO is more prevalent. Because LIFO generates lower taxable income during times of rising prices, it is estimated that eliminating LIFO would generate an estimated $102 billion in tax revenues in the US for the period 2017–2026. In creating IFRS, the IASB chose to eliminate LIFO, arguing that FIFO more closely matches the flow of goods. In the US, FASB believes the choice between LIFO and FIFO is a business model decision that should be left up to each company. In addition, there was significant pressure by some companies and industries to retain LIFO because of the significant tax liability that would arise for many companies from the elimination of LIFO.

Weighted-Average Cost Method

The **weighted-average cost method** (sometimes referred to as the average cost method) requires a calculation of the average cost of all units of each particular inventory items. The average is obtained by multiplying the number of units by the cost paid per unit for each lot of goods, then adding the calculated total value of all lots together, and finally dividing the total cost by the total number of units for that product. As a caveat relating to the average cost method, note that a new average cost must be calculated after every change in inventory to reassess the per-unit weighted-average value of the goods. This laborious requirement might make use of the average method cost-prohibitive.

Three separate lots of goods are purchased:

	Number of Units	Unit Cost
Lot 1	150	$21
Lot 2	225	27
Lot 3	210	33

Sales revenue	$36.00
– Cost, assuming average cost of units sold from Lots 1, 2, and 3*	27.62
= Gross margin for one unit	8.38

Note: one unit sold for $36, using the weighted average costing method

*[(150 × $21) + (225 × $27) + (210 × $33)]/585 = $27.62 average

Comparing the various costing methods for the sale of one unit in this simple example reveals a significant difference that the choice of cost allocation method can make. Note that the sales price is not affected by the cost assumptions; only the cost amount varies, depending on which method is chosen. Figure 10.4 depicts the different outcomes that the four methods produced.

	Sp ID	FIFO	LIFO	AVG
Sales revenue	36	36	36	36.00
– Cost, under each cost allocation method	27	21	33	27.62
= Gross margin for one unit	9	15	3	8.38

Figure 10.4 Comparison of the Four Costing Methods. One unit sold for $36. (attribution: Copyright Rice University, OpenStax, under CC BY-NC-SA 4.0 license)

Once the methods of costing are determined for the company, that methodology would typically be applied repeatedly over the remainder of the company's history to accomplish the generally accepted accounting principle of **consistency** from one period to another. It is possible to change methods if the company finds that a different method more accurately reflects results of operations, but the change requires disclosure in the company's notes to the financial statements, which alerts financial statement users of the impact of the change in methodology. Also, it is important to realize that although the Internal Revenue Service generally allows differing methods of accounting treatment for tax purposes than for financial statement purposes, an exception exists that prohibits the use of LIFO inventory costing on the company tax return unless LIFO is also used for the financial statement costing calculations.

ETHICAL CONSIDERATIONS

Auditors Look for Inventory Fraud

Inventory fraud can be used to book false revenue or to increase the amount of assets to obtain additional lending from a bank or other sources. In the typical chain of accounting events, inventory ultimately becomes an expense item known as cost of goods sold.[1] In a manipulated accounting system, a trail of fraudulent transactions can point to accounting misrepresentation in the sales cycle, which may include

- recording fictitious and nonexistent inventory,
- manipulation of inventory counts during a facility audit,
- recording of sales but no recording of purchases, and/or
- fraudulent inventory capitalization,

to list a few.[2] All these elaborate schemes have the same goal: to improperly manipulate inventory values to support the creation of a fraudulent financial statement. Accountants have an ethical, moral, and legal duty to not commit accounting and financial statement fraud. Auditors have a duty to look for such inventory fraud.

Auditors follow the Statement on Auditing Standards (SAS) No. 99 and AU Section 316 Consideration of Fraud in a Financial Statement Audit when auditing a company's books. Auditors are outside accountants hired to "obtain reasonable assurance about whether the financial statements are free of material misstatement, whether caused by error or fraud."[3] Ultimately, an auditor will prepare an audit report based on the testing of the balances in a company's books, and a review of the company's accounting system. The auditor is to perform "procedures at locations on a surprise or unannounced basis, for example, observing inventory on unexpected dates or at unexpected locations or counting cash on a surprise basis."[4] Such testing of a company's inventory system is used to catch accounting fraud. It is the responsibility of the accountant to present accurate accounting records to the auditor, and for the auditor to create auditing procedures that reasonably ensure that the inventory balances are free of material misstatements in the accounting balances.

Additional Inventory Issues

Various other issues that affect inventory accounting include consignment sales, transportation and ownership issues, inventory estimation tools, and the effects of inflationary versus deflationary cycles on various methods.

Consignment

Consigned goods refer to merchandise inventory that belongs to a third party but which is displayed for sale by the company. These goods are not owned by the company and thus must not be included on the company's balance sheet nor be used in the company's inventory calculations. The company's profit relating to consigned goods is normally limited to a percentage of the sales proceeds at the time of sale.

For example, assume that you sell your office and your current furniture doesn't match your new building.

1 "Inventory Fraud: Knowledge Is Your First Line of Defense." Weaver. Mar. 27, 2015. https://weaver.com/blog/inventory-fraud-knowledge-your-first-line-defense

2 Wells, Joseph T. "Ghost Goods: How to Spot Phantom Inventory." *Journal of Accountancy*. June 1, 2001. https://www.journalofaccountancy.com/issues/2001/jun/ghostgoodshowtospotphantominventory.html

3 American Institute of Certified Public Accountants (AICPA). *Consideration of Fraud in a Financial Statement Audit* (AU Section 316). https://www.aicpa.org/Research/Standards/AuditAttest/DownloadableDocuments/AU-00316.pdf

4 American Institute of Certified Public Accountants (AICPA). *Consideration of Fraud in a Financial Statement Audit* (AU Section 316). https://www.aicpa.org/Research/Standards/AuditAttest/DownloadableDocuments/AU-00316.pdf

One way to dispose of the furniture would be to have a consignment shop sell it. The shop would keep a percentage of the sales revenue and pay you the remaining balance. Assume in this example that the shop will keep one-third of the sales proceeds and pay you the remaining two-thirds balance. If the furniture sells for $15,000, you would receive $10,000 and the shop would keep the remaining $5,000 as its sales commission. A key point to remember is that until the inventory, in this case your office furniture, is sold, you still own it, and it is reported as an asset on your balance sheet and not an asset for the consignment shop. After the sale, the buyer is the owner, so the consignment shop is never the property's owner.

Free on Board (FOB) Shipping and Destination

Transportation costs are commonly assigned to either the buyer or the seller based on the free on board (FOB) terms, as the terms relate to the seller. Transportation costs are part of the responsibilities of the owner of the product, so determining the owner at the shipping point identifies who should pay for the shipping costs. The seller's responsibility and ownership of the goods ends at the point that is listed after the FOB designation. Thus, **FOB shipping point** means that the seller transfers title and responsibility to the buyer at the shipping point, so the buyer would owe the shipping costs. The purchased goods would be recorded on the buyer's balance sheet at this point.

Similarly, **FOB destination** means the seller transfers title and responsibility to the buyer at the destination, so the seller would owe the shipping costs. Ownership of the product is the trigger that mandates that the asset be included on the company's balance sheet. In summary, the goods belong to the seller until they transition to the location following the term FOB, making the seller responsible for everything about the goods to that point, including recording purchased goods on the balance sheet . If something happens to damage or destroy the goods before they reach the FOB location, the seller would be required to replace the product or reverse the sales transaction.

Lower-of-Cost-or-Market (LCM)

Reporting inventory values on the balance sheet using the accounting concept of **conservatism** (which discourages overstatement of net assets and net income) requires inventory to be calculated and adjusted to a value that is the lower of the cost calculated using the company's chosen valuation method or the market value based on the market or replacement value of the inventory items. Thus, if traditional cost calculations produce inventory values that are overstated, the **lower-of-cost-or-market (LCM)** concept requires that the balance in the inventory account should be decreased to the more conservative replacement value rather than be overstated on the balance sheet.

Estimating Inventory Costs: Gross Profit Method and Retail Inventory Method

Sometimes companies have a need to estimate inventory values. These estimates could be needed for interim reports, when physical counts are not taken. The need could be result from a natural disaster that destroys part or all of the inventory or from an error that causes inventory counts to be compromised or omitted. Some specific industries (such as select retail businesses) also regularly use these estimation tools to determine cost of goods sold. Although the method is predictable and simple, it is also less accurate since it is based on estimates rather than actual cost figures.

The **gross profit method** is used to estimate inventory values by applying a standard gross profit percentage to the company's sales totals when a physical count is not possible. The resulting gross profit can then be subtracted from sales, leaving an estimated cost of goods sold. Then the ending inventory can be calculated by subtracting cost of goods sold from the total goods available for sale. Likewise, the **retail inventory method** estimates the cost of goods sold, much like the gross profit method does, but uses the retail value of the portions of inventory rather than the cost figures used in the gross profit method.

Inflationary Versus Deflationary Cycles

As prices rise (inflationary times), FIFO ending inventory account balances grow larger even when inventory unit counts are constant, while the income statement reflects lower cost of goods sold than the current prices for those goods, which produces higher profits than if the goods were costed with current inventory prices. Conversely, when prices fall (deflationary times), FIFO ending inventory account balances decrease and the income statement reflects higher cost of goods sold and lower profits than if goods were costed at current inventory prices. The effect of inflationary and deflationary cycles on LIFO inventory valuation are the exact opposite of their effects on FIFO inventory valuation.

LINK TO LEARNING

Accounting Coach does a great job in explaining inventory issues (and so many other accounting topics too): Learn more about inventory and cost of goods sold (https://openstax.org/l/50inventory) on their website.

THINK IT THROUGH

First-in, First-out (FIFO)

Suppose you are the assistant controller for a retail establishment that is an independent bookseller. The company uses manual, periodic inventory updating, using physical counts at year end, and the FIFO method for inventory costing. How would you approach the subject of whether the company should consider switching to computerized perpetual inventory updating? Can you present a persuasive argument for the benefits of perpetual? Explain.

10.2 Calculate the Cost of Goods Sold and Ending Inventory Using the Periodic Method

As you've learned, the periodic inventory system is updated at the end of the period to adjust inventory numbers to match the physical count and provide accurate merchandise inventory values for the balance sheet. The adjustment ensures that only the inventory costs that remain on hand are recorded, and the remainder of the goods available for sale are expensed on the income statement as cost of goods sold. Here we will demonstrate the mechanics used to calculate the ending inventory values using the four cost allocation methods and the periodic inventory system.

Information Relating to All Cost Allocation Methods, but Specific to Periodic Inventory Updating

Let’s return to the example of The Spy Who Loves You Corporation to demonstrate the four cost allocation methods, assuming inventory is updated at the end of the period using the periodic system.

Cost Data for Calculations

Company: Spy Who Loves You Corporation

Product: Global Positioning System (GPS) Tracking Device

Description: This product is an economical real-time GPS tracking device, designed for individuals who wish to monitor others’ whereabouts. It is being marketed to parents of middle school and high school students as a safety measure. Parents benefit by being apprised of the child’s location, and the student benefits by not having to constantly check in with parents. Demand for the product has spiked during the current fiscal period, while supply is limited, causing the selling price to escalate rapidly. Note: For simplicity of demonstration, beginning inventory cost is assumed to be $21 per unit for all cost assumption methods.

SPY WHO LOVES YOU TRACKER			
	Number of Units	**Unit Cost**	**Sales Price**
Beginning Inventory Jul. 1	150	$21	
Sold Jul. 5	120		$36
Purchased Jul. 10	225	27	
Sold Jul. 15	180		39
Purchased Jul. 25	210	33	
Ending Inventory Jul. 31	285		

Specific Identification

The specific units assumed to be sold in this period are designated as follows, with the specific inventory distinction being associated with the lot numbers:

- Sold 120 units, all from Lot 1 (beginning inventory), costing $21 per unit
- Sold 180 units, 20 from Lot 1 (beginning inventory), costing $21 per unit; 160 from the Lot 2 (July 10 purchase), costing $27 per unit

The specific identification method of cost allocation directly tracks each of the units purchased and costs them out as they are actually sold. In this demonstration, assume that some sales were made by specifically tracked goods that are part of a lot, as previously stated for this method. So for The Spy Who Loves You, considering the entire period together, note that

- 140 of the 150 units that were purchased for $21 were sold, leaving 10 of $21 units remaining
- 160 of the 225 units that were purchased for $27 were sold, leaving 65 of the $27 units remaining
- none of the 210 units that were purchased for $33 were sold, leaving all 210 of the $33 units remaining

Ending inventory was made up of 10 units at $21 each, 65 units at $27 each, and 210 units at $33 each, for a total specific identification ending inventory value of $8,895. Subtracting this ending inventory from the $16,155 total of goods available for sale leaves $7,260 in cost of goods sold this period.

Calculations of Costs of Goods Sold, Ending Inventory, and Gross Margin, Specific Identification

The specific identification costing assumption tracks inventory items individually, so that when they are sold, the exact cost of the item is used to offset the revenue from the sale. The cost of goods sold, inventory, and gross margin shown in Figure 10.5 were determined from the previously-stated data, particular to specific identification costing.

Cost of Goods Sold	
Beginning Inventory	$ 3,150
+ Purchases	13,005
= Goods Available	16,155
- Ending Inventory	8,895
Cost of Goods Sold	7,260

Cost Value	
10 units at $21	$ 210
65 units at $27	1,755
210 units at $33	6,930
Total	8,895

Note: Purchases = (225 × $27) + (210 × $33)

Figure 10.5 Specific Identification Costing Assumption Cost of Goods Sold and Cost Value. (attribution: Copyright Rice University, OpenStax, under CC BY-NC-SA 4.0 license)

The gross margin, resulting from the specific identification periodic cost allocations of $7,260, is shown in Figure 10.6.

Gross Margin	
Sales	$11,340
– Cost of Goods Sold	7,260
= Gross Margin	4,080

(120 × $36) + (180 × 39)

Figure 10.6 Specific Identification Periodic Cost Allocations Gross Margin. (attribution: Copyright Rice University, OpenStax, under CC BY-NC-SA 4.0 license)

Calculation for the Ending Inventory Adjustment under Periodic/Specific Identification Methods

Merchandise inventory, before adjustment, had a balance of $3,150, which was the beginning inventory. Journal entries are not shown, but the following calculations provide the information that would be used in recording the necessary journal entries. The inventory at the end of the period should be $8,895, requiring an entry to increase merchandise inventory by $5,745. Cost of goods sold was calculated to be $7,260, which should be recorded as an expense. The credit entry to balance the adjustment is $13,005, which is the total amount that was recorded as purchases for the period. This entry distributes the balance in the purchases account between the inventory that was sold (cost of goods sold) and the amount of inventory that remains at period end (merchandise inventory).

First-in, First-out (FIFO)

The first-in, first-out method (FIFO) of cost allocation assumes that the earliest units purchased are also the first units sold. For The Spy Who Loves You, considering the entire period, 300 of the 585 units available for the period were sold, and if the earliest acquisitions are considered sold first, then the units that remain under FIFO are those that were purchased last. Following that logic, ending inventory included 210 units purchased at $33 and 75 units purchased at $27 each, for a total FIFO periodic ending inventory value of $8,955. Subtracting this ending inventory from the $16,155 total of goods available for sale leaves $7,200 in cost of goods sold this period.

FIFO Periodic Ending Inventory Value	
Units Sold (180 +120) = 300 units	
150 units x $21	$3,150
150 units x $27	4,050
Total Sold equals 300 units	
Cost of Goods Sold	$7,200
Ending Inventory	
210 units x $33	6,930
75 units x $27	2,025
Ending Inventory Value	$8,955

Calculations of Costs of Goods Sold, Ending Inventory, and Gross Margin, First-in, First-out (FIFO)

The FIFO costing assumption tracks inventory items based on segments or lots of goods that are tracked, in the order that they were acquired, so that when they are sold, the earliest acquired items are used to offset the revenue from the sale. The cost of goods sold, inventory, and gross margin shown in Figure 10.7 were determined from the previously-stated data, particular to FIFO costing.

Cost of Goods Sold	
Beginning Inventory	$ 3,150
+ Purchases	13,005
= Goods Available	16,155
- Ending Inventory	8,955
Cost of Goods Sold	7,200

Cost Value	
75 units at $27	$2,025
210 units at $33	6,930
Total	8,955

Note: Purchases = (225 × $27) + (210 × $33)

Figure 10.7 FIFO Costing Assumption Cost of Goods Sold and Cost Value. (attribution: Copyright Rice University, OpenStax, under CC BY-NC-SA 4.0 license)

The gross margin, resulting from the FIFO periodic cost allocations of $7,200, is shown in Figure 10.8.

Gross Margin	
Sales	$11,340
- Cost of Goods Sold	7,200
= Gross Margin	4,140

Figure 10.8 FIFO Periodic Cost Allocations Gross Margin. (attribution: Copyright Rice University, OpenStax, under CC BY-NC-SA 4.0 license)

Calculations for Inventory Adjustment, Periodic/First-in, First-out (FIFO)

Beginning merchandise inventory had a balance of $3,150 before adjustment. The inventory at period end should be $8,955, requiring an entry to increase merchandise inventory by $5,895. Journal entries are not shown, but the following calculations provide the information that would be used in recording the necessary journal entries. Cost of goods sold was calculated to be $7,200, which should be recorded as an expense. The credit entry to balance the adjustment is for $13,005, which is the total amount that was recorded as purchases for the period. This entry distributes the balance in the purchases account between the inventory that was sold (cost of goods sold) and the amount of inventory that remains at period end (merchandise inventory).

Last-in, First-out (LIFO)

The last-in, first-out method (LIFO) of cost allocation assumes that the last units purchased are the first units sold. For The Spy Who Loves You, considering the entire period together, 300 of the 585 units available for the period were sold, and if the latest acquisitions are considered sold first, then the units that remain under LIFO are those that were purchased first. Following that logic, ending inventory included 150 units purchased at $21 and 135 units purchased at $27 each, for a total LIFO periodic ending inventory value of $6,795. Subtracting this ending inventory from the $16,155 total of goods available for sale leaves $9,360 in cost of goods sold this period.

LIFO Periodic Ending Inventory Value	
Units Sold (210 + 90) = 300 Units	
210 units x $33	$6,930
90 units x $27	2,430
Total Sold equals 300 units	
Cost of Goods Sold	9,360
Ending Inventory	
150 units x $21	3,150
135 units x $27	3,645
Ending Inventory Value	$6,795

It is important to note that these answers can differ when calculated using the perpetual method. When perpetual methodology is utilized, the cost of goods sold and ending inventory are calculated at the time of each sale rather than at the end of the month. For example, in this case, when the first sale of 150 units is made, inventory will be removed and cost computed as of that date from the beginning inventory. The differences in timing as to when cost of goods sold is calculated can alter the order that costs are sequenced.

Calculations of Costs of Goods Sold, Ending Inventory, and Gross Margin, Last-in, First-out (LIFO)

The LIFO costing assumption tracks inventory items based on lots of goods that are tracked, in the order that they were acquired, so that when they are sold, the latest acquired items are used to offset the revenue from the sale. The following cost of goods sold, inventory, and gross margin were determined from the previously-stated data, particular to LIFO costing.

Cost of Goods Sold	
Beginning Inventory	$ 3,150
+ Purchases	13,005
= Goods Available	16,155
- Ending Inventory	6,795
Cost of Goods Sold	9,360

Note: Purchases = (225 × $27) + (210 × $33)

Cost Value	
150 units at $21	$3,150
135 units at $27	3,645
Total	6,795

Figure 10.9 LIFO Costing Assumption Cost of Goods Sold and Cost Value. (attribution: Copyright Rice University, OpenStax, under CC BY-NC-SA 4.0 license)

The gross margin, resulting from the LIFO periodic cost allocations of $9,360, is shown in Figure 10.10.

Gross Margin	
Sales	$11,340
– Cost of Goods Sold	9,360
= Gross Margin	1,980

Figure 10.10 LIFO Periodic Cost Allocations Gross Margin. (attribution: Copyright Rice University, OpenStax, under CC BY-NC-SA 4.0 license)

Calculations for Inventory Adjustment, Periodic/Last-in, First-out (LIFO)

Beginning merchandise inventory had a balance before adjustment of $3,150. The inventory at period end should be $6,795, requiring an entry to increase merchandise inventory by $3,645. Journal entries are not shown, but the following calculations provide the information that would be used in recording the necessary journal entries. Cost of goods sold was calculated to be $9,360, which should be recorded as an expense. The credit entry to balance the adjustment is for $13,005, which is the total amount that was recorded as purchases for the period. This entry distributes the balance in the purchases account between the inventory that was sold (cost of goods sold) and the amount of inventory that remains at period end (merchandise inventory).

Weighted-Average Cost (AVG)

Weighted-average cost allocation requires computation of the average cost of all units in goods available for sale at the time the sale is made. For The Spy Who Loves You, considering the entire period, the weighted-average cost is computed by dividing total cost of goods available for sale ($16,155) by the total number of available units (585) to get the average cost of $27.62. Note that 285 of the 585 units available for sale during the period remained in inventory at period end. Following that logic, ending inventory included 285 units at an average cost of $27.62 for a total AVG periodic ending inventory value of $7,872. Subtracting this ending inventory from the $16,155 total of goods available for sale leaves $8,283 in cost of goods sold this period. It is important to note that final numbers can often differ by one or two cents due to rounding of the calculations. In this case, the cost comes to $27.6154 but rounds up to the stated cost of $27.62.

Calculations of Costs of Goods Sold, Ending Inventory, and Gross Margin, Weighted Average (AVG)

The AVG costing assumption tracks inventory items based on lots of goods that are tracked but averages the cost of all units on hand every time an addition is made to inventory so that, when they are sold, the most recently averaged cost items are used to offset the revenue from the sale. The cost of goods sold, inventory, and gross margin shown in Figure 10.11 were determined from the previously-stated data, particular to AVG costing.

Cost of Goods Sold	
Beginning Inventory	$ 3,150
+ Purchases	13,005
= Goods Available	16,155
- Ending Inventory	7,872
Cost of Goods Sold	8,283

Note: Purchases = (225 × $27) + (210 × $33)

Cost Value	
285 units at $27.62	$7,872
Total	7,872

Figure 10.11 AVG Costing Assumption Cost of Goods Sold and Cost Value. (attribution: Copyright Rice University, OpenStax, under CC BY-NC-SA 4.0 license)

Figure 10.12 shows the gross margin resulting from the weighted-average periodic cost allocations of $8283.

Gross Margin	
Sales	$11,340
- Cost of Goods Sold	8,283
= Gross Margin	3,057

Figure 10.12 Weighted AVG Periodic Cost Allocations Gross Margin. (attribution: Copyright Rice University, OpenStax, under CC BY-NC-SA 4.0 license)

Journal Entries for Inventory Adjustment, Periodic/Weighted Average

Beginning merchandise inventory had a balance before adjustment of $3,150. The inventory at period end should be $7,872, requiring an entry to increase merchandise inventory by $4,722. Journal entries are not shown, but the following calculations provide the information that would be used in recording the necessary journal entries. Cost of goods sold was calculated to be $8,283, which should be recorded as an expense. The credit entry to balance the adjustment is for $13,005, which is the total amount that was recorded as purchases for the period. This entry distributes the balance in the purchases account between the inventory that was sold (cost of goods sold) and the amount of inventory that remains at period end (merchandise inventory).

10.3 Calculate the Cost of Goods Sold and Ending Inventory Using the Perpetual Method

As you've learned, the perpetual inventory system is updated continuously to reflect the current status of inventory on an ongoing basis. Modern sales activity commonly uses electronic identifiers—such as bar codes and RFID technology—to account for inventory as it is purchased, monitored, and sold. Specific identification inventory methods also commonly use a manual form of the perpetual system. Here we'll demonstrate the mechanics implemented when using perpetual inventory systems in inventory accounting, whether those calculations are orchestrated in a laborious manual system or electronically (in the latter, the inventory accounting operates effortlessly behind the scenes but nonetheless utilizes the same perpetual methodology).

CONCEPTS IN PRACTICE

Perpetual Inventory's Advancements through Technology

Perpetual inventory has been seen as the wave of the future for many years. It has grown since the 1970s alongside the development of affordable personal computers. Universal product codes, commonly known as UPC barcodes, have advanced inventory management for large and small retail organizations, allowing real-time inventory counts and reorder capability that increased popularity of the perpetual inventory system. These UPC codes identify specific products but are not specific to the particular batch of goods that were produced. Electronic product codes (EPCs) such as radio frequency identifiers (RFIDs) are essentially an evolved version of UPCs in which a chip/identifier is embedded in the EPC code that matches the goods to the actual batch of product that was produced. This more specific information allows better control, greater accountability, increased efficiency, and overall quality monitoring of goods in inventory. The technology advancements that are available for perpetual inventory systems make it nearly impossible for businesses to choose periodic inventory and forego the competitive advantages that the technology offers.

Information Relating to All Cost Allocation Methods, but Specific to Perpetual Inventory Updating

Let's return to The Spy Who Loves You Corporation data to demonstrate the four cost allocation methods, assuming inventory is updated on an ongoing basis in a perpetual system.

Cost Data for Calculations

Company: Spy Who Loves You Corporation

Product: Global Positioning System (GPS) Tracking Device

Description: This product is an economical real-time GPS tracking device, designed for individuals who wish to monitor others' whereabouts. It is being marketed to parents of middle school and high school students as a safety measure. Parents benefit by being apprised of the child's location, and the student benefits by not having to constantly check in with parents. Demand for the product has spiked during the current fiscal period, while supply is limited, causing the selling price to escalate rapidly. Note: For simplicity of demonstration, beginning inventory cost is assumed to be $21 per unit for all cost assumption methods.

SPY WHO LOVES YOU TRACKER			
	Number of Units	Unit Cost	Sales Price
Beginning Inventory Jul. 1	150	$21	
Sold Jul. 5	120		$36
Purchased Jul. 10	225	27	
Sold Jul. 15	180		39
Purchased Jul. 25	210	33	
Ending Inventory Jul. 31	185		

Calculations for Inventory Purchases and Sales during the Period, Perpetual Inventory Updating

Regardless of which cost assumption is chosen, recording inventory sales using the perpetual method involves recording both the revenue and the cost from the transaction for each individual sale. As additional inventory is purchased during the period, the cost of those goods is added to the merchandise inventory account. Normally, no significant adjustments are needed at the end of the period (before financial statements are prepared) since the inventory balance is maintained to continually parallel actual counts.

ETHICAL CONSIDERATIONS

Ethical Short-Term Decision Making

When management and executives participate in unethical or fraudulent short-term decision making, it can negatively impact a company on many levels. According to Antonia Chion, Associate Director of the SEC's Division of Enforcement, those who participate in such activities will be held accountable.[5] For example, in 2015, the Securities and Exchange Commission (SEC) charged two former top executives of OCZ Technology Group Inc. for accounting failures.[6] The SEC alleged that OCZ's former CEO Ryan Petersen engaged in a scheme to materially inflate OCZ's revenues and gross margins from 2010 to 2012, and that OCZ's former chief financial officer Arthur Knapp participated in certain accounting, disclosure, and internal accounting controls failures.

Petersen and Knapp allegedly participated in channel stuffing, which is the process of recognizing and recording revenue in a current period that actually will be legally earned in one or more future fiscal periods. A common example is to arrange for customers to submit purchase orders in the current year, often with the understanding that if they don't need the additional inventory then they may return the inventory received or cancel the order if delivery has not occurred.[7] When the intention behind channel stuffing is to mislead investors, it crosses the line into fraudulent practice. This and other unethical short-term accounting decisions made by Petersen and Knapp led to the bankruptcy of the company they were supposed to oversee and resulted in fraud charges from the SEC. Practicing ethical short-term decision making may have prevented both scenarios.

Specific Identification

For demonstration purposes, the specific units assumed to be sold in this period are designated as follows, with the specific inventory distinction being associated with the lot numbers:

- Sold 120 units, all from Lot 1 (beginning inventory), costing $21 per unit
- Sold 180 units, 20 from Lot 1 (beginning inventory), costing $21 per unit; 160 from Lot 2 (July 10 purchase), costing $27 per unit

The specific identification method of cost allocation directly tracks each of the units purchased and costs them out as they are sold. In this demonstration, assume that some sales were made by specifically tracked goods that are part of a lot, as previously stated for this method. For The Spy Who Loves You, the first sale of 120

5 U.S. Securities and Exchange Commission (SEC). "SEC Charges Former Executives with Accounting Fraud and Other Accounting Failures." October 6, 2015. https://www.sec.gov/news/pressrelease/2015-234.html

6 *SEC v. Ryan Petersen*, No. 15-cv-04599 (N.D. Cal. filed October 6, 2015). https://www.sec.gov/litigation/litreleases/2017/lr23874.htm

7 George B. Parizek and Madeleine V. Findley. *Charting a Course: Revenue Recognition Practices for Today's Business Environment*. 2008. https://www.sidley.com/-/media/files/publications/2008/10/charting-a-course-revenue-recognition-practices-__/files/view-article/fileattachment/chartingacourse.pdf

units is assumed to be the units from the beginning inventory, which had cost $21 per unit, bringing the total cost of these units to $2,520. Once those units were sold, there remained 30 more units of the beginning inventory. The company bought 225 more units for $27 per unit. The second sale of 180 units consisted of 20 units at $21 per unit and 160 units at $27 per unit for a total second-sale cost of $4,740. Thus, after two sales, there remained 10 units of inventory that had cost the company $21, and 65 units that had cost the company $27 each. The last transaction was an additional purchase of 210 units for $33 per unit. Ending inventory was made up of 10 units at $21 each, 65 units at $27 each, and 210 units at $33 each, for a total specific identification perpetual ending inventory value of $8,895.

Calculations of Costs of Goods Sold, Ending Inventory, and Gross Margin, Specific Identification

The specific identification costing assumption tracks inventory items individually so that, when they are sold, the exact cost of the item is used to offset the revenue from the sale. The cost of goods sold, inventory, and gross margin shown in Figure 10.13 were determined from the previously-stated data, particular to specific identification costing.

	Cost of Goods Purchased			Cost of Goods Sold			Cost of Inventory Remaining		
	Number of Units	Unit Cost	Total Cost	Number of Units	Unit Cost	Total Cost	Number of Units	Unit Cost	Total Cost
Beginning, Jul. 1							150	$21	$3,150
Sale, Jul. 5				120	$21	$2,520	30	21	630
Purchase, Jul. 10	225	$27	$6,075				30 225	21 27	630 6,075
Sale, Jul. 15				20 160	21 27	420 4,320	30 65	21 27	210 1,755
Purchase, Jul. 25	210	33	6,930				30 65 210	21 27 33	210 1,755 6,930
Total Purchases in Jul.			$13,005	Total COGS		$7,260			

Cost Value:	
10 units at $21	210
65 units at $27	1,755
210 units at $33	6,930
Total	8,895

Figure 10.13 Specific Identification Costing Assumption Cost of Goods Sold, Inventory, and Cost Value. (attribution: Copyright Rice University, OpenStax, under CC BY-NC-SA 4.0 license)

Figure 10.14 shows the gross margin, resulting from the specific identification perpetual cost allocations of $7,260.

Gross Margin	
Sales	$11,340
– Cost of Goods Sold	7,260
= Gross Margin	4,080

(120 × $36) + (180 × $39)

Figure 10.14 Specific Identification Perpetual Cost Allocations Gross Margin. (attribution: Copyright Rice University, OpenStax, under CC BY-NC-SA 4.0 license)

Description of Journal Entries for Inventory Sales, Perpetual, Specific Identification

Journal entries are not shown, but the following discussion provides the information that would be used in recording the necessary journal entries. Each time a product is sold, a revenue entry would be made to record the sales revenue and the corresponding accounts receivable or cash from the sale. Because of the choice to apply perpetual inventory updating, a second entry made at the same time would record the cost of the item based on the actual cost of the items, which would be shifted from merchandise inventory (an asset) to cost of goods sold (an expense).

First-in, First-out (FIFO)

The first-in, first-out method (FIFO) of cost allocation assumes that the earliest units purchased are also the first units sold. For The Spy Who Loves You, using perpetual inventory updating, the first sale of 120 units is assumed to be the units from the beginning inventory, which had cost $21 per unit, bringing the total cost of these units to $2,520. Once those units were sold, there remained 30 more units of beginning inventory. The company bought 225 more units for $27 per unit. At the time of the second sale of 180 units, the FIFO assumption directs the company to cost out the last 30 units of the beginning inventory, plus 150 of the units that had been purchased for $27. Thus, after two sales, there remained 75 units of inventory that had cost the company $27 each. The last transaction was an additional purchase of 210 units for $33 per unit. Ending inventory was made up of 75 units at $27 each, and 210 units at $33 each, for a total FIFO perpetual ending inventory value of $8,955.

Calculations of Costs of Goods Sold, Ending Inventory, and Gross Margin, First-in, First-out (FIFO)

The FIFO costing assumption tracks inventory items based on lots of goods that are tracked, in the order that they were acquired, so that when they are sold the earliest acquired items are used to offset the revenue from the sale. The cost of goods sold, inventory, and gross margin shown in Figure 10.15 were determined from the previously-stated data, particular to perpetual FIFO costing.

	Cost of Goods Purchased			Cost of Goods Sold			Cost of Inventory Remaining		
	Number of Units	Unit Cost	Total Cost	Number of Units	Unit Cost	Total Cost	Number of Units	Unit Cost	Total Cost
Beginning, Jul. 1							150	$21	$3,150
Sale, Jul. 5				120	$21	$2,520	30	21	630
Purchase, Jul. 10	225	$27	$6,075				30 225	21 27	630 6,075
Sale, Jul. 15				30 150	21 27	630 4,050	– 75	– 27	– 2,025
Purchase, Jul. 25	210	33	6,930				75 210	27 33	2,025 6,930
Total Purchases in Jul.			$13,005	Total COGS		$7,200			

Cost Value:	
75 units at $27	2,025
210 units at $33	6,930
Total	8,955

Figure 10.15 FIFO Costing Assumption Cost of Goods Purchased, Cost of Goods Sold, and Cost of Inventory Remaining. (attribution: Copyright Rice University, OpenStax, under CC BY-NC-SA 4.0 license)

Figure 10.16 shows the gross margin, resulting from the FIFO perpetual cost allocations of $7,200.

Gross Margin	
Sales	11,340
– Cost of Goods Sold	7,200
= Gross Margin	4,140

Figure 10.16 FIFO Perpetual Cost Allocations Gross Margin. (attribution: Copyright Rice University, OpenStax, under CC BY-NC-SA 4.0 license)

Description of Journal Entries for Inventory Sales, Perpetual, First-in, First-out (FIFO)

Journal entries are not shown, but the following discussion provides the information that would be used in recording the necessary journal entries. Each time a product is sold, a revenue entry would be made to record the sales revenue and the corresponding accounts receivable or cash from the sale. When applying perpetual inventory updating, a second entry made at the same time would record the cost of the item based on FIFO, which would be shifted from merchandise inventory (an asset) to cost of goods sold (an expense).

Last-in, First-out (LIFO)

The last-in, first-out method (LIFO) of cost allocation assumes that the last units purchased are the first units sold. For The Spy Who Loves You, using perpetual inventory updating, the first sale of 120 units is assumed to be the units from the beginning inventory (because this was the only lot of good available, so it represented the last purchased lot), which had cost $21 per unit, bringing the total cost of these units in the first sale to $2,520. Once those units were sold, there remained 30 more units of beginning inventory. The company bought 225 more units for $27 per unit. At the time of the second sale of 180 units, the LIFO assumption directs the company to cost out the 180 units from the latest purchased units, which had cost $27 for a total cost on the second sale of $4,860. Thus, after two sales, there remained 30 units of beginning inventory that had cost the company $21 each, plus 45 units of the goods purchased for $27 each. The last transaction was an additional purchase of 210 units for $33 per unit. Ending inventory was made up of 30 units at $21 each, 45 units at $27 each, and 210 units at $33 each, for a total LIFO perpetual ending inventory value of $8,775.

Calculations of Costs of Goods Sold, Ending Inventory, and Gross Margin, Last-in, First-out (LIFO)

The LIFO costing assumption tracks inventory items based on lots of goods that are tracked in the order that they were acquired, so that when they are sold, the latest acquired items are used to offset the revenue from the sale. The following cost of goods sold, inventory, and gross margin were determined from the previously-stated data, particular to perpetual, LIFO costing.

	Cost of Goods Purchased			Cost of Goods Sold			Cost of Inventory Remaining		
	Number of Units	Unit Cost	Total Cost	Number of Units	Unit Cost	Total Cost	Number of Units	Unit Cost	Total Cost
Beginning, Jul. 1							150	$21	$3,150
Sale, Jul. 5				120	$21	$2,520	30	21	630
Purchase, Jul. 10	225	$27	$6,075				30 225	21 27	630 6,075
Sale, Jul. 15				180	27	4,860	30 45	21 27	630 1,215
Purchase, Jul. 25	210	$33	6,930				30 45 210	21 27 33	630 1,215 6,930
Total Purchases in Jul.			$13,005	Total COGS		$7,380			

Cost Value:	
30 units at $21	$ 630
45 units at $27	1,215
210 units at $33	6,930
Total	8,775

Figure 10.17 LIFO Costing Assumption Cost of Goods Purchased, Cost of Goods Sold, and Cost of Inventory Remaining. (attribution: Copyright Rice University, OpenStax, under CC BY-NC-SA 4.0 license)

Figure 10.18 shows the gross margin resulting from the LIFO perpetual cost allocations of $7,380.

Gross Margin	
Sales	11,340
- Cost of Goods Sold	7,380
= Gross Margin	3,960

Figure 10.18 LIFO Perpetual Cost Allocations Gross Margin. (attribution: Copyright Rice University, OpenStax, under CC BY-NC-SA 4.0 license)

Description of Journal Entries for Inventory Sales, Perpetual, Last-in, First-out (LIFO)

Journal entries are not shown, but the following discussion provides the information that would be used in recording the necessary journal entries. Each time a product is sold, a revenue entry would be made to record the sales revenue and the corresponding accounts receivable or cash from the sale. When applying apply perpetual inventory updating, a second entry made at the same time would record the cost of the item based on LIFO, which would be shifted from merchandise inventory (an asset) to cost of goods sold (an expense).

LINK TO LEARNING

Visit this Amazon inventory video for a little insight into some of the inventory challenges experienced by retail giant Amazon (https://openstax.org/l/50Amazon) to learn more.

Weighted-Average Cost (AVG)

Weighted-average cost allocation requires computation of the average cost of all units in goods available for sale at the time the sale is made for perpetual inventory calculations. For The Spy Who Loves You, the first sale of 120 units is assumed to be the units from the beginning inventory (because this was the only lot of good available, so the price of these units also represents the average cost), which had cost $21 per unit, bringing the total cost of these units in the first sale to $2,520. Once those units were sold, there remained 30 more units of the inventory, which still had a $21 average cost. The company bought 225 more units for $27 per unit. Recalculating the average cost, after this purchase, is accomplished by dividing total cost of goods available for sale (which totaled $6,705 at that point) by the number of units held, which was 255 units, for an average cost of $26.29 per unit. At the time of the second sale of 180 units, the AVG assumption directs the company to cost out the 180 at $26.29 for a total cost on the second sale of $4,732. Thus, after two sales, there remained 75 units at an average cost of $26.29 each. The last transaction was an additional purchase of 210 units for $33 per unit. Recalculating the average cost again resulted in an average cost of $31.24 per unit. Ending inventory was made up of 285 units at $31.24 each for a total AVG perpetual ending inventory value of $8,902 (rounded).[8]

Calculations of Costs of Goods Sold, Ending Inventory, and Gross Margin, Weighted Average (AVG)

The AVG costing assumption tracks inventory items based on lots of goods that are combined and re-averaged after each new acquisition to determine a new average cost per unit so that, when they are sold, the latest averaged cost items are used to offset the revenue from the sale. The cost of goods sold, inventory, and gross margin shown in Figure 10.19 were determined from the previously-stated data, particular to perpetual, AVG costing.

8 Note that there is a $1 rounding difference due to the rounding of cents inherent in the cost determination chain process.

	Cost of Goods Purchased			Cost of Goods Sold			Cost of Inventory Remaining		
	Number of Units	Unit Cost	Total Cost	Number of Units	Unit Cost	Total Cost	Number of Units	Unit Cost	Total Cost
Beginning							150	$21.00	$3,150
Sale				120	$21.00	$2,520	30	21.00	630
Purchase	225	$27.00	$6,075				255	26.29	6,705
Sale				180	26.29	4,733	75	26.29	1,972
Purchase	210	33.00	6,930				285	31.24	8,902
Total Purchases			$13,005	Total COGS		$7,253			

Cost Value:	
285 units at $31.24	$8,902
Total	8,902

Figure 10.19 AVG Costing Assumption Cost of Goods Purchased, Cost of Goods Sold, and Cost of Inventory Remaining. (attribution: Copyright Rice University, OpenStax, under CC BY-NC-SA 4.0 license)

Figure 10.20 shows the gross margin, resulting from the weighted-average perpetual cost allocations of $7,253.

Gross Margin:	
Sales	$11,340
– Cost of Goods Sold	7,253
= Gross Margin	4,087

Figure 10.20 Weighted AVG Perpetual Cost Allocations Gross Margin. (attribution: Copyright Rice University, OpenStax, under CC BY-NC-SA 4.0 license)

Description of Journal Entries for Inventory Sales, Perpetual, Weighted Average (AVG)

Journal entries are not shown, but the following discussion provides the information that would be used in recording the necessary journal entries. Each time a product is sold, a revenue entry would be made to record the sales revenue and the corresponding accounts receivable or cash from the sale. When applying perpetual inventory updating, a second entry would be made at the same time to record the cost of the item based on the AVG costing assumptions, which would be shifted from merchandise inventory (an asset) to cost of goods sold (an expense).

Comparison of All Four Methods, Perpetual

The outcomes for gross margin, under each of these different cost assumptions, is summarized in Figure 10.21.

	Sp ID	FIFO	LIFO	AVG
Sales Revenue	$11,340	$11,340	$11,340	$11,340
- Cost	7,260	7,200	7,380	7,253
= Gross Margin	4,080	4,140	3,960	4,087

Figure 10.21 Gross Margin Comparison. (attribution: Copyright Rice University, OpenStax, under CC BY-NC-SA 4.0 license)

THINK IT THROUGH

Last-in, First-out (LIFO)

Two-part consideration: 1) Why do you think a company would ever choose to use perpetual LIFO as its costing method? It is clearly more trouble to calculate than other methods and doesn't really align with the natural flow of the merchandise, in most cases. 2) Should the order in which the items are actually sold determine which costs are used to offset sales revenues from those goods? Explain your understanding of these issues.

10.4 Explain and Demonstrate the Impact of Inventory Valuation Errors on the Income Statement and Balance Sheet

Because of the dynamic relationship between cost of goods sold and merchandise inventory, errors in inventory counts have a direct and significant impact on the financial statements of the company. Errors in inventory valuation cause mistaken values to be reported for merchandise inventory and cost of goods sold due to the toggle effect that changes in either one of the two accounts have on the other. As explained, the company has a finite amount of inventory that they can work with during a given period of business operations, such as a year. This limited quantity of goods is known as goods available for sale and is sourced from

1. beginning inventory (unsold goods left over from the previous period's operations); and
2. purchases of additional inventory during the current period.

These available inventory items (goods available for sale) will be handled in one of two ways:

1. be sold to customers (normally) or be lost due to shrinkage, spoilage, or theft (occasionally), and reported as cost of goods sold on the income statement; OR
2. be unsold and held in ending inventory, to be passed into the next period, and reported as merchandise inventory on the balance sheet.

Fundamentals of the Impact of Inventory Valuation Errors on the Income Statement and Balance Sheet

Understanding this interaction between inventory assets (merchandise inventory balances) and inventory expense (cost of goods sold) highlights the impact of errors. Errors in the valuation of ending merchandise inventory, which is on the balance sheet, produce an equivalent corresponding error in the company's cost of goods sold for the period, which is on the income statement. When cost of goods sold is overstated, inventory and net income are understated. When cost of goods sold is understated, inventory and net income are overstated. Further, an error in ending inventory carries into the next period, since ending inventory of one period becomes the beginning inventory of the next period, causing both the balance sheet and the income statement values to be wrong in year two as well as in the year of the error. Over a two-year period, misstatements of ending inventory will balance themselves out. For example, an overstatement to ending inventory overstates net income, but next year, since ending inventory becomes beginning inventory, it understates net income. So over a two-year period, this corrects itself. However, financial statements are prepared for one period, so all this means is that two years of cost of goods sold are misstated (the first year is overstated/understated, and the second year is understated/overstated.)

In periodic inventory systems, inventory errors commonly arise from careless oversight of physical counts. Another common cause of periodic inventory errors results from management neglecting to take the physical count. Both perpetual and periodic updating inventory systems also face potential errors relating to ownership transfers during transportation (relating to FOB shipping point and FOB destination terms); losses in value due to shrinkage, theft, or obsolescence; and consignment inventory, the goods for which should never be included in the retailer's inventory but should be recorded as an asset of the consignor, who remains the legal owner of the goods until they are sold.

Calculated Income Statement and Balance Sheet Effects for Two Years

Let's return to The Spy Who Loves You Company dataset to demonstrate the effects of an inventory error on the company's balance sheet and income statement. Example 1 (shown in Figure 10.22) depicts the balance sheet and income statement toggle when no inventory error is present. Example 2 (see Figure 10.23) shows the balance sheet and income statement inventory toggle, in a case when a $1,500 understatement error occurred at the end of year 1.

	Balance Sheet Year 1	Income Statement Year 1	Balance Sheet Year 2	Income Statement Year 2
Sales		$11,340		$12,474
Beginning Inventory	$ 3,150		$ 8,955	
+ Purchases	13,005		8,816	
= Goods Available for Sale	16,155		17,771	
- Ending Inventory	8,955		9,851	
= Cost of Goods Sold		7,200		7,920
Gross Margin		4,140		4,554
All other expenses		3,000		3,000
Net Income		1,140		1,554
Note: Year 2 correctly stated values for Sales, Goods Available, and Ending Inventory were estimated, based on 110% of Year 1's amounts.				

Figure 10.22 Example 1. Assume these values to be correct (no inventory error). This chart shows excerpted values from The Spy Who Loves You Company's financial statements without inventory errors. (attribution: Copyright Rice University, OpenStax, under CC BY-NC-SA 4.0 license)

	Balance Sheet Year 1	Income Statement Year 1	Balance Sheet Year 2	Income Statement Year 2
Sales		$11,340		$12,474
Beginning Inventory	$ 3,150		$ 7,455	
+ Purchases	13,005		8,816	
= Goods Available for Sale	16,155		16,271	
– Ending Inventory (understated by $1,500)	7,455		8,201	
= Cost of Goods Sold		8,700		6,420
Gross Margin		2,640		6,054
All other expenses		3,000		3,000
Net Income		(360)		3,054

Note: Year 2 correctly stated values for Sales, Goods Available, and Ending Inventory were estimated, based on 110% of Year 1's amounts.

Figure 10.23 Example 2. Assume these values to be incorrect (with inventory error). This chart shows excerpted values from The Spy Who Loves You Company's financial statements with inventory errors. (attribution: Copyright Rice University, OpenStax, under CC BY-NC-SA 4.0 license)

Comparing the two examples with and without the inventory error highlights the significant effect the error had on the net results reported on the balance sheet and income statements for the two years. Users of financial statements make important business and personal decisions based on the data they receive from the statements and errors of this sort provide those users with faulty information that could negatively affect the quality of their decisions. In these examples, the combined net income was identical for the two years and the error worked itself out at the end of the second year, yet year 1 and year 2 were incorrect and not representative of the true activity of the business for those periods of time. Extreme care should be taken to value inventories accurately.

10.5 Examine the Efficiency of Inventory Management Using Financial Ratios

Inventory is a large investment for many companies so it is important that this asset be managed wisely. Too little inventory means lost sales opportunities, whereas too much inventory means unproductive investment of resources as well as extra costs related to storage, care, and protection of the inventory. Ratio analysis is used to measure how well management is doing at maintaining just the right amount of inventory for the needs of their particular business.

Once calculated, these ratios should be compared to previous years' ratios for the company, direct competitors' ratios, industry ratios, and other industries' ratios. The insights gained from the ratio analysis should be used to augment analysis of the general strength and stability of the company, with the full data available in the annual report, including financial statements and notes to the financial statement.

Fundamentals of Inventory Ratios

Inventory ratio analysis relates to how well the inventory is being managed. Two ratios can be used to assess how efficiently management is handling inventory. The first ratio, inventory turnover, measures the number of times an average quantity of inventory was bought and sold during the period. The second ratio, number of days' sales in inventory, measures how many days it takes to complete the cycle between buying and selling inventory.

Calculating and Interpreting the Inventory Turnover Ratio

Inventory turnover ratio is computed by dividing cost of goods sold by average inventory. The ratio measures the number of times inventory rotated through the sales cycle for the period. Let's review how this works for The Spy Who Loves You dataset. This example scenario relates to the FIFO periodic cost allocation, using those previously calculated values for year 1 cost of goods sold, beginning inventory, and ending inventory, and assuming a 10% increase in inventory activity for year 2, as shown in Figure 10.24.

	Balance Sheet Year 1	Income Statement Year 1	Balance Sheet Year 2	Income Statement Year 2
Beginning Inventory	$ 3,150		$ 8,955	
+ Purchases	13,005		8,816	
= Goods Available for Sale	16,155		17,771	
– Ending Inventory	8,955		9,851	
= Cost of Goods Sold		7,200		7,920
Note: Year 2 values for Sales, Goods Available, and Ending Inventory were estimated, based on 110% of Year 1's amounts.				

Figure 10.24 Excerpts from Financial Statements of The Spy Who Loves You Company. (attribution: Copyright Rice University, OpenStax, under CC BY-NC-SA 4.0 license)

The inventory turnover ratio is calculated by dividing cost of goods sold by average inventory. The result for the Spy Who Loves You Company indicates that the inventory cycled through the sales cycle 1.19 times in year 1, and 0.84 times in year 2.

Inventory Turnover Ratio	Year 1	Year 2
Cost of Goods Sold	$7,200	$7,920
/ Average Inventory*	6,053	9,403
= Inventory Turnover	1.19	0.84
** Average Inventory Year 1 = (3,150 + 8,955) / 2; Average Inventory Year 2 = (8,955 + 9,851) / 2*		

The fact that the year 2 inventory turnover ratio is lower than the year 1 ratio is not a positive trend. This result would alert management that the inventory balance might be too high to be practical for this volume of sales. Comparison should also be made to competitor and industry ratios, while consideration should also be given to other factors affecting the company's financial health as well as the strength of the overall market economy.

Calculating and Interpreting the Days' Sales in Inventory Ratio

Number of days' sales in inventory ratio is computed by dividing average merchandise inventory by the average daily cost of goods sold. The ratio measures the number of days it would take to clear the remaining inventory. Let's review this using The Spy Who Loves You dataset. The example scenario relates to the FIFO periodic cost allocation, using those previously calculated values for year 1 cost of goods sold, beginning inventory, and ending inventory, and assuming a 10% increase in inventory activity for year 2, as in Figure 10.25.

	Balance Sheet Year 1	Income Statement Year 1	Balance Sheet Year 2	Income Statement Year 2
Beginning Inventory	$ 3,150		$ 8,955	
+ Purchases	13,005		8,816	
= Goods Available for Sale	16,155		17,771	
– Ending Inventory	8,955		9,851	
= Cost of Goods Sold		$7,200		$7,920

Note: Year 2 values for Sales, Goods Available, and Ending Inventory were estimated, based on 110% of Year 1's amounts.

Figure 10.25 Excerpts from Financial Statements of The Spy Who Loves You Company. (attribution: Copyright Rice University, OpenStax, under CC BY-NC-SA 4.0 license)

The number of days' sales in inventory ratio is calculated by dividing average inventory by average daily cost of goods sold. The result for the Spy Who Loves You indicates that it would take about 307 days to clear the average inventory held in year 1 and about 433 days to clear the average inventory held in year 2.

Number of Days' Sales in Inventory Ratio	Year 1	Year 2
Average Inventory*	$ 6,053	$ 9,403
/ Average Daily Cost of Goods Sold**	19.73	21.70
= Days' Sales in Inventory	306.79	433.32

** Average Inventory Year 1 = (3,150 + 8,955) / 2; Average Inventory Year 2 = (8,955 + 9,851) / 2*
*** Average Daily COGS Year 1 = (7,200 / 365): Average Daily COGS Year 2 = (7,920 / 365)*

Year 2's number of days' sales in inventory ratio increased over year 1's ratio results, indicating an unfavorable change. This result would alert management that it is taking much too long to sell the inventory, so reduction in the inventory balance might be appropriate, or as an alternative, increased sales efforts could turn the ratio toward a more positive trend. This ratio is useful to identify cases of obsolescence, which is especially prevalent in an evolving market, such as the technology sector of the economy. As with any ratio, comparison should also be made to competitor and industry ratios, while consideration should also be given to other factors affecting the company's financial health, as well as to the strength of the overall market economy.

LINK TO LEARNING

Check out Investopedia for help with calculation and analysis of ratios and their discussion about the inventory turnover ratio (https://openstax.org/l/50TurnoverRatio) to learn more.

Key Terms

conservatism concept that if there is uncertainty in a potential financial estimate, a company should err on the side of caution and report the most conservative amount

consignment arrangement whereby goods are available to sell by one party, but owned by another party, without transfer of ownership

consistency principle accounting methods applied in a like manner, across multiple periods, allow for contrast and comparison between periods

first-in, first-out method (FIFO) inventory cost allocation method that assumes the earliest acquired inventory items are the first to be sold

FOB destination point transportation terms whereby the seller transfers ownership and financial responsibility at the time of delivery

FOB shipping point transportation terms whereby the seller transfers ownership and financial responsibility at the time of shipment

goods available for sale total of all inventory (beginning inventory plus purchased inventory); will either be sold this period or held in period-end inventory

gross profit net profit from sale of goods; sales revenue minus cost of goods sold

gross profit method inventory estimation tool that uses a company's usual gross profit percentage, related to total sales revenue, to estimate the cost of the ending inventory

inventory turnover ratio computed by dividing cost of goods sold by average inventory; measures number of times inventory rotated through the sales cycle for the period

last-in, first-out method (LIFO) inventory cost allocation method that assumes the latest acquired inventory items are the first to sell

lower-of-cost-or-market (LCM) conservatism-based concept that mandates inventory be reported at the lower of the value of inventory reflected in the general ledger or replacement value

merchandise inventory goods held for sale at a given point in the period

number of days' sales in inventory ratio computed by dividing average merchandise inventory by average daily cost of goods sold; measures number of days it would take to clear remaining inventory

periodic inventory system system that is updated at the end of the period, to match the physical count of goods on hand

perpetual inventory system system that automatically updates and records the inventory account every time a sale or purchase of inventory occurs

purchases new acquisitions of merchandise inventory during the period

retail inventory method inventory estimation tool that uses a company's usual gross profit percentage, related to total sales revenue, to estimate the retail value of the ending inventory, which can then be reduced to an estimated cost figure

specific identification method inventory cost allocation method that traces actual cost of each specific item, whether sold or held in inventory; usually used for customized or differentiated products

weighted-average method inventory cost allocation method that calculates the average value inventory items by weighting each purchase lot's goods available for sale, before dividing by the total number of units of that item

Summary

10.1 Describe and Demonstrate the Basic Inventory Valuation Methods and Their Cost Flow Assumptions

- The total cost of goods available for sale is a combination of the beginning inventory plus new inventory purchases. These costs relating to goods available for sale are included in the ending inventory, reported on the balance sheet, or become part of the cost of goods sold reported on the income statement.
- Merchandise inventory is maintained using either the periodic or the perpetual updating system. Periodic updating is performed at the end of the period only, whereas perpetual updating is an ongoing activity that maintains inventory records that are approximately equal to the actual inventory on hand at any time.
- There are four basic inventory cost flow allocation methods, which are alternative ways to estimate the cost of the units that are sold and the value of the ending inventory. The costing methods are not indicative of the flow of the goods, which often moves in a different order than the flow of the costs.
- Utilizing different cost allocation options results in marked differences in reported cost of goods sold, net income, and inventory balances.

10.2 Calculate the Cost of Goods Sold and Ending Inventory Using the Periodic Method

- The periodic inventory system updates inventory at the end of a fixed accounting period. During the accounting period, inventory records are not changed, and at the end of the period, inventory records are adjusted for what was sold and added during the period.
- Companies using the periodic and perpetual method for inventory updating choose between the basic four cost flow assumption methods, which are first-in, first-out (FIFO); last-in, first-out (LIFO); specific identification (SI); and weighted average (AVG).
- Periodic inventory systems are still used in practice, but the prevalence of their use has greatly diminished, with advances in technology and as prices for inventory management software have significantly decreased.

10.3 Calculate the Cost of Goods Sold and Ending Inventory Using the Perpetual Method

- Perpetual inventory systems maintain inventory balance in the company records in a real-time or slightly delayed, continuously updated state. No significant adjustments are needed at the end of the period, before issuing the financial statements.
- Companies using the perpetual method for inventory updating choose between the basic four cost flow assumption methods, which are first-in, first-out (FIFO); last-in, first-out (LIFO); specific identification (SI); and weighted average (AVG).
- Most modern inventory systems utilize the perpetual inventory system, due to the benefits it offers for efficiency, ease of operation, availability of real-time updating, and accuracy.

10.4 Explain and Demonstrate the Impact of Inventory Valuation Errors on the Income Statement and Balance Sheet

- The value for cost of the goods available for sale is dependent on accurate beginning and ending inventory numbers. Because of the interrelationship between inventory values and cost of goods sold, when the inventory values are incorrect, the associated income statement and balance sheet accounts are also incorrect.
- Inventory errors at the beginning of a reporting period affect only the income statement. Overstatements of beginning inventory result in overstated cost of goods sold and understated net income. Conversely, understatements of beginning inventory result in understated cost of goods sold and overstated net income.
- Inventory errors at the end of a reporting period affect both the income statement and the balance sheet. Overstatements of ending inventory result in understated cost of goods sold, overstated net income, overstated assets, and overstated equity. Conversely, understatements of ending inventory result in overstated cost of goods sold, understated net income, understated assets, and understated equity.

10.5 Examine the Efficiency of Inventory Management Using Financial Ratios

- Inventory ratio analysis tools help management to identify inefficient management practices and pinpoint troublesome scenarios within their inventory operations processes.
- The inventory turnover ratio measures how fast the inventory sells, which can be useful for inter-period comparison as well as comparisons with competitor firms.
- The number of days' sales in inventory ratio indicates how long it takes for inventory to be sold, on average, which can help the firm identify instances of too much or too little inventory, indicating such cases as product obsolescence or excess stocking, or the reverse scenario: insufficient inventory, which could result in customer dissatisfaction and lost sales.

Multiple Choice

1. LO 10.1 If a company has four lots of products for sale, purchase 1 (earliest) for $17, purchase 2 (middle) for $15, purchase 3 (middle) for $12, and purchase 4 (latest) for $14, which cost would be assumed to be sold first using LIFO costing?

A. $17

B. $15

C. $12

D. $14

2. LO 10.1 If a company has three lots of products for sale, purchase 1 (earliest) for $17, purchase 2 (middle) for $15, purchase 3 (latest) for $12, which of the following statements is true?

A. This is an inflationary cost pattern.

B. This is a deflationary cost pattern.

C. The next purchase will cost less than $12.

D. None of these statements can be verified.

3. LO 10.1 When inventory items are highly specialized, the best inventory costing method is ________.

A. specific identification

B. first-in, first-out

C. last-in, first-out

D. weighted average

4. LO 10.1 If goods are shipped FOB destination, which of the following is true?

A. Title to the goods will transfer as soon as the goods are shipped.

B. FOB indicates that a price reduction has been applied to the order.

C. The seller must pay the shipping.

D. The seller and the buyer will each pay 50% of the cost.

5. LO 10.1 On which financial statement would the merchandise inventory account appear?

A. balance sheet

B. income statement

C. both balance sheet and income statement

D. neither balance sheet nor income statement

6. LO 10.1 When would using the FIFO inventory costing method produce higher inventory account balances than the LIFO method would?

A. inflationary times
B. deflationary times
C. always
D. never

7. LO 10.1 Which accounting rule serves as the primary basis for the lower-of-cost-or-market methodology for inventory valuation?

A. conservatism
B. consistency
C. optimism
D. pessimism

8. LO 10.1 Which type or types of inventory timing system (periodic or perpetual) requires the user to record two journal entries every time a sale is made.

A. periodic
B. perpetual
C. both periodic and perpetual
D. neither periodic nor perpetual

9. LO 10.2 Which of these statements is false?

A. If cost of goods sold is incorrect, ending inventory is usually incorrect too.
B. beginning inventory + purchases = cost of goods sold
C. ending inventory + cost of goods sold = goods available for sale
D. goods available for sale – beginning inventory = purchases

10. LO 10.3 Which inventory costing method is almost always done on a perpetual basis?

A. specific identification
B. first-in, first-out
C. last-in, first-out
D. weighted average

11. LO 10.3 Which of the following describes features of a perpetual inventory system?

A. Technology is normally used to record inventory changes.
B. Merchandise bought is recorded as purchases.
C. An adjusting journal entry is required at year end, to match physical counts to the asset account.
D. Inventory is updated at the end of the period.

12. LO 10.4 Which of the following financial statements would be impacted by a current-year ending inventory error, when using a periodic inventory updating system?

A. balance sheet
B. income statement
C. neither statement
D. both statements

13. LO 10.4 Which of the following would cause periodic ending inventory to be overstated?
   A. Goods held on consignment are omitted from the physical count.
   B. Goods purchased and delivered, but not yet paid for, are included in the physical count.
   C. Purchased goods shipped FOB destination and not yet delivered are included in the physical count.
   D. None of the above

14. LO 10.5 Which of the following indicates a positive trend for inventory management?
   A. increasing number of days' sales in inventory ratio
   B. increasing inventory turnover ratio
   C. increasing cost of goods sold
   D. increasing sales revenue

Questions

1. LO 10.1 What is meant by the term *gross margin*?

2. LO 10.1 Can a business change from one inventory costing method to another any time they wish? Explain.

3. LO 10.1 Why do consignment arrangements present a challenge in inventory management? Explain.

4. LO 10.1 Explain the difference between the terms *FOB destination* and *FOB shipping point*.

5. LO 10.1 When would a company use the specific identification method of inventory cost allocation?

6. LO 10.1 Explain why a company might want to utilize the gross profit method or the retail inventory method for inventory valuation.

7. LO 10.1 Describe the goal of the lower-of-cost-or-market concept.

8. LO 10.1 Describe two separate and distinct ways to calculate goods available for sale.

9. LO 10.3 Describe costing inventory using first-in, first-out. Address the different treatment, if any, that must be given for periodic and perpetual inventory updating.

10. LO 10.3 Describe costing inventory using last-in, first-out. Address the different treatment, if any, that must be given for periodic and perpetual inventory updating.

11. LO 10.3 Describe costing inventory using weighted average. Address the different treatment, if any, that must be given for periodic and perpetual inventory updating.

12. LO 10.4 How long does it take an inventory error affecting ending inventory to correct itself in the financial statements? Explain.

13. LO 10.4 What type of issues would arise that might cause inventory errors?

14. LO 10.5 Explain the difference between the flow of cost and the flow of goods as it relates to inventory.

15. LO 10.5 What insights can be gained from inventory ratio analysis, such as inventory turnover ratio and number of days' sales in inventory ratio?

Exercise Set A

EA1. LO 10.1 Calculate the goods available for sale for Atlantis Company, in units and in dollar amounts, given the following facts about their inventory for the period:

	Number of Units	Cost per Unit
Beginning inventory	140	$75
Purchased goods during the period	240	77
Sold goods during the period	80	125
Purchased goods during the period	220	80

EA2. LO 10.1 E Company accepts goods on consignment from R Company and also purchases goods from S Company during the current month. E Company plans to sell the merchandise to customers during the following month. In each of these independent situations, who owns the merchandise at the end of the current month and should therefore include it in their company's ending inventory? Choose E, R, or S.

A. Goods ordered from R, delivered and displayed on E's showroom floor at the end of the current month.
B. Goods ordered from S, in transit, with shipping terms FOB destination.
C. Goods ordered from R, in transit, with no stated shipping terms.
D. Goods ordered from S, delivered and displayed on E's showroom floor at the end of the current month, with shipping terms FOB destination.
E. Goods ordered from S, in transit, with shipping terms FOB shipping point.

EA3. LO 10.1 The following information is taken from a company's records. Applying the lower-of-cost-or-market approach, what is the correct value that should be reported on the balance sheet for the inventory?

	Cost per Unit	Market Value per Unit
Inventory item 1 (10 units)	$36	$35
Inventory item 2 (25 units)	20	20
Inventory item 3 (12 units)	6	8

EA4. LO 10.2 Complete the missing piece of information involving the changes in inventory, and their relationship to goods available for sale, for the two years shown:

	2021	2022
Beginning inventory	$10,000	$7,000
Purchases	25,000	3,000
Goods available for sale	35,000	
Ending inventory	7,000	
Cost of goods sold		8,500

EA5. LO 10.2 Akira Company had the following transactions for the month.

	Number of Units	Cost per Unit
Beginning inventory	150	$10
Purchased Mar. 31	160	12
Purchased Oct. 15	130	15
Ending inventory	50	?

Calculate the ending inventory dollar value for the period for each of the following cost allocation methods, using periodic inventory updating. Provide your calculations.

A. first-in, first-out (FIFO)
B. last-in, first-out (LIFO)
C. weighted average (AVG)

EA6. LO 10.2 Akira Company had the following transactions for the month.

	Number of Units	Cost per Unit
Beginning inventory	150	$1,500
Purchased Mar. 31	160	1,920
Purchased Oct. 15	130	1,950
Total goods available for sale	440	5,370
Ending inventory	50	?

Calculate the gross margin for the period for each of the following cost allocation methods, using periodic inventory updating. Assume that all units were sold for $25 each. Provide your calculations.

A. first-in, first-out (FIFO)
B. last-in, first-out (LIFO)
C. weighted average (AVG)

EA7. LO 10.2 Prepare journal entries to record the following transactions, assuming periodic inventory updating and first-in, first-out (FIFO) cost allocation.

	Number of Units	Cost per Unit
Jan. 2, purchased merchandise for resale	300	$21
Jan. 12, purchased merchandise for resale	200	24
Jan. 16, sold merchandise for $40 per unit	220	

EA8. LO 10.3 Calculate the cost of goods sold dollar value for A65 Company for the month, considering the following transactions under three different cost allocation methods and using perpetual inventory updating. Provide calculations for first-in, first-out (FIFO).

	Number of Units	Unit Cost	Sales
Beginning inventory	800	$50	
Purchased	600	52	
Sold	400		$80
Sold	350		90
Ending inventory	650		

EA9. LO 10.3 Calculate the cost of goods sold dollar value for A66 Company for the month, considering the following transactions under three different cost allocation methods and using perpetual inventory updating. Provide calculations for last-in, first-out (LIFO).

	Number of Units	Unit Cost	Sales
Beginning inventory	800	$50	
Purchased	600	52	
Sold	400		$80
Sold	350		90
Ending inventory	650		

EA10. LO 10.3 Calculate the cost of goods sold dollar value for A67 Company for the month, considering the following transactions under three different cost allocation methods and using perpetual inventory updating. Provide calculations for weighted average (AVG).

	Number of Units	Unit Cost	Sales
Beginning inventory	800	$50	
Purchased	600	52	
Sold	400		$80
Sold	350		90
Ending inventory	650		

EA11. LO 10.3 Prepare journal entries to record the following transactions, assuming perpetual inventory updating and first-in, first-out (FIFO) cost allocation. Assume no beginning inventory.

	Number of Units	Unit Cost
Jan. 2, purchased merchandise for resale	300	$21
Jan. 12, purchased merchandise for resale	200	24
Jan. 16, sold merchandise for $40 per unit	220	

EA12. LO 10.3 Prepare Journal entries to record the following transactions, assuming perpetual inventory updating, and last-in, first-out (LIFO) cost allocation. Assume no beginning inventory.

	Number of Units	Unit Cost
Mar. 12, purchased merchandise for resale	5,000	$ 90
Mar. 15, purchased merchandise for resale	3,500	100
Mar. 16, sold merchandise for $200 per unit	2,000	

EA13. LO 10.4 If a group of inventory items costing $15,000 had been omitted from the year-end inventory count, what impact would the error have on the following inventory calculations? Indicate the effect (and amount) as either (a) none, (b) understated $_____, or (c) overstated $_____.

Inventory Item	None or amount?	Understated or overstated?
Beginning Inventory		
Purchases		
Goods Available for Sale		
Ending Inventory		
Cost of Goods Sold		

Table 10.1

EA14. LO 10.4 If Wakowski Company's ending inventory was actually $86,000 but was adjusted at year end to a balance of $68,000 in error, what would be the impact on the presentation of the balance sheet and income statement for the year that the error occurred, if any?

EA15. LO 10.4 Shetland Company reported net income on the year-end financial statements of $125,000. However, errors in inventory were discovered after the reports were issued. If inventory was understated by $15,000, how much net income did the company actually earn?

EA16. LO 10.5 Compute Altoona Company's (a) inventory turnover ratio and (b) number of days' sales in inventory ratio, using the following information.

Cost of goods sold	$722,000
Beginning inventory	53,000
Ending inventory	67,000

EA17. LO 10.5 Complete the missing pieces of McCarthy Company's inventory calculations and ratios.

Beginning inventory	?
Purchases	$ 92,000
Goods available for sale	100,500
Ending inventory	9,400
Cost of goods sold	91,100
Turnover ratio	?
Days' sales in inventory	?

Exercise Set B

EB1. LO 10.1 Calculate the goods available for sale for Soros Company, in units and in $ (dollar amounts), given the following facts about their inventory for the period.

	Number of Units	Cost per Unit
Beginning inventory	1,100	$20
Purchased goods during the period	800	20
Sold goods during the period	700	37
Purchased goods during the period	650	21

EB2. LO 10.1 X Company accepts goods on consignment from C Company, and also purchases goods from P Company during the current month. X Company plans to sell the merchandise to customers during the following month. In each of these independent situations, who owns the merchandise at the end of the current month, and should therefore include it in their company's ending inventory? Choose X, C, or P.

A. Goods ordered from P, in transit, with shipping terms FOB destination.
B. Goods ordered from P, in transit, with shipping terms FOB shipping point.
C. Goods ordered from P, inventory in stock, held in storage until floor space is available.
D. Goods ordered from C, inventory in stock, set aside for customer pickup and payments to finalize sale.

EB3. LO 10.1 Considering the following information, and applying the lower-of-cost-or-market approach, what is the correct value that should be reported on the balance sheet for the inventory?

	Cost per unit	Market Value per Unit
Inventory item 1 (20 units)	$100	$95
Inventory item 2 (30 units)	75	70
Inventory item 3 (45 units)	50	55

EB4. LO 10.2 Complete the missing piece of information involving the changes in inventory, and their relationship to goods available for sale, for the two years shown.

	2021	2022
Beginning inventory		$200,000
Purchases	$700,000	
Goods available for sale	875,000	388,500
Ending inventory		75,000
Cost of goods sold	675,000	313,500

EB5. LO 10.2 Bleistine Company had the following transactions for the month.

	Number of Units	Cost per Unit
Beginning inventory	880	$35
Purchased Jun. 1	750	40
Purchased Nov. 1	800	43
Ending inventory	110	?

Calculate the ending inventory dollar value for each of the following cost allocation methods, using periodic inventory updating. Provide your calculations.

A. first-in, first-out (FIFO)
B. last-in, first-out (LIFO)
C. weighted average (AVG)

EB6. LO 10.2 Bleistine Company had the following transactions for the month.

	Number of Units	Cost per Unit
Beginning inventory	880	$30,800
Purchased Jun. 1	750	30,000
Purchased Nov. 1	800	34,400
Total goods available for sale	2,430	95,200
Ending inventory	110	?

Calculate the gross margin for the period for each of the following cost allocation methods, using periodic inventory updating. Assume that all units were sold for $50 each. Provide your calculations.

A. first-in, first-out (FIFO)
B. last-in, first-out (LIFO)
C. weighted average (AVG)

EB7. LO 10.2 Prepare journal entries to record the following transactions, assuming periodic inventory updating and first-in, first-out (FIFO) cost allocation.

	Number of Units	Cost per Unit
Nov. 19, purchased merchandise for resale	1,200	$6
Nov. 22, purchased merchandise for resale	980	5
Nov. 30, sold merchandise for $10 per unit	850	

EB8. LO 10.3 Calculate the cost of goods sold dollar value for B65 Company for the month, considering the following transactions under three different cost allocation methods and using perpetual inventory updating. Provide calculations for first-in, first-out (FIFO).

	Number of Units	Unit Cost	Sales
Beginning inventory	100	$66	
Purchased	80	75	
Sold	50		$120
Sold	25		125
Ending inventory	105		

EB9. LO 10.3 Calculate the cost of goods sold dollar value for B66 Company for the month, considering the following transactions under three different cost allocation methods and using perpetual inventory updating. Provide calculations for last-in, first-out (LIFO).

	Number of Units	Unit Cost	Sales
Beginning inventory	100	$66	
Purchased	80	75	
Sold	50		$120
Sold	25		125
Ending inventory	105		

EB10. LO 10.3 Calculate the cost of goods sold dollar value for B67 Company for the month, considering the following transactions under three different cost allocation methods and using perpetual inventory updating. Provide calculations for weighted average (AVG).

	Number of Units	Unit Cost	Sales
Beginning inventory	100	$66	
Purchased	80	75	
Sold	50		$120
Sold	25		125
Ending inventory	105		

EB11. LO 10.3 Prepare journal entries to record the following transactions, assuming perpetual inventory updating and first-in, first-out (FIFO) cost allocation. Assume no beginning inventory.

	Number of Units	Unit Cost
Nov. 19, purchased merchandise for resale	1,200	$6
Nov. 22, purchased merchandise for resale	980	5
Nov. 30, sold merchandise for $10 per unit	850	

EB12. LO 10.3 Prepare journal entries to record the following transactions, assuming perpetual inventory updating and last-in, first-out (LIFO) cost allocation. Assume no beginning inventory.

	Number of Units	Unit Cost
Mar. 12, purchased merchandise for resale	120	$52
Mar. 15, purchased merchandise for resale	180	56
Mar. 16, sold merchandise for $95 per unit	90	

EB13. LO 10.4 If a group of inventory items costing $3,200 had been double counted during the year-end inventory count, what impact would the error have on the following inventory calculations? Indicate the effect (and amount) as either (a) none, (b) understated $_____, or (c) overstated $_____.

Inventory Item	None or amount?	Understated or overstated?
Beginning Inventory		
Purchases		
Goods Available for Sale		
Ending Inventory		
Cost of Goods Sold		

Table 10.2

EB14. LO 10.4 If Barcelona Company's ending inventory was actually $122,000, but the cost of consigned goods, with a cost value of $20,000 were accidentally included with the company assets, when making the year-end inventory adjustment, what would be the impact on the presentation of the balance sheet and income statement for the year that the error occurred, if any?

EB15. LO 10.4 Tanke Company reported net income on the year-end financial statements of $850,200. However, errors in inventory were discovered after the reports were issued. If inventory was overstated by $21,000, how much net income did the company actually earn?

EB16. LO 10.5 Compute Westtown Company's (A) inventory turnover ratio and (B) number of days' sales in inventory ratio, using the following information.

Cost of goods sold	$156,000
Beginning inventory	14,500
Ending inventory	17,500

EB17. LO 10.5 Complete the missing pieces of Delgado Company's inventory calculations and ratios.

Beginning inventory	$ 25,000
Purchases	132,000
Goods available for sale	157,000
Ending inventory	27,000
Cost of goods sold	?
Turnover ratio	5.0
Days' sales in inventory	?

Problem Set A

PA1. LO 10.1 When prices are rising (inflation), which costing method would produce the *highest* value for gross margin? Choose between first-in, first-out (FIFO); last-in, first-out (LIFO); and weighted average (AVG).

Evansville Company had the following transactions for the month.

	Number of Units	Cost per Unit
Purchase	2	$6,000
Purchase	3	7,000
Purchase	4	7,500

Calculate the gross margin for each of the following cost allocation methods, assuming A62 sold just one unit of these goods for $10,000. Provide your calculations.

A. first-in, first-out (FIFO)
B. last-in, first-out (LIFO)
C. weighted average (AVG)

PA2. LO 10.2 Trini Company had the following transactions for the month.

	Number of Units	Cost per Unit	Total
Beginning inventory	1,050	$22	$ 23,100
Purchased May 31	1,020	23	23,460
Purchased Jul. 15	1,300	26	33,800
Purchased Nov. 1	1,200	27	32,400
Totals (goods available)	4,570		112,760
Ending inventory	900	?	

Calculate the ending inventory dollar value for each of the following cost allocation methods, using periodic inventory updating. Provide your calculations.

A. first-in, first-out (FIFO)
B. last-in, first-out (LIFO)
C. weighted average (AVG)

PA3. LO 10.2 Trini Company had the following transactions for the month.

	Number of Units	Cost per Unit	Total
Beginning inventory	1,050	$22	$ 23,100
Purchased May 31	1,020	23	23,460
Purchased Jul. 15	1,300	26	33,800
Purchased Nov. 1	1,200	27	32,400
Totals (goods available for sale)	4,570		112,760
Ending inventory	900	?	

Calculate the cost of goods sold dollar value for the period for each of the following cost allocation methods, using periodic inventory updating. Provide your calculations.

A. first-in, first-out (FIFO)
B. last-in, first-out (LIFO)
C. weighted average (AVG)

PA4. LO 10.3 Calculate the cost of goods sold dollar value for A74 Company for the sale on March 11, considering the following transactions under three different cost allocation methods and using perpetual inventory updating. Provide calculations for (a) first-in, first-out (FIFO); (b) last-in, first-out (LIFO); and (c) weighted average (AVG).

	Number of Units	Unit Cost
Beginning inventory Mar. 1	110	$87
Purchased Mar. 8	140	89
Sold Mar. 11 for $120 per unit	95	

PA5. LO 10.3 Use the first-in, first-out (FIFO) cost allocation method, with perpetual inventory updating, to calculate (a) sales revenue, (b) cost of goods sold, and c) gross margin for A75 Company, considering the following transactions.

	Number of Units	Unit Cost
Beginning inventory	105	$40
Purchased Mar. 2	150	42
Sold Mar. 31 for $75 per unit	88	

PA6. LO 10.3 Use the last-in, first-out (LIFO) cost allocation method, with perpetual inventory updating, to calculate (a) sales revenue, (b) cost of goods sold, and c) gross margin for A75 Company, considering the following transactions.

	Number of Units	Unit Cost
Beginning inventory	105	$40
Purchased Mar. 2	150	42
Sold Mar. 31 for $75 per unit	88	

PA7. LO 10.3 Use the weighted-average (AVG) cost allocation method, with perpetual inventory updating, to calculate (a) sales revenue, (b) cost of goods sold, and c) gross margin for A75 Company, considering the following transactions.

	Number of Units	Unit Cost
Beginning inventory	105	$40
Purchased Mar. 2	150	42
Sold Mar. 31 for $75 per unit	88	

PA8. LO 10.3 Prepare journal entries to record the following transactions, assuming perpetual inventory updating and first-in, first-out (FIFO) cost allocation. Assume no beginning inventory.

	Number of Units	Unit Cost	Sales
Purchased	165	$21	
Sold	120		$36
Purchased	225	27	
Sold	180		39
Purchased	210	33	

PA9. LO 10.3 Calculate a) cost of goods sold, b) ending inventory, and c) gross margin for A76 Company, considering the following transactions under three different cost allocation methods and using perpetual inventory updating. Provide calculations for first-in, first-out (FIFO).

	Number of Units	Unit Cost	Sales
Beginning inventory	240	$100	
Sold	160		$140
Purchased	520	103	
Sold	400		142
Purchased	400	110	
Sold	370		144
Ending inventory	230		

PA10. LO 10.3 Calculate a) cost of goods sold, b) ending inventory, and c) gross margin for A76 Company, considering the following transactions under three different cost allocation methods and using perpetual inventory updating. Provide calculations for last-in, first-out (LIFO).

	Number of Units	Unit Cost	Sales
Beginning inventory	240	$100	
Sold	160		$140
Purchased	520	103	
Sold	400		142
Purchased	400	110	
Sold	370		144
Ending inventory	230		

PA11. LO 10.3 Calculate a) cost of goods sold, b) ending inventory, and c) gross margin for A76 Company, considering the following transactions under three different cost allocation methods and using perpetual inventory updating. Provide calculations for weighted average (AVG).

	Number of Units	Unit Cost	Sales
Beginning inventory	240	$100	
Sold	160		$140
Purchased	520	103	
Sold	400		142
Purchased	400	110	
Sold	370		144
Ending inventory	230		

PA12. LO 10.3 Compare the calculations for gross margin for A76 Company, based on the results of the perpetual inventory calculations using FIFO, LIFO, and AVG.

PA13. LO 10.4 Company Elmira reported the following cost of goods sold but later realized that an error had been made in ending inventory for year 2021. The correct inventory amount for 2021 was 32,000. Once the error is corrected, (a) how much is the restated cost of goods sold for 2021? and (b) how much is the restated cost of goods sold for 2022?

	2021	2022
Beginning inventory	$ 31,000	$ 27,000
Purchases	185,000	188,000
Goods available for sale	216,000	215,000
Ending inventory	27,000	30,000
Cost of goods sold	189,000	185,000

PA14. LO 10.4 Assuming a company's year-end inventory were overstated by $5,000, indicate the effect (overstated/understated/no effect) of the error on the following balance sheet and income statement accounts.

A. Income Statement: Cost of Goods Sold
B. Income Statement: Net Income
C. Balance Sheet: Assets
D. Balance Sheet: Liabilities
E. Balance Sheet: Equity

PA15. LO 10.5 Use the following information relating to Shana Company to calculate the inventory turnover ratio and the number of days' sales in inventory ratio.

	Sales	Cost of Goods Sold	Average Inventory
Year 2021	$22,000	$16,500	$2,400
Year 2022	28,000	21,000	3,000
Year 2023	33,000	24,750	3,500
Year 2024	35,000	26,250	4,000

PA16. LO 10.5 Use the following information relating to Clover Company to calculate the inventory turnover ratio, gross margin, and the number of days' sales in inventory ratio, for years 2022 and 2023.

	Sales	Cost of Goods Sold	Average Inventory
Year 2021	$250,000	$187,500	$24,000
Year 2022	295,000	221,250	30,000
Year 2023	323,000	242,250	35,000

Problem Set B

PB1. LO 10.1 When prices are falling (deflation), which costing method would produce the *highest* gross margin for the following? Choose first-in, first-out (FIFO); last-in, first-out (LIFO); or weighted average, assuming that B62 Company had the following transactions for the month.

	Number of Units	Cost per Unit
Purchase	10	$200
Purchase	20	205
Purchase	10	230
	40	

Calculate the gross margin for each of the following cost allocation methods, assuming B62 sold just one unit of these goods for $400. Provide your calculations.

A. first-in, first-out (FIFO)
B. last-in, first-out (LIFO)
C. weighted average (AVG)

PB2. LO 10.2 DeForest Company had the following transactions for the month.

	Number of Units	Cost per Unit	Total
Beginning inventory	500	$40	$20,000
Purchased Apr. 30	600	45	27,000
Purchased Aug. 15	650	40	26,000
Purchased Dec. 10	700	35	24,500
Totals (goods available)	2,450		97,500
Ending inventory	550	?	

Calculate the ending inventory dollar value for the period for each of the following cost allocation methods, using periodic inventory updating. Provide your calculations.

A. first-in, first-out (FIFO)
B. last-in, first-out (LIFO)
C. weighted average (AVG)

PB3. LO 10.2 DeForest Company had the following transactions for the month.

	Number of Units	Cost per Unit	Total
Beginning inventory	500	$40	$20,000
Purchased Apr. 30	600	45	27,000
Purchased Aug. 15	650	40	26,000
Purchased Dec. 10	700	35	24,500
Totals (goods available for sale)	2,450		97,500
Ending inventory	550	?	

Calculate the ending inventory dollar value for the period for each of the following cost allocation methods, using periodic inventory updating. Provide your calculations.

A. first-in, first-out (FIFO)
B. last-in, first-out (LIFO)
C. weighted average (AVG)

PB4. LO 10.3 Calculate the cost of goods sold dollar value for B74 Company for the sale on November 20, considering the following transactions under three different cost allocation methods and using perpetual inventory updating. Provide calculations for (a) first-in, first-out (FIFO); (b) last-in, first-out (LIFO); and (c) weighted average (AVG).

	Number of Units	Unit Cost
Beginning inventory Nov. 1	650	$55
Purchased Nov. 15	500	52
Sold Nov. 20 for $80 per unit	400	

PB5. LO 10.3 Use the first-in, first-out method (FIFO) cost allocation method, with perpetual inventory updating, to calculate (a) sales revenue, (b) cost of goods sold, and c) gross margin for B75 Company, considering the following transactions.

	Number of Units	Unit Cost
Beginning inventory	7,500	$60
Purchased Sept. 18	8,000	55
Sold Sept. 28 for $100 per unit	500	

PB6. LO 10.3 Use the last-in, first-out method (LIFO) cost allocation method, with perpetual inventory updating, to calculate (a) sales revenue, (b) cost of goods sold, and c) gross margin for B75 Company, considering the following transactions.

	Number of Units	Unit Cost
Beginning inventory	7,500	$60
Purchased Sept. 18	8,000	55
Sold Sept. 28 for $100 per unit	500	

PB7. LO 10.3 Use the **weighted-average (AVG)** cost allocation method, with perpetual inventory updating, to calculate (a) sales revenue, (b) cost of goods sold, and c) gross margin for B75 Company, considering the following transactions.

	Number of Units	Unit Cost
Beginning inventory	7,500	$60
Purchased Sept. 18	8,000	55
Sold Sept. 28 for $100 per unit	500	

PB8. LO 10.3 Prepare journal entries to record the following transactions, assuming perpetual inventory updating, and last-in, first-out (LIFO) cost allocation. Assume no beginning inventory.

	Number of Units	Unit Cost	Sales
Purchased	165	$21	
Sold	120		$36
Purchased	225	27	
Sold	180		39
Purchased	210	33	

PB9. LO 10.3 Calculate a) cost of goods sold, b) ending inventory, and c) gross margin for B76 Company, considering the following transactions under three different cost allocation methods and using perpetual inventory updating. Provide calculations for first-in, first-out (FIFO).

	Number of Units	Unit Cost	Sales
Beginning inventory	420	$200	
Sold	150		$401
Purchased	250	205	
Sold	275		421
Purchased	200	215	
Sold	260		441
Ending inventory	185		

PB10. LO 10.3 Calculate a) cost of goods sold, b) ending inventory, and c) gross margin for B76 Company, considering the following transactions under three different cost allocation methods and using perpetual inventory updating. Provide calculations for last-in, first-out (LIFO).

	Number of Units	Unit Cost	Sales
Beginning inventory	420	$200	
Sold	150		$401
Purchased	250	205	
Sold	275		421
Purchased	200	215	
Sold	260		441
Ending inventory	185		

PB11. LO 10.3 Calculate a) cost of goods sold, b) ending inventory, and c) gross margin for B76 Company, considering the following transactions under three different cost allocation methods and using perpetual inventory updating. Provide calculations for weighted average (AVG).

	Number of Units	Unit Cost	Sales
Beginning inventory	420	$200	
Sold	150		$401
Purchased	250	205	
Sold	275		421
Purchased	200	215	
Sold	260		441
Ending inventory	185		

PB12. LO 10.3 Compare the calculations for gross margin for B76 Company, based on the results of the perpetual inventory calculations using FIFO, LIFO, and AVG.

PB13. LO 10.4 Company Edgar reported the following cost of goods sold but later realized that an error had been made in ending inventory for year 2021. The correct inventory amount for 2021 was 12,000. Once the error is corrected, (a) how much is the restated cost of goods sold for 2021? and (b) how much is the restated cost of goods sold for 2022?

	2021	2022
Beginning inventory	$ 11,000	$ 16,000
Purchases	135,000	140,000
Goods available for sale	146,000	156,000
Ending inventory	16,000	14,000
Cost of goods sold	130,000	142,000

PB14. LO 10.4 Assuming a company's year-end inventory were understated by $16,000, indicate the effect (overstated/understated/no effect) of the error on the following balance sheet and income statement accounts.

A. Income Statement: Cost of Goods Sold
B. Income Statement: Net Income
C. Balance Sheet: Assets
D. Balance Sheet: Liabilities
E. Balance Sheet: Equity

PB15. LO 10.5 Use the following information relating to Singh Company to calculate the inventory turnover ratio and the number of days' sales in inventory ratio.

	Sales	Cost of Goods Sold	Average Inventory
Year 2021	$12,500	$ 8,750	$1,750
Year 2022	14,000	9,800	2,200
Year 2023	19,500	13,650	2,800
Year 2024	20,500	14,350	3,000

PB16. LO 10.5 Use the following information relating to Medinas Company to calculate the inventory turnover ratio, gross margin, and the number of days' sales in inventory ratio, for years 2022 and 2023.

	Sales	Cost of Goods Sold	Average Inventory
Year 2021	$ 75,000	$52,500	$ 8,000
Year 2022	90,000	63,000	9,500
Year 2023	100,000	70,000	11,000

Thought Provokers

TP1. LO 10.1 Search the SEC website (https://www.sec.gov/edgar/searchedgar/companysearch.html) and locate the latest Form 10-K for a company you would like to analyze. When you are choosing, make sure the company sells a product (has inventory on the balance sheet and cost of goods sold on the income statement). Submit a short memo that states the following:

a. The name and ticker symbol of the company you have chosen.
b. Answer the following questions from the company's statement of Form 10-K financial statements:
    - What amount of merchandise inventory does the company report on their balance sheet?
    - What amount of cost of goods sold does the company report on their income statement?

Provide the weblink to the company's Form 10-K, to allow accurate verification of your answers.

TP2. LO 10.2 Assume your company uses the periodic inventory costing method, and the inventory count left out an entire warehouse of goods that were in stock at the end of the year, with a cost value of $222,000. How will this affect your net income in the current year? How will it affect next year's net income?

TP3. LO 10.3 Search the internet for recent news items (within the past year) relating to inventory issues. Submit a short memo describing what you found and explaining why it is important to the future of inventory accounting or management. For example, this can be related to technology, bar code, RFID, shipping, supply chain, logistics, or other inventory-related topics that are currently trending. Provide the weblink to the source of your information.

TP4. LO 10.3 Search the internet for information about the technological breakthrough relating to inventory issues, referred to as the Internet of Things (IoT). How do you think the development of such technology will change the way accountants manage inventory in the future? Provide the weblink to the source or sources of your information.

TP5. LO 10.4 Consider the dilemma you might someday face if you are the CFO of a company that is struggling to satisfy investors, creditors, stockholders, and internal company managers. All of these financial statement users are clamoring for higher profits and more net assets (also known as equity). If at some point, you suddenly found yourself not meeting the internal and external earnings and equity targets that these parties expect, you would probably search for some way to make the financial statements look better. What if your boss, the CEO, suggested that maybe you should make just one simple journal entry to record all the goods that your company is holding on consignment, as if that significant amount of goods were owned by your company? She might say that this action on your part would fix a lot of problems at once, since adding the consigned goods to merchandise inventory would simultaneously increase net assets on the balance sheet *and* increase net income on the income statement (since it would decrease cost of goods sold). How would you respond to this request?

Write a memo, detailing your willingness or not to embrace this suggestion, giving reasons behind your decision. Remember to exercise diplomacy, even if you must dissent from the opinion of a supervisor. Note that the challenge of the assignment is to keep your integrity intact while also keeping your job, if possible.

TP6. LO 10.5 Use a spreadsheet and the following excerpts from Hileah Company's financial information to build a template that automatically calculates (A) inventory turnover and (B) number of days' sales in inventory, for the year 2018.

	12/31/18	**12/31/17**
Cash	$10,000	$14,000
Accounts receivable	22,000	17,000
Merchandise inventory	15,900	14,200
Total assets	47,900	45,200
Accounts payable	4,500	5,500
Common stock	10,000	10,000
Retained earnings	33,400	29,700
Total liabilities and equity	47,900	45,200
Additional information		
Cost of goods sold	177,000	

TP7. LO 10.5 Search the SEC website (https://www.sec.gov/edgar/searchedgar/companysearch.html) and locate the latest Form 10-K for a company you would like to analyze. Submit a short memo that states the following:

a. The name and ticker symbol of the company you have chosen.
b. Describe two items relating to inventory from the company's notes to financial statements:
    - one familiar item that you expected to be in the notes to the financial statement, based on this chapter's coverage; and
    - one unfamiliar item that you did not expect to be in the notes to the financial statements.
c. Provide the weblink to the company's Form 10-K, to allow accurate verification of your answers.

11 Long-Term Assets

Figure 11.1 Long-Term Assets. A silk-screening machine used to create designs on clothing is a long-term asset. (credit: modification of "Flat Bed Silk Screen Printing Machine with LED UV Curing System2" by Benny Zheng/Flickr, Public Domain)

Chapter Outline

LO **11.1** Distinguish between Tangible and Intangible Assets

LO **11.2** Analyze and Classify Capitalized Costs versus Expenses

LO **11.3** Explain and Apply Depreciation Methods to Allocate Capitalized Costs

LO **11.4** Describe Accounting for Intangible Assets and Record Related Transactions

LO **11.5** Describe Some Special Issues in Accounting for Long-Term Assets

Why It Matters

Liam is excited to be graduating from his MBA program and looks forward to having more time to pursue his business venture. During one of his courses, Liam came up with the business idea of creating trendy workout attire. For his class project, he started silk-screening vintage album cover designs onto tanks, tees, and yoga pants. He tested the market by selling his wares on campus and was surprised how quickly and how often he sold out. In fact, sales were high enough that he decided to go into business for himself. One of his first decisions involved whether he should continue to pay someone else to silk-screen his designs or do his own silk-screening. To do his own silk-screening, he would need to invest in a silk-screening machine.

Liam will need to analyze the purchase of a silk-screening machine to determine the impact on his business in the short term as well as the long term, including the accounting implications related to the expense of this machine. Liam knows that over time, the value of the machine will decrease, but he also knows that an asset is supposed to be recorded on the books at its historical cost. He also wonders what costs are considered part of this asset. Additionally, Liam has learned about the matching principle (expense recognition) but needs to learn how that relates to a machine that is purchased in one year and used for many years to help generate revenue. Liam has a lot of information to consider before making this decision.

11.1 Distinguish between Tangible and Intangible Assets

Assets are items a business owns.[1] For accounting purposes, assets are categorized as current versus long term, and tangible versus intangible. Assets that are expected to be used by the business for more than one year are considered **long-term assets**. They are not intended for resale and are anticipated to help generate revenue for the business in the future. Some common long-term assets are computers and other office machines, buildings, vehicles, software, computer code, and copyrights. Although these are all considered long-term assets, some are tangible and some are intangible.

Tangible Assets

An asset is considered a **tangible asset** when it is an economic resource that has physical substance—it can be seen and touched. Tangible assets can be either short term, such as inventory and supplies, or long term, such as land, buildings, and equipment. To be considered a long-term tangible asset, the item needs to be used in the normal operation of the business for more than one year, not be near the end of its useful life, and the company must have no plan to sell the item in the near future. The **useful life** is the time period over which an asset cost is allocated. Long-term tangible assets are known as **fixed assets**.

Businesses typically need many different types of these assets to meet their objectives. These assets differ from the company's products. For example, the computers that Apple Inc. intends to sell are considered inventory (a short-term asset), whereas the computers Apple's employees use for day-to-day operations are long-term assets. In Liam's case, the new silk-screening machine would be considered a long-term tangible asset as he plans to use it over many years to help him generate revenue for his business. Long-term tangible assets are listed as noncurrent assets on a company's balance sheet. Typically, these assets are listed under the category of Property, Plant, and Equipment (PP&E), but they may be referred to as fixed assets or plant assets.

Apple Inc. lists a total of $33,783,000,000 in total Property, Plant and Equipment (net) on its 2017 consolidated balance sheet (see Figure 11.2).[2] As shown in the figure, this net total includes land and buildings, machinery, equipment and internal-use software, and leasehold improvements, resulting in a gross PP&E of $75,076,000,000—less accumulated depreciation and amortization of $41,293,000,000—to arrive at the net amount of $33,783,000,000.

1 The Financial Accounting Standards Board (FASB) defines assets as "probable future economic benefits obtained or controlled by a particular entity as a result of past transactions or events" (SFAC No. 6, p. 12).

2 Apple, Inc. U.S. Securities and Exchange Commission 10-K Filing. November 3, 2017. http://pdf.secdatabase.com/2624/0000320193-17-000070.pdf

PROPERTY Plant and Equipment, Net (in millions)	2017	2016
Land and Buildings	$ 13,587	$ 10,185
Machinery, Equipment and Internal-use Software	54,210	44,543
Leasehold Improvements	7,279	6,517
Gross Property, Plant and Equipment	75,076	61,245
Accumulated Depreciation and Amortization	(41,293)	(34,235)
Total Property, Plant and Equipment, net	$ 33,783	$ 27,010

Figure 11.2 Apple Inc.'s Property, Plant and Equipment, Net. This report shows the company's consolidated financial statement details as of September 30, 2017, and September 24, 2016 (in millions). (attribution:)

LINK TO LEARNING

Recently, there has been a trend involving an increase in the number of intangibles on companies' balance sheets. As a result, investors need a better understanding of how this will affect their valuation of these companies. Read this article on intangible assets from The Economist (https://openstax.org/l/50IntangAsset) for more information.

Intangible Assets

Companies may have other long-term assets used in the operations of the business that they do not intend to sell, but that do not have physical substance; these assets still provide specific rights to the owner and are called **intangible assets**. These assets typically appear on the balance sheet following long-term tangible assets (see Figure 11.3.)[3] Examples of intangible assets are patents, copyrights, franchises, licenses, goodwill, sometimes software, and trademarks (Table 11.1). Because the value of intangible assets is very subjective, it is usually not shown on the balance sheet until there is an event that indicates value objectively, such as the purchase of an intangible asset.

A company often records the costs of developing an intangible asset internally as expenses, not assets, especially if there is ambiguity in the expense amounts or economic life of the asset. However, there are also conditions under which the costs can be allocated over the anticipated life of the asset. (The treatment of intangible asset costs can be quite complex and is taught in advanced accounting courses.)

3 Apple, Inc. U.S. Securities and Exchange Commission 10-K Filing. November 3, 2017. http://pdf.secdatabase.com/2624/0000320193-17-000070.pdf

APPLE INC. Consolidated Balance Sheets (in millions)		
Assets	**2017**	**2016**
Current Assets:		
Cash and Cash Equivalents	$ 20,289	$ 20,484
Short-term Marketable Securities	53,892	46,671
Accounts Receivable, Allowances of $58 and $53, respectively	17,874	15,754
Inventories	4,855	2,132
Vendor Nontrade Receivables	17,799	13,545
Other Current Assets	13,936	8,283
Total Current Assets	128,645	106,869
Long-term Marketable Securities	194,714	170,430
Property, Plant, and Equipment, net	33,783	27,010
Goodwill	5,717	5,414
Acquired Intangible Assets, net	2,298	3,206
Other Noncurrent Assets	10,162	8,757
Total Assets	$375,319	$321,686

Figure 11.3 Consolidated Balance Sheets for Apple, Inc. in 2017 and 2016. (attribution: Copyright Rice University, OpenStax, under CC BY-NC-SA 4.0 license)

Types of Intangible Assets

Asset	Useful Life
Patents	Twenty years
Trademarks	Renewable every ten years
Copyrights	Seventy years beyond death of creator
Goodwill	Indefinite

Table 11.1

THINK IT THROUGH

Categorizing Intangible Assets

Your company has recently hired a star scientist who has a history of developing new technologies. The company president is excited with the new hire, and questions you, the company accountant, why the scientist cannot be recorded as an intangible asset, as the scientist will probably provide more value to the company in the future than any of its other assets. Discuss why the scientist, and employees in general, who often provide the greatest value for a company, are not recorded as intangible assets.

Patents

A **patent** is a contract that provides a company exclusive rights to produce and sell a unique product. The rights are granted to the inventor by the federal government and provide exclusivity from competition for twenty years. Patents are common within the pharmaceutical industry as they provide an opportunity for drug companies to recoup the significant financial investment on research and development of a new drug. Once the new drug is produced, the company can sell it for twenty years with no direct competition.

THINK IT THROUGH

Research and Development Costs

Jane works in product development for a technology company. She just heard that her employer is slashing research and development costs. When she asks why, the marketing senior vice president tells her that current research and development costs are reducing net income in the current year for a potential but unknown benefit in future years, and that management is concerned about the effect on stock price. Jane wonders why research and development costs are not capitalized so that the cost would be matched with the future revenues. Why do you think research and development costs are not capitalized?

Trademarks and Copyrights

A company's **trademark** is the exclusive right to the name, term, or symbol it uses to identify itself or its products. Federal law allows companies to register their trademarks to protect them from use by others. Trademark registration lasts for ten years with optional 10-year renewable periods. This protection helps prevent impersonators from selling a product similar to another or using its name. For example, a burger joint could not start selling the "Big Mac." Although it has no physical substance, the exclusive right to a term or logo has value to a company and is therefore recorded as an asset.

A **copyright** provides the exclusive right to reproduce and sell artistic, literary, or musical compositions. Anyone who owns the copyright to a specific piece of work has exclusive rights to that work. Copyrights in the United States last seventy years beyond the death of the original author. While you might not be overly interested in what seems to be an obscure law, it actually directly affects you and your fellow students. It is one of the primary reasons that your copy of the *Collected Works of William Shakespeare* costs about $40 in your bookstore or online, while a textbook, such as *Principles of Biology* or *Principles of Accounting*, can run in the hundreds of dollars.

Goodwill

Goodwill is a unique intangible asset. **Goodwill** refers to the value of certain favorable factors that a business possesses that allows it to generate a greater rate of return or profit. Such factors include superior management, a skilled workforce, quality products or service, great geographic location, and overall reputation. Companies typically record goodwill when they acquire another business in which the purchase price is in excess of the fair value of the identifiable net assets. The difference is recorded as goodwill on the purchaser's balance sheet. For example, the goodwill of $5,717,000,000 that we see on Apple's consolidated balance sheets for 2017 (see Figure 11.3) was created when Apple purchased another business for a purchase price exceeding the book value of its net assets.

YOUR TURN

Classifying Long-Term Assets as Tangible or Intangible

Your cousin started her own business and wants to get a small loan from a local bank to expand production in the next year. The bank has asked her to prepare a balance sheet, and she is having trouble classifying the assets properly. Help her sort through the list below and note the assets that are tangible long-term assets and those that are intangible long-term assets.

- Cash
- Patent
- Accounts Receivable
- Land
- Investments
- Software
- Inventory
- Note Receivable
- Machinery
- Equipment
- Marketable Securities
- Owner Capital
- Copyright
- Building
- Accounts Payable
- Mortgage Payable

Solution

Tangible long-term assets include land, machinery, equipment, and building. Intangible long-term assets include patent, software, and copyright.

11.2 Analyze and Classify Capitalized Costs versus Expenses

When a business purchases a long-term asset (used for more than one year), it classifies the asset based on whether the asset is used in the business's operations. If a long-term asset is used in the business operations, it will belong in property, plant, and equipment or intangible assets. In this situation the asset is typically capitalized. **Capitalization** is the process by which a long-term asset is recorded on the balance sheet and its allocated costs are expensed on the income statement over the asset's economic life. Explain and Apply Depreciation Methods to Allocate Capitalized Costs addresses the available methods that companies may choose for expensing capitalized assets.

Long-term assets that are not used in daily operations are typically classified as an investment. For example, if a business owns land on which it operates a store, warehouse, factory, or offices, the cost of that land would be included in property, plant, and equipment. However, if a business owns a vacant piece of land on which the business conducts no operations (and assuming no current or intermediate-term plans for development), the land would be considered an investment.

YOUR TURN

Classifying Assets and Related Expenditures

You work at a business consulting firm. Your new colleague, Marielena, is helping a client organize his accounting records by types of assets and expenditures. Marielena is a bit stumped on how to classify certain assets and related expenditures, such as capitalized costs versus expenses. She has given you the following list and asked for your help to sort through it. Help her classify the expenditures as either capitalized or expensed, and note which assets are property, plant, and equipment.

Expenditures:

- normal repair and maintenance on the manufacturing facility
- cost of taxes on new equipment used in business operations
- shipping costs on new equipment used in business operations
- cost of a minor repair on existing equipment used in business operations

Assets:

- land next to the production facility held for use next year as a place to build a warehouse
- land held for future resale when the value increases
- equipment used in the production process

Solution

Expenditures:

- normal repair and maintenance on the manufacturing facility: expensed
- cost of taxes on new equipment used in business operations: capitalized
- shipping costs on new equipment used in business operations: capitalized
- cost of a minor repair on existing equipment used in business operations: expensed

Assets:

- land next to the production facility held for use next year as a place to build a warehouse: property, plant, and equipment
- land held for future resale when the value increases: investment
- equipment used in the production process: property, plant, and equipment

Property, Plant, and Equipment (Fixed Assets)

Why are the costs of putting a long-term asset into service capitalized and written off as expenses (depreciated) over the economic life of the asset? Let's return to Liam's start-up business as an example. Liam plans to buy a silk-screening machine to help create clothing that he will sell. The machine is a long-term asset, because it will be used in the business's daily operation for many years. If the machine costs Liam $5,000 and it is expected to be used in his business for several years, generally accepted accounting principles (GAAP) require the allocation of the machine's costs over its useful life, which is the period over which it will produce revenues. Overall, in determining a company's financial performance, we would not expect that Liam should have an expense of $5,000 this year and $0 in expenses for this machine for future years in which it is being used. GAAP addressed this through the *expense recognition* (*matching*) principle, which states that expenses should be recorded in the same period with the revenues that the expense helped create. In Liam's case, the $5,000 for this machine should be allocated over the years in which it helps to generate revenue for the business. Capitalizing the machine allows this to occur. As stated previously, to capitalize is to record a long-term asset on the balance sheet and expense its allocated costs on the income statement over the asset's economic life. Therefore, when Liam purchases the machine, he will record it as an asset on the financial statements.

JOURNAL			
Date	Account	Debit	Credit
Jan. 1, 2019	Machine Cash	5,000	 5,000

When capitalizing an asset, the total cost of acquiring the asset is included in the cost of the asset. This includes additional costs beyond the purchase price, such as shipping costs, taxes, assembly, and legal fees. For example, if a real estate broker is paid $8,000 as part of a transaction to purchase land for $100,000, the land would be recorded at a cost of $108,000.

Over time as the asset is used to generate revenue, Liam will need to depreciate the asset.

Depreciation is the process of allocating the cost of a tangible asset over its useful life, or the period of time that the business believes it will use the asset to help generate revenue. This process will be described in Explain and Apply Depreciation Methods to Allocate Capitalized Costs.

ETHICAL CONSIDERATIONS

How WorldCom's Improper Capitalization of Costs Almost Shut Down the Internet

In 2002, telecommunications giant WorldCom filed for the largest Chapter 11 bankruptcy to date, a situation resulting from manipulation of its accounting records. At the time, WorldCom operated nearly a third of the bandwidth of the twenty largest US internet backbone routes, connecting over 3,400 global networks that serviced more than 70,000 businesses in 114 countries.[4]

WorldCom used a number of accounting gimmicks to defraud investors, mainly including capitalizing costs that should have been expensed. Under normal circumstances, this might have been considered just another account fiasco leading to the end of a company. However, WorldCom controlled a large percentage of backbone routes, a major component of the hardware supporting the internet, as even the Securities and Exchange Commission recognized.[5] If WorldCom's bankruptcy due to accounting malfeasance shut the company down, then the internet would no longer be functional.

If such an event was to happen today, it could shut down international commerce and would be

4 Cybertelecom. "WorldCom (UNNET)." n.d. http://www.cybertelecom.org/industry/wcom.htm

considered a national emergency. As demonstrated by WorldCom, the unethical behavior of a few accountants could have shut down the world's online businesses and international commerce. An accountant's job is fundamental and important: keep businesses operating in a transparent fashion.

Investments

A short-term or long-term asset that is not used in the day-to-day operations of the business is considered an **investment** and is not expensed, since the company does not expect to use up the asset over time. On the contrary, the company hopes that the assets (investment) would grow in value over time. Short-term investments are investments that are expected to be sold within a year and are recorded as current assets.

CONTINUING APPLICATION AT WORK

Investment in Property in the Grocery Industry

To remain viable, companies constantly look to invest in upgrades in long-term assets. Such acquisitions might include new machinery, buildings, warehouses, or even land in order to expand operations or make the work process more efficient. Think back to the last time you walked through a grocery store. Were you mostly focused on getting the food items on your list? Or did you plan to pick up a prescription and maybe a coffee once you finished?

Grocery stores have become a one-stop shopping environment, and investments encompass more than just shelving and floor arrangement. Some grocery chains purchase warehouses to distribute inventory as needed to various stores. Machinery upgrades can help automate various departments. Some supermarkets even purchase large parcels of land to build not only their stores, but also surrounding shopping plazas to draw in customers. All such investments help increase the company's net profit.

CONCEPTS IN PRACTICE

Vehicle Repairs and Enhancements

Automobiles are a useful way of looking at the difference between repair and maintenance expenses and capitalized modifications. Routine repairs such as brake pad replacements are recorded as repair and maintenance expense. They are an expected part of owning a vehicle. However, a car may be modified to change its appearance or performance. For example, if a supercharger is added to a car to increase its horsepower, the car's performance is increased, and the cost should be included as a part of the vehicle asset. Likewise, if replacing the engine of an older car extends its useful life, that cost would also be capitalized.

5 Dennis R. Beresford, Nicholas DeB. Katzenbach, and C.B. Rogers, Jr. "Special Investigative Committee of the Board of Directors of WorldCom." *Report of Investigation*. March 31, 2003. https://www.sec.gov/Archives/edgar/data/723527/000093176303001862/dex991.htm

Repair and Maintenance Costs of Property, Plant, and Equipment

Long-term assets may have additional costs associated with them over time. These additional costs may be capitalized or expensed based on the nature of the cost. For example, Walmart's financial statements explain that major improvements are capitalized, while costs of normal repairs and maintenance are charged to expense as incurred.

An amount spent is considered a **current expense**, or an amount charged in the current period, if the amount incurred did not help to extend the life of or improve the asset. For example, if a service company cleans and maintains Liam's silk-screening machine every six months, that service does not extend the useful life of the machine beyond the original estimate, increase the capacity of the machine, or improve the quality of the silk-screening performed by the machine. Therefore, this maintenance would be expensed within the current period. In contrast, if Liam had the company upgrade the circuit board of the silk-screening machine, thereby increasing the machine's future capabilities, this would be capitalized and depreciated over its useful life.

THINK IT THROUGH

Correcting Errors in Classifying Assets

You work at a business consulting firm. Your new colleague, Marielena, helped a client organize his accounting records last year by types of assets and expenditures. Even though Marielena was a bit stumped on how to classify certain assets and related expenditures, such as capitalized costs versus expenses, she did not come to you or any other more experienced colleagues for help. Instead, she made the following classifications and gave them to the client who used this as the basis for accounting transactions over the last year. Thankfully, you have been asked this year to help prepare the client's financial reports and correct errors that were made. Explain what impact these errors would have had over the last year and how you will correct them so you can prepare accurate financial statements.

Expenditures:

- Normal repair and maintenance on the manufacturing facility were capitalized.
- The cost of taxes on new equipment used in business operations was expensed.
- The shipping costs on new equipment used in business operations were expensed.
- The cost of a minor repair on existing equipment used in business operations was capitalized.

Assets:

- Land next to the production facility held for use next year as a place to build a warehouse was depreciated.
- Land held for future resale when the value increases was classified as Property, Plant, and Equipment but not depreciated.
- Equipment used in the production process was classified as an investment.

LINK TO LEARNING

Many businesses invest a lot of money in production facilities and operations. Some production processes are more automated than others, and they require a greater investment in property, plant, and equipment than production facilities that may be more labor intensive. Watch this video of the operation of a Georgia-Pacific lumber mill (https://openstax.org/l/50GPLumberMill) and note where you see all components of property, plant, and equipment in operations in this fascinating production process. There's even a reference to an intangible asset—if you watch and listen closely, you just might catch it.

11.3 Explain and Apply Depreciation Methods to Allocate Capitalized Costs

In this section, we concentrate on the major characteristics of determining capitalized costs and some of the options for allocating these costs on an annual basis using the depreciation process. In the determination of capitalized costs, we do not consider just the initial cost of the asset; instead, we determine all of the costs necessary to place the asset into service. For example, if our company purchased a drill press for $22,000, and spent $2,500 on sales taxes and $800 for delivery and setup, the depreciation calculation would be based on a cost of $22,000 plus $2,500 plus $800, for a total cost of $25,300.

We also address some of the terminology used in depreciation determination that you want to familiarize yourself with. Finally, in terms of allocating the costs, there are alternatives that are available to the company. We consider three of the most popular options, the *straight-line method*, the *units-of-production method*, and the *double-declining-balance method*.

YOUR TURN

Calculating Depreciation Costs

Liam buys his silk screen machine for $10,000. He estimates that he can use this machine for five years or 100,000 presses, and that the machine will only be worth $1,000 at the end of its life. He also estimates that he will make 20,000 clothing items in year one and 30,000 clothing items in year two. Determine Liam's depreciation costs for his first two years of business under straight-line, units-of-production, and double-declining-balance methods. Also, record the journal entries.

Solution

Straight-line method: ($10,000 – $1,000)/5 = $1,800 per year for both years.

JOURNAL			
Date	**Account**	**Debit**	**Credit**
Jan. 1, 2019	Depreciation Expense Accumulated Depreciation	1,800	 1,800

Units-of-production method: ($10,000 – $1,000)/100,000= $0.09 per press

Year 1 expense: $0.09 × 20,000 = $1,800

JOURNAL			
Date	**Account**	**Debit**	**Credit**
Jan. 1, 2019	Depreciation Expense Accumulated Depreciation	1,800	 1,800

Year 2 expense: $0.09 × 30,000 = $2,700

JOURNAL			
Date	**Account**	**Debit**	**Credit**
Jan. 1, 2019	Depreciation Expense Accumulated Depreciation	2,700	 2,700

Double-declining-balance method:

Year 1 expense: [($10,000 – 0)/5] × 2 = $4,000

JOURNAL			
Date	**Account**	**Debit**	**Credit**
Jan. 1, 2019	Depreciation Expense Accumulated Depreciation	4,000	 4,000

Year 2 expense: [($10,000 – $4,000)/5] × 2 = $2,400

JOURNAL			
Date	**Account**	**Debit**	**Credit**
Jan. 1, 2019	Depreciation Expense Accumulated Depreciation	2,400	 2,400

Fundamentals of Depreciation

As you have learned, when accounting for a long-term fixed asset, we cannot simply record an expense for the cost of the asset and record the entire outflow of cash in one accounting period. Like all other assets, when purchasing or acquiring a long-term asset, it must be recorded at the historical (initial) cost, which includes all costs to acquire the asset and put it into use. The initial recording of an asset has two steps:

1. Record the initial purchase on the date of purchase, which places the asset on the balance sheet (as property, plant, and equipment) at cost, and record the amount as notes payable, accounts payable, or an outflow of cash.
2. At the end of the period, make an adjusting entry to recognize the depreciation expense. Companies may record depreciation expense incurred annually, quarterly, or monthly.

Following GAAP and the expense recognition principle, the depreciation expense is recognized over the asset's estimated useful life.

Recording the Initial Purchase of an Asset

Assets are recorded on the balance sheet at cost, meaning that all costs to purchase the asset and to prepare the asset for operation should be included. Costs outside of the purchase price may include shipping, taxes, installation, and modifications to the asset.

The journal entry to record the purchase of a fixed asset (assuming that a note payable is used for financing and not a short-term account payable) is shown here.

JOURNAL			
Date	**Account**	**Debit**	**Credit**
Jan. 1, 2019	Fixed Asset (truck, building, etc.) Cash/Notes Payable *To record purchase of fixed asset*	XXX	 XXX

Applying this to Liam's silk-screening business, we learn that he purchased his silk-screening machine for $5,000 by paying $1,000 cash and the remainder in a note payable over five years. The journal entry to record the purchase is shown here.

JOURNAL			
Date	**Account**	**Debit**	**Credit**
Jan. 1, 2019	Equipment Cash Notes Payable *To recognize purchase of delivery truck*	5,000	 1,000 4,000

CONCEPTS IN PRACTICE

Estimating Useful Life and Salvage Value

Useful life and salvage value are estimates made at the time an asset is placed in service. It is common and expected that the estimates are inaccurate with the uncertainty involved in estimating the future. Sometimes, however, a company may attempt to take advantage of estimating salvage value and useful life to improve earnings. A larger salvage value and longer useful life decrease annual depreciation expense and increase annual net income. An example of this behavior is Waste Management, which was disciplined by the Securities and Exchange Commission for fraudulently altering its estimates to reduce depreciation expense and overstate net income by $1.7 billion.[6]

Components Used in Calculating Depreciation

The expense recognition principle that requires that the cost of the asset be allocated over the asset's useful life is the process of depreciation. For example, if we buy a delivery truck to use for the next five years, we would allocate the cost and record depreciation expense across the entire five-year period. The calculation of the depreciation expense for a period is not based on anticipated changes in the fair market value of the asset;

6 U.S. Securities and Exchange Commission. "Judge Enters Final Judgment against Former CFO of Waste Management, Inc. Following Jury Verdict in SEC's Favor." January 3, 2008. https://www.sec.gov/news/press/2008/2008-2.htm

instead, the depreciation is based on the allocation of the cost of owning the asset over the period of its useful life.

The following items are important in determining and recording depreciation:

- **Book value**: the asset's original cost less accumulated depreciation.
- **Useful life**: the length of time the asset will be productively used within operations.
- **Salvage (residual) value**: the price the asset will sell for or be worth as a trade-in when its useful life expires. The determination of salvage value can be an inexact science, since it requires anticipating what will occur in the future. Often, the salvage value is estimated based on past experiences with similar assets.
- **Depreciable base (cost)**: the depreciation expense over the asset's useful life. For example, if we paid $50,000 for an asset and anticipate a salvage value of $10,000, the depreciable base is $40,000. We expect $40,000 in depreciation over the time period in which the asset was used, and then it would be sold for $10,000.

Depreciation records an expense for the value of an asset consumed and removes that portion of the asset from the balance sheet. The journal entry to record depreciation is shown here.

JOURNAL			
Date	**Account**	**Debit**	**Credit**
Jan. 1, 2019	Depreciation Expense	XXX	
	Accumulated Depreciation		XXX
	To record depreciation on asset for period		

Depreciation expense is a common operating expense that appears on an income statement. **Accumulated depreciation** is a **contra account**, meaning it is attached to another account and is used to offset the main account balance that records the total depreciation expense for a fixed asset over its life. In this case, the asset account stays recorded at the historical value but is offset on the balance sheet by accumulated depreciation. Accumulated depreciation is subtracted from the historical cost of the asset on the balance sheet to show the asset at book value. Book value is the amount of the asset that has not been allocated to expense through depreciation.

HARRY COMPANY Partial Balance Sheet December 31, 2020	
Assets	
Property, Plant and Equipment:	
Truck	$25,000
− Accumulated Depreciation	(5,000)
	$20,000

In this case, the asset's book value is $20,000: the historical cost of $25,000 less the accumulated depreciation of $5,000.

It is important to note, however, that not all long-term assets are depreciated. For example, land is not depreciated because depreciation is the allocating of the expense of an asset over its useful life. How can one determine a useful life for land? It is assumed that land has an unlimited useful life; therefore, it is not depreciated, and it remains on the books at historical cost.

Once it is determined that depreciation should be accounted for, there are three methods that are most commonly used to calculate the allocation of depreciation expense: the *straight-line method*, the *units-of-production method*, and the *double-declining-balance method*. A fourth method, the *sum-of-the-years-digits method*, is another *accelerated* option that has been losing popularity and can be learned in intermediate accounting courses. Let's use the following scenario involving Kenzie Company to work through these three methods.

Assume that on January 1, 2019, Kenzie Company bought a printing press for $54,000. Kenzie pays shipping costs of $1,500 and setup costs of $2,500, assumes a useful life of five years or 960,000 pages. Based on experience, Kenzie Company anticipates a salvage value of $10,000.

Recall that determination of the costs to be depreciated requires including all costs that prepare the asset for use by the company. The Kenzie example would include shipping and setup costs. Any costs for maintaining or repairing the equipment would be treated as regular expenses, so the total cost would be $58,000, and, after allowing for an anticipated salvage value of $10,000 in five years, the business could take $48,000 in depreciation over the machine's economic life.

	Total Cost
Purchase Price	$ 54,000
Shipping Costs	1,500
Set-up Costs	2,500
Total Cost	$ 58,000
– Salvage Value	(10,000)
Depreciable Base	$ 48,000

CONCEPTS IN PRACTICE

Fixed Assets

You work for Georgia-Pacific as an accountant in charge of the fixed assets subsidiary ledger at a production and warehouse facility in Pennsylvania. The facility is in the process of updating and replacing several asset categories, including warehouse storage units, fork trucks, and equipment on the production line. It is your job to keep the information in the fixed assets subsidiary ledger up to date and accurate. You need information on original historical cost, estimated useful life, salvage value, depreciation methods, and additional capital expenditures. You are excited about the new purchases and upgrades to the facility and how they will help the company serve its customers better. However, you have been in your current position for only a few years and have never overseen extensive updates, and you realize that you will have to gather a lot of information at once to keep the accounting records accurate. You feel overwhelmed and take a minute to catch your breath and think through what you need. After a few minutes, you realize that you have many people and many resources to work with to tackle this project. Whom will you work with and how will you go about gathering what you need?

Straight-Line Depreciation

Straight-line depreciation is a method of depreciation that evenly splits the depreciable amount across the useful life of the asset. Therefore, we must determine the yearly depreciation expense by dividing the depreciable base of $48,000 by the economic life of five years, giving an annual depreciation expense of $9,600. The journal entries to record the first two years of expenses are shown, along with the balance sheet information. Here are the journal entry and information for year one:

JOURNAL			
Date	**Account**	**Debit**	**Credit**
Dec. 31, 2019	Depreciation Expense: Printing Press Accumulated Depreciation: Printing Press *To record depreciation on asset for period*	9,600	 9,600

Printing Press	$58,000
− Accumulated Depreciation: Printing Press	(9,600)
Net Book Value	$48,400

After the journal entry in year one, the press would have a book value of $48,400. This is the original cost of $58,000 less the accumulated depreciation of $9,600. Here are the journal entry and information for year two:

JOURNAL			
Date	**Account**	**Debit**	**Credit**
Dec. 31, 2020	Depreciation Expense: Printing Press Accumulated Depreciation: Printing Press *To record depreciation on asset for period*	9,600	 9,600

Printing Press	$ 58,000
− Accumulated Depreciation: Printing Press	(19,200)
Net Book Value	$ 38,800

Kenzie records an annual depreciation expense of $9,600. Each year, the accumulated depreciation balance increases by $9,600, and the press's book value decreases by the same $9,600. At the end of five years, the asset will have a book value of $10,000, which is calculated by subtracting the accumulated depreciation of $48,000 (5 × $9,600) from the cost of $58,000.

Units-of-Production Depreciation

Straight-line depreciation is efficient, accounting for assets used consistently over their lifetime, but what about assets that are used with less regularity? The **units-of-production depreciation method** bases depreciation on the actual usage of the asset, which is more appropriate when an asset's life is a function of usage instead of time. For example, this method could account for depreciation of a printing press for which the depreciable base is $48,000 (as in the straight-line method), but now the number of pages the press prints is important.

In our example, the press will have total depreciation of $48,000 over its useful life of 960,000 pages. Therefore, we would divide $48,000 by 960,000 pages to get a cost per page of $0.05. If Kenzie printed 180,000 pages in the first year, the depreciation expense would be 180,000 pages × $0.05 per page, or $9,000. The journal entry to record this expense would be the same as with straight-line depreciation: only the dollar amount would have changed. The presentation of accumulated depreciation and the calculation of the book value would also be the same. Kenzie would continue to depreciate the asset until a total of $48,000 in depreciation was taken after printing 960,000 total pages.

THINK IT THROUGH

Deciding on a Depreciation Method

Liam is struggling to determine which deprecation method he should use for his new silk-screening machine. He expects sales to increase over the next five years. He also expects (hopes) that in two years he will need to buy a second silk-screening machine to keep up with the demand for products of his growing company. Which depreciation method makes more sense for Liam: higher expenses in the first few years, or keeping expenses consistent over time? Or would it be better for him to not think in terms of time, but rather in the usage of the machine?

Double-Declining-Balance Depreciation

The **double-declining-balance depreciation method** is the most complex of the three methods because it accounts for both time and usage and takes more expense in the first few years of the asset's life. Double-declining considers time by determining the percentage of depreciation expense that would exist under straight-line depreciation. To calculate this, divide 100% by the estimated life in years. For example, a five-year asset would be 100/5, or 20% a year. A four-year asset would be 100/4, or 25% a year. Next, because assets are typically more efficient and "used" more heavily early in their life span, the double-declining method takes usage into account by doubling the straight-line percentage. For a four-year asset, multiply 25% (100%/4-year life) × 2, or 50%. For a five-year asset, multiply 20% (100%/5-year life) × 2, or 40%.

One unique feature of the double-declining-balance method is that in the first year, the estimated salvage value is not subtracted from the total asset cost before calculating the first year's depreciation expense. Instead the total cost is multiplied by the calculated percentage. However, depreciation expense is not permitted to take the book value below the estimated salvage value, as demonstrated in the following text.

Year	Depreciation Expense	Accumulated Depreciation	Book Value
			$58,000
1: $58,000 × 40% =	$23,200	$23,200	34,800
2: $34,800 × 40% =	13,920	37,120	20,880
3: $20,880 × 40% =	8,352	45,472	12,528
4: $12,528 – $10,000 =	2,528	48,000	10,000
5	0	48,000	10,000
Total	$48,000	$48,000	$10,000

Notice that in year four, the remaining book value of $12,528 was not multiplied by 40%. This is because the expense would have been $5,011.20, and since we cannot depreciate the asset below the estimated salvage value of $10,000, the expense cannot exceed $2,528, which is the amount left to depreciate (difference between the book value of $12,528 and the salvage value of $10,000). Since the asset has been depreciated to its salvage value at the end of year four, no depreciation can be taken in year five.

In our example, the first year's double-declining-balance depreciation expense would be $58,000 × 40%, or $23,200. For the remaining years, the double-declining percentage is multiplied by the remaining book value of the asset. Kenzie would continue to depreciate the asset until the book value and the estimated salvage value are the same (in this case $10,000).

The net effect of the differences in straight-line depreciation versus double-declining-balance depreciation is that under the double-declining-balance method, the allowable depreciation expenses are greater in the earlier years than those allowed for straight-line depreciation. However, over the depreciable life of the asset, the total depreciation expense taken will be the same, no matter which method the entity chooses. For example, in the current example both straight-line and double-declining-balance depreciation will provide a total depreciation expense of $48,000 over its five-year depreciable life.

IFRS CONNECTION

Accounting for Depreciation

Both US GAAP and International Financial Reporting Standards (IFRS) account for long-term assets (tangible and intangible) by recording the asset at the cost necessary to make the asset ready for its intended use. Additionally, both sets of standards require that the cost of the asset be recognized over the economic, useful, or legal life of the asset through an allocation process such as depreciation. However, there are some significant differences in how the allocation process is used as well as how the assets are carried on the balance sheet.

IFRS and US GAAP allow companies to choose between different methods of depreciation, such as even allocation (straight-line method), depreciation based on usage (production methods), or an accelerated method (double-declining balance). The mechanics of applying these methods do not differ between the two standards. However, IFRS requires companies to use “component depreciation” if it is feasible. Component depreciation would apply to assets with components that have differing lives. Consider the following example using a plane owned by Southwest Airlines. Let’s divide this plane into three components: the interior, the engines, and the fuselage. Suppose the average life of the interior of a plane is ten years, the average life of the engines is fifteen years, and the average life of the fuselage is twenty-five years. Given this, what should be the depreciable life of the asset? In that case, under IFRS, the costs associated with the interior would be depreciated over ten years, the costs associated with the engines would be depreciated over fifteen years, and the costs associated with the fuselage would be depreciated over twenty-five years. Under US GAAP, the total cost of the airplane would likely be depreciated over twenty years. Obviously, component depreciation involves more record keeping and differing amounts of depreciation per year for the life of the asset. But the same amount of total depreciation, the cost of the asset less residual value, would be taken over the life of the asset under both US GAAP and IFRS.

Probably one of the most significant differences between IFRS and US GAAP affects long-lived assets. This is the ability, under IFRS, to adjust the value of those assets to their fair value as of the balance sheet date. The adjustment to fair value is to be done by “class” of asset, such as real estate, for example. A company can adjust some classes of assets to fair value but not others. Under US GAAP, almost all long-lived assets are carried on the balance sheet at their depreciated historical cost, regardless of how the actual fair value of the asset changes. Consider the following example. Suppose your company owns a single building that you bought for $1,000,000. That building currently has $200,000 in accumulated depreciation. This building now has a book value of $800,000. Under US GAAP, this is how this building would appear in the balance sheet. Even if the fair value of the building is $875,000, the building would still appear on the balance sheet at its depreciated historical cost of $800,000 under US GAAP. Alternatively, if the company used IFRS and elected to carry real estate on the balance sheet at fair value, the building would appear on the company's balance sheet at its new fair value of $875,000.

It is difficult to determine an accurate fair value for long-lived assets. This is one reason US GAAP has not permitted the fair valuing of long-lived assets. Different appraisals can result in different determinations of "fair value." Thus, the Financial Accounting Standards Board (FASB) elected to continue with the current method of carrying assets at their depreciated historical cost. The thought process behind the adjustments to fair value under IFRS is that fair value more accurately represents true value. Even if the fair value reported is not known with certainty, reporting the class of assets at a reasonable representation of fair value enhances decision-making by users of the financial statements.

Summary of Depreciation

Table 11.2 compares the three methods discussed. Note that although each time-based (straight-line and double-declining balance) annual depreciation expense is different, after five years the total amount depreciated (accumulated depreciation) is the same. This occurs because at the end of the asset's useful life, it was expected to be worth $10,000: thus, both methods depreciated the asset's value by $48,000 over that time period.

The sum-of-the-years-digits is different from the two above methods in that while those methods are based on time factors, the sum-of-the-years-digits is based on usage. However, the total amount of depreciation taken over an asset's economic life will still be the same. In our example, the total depreciation will be $48,000, even though the sum-of-the-years-digits method could take only two or three years or possibly six or seven years to be allocated.

Calculation of Depreciation Expense

Depreciation Method	Calculation
Straight line	(Cost – salvage value)/Useful life
Units of production	(Cost – salvage value) × (Units produced in current period/Estimated total units to be produced)
Double declining balance	Book value × Straight-line annual depreciation percentage × 2

Table 11.2

Period	Straight-Line Depreciation Method	Units of Production Method	Double-Declining-Balance Method
Year 1	$ 9,600	(180,000 units) $ 9,000	$23,200
Year 2	9,600	(200,000 units) 10,000	13,920
Year 3	9,600	(210,000 units) 10,500	8,352
Year 4	9,600	(190,000 units) 9,500	2,528
Year 5	9,600	(180,000 units) 9,000	0
Total	$48,000	$48,000	$48,000

ETHICAL CONSIDERATIONS

Depreciation Analysis Requires Careful Evaluation

When analyzing depreciation, accountants are required to make a supportable estimate of an asset's useful life and its salvage value. However, "management teams typically fail to invest either time or attention into making or periodically revisiting and revising reasonably supportable estimates of asset lives or salvage values, or the selection of depreciation methods, as prescribed by GAAP."[7] This failure is not an ethical approach to properly accounting for the use of assets.

Accountants need to analyze depreciation of an asset over the entire useful life of the asset. As an asset supports the cash flow of the organization, expensing its cost needs to be allocated, not just recorded as an arbitrary calculation. An asset's depreciation may change over its life according to its use. If asset depreciation is arbitrarily determined, the recorded "gains or losses on the disposition of depreciable property assets seen in financial statements"[8] are not true best estimates. Due to operational changes, the depreciation expense needs to be periodically reevaluated and adjusted.

Any mischaracterization of asset usage is not proper GAAP and is not proper accrual accounting. Therefore, "financial statement preparers, as well as their accountants and auditors, should pay more attention to the quality of depreciation-related estimates and their possible mischaracterization and losses of credits and charges to operations as disposal gains."[9] An accountant should always follow GAAP guidelines and allocate the expense of an asset according to its usage.

Partial-Year Depreciation

A company will usually only own depreciable assets for a portion of a year in the year of purchase or disposal. Companies must be consistent in how they record depreciation for assets owned for a partial year. A common method is to allocate depreciation expense based on the number of months the asset is owned in a year. For example, a company purchases an asset with a total cost of $58,000, a five-year useful life, and a salvage value of $10,000. The annual depreciation is $9,600 ([$58,000 – 10,000]/5). However, the asset is purchased at the

7 Howard B. Levy. "Depreciable Asset Lives." *The CPA Journal*. September 2016. https://www.cpajournal.com/2016/09/08/depreciable-asset-lives/

8 Howard B. Levy. "Depreciable Asset Lives." *The CPA Journal*. September 2016. https://www.cpajournal.com/2016/09/08/depreciable-asset-lives/

9 Howard B. Levy. "Depreciable Asset Lives." *The CPA Journal*. September 2016. https://www.cpajournal.com/2016/09/08/depreciable-asset-lives/

beginning of the fourth month of the fiscal year. The company will own the asset for nine months of the first year. The depreciation expense of the first year is $7,200 ($9,600 × 9/12). The company will depreciate the asset $9,600 for the next four years, but only $2,400 in the sixth year so that the total depreciation of the asset over its useful life is the depreciable amount of $48,000 ($7,200 + 9,600 + 9,600 + 9,600 + 9,600 + 2,400).

THINK IT THROUGH

Choosing Appropriate Depreciation Methods

You are part of a team reviewing the financial statements of a new computer company. Looking over the fixed assets accounts, one long-term tangible asset sticks out. It is labeled "USB" and valued at $10,000. You ask the company's accountant for more detail, and he explains that the asset is a USB drive that holds the original coding for a game the company developed during the year. The company expects the game to be fairly popular for the next few years, and then sales are expected to trail off. Because of this, they are planning on depreciating this asset over the next five years using the double-declining method. Does this recording seem appropriate, or is there a better way to categorize the asset? How should this asset be expensed over time?

Special Issues in Depreciation

While you've now learned thebasic foundationof the major available depreciation methods, there are a few special issues. Until now, we have assumed a definite physical or economically functional useful life for the depreciable assets. However, in some situations, depreciable assets can be used beyond their useful life. If so desired, the company could continue to use the asset beyond the original estimated economic life. In this case, a new remaining depreciation expense would be calculated based on the remaining depreciable base and estimated remaining economic life.

Assume in the earlier Kenzie example that after five years and $48,000 in accumulated depreciation, the company estimated that it could use the asset for two more years, at which point the salvage value would be $0. The company would be able to take an additional $10,000 in depreciation over the extended two-year period, or $5,000 a year, using the straight-line method.

As with the straight-line example, the asset could be used for more than five years, with depreciation recalculated at the end of year five using the double-declining balance method. While the process of calculating the additional depreciation for the double-declining-balance method would differ from that of the straight-line method, it would also allow the company to take an additional $10,000 after year five, as with the other methods, so long as the cost of $58,000 is not exceeded.

As a side note, there often is a difference in useful lives for assets when following GAAP versus the guidelines for depreciation under federal tax law, as enforced by the Internal Revenue Service (IRS). This difference is not unexpected when you consider that tax law is typically determined by the United States Congress, and there often is an economic reason for tax policy.

For example, if we want to increase investment in real estate, shortening the economic lives of real estate for taxation calculations can have a positive increasing effect on new construction. If we want to slow down new production, extending the economic life can have the desired slowing effect. In this course, we concentrate on financial accounting depreciation principles rather than tax depreciation.

Fundamentals of Depletion of Natural Resources

Another type of fixed asset is **natural resources**, assets a company owns that are consumed when used. Examples include lumber, mineral deposits, and oil/gas fields. These assets are considered natural resources while they are still part of the land; as they are extracted from the land and converted into products, they are then accounted for as inventory (raw materials). Natural resources are recorded on the company's books like a fixed asset, at cost, with total costs including all expenses to acquire and prepare the resource for its intended use.

As the resource is consumed (converted to a product), the cost of the asset must be expensed: this process is called **depletion**. As with depreciation of nonnatural resource assets, a contra account called **accumulated depletion**, which records the total depletion expense for a natural resource over its life, offsets the natural resource asset account. Depletion expense is typically calculated based on the number of units extracted from cutting, mining, or pumping the resource from the land, similar to the units-of-production method. For example, assume a company has an oil well with an estimated 10,000 gallons of crude oil. The company purchased this well for $1,000,000, and the well is expected to have no salvage value once it is pumped dry. The depletion cost per gallon will be $1,000,000/10,000 = $100. If the company extracts 4,000 gallons of oil in a given year, the depletion expense will be $400,000.

Fundamentals of Amortization of an Intangible

Recall that intangible assets are recorded as long-term assets at their cost. As with tangible assets, many intangible assets have a finite (limited) life span so their costs must be allocated over their useful lives: this process is **amortization**. Depreciation and amortization are similar in nature but have some important differences. First, amortization is typically only done using the straight-line method. Second, there is usually no salvage value for intangible assets because they are completely used up over their life span. Finally, an accumulated amortization account is not required to record yearly expenses (as is needed with depreciation); instead, the intangible asset account is written down each period.

For example, a company called Patents-R-Us purchased a product patent for $10,000, granting the company exclusive use of that product for the next twenty years. Therefore, unless the company does not think the product will be useful for all twenty years (at that point the company would use the shorter useful life of the product), the company will record amortization expense of $500 a year ($10,000/20 years). Assuming that it was placed into service on October 1, 2019, the journal entry would be as follows:

JOURNAL			
Date	**Account**	**Debit**	**Credit**
Oct. 1, 2019	Amortization Expense	125	
	Patent		125
	To record amortization on patent for period		

LINK TO LEARNING

See Form 10-K that was filed with the SEC (https://openstax.org/l/50McDForm10K) to determine which depreciation method McDonald's Corporation used for its long-term assets in 2017.

11.4 Describe Accounting for Intangible Assets and Record Related Transactions

Intangible assets can be difficult to understand and incorporate into the decision-making process. In this section we explain them in more detail and provide examples of how to amortize each type of intangible asset.

Fundamentals of Intangible Assets

Intangibles are recorded at their acquisition cost, as are tangible assets. The costs of internally generated intangible assets, such as a patent developed through research and development, are recorded as expenses when incurred. An exception is legal costs to register or defend an intangible asset. For example, if a company incurs legal costs to defend a patent it has developed internally, the costs associated with developing the patent are recorded as an expense, but the legal costs associated with defending the patent would be capitalized as a patent intangible asset.

Amortization of intangible assets is handled differently than depreciation of tangible assets. Intangible assets are typically amortized using the straight-line method; there is typically no salvage value, as the usefulness of the asset is used up over its lifetime, and no accumulated amortization account is needed. Additionally, based on regulations, certain intangible assets are restricted and given limited life spans, while others are infinite in their economic life and not amortized.

Copyrights

While copyrights have a finite life span of 70 years beyond the author's death, they are amortized over their estimated useful life. Therefore, if a company acquired a copyright on a new graphic novel for $10,000 and estimated it would be able to sell that graphic novel for the next ten years, it would amortize $1,000 a year ($10,000/ten years), and the journal entry would be as shown. Assume that the novel began sales on January 1, 2019.

JOURNAL			
Date	**Account**	**Debit**	**Credit**
Dec. 31, 2019	Amortization Expense Copyright	1,000	 1,000

Patents

Patents are issued to the inventor of the product by the federal government and last twenty years. All costs associated with creating the product being patented (such as research and development costs) are expensed; however, direct costs to obtain the patent could be capitalized. Otherwise, patents are capitalized only when purchased. Like copyrights, patents are amortized over their useful life, which can be shorter than twenty years due to changing technology. Assume Mech Tech purchased the patent for a new pump system. The patent cost $20,000, and the company expects the pump to be a useful product for the next twenty years. Mech Tech will then amortize the $20,000 over the next twenty years, which is $1,000 a year.

JOURNAL			
Date	**Account**	**Debit**	**Credit**
Dec. 31, 2019	Amortization Expense Patent	1,000	 1,000

Trademarks

Companies can register their trademarks with the federal government for ten years with the opportunity to renew the trademark every ten years. Trademarks are recorded as assets only when they are purchased from another company and are valued based on market price at the time of purchase. In this case, these trademarks are amortized over the expected useful life. In some cases, the trademark may be seen as having an indefinite life, in which case there would be no amortization.

Goodwill

From an accounting standpoint, goodwill is internally generated and is not recorded as an asset unless it is purchased during the acquisition of another company. The purchase of goodwill occurs when one company buys another company for an amount greater than the total value of the company's net assets. The value difference between net assets and the purchase price is then recorded as goodwill on the purchaser's financial statements. For example, say the London Hoops professional basketball team was sold for $10 million. The new owner received net assets of $7 million, so the goodwill (value of the London Hoops above its net assets) is $3 million. The following journal entry shows how the new owner would record this purchase.

JOURNAL			
Date	**Account**	**Debit**	**Credit**
Jan. 1, 2019	Net Assets Goodwill Cash	7,000,000 3,000,000	 10,000,000

Goodwill does not have an expected life span and therefore is not amortized. However, a company is required to compare the book value of goodwill to its market value at least annually to determine if it needs to be adjusted. This comparison process is called *testing for impairment*. If the market value of goodwill is found to be lower than the book value, then goodwill needs to be reduced to its market value. If goodwill is impaired, it is reduced with a credit, and an impairment loss is debited. Goodwill is never increased beyond its original cost. For example, if the new owner of London Hoops assesses that London Hoops now has a fair value of $9,000,000 rather than the $10,000,000 of the original purchase, the owner would need to record the impairment as shown in the following journal entry.

JOURNAL			
Date	Account	Debit	Credit
Dec. 31, 2019	Impairment Loss Goodwill	1,000,000	 1,000,000

CONCEPTS IN PRACTICE

Microsoft's Goodwill

In 2016, Microsoft bought LinkedIn for $25 billion. Microsoft wanted the brand, website platform, and software, which are intangible assets of LinkedIn, and therefore Microsoft only received $4 billion in net assets. The overpayment by Microsoft is not necessarily a bad business decision, but rather the premium or value of those intangible assets that LinkedIn owned and Microsoft wanted. The $21 billion difference will be listed on Microsoft's balance sheet as goodwill.

LINK TO LEARNING

Apple Inc. had goodwill of $5,717,000,000 on its 2017 balance sheet. Explore Apple, Inc.'s U.S. Securities and Exchange Commission 10-K Filing (https://openstax.org/l/50AppleForm10K) for notes that discuss goodwill and whether Apple has had to adjust for the impairment of this asset in recent years.

11.5 Describe Some Special Issues in Accounting for Long-Term Assets

A company will account for some events for long-term assets that are less routine than recording purchase and depreciation or amortization. For example, a company may realize that its original estimate of useful life or salvage value is no longer accurate. A long-term asset may lose its value, or a company may sell a long-term asset.

Revision of Remaining Life or Salvage Value

As you have learned, depreciation is based on estimating both the useful life of an asset and the salvage value of that asset. Over time, these estimates may be proven inaccurate and need to be adjusted based on new information. When this occurs, the depreciation expense calculation should be changed to reflect the new (more accurate) estimates. For this entry, the remaining depreciable balance of the net book value is allocated over the new useful life of the asset. To work through this process with data, let's return to the example of Kenzie Company.

- Kenzie has a press worth $58,000.
- Its salvage value was originally estimated to be $10,000.
- Its economic life was originally estimated to be five years.

- Kenzie uses straight-line depreciation.

After three years, Kenzie determines that the estimated useful life would have been more accurately estimated at eight years, and the salvage value at that time would be $6,000. The revised depreciation expense is calculated as shown:

Original Cost	$ 58,000
Depreciation Previously Taken (3 × $9,600)	(28,800)
Book Value at Beginning of Year 4	$ 29,200
Revised Salvage Value	(6,000)
Revised Remaining Depreciable Cost	$ 23,200
Revised Remaining Useful Life	5 years
Revised Depreciation: $23,200/5 years = $4,640 per year	

These revised calculations show that Kenzie should now be recording a depreciation of $4,640 per year for the next five years.

YOUR TURN

Useful Life

Georgia-Pacific is a global company that employs a wide variety of property, plant, and equipment assets in its production facilities. You work for Georgia-Pacific as an accountant in charge of the fixed assets subsidiary ledger at a warehouse facility in Pennsylvania. You find out that the useful lives for the fork trucks need to be adjusted. As an asset category, the trucks were bought at the same time and had original useful lives of seven years. However, after depreciating them for two years, the company makes improvements to the trucks that allow them to be used outdoors in what can be harsh winters. The improvements also extend their useful lives by two additional years. What is the remaining useful life after the improvements?

Solution

Seven original years – two years depreciated + two additional years = seven years remaining.

Obsolescence

Obsolescence refers to the reduction in value and/or use of the asset. Obsolescence has traditionally resulted from the physical deterioration of the asset—called **physical obsolescence**. In current application—and considering the role of modern technology and tech assets—accounting for functional obsolescence is becoming more common. **Functional obsolescence** is the loss of value from all causes within a property *except* those due to physical deterioration. With functional obsolescence, the useful life still needs to be adjusted downward: although the asset physically still works, its functionality makes it less useful for the company. Also, an adjustment might be necessary in the salvage value. This potential adjustment depends on the specific details of each obsolescence determination or decision.

Sale of an Asset

When an asset is sold, the company must account for its depreciation up to the date of sale. This means companies may be required to record a depreciation entry before the sale of the asset to ensure it is current. After ensuring that the net book value of an asset is current, the company must determine if the asset has sold at a gain, at a loss, or at book value. We look at examples of each accounting alternative using the Kenzie Company data.

Recall that Kenzie's press has a depreciable base of $48,000 and an economic life of five years. If Kenzie sells the press at the end of the third year, the company would have taken three years of depreciation amounting to $28,800 ($9,600 × 3 years). With an original cost of $58,000, and after subtracting the accumulated depreciation of $28,800, the press would have a book value of $29,200. If the company sells the press for $31,000, it would realize a gain of $1,800, as shown.

Cost of Press	$ 58,000
− Accumulated Depreciation: Printing Press	(28,800)
Book Value	$ 29,200
Sales Price	$ 31,000
− Book Value	(29,200)
Gain on Sale of Printing Press	$ 1,800

The journal entry to record the sale is shown here.

JOURNAL			
Date	**Account**	**Debit**	**Credit**
Dec. 31, 2019	Cash	31,000	
	Accumulated Depreciation: Printing Press	28,800	
	Printing Press		58,000
	Gain on Sale: Printing Press		1,800

If Kenzie sells the printing press for $27,100, what would the journal entries be? The book value of the press is $29,200, so Kenzie would be selling the press at a loss. The journal entry to record the sale is shown here.

JOURNAL			
Date	**Account**	**Debit**	**Credit**
Dec. 31, 2019	Cash	27,100	
	Accumulated Depreciation: Printing Press	28,800	
	Loss on Sale of Printing Press	2,100	
	Printing Press		58,000

What if Kenzie sells the press at exactly book value? In this case, the company will realize neither a gain nor a loss. Here is the journal entry to record the sale.

JOURNAL			
Date	**Account**	**Debit**	**Credit**
Dec. 31, 2019	Cash	29,200	
	Accumulated Depreciation: Printing Press	28,800	
	Printing Press		58,000

While it would be ideal to estimate a salvage value that provides neither a gain nor a loss upon the retirement and sale of a long-term asset, this type of accuracy is virtually impossible to reach, unless you negotiate a fixed future sales price. For example, you might buy a truck for $80,000 and lock in a five-year life with 100,000 or fewer miles driven. Under these conditions, the dealer might agree to pay you $20,000 for the truck in five years.

Under these conditions, you could justify calculating your depreciation over a five-year period, using a depreciable base of $60,000. Under the straight-line method, this would provide an annual depreciation amount of $12,000. Also, when you sell the truck to the dealer after five years, the sales price will be $20,000, and the book value will be $20,000, so there would be neither a gain nor a loss on the sale.

In the Kenzie example where the asset was sold for $31,000 after three years, Kenzie should have recorded a total of $27,000 in depreciation (cost of $58,000 less the sales value of $31,000). However, the company recorded $28,800 in depreciation over the three-year period. Subtracting the gain of $1,800 from the total depreciation expense of $28,800 shows the true cost of using the asset as $27,000, and not the depreciation amount of $28,800.

When the asset was sold for $27,100, the accounting records would show $30,900 in depreciation (cost of $58,000 less the sales price of $27,100). However, depreciation is listed as $28,800 over the three-year period. Adding the loss of $2,100 to the total depreciation expense of $28,800 results in a cost of $30,900 for use of the asset rather than the $28,800 depreciation.

If the asset sells for exactly the book value, its depreciation expense was estimated perfectly, and there is no gain or loss. If it sells for $29,200 and had a book value of $29,200, its depreciation expense of $28,800 matches the original estimate.

THINK IT THROUGH

Depreciation of Long-Term Assets

You are a new staff accountant at a large construction company. After a rough year, management is seeking ways to minimize expenses or increase revenues before year-end to help increase the company's earnings per share. Your boss has asked staff to think "outside the box" and has asked to you look through the list of long-term assets to find ones that have been fully depreciated in value but may still have market value. Why would your manager be looking for these specific assets? How significantly might these items impact your company's overall performance? What ethical issues might come into play in the task you have been assigned?

LINK TO LEARNING

The management of fixed assets can be quite a challenge for any business, from sole proprietorships to global corporations. Not only do companies need to track their asset purchases, depreciation, sales, disposals, and capital expenditures, they also need to be able to generate a variety of reports. Read this Finances Online post for more details on software packages (https://openstax.org/l/50SoftwarePkg) that help companies steward their fixed assets no matter what their size.

Key Terms

accumulated depletion contra account that records the total depletion expense for a natural resource over its life

accumulated depreciation contra account that records the total depreciation expense for a fixed asset over its life

amortization allocation of the costs of intangible assets over their useful economic lives; also, process of separating the principal and interest in loan payments over the life of a loan

capitalization process in which a long-term asset is recorded on the balance sheet and its allocated costs are expensed on the income statement over the asset's economic life

contra account account paired with another account type, has an opposite normal balance to the paired account, and reduces the balance in the paired account at the end of a period

copyright exclusive rights to reproduce and sell an artistic, literary, or musical asset

current expense cost to the business that is charged in the current period

depletion expense associated with consuming a natural resource

depreciation process of allocating the costs of a tangible asset over the asset's economic life

double-declining-balance depreciation method accelerated depreciation method that accounts for both time and usage, so it takes more expense in the first few years of the asset's life

fixed asset tangible long-term asset

functional obsolescence reduction of an asset's value to the company, not including physical obsolescence

goodwill value of certain favorable factors that a business possesses that allows it to generate a greater rate of return or profit; includes price paid for an acquired company above the fair value of its identifiable net assets

intangible asset asset with financial value but no physical presence; examples include copyrights, patents, goodwill, and trademarks

investment short-term and long-term asset that is not used in the day-to-day operations of the business

long-term asset asset used ongoing in the normal course of business for more than one year that is not intended to be resold

natural resources assets a company owns that are consumed when used; they are typically taken out of the earth

patent contract providing exclusive rights to produce and sell a unique product without competition for twenty years

physical obsolescence reduction in the value of an asset to the company based on its physical deterioration

salvage (residual) value price that the asset will sell for or be worth as a trade-in when the useful life is over

straight-line depreciation depreciation method that evenly splits the depreciable amount across the useful life of the asset

tangible asset asset that has physical substance

trademark exclusive right to a name, term, or symbol a company uses to identify itself or its products

units-of-production depreciation method depreciation method that considers the actual usage of the asset to determine the depreciation expense

useful life time period over which an asset cost is allocated

Summary

11.1 Distinguish between Tangible and Intangible Assets

- Tangible assets are assets that have physical substance.
- Long-term tangible assets are assets used in the normal course of operation of businesses that last for more than one year and are not intended to be resold.
- Examples of long-term tangible assets are land, building, and machinery.
- Intangible assets lack physical substance but often have value and legal rights and protections, and therefore are still assets to the firm.
- Examples of intangible assets are patents, trademarks, copyrights, and goodwill.

11.2 Analyze and Classify Capitalized Costs versus Expenses

- Costs incurred to purchase an asset that will be used in the day-to-day operations of the business will be capitalized and then depreciated over the useful life of that asset.
- Costs incurred to purchase an asset that will not be used in the day-to-day operations, but was purchased for investment purposes, will be considered an investment asset.
- Investments are short term (can be converted to cash in one year) or long term (held for over a year).
- Costs incurred during the life of the asset are expensed right away if they do not extend the useful life of that asset or are capitalized if they extend the asset's useful life.

11.3 Explain and Apply Depreciation Methods to Allocate Capitalized Costs

- Fixed assets are recorded at the historical (initial) cost, including any costs to acquire the asset and get it ready for use.
- Depreciation is the process of allocating the cost of using a long-term asset over its anticipated economic (useful) life. To determine depreciation, one needs the fixed asset's historical cost, salvage value, and useful life (in years or units).
- There are three main methods to calculate depreciation: the straight-line method, units-of-production method, and double-declining-balance method.
- Natural resources are tangible assets occurring in nature that a company owns, which are consumed when used. Natural resources are depleted over the life of the asset, using a units-consumed method.
- Intangible assets are amortized over the life of the asset. Amortization is different from depreciation as there is typically no salvage value, the straight-line method is typically used, and no accumulated amortization account is required.

11.4 Describe Accounting for Intangible Assets and Record Related Transactions

- Intangible assets are expensed using amortization. This is similar to depreciation but is credited to the intangible asset rather than to a contra account.
- Finite intangible assets are typically amortized using the straight-line method over the useful life of the asset.
- Intangible assets with an indefinite life are not amortized but are assessed yearly for impairment.

11.5 Describe Some Special Issues in Accounting for Long-Term Assets

- Because estimates are used to calculate depreciation of fixed assets, sometimes adjustments may need to be made to the asset's useful life or to its salvage value.
- To make these adjustments, the asset's net book value is updated, and then the adjustments are made for the remaining years.
- Assets are sometimes sold before the end of their useful life. These sales can result in a gain, a loss, or neither, depending on the cash received and the asset's net book value.

Multiple Choice

1. LO 11.1 Property, Plant, and Equipment is considered why type of asset?

A. current assets
B. contra assets
C. tangible assets
D. intangible assets

2. LO 11.1 Which of the following would *not* be considered an intangible asset?

A. goodwill
B. patent
C. copyright
D. inventory

3. LO 11.1 The legal protection that provides a company exclusive rights to produce and sell a unique product is known as which of the following?

A. trademark
B. copyright
C. patent
D. goodwill

4. LO 11.2 Which of the following statements about capitalizing costs is correct?

A. Capitalizing costs refers to the process of converting assets to expenses.
B. Only the purchase price of the asset is capitalized.
C. Capitalizing a cost means to record it as an asset.
D. Capitalizing costs results in an immediate decrease in net income.

5. LO 11.2 Ngo Company purchased a truck for $54,000. Sales tax amounted to $5,400; shipping costs amounted to $1,200; and one-year registration of the truck was $100. What is the total amount of costs that should be capitalized?

A. $60,600
B. $66,100
C. $54,000
D. $59,400

6. LO 11.2 If a company capitalizes costs that should be expensed, how is its income statement for the current period impacted?

A. Assets understated
B. Net Income understated
C. Expenses understated
D. Revenues understated

7. LO 11.3 Depreciation of a plant asset is the process of ______.

A. asset valuation for statement of financial position purposes
B. allocation of the asset's cost to the periods of use
C. fund accumulation for the replacement of the asset
D. asset valuation based on current replacement cost data

8. LO 11.3 An accelerated depreciation method that takes more expense in the first few years of the asset's life is ______.

A. units-of-production depreciation
B. double-declining-balance depreciation
C. accumulated depreciation
D. straight-line depreciation

9. LO 11.3 The estimated economic life of an asset is also known as ______.

A. residual value
B. book value
C. salvage life
D. useful life

10. LO 11.4 The amortization process is like what other process?

A. depreciation
B. valuation
C. recognizing revenue
D. capitalization

11. LO 11.4 How are intangible assets with an indefinite life treated?

A. They are depreciated.
B. They are amortized.
C. They are depleted.
D. They are tested yearly for impairment.

12. LO 11.4 If the market value of goodwill is found to be lower than the book value, goodwill is ________ and must be adjusted by ________.

A. worthless; reducing it with a credit
B. impaired; reducing it with a credit
C. impaired; increasing it with a credit
D. worthless; increasing it with a credit

13. LO 11.5 Which of the following represents an event that is less routine when accounting for long-term assets?

A. recording an asset purchase
B. recording depreciation on an asset
C. recording accumulated depreciation for an asset or asset category
D. changing the estimated useful life of an asset

14. LO 11.5 Which of the following is true regarding special issues in accounting for long-term assets?

A. An asset's useful life can never be changed.
B. An asset's salvage value can never be changed.
C. Depreciation expense calculations may need to be updated using new and more accurate estimates.
D. Asset values are never reduced in value due to physical deterioration.

15. LO 11.5 The loss in value from all causes within a property *except* those due to physical deterioration is known as which of the following?

A. functional obsolescence
B. obsolescence
C. true obsolescence
D. deterioration

Questions

1. LO 11.1 What is the difference between tangible and intangible assets?

2. LO 11.1 Define intangible assets.

3. LO 11.1 What is the difference between a patent and a copyright?

4. LO 11.1 What is goodwill, and how is it generated?

5. LO 11.2 For each of the following transactions, state whether the cost would be capitalized (C) or recorded as an expense (E).

A. Purchased a machine, $100,000; gave long-term note
B. Paid $600 for ordinary repairs
C. Purchased a patent for $45,300 cash
D. Paid $200,000 cash for addition to old building
E. Paid $20,000 for monthly salaries
F. Paid $250 for routine maintenance
G. Paid $16,000 for major repairs

6. LO 11.2 What amounts should be recorded as a cost of a long-term asset?

7. LO 11.2 Describe the relationship between expense recognition and long-term assets.

8. LO 11.3 Define natural resources.

9. LO 11.3 Explain the difference between depreciation, depletion, and amortization.

10. LO 11.4 Explain the differences between the process of amortizing intangible assets and the process of depreciating tangible assets.

11. LO 11.4 What is goodwill, and what are the unique aspects of accounting for it?

12. LO 11.5 What are some examples of special issues in accounting for long-term assets? How are they handled?

13. LO 11.5 What is the difference between functional obsolescence and physical obsolescence?

Exercise Set A

EA1. LO 11.1 Fombell, Incorporated has the following assets in its trial balance:

Cash	$ 10,000
Equipment	60,000
Accounts receivable	3,000
Copyright	4,000
Inventory	16,000
Patent	10,000
Building	100,000

What is the total balance of its Property, Plant, and Equipment?

EA2. LO 11.2 Jada Company had the following transactions during the year:

- Purchased a machine for $500,000 using a long-term note to finance it
- Paid $500 for ordinary repair
- Purchased a patent for $45,000 cash
- Paid $200,000 cash for addition to an existing building
- Paid $60,000 for monthly salaries
- Paid $250 for routine maintenance on equipment
- Paid $10,000 for extraordinary repairs

If all transactions were recorded properly, what amount did Jada capitalize for the year, and what amount did Jada expense for the year?

EA3. LO 11.3 Montello Inc. purchases a delivery truck for $15,000. The truck has a salvage value of $3,000 and is expected to be driven for eight years. Montello uses the straight-line depreciation method. Calculate the annual depreciation expense.

EA4. LO 11.3 Montello Inc. purchases a delivery truck for $15,000. The truck has a salvage value of $3,000 and is expected to be driven for 120,000 miles. Montello uses the units-of-production depreciation method and in year one it expects to use the truck for 23,000 miles. Calculate the annual depreciation expense.

EA5. LO 11.3 Steele Corp. purchases equipment for $25,000. Regarding the purchase, Steele recorded the following transactions:

- Paid shipping of $1,000
- Paid installation fees of $2,000
- Pays annual maintenance cost of $200
- Received a 5% discount on $25,000 sales price

Determine the acquisition cost of the equipment.

EA6. LO 11.3 Calico Inc. purchased a patent on a new drug. The patent cost $21,000. The patent has a life of twenty years, but Calico only expects to be able to sell the drug for fifteen years. Calculate the amortization expense and record the journal for the first-year expense.

EA7. LO 11.3 Alfredo Company purchased a new 3-D printer for $900,000. Although this printer is expected to last for ten years, Alfredo knows the technology will become old quickly, and so they plan to replace this printer in three years. At that point, Alfredo believes it will be able to sell the printer for $15,000. Calculate yearly depreciation using the double-declining-balance method.

EA8. LO 11.3 Using the information from EA7, calculate depreciation using the straight-line method.

EA9. LO 11.3 Santa Rosa recently purchased a new boat to help ship product overseas. The following information is related to that purchase:

- Purchase price $4,500,000
- Cost to bring boat to production facility $25,000
- Yearly insurance cost $25,000
- Annual maintenance cost of $30,000
- Received 8% discount on sales price

Determine the acquisition cost of the boat, and record the journal entry needed.

EA10. LO 11.3 Warriors Productions recently purchased a copyright. Although the copyright is expected to last a minimum of twenty-five years, the chief executive officer of the company believes this B-list movie will only be useful for the next fifteen years. Calculate the amortization expense and record the journal for the first year's expense. The total cost of the copyright was $15,000.

EA11. LO 11.4 The following intangible assets were purchased by Goldstein Corporation:

A. A patent with a remaining legal life of twelve years is bought, and Goldstein expects to be able to use it for seven years.

B. A copyright with a remaining life of thirty years is purchased, and Goldstein expects to be able to use it for ten years.

For each of these situations, determine the useful life over which Goldstein will amortize the intangible assets.

EA12. LO 11.5 Sand River Sales has a fork truck used in its warehouse operations. The truck had an original useful life of five years. However, after depreciating the asset for three years, the company makes a major repair that extends the life by four years. What is the remaining useful life after the major repair?

Exercise Set B

EB1. LO 11.1 New Carlisle, Incorporated, has the following assets in its trial balance:

Cash	$ 15,000
Equipment	69,000
Accounts receivable	12,000
Copyright	14,000
Inventory	16,000
Patent	20,000
Building	150,000

What is New Carlisle's total amount of intangible assets?

EB2. LO 11.2 Johnson, Incorporated had the following transactions during the year:

- Purchased a building for $5,000,000 using a mortgage for financing
- Paid $2,000 for ordinary repair on a piece of equipment
- Sold product on account to customers for $1,500,600
- Purchased a copyright for $5,000 cash
- Paid $20,000 cash to add a storage shed in the corner of an existing building
- Paid $360,000 in monthly salaries
- Paid $25,000 for routine maintenance on equipment
- Paid $110,000 for major repairs

If all transactions were recorded properly, what amount did Johnson capitalize for the year, and what amount did Johnson expense for the year?

EB3. LO 11.3 Montello Inc. purchases a delivery truck for $25,000. The truck has a salvage value of $6,000 and is expected to be driven for ten years. Montello uses the straight-line depreciation method. Calculate the annual depreciation expense.

EB4. LO 11.3 Montello Inc. purchases a delivery truck for $25,000. The truck has a salvage value of $6,000 and is expected to be driven for 125,000 miles. Montello uses the units-of-production depreciation method, and in year one it expects to use the truck for 26,000 miles. Calculate the annual depreciation expense.

EB5. LO 11.3 Steele Corp. purchases equipment for $30,000. Regarding the purchase, Steele

- paid shipping of $1,200,
- paid installation fees of $2,750,
- pays annual maintenance cost of $250, and
- received a 10% discount on sales price.

Determine the acquisition cost of the equipment.

EB6. LO 11.3 Calico Inc. purchased a patent on a new drug it created. The patent cost $12,000. The patent has a life of twenty years, but Calico expects to be able to sell the drug for fifty years. Calculate the amortization expense and record the journal for the first year's expense.

EB7. LO 11.3 Kenzie purchased a new 3-D printer for $450,000. Although this printer is expected to last for ten years, Kenzie knows the technology will become old quickly and so she plans to replace this printer in three years. At that point, Kenzie believes she will be able to sell the printer for $30,000. Calculate yearly depreciation using the double-declining-balance method.

EB8. LO 11.3 Using the information from EB7, calculate depreciation using the straight-line method.

EB9. LO 11.3 Ronson recently purchased a new boat to help ship product overseas. The following information is related to that purchase:

- purchase price $4,500,000
- cost to bring boat to production facility $15,000
- yearly insurance cost $12,000
- pays annual maintenance cost of $22,000
- received a 10% discount on sales price

Determine the acquisition cost of the boat and record the journal entry needed.

EB10. LO 11.3 Warriors Production recently purchased a copyright on its new film. Although the copyright is expected to last a minimum of twenty-five years, the chief executive officer of the company believes this B-list movie will only be useful for the next five years. Calculate the amortization expense and record the journal for the first-year expense. The total cost of the copyright was $23,500.

EB11. LO 11.4 The following intangible assets were purchased by Hanna Unlimited:

A. A patent with a remaining legal life of twelve years is bought, and Hanna expects to be able to use it for six years. It is purchased at a cost of $48,000.

B. A copyright with a remaining life of thirty years is purchased, and Hanna expects to be able to use it for ten years. It is purchased for $70,000.

Determine the annual amortization amount for each intangible asset.

EB12. LO 11.5 Baglia's Wholesale Trinkets has a 3-D printer used in operations. The original useful life was estimated to be six years. However, after two years of use, the printer was overhauled, and its total useful life was extended to eight years. How many years of depreciation remain after the overhaul in year 2?

Problem Set A

PA1. LO 11.1 Selected accounts from Phipps Corporation's trial balance are as follows. Prepare the assets section of the company's balance sheet.

PHIPPS CORPORATION Trail Balance December 31		
(Selected Accounts)		
	Debit	**Credit**
Cash	$ 50,000	
Short-term Marketable Securities	25,000	
Accounts Receivable	13,000	
Inventories	45,000	
Other current Assets	10,000	
Land	100,000	
Equipment	45,000	
Accumulated Depreciation: Equipment		$5,000
Goodwill	20,000	
Other Intangible Assets	15,000	

PA2. LO 11.1 Selected accounts from Han Corporation's trial balance are as follows. Prepare the detailed schedule showing the Property, Plant, and Equipment.

HAN CORPORATION Trail Balance December 31		
(Selected Accounts)		
	Debit	**Credit**
Cash	$ 150,000	
Short-term Marketable Securities	145,000	
Accounts Receivable	26,000	
Inventories	90,000	
Other current Assets	10,000	
Land	350,000	
Buildings	300,000	
Accumulated Depreciation: Buildings		$40,000
Equipment	145,000	
Accumulated Depreciation: Equipment		10,000
Goodwill	40,000	
Other Intangible Assets	20,000	

PA3. LO 11.2 During the current year, Alanna Co. had the following transactions pertaining to its new office building.

Purchase price of land	$120,000
Legal fees for contracts to purchase land	4,000
Architect fees	16,000
Demolition of the old building on site	10,000
Sale of scrap from old building	6,000
Construction cost of new building	700,000

A. What should Alanna Co. record on its books for the land? The total cost of land includes all costs of preparing the land for use. The demolition cost of the old building is added to the land costs, and the sale of the old building scrap is subtracted from the land cost.

B. What should Alanna Co. record on its books for the building?

PA4. LO 11.2 During the current year, Arkells Inc. made the following expenditures relating to plant machinery.

- Renovated five machines for $100,000 to improve efficiency in production of their remaining useful life of five years
- Low-cost repairs throughout the year totaled $70,000
- Replaced a broken gear on a machine for $10,000

   A. What amount should be expensed during the period?

   B. What amount should be capitalized during the period?

PA5. LO 11.2 Jada Company had the following transactions during the year:

- Purchased a machine for $500,000 using a long-term note to finance it
- Paid $500 for ordinary repair
- Purchased a patent for $45,000 cash
- Paid $200,000 cash for addition to an existing building
- Paid $60,000 for monthly salaries
- Paid $250 for routine maintenance on equipment
- Paid $10,000 for major repairs
- Depreciation expense recorded for the year is $25,000

If all transactions were recorded properly, what is the amount of increase to the Property, Plant, and Equipment section of Jada's balance sheet resulting from this year's transactions? What amount did Jada report on the income statement for expenses for the year?

PA6. LO 11.3 Gimli Miners recently purchased the rights to a diamond mine. It is estimated that there are one million tons of ore within the mine. Gimli paid $23,100,000 for the rights and expects to harvest the ore over the next ten years. The following is the expected extraction for the next five years.

- Year 1: 50,000 tons
- Year 2: 90,000 tons
- Year 3: 100,000 tons
- Year 4: 110,000 tons
- Year 5: 130,000 tons

Calculate the depletion expense for the next five years, and create the journal entry for year one.

PA7. LO 11.3 Tree Lovers Inc. purchased 100 acres of woodland in which the company intends to harvest the complete forest, leaving the land barren and worthless. Tree Lovers paid $2,100,000 for the land. Tree Lovers will sell the lumber as it is harvested and expects to deplete it over five years (twenty acres in year one, thirty acres in year two, twenty-five acres in year three, fifteen acres in year four, and ten acres in year five). Calculate the depletion expense for the next five years and create the journal entry for year one.

PA8. LO 11.3 Referring to PA7 where Kenzie Company purchased a 3-D printer for $450,000, consider how the purchase of the printer impacts not only depreciation expense each year but also the asset's book value. What amount will be recorded as depreciation expense each year, and what will the book value be at the end of each year after depreciation is recorded?

PA9. LO 11.4 For each of the following unrelated situations, calculate the annual amortization expense and prepare a journal entry to record the expense:

A. A patent with a ten-year remaining legal life was purchased for $300,000. The patent will be usable for another eight years.
B. A patent was acquired on a new smartphone. The cost of the patent itself was only $24,000, but the market value of the patent is $600,000. The company expects to be able to use this patent for all twenty years of its life.

PA10. LO 11.4 Buchanan Imports purchased McLaren Corporation for $5,000,000 cash when McLaren had net assets worth $4,500,000.

A. What is the amount of goodwill in this transaction?
B. What is Buchanan's journal entry to record the purchase of McLaren?
C. What journal entry should Buchanan write when the company internally generates additional goodwill in the year following the purchase of McLaren?

PA11. LO 11.5 Montezuma Inc. purchases a delivery truck for $15,000. The truck has a salvage value of $3,000 and is expected to be driven for eight years. Montezuma uses the straight-line depreciation method. Calculate the annual depreciation expense. After three years of recording depreciation, Montezuma determines that the delivery truck will only be useful for another three years and that the salvage value will increase to $4,000. Determine the depreciation expense for the final three years of the asset's life, and create the journal entry for year four.

PA12. LO 11.5 Garcia Co. owns equipment that costs $76,800, with accumulated depreciation of $40,800. Garcia sells the equipment for cash. Record the journal entry for the sale of the equipment if Garcia were to sell the equipment for the following amounts:

A. $47,000 cash
B. $36,000 cash
C. $31,000 cash

PA13. LO 11.5 Colquhoun International purchases a warehouse for $300,000. The best estimate of the salvage value at the time of purchase was $15,000, and it is expected to be used for twenty-five years. Colquhoun uses the straight-line depreciation method for all warehouse buildings. After four years of recording depreciation, Colquhoun determines that the warehouse will be useful for only another fifteen years. Calculate annual depreciation expense for the first four years. Determine the depreciation expense for the final fifteen years of the asset's life, and create the journal entry for year five.

Problem Set B

PB1. LO 11.1 Selected accounts from Hanna Corporation's trial balance are as follows. Prepare the assets section of the company's balance sheet.

HANNA CORPORATION Trail Balance December 31		
(Selected Accounts)		
	Debit	**Credit**
Cash	$ 150,000	
Short-term Marketable Securities	145,000	
Accounts Receivable	26,000	
Inventories	90,000	
Other current Assets	10,000	
Land	350,000	
Equipment	145,000	
Accumulated Depreciation: Equipment		$10,000
Goodwill	40,000	
Other Intangible Assets	20,000	

PB2. LO 11.1 Selected accounts from Boxwood Corporation's trial balance are as follows. Prepare the detailed schedule showing the Property, Plant, and Equipment.

BOXWOOD CORPORATION Trail Balance December 31		
(Selected Accounts)		
	Debit	**Credit**
Cash	$ 500,000	
Short-term Marketable Securities	675,000	
Accounts Receivable	149,000	
Inventories	180,000	
Other current Assets	50,000	
Land	700,000	
Buildings	1,800,000	
Accumulated Depreciation: Buildings		$140,000
Equipment	1,150,000	
Accumulated Depreciation: Equipment		50,000
Goodwill	140,000	
Other Intangible Assets	200,000	

PB3. LO 11.2 During the current year, Alanna Co. had the following transactions pertaining to its new office building.

Purchase price of land	$240,000
Legal fees for contracts to purchase land	6,000
Architect fees	8,000
Demolition of the old building on site	15,000
Sale of scrap from old Building	10,000
Construction cost of new building	500,000

A. What should Alanna Co. record on its books for the land? The total cost of land includes all costs of preparing the land for use. The demolition cost of the old building is added to the land costs, and the sale of the old building scrap is subtracted from the land cost.

B. What should Alanna Co. record on its books for the building?

PB4. LO 11.2 During the current year, Arkells Inc. made the following expenditures relating to plant machinery.

- Renovated seven machines for $250,000 to improve efficiency in production of their remaining useful life of eight years
- Low-cost repairs throughout the year totaled $79,000
- Replaced a broken gear on a machine for $6,000

  A. What amount should be expensed during the period?

  B. What amount should be capitalized during the period?

PB5. LO 11.2 Johnson, Incorporated, had the following transactions during the year:

- Purchased a building for $5,000,000 using a mortgage for financing
- Paid $2,000 for ordinary repair on a piece of equipment
- Sold product on account to customers for $1,500,600
- Paid $20,000 cash to add a storage shed in the corner of an existing building
- Paid $360,000 in monthly salaries
- Paid $25,000 for routine maintenance on equipment
- Paid $110,000 for extraordinary repairs
- Depreciation expense recorded for the year is $15,000.

If all transactions were recorded properly, what is the amount of increase to the Property, Plant, and Equipment section of Johnson's balance sheet resulting from this year's transactions? What amount did Johnson report on the income statement for expenses for the year?

PB6. LO 11.3 Underwood's Miners recently purchased the rights to a diamond mine. It is estimated that there are two million tons of ore within the mine. Underwood's paid $46,000,000 for the rights and expects to harvest the ore over the next fifteen years. The following is the expected extraction for the next five years.

- Year 1: 50,000 tons
- Year 2: 900,000 tons
- Year 3: 400,000 tons
- Year 4: 210,000 tons
- Year 5: 150,000 tons

Calculate the depletion expense for the next five years and create the journal entry for year one.

PB7. LO 11.3 Tree Lovers Inc. purchased 2,500 acres of woodland in which it intends to harvest the complete forest, leaving the land barren and worthless. Tree Lovers paid $5,000,000 for the land. Tree Lovers will sell the lumber as it is harvested and it expects to deplete it over ten years (150 acres in year one, 300 acres in year two, 250 acres in year three, 150 acres in year four, and 100 acres in year five). Calculate the depletion expense for the next five years and create the journal entry for year one.

PB8. LO 11.3 Montello Inc. purchases a delivery truck for $25,000. The truck has a salvage value of $6,000 and is expected to be driven for 125,000 miles. Montello uses the units-of-production depreciation method, and in year one the company expects the truck to be driven for 26,000 miles; in year two, 30,000 miles; and in year three, 40,000 miles. Consider how the purchase of the truck will impact Montello's depreciation expense each year and what the truck's book value will be each year after depreciation expense is recorded.

PB9. LO 13.4 Prepare the assets section of the balance sheet as of December 31 for Hooper's International using the following information:

Cash	$ 900,000
Equipment	580,000
Accounts receivable	90,000
Copyright*	60,000
Copyright amortization expense	2,000
Inventory	120,000
Patent	20,000
Building	1,500,000
Depreciation expense building	56,000
Depreciation expense equipment	43,000
Accumulated depreciation building	112,000
Accumulated depreciation equipment	86,000
Sales revenue	590,000
Cost of goods sold	235,000
Selling, general, and administrative expenses	110,000
Goodwill	29,000
*after amortization expense entry was recorded	

PB10. LO 11.4 For each of the following unrelated situations, calculate the annual amortization expense and prepare a journal entry to record the expense:

A. A patent with a seventeen-year remaining legal life was purchased for $850,000. The patent will be usable for another six years.

B. A patent was acquired on a new tablet. The cost of the patent itself was only $12,000, but the market value of the patent is $150,000. The company expects to be able to use this patent for all twenty years of its life.

PB11. LO 11.4 On May 1, 2015, Zoe Inc. purchased Branta Corp. for $15,000,000 in cash. They only received $12,000,000 in net assets. In 2016, the market value of the goodwill obtained from Branta Corp. was valued at $4,000,000, but in 2017 it dropped to $2,000,000. Prepare the journal entry for the creation of goodwill and the entry to record any impairments to it in subsequent years.

PB12. LO 11.4 Farm Fresh Agriculture Company purchased Sunny Side Egg Distribution for $400,000 cash when Sunny Side had net assets worth $390,000.

A. What is the amount of goodwill in this transaction?

B. What is Farm Fresh Agriculture Company's journal entry to record the purchase of Sunny Side Egg Distribution?

C. What journal entry should Farm Fresh Agriculture Company write when the company tests for impairment and determines that goodwill is worth $1,000 in the year following the purchase of Sunny Side?

PB13. LO 11.5 Montezuma Inc. purchases a delivery truck for $20,000. The truck has a salvage value of $8,000 and is expected to be driven for ten years. Montezuma uses the straight-line depreciation method. Calculate the annual depreciation expense. After five years of recording depreciation, Montezuma determines that the delivery truck will be useful for another five years (ten years in total, as originally expected) and that the salvage value will increase to $10,000. Determine the depreciation expense for the final five years of the asset's life, and create the journal entry for years 6–10 (the entry will be the same for each of the five years).

PB14. LO 11.5 Garcia Co. owns equipment that costs $150,000, with accumulated depreciation of $65,000. Garcia sells the equipment for cash. Record the journal entry for the sale of the equipment if Garcia were to sell the equipment for the following amounts:

A. $90,000 cash
B. $85,000 cash
C. $80,000 cash

PB15. LO 11.5 Urquhart Global purchases a building to house its administrative offices for $500,000. The best estimate of the salvage value at the time of purchase was $45,000, and it is expected to be used for forty years. Urquhart uses the straight-line depreciation method for all buildings. After ten years of recording depreciation, Urquhart determines that the building will be useful for a total of fifty years instead of forty. Calculate annual depreciation expense for the first ten years. Determine the depreciation expense for the final forty years of the asset's life, and create the journal entry for year eleven.

Thought Provokers

TP1. LO 11.1 You are an accounting student at your local university. Your brother has recently managed to save $5,000, and he would like to invest some of this money in the stock market, so he's researching various global corporations that are listed on the stock exchange. He is reviewing a company that has "Goodwill" as an item on the balance sheet. He is quite perplexed about what this means, so he asks you for help, knowing that you are taking accounting classes. How would you explain the concept of goodwill to him by comparing it to other types of resources the company has available?

TP2. LO 11.2 Speedy delivery service recently hired a new accountant who discovered that the prior accountant had erroneously capitalized routine repair and maintenance costs on delivery trucks. The costs were added to the overall trucks' book values and depreciated over time. How should Speedy have recorded routine maintenance and repair costs? What effect did the error have on Speedy's balance sheet and income statement?

TP3. LO 11.3 Speedy Delivery has a very lazy accountant. When originally setting up the delivery trucks into the accounting system, the accountant did not want to calculate the expected salvage value for each vehicle. He left salvage value at $0 even though this is not the case. Explain what leaving the salvage value at $0 would do for depreciation. Discuss the differences, if any, between straight-line, double-declining, and units-of-production methods.

TP4. LO 11.4 Malone Industries has been in business for five years and has been very successful. In the past year, it expanded operations by buying Hot Metal Manufacturing for a price greater than the value of the net assets purchased. In the past year, the customer base has expanded much more than expected, and the company's owners want to increase the goodwill account. Your CPA firm has been hired to help Malone prepare year-end financial statements, and your boss has asked you to talk to Malone's managers about goodwill and whether an adjustment can be made to the goodwill account. How do you respond to the owners and managers?

TP5. LO 11.5 Your family started a new manufacturing business making outdoor benches for use in parks and outdoor venues two years ago. The business has been very successful, and sales are soaring. Because of this success, your family realizes that the equipment purchased to start the business will not last as long as expected because the company has needed to run twenty-four-hour production shifts for most of the past year. There has been a lot of wear and tear on the equipment. The original useful lives and salvage values are not as accurate as your family had hoped. Your aunt, who is the production manager for the family business, has approached you because she is concerned about this issue, and she knows you have had an accounting class. What advice do you have for her? How should the company readjust given the realities of the last few years?

12

Current Liabilities

Figure 12.1 Summer Eatery. Proper management of short-term obligations can lead to long-term business success. (credit: modification of “Hands Holding Plate” by unknown/Pixabay, CC0)

Chapter Outline

LO **12.1** Identify and Describe Current Liabilities

LO **12.2** Analyze, Journalize, and Report Current Liabilities

LO **12.3** Define and Apply Accounting Treatment for Contingent Liabilities

LO **12.4** Prepare Journal Entries to Record Short-Term Notes Payable

LO **12.5** Record Transactions Incurred in Preparing Payroll

Why It Matters

Willow knew from a young age that she had a future in food. She has just transformed her passion into a thriving business venture as the owner of a small restaurant called Summer Eatery.

To grow her business, Willow has decided to provide both restaurant dining and catering services. When Summer Eatery accepts catering orders, it requires a client deposit equal to 50% of the total order. Since Summer Eatery has not yet provided the catering services at the time of deposit, the deposit amount is recognized as unearned revenue. Once the catering services have been provided, this liability to the client is reclassified as revenue for the restaurant.

The catering service is a success, and Summer Eatery’s income increases twofold. The increase in business has allowed Willow to form a strong relationship with her vendors (suppliers). Because of this relationship, some suppliers will deliver the food and equipment she needs and allow the restaurant to defer payment until a later date. This helps Summer Eatery because it does not yet have enough cash on hand to pay for the food and equipment. Rather than incur more debt, or have to delay ordering, this arrangement allows Willow to grow and still meet her current obligations.

It takes more than an idea to make a business grow, and Willow will continue to experience the ebb and flow of running a restaurant and catering service. Her management of short-term obligations will be one of the keys to Summer Eatery's future success.

12.1 Identify and Describe Current Liabilities

To assist in understanding current liabilities, assume that you own a landscaping company that provides landscaping maintenance services to clients. As is common for landscaping companies in your area, you require clients to pay an initial deposit of 25% for services before you begin working on their property. Asking a customer to pay for services before you have provided them creates a current liability transaction for your business. As you've learned, liabilities require a future disbursement of assets or services resulting from a prior business activity or transaction. For companies to make more informed decisions, liabilities need to be classified into two specific categories: current liabilities and noncurrent (or long-term) liabilities. The differentiating factor between current and long-term is when the liability is due. The focus of this chapter is on current liabilities, while Long-Term Liabilities emphasizes long-term liabilities.

Fundamentals of Current Liabilities

A **current liability** is a debt or obligation due within a company's standard operating period, typically a year, although there are exceptions that are longer or shorter than a year. A company's typical operating period (sometimes called an operating cycle) is a year, which is used to delineate current and noncurrent liabilities, and current liabilities are considered short term and are typically due within a year or less.

Noncurrent liabilities are long-term obligations with payment typically due in a subsequent operating period. Current liabilities are reported on the classified balance sheet, listed before noncurrent liabilities. Changes in current liabilities from the beginning of an accounting period to the end are reported on the statement of cash flows as part of the cash flows from operations section. An increase in current liabilities over a period increases cash flow, while a decrease in current liabilities decreases cash flow.

Current vs. Noncurrent Liabilities

Current Liabilities	Noncurrent Liabilities
Due within one year or less for a typical one-year operating period	Due in more than one year or longer than one operating period

Table 12.1 A delineator between current and noncurrent liabilities is one year or the company's operating period, whichever is longer.

Current vs. Noncurrent Liabilities

Current Liabilities	Noncurrent Liabilities
Short-term accounts such as: • Accounts Payable • Salaries Payable • Unearned Revenues • Interest Payable • Taxes Payable • Notes Payable within one operating period • Current portion of a longer-term account such as Notes Payable or Bonds Payable	Long-term portion of obligations such as: • Noncurrent portion of a longer-term account such as Notes Payable or Bonds Payable

Table 12.1 A delineator between current and noncurrent liabilities is one year or the company's operating period, whichever is longer.

Examples of Current Liabilities

Common current liabilities include accounts payable, unearned revenues, the current portion of a note payable, and taxes payable. Each of these liabilities is current because it results from a past business activity, with a disbursement or payment due within a period of less than a year.

ETHICAL CONSIDERATIONS

Proper Current Liabilities Reporting and Calculating Burn Rate

When using financial information prepared by accountants, decision-makers rely on ethical accounting practices. For example, investors and creditors look to the current liabilities to assist in calculating a company's annual *burn rate*. The burn rate is the metric defining the monthly and annual cash needs of a company. It is used to help calculate how long the company can maintain operations before becoming insolvent. The proper classification of liabilities as current assists decision-makers in determining the short-term and long-term cash needs of a company.

Another way to think about burn rate is as the amount of cash a company uses that exceeds the amount of cash created by the company's business operations. The burn rate helps indicate how quickly a company is using its cash. Many start-ups have a high cash burn rate due to spending to start the business, resulting in low cash flow. At first, start-ups typically do not create enough cash flow to sustain operations.

Proper reporting of current liabilities helps decision-makers understand a company's burn rate and how much cash is needed for the company to meet its short-term and long-term cash obligations. If misrepresented, the cash needs of the company may not be met, and the company can quickly go out of business. Therefore, it is important that the accountant appropriately report current liabilities because a creditor, investor, or other decision-maker's understanding of a company's specific cash needs helps them make good financial decisions.

Accounts Payable

Accounts payable accounts for financial obligations owed to suppliers after purchasing products or services on credit. This account may be an open credit line between the supplier and the company. An open credit line is a borrowing agreement for an amount of money, supplies, or inventory. The option to borrow from the lender can be exercised at any time within the agreed time period.

An account payable is usually a less formal arrangement than a promissory note for a current note payable. Long-term debt is covered in depth in Long-Term Liabilities. For now, know that for some debt, including short-term or current, a formal contract might be created. This contract provides additional legal protection for the lender in the event of failure by the borrower to make timely payments. Also, the contract often provides an opportunity for the lender to actually sell the rights in the contract to another party.

An invoice from the supplier (such as the one shown in Figure 12.2) detailing the purchase, credit terms, invoice date, and shipping arrangements will suffice for this contractual relationship. In many cases, accounts payable agreements do not include interest payments, unlike notes payable.

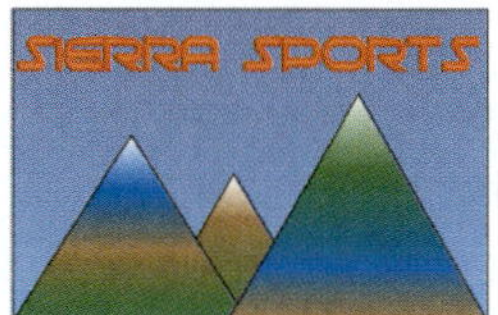

INVOICE

246 Sierra Road,
Anywhere,
USA 01234

Invoice No.: 00257
Invoice Date: 8/12/2016

Bill to:
Joe Johnson

SI NO.	DESCRIPTION	QUANTITY	UNIT PRICE	AMOUNT
1	Youth Snowboard	10	$45.99	$459.90
			Shipping Charges	$56.00
			TOTAL **Credit Term: Net 30**	**$515.90**

Figure 12.2 Accounts Payable. Contract terms for accounts payable transactions are usually listed on an invoice. (attribution: Copyright Rice University, OpenStax, under CC BY-NC-SA 4.0 license)

For example, assume the owner of a clothing boutique purchases hangers from a manufacturer on credit. The organizations may establish an ongoing purchase agreement, which includes purchase details (such as hanger prices and quantities), credit terms (2/10, n/60), an invoice date, and shipping charges (free on board [FOB] shipping) for each order. The basics of shipping charges and credit terms were addressed in Merchandising Transactions if you would like to refresh yourself on the mechanics. Also, to review accounts payable, you can also return to Merchandising Transactions for detailed explanations.

Unearned Revenue

Unearned revenue, also known as deferred revenue, is a customer's advance payment for a product or service that has yet to be provided by the company. Some common unearned revenue situations include subscription services, gift cards, advance ticket sales, lawyer retainer fees, and deposits for services. As you learned when studying the accounting cycle (Analyzing and Recording Transactions, The Adjustment Process, and Completing the Accounting Cycle), we are applying the principles of accrual accounting when revenues and expenses are recognized in different months or years. Under accrual accounting, a company does not record revenue as earned until it has provided a product or service, thus adhering to the revenue recognition principle. Until the customer is provided an obligated product or service, a liability exists, and the amount paid in advance is recognized in the Unearned Revenue account. As soon as the company provides all, or a portion, of the product or service, the value is then recognized as earned revenue.

For example, assume that a landscaping company provides services to clients. The company requires advance payment before rendering service. The customer's advance payment for landscaping is recognized in the Unearned Service Revenue account, which is a liability. Once the company has finished the client's landscaping, it may recognize all of the advance payment as earned revenue in the Service Revenue account. If the landscaping company provides part of the landscaping services within the operating period, it may recognize the value of the work completed at that time.

Perhaps at this point a simple example might help clarify the treatment of unearned revenue. Assume that the previous landscaping company has a three-part plan to prepare lawns of new clients for next year. The plan includes a treatment in November 2019, February 2020, and April 2020. The company has a special rate of $120 if the client prepays the entire $120 before the November treatment. In real life, the company would hope to have dozens or more customers. However, to simplify this example, we analyze the journal entries from one customer. Assume that the customer prepaid the service on October 15, 2019, and all three treatments occur on the first day of the month of service. We also assume that $40 in revenue is allocated to each of the three treatments.

Before examining the journal entries, we need some key information. Because part of the service will be provided in 2019 and the rest in 2020, we need to be careful to keep the recognition of revenue in its proper period. If all of the treatments occur, $40 in revenue will be recognized in 2019, with the remaining $80 recognized in 2020. Also, since the customer could request a refund before any of the services have been provided, we need to ensure that we do not recognize revenue until it has been earned. While it is nice to receive funding before you have performed the services, in essence, all you have received when you get the money is a liability (unearned service revenue), with the hope of it eventually becoming revenue. The following journal entries are built upon the client receiving all three treatments. First, for the prepayment of future services and for the revenue earned in 2019, the journal entries are shown.

JOURNAL			
Date	**Account**	**Debit**	**Credit**
Oct. 15, 2019	Cash	120	
	Unearned Revenue: Landscaping		120
	To recognize prepayment of future landscaping services		
Nov. 1, 2019	Unearned Revenue: Landscaping	40	
	Earned Revenue: Landscaping		40
	To record landscaping revenue earned		

For the revenue earned in 2020, the journal entries would be.

JOURNAL			
Date	**Account**	**Debit**	**Credit**
Feb. 1, 2020	Unearned Revenue: Landscaping	40	
	Earned Revenue: Landscaping		40
	To record landscaping revenue earned		
Apr. 1, 2020	Unearned Revenue: Landscaping	40	
	Earned Revenue: Landscaping		40
	To record landscaping revenue earned		

Figure 12.3 Advance Ticket Sales. Season ticket sales are considered unearned revenue because customers pay for them in advance of any games played. (credit: "Fans in Razorback Stadium (Fayetteville, AR)" by Rmcclen/Wikimedia Commons, Public Domain)

CONCEPTS IN PRACTICE

Thinking about Unearned Revenue

When thinking about unearned revenue, consider the example of Amazon.com, Inc. Amazon has a large business portfolio that includes a widening presence in the online product and service space. Amazon has two services in particular that contribute to their unearned revenue account: Amazon Web Services and Prime membership.

According to *Business Insider*, Amazon had $4.8 billion in unearned revenue recognized in their fourth quarter report (December 2016), with most of that contribution coming from Amazon Web Services.[1] This is an increase from prior quarters. The growth is due to larger and longer contracts for web services. The advance payment for web services is transferred to revenue over the term of the contract. The same is true for Prime membership. Amazon receives $99 in advance pay from customers, which is amortized over the twelve-month period of the service agreement. This means that each month, Amazon only recognizes $8.25 per Prime membership payment as earned revenue.

Current Portion of a Note Payable

A **note payable** is a debt to a lender with specific repayment terms, which can include principal and interest. A note payable has written contractual terms that make it available to sell to another party. The **principal** on a note refers to the initial borrowed amount, not including interest. In addition to repayment of principal, interest may accrue. **Interest** is a monetary incentive to the lender, which justifies loan risk.

Let's review the concept of interest. Interest is an expense that you might pay for the use of someone else's money. For example, if you have a credit card and you owe a balance at the end of the month it will typically charge you a percentage, such as 1.5% a month (which is the same as 18% annually) on the balance that you owe. Assuming that you owe $400, your interest charge for the month would be $400 × 1.5%, or $6.00. To pay your balance due on your monthly statement would require $406 (the $400 balance due plus the $6 interest expense).

We make one more observation about interest: interest rates are typically quoted in annual terms. For example, if you borrowed money to buy a car, your interest expense might be quoted as 9%. Note that this is an annual rate. If you are making monthly payments, the monthly charge for interest would be 9% divided by twelve, or 0.75% a month. For example, if you borrowed $20,000, and made sixty equal monthly payments, your monthly payment would be $415.17, and your interest expense component of the $415.17 payment would be $150.00. The formula to calculate interest on either an annual or partial-year basis is:

Interest = Principal (amount borrowed) × Interest Rate × Period of Time

In our example this would be

$$\$20{,}000 \times 9\% \times \frac{1}{12} = \$150$$

The good news is that for a loan such as our car loan or even a home loan, the loan is typically what is called *fully amortizing*. At this point, you just need to know that in our case the amount that you owe would go from a balance due of $20,000 down to $0 after the twentieth payment and the part of your $415.17 monthly payment allocated to interest would be less each month. For example, your last (sixtieth) payment would only incur $3.09 in interest, with the remaining payment covering the last of the principle owed. See Figure 13.7 for an exhibit that demonstrates this concept.

1 Eugene Kim. "An Overlooked Part of Amazon Will Be in the Spotlight When the Company Reports Earnings." *Business Insider*. April 28, 2016. https://www.businessinsider.com/amazon-unearned-revenue-growth-shows-why-it-spent-more-on-shipping-last-quarter-2016-4

CONCEPTS IN PRACTICE

Applying Amortization

Car loans, mortgages, and education loans have an amortization process to pay down debt. Amortization of a loan requires periodic scheduled payments of principal and interest until the loan is paid in full. Every period, the same payment amount is due, but interest expense is paid first, with the remainder of the payment going toward the principal balance. When a customer first takes out the loan, most of the scheduled payment is made up of interest, and a very small amount goes to reducing the principal balance. Over time, more of the payment goes toward reducing the principal balance rather than interest.

For example, let's say you take out a car loan in the amount of $10,000. The annual interest rate is 3%, and you are required to make scheduled payments each month in the amount of $400. You first need to determine the monthly interest rate by dividing 3% by twelve months (3%/12), which is 0.25%. The monthly interest rate of 0.25% is multiplied by the outstanding principal balance of $10,000 to get an interest expense of $25. The scheduled payment is $400; therefore, $25 is applied to interest, and the remaining $375 ($400 – $25) is applied to the outstanding principal balance. This leaves an outstanding principal balance of $9,625. Next month, interest expense is computed using the new principal balance outstanding of $9,625. The new interest expense is $24.06 ($9,625 × 0.25%). This means $24.06 of the $400 payment applies to interest, and the remaining $375.94 ($400 – $24.06) is applied to the outstanding principal balance to get a new balance of $9,249.06 ($9,625 – $375.94). These computations occur until the entire principal balance is paid in full.

A note payable is usually classified as a long-term (noncurrent) liability if the note period is longer than one year or the standard operating period of the company. However, during the company's current operating period, any portion of the long-term note due that will be paid in the current period is considered a **current portion of a note payable**. The outstanding balance note payable during the current period remains a noncurrent note payable. Note that this does not include the interest portion of the payments. On the balance sheet, the current portion of the noncurrent liability is separated from the remaining noncurrent liability. No journal entry is required for this distinction, but some companies choose to show the transfer from a noncurrent liability to a current liability.

For example, a bakery company may need to take out a $100,000 loan to continue business operations. The bakery's outstanding note principal is $100,000. Terms of the loan require equal annual principal repayments of $10,000 for the next ten years. Payments will be made on July 1 of each of the ten years. Even though the overall $100,000 note payable is considered long term, the $10,000 required repayment during the company's operating cycle is considered current (short term). This means $10,000 would be classified as the current portion of a noncurrent note payable, and the remaining $90,000 would remain a noncurrent note payable.

The portion of a note payable due in the current period is recognized as current, while the remaining outstanding balance is a noncurrent note payable. For example, Figure 12.4 shows that $18,000 of a $100,000 note payable is scheduled to be paid within the current period (typically within one year). The remaining $82,000 is considered a long-term liability and will be paid over its remaining life.

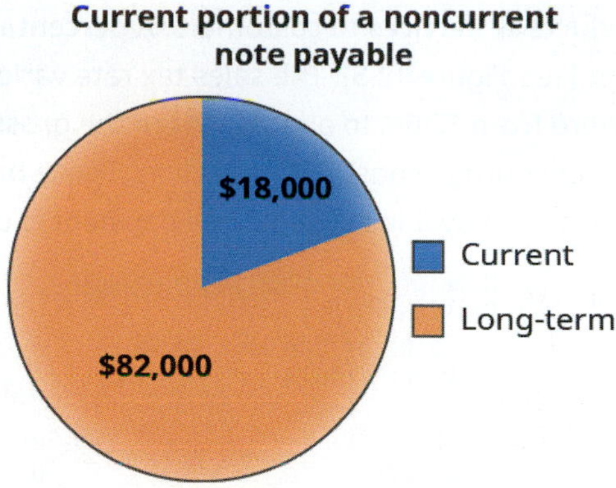

Figure 12.4 Current Portion of a Noncurrent Note Payable. (attribution: Copyright Rice University, OpenStax, under CC BY-NC-SA 4.0 license)

In addition to the $18,000 portion of the note payable that will be paid in the current year, any accrued interest on both the current portion and the long-term portion of the note payable that is due will also be paid. Assume, for example, that for the current year $7,000 of interest will be accrued. In the current year the debtor will pay a total of $25,000—that is, $7,000 in interest and $18,000 for the current portion of the note payable. A similar type of payment will be paid each year for as long as any of the note payable remains; however, the annual interest expense would be reduced since the remaining note payable owed will be reduced by the previous payments.

Interest payable can also be a current liability if accrual of interest occurs during the operating period but has yet to be paid. An annual interest rate is established as part of the loan terms. Interest accrued is recorded in Interest Payable (a credit) and Interest Expense (a debit). To calculate interest, the company can use the following equations. This method assumes a twelve-month denominator in the calculation, which means that we are using the calculation method based on a 360-day year. This method was more commonly used prior to the ability to do the calculations using calculators or computers, because the calculation was easier to perform. However, with today's technology, it is more common to see the interest calculation performed using a 365-day year. We will demonstrate both methods.

$$\textbf{Interest Payable} = \textbf{Annual Interest Rate} \times \textbf{Loan Principal} \times \textbf{Part of Year}$$

$$\textbf{Part of Year} = \frac{\textbf{Number of Months of Accrued Interest}}{\textbf{12 Months}}$$

For example, we assume the bakery has an annual interest rate on its loan of 7%. The loan interest began accruing on July 1 and it is now December 31. The bakery has accrued six months of interest and would compute the interest liability as

$$\$100{,}000 \times 7\% \times \frac{6}{12} = \$3{,}500$$

The $3,500 is recognized in Interest Payable (a credit) and Interest Expense (a debit).

Taxes Payable

Taxes payable refers to a liability created when a company collects taxes on behalf of employees and customers or for tax obligations owed by the company, such as sales taxes or income taxes. A future payment to a government agency is required for the amount collected. Some examples of taxes payable include sales tax and income taxes.

Sales taxes result from sales of products or services to customers. A percentage of the sale is charged to the customer to cover the tax obligation (see Figure 12.5). The sales tax rate varies by state and local municipalities but can range anywhere from 1.76% to almost 10% of the gross sales price. Some states do not have sales tax because they want to encourage consumer spending. Those businesses subject to sales taxation hold the sales tax in the Sales Tax Payable account until payment is due to the governing body.

Receipt: 001-190310-010-031468
Station: Station 7
Date: 3/10/2019 1:24 PM
Cashier: Erin D

Qty	Item	Amount
1	Fly High Party	299.99
12	Party Jumper	.00
12	Group 30 Minute Add-On	47.88
1	Birthday Shirt: Adult Smal	.00
1	Fly High Party Add On	18.99
4	Group 30 Minute Add-On	15.96
4	Party Jumper	.00
15	Bottled Water	29.85

Group Name:
Event No: 21273
Arrival Date: 3/10/2019
Description: Sam- Fly High

Group Total: $412.67
Less Discounts: $0.00
Sub Total: $412.67
WI Sales Tax: $22.70
Total Amount Due: $435.37

Figure 12.5 Sales Tax. Many businesses are required to charge a sales tax on products or services sold. (credit: modification of "Sales Tax" by Kerry Ceszyk/Flickr, CC BY 4.0)

For example, assume that each time a shoe store sells a $50 pair of shoes, it will charge the customer a sales tax of 8% of the sales price. The shoe store collects a total of $54 from the customer. The $4 sales tax is a current liability until distributed within the company's operating period to the government authority collecting sales tax.

Income taxes are required to be withheld from an employee's salary for payment to a federal, state, or local authority (hence they are known as *withholding taxes*). This withholding is a percentage of the employee's gross pay. Income taxes are discussed in greater detail in Record Transactions Incurred in Preparing Payroll.

LINK TO LEARNING

Businesses can use the Internal Revenue Service's Sales Tax Deduction Calculator and associated tips and guidance (https://openstax.org/l/50IRSTaxCalc) to determine their estimated sales tax obligation owed to the state and local government authority.

12.2 Analyze, Journalize, and Report Current Liabilities

To illustrate current liability entries, we use transaction information from Sierra Sports (see Figure 12.6). Sierra Sports owns and operates a sporting goods store in the Southwest specializing in sports apparel and equipment. The company engages in regular business activities with suppliers, creditors, customers, and employees.

Figure 12.6 Sierra Sports Logo. (attribution: Copyright Rice University, OpenStax, under CC BY-NC-SA 4.0 license)

Accounts Payable

On August 1, Sierra Sports purchases $12,000 of soccer equipment from a manufacturer (supplier) on credit. Assume for the following examples that Sierra Sports uses the perpetual inventory method, which uses the Inventory account when the company buys, sells, or adjusts the inventory balance, such as in the following example where they qualified for a discount. In the current transaction, credit terms are 2/10, n/30, the invoice date is August 1, and shipping charges are FOB shipping point (which is included in the purchase cost).

Recall from Merchandising Transactions, that credit terms of 2/10, n/30 signal the payment terms and discount, and FOB shipping point establishes the point of merchandise ownership, the responsibility during transit, and which entity pays shipping charges. Therefore, 2/10, n/30 means Sierra Sports has ten days to pay its balance due to receive a 2% discount, otherwise Sierra Sports has net thirty days, in this case August 31, to pay in full but not receive a discount. FOB shipping point signals that since Sierra Sports takes ownership of the merchandise when it leaves the manufacturer, it takes responsibility for the merchandise in transit and will pay the shipping charges.

Sierra Sports would make the following journal entry on August 1.

JOURNAL			
Date	**Account**	**Debit**	**Credit**
Aug. 1	Inventory	12,000	
	Accounts Payable		12,000
	To recognize the purchase of equipment on credit, terms 2/10, n/30, invoice date Aug. 1		

The merchandise is purchased from the supplier on credit. In this case, Accounts Payable would increase (a credit) for the full amount due. Inventory, the asset account, would increase (a debit) for the purchase price of the merchandise.

If Sierra Sports pays the full amount owed on August 10, it qualifies for the discount, and the following entry would occur.

JOURNAL			
Date	**Account**	**Debit**	**Credit**
Aug. 10	Accounts Payable Inventory Cash *To recognize payment of the amount due, less discount*	12,000	 240 11,760

Assume that the payment to the manufacturer occurs within the discount period of ten days (2/10, n/30) and is recognized in the entry. Accounts Payable decreases (debit) for the original amount due, Inventory decreases (credit) for the discount amount of $240 ($12,000 × 2%), and Cash decreases (credit) for the remaining balance due after discount.

Note that Inventory is decreased in this entry because the value of the merchandise (soccer equipment) is reduced. When applying the perpetual inventory method, this reduction is required by generally accepted accounting principles (GAAP) (under the cost principle) to reflect the actual cost of the merchandise.

A second possibility is that Sierra will return part of the purchase before the ten-day discount window has expired. Assume in this example that $1,000 of the $12,000 purchase was returned to the seller on August 8 and the remaining account payable due was paid by Sierra to the seller on August 10, which means that Sierra qualified for the remaining eligible discount. The following two journal entries represent the return of inventory and the subsequent payment for the remaining account payable owed. The initial journal entry from August 1 will still apply, because we assume that Sierra intended to keep the full $12,000 of inventory when the purchase was made.

When the $1,000 in inventory was returned on August 8, the accounts payable account and the inventory accounts should be reduced by $1,000 as demonstrated in this journal entry.

JOURNAL			
Date	**Account**	**Debit**	**Credit**
Aug. 8	Accounts Payable Inventory *To recognize return of inventory purchased*	1,000	 1,000

After this transaction, Sierra still owed $11,000 and still had $11,000 in inventory from the purchase, assuming that Sierra had not sold any of it yet.

When Sierra paid the remaining balance on August 10, the company qualified for the discount. However, since Sierra only owed a remaining balance of $11,000 and not the original $12,000, the discount received was 2% of $11,000, or $220, as demonstrated in this journal entry. Since Sierra owed $11,000 and received a discount of $220, the supplier was paid $10,780. This second journal entry is the same as the one that would have recognized an original purchase of $11,000 that qualified for a discount.

JOURNAL			
Date	**Account**	**Debit**	**Credit**
Aug. 8	Accounts Payable Inventory Cash *To recognize payment of remaining accounts payable balance after qualifying for the discount*	11,000	 220 10,780

Remember that since we are assuming that Sierra was using the perpetual inventory method, purchases, payments, and adjustments in goods available for sale are reflected in the company's Inventory account. In our example, one of the potential adjustments is that discounts received are recorded as reductions to the Inventory account.

To demonstrate this concept, after buying $12,000 in inventory, returning $1,000 in inventory, and then paying for the remaining balance and qualifying for the discount, Sierra's Inventory balance increased by $10,780, as shown.

SIERRA SPORTS Inventory Account	
Initial inventory purchase (Aug. 1)	$12,000
Return of inventory (Aug. 8)	(1,000)
Subtotal (Aug. 8)	$11,000
Discount allowed Aug. 10 (reduction in inventory)	(220)
Final Inventory after Account Payable	$10,780

If Sierra had bought $11,000 of inventory on August 1 and paid cash and taken the discount, after taking the $220 discount, the increase of Inventory on their balance sheet would have been $10,780, as it finally ended up being in our more complicated set of transactions on three different days. The important factor is that the company qualified for a 2% discount on inventory that had a retail price before discounts of $11,000.

In a final possible scenario, assume that Sierra Sports remitted payment outside of the discount window on August 28, but inside of thirty days. In this case, they did not qualify for the discount, and assuming that they made no returns they paid the full, undiscounted balance of $12,000.

JOURNAL			
Date	**Account**	**Debit**	**Credit**
Aug. 28	Accounts Payable	12,000	
	Cash		12,000
	To recognize payment of the amount due, no discount applied		

If this occurred, both Accounts Payable and Cash decreased by $12,000. Inventory is not affected in this instance because the full cost of the merchandise was paid; so, the increase in value for the inventory was $12,000, and not the $11,760 value determined in our beginning transactions where they qualified for the discount.

YOUR TURN

Accounting for Advance Payments

You are the owner of a catering company and require advance payments from clients before providing catering services. You receive an order from the Coopers, who would like you to cater their wedding on June 10. The Coopers pay you $5,500 cash on March 25. Record your journal entries for the initial payment from the Coopers, and when the catering service has been provided on June 10.

Solution

JOURNAL			
Date	**Account**	**Debit**	**Credit**
Mar. 25	Cash	5,500	
	Unearned Revenue: Catering		5,500
	To recognize advanced payment from client		
Jun. 10	Unearned Revenue: Catering	5,500	
	Revenue: Catering		5,500
	To recognize catering revenue earned		

Unearned Revenue

Sierra Sports has contracted with a local youth football league to provide all uniforms for participating teams. The league pays for the uniforms in advance, and Sierra Sports provides the customized uniforms shortly after purchase. The following situation shows the journal entry for the initial purchase with cash. Assume the league pays Sierra Sports for twenty uniforms (cost per uniform is $30, for a total of $600) on April 3.

JOURNAL			
Date	**Account**	**Debit**	**Credit**
Apr. 3	Cash	600	
	Unearned Uniform Revenue		600
	To recognize advanced payment for 20 uniforms at $30 each		

Sierra Sports would see an increase to Cash (debit) for the payment made from the football league. The revenue from the sale of the uniforms is $600 (20 uniforms × $30 per uniform). Unearned Uniform Revenue accounts reflect the prepayment from the league, which cannot be recognized as earned revenue until the uniforms are provided. Unearned Uniform Revenue is a current liability account that increases (credit) with the increase in outstanding product debt.

Sierra provides the uniforms on May 6 and records the following entry.

JOURNAL			
Date	**Account**	**Debit**	**Credit**
May 6	Unearned Revenue: Uniforms	600	
	Revenue: Uniforms		600
	To recognize uniform revenue as earned		
May 6	Cost of Goods Sold	280	
	Inventory		280
	To recognize cost of goods sold of uniform sales		

Now that Sierra has provided all of the uniforms, the unearned revenue can be recognized as earned. This satisfies the revenue recognition principle. Therefore, Unearned Uniform Revenue would decrease (debit), and Uniform Revenue would increase (credit) for the total amount.

Let's say that Sierra only provides half the uniforms on May 6 and supplies the rest of the order on June 2. The company may not recognize revenue until a product (or a portion of a product) has been provided. This means only half the revenue can be recognized on May 6 ($300) because only half of the uniforms were provided. The rest of the revenue recognition will have to wait until June 2. Since only half of the uniforms were delivered on

May 6, only half of the costs of goods sold would be recognized on May 6. The other half of the costs of goods sold would be recognized on June 2 when the other half of the uniforms were delivered. The following entries show the separate entries for partial revenue recognition.

JOURNAL			
Date	**Account**	**Debit**	**Credit**
May 6	Unearned Revenue: Uniforms Revenue: Uniforms *To recognize partial uniform revenue as earned*	300	 300
May 6	Cost of Goods Sold Inventory *To recognize cost of goods sold of uniform sales*	140	 140
Jun. 2	Unearned Revenue: Uniforms Revenue: Uniforms *To recognize partial uniform revenue as earned*	300	 300
Jun. 2	Cost of Goods Sold Inventory *To recognize cost of goods sold of uniform sales*	140	 140

In another scenario using the same cost information, assume that on April 3, the league contracted for the production of the uniforms on credit with terms 5/10, n/30. They signed a contract for the production of the uniforms, so an account receivable was created for Sierra, as shown.

JOURNAL			
Date	**Account**	**Debit**	**Credit**
Apr. 3	Accounts Receivable Unearned Revenue: Uniforms *To recognize advanced payment on credit for 20 uniforms (5/10, n/30)*	600	 600

Sierra and the league have worked out credit terms and a discount agreement. As such, the league can delay cash payment for ten days and receive a discount, or for thirty days with no discount assessed. Instead of cash increasing for Sierra, Accounts Receivable increases (debit) for the amount the football league owes.

The league pays for the uniforms on April 15, and Sierra provides all uniforms on May 6. The following entry shows the payment on credit.

JOURNAL			
Date	**Account**	**Debit**	**Credit**
Apr. 15	Cash Accounts Receivable *To recognize payment of the amount due; no discount applied*	600	 600

The football league made payment outside of the discount period, since April 15 is more than ten days from the invoice date. Thus, they do not receive the 5% discount. Cash increases (debit) for the $600 paid by the football league, and Accounts Receivable decreases (credit).

In the next example, let’s assume that the league made payment within the discount window, on April 13. The following entry occurs.

JOURNAL			
Date	**Account**	**Debit**	**Credit**
Apr. 13	Cash Sales Discount Accounts Receivable *To recognize league payment with 5 percent discount*	570 30	 600

In this case, Accounts Receivable decreases (credit) for the original amount owed, Sales Discount increases (debit) for the discount amount of $30 ($600 × 5%), and Cash increases (debit) for the $570 paid by the football league less discount.

When the company provides the uniforms on May 6, Unearned Uniform Revenue decreases (debit) and Uniform Revenue increases (credit) for $600.

JOURNAL			
Date	**Account**	**Debit**	**Credit**
May 6	Unearned Revenue: Uniforms Revenue: Uniforms *To recognize uniform revenue as earned*	600	 600

ETHICAL CONSIDERATIONS

Stock Options and Unearned Revenue Manipulation

The anticipated income of public companies is projected by stock market analysts through *whisper-earnings*, or forecasted earnings. It can be advantageous for a company to have its stock beat the stock market's expectation of earnings. Likewise, falling below the market's expectation can be a disadvantage. If a company's whisper-earnings are not going to be met, there could be pressure on the chief financial officer to misrepresent earnings through manipulation of unearned revenue accounts to better match the stock market's expectation.

Because many executives, other top management, and even employees have stock options, this can also provide incentive to manipulate earnings. A stock option sets a minimum price for the stock on a certain date. This is the date the option vests, at what is commonly called the *strike price*. Options are worthless if the stock price on the vesting date is lower than the price at which they were granted. This could result in a loss of income, potentially incentivizing earnings manipulation to meet the stock market's expectations and exceed the vested stock price in the option.

Researchers have found that when executive options are about to vest, companies are more likely to present financial statements meeting or just slightly beating the earnings forecasts of analysts. The proximity of the actual earnings to earnings forecasts suggests they were manipulated because of the vesting.[2] As Douglas R. Carmichael points out, "public companies that fail to report quarterly earnings which meet or exceed analysts' expectations often experience a drop in their stock prices. This can lead to practices that sometimes include fraudulent overstatement of quarterly revenue."[3] If earnings meet or exceed expectations, a stock price can hit or surpass the vested stock price in the option. For company members with stock options, this could result in higher income. Thus, financial statements that align closely with analysts' estimates, rather than showing large projections above or below whisper-earnings, could indicate that accounting information has possibly been adjusted to meet the expected numbers. Such manipulations can be made in unearned revenue accounts.

In November 1998, the Securities and Exchange Commission (SEC) issued Practice Alert 98-3, Revenue Recognition Issues, SEC Practice Section Professional Issues Task Force, recognizing and discussing the manipulation of earnings used to exceed stock market and analysts' expectations. Accountants should watch for revenue recognition related issues in preparing the financial statements of their company or client, especially when employees' or management's stock options are about to vest.

Current Portion of a Noncurrent Note Payable

Sierra Sports takes out a bank loan on January 1, 2017 to cover expansion costs for a new store. The note amount is $360,000. The note has terms of repayment that include equal principal payments annually over the next twenty years. The annual interest rate on the loan is 9%. Interest accumulates each month based on the standard interest rate formula discussed previously, and on the current outstanding principal balance of the loan. Sierra records interest accumulation every three months, at the end of each third month. The initial loan (note) entry follows.

JOURNAL			
Date	**Account**	**Debit**	**Credit**
Jan. 1	Cash Notes Payable *To recognize long-term loan, interest rate 9%*	360,000	 360,000

Notes Payable increases (credit) for the full loan principal amount. Cash increases (debit) as well. On March 31, the end of the first three months, Sierra records their first interest accumulation.

JOURNAL			
Date	**Account**	**Debit**	**Credit**
Mar. 31	Interest Expense Interest Payable *To recognize interest accumulated after three months*	8,100	 8,100

Interest Expense increases (debit) as does Interest Payable (credit) for the amount of interest accumulated but unpaid at the end of the three-month period. The amount $8,100 is found by using the interest formula, where the outstanding principal balance is $360,000, interest rate of 9%, and the part of the year being three out of twelve months: $360,000 × 9% × (3/12).

The same entry for interest will occur every three months until year-end. When accumulated interest is paid on January 1 of the following year, Sierra would record this entry.

2 Jena McGregor. "How Stock Options Lead CEOs to Put Their Own Interests First." *Washington Post*. February 11, 2014. https://www.washingtonpost.com/news/on-leadership/wp/2014/02/11/how-stock-options-lead-ceos-to-put-their-own-interests-first/?utm_term=.24d99a4fb1a5

3 Douglas R. Carmichael. "Hocus-Pocus Accounting." *Journal of Accountancy*. October 1, 1999. https://www.journalofaccountancy.com/issues/1999/oct/carmichl.html

JOURNAL			
Date	**Account**	**Debit**	**Credit**
Jan. 1	Interest Payable Cash *To recognize interest payment for 2017*	32,400	 32,400

Both Interest Payable and Cash decrease for the total interest amount accumulated during 2017. This is calculated by taking each three-month interest accumulation of $8,100 and multiplying by the four recorded interest entries for the periods. You could also compute this by taking the original principal balance and multiplying by 9%.

On December 31, 2017, the first principal payment is due. The following entry occurs to show payment of this principal amount due in the current period.

JOURNAL			
Date	**Account**	**Debit**	**Credit**
Dec. 31	Notes Payable Cash *To recognize current principal payment for 2017*	18,000	 18,000

Notes Payable decreases (debit), as does Cash (credit), for the amount of the noncurrent note payable due in the current period. This amount is calculated by dividing the original principal amount ($360,000) by twenty years to get an annual current principal payment of $18,000 ($360,000/20).

While the accounts used to record a reduction in Notes Payable are the same as the accounts used for a noncurrent note, the reporting on the balance sheet is classified in a different area. The current portion of the noncurrent note payable ($18,000) is reported under Current Liabilities, and the remaining noncurrent balance of $342,000 ($360,000 – $18,000) is classified and displayed under noncurrent liabilities, as shown in Figure 12.7.

SIERRA SPORTS Balance Sheet December 31, 2017			
Assets		**Liabilities and Stockholders Equity**	
Current Assets		Current Liabilities	
Cash	$ 21,580	Note Payable: Current	$ 18,000
Account Receivable	2,000	Accounts Payable	9,000
Total Current Assets	23,580	Unearned Revenue	4,000
		Total Current Liabilities	31,000
Property, Plant, and Equipment			
Buildings	300,000	Long-term Liabilities	
Sporting Equipment	60,000	Notes Payable	342,000
Total Property, Plant, and Equipment	360,000		
		Stockholders' Equity	
		Common Stock	5,000
		Retained Earnings	5,580
		Total Stockholders' Equity	10,580
Total Assets	$383,580	Total Liabilities and Stockholders' Equity	$383,580

Figure 12.7 Sierra Sports Balance Sheet. (attribution: Copyright Rice University, OpenStax, under CC BY-NC-SA 4.0 license)

Taxes Payable

Let's consider our previous example where Sierra Sports purchased $12,000 of soccer equipment in August. Sierra now sells the soccer equipment to a local soccer league for $18,000 cash on August 20. The sales tax rate is 6%. The following revenue entry would occur.

JOURNAL			
Date	**Account**	**Debit**	**Credit**
Aug. 20	Cash	19,080	
	Sales Tax Payable		1,080
	Sales		18,000
	To recognize soccer equipment sale, tax rate 6%		

Cash increases (debit) for the sales amount plus sales tax. Sales Tax Payable increases (credit) for the 6% tax rate ($18,000 × 6%). Sierra's tax liability is owed to the State Tax Board. Sales increases (credit) for the original amount of the sale, not including sales tax. If Sierra's customer pays on credit, Accounts Receivable would increase (debit) for $19,080 rather than Cash.

When Sierra remits payment to the State Tax Board on October 1, the following entry occurs.

JOURNAL			
Date	**Account**	**Debit**	**Credit**
Oct. 1	Sales Tax Payable	1,080	
	Cash		1,080
	To recognize State Tax Board payment		

Sales Tax Payable and Cash decrease for the payment amount of $1,080. Sales tax is not an expense to the business because the company is holding it on account for another entity.

Sierra Sports payroll tax journal entries will appear in Record Transactions Incurred in Preparing Payroll.

YOUR TURN

Accounting for Purchase Discounts

You own a shipping and packaging facility and provide shipping services to customers. You have worked out a contract with a local supplier to provide your business with packing materials on an ongoing basis. Terms of your agreement allow for delayed payment of up to thirty days from the invoice date, with an incentive to pay within ten days to receive a 5% discount on the packing materials. On April 3, you purchase 1,000 boxes (Box Inventory) from this supplier at a cost per box of $1.25. You pay the amount due to the supplier on April 11. Record the journal entries to recognize the initial purchase on April 3, and payment of the amount due on April 11.

Solution

JOURNAL			
Date	Account	Debit	Credit
Apr. 3	Box Inventory	1,250	
	Accounts Payable		1,250
	To recognize purchases of boxes, 5/10, n/30		
Apr. 11	Accounts Payable	1,250	
	Box Inventory		62.50
	Cash		1,187.50
	To recognize payment, less discount		

12.3 Define and Apply Accounting Treatment for Contingent Liabilities

What happens if your business anticipates incurring a loss or debt? Do you need to report this if you are uncertain it will occur? What if you know the loss or debt will occur but it has not happened yet? Do you have to report this event now, or in the future? These are questions businesses must ask themselves when exploring contingencies and their effect on liabilities.

A **contingency** occurs when a current situation has an outcome that is unknown or uncertain and will not be resolved until a future point in time. The outcome could be positive or negative. A **contingent liability** can produce a future debt or negative obligation for the company. Some examples of contingent liabilities include pending litigation (legal action), warranties, customer insurance claims, and bankruptcy.

While a contingency may be positive or negative, we only focus on outcomes that may produce a liability for the company (negative outcome), since these might lead to adjustments in the financial statements in certain cases. Positive contingencies do not require or allow the same types of adjustments to the company's financial statements as do negative contingencies, since accounting standards do not permit positive contingencies to be recorded.

Pending litigation involves legal claims against the business that may be resolved at a future point in time. The outcome of the lawsuit has yet to be determined but could have negative future impact on the business.

Warranties arise from products or services sold to customers that cover certain defects (see Figure 12.8). It is unclear if a customer will need to use a warranty, and when, but this is a possibility for each product or service sold that includes a warranty. The same idea applies to insurance claims (car, life, and fire, for example), and bankruptcy. There is an uncertainty that a claim will transpire, or bankruptcy will occur. If the contingencies do occur, it may still be uncertain when they will come to fruition, or the financial implications.

Figure 12.8 One-Year Warranty. Companies may offer product or service warranties. (credit: modification of "Seal Guaranteed" by "harshahars"/Pixabay, CC0)

The answer to whether or not uncertainties must be reported comes from Financial Accounting Standards Board (FASB) pronouncements.

Two Financial Accounting Standards Board (FASB) Requirements for Recognition of a Contingent Liability

There are two requirements for contingent liability recognition:

1. There is a likelihood of occurrence.
2. Measurement of the occurrence is classified as either estimable or inestimable.

Application of Likelihood of Occurrence Requirement

Let's explore the likelihood of occurrence requirement in more detail.

According to the FASB, if there is a probable liability determination before the preparation of financial statements has occurred, there is a **likelihood of occurrence**, and the liability must be disclosed and recognized. This financial recognition and disclosure are recognized in the current financial statements. The income statement and balance sheet are typically impacted by contingent liabilities.

For example, Sierra Sports has a one-year warranty on part repairs and replacements for a soccer goal they sell. The warranty is good for one year. Sierra Sports notices that some of its soccer goals have rusted screws that require replacement, but they have already sold goals with this problem to customers. There is a probability that someone who purchased the soccer goal may bring it in to have the screws replaced. Not only does the contingent liability meet the probability requirement, it also meets the measurement requirement.

Application of Measurement Requirement

The **measurement requirement** refers to the company's ability to reasonably estimate the amount of loss. Even though a reasonable estimate is the company's best guess, it should not be a frivolous number. For a financial figure to be reasonably estimated, it could be based on past experience or industry standards (see Figure 12.9). It could also be determined by the potential future, known financial outcome.

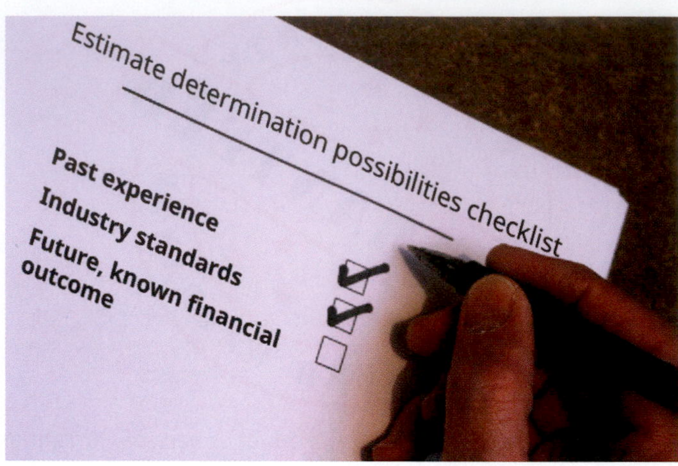

Figure 12.9 Contingent Liabilities Estimation Checklist. These are possible ways to determine a contingent liability financial estimate. (credit: modification of "Checklist" by Alan Cleaver/Flickr, CC BY 2.0)

Let's continue to use Sierra Sports' soccer goal warranty as our example. If the warranties are honored, the company should know how much each screw costs, labor cost required, time commitment, and any overhead costs incurred. This amount could be a reasonable estimate for the parts repair cost per soccer goal. Since not all warranties may be honored (warranty expired), the company needs to make a reasonable determination for the amount of honored warranties to get a more accurate figure.

Another way to establish the warranty liability could be an estimation of honored warranties as a percentage of sales. In this instance, Sierra could estimate warranty claims at 10% of its soccer goal sales.

When determining if the contingent liability should be recognized, there are four potential treatments to consider.

Let's expand our discussion and add a brief example of the calculation and application of warranty expenses. To begin, in many ways a warranty expense works similarly to the bad debt expense concept covered in Accounting for Receivables in that the anticipated expense is determined by examining past period expense experiences and then basing the current expense on current sales data. Also, as with bad debts, the warranty repairs typically are made in an accounting period sometimes months or even years after the initial sale of the product, which means that we need to estimate future costs to comply with the revenue recognition and matching principles of generally accepted accounting principles (GAAP).

Some industries have such a large number of transactions and a vast data bank of past warranty claims that they have an easier time estimating potential warranty claims, while other companies have a harder time estimating future claims. In our case, we make assumptions about Sierra Sports and build our discussion on the estimated experiences.

For our purposes, assume that Sierra Sports has a line of soccer goals that sell for $800, and the company anticipates selling 500 goals this year (2019). Past experience for the goals that the company has sold is that 5% of them will need to be repaired under their three-year warranty program, and the cost of the average repair is $200. To simplify our example, we concentrate strictly on the journal entries for the warranty expense recognition and the application of the warranty repair pool. If the company sells 500 goals in 2019 and 5% need to be repaired, then 25 goals will be repaired at an average cost of $200. The average cost of $200 × 25 goals gives an anticipated future repair cost of $5,000 for 2019. Assume for the sake of our example that in

2020 Sierra Sports made repairs that cost $2,800. Following are the necessary journal entries to record the expense in 2019 and the repairs in 2020. The resources used in the warranty repair work could have included several options, such as parts and labor, but to keep it simple we allocated all of the expenses to repair parts inventory. Since the company's inventory of supply parts (an asset) went down by $2,800, the reduction is reflected with a credit entry to repair parts inventory. First, following is the necessary journal entry to record the expense in 2019.

JOURNAL			
Date	**Account**	**Debit**	**Credit**
2019	Warranty Expense Allowance for Warranty Expense *Anticipated future warranty expense allowance*	5,000	 5,000

Next, here is the journal entry to record the repairs in 2020.

JOURNAL			
Date	**Account**	**Debit**	**Credit**
2020	Allowance for Warranty Expense Repair Parts Inventory *To reflect the repair of goals under warranty*	2,800	 2,800

Before we finish, we need to address one more issue. Our example only covered the warranty expenses anticipated from the 2019 sales. Since the company has a three-year warranty, and it estimated repair costs of $5,000 for the goals sold in 2019, there is still a balance of $2,200 left from the original $5,000. However, its actual experiences could be more, the same, or less than $2,200. If it is determined that too much is being set aside in the allowance, then future annual warranty expenses can be adjusted downward. If it is determined that not enough is being accumulated, then the warranty expense allowance can be increased.

Since this warranty expense allocation will probably be carried on for many years, adjustments in the estimated warranty expenses can be made to reflect actual experiences. Also, sales for 2020, 2021, 2022, and all subsequent years will need to reflect the same types of journal entries for their sales. In essence, as long as Sierra Sports sells the goals or other equipment and provides a warranty, it will need to account for the warranty expenses in a manner similar to the one we demonstrated.

THINK IT THROUGH

Product Recalls: Contingent Liabilities?

Consider the following scenario: A hoverboard is a self-balancing scooter that uses body position and weight transfer to control the device. Hoverboards use a lithium-ion battery pack, which was found to overheat causing an increased risk for the product to catch fire or explode. Several people were badly injured from these fires and explosions. As a result, a recall was issued in mid-2016 on most hoverboard models. Customers were asked to return the product to the original point of sale (the retailer). Retailers were required to accept returns and provide repair when available. In some cases, retailers were held accountable by consumers, and not the manufacturer of the hoverboards. You are the retailer in this situation and must decide if the hoverboard scenario creates any contingent liabilities. If so, what are the contingent liabilities? Do the conditions meet FASB requirements for contingent liability reporting? Which of the four possible treatments are best suited for the potential liabilities identified? Are there any journal entries or note disclosures necessary?

Four Potential Treatments for Contingent Liabilities

If the contingency is **probable and estimable**, it is likely to occur and can be reasonably estimated. In this case, the liability and associated expense must be journalized and included in the current period's financial statements (balance sheet and income statement) along with note disclosures explaining the reason for recognition. The note disclosures are a GAAP requirement pertaining to the full disclosure principle, as detailed in Analyzing and Recording Transactions.

If the contingent liability is **probable and inestimable**, it is likely to occur but cannot be reasonably estimated. In this case, a note disclosure is required in financial statements, but a journal entry and financial recognition should not occur until a reasonable estimate is possible.

If the contingency is **reasonably possible**, it could occur but is not probable. The amount may or may not be estimable. Since this condition does not meet the requirement of likelihood, it should not be journalized or financially represented within the financial statements. Rather, it is disclosed in the notes only with any available details, financial or otherwise.

If the contingent liability is considered **remote**, it is unlikely to occur and may or may not be estimable. This does not meet the likelihood requirement, and the possibility of actualization is minimal. In this situation, no journal entry or note disclosure in financial statements is necessary.

Financial Statement Treatments

	Journalize	Note Disclosure
Probable and estimable	Yes	Yes
Probable and inestimable	No	Yes
Reasonably possible	No	Yes
Remote	No	No

Table 12.2 Four Treatments of Contingent Liabilities. Proper recognition of the four contingent liability treatments.

LINK TO LEARNING

Google, a subsidiary of Alphabet Inc., has expanded from a search engine to a global brand with a variety of product and service offerings. Like many other companies, contingent liabilities are carried on Google's balance sheet, report expenses related to these contingencies on its income statement, and note disclosures are provided to explain its contingent liability treatments. Check out Google's contingent liability considerations in this press release for Alphabet Inc.'s First Quarter 2017 Results (https://openstax.org/l/50Alphabet2017) to see a financial statement package, including note disclosures.

Let's review some contingent liability treatment examples as they relate to our fictitious company, Sierra Sports.

Probable and Estimable

If Sierra Sports determines the cost of the soccer goal screws are $30, the labor requirement is one hour at a rate of $40 per hour, and there is no extra overhead applied, then the total estimated warranty repair cost would be $70 per goal: $30 + (1 hour × $40 per hour). Sierra Sports sold ten goals before it discovered the rusty screw issue. The company believes that only six of those goals will have their warranties honored, based on past experience. This means Sierra will incur a warranty liability of $420 ($70 × 6 goals). The $420 is considered probable and estimable and is recorded in Warranty Liability and Warranty Expense accounts during the period of discovery (current period).

JOURNAL			
Date	**Account**	**Debit**	**Credit**
	Warranty Expense Warranty Liability *To recognize estimated warranty liability for soccer goals*	420	 420

An example of determining a warranty liability based on a percentage of sales follows. The sales price per soccer goal is $1,200, and Sierra Sports believes 10% of sales will result in honored warranties. The company would record this warranty liability of $120 ($1,200 × 10%) to Warranty Liability and Warranty Expense accounts.

JOURNAL			
Date	**Account**	**Debit**	**Credit**
	Warranty Expense Warranty Liability *To recognize estimated warranty liabilities for soccer goals as a percentage of sales*	120	 120

When the warranty is honored, this would reduce the Warranty Liability account and decrease the asset used for repair (Parts: Screws account) or Cash, if applicable. The recognition would happen as soon as the warranty is honored. This first entry shown is to recognize honored warranties for all six goals.

JOURNAL			
Date	Account	Debit	Credit
	Warranty Liability Parts: Screws *To record an honored warranty for soccer goals*	420	420

This second entry recognizes an honored warranty for a soccer goal based on 10% of sales from the period.

JOURNAL			
Date	Account	Debit	Credit
	Warranty Liability Parts: Screws *To recognize an honored warranty for soccer goals at 10% of sales*	120	120

As you've learned, not only are warranty expense and warranty liability journalized, but they are also recognized on the income statement and balance sheet. The following examples show recognition of Warranty Expense on the income statement Figure 12.10 and Warranty Liability on the balance sheet Figure 12.11 for Sierra Sports.

SIERRA SPORTS Income Statement Year Ended December 31, 2017		
Revenue	$19,500	
Cost of Goods Sold	9,000	
Gross Profit		10,500
Expenses		
Salaries Expense	2,700	
Administrative Expense	1,500	
Warranty Expense	420	
Utilities Expense	300	
Total Expenses		4,920
Net Income		$ 5,580

Figure 12.10 Sierra Sports' Income Statement. Warranty Expense is recognized on the income statement. (attribution: Copyright Rice University, OpenStax, under CC BY-NC-SA 4.0 license)

SIERRA SPORTS Balance Sheet December 31, 2017			
Assets		**Liabilities and Stockholders Equity**	
Current Assets		Current Liabilities	
Cash	$ 21,580	Note Payable: Current	$ 18,000
Accounts Receivable	2,000	Accounts Payable	8,580
Total Current Assets	23,580	Warranty Liability	420
		Unearned Revenue	4,000
Property, Plant, and Equipment		Total Current Liabilities	31,000
Buildings	300,000		
Sporting Equipment	60,000	Long-term Liabilities	
Total Property, Plant, and Equipment	360,000	Notes Payable	342,000
		Stockholders' Equity	
		Common Stock	5,000
		Retained Earnings	5,580
		Total Stockholders' Equity	10,580
Total Assets	$383,580	Total Liabilities and Stockholders' Equity	$383,580

Figure 12.11 Sierra Sports' Balance Sheet. Warranty Liability is recognized on the balance sheet. (attribution: Copyright Rice University, OpenStax, under CC BY-NC-SA 4.0 license)

Probable and Not Estimable

Assume that Sierra Sports is sued by one of the customers who purchased the faulty soccer goals. A settlement of responsibility in the case has been reached, but the actual damages have not been determined and cannot be reasonably estimated. This is considered probable but inestimable, because the lawsuit is very likely to occur (given a settlement is agreed upon) but the actual damages are unknown. No journal entry or financial adjustment in the financial statements will occur. Instead, Sierra Sports will include a note describing any details available about the lawsuit. When damages have been determined, or have been reasonably estimated, then journalizing would be appropriate.

Sierra Sports could say the following in its financial statement disclosures: "There is pending litigation against our company with the likelihood of settlement probable. Detailed terms and damages have not yet reached agreement, and a reasonable assessment of financial impact is currently unknown."

Reasonably Possible

Sierra Sports may have more litigation in the future surrounding the soccer goals. These lawsuits have not yet been filed or are in the very early stages of the litigation process. Since there is a past precedent for lawsuits of this nature but no establishment of guilt or formal arrangement of damages or timeline, the likelihood of occurrence is reasonably possible. The outcome is not probable but is not remote either. Since the outcome is possible, the contingent liability is disclosed in Sierra Sports' financial statement notes.

Sierra Sports could say the following in their financial statement disclosures: "We anticipate more claimants filing legal action against our company with the likelihood of settlement reasonably possible. Assignment of guilt, detailed terms, and potential damages have not been established. A reasonable assessment of financial impact is currently unknown."

Remote

Sierra Sports worries that as a result of pending litigation and losses associated with the faulty soccer goals, the company might have to file for bankruptcy. After consulting with a financial advisor, the company is pretty certain it can continue operating in the long term without restructuring. The chances are remote that a bankruptcy would occur. Sierra Sports would not recognize this remote occurrence on the financial statements or provide a note disclosure.

IFRS CONNECTION

Current Liabilities

US GAAP and International Financial Reporting Standards (IFRS) define “current liabilities” similarly and use the same reporting criteria for most all types of current liabilities. However, two primary differences exist between US GAAP and IFRS: the reporting of (1) debt due on demand and (2) contingencies.

Liquidity and solvency are measures of a company’s ability to pay debts as they come due. Liquidity measures evaluate a company’s ability to pay current debts as they come due, while solvency measures evaluate the ability to pay debts long term. One common liquidity measure is the current ratio, and a higher ratio is preferred over a lower one. This ratio—current assets divided by current liabilities—is lowered by an increase in current liabilities (the denominator increases while we assume that the numerator remains the same). When lenders arrange loans with their corporate customers, limits are typically set on how low certain liquidity ratios (such as the current ratio) can go before the bank can demand that the loan be repaid immediately.

In theory, debt that has not been paid and that has become “on demand” would be considered a current liability. However, in determining how to report a loan that has become “on-demand,” US GAAP and IFRS differ:

- Under US GAAP, debts on which payment has been demanded because of violations of the contractual agreement between the lender and creditor are only included in current liabilities if, by the financial statement presentation date, there have been no arrangements made to pay off or restructure the debt. This allows companies time between the end of the fiscal year and the actual publication of the financial statements (typically two months) to make arrangements for repayment of the loan. Most often these loans are refinanced.
- Under IFRS, any payment or refinancing arrangements must be made by the fiscal year-end of the debtor. This difference means that companies reporting under IFRS must be proactive in assessing whether their debt agreements will be violated and make appropriate arrangements for refinancing or differing payment options prior to final year-end numbers being reported.

A second set of differences exist regarding reporting contingencies. Where US GAAP uses the term “contingencies,” IFRS uses “provisions.” In both cases, gain contingencies are not recorded until they are essentially realized. Both systems want to avoid prematurely recording or overstating gains based on the principles of conservatism. Loss contingencies are recorded (accrued) if certain conditions are met:

- Under US GAAP, loss contingencies are accrued if they are probable and can be estimated. Probable means “likely” to occur and is often assessed as an 80% likelihood by practitioners.

- Under IFRS, probable is defined as “more likely than not” and is typically assessed at 50% by practitioners.

The determination of whether a contingency is probable is based on the judgment of auditors and management in both situations. This means a contingent situation such as a lawsuit might be accrued under IFRS but not accrued under US GAAP. Finally, how a loss contingency is measured varies between the two options as well. For example, if a company is told it will be probable that it will lose an active lawsuit, and the legal team gives a range of the dollar value of that loss, under IFRS, the discounted midpoint of that range would be accrued, and the range disclosed. Under US GAAP, the low end of the range would be accrued, and the range disclosed.

12.4 Prepare Journal Entries to Record Short-Term Notes Payable

If you have ever taken out a payday loan, you may have experienced a situation where your living expenses temporarily exceeded your assets. You need enough money to cover your expenses until you get your next paycheck. Once you receive that paycheck, you can repay the lender the amount you borrowed, plus a little extra for the lender’s assistance.

There is an ebb and flow to business that can sometimes produce this same situation, where business expenses temporarily exceed revenues. Even if a company finds itself in this situation, bills still need to be paid. The company may consider a short-term note payable to cover the difference.

A **short-term note payable** is a debt created and due within a company’s operating period (less than a year). Some key characteristics of this written promise to pay (see Figure 12.12) include an established date for repayment, a specific payable amount, interest terms, and the possibility of debt resale to another party. A short-term note is classified as a current liability because it is wholly honored within a company’s operating period. This payable account would appear on the balance sheet under Current Liabilities.

PROMISSORY NOTE

I, (Borrower) ______________________ agree and promise to pay the amount of ($________)

to (Lender) ______________________ for value received at an annual interest rate of (%____).

First Payment Due Date (30 days after date of this promissory note) ______________.

Final Payment Due Date (120 days after date of this promissory note) ______________.

Witnessed by ______________________ Notary Public: (Seal)

City ____________ State ____________ Date ____________

Figure 12.12 Short-Term Promissory Note. A promissory note includes terms of repayment, such as the date and interest rate. (attribution: Copyright Rice University, OpenStax, under CC BY-NC-SA 4.0 license)

Debt sale to a third party is a possibility with any loan, which includes a short-term note payable. The terms of the agreement will state this resale possibility, and the new debt owner honors the agreement terms of the original parties. A lender may choose this option to collect cash quickly and reduce the overall outstanding debt.

We now consider two short-term notes payable situations; one is created by a purchase, and the other is created by a loan.

THINK IT THROUGH

Promissory Notes: Time to Issue More Debt?

A common practice for government entities, particularly schools, is to issue short-term (promissory) notes to cover daily expenditures until revenues are received from tax collection, lottery funds, and other sources. School boards approve the note issuances, with repayments of principal and interest typically met within a few months.

The goal is to fully cover all expenses until revenues are distributed from the state. However, revenues distributed fluctuate due to changes in collection expectations, and schools may not be able to cover their expenditures in the current period. This leads to a dilemma—whether or not to issue more short-term notes to cover the deficit.

Short-term debt may be preferred over long-term debt when the entity does not want to devote resources to pay interest over an extended period of time. In many cases, the interest rate is lower than long-term debt, because the loan is considered less risky with the shorter payback period. This shorter payback period is also beneficial with amortization expenses; short-term debt typically does not amortize, unlike long-term debt.

What would you do if you found your school in this situation? Would you issue more debt? Are there alternatives? What are some positives and negatives to the promissory note practice?

Recording Short-Term Notes Payable Created by a Purchase

A short-term notes payable created by a purchase typically occurs when a payment to a supplier does not occur within the established time frame. The supplier might require a new agreement that converts the overdue accounts payable into a short-term note payable (see Figure 12.13), with interest added. This gives the company more time to make good on outstanding debt and gives the supplier an incentive for delaying payment. Also, the creation of the note payable creates a stronger legal position for the owner of the note, since the note is a negotiable legal instrument that can be more easily enforced in court actions.

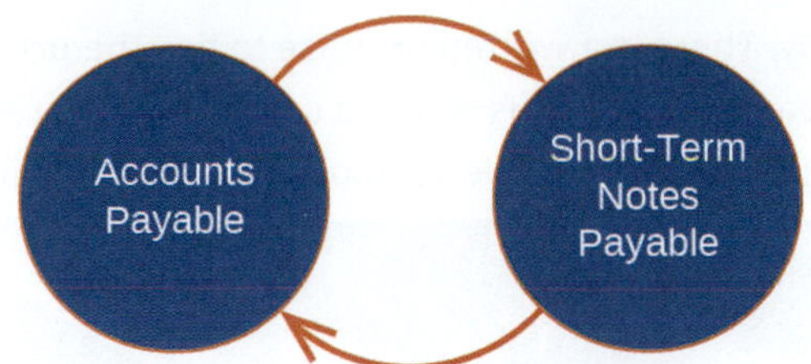

Figure 12.13 Accounts Payable Conversion. Accounts Payable may be converted into a short-term notes payable, if there is a default on payment. (attribution: Copyright Rice University, OpenStax, under CC BY-NC-SA 4.0 license)

To illustrate, let's revisit Sierra Sports' purchase of soccer equipment on August 1. Sierra Sports purchased $12,000 of soccer equipment from a supplier on credit. Credit terms were 2/10, n/30, invoice date August 1. Let's assume that Sierra Sports was unable to make the payment due within 30 days. On August 31, the supplier renegotiates terms with Sierra and converts the accounts payable into a written note, requiring full payment in two months, beginning September 1. Interest is now included as part of the payment terms at an annual rate of 10%. The conversion entry from an account payable to a Short-Term Note Payable in Sierra's journal is shown.

JOURNAL			
Date	**Account**	**Debit**	**Credit**
Aug. 31	Accounts Payable Short-Term Notes Payable *To record conversion of Accounts Payable to short-term note, terms two-month repayment, 10% interest*	12,000	 12,000

Accounts Payable decreases (debit) and Short-Term Notes Payable increases (credit) for the original amount owed of $12,000. When Sierra pays cash for the full amount due, including interest, on October 31, the following entry occurs.

JOURNAL			
Date	**Account**	**Debit**	**Credit**
Oct. 31	Short-Term Notes Payable Interest Expense Cash *To record payment for short-term note, with interest*	12,000 200	 12,200

Since Sierra paid the full amount due, Short-Term Notes Payable decreases (debit) for the principal amount of the debt. Interest Expense increases (debit) for two months of interest accumulation. Interest Expense is found from our earlier equation, where Interest = Principal × Annual interest rate × Part of year ($12,000 × 10% × [2/12]), which is $200. Cash decreases (credit) for $12,200, which is the principal plus the interest due.

The other short-term note scenario is created by a loan.

Recording Short-Term Notes Payable Created by a Loan

A short-term notes payable created by a loan transpires when a business incurs debt with a lender Figure 12.14. A business may choose this path when it does not have enough cash on hand to finance a capital expenditure immediately but does not need long-term financing. The business may also require an influx of cash to cover expenses temporarily. There is a written promise to pay the principal balance and interest due on or before a specific date. This payment period is within a company's operating period (less than a year). Consider a short-term notes payable scenario for Sierra Sports.

Figure 12.14 Bank Loan. A short-term note can be created from a loan. (credit: "Business Paperwork Deal" by "rawpixel"/Pixabay, CC0)

Sierra Sports requires a new apparel printing machine after experiencing an increase in custom uniform orders. Sierra does not have enough cash on hand currently to pay for the machine, but the company does not need long-term financing. Sierra borrows $150,000 from the bank on October 1, with payment due within three months (December 31), at a 12% annual interest rate. The following entry occurs when Sierra initially takes out the loan.

JOURNAL			
Date	**Account**	**Debit**	**Credit**
Oct. 1	Cash Short-Term Notes Payable *To record short-term loan, 12% interest, payable in three months*	150,000	 150,000

Cash increases (debit) as does Short-Term Notes Payable (credit) for the principal amount of the loan, which is $150,000. When Sierra pays in full on December 31, the following entry occurs.

JOURNAL			
Date	**Account**	**Debit**	**Credit**
Dec. 31	Short-Term Notes Payable Interest Expense Cash *To record short-term loan, 12% interest, payable in three months*	150,000 4,500	 154,500

Short-Term Notes Payable decreases (a debit) for the principal amount of the loan ($150,000). Interest Expense increases (a debit) for $4,500 (calculated as $150,000 principal × 12% annual interest rate × [3/12 months]). Cash decreases (a credit) for the principal amount plus interest due.

LINK TO LEARNING

Loan calculators can help businesses determine the amount they are able to borrow from a lender given certain factors, such as loan amount, terms, interest rate, and payback categorization (payback periodically or at the end of the loan, for example). A group of information technology professionals provides one such loan calculator with definitions and additional information and tools (https://openstax.org/l/50LoanCalc) to provide more information.

12.5 Record Transactions Incurred in Preparing Payroll

Have you ever looked at your paycheck and wondered where all the money went? Well, it did not disappear; the money was used to contribute required and optional financial payments to various entities.

Payroll can be one of the largest expenses and potential liabilities for a business. Payroll liabilities include employee salaries and wages, and deductions for taxes, benefits, and employer contributions. In this section, we explain these elements of payroll and the required journal entries.

Employee Compensation and Deductions

As an employee working in a business, you receive compensation for your work. This pay could be a monthly salary or hourly wages paid periodically. The amount earned by the employee before any reductions in pay occur is considered **gross income (pay)**. These reductions include involuntary and voluntary deductions. The remaining balance after deductions is considered **net income (pay)**, or “take-home-pay.” The take-home-pay is what employees receive and deposit in their bank accounts.

Involuntary Deductions

Involuntary deductions are withholdings that neither the employer nor the employee have control over and are required by law.

Federal, state, and local income taxes are considered involuntary deductions. Income taxes imposed are different for every employee and are based on their W-4 Form, the Employee’s Withholding Allowance Certificate. An employee will fill in his or her marital status, number of allowances requested, and any additional reduction amounts. The employer will use this information to determine the **federal income tax withholding** amount from each paycheck. **State income tax withholding** may also use W-4 information or the state’s withholdings certificate. The federal income tax withholding and state income tax withholding amounts can be established with tax tables published annually by the Internal Revenue Service (IRS) (see Figure 12.15) and state government offices, respectively. Some states though do not require an income tax withholding, since they do not impose a state income tax. Federal and state income liabilities are held in payable accounts until disbursement to the governmental bodies that administer the tax compliance process for their particular governmental entity.

Wage Bracket Method Tables for Income Tax Withholding

SINGLE Persons—**MONTHLY** Payroll Period

(For Wages Paid through December 31, 2018)

And the wages are–		And the number of withholding allowances claimed is—										
At least	But less than	0	1	2	3	4	5	6	7	8	9	10
		The amount of income tax to be withheld is—										
$ 0	$305	$0	$0	$0	$0	$0	$0	$0	$0	$0	$0	$0
305	325	1	0	0	0	0	0	0	0	0	0	0
325	345	3	0	0	0	0	0	0	0	0	0	0
345	365	5	0	0	0	0	0	0	0	0	0	0
365	385	7	0	0	0	0	0	0	0	0	0	0
385	405	9	0	0	0	0	0	0	0	0	0	0
405	425	11	0	0	0	0	0	0	0	0	0	0
425	445	13	0	0	0	0	0	0	0	0	0	0
445	465	15	0	0	0	0	0	0	0	0	0	0
465	485	17	0	0	0	0	0	0	0	0	0	0
485	505	19	0	0	0	0	0	0	0	0	0	0
505	525	21	0	0	0	0	0	0	0	0	0	0
525	545	23	0	0	0	0	0	0	0	0	0	0
545	565	25	0	0	0	0	0	0	0	0	0	0
565	585	27	0	0	0	0	0	0	0	0	0	0
585	605	29	0	0	0	0	0	0	0	0	0	0
605	645	32	0	0	0	0	0	0	0	0	0	0
645	685	36	1	0	0	0	0	0	0	0	0	0
685	725	40	5	0	0	0	0	0	0	0	0	0
725	765	44	9	0	0	0	0	0	0	0	0	0
765	805	48	13	0	0	0	0	0	0	0	0	0
805	845	52	17	0	0	0	0	0	0	0	0	0
845	885	56	21	0	0	0	0	0	0	0	0	0
885	925	60	25	0	0	0	0	0	0	0	0	0
925	965	64	29	0	0	0	0	0	0	0	0	0
965	1,005	68	33	0	0	0	0	0	0	0	0	0
1,005	1,045	72	37	3	0	0	0	0	0	0	0	0
1,045	1,085	76	41	7	0	0	0	0	0	0	0	0
1,085	1,125	80	45	11	0	0	0	0	0	0	0	0
1,125	1,165	85	49	15	0	0	0	0	0	0	0	0
1,165	1,205	89	53	19	0	0	0	0	0	0	0	0
1,205	1,245	94	57	23	0	0	0	0	0	0	0	0
1,245	1,285	99	61	27	0	0	0	0	0	0	0	0
1,285	1,325	104	65	31	0	0	0	0	0	0	0	0
1,325	1,365	109	69	35	0	0	0	0	0	0	0	0
1,365	1,405	113	73	39	4	0	0	0	0	0	0	0
1,405	1,445	118	77	43	8	0	0	0	0	0	0	0
1,445	1,485	123	81	47	12	0	0	0	0	0	0	0
1,485	1,525	128	86	51	16	0	0	0	0	0	0	0
1,525	1,565	133	91	55	20	0	0	0	0	0	0	0
1,565	1,605	137	96	59	24	0	0	0	0	0	0	0
1,605	1,645	142	101	63	28	0	0	0	0	0	0	0
1,645	1,685	147	105	67	32	0	0	0	0	0	0	0
1,685	1,725	152	110	71	36	1	0	0	0	0	0	0
1,725	1,765	157	115	75	40	5	0	0	0	0	0	0
1,765	1,805	161	120	79	44	9	0	0	0	0	0	0
1,805	1,845	166	125	83	48	13	0	0	0	0	0	0
1,845	1,885	171	129	88	52	17	0	0	0	0	0	0
1,885	1,925	176	134	93	56	21	0	0	0	0	0	0
1,925	1,965	181	139	98	60	25	0	0	0	0	0	0
1,965	2,005	185	144	102	64	29	0	0	0	0	0	0
2,005	2,045	190	149	107	68	33	0	0	0	0	0	0
2,045	2,085	195	153	112	72	37	3	0	0	0	0	0
2,085	2,125	200	158	117	76	41	7	0	0	0	0	0
2,125	2,165	205	163	122	80	45	11	0	0	0	0	0
2,165	2,205	209	168	126	85	49	15	0	0	0	0	0
2,205	2,245	214	173	131	90	53	19	0	0	0	0	0
2,245	2,285	219	177	136	94	57	23	0	0	0	0	0
2,285	2,325	224	182	141	99	61	27	0	0	0	0	0
2,325	2,365	229	187	146	104	65	31	0	0	0	0	0
2,365	2,405	233	192	150	109	69	35	0	0	0	0	0
2,405	2,445	238	197	155	114	73	39	4	0	0	0	0
2,445	2,485	243	201	160	118	77	43	8	0	0	0	0
2,485	2,525	248	206	165	123	82	47	12	0	0	0	0
2,525	2,565	253	211	170	128	87	51	16	0	0	0	0
2,565	2,605	257	216	174	133	91	55	20	0	0	0	0
2,605	2,645	262	221	179	138	96	59	24	0	0	0	0
2,645	2,685	267	225	184	142	101	63	28	0	0	0	0
2,685	2,725	272	230	189	147	106	67	32	0	0	0	0
2,725	2,765	277	235	194	152	111	71	36	2	0	0	0

Page 60 **Publication 15 (2018)**

Figure 12.15 Wage Bracket Tax Withholding Table: Single Persons (2017). These are the monthly tax withholding amounts recommended by the IRS for wages earned by single persons in 2017. (credit:

"Employer's Tax Guide" by Department of the Treasury Internal Revenue Service, Public Domain)

While not a common occurrence, **local income tax withholding** is applied to those living or working within a jurisdiction to cover schooling, social services, park maintenance, and law enforcement. If local income taxes are withheld, these remain current liabilities until paid.

Other involuntary deductions involve **Federal Insurance Contribution Act (FICA) taxes** for Social Security and Medicare. FICA mandates employers to withhold taxes from employee wages "to provide benefits for retirees, the disabled, and children." The **Social Security tax rate** is 6.2% of employee gross wages. As of 2017, there is a maximum taxable earnings amount of $127,200. Meaning, only the first $127,200 of each employee's gross wages has the Social Security tax applied. In 2018, the maximum taxable earnings amount increased to $128,400. The **Medicare tax rate** is 1.45% of employee gross income. There is no taxable earnings cap for Medicare tax. The two taxes combined equal 7.65% (6.2% + 1.45%). Both the employer and the employee pay the two taxes on behalf of the employee.

More recent health-care legislation, the Affordable Care Act (ACA), requires an **additional medicare tax** withholding from employee pay of 0.9% for individuals who exceed an income threshold based on their filing status (married, single, or head of household, for example). This Additional Medicare Tax withholding is only applied to employee payroll.

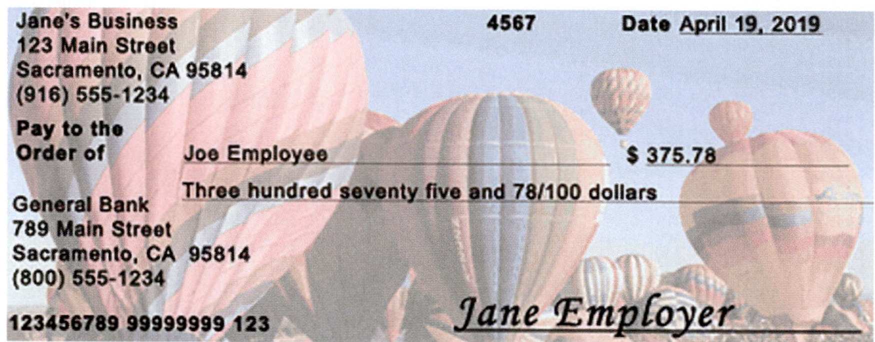
Jane's Business
123 Main Street
Sacramento, CA 95814
(916) 555-1234
4567
Date April 19, 2019
Pay to the Order of Joe Employee $ 375.78
Three hundred seventy five and 78/100 dollars
General Bank
789 Main Street
Sacramento, CA 95814
(800) 555-1234
Jane Employer
123456789 99999999 123

Payroll Check Stub

Jane's Business
123 Main Street
Sacramento, CA 95814

Week of April 7-13, 2019
Joe Employee
123-45-6789

Salary	$500.00
Taxes	
1. Federal Withholding	68.00
2. Social Security (6.2%)	31.00
3. Medicare (1.45%)	7.25
4. State Disability Insurance (.9%)	4.50
5. State Withholding	13.47
Net	$375.78

Figure 12.16 FICA Social Security and FICA Medicare Taxes. Deductions to payroll include FICA Social Security and FICA Medicare taxes. (credit: modification of work by California Tax Service Center, State of California/ CA.gov, Public Domain)

Last, involuntary deductions may also include child support payments, IRS federal tax levies, court-ordered wage garnishments, and bankruptcy judgments. All involuntary deductions are an employer's liability until they are paid.

Voluntary Deductions

In addition to involuntary deductions, employers may withhold certain **voluntary deductions** from employee wages. Voluntary deductions are not required to be removed from employee pay unless the employee designates reduction of these amounts. Voluntary deductions may include, but are not limited to, health-care coverage, life insurance, retirement contributions, charitable contributions, pension funds, and union dues. Employees can cover the full cost of these benefits or they may cost-share with the employer.

Health-care coverage is a requirement for many businesses to provide as a result of the ACA. Employers may provide partial benefit coverage and request the employee to pay the remainder. For example, the employer would cover 30% of health-care cost, and 70% would be the employee's responsibility.

Retirement contributions may include those made to an employer-sponsored plan, such as a **defined contribution plan**, which "shelters" the income in a 401(k) or a 403(b). In simple terms, a defined contribution plan allows an employee to voluntarily contribute a specified amount or percentage of his or her pretax wages to a special account in order to defer the tax on those earnings. Usually, a portion of the employee's contribution is matched by his or her employer; employers often use this as an incentive to attract and keep highly skilled and valuable employees. Only when the employee eventually withdraws funds from the plan will he or she be required to pay the tax on those earnings. Because the amount contributed to the plan is not immediately taxed by the IRS, it enables the employee to accumulate funds for his or her retirement. This deferred income may be excluded from the employee's current federal taxable income but not FICA taxes. All voluntary deductions are considered employer liabilities until remitted. For more in-depth information on retirement planning, and using a 401(k) or a 403(b), refer to Appendix C.

Figure 12.17 Retirement Savings. Defined contribution plans can help you save for retirement. (credit: modification of "Money Coin Investment" by "nattanan23"/Pixabay, CC0)

As with involuntary deductions, voluntary deductions are held as a current liability until paid. When payroll is disbursed, journal entries are required.

CONCEPTS IN PRACTICE

Should You Start Saving for Retirement?

Should you save for retirement now or wait? As a student, you may be inclined to put off saving for retirement for many reasons. You may not be in a financial position to do so, you believe Social Security will be enough to cover your needs, or you may not have even thought about it up to this point.

According to a 2012 survey from the Bureau of Labor Statistics, of those who had access to a defined contribution plan, only 68% of employees contributed to their retirement plan. Many employees wait until their mid-thirties or forties to begin saving, and this can delay retirement, or may leave the retiree unable to cover his or her annual expenses. Some pitfalls contributing to this lack of saving are short-term negative spending practices such as high-interest loan debt, credit card purchases, and discretionary spending (optional expenses such as eating out or entertainment). To avoid these hazards, you should

1. Analyze your spending habits and make changes where possible.
2. Develop a financial plan with the help of a finance specialist.
3. Join a defined contribution plan and stick with the plan (do not withdraw funds early).
4. Try to contribute at least as much as your employer is willing to match.
5. Consider other short-term savings options like bonds, or high-interest bank accounts.
6. Have a specific savings goal for your retirement account. For example, many financial advisors recommend saving at least 15% of your monthly income for retirement. However, they usually include both the employee's contribution and the employer's. For example, assume that the company matches each dollar invested by the employee with a $0.50 contribution from the employer, up to 8% for the employee. In this case, if the employee contributes 8% and the company provides 4%, that takes the employee to 80% of the recommended goal (12% of the recommended 15%).

Remember, the longer you wait to begin investing, the more you will have to save later on to have enough for retirement.

Journal Entries to Report Employee Compensation and Deductions

We continue to use Sierra Sports as our example company to prepare journal entries.

Sierra Sports employs several people, but our focus is on one specific employee for this example. Billie Sanders works for Sierra Sports and earns a salary each month of $2,000. She claims two withholdings allowances (see Figure 12.15). This amount is paid on the first of the following month. Withholdings for federal and state income taxes are assessed in the amount of $102 and $25, respectively. FICA Social Security is taxed at the 6.2% rate, and FICA Medicare is taxed at the 1.45% rate. Billie has voluntary deductions for health insurance and a 401(k) retirement contribution. She is responsible for 40% of her $500 health-care insurance premium;

Sierra Sports pays the remaining 60% (as explained in employer payroll). The 401(k) contributions total $150. The first entry records the salaries liability during the month of August.

JOURNAL			
Date	**Account**	**Debit**	**Credit**
Aug. 31	Salaries Expense	2,000	
	FICA Social Security Tax Payable		124
	FICA Medicare Tax Payable		29
	Federal Income Tax Payable		102
	State Income Tax Payable		25
	Health Insurance Payable		200
	401(k) Retirement Plan Payable		150
	Salaries Payable		1,370
	To recognize employee payroll for August		

Salaries Expense is an equity account used to recognize the accumulated (accrued) expense to the business during August (increase on the debit side). Salaries Expense represents the employee's gross income (pay) before any deductions. Each deduction liability is listed in its own account; this will help for ease of payment to the different entities. Note that Health Insurance Payable is in the amount of $200, which is 40% of the employee's responsibility for the premium ($500 × 0.40 = $200). Salaries Payable represents net income (pay) or the "take-home pay" for Billie. Salaries Payable is $1,370, which is found by taking gross income and subtracting the sum of the liabilities ($2,000 – $630 = $1,370). Since salaries are not paid until the first of the following month, this liability will remain during the month of August. All liabilities (payables) increase due to the company's outstanding debt (increase on the credit side).

The second entry records cash payment of accumulated salaries on September 1.

JOURNAL			
Date	**Account**	**Debit**	**Credit**
Aug. 31	Salaries Payable	1,370	
	Cash		1,370
	To record payment of accrued salaries		

Payment to Billie Sanders occurs on September 1. The payment is for salaries accumulated from the month of August. The payment decreases Salaries Payable (debit side) since the liability was paid and decreases Cash (credit side), because cash is the asset used for payment.

LINK TO LEARNING

The IRS has developed a simulation database with twenty different taxpayer simulations (https://openstax.org/l/50TaxSim) to help taxpayers understand their tax returns and withholdings.

Employer Compensation and Deductions

At this point you might be asking yourself, "why am I having to pay all of this money and my employer isn't?" Your employer also has a fiscal and legal responsibility to contribute and match funds to certain payroll liability accounts.

Involuntary Payroll Taxes

Employers must match employee contributions to FICA Social Security (6.2% rate) on the first $127,200 of employee wages for 2017, and FICA Medicare (1.45% rate) on all employee earnings. Withholdings for these taxes are forwarded to the same place as employee contributions; thus, the same accounts are used when recording journal entries.

Employers are required by law to pay into an unemployment insurance system that covers employees in case of job disruption due to factors outside of their control (job elimination from company bankruptcy, for example). The tax recognizing this required payment is the **Federal Unemployment Tax Act (FUTA)**. FUTA is at a rate of 6%. This tax applies to the initial $7,000 of each employee's wages earned during the year. This rate may be reduced by as much as 5.4% as a credit for paying into state unemployment on time, producing a lower rate of 0.6%. The **State Unemployment Tax Act (SUTA)** is similar to the FUTA process, but tax rates and minimum taxable earnings vary by state.

Figure 12.18 Unemployment Support. Two common employer payroll deductions are federal and state unemployment taxes. (credit: "Laptop" by Unknown/pxhere, CC0)

Voluntary Benefits Provided by the Employer

Employers offer competitive advantages (benefits) to employees in an effort to improve job satisfaction and increase employee morale. There is no statute mandating the employer cover these benefits financially. Some possible benefits are health-care coverage, life insurance, contributions to retirement plans, paid sick leave, paid maternity/paternity leave, and **vacation compensation**.

Paid sick leave, paid maternity/paternity leave, and vacation compensation help employees take time off when needed or required by providing a stipend while the employee is away. This compensation is often comparable to the wages or salary for the covered period. Some companies have policies that require vacation and paid sick leave to be used within the year or the employee risks losing that benefit in the current period. These benefits are considered estimated liabilities since it is not clear when, if, or how much the employee will use them. Let's now see the process for journalizing employer compensation and deductions.

Figure 12.19 Employer-Provided Benefit. Providing employees with vacation benefits can increase job satisfaction. (credit: "Ellie relaxes by the palm tree" Darren Foreman/Flickr, CC BY 2.0)

Journal Entries to Report Employer Compensation and Deductions

In addition to the employee payroll entries for Billie Sanders, Sierra Sports has an obligation to contribute taxes to federal unemployment, state unemployment, FICA Social Security, and FICA Medicare. They are also responsible for 60% of Billie's health insurance premium payment. Assume Sierra Sports receives the FUTA credit and is only taxed at the rate of 0.6%, and SUTA taxes are $100. August is Billie Sanders' first month of pay for the year. The following entry represents the employer payroll liabilities and expense for the month of August. The second entry records the health insurance premium liability.

JOURNAL			
Date	**Account**	**Debit**	**Credit**
Aug. 31	Employer Payroll Taxes Expense	265	
	Federal Unemployment Tax Payable		12
	State Unemployment Tax Payable		100
	FICA Social Security Tax Payable		124
	FICA Medicare Tax Payable		29
	To recognize employer payroll liabilities for August		
Aug. 31	Benefits Expense	300	
	Health Insurance Payable		300
	To recognize employer benefit liabilities for August		

Employer Payroll Tax Expense is the equity account used to recognize payroll expenses during the period (increases on the debit side). The amount of $265 is the sum of all liabilities from that period. Notice that FICA Social Security Tax Payable and FICA Medicare Tax Payable were used in the employee payroll entry earlier and again here in the employer payroll. You only need to use one account if the payments are for the same recipient and purpose. The amounts of Social Security ($124) and Medicare ($29) taxes withheld match the amounts withheld from employee payroll. Federal Unemployment Tax Payable and State Unemployment Tax Payable recognize the liabilities for federal and state unemployment deductions, respectively. The federal unemployment tax ($12) is computed by multiplying the federal unemployment tax rate of 0.6% by $2,000. These liability accounts increase (credit side) when the amount owed increases.

The second entry recognizes the liability created from providing the voluntary benefit, health insurance coverage. Voluntary and involuntary employer payroll items should be separated. It is also important to separate estimated liabilities from certain voluntary benefits due to their uncertainty. Benefits Expense recognizes the health insurance expense from August. Health Insurance Payable recognizes the outstanding liability for health-care coverage covered by the employer ($500 × 60% = $300).

The following entries represent payment of the employer payroll and benefit liabilities in the following period.

JOURNAL			
Date	**Account**	**Debit**	**Credit**
Aug. 31	Federal Unemployment Tax Payable	12	
	State Unemployment Tax Payable	100	
	FICA Social Security Tax Payable	124	
	FICA Medicare Tax Payable	29	
	Cash		265
	To recognize payment of employer payroll liabilities		
Aug. 31	Health Insurance Payable	300	
	Cash		300
	To record payment of accrued health insurance premiums		

When payment occurs, all payable accounts decrease (debit) because the company paid all taxes and benefits owed for those liabilities. Cash is the accepted form of payment at the payee organizations (Social Security Administration, and health plan administrator, for example).

LINK TO LEARNING

The IRS oversees all tax-related activities on behalf of the US Department of the Treasury. In an effort to assist taxpayers with determining amounts they may owe, the IRS has established a withholdings calculator (https://openstax.org/l/50WitholdCalc) that can let an employee know if he or she needs to submit a new W-4 form to the employer based on the results.

Key Terms

account payable account for financial obligations to suppliers after purchasing products or services on credit

Additional Medicare Tax requirement for employers to withhold 0.9% from employee pay for individuals who exceed an income threshold based on their filing status

contingency current situation, where the outcome is unknown or uncertain and will not be resolved until a future point in time

contingent liability uncertain outcome to a current condition that could produce a future debt or negative obligation for the company

current liability debt or obligation due within one year or, in rare cases, a company's standard operating cycle, whichever is greater

current portion of a note payable portion of a long-term note due during the company's current operating period

defined contribution plans money set aside and held in account for employee's retirement with possible contribution from employers

federal income tax withholding amount withheld from employee pay based on employee responses given on Form W-4

Federal Insurance Contribution Act (FICA) tax involuntary tax mandated by FICA that requires employers to withhold taxes from employee wages "to provide benefits for retirees, the disabled, and children"

Federal Unemployment Tax Act (FUTA) response to a law requiring employers to pay into a federal unemployment insurance system that covers employees in case of job disruption due to factors outside of their control

gross income (pay) amount earned by the employee before any reductions in pay occur due to involuntary and voluntary deductions

interest monetary incentive to the lender, which justifies loan risk; interest is paid to the lender by the borrower

involuntary deduction withholding that neither the employer nor the employee have control over, and is required by law

likelihood of occurrence contingent liability must be recognized and disclosed if there is a probable liability determination before the preparation of financial statements has occurred

local income tax withholding applied to those living or working within a jurisdiction to cover schooling, social services, park maintenance, and law enforcement

measurement requirement company's ability to reasonably estimate the amount of loss

Medicare tax rate currently 1.45% of employee gross income with no taxable earnings cap

net income (pay) (also, take home pay) remaining employee earnings balance after involuntary and voluntary deductions from employee pay

note payable legal document between a borrower and a lender specifying terms of a financial arrangement; in most situations, the debt is long-term

principal initial borrowed amount of a loan, not including interest; also, face value or maturity value of a bond (the amount to be paid at maturity)

probable and estimable contingent liability is likely to occur and can be reasonably estimated

probable and inestimable contingent liability is likely to occur but cannot be reasonably estimated

reasonably possible contingent liability could occur but is not probable

remote contingent liability is unlikely to occur

short-term note payable debt created and due within a company's operating period (less than a year)

Social Security tax rate currently 6.2% of employees gross wage earnings with a maximum taxable earnings amount of $127,200 in 2017 and $128,400 in 2018

state income tax withholding reduction to employee pay determined by responses given on Form W-4, or on a state withholdings certificate

State Unemployment Tax Act (SUTA) response to a law requiring employers to pay into a state unemployment insurance system that covers employees in case of job disruption due to factors outside of their control

taxes payable liability created when a company collects taxes on behalf of employees and customers

unearned revenue advance payment for a product or service that has yet to be provided by the company; the transaction is a liability until the product or service is provided

vacation compensation stipend provided by the employer to employees when they take time off for vacation

voluntary deduction not required to be removed from employee pay unless the employee designates reduction of this amount

Summary

12.1 Identify and Describe Current Liabilities

- Current liabilities are debts or obligations that arise from past business activities and are due for payment within a company's operating period (one year). Common examples of current liabilities include accounts payable, unearned revenue, the current portion of a noncurrent note payable, and taxes payable.
- Accounts payable is used to record purchases from suppliers on credit. Accounts payable typically does not include interest payments.
- Unearned revenue is recorded when customers pay in advance for products or services before receiving their benefits. The company maintains the liability until services or products are rendered.
- Notes payable is a debt to a lender with specific repayment terms, which can include principal and interest. Interest accrued can be computed with the annual interest rate, principal loan amount, and portion of the year accrued.
- Employers withhold taxes from employees and customers for payment to government agencies at a later date, but within the business operating period. Common taxes are sales tax and federal, state, and local income taxes.

12.2 Analyze, Journalize, and Report Current Liabilities

- When the merchandiser initially pays the supplier on credit, it increases both Accounts Payable (a credit) and the appropriate merchandise Inventory account (a debit). When the amount due is later paid, it decreases both Accounts Payable (a debit) and Cash (a credit).
- When the company collects payment from a customer in advance of providing a product or service, it increases both Unearned Revenue (a credit) and Cash (a debit). When the company provides the product or service, Unearned Revenue decreases (a debit), and Revenue increases (a credit) to realize the amount earned.
- To recognize payment of the current portion of a noncurrent note payable, both Notes Payable and Cash would decrease, resulting in a debit and a credit, respectively. To recognize interest accumulation, both Interest Expense and Interest Payable would increase, resulting in a debit and a credit, respectively.
- To recognize sales tax in the initial sale to a customer, Cash or Accounts Receivable increases (a debit), and Sales Tax Payable increases (a credit), as does Sales (a credit). When the company remits the sales tax

payment to the governing body, Sales Tax Payable decreases (a debit), as does Cash (a credit).

12.3 Define and Apply Accounting Treatment for Contingent Liabilities

- Contingent liabilities arise from a current situation with an uncertain outcome that may occur in the future. Contingent liabilities may include litigation, warranties, insurance claims, and bankruptcy.
- Two FASB recognition requirements must be met before declaring a contingent liability. There must be a probable likelihood of occurrence, and the loss amount is reasonably estimated.
- The four contingent liability treatments are probable and estimable, probable and inestimable, reasonably possible, and remote.
- Recognition in financial statements, as well as a note disclosure, occurs when the outcome is probable and estimable. Probable and not estimable and reasonably possible outcomes require note disclosures only. There is not recognition or note disclosure for a remote outcome.

12.4 Prepare Journal Entries to Record Short-Term Notes Payable

- Short-term notes payable is a debt created and due within a company's operating period (less than a year). This debt includes a written promise to pay principal and interest.
- If a company does not pay for its purchases within a specified time frame, a supplier will convert the accounts payable into a short-term note payable with interest. When the company pays the amount owed, short-term notes payable and Cash will decrease, while interest expense increases.
- A company may borrow from a bank because it does not have enough cash on hand to pay for a capital expenditure or cover temporary expenses. The loan will consist of short-term repayment with interest, affecting short-term notes payable, cash, and interest expense.

12.5 Record Transactions Incurred in Preparing Payroll

- An employee's net income (pay) results from gross income (pay) minus any involuntary and voluntary deductions. Employee payroll deductions may include federal, state, and local income taxes; FICA Social Security; FICA Medicare; and voluntary deductions such as health insurance, retirement plan contributions, and union dues.
- When recording employee payroll liabilities, Salaries Expense, Salaries Payable, and all payables for income taxes, Social Security, Medicare, and voluntary deductions, are reported. When the company pays the accrued salaries, Salaries Payable is reduced, as is cash.
- Employers are required to match employee withholdings for Social Security and Medicare. They must also remit FUTA and SUTA taxes, as well as voluntary deductions and benefits provided to employees.
- When recording employer payroll liabilities, Employer Payroll Taxes Expense and all payables associated with FUTA, SUTA, Social Security, Medicare, and voluntary deductions are required. When the company pays all employer liabilities, each payable and cash account decreases.

Multiple Choice

1. LO 12.1 Which of the following is *not* considered a current liability?

A. Accounts Payable
B. Unearned Revenue
C. the component of a twenty-year note payable due in year 20
D. current portion of a noncurrent note payable

2. LO 12.1 A company regularly purchases materials from a manufacturer on credit. Payments for these purchases occur within the company's operating cycle. They do not include interest and are established with an invoice outlining purchase details, credit terms, and shipping charges. Which current liability situation does this best describe?

A. sales tax payable
B. accounts payable
C. unearned revenue
D. income taxes payable

3. LO 12.1 The following is selected financial data from Block Industries:

Cash	$20,000
Accounts receivable	13,400
Equipment	10,650
Prepaid expenses	5,000
Accounts payable	12,300
Unearned revenue	7,500
Long-term notes payable	10,000
Common stock	18,000
Revenue	11,700
Sales tax payable	6,000
Interest expense	4,500
Depreciation expense	1,000

How much does Block Industries have in current liabilities?

A. $19,800
B. $18,300
C. $12,300
D. $25,800

4. LO 12.1 A ski company takes out a $400,000 loan from a bank. The bank requires eight equal repayments of the loan principal, paid annually. Assume no interest is paid or accumulated on the loan until the final repayment. How much of the loan principal is considered a current portion of a noncurrent note payable in year 3?

A. $50,000
B. $150,000
C. $100,000
D. $250,000

5. LO 12.2 Nido Co. has a standing agreement with a supplier for purchasing car parts. The terms of the agreement are 3/15, n/30 from the invoice date of September 1. The company makes a purchase on September 1 for $5,000 and pays the amount due on September 13. What amount does Nido Co. pay in cash on September 13?

A. $5,000
B. $4,850
C. $150
D. $4,250

6. LO 12.2 A client pays cash in advance for a magazine subscription to *Living Daily*. *Living Daily* has yet to provide the magazine to the client. What accounts would *Living Daily* use to recognize this advance payment?

A. unearned subscription revenue, cash
B. cash, subscription revenue
C. subscription revenue, unearned subscription revenue
D. unearned subscription revenue, subscription revenue, cash

7. LO 12.2 Lime Co. incurs a $4,000 note with equal principal installment payments due for the next eight years. What is the amount of the current portion of the noncurrent note payable due in the second year?

A. $800
B. $1,000
C. $500
D. nothing, since this is a noncurrent note payable

8. LO 12.3 Which of the following best describes a contingent liability that is likely to occur but cannot be reasonably estimated?

A. reasonably possible
B. probable and estimable
C. probable and inestimable
D. remote

9. LO 12.3 Blake Department Store sells television sets with one-year warranties that cover repair and replacement of television parts. In the month of June, Blake sells forty television sets with a per unit cost of $500. If Blake estimates warranty fulfillment at 10% of sales, what would be the warranty liability reported in June?

A. $1,000
B. $2,000
C. $500
D. $20,000

10. LO 12.3 What accounts are used to record a contingent warranty liability that is probable and estimable but has yet to be fulfilled?

A. warranty liability and cash
B. warranty expense and cash
C. warranty liability and warranty expense, cash
D. warranty expense and warranty liability

11. LO 12.3 Which of the following best describes a contingent liability that is unlikely to occur?

A. remote
B. probable and estimable
C. reasonably possible
D. probable and inestimable

12. LO 12.4 Which of the following accounts are used when a short-term note payable with 5% interest is honored (paid)?

A. short-term notes payable, cash
B. short-term notes payable, cash, interest expense
C. interest expense, cash
D. short-term notes payable, interest expense, interest payable

13. LO 12.4 Which of the following is not a characteristic of a short-term note payable?

A. Payment is due in less than a year.
B. It bears interest.
C. It can result from an accounts payable conversion.
D. It is reported on the balance sheet under noncurrent liabilities.

14. LO 12.4 Sunlight Growers borrows $250,000 from a bank at a 4% annual interest rate. The loan is due in three months. At the end of the three months, the company pays the amount due in full. How much did the company remit to the bank?

A. $250,000
B. $10,000
C. $252,500
D. $2,500

15. LO 12.4 Marathon Peanuts converts a $130,000 account payable into a short-term note payable, with an annual interest rate of 6%, and payable in four months. How much interest will Marathon Peanuts owe at the end of four months?

A. $2,600
B. $7,800
C. $137,800
D. $132,600

16. LO 12.5 An employee earns $8,000 in the first pay period. The FICA Social Security Tax rate is 6.2%, and the FICA Medicare tax rate is 1.45%. What is the employee's FICA taxes responsibility?

A. $535.50
B. $612
C. None, only the employer pays FICA taxes
D. $597.50
E. $550

17. LO 12.5 Which of the following is considered an employer payroll tax?

A. FICA Medicare
B. FUTA
C. SUTA
D. A and B only
E. B and C only
F. A, B, and C

18. LO 12.5 Employees at Rayon Enterprises earn one day a month of vacation compensation (twelve days total each year). Vacation compensation is paid at an hourly rate of $45, based on an eight-hour work day. Rayon's first pay period is January. It is now April 30, how much vacation liability has accumulated if the company has four employees and no vacation compensation has been paid?

A. $1,440
B. $4,320
C. $5,760
D. $7,200

19. LO 12.5 An employee and employer cost-share health insurance. If the employee covers three-fourths of the cost and the employer covers the rest, what would be the employee's responsibility if the total premium was $825?

A. $618.75
B. $206.25
C. $412.50
D. $275

Questions

1. LO 12.1 Why is Accounts Payable classified as a current liability?

2. LO 12.1 On which financial statement are current liabilities reported?

3. LO 12.1 What is the difference between a noncurrent liability and a current liability?

4. LO 12.1 How is the sales tax rate usually determined? Does the company get to keep the sales tax as earned revenue?

5. LO 12.2 If Bergen Air Systems takes out a $100,000 loan, with eight equal principal payments due over the next eight years, how much will be accounted for as a current portion of a noncurrent note payable each year?

6. LO 12.2 What amount is payable to a state tax board if the original sales price is $3,000, and the tax rate is 3.5%?

7. LO 12.2 What specific accounts are recognized when a business purchases equipment on credit?

8. LO 12.3 What is a contingent liability?

9. LO 12.3 What are the two FASB required conditions for a contingent liability to be recognized?

10. LO 12.3 If a bankruptcy is deemed likely to occur and is reasonably estimated, what would be the recognition and disclosure requirements for the company?

11. LO 12.3 Name the four contingent liability treatments.

12. LO 12.3 A company's sales for January are $250,000. If the company projects warranty obligations to be 5% of sales, what is the warranty liability amount for January?

13. LO 12.4 What is a key difference between a short-term note payable and a current portion of a noncurrent note payable?

14. LO 12.4 What business circumstance could bring about a short-term note payable created from a purchase?

15. LO 12.4 What business circumstance could produce a short-term notes payable created from a loan?

16. LO 12.4 Jain Enterprises honors a short-term note payable. Principal on the note is $425,000, with an annual interest rate of 3.5%, due in 6 months. What journal entry is created when Jain honors the note?

17. LO 12.5 What are examples of involuntary deductions employers are required to collect for employee and employer payroll liabilities?

18. LO 12.5 What are the tax rates for FICA Social Security and FICA Medicare? What are the maximum taxable earnings amounts for each of these taxes?

19. LO 12.5 What are FUTA and SUTA taxes? Is there any possible reduction in the FUTA tax rate? If so, what is the reduction, and how is this determined?

20. LO 12.5 Use Figure 12.15 as a reference to answer the following questions.

A. If an employee makes $1,400 per month and files as single with no withholding allowances, what would be his monthly income tax withholding?

B. What would it be if an employee makes $2,500 per month and files as single with two withholding allowances?

Exercise Set A

EA1. LO 12.1 Campus Flights takes out a bank loan in the amount of $200,500 on March 1. The terms of the loan include a repayment of principal in ten equal installments, paid annually from March 1. The annual interest rate on the loan is 8%, recognized on December 31. (Round answers to the nearest whole dollar if needed.)

A. Compute the interest recognized as of December 31 in year 1 rounded to the whole dollar.

B. Compute the principal due in year 1.

EA2. LO 12.1 Consider the following accounts and determine if the account is a current liability, a noncurrent liability, or neither.

A. cash

B. federal income tax payable this year

C. long-term note payable

D. current portion of a long-term note payable

E. note payable due in four years

F. interest expense

G. state income tax

EA3. LO 12.1 Lamplight Plus sells lamps to consumers. The company contracts with a supplier who provides them with lamp fixtures. There is an agreement that Lamplight Plus is not required to provide cash payment immediately and instead will provide payment within thirty days of the invoice date.

Additional information:

- Lamplight purchases thirty light fixtures for $20 each on August 1, invoice date August 1, with no discount terms
- Lamplight returns ten light fixtures (receiving a credit amount for the total purchase price per fixture of $20 each) on August 3.
- Lamplight purchases an additional fifteen light fixtures for $15 each on August 19, invoice date August 19, with no discount terms.
- Lamplight pays $100 toward its account on August 22.

What amount does Lamplight Plus still owe to the supplier on August 30? What account is used to recognize this outstanding amount?

EA4. LO 12.2 Review the following transactions and prepare any necessary journal entries for Olinda Pet Supplies.

A. On March 2, Olinda Pet Supplies receives advance cash payment from a customer for forty dog food dishes (from their Dish inventory), costing $25 each. Olinda had yet to supply the dog food bowls as of March 2.

B. On April 4, Olinda provides all of the dog food bowls to the customer.

EA5. LO 12.2 Review the following transactions and prepare any necessary journal entries for Tolbert Enterprises.

A. On April 7, Tolbert Enterprises contracts with a supplier to purchase 300 water bottles for their merchandise inventory, on credit, for $10 each. Credit terms are 2/10, n/60 from the invoice date of April 7.

B. On April 15, Tolbert pays the amount due in cash to the supplier.

EA6. LO 12.2 Elegant Electronics sells a cellular phone on September 2 for $450. On September 6, Elegant sells another cellular phone for $500. Sales tax is computed at 3.5% of the total sale. Prepare journal entries for each sale, including sales tax, and the remittance of all sales tax to the tax board on October 23.

EA7. LO 12.2 Homeland Plus specializes in home goods and accessories. In order for the company to expand its business, the company takes out a long-term loan in the amount of $650,000. Assume that any loans are created on January 1. The terms of the loan include a periodic payment plan, where interest payments are accumulated each year but are only computed against the outstanding principal balance during that current period. The annual interest rate is 8.5%. Each year on December 31, the company pays down the principal balance by $80,000. This payment is considered part of the outstanding principal balance when computing the interest accumulation that also occurs on December 31 of that year.

A. Determine the outstanding principal balance on December 31 of the first year that is computed for interest.

B. Compute the interest accrued on December 31 of the first year.

C. Make a journal entry to record interest accumulated during the first year, but not paid as of December 31 of that first year.

EA8. LO 12.2 Bhakti Games is a chain of board game stores. Record entries for the following transactions related to Bhakti's purchase of inventory.

A. On October 5, Bhakti purchases and receives inventory from XYZ Entertainment for $5,000 with credit terms of 2/10 net 30.

B. On October 7, Bhakti returns $1,000 worth of the inventory purchased from XYZ.

C. Bhakti makes payment in full on its purchase from XYZ on October 14.

EA9. LO 12.3 Following is the unadjusted trial balance for Sun Energy Co. on December 31, 2017.

SUN ENERGY CO. Unadjusted Trial Balance Year Ended December 31, 2017		
Account	**Debit**	**Credit**
Cash	$ 5,000	
Account Receivable	2,000	
Merchandise Inventory	4,500	
Buildings	2,400	
Equipment	3,200	
Accounts Payable		$ 5,700
Salaries Payable		2,500
Common Stock		1,500
Dividends		
Sales Revenue		13,700
COGS	3,800	
Salaries Expense	2,500	
Totals	$23,400	$23,400

You are also given the following supplemental information: A pending lawsuit, claiming $2,700 in damages, is considered likely to favor the plaintiff and can be reasonably estimated. Sun Energy Co. believes a customer may win a lawsuit for $3,500 in damages, but the outcome is only reasonably possible to occur. Sun Energy calculated warranty expense estimates of $210.

A. Using the unadjusted trial balance and supplemental information for Sun Energy Co., construct an income statement for the year ended December 31, 2017. Pay particular attention to expenses resulting from contingencies.
B. Construct a balance sheet, for December 31, 2017, from the given unadjusted trial balance, supplemental information, and income statement for Sun Energy Co., paying particular attention to contingent liabilities.
C. Prepare any necessary contingent liability note disclosures for Sun Energy Co. Only give one to three sentences for each contingency note disclosure.

EA10. LO 12.4 Barkers Baked Goods purchases dog treats from a supplier on February 2 at a quantity of 6,000 treats at $1 per treat. Terms of the purchase are 2/10, n/30. Barkers pays half the amount due in cash on February 28 but cannot pay the remaining balance due in four days. The supplier renegotiates the terms on March 4 and allows Barkers to convert its purchase payment into a short-term note, with an annual interest rate of 6%, payable in 9 months.

Show the entries for the initial purchase, the partial payment, and the conversion.

EA11. LO 12.4 Use information from EA10. Compute the interest expense due when Barkers honors the note. Show the journal entry to recognize payment of the short-term note on December 4.

EA12. LO 12.4 Scrimiger Paints wants to upgrade its machinery and on September 20 takes out a loan from the bank in the amount of $500,000. The terms of the loan are 2.9% annual interest rate and payable in 8 months. Interest is due in equal payments each month.

Compute the interest expense due each month. Show the journal entry to recognize the interest payment on October 20, and the entry for payment of the short-term note and final interest payment on May 20. Round to the nearest cent if required.

EA13. LO 12.5 Following are payroll deductions for Mars Co. Classify each payroll deduction as either a voluntary or involuntary deduction. Record a (V) for voluntary and an (I) for involuntary.

Payroll Deductions

Payroll Deduction	Voluntary (V) or Involuntary (I)?
FICA Social Security Tax	
Vacation pay	
401(k) retirement plan contribution	
Charitable contributions	
Federal Unemployment Tax (FUTA)	
Health insurance plan contribution	
FICA Medicare Tax	
State Unemployment Tax (SUTA)	

Table 12.3

EA14. LO 12.5 Toren Inc. employs one person to run its solar management company. The employee's gross income for the month of May is $6,000. Payroll for the month of May is as follows: FICA Social Security tax rate at 6.2%, FICA Medicare tax rate at 1.45%, federal income tax of $400, state income tax of $75, health-care insurance premium of $200, and union dues of $50. The employee is responsible for covering 30% of his or her health insurance premium.

A. Record the journal entry to recognize employee payroll for the month of May, dated May 31, 2017.
B. Record remittance of the employee's salary with cash on June 1.

EA15. LO 12.5 In EA14, you prepared the journal entries for the employee of Toren Inc. You have now been given the following additional information:

- May is the first pay period for this employee. FUTA taxes are 0.6% and SUTA taxes are 5.4% of the first $7,000 paid to the employee. FICA Social Security and FICA Medicare match employee deductions. The employer is responsible for 70% of the health insurance premium.

Using the information from EA14 and the additional information provided:

A. Record the employer payroll for the month of May, dated May 31, 2017.
B. Record the payment in cash of all employer liabilities only on June 1.

EA16. LO 12.5 An employee and employer cost-share pension plan contributions and health insurance premium payments. If the employee covers 35% of the pension plan contribution and 25% of the health insurance premium, what would be the employee's total benefits responsibility if the total pension contribution was $900, and the health insurance premium was $375?

Include the journal entry representing the payroll benefits accumulation for the employer in the month of February.

 Exercise Set B

EB1. LO 12.1 Everglades Consultants takes out a loan in the amount of $375,000 on April 1. The terms of the loan include a repayment of principal in eight, equal installments, paid annually from the April 1 date. The annual interest rate on the loan is 5%, recognized on December 31. (Round answers to the nearest cent, if needed.)

A. Compute the interest recognized as of December 31 in year 1.
B. Compute the principal due in year 1.

EB2. LO 12.1 Match each of the following accounts with the appropriate transaction or description.

A. Sales Tax Payable	i. A customer pays in advance for services
B. Income Taxes Payable	ii. A risk incentive rate for a loan
C. Current portion of a long-term note payable	iii. State withholding from an employee's paycheck
D. Interest Payable	iv. The portion of a note due within the operating period
E. Accounts Payable	v. A credit line between a purchaser and a supplier
F. Unearned Revenue	vi. Extra tax collected on the sale of a product

EB3. LO 12.1 Pianos Unlimited sells pianos to customers. The company contracts with a supplier who provides it with replacement piano keys. There is an agreement that Pianos Unlimited is not required to provide cash payment immediately, and instead will provide payment within thirty days of the invoice date.

Additional information:

- Pianos Unlimited purchases 400 piano keys for $7 each on September 1, invoice date September 1, with discount terms 2/10, n/30.
- Pianos Unlimited returns 150 piano keys (receiving a credit amount for the total purchase price per key of $7 each) on September 8.
- The company purchases an additional 230 keys for $5 each on September 15, invoice date September 15, with no discount terms.
- The company pays 50% of the total amount due to the supplier on September 24.

What amount does Pianos Unlimited still owe to the supplier on September 30? What account is used to recognize this outstanding amount?

EB4. LO 12.2 Review the following transactions and prepare any necessary journal entries for Bernard Law Offices.

A. On June 1, Bernard Law Offices receives an advance cash payment of $4,500 from a client for three months of legal services.
B. On July 31, Bernard recognizes legal services provided.

EB5. LO 12.2 Review the following transactions and prepare any necessary journal entries for Lands Inc.

A. On December 10, Lands Inc. contracts with a supplier to purchase 450 plants for its merchandise inventory, on credit, for $12.50 each. Credit terms are 4/15, n/30 from the invoice date of December 10.
B. On December 28, Lands pays the amount due in cash to the supplier.

EB6. LO 12.2 Monster Drinks sells twenty-four cases of beverages on October 18 for $120 per case. On October 25, Monster sells another thirty-five cases for $140 per case. Sales tax is computed at 4% of the total sale. Prepare journal entries for each sale, including sales tax, and the remittance of all sales tax to the tax board on November 5.

EB7. LO 12.2 McMasters Inc. specializes in BBQ accessories. In order for the company to expand its business, they take out a long-term loan in the amount of $800,000. Assume that any loans are created on January 1. The terms of the loan include a periodic payment plan, where interest payments are accumulated each year but are only computed against the outstanding principal balance during that current period. The annual interest rate is 9%. Each year on December 31, the company pays down the principal balance by $50,000. This payment is considered part of the outstanding principal balance when computing the interest accumulation that also occurs on December 31 of that year.

A. Determine the outstanding principal balance on December 31 of the first year that is computed for interest.
B. Compute the interest accrued on December 31 of the first year.
C. Make a journal entry to record interest accumulated during the first year, but not paid as of December 31 of that first year.

EB8. LO 12.3 Following is the unadjusted trial balance for Pens Unlimited on December 31, 2017.

PENS UNLIMITED Unadjusted Trial Balance Year Ended December 31, 2017		
Account	**Debit**	**Credit**
Cash	$ 8,500	
Account Receivable	3,000	
Merchandise Inventory	6,750	
Buildings	5,600	
Equipment	4,000	
Accounts Payable		$ 7,500
Salaries Payable		4,250
Common Stock		5,000
Dividends		
Sales Revenue		20,750
COGS	5,400	
Salaries Expense	4,250	
Totals	$37,500	$37,500

You are also given the following supplemental information: A pending lawsuit, claiming $4,200 in damages, is considered likely to favor the plaintiff and can be reasonably estimated. Pens Unlimited believes a customer may win a lawsuit for $5,000 in damages, but the outcome is only reasonably possible to occur. Pens Unlimited records warranty estimates on the basis of 2% of annual sales revenue.

A. Using the unadjusted trial balance and supplemental information for Pens Unlimited, construct an income statement for the year ended December 31, 2017. Pay particular attention to expenses resulting from contingencies.
B. Construct a balance sheet, for December 31, 2017, from the given unadjusted trial balance, supplemental information, and income statement for Pens Unlimited. Pay particular attention to contingent liabilities.
C. Prepare any necessary contingent liability note disclosures for Pens Unlimited. Only give one to three sentences for each contingency note disclosure.

EB9. LO 12.4 Airplanes Unlimited purchases airplane parts from a supplier on March 19 at a quantity of 4,800 parts at $12.50 per part. Terms of the purchase are 3/10, n/30. Airplanes pays one-third of the amount due in cash on March 30 but cannot pay the remaining balance due. The supplier renegotiates the terms on April 18 and allows Airplanes to convert its purchase payment into a short-term note, with an annual interest rate of 9%, payable in six months.

Show the entries for the initial purchase, the partial payment, and the conversion.

EB10. LO 12.4 Use information from EB9. Compute the interest expense due when Airplanes Unlimited honors the note. Show the journal entry to recognize payment of the short-term note on October 18.

EB11. LO 12.4 Whole Leaves wants to upgrade their equipment, and on January 24 the company takes out a loan from the bank in the amount of $310,000. The terms of the loan are 6.5% annual interest rate, payable in three months. Interest is due in equal payments each month.

Compute the interest expense due each month. Show the journal entry to recognize the interest payment on February 24, and the entry for payment of the short-term note and final interest payment on April 24. Round to the nearest cent if required.

EB12. LO 12.5 Reference Figure 12.15 and use the following information to complete the requirements.

Employee	Monthly Gross Income	Withholding Allowances
Debbie	$1,150	0
Michael	$1,270	2
Karen	$2,600	1

A. Determine the federal income tax withholdings amount per monthly pay period for each employee.
B. Record the employee payroll entry (all employees) for the month of January assuming FICA Social Security is 6.2%, FICA Medicare is 1.45%, and state income tax is equal to 3% of gross income. (Round to the nearest cent if necessary.)

EB13. LO 12.5 Marc & Associates employs Janet Evanovich at its law firm. Her gross income for June is $7,500. Payroll for the month of June follows: federal income tax of $650, state income tax of $60, local income tax of $30, FICA Social Security tax rate at 6.2%, FICA Medicare tax rate at 1.45%, health-care insurance premium of $300, donations to a charity of $50, and pension plan contribution of $200. The employee is responsible for covering 40% of his or her health insurance premium.

A. Record the journal entry to recognize employee payroll for the month of June; dated June 30, 2017.
B. Record remittance of the employee's salary with cash on July 1.

EB14. LO 12.5 In EB13, you prepared the journal entries for Janet Evanovich, an employee of Marc & Associates. You have now been given the following additional information: June is the first pay period for this employee. FUTA taxes are 0.6% and SUTA taxes are 5.4% of the first $7,000 paid to the employee. FICA Social Security and FICA Medicare match employee deductions. The employer is responsible for 60% of the health insurance premium. The employer matches 50% of employee pension plan contributions.

Using the information from EB13 and the additional information provided:

A. Record the employer payroll for the month of June, dated June 30, 2017.
B. Record the payment in cash of all employer liabilities only on July 1.

EB15. LO 12.5 An employee and employer cost-share 401(k) plan contributions, health insurance premium payments, and charitable donations. The employer also provides annual vacation compensation equal to ten days of pay at a rate of $30 per hour, eight-hour work day. The employee makes a gross wage of $3,000 monthly. The employee decides to use five days of vacation during the current pay period. Employees cover 30% of the 401(k) plan contribution and 30% of the health insurance premium. The employee also donates 1% of gross pay to a charitable organization.

A. What would be the employee's total benefits responsibility if the total 401(k) contribution is $700 and the health insurance premium is $260?

B. Include the journal entry representing the payroll benefits accumulation for the employer in the month of March, if the employer matches the employee's charitable donation of 1%.

Problem Set A

PA1. LO 12.1 Consider the following situations and determine (1) which type of liability should be recognized (specific account), and (2) how much should be recognized in the current period (year).

A. A business sets up a line of credit with a supplier. The company purchases $10,000 worth of equipment on credit. Terms of purchase are 5/10, n/30.

B. A customer purchases a watering hose for $25. The sales tax rate is 5%.

C. Customers pay in advance for season tickets to a soccer game. There are fourteen customers, each paying $250 per season ticket. Each customer purchased two season tickets.

D. A company issues 2,000 shares of its common stock with a price per share of $15.

PA2. LO 12.1 Stork Enterprises delivers care packages for special occasions. They charge $45 for a small package, and $80 for a large package. The sales tax rate is 6%. During the month of May, Stork delivers 38 small packages and 22 large packages.

A. What is the total tax charged to the customer per small package? What is the overall charge per small package?

B. What is the total tax charged to the customer per large package? What is the overall charge per large package?

C. How much sales tax liability does Stork Enterprises have for the month of May?

D. What accounts are used to recognize this tax situation for the month of May?

E. When Stork remits payment to the sales tax governing body, what happens to the sales tax liability?

PA3. LO 12.2 Review the following transactions, and prepare any necessary journal entries for Renovation Goods.

A. On May 12, Renovation Goods purchases 750 square feet of flooring (Flooring Inventory) at $3.00 per square foot from a supplier, on credit. Terms of the purchase are 2/10, n/30 from the invoice date of May 12.

B. On May 15, Renovation Goods purchases 200 measuring tapes (Tape Inventory) at $5.75 per tape from a supplier, on credit. Terms of the purchase are 4/15, n/60 from the invoice date of May 15.

C. On May 22, Renovation Goods pays cash for the amount due to the flooring supplier from the May 12 transaction.

D. On June 3, Renovation Goods pays cash for the amount due to the tape supplier from the May 15 transaction.

PA4. LO 12.2 Review the following transactions, and prepare any necessary journal entries for Juniper Landscaping Services.

A. On November 5, Juniper receives advance cash payment from a customer for landscaping services in the amount of $3,500. Juniper had yet to provide landscaping services as of November 5.
B. On December 11, Juniper provides all of the landscaping services to the customer from November 5.
C. On December 14, Juniper receives advance payment from another customer for landscaping services in the amount of $4,400. Juniper has yet to provide landscaping services as of December 14.
D. On January 19 of the following year, Juniper provides and recognizes 80% of landscaping services to the customer from December 14.

PA5. LO 12.2 Review the following transactions, and prepare any necessary journal entries.

A. On July 16, Arrow Corp. purchases 200 computers (Equipment) at $500 per computer from a supplier, on credit. Terms of the purchase are 4/10, n/50 from the invoice date of July 16.
B. On August 10, Hondo Inc. receives advance cash payment from a client for legal services in the amount of $9,000. Hondo had yet to provide legal services as of August 10.
C. On September 22, Jack Pies sells thirty pies for $25 cash per pie. The sales tax rate is 8%.
D. On November 8, More Supplies paid a portion of their noncurrent note in the amount of $3,250 cash.

PA6. LO 12.3 Machine Corp. has several pending lawsuits against its company. Review each situation and (1) determine the treatment for each situation as probable and estimable, probable and inestimable, reasonably possible, or remote; (2) determine what, if any, recognition or note disclosure is required; and (3) prepare any journal entries required to recognize a contingent liability.

A. A pending lawsuit, claiming $100,000 in damages, is considered likely to favor the plaintiff and can be reasonably estimated.
B. Machine Corp. believes there might be other potential lawsuits about this faulty machinery, but this is unlikely to occur.
C. A claimant sues Machine Corp. for damages, from a dishonored service contract agreement; the plaintiff will likely win the case but damages cannot be reasonably estimated.
D. Machine Corp. believes a customer will win a lawsuit it filed, but the outcome is not likely and is not remote. It is possible the customer will win.

PA7. LO 12.3 Emperor Pool Services provides pool cleaning and maintenance services to residential clients. It offers a one-year warranty on all services. Review each of the transactions, and prepare any necessary journal entries for each situation.

A. March 31: Emperor provides cleaning services for fifteen pools during the month of March at a sales price per pool of $550 cash. Emperor records warranty estimates when sales are recognized and bases warranty estimates on 2% of sales.
B. April 5: A customer files a warranty claim that Emperor honors in the amount of $100 cash.
C. April 13: Another customer, J. Jones, files a warranty claim that Emperor does not honor due to customer negligence.
D. June 8: J. Jones files a lawsuit requesting damages related to the dishonored warranty in the amount of $1,500. Emperor determines that the lawsuit is likely to end in the plaintiff's favor and the $1,500 is a reasonable estimate for damages.

PA8. LO 12.4 Serene Company purchases fountains for its inventory from Kirkland Inc. The following transactions take place during the current year.

A. On July 3, the company purchases thirty fountains for $1,200 per fountain, on credit. Terms of the purchase are 2/10, n/30, invoice dated July 3.
B. On August 3, Serene does not pay the amount due and renegotiates with Kirkland. Kirkland agrees to convert the debt owed into a short-term note, with an 8% annual interest rate, payable in two months from August 3.
C. On October 3, Serene Company pays its account in full.

Record the journal entries to recognize the initial purchase, the conversion, and the payment.

PA9. LO 12.4 Mohammed LLC is a growing consulting firm. The following transactions take place during the current year.

A. On June 10, Mohammed borrows $270,000 from a bank to cover the initial cost of expansion. Terms of the loan are payment due in four months from June 10, and annual interest rate of 5%.
B. On July 9, Mohammed borrows an additional $100,000 with payment due in four months from July 9, and an annual interest rate of 12%.
C. Mohammed pays their accounts in full on October 10 for the June 10 loan, and on November 9 for the July 9 loan.

Record the journal entries to recognize the initial borrowings, and the two payments for Mohammed.

PA10. LO 12.5 Lemur Corp. is going to pay three employees a year-end bonus. The amount of the year-end bonus and the amount of federal income tax withholding are as follows.

Employee	Filing Status	Allowances	Gross Income	Federal Income Withholding
Sarah	Married	4	$10,000	$ 962
Joe	Single	2	$ 9,000	$1,362
Kevin	Single	1	$ 4,000	$ 357

Lemur's payroll deductions include FICA Social Security at 6.2%, FICA Medicare at 1.45%, FUTA at 0.6%, SUTA at 5.4%, federal income tax as previously shown, state income tax at 5% of gross pay, and 401(k) employee contributions at 2% of gross pay.

Record the entry for the employee payroll on December 31.

PA11. LO 12.5 Record the journal entries for each of the following payroll transactions.

Apr. 2	Paid $650 and $340 cash to a federal depository for FICA Social Security and FICA Medicare, respectively
Apr. 4	Paid accumulated employee salaries of $15,220
Apr. 11	Issued checks in the amounts of $480 for federal income tax and $300 for state income tax to an IRS-approved bank
Apr. 14	Paid cash to health insurance carrier for total outstanding health insurance liability of $800
Apr. 22	Remitted cash payments for FUTA and SUTA to federal and state unemployment agencies in the amounts of $130 and $250, respectively

Problem Set B

PB1. LO 12.1 Consider the following situations and determine (1) which type of liability should be recognized (specific account), and (2) how much should be recognized in the current period (year).

A. A business depreciates a building with a book value of $12,000, using straight-line depreciation, no salvage value, and a remaining useful life of six years.
B. An organization has a line of credit with a supplier. The company purchases $35,500 worth of inventory on credit. Terms of purchase are 3/20, n/60.
C. An employee earns $1,000 in pay and the employer withholds $46 for federal income tax.
D. A customer pays $4,000 in advance for legal services. The lawyer has previously recognized 30% of the services as revenue. The remainder is outstanding.

PB2. LO 12.1 Perfume Depot sells two different tiers of perfume products to customers. They charge $30 for tier 1 perfume and $100 for tier 2 perfume. The sales tax rate is 4.5%. During the month of October, Perfume Depot sells 75 tier 1 perfumes, and 60 tier 2 perfumes.

A. What is the total tax charged to the customer per tier 1 perfume? What is the overall charge per tier 1 category perfume?
B. What is the total tax charged to the customer per tier 2 perfume? What is the overall charge per tier 2 category perfume?
C. How much sales tax liability does Perfume Depot have for the month of October?
D. What accounts are used to recognize this tax situation for the month of October?
E. When Perfume Depot remits payment to the sales tax governing body, what happens to the sales tax liability?

PB3. LO 12.2 Review the following transactions, and prepare any necessary journal entries for Sewing Masters Inc.

A. On October 3, Sewing Masters Inc. purchases 800 yards of fabric (Fabric Inventory) at $9.00 per yard from a supplier, on credit. Terms of the purchase are 1/5, n/40 from the invoice date of October 3.
B. On October 8, Sewing Masters Inc. purchases 300 more yards of fabric from the same supplier at an increased price of $9.25 per yard, on credit. Terms of the purchase are 5/10, n/20 from the invoice date of October 8.
C. On October 18, Sewing Masters pays cash for the amount due to the fabric supplier from the October 8 transaction.
D. On October 23, Sewing Masters pays cash for the amount due to the fabric supplier from the October 3 transaction.

PB4. LO 12.2 Review the following transactions and prepare any necessary journal entries for *Woodworking Magazine*. *Woodworking Magazine* provides one issue per month to subscribers for a service fee of $240 per year. Assume January 1 is the first day of operations for this company, and no new customers join during the year.

A. On January 1, *Woodworking Magazine* receives advance cash payment from forty customers for magazine subscription services. Handyman had yet to provide subscription services as of January 1.
B. On April 30, *Woodworking* recognizes subscription revenues earned.
C. On October 31, *Woodworking* recognizes subscription revenues earned.
D. On December 31, *Woodworking* recognizes subscription revenues earned.

PB5. LO 12.2 Review the following transactions and prepare any necessary journal entries.

A. On January 5, Bunnet Co. purchases 350 aprons (Supplies) at $25 per apron from a supplier, on credit. Terms of the purchase are 3/10, n/30 from the invoice date of January 5.

B. On February 18, Melon Construction receives advance cash payment from a client for construction services in the amount of $20,000. Melon had yet to provide construction services as of February 18.

C. On March 21, Noonan Smoothies sells 875 smoothies for $4 cash per smoothie. The sales tax rate is 6.5%.

D. On June 7, Organic Methods paid a portion of their noncurrent note in the amount of $9,340 cash.

PB6. LO 12.3 Roundhouse Tools has several potential warranty claims as a result of damaged tool kits. Review each situation and (1) determine the treatment for each situation as probable and estimable, probable and inestimable, reasonably possible, or remote; (2) determine what, if any, recognition or note disclosure is required; and (3) prepare any journal entries required to recognize a contingent liability.

A. Roundhouse Tools has several claims for replacement of another tool kit not listed as one of their damaged tool kits. The honored warranty for these tool kits is not likely but is not remote. It is possible.

B. A pending warranty claim has been received with the projected cost to be $450. Roundhouse Tools believes honoring that warranty claim is likely to occur and that figure is reasonably estimated.

C. Roundhouse Tools believes other potential warranties may have to be honored outside of the warranty period, but this is unlikely to occur.

D. Warranty replacements will cost the company a percentage of sales for the period. This amount allotted for warranty replacements cannot be reasonably estimated but is likely to occur.

PB7. LO 12.3 Shoe Hut sells custom, handmade shoes. It offers a one-year warranty on all shoes for repair or replacement. Review each of the transactions and prepare any necessary journal entries for each situation.

A. May 31: Shoe Hut sells 100 pairs of shoes during the month of May at a sales price per pair of shoes of $240 cash. Shoe Hut records warranty estimates when sales are recognized and bases warranty estimates on 4% of sales.

B. June 2: A customer files a warranty claim that Shoe Hut honors in the amount of $30 for repair to laces. Laces Inventory corresponds to shoelace inventory used for repairs.

C. June 4: Another customer files a warranty claim that Shoe Hut honors. Shoe Hut replaces the damaged shoes at a cost of $200, affecting their Shoe Replacement Inventory account.

D. August 10: Shoe Hut explores the possibility of bankruptcy, given the current economic conditions (recession). It determines the bankruptcy is unlikely to occur (remote).

PB8. LO 12.4 Air Compressors Inc. purchases compressor parts for its inventory from a supplier. The following transactions take place during the current year:

A. On April 5, the company purchases 400 parts for $8.30 per part, on credit. Terms of the purchase are 4/10, n/30, invoice dated April 5.

B. On May 5, Air Compressors does not pay the amount due and renegotiates with the supplier. The supplier agrees to $400 cash immediately as partial payment on note payable due, converting the debt owed into a short-term note, with a 7% annual interest rate, payable in three months from May 5.

C. On August 5, Air Compressors pays its account in full.

Record the journal entries to recognize the initial purchase, the conversion plus cash, and the payment.

PB9. LO 12.4 Pickles R Us is a pickle farm located in the Northeast. The following transactions take place:

A. On November 6, Pickles borrows $820,000 from a bank to cover the initial cost of expansion. Terms of the loan are payment due in six months from November 6, and annual interest rate of 3%.
B. On December 12, Pickles borrows an additional $200,000 with payment due in three months from December 12, and an annual interest rate of 10%.
C. Pickles pays its accounts in full on March 12, for the December 12 loan, and on May 6 for the November 6 loan.

Record the journal entries to recognize the initial borrowings, and the two payments for Pickles.

PB10. LO 12.5 Use Figure 12.15 to complete the following problem. Roland Inc. employees' monthly gross pay information and their W-4 Form withholding allowances follow.

Employee	Monthly Gross Income	Withholding Allowances
Jim	$1,000	1
Amy	$1,200	2
Stephanie	$2,300	3

Roland's payroll deductions include FICA Social Security at 6.2%, FICA Medicare at 1.45%, FUTA at 0.6%, SUTA at 5.4%, federal income tax (based on withholdings table) of gross pay, state income tax at 3% of gross pay, and health insurance coverage premiums of $1,000 split 50% employees and 50% employer. Assume each employee files as single, gross income is the same amount each month, October is the first month of business operation for the company, and salaries have yet to be paid.

Record the entry or entries for accumulated employee and employer payroll for the month of October; dated October 31.

PB11. LO 12.5 Use the information from PB10 to complete this problem. Record entries for each transaction listed.

Nov. 1	Paid cash to a federal depository for FICA Social Security and FICA Medicare; paid accumulated salaries
Nov. 3	Remitted cash payment for FUTA and SUTA to federal and state unemployment agencies
Nov. 10	Issued a check to an IRS-approved bank for federal and state income taxes
Nov. 12	Paid cash to health insurance carrier for total outstanding health insurance liability

Thought Provokers

TP1. LO 12.1 Research a Major League Baseball team's season ticket prices. Pick one season ticket price level and answer the following questions:

- What team did you choose, and what are the ticket prices for a season?
- What is the sales tax rate for the purchase of season tickets?
- How many games are included in the season package?
- What are the refund and exchange policies for purchases?
- What are some benefits to the team with customers paying in advance for season tickets?
- Explain in detail the unearned revenue liability created from season ticket sales.
- When does the team recognize this future revenue as earned?
- What effect does the refund or exchange policy have on the unearned revenue account, and the ability of the team to recognize revenue?
- If unearned revenue was split equally among all games (not including playoff games), how much would be recognized per game?
- Explain in detail the sales tax liability created from season ticket sales.
- When does the team collect sales tax?
- What is the final purchase price of the season ticket with sales tax?
- Where does the team recognize the sales tax liability (which statement and account[s])?
- To whom does the team pay the sales tax collected?
- When is sales tax payment required?

TP2. LO 12.2 Review TP1. Review current season ticket prices for one Major League Baseball team. Choose one season ticket price area to review.

A. Determine what is recognized as per ticket revenue after each game is played for your chosen season ticket price area. Assume an equal amount is distributed per game. Do not include playoff games or preseason games in your computations. If parking and other amenities are factored into the season ticket price, please continue to include them in your calculations.

B. Determine an average attendance figure for this team during the 2016 season for all seating areas, and per game (assume equal distribution of game attendance), and use this as a projection for future attendance. You may use Ballparks of Baseball http://www.ballparksofbaseball.com/2010s-ballpark-attendance/ for attendance figures.

C. Assume that attendance is distributed equally between all season ticket areas. Determine the attendance for your season ticket area for the season and per game.

D. Determine the total unearned ticket revenue amount before the season begins. Assume all season ticket holders paid with cash, in full.

E. Prepare the journal entry to recognize unearned ticket revenue at the beginning of the season for your chosen season ticket area. Assume all seats are filled by season ticket holders. Show any support calculations and documentation used.

F. Prepare the journal entry to recognize ticket revenue earned after the first game is played in your chosen season ticket area.

G. Suppose the team only records revenues every three months (at the end of each month), record the journal entry to recognize the first three months of ticket revenue earned during the season in your chosen season ticket area.

TP3. LO 12.3 Toyota is a car manufacturer that has issued several recalls over the years. One major recall centered on faulty air bags from Takata. A prior recall focused on unintentional pedal acceleration. Research information about the car manufacturer, and one of the two recall situations described. Answer the following questions:

- What are some of the main points discussed in the supplements you researched?
- What negative impact did this recall have on Toyota?
- As a result of the recall, what contingent liabilities were (or could be) created?
- How did Toyota handle the reporting of these contingent liabilities?
- How did Toyota determine the estimated liability amounts?
- Do you agree with Toyota's treatment assignment for reported liabilities (probable and estimable, probable and inestimable, for example)?
- What note disclosures accompanied the recognized contingent liabilities?
- What long-term effect, if any, did the recall have on Toyota's financials and reputation?

TP4. LO 12.4 You own a farm and grow seasonal products such as pumpkins, squash, and pine trees. Most of your business revenues are earned during the months of October to December. The rest of your year supports the growing process, where revenues are minimal and expenses are high. In order to cover the expenses from January to September, you consider borrowing a short-term note from a bank for $300,000.

- Research the lending practices of a local bank.
- Determine the interest rate charged for a $300,000 loan.
- What collateral does the bank require to secure the loan?
- Determine your overall payback amount if you were to repay the loan in less than one year. Choose either a payback with periodic payments or all at the end of the loan term, and compare the outcomes.
- After conducting your research, would you consider borrowing the money?
- What positive and negative outcomes accompany borrowing the money?

TP5. LO 12.5 Payroll Comparison Research Paper: Search the Internet for local public K–12 school districts, community colleges, and public universities that publish their employees' salary (pay) schedules. Also research any available data on employee benefits provided to each of these schools. Review federal and state taxation rates on income, unemployment, Social Security, and Medicare. Write a comprehensive paper addressing the following questions and situations. You must provide scholarly data and source information to support your claims.

- Which schools did you compare?
- How do the salaries compare for each school entity?
- What voluntary benefits were provided by the employer (school district)?
- What involuntary deductions would be taken out of these salaries?
- What would your federal, state, and local income tax rates be if you worked for one of these schools? Hint: Choose one of the salaries from the schedule.
- Create a Form W-4 to determine your tax liability.
- Assume you are the employer for your chosen school. Prepare journal entries to record January's employee and employer payroll (assume January is the first pay period and you are preparing the entry for one employee). You must record the liabilities from the January 31 payroll, along with the payment of these liabilities on February 1.
- Record any observations you have made at the culmination of your research, and connect these observations to what you've learned about current liabilities.

13 Long-Term Liabilities

Figure 13.1 Car Purchase. Purchasing a vehicle can be an exciting experience. A vehicle is a significant financial investment and buyers want to ensure they are getting a good value for their money. (credit left: modification of "Auto" by unknown/Pixabay, CC0; credit right: modification of "Guy" by unknown/Pixabay, CC0)

Chapter Outline

Why It Matters

Olivia is excited to be shopping for her very first car. She has saved up money from birthdays, holidays, and household chores and would like to get a vehicle so she can get a summer job. Her mother mentioned that a coworker is selling one of their vehicles.

Olivia and her family decide to go look at the vehicle and take it for a test drive. After inspecting the vehicle and taking it for a test drive, Olivia decides she would like to purchase the car. Olivia planned on spending up to $6,000 (the amount that she has saved), but the seller is asking $9,000 for this particular vehicle. Because the car has been well-maintained and has many extra features, Olivia decides it is worth spending the extra money in order to get reliable transportation. However, she is not sure how to come up with the additional $3,000. Olivia's parents tell her she can get a bank loan of $3,000 to cover the difference, but she will have to repay the bank more than the $3,000 she is borrowing. This is because the loan will be repaid over a period of time, say twelve months, and the loan will require that she pay interest in addition to repaying the $3,000 in principal that she is borrowing. After meeting with the bank and signing the necessary paperwork to secure the $3,000 loan, a few days later Olivia returns to the seller with a check for $9,000 and is overjoyed to have purchased her first vehicle.

13.1 Explain the Pricing of Long-Term Liabilities

Businesses have several ways to secure financing and, in practice, will use a combination of these methods to finance the business. As you've learned, net income does not necessarily mean cash. In some cases, in the long-run, profitable operations will provide businesses with sufficient cash to finance current operations and to invest in new opportunities. However, situations might arise where the cash flow generated is insufficient to cover future anticipated expenses or expansion, and the company might need to secure additional funding.

If the extra amount needed is somewhat temporary or small, a short-term source, such as a loan, might be appropriate. Short-term (current) liabilities were covered in Current Liabilities. When additional long-term funding needs arise, a business can choose to sell stock in the company (equity-based financing) or obtain a **long-term liability** (debt-based financing), such as a loan that is spread over a period longer than a year.

Types of Long-Term Funding

If a company needs additional funding for a major expenditure, such as expansion, the source of funding would typically be repaid over several years, or in the case of equity-based financing, over an indefinite period of time. With equity-based financing, the company sells an interest in the company's ownership by issuing shares of the company's common stock. This financing option is equity financing, and it will be addressed in detail in Corporation Accounting. Here, we will focus on two major long-term debt-based options: long-term loans and bonds.

Debt as an option for financing is an important source of funding for businesses. If a company chooses a debt-based option, the business can borrow money on an intermediate (typically two to four years) or long-term (longer than four years) basis from lenders. In the case of bonds, the funds would be provided by investors. While loans and bonds are similar in that they borrow money on which the borrower will pay interest and eventually repay the lenders, they have some important differences. First, a company can raise funds by borrowing from an individual, bank, or other lender, while a bond is typically sold to numerous investors. When a company chooses a loan, the business signs what is known as a note, and a legal relationship called a **note payable** is created between the borrower and the lender. The document lists the conditions of the financial arrangement, a fixed predetermined interest rate (or, if the agreement allows, a variable interest rate), the amount borrowed, the borrowing costs to be charged, and the timing of the payments. In some cases, companies will secure an **interest-only loan**, which means that for the life of the loan the organization pays only the interest expense that has accrued and upon maturity repays the original amount that it borrowed and still owes. For individuals a student loan, car loan, or a mortgage can all be types of notes payable. For Olivia's car purchase in Why It Matters, a document such as a **promissory note** is typically created, representing a personal loan agreement between a lender and borrower. Figure 13.2 shows a sample promissory note that might be used for a simple, relatively intermediate-term loan. If we were considering a loan that would be repaid over a several-year period the document might be a little more complicated, although it would still have many of the same components of Olivia's loan document.

PROMISSORY NOTE

Loan Agreement Effective Date: *[DD/MM/YYYY]*

Borrower: ______________________________ **Lender:** ______________________________

______________________________ ______________________________

Address Line 1 (street address) *Address Line 1 (street address)*

______________________________ ______________________________

Address Line 2 (city/state/zip code) *Address Line 2 (city/state/zip code)*

Promise to pay: in U.S. Dollars $ ______________________ within _________ months from today, in equal continuous monthly payments of $___________each on the ___________ day of each month, beginning on ___________ and ending on _____________.

Borrower promises to pay the Lender the principal listed above plus interest at the APR % rate of: _______________.

Value Received for Property as described:

____.

If this note is not paid in full upon date due, I/we agree to pay all reasonable costs for collection, including all attorney fees.

Figure 13.2 Promissary Note. A personal loan agreement is a formal contract between a lender and borrower. The document lists the conditions of the loan, including the amount borrowed, the borrowing costs to be charged, and the timing of the payments. (attribution: Copyright Rice University, OpenStax, under CC BY-NC-SA 4.0 license)

If debt instruments are created with a variable interest rate that can fluctuate up or down, depending upon predetermined factors, an inflation measurement must also be included in the documentation. The Federal Funds Rate, for example, is a commonly used tool for potential adjustments in interest rates. To keep our discussion simple, we will use a fixed interest rate in our subsequent calculations.

Another difference between loans and bonds is that the note payable creates an obligation for the borrower to repay the lender on a specified date. To demonstrate the mechanics of a loan,with loans, a note payable is created for the borrower when the loan is initiated. This example assumes the loan will be paid in full by the maturity or due date. Typically, over the life of the loan, payments will be composed of both principal and interest components. The principal component paid typically reduces the amount that the borrower owes the lender. For example, assume that a company borrowed $10,000 from a lender under the following terms: a five-year life, an annual interest rate of 10%, and five annual payments at the end of the year.

Under these terms, the annual payment would be $2,637.97. The first year's payment would be allocated to an interest expense of $1,000, and the remaining amount of the payment would go to reduce the amount borrowed (principal) by $1,637.97. After the first year's payment, the company would owe a remaining balance of $8,362.03 ($10,000 – $1637.97.) Additional detail on this type of calculation will be provided in Compute Amortization of Long-Term Liabilities Using the Effective-Interest Method.

Typical long-term loans have other characteristics. For example, most long-term notes are held by one entity, meaning one party provides all of the financing. If a company bought heavy-duty equipment from Caterpillar, it would be common for the seller of the equipment to also have a division that would provide the financing for the transaction. An additional characteristic of a long-term loan is that in many, if not most, situations, the initial creator of the loan will hold it and receive and process payments until it matures.

Returning to the differences between long-term debt and bonds, another difference is that the process for issuing (selling) bonds can be very complicated, especially for companies that are subject to regulation. The bond issue must be approved by the appropriate regulatory agency, and then outside parties such as investment banks sell the bonds to, typically, a large audience of investors. It is not unusual for several months to pass between the time that the company's board of directors approves the bond offering, gets regulatory approval, and then markets and issues the bonds. This additional time is often the reason that the market rate for similar bonds in the outside business environment is higher or lower than the stated interest rate that the company committed to pay when the bond process was first begun. This difference can lead to bonds being issued (sold) at a discount or premium.

Finally, while loans can normally be paid off before they are due, in most cases bonds must be held by an owner until they mature. Because of this last characteristic, a bond,such as a thirty-year bond, might have several owners over its lifetime, while most long-term notes payable will only have one owner.

ETHICAL CONSIDERATIONS

Bond Fraud

The U.S. Department of the Treasury (DOT) defines historical bonds as "those bonds that were once valid obligations of American entities but are now worthless as securities and are quickly becoming a favorite tool of scam artists."[1] The DOT also warns against scams selling non-existent "limited edition" U.S. Treasury securities. The scam involves approaching broker-dealers and banks to act as fiduciaries for transactions. Further, the DOT notes: "The proposal to sell these fictitious securities makes misrepresentations about the way marketable securities are bought and sold, and it also misrepresents the role that we play in the original sale and issuance of our securities."[2] Many fraudulent attempts are made to sell such bonds.

According to *Business Insider*, in the commonest scam, a fake bearer bond is offered for sale for far less than its stated cover price. The difference in the cost and the cover price entices the victim to buy the bond. Again, from *Business Insider*: "Another variation is a flavor of the 'Nigerian prince' scheme; the fraudster will ask for the victim's help in depositing a recently obtained 'fortune' in bonds, promising the victim a cut in return."[3]

A diligent accountant is both educated about the investments of their company or organization and is skeptical about any investment that looks too good to be true.

---

1 U.S. Department of the Treasury. "Historical Bond Fraud." September 21, 2012. https://www.treasury.gov/about/organizational-structure/ig/Pages/Scams/Historical-Bond-Fraud.aspx

2 U.S. Department of the Treasury. "Examples of Known Phony Securities." April 5, 2013. https://www.treasury.gov/about/organizational-structure/ig/Pages/Scams/Examples-of-Known-Phony-Securities.aspx

3 Lawrence Delavigne. "Fake Bearer Bonds Were Just the Beginning of Huge Wave of Bond-Fraud." *Business Insider*. October 12, 2009. https://www.businessinsider.com/bond-fraud-is-on-the-rise-2009-10

YOUR TURN

Current versus Long-Term Liabilities

Below is a portion of the 2017 Balance Sheet of Emerson, Inc. (shown in millions of dollars).[4] There are several observations we can make from this information.

	2016	2017
Current liabilities		
Short-term borrowings and current maturities of long-term debt	$2,584	862
Long-term debt	4,051	3,794

Notice the company lists separately the Current Liabilities (listed as "Short-term borrowings and current maturities of long-term debt") and Long-term Liabilities (listed as "Long-term debt"). Also, under the "Current liabilities" heading, notice the "Short-term borrowings and current maturities of long-term debt" decreased significantly from 2016 to 2017. In 2016, Emerson held $2.584 billion in short-term borrowings and current maturities of long-term debt. This amount decreased by $1.722 billion in 2017, which is a 67% decrease. During the same timeframe, long-term debt decreased $257 million, going from $4.051 billion to $3.794 billion, which is a 6.3% decrease.

Thinking about the primary purpose of accounting, why do you think accountants separate liabilities into current liabilities and long-term liabilities?

Solution

The primary purpose of accounting is to provide stakeholders with financial information that is useful for decision making. It is important for stakeholders to understand how much cash will be required to satisfy liabilities within the next year (liquidity) as well as how much will be required to satisfy long-term liabilities (solvency). Stakeholders, especially lenders and owners, are concerned with both liquidity and solvency of the business.

Fundamentals of Bonds

Now let us look at bonds in more depth. A **bond** is a type of financial instrument that a company issues directly to investors, bypassing banks or other lending institutions, with a promise to pay the investor a specified rate of interest over a specified period of time. When a company borrows money by selling bonds, it is said the company is "issuing" bonds. This means the company exchanges cash for a promise to repay the cash, along with interest, over a set period of time. As you've learned, bonds are formal legal documents that contain specific information related to the bond. In short, it is a legal contract—called a bond certificate (as shown in Figure 13.3) or an indenture—between the issuer (the business borrowing the money) and the lender (the investor lending the money). Bonds are typically issued in relatively small denominations, such as $1,000 so they can be placed in the market and are accessible to a greater market of investors compared to notes. The

4 Emerson. *2017 Annual Report*. Emerson Electric Company. 2017. https://www.emerson.com/documents/corporate/2017emersonannualreport-en-2883292.pdf

bond indenture is a contract that lists the features of the bond, such as the amount of money that will be repaid in the future, called the **principal** (also called face value or maturity value); the **maturity date**, the day the bond holder will receive the principal amount; and the **stated interest rate**, which is the rate of interest the issuer agrees to pay the bondholder throughout the term of the bond.

Figure 13.3 Bond Certificate. If you bought this $1,000 bond on July 1, 2018 and received this bond certificate, it had three important pieces of information: the maturity date (June 30, 2023, 5 years from the issue date when the company will pay back the $1,000; the principal amount ($1,000) which is the amount you will receive in 2023; and the stated annual interest rate (5%) which they will use to determine how much cash to send you each year (0.05 × $1,000 = $50 interest a year for 5 years). (attribution: Copyright Rice University, OpenStax, under CC BY-NC-SA 4.0 license)

For a typical bond, the issuer commits to paying a stated interest rate either once a year (annually) or twice a year (semiannually). It is important to understand that the stated rate will not go up or down over the life of the bond. This means the borrower will pay the same semiannual or annual interest payment on the same dates for the life of the bond. In other words, when an investor buys a typical bond, the investor will receive, in the future, two major cash flows: periodic interest payments paid either annually or semiannually based on the stated rate of the bond, and the maturity value, which is the total amount paid to the owner of the bond on the maturity date.

LINK TO LEARNING

The website for the nonprofit Kiva (https://openstax.org/l/50Kiva) allows you to lend money to people around the world. The borrower makes monthly payments to pay the loan back. The companies Prosper (https://openstax.org/l/50Prosper) and LendingClub (https://openstax.org/l/50LendingClub) let you borrow or lend money to people in the U.S. who then make monthly payments, with interest, to pay it back.

The process of preparing a bond issuance for sale and then selling on the primary market is lengthy, complex, and is usually performed by underwriters—finance professionals who specialize in issuing bonds and other financial instruments. Here, we will only examine transactions concerning issuance, interest payments, and the sale of existing bonds.

There are two other important characteristics of bonds to discuss. First, for most companies, the total value of bonds issued can often range from hundreds of thousands to several million dollars. The primary reason for this is that bonds are typically used to help finance significant long-term projects or activities, such as the purchase of equipment, land, buildings, or another company.

CONCEPTS IN PRACTICE

Apple Inc. Issues Bonds

On May 11, 2017, Apple Inc. issued bonds to get cash. Apple Inc. submitted a form to the Securities and Exchange Commission (www.sec.gov) to announce their intentions.

Apple Bonds Issued May 11, 2017		
Maturity	**Interest Rate**	**Bond Amount**
2020	Floating rate (variable)	$ 500,000,000.00
2022	Floating rate (variable)	750,000,000.00
2020	1.80% fixed	1,000,000,000.00
2022	2.30% fixed	1,000,000,000.00
2024	2.85% fixed	1,750,000,000.00
2027	3.20% fixed	2,000,000,000.00
		$7,000,000,000.00

On May 3 of the same year, Apple Inc. had issued their 10-Q (quarterly report) that showed the following assets.

APPLE INC. Condensed Consolidated Balance Sheets (Unaudited) (In millions, except number of shares which are reflected in thousands and par value)		
Assets	**April 1, 2017**	**September 24, 2016**
Current assets:		
Cash and cash equivalents	$15,157	$20,484

Apple Inc. reported it had $15 billion dollars in cash and a total of $101 billion in Current Assets. Why did it need to issue bonds to raise $7 billion more?

Analysts suggested that Apple would use the cash to pay shareholder dividends. Even though Apple reported billions of dollars in cash, most of the cash was in foreign countries because that was where the products had been sold. Tax laws vary by country, but if Apple transferred the cash to a US bank account, they would have to pay US income tax on it, at a tax rate as high as 39%. So, Apple was much better off borrowing and paying 3.2% interest, which is tax deductible, than bringing the cash to the US and paying a 39% income tax.

However, it's important to remember that in the United States, Congress can change tax laws at any time, so what was then current tax law when this transaction occurred could change in the future.

The second characteristic of bonds is that bonds are often sold to several investors instead of to one individual investor.

When establishing the stated rate of interest the business will pay on a bond, bond underwriters consider many factors, including the interest rates on government treasury bonds (which are assumed to be risk-free), rates on comparable bond offerings, and firm-specific factors related to the business's risk (including its ability to repay the bond). The more likely the possibility that a company will default on the bond, meaning they either miss an interest payment or do not return the maturity amount to the bond's owner when it matures, the higher the interest rate is on the bond. It is important to understand that the stated rate will not change over the life of any one bond once it is issued. However, the stated rate on future new bonds may change as economic circumstances and the company's financial position changes.

Bonds themselves can have different characteristics. For example, a **debenture** is an unsecured bond issued based on the good name and reputation of the company. These companies are not pledging other assets to cover the amount in case they fail to pay the debt, or **default**. The opposite of a debenture is a **secured bond**, meaning the company is pledging a specific asset as collateral for the bond. With a secured bond, if the company goes under and cannot pay back the bond, the pledged asset would be sold, and the proceeds would be distributed to the bondholders.

There are **term bonds**, or single-payment bonds, meaning the entire bond will be repaid all at once, rather than in a series of payments. And there are **serial bonds**, or bonds that will mature over a period of time and will be repaid in a series of payments.

A **callable bond** (also known as a redeemable bond) is one that can be repurchased or "called" by the issuer of the bond. If a company sells callable bonds with an 8% interest rate and the interest rate the bank is offering subsequently drops to 5%, the company can borrow at that new rate of 5%, call the 8% bonds, and pay them off (even if the purchaser does not want to sell them back). In essence, the institution would be lowering its rate of interest to borrow money from 8% to 5% by calling the bond.

Putable bonds give the bondholder the right to decide whether to sell it back early or keep it until it matures. It is essentially the opposite of a callable bond.

A **convertible bond** can be converted to common stock in a one-way, one-time conversion. Under what conditions would it make sense to convert? Suppose the face-value interest rate of the bond is 8%. If the company is doing well this year, such that there is an expectation that shareholders will receive a significant dividend and the stock price will rise, the stock might appear to be more valuable than the return on the bond.

THINK IT THROUGH

Callable versus Putable Bonds

Which type of bond is better for the corporation issuing the bond: callable or putable?

ETHICAL CONSIDERATIONS

Junk Bonds

Junk bonds, which are also called speculative or high-yield bonds, are a specific type of bond that can be attractive to certain investors. On one hand, junk bonds are attractive because the bonds pay a rate of interest that is significantly higher than the average market rate. On the other hand, the bonds are riskier because the issuing company is deemed to have a higher risk of defaulting on the bonds. If the economy or the company's financial condition deteriorates, the company will be unable to repay the money borrowed. In short, junk bonds are deemed to be high risk, high reward investments.

The development of the junk bond market, which occurred during the 1970s and 1980s, is attributed to Michael Milken, the so-called "junk bond king." Milken amassed a large fortune by using junk bonds as a means of financing corporate mergers and acquisitions. It is estimated that during the 1980s, Milken earned between $200 million and $550 million per year.[5] In 1990, however, Milken's winning streak came to an end when, according to the *New York Times*, he was indicted on "98 counts of racketeering, securities fraud, mail fraud and other crimes."[6] He later pleaded guilty to six charges, resulting in a 10-year prison sentence, of which he served two, and was as also forced to pay over $600 million in fines and settlements.[7]

Today, Milken remains active in philanthropic activities and, as a cancer survivor, remains committed to medical research.

Pricing Bonds

Imagine a concert-goer who has an extra ticket for a good seat at a popular concert that is sold out. The concert-goer purchased the ticket from the box office at its face value of $100. Because the show is sold out, the ticket could be resold at a premium. But what happens if the concert-goer paid $100 for the ticket and the show is not popular and does not sell out? To convince someone to purchase the ticket from her instead of the box office, the concert-goer will need to sell the ticket at a discount. Bonds behave in the same way as this concert ticket.

Bond quotes can be found in the financial sections of newspapers or on the Internet on many financial websites. Bonds are quoted as a percentage of the bond's maturity value. The percentage is determined by

5 James Chen. "Micheal Milken." January 22, 2018. https://www.investopedia.com/terms/m/michaelmilken.asp

6 Kurt Eichenwald. "Milken Set to Pay a $600 Million Fine in Wall St. Fraud." April 21, 1990. https://www.nytimes.com/1990/04/21/business/milken-set-to-pay-a-600-million-fine-in-wall-st-fraud.html?pagewanted=all

7 Michael Buchanan. "November 21, 1990, Michael Milken Sentenced to 10 Years for Security Law Violations." November 20, 2011. http://reasonabledoubt.org/criminallawblog/entry/november-21-1990-michael-milken-sentenced-to-10-years-for-security-law-violations-today-in-crime-history-1

dividing the current market (selling) price by the maturity value, and then multiplying the value by 100 to convert the decimal into a percentage. In the case of a $30,000 bond discounted to $27,591.94 because of an increase in the market rate of interest, the bond quote would be $27,591.24/$30,000 × 100, or 91.9708. Using another example, a quote of 88.50 would mean that the bonds in question are selling for 88.50% of the maturity value. If an investor were considering buying a bond with a $10,000 maturity value, the investor would pay 88.50% of the maturity value of $10,000, or $8,850.00. If the investor was considering bonds with a maturity value of $100,000, the price would be $88,500. If the quote were over 100, this would indicate that the market interest rate has decreased from its initial rate. For example, a quote of 123.45 indicates that the investor would pay $123,450 for a $100,000 bond.

Figure 13.4 shows a bond issued on July 1, 2018. It is a promise to pay the holder of the bond $1,000 on June 30, 2023, and 5% of $1,000 every year. We will use this bond to explore how a company addresses interest rate changes when issuing bonds.

Figure 13.4 Bond Certificate. A bond certificate shows the terms of the bond. (attribution: Copyright Rice University, OpenStax, under CC BY-NC-SA 4.0 license)

On this bond certificate, we see the following:

- The $1,000 principal or maturity value.
- The interest rate printed on the face of the bond is the stated interest rate, the contract rate, the face rate, or the **coupon rate**. This rate is the interest rate used to calculate the interest payment on bonds.

Issuing Bonds When the Contract and Market Rates Are the Same

If the stated rate and the market rate are both 5%, the bond will be issued at **par value**, which is the value assigned to stock in the company's charter, typically set at a very small arbitrary amount, which serves as legal capital; in our example, the part value is $1,000. The purchaser will give the company $1,000 today and will receive $50 at the end of every year for 5 years. In 5 years, the purchaser will receive the maturity value of the $1,000. The bond's quoted price is 100.00. That is, the bond will sell at 100% of the $1,000 face value, which means the seller of the bond will receive (and the investor will pay) $1,000.00. You will learn the calculations used to determine a bond's quoted price later; here, we will provide the quoted price for any calculations.

LINK TO LEARNING

The Securities and Exchange Commission website Investor.gov provides an explanation of corporate bonds (https://openstax.org/l/50SECBonds) to learn more.

Issuing Bonds at a Premium

The stated interest rate is not the only rate affecting bonds. There is also the market interest rate, also called the effective interest rate or bond yield. The amount of money that borrowers receive on the date the bonds are issued is influenced by the terms stated on the bond indenture *and* on the market interest rate, which is the rate of interest that investors can earn on similar investments. The market interest rate is influenced by many factors external to the business, such as the overall strength of the economy, the value of the U.S. dollar, and geopolitical factors.

This **market interest rate** is the rate determined by supply and demand, the current overall economic conditions, and the credit worthiness of the borrower, among other factors. Suppose that, while a company has been busy during the long process of getting its bonds approved and issued (it might take several months), the interest rate changed because circumstances in the market changed. At this point, the company cannot change the rate used to market the bond issue. Instead, the company might have to sell the bonds at a price that will be the equivalent of having a different stated rate (one that is equivalent to a market rate based on the company's financial characteristics at the time of the issuance (sale) of the bonds).

If the company offers 5% (the bond rate used to market the bond issue) and the market rate prior to issuance drops to 4%, the bonds will be in high demand. The company is scheduled to pay a higher interest rate than everyone else, so it can issue them for more than face value, or at a premium. In this example, where the stated interest rate is higher than the market interest rate, let's say the bond's quoted price is 104.46. That is, the bond will sell at 104.46% of the $1,000 face value, which means the seller of the bond will receive and the investor will pay $1,044.60.

Issuing Bonds at a Discount

Now let's consider a situation when the company's bonds prior to issuance are scheduled to pay 5% and the market rate jumps to 7% at issuance. No one will want to buy the bonds at 5% when they can earn more interest elsewhere. The company will have to sell the $1,000 bond for less than $1,000, or at a discount. In this example, where the stated interest rate is lower than the market interest rate, the bond's quoted price is 91.80. That is, the bond will sell at 91.80% of the $1,000 face value, which means the seller of the bond will receive (and the investor will pay) $918.00.

Sale of Bonds before Maturity

Let's look at bonds from the perspective of the issuer and the investor. As we previously discussed, bonds are often classified as long-term liabilities because the money is borrowed for long periods of time, up to 30 years in some cases. This provides the business with the money necessary to fund long-term projects and investments in the business. Due to unanticipated circumstances, the investors, on the other hand, may not want to wait up to 30 years to receive the maturity value of the bond. While the investor will receive periodic interest payments while the bond is held, investors may want to receive the current market value prior to the maturity date. Therefore, from the investor's perspective, one of the advantages of investing in bonds is that they are typically easy to sell in the secondary market should the investor need the money before the maturity date, which may be many years in the future. The **secondary market** is an organized market where previously issued stocks and bonds can be traded after they are issued.

If a bond sells on the secondary market after it has been issued, the terms of the bond (a particular interest rate, at a determined timeframe, and a given maturity value) do not change. If an investor buys a bond after it is issued or sells it before it matures, there is the possibility that the investor will receive more or less for the bond than the amount the bond was originally sold for. This change in value may occur if the market interest rate differs from the stated interest rate.

CONTINUING APPLICATION AT WORK

Debt Considerations for Grocery Stores

Every company faces internal decisions when it comes to borrowing funds for improvements and/or expansions. Consider the improvements your local grocery stores have made over the past couple of years. Just like any large retail business, if grocery stores don't invest in each property by adding services, upgrading the storefront, or even making more energy efficient changes, the location can fall out of popularity.

Such investments require large amounts of capital infusion. The primary available investment funds for privately-owned grocery chains are bank loans or owners' capital. This limitation often restricts the expansions or upgrades such a company can do at any one time. Publicly-traded grocery chains can also borrow funds from a bank, but other options, like issuing bonds or more stock can also help fund development. Thus publicly-traded grocery chains have more options to fund improvements and can therefore expand their share of the market more easily, unlike their private smaller counterparts who must decide what improvement is the most critical.

Fundamentals of Interest Calculation

Since interest is paid on long-term liabilities, we now need to examine the process of calculating interest. Interest can be calculated in several ways, some more common than others. For our purposes, we will explore interest calculations using the simple method and the compounded method. Regardless of the method involved, there are three components that we need when calculating interest:

1. Amount of money borrowed (called the principal).
2. Interest rate for the time frame of the loan. Note that interest rates are usually stated in annual terms (e.g., 8% per year). If the timeframe is excluded, an annual rate should be assumed. Pay particular attention to how often the interest is to be paid because this will affect the rate used in the calculation:

Interest rate = Annual rate / Payments per period

For example, if the rate on a bond is 6% per year but the interest is paid semi-annually, the rate used in the interest calculation should be 3% because the interest applies to a 6-month timeframe (6% ÷ 2). Similarly, if the rate on a bond is 8% per year but the interest is paid quarterly, the rate used in the interest calculation should be 2% (8% ÷ 4).

3. Time period for which we are calculating the interest.

Let's explore simple interest first. We use the following formula to calculate interest in dollars:

Interest in $ = Principal × Interest Rate × Time

Principal is the amount of money invested or borrowed, *interest rate* is the interest rate paid or earned, and *time* is the length of time the principal is borrowed or invested. Consider a bank deposit of $100 that remains in the account for 3 years, earning 6% per year with the bank paying simple interest. In this calculation, the interest rate is 6% a year, paid once at the end of the year. Using the interest rate formula from above, the interest rate remains 6% (6% ÷ 1). Using 6% interest per year earned on a $100 principal provides the following results in the first three years (Figure 13.5):

- Year 1: The $100 in the bank earns 6% interest, and at the end of the year, the bank pays $6.00 in interest, making the amount in the bank account $106 ($100 principal + $6 interest).
- Year 2: Assuming we do not withdraw the interest, the $106 in the bank earns 6% interest on the principal ($100), and at the end of the year, the bank pays $6 in interest, making the total amount $112.
- Year 3: Again, assuming we do not withdraw the interest, $112 in the bank earns 6% interest on the principal ($100), and at the end of the year, the bank pays $6 in interest, making the total amount $118.

Year	1	2	3
Initial investment	$ 100.00	$ 100.00	$ 100.00
Annual interest rate, 6%	0.06	0.06	0.06
Interest earned	$ 6.00	$ 6.00	$ 6.00
Add amount to date	$100.00	$106.00	$112.00
= Total cash	$106.00	$112.00	$118.00

Figure 13.5 Simple Interest. Simple interest earns money only on the principal. (attribution: Copyright Rice University, OpenStax, under CC BY-NC-SA 4.0 license)

With simple interest, the amount paid is always based on the principal, not on any interest earned.

Another method commonly used for calculating interest involves compound interest. **Compound interest** means that the interest earned also earns interest. Figure 13.6 shows the same deposit with compounded interest.

Year	1	2	3
Initial investment	$100.00	$106.00	$112.36
Annual interest rate, 6%	0.06	0.06	0.06
Interest earned	$ 6.00	$ 6.36	$ 6.74
Add amount to date	$100.00	$106.00	$112.36
= Total cash	$106.00	$112.36	$119.10

Figure 13.6 Compund Interest. Compound interest earns money on the principal plus interest earned in a previous period. (attribution: Copyright Rice University, OpenStax, under CC BY-NC-SA 4.0 license)

In this case, investing $100 today in a bank that pays 6% per year for 3 years with compound interest will produce $119.10 at the end of the three years, instead of $118.00, which was earned with simple interest.

At this point, we need to provide an assumption we make in this chapter. Since financial institutions typically cannot deal in fractions of a cent, in calculations such as the above, we will round the final answer to the nearest cent, if necessary. For example, the final cash total at the end of the third year in the above example would be $119.1016. However, we rounded the answer to the nearest cent for convenience. In the case of a car or home loan, the rounding can lead to a higher or lower adjustment in your final payment. For example, you might finance a car loan by borrowing $20,000 for 48 months with monthly payments of $469.70 for the first 47 months and $469.74 for the final payment.

LINK TO LEARNING

Go to the Securities and Exchange Commission website for an explanation of US Savings Bonds (https://openstax.org/l/50SECSaveBond) to learn more.

13.2 Compute Amortization of Long-Term Liabilities Using the Effective-Interest Method

In our discussion of long-term debt amortization, we will examine both notes payable and bonds. While they have some structural differences, they are similar in the creation of their amortization documentation.

Pricing of Long-Term Notes Payable

When a consumer borrows money, she can expect to not only repay the amount borrowed, but also to pay interest on the amount borrowed. When she makes periodic loan payments that pay back the principal and interest over time with payments of equal amounts, these are considered **fully amortized notes**. In these timed payments, part of what she pays is interest. The amount borrowed that is still due is often called the principal. After she has made her final payment, she no longer owes anything, and the loan is fully repaid, or amortized. **Amortization** is the process of separating the principal and interest in the loan payments over the life of a loan. A fully amortized loan is fully paid by the end of the maturity period.

In the following example, assume that the borrower acquired a five-year, $10,000 loan from a bank. She will repay the loan with five equal payments at the end of the year for the next five years. The bank's required interest rate is an annual rate of 12%.

Interest rates are typically quoted in annual terms. Since her interest rate is 12% a year, the borrower must pay 12% interest each year on the principal that she owes. As stated above, these are equal annual payments, and each payment is first applied to any applicable interest expenses, with the remaining funds reducing the principal balance of the loan.

After each payment in a fully amortizing loan, the principal is reduced, which means that since the five payment amounts are equal, the portion allocated to interest is reduced each year, and the amount allocated to principal reduction increases an equal amount.

We can use an amortization table, or schedule, prepared using Microsoft Excel or other financial software, to show the loan balance for the duration of the loan. An amortization table calculates the allocation of interest and principal for each payment and is used by accountants to make journal entries. These journal entrieswill be discussed later in this chapter.

The first step in preparing an amortization table is to determine the annual loan payment. The $10,000 loan amount is the value today and, in financial terms, is called the present value (PV). Since repayment will be in a series of five equal payments, it is an annuity. Look up the PV from an annuity table for 5 periods and 12% interest. The factor is 3.605. Dividing the principal, $10,000, by the factor 3.605 gives us $2,773.93, which is the amount of each yearly payment. For the rest of the chapter, we will provide the necessary data, such as bond prices and payment amounts; you will not need to use the present value tables.

When the first payment is made, part of it is interest and part is principal. To determine the amount of the payment that is interest, multiply the principal by the interest rate ($10,000 × 0.12), which gives us $1,200. This is the amount of interest charged that year. The payment itself ($2,773.93) is larger than the interest owed for that period of time, so the remainder of the payment is applied against the principal.

Figure 13.7 shows an amortization table for this $10,000 loan, over five years at 12% annual interest. Assume that the final payment will be $2,774.99 in order to eliminate the potential rounding error of $1.06.

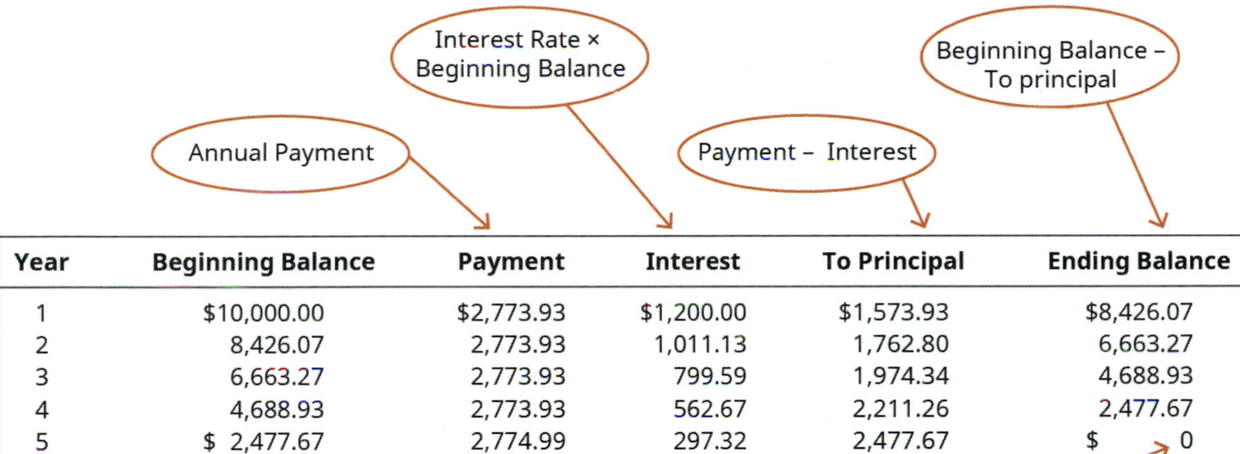

Year	Beginning Balance	Payment	Interest	To Principal	Ending Balance
1	$10,000.00	$2,773.93	$1,200.00	$1,573.93	$8,426.07
2	8,426.07	2,773.93	1,011.13	1,762.80	6,663.27
3	6,663.27	2,773.93	799.59	1,974.34	4,688.93
4	4,688.93	2,773.93	562.67	2,211.26	2,477.67
5	$ 2,477.67	2,774.99	297.32	2,477.67	$ 0

Figure 13.7 Amortization Table. An amortization table shows how payments are applied to interest in principal for the life of the loan. (attribution: Copyright Rice University, OpenStax, under CC BY-NC-SA 4.0 license)

YOUR TURN

Creating Your Own Amortization Table

You want to borrow $100,000 for five years when the interest rate is 5%. You will make yearly payments of $23,097.48 for 5 years. Fill in the blanks in the amortization table below. Assume that the loan was created on January 1, 2018 and totally repaid by December 31, 2022, after five equal, annual payments.

Date	Beginning Balance	Cash Payment	Interest Expense	To Principal	Ending Balance
Year 1	$100,000.00	$ 23,097.48			
Year 2		23,097.48			
Year 3		23,097.48			
Year 4		23,097.48			
Year 5		23,097.48			

Solution

Multiply the $100,000 by the 5% interest rate and $5,000 is the amount of interest you owe for year 1. Subtract the interest from the payment of $23,097.48 to find $18,097.48 is applied toward the principal ($100,000), leaving $81,902.52 as the ending balance. In year 2, $81,902.52 is charged 5% interest ($4,095.13), but the rest of the 23,097.48 payment goes toward the loan balance. Follow the same process for years 3 through 5.

Date	Beginning Balance	Cash Payment	5% Interest Expense	To Principal	Ending Balance
12/31/2018	$100,000.00	$ 23,097.48	$ 5,000.00	$ 18,097.48	$81,902.52
12/31/2019	81,902.52	23,097.48	4,095.13	19,002.35	62,900.17
12/31/2020	62,900.17	23,097.48	3,145.01	19,952.47	42,947.69
12/31/2021	42,947.69	23,097.48	2,147.38	20,950.10	21,997.60
12/31/2022	21,997.60	23,097.48	1,099.88	21,997.60	(0.00)
		115,487.40	15,487.40	$100,000.00	

Bonds Payable

As you've learned, each time a company issues an interest payment to bondholders, amortization of the discount or premium, if one exists, impacts the amount of interest expense that is recorded. Amortization of the discounts increases the amount of interest expense and premiums reduce the amount of interest expense. There are two methods used to amortize bond discounts or premiums: the effective-interest method and the straight-line method.

Our calculations have used what is known as the **effective-interest method**, a method that calculates interest expense based on the carrying value of the bond and the market interest rate. Generally accepted accounting principles (GAAP) require the use of the effective-interest method unless there is no significant difference between the effective-interest method and the straight-line method, a method that allocates the same amount of the bond discount or premium for each interest payment. The effective interest amortization method is more accurate than the straight-line method. International Financial Reporting Standards (IFRS) require the use of the effective-interest method, with no exceptions.

The **straight-line method** doesn't base its calculation of amortization for a period base on a changing carrying value like the effective-interest method does; instead, it allocates the same amount of premium or discount amortation for each of the bond's payment periods.

For example, assume that $500,000 in bonds were issued at a price of $540,000 on January 1, 2019, with the first annual interest payment to be made on December 31, 2019. Assume that the stated interest rate is 10% and the bond has a four-year life. If the straight-line method is used to amortize the $40,000 premium, you would divide the premium of $40,000 by the number of payments, in this case four, giving a $10,000 per year amortization of the premium. Figure 13.8 shows the effects of the premium amortization after all of the 2019 transactions are considered. The net effect of creating the $40,000 premium and writing off $10,000 of it gives the company an interest expense of $40,000 instead of $50,000, since the $50,000 expense is reduced by the $10,000 premium write down at the end of the year.

JOURNAL			
Date	**Account**	**Debit**	**Credit**
Jan. 1, 2019	Cash	540,000	
	Bonds Payable		500,000
	Premium on Bonds Payable		40,000
Jan. 1, 2019	Interest Expense	50,000	
	Cash		50,000
Jan. 1, 2019	Premium on Bonds Payable	10,000	
	Interest Expense		10,000

Figure 13.8 Premium Amortization Using the Straight-Line Method. (attribution: Copyright Rice University, OpenStax, under CC BY-NC-SA 4.0 license)

Issued When Market Rate Equals Contract Rate

Assume a company issues a $100,000 bond with a 5% stated rate when the market rate is also 5%. The bond was issued at par, meaning it sold for $100,000. There was no premium or discount to amortize, so there is no application of the effective-interest method in this example.

Issued at a Premium

The same company also issued a 5-year, $100,000 bond with a stated rate of 5% when the market rate was 4%. This bond was issued at a premium, for $104,460. The amount of the premium is $4,460, which will be amortized over the life of the bond using the effective-interest method. This method of amortizing the interest expense associated with a bond is similar to the amortization of the note payable described earlier, in which the principal was separated from the interest payments using the interest rate times the principal.

Begin by assuming the company issued all the bonds on January 1 of year 1 and the first interest payment will be made on December 31 of year 1. The amortization table begins on January 1, year 1, with the carrying value of the bond: the face value of the bond plus the bond premium.

On December 31, year 1, the company will have to pay the bondholders $5,000 (0.05 × $100,000). The *cash interest payment* is the amount of interest the company must pay the bondholder. The company promised 5% when the market rate was 4% so it received more money. But the company is only paying interest on $100,000—not on the full amount received. The difference in the sale price was a result of the difference in the interest rates so both rates are used to compute the true interest expense.

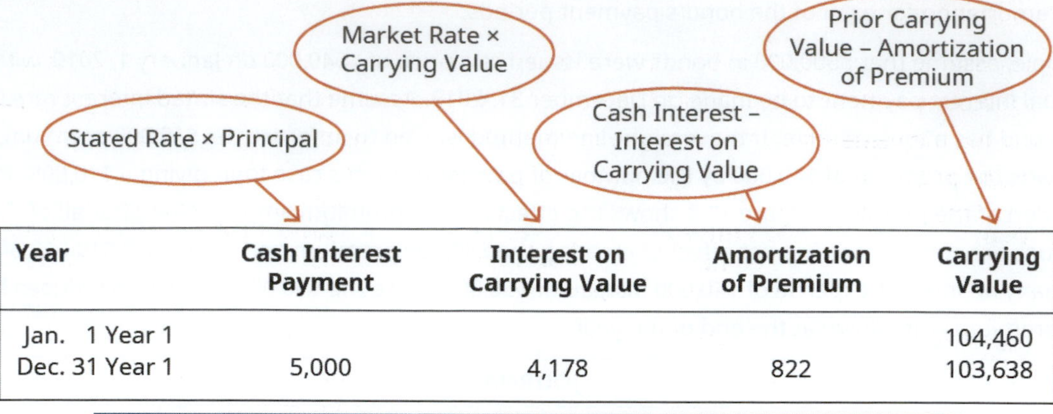

Year	Cash Interest Payment	Interest on Carrying Value	Amortization of Premium	Carrying Value
Jan. 1 Year 1				104,460
Dec. 31 Year 1	5,000	4,178	822	103,638

Assets	=	Liabilities	+	Equity	+	Revenue	–	Expenses

Cash (Dr.)	Cash (Cr.)	=	Bonds Payable (Dr.)	Bonds Payable (Cr.)	Premium on Bonds Payable (Dr.)	Premium on Bonds Payable (Cr.)	Interest Expense (Dr.)	Interest Expense (Cr.)
				100,000		4,460		
	5,000						5,000	
					822			822
						3,638	4,178	

The interest on the carrying value is the market rate of interest times the carrying value: 0.04 × $104,460 = $4,178. If the company had issued the bonds with a stated rate of 4%, and received $104,460, it would be paying $4,178 in interest. The difference between the cash interest payment and the interest on the carrying value is the amount to be amortized the first year. The complete amortization table for the bond is shown in Figure 13.9. The table is necessary to provide the calculations needed for the adjusting journal entries.

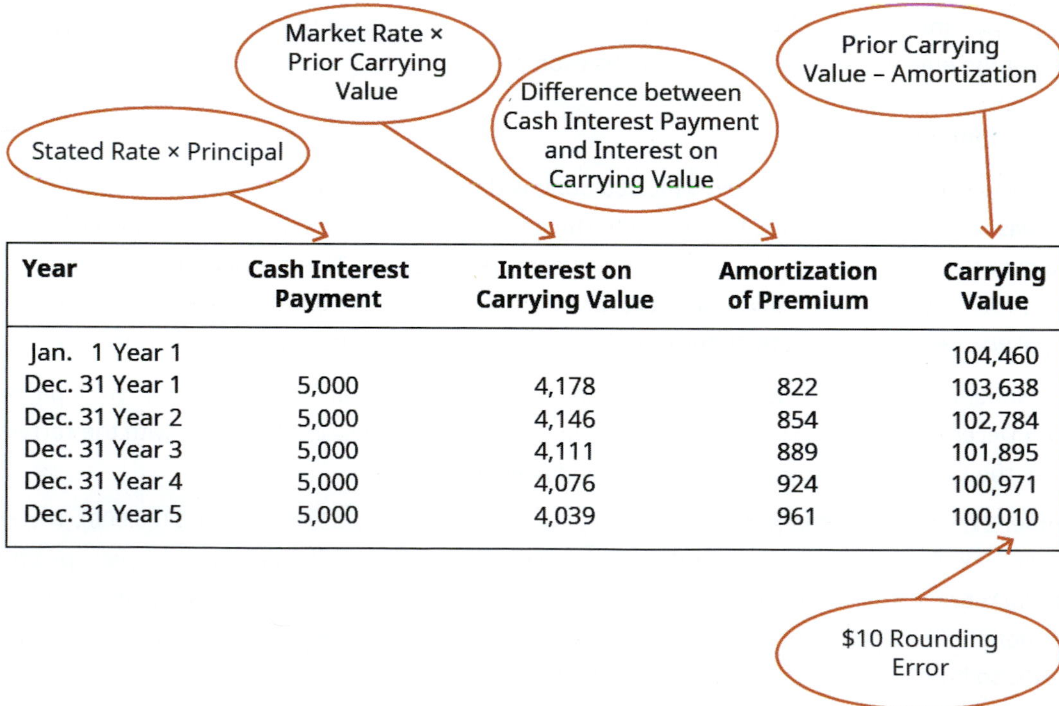

Year	Cash Interest Payment	Interest on Carrying Value	Amortization of Premium	Carrying Value
Jan. 1 Year 1				104,460
Dec. 31 Year 1	5,000	4,178	822	103,638
Dec. 31 Year 2	5,000	4,146	854	102,784
Dec. 31 Year 3	5,000	4,111	889	101,895
Dec. 31 Year 4	5,000	4,076	924	100,971
Dec. 31 Year 5	5,000	4,039	961	100,010

Figure 13.9 Bond Amortization Table. (attribution: Copyright Rice University, OpenStax, under CC BY-NC-SA 4.0 license)

Issued at a Discount

The company also issued $100,000 of 5% bonds when the market rate was 7%. It received $91,800 cash and recorded a Discount on Bonds Payable of $8,200. This amount will need to be amortized over the 5-year life of the bonds. Using the same format for an amortization table, but having received $91,800, interest payments are being made on $100,000.

Year	Cash Interest Payment	Interest on Carrying Value	Amortization of Discount	Carrying Value
Jan. 1 Year 1				91,800
Dec. 31 Year 1	5,000	6,426	1,426	93,226

The cash interest payment is still the stated rate times the principal. The interest on carrying value is still the market rate times the carrying value. The difference in the two interest amounts is used to amortize the discount, but now the amortization of discount amount is added to the carrying value.

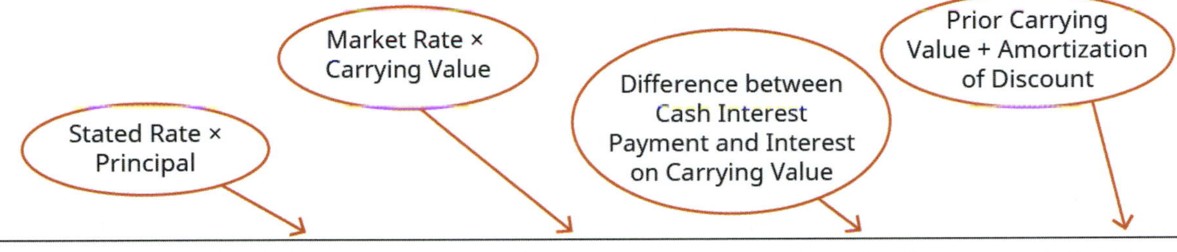

Year	Cash Interest Payment	Interest on Carrying Value	Amortization of Discount	Carrying Value
Jan. 1 Year 1				91,800
Dec. 31 Year 1	5,000	6,426	1,426	93,226
Dec. 31 Year 2	5,000	6,526	1,526	94,752
Dec. 31 Year 3	5,000	6,633	1,633	96,384
Dec. 31 Year 4	5,000	6,747	1,747	98,131
Dec. 31 Year 5	5,000	6,869	1,869	100,000

Figure 13.10 illustrates the relationship between rates whenever a premium or discount is created at bond issuance.

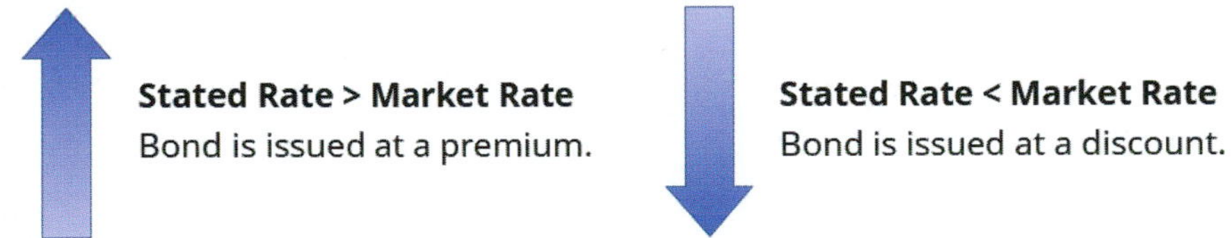

Figure 13.10 Stated Rate and Market Rate. When the stated rate is higher than the market rate, the bond is issued at a premium. When the stated rate is lower than the market rate, the bond is issued at a discount. (attribution: Copyright Rice University, OpenStax, under CC BY-NC-SA 4.0 license)

CONCEPTS IN PRACTICE

Bond Ratings

Investors intending to purchase corporate bonds may find it overwhelming to decide which company would be the best to invest in. Investors are concerned with two primary factors: the return *on* the investment (meaning, the periodic interest payments) and the return *of* the investment (meaning, payment of the face value on the maturity date). While there are risks with any investment, attempting to maximize the return *on* the investment and maximizing the likelihood receiving the return *of* the investment would take a significant amount of time for the investor. To become informed and make a wise investment, the investor would have to spend many hours analyzing the financial statements of potential companies to invest in.

One resource investors find useful when screening investment opportunities is through the use of rating agencies. Rating agencies specialize in analyzing financial and other company information in order to assess and rate a company's riskiness as an investment. A particularly useful website is Investopedia (https://openstax.org/l/50Investopedia) which highlights the rating system for three large rating agencies—Moody's, Standard & Poor's, and Fitch Ratings. The rating systems, shown below, are somewhat similar to academic grading scales, with rankings ranging from A (highest quality) to D (lowest quality):

Rating Agencies[8]

Credit Risk	Moody's	Standard & Poor's	Fitch Ratings
Investment Grade	—	—	—
Highest Quality	Aaa	AAA	AAA
High Quality	Aa1, Aa2, Aa3	AA+, AA, AA–	AA+, AA, A–
Upper Medium	A1, A2, A3	A+, A, A–	A+, A, A–
Medium	Baa1, Baa2, Baa3	BBB+, BBB, BBB–	BBB+, BBB, BBB–
Not Investment Grade	Ba1	BB+	BB+
Speculative Medium	Ba2, Ba3	BB, BB–	BB, BB–
Speculative Lower Grade	B1, B2, B3	B+, B, B–	B+, B, B–
Speculative Risky	Caa1	CCC+	CCC
Speculative Poor Standing	Caa2, Caa3	CCC, CCC–	—
No Payments / Bankruptcy	Ca / C	—	—
In Default	—	D	DDD, DD, D

Table 13.1

8 Michael Schmidt. "When to Trust Bond Rating Agencies." Investopedia. September 29, 2018. https://www.investopedia.com/articles/bonds/09/bond-rating-agencies.asp

13.3 Prepare Journal Entries to Reflect the Life Cycle of Bonds

Recall from the discussion in Explain the Pricing of Long-Term Liabilities that one way businesses can generate long-term financing is by borrowing from lenders.

In this section, we will explore the journal entries related to bonds. Earlier, we found that cash flows related to a bond include the following:

1. The receipt of cash when the bond is issued
2. Payment of interest each period
3. Repayment of the bond at maturity

A journal entry must be made for each of these transactions. As we go through the journal entries, it is important to understand that we are analyzing the accounting transactions from the perspective of the issuer of the bond. These are considered long-term liabilities. The investor would make the opposite journal entries. For example, on the issue date of a bond, the borrower receives cash while the lender pays cash.

A final point to consider relates to accounting for the interest costs on the bond. Recall that the bond indenture specifies how much interest the borrower will pay with each periodic payment based on the stated rate of interest. The periodic interest payments to the buyer (investor) will be the same over the course of the bond. It may help to think of personal loan examples. For example, if you or your family have ever borrowed money from a bank for a car or home, the payments are typically the same each month. The interest payments will be the same because of the rate stipulated in the bond indenture, regardless of what the market rate does. The amount of interest cost that we will recognize in the journal entries, however, will change over the course of the bond term, assuming that we are using the effective interest.

IFRS CONNECTION

Defining Long-Term Liabilities

Under both IFRS and US GAAP, the general definition of a long-term liability is similar. However, there are many types of long-term liabilities, and various types have specific measurement and reporting criteria that may differ between the two sets of accounting standards. With two exceptions, bonds payable are primarily the same under the two sets of standards.

The first difference pertains to the method of interest amortization. Beyond FASB's preferred method of interest amortization discussed here, there is another method, the straight-line method. This method is permitted under US GAAP if the results produced by its use would not be materially different than if the effective-interest method were used. IFRS does not permit straight-line amortization and only allows the effective-interest method.

The second difference pertains to how the bonds are reported on the books. Under US GAAP, bonds are recorded at face value and the premium or discount is recorded in a separate account. IFRS does not use "premium" or "discount" accounts. Instead, under IFRS, the carrying value of bonds issued at either a premium or discount is shown on the balance sheet at its net. For example, $100,000 bonds issued at a discount of $4,000 would be recorded under US GAAP as

JOURNAL			
Date	**Account**	**Debit**	**Credit**
	Cash Discount on Bonds Payable Bonds Payable	94,000 6,000	 100,000

Under IFRS, these bonds would be reported as

JOURNAL			
Date	**Account**	**Debit**	**Credit**
	Cash Bonds Payable	94,000	 94,000

Obviously, the above example implies that, in the subsequent entries to recognize interest expense, under IFRS, the Bonds Payable account is amortized directly for the increase or reduction in bond principal. Suppose in this example that the cash interest was $200 and the interest expense for the first interest period was $250. The entry to record the transaction under the two different standards would be as follows:

Under US GAAP:

JOURNAL			
Date	**Account**	**Debit**	**Credit**

	Bond Interest Expense
	    Discount on Bonds Payable
	    Cash
		250	
			50
			200

Under IFRS:

JOURNAL			
Date	**Account**	**Debit**	**Credit**

	Bond Interest Expense
	    Bonds Payable
	    Cash
		250	
			50
			200

Note that under either method, the interest expense and the carrying value of the bonds stays the same.

Issuance of Bonds

Since the process of underwriting a bond issuance is lengthy and extensive, there can be several months between the determination of the specific characteristics of a bond issue and the actual issuance of the bond. Before the bonds can be issued, the underwriters perform many time-consuming tasks, including setting the bond interest rate. The bond interest rate is influenced by specific factors relating to the company, such as existing debt balances and the ability of the company to repay the funds, as well as the market rate, which is influenced by many external economic factors.

Because of the time lag caused by underwriting, it is not unusual for the market rate of the bond to be different from the stated interest rate. The difference in the stated rate and the market rate determine the accounting treatment of the transactions involving bonds. When the bond is issued at par, the accounting treatment is simplest. It becomes more complicated when the stated rate and the market rate differ.

Issued When Market Rate Equals Contract Rate

First, we will explore the case when the stated interest rate is equal to the market interest rate when the bonds are issued.

Returning to our example of a $1,000, 5-year bond with a stated interest rate of 5%, at issuance, the market rate was 5% and the sales price was quoted at 100, which means the seller of the bond will receive (and the investor will pay) 100% of the $1,000 face value of the bond. The journal entry to record the sale of 100 of these bonds is:

JOURNAL			
Date	**Account**	**Debit**	**Credit**
	Cash Bonds Payable *To record issuance of 100, $1,000, 5% bonds with an effective interest rate of 5%*	100,000	 100,000

Since the book value is equal to the amount that will be owed in the future, no other account is included in the journal entry.

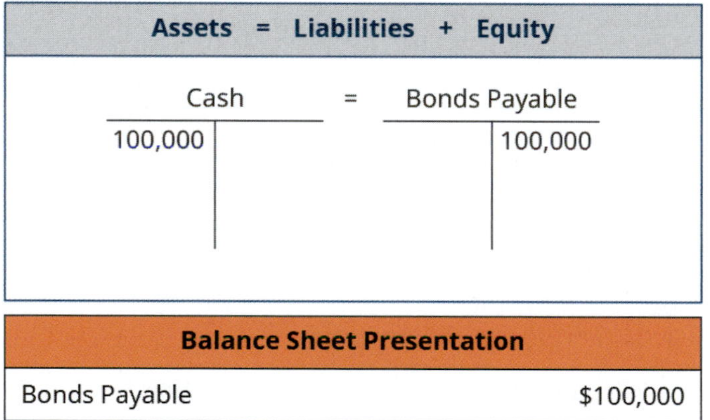

Issued at a Premium

If, during the timeframe of establishing the bond stated rate and issuing the bonds, the market rate drops below the stated interest, the bonds would become more valuable. In other words, the investors will earn a higher rate on these bonds than if the investors purchased similar bonds elsewhere in the market. Naturally, investors would want to purchase these bonds and earn a higher interest rate. The increased demand drives up the bond price to a point where investors earn the same interest as similar bonds. Earlier, we found that the sale price of a $1,000, 5-year bond with a stated rate of 5% and a market rate of 4% is 104.46. That is, the bond will sell at 104.46% of the $1,000 face value, which means the seller of the bond will receive (and the investor will pay) $1,044.60.

Selling 100 of these bonds, would yield $104,460.

JOURNAL			
Date	**Account**	**Debit**	**Credit**
	Cash	104,460	
	Premium on Bonds Payable		4,460
	Bonds Payable		100,000
	To record issuance of 100, $1,000, 5% bonds with an effective interest rate of 4%		

The financial statement presentation looks like this:

Balance Sheet Presentation	
Bonds Payable	$100,000
Premium on Bonds Payable	4,460
Carrying (Book) Value	$104,460

On the date that the bonds were issued, the company received cash of $104,460.00 but agreed to pay $100,000.00 in the future for 100 bonds with a $1,000 face value. The difference in the amount received and the amount owed is called the *premium*. Since they promised to pay 5% while similar bonds earn 4%, the company received more cash up front. In other words, they sold the bond at a premium. They did this because the cost of the premium plus the 5% interest on the face value is mathematically the same as receiving the face value but paying 4% interest. The interest rate was effectively the same.

The **premium on bonds payable** account is a contra liability account. It is contra because it increases the amount of the Bonds Payable liability account. It is "married" to the Bonds Payable account on the balance sheet. If one of the accounts appears, both must appear. The Premium will disappear over time as it is amortized, but it will decrease the interest expense, which we will see in subsequent journal entries.

Taken together, the Bond Payable liability of $100,000 and the Premium on Bond Payable contra liability of $4,460 show the bond's carrying value or **book value**—the value that assets or liabilities are recorded at in the company's financial statements.

The effect on the accounting equation looks like this:

Assets	=	Liabilities	+ Equity
Cash	=	Bonds Payable	Premium on Bonds Payable
104,460 (debit)		100,000 (credit)	4,460 (credit)

It looks like the issuer will have to pay back $104,460, but this is not quite true. If the bonds were to be paid off today, the full $104,460 would have to be paid back. But as time passes, the Premium account is amortized until it is zero. The bondholders have bonds that say the issuer will pay them $100,000, so that is all that is owed at maturity. The premium will disappear over time and will reduce the amount of interest incurred.

Issued at a Discount

Bonds issued at a discount are the exact opposite in concept as bonds issued at a premium. If, during the timeframe of establishing the bond stated rate and issuing the bonds, the market rate rises above the stated interest on the bonds, the bonds become less valuable because investors can earn a higher rate of interest on other similar bonds. In other words, the investors will earn a lower rate on these bonds than if the investors purchased similar bonds elsewhere in the market. Naturally, investors would not want to purchase these bonds and earn a lower interest rate than could be earned elsewhere. The decreased demand drives down the bond price to a point where investors earn the same interest for similar bonds. Earlier, we found the sale price of a $1,000, 5-year bond with a stated interest rate of 5% and a market rate of 7% is 91.80. That is, the bond will sell at 91.80% of the $1,000 face value, which means the seller of the bond will receive (and the investor will pay) $918.00. On selling 100 of the $1,000 bonds today, the journal entry would be:

JOURNAL			
Date	**Account**	**Debit**	**Credit**
	Cash	91,800	
	Discount on Bonds Payable	8,200	
	Bonds Payable		100,000
	To record issuance of 100, $1,000, 5% bonds with an effective interest rate of 7%		

Balance Sheet Presentation	
Bonds Payable	$100,000
Premium on Bonds Payable	4,460
Carrying (Book) Value	$104,460

Today, the company receives cash of $91,800.00, and it agrees to pay $100,000.00 in the future for 100 bonds with a $1,000 face value. The difference in the amount received and the amount owed is called the *discount*. Since they promised to pay 5% while similar bonds earn 7%, the company, accepted less cash up front. In other words, they sold the bond at a discount. They did this because giving a discount but still paying only 5% interest on the face value is mathematically the same as receiving the face value but paying 7% interest. The interest rate was effectively the same.

Like the Premium on Bonds Payable account, the **discount on bonds payable** account is a contra liability account and is "married" to the Bonds Payable account on the balance sheet. The Discount will disappear over time as it is amortized, but it will increase the interest expense, which we will see in subsequent journal entries.

The effect on the accounting equation looks like this:

Assets	=	Liabilities	+ Equity
Cash	=	Bonds Payable	Discount on Bonds Payable
91,800 (debit)		100,000 (credit)	8,200 (debit)

First and Second Semiannual Interest Payment

When a company issues bonds, they make a promise to pay interest annually or sometimes more often. If the interest is paid annually, the journal entry is made on the last day of the bond's year. If interest was promised semiannually, entries are made twice a year.

CONCEPTS IN PRACTICE

Municipal Bonds

Municipal bonds are a specific type of bonds that are issued by governmental entities such as towns and school districts. These bonds are issued in order to finance specific projects (such as water treatment plants and school building construction) that require a large investment of cash. The primary benefit to the issuing entity (i.e., the town or school district) is that cash can be obtained more quickly than, for example, collecting taxes and fees over a long period of time. This allows the project to be completed sooner, which is a benefit to the community.

Municipal bonds, like other bonds, pay periodic interest based on the stated interest rate and the face value at the end of the bond term. However, corporate bonds often pay a higher rate of interest than municipal bonds. Despite the lower interest rate, one benefit of municipal bonds relates to the tax treatment of the periodic interest payments for investors. With corporate bonds, the periodic interest payments are considered taxable income to the investor. For example, if an investor receives $1,000 of interest and is in the 25% tax bracket, the investor will have to pay $250 of taxes on the interest, leaving the investor with an after-tax payment of $750. With municipal bonds, interest payments are exempt from federal tax. So the same investor receiving $1,000 of interest from a municipal bond would pay no income tax on the interest income. This tax-exempt status of municipal bonds allows the entity to attract investors and fund projects more easily.

Interest Payment: Issued When Market Rate Equals Contract Rate

Recall that the Balance Sheet presentation of the bond when the market rate equals the stated rate is as follows:

Balance Sheet Presentation	
Bonds Payable	$100,000

In this example, the company issued 100 bonds with a face value of $1,000, a 5-year term, and a stated interest rate of 5% when the market rate was 5% and received $100,000. As previously discussed, since the bonds were sold when the market rate equals the stated rate, the carrying value of the bonds is $100,000. These bonds did not specify when interest was paid, so we can assume that it is an annual payment. If the bonds were issued on January 1, the company would pay interest on December 31 and the journal entry would be:

JOURNAL			
Date	**Account**	**Debit**	**Credit**
	Interest Expense (0.05 × $100,000)	5,000	
	Cash (0.05 × $100,000)		5,000
	To record interest expense on 5% bonds sold with effective interest rate of 5%		

The interest expense is calculated by taking the Carrying Value ($100,000) multiplied by the market interest rate (5%). The stated rate is used when calculating the interest cash payment. The company is obligated by the bond indenture to pay 5% per year based on the face value of the bond. When the situation changes and the bond is sold at a discount or premium, it is easy to get confused and incorrectly use the market rate here. Since the market rate and the stated rate are the same in this example, we do not have to worry about any differences between the amount of interest expense and the cash paid to bondholders. This journal entry will be made every year for the 5-year life of the bond.

When performing these calculations, the rate is adjusted for more frequent interest payments. If the company had issued 5% bonds that paid interest semiannually, interest payments would be made twice a year, but each interest payment would only be half an annual interest payment. Earning interest for a full year at 5% annually is the equivalent of receiving half of that amount each six months. So, for semiannual payments, we would divide 5% by 2 and pay 2.5% every six months.

CONCEPTS IN PRACTICE

Mortgage Debt

According to Statista (https://openstax.org/l/50Statista) the amount of mortgage debt—debt incurred to purchase homes—in the United States was $14.9 trillion on 2017. This value does not include the interest cost—the cost of borrowing—related to the debt.

A common loan term for those borrowing money to buy a house is 30 years. Each month, the borrower must make payments on the loan, which would add up to 360 payments for a 30-year loan. Recall from previous discussions on amortization that each payment can be divided into two components: the interest expense and the amount that is applied to reduce the principal.

In order to calculate the amount of interest and principal reduction for each payment, banks and borrowers often use amortization tables. While amortization tables are easily created in Microsoft Excel or other spreadsheet applications, there are many websites that have easy-to-use amortization tables. The popular lending website Zillow (https://openstax.org/l/50Zillow) has a loan calculator to calculate the monthly payments of a loan as well as an amortization table that shows how much interest and principal reduction is applied for each payment.

For example, borrowing $200,000 for 30 years at an interest rate of 5% would require the borrow to repay a total $386,513. The monthly payment on this loan is $1,073.64. This amount represents the $200,000 borrowed and $186,513 of interest cost. If the borrower chose a 15-year loan, the total payments drops significantly to $266,757, but the monthly payments increase to $1,581.59.

Because interest is calculated based on the outstanding loan balance, the amount of interest paid in the first payment is much more than the amount of interest in the final payment. The pie charts below show the amount of the $1,073.64 payment allocated to interest and loan reduction for the first and final payments, respectively, on the 30-year loan.

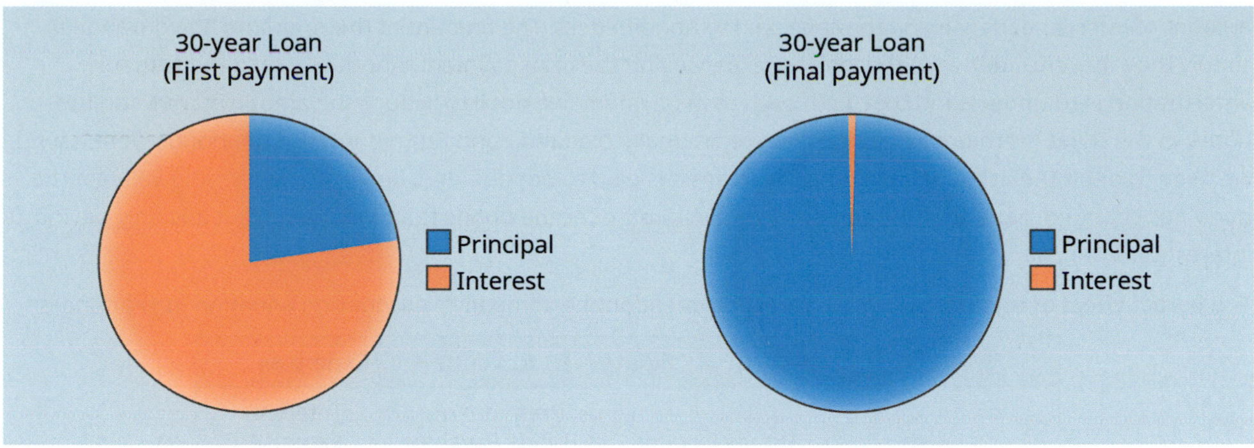

Interest Payment: Issued at a Premium

Recall that the Balance Sheet presentation of the bond when the market rate at issue is lower than the stated rate is as follows:

Balance Sheet Presentation	
Bonds Payable	$100,000
Premium on Bonds Payable	4,460
Carrying (Book) Value	$104,460

In this scenario, the sale price of a $1,000, 5-year bond with a stated rate of 5% and a market rate of 4% was $1,044.60. If the company sold 100 of these bonds, it would receive $104,460 and the journal entry would be:

JOURNAL			
Date	Account	Debit	Credit
	Cash	104,460	
	Premium on Bonds Payable		4,460
	Bonds Payable		100,000
	To record issuance of 100, $1,000, 5% bonds with an effective interest rate of 4%		

Again, let's assume that the bonds pay interest annually. At the end of the bond's year, we would record the interest expense:

JOURNAL			
Date	Account	Debit	Credit
	Interest Expense (0.04 × $104,460)	4,178	
	Premium on Bonds Payable (Difference)	822	
	Cash (0.05 × $100,000)		5,000
	To record payment of interest on bonds payable		

The interest expense determination is calculated using the *effective interest* amortization interest method. Under the effective-interest method, the interest expense is calculated by taking the Carrying (or Book) Value ($104,460) multiplied by the market interest rate (4%). The amount of the cash payment in this example is calculated by taking the face value of the bond ($100,000) multiplied by the stated rate.

Since the market rate and the stated rate are different, we need to account for the difference between the amount of interest expense and the cash paid to bondholders. The amount of the premium amortization is simply the difference between the interest expense and the cash payment. Another way to think about amortization is to understand that, with each cash payment, we need to reduce the amount carried on the books in the Bond Premium account. Since we originally credited Bond Premium when the bonds were issued, we need to debit the account each time the interest is paid to bondholders because the carrying value of the bond has changed. Note that the company received more for the bonds than face value, but it is only paying interest on $100,000.

The partial effect of the first period's interest payment on the company's accounting equation in year one is:

Assets	=	Liabilities		+ Equity		+ Revenue – Expenses	
Cash		= Bonds Payable		Premium on Bonds Payable		Interest Expense	
			100,000		4,460		
	5,000					5,000	
				822			822
					3,638	4,178	

And the financial-statement presentation at the end of year 1 is:

Balance Sheet Presentation	
Bonds Payable	$100,000
Bond Premium	3,638
Carrying (Book) Value	$103,638

Income Statement Presentation	
Bonds Interest Expense	$4,178

The journal entry for year 2 is:

JOURNAL			
Date	**Account**	**Debit**	**Credit**
	Interest Expense (0.04 × $103,638)	4,146	
	Premium on Bonds Payable (Difference)	854	
	Cash (0.05 × $100,000)		5,000
	To record payment of interest to bondholders and to amortize the bond premium		

The interest expense is calculated by taking the Carrying (or Book) Value ($103,638) multiplied by the market interest rate (4%). The amount of the cash payment in this example is calculated by taking the face value of the bond ($100,000) multiplied by the stated rate (5%). Since the market rate and the stated rate are different, we again need to account for the difference between the amount of interest expense and the cash paid to bondholders.

The partial effect on the accounting equation in year two is:

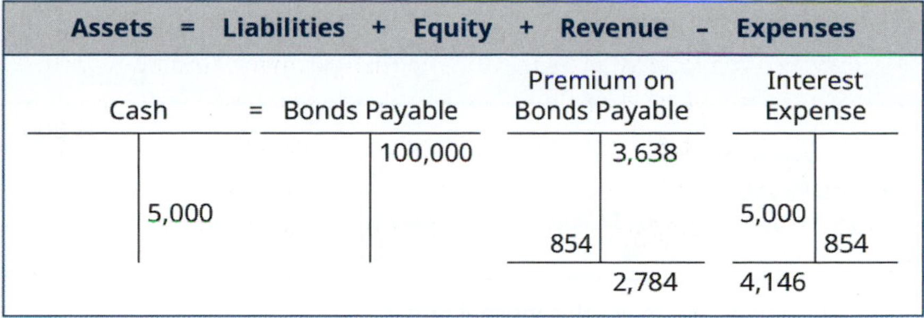

And the financial-statement presentation at the end of year 2 is:

Balance Sheet Presentation	
Bonds Payable	$100,000
Bond Premium	2,784
Carrying (Book) Value	$102,784

Income Statement Presentation	
Bonds Interest Expense	$4,146

By the end of the 5th year, the bond premium will be zero, and the company will only owe the Bonds Payable amount of $100,000.

LINK TO LEARNING

A mortgage calculator (https://openstax.org/l/50MortgageCalc) provides monthly payment estimates for a long-term loan like a mortgage. To use the calculator, enter the cost of the house to be purchased, the amount of cash to be borrowed, the number of years over which the mortgage is to be paid back (generally 30 years), and the current interest rate. The calculator returns the amount of the mortgage payment. Mortgages are long-term liabilities that are used to finance real estate purchases. We tend to think of them as home loans, but they can also be used for commercial real estate purchases.

Interest Payment: Issued at a Discount

Recall that the Balance Sheet presentation of the bond when the market rate at issue was higher than the stated rate is as follows:

Balance Sheet Presentation	
Bonds Payable	$100,000
Discount on Bonds Payable	(8,200)
Carrying (Book) Value	$ 91,800

We found the sale price of a $1,000, 5-year bond with a stated interest rate of 5% and a market rate of 7% was $918.00. We then showed the journal entry to record sale of 100 bonds:

JOURNAL			
Date	Account	Debit	Credit
	Cash	91,800	
	Discount on Bonds Payable	8,200	
	Bonds Payable		100,000
	To record issuance of 100, $1,000, 5% bonds with an effective interest rate of 7%		

At the end of the bond's first year, we make this journal entry:

JOURNAL			
Date	Account	Debit	Credit
	Interest Expense (0.07 × $91,800)	6,426	
	Cash (0.05 × $100,000)		5,000
	Discount on Bonds Payable (Difference)		1,426
	To record payment of interest on bonds payable		

The interest expense is calculated by taking the Carrying Value ($91,800) multiplied by the market interest rate (7%). The amount of the cash payment in this example is calculated by taking the face value of the bond ($100,000) and multiplying it by the stated rate (5%). Since the market rate and the stated rate are different, we need to account for the difference between the amount of interest expense and the cash paid to bondholders. The amount of the discount amortization is simply the difference between the interest expense and the cash payment. Since we originally debited Bond Discount when the bonds were issued, we need to credit the account each time the interest is paid to bondholders because the carrying value of the bond has changed. Note that the company received less for the bonds than face value but is paying interest on the $100,000.

The partial effect on the accounting equation in year one is:

Assets	=	Liabilities	+ Equity + Revenue – Expenses	
Cash	=	Bonds Payable	Discount on Bonds Payable	Interest Expense
Credit: 5,000		Credit: 100,000	Debit: 8,200; Credit: 1,426	Debit: 5,000; Debit: 1,426
			Balance: 6,774	Balance: 6,426

And the financial-statement presentation at the end of year 1 is:

Balance Sheet Presentation	
Bonds Payable	$100,000
Discount on Bonds Payable	(6,774)
Carrying (Book) Value	$ 93,226

Income Statement Presentation	
Bonds Interest Expense	$6,426

The journal entry for year 2 is:

JOURNAL			
Date	Account	Debit	Credit
	Interest Expense (0.07 × $93,226)	6,526	
	Cash (0.05 × $100,000)		5,000
	Discount on Bonds Payable (Difference)		1,526
	To record payment of interest on bonds payable		

The interest expense is calculated by taking the Carrying Value ($93,226) multiplied by the market interest rate (7%). The amount of the cash payment in this example is calculated by taking the face value of the bond ($100,000) multiplied by the stated rate (5%). Again, we need to account for the difference between the amount of interest expense and the cash paid to bondholders by crediting the Bond Discount account.

The partial effect on the accounting equation in year two is:

Assets	=	Liabilities	+	Equity	+	Revenue	–	Expenses

Cash (Dr)	Cash (Cr)	=	Bonds Payable (Dr)	Bonds Payable (Cr)	Discount on Bonds Payable (Dr)	Discount on Bonds Payable (Cr)	Interest Expense (Dr)	Interest Expense (Cr)
				100,000	6,774			
	5,000						5,000	
						1,526	1,526	
					5,248		6,526	

And the financial statement presentation at the end of year 2 is:

Balance Sheet Presentation	
Bonds Payable	$100,000
Discount on Bonds Payable	(5,248)
Carrying (Book) Value	$ 94,752

Income Statement Presentation	
Bonds Interest Expense	$6,526

By the end of the 5th year, the bond premium will be zero and the company will only owe the Bonds Payable amount of $100,000.

Retirement of Bonds When the Bonds Were Issued at Par

At some point, a company will need to record **bond retirement**, when the company pays the obligation. Often, they will retire bonds when they mature. For example, earlier we demonstrated the issuance of a five-year bond, along with its first two interest payments. If we had carried out recording all five interest payments, the next step would have been the maturity and retirement of the bond. At this stage, the bond issuer would pay the maturity value of the bond to the owner of the bond, whether that is the original owner or a secondary investor.

This example demonstrates the least complicated method of a bond issuance and retirement at maturity. There are other possibilities that can be much more complicated and beyond the scope of this course. For example, a bond might be callable by the issuing company, in which the company may pay a call premium paid to the current owner of the bond. Also, a bond might be called while there is still a premium or discount on the bond, and that can complicate the retirement process. Situations like these will be addressed in later accounting courses.

To continue with our example, assume that the company issued 100 bonds with a face value of $1,000, a 5-year term, and a stated interest rate of 5% when the market rate was 5% and received $100,000. It was recorded in this way:

JOURNAL			
Date	Account	Debit	Credit
	Cash Bonds Payable *To record issuance of 100, $1,000, 5% bonds with an effective interest rate of 5%*	100,000	 100,000

At the end of 5 years, the company will retire the bonds by paying the amount owed. To record this action, the company would debit Bonds Payable and credit Cash. Remember that the bond payable retirement debit entry will always be the face amount of the bonds since, when the bond matures, any discount or premium will have been completely amortized.

JOURNAL			
Date	Account	Debit	Credit
	Bonds Payable Cash *To record the retirement of bonds payable*	100,000	 100,000

13.4 Appendix: Special Topics Related to Long-Term Liabilities

Here we will address some special topics related to long-term liabilities.

Brief Comparison between Equity and Debt Financing

Although we briefly addressed equity versus debt financing in Explain the Pricing of Long-Term Liabilities, we will now review the two options. Let's consider Maria, who wants to buy a business. The venture is for sale for $1 million, but she only has $200,000. What are her options? In this situation, a business owner can use debt financing by borrowing money or equity financing by selling part of the company, or she can use a combination of both.

Debt financing means borrowing money that will be repaid on a specific date in the future. Many companies have started by incurring debt. To decide whether this is a viable option, the owners need to determine whether they can afford the monthly payments to repay the debt. One positive to this scenario is that interest paid on the debt is tax deductible and can lower the company's tax liability. On the other hand, businesses can struggle to make these payments every month, especially as they are starting out.

With **equity financing**, a business owner sells part of the business to obtain money to finance business operations. With this type of financing, the original owner gives up some portion of ownership in the company in return for cash. In Maria's case, partners would supplement her $200,000 and would then own a share of the business. Each partner's share is based on their financial or other contributions.

If a business owner forms a corporation, each owner will receive shares of stock. Typically, those making the largest financial investment have the largest say in decisions about business operations. The issuance of dividends should also be considered in this set-up. Paying dividends to shareholders is not tax deductible, but dividend payments are also not required. Additionally, a company does not have to buy back any stock it sells.

ETHICAL CONSIDERATIONS

Debt versus Equity Financing

Many start-ups and small companies with just one or two owners struggle to obtain the cash to run their operations. Owners may want to use lending, or debt financing, to obtain the money to run operations, but have to turn to investors, or equity financing. Ethical and legal obligations to investors are typically greater than ethical and legal obligations to lenders. This is because a company's owners have an ethical and legal responsibility to take investors' interests into account when making business decisions, even if the decision is not in the founding owners' best interest. The primary obligation to lenders, however, is only to pay back the money borrowed with interest. When determining which type of financing is appropriate for a business operation, the different ethical and legal obligations between having lenders or investors need to be considered.[9]

Equity Financing

For a corporation, equity financing involves trading or selling shares of stock in the business to raise funds to run the business. For a sole proprietorship, selling part of the business means it is no longer a sole proprietorship: the subsequent transaction could create either a corporation or partnership. The owners would choose which of the two to create. Equity means ownership. However, business owners can be creative in selling interest in their venture. For example, Maria might sell interest in the building housing her candy store and retain all revenues for herself, or she may decide to share interest in the operations (sales revenues) and retain sole ownership of the building.

The main benefit of financing with equity is that the business owner is not required to pay back the invested funds, so revenue can be re-invested in the company's growth. Companies funded this way are also more likely to succeed through their initial years. The Small Business Administration suggests a new business should have access to enough cash to operate for six months without having to borrow. The disadvantages of this funding method are that someone else owns part of the business and, depending on the arrangement, may have ideas that conflict with the original owner's ideas but that cannot be disregarded.

The following characteristics are specific to equity financing:

1. No required payment to owners or shareholders; dividends or other distributions are optional. Stock owners typically invest in stocks for two reasons: the dividends that many stocks pay or the appreciation in the market value of the stocks. For example, a stock holder might buy Walmart stock for $100 per share with the expectation of selling it for much more than $100 per share at some point in the future.
2. Ownership interest held by the original or current owners can be diluted by issuing additional new shares of common stock.
3. Unlike bonds that mature, common stocks do not have a definite life. To convert the stock to cash, some of the shares must be sold.
4. In the past, common stocks were typically sold in even 100-share lots at a given market price per share. However, with Internet brokerages today, investors can buy any particular quantity they want.

9 Nolo. "Financing a Small Business: Equity or Debt?" *Forbes*. January 5, 2007. https://www.forbes.com/2007/01/05/equity-debt-smallbusiness-ent-fin-cx_nl_0105nolofinancing.html#bd27de55819f

Debt Financing

As you have learned, debt is an obligation to pay back an amount of money at some point in the future. Generally, a term of less than one year is considered short-term, and a term of one year or longer is considered long-term. Borrowing money for college or a car with a promise to pay back the amount to the lender generates debt. Formal debt involves a signed written document with a due date, an interest rate, and the amount of the loan. A student loan is an example of a formal debt.

The following characteristics are specific to debt financing:

1. The company is required to make timely interest payments to the holders of the bonds or notes payable.
2. The interest in cash that is to be paid by the company is generally locked in at the agreed-upon rate, and thus the same dollar payments will be made over the life of the bond. Virtually all bonds will have a maturity point. When the bond matures, the maturity value, which was the same as the contract or issuance value, is paid to whoever owns the bond.
3. The interest paid is deductible on the company's income tax return.
4. Bonds or notes payable do not dilute the company's ownership interest. The holders of the long-term liabilities do not have an ownership interest.
5. Bonds are typically sold in $1,000 increments.

CONCEPTS IN PRACTICE

Short-Term Debt

Businesses sometimes offer lines of credit (short-term debt) to their customers. For example, Wilson Sporting Goods offers open credit to tennis clubs around the country. When the club needs more tennis balls, a club manager calls Wilson and says, "I'd like to order some tennis balls." The person at Wilson says, "What's your account number," and takes the order. Wilson does not ask the manager to sign a note but does expect to be paid back. If the club does not pay within 120 days, Wilson will not let them order more items until the bill is paid. Ordering on open credit makes transactions simpler for the club and for Wilson, since there is not a need to formalize every order. But collecting on the amount might be difficult for Wilson if the club delays payment. For this reason, typically customers must fill out applications, or have a history with the vendor to go on open credit.

Effect of Interest Points and Loan Term in Years on a Loan

A mortgage loan is typically a long-term loan initiated by a potential home buyer through a mortgage lender. These lenders can be banks and other financial institutions or specialized mortgage lenders. Figure 13.11 shows some examples of the major categories of loans. The table demonstrates some interesting characteristics of home loans.

TODAY'S MORTGAGE RATES AND REFINANCE RATES		
Product	**Interest Rate**	**APR**
Conforming and Government Loans		
30-Year Fixed Rate	4.375%	4.435%
30-Year Fixed-Rate VA	4.375%	4.681%
20-Year Fixed Rate	4.250%	4.297%
15-Year Fixed Rate	3.875%	3.978%
7/1 ARM	4.125%	4.379%
5/1 ARM	4.000%	4.397%
Jumbo Loans-Amounts that exceed conforming loan limits		
30-Year Fixed — Rate Jumbo	4.375%	4.386%
15-Year Fixed-Rate Jumbo	4.250%	4.266%
7/1 ARM Jumbo	4.000%	4.269%
10/1 ARM Jumbo	4.125%	4.276%

Source: www.wellsfargo.com/mortgage/rates/

Figure 13.11 Home Loans. There are a number of different types of mortgages, each with varying interest rates, based on the individual loan characteristics. (attribution: Copyright Rice University, OpenStax, under CC BY-NC-SA 4.0 license)

The first characteristic is that loans can be classified into several categories. One category is the length of the loan, usually 15 years, 20 years, or 30 years. Some mortgages lock in a fixed interest rate for the life of the loan, while others only lock in the rate for a period of time. An adjustable rate mortgage (ARM), such as a 5-year or 7-year ARM, locks in the interest rate for 5 or 7 years. After that period, the interest rate adjusts to the market rate, which could be higher or lower. Some loans are based on the fair market value (FMV) of the home. For example, above a certain purchase price, the mortgage would be considered a *jumbo loan*, with a slightly higher interest rate than a conforming loan with a lower FMV.

The second characteristic demonstrated by the table is the concept of *points*. People pay points up front (at the beginning of the loan) to secure a lower interest rate when they take out a home loan. For example, potential borrowers might be informed by their loan officer that they could secure a 30-year loan at 5.0%, with no points or a 30-year loan at 4.75% by paying one point. A point is 1% of the amount of the loan. For example, one point on a $100,000 loan would be $1,000.

Whether or not buying down a lower interest rate by paying points is a smart financial move is beyond the scope of this course. However, when you take a real estate course or decide to buy and finance a home, you will want to conduct your own research on the function of points in a mortgage.

The third and final characteristic is that when you apply for and secure a home loan, there will typically be an assortment of other costs that you will pay, such as loan origination fees and a survey fee, for example. These additional costs are reflected in the loan's annual percentage rate (or APR). These additional costs are considered part of the costs of the loan and explain why the APR rates in the table are higher than the interest rates listed for each loan.

Figure 13.11 shows data from the Wells Fargo website. You will notice that there is a column for "Interest Rate" and a column for "APR." Why does a 30-year loan have an interest rate of 4.375% with an APR of 4.435%? The difference results from compound interest.

Borrowing $100,000 for one year at 4.0%, with interest compounded yearly, would lead to $4,000 owed in interest. But since mortgages are compounded monthly, a mortgage of $100,000 would generate $4,073.70 in interest in a year.

Summary of Bond Principles

As we conclude our discussion of bonds, there are two principles that are worth noting. The first principle is there is an inverse relationship between the market rate of interest and the price of the bond. That is, when the market interest rate increases, the price of the bond decreases. This is due to the fact that the stated rate of the bond does not change.[10] As we discussed, when the market interest rate is higher than the stated interest rate of the bond, the bond will sell at a discount to attract investors and to compensate for the interest rate earned between similar bonds. When, on the other hand, the market interest rate is lower than the stated interest rate, the bond will sell at a premium, which also compensates for the interest rate earned between similar bonds. It may be helpful to think of the inverse relationship between the market interest rate and the bond price in terms of analogies such as a teeter-totter in a park or a balance scale, as shown in Figure 13.12.

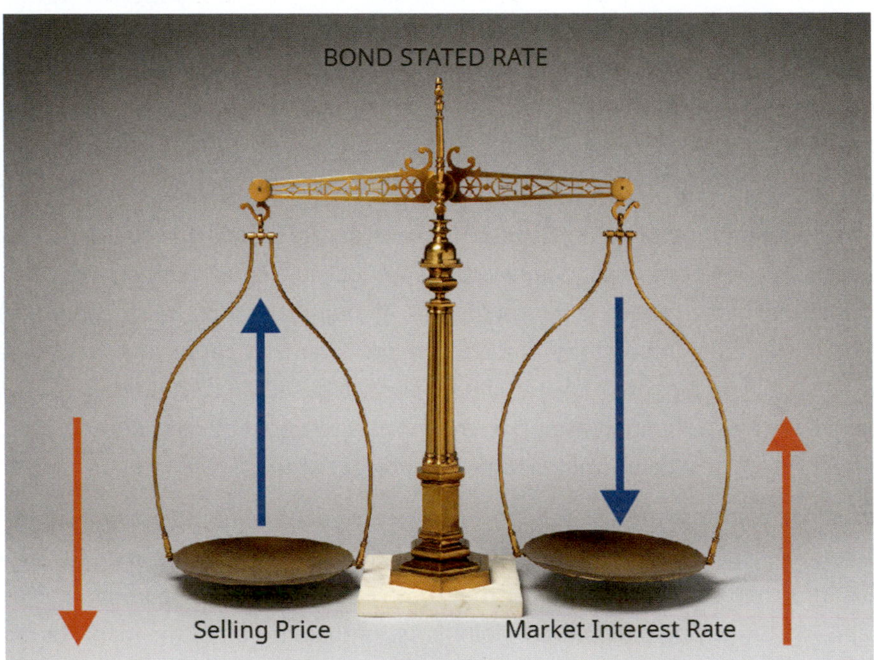

Figure 13.12 Bond Stated Rate. This illustration demonstrates the relationship between the market interest rate and the selling price of bonds. When the market interest rate goes down, the selling price goes up. The opposite is also true. (credit: modification of "Balance scale MET DP318014" gift of Mr. and Mrs. Stuart P. Feld, 2013 to Metropolitan Museum of Art/Wikimedia Commons, CC0 1.0)

In reality, the market interest rate will be above or below the stated interest rate and is rarely equal to the stated rate. The point of this illustration is to help demonstrate the inverse relationship between the market interest rate and the bond selling price.

A second principle relating to bonds involves the relationship of the bond carrying value relative to its face value. By reviewing the amortization tables for bonds sold at a discount and bonds sold at a premium it is clear that the carrying value of bonds will always move toward the face value of the bond. This occurs because interest expense (using the effective-interest method) is calculated using the bond carrying value, which changes each period.

10 Another reason for the inverse relationship between the market interest rate and bond prices is due to the time value of money.

For example, earlier we explored a 5-year, $100,000 bond that sold for $104,460. Return to the amortization table in Figure 13.9 and notice the ending value on the bond is equal to the bond face value of $100,000 (ignoring the rounding difference). The same is true for bonds sold at a discount. In our example, the $100,000 bond sold at $91,800 and the carrying value in year five was $100,000. Understanding that the carrying value of bonds will always move toward the bond face value is one trick students can use to ensure the amortization table and related accounting are correct. If, on the maturity date, the bond carrying value does not equal the bond face value, something is incorrect.

Let’s summmarize bond characteristics, When businesses borrow money from banks or other investors, the terms of the arrangement, which include the frequency of the periodic interest payments, the interest rate, and the maturity value, are specified in the bond indentures or loan documents. Recall, too, that when the bonds are issued, the bond indenture only specifies how much the borrower will repay the lender on the maturity date. The amount of money received by the business (borrower) during the issue is called the bond proceeds. The bond proceeds can be impacted by the market interest rate at the time the bonds are sold. Also, because of the lag time between preparing a bond issuance and selling the bonds, the market dynamics may cause the stated interest rate to change. Rarely, the market rate is equal to the stated rate when the bonds are sold, and the bond proceeds will equal the face value of the bonds. More commonly, the market rate is not equal to the stated rate. If the market rate is higher than the stated rate when the bonds are sold, the bonds will be sold at a discount. If the market rate is lower than the stated rate when the bonds are sold, the bonds will be sold at a premium. Figure 13.10 illustrates this rule: that bond prices are inversely related to the market interest rate.

Key Terms

amortization allocation of the costs of intangible assets over their useful economic lives; also, process of separating the principal and interest in loan payments over the life of a loan

bond type of financial instrument that a company issues directly to investors, bypassing banks or other lending institutions, with a promise to pay the investor a specified rate of interest over a specified period of time

bond indenture contract that lists the features of the bond, such as the principal, the maturity date, and the interest rate

bond retirement when the company that issued the bonds pays their obligation

book value difference between the asset's value (cost) and accumulated depreciation; also, value at which assets or liabilities are recorded in a company's financial statements

callable bond (also, redeemable bond) bond that can be repurchased or "called" by the issuer of the bond before its due date

carrying value (also, book value) value that assets or liabilities are recorded at in the company's financial statements

compound interest in a loan, when interest earned also earns interest

convertible bond bond that can be converted into common stock at the option of the bond holder

coupon rate (also, stated interest rate or face rate) interest rate printed on the certificate, used to determine the amount of interest paid to the holder of the bond

debenture bond backed by the general credit worthiness of a company rather than specific assets

debt financing borrowing money that will be repaid on a specific date in the future in order to finance business operations

default failure to pay a debt as promised

discount on bonds payable contra liability account associated with a bond that has a stated rate that is lower than the market rate and is sold at a discount

effective-interest method method of calculating interest expense based on multiplying the carrying value of the bond by the market interest rate

equity financing selling part of the business to obtain money to finance business operations

fully amortized notes periodic loan payments that pay back the principal and interest over time with payments of equal amounts

interest-only loan type of loan that only requires regular interest payments with all the principal due at maturity

long-term liability debt settled outside one year or one operating cycle, whichever is longer

market interest rate (also, effective interest rate) rate determined by supply and demand and by the credit worthiness of the borrower

maturity date date a bond or note becomes due and payable

maturity value amount to be paid at the maturity date

note payable legal document between a borrower and a lender specifying terms of a financial arrangement; in most situations, the debt is long-term

par value value assigned to stock in the company's charter, typically set at a very small arbitrary amount; serves as legal capital

premium on bonds payable contra account associated with a bond that has a stated rate that is higher than the market rate and is sold at a premium

principal face value or maturity value of a bond (the amount to be paid at maturity); also, initial borrowed amount of a loan, not including interest

promissory note represents a personal loan agreement that is a formal contract between a lender and borrower

putable bond bond that give the bondholder the right to decide whether to sell it back early or keep it until it matures

secondary market organized market where previously issued stocks and bonds can be traded after they are issued

secured bond bond backed by specific assets as collateral for the bond

serial bond bond that will mature over a period of time and will be repaid in a series of payments

stated interest rate (also, contract interest rate) interest rate printed on the face of the bond that the issuer agrees to pay the bondholder throughout the term of the bond; also known as the *coupon rate* and *face rate*

straight-line method method of calculating interest expense that allocates the same amount of premium or discount amortization for each of the bond's payment periods

term bond bond that will be repaid all at once, rather than in a series of payments

Summary

13.1 Explain the Pricing of Long-Term Liabilities

- Businesses can obtain financing (cash) through profitable operations, issuing (selling) debt, and by selling ownership (equity).
- Notes payable and bonds payable are specific types of debt that businesses issue in order to generate financial capital.
- Liabilities are categorized as either current or noncurrent based on when the liability will be settled relative to the operating period of the business.
- A bond indenture is a legal document containing the principal amount, maturity date, stated interest rate and other requirements of the bond issuer.
- Bonds can be issued under different structures and include different features.
- Periodic interest payments are based on the amount borrowed, the interest rate, and the time period for which interest is calculated.
- Bond selling prices are determined by the market interest rate at the time of the sale and the stated interest rate of the bond.
- Bonds can be sold at face value, at a premium, or at a discount.

13.2 Compute Amortization of Long-Term Liabilities Using the Effective-Interest Method

- The effective-interest method is a common method used to calculate the interest expense for a given interest payment.
- There is an inverse relationship between the price of a bond and the market interest rate.
- The carrying value of a bond sold at a discount will increase during the life of a bond until the maturity or face value is reached.
- The carrying value of a bond sold at a premium will decrease during the life of a bond until the maturity or face value is reached.
- The amount of cash to be paid, the interest expense, and the premium or discount amortization (when applicable) with each periodic payment are calculated based on an amortization table or schedule.

13.3 Prepare Journal Entries to Reflect the Life Cycle of Bonds

- When a company issues a bond, the specific terms of the bond are contained in the bond indenture.

- Journal entries are recorded at various stages of a bond, including when the bond is issued, for periodic interest payments, and for payment of the bond at maturity.
- The difference between the face value of a bond and the cash proceeds are recorded in the discount (when the proceeds are lower than the face value) and premium (when the proceeds are higher than the face value) accounts.
- The carrying or book value of a bond is determined by the balances of the Bond Payable and Discount and/or Premium accounts.
- Interest expense associated with a bond interest payment is calculated by the bond's carrying or book value multiplied by the market interest rate.

Multiple Choice

1. LO 13.1 An amortization table _______.

A. breaks each payment into the amount that goes toward interest and the amount that goes toward the principal
B. is a special table used in a break room to make people feel equitable
C. separates time value of money tables into present value and future value
D. separates time value of money tables into single amounts and streams of cash

2. LO 13.1 A debenture is _______.

A. the interest paid on a bond
B. a type of bond that can be sold back to the issuing company whenever the bondholder wishes
C. a bond with only the company's word that they will pay it back
D. a bond with assets such as land to back their word that they will pay it back

3. LO 13.1 The principal of a bond is _______.

A. the person who sold the bond for the company
B. the person who bought the bond
C. the interest rate printed on the front of the bond
D. the face amount of the bond that will be paid back at maturity

4. LO 13.1 A convertible bond can be converted into _______.

A. preferred stock
B. common stock and then converted into preferred stock
C. common stock of a different company
D. common stock of the company

5. LO 13.1 On January 1, a company issued a 5-year $100,000 bond at 6%. Interest payments on the bond of $6,000 are to be made annually. If the company received proceeds of $112,300, how would the bond's issuance be quoted?

A. 1.123
B. 112.30
C. 0.890
D. 89.05

6. LO 13.1 On July 1, a company sells 8-year $250,000 bonds with a stated interest rate of 6%. If interest payments are paid annually, each interest payment will be _______.

A. $120,000
B. $60,000
C. $7,500
D. $15,000

7. LO 13.1 On January 1 a company issues a $75,000 bond that pays interest semi-annually. The first interest payment of $1,875 is paid on July 1. What is the stated annual interest rate on the bond?

A. 5.00%
B. 2.50%
C. 1.25%
D. 10.00%

8. LO 13.1 On October 1 a company sells a 3-year, $2,500,000 bond with an 8% stated interest rate. Interest is paid quarterly and the bond is sold at 89.35. On October 1 the company would collect _______.

A. $200,000
B. $558,438
C. $2,233,750
D. $6,701,250

9. LO 13.1 On April 1 a company sells a 5-year, $60,000 bond with a 7% stated interest rate. The market interest on that day was also 7%. If interest is paid quarterly, the company makes interest payments of _______.

A. $1,050
B. $3,150
C. $4,200
D. $5,250

10. LO 13.2 The effective-interest method of bond amortization finds the difference between the _______ times the _______ and the _______ times the _______.

A. stated interest rate, principal, stated interest rate, carrying value
B. stated interest rate, principal, market interest rate, carrying value
C. stated interest rate, carrying value, market interest rate, principal
D. market interest rate, carrying value, market interest rate, principal

11. LO 13.2 When a bond sells at a discount, the carrying value _______ after each amortization entry.

A. increases
B. decreases
C. stays the same
D. cannot be determined

12. LO 13.2 The International Financial Reporting Standards require the use of _______.

A. any method of amortization of bond premiums
B. the straight-line method of amortization of bond discounts
C. the effective-interest method of amortization of bond premiums and discounts
D. any method approved by US GAAP

13. LO 13.2 The cash interest payment a corporation makes to its bondholders is based on _______.

A. the market rate times the carrying value
B. the stated rate times the principal
C. the stated rate times the carrying value
D. the market rate times the principal

14. LO 13.2 Whirlie Inc. issued $300,000 face value, 10% paid annually, 10-year bonds for $319,251 when the market of interest was 9%. The company uses the effective-interest method of amortization. At the end of the year, the company will record _______.

A. a credit to cash for $28,733
B. a debit to interest expense for $31,267
C. a debit to Discount on Bonds Payable for $1,267
D. a debit to Premium on Bonds Payable for $1.267

15. LO 13.3 Naval Inc. issued $200,000 face value bonds at a discount and received $190,000. At the end of 2018, the balance in the Discount on Bonds Payable account is $5,000. This year's balance sheet will show a net liability of _______.

A. $200,000
B. $180,000
C. $195,000
D. $205,000

16. LO 13.3 Keys Inc. issued 100 bonds with a face value of $1,000 and a rate of 8% at $1,025 each. The journal entry to record this transaction includes _______.

A. a credit to Bonds Payable for $102,500
B. a credit to cash for $102,500
C. a debit to cash for $100,000
D. a credit to Premium on Bonds Payable for $2,500

17. LO 13.3 Huang Inc. issued 100 bonds with a face value of $1,000 and a 5-year term at $960 each. The journal entry to record this transaction includes _______.

A. a debit to Bonds Payable for $100,000
B. a debit to Discount on Bonds Payable for $4,000
C. a credit to cash for $96,000
D. a credit to Discount on Bonds Payable for $4,000

18. LO 13.3 O'Shea Inc. issued bonds at a face value of $100,000, a rate of 6%, and a 5-year term for $98,000. From this information, we know that the market rate of interest was _______.

A. more than 6%
B. less than 6%
C. equal to 6%
D. cannot be determined from the information given.

19. LO 13.3 Gingko Inc. issued bonds with a face value of $100,000, a rate of 7%, and a 10-yearterm for $103,000. From this information, we know that the market rate of interest was _______.

A. more than 7%
B. less than 7%
C. equal to 7%
D. equal to 1.3%

20. LO 13.4 The difference between equity financing and debt financing is that

A. equity financing involves borrowing money.
B. equity financing involves selling part of the company.
C. debt financing involves selling part of the company.
D. debt financing means the company has no debt.

Questions

1. LO 13.1 What is the difference between callable and putable bonds?

2. LO 13.1 What is the difference between serial bonds and term bonds?

3. LO 13.1 What is a junk bond?

4. LO 13.1 How are savings bonds different from a corporate bond?

5. LO 13.1 What do you have to do to the interest rate and years of maturity if a bond pricing problem tells you that interest is compounded quarterly?

6. LO 13.2 An amortization table/schedule is created to compute the amount to be amortized each year. What are the four columns needed to prepare the table?

7. LO 13.2 In the amortization table, how is the amortization of discount of premium computed?

8. LO 13.2 Does issuing a bond at a discount increase or decrease interest expense over the life of the bond?

9. LO 13.2 What kind of account is the Discount on Bonds Payable? What kind of account is the Premium on Bonds Payable?

10. LO 13.2 Why is the effective-interest method of amortization required under the International Financial Reporting Standards?

11. LO 13.3 If there is neither a premium nor discount present, the journal entry to record bond interest payments is ______.

12. LO 13.3 When do you use the Bond Discount Account?

13. LO 13.3 A company issued bonds with a $100,000 face value, a 5-year term, a stated rate of 6%, and a market rate of 7%. Interest is paid annually. What is the amount of interest the bondholders will receive at the end of the year?

14. LO 13.3 A company issued $100,000, 5-year bonds, receiving $97,000. What is the balance sheet presentation immediately after the sale?

15. LO 13.3 Does interest expense increase or decrease when a bond premium is amortized?

Exercise Set A

EA1. LO 13.1 Halep Inc. borrowed $30,000 from Davis Bank and signed a 4-year note payable stating the interest rate was 4% compounded annually. Halep Inc. will make payments of $8,264.70 at the end of each year. Prepare an amortization table showing the principal and interest in each payment.

EA2. LO 13.1 Beluga Inc. issued 10-year bonds with a face value of $100,000 and a stated rate of 3% when the market rate was 4%. Interest was paid annually. The bonds were sold at 87.5. What was the sales price of the bonds? Were they issued at a discount, a premium, or at par?

EA3. LO 13.1 Krystian Inc. issued 10-year bonds with a face value of $100,000 and a stated rate of 4% when the market rate was 6%. Interest was paid semi-annually. Calculate and explain the timing of the cash flows the purchaser of the bonds (the investor) will receive throughout the bond term. Would an investor be willing to pay more or less than face value for this bond?

EA4. LO 13.1 On January 1, 2018, Wawatosa Inc. issued 5-year bonds with a face value of $200,000 and a stated interest rate of 12% payable semi-annually on July 1 and January 1. The bonds were sold to yield 10%. Assuming the bonds were sold at 107.732, what is the selling price of the bonds? Were they issued at a discount or a premium?

EA5. LO 13.2 Diana Inc. issued $100,000 of its 9%, 5-year bonds for $96,149 when the market rate was 10%. The bonds pay interest semi-annually. Prepare an amortization table for the first three payments.

EA6. LO 13.2 Oak Branch Inc. issued $700,000 of 5%, 10-year bonds when the market rate was 4%. They received $757,243. Interest was paid semi-annually. Prepare an amortization table for the first three years of the bonds.

EA7. LO 13.3 On Jan. 1, Year 1, Foxcroft Inc. issued 100 bonds with a face value of $1,000 for $104,000. The bonds had a stated rate of 6% and paid interest semiannually. What is the journal entry to record the issuance of the bonds?

EA8. LO 13.3 Medhurst Corporation issued $90,000 in bonds for $87,000. The bonds had a stated rate of 8% and pay interest quarterly. What is the journal entry to record the sale of the bonds?

EA9. LO 13.3 On Jan. 1, Year 1, Foxcroft Inc. issued 100 bonds with a face value of $1,000 for $104,000. The bonds had a stated rate of 6% and paid interest semi-annually. What is the journal entry to record the first payment to the bondholders?

EA10. LO 13.3 Pinetop Corporation issued $150,000 10-year bonds at par. The bonds have a stated rate of 6% and pay interest annually. What is the journal entry to record the sale of the bonds?

EA11. LO 13.3 Medhurst Corporation issued $90,000 in bonds for $87,000. The bonds had a stated rate of 8% and pay interest quarterly. What is the journal entry to record the first interest payment?

Exercise Set B

EB1. LO 13.1 Sharapovich Inc. borrowed $50,000 from Kerber Bank and signed a 5-year note payable stating the interest rate was 5% compounded annually. Sharapovich Inc. will make payments of $11,548.74 at the end of each year. Prepare an amortization table showing the principal and interest in each payment.

EB2. LO 13.1 Waylan Sisters Inc. issued 3-year bonds with a par value of $100,000 and a 6% annual coupon when the market rate of interest was 5%. If the bonds sold at 102.438, how much cash did Williams Sisters Inc. receive from issuing the bonds?

EB3. LO 13.1 Smashing Cantaloupes Inc. issued 5-year bonds with a par value of $35,000 and an 8% semi-annual coupon (payable June 30 and December 31) on January 1, 2018, when the market rate of interest was 10%. Were the bonds issued at a discount or premium? Assuming the bonds sold at 92.288, what was the sales price of the bonds?

EB4. LO 13.1 Chung Inc. issued $50,000 of 3-year bonds on January 1, 2018, with a stated rate of 4% and a market rate of 4%. The bonds paid interest semi-annually on June 30 and Dec. 31. How much money did the company receive when the bonds were issued? The bonds would be quoted at what rate?

EB5. LO 13.2 Haiku Inc. issued $600,000 of 10-year bonds with a stated rate of 11% when the market rate was 12%. The bonds pay interest semi-annually. Prepare the first three years of an amortization schedule. Assume that the bonds were issued for $565,710.

EB6. LO 13.2 Waldron Inc. issued $400,000 bonds with a stated rate of 7% when the market rate was 5%. They are 3-year bonds with interest to be paid annually. Prepare a table to amortize the premium of the bonds. Assume that the bonds were issued for $421,844.

EB7. LO 13.3 Willoughby Inc. issued 100 bonds with a face value of $1,000 and a stated rate of 4% and received $105,000. What is the journal entry to record the sale of the bonds?

EB8. LO 13.3 Allante Corporate issued 50 bonds with a face value of $1,000 and a stated rate of 4% and received $45,000. What is the journal entry to record the sale of the bonds?

EB9. LO 13.3 Roo Incorporated issued 50 bonds with a face value of $1,000 and a stated rate of 6% when the market rate was 6%. What is the journal entry to record the sale of the bonds?

EB10. LO 13.3 Piedmont Corporation issued $200,000 of 10-year bonds at par. The bonds have a stated rate of 6% and pay interest annually. What is the journal entry to record the first interest payment to the bondholders?

EB11. LO 13.3 Lunar Corporation issued $80,000 in bonds for $87,000 on Jan. 1. The bonds had a stated rate of 8% and pay interest quarterly. What is the journal entry to record the first interest payment?

Problem Set A

PA1. LO 13.3 On January 1, 2018, King Inc. borrowed $150,000 and signed a 5-year, note payable with a 10% interest rate. Each annual payment is in the amount of $39,569 and payment is due each Dec. 31. What is the journal entry on Jan. 1 to record the cash received and on Dec. 31 to record the annual payment? (You will need to prepare the first row in the amortization table to determine the amounts.)

PA2. LO 13.1 On July 1, Somerset Inc. issued $200,000 of 10%, 10-year bonds when the market rate was 12%. The bonds paid interest semi-annually. Assuming the bonds sold at 58.55, what was the selling price of the bonds? Explain why the cash received from selling this bond is different from the $200,000 face value of the bond.

PA3. LO 13.2 Eli Inc. issued $100,000 of 8% annual, 5-year bonds for $103,000. What is the total amount of interest expense over the life of the bonds?

PA4. LO 13.2 Evie Inc. issued 50 bonds with a $1,000 face value, a five-year life, and a stated annual coupon of 6% for $980 each. What is the total amount of interest expense over the life of the bonds?

PA5. LO 13.3 Volunteer Inc. issued bonds with a $500,000 face value, 10% interest rate, and a 4-year term on July 1, 2018 and received $540,000. Interest is payable annually. The premium is amortized using the straight-line method. Prepare journal entries for the following transactions.

A. July 1, 2018: entry to record issuing the bonds
B. June 30, 2019: entry to record payment of interest to bondholders
C. June 30, 2019: entry to record amortization of premium
D. June 30, 2020: entry to record payment of interest to bondholders
E. June 30, 2020: entry to record amortization of premium

PA6. LO 13.3 Aggies Inc. issued bonds with a $500,000 face value, 10% interest rate, and a 4-year term on July 1, 2018, and received $540,000. Interest is payable semi-annually. The premium is amortized using the straight-line method. Prepare journal entries for the following transactions.

A. July 1, 2018: entry to record issuing the bonds
B. Dec. 31, 2018: entry to record payment of interest to bondholders
C. Dec. 31, 2018: entry to record amortization of premium

Problem Set B

PB1. LO 13.3 Sub-Cinema Inc. borrowed $10,000 on Jan. 1 and will repay the loan with 12 equal payments made at the end of the month for 12 months. The interest rate is 12% annually. If the monthly payments are $888.49, what is the journal entry to record the cash received on Jan. 1 and the first payment made on Jan. 31?

PB2. LO 13.1 Charleston Inc. issued $200,000 bonds with a stated rate of 10%. The bonds had a 10-year maturity date. Interest is to be paid semi-annually and the market rate of interest is 8%. If the bonds sold at 113.55, what amount was received upon issuance?

PB3. LO 13.2 Starmount Inc. sold bonds with a $50,000 face value, 12% interest, and 10-year term at $48,000. What is the total amount of interest expense over the life of the bonds?

PB4. LO 13.2 Irving Inc. sold bonds with a $50,000, 10% interest, and 10-year term at $52,000. What is the total amount of interest expense over the life of the bonds?

PB5. LO 13.3 Dixon Inc. issued bonds with a $500,000 face value, 10% interest rate, and a 4-year term on July 1, 2018 and received $480,000. Interest is payable annually. The discount is amortized using the straight-line method. Prepare journal entries for the following transactions.

A. July 1, 2018: entry to record issuing the bonds
B. June 30, 2019: entry to record payment of interest to bondholders
C. June 30, 2019: entry to record amortization of discount
D. June 30, 2020: entry to record payment of interest to bondholders
E. June 30, 2020: entry to record amortization of discount

PB6. LO 13.3 Edward Inc. issued bonds with a $500,000 face value, 10% interest rate, and a 4-year term on July 1, 2018 and received $480,000. Interest is payable semiannually. The discount is amortized using the straight-line method. Prepare journal entries for the following transactions.

A. July 1, 2018: entry to record issuing the bonds
B. Dec. 31, 2018: entry to record payment of interest to bondholders
C. Dec. 31, 2018: entry to record amortization of discount

Thought Provokers

TP1. LO 13.1 It is somewhat difficult to find current quotes on corporate bonds, but one source is the Financial Industry Regulatory Authority. Using the link http://finra-markets.morningstar.com/BondCenter/Default.jsp, click on the “Search” tab. Make sure “Bond Type” is set to “Corporate” and enter “Nike” in the “Issuer Name” field and hit enter.

Write a brief summary explaining the results, including an explanation of each of the fields. Assume that an investor purchases a $1,000 bond and interest payments are made semi-annually. Be sure to include the price the investor would pay for the bond.

TP2. LO 13.2 Below is select information from two, independent companies.

	Company A	Company B
Sales	$2,300,000	$2,300,000
Cost of goods sold	1,081,000	1,081,000
Depreciation	575,000	575,000
Utilities	32,000	32,000
Sales, general, and administrative expenses	175,000	175,000
Other expenses	235,000	235,000

Additional information includes:

- On January 1, Company A issued a 5-year $1,500,000 bond with at 6% stated rate. Interest is paid semiannually and the bond was sold at 105.5055 to yield a market rate of 4.75%.
- On January 1, Company B sold $1,500,000 of common stock and paid dividends of $75,000.

A. Prepare an income statement for each company (ignore taxes)

B. Explain why the net income amounts are different, paying particular attention to the operational performance and financing performance of each company. (Hint: it may be helpful for you to create an amortization table).

TP3. LO 13.3 Assume you are a newly-hired accountant for a local manufacturing firm. You have enjoyed working for the company and are looking forward to your first experience participating in the preparation of the company’s financial statements for the year-ending December 31, the end of the company’s fiscal year.

As you are preparing your assigned journal entries, your supervisor approaches you and asks to speak with you. Your supervisor is concerned because, based on her preliminary estimates, the company will fall just shy of its financial targets for the year. If the estimates are true, this means that all 176 employees of the company will not receive year-end bonuses, which represent a significant portion of their pay.

One of the entries that you will prepare involves the upcoming bond interest payment that will be paid on January 15 of the next year. Your supervisor has calculated that, if the journal entry is dated on January 1 of the following year rather than on December 31 of the current year, the company will likely meet its financial goals thereby allowing all employees to receive year-end bonuses. Your supervisor asks you if you will consider dating the journal entry on January 1 instead of December 31 of the current year. Assess the implications of the various stakeholders and explain what your answer will be.

14

Corporation Accounting

Figure 14.1 Stocks. Company stocks are traded daily across the globe. (credit: modification of "E-ticker" by "klip game"/Wikimedia Commons, Public Domain)

Chapter Outline

LO **14.1** Explain the Process of Securing Equity Financing through the Issuance of Stock

LO **14.2** Analyze and Record Transactions for the Issuance and Repurchase of Stock

LO **14.3** Record Transactions and the Effects on Financial Statements for Cash Dividends, Property Dividends, Stock Dividends, and Stock Splits

LO **14.4** Compare and Contrast Owners' Equity versus Retained Earnings

LO **14.5** Discuss the Applicability of Earnings per Share as a Method to Measure Performance

Why It Matters

Chad and Rick have experienced resounding success operating their three Mexican restaurants named La Cantina. They are now ready to expand and open two more restaurants. The partners realize this will require significant funds for leasing locations, purchasing and installing equipment, and setting up operations. They have tentatively decided to form a new corporation for their future restaurant operations. The partners researched some of the characteristics of corporations and have learned that a corporation can sell shares of stock in exchange for funding their operations and buying new equipment. The sale of shares will dilute the partners' ownership interest in the restaurants but will enable them to finance the expansion without borrowing any money.

Chad and Rick are not ready to go public with the offering of their shares because the three current restaurants are not widely recognized. A public offering of the shares in a corporation is typically done when a company is recognized and investment banks and venture capitalists can create enough interest for a large number of investors. When a corporation is starting up, it shares are typically sold to friends and family, and then to angel investors. Many successful companies, like Amazon and Dell, started this way.

Partners Chad and Rick locate possible investors and then share their restaurant's financial information and business plan. The investors will not participate in management or work at the restaurants, but they will be stockholders along with Chad and Rick. Stockholders own part of the corporation by holding ownership in shares of the corporation's stock. The corporate form of business will enable Chad, Rick, and other shareholders to minimize their liability. The most that the investors can lose is the amount they have invested in the corporation. In addition, Chad and Rick will be able to receive a salary from the new corporation because they will manage the operations, and all of the shareholders will be able to share in the corporation's profits through the receipt of dividends.

14.1 Explain the Process of Securing Equity Financing through the Issuance of Stock

A **corporation** is a legal business structure involving one or more individuals (owners) who are legally distinct (separate) from the business that is created under state laws. The owners of a corporation are called **stockholders** (or shareholders) and may or may not be employees of the corporation. Most corporations rely on a combination of debt (liabilities) and equity (stock) to raise capital. Both debt and equity financing have the goal of obtaining funding, often referred to as capital, to be used to acquire other assets needed for operations or expansion. **Capital** consists of the total cash and other assets owned by a company found on the left side of the accounting equation. The method of financing these assets is evidenced by looking at the right side of the accounting equation, either recorded as liabilities or shareholders' equity.

The Organization of a Corporation

Incorporation is the process of forming a company into a corporate legal entity. The advantages of incorporating are available to a corporation regardless of size, from a corporation with one shareholder to those with hundreds of thousands of shareholders. To issue stock, an entity must first be incorporated in a state.

The process of incorporating requires filing the appropriate paperwork and receiving approval from a governmental entity to operate as a corporation. Each state has separate requirements for creating a corporation, but ultimately, each state grants a corporation the right to conduct business in the respective state in which the corporation is formed. The steps to incorporate are similar in most states:

1. The founders (incorporators) choose an available business name that complies with the state's corporation rules. A state will not allow a corporation to choose a name that is already in use or that has been in use in recent years. Also, similar names might be disallowed.
2. The founders of a corporation prepare **articles of incorporation** called a "charter," which defines the basic structure and purpose of the corporation and the amount of capital stock that can be issued or sold.
3. The founders file the articles of incorporation with the Department of State of the state in which the incorporation is desired. Once the articles are filed and any required fees are paid, the government approves the incorporation.
4. The incorporators hold an organizational meeting to elect the board of directors. Board meetings must be documented with formal board minutes (a written record of the items discussed, decisions made, and action plans resulting from the meeting). The board of directors generally meets at least annually. Microsoft, for example, has 14 directors on its board.[1] Boards may have more or fewer directors than this, but most boards have a minimum of at least three directors.

5. The board of directors prepares and adopts corporate bylaws. These bylaws lay out the operating rules for the corporation. Templates for drawing up corporate bylaws are usually available from the state to ensure that they conform with that state's requirements.
6. The board of directors agrees upon a par value price for the stock. Par value is a legal concept discussed later in this section. The price that the company receives (the initial market value) will be determined by what the purchasing public is willing to pay. For example, the company might set the par value at $1 per share, while the investing public on the day of issuance might be willing to pay $30 per share for the stock.

CONCEPTS IN PRACTICE

Deciding Where to Incorporate

With 50 states to choose from, how do corporations decide where to incorporate? Many corporations are formed in either Delaware or Nevada for several reasons. Delaware is especially advantageous for large corporations because it has some of the most flexible business laws in the nation and its court system has a division specifically for handling business cases that operates without juries. Additionally, companies formed in Delaware that do not transact business in the state do not need to pay state corporate income tax. Delaware imposes no personal tax for non-residents, and shareholders can be non-residents. In addition, stock shares owned by non-Delaware residents are not subject to Delaware state taxation.

Because of these advantages, Delaware dominated the share of business incorporation for several decades. In recent years, though, other states are seeking to compete for these businesses by offering similarly attractive benefits of incorporation. Nevada in particular has made headway. It has no state corporate income tax and does not impose any fees on shares or shareholders. After the initial set up fees, Nevada has no personal or franchise tax for corporations or their shareholders. Nevada, like Delaware, does not require shareholders to be state residents. If a corporation chooses to incorporate in Delaware, Nevada, or any state that is not its home state, it will need to register to do business in its home state. Corporations that transact in states other than their state of incorporation are considered *foreign* and may be subject to fees, local taxes, and annual reporting requirements that can be time consuming and expensive.

Advantages of the Corporate Form

Compared to other forms of organization for businesses, corporations have several advantages. A corporation is a separate legal entity, it provides limited liability for its owner or owners, ownership is transferable, it has a continuing existence, and capital is generally easy to raise.

Separate Legal Entity

A sole proprietorship, a partnership, and a corporation are different types of business entities. However, only a

1 Microsoft Corporation. "Board of Directors." https://www.microsoft.com/en-us/Investor/corporate-governance/board-of-directors.aspx

corporation is a legal entity. As a separate legal entity, a corporation can obtain funds by selling shares of stock, it can incur debt, it can become a party to a contract, it can sue other parties, and it can be sued. The owners are separate from the corporation. This separate legal status complies with one of the basic accounting concepts—the **accounting entity concept**, which indicates that the economic activity of an entity (the corporation) must be kept separate from the personal financial affairs of the owners.

Limited Liability

Many individuals seek to incorporate a business because they want the protection of limited liability. A corporation usually limits the liability of an investor to the amount of his or her investment in the corporation. For example, if a corporation enters into a loan agreement to borrow a sum of money and is unable to repay the loan, the lender cannot recover the amount owed from the shareholders (owners) unless the owners signed a personal guarantee. This is the opposite of partnerships and sole proprietorships. In partnerships and sole proprietorships, the owners can be held responsible for any unpaid financial obligations of the business and can be sued to pay obligations.

Transferable Ownership

Shareholders in a corporation can transfer shares to other parties without affecting the corporation's operations. In effect, the transfer takes place between the parties outside of the corporation. In most corporations, the company generally does not have to give permission for shares to be transferred to another party. No journal entry is recorded in the corporation's accounting records when a shareholder sells his or her stock to another shareholder. However, a memo entry must be made in the corporate stock ownership records so any dividends can be issued to the correct shareholder.

Continuing Existence

From a legal perspective, a corporation is granted existence forever with no termination date. This legal aspect falls in line with the basic accounting concept of the **going concern assumption**, which states that absent any evidence to the contrary, a business will continue to operate in the indefinite future. Because ownership of shares in a corporation is transferrable, re-incorporation is not necessary when ownership changes hands. This differs from a partnership, which ends when a partner dies, or from a sole proprietorship, which ends when the owner terminates the business.

Ease of Raising Capital

Because shares of stock can be easily transferred, corporations have a sizeable market of investors from whom to obtain capital. More than 65 million American households[2] hold investments in the securities markets. Compared to sole proprietorships (whose owners must obtain loans or invest their own funds) or to partnerships (which must typically obtain funds from the existing partners or seek other partners to join; although some partnerships are able borrow from outside parties), a corporation will find that capital is relatively easy to raise.

---

2 Financial Samurai. "What Percent of Americans Hold Stocks?" February 18, 2019. https://www.financialsamurai.com/what-percent-of-americans-own-stocks/

Disadvantages of the Corporate Form

As compared to other organizations for businesses, there are also disadvantages to operating as a corporation. They include the costs of organization, regulation, and taxation.

Costs of Organization

Corporations incur costs associated with organizing the corporate entity, which include attorney fees, promotion costs, and filing fees paid to the state. These costs are debited to an account called **organization costs**. Assume that on January 1, Rayco Corporation made a payment for $750 to its attorney to prepare the incorporation documents and paid $450 to the state for filing fees. Rayco also incurred and paid $1,200 to advertise and promote the stock offering. The total organization costs are $2,400 ($750 + $450 + $1,200). The journal entry recorded by Rayco is a $2,400 debit to Organization Costs and a $2,400 credit to Cash.

JOURNAL			
Date	**Account**	**Debit**	**Credit**
Jan. 1	Organization Costs Expense Cash *To record organization costs*	2,400	 2,400

Organization costs are reported as part of the operating expenses on the corporation's income statement.

Regulation

Compared to partnerships and sole proprietorships, corporations are subject to considerably more regulation both by the states in which they are incorporated and the states in which they operate. Each state provides limits to the powers that a corporation may exercise and specifies the rights and liabilities of shareholders. The **Securities and Exchange Commission (SEC)** is a federal agency that regulates corporations whose shares are listed and traded on security exchanges such as the New York Stock Exchange (NYSE), the National Association of Securities Dealers Automated Quotations Exchange (NASDAQ), and others; it accomplishes this through required periodic filings and other regulations. States also require the filing of periodic reports and payment of annual fees.

Taxation

As legal entities, typical corporations (C corporations, named after the specific subchapter of the Internal Revenue Service code under which they are taxed), are subject to federal and state income taxes (in those states with corporate taxes) based on the income they earn. Stockholders are also subject to income taxes, both on the dividends they receive from corporations and any gains they realize when they dispose of their stock. The income taxation of both the corporate entity's income and the stockholder's dividend is referred to as **double taxation** because the income is taxed to the corporation that earned the income and then taxed again to stockholders when they receive a distribution of the corporation's income.

Corporations that are closely held (with fewer than 100 stockholders) can be classified as S corporations, so named because they have elected to be taxed under subchapter S of the Internal Revenue Service code. For the most part, S corporations pay no income taxes because the income of the corporation is divided among and passed through to each of the stockholders, each of whom pays income taxes on his or her share. Both Subchapter S (Sub S) and similar Limited Liability Companies (LLCs) are not taxed at the business entity but instead pass their taxable income to their owners.

Financing Options: Debt versus Equity

Before exploring the process for securing corporate financing through equity, it is important to review the advantages and disadvantages of acquiring capital through debt. When deciding whether to raise capital by issuing debt or equity, a corporation needs to consider dilution of ownership, repayment of debt, cash obligations, budgeting impacts, administrative costs, and credit risks.

Dilution of Ownership

The most significant consideration of whether a company should seek funding using debt or equity financing is the effect on the company's financial position. Issuance of debt does not dilute the company's ownership as no additional ownership shares are issued. Issuing debt, or borrowing, creates an increase in cash, an asset, and an increase in a liability, such as notes payable or bonds payable. Because borrowing is independent of an owner's ownership interest in the business, it has no effect on stockholders' equity, and ownership of the corporation remains the same as illustrated in the accounting equation in Figure 14.2.

Assets	=	Liabilities	+	Stockholders' Equity
↑		↑		No effect

Figure 14.2 Debt Financing. Debt financing increases assets and liabilities but has no effect on stockholders' equity. (attribution: Copyright Rice University, OpenStax, under CC BY-NC-SA 4.0 license)

On the other hand, when a corporation issues stock, it is financing with equity. The same increase in cash occurs, but financing causes an increase in a capital stock account in stockholders' equity as illustrated in the accounting equation in Figure 14.3.

Assets	=	Liabilities	+	Stockholders' Equity
↑		No effect		↑

Figure 14.3 Equity Financing. Equity financing increases assets and stockholders' equity but has no effect on liabilities. (attribution: Copyright Rice University, OpenStax, under CC BY-NC-SA 4.0 license)

This increase in stockholders' equity implies that more shareholders will be allowed to vote and will participate in the distribution of profits and assets upon liquidation.

Repayment of Debt

A second concern when choosing between debt and equity financing relates to the repayment to the lender. A lender is a debt holder entitled to repayment of the original principal amount of the loan plus interest. Once the debt is paid, the corporation has no additional obligation to the lender. This allows owners of a corporation to claim a larger portion of the future earnings than would be possible if more stock were sold to investors. In addition, the interest component of the debt is an expense, which reduces the amount of income on which a company's income tax liability is calculated, thereby lowering the corporation's tax liability and the actual cost of the loan to the company.

Cash Obligations

The most obvious difference between debt and equity financing is that with debt, the principal and interest must be repaid, whereas with equity, there is no repayment requirement. The decision to declare dividends is solely up to the board of directors, so if a company has limitations on cash, it can skip or defer the declaration of dividends. When a company obtains capital through debt, it must have sufficient cash available to cover the repayment. This can put pressure on the company to meet debt obligations when cash is needed for other uses.

Budgeting

Except in the case of variable interest loans, loan and interest payments are easy to estimate for the purpose of budgeting cash payments. Loan payments do not tend to be flexible; instead the principal payment is required month after month. Moreover, interest costs incurred with debt are an additional fixed cost to the company, which raises the company's break-even point (total revenue equals total costs) as well as its cash flow demands.

Cost Differences

Issuing debt rather than equity may reduce additional administration costs associated with having additional shareholders. These costs may include the costs for informational mailings, processing and direct-depositing dividend payments, and holding shareholder meetings. Issuing debt also saves the time associated with shareholder controversies, which can often defer certain management actions until a shareholder vote can be conducted.

Risk Assessment by Creditors

Borrowing commits the borrower to comply with debt covenants that can restrict both the financing options and the opportunities that extend beyond the main business function. This can limit a company's vision or opportunities for change. For example, many debt covenants restrict a corporation's **debt-to-equity ratio**, which measures the portion of debt used by a company relative to the amount of stockholders' equity, calculated by dividing total debt by total equity.

$$\text{Debt-to-Equity Ratio} = \frac{\text{Total Debt}}{\text{Total Equity}}$$

When a company borrows additional funds, its total debt (the numerator) rises. Because there is no change in total equity, the denominator remains the same, causing the debt-to-equity ratio to increase. Because an increase in this ratio usually means that the company will have more difficulty in repaying the debt, lenders and investors consider this an added risk. Accordingly, a business is limited in the amount of debt it can carry. A debt agreement may also restrict the company from borrowing additional funds.

To increase the likelihood of debt repayment, a debt agreement often requires that a company's assets serve as collateral, or for the company's owners to guarantee repayment. Increased risks to the company from high-interest debt and high amounts of debt, particularly when the economy is unstable, include obstacles to growth and the potential for insolvency resulting from the costs of holding debt. These important considerations should be assessed prior to determining whether a company should choose debt or equity financing.

THINK IT THROUGH

Financing a Business Expansion

You are the CFO of a small corporation. The president, who is one of five shareholders, has created an innovative new product that is testing well with substantial demand. To begin manufacturing, $400,000 is needed to acquire the equipment. The corporation's balance sheet shows total assets of $2,400,000 and total liabilities of $600,000. Most of the liabilities relate to debt that carries a covenant requiring that the company maintain a debt-to-equity ratio not exceeding 0.50 times. Determine the effect that each of the two options of obtaining additional capital will have on the debt covenant. Prepare a brief memo outlining the advantages of issuing shares of common stock.

How Stocks Work

The Securities and Exchange Commission (SEC) (www.sec.gov) is a government agency that regulates large and small public corporations. Its mission is "to protect investors, maintain fair, orderly, and efficient markets, and facilitate capital formation."[3] The SEC identifies these as its five primary responsibilities:

- Inform and protect investors
- Facilitate capital information
- Enforce federal securities laws
- Regulate securities markets
- Provide data

Under the Securities Act of 1933,[4] all corporations that make their shares available for sale publicly in the United States are expected to register with the SEC. The SEC's registration requirement covers all securities—not simply shares of stock—including most tradable financial instruments. The Securities Act of 1933, also known as the "truth in securities law," aims to provide investors with the financial data they need to make informed decisions. While some companies are exempt from filing documents with the SEC, those that offer securities for sale in the U.S. and that are not exempt must file a number of forms along with financial statements audited by certified public accountants.

Private versus Public Corporations

Both private and public corporations become incorporated in the same manner through the state governmental agencies that handles incorporation. The journal entries and financial reporting are the same whether a company is a public or a private corporation. A **private corporation** is usually owned by a relatively small number of investors. Its shares are not publicly traded, and the ownership of the stock is restricted to only those allowed by the board of directors.

The SEC defines a **publicly traded company** as a company that "discloses certain business and financial information regularly to the public" and whose "securities trade on public markets."[5] A company can initially

3 U.S. Securities and Exchange Commission. "What We Do." June 10, 2013. https://www.sec.gov/Article/whatwedo.html

4 U.S. Securities and Exchange Commission. "Registration under the Securities Act of 1933." https://www.investor.gov/additional-resources/general-resources/glossary/registration-under-securities-act-1933

operate as private and later decide to "go public," while other companies go public at the point of incorporation. The process of going public refers to a company undertaking an **initial public offering (IPO)** by issuing shares of its stock to the public for the first time. After its IPO, the corporation becomes subject to public reporting requirements and its shares are frequently listed on a stock exchange.[6]

CONCEPTS IN PRACTICE

Spreading the Risk

The East India Company became the world's first publicly traded company as the result of a single factor—risk. During the 1600s, single companies felt it was too risky to sail from the European mainland to the East Indies. These islands held vast resources and trade opportunities, enticing explorers to cross the Atlantic Ocean in search of fortunes. In 1600, several shipping companies joined forces and formed "Governor and Company of Merchants of London trading with the East Indies," which was referred to as the East India Company. This arrangement allowed the shipping companies—the investors—to purchase shares in multiple companies rather than investing in a single voyage. If a single ship out of a fleet was lost at sea, investors could still generate a profit from ships that successfully completely their voyages.[7]

The Secondary Market

A corporation's shares continue to be bought and sold by the public after the initial public offering. Investors interested in purchasing shares of a corporation's stock have several options. One option is to buy stock on the **secondary market**, an organized market where previously issued stocks and bonds can be traded after they are issued. Many investors purchase through stock exchanges like the New York Stock Exchange or NASDAQ using a brokerage firm. A full-service brokerage firm provides investment advice as well as a variety of financial planning services, whereas a discount brokerage offers a reduced commission and often does not provide investment advice. Most of the **stock trading**—buying and selling of shares by investors—takes place through **brokers**, registered members of the stock exchange who buy and sell stock on behalf of others. Online access to trading has broadened the secondary market significantly over the past few decades. Alternatively, stocks can be purchased from **investment bankers**, who provide advice to companies wishing to issue new stock, purchase the stock from the company issuing the stock, and then resell the securities to the public.[8]

Marketing a Company's Stock

Once a corporation has completed the incorporation process, it can issue stock. Each share of stock sold entitles the shareholder (the investor) to a percentage of ownership in the company. Private corporations are

5 U. S. Securities and Exchange Commission. "Public Companies." https://www.investor.gov/introduction-investing/basics/how-market-works/public-companies

6 U.S. Securities and Exchange Commission. "Companies, Going Public." October 14, 2014. https://www.sec.gov/fast-answers/answers-comppublichtm.html

7 Johnson Hur. "History of The Stock Market." BeBusinessed.com. October 2016. https://bebusinessed.com/history/history-of-the-stock-market/

8 Dr. Econ. "Why Do Investment Banks Syndicate a New Securities Issue (and Related Questions)." Federal Reserve Bank of San Francisco. December 1999. https://www.frbsf.org/education/publications/doctor-econ/1999/december/investment-bank-securities-retirement-insurance/

usually owned by a small number of investors and are not traded on a public exchange. Regardless of whether the corporation is public or private, the steps to finding investors are similar:

1. Have a trusted and reliable management team. These should be experienced professionals who can guide the corporation.
2. Have a financial reporting system in place. Accurate financial reporting is key to providing potential investors with reliable information.
3. Choose an investment banker to provide advice and to assist in raising capital. Investment bankers are individuals who work in a financial institution that is primarily in the business of raising capital for corporations.
4. Write the company's story. This adds personality to the corporation. What is the mission, why it will be successful, and what sets the corporation apart?
5. Approach potential investors. Selecting the right investment bankers will be extremely helpful with this step.

Capital Stock

A company's corporate charter specifies the classes of shares and the number of shares of each class that a company can issue. There are two classes of capital stock—common stock and preferred stock. The two classes of stock enable a company to attract capital from investors with different risk preferences. Both classes of stock can be sold by either public or non-public companies; however, if a company issues only one class, it must be common stock. Companies report both common and preferred stock in the stockholders' equity section of the balance sheet.

Common Stock

A company's primary class of stock issued is **common stock**, and each share represents a partial claim to ownership or a share of the company's business. For many companies, this is the only class of stock they have authorized. Common stockholders have four basic rights.

1. Common stockholders have the right to vote on corporate matters, including the selection of corporate directors and other issues requiring the approval of owners. Each share of stock owned by an investor generally grants the investor one vote.
2. Common stockholders have the right to share in corporate net income proportionally through dividends.
3. If the corporation should have to liquidate, common stockholders have the right to share in any distribution of assets after all creditors and any preferred stockholders have been paid.
4. In some jurisdictions, common shareholders have a **preemptive right**, which allows shareholders the option to maintain their ownership percentage when new shares of stock are issued by the company. For example, suppose a company has 1,000 shares of stock issued and plans to issue 200 more shares. A shareholder who currently owns 50 shares will be given the right to buy a percentage of the new issue equal to his current percentage of ownership. His current percentage of ownership is 5%:

$$\text{Original ownership percentage} = \frac{50}{1{,}000} = 5\%$$

This shareholder will be given the right to buy 5% of the new issue, or 10 new shares.

$$\text{Number of new shares to be purchases} = 5\% \times 200 \text{ shares} = 10 \text{ shares}$$

Should the shareholder choose not to buy the shares, the company can offer the shares to other investors. The purpose of the preemptive right is to prevent new issuances of stock from reducing the ownership percentage of the current shareholders. If the shareholder in our example is not offered the opportunity to buy 5% of the additional shares (his current ownership percentage) and the new shares are sold to other investors, the shareholder's ownership percentage will drop because the total shares issued will increase.

$$\text{Total number of issues shares after the new issue} = 1{,}000 + 200 = 1{,}200 \text{ shares}$$

$$\text{New ownership percentage} = \frac{50}{1{,}200} = 4.17\%$$

The shareholder would now own only 4.17% of the corporation, compared to the previous 5%.

Preferred Stock

A company's charter may authorize more than one class of stock. **Preferred stock** has unique rights that are "preferred," or more advantageous, to shareholders than common stock. The classification of preferred stock is often a controversial area in accounting as some researchers believe preferred stock has characteristics closer to that of a stock/bond hybrid security, with characteristics of debt rather than a true equity item. For example, unlike common stockholders, preferred shareholders typically do not have voting rights; in this way, they are similar to bondholders. In addition, preferred shares do not share in the common stock dividend distributions. Instead, the "preferred" classification entitles shareholders to a dividend that is fixed (assuming sufficient dividends are declared), similar to the fixed interest rate associated with bonds and other debt items. Preferred stock also mimics debt in that preferred shareholders have a priority of dividend payments over common stockholders. While there may be characteristics of both debt and equity, preferred stock is still reported as part of stockholders' equity on the balance sheet.

Not every corporation authorizes and issues preferred stock, and there are some important characteristics that corporations should consider when deciding to issue preferred stock. The price of preferred stock typically has less volatility in the stock market. This makes it easier for companies to more reliably budget the amount of the expected capital contribution since the share price is not expected to fluctuate as freely as for common stock. For the investor, this means there is less chance of large gains or losses on the sale of preferred stock.

The Status of Shares of Stock

The corporate charter specifies the number of **authorized shares**, which is the maximum number of shares that a corporation can issue to its investors as approved by the state in which the company is incorporated. Once shares are sold to investors, they are considered **issued shares**. Shares that are issued and are currently held by investors are called **outstanding shares** because they are "out" in the hands of investors. Occasionally, a company repurchases shares from investors. While these shares are still issued, they are no longer considered to be outstanding. These repurchased shares are called **treasury stock**.

Assume that Waystar Corporation has 2,000 shares of capital stock authorized in its corporate charter. During May, Waystar issues 1,500 of these shares to investors. These investors are now called stockholders because they "hold" shares of stock. Because the other 500 authorized shares have not been issued they are considered unissued shares. Now assume that Waystar buys back 100 shares of stock from the investors who own the 1,500 shares. Only 1,400 of the issued shares are considered outstanding, because 100 shares are now held by the company as treasury shares.

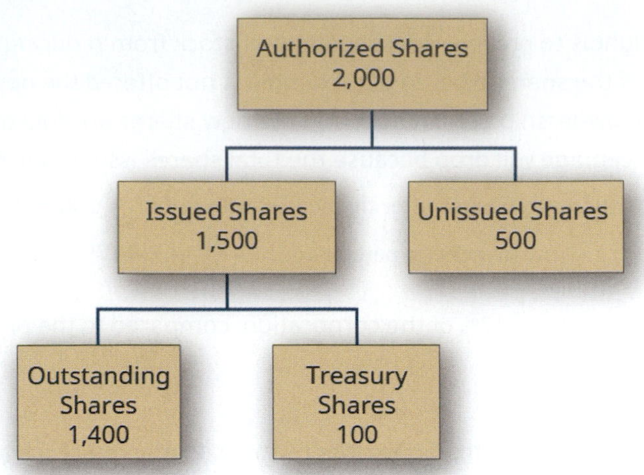

Stock Values

Two of the most important values associated with stock are market value and par value. The **market value of stock** is the price at which the stock of a public company trades on the stock market. This amount does not appear in the corporation's accounting records, nor in the company's financial statements.

Most corporate charters specify the **par value** assigned to each share of stock. This value is printed on the stock certificates and is often referred to as a face value because it is printed on the "face" of the certificate. Incorporators typically set the par value at a very small arbitrary amount because it is used internally for accounting purposes and has no economic significance. Because par value often has some legal significance, it is considered to be legal capital. In some states, par value is the minimum price at which the stock can be sold. If for some reason a share of stock with a par value of one dollar was issued for less than its par value of one dollar known as issuing at a **stock discount**, the shareholder could be held liable for the difference between the issue price and the par value if liquidation occurs and any creditors remain unpaid.

Under some state laws, corporations are sometimes allowed to issue **no-par stock**—a stock with no par value assigned. When this occurs, the company's board of directors typically assigns a **stated value** to each share of stock, which serves as the company's legal capital. Companies generally account for stated value in the accounting records in the same manner as par value. If the company's board fails to assign a stated value to no-par stock, the entire proceeds of the stock sale are treated as legal capital. A portion of the stockholders' equity section of Frontier Communications Corporation's balance sheet as of December 31, 2017 displays the reported preferred and common stock. The par value of the preferred stock is \$0.01 per share and \$0.25 per share for common stock. The legal capital of the preferred stock is \$192.50, while the legal capital of the common stock is \$19,883.[9]

FRONTIER COMMUNICATIONS CORPORATION Stockholders' Equity For the Month Ended December 31, 2017	
Preferred Stock, \$0.01 par value (50,000 authorized shares, 11.125%, Series A, 19,250 shares issued and outstanding)	\$ 192.50
Common Stock, \$0.25 par value (175,000 authorized shares, 79,532 issued, and 78,441 and 78,170 outstanding, at December 31, 2017 and 2016, respectively)	19,883.00

9 Frontier Communications Corporation. 10-K Filing. February 28, 2018. https://www.sec.gov/Archives/edgar/data/20520/000002052018000007/ftr-20171231x10k.htm#Exhibits_and_Financial_Statement_Schedul

ETHICAL CONSIDERATIONS

Shareholders, Stakeholders, and the Business Judgment Rule

Shareholders are the owners of a corporation, whereas stakeholders have an interest in the outcome of decisions of the corporation. Courts have ruled that, "A business corporation is organized and carried on primarily for the profit of the stockholders" as initially ruled in the early case *Dodge v. Ford Motor Co.*, 204 Mich. 459, 170 N.W. 668 (Mich. 1919). This early case outlined the "business judgment rule." It allows for a corporation to use its judgment in how to run the company in the best interests of the shareholders, but also allows the corporation the ability to make decisions for the benefit of the company's stakeholders. The term known as the "business judgment rule" has been expanded in numerous cases to include making decisions directly for the benefit of stakeholders, thereby allowing management to run a company in a prudent fashion. The stakeholder theories started in the *Dodge* case have been expended to allow corporations to make decisions for the corporation's benefit, including decisions that support stakeholder rights.

Prudent management of a corporation includes making decisions that support stakeholders and shareholders. A shareholder is also a stakeholder in any decision. A stakeholder is anyone with an interest in the outcome in the corporation's decision, even if the person owns no financial interest in the corporation. Corporations need to take a proactive step in managing stakeholder concerns and issues. Strategies on how to manage stakeholder needs have been developed from both a moral perspective and a risk management perspective. Both approaches allow management to understand the issues related to their stakeholders and to make decisions in the best interest of the corporation and its owners. Proper stakeholder management should allow corporations to develop profitable long-term plans that lead to greater viability of the corporation.

14.2 Analyze and Record Transactions for the Issuance and Repurchase of Stock

Chad and Rick have successfully incorporated La Cantina and are ready to issue common stock to themselves and the newly recruited investors. The proceeds will be used to open new locations. The corporate charter of the corporation indicates that the par value of its common stock is $1.50 per share. When stock is sold to investors, it is very rarely sold at par value. Most often, shares are issued at a value in excess of par. This is referred to as issuing stock at a premium. Stock with no par value that has been assigned a stated value is treated very similarly to stock with a par value.

Stock can be issued in exchange for cash, property, or services provided to the corporation. For example, an investor could give a delivery truck in exchange for a company's stock. Another investor could provide legal fees in exchange for stock. The general rule is to recognize the assets received in exchange for stock at the asset's fair market value.

Typical Common Stock Transactions

The company plans to issue most of the shares in exchange for cash, and other shares in exchange for kitchen equipment provided to the corporation by one of the new investors. Two common accounts in the equity section of the balance sheet are used when issuing stock—Common Stock and Additional Paid-in Capital from Common Stock. Common Stock consists of the par value of all shares of common stock issued. **Additional paid-in capital** from common stock consists of the excess of the proceeds received from the issuance of the stock over the stock's par value. When a company has more than one class of stock, it usually keeps a separate additional paid-in capital account for each class.

Issuing Common Stock with a Par Value in Exchange for Cash

When a company issues new stock for cash, assets increase with a debit, and equity accounts increase with a credit. To illustrate, assume that La Cantina issues 8,000 shares of common stock to investors on January 1 for cash, with the investors paying cash of $21.50 per share. The total cash to be received is $172,000.

$$8{,}000 \text{ shares} \times \$21.50 = \$172{,}000$$

The transaction causes Cash to increase (debit) for the total cash received. The Common Stock account increases (credit) with a credit for the par value of the 8,000 shares issued: 8,000 × $1.50, or $12,000. The excess received over the par value is reported in the Additional Paid-in Capital from Common Stock account. Since the shares were issued for $21.50 per share, the excess over par value per share of $20 ($21.50 – $1.50) is multiplied by the number of shares issued to arrive at the Additional Paid-in Capital from Common Stock credit.

$$(\$21.50 - \$1.50) \times 8{,}000 = \$160{,}000$$

JOURNAL			
Date	**Account**	**Debit**	**Credit**
Jan. 1	Cash	172,000	
	Common Stock		12,000
	Additional Paid-in Capital from Common Stock		160,000
	To record the issuance of $1.50 par value common stock for cash		

Issuing Common Stock with a Par Value in Exchange for Property or Services

When a company issues stock for property or services, the company increases the respective asset account with a debit and the respective equity accounts with credits. The asset received in the exchange—such as land, equipment, inventory, or any services provided to the corporation such as legal or accounting services—is recorded at the fair market value of the stock or the asset or services received, whichever is more clearly determinable.

To illustrate, assume that La Cantina issues 2,000 shares of authorized common stock in exchange for legal services provided by an attorney. The legal services have a value of $8,000 based on the amount the attorney would charge. Because La Cantina's stock is not actively traded, the asset will be valued at the more easily determinable market value of the legal services. La Cantina must recognize the market value of the legal services as an increase (debit) of $8,000 to its Legal Services Expense account. Similar to recording the stock issued for cash, the Common Stock account is increased by the par value of the issued stock, $1.50 × 2,000 shares, or $3,000. The excess of the value of the legal services over the par value of the stock appears as an increase (credit) to the Additional Paid-in Capital from Common Stock account:

$$\$8,000 - \$3,000 = \$5,000$$

JOURNAL			
Date	**Account**	**Debit**	**Credit**
Jan. 1	Legal Services Expense Common Stock Additional Paid-in Capital from Common Stock *To record the issuance of $1.50 par value common stock in exchange for legal services provided*	8,000	 3,000 5,000

Just after the issuance of both investments, the stockholders' equity account, Common Stock, reflects the total par value of the issued stock; in this case, $3,000 + $12,000, or a total of $15,000. The amounts received in excess of the par value are accumulated in the Additional Paid-in Capital from Common Stock account in the amount of $5,000 + $160,000, or $165,000. A portion of the equity section of the balance sheet just after the two stock issuances by La Cantina will reflect the Common Stock account stock issuances as shown in Figure 14.4.

LA CANTINA Partial Stockholders' Equity Section of the Balance Sheet For the Month Ended December 31, 2020	
Stockholders' Equity	
Common Stock, $1.50 par value, 20,000 shares authorized, 10,000 issued and outstanding	$ 15,000
Additional Paid-in Capital from Common Stock	165,000

Figure 14.4 Partial Stockholder's Equity for La Cantina. (attribution: Copyright Rice University, OpenStax, under CC BY-NC-SA 4.0 license)

Issuing No-Par Common Stock with a Stated Value

Not all stock has a par value specified in the company's charter. In most cases, no-par stock is assigned a stated value by the board of directors, which then becomes the legal capital value. Stock with a stated value is treated as if the stated value is a par value. Assume that La Cantina's 8,000 shares of common stock issued on June 1 for $21.50 were issued at a stated value of $1.50 rather than at a par value. The total cash to be received remains $172,000 (8,000 shares × $21.50), which is recorded as an increase (debit) to Cash. The Common Stock account increases with a credit for the stated value of the 8,000 shares issued: 8,000 × $1.50, or $12,000. The excess received over the stated value is reported in the Additional Paid-in Capital from Common Stock account at $160,000, based on the issue price of $21.50 per share less the stated value of $1.50, or $20, times the 8,000 shares issued:

$$(\$21.50 - \$1.50) \times 8,000 = \$160,000$$

The transaction looks identical except for the explanation.

JOURNAL			
Date	**Account**	**Debit**	**Credit**
Jan. 1	Cash	172,000	
	Common Stock		12,000
	Additional Paid-in Capital from Common Stock		160,000
	To record the issuance of $1.50 stated value common stock for cash		

If the 8,000 shares of La Cantina's common stock had been no-par, and no stated value had been assigned, the $172,000 would be debited to Cash, with a corresponding increase in the Common Stock account as a credit of $172,000. No entry would be made to Additional Paid-in Capital account as it is reserved for stock issue amounts above par or stated value. The entry would appear as:

JOURNAL			
Date	**Account**	**Debit**	**Credit**
Jan. 1	Cash	172,000	
	Common Stock		172,000
	To record the issuance of no-par common stock for cash		

Issuing Preferred Stock

A few months later, Chad and Rick need additional capital to develop a website to add an online presence and decide to issue all 1,000 of the company's authorized preferred shares. The 5%, $8 par value, preferred shares are sold at $45 each. The Cash account increases with a debit for $45 times 1,000 shares, or $45,000. The Preferred Stock account increases for the par value of the preferred stock, $8 times 1,000 shares, or $8,000. The excess of the issue price of $45 per share over the $8 par value, times the 1,000 shares, is credited as an increase to Additional Paid-in Capital from Preferred Stock, resulting in a credit of $37,000.

$$(\$45 - \$8) \times 1{,}000 = \$37{,}000$$

The journal entry is:

JOURNAL			
Date	**Account**	**Debit**	**Credit**
Jan. 1	Cash	45,000	
	Preferred Stock		8,000
	Additional Paid-in Capital from Preferred Stock		37,000
	To record the issuance of $8 par value preferred stock for cash		

Figure 14.5 shows what the equity section of the balance sheet will reflect after the preferred stock is issued.

LA CANTINA Partial Stockholders' Equity Section of the Balance Sheet For the Month Ended December 31, 2020	
Stockholders' Equity	
5% Preferred Stock. $8 par value, 1,000 shares authorized, 1,000 shares issued and outstanding	$ 8,000
Additional Paid-in Capital from Preferred Stock	37,000
Common Stock, $1.50 par value, 20,000 shares authorized, 10,000 shares issued and outstanding	15,000
Additional Paid-in Capital from Common Stock	165,000
Retained Earnings	xx

Figure 14.5 Partial Stockholders' Equity for La Cantina. (attribution: Copyright Rice University, OpenStax, under CC BY-NC-SA 4.0 license)

Notice that the corporation presents preferred stock before common stock in the Stockholders' Equity section of the balance sheet because preferred stock has preference over common stock in the case of liquidation. GAAP requires that each class of stock displayed in this section of the balance sheet includes several items that must be disclosed along with the respective account names. The required items to be disclosed are:

- Par or stated value
- Number of shares authorized
- Number of shares issued
- Number of shares outstanding
- If preferred stock, the dividend rate

Treasury Stock

Sometimes a corporation decides to purchase its own stock in the market. These shares are referred to as treasury stock. A company might purchase its own outstanding stock for a number of possible reasons. It can be a strategic maneuver to prevent another company from acquiring a majority interest or preventing a hostile takeover. A purchase can also create demand for the stock, which in turn raises the market price of the stock. Sometimes companies buy back shares to be used for employee stock options or profit-sharing plans.

THINK IT THROUGH

Walt Disney Buys Back Stock

The Walt Disney Company has consistently spent a large portion of its cash flows in buying back its own stock. According to *The Motley Fool*, the Walt Disney Company bought back 74 million shares in 2016 alone. Read the Motley Fool article (https://openstax.org/l/50DisneyShares) and comment on other options that Walt Disney may have had to obtain financing.

Acquiring Treasury Stock

When a company purchases treasury stock, it is reflected on the balance sheet in a contra equity account. As a contra equity account, Treasury Stock has a debit balance, rather than the normal credit balances of other equity accounts. The total cost of treasury stock reduces total equity. In substance, treasury stock implies that a company owns shares of itself. However, owning a portion of one's self is not possible. Treasury shares do not carry the basic common shareholder rights because they are not outstanding. Dividends are not paid on treasury shares, they provide no voting rights, and they do not receive a share of assets upon liquidation of the company. There are two methods possible to account for treasury stock—the cost method, which is discussed here, and the par value method, which is a more advanced accounting topic. The cost method is so named because the amount in the Treasury Stock account at any point in time represents the number of shares held in treasury times the original cost paid to acquire each treasury share.

Assume Duratech's net income for the first year was $3,100,000, and that the company has 12,500 shares of common stock issued. During May, the company's board of directors authorizes the repurchase of 800 shares of the company's own common stock as treasury stock. Each share of the company's common stock is selling for $25 on the open market on May 1, the date that Duratech purchases the stock. Duratech will pay the market price of the stock at $25 per share times the 800 shares it purchased, for a total cost of $20,000. The following journal entry is recorded for the purchase of the treasury stock under the cost method.

JOURNAL			
Date	**Account**	**Debit**	**Credit**
May 1	Treasury Stock	20,000	
	Cash		20,000
	To record the purchase of treasury stock for cash		

Even though the company is purchasing stock, there is no asset recognized for the purchase. An entity cannot own part of itself, so no asset is acquired. Immediately after the purchase, the equity section of the balance sheet (Figure 14.6) will show the total cost of the treasury shares as a deduction from total stockholders' equity.

DURATECH Partial Stockholders' Equity Section of the Balance Sheet For the Month Ended December 31, 2020	
Stockholders' Equity	
5% Preferred Stock. $8 par value, 1,000 shares authorized, 1,000 shares issued and outstanding	$ 8,000
Additional Paid-in Capital from Preferred Stock	37,000
Common Stock, $1.50 par value, 20,000 shares authorized, 10,000 shares issued, 9,200 shares outstanding	15,000
Additional Paid-in Capital from Common Stock	70,000
Retained Earnings	31,000
	161,000
Treasury Stock (800 shares) at cost	(20,000)
Total Stockholders' Equity	$141,000

Figure 14.6 Partial Stockholders' Equity Section of the Balance Sheet for Duratech. After the purchase of treasury stock, the stockholders' equity section of the balance sheet is shown as a deduction from total stockholders' equity. (attribution: Copyright Rice University, OpenStax, under CC BY-NC-SA 4.0 license)

Notice on the partial balance sheet that the number of common shares outstanding changes when treasury stock transactions occur. Initially, the company had 10,000 common shares issued and outstanding. The 800 repurchased shares are no longer outstanding, reducing the total outstanding to 9,200 shares.

CONCEPTS IN PRACTICE

Reporting Treasury Stock for Nestlé Holdings Group

Nestlé Holdings Group sells a number of major brands of food and beverages including Gerber, Häagen-Dazs, Purina, and Lean Cuisine. The company's statement of stockholders' equity shows that it began with 990 million Swiss francs (CHF) in treasury stock at the beginning of 2016. In 2017, it acquired additional shares at a cost of 3,547 million CHF, raising its total treasury stock to 4,537 million CHF at the end of 2017, primarily due to a share buy-back program.[10]

NESTLE HOLDING GROUP Consolidated Statement of Changes in Equity For the Year Ended December 31, 2017					
Millions (CHF)	**Share Capital**	**Treasury Shares**	**Paid-in Capital**	**Other**	**Total Equity**
Equity as of December 31, 2016	311	(990)	82,870	(16,210)	65,981
Profit for the year			7,538		7,538
Other comprehensive income			252		252
Dividends			(7,468)		(7,468)
Treasury Shares		(3,719)	113		(3,606)
Other		172	869	(961)	80
Equity at December 31, 2017	311	(4,537)	84,174	(17,171)	62,777

Reissuing Treasury Stock above Cost

Management typically does not hold treasury stock forever. The company can resell the treasury stock at cost, above cost, below cost, or retire it. If La Cantina reissues 100 of its treasury shares at cost ($25 per share) on July 3, a reversal of the original purchase for the 100 shares is recorded. This has the effect of increasing an asset, Cash, with a debit, and decreasing the Treasury Stock account with a credit. The original cost paid for each treasury share, $25, is multiplied by the 100 shares to be resold, or $2,500. The journal entry to record this sale of the treasury shares at cost is:

JOURNAL			
Date	**Account**	**Debit**	**Credit**
July 3	Cash	2,500	
	Treasury Stock		2,500
	To record the sale of 100 shares of treasury stock at cost		

If the treasury stock is resold at a price higher than its original purchase price, the company debits the Cash account for the amount of cash proceeds, reduces the Treasury Stock account with a credit for the cost of the

10 Nestlé. "Annual Report 2017." 2017. https://www.nestle.com/investors/annual-report

treasury shares being sold, and credits the Paid-in Capital from Treasury Stock account for the difference. Even though the difference—the selling price less the cost—looks like a gain, it is treated as additional capital because gains and losses only result from the disposition of economic resources (assets). Treasury Stock is not an asset. Assume that on August 1, La Cantina sells another 100 shares of its treasury stock, but this time the selling price is $28 per share. The Cash Account is increased by the selling price, $28 per share times the number of shares resold, 100, for a total debit to Cash of $2,800. The Treasury Stock account decreases by the cost of the 100 shares sold, 100 × $25 per share, for a total credit of $2,500, just as it did in the sale at cost. The difference is recorded as a credit of $300 to Additional Paid-in Capital from Treasury Stock.

JOURNAL			
Date	**Account**	**Debit**	**Credit**
Aug. 1	Cash Treasury Stock Additional Paid-in Capital from Treasury Stock *To record the sale of 100 shares of treasury stock above cost*	2,800	 2,500 300

Reissuing Treasury Stock Below Cost

If the treasury stock is reissued at a price below cost, the account used for the difference between the cash received from the resale and the original cost of the treasury stock depends on the balance in the Paid-in Capital from Treasury Stock account. Any balance that exists in this account will be a credit. The transaction will require a debit to the Paid-in Capital from Treasury Stock account to the extent of the balance. If the transaction requires a debit greater than the balance in the Paid-in Capital account, any additional difference between the cost of the treasury stock and its selling price is recorded as a reduction of the Retained Earnings account as a debit. If there is no balance in the Additional Paid-in Capital from Treasury Stock account, the entire debit will reduce retained earnings.

Assume that on October 9, La Cantina sells another 100 shares of its treasury stock, but this time at $23 per share. Cash is increased for the selling price, $23 per share times the number of shares resold, 100, for a total debit to Cash of $2,300. The Treasury Stock account decreases by the cost of the 100 shares sold, 100 × $25 per share, for a total credit of $2,500. The difference is recorded as a debit of $200 to the Additional Paid-in Capital from Treasury Stock account. Notice that the balance in this account from the August 1 transaction was $300, which was sufficient to offset the $200 debit. The transaction is recorded as:

JOURNAL			
Date	**Account**	**Debit**	**Credit**
Oct. 9	Cash Additional Paid-in Capital from Treasury Stock Treasury Stock *To record the sale of 100 shares of treasury stock below cost*	2,300 200	 2,500

Treasury stock transactions have no effect on the number of shares authorized or issued. Because shares held in treasury are not outstanding, each treasury stock transaction will impact the number of shares outstanding. A corporation may also purchase its own stock and retire it. Retired stock reduces the number of shares issued. When stock is repurchased for retirement, the stock must be removed from the accounts so that it is not reported on the balance sheet. The balance sheet will appear as if the stock was never issued in the first place.

YOUR TURN

Understanding Stockholders' Equity

Wilson Enterprises reports the following stockholders' equity:

WILSON ENTERPRISES, INC. Stockholders' Equity Section of the Balance Sheet For the Month Ended December 31, 2020	
Stockholders' Equity	
Preferred Stock, $100 par value, 10,000 shares authorized, 10,000 shares issued and outstanding	$ 1,000,000
Common Stock, $1 par value, 2,000,000 shares authorized, 1,200,000 shares issued, and 1,180,000 shares outstanding	1,200,000
Additional Paid-in Capital	16,800,000
Retained Earnings	3,670,000
	22,670,000
Treasury Stock (20,000 shares)	(240,000)
Total Stockholders' Equity	$22,430,000

Figure 14.7 Wilson Enterprises, Inc., Stockholders' Equity Section of the Balance Sheet, For the Month Ended December 31, 2020. (attribution: Copyright Rice University, OpenStax, under CC BY-NC-SA 4.0 license)

Based on the partial balance sheet presented, answer the following questions:

A. At what price was each share of treasury stock purchased?
B. What is reflected in the additional paid-in capital account?
C. Why is there a difference between the common stock shares issued and the shares outstanding?

Solution

A. $240,000 ÷ 20,000 = $12 per share. B. The difference between the market price and the par value when the stock was issued. C. Treasury stock.

14.3 Record Transactions and the Effects on Financial Statements for Cash Dividends, Property Dividends, Stock Dividends, and Stock Splits

Do you remember playing the board game Monopoly when you were younger? If you landed on the Chance space, you picked a card. The Chance card may have paid a $50 dividend. At the time, you probably were just excited for the additional funds.

Figure 14.8 Chance Card. A Chance card from a Monopoly game indicates that the bank pays you a dividend of $50. (credit: modification of "Monopoly Chance Card" by Kerry Ceszyk/Flickr, CC BY 4.0)

For corporations, there are several reasons to consider sharing some of their earnings with investors in the form of dividends. Many investors view a dividend payment as a sign of a company's financial health and are more likely to purchase its stock. In addition, corporations use dividends as a marketing tool to remind investors that their stock is a profit generator.

This section explains the three types of dividends—cash dividends, property dividends, and stock dividends—along with stock splits, showing the journal entries involved and the reason why companies declare and pay dividends.

The Nature and Purposes of Dividends

Stock investors are typically driven by two factors—a desire to earn income in the form of dividends and a desire to benefit from the growth in the value of their investment. Members of a corporation's board of directors understand the need to provide investors with a periodic return, and as a result, often declare dividends up to four times per year. However, companies can declare dividends whenever they want and are not limited in the number of annual declarations. Dividends are a distribution of a corporation's earnings. They are not considered expenses, and they are not reported on the income statement. They are a distribution of the net income of a company and are not a cost of business operations.

CONCEPTS IN PRACTICE

So Many Dividends

The declaration and payment of dividends varies among companies. In December 2017 alone, 4,506 U.S. companies declared either cash, stock, or property dividends—the largest number of declarations since 2004.[11] It is likely that these companies waited to declare dividends until after financial statements were prepared, so that the board and other executives involved in the process were able to provide estimates of the 2017 earnings.

Some companies choose not to pay dividends and instead reinvest all of their earnings back into the company. One common scenario for situation occurs when a company experiencing rapid growth. The company may

11 Ironman at Political Calculations. "Dividends by the Numbers through January 2018." Seeking Alpha. February 9, 2018. https://seekingalpha.com/article/4145079-dividends-numbers-january-2018

want to invest all their retained earnings to support and continue that growth. Another scenario is a mature business that believes retaining its earnings is more likely to result in an increased market value and stock price. In other instances, a business may want to use its earnings to purchase new assets or branch out into new areas. Most companies attempt **dividend smoothing**, the practice of paying dividends that are relatively equal period after period, even when earnings fluctuate. In exceptional circumstances, some corporations pay a **special dividend**, which is a one-time extra distribution of corporate earnings. A special dividend usually stems from a period of extraordinary earnings or a special transaction, such as the sale of a division. Some companies, such as Costco Wholesale Corporation, pay recurring dividends and periodically offer a special dividend. While Costco's regular quarterly dividend is $0.57 per share, the company issued a $7.00 per share cash dividend in 2017.[12] Companies that have both common and preferred stock must consider the characteristics of each class of stock.

Note that dividends are distributed or paid only to shares of stock that are outstanding. Treasury shares are not outstanding, so no dividends are declared or distributed for these shares. Regardless of the type of dividend, the declaration always causes a decrease in the retained earnings account.

Dividend Dates

A company's board of directors has the power to formally vote to declare dividends. The **date of declaration** is the date on which the dividends become a legal liability, the date on which the board of directors votes to distribute the dividends. Cash and property dividends become liabilities on the declaration date because they represent a formal obligation to distribute economic resources (assets) to stockholders. On the other hand, stock dividends distribute additional shares of stock, and because stock is part of equity and not an asset, stock dividends do not become liabilities when declared.

At the time dividends are declared, the board establishes a date of record and a date of payment. The **date of record** establishes who is entitled to receive a dividend; stockholders who own stock on the date of record are entitled to receive a dividend even if they sell it prior to the date of payment. Investors who purchase shares after the date of record but before the payment date are not entitled to receive dividends since they did not own the stock on the date of record. These shares are said to be sold **ex dividend**. The **date of payment** is the date that payment is issued to the investor for the amount of the dividend declared.

Cash Dividends

Cash dividends are corporate earnings that companies pass along to their shareholders. To pay a cash dividend, the corporation must meet two criteria. First, there must be sufficient cash on hand to fulfill the dividend payment. Second, the company must have sufficient retained earnings; that is, it must have enough residual assets to cover the dividend such that the Retained Earnings account does not become a negative (debit) amount upon declaration. On the day the board of directors votes to declare a cash dividend, a journal entry is required to record the declaration as a liability.

Accounting for Cash Dividends When Only Common Stock Is Issued

Small private companies like La Cantina often have only one class of stock issued, common stock. Assume that

12 Jing Pan. "Will Costco Wholesale Corporation Pay a Special Dividend in 2018?" Income Investors. May 9, 2018. https://www.incomeinvestors.com/will-costco-wholesale-corporation-pay-special-dividend-2018/38865/

on December 16, La Cantina's board of directors declares a $0.50 per share dividend on common stock. As of the date of declaration, the company has 10,000 shares of common stock issued and holds 800 shares as treasury stock. The total cash dividend to be paid is based on the number of shares outstanding, which is the total shares issued less those in treasury. Outstanding shares are 10,000 – 800, or 9,200 shares. The cash dividend is:

$$9{,}200 \text{ shares} \times \$0.50 = \$4{,}600$$

The journal entry to record the declaration of the cash dividends involves a decrease (debit) to Retained Earnings (a stockholders' equity account) and an increase (credit) to Cash Dividends Payable (a liability account).

JOURNAL			
Date	**Account**	**Debit**	**Credit**
Oct. 9	Retained Earnings	4,600	
	Cash Dividends Payable		4,600
	To record the declaration of a cash dividend		

While a few companies may use a temporary account, Dividends Declared, rather than Retained Earnings, most companies debit Retained Earnings directly. Ultimately, any dividends declared cause a decrease to Retained Earnings.

The second significant dividend date is the date of record. The date of record determines which shareholders will receive the dividends. There is no journal entry recorded; the company creates a list of the stockholders that will receive dividends.

The date of payment is the third important date related to dividends. This is the date that dividend payments are prepared and sent to shareholders who owned stock on the date of record. The related journal entry is a fulfillment of the obligation established on the declaration date; it reduces the Cash Dividends Payable account (with a debit) and the Cash account (with a credit).

JOURNAL			
Date	**Account**	**Debit**	**Credit**
Oct. 15	Cash Dividends Payable	4,600	
	Cash		4,600
	To record the payment of a cash dividend		

Property Dividends

A **property dividend** occurs when a company declares and distributes assets other than cash. The dividend typically involves either the distribution of shares of another company that the issuing corporation owns (one of its assets) or a distribution of inventory. For example, Walt Disney Company may choose to distribute tickets to visit its theme parks. Anheuser-Busch InBev, the company that owns the Budweiser and Michelob brands, may choose to distribute a case of beer to each shareholder. A property dividend may be declared when a company wants to reward its investors but doesn't have the cash to distribute, or if it needs to hold onto its existing cash for other investments. Property dividends are not as common as cash or stock dividends. They are recorded at the fair market value of the asset being distributed. To illustrate accounting for a property dividend, assume that Duratech Corporation has 60,000 shares of $0.50 par value common stock outstanding at the end of its second year of operations, and the company's board of directors declares a property dividend consisting of a package of soft drinks that it produces to each holder of common stock. The retail value of each case is $3.50. The amount of the dividend is calculated by multiplying the number of shares by the market value of each package:

$$60{,}000 \text{ shares} \times \$3.50 = \$210{,}000$$

The declaration to record the property dividend is a decrease (debit) to Retained Earnings for the value of the dividend and an increase (credit) to Property Dividends Payable for the $210,000.

JOURNAL			
Date	**Account**	**Debit**	**Credit**
Dec. 31	Retained Earnings Property Dividends Payable *To record the declaration of a property dividend*	210,000	 210,000

The journal entry to distribute the soft drinks on January 14 decreases both the Property Dividends Payable account (debit) and the Cash account (credit).

JOURNAL			
Date	**Account**	**Debit**	**Credit**
Jan. 14	Property Dividends Payable Inventory *To record the distribution of a property dividend*	210,000	 210,000

Comparing Small Stock Dividends, Large Stock Dividends, and Stock Splits

Companies that do not want to issue cash or property dividends but still want to provide some benefit to shareholders may choose between small stock dividends, large stock dividends, and stock splits. Both small and large stock dividends occur when a company distributes additional shares of stock to existing stockholders.

There is no change in total assets, total liabilities, or total stockholders' equity when a small stock dividend, a large stock dividend, or a stock split occurs. Both types of stock dividends impact the accounts in stockholders' equity. A stock split causes no change in any of the accounts within stockholders' equity. The impact on the financial statement usually does not drive the decision to choose between one of the stock dividend types or a stock split. Instead, the decision is typically based on its effect on the market. Large stock dividends and stock splits are done in an attempt to lower the market price of the stock so that it is more affordable to potential investors. A small stock dividend is viewed by investors as a distribution of the company's earnings. Both small and large stock dividends cause an increase in common stock and a decrease to retained earnings. This is a method of capitalizing (increasing stock) a portion of the company's earnings (retained earnings).

Stock Dividends

Some companies issue shares of stock as a dividend rather than cash or property. This often occurs when the company has insufficient cash but wants to keep its investors happy. When a company issues a **stock dividend**, it distributes additional shares of stock to existing shareholders. These shareholders do not have to pay income taxes on stock dividends when they receive them; instead, they are taxed when the investor sells them in the future.

A stock dividend distributes shares so that after the distribution, all stockholders have the exact same percentage of ownership that they held prior to the dividend. There are two types of stock dividends—small stock dividends and large stock dividends. The key difference is that small dividends are recorded at market value and large dividends are recorded at the stated or par value.

Small Stock Dividends

A **small stock dividend** occurs when a stock dividend distribution is less than 25% of the total outstanding shares based on the shares outstanding prior to the dividend distribution. To illustrate, assume that Duratech Corporation has 60,000 shares of $0.50 par value common stock outstanding at the end of its second year of operations. Duratech's board of directors declares a 5% stock dividend on the last day of the year, and the market value of each share of stock on the same day was $9. Figure 14.9 shows the stockholders' equity section of Duratech's balance sheet just prior to the stock declaration.

DURATECH Stockholders' Equity Section of the Balance Sheet For the Month Ended December 31, 2020	
Stockholders' Equity	
Common Stock, $0.50 par value, 100,000 shares authorized, 60,000 shares issued and outstanding	$ 30,000
Additional Paid-in Capital	44,000
Retained Earnings	51,000
Total Stockholders' Equity	$125,000

Figure 14.9 Stockholders' Equity for Duratech. (attribution: Copyright Rice University, OpenStax, under CC BY-NC-SA 4.0 license)

The 5% common stock dividend will require the distribution of 60,000 shares times 5%, or 3,000 additional shares of stock. An investor who owns 100 shares will receive 5 shares in the dividend distribution (5% × 100 shares). The journal entry to record the stock dividend declaration requires a decrease (debit) to Retained Earnings for the market value of the shares to be distributed: 3,000 shares × $9, or $27,000. An increase (credit) to the Common Stock Dividends Distributable is recorded for the par value of the stock to be distributed: 3,000 × $0.50, or $1,500. The excess of the market value over the par value is reported as an increase (credit) to the Additional Paid-in Capital from Common Stock account in the amount of $25,500.

JOURNAL			
Date	**Account**	**Debit**	**Credit**
Dec. 31	Retained Earnings	27,000	
	Common Stock Dividend Distributable		1,500
	Additional Paid-in Capital from Common Stock		25,500
	To record the declaration of a 5% stock dividend		

If the company prepares a balance sheet prior to distributing the stock dividend, the Common Stock Dividend Distributable account is reported in the equity section of the balance sheet beneath the Common Stock account. The journal entry to record the stock dividend distribution requires a decrease (debit) to Common Stock Dividend Distributable to remove the distributable amount from that account, $1,500, and an increase (credit) to Common Stock for the same par value amount.

JOURNAL			
Date	**Account**	**Debit**	**Credit**
Jan. 7	Common Stock Dividend Distributable Common Stock *To record the distribution of a 5% stock dividend*	1,500	 1,500

To see the effects on the balance sheet, it is helpful to compare the stockholders' equity section of the balance sheet before and after the small stock dividend.

DURATECH Stockholders' Equity Section of the Balance Sheet For the Month Ended December 31, 2020			
Stockholders' Equity	**Before the Stock Dividend**	**Stock Dividend Effect**	**After the Stock Dividend**
Common Stock, $0.50 par value	$ 30,000	$ 1,500	$ 31,500
Additional Paid-in Capital	44,000	25,500	69,500
Retained Earnings	51,000	(27,000)	24,000
Total Stockholders' Equity	$125,000	$ 0	$125,000

After the distribution, the total stockholders' equity remains the same as it was prior to the distribution. The amounts within the accounts are merely shifted from the earned capital account (Retained Earnings) to the contributed capital accounts (Common Stock and Additional Paid-in Capital). However, the number of shares outstanding has changed. Prior to the distribution, the company had 60,000 shares outstanding. Just after the distribution, there are 63,000 outstanding. The difference is the 3,000 additional shares of the stock dividend distribution. The company still has the same total value of assets, so its value does not change at the time a stock distribution occurs. The increase in the number of outstanding shares does not dilute the value of the shares held by the existing shareholders. The market value of the original shares plus the newly issued shares is the same as the market value of the original shares before the stock dividend. For example, assume an investor owns 200 shares with a market value of $10 each for a total market value of $2,000. She receives 10 shares as a stock dividend from the company. She now has 210 shares with a total market value of $2,000. Each share now has a theoretical market value of about $9.52.

Large Stock Dividends

A **large stock dividend** occurs when a distribution of stock to existing shareholders is greater than 25% of the total outstanding shares just before the distribution. The accounting for large stock dividends differs from that of small stock dividends because a large dividend impacts the stock's market value per share. While there may be a subsequent change in the market price of the stock after a small dividend, it is not as abrupt as that with a large dividend.

To illustrate, assume that Duratech Corporation's balance sheet at the end of its second year of operations shows the following in the stockholders' equity section prior to the declaration of a large stock dividend.

DURATECH Stockholders' Equity Section of the Balance Sheet For the Month Ended December 31, 2020	
Stockholders' Equity	
Common Stock, $0.50 par value, 100,000 shares authorized, 60,000 shares issued and outstanding	$ 30,000
Additional Paid-in Capital	44,000
Retained Earnings	51,000
Total Stockholders' Equity	$125,000

Also assume that Duratech's board of directors declares a 30% stock dividend on the last day of the year, when the market value of each share of stock was $9. The 30% stock dividend will require the distribution of 60,000 shares times 30%, or 18,000 additional shares of stock. An investor who owns 100 shares will receive 30 shares in the dividend distribution (30% × 100 shares). The journal entry to record the stock dividend declaration requires a decrease (debit) to Retained Earnings and an increase (credit) to Common Stock Dividends Distributable for the par or stated value of the shares to be distributed: 18,000 shares × $0.50, or $9,000. The journal entry is:

JOURNAL			
Date	**Account**	**Debit**	**Credit**
Dec. 31	Retained Earnings	9,000	
	Common Stock Dividends Distributable		9,000
	To record the declaration of a 30% stock dividend		

The subsequent distribution will reduce the Common Stock Dividends Distributable account with a debit and increase the Common Stock account with a credit for the $9,000.

JOURNAL			
Date	**Account**	**Debit**	**Credit**
Dec. 31	Common Stock Dividends Distributable	9,000	
	Common Stock		9,000
	To record the distribution of a 30% stock dividend		

There is no consideration of the market value in the accounting records for a large stock dividend because the number of shares issued in a large dividend is large enough to impact the market; as such, it causes an immediate reduction of the market price of the company's stock.

In comparing the stockholders' equity section of the balance sheet before and after the large stock dividend, we can see that the total stockholders' equity is the same before and after the stock dividend, just as it was with a small dividend (Figure 14.10).

DURATECH Stockholders' Equity Section of the Balance Sheet For the Month Ended December 31, 2020			
Stockholders' Equity	Before the Stock Dividend	Stock Dividend Effect	After the Stock Dividend
Common Stock, $0.50 par value	$ 30,000	$ 9,000	$ 39,000
Additional Paid-in Capital	44,000		44,000
Retained Earnings	51,000	(9,000)	42,000
Total Stockholders' Equity	$125,000	$ 0	$125,000

Figure 14.10 Stockholders' Equity Section of the Balance Sheet for Duratech. (attribution: Copyright Rice University, OpenStax, under CC BY-NC-SA 4.0 license)

Similar to distribution of a small dividend, the amounts within the accounts are shifted from the earned capital account (Retained Earnings) to the contributed capital account (Common Stock) though in different amounts. The number of shares outstanding has increased from the 60,000 shares prior to the distribution, to the 78,000 outstanding shares after the distribution. The difference is the 18,000 additional shares in the stock dividend distribution. No change to the company's assets occurred; however, the potential subsequent increase in market value of the company's stock will increase the investor's perception of the value of the company.

Stock Splits

A traditional **stock split** occurs when a company's board of directors issue new shares to existing shareholders in place of the old shares by increasing the number of shares and reducing the par value of each share. For example, in a 2-for-1 stock split, two shares of stock are distributed for each share held by a shareholder. From a practical perspective, shareholders return the old shares and receive two shares for each share they previously owned. The new shares have half the par value of the original shares, but now the shareholder owns twice as many. If a 5-for-1 split occurs, shareholders receive 5 new shares for each of the original shares they owned, and the new par value results in one-fifth of the original par value per share.

While a company technically has no control over its common stock price, a stock's market value is often affected by a stock split. When a split occurs, the market value per share is reduced to balance the increase in the number of outstanding shares. In a 2-for-1 split, for example, the value per share typically will be reduced by half. As such, although the number of outstanding shares and the price change, the total market value remains constant. If you buy a candy bar for $1 and cut it in half, each half is now worth $0.50. The total value of the candy does not increase just because there are more pieces.

A stock split is much like a large stock dividend in that both are large enough to cause a change in the market price of the stock. Additionally, the split indicates that share value has been increasing, suggesting growth is likely to continue and result in further increase in demand and value. Companies often make the decision to split stock when the stock price has increased enough to be out of line with competitors, and the business wants to continue to offer shares at an attractive price for small investors.

CONCEPTS IN PRACTICE

Samsung Boasts a 50-to-1 Stock Split

In May of 2018, Samsung Electronics[13] had a 50-to-1 stock split in an attempt to make it easier for investors to buy its stock. Samsung's market price of each share prior to the split was an incredible 2.65 won ("won" is a Japanese currency), or $2,467.48. Buying one share of stock at this price is rather expensive for most people. As might be expected, even after a slight drop in trading activity just after the split announcement, the reduced market price of the stock generated a significant increase to investors by making the price per share less expensive. The split caused the price to drop to 0.053 won, or $49.35 per share. This made the stock more accessible to potential investors who were previously unable to afford a share at $2,467.

A **reverse stock split** occurs when a company attempts to increase the market price per share by reducing the number of shares of stock. For example, a 1-for-3 stock split is called a reverse split since it reduces the number of shares of stock outstanding by two-thirds and triples the par or stated value per share. The effect on the market is to increase the market value per share. A primary motivator of companies invoking reverse splits is to avoid being delisted and taken off a stock exchange for failure to maintain the exchange's minimum share price.

Accounting for stock splits is quite simple. No journal entry is recorded for a stock split. Instead, the company prepares a memo entry in its journal that indicates the nature of the stock split and indicates the new par value. The balance sheet will reflect the new par value and the new number of shares authorized, issued, and outstanding after the stock split. To illustrate, assume that Duratech's board of directors declares a 4-for-1 common stock split on its $0.50 par value stock. Just before the split, the company has 60,000 shares of common stock outstanding, and its stock was selling at $24 per share. The split causes the number of shares outstanding to increase by four times to 240,000 shares (4 × 60,000), and the par value to decline to one-fourth of its original value, to $0.125 per share ($0.50 ÷ 4). No change occurs to the dollar amount of any general ledger account.

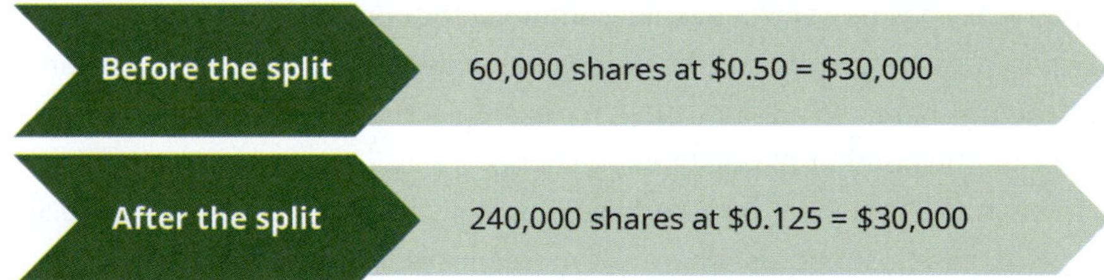

The split typically causes the market price of stock to decline immediately to one-fourth of the original value—from the $24 per share pre-split price to approximately $6 per share post-split ($24 ÷ 4), because the total value of the company did not change as a result of the split. The total stockholders' equity on the company's balance sheet before and after the split remain the same.

13 Joyce Lee. "Trading in Samsung Electronics Shares Surges after Stock Split." *Reuters*. May 3, 2018. https://www.reuters.com/article/us-samsung-elec-stocks/samsung-elec-shares-open-at-53000-won-each-after-501-stock-split-idUSKBN1I500B

DURATECH Stockholders' Equity Section of the Balance Sheet For the Month Ended December 31, 2020			
Stockholders' Equity	**Before the Stock Split**	**Stock Split Effect**	**After the Stock Split**
Common Stock	$ 30,000	$ 0	$ 30,000
Additional Paid-in Capital	44,000		44,000
Retained Earnings	51,000	0	51,000
Total Stockholders' Equity	$125,000	$ 0	$125,000

THINK IT THROUGH

Accounting for a Stock Split

You have just obtained your MBA and obtained your dream job with a large corporation as a manager trainee in the corporate accounting department. Your employer plans to offer a 3-for-2 stock split. Briefly indicate the accounting entries necessary to recognize the split in the company's accounting records and the effect the split will have on the company's balance sheet.

YOUR TURN

Dividend Accounting

Cynadyne, Inc.'s has 4,000 shares of $0.20 par value common stock authorized, 2,800 issued, and 400 shares held in treasury at the end of its first year of operations. On May 1, the company declared a $1 per share cash dividend, with a date of record on May 12, to be paid on May 25. What journal entries will be prepared to record the dividends?

Solution

A journal entry for the dividend declaration and a journal entry for the cash payout:

To record the declaration:

May 1	Retained Earnings Dividends Payable *To record board of directors authorizing cash dividends*	2,400	2,400

Date of declaration, May 12, no entry.

To record the payment:

May 25	Dividends Payable Cash *To record cash payout of dividends*	2,400	2,400

THINK IT THROUGH

Recording Stock Transactions

In your first year of operations the following transactions occur for a company:

- Net profit for the year is $16,000
- 100 shares of $1 par value common stock are issued for $32 per share
- The company purchases 10 shares at $35 per share
- The company pays a cash dividend of $1.50 per share

Prepare journal entries for the above transactions and provide the balance in the following accounts: Common Stock, Dividends, Paid-in Capital, Retained Earnings, and Treasury Stock.

14.4 Compare and Contrast Owners' Equity versus Retained Earnings

Owners' equity represents the business owners' share of the company. It is often referred to as net worth or net assets in the financial world and as stockholders' equity or shareholders' equity when discussing businesses operations of corporations. From a practical perspective, it represents everything a company owns (the company's assets) minus all the company owes (its liabilities). While "owners' equity" is used for all three types of business organizations (corporations, partnerships, and sole proprietorships), only sole proprietorships name the balance sheet account "owner's equity" as the entire equity of the company belongs to the sole owner. Partnerships (to be covered more thoroughly in Partnership Accounting) often label this section of their balance sheet as "partners' equity." All three forms of business utilize different accounting for the respective equity transactions and use different equity accounts, but they all rely on the same relationship represented by the basic accounting equation (Figure 14.11).

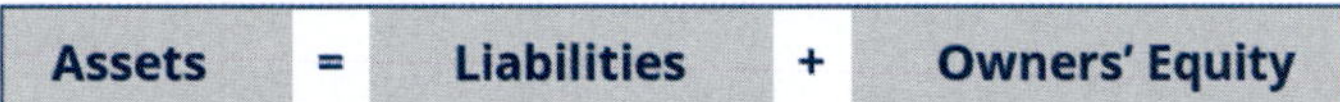

Figure 14.11 Accounting Equation. The relationship among assets, liabilities, and equity is represented in the accounting equation. (attribution: Copyright Rice University, OpenStax, under CC BY-NC-SA 4.0 license)

Three Forms of Business Ownership

Businesses operate in one of three forms—sole proprietorships, partnerships, or corporations. Sole proprietorships utilize a single account in owners' equity in which the owner's investments and net income of the company are accumulated and distributions to the owner are withdrawn. Partnerships utilize a separate capital account for each partner, with each capital account holding the respective partner's investments and the partner's respective share of net income, with reductions for the distributions to the respective partners. Corporations differ from sole proprietorships and partnerships in that their operations are more complex, often due to size. Unlike these other entity forms, owners of a corporation usually change continuously.

The stockholders' equity section of the balance sheet for corporations contains two primary categories of accounts. The first is paid-in capital, or **contributed capital**—consisting of amounts paid in by owners. The second category is **earned capital**, consisting of amounts earned by the corporation as part of business operations. On the balance sheet, retained earnings is a key component of the earned capital section, while the stock accounts such as common stock, preferred stock, and additional paid-in capital are the primary components of the contributed capital section.

CONCEPTS IN PRACTICE

Contributed Capital and Earned Capital

The stockholders' equity section of Cracker Barrel Old Country Store, Inc.'s consolidated balance sheet as of July 28, 2017, and July 29, 2016, shows the company's contributed capital and the earned capital accounts.[14]

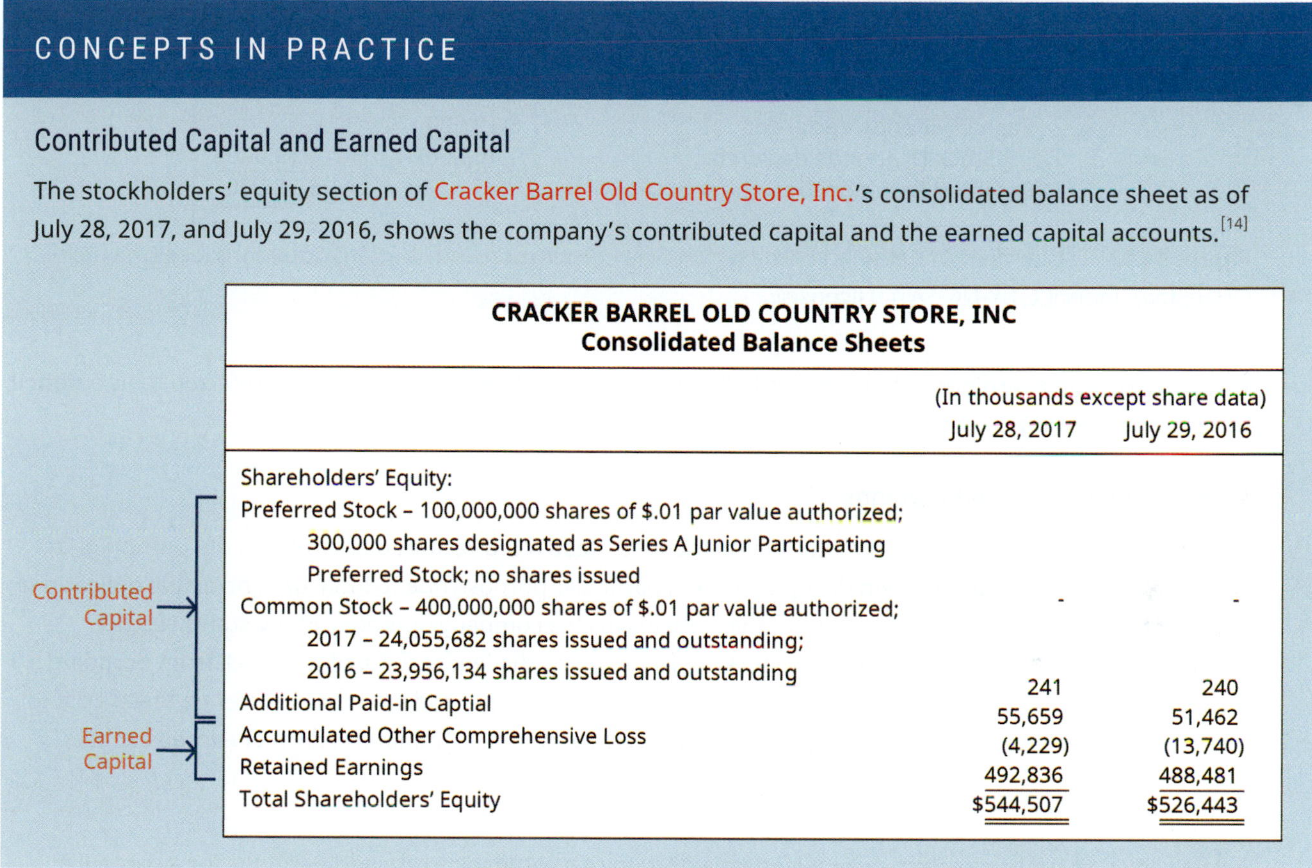

CRACKER BARREL OLD COUNTRY STORE, INC
Consolidated Balance Sheets

	(In thousands except share data) July 28, 2017	July 29, 2016
Shareholders' Equity:		
Preferred Stock – 100,000,000 shares of $.01 par value authorized; 300,000 shares designated as Series A Junior Participating Preferred Stock; no shares issued	-	-
Common Stock – 400,000,000 shares of $.01 par value authorized; 2017 – 24,055,682 shares issued and outstanding; 2016 – 23,956,134 shares issued and outstanding	241	240
Additional Paid-in Captial	55,659	51,462
Accumulated Other Comprehensive Loss	(4,229)	(13,740)
Retained Earnings	492,836	488,481
Total Shareholders' Equity	$544,507	$526,443

Characteristics and Functions of the Retained Earnings Account

Retained earnings is the primary component of a company's earned capital. It generally consists of the cumulative net income minus any cumulative losses less dividends declared. A basic statement of retained earnings is referred to as an analysis of retained earnings because it shows the changes in the retained earnings account during the period. A company preparing a full set of financial statements may choose between preparing a statement of retained earnings, if the activity in its stock accounts is negligible, or a statement of stockholders' equity, for corporations with activity in their stock accounts. A statement of retained earnings for Clay Corporation for its second year of operations (Figure 14.12) shows the company generated more net income than the amount of dividends it declared.

14 Cracker Barrel. *Cracker Barrel Old Country Store Annual Report 2017.* September 22, 2017. http://investor.crackerbarrel.com/static-files/c05f90b8-1214-4f50-8508-d9a70301f51f

CLAY CORPORATION Statement of Retained Earnings For the Year Ended December 31, 2020		
Retained Earnings, January 1, 2020		$ 24,000
Net Income		33,000
		57,000
Cash Dividends declared	$(12,500)	
Stock Dividends declared	(6,500)	(19,000)
Retained Earnings, December 31, 2020		$ 38,000

Figure 14.12 Statement of Retained Earnings for Clay Corporation. (attribution: Copyright Rice University, OpenStax, under CC BY-NC-SA 4.0 license)

When the retained earnings balance drops below zero, this negative or debit balance is referred to as a **deficit in retained earnings**.

Restrictions to Retained Earnings

Retained earnings is often subject to certain restrictions. **Restricted retained earnings** is the portion of a company's earnings that has been designated for a particular purpose due to legal or contractual obligations. Some of the restrictions reflect the laws of the state in which a company operates. Many states restrict retained earnings by the cost of treasury stock, which prevents the legal capital of the stock from dropping below zero. Other restrictions are contractual, such as debt covenants and loan arrangements; these exist to protect creditors, often limiting the payment of dividends to maintain a minimum level of earned capital.

Appropriations of Retained Earnings

A company's board of directors may designate a portion of a company's retained earnings for a particular purpose such as future expansion, special projects, or as part of a company's risk management plan. The amount designated for a particular purpose is classified as **appropriated retained earnings**.

There are two options in accounting for appropriated retained earnings, both of which allow the corporation to inform the financial statement users of the company's future plans. The first accounting option is to make no journal entry and disclose the amount of appropriation in the notes to the financial statement. The second option is to record a journal entry that transfers part of the unappropriated retained earnings into an Appropriated Retained Earnings account. To illustrate, assume that on March 3, Clay Corporation's board of directors appropriates $12,000 of its retained earnings for future expansion. The company's retained earnings account is first renamed as Unappropriated Retained Earnings. The journal entry decreases the Unappropriated Retained Earnings account with a debit and increases the Appropriated Retained Earnings account with a credit for $12,000.

JOURNAL			
Date	Account	Debit	Credit
Mar. 3	Unappropriated Retained Earnings	12,000	
	Appropriated Retained Earnings		12,000
	To record the appropriation of retained earnings		

The company will report the appropriate retained earnings in the earned capital section of its balance sheet. It should be noted that an appropriation does not set aside funds nor designate an income statement, asset, or liability effect for the appropriated amount. The appropriation simply designates a portion of the company's retained earnings for a specific purpose, while signaling that the earnings are being retained in the company and are not available for dividend distributions.

Statement of Stockholders' Equity

The statement of retained earnings is a subsection of the statement of stockholders' equity. While the retained earnings statement shows the changes between the beginning and ending balances of the retained earnings account during the period, the **statement of stockholders' equity** provides the changes between the beginning and ending balances of each of the stockholders' equity accounts, including retained earnings. The format typically displays a separate column for each stockholders' equity account, as shown for Clay Corporation in Figure 14.13. The key events that occurred during the year—including net income, stock issuances, and dividends—are listed vertically. The stockholders' equity section of the company's balance sheet displays only the ending balances of the accounts and does not provide the activity or changes during the period.

CLAY CORPORATION Statement of Stockholders' Equity For the Year Ended December 31, 2020					
	Common Stock, $1 par	Additional Paid-in Capital	Treasury Stock, at cost $3	Retained Earnings	Totals
Beginning balance, January 1, 2020	$5,000	$64,000	$(1,200)	$ 24,000	$ 91,800
Net Income				33,000	33,000
Common Stock issued, 800 shares	800	3,600			4,400
Cash Dividends declared				(12,500)	(12,500)
Stock Dividends declared				(6,500)	(6,500)
Treasury Stock acquired, 600 shares			(4,200)		(4,200)
Ending balance, December 31, 2020	$5,800	$67,600	$(5,400)	$ 38,000	$106,000

Figure 14.13 Statement of Stockholders' Equity for Clay Corporation. (attribution: Copyright Rice University, OpenStax, under CC BY-NC-SA 4.0 license)

Nearly all public companies report a statement of stockholders' equity rather than a statement of retained earnings because GAAP requires disclosure of the changes in stockholders' equity accounts during each accounting period. It is significantly easier to see the changes in the accounts on a statement of stockholders' equity rather than as a paragraph note to the financial statements.

IFRS CONNECTION

Corporate Accounting and IFRS

Both U.S. GAAP and IFRS require the reporting of the various owners' accounts. Under U.S. GAAP, these accounts are presented in a statement that is most often called the Statement of Stockholders' Equity. Under IFRS, this statement is usually called the Statement of Changes in Equity. Some of the biggest differences between U.S. GAAP and IFRS that arise in reporting the various accounts that appear in those statements relate to either categorization or terminology differences.

U.S. GAAP divides owners' accounts into two categories: contributed capital and retained earnings. IFRS uses three categories: share capital, accumulated profits and losses, and reserves. The first two IFRS categories correspond to the two categories used under U.S. GAAP. What about the third category, reserves? Reserves is a category that is used to report items such as revaluation surpluses from revaluing long-term assets (see the Long-Term Assets Feature Box: IFRS Connection for details), as well as other equity transactions such as unrealized gains and losses on available-for-sale securities and transactions that fall under Other Comprehensive Income (topics typically covered in more advanced accounting classes). U.S. GAAP does not use the term "reserves" for any reporting.

There are also differences in terminology between U.S. GAAP and IFRS shown in Table 14.1.

Terminology Differences between U.S. GAAP and IFRS

U.S. GAAP	IFRS
Common stock	Share capital
Preferred stock	Preference shares
Additional paid-in capital	Share premium
Stockholders	Shareholders
Retained earnings	Retained profits or accumulated profits
Retained earnings deficit	Accumulated losses

Table 14.1

All of this information pertains to publicly traded corporations, but what about corporations that are not publicly traded? Most corporations in the U.S. are not publicly traded, so do these corporations use U.S. GAAP? Some do; some do not. A non-public corporation can use cash basis, tax basis, or full accrual basis of accounting. Most corporations would use a full accrual basis of accounting such as U.S. GAAP. Cash and tax basis are most likely used only by sole proprietors or small partnerships.

However, U.S. GAAP is not the only full accrual method available to non-public corporations. Two alternatives are IFRS and a simpler form of IFRS, known as IFRS for Small and Medium Sized Entities, or SMEs for short. In 2008, the AICPA recognized the IASB as a standard setter of acceptable GAAP and designated IFRS and IFRS for SMEs as an acceptable set of generally accepted accounting principles. However, it is up to each State Board of Accountancy to determine if that state will allow the use of IFRS or IFRS for SMEs by non-public entities incorporated in that state.

What is a SME? Despite the use of size descriptors in the title, qualifying as a small or medium-sized entity has nothing to do with size. A SME is any entity that publishes general purpose financial statements for public use but does not have public accountability. In other words, the entity is not publicly traded. In addition, the entity, even if it is a partnership, cannot act as a fiduciary; for example, it cannot be a bank or insurance company and use SME rules.

Why might a non-public corporation want to use IFRS for SMEs? First, IFRS for SMEs contains fewer and simpler standards. IFRS for SMEs has only about 300 pages of requirements, whereas regular IFRS is over 2,500 pages and U.S. GAAP is over 25,000 pages. Second, IFRS for SMEs is only modified every three years. This means entities using IFRS for SMEs don't have to frequently adjust their accounting systems and reporting to new standards, whereas U.S. GAAP and IFRS are modified more frequently. Finally, if a corporation transacts business with international businesses, or hopes to attract international partners, seek capital from international sources, or be bought out by an international company, then having their financial statements in IFRS form would make these transactions easier.

Prior Period Adjustments

Prior period adjustments are corrections of errors that appeared on previous periods' financial statements. These errors can stem from mathematical errors, misinterpretation of GAAP, or a misunderstanding of facts at the time the financial statements were prepared. Many errors impact the retained earnings account whose balance is carried forward from the previous period. Since the financial statements have already been issued, they must be corrected. The correction involves changing the financial statement amounts to the amounts they would have been had no errors occurred, a process known as **restatement**. The correction may impact both balance sheet and income statement accounts, requiring the company to record a transaction that corrects both. Since income statement accounts are closed at the end of every period, the journal entry will contain an entry to the Retained Earnings account. As such, prior period adjustments are reported on a company's statement of retained earnings as an adjustment to the beginning balance of retained earnings. By directly adjusting beginning retained earnings, the adjustment has no effect on current period net income. The goal is to separate the error correction from the current period's net income to avoid distorting the current period's profitability. In other words, prior period adjustments are a way to go back and correct past financial statements that were misstated because of a reporting error.

CONCEPTS IN PRACTICE

Are Companies Making Fewer Errors in Financial Reporting?

According to Kevin LaCroix, additional reporting requirements created by the Sarbanes Oxley Act prompted a surge in 2005 and 2006 of the number of companies that had to make corrections and reissue financial statements. However, since that time, the number of companies making corrections has dropped over 60%, partially due to the number of U.S. companies listed on stock exchanges, and partially due to tighter regulations. The severity of the errors that caused restatements has declined as well, primarily due to tighter regulation, which has forced companies to improve their internal controls.[15]

To illustrate how to correct an error requiring a prior period adjustment, assume that in early 2020, Clay Corporation's controller determined it had made an error when calculating depreciation in the preceding year,

15 Kevin M. LaCroix. "Financial Statements Continue to Decline for U.S. Reporting Companies." The D & O Diary. June 12, 2017. https://www.dandodiary.com/2017/06/articles/sox-generally/financial-restatements-continue-decline-u-s-reporting-companies/

resulting in an understatement of depreciation of $1,000. The entry to correct the error contains a decrease to Retained Earnings on the statement of retained earnings for $1,000. Depreciation expense would have been $1,000 higher if the correct depreciation had been recorded. The entry to Retained Earnings adds an additional debit to the total debits that were previously part of the closing entry for the previous year. The credit is to the balance sheet account in which the $1,000 would have been recorded had the correct depreciation entry occurred, in this case, Accumulated Depreciation.

JOURNAL			
Date	**Account**	**Debit**	**Credit**
Jan. 2	Retained Earnings	1,000	
	Accumulated Depreciation		1,000
	To record the correction of depreciation expense for a prior period		

Because the adjustment to retained earnings is due to an income statement amount that was recorded incorrectly, there will also be an income tax effect. The tax effect is shown in the statement of retained earnings in presenting the prior period adjustment. Assuming that Clay Corporation's income tax rate is 30%, the tax effect of the $1,000 is a $300 (30% × $1,000) reduction in income taxes. The increase in expenses in the amount of $1,000 combined with the $300 decrease in income tax expense results in a net $700 decrease in net income for the prior period. The $700 prior period correction is reported as an adjustment to beginning retained earnings, net of income taxes, as shown in Figure 14.14.

CLAY CORPORATION Statement of Retained Earnings For the Year Ended December 31, 2020		
Retained Earnings, January 1, 2020		$ 24,000
Prior period adjustment, net of income taxes		700
Adjusted Retained Earnings, January 1, 2020		24,700
Net Income		33,000
		57,700
Cash Dividends declared	$(12,500)	
Stock Dividends declared	(6,500)	(19,000)
Retained Earnings, December 31, 2020		$ 38,700

Figure 14.14 Statement of Retained Earnings for Clay Corporation. (attribution: Copyright Rice University, OpenStax, under CC BY-NC-SA 4.0 license)

Generally accepted accounting principles (GAAP), the set of accounting rules that companies are required to follow for financial reporting, requires companies to disclose in the notes to the financial statements the nature of any prior period adjustment and the related impact on the financial statement amounts.

LINK TO LEARNING

The correction of errors in financial statements is a complicated situation. Both shareholders and investors tend to view these with deep suspicion. Many believe corporations are attempting to smooth earnings, hide possible problems, or cover up mistakes. The *Journal of Accountancy*, a periodical published by the AICPA, offers guidance in how to manage this process. Browse the Journal of Accountancy website (https://openstax.org/l/50JournofAcct) for articles and cases of prior period adjustment issues.

CONCEPTS IN PRACTICE

Tune into Financial News

Tune into a financial news program like *Squawk Box* or *Mad Money* on CNBC or *Bloomberg's*. Notice the terminology used to describe the corporations being analyzed. Notice the speed at which topics are discussed. Are these shows for the novice investor? How could this information impact potential investors?

LINK TO LEARNING

Log onto the Annual Reports website (https://openstax.org/l/50AnnualReports) to access a comprehensive collection of more than 5,000 annual reports produced by publicly-traded companies. The site is a tremendous resource for both school and investment-related research. Reading annual reports provides a different type of insight into corporations. Beyond the financial statements, annual reports give shareholders and the public a glimpse into the operations, mission, and charitable giving of a corporation.

14.5 Discuss the Applicability of Earnings per Share as a Method to Measure Performance

Earnings per share (EPS) measures the portion of a corporation's profit allocated to each outstanding share of common stock. Many financial analysts believe that EPS is the single most important tool in assessing a stock's market price. A high or increasing earnings per share can drive up a stock price. Conversely, falling earnings per share can lower a stock's market price. EPS is also a component in calculating the price-to-earnings ratio (the market price of the stock divided by its earnings per share), which many investors find to be a key indicator of the value of a company's stock.

CONCEPTS IN PRACTICE

Microsoft Earnings Announcements Exceeds Wall Street Targets

While a company's board of directors makes the final approval of the reports, a key goal of each company is to look favorable to investors while providing financial statements that accurately reflect the financial condition of the company. Each quarter, public companies report EPS through a public announcement as one of the key measures of their profitability. These announcements are highly anticipated by investors and analysts. The suspense is heightened because analysts provide earnings estimates to the public prior to each announcement release. According to Matt Weinberger of *Business Insider*, the announcement by Microsoft of its first quarter 2018 EPS reported at $0.95 per share, higher than analysts' estimates of $0.85 per share, caused the value of its stock to rise by more than 3% within hours of the announcement.[16] While revenue was the other key metric in Microsoft's earnings announcement, EPS carried more weight in the surge of the company's market price.

Calculating Earnings per Share

Earnings per share is the profit a company earns for each of its outstanding common shares. Both the balance sheet and income statement are needed to calculate EPS. The balance sheet provides details on the preferred dividend rate, the total par value of the preferred stock, and the number of common shares outstanding. The income statement indicates the net income for the period. The formula to calculate basic earnings per share is:

$$\text{Earnings per Share} = \frac{\text{Net Income} - \text{Preferred Dividends}}{\text{Weighted Average Common Shares Outstanding}}$$

By removing the preferred dividends from net income, the numerator represents the profit available to common shareholders. Because preferred dividends represent the amount of net income to be distributed to preferred shareholders, this portion of the income is obviously not available for common shareholders. While there are a number of variations of measuring a company's profit used in the financial world, such as NOPAT (net operating profit after taxes) and EBITDA (earnings before interest, taxes, depreciation, and amortization), GAAP requires companies to calculate EPS based on a corporation's net income, as this amount appears directly on a company's income statement, which for public companies must be audited.

In the denominator, only common shares are used to determine earnings per share because EPS is a measure of earnings for each common share of stock. The denominator can fluctuate throughout the year as a company issues and buys back shares of its own stock. The weighted average number of shares is used on the denominator because of this fluctuation. To illustrate, assume that a corporation began the year with 600 shares of common stock outstanding and then on April 1 issued 1,000 more shares. During the period January 1 to March 31, the company had the original 600 shares outstanding. Once the new shares were issued, the company had the original 600 plus the new 1,000 shares, for a total of 1,600 shares for each of the next nine months—from April 1 to December 31. To determine the weighted average shares, apply these fractional weights to both of the stock amounts, as shown in Figure 14.15.

16 Matt Weinberger. "Microsoft's Cloud Business Is Driving a Revenue Surge That's Well above Wall Street Targets." *Business Insider*. April 26, 2018. https://www.businessinsider.com/microsoft-q3-fy18-earnings-revenue-eps-analysis-2018-4

Number of Shares	×	Portion of Year	=	Weighted Shares
600	×	3/12	=	150
1,600	×	9/12	=	1,200
Weighted average shares				1,350

Figure 14.15 Weighted Shares. (attribution: Copyright Rice University, OpenStax, under CC BY-NC-SA 4.0 license)

If the shares were not weighted, the calculation would not consider the time period during which the shares were outstanding.

To illustrate how EPS is calculated, assume Sanaron Company earns $50,000 in net income during 2020. During the year, the company also declared a $10,000 dividend on preferred stock and a $14,000 dividend on common stock. The company had 5,000 common shares outstanding the entire year along with 2,000 preferred shares. Sanaron has generated $8 of earnings ($50,000 less the $10,000 of preferred dividends) for each of the 5,000 common shares of stock it has outstanding.

$$\text{Earnings per share} = \frac{\$50{,}000 - \$10{,}000}{5{,}000} = \$8.00$$

THINK IT THROUGH

When a company issued new shares of stock and buys other back as treasury stock, EPS can be manipulated because both of these transactions affect the number of shares of stock outstanding. What are ethical considerations involved in calculating EPS?

Measuring Performance with EPS

EPS is a key profitability measure that both current and potential common stockholders monitor. Its importance is accentuated by the fact that GAAP requires public companies to report EPS on the face of a company's income statement. This is only ratio that requires such prominent reporting. If fact, public companies are required to report two different earnings per share amounts on their income statements—basic and diluted. We've illustrated the calculation of basic EPS. Diluted EPS, which is not demonstrated here, involves the consideration of all securities such as stocks and bonds that could potentially dilute, or reduce, the basic EPS.

LINK TO LEARNING

Where can you find EPS information on public companies? Check out the Yahoo Finance website (https://openstax.org/l/50YahooFinance) and search for EPS data for your favorite corporation.

Common stock shares are normally purchased by investors to generate income through dividends or to sell at a profit in the future. Investors realize that inadequate EPS can result in poor or inconsistent dividend payments and fluctuating stock prices. As such, companies seek to produce EPS amounts that rise each period. However, an increase in EPS may not always reflect favorable performance, as there are multiple reasons that EPS may increase. One way EPS can increase is because of increased net income. On the other hand, it can also increase when a company buys back its own shares of stock. For example, assume that Ranadune Enterprises generated net income of $15,000 in 2020. In addition, 20,000 shares of common stock and no preferred stock were outstanding throughout 2020. On January 1, 2020, the company buys back 2,500 shares of its common stock and holds them as treasury shares. Net income for 2020 stayed static at $15,000. Just before the repurchasing of the stock, the company's EPS is $0.75 per share:

$$\text{Earnings per share} = \frac{\$15,000}{20,000 \text{ shares}} = \$0.75 \text{ per share}$$

The purchase of treasury stock in 2020 reduces the common shares outstanding to 17,500 because treasury shares are considered issued but not outstanding (20,000 – 2,500). EPS for 2020 is now $0.86 per share even though earnings remains the same.

$$\text{Earnings per share} = \frac{\$15,000}{17,500 \text{ shares}} = \$0.86 \text{ per share}$$

This increase in EPS occurred because the net income is now spread over fewer shares of stock. Similarly, EPS can decline even when a company's net income increases if the number of shares increases at a higher degree than net income. Unfortunately, managers understand how the number of shares outstanding can affect EPS and are often in position to manipulate EPS by creating transactions that target a desired EPS number.

ETHICAL CONSIDERATIONS

Stock Buybacks Drive Up Earnings per Share: Ethical?

Public companies can increase their earnings per share by buying their own stock in the open market. The increase in earnings per share results because the number of shares is reduced by the purchase even though the earnings remain the same. With fewer shares and the same amount of earnings, the earnings per share increases without any change in overall profitability or operational efficiency. A *Market Watch* article attributing Goldman Sachs states, "S&P 500 companies will spend about $780 billion on share buybacks in 2017, marking a 30% rise from 2016."[17] An article in *Forbes* provides some perspective by pointing out that buying back shares was legalized in 1982, but for the majority of the twentieth century, corporate buybacks of shares was considered illegal because "they were thought to be a form of stock market manipulation. . . . Buying back company stock can inflate a company's share price and boost its earnings per share—metrics that often guide lucrative executive bonuses."[18] Is a corporation buying back its shares an ethical way in which to raise or maintain the price of a company's shares?

Earnings per share is interpreted differently by different analysts. Some financial experts favor companies with higher EPS values. The reasoning is that a higher EPS is a reflection of strong earnings and therefore a good

17 C. Linnane and T. Kilgore. "Share Buybacks Will Rise 30% to $780 Billion Next Year, says Goldman Sachs." Market Watch. November 22, 2016 https://www.marketwatch.com/story/share-buybacks-will-return-with-a-vengeance-next-year-2016-11-21.

18 Arne Alsin. "The Ugly Truth Behind Stock Buybacks." *Forbes*. Feb. 28, 2017. https://www.forbes.com/sites/aalsin/2017/02/28/shareholders-should-be-required-to-vote-on-stock-buybacks/#69b300816b1e

investment prospect. A more meaningful analysis occurs when EPS is tracked over a number of years, such as when presented in the comparative income statements for Cracker Barrel Old Country Store, Inc.'s respective year ends in 2017, 2016, and 2015 shown in Figure 14.16.[19] Cracker Barrel's basic EPS is labeled as "net income per share: basic."

CRACKER BARREL OLD COUNTRY STORE, INC. Consolidated Statements of Income			
	(In thousands except share data) Fiscal years ended		
	July 28, 2017	**July 29, 2016**	**July 31, 2015**
Total Revenue	$ 2,926,289	$ 2,912,351	$ 2,842,284
Cost of Goods Sold (exclusive of depreciation and rent)	891,293	928,176	924,171
Labor and other related expenses	1,017,124	1,006,188	992,382
Other Store Operating Expenses	563,300	554,534	523,307
Store Operating Income	454,572	423,453	402,424
General and Adminstrative Expenses	141,414	142,982	147,544
Operating Income	313,158	280,471	254,880
Interest Expense	14,271	14,052	16,679
Income before income taxes	298,887	266,419	238,201
Provision for income taxes	96,988	77,120	74,298
Net Income	$ 201,899	$ 189,299	$ 163,903
Net Income per share: basic	$ 8.40	$ 7.91	$ 6.85
Net Income per share: diluted	$ 8.37	$ 7.86	$ 6.82
Basic weighted average shares outstanding	**24,031,810**	**23,945,041**	**23,918,368**
Diluted weighted average shares outstanding	**24,118,288**	**24,074,273**	**24,048,924**

Figure 14.16 Consolidated Statements of Income for Cracker Barrel. (attribution: Copyright Rice University, OpenStax, under CC BY-NC-SA 4.0 license)

Most analysts believe that a consistent improvement in EPS year after year is the indication of continuous improvement in the earning power of a company. This is what is seen in Cracker Barrel's EPS amounts over each of the three years reported, moving from $6.85 to $7.91 to $8.40. However, it is important to remember that EPS is calculated on historical data, which is not always predictive of the future. In addition, when EPS is used to compare different companies, significant differences may exist. If companies are in the same industry, that comparison may be more valuable than if they are in different industries. Basically, EPS should be a tool used in decision-making, utilized alongside other analytic tools.

YOUR TURN

Would You Have Invested?

What if, in 1997, you invested $5,000 in Amazon? Today, your investment would be worth nearly $1 million. Potential investors viewing Amazon's income statement in 1997 would have seen an EPS of a negative $0.11. In other words, Amazon lost $0.11 for each share of common stock outstanding. Would

19 Cracker Barrel. *Cracker Barrel Old Country Store 2017 Annual Report.* September 22, 2017. http://investor.crackerbarrel.com/static-files/c05f90b8-1214-4f50-8508-d9a70301f51f

you have invested?

Solution

Answers will vary. A strong response would include the idea that a negative or small EPS reflects upon the past historical operations of a company. EPS does not predict the future. Investors in 1997 looked beyond Amazon's profitability and saw its business model having strong future potential.

THINK IT THROUGH

Using Earnings per Share in Decision Making

As a valued employee, you have been awarded 10 shares of the company's stock. Congratulations! How could you use earnings per share to help you decide whether to hold on to the stock or keep it for the future?

Key Terms

accounting entity concept concept indicating that the financial activity of an entity (corporation) must be kept separate from that of the owners

additional paid-in capital account for recording excess of the proceeds received from the issuance of the stock over the stock's par value

appropriated retained earnings portion of a company's retained earnings designated for a particular purpose such as future expansion, special projects, or as part of a company's risk management plan

articles of incorporation (also, charter) define the basic structure and purpose of a corporation and the amount of capital stock that can be issued or sold

authorized shares maximum number of shares that a corporation can issue to investors; approved by state in which company is incorporated and specified in the corporate charter

brokers buy and sell issues of stock on behalf of others

capital cash and other assets owned by a company

cash dividend corporate earnings that companies pass along to their shareholders in the form of cash payments

common stock corporation's primary class of stock issued, with each share representing a partial claim to ownership or a share of the company's business

contributed capital owner's investment (cash and other assets) in the business, which typically comes in the form of common stock

corporation legal business structure involving one or more individuals (owners) who are legally distinct (separate) from the business

date of declaration date upon which a company's board of directors votes and decides to give a cash dividend to all the company shareholders; the date on which the dividends become a legal liability

date of payment date that cash dividends are paid to shareholders

date of record date the list of dividend eligible shareholders is prepared; no journal entry is required

debt-to-equity ratio measures the portion of debt used by a company relative to the amount of stockholders' equity, calculated by dividing total debt by total equity

deficit in retained earnings negative or debit balance

dividend smoothing practice of paying dividends that are relatively equal period after period even when earnings fluctuate

double taxation occurs when income is taxed to the corporation that earned the income, and then taxed again to stockholders when they receive a distribution of the corporation's income as dividends

earned capital capital earned by the corporation as part of business operations

earnings per share (EPS) measurement of the portion of a corporation's profit allocated to each outstanding share of common stock

ex dividend status of stock sold between the record date and payment date during which the investor is not entitled to receive dividends

going concern assumption absent any evidence to the contrary, assumption that a business will continue to operate in the indefinite future

incorporation process of constituting a company into a legal entity

initial public offering (IPO) when a company issues shares of its stock to the public for the first time

investment banker financial professional who provides advice to companies wishing to issue new stock, then purchase the stock from the company issuing the stock and resell the securities to the public

issued shares authorized shares that have been sold to shareholders

large stock dividend stock dividend distribution that is larger than 25% of the total outstanding shares just before the distribution

market value of stock price at which the stock of public companies trades on the stock market

no-par stock stock issued with no par value assigned to it in a corporate charter

organization costs costs of organizing the corporate entity that include attorney fees, promotion costs, and filing fees paid to the state

outstanding shares shares that have been issues and are currently held by shareholders

owners' equity business owners' share of the company

par value value assigned to stock in the company's charter and is typically set at a very small arbitrary amount; serves as legal capital

preemptive right allows stockholders the option to maintain their ownership percentage when new shares of stock are issued by the company

preferred stock type of stock that entitles the holder to unique preferences that are advantageous over common stock features

prior period adjustments corrections of errors that occurred on previous periods' financial statements

private corporation corporation usually owned by a relatively small number of investors; shares are not traded publicly, and the ownership of the stock is restricted to only those allowed by the board of directors

property dividend stock dividend distribution of assets other than cash

publicly traded company company whose stock is traded (bought and sold) on an organized stock exchange

restatement correction of financial statement amounts due to an accounting error in a prior period

restricted retained earnings portion of a company's earnings that has been designated for a particular purpose due to legal or contractual obligations

reverse stock split issuance of new shares to existing shareholders in place of the old shares by decreasing the number of shares and increasing the par value of each share

secondary market organized market where previously issued stocks and bonds can be traded after they are issued

Securities and Exchange Commission (SEC) federal regulatory agency that regulates corporations with shares listed and traded on security exchanges through required periodic filings

small stock dividend stock dividend distribution that is less than 25% of the total outstanding shares just before the distribution

special dividend one-time extra distribution of corporate earnings to shareholders, usually stemming from a period of extraordinary earnings or special transaction, such as the sale of a company division

stated value is an amount a board of director's assigns to each share of a company's stock; functions as the legal capital

statement of stockholders' equity provides the changes between the beginning and ending balances of each of the stockholders' equity accounts during the period

stock discount amount at which stock is issued below the par value of stock

stock dividend dividend payment consisting of additional shares rather than cash

stock split issuance of new shares to existing shareholders in place of the old shares by increasing the number of shares and reducing the par value of each share

stock trading buying and selling of shares by investors and brokers

stockholder owner of stock, or shares, in a business

treasury stock company's own shares that it has repurchased from investors

Summary

14.1 Explain the Process of Securing Equity Financing through the Issuance of Stock

- The process of forming a corporation involves several steps, which result in a legal entity that can issue stock, enter into contracts, buy and sell assets, and borrow funds.
- The corporate form has several advantages, which include the ability to function as a separate legal entity, limited liability, transferable ownership, continuing existence, and ease of raising capital.
- The disadvantages of operating as a corporation include the costs of organization, regulation, and potential double taxation.
- There are a number of considerations when choosing whether to finance with debt or equity as a means to raise capital, including dilution of ownership, the repayment obligation, the cash obligation, budgeting reliability, cost savings, and the risk assessment by creditors.
- The Securities and Exchange Commission regulates large and small public corporations.
- There are key differences between public corporations that experience an IPO and private corporations.
- A corporation's shares continue to be bought and sold by the public in the secondary market after an IPO.
- The process of marketing a company's stock involves several steps.
- Capital stock consists of two classes of stock—common and preferred, each providing the company with the ability to attract capital from investors.
- Shares of stock are categorized as authorized, issued, and outstanding.
- Shares of stock are measured based on their market or par value. Some stock is no-par, which carries a stated value.
- A company's primary class of stock issued is common stock, and each share represents a partial claim to ownership or a share of the company's business. Common shareholders have four rights: right to vote, the right to share in corporate net income through dividends, the right to share in any distribution of assets upon liquidation, and a preemptive right.
- Preferred stock, by definition, has preferred characteristics, which are more advantageous to shareholders over common stock characteristics. These include dividend preferences such as cumulative and participating and a preference for asset distribution upon liquidation. These shares can also be callable or convertible.

14.2 Analyze and Record Transactions for the Issuance and Repurchase of Stock

- The initial issuance of common stock reflects the sale of the first stock by a corporation.
- Common stock issued at par value for cash creates an additional paid-in capital account for the excess of the issue price over the par value.
- Stock issued in exchange for property or services is recorded at the fair market value of the stock or the asset or services received, whichever is more clearly determinable.
- Stock with a stated value is treated as if the stated value is a par value. The entire issue price of no-par stock with no stated value is credited to the capital stock account.
- Preferred stock issued at par or stated value creates an additional paid-in capital account for the excess of the issue price over the par value.
- A corporation reports a stock's par or stated value, the number of shares authorized, issued, and outstanding, and if preferred, the dividend rate on the face of the balance sheet.
- Treasury stock is a corporation's stock that the corporation purchased back. A company may buy back its stock for strategic purposes against competitors, to create demand, or to use for employee stock option plans.
- The acquisition of treasury stock creates a contra equity account, Treasury Stock, reported in the

stockholders' equity section of the balance sheet.

- When a corporation reissues its treasury stock at an amount above the cost, it generates a credit to the Additional Paid-in Capital from Treasury stock account.
- When a corporation reissues its treasury stock at an amount below cost, the Additional Paid-in Capital from Treasury stock account is reduced first, then any excess is debited to Retained Earnings.

14.3 Record Transactions and the Effects on Financial Statements for Cash Dividends, Property Dividends, Stock Dividends, and Stock Splits

- Dividends are a distribution of corporate earnings, though some companies reinvest earnings rather than declare dividends.
- There are three dividend dates: date of declaration, date of record, and date of payment.
- Cash dividends are accounted for as a reduction of retained earnings and create a liability when declared.
- When dividends are declared and a company has only common stock issued, the reduction of retained earnings is the amount per share times the number of outstanding shares.
- A property dividend occurs when a company declares and distributes assets other than cash. They are recorded at the fair market value of the asset being distributed.
- A stock dividend is a distribution of shares of stock to existing shareholders in lieu of a cash dividend.
- A small stock dividend occurs when a stock dividend distribution is less than 25% of the total outstanding shares based on the outstanding shares prior to the dividend distribution. The entry requires a decrease to Retained Earnings for the market value of the shares to be distributed.
- A large stock dividend involves a distribution of stock to existing shareholders that is larger than 25% of the total outstanding shares just before the distribution. The journal entry requires a decrease to Retained Earnings and a credit to Stock Dividends Distributable for the par or stated value of the shares to be distributed.
- Some corporations employ stock splits to keep their stock price competitive in the market. A traditional stock split occurs when a company's board of directors issues new shares to existing shareholders in place of the old shares by increasing the number of shares and reducing the par value of each share.

14.4 Compare and Contrast Owners' Equity versus Retained Earnings

- Owner's equity reflects an owner's investment value in a company.
- The three forms of business utilize different accounts and transactions relative to owners' equity.
- Retained earnings is the primary component of a company's earned capital. It generally consists of the cumulative net income minus any cumulative losses less dividends declared. A statement of retained earnings shows the changes in the retained earnings account during the period.
- Restricted retained earnings is the portion of a company's earnings that has been designated for a particular purpose due to legal or contractual obligations.
- A company's board of directors may designate a portion of a company's retained earnings for a particular purpose such as future expansion, special projects, or as part of a company's risk management plan. The amount designated is classified as appropriated retained earnings.
- The statement of stockholders' equity provides the changes between the beginning and ending balances of each of the stockholders' equity accounts, including retained earnings.
- Prior period adjustments are corrections of errors that occurred on previous periods' financial statements. They are reported on a company's statement of retained earnings as an adjustment to the beginning balance.

14.5 Discuss the Applicability of Earnings per Share as a Method to Measure Performance

- Earnings per share (EPS) measures the portion of a corporation's profit allocated to each outstanding share of common stock.

- EPS is calculated by dividing the profit earned for common shareholders by the weighted average common shares of stock outstanding.
- Because EPS is a key profitability measure that both current and potential common stockholders monitor, it is important to understand how to interpret it.

Multiple Choice

1. LO 14.1 Which of the following is *not* a characteristic that sets preferred stock apart from common stock?

A. voting rights
B. dividend payments
C. transferability
D. ownership

2. LO 14.1 Issued stock is defined as stock that _______.

A. is available for sale
B. that is held by the corporation
C. has been sold to investors
D. has no voting rights

3. LO 14.1 Your friend is considering incorporating and asks for advice. Which of the following is *not* a major concern?

A. colors for the logo
B. which state in which to incorporate
C. number of shares of stock to authorize
D. selection of the corporation name

4. LO 14.1 Par value of a stock refers to the _______.

A. issue price of a stock
B. value assigned by the incorporation documents
C. maximum selling price of a stock
D. dividend to be paid by the corporation

5. LO 14.1 Which of the following is not one of the five primary responsibilities of the Securities and Exchange Commission (the SEC)?

A. inform and protect investors
B. regulate securities law
C. facilitate capital formation
D. assure that dividends are paid by corporations

6. LO 14.1 When a C corporation has only one class of stock it is referred to as _______.

A. stated value stock
B. par value stock
C. common stock
D. preferred stock

7. LO 14.1 The number of shares that a corporation's incorporation documents allows it to sell is referred to as _______.

A. issued stock
B. outstanding stock
C. common stock
D. authorized stock

8. LO 14.2 The total amount of cash and other assets received by a corporation from the stockholders in exchange for the shares is _______.

A. always equal to par value
B. referred to as retained earnings
C. always below its stated value
D. referred to as paid-in capital

9. LO 14.2 Stock can be issued for all *except* which of the following?

A. accounts payable
B. state income tax payments
C. property such as a delivery truck
D. services provided to the corporation such as legal fees

10. LO 14.3 A company issued 40 shares of $1 par value common stock for $5,000. The journal entry to record the transaction would include which of the following?

A. debit of $4,000 to common stock
B. credit of $20,000 to common stock
C. credit of $40 to common stock
D. debit of $20,000 to common stock

11. LO 14.3 A company issued 30 shares of $.50 par value common stock for $12,000. The credit to additional paid-in capital would be _______.

A. $11,985
B. $12,000
C. $15
D. $10,150

12. LO 14.3 A corporation issued 100 shares of $100 par value preferred stock for $150 per share. The resulting journal entry would include which of the following?

A. a credit to common stock
B. a credit to cash
C. a debit to paid-in capital in excess of preferred stock
D. a debit to cash

13. LO 14.3 The date the board of directors votes to declare and pay a cash dividend is called the:

A. date of stockholder's meeting
B. date of payment
C. date of declaration
D. date of liquidation

14. LO 14.3 Which of the following is true of a stock dividend?

A. It is a liability.

B. The decision to issue a stock dividend resides with shareholders.

C. It does not affect total equity but transfers amounts between equity components.

D. It creates a cash reserve for shareholders.

15. LO 14.4 Stockholders' equity consists of which of the following?

A. bonds payable

B. retained earnings and accounts receivable

C. retained earnings and paid-in capital

D. discounts and premiums on bond payable

16. LO 14.4 Retained earnings is accurately described by all *except* which of the following statements?

A. Retained earnings is the primary component of a company's earned capital.

B. Dividends declared are added to retained earnings.

C. Net income is added to retained earnings.

D. Net losses are accumulated in the retained earnings account.

17. LO 14.4 If a company's board of directors designates a portion of earnings for a particular purpose due to legal or contractual obligations, they are designated as _______.

A. retained earnings payable

B. appropriated retained earnings

C. cumulative retained earnings

D. restricted retained earnings

18. LO 14.4 Corrections of errors that occurred on a previous period's financial statements are called _______.

A. restrictions

B. deficits

C. prior period adjustments

D. restatements

19. LO 14.4 Owner's equity represents which of the following?

A. the amount of funding the company has from issuing bonds

B. the sum of the retained earnings and accounts receivable account balances

C. the total of retained earnings plus paid-in capital

D. the business owner's/owners' share of the company, also known as net worth or net assets

20. LO 14.5 Which of the following is a measurement of earnings that represents the profit before interest, taxes, depreciation and amortization are subtracted?

A. net income

B. retained earnings

C. EBITDA

D. EPS

21. LO 14.5 Which of the following measures the portion of a corporation's profit allocated to each outstanding share of common stock?

A. retained earnings

B. EPS

C. EBITDA

D. NOPAT

22. LO 14.5 The measurement of earnings concept that consists of a company's profit from operations after taxed are subtracted is ______.

A. ROI
B. EPS
C. EBITDA
D. NOPAT

23. LO 14.5 The correct formula for the calculation of earnings per share is ______.

A. (Net income + Preferred dividends) / Weighted average common shares outstanding
B. Net income / Weighted average common shares outstanding
C. (Net income – Preferred dividends) / Weighted average common shares outstanding
D. (Net income – Preferred dividends) / Treasury shares outstanding

24. LO 14.5 Most analysts believe which of the following is true about EPS?

A. Consistent improvement in EPS year after year is the indication of continuous improvement in the company's earning power.
B. Consistent improvement in EPS year after year is the indication of continuous decline in the company's earning power.
C. Consistent improvement in EPS year after year is the indication of fraud within the company.
D. Consistent improvement in EPS year after year is the indication that the company will never suffer a year of net loss rather than net income.

Questions

1. LO 14.1 Your corporation needs additional capital to fund an expansion. Discuss the advantages and disadvantages of raising capital through the issuance of stock. Would debt be a better option? Why or why not?

2. LO 14.1 How many shares of stock should your new corporation authorize? How did you arrive at your number?

3. LO 14.1 What factors should a new company consider in deciding in which state to incorporate?

4. LO 14.1 What are some of the reasons a business owner might choose the corporate form of business?

5. LO 14.2 Why would a company repurchase its own stock?

6. LO 14.2 The following data was reported by Saturday Corporation:

- Authorized shares: 30,000
- Issued shares: 25,000
- Treasury shares: 5,000

How many shares are outstanding?

7. LO 14.2 A corporation issues 6,000 shares of $1 par value stock for a parcel of land valued at $12,000. Prepare the journal entry to reflect this transaction.

8. LO 14.2 When corporations issue stock in exchange for professional services, what account(s) should be debited and what account(s) should be credited?

9. LO 14.2 A corporation issues 5,000 shares of $1 par value stock for some equipment with a clearly determined value of $10,000. Prepare the journal entry to reflect this transaction.

10. LO 14.3 On April 2, West Company declared a cash dividend of $0.50 per share. There are 50,000 shares outstanding. What is the journal entry that should be recorded?

11. LO 14.3 Assuming the same facts as Exercise 59., what is the journal that should be recorded on May 5, the date of payment?

12. LO 14.3 When does a corporation incur a liability for a dividend?

13. LO 14.3 How does a stock split affect the balance sheet of a corporation?

14. LO 14.4 Your friend has questions about retained earnings and dividends. How do you explain to him that dividends are paid out of retained earnings?

15. LO 14.4 What does owners' equity mean for the owner?

16. LO 14.4 What types of transactions reduce owner's equity? What types of transactions reduce retained earnings? What do they have in common?

17. LO 14.4 Sometimes financial statements contain errors. What type of liabilities may need correction as a prior period adjustment?

18. LO 14.4 Retained earnings may be restricted or appropriated. Explain the difference between the two and give an example of when each may be used.

19. LO 14.5 Which financial statements do you need to calculate EPS?

20. LO 14.5 Where is EPS disclosed for publicly traded companies?

21. LO 14.5 Should investors rely on EPS as an investing tool? Why or why not?

22. LO 14.5 What information do you need to calculate the weighted average common shares outstanding?

23. LO 14.5 Which is the only ratio required to be reported on the face of a company's financial statements? What are the two ways the ratio is required to be reported?

Exercise Set A

EA1. LO 14.1 You are an accountant working for a company that has recently decided to incorporate. The company has incurred $4,300 for attorney's fees, promotion costs, and filing fees with the state of incorporation as a part of organizing the corporate entity. What is the journal entry to record these costs on March 13, assuming they are paid in cash?

EA2. LO 14.1 What is the impact on stockholders' equity when a company uses debt financing as a source of funding?

EA3. LO 14.1 What is the most obvious difference between debt and equity financing?

EA4. LO 14.1 How do creditors assess risk when lending funds to a company?

EA5. LO 14.2 Fortuna Company is authorized to issue 1,000,000 shares of $1 par value common stock. In its first year, the company has the following transactions:

Jan. 31	Issued 40,000 shares at $10 share
Jun. 10	Issued 100,000 shares in exchange for land with a clearly determined value of $850,000
Aug. 3	Purchased 10,000 shares of treasury stock at $9 per share

Journalize the transactions and calculate how many shares of stock are outstanding at August 3.

EA6. LO 14.2 James Incorporated is authorized to issue 5,000,000 shares of $1 par value common stock. In its second year of business, the company has the following transactions:

Mar. 31	Issued 30,000 shares at $10 share
Jul. 9	Issued 100,000 shares in exchange for a building with a clearly determined value of $700,000
Aug. 30	Purchased 7,000 shares of treasury stock at $9 per share

Journalize the transactions.

EA7. LO 14.2 McVie Corporation's stock has a par value of $2. The company has the following transactions during the year:

Feb. 28	Issued 300,000 shares at $5 share
Jun. 7	Issued 90,000 shares in exchange for equipment with a clearly determined value of $200,000
Sep. 19	Purchased 3,000 shares of treasury stock at $7 per share

Journalize the transactions.

EA8. LO 14.2 Anslo Fabricating, Inc. is authorized to issue 10,000,000 shares of $5 stated value common stock. During the year, the company has the following transactions:

Jan. 3	Issued 60,000 shares at $10 share
Jun. 15	Issued 5,000 shares in exchange for office equipment with a clearly determined value of $50,000
Aug. 16	Purchased 4,000 shares of treasury stock at $20 per share

Journalize the transactions.

EA9. LO 14.2 St. Marie Company is authorized to issue 1,000,000 shares of $5 par value preferred stock, and 5,000,000 shares of $1 stated value common stock. During the year, the company has the following transactions:

Jan. 31	Issued 140,000 common shares at $10 share
Jun. 10	Issued 160,000 preferred shares in exchange for land with a clearly determined value of $850,000
Aug. 3	Issued 10,000 shares of common stock for $9 per share

Journalize the transactions.

EA10. LO 14.3 Nutritious Pet Food Company's board of directors declares a cash dividend of $1.00 per common share on November 12. On this date, the company has issued 12,000 shares but 2,000 shares are held as treasury shares. What is the journal entry to record the declaration of this dividend?

EA11. LO 14.3 Nutritious Pet Food Company's board of directors declares a cash dividend of $1.00 per common share on November 12. On this date, the company has issued 12,000 shares but 2,000 shares are held as treasury shares. The company pays the dividend on December 14. What is the journal entry to record the payment of the dividend?

EA12. LO 14.3 Nutritious Pet Food Company's board of directors declares a cash dividend of $5,000 on June 30. At that time, there are 3,000 shares of $5 par value 5% preferred stock outstanding and 7,000 shares of $1 par value common stock outstanding (none held in treasury). What is the journal entry to record the declaration of the dividend?

EA13. LO 14.3 Nutritious Pet Food Company's board of directors declares a small stock dividend (20%) on June 30 when the stock's market value per share is $30. At that time, there are 10,000 shares of $1 par value common stock outstanding (none held in treasury). What is the journal entry to record the declaration of the dividend?

EA14. LO 14.4 Blanket Company has paid quarterly dividends every quarter for the past 15 years. Lately, slowing sales have created a cash crunch for the company. While the company still has positive retained earnings, the retained earnings balance is close to zero. Should the company borrow to continue to pay dividends? Why or why not?

EA15. LO 14.4 Farmington Corporation began the year with a retained earnings balance of $20,000. The company paid a total of $3,000 in dividends and earned a net income of $60,000 this year. What is the ending retained earnings balance?

EA16. LO 14.4 Montana Incorporated began the year with a retained earnings balance of $50,000. The company paid a total of $5,000 in dividends and experienced a net loss of $25,000 this year. What is the ending retained earnings balance?

EA17. LO 14.4 Jesse and Mason Fabricating, Inc. general ledger has the following account balances at the end of the year:

Cash	9,000
Common stock	5,000
Accounts receivable	7,000
Accounts payable	2,000
Additional paid-in capital	4,000
Prepaid insurance	5,000
Unearned revenue	4,000
Retained earnings	6,000

What is the total ending balance as reported on the company's Statement of Stockholder's Equity?

EA18. LO 14.4 Roxanne's Delightful Candies, Inc. began the year with a retained earnings balance of $45,000. The company had a great year and earned a net income of $80,000. However, the company's controller determined that it had made an error when calculating depreciation in the preceding year, resulting in an understated depreciation expense amount of $2,000. What is the ending retained earnings balance?

EA19. LO 14.5 Jupiter Corporation earned net income of $90,000 this year. The company began the year with 600 shares of common stock and issued 500 more on April 1. They issued $5,000 in preferred dividends for the year. What is Jupiter Corporation's weighted average number of shares for the year?

EA20. LO 14.5 Longmont Corporation earned net income of $90,000 this year. The company began the year with 600 shares of common stock and issued 500 more on April 1. They issued $5,000 in preferred dividends for the year. What is the numerator of the EPS calculation for Longmont?

EA21. LO 14.5 James Corporation earned net income of $90,000 this year. The company began the year with 600 shares of common stock and issued 500 more on April 1. They issued $5,000 in preferred dividends for the year. What is the EPS for the year for James (rounded to the nearest dollar)?

Exercise Set B

EB1. LO 14.1 Your high school friend started a business that has blossomed over the years, and she is considering incorporating so she can sell shares of stock and expand. She has asked you for help understanding the process she will need to undertake. How do you explain the process of incorporation to her?

EB2. LO 14.1 You are an accountant working for a manufacturing company that makes personal care products and has recently decided to incorporate. The company incurred a total of $7,900 for attorney's fees, promotion costs, and filing fees with the state of incorporation as a part of organizing the corporate entity. What is the journal entry to record these costs on February 28, assuming they are paid in cash?

EB3. LO 14.1 What is the impact on stockholders' equity when a company uses equity financing as a source of funding?

EB4. LO 14.1 What is the biggest disadvantage to be considered when exploring the option of equity financing versus debt financing?

EB5. LO 14.1 Your high school friend started a business that has blossomed over the years, and he is considering incorporating so he can sell shares of stock and expand. He has asked you for help understanding the costs of incorporating. What are some of the costs that he will face as he organizes the corporation and begins to sell shares of stock?

EB6. LO 14.2 Spring Company is authorized to issue 500,000 shares of $2 par value common stock. In its first year, the company has the following transactions:

Mar. 1	Issued 40,000 shares of stock at $9.75 per share
Apr. 10	Issued 1,000 shares of stock for legal services valued at $10,000.
Oct. 3	Purchased 1,000 shares of treasury stock at $9 per share

Journalize the transactions and calculate how many shares of stock are outstanding at August 3.

EB7. LO 14.2 Silva Company is authorized to issue 5,000,000 shares of $2 par value common stock. In its IPO, the company has the following transaction: Mar. 1, issued 500,000 shares of stock at $15.75 per share for cash to investors. Journalize this transaction.

EB8. LO 14.2 Juniper Company is authorized to issue 5,000,000 shares of $2 par value common stock. In conjunction with its incorporation process and the IPO, the company has the following transaction: Mar. 1, issued 4,000 shares of stock in exchange for equipment worth $250,000. Journalize the transaction.

EB9. LO 14.2 Vishnu Company is authorized to issue 500,000 shares of $2 par value common stock. In conjunction with its incorporation process and the IPO, the company has the following transaction: Apr. 10, issued 1,000 shares of stock for legal services valued at $15,000. Journalize the transaction.

EB10. LO 14.2 Ammon Company is authorized to issue 500,000 shares of $5 par value preferred stock. In its first year, the company has the following transaction: Mar. 1, issued 40,000 shares of preferred stock at $20.50 per share. Journalize the transaction.

EB11. LO 14.3 Nutritious Pet Food Company's board of directors declares a small stock dividend (20%) on June 30 when the stock's market value per share is $30. At that time, there are 10,000 shares of $1 par value common stock outstanding (none held in treasury). What is the journal entry to record the stock dividend distribution on July 31?

EB12. LO 14.3 Nutritious Pet Food Company's board of directors declares a large stock dividend (50%) on June 30 when the stock's market value per share is $30. At that time, there are 10,000 shares of $1 par value common stock outstanding (none held in treasury). What is the journal entry to record the declaration of the dividend?

EB13. LO 14.3 Nutritious Pet Food Company's board of directors declares a large stock dividend (50%) on June 30 when the stock's market value per share is $30. At that time, there are 10,000 shares of $1 par value common stock outstanding (none held in treasury). What is the journal entry to record the stock dividend distribution on July 31?

EB14. LO 14.3 Nutritious Pet Food Company's board of directors declares a 2-for-1 stock split on June 30 when the stock's market value per share is $30. At that time, there are 10,000 shares of $1 par value common stock outstanding (none held in treasury). What is the new par value of the shares and how many shares are outstanding after the split?

EB15. LO 14.3 Nutritious Pet Food Company's board of directors declares a 2-for-1 stock split on June 30 when the stock's market value per share is $30. At that time, there are 10,000 shares of $1 par value common stock outstanding (none held in treasury). What is the new par value of the shares and how many shares are outstanding after the split? What is the total amount of equity before and after the split?

EB16. LO 14.4 Birmingham Company has been in business for five years. Last year, it experienced rapid growth and hired a new accountant to oversee the physical assets and record acquisitions and depreciation. This year, the controller discovered that the accounting records were not in order when the new accountant took over, and a $3,000 depreciation entry was omitted resulting in depreciation expense being understated last year. How does the company make this type of correction and where is it reported?

EB17. LO 14.4 Chelsea Company is a sole proprietorship. Ashley, Incorporated is a corporation. Which company would report stockholder's equity and retained earnings and not simply owner's equity? Why? What is the difference between these accounts?

EB18. LO 14.4 Tart Restaurant Holdings, Incorporated began the year with a retained earnings balance of $950,000. The company paid a total of $14,000 in dividends and experienced a net loss of $20,000 this year. What is the ending retained earnings balance?

EB19. LO 14.4 Josue Fabricating, Inc.'s accountant has the following information available to prepare the Statement of Stockholder's Equity for the year just ended.

Cash	19,000
Common stock	15,000
Accounts receivable	17,000
Accounts payable	12,000
Preferred stock	18,000
Additional paid-in capital	14,000
Prepaid insurance	15,000
Unearned revenue	14,000
Retained earnings	16,000

What is the total balance on the company's Statement of Stockholder's Equity? What is the amount of the contributed capital?

EB20. LO 14.4 Trumpet and Trombone Manufacturing, Inc. began the year with a retained earnings balance of $545,000. The company had a great year and earned a net income of $190,000 this year and paid dividends of $14,000. Additionally, the company's controller determined that it had made an error when calculating tax expense in the preceding year, resulting in an understated expense amount of $22,000. What is the ending retained earnings balance?

EB21. LO 14.5 Brunleigh Corporation earned net income of $200,000 this year. The company began the year with 10,000 shares of common stock and issued 5,000 more on April 1. They issued $7,500 in preferred dividends for the year. What is Brunleigh Corporation's weighted average number of shares for the year?

EB22. LO 14.5 Errol Corporation earned net income of $200,000 this year. The company began the year with 10,000 shares of common stock and issued 5,000 more on April 1. They issued $7,500 in preferred dividends for the year. What is the numerator of the EPS calculation for Errol?

EB23. LO 14.5 Bastion Corporation earned net income of $200,000 this year. The company began the year with 10,000 shares of common stock and issued 5,000 more on April 1. They issued $7,500 in preferred dividends for the year. What is the EPS for the year for Bastion?

Problem Set A

PA1. LO 14.1 You are a CPA who has been hired by DEF Company to assist with their initial public offering. Prepare a memo to the president of DEF outlining the steps you will take to launch the IPO.

PA2. LO 14.1 You are a CPA who has been hired by DEF Company to assist with their incorporation process. Prepare a memo to the president of DEF explaining the different statuses of shares of stock: authorized shares, issued shares, outstanding shares, and treasury shares.

PA3. LO 14.1 You are a CPA who has been hired by DEF Company to assist with their initial public offering. Prepare a memo to the president of DEF outlining the two most significant values, market value and par value, associated with stock.

PA4. LO 14.2 Wingra Corporation was organized in March. It is authorized to issue 500,000 shares of $100 par value 8% preferred stock. It is also authorized to issue 750,000 shares of $1 par value common stock. In its first year, the corporation has the following transactions:

Mar. 1	Issued 10,000 shares of preferred stock at $115 per share
Mar. 2	Issued 120,000 shares of common stock at $12.50 per share
Apr. 10	Issued 15,000 shares of common stock for equipment valued at $196,000. The stock is currently trading at $12 per share, and is a more reliable indicator of the value of the equipment.
Jun. 12	Issued 10,000 shares of common stock at $15 per share
Aug. 5	Issued 1,000 shares of preferred stock at $112 per share

Journalize the transactions.

PA5. LO 14.2 Copper Corporation was organized in May. It is authorized to issue 50,000,000 shares of $200 par value 7% preferred stock. It is also authorized to issue 75,000,000 shares of $5 par value common stock. In its first year, the corporation has the following transactions:

May 1	Issued 1,000 shares of preferred stock for cash at $250 per share
May 23	Issued 2,000 shares of common stock at $15.50 per share
Jun. 10	Issued 15,000 shares of common stock for equipment without a readily determinable value. The stock is currently trading at $15 per share.

Journalize the transactions.

PA6. LO 14.2 EllaJane Corporation was organized several years ago and was authorized to issue 4,000,000 shares of $50 par value 6% preferred stock. It is also authorized to issue 1,750,000 shares of $1 par value common stock. In its fifth year, the corporation has the following transactions:

Mar. 1	Purchased 1,000 shares of its own common stock at $11 per share
Apr. 10	Reissued 500 shares of its common stock held in the treasury for $15 per share.
Jun. 12	Reissued 500 shares of common stock at $9 per share

Journalize the transactions.

PA7. LO 14.3 Aggregate Mining Corporation was incorporated five years ago. It is authorized to issue 500,000 shares of $100 par value 8% preferred stock. It is also authorized to issue 750,000 shares of $1 par value common stock. It has issued only 50,000 of the common shares and none of the preferred shares. In its sixth year, the corporation has the following transactions:

Mar. 1	Declares a cash dividend of $2 per share
Mar. 30	Pays the cash dividend
Jul. 10	Declares a 5% stock dividend when the stock is trading at $15 per share
Aug. 5	Issues the stock dividend

Journalize these transactions.

PA8. LO 14.3 Aggregate Mining Corporation was incorporated five years ago. It is authorized to issue 500,000 shares of $100 par value 8% preferred stock. It is also authorized to issue 750,000 shares of $1 par value common stock. It has issued only 50,000 of the common shares and none of the preferred shares. In its seventh year, the corporation has the following transactions:

Mar. 1	Declares a cash dividend of $5 per share
Mar. 30	Pays the cash dividend
Jul. 10	Declares a property dividend of 1/2 ton of limestone per share when the price of limestone is $25 per ton

Journalize these transactions.

PA9. LO 14.3 Aggregate Mining Corporation was incorporated five years ago. It is authorized to issue 500,000 shares of $100 par value 8% cumulative preferred stock. It is also authorized to issue 750,000 shares of $6 par value common stock. It has issued 50,000 of the common shares and 1,000 of the cumulative preferred shares. The corporation has never declared a dividend and the preferred shares are one years in arrears. Aggregate Mining has the following transactions this year:

Mar. 1	Declares a cash dividend of $20,000
Mar. 30	Pays the cash dividend
Jul. 10	Declares a 3-for-1 stock split of its common shares

Journalize these transactions. For the stock split, show the calculation for how many shares are outstanding after the split and the par value per share after the split

PA10. LO 14.4 The board of directors is interested in investing in a new technology. Appropriating existing retained earnings is a choice for funding the new technology. You are a consultant to the board. How would you explain this option to the board members so that they could make an educated decision?

PA11. LO 14.4 You are a consultant for several emerging, high-growth technology firms that were started locally and have been a part of a business incubator in your area. These firms start out as sole proprietorships but quickly realize the need for more capital and often incorporate. One of the common questions you are asked is about stockholder's equity. Explain the characteristics and functions of the retained earnings account and how the account is different from contributed capital.

PA12. LO 14.4 You are the accountant for Kamal Fabricating, Inc. and you oversee the preparation of financial statements for the year just ended 6/30/2020. You have the following information from the company's general ledger and other financial reports (all balances are end-of-year except for those noted otherwise:

Cash	$9,000
Common stock	5,000
Accounts receivable	7,000
Accounts payable	2,000
Cash dividends declared for the year	1,000
Additional paid-in capital	4,000
Prepaid insurance	5,000
Prior period adjustment net of income tax	(2,000)
Unearned revenue	4,000
Retained earnings, beginning of the year	6,000
Net income for the year	9,000

Prepare the company's Statement of Retained Earnings.

PA13. LO 14.5 You have some funds that you would like to invest. Do some internet research to find two publicly traded companies in the same industry and compare their earnings per share. Would the earnings per share reported by each company influence your decision in selecting which company to invest in?

PA14. LO 14.5 You are a consultant working with various companies that are considering incorporating and listing shares on a stock exchange. Explain the importance of the EPS calculation to financial analysts who follow companies on the stock exchanges.

Problem Set B

PB1. LO 14.1 You are the president of Duke Company and are leading the company through the process of incorporation. The next step is determining the type of stock the company should offer. You are relying on feedback from several key executives at Duke to help you assess the wisdom in this decision. Prepare a memo to your executive team outlining the differences between common stock and preferred stock. The memo should be complete enough to assist them with assessing differences and providing you with robust feedback.

PB2. LO 14.1 You are the president of Duke Company and are leading the company through the process of incorporation. The company has determined that common stock shares will be issued, but several key executives at Duke are not quite sure they understand the preemptive right feature associated with common shares. Prepare a memo to your executive team outlining the meaning of this right.

PB3. LO 14.2 Autumn Corporation was organized in August. It is authorized to issue 100,000 shares of $100 par value 7% preferred stock. It is also authorized to issue 500,000 shares of $5 par value common stock. During the year, the corporation had the following transactions:

Aug. 22	Issued 2,000 shares of preferred stock at $105 per share
Sep. 3	Issued 80,000 shares of common stock at $13.25 per share
Oct. 11	Issued 12,000 shares of common stock for land valued at $156,000. The stock is currently trading at $12 per share, and the stock's trading value is a more accurate determinant of the land's value.
Nov. 12	Issued 5,000 shares of common stock at $15 per share
Dec. 5	Issued 1,000 shares of preferred stock at $112 per share

Journalize the transactions.

PB4. LO 14.2 MacKenzie Mining Corporation is authorized to issue 50,000 shares of $500 par value 7% preferred stock. It is also authorized to issue 5,000,000 shares of $3 par value common stock. In its first year, the corporation has the following transactions:

May 1	Issued 3,000 shares of preferred stock for cash at $750 per share
May 23	Issued 6,000 shares of common stock at $12.50 per share
Jun. 10	Issued 5,000 shares of common stock for equipment without a readily determinable value. The stock is currently trading at $11 per share

Journalize the transactions.

PB5. LO 14.2 Paydirt Limestone, Incorporated was organized several years ago and was authorized to issue 3,000,000 shares of $40 par value 9% preferred stock. It is also authorized to issue 3,750,000 shares of $2 par value common stock. In its fifth year, the corporation has the following transactions:

Mar. 1	Purchased 2,000 shares of its own common stock at $15 per share
Apr. 10	Reissued 1,000 shares of its common stock held in the treasury for $18 per share.
Jun. 12	Reissued 1,000 shares of common stock at $12 per share

Journalize the transactions.

PB6. LO 14.3 Tent & Tarp Corporation is a manufacturer of outdoor camping equipment. The company was incorporated ten years ago. It is authorized to issue 50,000 shares of $10 par value 5% preferred stock. It is also authorized to issue 500,000 shares of $1 par value common stock. It has issued 5,000 common shares and none of the preferred shares. Tent & Tarp has the following transactions:

Mar. 1	Declares a cash dividend of $3 per share
Mar. 30	Pays the cash dividend
Jul. 10	Declares a 35% stock dividend when the stock is trading at $15 per share
Aug. 5	Issues the stock dividend

Journalize these transactions.

PB7. LO 14.3 Tent & Tarp Corporation is a manufacturer of outdoor camping equipment. The company was incorporated ten years ago. It is authorized to issue 50,000 shares of $10 par value 5% preferred stock. It is also authorized to issue 500,000 shares of $1 par value common stock. It has issued 5,000 common shares and none of the preferred shares. Tent & Tarp has the following transactions:

Mar. 1	Declares a cash dividend of $5 per share
Mar. 30	Pays the cash dividend
Jul. 10	Declares a property dividend of one 6-person camping tent per share of stock when the price per tent is $150.

Journalize these transactions.

PB8. LO 14.3 Tent & Tarp Corporation is a manufacturer of outdoor camping equipment. The company was incorporated ten years ago. It is authorized to issue 50,000 shares of $10 par value 5% preferred stock. It is also authorized to issue 500,000 shares of $1 par value common stock. It has issued 5,000 common shares and 2,000 of the preferred shares. The corporation has never declared a dividend and the preferred shares are one years in arrears. Tent & Tarp has the following transactions:

Mar. 1	Declares a cash dividend of $10,000
Mar. 30	Pays the cash dividend
Jul. 10	Declares a 5-for-1 stock split of its common shares

Journalize these transactions. For the stock split, show the calculation for how many shares are outstanding after the split and the par value per share after the split

PB9. LO 14.4 You are a CPA working with sole proprietors. Several of your clients are considering incorporating because they need to expand and grow. One client is curious about how her financial reports will change. She's heard that she may need to prepare a statement of retained earnings and a statement of stockholder's equity. She's confused about the difference between the two and what they report. How would you explain the characteristics and functions of the two types of statements?

PB10. LO 14.4 You are a consultant for several emerging, high growth technology firms that were started locally and have been a part of a business incubator in your area. These firms start out as sole proprietorships but quickly realize the need for more capital and often incorporate. One of the common questions you get is about stockholder's equity. Explain the key ways the companies need to view retained earnings if they want to use it as a source of capital for future expansion and growth after incorporating.

PB11. LO 14.4 You are the accountant for Trumpet and Trombone Manufacturing, Inc. and you oversee the preparation of financial statements for the year just ended 6/30/2020. You have the following information from the company's general ledger and other financial reports (all balances are end-of-year except for those noted otherwise):

Cash	18,000
Common stock	16,000
Accounts receivable	19,000
Accounts payable	11,000
Cash dividends declared for the year	12,000
Additional paid-in capital	17,000
Prepaid insurance	15,000
Unearned revenue	14,000
Retained earnings, beginning of the year	26,000
Net income for the year	39,000

Prepare the company's Statement of Retained Earnings

PB12. LO 14.5 You have some funds that you would like to invest and you are relying heavily on the EPS calculation to help you make your decision. Initially you are baffled about why preferred dividends are subtracted in the numerator and why a weighted average is used in the denominator, so you do some research and reflection and come to understand why. Your friend is interested in hearing about your thought process. How would you explain to your friend why it's important to subtract preferred dividends and to use weighted averages?

PB13. LO 14.5 You are a consultant working with various companies that are considering incorporating and listing shares on a stock exchange. One of your clients asks you about the various acronyms she has been hearing in conjunction with financial analysis. Explain the following acronyms and how they measure different things but may complement each other: EPS (earnings per share), EBITDA (earnings before interest, taxes, depreciation, and amortization), and NOPAT (net operating profit after taxes).

Thought Provokers

TP1. LO 14.1 Your bakery is incorporated and is looking for investors. Write a one paragraph story of why investors should buy stock in your company. What makes your bakery special?

TP2. LO 14.1 Do some research: why did Facebook choose to reincorporate in Delaware?

TP3. LO 14.1 Do some research: why is Comcast incorporated in Pennsylvania?

TP4. LO 14.2 On November 7, 2013, Twitter released its initial public offering (IPO) priced at $26 per share. When the day ended, it was priced at $44.90, reportedly making about 1600 people into millionaires in a single day.[20] At the time it was considered a successful IPO. Four years later, Twitter is trading at around $18 per share. Why do you think that occurred? Is Twitter profitable? How can you find out?

TP5. LO 14.2 Research online to find a company that bought back shares of its own stock (treasury stock) within the last 6–12 months. Why did it repurchase the shares? What happened to the company's stock price immediately after the repurchase and in the months since then? Is there any reason to think the repurchase impacted the price?

TP6. LO 14.3 As a bakery business continues to grow, cash flow has become more of a concern. The board of directors would like to maintain the market share price, so a discussion ensues about issuing a stock dividend versus a cash dividend. As a newly appointed board member you listen to the conversation and need to cast your vote. Which do you vote for: stock dividend or cash dividend?

TP7. LO 14.3 Use the internet to find a company that declared a stock split within the last 1–2 years. Why did it declare the split? What happened to the company's stock price immediately after the split and in the months since then? Is there any reason to think the split impacted the price?

TP8. LO 14.4 Use the internet to find a publicly-held company's annual report. Locate the section reporting Stockholder's Equity. Assume that you work for a consulting firm that has recently taken on this firm as a client, and it is your job to brief your boss on the financial health of the company. Write a short memo noting what insights you gather by looking at the Stockholder's Equity section of the financial reports.

TP9. LO 14.4 Use the internet to find a publicly-held company's annual report. Locate the section that comments on the Stockholder's Equity section of the financial reports. What additional insights are you able to learn by looking further into the commentary? Is there anything that surprised you or that you think is missing and could help you if you were deciding whether to invest $100,000 of your savings in this company's stock?

20 Julie Bort. "Twitter's IPO Created 1,600 New Millionaires and a $2.2 Billion Tax Bill, Analyst Says." *Business Insider*. November 11, 2013. http://www.businessinsider.com/twitter-ipo-created-1600-millionaires-2013-11

15 Partnership Accounting

Figure 15.1 Partnership. Dale, Ciara, and Remi discuss operations of a landscape architecture company and need to decide on a business model. Should they choose a partnership? (credit: modification of “Business Meeting Architect” by “889520”/Pixabay, CC0)

Chapter Outline

LO **15.1** Describe the Advantages and Disadvantages of Organizing as a Partnership

LO **15.2** Describe How a Partnership Is Created, Including the Associated Journal Entries

LO **15.3** Compute and Allocate Partners’ Share of Income and Loss

LO **15.4** Prepare Journal Entries to Record the Admission and Withdrawal of a Partner

LO **15.5** Discuss and Record Entries for the Dissolution of a Partnership

Why It Matters

As a recent graduate of a landscape architecture program, Ciara is ready to start her professional career. Dale, her friend from high school, has started a small lawn mowing and hardscape business and wants to expand his services. Ciara and Dale sit down and work out that if they combine their talents, they will be able to take advantage of a growing need in their local housing market. They agree to form a partnership, and together they decide what each person will contribute to the business. Ciara has committed to invest cash, and Dale will contribute assets he has acquired in his business. In addition to the assets that each will provide, Ciara will contribute her expertise in landscape design, while Dale will contribute his experience in property maintenance and stonework/wood design and construction.

They set out on their adventure, creating a partnership agreement and detailing the roles each will play in this newly created partnership. At first, business is great and they work well together. There is one problem: they have more business than they can handle, and they are getting requests for services they currently don’t provide. However, Ciara’s friend Remi is a pond installer. From speaking with Remi, she knows he is very dedicated and has a vast customer base. She realizes that if he joins the partnership, the company can handle all the business demand better. Therefore, Ciara and Dale decide to amend the partnership agreement and admit Remi as a new one-third partner.

15.1 Describe the Advantages and Disadvantages of Organizing as a Partnership

A **partnership** is legal business structure consisting of an association of two or more people who contribute money, property, or services to operate as co-owners of a business. When discussing partnerships as a form of business ownership, the term *person* can refer to individuals, corporations, or even other partnerships. However, in this chapter, all the partners are individuals.

THINK IT THROUGH

Choosing a Partner

In some ways, a partnership is like a marriage; choosing a partner requires a great deal of thought. How do you know whether you and your potential partner or partners will be a good fit? A strong partnership agreement is one way to help settle future disagreements.

But before you get that far, it is really important to take a hard look at future partners. How do they deal with stressful situations? What skills and assets do they possess that you do not, and vice versa? What work ethic do they exemplify? Do they procrastinate? Are they planners? Do they get along with others? Do the two of you work well with each other?

All these questions and many more should be explored before choosing business partners. While you cannot predict the future or see all possible issues, doing your due diligence will help.

What other questions can you think of that would help you decide whether someone will be a good business partner for you?

Characteristics of a Partnership

Just like a corporation, a partnership is a legal entity. It can own property and can be held legally liable for its actions. It is a separate entity from its owners, the **partners**. Partnerships have several distinct characteristics that set them apart from other entity types. The most common characteristics of a partnership are the following:

- **Formation by agreement.** A partnership is formed by voluntary membership or association. The partners must have an agreement about who contributes assets or services, who performs what functions of the business, and how profits and losses and any additional compensation are shared. Ideally, this agreement should be in writing; however, if not, the Uniform Partnership Act or the Revised Uniform Partnership Act (RUPA) governs in areas of disagreement, depending on the state in which the partnership is located.
- **Defined or limited life.** Typically, the life term of the partnership is established by agreement. Unlike corporations, which have an unlimited life, partnerships end when a new partner is accepted or a partner leaves (and a new partnership may be created), or the partnership dissolves.

- **Mutual agency.** In a partnership, partners are considered agents of the entity. **Mutual agency** give each partner the ability to act as an agent for the partnership in dealing with outside entities such as vendors and lenders. The partnership is then bound by the actions of each partner acting within the scope of partnership activities.
- **Unlimited liability.** Due to mutual agency, any partner has the ability to incur debt for the partnership. Regardless of who negotiated the debt, each partner is liable to pay it if the debt was incurred to further partnership activities. There are exceptions to this, but only for partners who meet limited partnership standards (which you will learn about later in this chapter). If you are considered a general partner, you are liable for the business's debt.
- **Non-taxable income at partnership level.** The net income of a partnership is not subject to federal taxation at the partnership level, despite the company's being a separate legal entity from its partners. Instead, its income or loss is allocated among the partners based upon the partnership agreement and tax legislation, and the allocation is reported on each partner's Tax Form K-1. The tax information on each partner's K-1 is then incorporated into each partner's individual tax return, and tax is paid at each individual partner's relevant tax rate.

  Income tax is levied on the partners regardless of how much of that taxable income is actually withdrawn by the partner in a given year. For example, assume that a partner earned $20,000 in taxable income from a partnership in 2019 and withdrew $25,000 as a draw. The partner's taxable income from the partnership for the year is $20,000. Draws are not considered taxable income. Instead, they are withdrawals from a partner's capital account. However, the $25,000 draw in this example reduces the partner's capital account by $25,000.
- **Co-ownership of property.** In a partnership, assets are jointly owned by all partners. If a dissolution occurs, each partner retains a claim on the total assets proportional to that partner's equity in the organization. The rule presented herein does not apply to specific assets.
- **Limited capital investment.** Unlike a corporation, which is able to raise capital investments by issuing stock, partners do not have the ability to raise capital except by incurring additional debt or agreeing to contribute more of their personal assets. This limits the partnerships' ability for rapid expansion.
- **Participation in both income and loss.** The net income or loss of the partnership is distributed as specified in the partnership agreement. If the arrangement is not specified in the partnership agreement, all partners participate equally in net income or losses.

IFRS CONNECTION

Partnerships and IFRS

You've learned how partnerships are formed, and you will soon learn how partnership capital and income can be allocated and what happens to the capital structure when a partner is added or subtracted. But how does a partnership account for normal day-to-day business transactions?

Partnership organizations can be very small, very large, or any size in between. What type of accounting rules do partnerships use to record their daily business activities? Partnerships can choose among various forms of accounting. The options broadly include using a cash basis, a tax basis, and a full accrual basis to track transactions. When choosing to use the full accrual basis of accounting, partnerships apply U.S. GAAP rules in their accounting processes. But you may be surprised to learn that some non-publicly traded partnerships in the United States can use IFRS, or a simpler form of IFRS known as IFRS for Small and Medium Sized Entities (SMEs). In 2008, the AICPA designated IFRS and IFRS for SMEs as acceptable sets of generally accepted accounting principles. However, it is up to each State Board of Accountancy to determine whether that state will allow the use of IFRS or IFRS for SMEs by non-public entities incorporated in that state.

Despite the use of size descriptors in the title, qualifying as a small- or medium-sized entity has nothing to do with size. A SME is any entity that publishes general purpose financial statements for public use but does not have public accountability. In other words, the entity is not publicly traded. In addition, the entity, even if it is a partnership, cannot act as a fiduciary; for example, it cannot be a bank or insurance company and use SME rules.

Why might a partnership want to use IFRS for SMEs? First, IFRS for SMEs contains fewer and simpler standards. IFRS for SMEs is only about 300 pages in length, whereas regular IFRS is over 2,500 pages long and U.S. GAAP is over 25,000 pages. Second, IFRS for SMEs is modified only every three years, whereas U.S. GAAP and IFRS are modified more frequently. This means entities using IFRS for SMEs don't have to adjust their accounting systems and reporting to new standards as frequently. Finally, if a partnership transacts business with international businesses or hopes to attract international partners, seek capital from international sources, or be bought out by an international company, having its financial statements in IFRS form can make these transactions easier.

Advantages of Organizing as a Partnership

When it comes to choosing a legal structure or form for your business, the most common options are sole proprietorships, partnerships, and different forms of corporations, each with advantages and disadvantages. Partnerships have several advantages over other forms of business entities, as follows:

- **Exemption from taxation at the partnership level.** A significant advantage to forming a partnership is the exemption from taxation as a business entity. In other words, although the individual partners are taxed at the individual level, the partnership itself (as a business unit) is not subject to income tax. The tax characteristics of a partnership "flow through" to the individual partners.
- **Ease and lower cost of formation.** Most business regulations tend to be written for corporations, which is to be expected given the complexities of many such companies. Partnerships, on the other hand, are simpler and have to comply with fewer regulations. Also, without shareholders, partnerships have fewer reporting requirements. The partnership formation paperwork also tends to be less cumbersome than that for other entities in most states. Overall, partnerships are simple to form, alter, and terminate.
- **Combined skills and financial resources.** Combining business acumen and financial assets can give a partnership an advantage over sole proprietorships.
- **Flexibility in managing and running the business.** Partnerships are often simpler to manage and run than other business structures (except for most sole proprietorships), and they can offer more management flexibility as well if the partners generally agree on management issues. Since there is no board of directors overseeing operations, partnerships can be nimble and make speedy changes—again, as long as the partners agree.
- **Easily changed business structure.** It is a relatively easy process to convert a partnership to a corporation in the future. With no shareholders to consider, a partnership's capital can be converted to shares of common stock.

- **Informality.** Unlike publicly traded corporations, partnerships do not need to prepare articles of incorporation, write bylaws, issue stock certificates to owners, document minutes or board meetings, pay incorporation fees to states, or file quarterly financial statements with the SEC. However, it is advised that partners create a written document detailing decision on issues such as profit sharing, dispute resolution procedures, partnership changes, and other terms that the partners might agree upon to prevent future complications.

YOUR TURN

All in the Family

Family partnerships are frequently utilized to allow family members to pool resources for investment purposes and to transfer assets in a tax-efficient manner. In what ways can you imagine using a family partnership?

Solution

Cash can be combined to purchase income-producing properties or other investments without having to sell assets, thus keeping costly investments all in the family. Through a family partnership, it becomes possible for those in high net worth tax brackets to transfer assets and wealth to younger generations in a way that reduces potential estate and gift taxes. For example, a family partnership can be formed by a grandparent who owns an apartment building. Children and grandchildren can be partners to share in profits of the building. As they earn the income from the building while living, this can be a very tax efficient way to transfer wealth.

Disadvantages of Organizing as a Partnership

While partnerships carry some clear advantages, there are also several disadvantages to consider. For example, due to unlimited liability, each partner in a general partnership is equally and personally liable for all the debts of the partnership. Following are some of the disadvantages of the partnership form of business organization:

- **Difficulty of ownership transfer.** Since a partnership dissolves when there is a change in ownership, it tends to be difficult to transfer ownership. It is a complicated process when a new partner is added or a partnership interest is sold, requiring asset valuation and negotiation of previously agreed upon partnership operating terms.
- **Relative lack of regulation.** You learned, for example, that a partnership's informal agreement not need be in writing. But this could lead to legal disputes between partners and expose them to unlimited liability, something individuals in corporations do not need to worry about (they are liable only for the amount of their investment in the corporation's stock).
- **Taxation subject to individual's tax rate.** Individual partners often have other sources of income outside the partnership; this can make their allocated partnership income taxable at a higher rate than if the partnership were liable for the income taxes instead.
- **Limited life.** The partnership ends when a new partner is accepted into the partnership, a partner leaves, a partner dies, or the partnership dissolves. Therefore, most partnerships tend to have limited lives.

- **Unlimited liability. Unlimited liability** is the legal obligation of all general partners for the partnership's debts regardless of which partner incurred them. This liability can extend to the partners' personal assets.
- **Mutual agency and partnership disagreements.** Mutual agency is the right of all partners to represent the business and bind the partnership to contracts and agreements. This rule applies regardless of whether all the partners agree with the contract or agreement. Mutual agency could cause tension among the partners, since any of them can bind the partnership and make everyone liable as long as the action is taken in the interest of furthering the partnership.
- **Limited ability to raise capital.** A partnership is often limited in its ability to raise capital or additional funds, whether from the individual partners themselves or from a financial institution making a loan.

CONCEPTS IN PRACTICE

Sports Memorabilia Store

Farah and David decide to form a sports memorabilia retail partnership. They have known each other since business graduate school and have always worked well together on various projects. The business is doing well but cash flow is very tight. Farah takes several calls from vendors asking for payment. He believed David had been paying the bills. When he asks about this, David admits to embezzling from the partnership. What liability does Farah face as a result of the theft?

Table 15.1 summarizes some of the main advantages and disadvantages of the partnership form of business organization.

Advantages and Disadvantages of Forming a Partnership

Potential Advantages	Potential Disadvantages
• No taxation at the partnership level • Ease and lower cost of formation • Combined skills and financial resources • Flexibility in managing and running the business • Easily changed business structure • Informality	• Difficulty of ownership transfer • Relative lack of oversight/regulation • Number of partners needed • Taxation subject to individual's tax rate • Limited life • Unlimited liability • Mutual agency and potential for partnership disagreements • Limited ability to raise capital

Table 15.1

Types of Partnerships

A **general partnership** is an association in which each partner is personally liable to the partnership's creditors if the partnership has insufficient assets to pay its creditors. These partners are often referred to as general partners. A **limited partnership (LP)** is an association in which at least one partner is a general partner but the remaining partners can be limited partners, which means they are liable only for their own investment in the firm if the partnership cannot pay its creditors. Thus, their personal assets are not at risk.

Finally, the third type is a **limited liability partnership (LLP)**, which provides all partners with limited personal liability against another partner's obligations. **Limited liability** is a form of legal liability in which a partner's obligation to creditors is limited to his or her capital contributions to the firm. These types of partnerships include "LLP" or partnership in their names and are usually formed by professional groups such as lawyers and accountants. Each partner is at risk however, for his or her own negligence and wrongdoing as well as the negligence and wrongdoing of those who are under the partners' control or direction. Table 15.2 summarizes the advantages and disadvantages of different types of partnerships.

Advantages and Disadvantages of Types of Partnerships

Type of partnership	Advantages	Disadvantages
General partnership	Business is simple to form	All partners have personal liability
Limited partnership (LP)	Limited partners have limited liability	General partners are personally liable
Limited liability partnership (LLP)	Partners are protected from other partners' malpractice	Some partners remain personally liable

Table 15.2

LINK TO LEARNING

Arthur Andersen was one of the "Big 5" accounting firms until it was implicated in the Enron scandal. Arthur Andersen had been formed as an LLP. Read this CNN Money article about the Arthur Andersen case (https://openstax.org/l/50AACaseLiable) to see how courts can hold partners liable.

Dissolution of a Partnership

Dissolution occurs when a partner withdraws (due to illness or any other reason), a partner dies, a new partner is admitted, or the business declares bankruptcy. Whenever there is a change in partners for any reason, the partnership must be dissolved and a new agreement must be reached. This does not preclude the partnership from continuing business operations; it only changes the document underlying the business. In some cases, the new partnership may also require the revaluation of partnerships assets and, possibly, their sale. Ideally, the partnership agreement has been written to address dissolution.

15.2 Describe How a Partnership Is Created, Including the Associated Journal Entries

After examining all the relevant factors, Dale and Ciara decide to create their landscaping partnership. After much discussion, they agree on the name Acorn Lawn & Hardscapes. The first step is to formally document the actual partnership agreement. While a handshake would work, it is far more sensible to document it in case of disagreement.

Creation of a Partnership

Ideally, the agreement to form a partnership should be in the form of a written contract. This **partnership agreement** details the partners' roles, the way profits and losses are shared, and the contributions each partner makes to the partnership. It also should contain basic information such as the business's name, its location, its purpose or mission, the names of the partners, and the date of inception. Even more importantly, it should outline the following information. There is no legal requirement for a written partnership agreement. In fact, individuals can end up in court after forming a partnership agreement by accident with no written documentation. It is strongly suggested that any business relationship has a written agreement. A properly drafted agreement will often contain the following details:

- capital contributions of each partner
- allocation of profit, losses, and draws (withdrawals) among the partners
- partners' authority and decision-making role
- process for change in partners
- process for partnership dissolutions
- process for settling disputes

The partners should also consider the following items:

- **Name of the partnership.** The business needs a name. Many partnerships are named for the partners or the location, or the partners can choose and register an invented name. In many situations, if you are using an invented name you must file a *Doing Business As* (DBA) statement with the appropriate governmental agency.
- **Contributions to the partnership.** Important to the start of any business is finding the capital and equipment with which to begin. The partners should agree up front about what each partner will contribute, how the contribution will be recorded, and how the investment will affect each partner's share of ownership. For example, it is common for a partnership to allocate an ownership interest to a partner who has valuable experience or contacts in an area of interest to a partnership. Partners can also contribute service to the partnership rather than assets. Failure to address these details can derail a business before it even starts.
- **Partners' authority.** As you've learned, mutual agency can allow every partner to bind the partnership in agreements with outside vendors or lenders. If the authority of each partner has not been documented, problems can arise. Thus, it is important to outline who is responsible for what. The same goes for decision making. A strong agreement will outline how decision are made and at what thresholds all the partners need to be involved. A final point to cover is how management responsibilities will be divided up.
- **Allocation of profits, losses, and draws.** How will the partners share in the profits or losses of the partnership? Will any of the partners receive a guaranteed payment (salary)? If so, how much? Each partner is going to have different needs and requirements, and these should be agreed upon to avoid

dispute.

- **Change in Partners.** At some point there may be a change in partners – whether it is an addition or a withdrawal. A well-drafted partnership agreement will create rules for how that can happen.
- **Dispute resolution.** Selecting a means to resolve conflicts may one may be the most important choices for the new partners to make. It is human nature to disagree; the partnership agreement should cover how disputes will be handled so they do not interrupt business in the future.

Once the partnership agreement is complete, there are other steps to take to create the business as a legal entity.

1. Select the state in which you plan to operate. Typically, partnerships choose the state in which they are located. Since the partnership does not pay taxes and regulations are limited, state selection is not as important as it is for a corporation.
2. Register the name with the authorities required by the state in which the partnership is formed. This allows the partnership to use the name and prevents others from selecting it.
3. Obtain the required business licenses. If your partnership will be selling items subject to sales tax, you will need to obtain a sales tax license. If you are operating as a professional services firm, there may be state licensing requirements – attorneys, physicians, and certified public accountants (CPAs) are especially subject to license requirements.

ETHICAL CONSIDERATIONS

Ethical Obligations to Partners

Recall that each partner is jointly and severally liable for all the debts of the partnership, meaning each partner is personally liable for these obligations. As a result, in most business settings and jurisdictions, the actions of any partner are attributed to the partnership and each of its partners, whether the actions were approved by all partners or not. For example, if partner A signs a loan agreement on behalf of the partnership and the partnership defaults on the loan, partner B can be personally liable for the loan, even though this partner had no role in signing the initial agreement.

Due to this unlimited liability, whether there is a written partnership agreement or not, partners have an ethical duty to act in the best interests of the partnership and of each of their partners. This is generally called a fiduciary duty. A fiduciary is someone who has a legal and/or ethical obligation to act in the best interest of others in order to maintain a relationship of trust and confidence. What this means in practice is that partners are to avoid actual and potential conflicts of interests, and there is to be no self-dealing. Partners are expected to put the partnership's interest ahead of their own.

Formation of the Partnership

Each partner's initial contribution is recorded on the partnership's books. These contributions are recorded at the fair value of the asset at the date of transfer. All partners must agree to the valuation being recorded.

As an example, let's go back to Dale and Ciara. On January 1, 2019 they combined their resources into a general partnership named Acorn Lawn & Hardscapes. They agree to a 50:50 split of income and losses. As stated earlier, Ciara will invest cash and Dale has real assets to contribute to the partnership.

Dale's contributed assets include lawn equipment that he bought or created based on his specific needs. The equipment had a book value (determined in the process of filing Dale's past individual income taxes) of $5,600 and a fair market value (the current price at which it would sell) of $6,400. He also contributed accounts receivable from his business with a book value of $2,000. However, he expects to collect only $1,600 of it, so he is contributing accounts receivable with a market value of $1,600. Since Ciara contributed cash of $8,000 and no other assets, her contribution has a book value and a fair market value of $8,000 (Figure 15.2).

Note this point about the formation of a partnership when its assets' fair market value differs from their book value: it wouldn't make sense to base the value of the capital contribution of assets (or liabilities) on their book value. To see why, consider the equipment and accounts receivable contributions made by Dale. The equipment had a book value of $5,600 and a fair value of $6,400. Why should Dale get credit for a contribution of only the $5,600 book value when he could have sold the equipment for $6,400 and contributed $6,400 in cash, instead of the equipment with a fair value of $6,400?

The same principle applies to Dale's Accounts Receivable but in the opposite direction. Dale is contributing Accounts Receivable with a book value of $2,000, but since the partnership expects to collect only $1,600, that is the amount of capital contribution credit he will receive.

	Book value		Fair value	
	Ciara	Dale	Ciara	Dale
Cash	$8,000	$ 0	$8,000	$ 0
Equipment	0	5,600	0	6,400
Accounts receivable	0	2,000	0	1,600
Total	$8,000	$7,600	$8,000	$8,000

Figure 15.2 Assets Invested by Partners at Book Value and Fair Value. (attribution: Copyright Rice University, OpenStax, under CC BY-NC-SA 4.0 license)

The journal entries would be as follows:

JOURNAL			
Date	Account	Debit	Credit
2019			
Jan. 1	Equipment	6,400	
	Accounts receivable	1,600	
	Dale, Capital		8,000
	To record partner assets contributed		
Jan. 1	Cash	8,000	
	Ciara, Capital		8,000
	To record partner assets contributed		

When used fixed assets are contributed, depreciation is calculated based on their fair value and the partnership's estimate of their useful life. Fixed assets are contributed at their fair value, not the book value on the partner's individual books before the formation of the partnership. (In our examples, assume all the partners were sole proprietors before the formation of the partnership.)

Likewise, if the partnership were to assume liabilities from one of the partners, the liability would be recorded at the current value. And, as demonstrated above, any non-cash assets contributed to the partnership should be valued at their current values.

15.3 Compute and Allocate Partners' Share of Income and Loss

The landscaping partnership is going well and has realized increases in the number of jobs performed as well as in the partnership's earnings. At the end of the year, the partners meet to review the income and expenses. Once that has been done, they need to allocate the profit or loss based upon their agreement.

Allocation of Income and Loss

Just like sole proprietorships, partnerships make four entries to close the books at the end of the year. The entries for a partnership are:

1. Debit each revenue account and credit the income section account for total revenue.
2. Credit each expense account and debit the income section account for total expenses.
3. If the partnership had income, debit the income section for its balance and credit each partner's capital account based on his or her share of the income. If the partnership realized a loss, credit the income section and debit each partner's capital account based on his or her share of the loss.
4. Credit each partner's drawing account and debit each partner's capital account for the balance in that same partner's drawing account.

The first two entries are the same as for a proprietorship. Both revenue and expense accounts are temporary accounts. The last two entries are different because there is more than one equity account and more than one drawing account. **Capital accounts** are equity accounts for each partner that track all activities, such as profit sharing, reductions due to distributions, and contributions by partners to the partnership. Capital accounts are permanent while drawing accounts must be zeroed out for each accounting period.

By December 31 at the end of the first year, the partnership realized net income of $50,000. Since Dale and Ciara had agreed to a 50:50 split in their partnership agreement, each partner will record an increase to their capital accounts of $25,000. The journal records the entries to allocate year end net income to the partner capital accounts.

JOURNAL			
Date	**Account**	**Debit**	**Credit**
2019			
Dec. 31	Income summary	25,000	
	Dale, Capital		25,000
	To record 50:50 split of net income		
	Income summary	25,000	
	Ciara, Capital		25,000
	To record 50:50 split of net income		

Income Allocations

Not every partnership allocates profit and losses on an even basis. As you've learned, the partnership agreement should delineate how the partners will share net income and net losses. The partnership needs to find a methodology that is fair and will equitably reflect each partner's service and financial commitment to the partnership. The following are examples of typical ways to allocate income:

1. A fixed ratio where income is allocated in the same way every period. The ratio can be expressed as a percentage (80% and 20%), a proportion (7:3) or a fraction (1/4, 3/4).
2. A ratio based on beginning-of-year capital balances, end-of-year capital balances, or an average capital

balance during the year.

3. Partners may receive a guaranteed salary, and the remaining profit or loss is allocated on a fixed ratio.
4. Income can be allocated based on the proportion of interest in the capital account. If one partner has a capital account that equates to 75% of capital, that partner would take 75% of the income.
5. Some combination of all or some of the above methods.

A fixed ratio is the easiest approach because it is the most straightforward. As an example, assume that Jeffers and Singh are partners. Each contributed the same amount of capital. However, Jeffers works full time for the partnership and Singh works part time. As a result, the partners agree to a fixed ratio of 0.75:0.25 to share the net income.

Selecting a ratio based on capital balances may be the most logical basis when the capital investment is the most important factor to a partnership. These types of ratios are also appropriate when the partners hire managers to run the partnership in their place and do not take an active role in daily operations. The last three approaches on the list recognize differences among partners based upon factors such as time spent on the business or funds invested in it.

Salaries and interest paid to partners are considered expenses of the partnership and therefore deducted prior to income distribution. Partners are not considered employees or creditors of the partnership, but these transactions affect their capital accounts and the net income of the partnership.

Let's return to the partnership with Dale and Ciara to see how income and salaries can affect the split of net income (Figure 15.3). Acorn Lawn & Hardscapes reports net income of $68,000. The partnership agreement has defined an income sharing ratio, which provides for salaries of $15,000 to Dale and $10,000 to Ciara. They will share in the net income on a 50:50 basis. The calculation for income sharing between the partners is as follows:

	Dale	Ciara	Total	Total Remaining
Income Realized			$68,000	$68,000
Salaries	$15,000	$10,000	(25,000)	43,000
Income allocation	21,500	21,500	(43,000)	0
Total Division of Income	$36,500	$31,500		$ 0

Figure 15.3 Income Allocation for Acorn Lawn & Hardscapes. (attribution: Copyright Rice University, OpenStax, under CC BY-NC-SA 4.0 license)

Now, consider the same scenario for Acorn Lawn & Hardscapes, but instead of net income, they realize a net loss of $32,000. The salaries for Dale and Ciara remain the same. Also, the distribution process for allocating a loss is the same as the allocation process for distributing a gain, as demonstrated above. The partners will share in the net loss on a 50:50 basis. The calculation for the sharing of the loss between the partners is shown in Figure 15.4

	Dale	Ciara	Total	Total Remaining
Loss Realized			$(32,000)	$(32,000)
Salaries	$ 15,000	$ 10,000	(25,000)	(57,000)
Loss allocation	(28,500)	(28,500)	$(57,000)	0
Total division of Loss	$(13,500)	$(18,500)		$ 0

Figure 15.4 Loss sharing Allocation for Acorn Lawn & Hardscapes. (attribution: Copyright Rice University, OpenStax, under CC BY-NC-SA 4.0 license)

CONCEPTS IN PRACTICE

Spidell and Diaz: A Partnership

For several years, Theo Spidell has operated a consulting company as a sole proprietor. On January 1, 2017 he formed a partnership with Juanita Diaz called Insect Management.

The facts are as follows:

- Spidell was to transfer the cash, accounts receivable, furniture and equipment, and all the liabilities of the sole proprietorship in return for 60% of the partnership capital.
- The fair market value in the relevant accounts of the sole proprietorship at the close of business on December 31, 2016 are shown in Figure 15.5.

Cash	$ 52,000
Accounts receivable	120,000
Furniture and equipment	34,000
Accounts payable	10,000

Figure 15.5 Fair Market Values of Sole Proprietorship. (attribution: Copyright Rice University, OpenStax, under CC BY-NC-SA 4.0 license)

- In exchange for 40% of the partnership, Diaz will invest $130,667 in cash.
- Each partner will be paid a salary – Spidell $3,000 per month and Diaz $2,000 per month.
- The partnership's net income for 2016 was $300,000. The partnership agreement dictates an income-sharing ratio.
- Assume that all allocations are 60% Spidell and 40% Diaz.

Record the following transactions as journal entries in the partnership's records.

A. Receipt of assets and liabilities from Spidell
B. Investment of cash by Diaz
C. Profit or loss allocation including salary allowances and the closing balance in the Income Section account

THINK IT THROUGH

Sharing Profits and Losses in a Partnership

Michael Wingra has operated a very successful hair salon for the past 7 years. It is almost too successful because Michael does not have any free time. One of his best customers, Jesse Tyree, would like to get involved, and they have had several conversations about forming a partnership. They have asked you to provide some guidance about how to share in the profits and losses.

Michael plans to contribute the assets from his salon, which have been appraised at $500,000.

Jesse will invest cash of $300,000. Michael will work full time at the salon and Jesse will work part time. Assume the salon will earn a profit of $120,000.

Instructions:

1. What division of profits would you recommend to Michael and Jesse?
2. Using your recommendation, prepare a schedule sharing the net income.

15.4 Prepare Journal Entries to Record the Admission and Withdrawal of a Partner

So far we have demonstrated how to create a partnership, distribute the income or loss, and calculate income distributed at the end of the year after salaries have been paid. Acorn Lawn & Hardscapes has been doing well, but what if the opportunity arises to add another partner to handle more business? Or what happens if one partner wants to leave the partnership or sell his or her interest to someone else? This section will discuss those situations.

Admission of New Partner

There are two ways for a new partner to join a partnership. In both, a new partnership agreement should be drawn up because the existing partnership will come to an end.

1. The new partner can invest cash or other assets into an existing partnership while the current partners remain in the partnership.
2. The new partner can purchase all or part of the interest of a current partner, making payment directly to the partner and not to the partnership. If the new partner buys an existing partner's entire interest, the existing partner leaves the partnership.

The new partner's investment, share of ownership capital, and share of the net income or loss are all negotiated in the process of developing the new partnership agreement. Based on how a partner is admitted, oftentimes the admission can create a situation to be illustrated called a bonus to those in the partnership. A **bonus** is the difference between the value of a partner's capital account and the cash payment made at the time of that partner's or another partner's withdrawal.

Admission of New Partner—No Bonus

Whenever a new partner is admitted to the partnership, a new capital account must be opened for him or her. This will allow the partnership to reflect the new members of the partnership.

The purchase of an existing partner's ownership by a new partner is a personal transaction that involves the existing partner and the new partner without otherwise affecting the records of the partnership. Accounting for this method is very straightforward. The only changes that are recorded on the partnership's books occur in the two partners' capital accounts. The existing partner's capital account is debited and, after being created, the new partner's capital account is credited.

To illustrate, Dale decides to sell his interest in Acorn Lawn & Hardscapes to Remi. Since this is a personal transaction, the only entry Acorn needs to make is to record the transfer of partner interest from Dale to Remi on its books.

JOURNAL			
Date	**Account**	**Debit**	**Credit**
2021			
Jan. 1	Dale, Capital	55,000	
	Remi, Capital		55,000
	To record transfer of partner interest		

No other entry needs to be made. Note that the entry is a paper transfer—it is to move the balance in the capital account. The amount paid by Remi to Dale does not affect this entry.

If instead the new partner invests directly into the partnership, the change increases the assets of the partnership as well as the capital accounts. Suppose that, instead of buying Dale's interest, Remi will join Dale and Ciara in the partnership. The following journal entry will be made to record the admission of Remi as a partner in Acorn Lawn & Hardscapes.

JOURNAL			
Date	**Account**	**Debit**	**Credit**
2021			
Jan. 1	Cash	55,000	
	Remi, Capital		55,000
	To record new partner investment		

Admission of New Partner—Bonus to Old Partners

A bonus to the old partners can come about when the new partner's investment in the partnership creates an inequity in the capital of the new partnership, such as when a new partner's capital account is not proportionate to that of a previous partner. Because a change in ownership of a partnership produces a new partnership agreement, a bonus may be used to record the change in the ownership capital to prevent inequities among the partners.

A bonus to the old partner or partners increases (or credits) their capital balances. The amount of the increase depends on the income ratio before the new partner's admission.

As an illustration, Remi is a skilled machine operator who will aid Acorn Lawn & Hardscapes in the building of larger projects. Assume the following information (Figure 15.6) for the partnership on the day Remi becomes a partner.

Total capital of Acorn Lawn & Hardscapes	$100,000
Investment by new partner, Remi	65,000
Total capital of new partnership	165,000
Remi's capital credit (1/3 of $165,000)	55,000
Total bonus to Dale and Ciara	10,000

Figure 15.6 Breakdown of Allocation of Bonus to Old Partners. (attribution: Copyright Rice University, OpenStax, under CC BY-NC-SA 4.0 license)

To allocate the $10,000 bonus to the old partners, Dale and Ciara, make the following calculations:

$$\text{Dale: } (\$10{,}000 \times 50\%) = \$5{,}000$$
$$\text{Ciara: } (\$10{,}000 \times 50\%) = \$5{,}000$$

The journal entry to record Remi's admission to the partnership and the allocation of the bonus to Dale and Ciara is as shown.

JOURNAL			
Date	**Account**	**Debit**	**Credit**
2021			
Jan. 1	Cash	65,000	
	Dale, Capital		5,000
	Ciara, Capital		5,000
	Remi, Capital		55,000
	To record bonus to old partners		

Admission of New Partner—Bonus to New Partner

When the new partner's investment may be less than his or her capital credit, a bonus to the new partner may be considered. Sometimes the partnership is more interested in the skills the new partner possesses than in any assets brought to the business. For instance, the new partner may have expertise in a particular field that would be beneficial to the partnership, or the new partner may be famous and can draw attention to the partnership as a result. This frequently happens with restaurants; many are named after sports celebrity partners. A bonus to a newly admitted partner can also occur when the book values of assets currently on the partnership's books have a higher value than their fair market values.

A bonus to a new admitted partner decreases (or debits) the capital balances of the old partners. The amount of the decrease depends on the income ratio defined by the old partnership agreement in place before the new partner's admission.

In our landscaping business example, suppose Remi receives a bonus based on his skills as a machine operator. Assume the following information (Figure 15.7) for the partnership on the day he becomes a partner.

Total capital of Acorn Lawn & Hardscapes	$110,000
Investment by new partner, Remi	40,000
Total capital of new partnership	150,000
Remi's capital credit (1/3 of $150,000)	50,000
Total bonus to Remi	10,000

Figure 15.7 Breakdown of Allocation of Bonus to New Partner. (attribution: Copyright Rice University, OpenStax, under CC BY-NC-SA 4.0 license)

To allocate the $10,000 bonus that each of the old partners will contribute to the new partner, Remi, make the following calculations.

$$\text{Dale: } (\$10{,}000 \times 50\%) = \$5{,}000$$
$$\text{Ciara: } (\$10{,}000 \times 50\%) = \$5{,}000$$

The journal entry to record Remi's admission and the payment of his bonus in the partnership records is as follows:

JOURNAL			
Date	**Account**	**Debit**	**Credit**
2021			
Jan. 1	Cash	40,000	
	Dale, Capital	5,000	
	Ciara, Capital	5,000	
	Remi, Capital		50,000
	To record payment of bonus from old partners to new partner		

Withdrawal of Partner

Now, let's explore the opposite situation—when a partner withdraws from a partnership. Partners may withdraw by selling their equity in the business, through retirement, or upon death. The withdrawal of a partner, just like the admission of a new partner, dissolves the partnership, and a new agreement must be reached. As with a new partner, only the economic effect of the change in ownership is reflected on the books.

When existing partners buy out a retiring partner, the case is the opposite of admitting a new partner, but the transaction is similar. The existing partners use personal assets to acquire the withdrawing partner's equity and, as a result, the partnership's assets are not affected. The only effect in the partnership's records is the change in capital accounts. For example, assume that, after much discussion, Dale is ready to retire. Each partner has capital account balances of $60,000. Ciara and Remi agree to pay Dale $30,000 each to close out his partnership account. To record the withdrawal of Dale from the partnership, the journal entry is as follows:

JOURNAL			
Date	**Account**	**Debit**	**Credit**
2021			
Jan. 1	Dale, Capital	60,000	
	Ciara, Capital		30,000
	Remi, Capital		30,000
	To record withdrawal of a partner		

Note that there is no change to the net assets of Acorn Lawn & Hardscapes—only a change in the capital accounts. Ciara and Remi now have to create a new partnership agreement to reflect their new situation.

Partnership Buys Out Withdrawing Partner

When a partnership buys out a withdrawing partner, the terms of the buy-out should follow the partnership agreement. Using partnership assets to pay for a withdrawing partner is the opposite of having a new partner invest in the partnership. In accounting for the withdrawal by payment from partnership assets, the partnership should consider the difference, if any, between the agreed-upon buy-out dollar amount and the balance in the withdrawing partner's capital account. That difference is a bonus to the retiring partner.

This situation occurs when:

1. The partnership's fair market value of assets exceeds the book value.
2. Goodwill resulting from the partnership has not been accounted for.
3. The remaining partners urgently want the withdrawing partner to exit or want to show their appreciation of the partner's contributions.

The partnership debits (or reduces) the bonus from the remaining partners' capital balances on the basis of their income ratio at the time of the buy-out. To illustrate, Acorn Lawn & Hardscapes is appreciative of the hard work that Dale has put into its success and would like to pay him a bonus. Dale, Ciara, and Remi each have capital account balances of $60,000 at the time of Dale's retirement. Acorn Lawn & Hardscapes intends to pay Dale $80,000 for his interest. Ciara and Remi will do this as follows:

1. Calculate the amount of the bonus. This is done by subtracting Dale's capital account balance from the cash payment: ($80,000 – $60,000) = $20,000.
2. Allocate the cost of the bonus to the remaining partners on the basis of their income ratio. This calculation comes to $10,000 each for Ciara and Remi ($20,000 × 50%).

The journal entry to record Dale's retirement from the partnership and the bonus payment to reflect his withdrawal is as shown:

JOURNAL			
Date	**Account**	**Debit**	**Credit**
2021			
Jan. 1	Dale, Capital	60,000	
	Ciara, Capital	10,000	
	Remi, Capital	10,000	
	Cash		80,000
	To record retirement of a partner with a bonus payment		

In some cases, the retiring partner may give a bonus to the remaining partners. This can happen when:

1. Recorded assets are overvalued.
2. The partnership is not performing well.
3. The partner urgently wants to leave the partnership

In these cases, the cash paid by the partnership to the retiring partner is less than the balance in his or her capital account. As a result, the other partners receive a bonus to their capital accounts based on the income-sharing ratio established prior to the withdrawal.

As an example, each of three partners of Acorn Lawn & Hardscapes has a capital balance of $60,000. Dale has another opportunity and is eager to move on. He is willing to accept $50,000 cash in order to retire. The difference between this cash amount and Dale's capital account is a bonus to the remaining partners. The bonus will be allocated to Ciara and Remi based on the income ratio at the time of Dale's departure.

The journal entry to record Dale's withdrawal and the bonus to Ciara and Remi is as shown:

JOURNAL			
Date	**Account**	**Debit**	**Credit**
2021			
Jan. 1	Dale, Capital	60,000	
	Cash		50,000
	Ciara, Capital		5,000
	Remi, Capital		5,000
	To record withdrawal of a partner and a bonus payment to remaining partners		

When a partner passes away, the partnership dissolves. Most partnership agreements have provisions for the surviving partners to continue operating the partnership. Typically, a valuation is performed at the date of death, and the remaining partners settle with the deceased partner's estate either directly with cash or through distribution of the partnership's assets.

15.5 Discuss and Record Entries for the Dissolution of a Partnership

Partnerships dissolve. Sometime the decision is made to close the business. Sometimes there is a bankruptcy. Partner negligence, retirement, death, poor cash flow, and change in business practices are just some of the reasons for closing down.

ETHICAL CONSIDERATIONS

Ethical Partnership Dissolution

In most dissolutions of a partnership, the business partners need to decide what will happen to the partnership itself. A partnership may be dissolved, but that may not end business operations. If the partnership's business operations are to continue, the partnership must decide what to do with its customers or clients, particularly those primarily served by a partner leaving the business. An ethical partnership will notify its customers and clients of the change and whether and how the partnership is going to continue as a business under a new partnership agreement. Partners who are unable to agree on how to notify their customers and clients should look to the Uniform Partnership Act, Article 8, which outlines the general obligations and duties of partners when a partnership is dissolved.

A partner's duties and obligation upon dissolution describe what the departing partner owes to the partnership and the other partners in duties of loyalty and care, which are the basic fiduciary duties of a partner prior to dissolution, as outlined in Section 409 of the Uniform Partnership Act. The one change upon dissolution is that "each partner's duty not to compete ends when the partnership dissolves." The Act states that "the dissolution of a partnership is the change in the relation of the partners caused by any partner ceasing to be associated in the carrying on as distinguished from the winding up of the business."[1] This may not terminate the partnership's business operations, but the partner's obligations under the dissolved partnership agreement will end, regardless of how the remaining partners create a new partnership.

The departure or removal of a partner or partners and the resulting creation of a new partnership may be tricky, because all original partners owe each other the duty of fairness and loyalty until the dissolution has been completed. All the partners, departing or otherwise, are required to behave in a fashion that does not hurt business operations and avoid putting their individual interests ahead of the interests of the soon-to-be-dissolved partnership. Once the partnership has been dissolved, the departing partners no longer have an obligation to their old business partners.

Fundamentals of Partnership Dissolution

The **liquidation** or dissolution process for partnerships is similar to the liquidation process for corporations. Over a period of time, the partnership's non-cash assets are converted to cash, creditors are paid to the extent possible, and remaining funds, if any, are distributed to the partners. Partnership liquidations differ from corporate liquidations in some respects, however:

1. General partners, as you may recall, have unlimited liability. Any general partner may be asked to contribute additional funds to the partnership if its assets are insufficient to satisfy creditors' claims.
2. If a general partner does not make good on his or her deficit capital balance, the remaining partners must absorb that deficit balance. Absorption of the partner's deficit balance gives the absorbing partner legal recourse against the deficit partner.

Recording the Dissolution Process

As discussed above, the liquidation or dissolution of a partnership is synonymous with closing the business. This may occur due to mutual partner agreement to sell the business, the death of a partner, or bankruptcy. Before proceeding with liquidation, the partnership should complete the accounting cycle for its final operational period. This will require closing the books with only balance sheet accounts remaining. Once that process has been completed, four steps remain in the accounting for the liquidation, each requiring an accounting entry. They are:

- Step 1: Sell noncash assets for cash and recognize a gain or loss on **realization**. Realization is the sale of noncash assets for cash.
- Step 2: Allocate the gain or loss from realization to the partners based on their income ratios.
- Step 3: Pay partnership liabilities in cash.
- Step 4: Distribute any remaining cash to the partners on the basis of their capital balances.

These steps must be performed in sequence. Partnerships must pay creditors prior to distributing funds to partners. At liquidation, some partners may have a deficiency in their capital accounts, or a debit balance.

Let's consider an example. Football Partnership is liquidated; its balance sheet after closing the books is shown in Figure 15.8.

1 Uniform Law Commission. *Uniform Partnership Act* (1997) (Last Amended 2013). https://www.uniformlaws.org/viewdocument/final-act-with-comments-118?CommunityKey=52456941-7883-47a5-91b6-d2f086d0bb44&tab=librarydocuments

FOOTBALL PARTNERSHIP Balance Sheet For the Month Ended December 31, 2019	
Assets	
Cash	$ 5,000
Accounts Receivable	10,000
Inventory	22,000
Equipment	30,000
Accumulated Depreciation	(5,000)
Total Assets	$62,000
Liabilities and Partner Capital	
Notes Payable	$15,000
Accounts Payable	15,000
Raven, Capital	15,000
Brown, Capital	10,000
Eagle, Capital	7,000
Total Liabilities and Partner Capital	$62,000

Figure 15.8 Balance Sheet for Football Partnership. (attribution: Copyright Rice University, OpenStax, under CC BY-NC-SA 4.0 license)

The partners of Football Partnership agree to liquidate the partnership on the following terms:

1. All the partnership assets will be sold to Hockey Partnership for $60,000 cash.
2. The partnership will satisfy the liabilities.
3. The income ratio will be 3:2:1 to partners Raven, Brown, and Eagle respectively. (Another way of saying this is 3/6:2/6:1/6.)
4. The remaining cash will be distributed to the partners based on their capital account basis.

The journal entry to record the sale of assets to Hockey Partnership (Step 1) is as shown:

JOURNAL			
Date	**Account**	**Debit**	**Credit**
2020 Jan. 1	Cash	60,000	
	Accumulated depreciation	5,000	
	Accounts receivable		10,000
	Inventory		22,000
	Equipment		30,000
	Gain on realization		3,000
	To record the sale of assets to Hockey Partnership		

The journal entry to allocate the gain on realization among the partners' capital accounts in the income ratio of 3:2:1 to Raven, Brown, and Eagle, respectively (Step 2), is as shown:

JOURNAL			
Date	**Account**	**Debit**	**Credit**
2020 Jan. 1	Gain on realization Raven, Capital (3/6 × $3,000) Brown, Capital (2/6 × $3,000) Eagle, Capital (1/6 × $3,000) *To allocate gain on realization among partner capital accounts*	3,000	 1,500 1,000 500

The journal entry for Football Partnership to pay off the liabilities (Step 3) is as shown:

JOURNAL			
Date	**Account**	**Debit**	**Credit**
2020 Jan. 1	Notes payable Accounts payable Cash *To record payment of liabilities*	15,000 15,000	 30,000

The journal entry to distribute the remaining cash to the partners based on their capital account basis (Step 4) is as shown:

JOURNAL			
Date	**Account**	**Debit**	**Credit**
2020 Jan. 1	Raven, Capital Brown, Capital Eagle, Capital Cash *To allocate gain on realization among partner capital accounts*	16,500 11,000 7,500	 35,000

Key Terms

bonus difference between the value of a partner's capital account and the cash payment made at the time of that partner's or another partner's withdrawal

capital account equity account for each partner that tracks all activities such as profit sharing, reductions due to distributions, and contributions by partners to partnership

dissolution closing down of a partnership for economic, personal, or other reasons that may be unique to the particular partnership

general partnership partnership in which each partner is personally liable to the partnership's creditors if the partnership has insufficient assets to pay its creditors

limited liability form of legal liability in which a partner's obligation to creditors is limited to his or her capital contributions to the firm

limited liability partnership (LLP) partnership that provides all partners with limited personal liability against all other partners' obligations

limited partnership (LP) partnership in which at least one partner is a general partner but the remaining partners can be limited partners, which means they are liable only for their own investment in the firm if the partnership cannot pay its creditors; thus, their personal assets are not at risk

liquidation (also, dissolution) process of selling off non-cash assets

mutual agency ability of each partner to act as an agent of the partnership in dealing with persons outside the partnership

partner individuals, corporations, and even other partnerships participating in a partnership entity

partnership legal business structure consisting of an association of two or more people who contribute money, property, or services to operate as co-owners of a business

partnership agreement document that details the partners' role, the way profits and loss are shared, and the contributions each partner makes to the partnership

realization the sale of noncash assets for cash

unlimited liability form of legal liability in which general partners are liable for all business debts if the business cannot meet its liabilities

Summary

15.1 Describe the Advantages and Disadvantages of Organizing as a Partnership

- There are many advantages and disadvantages of partnership as a form of business entity and they should be carefully considered.
- The most significant advantage of partnerships is the exemption from tax at the business level. Partners are taxed on their share of the profit or loss at their individual tax rates.
- Mutual agency and unlimited liability should be weighed against the tax benefits of partnership.
- There are other entity forms that have many of the characteristics of standard partnerships. These other entity forms often share the legal liability protection of corporations, and the tax and personal benefits of a partnership.

15.2 Describe How a Partnership Is Created, Including the Associated Journal Entries

- Partners must consider several factors when developing their partnership agreement, such as the contributions and authority of each partner and a means to resolve disputes.
- Non-cash assets such as equipment and prepaid expenses should be recorded at current market values.

- Partners are sometimes given an ownership interest based on their expertise or experience instead of any contributed assets.
- Liabilities assumed by the partnership should be recorded at their current value.

15.3 Compute and Allocate Partners' Share of Income and Loss

- There are several different approaches to sharing the income or loss of a partnership, including fixed ratios, capital account balances, and combinations of the two.

15.4 Prepare Journal Entries to Record the Admission and Withdrawal of a Partner

- There are two different methods for admitting a new partner to a partnership—direct investment to the partnership (affects partnership assets) and transaction among partners (does not affect partnership assets).
- There are two different methods for a partner to withdraw from a partnership—direct payment from the partnership and direct payment from the partners.

15.5 Discuss and Record Entries for the Dissolution of a Partnership

- There are times, such as following bankruptcy, death, or retirement, when a partnership ceases operation.
- The following four accounting steps must be taken, in order, to dissolve a partnership: sell noncash assets; allocate any gain or loss on the sale based on the income-sharing ratio in the partnership agreement; pay off liabilities; distribute any remaining cash to partners based on their capital account balances.

Multiple Choice

1. LO 15.1 A partnership ______.

A. has one owner
B. can issue stock
C. pays taxes on partnership income
D. can have more than one general partner

2. LO 15.1 Any assets invested by a particular partner in a partnership ______.

A. do not become a partnership asset but instead remain with the partner
B. can be used only by the investing partner
C. become the property of all the partners
D. are the basis for all profit sharing

3. LO 15.1 Which of the following is a *disadvantage* of the partnership form of organization?

A. limited life
B. no taxation at the partnership level
C. flexibility in business operations
D. combining of financial resources

4. LO 15.1 Mutual agency is defined as:

A. a mutual agreement

B. the right of all partners to represent the company's normal business operations

C. a synonym for partnership

D. a partnership between two partnerships

5. LO 15.2 Chani contributes equipment to a partnership that she purchased 2 years ago for $10,000. The current book value is $7,500 and the market value is $9,000. At what value should the partnership record the equipment?

A. $10,000

B. $9,000

C. $7,500

D. none of the above

6. LO 15.2 Juan contributes marketable securities to a partnership. The book value of the securities is $7,000 and they have a current market value of $10,000. What amount should the partnership record in Juan's Capital account due to this contribution?

A. $10,000

B. $7,000

C. $3,000

D. none of the above

7. LO 15.2 Which one of the following would *not* be considered in the development of a partnership agreement?

A. profit and loss levels

B. processing disputes

C. stock options

D. asset contributions

8. LO 15.3 A well written partnership agreement should include each of the following *except* ______.

A. how to settle disputes

B. the name of the partnership

C. division of responsibilities

D. Partner's individual tax rate

9. LO 15.3 What type of assets may a partner *not* contribute to a partnership?

A. accounts receivable

B. furniture

C. equipment

D. personal credit cards

10. LO 15.3 How does a newly formed partnership handle the contribution of previously depreciated assets?

A. continues the depreciation life as if the owner had not changed

B. starts over, using the contributed value as the new cost basis

C. shortens the useful life of the asset per the partnership agreement

D. does not depreciate the contributed asset

11. LO 15.4 Thandie and Marco are partners with capital balances of $60,000. They share profits and losses at 50% each. Chris contributes $30,000 to the partnership for a 1/3 share. What amount should the partnership record as a bonus to Chris?

A. $20,000
B. $15,000
C. $10.500
D. $5,000

12. LO 15.4 Thandie and Marco are partners with capital balances of $60,000. They share profits and losses at 50%. Chris contributes $30,000 to the partnership for a 1/3 share. What amount should Thandie's capital balance in the partnership be?

A. $60,000
B. $50,000
C. $45,000
D. $30,000

13. LO 15.4 Thandie and Marco are partners with capital balances of $60,000. They share profits and losses at 50%. Chris contributes $90,000 to the partnership for a 1/3 share. What amount should the partnership record as an individual bonus to each of the old partners?

A. $10,000
B. $7,000
C. $3,000
D. $20,000

14. LO 15.4 Thandie and Marco are partners with capital balances of $60,000. They share profits and losses at 50%. Chris contributes $60,000 to the partnership for a 1/3 share. What amount should the partnership record as an individual bonus to each of the old partners?

A. $10,000
B. $7,000
C. $0
D. $5,000

15. LO 15.5 When a partnership dissolves, the first step in the dissolution process is to ______.

A. allocate the gain or loss on sale based on income sharing ratio
B. pay off liabilities
C. sell noncash assets
D. divide the remaining cash among the partners

16. LO 15.5 When a partnership dissolves, the last step in the dissolution process is to ______.

A. allocate the gain or loss on sale based on income sharing ratio
B. pay off liabilities
C. sell noncash assets
D. divide the remaining cash among the partners

17. LO 15.5 Prior to proceeding with the liquidation, the partnership should ______.

A. prepare adjusting entries without closing
B. complete the accounting cycle for final operational period
C. prepare only closing entries
D. complete financial statements only

Questions

1. LO 15.1 Does a partnership pay income tax?

2. LO 15.1 Can a partner's personal assets in a limited liability partnership be at risk?

3. LO 15.2 Can a partnership assume liabilities as part of one of the partner's contributions?

4. LO 15.2 Does each partner have to contribute an equal amount of assets in order to split profit and losses?

5. LO 15.3 What types of bases for dividing partnership net income or net loss are available?

6. LO 15.3 Angela and Agatha are partners in Double A Partners. When they withdraw cash for personal use, how should that be recorded in the accounting records?

7. LO 15.3 On February 3, 2016 Sam Singh invested $90,000 cash for a 1/3 interest in a newly formed partnership. Prepare the journal entry to record the transaction.

8. LO 15.5 Why do partnerships dissolve?

9. LO 15.5 What are the four steps involved in liquidating a partnership?

10. LO 15.5 When a partner withdraws from the firm, which accounts are affected?

11. LO 15.5 What is the first step in a partnership liquidation (termination and sale of assets)?

12. LO 15.5 When a partnership liquidates, do partners get paid first or do creditors get paid first?

13. LO 15.5 Coffee Partners decides to close due to the increased competition from the national chains. If after liquidating the noncash assets there is not enough cash to cover accounts payable, what happens?

Exercise Set A

EA1. LO 15.2 On May 1, 2017, BJ and Paige formed a partnership. Each contributed assets with the following agreed-upon valuations.

	BJ	Paige
Cash	$80,000	$20,000
Equipment	50,000	60,000
Building	0	240,000
Loan payable	0	100,000

Prepare a separate journal entry to record each partner's contributions.

EA2. LO 15.3 The partnership of Chase and Chloe shares profits and losses in a 70:30 ratio respectively after Chloe receives a $10,000 salary. Prepare a schedule showing how the profit and loss should be divided, assuming the profit or loss for the year is:

A. $ 30,000
B. $ 6,000
C. ($10,000)

EA3. LO 15.4 The partnership of Tasha and Bill shares profits and losses in a 50:50 ratio, and the partners have capital balances of $45,000 each. Prepare a schedule showing how the bonus should be divided if Ashanti joins the partnership with a $60,000 investment. The partner's new agreement will share profit and loss in a 1:3 ratio.

EA4. LO 15.5 Cheese Partners has decided to close the store. At the date of closing, Cheese Partners had the following account balances:

Capital	$ 9,000
Cash	$ 6,000
Inventory	$15,000
Store fixtures	$10,000
Accounts payable	$22,000

A competitor agrees to buy the inventory and store fixtures for $20,000. Prepare the journal entries detailing the liquidation, assuming that partners Colette and Swarma are sharing profits on a 50:50 basis:

Exercise Set B

EB1. LO 15.4 The partnership of Michelle, Amal, and Maureen has done well. The three partners have shared profits and losses in a 1:3 ratio, with capital balances of $60,000 each. Maureen wants to retire and withdraw. Prepare a schedule showing how the cost should be divided if Amal and Michelle decide to pay Maureen $70,000 for retirement of her capital account and the new agreement will share profits and losses 50:50.

Problem Set A

PA1. LO 15.3 The partnership of Tatum and Brook shares profits and losses in a 60:40 ratio respectively after Tatum receives a 10,000 salary and Brook receives a 15,000 salary. Prepare a schedule showing how the profit and loss should be divided, assuming the profit or loss for the year is:

A. $40,000
B. $25,000
C. ($5,000)

In addition, show the resulting entries to each partner's capital account. Tatum's capital account balance is $50,000 and Brook's is $60,000.

PA2. LO 15.4 Arun and Margot want to admit Tammy as a third partner for their partnership. Their capital balances prior to Tammy's admission are $50,000 each. Prepare a schedule showing how the bonus should be divided among the three, assuming the profit or loss agreement will be 1:3 once Tammy has been admitted and her contribution is:

A. $20,000
B. $80,000
C. $50,000.

In addition, show the resulting journal entries to each of the three partners' capital accounts.

PA3. LO 15.5 When a partnership is liquidated, any gains or losses realized by the sale of noncash assets are allocated to the partners based on their income sharing ratio. Why?

Problem Set B

PB1. LO 15.3 The partnership of Magda and Sue shares profits and losses in a 50:50 ratio after Mary receives a $7,000 salary and Sue receives a $6,500 salary. Prepare a schedule showing how the profit and loss should be divided, assuming the profit or loss for the year is:

A. $10,000
B. $5,000
C. ($12,000)

In addition, show the resulting entries to each partner's capital account.

PB2. LO 15.4 The partnership of Arun, Margot, and Tammy has been doing well. Arun wants to retire and move to another state for a once-in-a-lifetime opportunity. The partners' capital balances prior to Arun's retirement are $60,000 each. Prepare a schedule showing how Arun's withdrawal should be divided assuming his buyout is:

A. $70,000
B. $45,000
C. $60,000.

In addition, show the resulting entries to the capital accounts of each of the three.

PB3. LO 15.5 Match each of the following descriptions with the appropriate term related to partnership accounting.

A. Each and every partner can enter into contracts on behalf of the partnership	i. liquidation
B. The business ceases operations.	ii. capital deficiency
C. How partners share in income and loss	iii. admission of a new partner
D. Adding a new partner by contributing cash	iv. mutual agency
E. A partner account with a debit balance	v. income sharing ratio

Thought Provokers

TP1. LO 15.1 While sole proprietorships and corporations are the most popular forms of business organization, the limited liability company (LLC) is a close third. Limited liability companies are treated like partnerships in the majority of situations. Why do you think LLCs are gaining in popularity?

TP2. LO 15.5 A partnership is thriving. The three partners get along well; they complement each other's skill sets and enjoy each other's company. One of the partners, Melinda, begins to behave differently. She begins coming to work late or not at all. On several occasions she is spotted leaving the hotel next door in the afternoon. The other partners are concerned about the change in her behavior. They confront her and Melinda denies that anything is different. She points out that her work is still getting done and that she wants a little more flexibility in her hours. The other partners are not convinced and decide to terminate the partnership agreement. Can the other partners break the agreement? What considerations must the partners take into account?

16

Statement of Cash Flows

Figure 16.1 Cash. (credit: modification of "Money" by "Tax Credits"/Flickr, CC BY 2.0)

Chapter Outline

LO **16.1** Explain the Purpose of the Statement of Cash Flows

LO **16.2** Differentiate between Operating, Investing, and Financing Activities

LO **16.3** Prepare the Statement of Cash Flows Using the Indirect Method

LO **16.4** Prepare the Completed Statement of Cash Flows Using the Indirect Method

LO **16.5** Use Information from the Statement of Cash Flows to Prepare Ratios to Assess Liquidity and Solvency

LO **16.6** Appendix: Prepare a Completed Statement of Cash Flows Using the Direct Method

Why It Matters

Most financial accounting processes focus on the accrual basis of accounting, which reflects revenue earned, regardless of whether that revenue has been collected or not, and the related costs involved in producing that revenue, whether those costs have been paid or not. Yet the single-minded focus on accrued revenues and expenses, without consideration of the cash impact of these transactions, can jeopardize the ability of users of the financial statements to make well-informed decisions. Some investors say that "cash is king," meaning that they think a company's cash flow is more important than its net income in determining investment opportunities. Companies go bankrupt because they run out of cash. Financial statement users should be able to develop a picture of how well a company's net income generates cash and the sources and uses of a company's cash. From the statement of cash flows, it becomes possible to reconcile income on the income statement to the cash actually generated during the same period. Having cash alone is not important, but the source and use of cash are also important, specifically where the cash is coming from. If the business is generating cash from operations (selling products and services), that is positive. If the company only has cash as it is taking out loans and selling assets, one must be careful in their analysis.

16.1 Explain the Purpose of the Statement of Cash Flows

The **statement of cash flows** is a financial statement listing the cash inflows and cash outflows for the business for a period of time. **Cash flow** represents the cash receipts and cash disbursements as a result of business activity. The statement of cash flows enables users of the financial statements to determine how well a company's income generates cash and to predict the potential of a company to generate cash in the future.

Accrual accounting creates timing differences between income statement accounts and cash. A revenue transaction may be recorded in a different fiscal year than the year the cash related to that revenue is received. One purpose of the statement of cash flows is that users of the financial statements can see the amount of cash inflows and outflows during a year in addition to the amount of revenue and expense shown on the income statement. This is important because cash flows often differ significantly from accrual basis net income. For example, assume in 2019 that Amazon showed a loss of approximately $720 million, yet Amazon's cash balance increased by more than $91 million. Much of the change can be explained by timing differences between income statement accounts and cash receipts and distributions.

A related use of the statement of cash flows is that it provides information about the quality of a company's net income. A company that has records that show significantly less cash inflow on the statement of cash flows than the reported net income on the income statement could very well be reporting revenue for which cash will never be received from the customer or underreporting expenses.

A third use of the statement of cash flows is that it provides information about a company's sources and uses of cash not related to the income statement. For example, assume in 2019 that Amazon spent $287 million on purchasing fixed assets and almost $370 million acquiring other businesses. This indicated to financial statement users that Amazon was expanding even as it was losing money. Investors must have thought that spending was good news as Amazon was able to raise more than $1 billion in borrowings or stock issuances in 2019.

ETHICAL CONSIDERATIONS

Cash Flow Statement Reporting

US generally accepted accounting principles (GAAP) has codified how cash flow statements are to be presented to users of financial statements. This was codified in Topic 230: Statement of Cash Flows as part of US GAAP.[1] Accountants in the United States should follow US GAAP. Accountants working internationally must report in accordance with International Accounting Standard (IAS) 7 Statement of Cash Flows.[2] The ethical accountant understands the users of a company's financial statement and properly prepares a Statement of Cash Flow. There is often more than one way that financial statements can be presented, such as US GAAP and International Financial Reporting Standards (IFRS). What if a company under US GAAP showed reporting issues on their financial statements and switched to IFRS where results looked better. Is this proper? Does this occur?

---

1 Financial Accounting Standards Board (FASB). "Statement of Cash Flows (Topic 230) Classification of Certain Cash Receipts and Cash Payments." An Amendment of the **FASB Accounting Standards Codification**. August 2016. https://asc.fasb.org/imageRoot/55/95454355.pdf
2 International Financial Reporting Standards (IFRS). "IAS 7 Statement of Cash Flows." n.d. https://www.ifrs.org/issued-standards/list-of-standards/ias-7-statement-of-cash-flows/

The statement of cash flows identifies the sources of cash as well as the uses of cash, for the period being reported, which leads the user of the financial statement to the period's **net cash flows**, which is a method used to determine profitability by measuring the difference between an entity's cash inflows and cash outflows. The statement answers the following two questions: What are the sources of cash (where does the cash come from)? What are the uses of cash (where does the cash go)? A positive net cash flow indicates an increase in cash during the reporting period, whereas a negative net cash flow indicates a decrease in cash during the reporting period. The statement of cash flows is also used as a predictive tool for external users of the financial statements, for estimated future cash flows, based on cash flow results in the past.

LINK TO LEARNING

This video from Khan Academy explains cash flows (https://openstax.org/l/50CashFlowsVid) in a unique way.

Approaches to Preparing the Statement of Cash Flows

The statement of cash flows can be prepared using the indirect approach or the direct approach. The **indirect method** approach reconciles net income to cash flows by subtracting noncash expenses and adjusting for changes in current assets and liabilities, which reflects timing differences between accrual-based net income and cash flows. A **noncash expense** is an expense that reduces net income but is not associated with a cash flow; the most common example is depreciation expense. The **direct method** lists net cash flows from revenue and expenses, whereby accrual basis revenue and expenses are converted to cash basis collections and payments. Because the vast majority of financial statements are presented using the indirect method, the indirect approach will be demonstrated within the chapter, and the direct method will be demonstrated in Appendix: Prepare a Completed Statement of Cash Flows Using the Direct Method.

LINK TO LEARNING

AccountingCoach (https://openstax.org/l/50AccountCoach) is a great resource for many accounting topics, including cash flow issues.

16.2 Differentiate between Operating, Investing, and Financing Activities

The statement of cash flows presents sources and uses of cash in three distinct categories: *cash flows from operating activities*, *cash flows from investing activities*, and *cash flows from financing activities*. Financial statement users are able to assess a company's strategy and ability to generate a profit and stay in business by assessing how much a company relies on operating, investing, and financing activities to produce its cash flows.

THINK IT THROUGH

Classification of Cash Flows Makes a Difference

Assume you are the chief financial officer of T-Shirt Pros, a small business that makes custom-printed T-shirts. While reviewing the financial statements that were prepared by company accountants, you discover an error. During this period, the company had purchased a warehouse building, in exchange for a $200,000 note payable. The company's policy is to report noncash investing and financing activities in a separate statement, after the presentation of the statement of cash flows. This noncash investing and financing transaction was inadvertently included in both the financing section as a source of cash, and the investing section as a use of cash.

T-Shirt Pros' statement of cash flows, as it was prepared by the company accountants, reported the following for the period, and had no other capital expenditures.

Cash flows from operating activities	$195,000
Cash flows from investing activities	(120,000)
Cash flows from financing activities	120,000
Total net cash flows	195,000

Because of the misplacement of the transaction, the calculation of free cash flow by outside analysts could be affected significantly. Free cash flow is calculated as cash flow from operating activities, reduced by capital expenditures, the value for which is normally obtained from the investing section of the statement of cash flows. As their manager, would you treat the accountants' error as a harmless misclassification, or as a major blunder on their part? Explain.

Cash Flows from Operating Activities

Cash flows from **operating activities** arise from the activities a business uses to produce net income. For example, operating cash flows include cash sources from sales and cash used to purchase inventory and to pay for operating expenses such as salaries and utilities. Operating cash flows also include cash flows from interest and dividend revenue interest expense, and income tax.

Cash Flows from Investing Activities

Cash flows from **investing activities** are cash business transactions related to a business' investments in long-term assets. They can usually be identified from changes in the Fixed Assets section of the long-term assets section of the balance sheet. Some examples of investing cash flows are payments for the purchase of land, buildings, equipment, and other investment assets and cash receipts from the sale of land, buildings, equipment, and other investment assets.

Cash Flows from Financing Activities

Cash flows from **financing activities** are cash transactions related to the business raising money from debt or stock, or repaying that debt. They can be identified from changes in long-term liabilities and equity. Examples of financing cash flows include cash proceeds from issuance of debt instruments such as notes or bonds payable, cash proceeds from issuance of capital stock, cash payments for dividend distributions, principal repayment or redemption of notes or bonds payable, or purchase of treasury stock. Cash flows related to changes in equity can be identified on the Statement of Stockholder's Equity, and cash flows related to long-term liabilities can be identified by changes in long-term liabilities on the balance sheet.

CONCEPTS IN PRACTICE

Can a Negative Be Positive?

Investors do not always take a negative cash flow as a negative. For example, assume in 2018 Amazon showed a loss of $124 billion and a net cash outflow of $262 billion from investing activities. Yet during the same year, Amazon was able to raise a net $254 billion through financing. Why would investors and lenders be willing to place money with Amazon? For one thing, despite having a net loss, Amazon produced $31 billion cash from operating activities. Much of this was through delaying payment on inventories. Amazon's accounts payable increased by $78 billion, while its inventory increased by $20 billion.

Another reason lenders and investors were willing to fund Amazon is that investing payments are often signs of a company growing. Assume that in 2018 Amazon paid almost $50 billion to purchase fixed assets and to acquire other businesses; this is a signal of a company that is growing. Lenders and investors interpreted Amazon's cash flows as evidence that Amazon would be able to produce positive net income in the future. In fact, Amazon had net income of $19 billion in 2017. Furthermore, Amazon is still showing growth through its statement of cash flows; it spent about $26 billion in fixed equipment and acquisitions.

16.3 Prepare the Statement of Cash Flows Using the Indirect Method

The statement of cash flows is prepared by following these steps:

Step 1: Determine Net Cash Flows from Operating Activities

Using the indirect method, operating net cash flow is calculated as follows:

- Begin with net income from the income statement.
- Add back noncash expenses, such as depreciation, amortization, and depletion.
- Remove the effect of gains and/or losses from disposal of long-term assets, as cash from the disposal of long-term assets is shown under investing cash flows.
- Adjust for changes in current assets and liabilities to remove accruals from operating activities.

Step 2: Determine Net Cash Flows from Investing Activities

Investing net cash flow includes cash received and cash paid relating to long-term assets.

Step 3: Present Net Cash Flows from Financing Activities

Financing net cash flow includes cash received and cash paid relating to long-term liabilities and equity.

Step 4: Reconcile Total Net Cash Flows to Change in Cash Balance during the Period

To reconcile beginning and ending cash balances:

- The net cash flows from the first three steps are combined to be total net cash flow.
- The beginning cash balance is presented from the prior year balance sheet.
- Total net cash flow added to the beginning cash balance equals the ending cash balance.

Step 5: Present Noncash Investing and Financing Transactions

Transactions that do not affect cash but do affect long-term assets, long-term debt, and/or equity are disclosed, either as a notation at the bottom of the statement of cash flow, or in the notes to the financial statements.

The remainder of this section demonstrates preparation of the statement of cash flows of the company whose financial statements are shown in Figure 16.2, Figure 16.3, and Figure 16.4.

PROPENSITY COMPANY Comparative Balance Sheet December 31			
	2018	**2017**	**Change increase/ (decrease)**
Assets			
Cash	$ 47,500	$ 24,300	$ 23,200
Accounts Receivable	21,500	26,000	(4,500)
Prepaid Insurance	2,500	1,800	700
Inventory	48,000	45,500	2,500
Land	20,000	10,000	10,000
Plant Assets	230,000	190,000	40,000
Accumulated Depreciation	(85,500)	(71,100)	(14,400)
Total Assets	$284,000	$226,500	$ 57,500
Liabilities and Equity			
Liabilities:			
Accounts Payable	$ 17,200	$ 19,000	$ (1,800)
Salaries Payable	1,900	1,500	400
Notes Payable	85,000	75,000	10,000
Total Liabilities	104,100	95,500	8,600
Equity:			
Common Stock	115,000	70,000	45,000
Retained Earnings	64,900	61,000	3,900
Total Equity	179,900	131,000	48,900
Total Liabilities and Equity	$284,000	$226,500	$ 57,500

Figure 16.2 Comparative Balance Sheet. (attribution: Copyright Rice University, OpenStax, under CC BY-NC-SA 4.0 license)

PROPENSITY COMPANY Income Statement Year Ended December 31, 2018		
Sales Revenue		$238,000
Cost of Goods Sold		153,000
Gross Profit		85,000
Operating Expenses:		
Depreciation Expense	$14,400	
Insurance Expense	12,000	
Salaries Expense	42,600	
Other Operating Expenses	11,100	
Total Operating Expenses		80,100
Operating Income		4,900
Other Revenue and (Expenses):		
Gain on Sale of Land	4,800	
Interest Expense	(3,500)	
Total Other Revenue and Expenses		1,300
Income Before Income Tax		6,200
Income Tax Expense		1,860
Net Income		$ 4,340

Figure 16.3 Income Statement. (attribution: Copyright Rice University, OpenStax, under CC BY-NC-SA 4.0 license)

Additional Information:

1. Propensity Company sold land with an original cost of $10,000, for $14,800 cash.
2. A new parcel of land was purchased for $20,000, in exchange for a note payable.
3. Plant assets were purchased for $40,000 cash.
4. Propensity declared and paid a $440 cash dividend to shareholders.
5. Propensity issued common stock in exchange for $45,000 cash.

PROPENSITY COMPANY Statement of Cash Flows Indirect Method For the Year Ended December 31, 2018		
Cash Flow from Operating Activities:		
Net Income		$ 4,340
Adjustments to Reconcile Net Income to Net Cash Flow from Operating Activities:		
Depreciation	$ 14,400	
Gain on Sale of Plant Assets	(4,800)	
Accounts Receivable decrease	4,500	
Prepaid Insurance increase	(700)	
Inventory increase	(2,500)	
Accounts Payable decrease	(1,800)	
Salaries Payable increase	400	9,500
Net Cash Flow: Operating Activities		13,840
Cash Flow from Investing Activities:		
Proceeds from Sale of Land	14,800	
Cost of New Plant Assets (Equipment)	(40,000)	
Net Cash Flow: Investing Activities		(25,200)
Cash Flow from Financing Activities:		
Payment of Notes Payable (principal)	(10,000)	
Issuance of Common Stock	45,000	
Payment of Dividends	(440)	
Net Cash Flow: Financing Activities		34,560
Total Cash Flow increase/(decrease)		23,200
Cash Balance, December 31, 2017		24,300
Cash Balance, December 31, 2018		$ 47,500
Noncash Investing and Financing Activities		
Land Acquired in Exchange for Note Payable		$ 20,000

Figure 16.4 Statement of Cash Flows. (attribution: Copyright Rice University, OpenStax, under CC BY-NC-SA 4.0 license)

Prepare the Operating Activities Section of the Statement of Cash Flows Using the Indirect Method

In the following sections, specific entries are explained to demonstrate the items that support the preparation of the operating activities section of the Statement of Cash Flows (Indirect Method) for the Propensity Company example financial statements.

- Begin with net income from the income statement.
- Add back noncash expenses, such as depreciation, amortization, and depletion.
- Reverse the effect of gains and/or losses from investing activities.
- Adjust for changes in current assets and liabilities, to reflect how those changes impact cash in a way that is different than is reported in net income.0

Start with Net Income

The operating activities cash flow is based on the company's net income, with adjustments for items that affect cash differently than they affect net income. The net income on the Propensity Company income statement for December 31, 2018, is $4,340. On Propensity's statement of cash flows, this amount is shown in the Cash Flows from Operating Activities section as Net Income.

Cash Flow from Operating Activities:	
Net Income	$ 4,340

Add Back Noncash Expenses

Net income includes deductions for noncash expenses. To reconcile net income to cash flow from operating activities, these noncash items must be added back, because no cash was expended relating to that expense. The sole noncash expense on Propensity Company's income statement, which must be *added back*, is the depreciation expense of $14,400. On Propensity's statement of cash flows, this amount is shown in the Cash Flows from Operating Activities section as an adjustment to reconcile net income to net cash flow from operating activities.

Adjustments to Reconcile Net Income to Net Cash Flow from Operating Activities:	
Depreciation	$14,400
Gain on Sale of Plant Assets	(4,800)
Accounts Receivable decrease	4,500
Prepaid Insurance increase	(700)
Inventory increase	(2,500)
Accounts Payable decrease	(1,800)
Salaries Payable decrease	400

Reverse the Effect of Gains and/or Losses

Gains and/or losses on the disposal of long-term assets are included in the calculation of net income, but cash obtained from disposing of long-term assets is a cash flow from an investing activity. Because the disposition gain or loss is not related to normal operations, the adjustment needed to arrive at cash flow from operating activities is a reversal of any gains or losses that are included in the net income total. A gain is subtracted from net income and a loss is added to net income to reconcile to cash from operating activities. Propensity's income statement for the year 2018 includes a gain on sale of land, in the amount of $4,800, so a reversal is accomplished by *subtracting* the gain from net income. On Propensity's statement of cash flows, this amount is shown in the Cash Flows from Operating Activities section as Gain on Sale of Plant Assets.

Adjustments to Reconcile Net Income to Net Cash Flow from Operating Activities:	
Depreciation	$14,400
Gain on Sale of Plant Assets	(4,800)
Accounts Receivable decrease	4,500
Prepaid Insurance increase	(700)
Inventory increase	(2,500)
Accounts Payable decrease	(1,800)
Salaries Payable decrease	400

Adjust for Changes in Current Assets and Liabilities

Because the Balance Sheet and Income Statement reflect the accrual basis of accounting, whereas the statement of cash flows considers the incoming and outgoing cash transactions, there are continual differences between (1) cash collected and paid and (2) reported revenue and expense on these statements.

Changes in the various current assets and liabilities can be determined from analysis of the company's comparative balance sheet, which lists the current period and previous period balances for all assets and liabilities. The following four possibilities offer explanations of the type of difference that might arise, and demonstrate examples from Propensity Company's statement of cash flows, which represent typical differences that arise relating to these current assets and liabilities.

Increase in Noncash Current Assets

Increases in current assets indicate a decrease in cash, because either (1) cash was paid to generate another current asset, such as inventory, or (2) revenue was accrued, but not yet collected, such as accounts receivable. In the first scenario, the use of cash to increase the current assets is not reflected in the net income reported on the income statement. In the second scenario, revenue is included in the net income on the income statement, but the cash has not been received by the end of the period. In both cases, current assets increased and net income was reported on the income statement greater than the actual net cash impact from the related operating activities. To reconcile net income to cash flow from operating activities, *subtract* increases in current assets.

Propensity Company had two instances of increases in current assets. One was an increase of $700 in prepaid insurance, and the other was an increase of $2,500 in inventory. In both cases, the increases can be explained as additional cash that was spent, but which was not reflected in the expenses reported on the income statement.

Adjustments to Reconcile Net Income to Net Cash Flow from Operating Activities:	
Depreciation	$14,400
Gain on Sale of Plant Assets	(4,800)
Accounts Receivable decrease	4,500
Prepaid Insurance increase	(700)
Inventory increase	(2,500)
Accounts Payable decrease	(1,800)
Salaries Payable decrease	400

Decrease in Noncash Current Assets

Decreases in current assets indicate lower net income compared to cash flows from (1) prepaid assets and (2) accrued revenues. For decreases in prepaid assets, using up these assets shifts these costs that were recorded as assets over to current period expenses that then reduce net income for the period. Cash was paid to obtain the prepaid asset in a prior period. Thus, cash from operating activities must be increased to reflect the fact that these expenses reduced net income on the income statement, but cash was not paid this period. Secondarily, decreases in accrued revenue accounts indicates that cash was collected in the current period but was recorded as revenue on a previous period's income statement. In both scenarios, the net income reported on the income statement was lower than the actual net cash effect of the transactions. To reconcile net income to cash flow from operating activities, *add* decreases in current assets.

Propensity Company had a decrease of $4,500 in accounts receivable during the period, which normally results only when customers pay the balance, they owe the company at a faster rate than they charge new account balances. Thus, the decrease in receivable identifies that more cash was collected than was reported as revenue on the income statement. Thus, an addback is necessary to calculate the cash flow from operating activities.

Adjustments to Reconcile Net Income to Net Cash Flow from Operating Activities:	
Depreciation	$14,400
Gain on Sale of Plant Assets	(4,800)
Accounts Receivable decrease	4,500
Prepaid Insurance increase	(700)
Inventory increase	(2,500)
Accounts Payable decrease	(1,800)
Salaries Payable increase	400

Current Operating Liability Increase

Increases in current liabilities indicate an increase in cash, since these liabilities generally represent (1) expenses that have been accrued, but not yet paid, or (2) deferred revenues that have been collected, but not yet recorded as revenue. In the case of accrued expenses, costs have been reported as expenses on the income statement, whereas the deferred revenues would arise when cash was collected in advance, but the revenue was not yet earned, so the payment would not be reflected on the income statement. In both cases, these increases in current liabilities signify cash collections that exceed net income from related activities. To reconcile net income to cash flow from operating activities, *add* increases in current liabilities.

Propensity Company had an increase in the current operating liability for salaries payable, in the amount of $400. The payable arises, or increases, when an expense is recorded but the balance due is not paid at that time. An increase in salaries payable therefore reflects the fact that salaries expenses on the income statement are greater than the cash outgo relating to that expense. This means that net cash flow from operating is greater than the reported net income, regarding this cost.

Adjustments to Reconcile Net Income to Net Cash Flow from Operating Activities:	
Depreciation	$14,400
Gain on Sale of Plant Assets	(4,800)
Accounts Receivable decrease	4,500
Prepaid Insurance increase	(700)
Inventory increase	(2,500)
Accounts Payable decrease	(1,800)
Salaries Payable decrease	400

Current Operating Liability Decrease

Decreases in current liabilities indicate a decrease in cash relating to (1) accrued expenses, or (2) deferred revenues. In the first instance, cash would have been expended to accomplish a decrease in liabilities arising from accrued expenses, yet these cash payments would not be reflected in the net income on the income statement. In the second instance, a decrease in deferred revenue means that some revenue would have been reported on the income statement that was collected in a previous period. As a result, cash flows from operating activities must be decreased by any reduction in current liabilities, to account for (1) cash payments to creditors that are higher than the expense amounts on the income statement, or (2) amounts collected that are lower than the amounts reflected as income on the income statement. To reconcile net income to cash flow from operating activities, *subtract* decreases in current liabilities.

Propensity Company had a decrease of $1,800 in the current operating liability for accounts payable. The fact that the payable decreased indicates that Propensity paid enough payments during the period to keep up with new charges, and also to pay down on amounts payable from previous periods. Therefore, the company had to have paid more in cash payments than the amounts shown as expense on the Income Statements, which means net cash flow from operating activities is lower than the related net income.

Adjustments to Reconcile Net Income to Net Cash Flow from Operating Activities:	
Depreciation	$14,400
Gain on Sale of Plant Assets	(4,800)
Accounts Receivable decrease	4,500
Prepaid Insurance increase	(700)
Inventory increase	(2,500)
Accounts Payable decrease	(1,800)
Salaries Payable decrease	400

Analysis of Change in Cash

Although the net income reported on the income statement is an important tool for evaluating the success of the company's efforts for the current period and their viability for future periods, the practical effectiveness of management is not adequately revealed by the net income alone. The net cash flows from operating activities adds this essential facet of information to the analysis, by illuminating whether the company's operating cash sources were adequate to cover their operating cash uses. When combined with the cash flows produced by investing and financing activities, the operating activity cash flow indicates the feasibility of continuance and advancement of company plans.

Determining Net Cash Flow from Operating Activities (Indirect Method)

Net cash flow from operating activities is the net income of the company, adjusted to reflect the cash impact of operating activities. Positive net cash flow generally indicates adequate cash flow margins exist to provide continuity or ensure survival of the company. The magnitude of the net cash flow, if large, suggests a comfortable cash flow cushion, while a smaller net cash flow would signify an uneasy comfort cash flow zone. When a company's net cash flow from operations reflects a substantial negative value, this indicates that the company's operations are not supporting themselves and could be a warning sign of possible impending doom for the company. Alternatively, a small negative cash flow from operating might serve as an early warning that allows management to make needed corrections, to ensure that cash sources are increased to amounts in excess of cash uses, for future periods.

For Propensity Company, beginning with net income of $4,340, and reflecting adjustments of $9,500, delivers a net cash flow from operating activities of $13,840.

Cash Flow from Operating Activities:		
Net Income		$ 4,340
Adjustments to Reconcile Net Income to Net Cash Flow from Operating Activities:		
Depreciation	$14,400	
Gain on Sale of Plant Assets	(4,800)	
Accounts Receivable decrease	4,500	
Prepaid Insurance increase	(700)	
Inventory increase	(2,500)	
Accounts Payable decrease	(1,800)	
Salaries Payable increase	400	9,500
Net Cash Flow: Operating Activities		$13,840

Figure 16.5 Cash from Operating. (attribution: Copyright Rice University, OpenStax, under CC BY-NC-SA 4.0 license)

YOUR TURN

Cash Flow from Operating Activities

Assume you own a specialty bakery that makes gourmet cupcakes. Excerpts from your company's financial statements are shown.

	Income Statement	Balance Sheets
Sales	$189,000	
Cost of Goods Sold	(75,600)	
Operating Expense (except depreciation)	(81,500)	
Depreciation Expense	(12,000)	
Net Income	19,900	
Accounts Receivable decrease		$2,000
Merchandise Inventory increase		1,600
Accounts Payable decrease		5,500

How much cash flow from operating activities did your company generate?

Solution

Cash flows from operating activities:	
Net income	$19,900
Depreciation add back	12,000
Accounts Receivable decrease	2,000
Merchandise Inventory increase	(1,600)
Accounts Payable decrease	(5,500)
= Net cash flows from operating activities	26,800

THINK IT THROUGH

Explaining Changes in Cash Balance

Assume that you are the chief financial officer of a company that provides accounting services to small businesses. You are called upon by the board of directors to explain why your cash balance did not increase much from the beginning of 2018 until the end of 2018, since the company produced a reasonably strong profit for the year, with a net income of $88,000. Further assume that there were no investing or financing transactions, and no depreciation expense for 2018. What is your response? Provide the calculations to back up your answer.

	Dec. 31, 2018	Dec. 31, 2017
Cash	$195,700	$146,000
Accounts Receivable	216,000	198,500
Prepaid Costs (Insurance and Office Rent)	6,000	7,200
Accounts Payable	80,500	102,500

Operating Activities:	
Net Income	$ 88,000
Increase in Accounts Receivable	(17,500)
Decrease in Prepaid Costs	1,200
Decrease in Accounts Payable	(22,000)
Net cash flow from operating activities	49,700

Prepare the Investing and Financing Activities Sections of the Statement of Cash Flows

Preparation of the investing and financing sections of the statement of cash flows is an identical process for both the direct and indirect methods, since only the technique used to arrive at net cash flow from operating activities is affected by the choice of the direct or indirect approach. The following sections discuss specifics regarding preparation of these two nonoperating sections, as well as notations about disclosure of long-term noncash investing and/or financing activities. Changes in the various long-term assets, long-term liabilities, and equity can be determined from analysis of the company's comparative balance sheet, which lists the current period and previous period balances for all assets and liabilities.

Investing Activities

Cash flows from investing activities always relate to long-term asset transactions and may involve increases or decreases in cash relating to these transactions. The most common of these activities involve purchase or sale of property, plant, and equipment, but other activities, such as those involving investment assets and notes receivable, also represent cash flows from investing. Changes in long-term assets for the period can be identified in the Noncurrent Assets section of the company's comparative balance sheet, combined with any related gain or loss that is included on the income statement.

In the Propensity Company example, the investing section included two transactions involving long-term assets, one of which increased cash, while the other one decreased cash, for a total net cash flow from investing of ($25,200). Analysis of Propensity Company's comparative balance sheet revealed changes in land and plant assets. Further investigation identified that the change in long-term assets arose from three transactions:

1. Investing activity: A tract of land that had an original cost of $10,000 was sold for $14,800.
2. Investing activity: Plant assets were purchased, for $40,000 cash.
3. Noncash investing and financing activity: A new parcel of land was acquired, in exchange for a $20,000 note payable.

Details relating to the treatment of each of these transactions are provided in the following sections.

Cash Flow from Investing Activities:		
Proceeds from Sale of Land	$ 14,800	
Cost of New Plant Assets (Equipment)	(40,000)	
Net Cash Flow: Investing Activities		$(25,200)

Cash Flow from Investing Activities:		
Proceeds from Sale of Land	$ 14,800	
Cost of New Plant Assets (Equipment)	(40,000)	
Net Cash Flow: Investing Activities		$(25,200)

Noncash Investing and Financing Activities	
Land Acquired in Exchange for Note Payable	$ 20,000

Investing Activities Leading to an Increase in Cash

Increases in net cash flow from investing usually arise from the sale of long-term assets. The cash impact is the cash proceeds received from the transaction, which is not the same amount as the gain or loss that is reported on the income statement. Gain or loss is computed by subtracting the asset's net book value from the cash proceeds. Net book value is the asset's original cost, less any related accumulated depreciation. Propensity Company sold land, which was carried on the balance sheet at a net book value of $10,000, representing the original purchase price of the land, in exchange for a cash payment of $14,800. The data set explained these net book value and cash proceeds facts for Propensity Company. However, had these facts not been stipulated in the data set, the cash proceeds could have been determined by adding the reported $4,800 gain on the sale to the $10,000 net book value of the asset given up, to arrive at cash proceeds from the sale.

Proceeds from Sale of Land	$ 14,800

Investing Activities Leading to a Decrease in Cash

Decreases in net cash flow from investing normally occur when long-term assets are purchased using cash. For example, in the Propensity Company example, there was a decrease in cash for the period relating to a simple purchase of new plant assets, in the amount of $40,000.

Cost of New Plant Assets (Equipment)	$(40,000)

Financing Activities

Cash flows from financing activities always relate to either long-term debt or equity transactions and may involve increases or decreases in cash relating to these transactions. Stockholders' equity transactions, like stock issuance, dividend payments, and treasury stock buybacks are very common financing activities. Debt transactions, such as issuance of bonds payable or notes payable, and the related principal payback of them, are also frequent financing events. Changes in long-term liabilities and equity for the period can be identified in the Noncurrent Liabilities section and the Stockholders' Equity section of the company's Comparative Balance Sheet, and in the retained earnings statement.

In the Propensity Company example, the financing section included three transactions. One long-term debt transaction decreased cash. Two transactions related to equity, one of which increased cash, while the other one decreased cash, for a total net cash flow from financing of $34,560. Analysis of Propensity Company's Comparative Balance Sheet revealed changes in notes payable and common stock, while the retained earnings statement indicated that dividends were distributed to stockholders. Further investigation identified that the change in long-term liabilities and equity arose from three transactions:

1. Financing activity: Principal payments of $10,000 were paid on notes payable.
2. Financing activity: New shares of common stock were issued, in the amount of $45,000.
3. Financing activity: Dividends of $440 were paid to shareholders.

Specifics about each of these three transactions are provided in the following sections.

Cash Flow from Financing Activities:		
Payment of Notes Payable (principal)	$(10,000)	
Issuance of Common Stock	45,000	
Payment of Dividends	(440)	
Net Cash Flow: Financing Activities		$34,560

Financing Activities Leading to an Increase in Cash

Increases in net cash flow from financing usually arise when the company issues share of stock, bonds, or notes payable to raise capital for cash flow. Propensity Company had one example of an increase in cash flows, from the issuance of common stock.

Issuance of Common Stock	$45,000

Financing Activities Leading to a Decrease in Cash

Decreases in net cash flow from financing normally occur when (1) long-term liabilities, such as notes payable or bonds payable are repaid, (2) when the company reacquires some of its own stock (treasury stock), or (3) when the company pays dividends to shareholders. In the case of Propensity Company, the decreases in cash resulted from notes payable principal repayments and cash dividend payments.

Payment of Notes Payable (principal)	$(10,000)
Payment of Dividends	(440)

Noncash Investing and Financing Activities

Sometimes transactions can be very important to the company, yet not involve any initial change to cash. Disclosure of these noncash investing and financing transactions can be included in the notes to the financial statements, or as a notation at the bottom of the statement of cash flows, after the entire statement has been completed. These noncash activities usually involve one of the following scenarios:

- exchanges of long-term assets for long-term liabilities or equity, or
- exchanges of long-term liabilities for equity.

Propensity Company had a noncash investing and financing activity, involving the purchase of land (investing activity) in exchange for a $20,000 note payable (financing activity).

Noncash Investing and Financing Activities	
Land Acquired in Exchange for Note Payable	$20,000

Summary of Investing and Financing Transactions on the Cash Flow Statement

Investing and financing transactions are critical activities of business, and they often represent significant amounts of company equity, either as sources or uses of cash. Common activities that must be reported as investing activities are purchases of land, equipment, stocks, and bonds, while financing activities normally relate to the company's funding sources, namely, creditors and investors. These financing activities could include transactions such as borrowing or repaying notes payable, issuing or retiring bonds payable, or issuing stock or reacquiring treasury stock, to name a few instances.

YOUR TURN

Cash Flow from Investing Activities

Assume your specialty bakery makes gourmet cupcakes and has been operating out of rented facilities in the past. You owned a piece of land that you had planned to someday use to build a sales storefront. This year your company decided to sell the land and instead buy a building, resulting in the following transactions.

Acquired new building, to be used as the storefront for the bakery	$85,000
Collected interest on investment assets	2,250
Gain on the sale of land	25,200
Additional information: Original cost of land	22,000

What are the cash flows from investing activities relating to these transactions?

Solution

Investing activities:	
Cash proceeds from sale of land	$ 47,200
Cash paid for purchase of building	(85,000)
Net cash flows from investing activities	(37,800)

Note: Interest earned on investments is an operating activity.

16.4 Prepare the Completed Statement of Cash Flows Using the Indirect Method

In this section, we use the example of Virtual Co. to work through the entire process of preparing the company's statement of cash flows using the indirect method. Virtual's comparative balance sheet and income statement are provided as a base for the preparation of the statement of cash flows.

Review Problem: Preparing the Virtual Co. Statement of Cash Flows

VIRTUAL CO. Comparative Balance Sheet December 31			
	2018	2017	Change increase/ (decrease)
Assets			
Cash	$ 66,700	$ 83,250	$(16,550)
Accounts Receivable	55,400	54,220	1,180
Prepaid Insurance	2,400	3,600	(1,200)
Investments	95,000	75,000	20,000
Plant Assets	356,000	290,000	66,000
Accumulated Depreciation	(65,700)	(36,700)	(29,000)
Total Assets	$509,800	$469,370	$ 40,430
Liabilities and Equity			
Liabilities:			
Accounts Payable	$ 48,100	$ 47,300	$ 800
Notes Payable	160,000	185,000	(25,000)
Total Liabilities	208,100	232,300	(24,200)
Equity:			
Common Stock	130,000	100,000	30,000
Retained Earnings	171,700	137,070	34,630
Total Equity	301,700	237,070	64,630
Total Liabilities and Equity	$509,800	$469,370	$ 40,430

Figure 16.6 Comparative Balance Sheet. (attribution: Copyright Rice University, OpenStax, under CC BY-NC-SA 4.0 license)

VIRTUAL CO. Income Statement For the Year Ended December 31, 2018		
Sales Revenue		$433,000
Cost of Goods Sold		289,000
Gross Profit		144,000
Operating Expenses:		
Depreciation Expense	$29,000	
Insurance Expense	14,400	
Other Operating Expenses	57,200	
Total Operating Expenses		100,600
Operating Income		43,400
Other Revenue and (Expenses):		
Gain on Sale of Land	17,500	
Total Other Revenue and Expenses		17,500
Income Before Income Tax		60,900
Income Tax Expense		18,270
Net Income		$ 42,630

Figure 16.7 Income Statement. (attribution: Copyright Rice University, OpenStax, under CC BY-NC-SA 4.0 license)

Additional Information

The following additional information is provided:

1. Investments that originally cost $30,000 were sold for $47,500 cash.
2. Investments were purchased for $50,000 cash.
3. Plant assets were purchased for $66,000 cash.
4. Cash dividends were declared and paid to shareholders in the amount of $8,000.

Directions:

Prepare the statement of cash flows (indirect method), for the year ended December 31, 2018.

VIRTUAL CO. Statement of Cash Flows: Indirect Method For the Year Ended December 31, 2018		
Cash Flow from Operating Activities:		
Net Income		$ 42,630
Adjustments to Reconcile Net Income to Net Cash Flow from Operating Activities:		
Depreciation	$ 29,000	
Gain on Sale of Plant Assets	(17,500)	
Accounts Receivable decrease	(1,180)	
Prepaid Insurance decrease	1,200	
Accounts Payable increase	800	12,320
Net Cash Flow: Operating Activities		54,950
Cash Flow from Investing Activities:		
Proceeds from Sale of Investments	47,500	
Cost of Investments Purchased	(50,000)	
Cost of New Plant Assets	(66,000)	
Net Cash Flow: Investing Activities		(68,500)
Cash Flow from Financing Activities:		
Payment of Notes Payable (principal)	(25,000)	
Issuance of Common Stock	30,000	
Payment of Dividends	(8,000)	
Net Cash Flow: Financing Activities		(3,000)
Total Cash Flow increase/(decrease)		(16,550)
Cash Balance, December 31, 2017		83,250
Cash Balance, December 31, 2018		$ 66,700

Figure 16.8 Statement of Cash Flows. (attribution: Copyright Rice University, OpenStax, under CC BY-NC-SA 4.0 license)

16.5 Use Information from the Statement of Cash Flows to Prepare Ratios to Assess Liquidity and Solvency

Cash flow ratio analysis allows financial statement users to see the company's liquidity position from a clearer perspective. The ratios presented in this section focus on **free cash flow**, calculated as operating cash, reduced by expected capital expenditures and by cash dividends payments. The free cash flow value is thus an adaptation of cash flow from operating activities. The result obtained in the initial free cash flow calculation is then used to calculate the **free cash flow to sales ratio**, which is the ratio of free cash flow to sales revenue, and the **free cash flow to assets ratio**, which is the ratio of free cash flow to total assets. These three tools give indicators about the company's flexibility and agility, which equates to their ability to seize opportunities in the future, as they arise.

ETHICAL CONSIDERATIONS

Cash Flow Analysis

Cash is required to pay the bills. All businesses need to have a clear picture of available cash so they can plan and pay their bills. The statement of cash flows allows investors direct insight into the actual activity on the company's cash balances. Mark A. Siegel wrote in *The CPA Journal* that "as Wall Street analysts have lost faith in earnings-based metrics in the wake of Enron, WorldCom, and others, many have gravitated toward the cash flow statement. Companies are regularly evaluated on the basis of free cash flow yield and other measures of cash generation."[3] The operating cash flow ratio, and the cash flow margin ratio, and the other cash flow–related metrics discussed allow an investor and other users of the financial statements to analyze financial statement data to see a company's ability to pay for current debt and assess its operational cash flow to function as a going concern.[4] This helps investors and other users of the financial statements ensure the veracity of a company's financial statements and its ability to pay its bills.

Free Cash Flow

Free cash flow calculations start with cash flows from operating activities, reduced by planned capital expenditures and planned cash dividend payments. In the example case demonstrated, free cash flow would be as follows:

Free cash flow calculation:

Cash flow from operating	$ 13,840
– Cash planned for capital expenditures	(40,000)
– Cash dividends	(440)
= Free Cash Flow	(26,600)

The absence of free cash flow is an indicator of severe liquidity concern for Propensity Company and could be an early indicator that the company may not be able to continue operations. This could also be a one-time occurrence, in a year where a large capital investment was planned, to be financed with resources from the company's capital reserves from previous years' profits. In such a case, the negative free cash flow would not be an issue of concern.

LINK TO LEARNING

This article by Investopedia presents information about how to use free cash flow (https://openstax.org/l/50FreeCashFlow) to evaluate strengths of various businesses:

3 Marc A. Siegel. "Accounting Shenanigans on the Cash Flow Statement." *CPA Journal*. March 2006. http://archives.cpajournal.com/2006/306/essentials/p38.htm

4 Steven D. Jones. "Why Cash Flow Matters in Evaluating a Company." *The Wall Street Journal*. August 11, 2016. https://www.wsj.com/articles/SB997466275287616386. Miriam Gottfried. "Spoiler Alert for Netflix: Debt and Cash Flow Matter." *The Wall Street Journal*. April 17, 2017. https://www.wsj.com/articles/spoiler-alert-for-netflix-debt-and-cash-flow-matter-1492468397

Cash Flows to Sales

The cash flows to sales ratio is computed by dividing free cash flow by sales revenue. In the Propensity Company case, free cash flow had a negative outcome, so the calculation would not be useful in this case.

Cash Flows to Assets

The cash flows to assets ratio is computed by dividing free cash flow by total assets. Again, when the free cash flow had a negative outcome, as it did in the Propensity Company example scenario, the calculation would not be useful

CONCEPTS IN PRACTICE

Lehman Brothers: Would You Have Invested?

Between 2005 and 2007, Lehman Brothers (an investment bank) increased its net income from $3.1 billion to $4.1 billion. It received nearly $42 billion interest and dividends on its investments, a primary part of its business model, in 2007 alone. It also had $7.2 billion available in cash at the end of 2007. Would you be interested in investing in Lehman Brothers? However, Lehman Brothers went bankrupt in September 2008; it was the biggest corporate bankruptcy in history. Could investors have known?

A clue would be its free cash ratio. Assuming that you would expect Lehman Brothers' actual capital expenditures and dividend payments from 2007 be expected in 2008, Lehman's free cash ratio would be calculated as, in millions:

Cash flows from operating activities	$(45,595)
Cash planned for capital expenditures	(1,931)
Cash dividends:	(418)
Free cash flow	$(47,944)

Lehman Brothers invested heavily in securities created from subprime mortgages. When the subprime mortgage market collapsed in 2008, Lehman Brothers was not able to generate enough cash to stay in business. The large negative free cash flow gave warning that Lehman Brothers was a risky investment.

IFRS CONNECTION

Statement of Cash Flows

In every type of business across the globe, it is important to understand the business's cash position. Analyzing cash inflows and outflows, current cash flow, and cash flow trends, and predicting future cash flows all importantly inform decision-making. The US Securities and Exchange Commission (SEC) requires the statement of cash flows as the mechanism that allows users to better assess a company's cash position. US generally accepted accounting principles (GAAP) and International Financial Reporting

Standards (IFRS) set forth rules regarding the composition and presentation of the statement of cash flows.

- Method: Both GAAP and IFRS recommend and encourage the direct method of preparing the statement of cash flows but allow the indirect method. Under US GAAP, if the direct method is used, a reconciliation between net income and operating income must also be presented. This reconciliation is not required under IFRS.
- Presentation: The three categories—Cash Flows from Operating Activities, Cash Flows from Investing Activities, and Cash Flows from Financing Activities—are required under both US GAAP and IFRS. US GAAP requires the presentation of only one year of information, while IFRS requires two years of data.
- Categorizing Transactions: IFRS is more flexible in where to present certain cash flow transactions than is US GAAP. This flexibility occurs around interest, dividends, and taxes. As shown in Table 16.1, US GAAP is more rigid in reporting.

Comparing GAAP and IFRS

	US GAAP	IFRS
Interest paid	Operating	Operating or financing
Interest received	Operating	Operating or investing
Dividends paid	Financing	Operating or financing
Dividends received	Operating	Operating or investing
Taxes	Operating	Usually operating but option to dissect tax into operating and financing components

Table 16.1

Understanding the impact of these potential differences is important. The statement of cash flows is used not only to evaluate from where a company receives and spends its cash, but also to predict future cash flows. The flexibility of these reporting items in the statement of cash flows can result in decreased comparability between similar companies using different reporting methods. For example, Free Cash Flow (Operating Cash Flows less Capital Expenditures), will have different results if interest and dividends are classified in sections other than operating activities.

Let's consider an example: World-Wide Co. is headquartered in London and currently reports under US GAAP because it is traded on the New York Stock Exchange (NYSE). World-Wide is considering switching to reporting under IFRS to make the company more comparable to its competitors, since most of them use IFRS. World-Wide has the following information in the operating activities section of its most recent statement of cash flows.

Cash flows from operating activities	$2,500,000
Cash interest payments	200,000
Cash interest received	90,000
Taxes paid	125,000
Cash dividends received	50,000

World-Wide had $1,000,000 in capital expenditures during the year, and they paid dividends of $80,000 to shareholders.

Based on this information, World-Wide's Free Cash Flow would be as follows:

Free Cash Flow = Cash from Operating Activities – Capital Expenditures

or

$2,500,000 – $1,000,000 = $1,500,000

If World-Wide switches to IFRS reporting, it has determined that its cash interest payments would be classified as financing activities because the payments are related to long-term debt. The interest received is from a short-term receivable and thus will remain classified as an operating activity, but the dividends received are from a long-term investment and will be reclassified to an investing activity. And, $60,000 of the taxes have been identified as being associated with tax consequences of an investing opportunity and therefore will be reclassified as an investing activity. With these reclassifications, the free cash flow of World-Wide would be as follows:

FCF = ($2,500,000 + $200,000 – $50,000 + $60,000) – 1,000,000 = $1,710,000

The take-away from this example is that the flexibility afforded by IFRS can have an impact on comparability between companies.

These, and other differences, between US GAAP and IFRS arise because of the more rules-based nature of the standards put forth by FASB versus the more principles-based rules set forth by IASB. The IASB, in creating IFRS standards, follows a substance-over-form viewpoint that allows firms more flexibility in assessing the intent of transactions. Anytime more judgement is allowed and/or utilized, there must be adequate disclosure to explain the chosen reporting methodology.

16.6 Appendix: Prepare a Completed Statement of Cash Flows Using the Direct Method

PROPENSITY COMPANY Statement of Cash Flows: Direct Method For the Year Ended December 31, 2018		
Cash Flow from Operating Activities:		
Cash Collected from Customers		$242,500
Cash Payments:		
To Suppliers for Inventory	$157,300	
For Salaries	42,200	
For Insurance	12,700	
For Interest	3,500	
For Income Taxes	1,860	
For Other Operating Expenses	11,100	228,660
Net Cash Flow: Operating Activities		13,840
Cash Flow from Investing Activities:		
Proceeds from Sale of Land	14,800	
Cost of New Plant Assets (Equipment)	(40,000)	
Net Cash Flow: Investing Activities		(25,200)
Cash Flow from Financing Activities:		
Payment of Notes Payable (principal)	(10,000)	
Issuance of Common Stock	45,000	
Payment of Dividends	(440)	
Net Cash Flow: Financing Activities		34,560
Total Cash Flow increase/(decrease)		23,200
Cash Balance, December 31, 2017		24,300
Cash Balance, December 31, 2018		$ 47,500
Noncash Investing and Financing Activities		
Land Acquired in Exchange for Note Payable		$ 20,000

Figure 16.9 Statement of Cash Flows. (attribution: Copyright Rice University, OpenStax, under CC BY-NC-SA 4.0 license)

As previously mentioned, the net cash flows for all sections of the statement of cash flows are identical when using the direct method or the indirect method. The difference is just in the way that net cash flows from operating activities are calculated and presented. The direct approach requires that each item of income and expense be converted from the accrual basis value to the cash basis value for that item. This is accomplished by adjusting the accrual amount for the revenue or expense by any related current operating asset or liability. Revenue and expense items that are not related to those current asset and liability accounts would not need an adjustment.

In the following section, we demonstrate the calculations needed to assess the component pieces of the operating section using the direct approach.

Cash Collected from Customers

Cash collected from customers is different from the sales revenue that is recorded on the accrual basis financial statements. To reconcile the amount of sales revenue reported on the income statement to the cash collected from sales, calculate the maximum amount of cash that could have been collected this period (potential cash collected) by combining (a) the amount that was due from customers on the first day of the period (beginning accounts receivable) and (b) total sales revenue recorded this period. If there were no outstanding accounts receivable balance at the end of the period, then one could reasonably assume that this total was collected in full during this period. Thus, the amount collected for sales can be determined by subtracting the ending accounts receivable balance from the total potential cash that could have been collected.

Cash Collected from Sales Revenue	
Beginning balance, Accounts Receivable	$ 26,000
+ Accrual Basis Sales	238,000
= Potential Cash Collected	264,000
– Ending balance, Accounts Receivable	21,500
= Cash Collected from Customers this Period	**$242,500**

Cash Paid to Suppliers for Inventory

Cash paid for inventory is different from the cost of goods sold that is recorded on the accrual basis financial statements. To reconcile the amount of cost of goods sold reported on the income statement to the cash paid for inventory, it is necessary to perform two calculations. The first part of the calculation determines how much inventory was purchased, and the second part of the calculation determines how much of those purchases were paid for during the current period.

First, calculate the maximum amount of inventory that was available for sale this period by combining (a) the amount of inventory that was on hand on the last day of the period (ending inventory) and (b) total cost of goods sold recorded this period. If there were no inventory balance at the beginning of the period, then one could reasonably assume that this total was purchased entirely during the current period. Thus, the amount of inventory purchased this period can be determined by subtracting the beginning inventory balance from the total goods (inventory) available for sale.

Second, calculate the maximum amount of cash that could have been paid for inventory this period (total obligation to pay inventory costs) by combining (a) the amount that was due to suppliers on the first day of the period (beginning accounts payable) and (b) total inventory purchases this period, from the first inventory calculation. If there were no outstanding accounts payable balance at the end of the period, then one could reasonably assume that this total was paid in full during this current period. Thus, the amount paid for inventory can be determined by subtracting the ending accounts payable balance from the total obligation to pay inventory costs that could have been paid. The final number of the second calculation is the actual cash paid for inventory.

Cash Paid for Inventory Purchases: Part 1	
Ending balance, Inventory	$ 48,000
+ Cost of Goods Sold	153,000
= Goods Available for Sale	201,000
- Beginning balance, Inventory	45,500
= Inventory Purchased this Period	155,500
Cash Paid for Inventory Purchases: Part 2	
Beginning balance, Accounts Payable	19,000
+ Inventory Purchased (from Part 1)	155,500
= Total Obligation to Pay Inventory Costs	174,500
- Ending balance, Accounts Payable	17,200
= Cash Paid for Inventory this Period	**$157,300**

Cash Paid for Salaries

Cash paid for salaries is different from the salaries expense that is recorded on the accrual basis financial statements. To reconcile the amount of salaries expense reported on the income statement to the cash paid for salaries, calculate the maximum amount of cash that could have been paid for salaries this period (total obligation to pay salaries) by combining (a) the amount that was due to employees on the first day of the period (beginning salaries payable) and (b) total salaries expense recorded this period. If there were no outstanding salaries payable balance at the end of the period, then one could reasonably assume that this total was paid in full during this current period. Thus, the amount paid for salaries can be determined by subtracting the ending salaries payable balance from the total obligation to pay salaries that could have been paid.

Cash Paid for Expense Related to a Current Liability	
Beginning balance, Salaries Payable	$ 1,500
+ Expense on Income Statement	42,600
= Total Obligation to Pay Salaries	44,100
- Ending balance, Salaries Payable	1,900
= Cash paid for Salaries this Period	**$42,200**

Cash Paid for Insurance

Cash paid for insurance is different from the insurance expense that is recorded on the accrual basis financial statements. To reconcile the amount of insurance expense reported on the income statement to the cash paid for insurance premiums, calculate the maximum amount of cash that could have been paid for insurance this period (total insurance premiums expended) by combining (a) the amount of insurance premiums that were prepaid on the last day of the period (ending prepaid insurance) and (b) total insurance expense recorded this period. If there were no prepaid insurance balance at the beginning of the period, then one could reasonably assume that this total was paid entirely during the current period. Thus, the amount paid for insurance this period can be determined by subtracting the beginning prepaid insurance balance from the total insurance premiums that had been recorded as expended.

Cash Paid for Expense Related to a Prepaid Asset	
Ending balance, Prepaid Insurance	$ 2,500
+ Insurance Expense on Income Statement	12,000
= Total Insurance Premiums Expended	14,500
– Beginning balance, Prepaid Insurance	1,800
= Insurance Paid this Period	**$12,700**

Key Terms

cash flow cash receipts and cash disbursements as a result of business activity

direct method approach used to determine net cash flows from operating activities, whereby accrual basis revenue and expenses are converted to cash basis collections and payments

financing activity cash business transaction reported on the statement of cash flows that obtains or retires financing

free cash flow operating cash, reduced by expected capital expenditures and by cash dividends payments

free cash flow to assets ratio ratio of free cash flow to total assets

free cash flow to sales ratio ratio of free cash flow to sales revenue

indirect method approach used to determine net cash flows from operating activities, starting with net income and adjusting for items that impact new income but do not require outlay of cash

investing activity cash business transaction reported on the statement of cash flows from the acquisition or disposal of a long-term asset

net cash flow method used to determine profitability by measuring the difference between an entity's cash inflows and cash outflows

noncash expense expense that reduces net income but is not associated with a cash flow; most common example is depreciation expense

operating activity cash business transaction reported on the statement of cash flows that relates to ongoing day-to-day operations

statement of cash flows financial statement listing the cash inflows and cash outflows for the business for a period of time

Summary

16.1 Explain the Purpose of the Statement of Cash Flows

- The statement of cash flows presents the sources and uses of cash.
- The statement of cash flows is used to predict future cash flows and to assess the quality of an entity's earnings.
- There are two approaches utilized to prepare the statement of cash flow: the indirect method and the direct method.

16.2 Differentiate between Operating, Investing, and Financing Activities

- Transactions must be segregated into the three types of activities presented on the statement of cash flows: operating, investing, and financing.
- Operating cash flows arise from the normal operations of producing income, such as cash receipts from revenue and cash disbursements to pay for expenses.
- Investing cash flows arise from a company investing in or disposing of long-term assets.
- Financing cash flows arise from a company raising funds through debt or equity and repaying debt.

16.3 Prepare the Statement of Cash Flows Using the Indirect Method

- Preparing the operating section of statement of cash flows by the indirect method starts with net income from the income statement and adjusts for items that affect cash flows differently than they affect net income.
- Multiple levels of adjustments are required to reconcile accrual-based net income to cash flows from operating activities.

- The investing section of statement of cash flows relates to changes in long-term assets.
- The financing section of statement of cash flows relates to changes in long-term liabilities and changes in equity.
- Company activities that reflect changes in long-term assets, long-term liabilities, or equity, but have no cash impact, require special reporting treatment, as noncash investing and financing transactions.

16.4 Prepare the Completed Statement of Cash Flows Using the Indirect Method

- Preparing the operating section of statement of cash flows by the indirect method starts with net income from the income statement and adjusts for items that affect cash flows differently than they affect net income.
- Multiple levels of adjustments are required to reconcile accrual-based net income to cash flows from operating activities.
- The investing section of the statement of cash flows relates to changes in long-term assets.
- The financing section of statement of cash flows relates to changes in long-term liabilities and changes in equity.
- Company activities that reflect changes in long-term assets, long-term liabilities, or equity, but have no cash impact, require special reporting treatment, as noncash investing and financing transactions.

16.5 Use Information from the Statement of Cash Flows to Prepare Ratios to Assess Liquidity and Solvency

- Free cash flow relates to the amount of expected cash from operations which is left over after planned capital expenditures and dividends are paid.
- The cash flow to assets ratio correlates the company's free cash flow to its total asset value.
- The cash flow to sales ratio considers free cash flow in relation to the company's sales revenue.

16.6 Appendix: Prepare a Completed Statement of Cash Flows Using the Direct Method

- This section included an example of a statement of cash flows, prepared under the direct method, using the continuing example for Propensity Company.
- The direct method of preparing the statement of cash flows is identical to the indirect method except for the cash flows from the operating section.
- To complete the cash flows from operating activities, the direct method directly shows the cash collected from customers from revenue activities and the cash spent on operations, rather than reconciling net income to cash flows from operating activities as done using the indirect method. Calculating the amounts directly collected from revenues and spent on expenditures involves calculating the cash effect of the accrual amounts reported on the income statement.

Multiple Choice

1. LO 16.1 Which of the following statements is false?

A. Noncash activities should be reported in accrual basis financial statements.
B. Net cash flow from operating activities relates to normal business operations.
C. Net income usually equals net cash flow from operating activities.
D. The statement of cash flows is an essential part of the basic financial statements.

2. LO 16.2 Which of these transactions would *not* be part of the cash flows from the operating activities section of the statement of cash flows?

A. credit purchase of inventory
B. sales of product, for cash
C. cash paid for purchase of equipment
D. salary payments to employees

3. LO 16.2 Which is the proper order of the sections of the statement of cash flows?

A. financing, investing, operating
B. operating, investing, financing
C. investing, operating, financing
D. operating, financing, investing

4. LO 16.2 Which of these transactions would be part of the financing section?

A. inventory purchased for cash
B. sales of product, for cash
C. cash paid for purchase of equipment
D. dividend payments to shareholders, paid in cash

5. LO 16.2 Which of these transactions would be part of the operating section?

A. land purchased, with note payable
B. sales of product, for cash
C. cash paid for purchase of equipment
D. dividend payments to shareholders, paid in cash

6. LO 16.2 Which of these transactions would be part of the investing section?

A. land purchased, with note payable
B. sales of product, for cash
C. cash paid for purchase of equipment
D. dividend payments to shareholders, paid in cash

7. LO 16.3 What is the effect on cash when current noncash operating assets increase?

A. Cash increases by the same amount.
B. Cash decreases by the same amount.
C. Cash decreases by twice as much.
D. Cash does not change.

8. LO 16.3 What is the effect on cash when current liabilities increase?

A. Cash increases by the same amount.
B. Cash decreases by the same amount.
C. Cash decreases by twice as much.
D. Cash does not change.

9. LO 16.3 What is the effect on cash when current noncash operating assets decrease?

A. Cash increases by the same amount.
B. Cash decreases by the same amount.
C. Cash decreases by twice as much.
D. Cash does not change.

10. LO 16.3 What is the effect on cash when current liabilities decrease?

A. Cash increases by the same amount.
B. Cash decreases by the same amount.
C. Cash decreases by twice as much.
D. Cash does not change.

11. LO 16.3 Which of the following would trigger a subtraction in the indirect operating section?

A. gain on sale of investments
B. depreciation expense
C. decrease in accounts receivable
D. decrease in bonds payable

12. LO 16.3 Which of the following represents a source of cash in the investing section?

A. sale of investments
B. depreciation expense
C. decrease in accounts receivable
D. decrease in bonds payable

13. LO 16.3 Which of the following would be included in the financing section?

A. loss on sale of investments
B. depreciation expense
C. increase in notes receivable
D. decrease in notes payable

14. LO 16.4 If beginning cash equaled $10,000 and ending cash equals $19,000, which is true?

A. Operating cash flow 9,000; Investing cash flow (3,500); Financing cash flow (2,500)
B. Operating cash flow 4,500; Investing cash flow 9,000; Financing cash flow (4,500)
C. Operating cash flow 2,000; Investing cash flow (13,000); Financing cash flow 2,000
D. none of the above

15. LO 16.5 Which of the following is a stronger indicator of cash flow flexibility?

A. cash flow from operating activities
B. cash flow to sales ratio
C. free cash flow
D. all three indicate comparable degrees of flexibility

Questions

1. LO 16.1 What function does the statement of cash flows serve, as one of the four basic financial statements?

2. LO 16.1 Is it possible for a company to have significant net income in the same time period that net cash flows are negative? Explain.

3. LO 16.2 What categories of activities are reported on the statement of cash flows? Does it matter in what order these sections are presented?

4. LO 16.2 Describe three examples of operating activities, and identify whether each of them represents cash collected or cash spent.

5. LO 16.2 Describe three examples of investing activities, and identify whether each of them represents cash collected or cash spent.

6. LO 16.2 Describe three examples of financing activities, and identify whether each of them represents cash collected or cash spent.

7. LO 16.3 Explain the difference between the two methods used to prepare the operating section of the statement of cash flows. How do the results of these two approaches compare?

8. LO 16.3 Why is depreciation an addition in the operating section of the statement of cash flows, when prepared by the indirect method?

9. LO 16.3 When preparing the operating section of the statement of cash flows, using the indirect method, how must gains and losses be handled? Why?

10. LO 16.3 If a company reports a gain/(loss) from the sale of assets, as part of the net income on the income statement, and the net book value of those assets on the date of the sale is known, can the amount of the cash proceeds from the sale be determined? If so, how?

11. LO 16.3 Note payments reduce cash and are related to long-term debt. Do these facts automatically lead to their inclusion as elements of the financing section of the statement of cash flows? Explain.

12. LO 16.4 Is there any significance that can be attributed to whether net cash flows are generated from operating activities, versus investing and/or financing activities? Explain.

13. LO 16.4 Would there ever be activities that relate to operating, investing, or financing activities that would not be reported in their respective sections of the statement of cash flows? Explain. If a company had any such activities, how would they be reported in the financial statements, if at all?

14. LO 16.5 What insight does the calculation of free cash flow provide about the company's cash flow position?

15. LO 16.6 Why is using the direct method to prepare the operating section of the statement of cash flows more challenging for accountants than preparing the balance sheet, income statement, and retained earnings statement?

Exercise Set A

EA1. LO 16.1 Provide journal entries to record each of the following transactions. For each, identify whether the transaction represents a source of cash (S), a use of cash (U), or neither (N).

A. Declared and paid to shareholders, a dividend of $24,000.
B. Issued common stock at par value for $12,000 cash.
C. Sold a tract of land that had cost $10,000, for $16,000.
D. Purchased a company truck, with a note payable of $38,000.
E. Collected $8,000 from customer accounts receivable.

EA2. LO 16.2 In which section of the statement of cash flows would each of the following transactions be included? For each, identify the appropriate section of the statement of cash flows as operating (O), investing (I), financing (F), or none (N). (Note: some transactions might involve two sections.)

A. paid advertising expense
B. paid dividends to shareholders
C. purchased business equipment
D. sold merchandise to customers
E. purchased plant assets

EA3. LO 16.2 In which section of the statement of cash flows would each of the following transactions be included? For each, identify the appropriate section of the statement of cash flows as operating (O), investing (I), financing (F), or none (N). (Note: some transactions might involve two sections.)

A. borrowed from the bank for business loan
B. declared dividends, to be paid next year
C. purchased treasury stock
D. purchased a two-year insurance policy
E. purchased plant assets

EA4. LO 16.3 Use the following information from Albuquerque Company's financial statements to determine operating net cash flows (indirect method).

Net income	$325,000
Change in accumulated depreciation (no sale of depreciable assets this year)	26,200
Loss on sale of company truck	7,800

EA5. LO 16.3 What adjustment(s) should be made to reconcile net income to net cash flows from operating activities (indirect method) considering the following balances in current assets?

Accounts receivable, beginning of year	$20,000
Accounts receivable, end of year	25,000
Prepaid insurance, beginning of year	12,000
Prepaid insurance, end of year	9,000

EA6. LO 16.3 Use the following information from Birch Company's balance sheets to determine net cash flows from operating activities (indirect method), assuming net income for 2018 of $122,000.

	Dec. 31, 2018	Dec. 31, 2017
Accounts Receivable	$12,800	$15,000
Prepaid Insurance	4,000	3,500
Accounts Payable	9,000	8,200
Accrued Liabilities	2,500	2,800

EA7. LO 16.3 Use the following information from Chocolate Company's financial statements to determine operating net cash flows (indirect method).

	Income Statement	Balance Sheet
Sales	$ 98,500	
Cost of Goods Sold	(62,000)	
Salaries Expense	(18,000)	
Depreciation Expense	(9,000)	
Net Income	9,500	
Accounts Receivable decrease		$2,000
Merchandise Inventory increase		1,600
Salaries Payable increase		450

EA8. LO 16.3 Use the following information from Denmark Company's financial statements to determine operating net cash flows (indirect method).

Net income	$145,000
Depreciation expense	16,500
Loss on sale of land	5,000
Decrease in accounts receivable	1,500
Decrease in accounts payable	1,250

EA9. LO 16.3 Use the following excerpts from Eagle Company's financial records to determine net cash flows from financing activities.

Acquired new plant assets	$18,000
Borrowed from bank, note payable	40,000
Declared and paid dividends to shareholders	15,000

EA10. LO 16.3 Use the following excerpts from Fruitcake Company's financial records to determine net cash flows from investing activities.

Acquired new plant assets	$18,000
Collected interest on investment assets	4,000
Sold land used in business	36,500

EA11. LO 16.3 Use the following excerpts from Grenada Company's financial records to determine net cash flows from operating activities and net cash flows from investing activities.

Net income this year	$158,750
Purchased plant assets this year	40,000
Sold tract of land this year	35,000
Original cost of land that was sold	25,000

EA12. LO 16.4 Provide the missing piece of information for the following statement of cash flows puzzle.

Cash flows from operating activities	$ 60,000
Cash flows from investing activities	(28,500)
Cash flows from financing activities	?
Cash at the beginning of the year	12,000
Cash at the end of the year	19,500

EA13. LO 16.4 Provide the missing piece of information for the following statement of cash flows puzzle.

Cash flows from operating activities	$?
Cash flows from investing activities	8,900
Cash flows from financing activities	(25,000)
Cash at the beginning of the year	24,000
Cash at the end of the year	22,100

EA14. LO 16.5 Use the following excerpts from Kirsten Company's Statement of Cash Flows and other financial records to determine the company's free cash flow.

From Statement of Cash Flows:	
Cash flows from operating activities	$135,000
Cash flows from investing activities	(50,000)
Cash flows from financing activities	65,000
From other records:	
Cash capital expenditures	75,000
Cash dividends paid	15,000

EA15. LO 16.5 Use the following excerpts from Franklin Company's statement of cash flows and other financial records to determine the company's free cash flow for 2018 and 2017.

	2018	2017
Cash flows from operating activities	$222,000	$200,000
Cash flows from investing activities	(33,000)	(35,000)
Cash flows from financing activities	66,000	60,000
Capital expenditures were 50% of investing activities, both years		
Cash dividends paid were $15,000, both years		

EA16. LO 16.5 The following are excerpts from Hamburg Company's statement of cash flows and other financial records.

From Statement of Cash Flows:	
Cash flows from operating activities	$100,000
Cash flows from investing activities	(50,000)
Cash flows from financing activities	(25,000)
From other records:	
Capital expenditure costs	20,000
Cash dividends payments	22,500
Sales revenue	221,000
Total assets	302,500

Compute the following for the company:

A. free cash flow
B. cash flows to sales ratio
C. cash flows to assets ratio

EA17. LO 16.6 Use the following excerpts from Algona Company's financial statements to determine cash received from customers in 2018.

From Balance Sheets	Dec. 31, 2018	Dec. 31, 2017
Accounts Receivable	$ 85,000	$105,000
From Income Statement:	2018	
Sales	700,000	

EA18. LO 16.6 Use the following excerpts from Huckleberry Company's financial statements to determine cash paid to suppliers for inventory in 2018.

From Balance Sheets:	Dec. 31, 2018	Dec. 31, 2017
Inventory	$ 74,000	$82,000
Accounts Payable	55,000	58,000
From Income Statement:	2018	
Cost of Goods Sold	$520,000	

Exercise Set B

EB1. LO 16.1 Provide journal entries to record each of the following transactions. For each, identify whether the transaction represents a source of cash (S), a use of cash (U), or neither (N).

A. Paid $22,000 cash on bonds payable.
B. Collected $12,600 cash for a note receivable.
C. Declared a dividend to shareholders for $16,000, to be paid in the future.
D. Paid $26,500 to suppliers for purchases on account.
E. Purchased treasury stock for $18,000 cash.

EB2. LO 16.2 In which section of the statement of cash flows would each of the following transactions be included? For each, identify the appropriate section of the statement of cash flows as operating (O), investing (I), financing (F), or none (N). (Note: some transactions might involve two sections.)

A. collected accounts receivable from customers
B. issued common stock for cash
C. declared and paid dividends
D. paid accounts payable balance
E. sold a long-term asset for the same amount as purchased

EB3. LO 16.2 In which section of the statement of cash flows would each of the following transactions be included? For each, identify the appropriate section of the statement of cash flows as operating (O), investing (I), financing (F), or none (N). (Note: some transactions might involve two sections.)

A. purchased stock in Xerox Corporation
B. purchased office supplies
C. issued common stock
D. sold plant assets for cash
E. sold equipment for cash

EB4. LO 16.3 Use the following information from Hamlin Company's financial statements to determine operating net cash flows (indirect method).

Net income	$113,750
Change in accumulated depreciation (no sale of depreciable assets this year)	9,800
Gain on sale of investments	11,400

EB5. LO 16.3 What adjustment(s) should be made to reconcile net income to net cash flows from operating activities (indirect method) considering the following balances in current assets?

Accounts payable, beginning of year	$18,000
Accounts payable, end of year	28,000
Salaries payable, beginning of year	6,000
Salaries payable, end of year	4,000

EB6. LO 16.3 Use the following excerpts from Indigo Company's balance sheets to determine net cash flows from operating activities (indirect method), assuming net income for 2018 of $225,000.

	Dec. 31, 2018	Dec. 31, 2017
Accounts Receivable	$33,000	$31,500
Prepaid Insurance	17,000	18,000
Accounts Payable	19,000	19,500
Accrued Liabilities	11,700	11,000

EB7. LO 16.3 Use the following information from Jumper Company's financial statements to determine operating net cash flows (indirect method).

	Income Statement	Balance Sheet
Sales	$111,000	
Cost of Goods Sold	(73,000)	
Salaries Expense	(12,000)	
Depreciation Expense	(8,000)	
Net Income	18,000	
Accounts Receivable decrease		$3,500
Merchandise Inventory increase		2,200
Salaries Payable increase		925

EB8. LO 16.3 Use the following information from Kentucky Company's financial statements to determine operating net cash flows (indirect method).

Net income	$176,000
Depreciation expense	18,750
Gain on sale of plant assets	15,000
Increase in accounts receivable	12,000
Decrease in accounts payable	5,500

EB9. LO 16.3 Use the following excerpts from Leopard Company's financial records to determine net cash flows from investing activities.

Collected payments on a customer note receivable	$27,500
Purchased plant assets	19,000
Received dividend income from stocks owned	2,500

EB10. LO 16.3 Use the following information from Manuscript Company's financial records to determine net cash flows from financing activities.

Repaid principal on bank loan	$16,500
Issued common stock, at par value	32,000
Declared dividends, to be paid to shareholders next year	9,000

EB11. LO 16.3 Use the following excerpts from Nutmeg Company's financial records to determine net cash flows from operating activities and net cash flows from investing activities.

Net income this year	$83,700
Purchased land this year	20,000
Sold investments this year	31,500
Original cost of investments that were sold	33,000

EB12. LO 16.4 Provide the missing piece of information for the following statement of cash flows puzzle.

Cash flows from operating activities	$ 75,000
Cash flows from investing activities	13,300
Cash flows from financing activities	(33,000)
Cash at the beginning of the year	?
Cash at the end of the year	65,000

EB13. LO 16.4 Provide the missing piece of information for the following statement of cash flows puzzle.

Cash flows from operating activities	$ 88,000
Cash flows from investing activities	?
Cash flows from financing activities	(45,000)
Cash at the beginning of the year	77,000
Cash at the end of the year	113,000

EB14. LO 16.5 Use the following excerpts from Indira Company's Statement of Cash Flows and other financial records to determine the company's free cash flow.

From Statement of Cash Flows:	
Cash flows from operating activities	$ 98,700
Cash flows from investing activities	125,000
Cash flows from financing activities	(16,500)
From other records:	
Cash capital expenditures	40,000
Cash dividends paid	12,000

EB15. LO 16.5 Use the following excerpts from Bolognese Company's statement of cash flows and other financial records to determine the company's free cash flow for 2018 and 2017.

	2018	2017
Cash flows from operating activities	$121,000	$114,000
Cash flows from investing activities	(56,000)	(40,000)
Cash flows from financing activities	(12,000)	(15,000)
Capital expenditures were 40% of investing activities, both years		
Cash dividends paid were $20,000, both years		

EB16. LO 16.5 The following shows excerpts from Camole Company's statement of cash flows and other financial records.

From Statement of Cash Flows:	
Cash flows from operating activities	$225,000
Cash flows from investing activities	(75,000)
Cash flows from financing activities	61,500
From other records:	
Capital expenditure costs	144,000
Cash dividends payments	36,000
Sales revenue	642,000
Total assets	450,000

Compute the following for the company:

A. free cash flow
B. cash flows to sales ratio
C. cash flows to assets ratio

EB17. LO 16.6 Use the following excerpts from Brownstone Company's financial statements to determine cash received from customers in 2018.

From Balance Sheets	**Dec. 31, 2018**	**Dec. 31, 2017**
Accounts Receivable	$ 25,000	$20,000
From Income Statement:	**2018**	
Sales	220,000	

EB18. LO 16.6 Use the following excerpts from Jasper Company's financial statements to determine cash paid to suppliers for inventory in 2018.

From Balance Sheets:	**Dec. 31, 2018**	**Dec. 31, 2017**
Inventory	$ 35,000	$31,000
Accounts Payable	22,000	20,500
From Income Statement:	**2018**	
Cost of Goods Sold	175,900	

Problem Set A

PA1. LO 16.2 Provide journal entries to record each of the following transactions. For each, also identify *the appropriate section of the statement of cash flows, and **whether the transaction represents a source of cash (S), a use of cash (U), or neither (N).

A. paid $12,000 of accounts payable
B. collected $6,000 from a customer
C. issued common stock at par for $24,000 cash
D. paid $6,000 cash dividend to shareholders
E. sold products to customers for $15,000
F. paid current month's utility bill, $1,500

PA2. LO 16.3 Use the following information from Acorn Company's financial statements to determine operating net cash flows (indirect method).

	2018 Income Statement	Balance Sheets
Sales	$ 453,000	
Cost of Goods Sold	(359,000)	
Operating Expenses, other than depreciation expense	(65,000)	
Depreciation Expense	(8,000)	
Loss on sale of plant assets	(11,900)	
Net Income	9,100	
		Dec. 31, 2018
Accounts Receivable		$29,500
Accounts Payable		13,250
		Dec. 31, 2017
Accounts Receivable		$26,500
Accounts Payable		11,750

PA3. LO 16.3 Use the following information from Berlin Company's financial statements to prepare the operating activities section of the statement of cash flows (indirect method) for the year 2018.

	Dec. 31, 2018	Dec. 31, 2017
Cash	$29,000	$24,000
Accounts Receivable	11,500	12,000
Prepaid Assets	1,200	1,000
Total Assets	41,700	37,000
Accrued Liabilities	1,700	1,800
Common Stock	33,000	30,000
Retained Earnings	7,000	5,200
Total Liabilities and Equity	41,700	37,000
Additional information:		
Net income	5,800	
Dividends paid	4,000	

PA4. LO 16.3 Use the following information from Coconut Company's financial statements to prepare the operating activities section of the statement of cash flows (indirect method) for the year 2018.

	Dec. 31, 2018	Dec. 31, 2017
Cash	$201,000	$175,000
Accounts Receivable	22,000	21,500
Inventory	33,750	30,500
Prepaid Rent	6,000	2,000
Accounts Payable	19,500	28,750
Additional information:		
Net income	55,000	
Depreciation expense	11,500	

PA5. LO 16.3 Use the following information from Dubuque Company's financial statements to prepare the operating activities section of the statement of cash flows (indirect method) for the year 2018.

From the Dec. 31, 2018, balance sheet, changes from prior year:	
Accounts Receivable	$ 7,600
Inventory	3,200
Prepaid Insurance	(2,000)
Accounts Payable	(4,000)
Sales Tax Payable	1,900
From the 2018 Income Statement:	
Gain from sale of investments	12,000
Depreciation Expense	26,500
Net Income	79,300

PA6. LO 16.3 Use the following information from Eiffel Company's financial statements to prepare the operating activities section of the statement of cash flows (indirect method) for the year 2018.

	2018 Income Statement	**Balance Sheets**
Sales	$ 299,000	
Cost of Goods Sold	(135,000)	
Operating Expenses, other than depreciation expense	(27,000)	
Depreciation Expense	(17,000)	
Gain on Sale of Plant Assets	16,500	
Net Income	136,500	
		Dec. 31, 2018
Accounts Receivable		$45,300
Inventory		1,600
Accounts Payable		22,500
Accrued Liabilities		900
		Dec. 31, 2017
Accounts Receivable		$43,400
Inventory		1,800
Accounts Payable		21,250
Accrued Liabilities		1,150

PA7. LO 16.3 Analysis of Forest Company's accounts revealed the following activity for its Land account, with descriptions added for clarity of analysis. How would these two transactions be reported for cash flow purposes? Note the section of the statement of cash flow, if applicable, and if the transaction represents a cash source, cash use, or noncash transaction.

	Land
Account balance, beginning of year	$220,000
Purchase of land this year, for cash	95,000
Purchase of land this year, with note payable	75,000
Account balance, end of year	390,000

PA8. LO 16.4 Use the following excerpts from Zowleski Company's financial information to prepare a statement of cash flows (indirect method) for the year 2018.

	Dec. 31, 2018	Dec. 31, 2017
Cash	$ 92,300	$ 85,000
Account Receivable	22,000	22,900
Merchandise Inventory	140,000	131,000
Plant Assets	180,000	150,000
Accumulated Depreciation	(25,000)	(21,000)
Total Assets	409,300	367,900
Accounts Payable	18,500	21,000
Notes Payable	135,500	120,000
Common Stock	20,000	20,000
Retained Earnings	235,300	206,900
Total Liabilities and Equity	409,300	367,900
Additional information:		
Net income for 2018	28,400	
Depreciation expense for 2018 (accumulated depreciation increase)	4,000	
Plant assets purchased (plant assets increase), financed by note	30,000	
Notes payable increased by amount of plant asset purchase	30,000	
Notes payable decreased by amount of principal note payments	14,500	

PA9. LO 16.4 Use the following excerpts from Yardley Company's financial information to prepare a statement of cash flows (indirect method) for the year 2018.

	2018 Income Statement	Balance Sheets
Sales	$ 455,000	
Cost of Goods Sold	(221,500)	
Operating Expenses, other than depreciation expense	(58,600)	
Depreciation Expense	(24,000)	
Gain on Sale of Plant Assets	23,500	
Net Income	174,400	
		Dec. 31, 2018
Cash		$321,450
Accounts Receivable		39,750
Inventory		33,000
Accounts Payable		17,550
Accrued Liabilities		3,500
		Dec. 31, 2017
Cash		$133,500
Accounts Receivable		36,500
Inventory		35,000
Accounts Payable		19,550
Accrued Liabilities		2,200
Additional information:		
Plant assets were sold for $40,000; book value $16,500		
Dividends of $25,000 were declared and paid		

PA10. LO 16.4 Use the following excerpts from Wickham Company's financial information to prepare a statement of cash flows (indirect method) for the year 2018.

	Dec. 31, 2018	Dec. 31, 2017
Cash	$225,000	$200,000
Account Receivable	38,350	35,350
Merchandise Inventory	59,500	58,200
Land	150,000	50,000
Plant Assets	160,000	160,000
Accumulated Depreciation	(49,000)	(37,000)
Total Assets	583,850	466,550
Accounts Payable	29,100	27,300
Accrued Liabilities	15,500	12,000
Common Stock	45,000	20,000
Retained Earnings	494,250	407,250
Total Liabilities and Equity	583,850	466,550
Additional information:		
Net income for 2018	98,000	
Depreciation expense for 2018	12,000	
Land purchased, for cash	100,000	
Stock issued in exchange for cash, at par value	25,000	
Dividends declared and paid	11,000	

PA11. LO 16.4 Use the following excerpts from Tungsten Company's financial information to prepare a statement of cash flows (indirect method) for the year 2018.

Beginning cash	$18,444
Net income	36,500
Depreciation expense	11,000
Accounts receivable change	(8,300)
Inventory change	4,900
Prepaid assets change	3,400
Investments change (no asset sales)	10,000
Accounts payable change	450
Note payable principal balance change (no new loans)	(9,400)
Common stock balance change (due to stock issuance)	20,000

PA12. LO 16.5 The following shows excerpts from financial information relating to Aspen Company and Bergamot Company.

	Aspen	Bergamot
Net Cash Flows from Operating Activities	$320,000	$486,900
Total Assets	450,400	625,000
Net Income	300,000	550,200
Sales Revenue	463,500	875,000
Capital Expenditures	120,750	250,000
Dividend Payments	25,000	65,700

Compute the following for both companies. Compare your results.

A. free cash flow

B. cash flows to sales ratio

C. cash flows to assets ratio

PA13. LO 16.6 Use the following excerpts from Fromera Company's financial information to prepare the operating section of the statement of cash flows (direct method) for the year 2018.

	2018 Income Statement	Balance Sheets
Sales	$ 299,000	
Cost of Goods Sold	(135,000)	
Operating Expenses, other than depreciation expense	(27,000)	
Depreciation Expense	(17,000)	
Gain on Sale of Plant Assets	16,500	
Net Income	136,500	
		Dec. 31, 2018
Accounts Receivable (associated with Sales)		$45,300
Inventory (associated with Inventory)		1,600
Accounts Payable (associated with Inventory)		22,500
Accrued Liabilities (associated with Other Expense)		900
		Dec. 31, 2017
Accounts Receivable (associated with Sales)		$43,400
Inventory (associated with Inventory)		1,800
Accounts Payable (associated with Inventory)		21,250
Accrued Liabilities (associated with Other Expense)		1,150

PA14. LO 16.6 Use the following excerpts from Victrolia Company's financial information to prepare a statement of cash flows (direct method) for the year 2018.

	2018 Income Statement	Balance Sheets
Sales	$ 455,000	
Cost of Goods Sold	(221,500)	
Operating Expenses, other than depreciation expense	(58,600)	
Depreciation Expense	(24,000)	
Gain on Sale of Plant Assets	23,500	
Net Income	174,400	
		Dec. 31, 2018
Cash		$321,450
Accounts Receivable		39,750
Inventory		33,000
Accounts Payable		17,550
Accrued Liabilities		3,500
		Dec. 31, 2017
Cash		$133,500
Accounts Receivable		36,500
Inventory		35,000
Accounts Payable		19,550
Accrued Liabilities		2,200

Additional information:
Plant assets were sold for $40,000; book value $16,500
Dividends of $25,000 were declared and paid

PA15. LO 16.6 Use the following cash transactions relating to Lucknow Company to determine the cash flows from operating, using the direct method.

Beginning cash balance	$122,000
Collected from customers	33,000
Paid dividends to stockholders	3,000
Paid for interest on notes payable	4,750
Collected dividends from stock owned	3,500
Collected cash from sale of land	20,000
Paid principal payments on notes payable	12,000
Collected cash from issuance of stock	40,000
Paid suppliers for merchandise	29,400
Ending cash balance	169,350

Problem Set B

PB1. LO 16.2 Provide journal entries to record each of the following transactions. For each, also identify: *the appropriate section of the statement of cash flows, and **whether the transaction represents a source of cash (S), a use of cash (U), or neither (N).

A. reacquired $30,000 treasury stock
B. purchased inventory for $20,000
C. issued common stock of $40,000 at par
D. purchased land for $25,000
E. collected $22,000 from customers for accounts receivable
F. paid $33,000 principal payment toward note payable to bank

PB2. LO 16.3 Use the following information from Grenada Company's financial statements to prepare the operating activities section of the statement of cash flows (indirect method) for the year 2018.

	2018 Income Statement	Balance Sheets
Sales	$ 286,000	
Cost of Goods Sold	(159,000)	
Operating Expenses, other than depreciation expense	(77,500)	
Depreciation Expense	(9,500)	
Gain on Sale of Investments	14,200	
Net Income	54,200	
		Dec. 31, 2018
Accounts Receivable		$16,500
Accounts Payable		7,400
		Dec. 31, 2017
Accounts Receivable		$18,250
Accounts Payable		8,800

PB3. LO 16.3 Use the following information from Honolulu Company's financial statements to prepare the operating activities section of the statement of cash flows (indirect method) for the year 2018.

	Dec. 31, 2018	Dec. 31, 2017
Cash	$275,000	$254,000
Accounts Receivable	143,000	132,000
Prepaid Assets	8,500	9,000
Total Assets	426,500	395,000
Accrued Liabilities	120,000	112,000
Common Stock	285,000	270,000
Retained Earnings	21,500	13,000
Total Liabilities and Equity	426,500	395,000
Additional information:		
Net income	20,500	
Dividends paid	12,000	

PB4. LO 16.3 Use the following information from Isthmus Company's financial statements to prepare the operating activities section of the statement of cash flows (indirect method) for the year 2018.

	Dec. 31, 2018	Dec. 31, 2017
Cash	$295,000	$259,000
Account Receivable	45,300	48,700
Inventory	92,200	91,000
Accounts Payable	23,000	26,300
Salaries Payable	1,700	1,500
Additional information:		
Net income	45,200	
Depreciation expense	33,300	

PB5. LO 16.3 Use the following information from Juniper Company's financial statements to prepare the operating activities section of the statement of cash flows (indirect method) for the year 2018.

From the Dec. 31, 2018, balance sheet, changes from prior year:	
Account Receivable	$ 4,000
Inventory	(5,500)
Prepaid Insurance	4,000
Accounts Payable	3,000
Sales Tax Payable	(200)
From the 2018 Income Statement:	
Loss from sale of land	4,200
Depreciation Expense	17,250
Net Income	22,222

PB6. LO 16.3 Use the following excerpts from Kayak Company's financial information to prepare the operating section of the statement of cash flows (indirect method) for the year 2018.

	2018 Income Statement	Balance Sheets
Sales	$ 777,000	
Cost of Goods Sold	(555,000)	
Operating Expenses, other than depreciation expense	(22,000)	
Depreciation Expense	(44,000)	
Loss on Sale of Plant Assets	(11,000)	
Net Income	145,000	
		Dec. 31, 2018
Accounts Receivable		$63,300
Inventory		2,400
Accounts Payable		35,000
Accrued Liabilities		2,100
		Dec. 31, 2017
Accounts Receivable		$63,000
Inventory		2,800
Accounts Payable		37,400
Accrued Liabilities		2,650

PB7. LO 16.3 Analysis of Longmind Company's accounts revealed the following activity for Equipment, with descriptions added for clarity of analysis. How would these two transactions be reported for cash flow purposes? Note the section of the statement of cash flow, if applicable, and if the transaction represents a cash source, cash use, or noncash transaction.

	Equipment
Account balance, beginning of year	$ 88,000
Purchase of equipment this year, for cash	29,500
Purchase of equipment this year, with note payable	34,750
Account balance, end of year	152,250

	Equipment
Account balance, beginning of year	$ 88,000
• Purchase of equipment this year, for cash	29,500
• Purchase of equipment this year, with note payable	34,750
Account balance, end of year	152,250

PB8. LO 16.4 Use the following excerpts from Stern Company's financial information to prepare a statement of cash flows (indirect method) for the year 2018.

	Dec. 31, 2018	Dec. 31, 2017
Cash	$121,000	$101,000
Account Receivable	37,200	35,300
Merchandise Inventory	120,000	128,700
Plant Assets	304,000	254,000
Accumulated Depreciation	(85,000)	(64,000)
Total Assets	497,200	455,000
Accounts Payable	23,200	19,900
Notes Payable	179,500	144,000
Common Stock	30,000	30,000
Retained Earnings	264,500	261,100
Total Liabilities and Equity	497,200	455,000
Additional information:		
Net income for 2018	3,400	
Depreciation expense for 2018 (accumulated depreciation increase)	21,000	
Plant assets purchased (plant assets increase), financed by note	50,000	
Notes payable increased by amount of plant asset purchase	50,000	
Notes payable decreased by amount of principal note payments	14,500	

PB9. LO 16.4 Use the following excerpts from Unigen Company's financial information to prepare the operating section of the statement of cash flows (indirect method) for the year 2018.

	2018 Income Statement	Balance Sheets
Sales	$ 777,000	
Cost of Goods Sold	(555,000)	
Operating Expenses, other than depreciation expense	(22,000)	
Depreciation Expense	(44,000)	
Loss on Sale of Plant Assets	(11,000)	
Net Income	145,000	
		Dec. 31, 2018
Cash		$429,850
Accounts Receivable		63,300
Inventory		2,400
Accounts Payable		35,000
Accrued Liabilities		2,100
		Dec. 31, 2017
Cash		$228,700
Accounts Receivable		63,000
Inventory		2,800
Accounts Payable		37,400
Accrued Liabilities		2,650
Additional information:		
Plant assets were sold for $22,000; book value $33,000		
Dividends of $18,000 were declared and paid		

PB10. LO 16.4 Use the following excerpts from Mountain Company's financial information to prepare a statement of cash flows (indirect method) for the year 2018.

	Dec. 31, 2018	Dec. 31, 2017
Cash	$100,000	$ 93,000
Account Receivable	19,000	18,000
Merchandise Inventory	29,000	31,500
Investments	132,000	120,000
Plant Assets	90,000	90,000
Accumulated Depreciation	(37,000)	(23,000)
Total Assets	333,000	329,500
Accounts Payable	12,100	13,400
Accrued Liabilities	2,400	1,900
Common Stock	81,000	63,000
Retained Earnings	237,500	251,200
Total Liabilities and Equity	333,000	329,500
Additional information:		
Net income (loss) for 2018	(5,700)	
Depreciation expense for 2018	14,000	
Investments purchased, for cash	12,000	
Common stock issued for cash, at par value	18,000	
Dividends declared and paid	8,000	

PB11. LO 16.4 Use the following excerpts from OpenAir Company's financial information to prepare a statement of cash flows (indirect method) for the year 2018.

Beginning cash	$120,000
Net income	87,500
Depreciation expense	22,000
Accounts receivable change	8,900
Inventory change	(6,500)
Prepaid assets change	2,400
Investments change (no asset sales)	30,000
Accounts payable change	(800)
Note payable principal balance change (no new loans)	(21,000)
Common stock balance change (due to stock issuance)	36,000

PB12. LO 16.5 The following shows excerpts from financial information relating to Stanwell Company and Thodes Company.

	Stanwell	Thodes
Net Cash Flows from Operating Activities	$138,000	$115,000
Total Assets	272,000	350,000
Net Income	35,000	32,000
Sales Revenue	385,000	250,000
Capital Expenditures	28,000	60,000
Dividend Payments	17,000	13,000

Compute the following for both companies. Compare your results.

A. free cash flow
B. cash flows to sales ratio
C. cash flows to assets ratio

PB13. LO 16.6 Use the following excerpts from Swansea Company's financial information to prepare the operating section of the statement of cash flows (direct method) for the year 2018.

	2018 Income Statement	Balance Sheets
Sales	$ 777,000	
Cost of Goods Sold	(555,000)	
Operating Expenses, other than depreciation expense	(22,000)	
Depreciation Expense	(44,000)	
Loss on Sale of Plant Assets	(11,000)	
Net Income	145,000	
		Dec. 31, 2018
Accounts Receivable (associated with Sales)		$63,300
Inventory (associated with Inventory)		2,400
Accounts Payable (associated with Inventory)		35,000
Accrued Liabilities (associated with Other Expense)		2,100
		Dec. 31, 2017
Accounts Receivable (associated with Sales)		$63,000
Inventory (associated with Inventory)		2,800
Accounts Payable (associated with Inventory)		37,400
Accrued Liabilities (associated with Other Expense)		2,650

PB14. LO 16.6 Use the following excerpts from Swahilia Company's financial information to prepare a statement of cash flows (direct method) for the year 2018.

	2018 Income Statement	Balance Sheets
Sales	$ 777,000	
Cost of Goods Sold	(555,000)	
Operating Expenses, other than depreciation expense	(22,000)	
Depreciation Expense	(44,000)	
Loss on Sale of Plant Assets	(11,000)	
Net Income	145,000	
		Dec. 31, 2018
Cash		$429,850
Accounts Receivable		63,300
Inventory		2,400
Accounts Payable		35,000
Accrued Liabilities		2,100
		Dec. 31, 2017
Cash		$228,700
Accounts Receivable		63,000
Inventory		2,800
Accounts Payable		37,400
Accrued Liabilities		2,650
Additional information:		
Plant assets were sold for $22,000; book value $33,000		
Dividends of $18,000 were declared and paid		

PB15. LO 16.6 Use the following cash transactions relating to Warthoff Company to determine the cash flows from operating, using the direct method.

Beginning cash balance	$45,000
Collected from customers	24,500
Paid dividends to stockholders	5,000
Paid for interest on notes payable	3,200
Collected dividends from stock owned	1,800
Collected cash from sale of land	15,000
Paid principal payments on notes payable	18,800
Collected cash from issuance of stock	25,000
Paid suppliers for merchandise	31,000
Ending cash balance	53,300

Thought Provokers

TP1. LO 16.2 Use the EDGAR (Electronic Data Gathering, Analysis, and Retrieval system) search tools on the US Securities and Exchange Commission website (https://openstax.org/l/50EDGAR) to locate the latest Form 10-K for a company you would like to analyze. Submit a short memo that provides the following information:

- the name and ticker symbol of the company you have chosen
- the following information from the company's statement of cash flows:
  - A. amount of cash flows from operating activities
  - B. amount of cash flows from investing activities
  - C. amount of cash flows from financing activities
- the URL to the company's Form 10-K to allow accurate verification of your answers

TP2. LO 16.3 Use a spreadsheet and the following financial information from Mineola Company's financial statements to build a template that automatically calculates the net operating cash flow. It should be suitable for use in preparing the operating section of the statement of cash flows (indirect method) for the year 2018.

	Dec. 31, 2018	**Dec. 31, 2017**
Cash	$57,000	$42,000
Account Receivable	12,500	15,000
Prepaid Assets	1,500	1,100
Total Assets	71,000	58,100
Accounts Payable	2,700	1,800
Common Stock	39,000	30,000
Retained Earnings	29,300	26,300
Total Liabilities and Equity	71,000	58,100
Additional information:		
Net income	7,000	
Dividends paid	4,000	

TP3. LO 16.3 Consider the dilemma you might someday face if you are the chief financial officer of a company that is struggling to maintain a positive cash flow, despite the fact that the company is reporting a substantial positive net income. Maybe the problem is so severe that there is often insufficient cash to pay ordinary business expenses, like utilities, salaries, and payments to suppliers. Assume that you have been asked to communicate to your board of directors about your company's year, in retrospect, as well as your vision for the company's future. Write a memo that expresses your insights about past experience and present prospects for the company. Note that the challenge of the assignment is to keep your integrity intact, while putting a positive spin on the situation, as much as is reasonably possible. How can you envision the situation turning into a success story?

TP4. LO 16.4 Use the EDGAR (Electronic Data Gathering, Analysis, and Retrieval system) search tools on the US Securities and Exchange Commission website (https://openstax.org/l/50EDGAR) to locate the latest Form 10-K for a company you would like to analyze. Pick a company and submit a short memo that provides the following information:

- The name and ticker symbol of the company you have chosen.
- A description of two items from the company's statement of cash flows:
    - One familiar item that you expected to be reported on the statement, based on what you've learned about cash flows
    - One unfamiliar item that you did not expect to be on the statement, based on what you've learned about cash flows
- The URL to the company's Form 10-K to allow accurate verification of your answers

TP5. LO 16.5 If you had $100,000 available for investing, which of these companies would you choose to invest with? Support your answer with analysis of free cash flow, based on the data provided, and include in your decision whatever other reasoning you chose to utilize.

	Aswan	Merrick
From Statement of Cash Flows:		
Cash flows from operating activities	$ 88,000	$146,500
Cash flows from investing activities	(30,000)	(50,000)
Cash flows from financing activities	58,000	(24,750)
From other records:		
Capital expenditure costs	30,000	50,000
Cash dividends payments	32,000	52,000
Sales Revenue	326,000	542,000
Net Income	65,000	160,500
Total Assets	150,000	350,000

A Financial Statement Analysis

Financial Statement Analysis

Financial statement analysis reviews financial information found on financial statements to make informed decisions about the business. The income statement, statement of retained earnings, balance sheet, and statement of cash flows, among other financial information, can be analyzed. The information obtained from this analysis can benefit decision-making for internal and external stakeholders and can give a company valuable information on overall performance and specific areas for improvement. The analysis can help them with budgeting, deciding where to cut costs, how to increase revenues, and future capital investments opportunities.

When considering the outcomes from analysis, it is important for a company to understand that data produced needs to be compared to others within industry and close competitors. The company should also consider their past experience and how it corresponds to current and future performance expectations. Three common analysis tools are used for decision-making; horizontal analysis, vertical analysis, and financial ratios.

For our discussion of financial statement analysis, we will use Banyan Goods. Banyan Goods is a merchandising company that sells a variety of products. Figure A.1 shows the comparative income statements and balance sheets for the past two years.

BARRY'S SUPERSTORE
Comparative Year-End Income Statements

	Prior Year	Current Year
Net Sales	$100,000	$120,000
Cost of Goods Sold	50,000	60,000
Gross Profit	50,000	60,000
Rent Expense	5,000	5,500
Depreciation Expense	2,500	3,600
Salaries Expense	3,000	5,400
Utility Expense	1,500	2,500
Operating Income	38,000	43,000
Interest Expense	3,000	2,000
Income Tax Expense	5,000	6,000
Net Income	$ 30,000	$ 35,000

BARRY'S SUPERSTORE
Comparative Year-End Balance Sheets

	Prior Year	Current Year
Assets:		
Cash	$90,000	$110,000
Accounts Receivable	20,000	30,000
Inventory	35,000	40,000
Short-Term Investments	15,000	20,000
Total Current Asstes	160,000	200,000
Equipment	40,000	50,000
Total Assets	$200,000	$250,000
Liabilities:		
Accounts Payable	$ 60,000	$ 75,000
Unearned Revenue	10,000	25,000
Total Current Liabilities	70,000	100,000
Notes Payable	40,000	50,000
Total Liabilities	110,000	150,000
Stockholder Equity		
Common Stock	75,000	80,000
Ending Retained Earnings	15,000	20,000
Total Stockholder Equity	90,000	100,000
Total Liabilities and Stockholder Equity	$200,000	$250,000

Figure A.1 Comparative Income Statements and Balance Sheets.

Keep in mind that the comparative income statements and balance sheets for Banyan Goods are simplified for our calculations and do not fully represent all the accounts a company could maintain. Let's begin our analysis discussion by looking at horizontal analysis.

Horizontal Analysis

Horizontal analysis (also known as trend analysis) looks at trends over time on various financial statement line items. A company will look at one period (usually a year) and compare it to another period. For example, a company may compare sales from their current year to sales from the prior year. The trending of items on these financial statements can give a company valuable information on overall performance and specific areas for improvement. It is most valuable to do horizontal analysis for information over multiple periods to see how change is occurring for each line item. If multiple periods are not used, it can be difficult to identify a trend. The year being used for comparison purposes is called the base year (usually the prior period). The year of comparison for horizontal analysis is analyzed for dollar and percent changes against the base year.

The dollar change is found by taking the dollar amount in the base year and subtracting that from the year of analysis.

Dollar Change = Year of Analysis Amount – Base Year Amount

Using Banyan Goods as our example, if Banyan wanted to compare net sales in the current year (year of analysis) of $120,000 to the prior year (base year) of $100,000, the dollar change would be as follows:

$$\text{Dollar change} = \$120{,}000 - \$1000{,}000 = \$20{,}000 \quad \text{(A1)}$$

The percentage change is found by taking the dollar change, dividing by the base year amount, and then multiplying by 100.

$$\textbf{Percent Change} = \left(\frac{\textbf{Dollar Change}}{\textbf{Base Year Amount}}\right) \times 100$$

Let's compute the percentage change for Banyan Goods' net sales.

$$\text{Percentage change} = \left(\frac{\$20{,}000}{\$100{,}000}\right) \times 100 = 20\% \quad \text{(A2)}$$

This means Banyan Goods saw an increase of $20,000 in net sales in the current year as compared to the prior year, which was a 20% increase. The same dollar change and percentage change calculations would be used for the income statement line items as well as the balance sheet line items. Figure A.2 shows the complete horizontal analysis of the income statement and balance sheet for Banyan Goods.

BARRY'S SUPERSTORE Comparative Year-End Income Statements Horizontal Analysis				
	Prior Year	Current Year	Dollar Change	% Change
Net Sales	$100,000	$120,000	$20,000	20%
Cost of Goods Sold	50,000	60,000	$10,000	20%
Gross Profit	50,000	60,000	$10,000	20%
Rent Expense	5,000	5,500	$ 500	10%
Depreciation Expense	2,500	3,600	$ 1,100	44%
Salaries Expense	3,000	5,400	$ 2,400	80%
Utility Expense	1,500	2,500	$ 1,000	67% *
Operating Income	38,000	43,000	$ 5,000	13% *
Interest Expense	3,000	2,000	($ 1,000)	(33%)*
Income Tax Expense	5,000	6,000	$ 1,000	20%
Net Income	$ 30,000	$ 35,000	$ 5,000	17% *

*Rounded to nearest whole percent

BARRY'S SUPERSTORE Comparative Year-End Balance Sheets Horizontal Analysis				
	Prior Year	Current Year	Dollar Change	% Change
Assets:				
Cash	$90,000	$110,000	$20,000	22%*
Accounts Receivable	20,000	30,000	$10,000	50%
Inventory	35,000	40,000	$ 5,000	14%*
Short-Term Investments	15,000	20,000	$ 5,000	33%*
Total Current Asstes	160,000	200,000	$40,000	25%
Equipment	40,000	50,000	$10,000	25%
Total Assets	$200,000	$250,000	$50,000	25%
Liabilities:				
Accounts Payable	$ 60,000	$ 75,000	$15,000	25%
Unearned Revenue	10,000	25,000	$15,000	150%
Total Current Liabilities	70,000	100,000	$30,000	43%*
Notes Payable	40,000	50,000	$10,000	25%
Total Liabilities	110,000	150,000	$40,000	36%*
Stockholder Equity				
Common Stock	75,000	80,000	$ 5,000	7%*
Ending Retained Earnings	15,000	20,000	$ 5,000	33%*
Total Stockholder Equity	90,000	100,000	$10,000	11%*
Total Liabilities and Stockholder Equity	$200,000	$250,000	$50,000	25%

*Rounded to nearest whole percent

Figure A.2 Income Statements and Horizontal Analysis.

Depending on their expectations, Banyan Goods could make decisions to alter operations to produce expected outcomes. For example, Banyan saw a 50% accounts receivable increase from the prior year to the current year. If they were only expecting a 20% increase, they may need to explore this line item further to determine what caused this difference and how to correct it going forward. It could possibly be that they are extending credit more readily than anticipated or not collecting as rapidly on outstanding accounts receivable. The company will need to further examine this difference before deciding on a course of action. Another method of analysis Banyan might consider before making a decision is vertical analysis.

Vertical Analysis

Vertical analysis shows a comparison of a line item within a statement to another line item within that same statement. For example, a company may compare cash to total assets in the current year. This allows a company to see what percentage of cash (the comparison line item) makes up total assets (the other line item) during the period. This is different from horizontal analysis, which compares across years. Vertical analysis compares line items within a statement in the current year. This can help a business to know how much of one item is contributing to overall operations. For example, a company may want to know how much inventory contributes to total assets. They can then use this information to make business decisions such as preparing the budget, cutting costs, increasing revenues, or capital investments.

The company will need to determine which line item they are comparing all items to within that statement and then calculate the percentage makeup. These percentages are considered *common-size* because they make businesses within industry comparable by taking out fluctuations for size. It is typical for an income statement to use net sales (or sales) as the comparison line item. This means net sales will be set at 100% and all other line items within the income statement will represent a percentage of net sales.

On the balance sheet, a company will typically look at two areas: (1) total assets, and (2) total liabilities and stockholders' equity. Total assets will be set at 100% and all assets will represent a percentage of total assets. Total liabilities and stockholders' equity will also be set at 100% and all line items within liabilities and equity will be represented as a percentage of total liabilities and stockholders' equity. The line item set at 100% is considered the base amount and the comparison line item is considered the comparison amount. The formula to determine the common-size percentage is:

$$\text{Common-Size Percentage} = \left(\frac{\text{Comparision Amount}}{\text{Base Amount}}\right) \times 100$$

For example, if Banyan Goods set total assets as the base amount and wanted to see what percentage of total assets were made up of cash in the current year, the following calculation would occur.

$$\text{Common-size percentage} = \left(\frac{\$110{,}000}{\$250{,}000}\right) \times 100 = 44\% \tag{A3}$$

Cash in the current year is $110,000 and total assets equal $250,000, giving a common-size percentage of 44%. If the company had an expected cash balance of 40% of total assets, they would be exceeding expectations. This may not be enough of a difference to make a change, but if they notice this deviates from industry standards, they may need to make adjustments, such as reducing the amount of cash on hand to reinvest in the business. Figure A.3 shows the common-size calculations on the comparative income statements and comparative balance sheets for Banyan Goods.

BARRY'S SUPERSTORE
Comparative Year-End Income Statements
Vertical Analysis

	Prior Year	Current Year	Common Size* Prior Year	Common Size* Current Year
Net Sales	$100,000	$120,000	100%	100%
Cost of Goods Sold	50,000	60,000	50%	50%
Gross Profit	50,000	60,000	50%	50%
Rent Expense	5,000	5,500	5%	5%
Depreciation Expense - Eq.	2,500	3,600	3%	3%
Salaries Expense	3,000	5,400	3%	5%
Utility Expense	1,500	2,500	2%	2%
Operating Income	38,000	43,000	38%	36%
Interest Expense	3,000	2,000	3%	2%
Income Tax Expense	5,000	6,000	5%	5%
Net Income	$ 30,000	$ 35,000	30%	29%

*Some figures rounded to the nearest whole percent, which may alter the total percentage to +/– 1% of 100%

BARRY'S SUPERSTORE
Comparative Year-End Balance Sheets
Vertical Analysis

	Prior Year	Current Year	Common Size Prior Year	Common Size Current Year
Assets:				
Cash	$90,000	$110,000	45%	44%
Accounts Receivable	20,000	30,000	10%	12%
Inventory	35,000	40,000	17.5%	16%
Short-Term Investments	15,000	20,000	7.5%	8%
Total Current Asstes	160,000	200,000	80%	80%
Equipment	40,000	50,000	20%	20%
Total Assets	$200,000	$250,000	100%	100%
Liabilities:				
Accounts Payable	$ 60,000	$ 75,000	30%	30%
Unearned Revenue	10,000	25,000	5%	10%
Total Current Liabilities	70,000	100,000	35%	40%
Notes Payable	40,000	50,000	20%	20%
Total Liabilities	110,000	150,000	55%	60%
Stockholder Equity				
Common Stock	75,000	80,000	37.5%	32%
Ending Retained Earnings	15,000	20,000	7.5%	8%
Total Stockholder Equity	90,000	100,000	45%	40%
Total Liabilities and Stockholder Equity	$200,000	$250,000	100%	100%

Figure A.3 Income Statements and Vertical Analysis.

Even though vertical analysis is a statement comparison within the same year, Banyan can use information from the prior year's vertical analysis to make sure the business is operating as expected. For example, unearned revenues increased from the prior year to the current year and made up a larger portion of total liabilities and stockholders' equity. This could be due to many factors, and Banyan Goods will need to examine this further to see why this change has occurred. Let's turn to financial statement analysis using financial ratios.

Overview of Financial Ratios

Financial ratios help both internal and external users of information make informed decisions about a company. A stakeholder could be looking to invest, become a supplier, make a loan, or alter internal operations, among other things, based in part on the outcomes of ratio analysis. The information resulting from ratio analysis can be used to examine trends in performance, establish benchmarks for success, set budget expectations, and compare industry competitors. There are four main categories of ratios: liquidity, solvency, efficiency, and profitability. Note that while there are more ideal outcomes for some ratios, the industry in which the business operates can change the influence each of these outcomes has over stakeholder decisions. (You will learn more about ratios, industry standards, and ratio interpretation in advanced accounting courses.)

Liquidity Ratios

Liquidity ratios show the ability of the company to pay short-term obligations if they came due immediately with assets that can be quickly converted to cash. This is done by comparing current assets to current liabilities. Lenders, for example, may consider the outcomes of liquidity ratios when deciding whether to extend a loan to a company. A company would like to be liquid enough to manage any currently due obligations but not too liquid where they may not be effectively investing in growth opportunities. Three common liquidity measurements are working capital, current ratio, and quick ratio.

Working Capital

Working capital measures the financial health of an organization in the short-term by finding the difference between current assets and current liabilities. A company will need enough current assets to cover current liabilities; otherwise, they may not be able to continue operations in the future. Before a lender extends credit, they will review the working capital of the company to see if the company can meet their obligations. A larger difference signals that a company can cover their short-term debts and a lender may be more willing to extend the loan. On the other hand, too large of a difference may indicate that the company may not be correctly using their assets to grow the business. The formula for working capital is:

Working Capital = Current Assets – Current Liabilities

Using Banyan Goods, working capital is computed as follows for the current year:

$$\text{Working capital} = \$200{,}000 - \$100{,}000 = \$100{,}000 \qquad \text{(A4)}$$

In this case, current assets were $200,000, and current liabilities were $100,000. Current assets were far greater than current liabilities for Banyan Goods and they would easily be able to cover short-term debt.

The dollar value of the difference for working capital is limited given company size and scope. It is most useful to convert this information to a ratio to determine the company's current financial health. This ratio is the current ratio.

Current Ratio

Working capital expressed as a ratio is the current ratio. The current ratio considers the amount of current assets available to cover current liabilities. The higher the current ratio, the more likely the company can cover its short-term debt. The formula for current ratio is:

$$\textbf{Current Ratio} = \left(\frac{\textbf{Current Assets}}{\textbf{Current Liabilities}}\right)$$

The current ratio in the current year for Banyan Goods is:

$$\text{Current ratio} = \left(\frac{\$200{,}000}{\$100{,}000}\right) = 2 \text{ or } 2{:}1 \qquad \text{(A5)}$$

A 2:1 ratio means the company has twice as many current assets as current liabilities; typically, this would be plenty to cover obligations. This may be an acceptable ratio for Banyan Goods, but if it is too high, they may want to consider using those assets in a different way to grow the company.

Quick Ratio

The quick ratio, also known as the acid-test ratio, is similar to the current ratio except current assets are more narrowly defined as the most liquid assets, which exclude inventory and prepaid expenses. The conversion of inventory and prepaid expenses to cash can sometimes take more time than the liquidation of other current assets. A company will want to know what they have on hand and can use quickly if an immediate obligation is due. The formula for the quick ratio is:

$$\textbf{Quick Ratio} = \left(\frac{\textbf{Cash + Short-Term Investments + Accounts Receivable}}{\textbf{Current Liabilities}}\right)$$

The quick ratio for Banyan Goods in the current year is:

$$\text{Quick ratio} = \left(\frac{\$110{,}000 + \$20{,}000 + \$30{,}000}{\$100{,}000}\right) = 1.6 \text{ or } 1.6{:}1 \qquad \text{(A6)}$$

A 1.6:1 ratio means the company has enough quick assets to cover current liabilities.

Another category of financial measurement uses solvency ratios.

Solvency Ratios

Solvency implies that a company can meet its long-term obligations and will likely stay in business in the future. To stay in business the company must generate more revenue than debt in the long-term. Meeting long-term obligations includes the ability to pay any interest incurred on long-term debt. Two main solvency ratios are the debt-to-equity ratio and the times interest earned ratio.

Debt to Equity Ratio

The debt-to-equity ratio shows the relationship between debt and equity as it relates to business financing. A company can take out loans, issue stock, and retain earnings to be used in future periods to keep operations running. It is less risky and less costly to use equity sources for financing as compared to debt resources. This is mainly due to interest expense repayment that a loan carries as opposed to equity, which does not have this requirement. Therefore, a company wants to know how much debt and equity contribute to its financing. Ideally, a company would prefer more equity than debt financing. The formula for the debt to equity ratio is:

$$\textbf{Debt-to-Equity Ratio} = \left(\frac{\textbf{Total Liabilities}}{\textbf{Total Stockholder Equity}}\right)$$

The information needed to compute the debt-to-equity ratio for Banyan Goods in the current year can be found on the balance sheet.

$$\text{Debt-to-equity ratio} = \left(\frac{\$150{,}000}{\$100{,}000}\right) = 1.5 \text{ or } 1.5{:}1 \tag{A7}$$

This means that for every $1 of equity contributed toward financing, $1.50 is contributed from lenders. This would be a concern for Banyan Goods. This could be a red flag for potential investors that the company could be trending toward insolvency. Banyan Goods might want to get the ratio below 1:1 to improve their long-term business viability.

Times Interest Earned Ratio

Time interest earned measures the company's ability to pay interest expense on long-term debt incurred. This ability to pay is determined by the available earnings before interest and taxes (EBIT) are deducted. These earnings are considered the operating income. Lenders will pay attention to this ratio before extending credit. The more times over a company can cover interest, the more likely a lender will extend long-term credit. The formula for times interest earned is:

$$\textbf{Times Interest Earned} = \left(\frac{\textbf{Earnings before Interest and Taxes}}{\textbf{Interest Expense}}\right)$$

The information needed to compute times interest earned for Banyan Goods in the current year can be found on the income statement.

$$\text{Times interest earned} = \left(\frac{\$43{,}000}{\$2{,}000}\right) = 21.5 \text{ times} \tag{A8}$$

The $43,000 is the operating income, representing earnings before interest and taxes. The 21.5 times outcome suggests that Banyan Goods can easily repay interest on an outstanding loan and creditors would have little risk that Banyan Goods would be unable to pay.

Another category of financial measurement uses efficiency ratios.

Efficiency Ratios

Efficiency shows how well a company uses and manages their assets. Areas of importance with efficiency are management of sales, accounts receivable, and inventory. A company that is efficient typically will be able to generate revenues quickly using the assets it acquires. Let's examine four efficiency ratios: accounts receivable turnover, total asset turnover, inventory turnover, and days' sales in inventory.

Accounts Receivable Turnover

Accounts receivable turnover measures how many times in a period (usually a year) a company will collect cash from accounts receivable. A higher number of times could mean cash is collected more quickly and that credit customers are of high quality. A higher number is usually preferable because the cash collected can be reinvested in the business at a quicker rate. A lower number of times could mean cash is collected slowly on these accounts and customers may not be properly qualified to accept the debt. The formula for accounts receivable turnover is:

$$\text{Accounts Receivable Turnover} = \left(\frac{\text{Net Credit Sales}}{\text{Average Accounts Receivable}}\right)$$

$$\text{Average Accounts Receivable} = \left(\frac{\text{Beginning Accounts Receivable + Ending Accounts Receivable}}{2}\right)$$

Many companies do not split credit and cash sales, in which case net sales would be used to compute accounts receivable turnover. Average accounts receivable is found by dividing the sum of beginning and ending accounts receivable balances found on the balance sheet. The beginning accounts receivable balance in the current year is taken from the ending accounts receivable balance in the prior year.

When computing the accounts receivable turnover for Banyan Goods, let's assume net credit sales make up $100,000 of the $120,000 of the net sales found on the income statement in the current year.

$$\begin{aligned} \text{Average accounts receivable} &= \frac{\$20,000 + \$30,000}{2} = \$25,000 \\ \text{Accounts receivable turnover} &= \frac{\$100,000}{\$25,000} = 4 \text{ times} \end{aligned} \tag{A9}$$

An accounts receivable turnover of four times per year may be low for Banyan Goods. Given this outcome, they may want to consider stricter credit lending practices to make sure credit customers are of a higher quality. They may also need to be more aggressive with collecting any outstanding accounts.

Total Asset Turnover

Total asset turnover measures the ability of a company to use their assets to generate revenues. A company would like to use as few assets as possible to generate the most net sales. Therefore, a higher total asset turnover means the company is using their assets very efficiently to produce net sales. The formula for total asset turnover is:

$$\text{Total Asset Turnover} = \left(\frac{\text{Net Sales}}{\text{Average Total Assets}}\right)$$

$$\text{Average Total Assets} = \left(\frac{\text{Beginning Total Assets + Ending Total Assets}}{2}\right)$$

Average total assets are found by dividing the sum of beginning and ending total assets balances found on the balance sheet. The beginning total assets balance in the current year is taken from the ending total assets balance in the prior year.

Banyan Goods' total asset turnover is:

$$\begin{aligned} \text{Average total assets} &= \frac{\$200,000 + \$250,000}{2} = \$225,000 \\ \text{Total assets turnover} &= \frac{\$120,000}{\$225,000} = 0.53 \text{ times (rounded)} \end{aligned} \tag{A10}$$

The outcome of 0.53 means that for every $1 of assets, $0.53 of net sales are generated. Over time, Banyan Goods would like to see this turnover ratio increase.

Inventory Turnover

Inventory turnover measures how many times during the year a company has sold and replaced inventory.

This can tell a company how well inventory is managed. A higher ratio is preferable; however, an extremely high turnover may mean that the company does not have enough inventory available to meet demand. A low turnover may mean the company has too much supply of inventory on hand. The formula for inventory turnover is:

$$\textbf{Inventory Turnover} = \left(\frac{\textbf{Cost of Goods Sold}}{\textbf{Average Inventory}}\right)$$

$$\textbf{Average Inventory} = \left(\frac{\textbf{Beginning Inventory + Ending Inventory}}{\textbf{2}}\right)$$

Cost of goods sold for the current year is found on the income statement. Average inventory is found by dividing the sum of beginning and ending inventory balances found on the balance sheet. The beginning inventory balance in the current year is taken from the ending inventory balance in the prior year.

Banyan Goods' inventory turnover is:

$$\begin{aligned} \text{Average inventory} &= \frac{\$35{,}000 + \$40{,}000}{2} = \$37{,}500 \\ \text{Inventory turnover} &= \frac{\$60{,}000}{\$37{,}500} = 1.6 \text{ times} \end{aligned} \tag{A11}$$

1.6 times is a very low turnover rate for Banyan Goods. This may mean the company is maintaining too high an inventory supply to meet a low demand from customers. They may want to decrease their on-hand inventory to free up more liquid assets to use in other ways.

Days' Sales in Inventory

Days' sales in inventory expresses the number of days it takes a company to turn inventory into sales. This assumes that no new purchase of inventory occurred within that time period. The fewer the number of days, the more quickly the company can sell its inventory. The higher the number of days, the longer it takes to sell its inventory. The formula for days' sales in inventory is:

$$\textbf{Days' Sales in Inventory} = \left(\frac{\textbf{Ending Inventory}}{\textbf{Cost of Goods Sold}}\right) \times \textbf{365}$$

Banyan Goods' days' sales in inventory is:

$$\text{Days' sales in inventory} = \left(\frac{\$40{,}000}{\$60{,}000}\right) \times 365 = 243 \text{ days (rounded)} \tag{A12}$$

243 days is a long time to sell inventory. While industry dictates what is an acceptable number of days to sell inventory, 243 days is unsustainable long-term. Banyan Goods will need to better manage their inventory and sales strategies to move inventory more quickly.

The last category of financial measurement examines profitability ratios.

Profitability Ratios

Profitability considers how well a company produces returns given their operational performance. The company needs to leverage its operations to increase profit. To assist with profit goal attainment, company revenues need to outweigh expenses. Let's consider three profitability measurements and ratios: profit margin, return on total assets, and return on equity.

Profit Margin

Profit margin represents how much of sales revenue has translated into income. This ratio shows how much of each $1 of sales is returned as profit. The larger the ratio figure (the closer it gets to 1), the more of each sales dollar is returned as profit. The portion of the sales dollar not returned as profit goes toward expenses. The formula for profit margin is:

$$\textbf{Profit Margin} = \left(\frac{\textbf{Net Income}}{\textbf{Net Sales}}\right)$$

For Banyan Goods, the profit margin in the current year is:

$$\text{Profit margin} = \left(\frac{\$35{,}000}{\$120{,}000}\right) = 0.29 \text{ (rounded) or } 29\% \qquad \text{(A13)}$$

This means that for every dollar of sales, $0.29 returns as profit. If Banyan Goods thinks this is too low, the company would try and find ways to reduce expenses and increase sales.

Return on Total Assets

The return on total assets measures the company's ability to use its assets successfully to generate a profit. The higher the return (ratio outcome), the more profit is created from asset use. Average total assets are found by dividing the sum of beginning and ending total assets balances found on the balance sheet. The beginning total assets balance in the current year is taken from the ending total assets balance in the prior year. The formula for return on total assets is:

$$\textbf{Return on Total Assets} = \left(\frac{\textbf{Net Income}}{\textbf{Average Total Assets}}\right)$$

$$\textbf{Average Total Assets} = \left(\frac{\textbf{Beginning Total Assets + Ending Total Assets}}{\textbf{2}}\right)$$

For Banyan Goods, the return on total assets for the current year is:

$$\begin{aligned} \text{Average total assets} &= \frac{\$200{,}000 + \$250{,}000}{2} = \$225{,}000 \\ \text{Return on total assets} &= \frac{\$35{,}000}{\$225{,}000} = 0.16 \text{ (rounded) or } 16\% \end{aligned} \qquad \text{(A14)}$$

The higher the figure, the better the company is using its assets to create a profit. Industry standards can dictate what is an acceptable return.

Return on Equity

Return on equity measures the company's ability to use its invested capital to generate income. The invested capital comes from stockholders investments in the company's stock and its retained earnings and is leveraged to create profit. The higher the return, the better the company is doing at using its investments to yield a profit. The formula for return on equity is:

$$\text{Return on Equity} = \left(\frac{\text{Net Income}}{\text{Average Stockholder Equity}}\right)$$

$$\text{Average Stockholder Equity} = \left(\frac{\text{Beginning Stockholder Equity} + \text{Ending Stockholder Equity}}{2}\right)$$

Average stockholders' equity is found by dividing the sum of beginning and ending stockholders' equity balances found on the balance sheet. The beginning stockholders' equity balance in the current year is taken from the ending stockholders' equity balance in the prior year. Keep in mind that the net income is calculated after preferred dividends have been paid.

For Banyan Goods, we will use the net income figure and assume no preferred dividends have been paid. The return on equity for the current year is:

$$\begin{aligned} \text{Average stockholder equity} &= \frac{\$90{,}000 + \$100{,}000}{2} = \$95{,}000 \\ \text{Return on equity} &= \frac{\$35{,}000}{\$95{,}000} = 0.37 \text{ (rounded) or } 37\% \end{aligned} \tag{A15}$$

The higher the figure, the better the company is using its investments to create a profit. Industry standards can dictate what is an acceptable return.

Advantages and Disadvantages of Financial Statement Analysis

There are several advantages and disadvantages to financial statement analysis. Financial statement analysis can show trends over time, which can be helpful in making future business decisions. Converting information to percentages or ratios eliminates some of the disparity between competitor sizes and operating abilities, making it easier for stakeholders to make informed decisions. It can assist with understanding the makeup of current operations within the business, and which shifts need to occur internally to increase productivity.

A stakeholder needs to keep in mind that past performance does not always dictate future performance. Attention must be given to possible economic influences that could skew the numbers being analyzed, such as inflation or a recession. Additionally, the way a company reports information within accounts may change over time. For example, where and when certain transactions are recorded may shift, which may not be readily evident in the financial statements.

A company that wants to budget properly, control costs, increase revenues, and make long-term expenditure decisions may want to use financial statement analysis to guide future operations. As long as the company understands the limitations of the information provided, financial statement analysis is a good tool to predict growth and company financial strength.

B Time Value of Money

Present Value of $1 Table

Present Value of $1 Table

$$\text{Factor} = \frac{1}{(1+i)^n}$$

Period (*n*)	1%	2%	3%	5%	8%	10%	12%	15%	20%
	Rate (*i*)								
1	0.990	0.980	0.971	0.952	0.926	0.909	0.893	0.870	0.833
2	0.980	0.961	0.943	0.907	0.857	0.826	0.797	0.756	0.694
3	0.971	0.942	0.915	0.864	0.794	0.751	0.712	0.658	0.579
4	0.961	0.924	0.888	0.823	0.735	0.683	0.636	0.572	0.482
5	0.952	0.906	0.863	0.784	0.681	0.621	0.567	0.497	0.402
6	0.942	0.888	0.837	0.746	0.630	0.564	0.507	0.432	0.335
7	0.933	0.871	0.813	0.711	0.583	0.513	0.452	0.376	0.279
8	0.924	0.853	0.789	0.677	0.540	0.467	0.404	0.327	0.233
9	0.914	0.837	0.766	0.645	0.500	0.424	0.361	0.284	0.194
10	0.905	0.820	0.744	0.614	0.463	0.386	0.322	0.247	0.162
11	0.896	0.804	0.722	0.585	0.429	0.350	0.287	0.215	0.135
12	0.888	0.788	0.701	0.557	0.397	0.319	0.257	0.187	0.112
13	0.879	0.773	0.681	0.530	0.368	0.290	0.229	0.163	0.093
14	0.861	0.758	0.661	0.505	0.340	0.263	0.205	0.141	0.078
15	0.861	0.743	0.642	0.481	0.315	0.239	0.183	0.123	0.065
16	0.853	0.728	0.623	0.458	0.292	0.218	0.163	0.107	0.054
17	0.844	0.714	0.605	0.436	0.270	0.198	0.146	0.093	0.045
18	0.836	0.700	0.587	0.416	0.250	0.180	0.130	0.081	0.038
19	0.828	0.686	0.570	0.396	0.232	0.164	0.116	0.070	0.031
20	0.820	0.673	0.554	0.377	0.215	0.149	0.104	0.061	0.026

Figure B.1 Present Value of $1 Table.

Present Value of an Ordinary Annuity Table

Future Value of an Ordinary Annuity Table

$$\text{Factor} = \frac{[1 - 1/(1+i)^n]}{i}$$

Period (n)	Rate (i)								
	1%	2%	3%	5%	8%	10%	12%	15%	20%
1	0.990	0.980	0.971	0.952	0.926	0.909	0.893	0.870	0.833
2	1.970	1.942	1.913	1.859	1.783	1.736	1.690	1.626	1.528
3	2.941	2.884	2.829	2.723	2.577	2.487	2.402	2.283	2.106
4	3.902	3.808	3.717	3.546	3.312	3.170	3.037	2.855	2.589
5	4.853	4.713	4.580	4.329	3.993	3.791	3.605	3.352	2.991
6	5.795	5.601	5.417	5.076	4.623	4.355	4.111	3.785	3.326
7	6.728	6.472	6.230	5.786	5.206	4.868	4.564	4.160	3.605
8	7.652	7.325	7.020	6.463	5.747	5.335	4.968	4.487	3.837
9	8.566	8.162	7.786	7.108	6.247	5.759	5.328	4.772	4.031
10	9.471	8.983	8.530	7.722	6.710	6.145	5.650	5.019	4.192
11	10.368	9.787	9.253	8.306	7.139	6.495	5.938	5.234	4.327
12	11.255	10.575	9.954	8.863	7.536	6.814	6.194	5.421	4.439
13	12.134	11.348	10.635	9.394	7.904	7.103	6.424	5.583	4.533
14	13.004	12.106	11.296	9.899	8.244	7.367	6.628	5.725	4.611
15	13.865	12.849	11.938	10.380	8.559	7.606	6.811	5.847	4.675
16	14.718	13.578	12.561	10.838	8.851	7.824	6.974	5.954	4.730
17	15.562	14.292	13.166	11.274	9.122	8.022	7.120	6.047	4.775
18	16.398	14.992	13.754	11.690	9.372	8.201	7.250	6.128	4.812
19	17.226	15.678	14.324	12.085	9.604	8.365	7.366	6.198	4.844
20	18.046	16.351	14.877	12.462	9.818	8.514	7.469	6.259	4.870

Figure B.2 Present Value of an Ordinary Annuity Table.

Future Value of $1 Table

Future Value of $1 Table Factor = $(1 + i)^n$ Rate (i)									
Period (n)	1%	2%	3%	5%	8%	10%	12%	15%	20%
1	1.010	1.020	1.030	1.050	1.080	1.100	1.120	1.150	1.200
2	1.020	1.040	1.061	1.103	1.166	1.210	1.254	1.323	1.440
3	1.030	1.061	1.093	1.158	1.260	1.331	1.405	1.521	1.728
4	1.041	1.082	1.126	1.216	1.360	1.464	1.574	1.749	2.074
5	1.051	1.104	1.159	1.276	1.469	1.611	1.762	2.011	2.488
6	1.062	1.126	1.194	1.340	1.587	1.772	1.974	2.313	2.986
7	1.072	1.149	1.230	1.407	1.714	1.949	2.211	2.660	3.583
8	1.083	1.172	1.267	1.477	1.851	2.144	2.476	3.059	4.300
9	1.094	1.195	1.305	1.551	1.999	2.358	2.773	3.518	5.160
10	1.105	1.219	1.344	1.629	2.159	2.594	3.106	4.046	6.192
11	1.116	1.243	1.384	1.710	2.332	2.853	3.479	4.652	7.430
12	1.127	1.268	1.426	1.796	2.518	3.138	3.896	5.350	8.916
13	1.138	1.294	1.469	1.886	2.720	3.452	4.363	6.153	10.699
14	1.149	1.319	1.513	1.980	2.937	3.797	4.887	7.076	12.839
15	1.161	1.346	1.558	2.079	3.172	4.177	5.474	8.137	15.407
16	1.173	1.373	1.605	2.183	3.426	4.595	6.130	9.358	18.488
17	1.184	1.400	1.653	2.292	3.700	5.054	6.866	10.761	22.186
18	1.196	1.428	1.702	2.407	3.996	5.560	7.690	12.375	26.623
19	1.208	1.457	1.754	2.527	4.316	6.116	8.613	14.232	31.948
20	1.220	1.486	1.806	2.653	4.661	6.727	9.646	16.367	38.338

Figure B.3 Future Value of $1 Table.

Future Value of an Ordinary Annuity Table

Future Value of an Ordinary Annuity Table

$$\text{Factor} = \frac{[(1+i)^n - 1]}{i}$$

Rate (i)

Period (n)	1%	2%	3%	5%	8%	10%	12%	15%	20%
1	1.000	1.000	1.000	1.000	1.000	1.000	1.000	1.000	1.000
2	2.010	2.020	2.030	2.050	2.080	2.100	2.120	2.150	2.200
3	3.030	3.060	3.091	3.153	3.246	3.310	3.374	3.473	3.640
4	4.060	4.122	4.184	4.310	4.506	4.641	4.779	4.993	5.368
5	5.101	5.204	5.309	5.526	5.867	6.105	6.353	6.742	7.442
6	6.152	6.308	6.468	6.802	7.336	7.716	8.115	8.754	9.930
7	7.214	7.434	7.662	8.142	8.923	9.487	10.089	11.067	12.916
8	8.286	8.583	8.892	9.549	10.637	11.436	12.300	13.727	16.499
9	9.369	9.755	10.159	11.027	12.488	13.579	14.776	16.786	20.799
10	10.462	10.950	11.464	12.578	14.487	15.937	17.549	20.304	25.959
11	11.567	12.169	12.808	14.207	16.645	18.531	20.655	24.349	32.150
12	12.683	13.412	14.192	15.917	18.977	21.384	24.133	29.002	39.581
13	13.809	14.680	15.618	17.713	21.495	24.523	28.029	34.352	48.497
14	14.947	15.974	17.086	19.599	24.215	27.975	32.393	40.505	59.196
15	16.097	17.293	18.599	21.579	27.152	31.772	37.280	47.580	72.035
16	17.258	18.639	20.157	23.657	30.324	35.950	42.753	55.717	87.442
17	18.430	20.012	21.762	25.840	33.750	40.545	48.884	65.075	105.930
18	19.615	21.412	23.414	28.132	37.450	45.599	55.750	75.836	128.120
19	20.811	22.841	25.117	30.539	41.446	51.159	63.440	88.212	154.740
20	22.019	24.297	26.870	33.066	45.762	57.275	72.052	102.440	186.690

Figure B.4 Future Value of an Ordinary Annuity Table.

C Suggested Resources

The resources listed provide further information on several topics: financial statements from real-world companies, accounting software and tools, personal finance, accounting organizations, and exams and professional certifications for accountants.

Sample Financial Statements

The following income statements and balance sheets show the finances of companies representing the manufacturing, retail, and service industries.

Manufacturing Company: General Motors

- Income statement: https://www.nasdaq.com/symbol/gm/financials?query=income-statement
- Balance sheet: https://www.nasdaq.com/symbol/gm/financials?query=balance-sheet

Retail Company: Costco Wholesale

- Income statement: https://www.nasdaq.com/symbol/cost/financials
- Balance sheet: https://www.nasdaq.com/symbol/cost/financials?query=balance-sheet

Service Company: Prudential

- Income statement https://www.marketwatch.com/investing/stock/pru/financials
- Balance sheet: https://www.marketwatch.com/investing/stock/pru/financials/balance-sheet

Accounting Software and Tools

The resources listed offer a variety of tutorials, training videos, and practice activities using software and tools common in accounting.

QuickBooks

- QuickBooks tutorials: https://quickbooks.intuit.com/tutorials/

Peachtree/Sage 50

- Peachtree 2011 guide: https://www.perdisco.com/peachtreeLearning/quickReferenceGuide/2011.aspx
- Sage 50 training course with videos: https://www.freebookkeepingaccounting.com/single-post/Sage-50-Accounts-Training-Course-Part-1

Microsoft Excel

- Excel tutorials, video guides, trainings, and worksheets: https://chandoo.org/wp/welcome/
- YouTube channel with accounting-specific video tutorials: https://www.youtube.com/user/ExcelIsFun

Financial Calculators

- HP10B setup video guide: https://www.youtube.com/watch?v=lmMdRfKre44
- HP10BII video introduction and examples: https://www.youtube.com/watch?v=fTqkkeG1xlw
- HP10B and HP12C time value of money calculations video guides: https://www.youtube.com/user/mssuprof/videos

Personal Finance

These resources can assist you with personal financial planning.

Earnings

- Current starting salaries for recent college graduates for various majors and degrees: https://careers.kennesaw.edu/employers/docs/2018-nace-salary-survey-winter.pdf
- Accounting-specific salaries and positions: https://www.roberthalf.com/blog/salaries-and-skills/the-rise-of-the-accountant-salary-and-10-top-accounting-jobs

Take-Home Pay

- Salary calculator that determines your net pay—the amount you'll take home in your paycheck that you need to plan your budget around. In addition to calculating state and federal taxes, this resource allows you to input other withholdings such as health insurance or 401K contributions: https://www.paycheckcity.com/

Saving and Retirement Planning

Determining how much your savings will grow and how much you will have in retirement are very important components of personal financial planning. These links will help you better plan for those aspects of saving.

- This basic savings growth calculator includes graphs that provide helpful visuals of the impact of changing any assumptions such as the timing or amount of contributions or the interest rate earned: https://smartasset.com/investing/investment-calculator
- To estimate retirement savings growth, use this calculator that allows you to see the impact of saving now (enter your current age) versus saving later (enter a future age): https://www.daveramsey.com/smartvestor/investment-calculator
- This calculator lets you more accurately plan how your retirement savings will grow by allowing you to input any matching amounts contributed by employers: https://nb.fidelity.com/public/nb/401k/tools/calculators/contributioncalculator

Budgeting

- A well-planned budget is the cornerstone of personal financial planning. Using the salary, pay and savings numbers obtained from the resources above, this calculator will help you create a detailed financial budget: https://www.clearpoint.org/tools/budget-calculator/

Debt Reduction

- Whether it is student loans, credit cards, car loans or any other kind of debt, it is always beneficial to understand the impact of differing payments on paying off debt. This resource will help you see the impact of changing the amount paid on the payoff timing and interest paid on the debt: https://www.money-zine.com/calculators/loan-calculators/debt-reduction-calculator/

Accounting-Related Organizations

A number of organizations are dedicated to regulating and supporting the variety of work undertaken in the discipline of accounting.

- Governmental Accounting Standards Board (GASB): https://www.gasb.org
- Financial Accounting Standards Board (FASB): https://www.fasb.org
- U.S. Securities and Exchange Commission (SEC): https://www.sec.gov
- Association of Chartered Certified Accountants (ACCA): https://www.accaglobal.com
- Institute of Management Accountants (IMA): https://www.imanet.org

Accounting Exams and Certificates

These sites provide information on exams and professional certifications.

Certified Public Accountant (CPA)

- American Institute of Certified Public Accountants (AICPA): https://www.aicpa.org/content/aicpa/
- National Association of State Boards of Accountancy (NASBA): https://nasba.org/
- This Way to the CPA: https://thiswaytocpa.com/

Certified Management Accountant (CMA)

- Institute of Management Accountants (IMA): https://www.imanet.org/cma-certification?ssopc=1

Certified Internal Auditor (CIA)

- Institute of Internal Auditors (IIA)-Global: https://global.theiia.org/Pages/globaliiaHome.aspx
- Institute of Internal Auditors (IIA)-North America: https://na.theiia.org/Pages/IIAHome.aspx

Certified Fraud Examiner (CFE)

- Association of Certified Fraud Examiners (ACFE): http://www.acfe.com/default.aspx

Chartered Financial Analyst (CFA)

- CFA Institute: https://www.cfainstitute.org/Pages/index.aspx

Certified Financial Planner (CFP)

- Certified Financial Planners (CFP) Board: https://www.cfp.net/home

Answer Key

Chapter 1

Multiple Choice

1. B
3. C
5. A
7. B
9. B
11. E
13. A
15. D
17. A
19. B

Questions

1. Answers will vary but should include factors such as starting salaries, value of fringe benefits, cost of living, and other monetary factors.
3. Answers will vary but should include considerations such as price, convenience, features, ease of purchase, availability, and other decision-making factors.
5. Responses should comment on the growth Netflix has experienced. Although this may have been due to subscription price increases, the biggest driver of these increases is the number of subscriptions. While this is only a few data points, it does appear likely that Netflix will continue to grow sales in the next year or so. Factors influencing this prediction would be competition, changes in the streaming market, and economic considerations.
7. Answers will vary, but responses should state, in a sentence or two, the primary purpose of the entity. The goal of this exercise is to have students clearly communicate why the entity exists, the stakeholders served by the entity, and the role accounting plays in the organization.
9. Answers will vary but should highlight aspects of each model: *Brick-and-mortar*: higher investment in physical storefront, interior, etc., to attain visual appeal; insurance and regulatory requirements; space/storage considerations; lower delivery costs; no delivery time. *Online*: less overhead costs, higher delivery costs, higher website and technology costs, competition.
11. Manufacturer: movies; service: hotels, restaurants, waste removal, entertainment; retail: shopDisney, clothes and apparel.
13. Answers will vary but should include the key services of the SEC related to regulation and enforcement. You may be particularly interested to explore the SEC's whistle-blowing initiatives. Responses regarding required filings for publicly traded companies should include a discussion about the relationship between transparency and protecting the public interest. The significant amount of invested capital by the investing public is also relevant to the discussion.
15. Answers will vary but should include the increase in popularity of energy drinks and Monster's partnership with the Coca-Cola Company (which now owns close to a 17% stake in Monster). Considerations as to whether or not to purchase Monster shares today would include the estimated future performance of the company, the energy drink market, purchasing at a high point, etc.
17. Answers will vary but should include a discussion of the importance for accountants to provide information that is unbiased. Accountants have an obligation to protect the public interest by reporting information that is useful for decision-making but does not sway the user in a particular way. Accountants are in a unique position where they serve many stakeholders, including their employer, clients, and the public. The interests of all stakeholders must be considered while maintaining the highest level of integrity.
19. Answers will vary and may include certifications/licensing in nursing, information technology, engineering, human resources management, counseling, medicine, and many other occupations.

Chapter 2

Multiple Choice

1. D
3. A
5. B
7. A
9. B

11. D
13. B
15. C
17. C

Questions

1. Income statement shows the financial performance of a business for a period of time; statement of owner's equity shows the change in net worth of a business for a period of time; balance sheet shows the financial position of a business on a specific date; statement of cash flows shows the cash inflows and outflows of the business for a period of time.
3. Both revenues and gains represent inflows to the business, making it more valuable. Revenues relate to the primary purpose of the business, while gains represent incidental or peripheral activities. This is important to stakeholders because revenues represent ongoing or permanent activities, while gains represent infrequent or transient activities. Stakeholders should focus on permanent earnings and put peripheral or incidental earnings into the proper context.
5. Equity is the net worth of the business. It can also be thought of as the net assets (assets minus liabilities) of the business. Activities that affect equity include revenues, expenses, gains, losses, and investment by and distributions to owners.
7. Both tangible and intangible assets have value to the company and can be bought, sold, or impaired; tangible assets have physical substance, while intangible assets do not.
9. Assets = Liabilities + Owner's Equity. Answers will vary and should include a combination of revenues/gains (increases), expenses/losses (decreases), investments (increases), and distributions (decreases). It is important to understand the following transactions/exchanges will not change equity: an asset for an asset, liability for liability, asset acquisitions by incurring liabilities, and asset reductions to reduce liabilities.
11. Revenues and investments increase equity, while expenses and distributions decrease equity.

Chapter 3

Multiple Choice

1. A
3. B
5. A
7. D
9. A
11. C
13. D
15. B
17. A
19. B
21. B
23. D
25. B
27. A
29. C
31. D
33. C
35. A
37. C
39. C
41. B

Questions

1. Conservatism means that if there is uncertainty in a potential financial estimate, a company should err on the side of caution and report the most conservative amount. For the example, answers will vary. Sample answer: When I am budgeting for revenue in our household, I estimate what amount we will be paid, and I always round slightly down and with the expenses round up slightly so that there is a little leftover.
3. Assets = Liabilities + Equity; Revenues increase equity, while expenses decrease equity.
5. The general journal.
7. Decreasing cash decreases assets; decreasing accounts payable decreases liabilities. Assets (decrease) = Liabilities (decrease) + Equity (no change).
9. The combined total of liabilities and equity equals the total of assets because there is a claim against every asset that the company owns. Creditors have claims against some of the company's assets, in the amount of

the liabilities owed to them; owners (stockholders) have claims against all the rest of the company's assets. Equity is the total of assets minus liabilities, which is sometimes referred to as net assets.
11. The total in accounts receivable will increase with a debit. We know this because accounts receivable is an asset account, and asset balances increase with debit entries.
13. A journal is a chronological listing of all of the recordable transactions that have occurred in a company.
15. Recognize means to make a journal entry.
17. It is a comprehensive listing for all accounts a company has and their balances.
19. T-accounts represent the changes made to the general ledger. They are used as an illustrative tool when planning or discussing the effects a particular transaction will have on the accounting records. T-accounts are used in academic and business situations, as they are easier to sketch out than general journals.
21. A prepaid account is an account that shows the balance of money we have paid in advance of an expense being incurred. Prepaid accounts are assets.
23. A T-account is a visual depiction of the activity in an account. Entries made on the left side of the T-account represent debits, while entries on the right side represent credits. The ending account balance is the total net combined debits and credits for that account.
25. Asset accounts, dividend accounts, and expense accounts are increased with a debit. (Also, contra-liability accounts, contra-equity accounts, and contra-revenue accounts are increased with a debit.)
27. Normal balance refers to the expected ending balance for an account, based on the way that the account balance increases (either debit or credit.)
29. The purpose of the trial balance is to recap the account balances, to ensure that debits equal credits. The trial balance is used to prepare the financial statements, in this order: Income Statement, Retained Earnings Statement, and Balance Sheet.

Chapter 4

Multiple Choice

1. B
3. A
5. D
7. A
9. B
11. C
13. B
15. D
17. C
19. C
21. A and C

Questions

1. The revenue recognition principle mandates that revenue be reported when earned, regardless of when the revenue is collected. For this reason, when revenue is earned but not yet collected, an accrual entry is required to accurately report revenue earned. For the same reason, when cash is collected, in advance of the earnings process, a deferral entry is required, to accurately report revenue earned.
3. Analyzing transactions (to enable journal entries) is the only analytical part of the accounting cycle. Analysis is required for both the original transaction entries and the adjusting entries. All of the other steps are just methodical posting of the entries, summarizing of the balances, regrouping of the accounts for financial reports, and closing of the accounts for year-end. Only the journal entries require decision-making processes.
5. Accruals—when cash has not moved, but it is time to record the transaction (examples: Accounts Payable or Accounts Receivable). Deferrals—when cash has moved, but it is not time to record the transaction (examples: Prepaid Insurance or Unearned Revenue).
7. Adjusting entries always include at least one income statement account and at least one balance sheet account, because the adjustment process is done to shift revenues and expenses between the Balance Sheet and the Income Statement, depending on whether it is the correct period to include that income or expense (report on the Income Statement) or not (report on the Balance Sheet).
9. An entry to adjust the supplies account to the $400 balance is needed; Debit Supplies Expense for 800; Credit Supplies for 800.
11. An entry to adjust the Prepaid Insurance account to $6,000 balance is needed; Debit Insurance Expense for 6,000; Credit Prepaid Insurance for 6,000.
13. The adjusted trial balance is the summary of account balances after the adjustments have been posted, so it reflects the corrected balances of all accounts.
15. (A) Income Statement; (B) Balance Sheet; (C) Balance Sheet; (D) Income Statement; (E) Retained Earnings Statement; (F) Balance Sheet

Chapter 5

Multiple Choice

1. A
3. C
5. A
7. B
9. D
11. C
13. C
15. C

Questions

1. Real/permanent accounts are those that carry over from one period to the next, with a continuing balance in the account. Examples are asset accounts, liability accounts, and equity accounts. In contrast, revenue accounts, expense accounts, and dividend accounts are *not* real/permanent accounts.
3. Closing entries are used to transfer the contents of the temporary accounts into the permanent account, Retained Earnings, which resets the temporary balances to zero, enabling tracking of revenues, expenses, and dividends in the next period.
5. Expense accounts and dividend accounts are credited during closing. This is because closing requires that the account balances be cleared, to prepare for the next accounting period.
7. Income Summary is a super-temporary account that is only used for closing. The revenue accounts are closed by a debit to each account and a corresponding credit to Income Summary. Then the expense accounts are closed by a credit to each account and a corresponding debit to Income Summary. Finally, the balance in Income Summary is cleared by an entry that transfers its balance to Retained Earnings. Thus, it is used in three journal entries, as part of the closing process, and has no other purpose in the accounting records.
9. The fact that Income Summary has a credit balance (of any size) after the first two closing entries are made indicates that the company made a net profit for the period. In this case, a credit of $125,500 reflects the fact that the company earned net income of $125,500 for the period.
11. The post-closing trial balance will include only the permanent/real accounts, which are assets, liabilities, and equity. All of the other accounts (temporary/nominal accounts: revenue, expense, dividend) would have been cleared to zero by the closing entries.
13. Working capital is calculated by subtracting current liabilities from current assets. The result indicates how well the company can pay bills as they come due, which is sometimes referred to as the company's liquidity position.
15. (1) First is the Unadjusted Trial Balance, which summarizes the account balances of all accounts in the ledger, *before period-end adjustments*. (2) Next, the Adjusted Trial Balance summarizes the account balances of all accounts in the ledger, *after adjusting entries* have been posted. (3) Finally, the Post-Closing Trial Balance summarizes the account balances of all accounts in the ledger, *after closing entries* have been posted.

Chapter 6

Multiple Choice

1. C
3. A
5. D
7. D
9. C
11. A
13. C
15. A
17. C
19. D
21. B
23. D
25. B
27. B

Questions

1. It helps solidify a long-term relationship with the customer, encourages the customer to purchase more, and decreases the time it takes for the company to see a liquid asset (cash). Cash can be used for other

purposes immediately, such as reinvesting the business, paying down loans quicker, and distributing dividends to shareholders.
3. A sales return occurs when a customer returns merchandise for a full refund. A sales allowance occurs when a customer keeps the merchandise and is issued a partial refund.
5. Advantages could include real-time data and more robust information. Disadvantages could include fewer inventory counts with opportunity for mismanagement of inventory. It is also costly, and time consuming.
7.

Oct 18	Accounts Receivable	130	
	Sales		130
	To recognize sale under periodic inventory system		
Note: No cost of sale entry is required currently, only at the end of the period under periodic.			

9. Cash would be remitted to a retainer if the retailer returns merchandise to a manufacturer after payment, or if the retailer receives an allowance for damaged merchandise after payment.
11. $110; $1,100 × 50% = $550, $550 × 20% = $110
13. $6.15; $205 × 3%
15. With FOB Destination, the seller is responsible for goods in transit, the seller pays for shipping, and the point of transfer is when the goods reach the buyer's place of business. With FOB Shipping Point, the buyer is responsible for goods in transit, the buyer pays for shipping, and the point of transfer is when the goods leave the seller's place of business.
17.

Accounts Receivable	800	
Sales		800
To recognize sale on credit, 2/10, n/30, FOB Destination		
COGS	300	
Merchandise Inventory		300
To recognize cost of sale		
Delivery Expense	100	
Cash		100
To recognize shipping charge, FOB Destination		

19. 32% or $.32; ($176,750 – 120,470) / $176,750
21. The gross profit margin ratio shows the company's margin over costs of sales to cover operating expenses and profit. If margin continue to increase over time, an investor or lender might consider the financial contribution less risky. If the ratio decreases, the stakeholder may perceive an increased risk that the company may not have enough revenue to service debt.
23. $14.70; $490 × 3%
25. Recognizing the return of merchandise to inventory occurs under the perpetual inventory system but not under the periodic inventory system.

Chapter 7

Multiple Choice

1. D
3. C
5. D
7. E
9. C
11. D

13. C
15. C
17. A
19. C
21. A
23. B
25. B
27. B
29. B
31. B

Questions

1. A computerized accounting information system performs the same steps in the accounting cycle as a manual accounting system. Therefore, understanding how a manual system works helps us understand what a computerized system does. We cannot take a computer apart and show how the accounting information fits together, but we can show the different pieces in a paper-based system. We want an accounting information system to be more than just a black box.
3. Scanners can input data faster and typically would produce fewer input errors.
5. All of these areas need an accounting information system. Keeping up with all of the data for an entire year without it would be difficult. Some companies have their own accounting information to process all of their transactions except for payroll. They sometimes use a payroll processing company that specializes in processing payroll transactions for many companies. However, that payroll company also uses computers.
7. Any special journal can require an entry to the subsidiary ledger if the entry involves accounts receivable or accounts payable.
9. The cash column is not posted to the subsidiary ledger. Only the accounts receivable and accounts payable columns are posted to the subsidiary ledgers.
11. Any amounts posted to Accounts Receivable or Accounts Payable should be posted daily (to the subsidiary ledger), and the account totals should be posted monthly. We also post the accounts in the Other Accounts column individually and may post daily or at the end of the month. We post all other total column amounts monthly.
13. The four main special journals are sales journal, purchases journal, cash receipts journal, and cash disbursements journal.
15. We would record the purchase of equipment for cash in the cash disbursements journal.
17. We post entries from the sales journal daily to the accounts receivable subsidiary ledger but monthly to Sales and to the Accounts Receivable general ledger account.
19. We record purchases of inventory for cash in the cash disbursements journal.
21. Forensic accountants analyze a company's transactions to determine if a crime has been committed. If they find evidence, they can testify in court as to their findings.

Chapter 8

Multiple Choice

1. C
3. A
5. D
7. C
9. A
11. A
13. C
15. C
17. B
19. C

Questions

1. Examples include weak internal controls, improper or nonexistent management oversight, and lack of an internal audit function or other opportunities that create the perception that the fraudster will be successful in committing a fraudulent act.
3. Examples include vices such as gambling, living beyond one's means, high debts, employer pressures to report fictitious accounting results, or alcohol/drug use.
5. Protect data from corruption or damage. Have their servers mirrored at various locations around the world. Ensure that no unauthorized parties have access to the data. Ensure that all transactions are entered into the accounting system properly and accurately. If fraud or illegal access to data occurs, a good internal control will

help identify the responsible party or parties.
8. To ensure that large companies are consistent with internal controls, properly documented, and tested.
10. One person should be responsible for the fund. If one person is in charge and the fund is short, then the petty cashier is the only one responsible for the shortage.
11. Records all sales and inventory reduction and ensures that correct prices are charged.
13. All differences must be researched, explained, and corrected. Differences pertaining to the bank must be reported. If fraud is suspected, a complete investigation must be performed.

Chapter 9

Multiple Choice

1. C
3. B
5. C
7. B
9. C
11. A
13. A
15. D
17. B
19. B
21. A
23. B

Questions

1. The matching principle states that expenses must be matched to revenues in the period in which they were incurred.
3. Nothing will be recognized as revenue, since the flower shop will not provide flowers until June. Until then, all revenue is considered unearned.
5. Allowance for Doubtful Accounts
7. $22,008.88; $323,660 × 6.8%
9. $11,393.10; ($22,480 × 6%) + ($36,540 × 17%) + ($15,330 × 25%)
11. The receivables cycle takes a while to convert into cash, which means that cash is tied up and cannot be used for other business investments. This could also mean that the company has to borrow money from a lender to meet its cash flow demands, or that credit extensions are too tight, and good credit candidates are lost to competitors.
13. Accounts receivable turnover ratio and number of days' sales in receivables ratio; these ratios can tell a stakeholder how credit extension policies affect sales, and how quickly current debt is collected
15. A decrease to bad debt expense increases net income, which can show a higher income level and improve opportunities for borrowing.
17. A higher bad debt expense figure reduces net income, which could have a positive impact on reducing business income and other taxes.
19. The installment method takes into account risk associated with long-term periodic payments, and it distributes revenue based on a gross profit percentage over the life of the contract.
21. The completed contract method is used in contracts and delays reporting of both revenues and expenses until the entire contract is complete
23.

Accounts Receivable		215,465	
	Notes Receivable		215,000
	Interest Revenue		465

25. The principal of a note is the initial borrowed amount, not including interest, requested by the customer.
27. Accounts receivable is an informal, short-term payment and usually no interest, whereas notes receivable is a legal contract, long-term payment, and usually has interest.

Chapter 10

Multiple Choice

1. D

3. A
5. A
7. A
9. B
11. A
13. C

Questions

1. Gross margin refers to the net profit from sale of goods. It is calculated by subtracting cost of goods sold from sales revenue.
3. Consigned goods are owned by the consignor, but the goods are physically present in the business of the consignee. Care must be taken not to count goods held on consignment in the company's physical inventory tally.
5. Specific identification works best for highly differentiated goods, large ticket items, customization, and small lot sizes. In all these cases, it is reasonably easy to keep track of the actual cost of each item, to be used to offset the sales price, when the goods are sold.
7. LCM sets out to record a conservative value for inventory by ensuring that goods that have decreased in value since their purchase can be revalued to match their current replacement market value.
9. The FIFO method assumes the first units acquired are sold first. On a periodic basis, that means that ending inventory can be determined by calculating the number of units remaining, and assuming that the cost of those units is the amount paid for the latest purchase; cost of goods sold is all inventory cost that is not in the ending inventory. For perpetual, inventory held at the time of each sale is evaluated and units acquired earliest are costed out against that particular sale.
11. The weighted-average method requires that the average cost be computed for all units that are available for sale. For periodic weighted average, the total dollar amount of goods available for sale should be divided by the total number of units available for sale, to obtain the average cost for the entire period. For perpetual, the average cost would be recalculated each time the total number of units changes, using the same strategy as described for periodic, but using the cost and number of units that are available at the time of sale.
13. Causes of inventory errors might be related to consigned goods, goods delivered before or after the title transfers, sloppy inventory counts, lost records, calculation errors, and any other circumstance that causes inaccuracy in the counts.
15. The inventory turnover ratio reveals the liquidity of the inventory by highlighting how many times during the year the entire inventory cycle could be rotated, based on the cost of the inventory sold, compared to the average cost of the unsold inventory. Days' sales in inventory reveals how many days it typically takes to turn inventory around, from date of purchase to date of sale.

Chapter 11

Multiple Choice

1. C
3. C
5. A
7. B
9. D
11. D
13. D
15. A

Questions

1. The main difference between tangible and intangible assets is that tangible assets have a physical substance to them. This means they can be touched and have some physical form.
3. A patent is a contract that provides a company with exclusive rights to produce and sell a unique product. It is granted by the federal government and provides exclusivity from competition for twenty years. A copyright provides the exclusive right to reproduce and sell artistic, literary, or musical compositions for a period of seventy years beyond the death of the original author.
5. A. capitalized. B. expense. C. capitalized. D. capitalized. E. expense. F. expense. G. capitalized.
7. In measuring and reporting long-term assets, the expense recognition ("matching") principle is applied. Under the expense recognition or "matching" principle, the acquisition cost of the asset must be allocated to the periods in which it is used to earn revenue. In this way, the cost of the asset is matched, as an expense, with the revenues that are earned from period to period through the use of the asset.
9. Depreciation is the process of allocating the cost of using a long-term asset over its anticipated economic (useful) life, whereas depletion is the process of expensing the cost of natural resources over the life of the

asset, typically using a unit-consumed method. Amortization is specifically for intangible assets and typically is calculated using straight-line with no salvage value.
11. Goodwill is internally generated, but it is not recorded as an asset unless (and only when) one company acquires another company at a price greater than the total value of the net assets being purchased. The purchaser will record goodwill for the difference between the fair value of net assets acquired and the purchase price. Goodwill is not amortized and will be tested annually for impairment.
13. Obsolescence refers to the reduction in value and/or use of an asset. It may refer to the actual physical deterioration of the asset, which is known as physical obsolescence, or to the loss of value from causes other than physical deterioration, which is functional obsolescence. Functional obsolescence is specific to the organization and the usefulness the asset has for the company going forward. This type of obsolescence could be the result of simply not needing the asset any longer.

Chapter 12

Multiple Choice

1. C
3. D
5. B
7. C
9. B
11. A
13. D
15. A
17. F
19. A

Questions

1. Accounts Payable can be set up as a line of credit between a purchaser and a supplier. The terms of the invoice usually state that payment is due within a year, or a shorter time frame. Since accounts payable amounts are due within a company's operating cycle, this account type would be considered a current liability.
3. A noncurrent liability is due in more than one year or outside a standard company operating period. A current liability is payable within a company's operating period, or less than a year.
5. $12,500
7. Accounts Payable and Equipment
9. The likelihood of occurrence and the measurement requirement are the FASB required conditions. A contingent liability must be recognized and disclosed if there is a probable liability determination before the preparation of financial statements has occurred, and the company can reasonably estimate the amount of loss.
11. They are probable and estimable, probable and inestimable, reasonably possible, and remote.
13. A short-term notes payable does not have any long-term characteristics and is meant to be paid in full within the company's operating period (less than a year). The current portion of a noncurrent note payable is based off of a long-term debt but is only recognized as a current liability when a portion of the long-term note payable is due. The remainder stays a long-term liability.
15. A business borrows money from a bank, and the bank makes the note payable within a year, with interest. For example, this could come from a capital expenditure need or when expenses exceed revenues.
17. Examples include FICA Social Security, FICA Medicare, Federal Unemployment Compensation Tax (FUTA), State Unemployment Compensation Tax (SUTA), federal income tax, state income tax, Additional Medicare Tax, and local income tax.
19. FUTA and SUTA are the acronyms for the Federal Unemployment Tax Act and the State Unemployment Tax Act. They are unemployment insurance systems that collect funds from employers to cover employees in case of job disruption beyond their control. The FUTA tax rate is 6% but can be reduced by paying on time to the state unemployment system. This rate can be reduced down to as low as 0.6%.

Chapter 13

Multiple Choice

1. A
3. D
5. B
7. A
9. A

11. A
13. B
15. C
17. B
19. B

Questions

1. Callable bonds can be bought back by the issuing company whenever they want to, but putable bonds can be cashed in by the holder whenever the holder wants to.
3. A junk bond is typically titled as a high-yield bond; it sounds less unfavorable than junk. Its rating is below what is typically expected for investment-grade bonds. Investors and speculators might buy these bonds because if they don't default, the rate of return could be significantly higher than investment grade bonds. However, the possibility of the bonds defaulting and neither paying the interest nor principle at maturity is higher than with investment-grade bonds.
5. In bond pricing problems, if the interest compounds more than one a year, divide the interest rate by the number of compounding periods per year, and multiply the number of years by the number of compounding periods per year. If it is paid quarterly, divide the interest rate by 4 and multiply the number of years by 4.
7. It is the difference between the cash interest payment and the interest on the carrying value.
9. The Discount on Bonds Payable is a contra liability account and reduces the associated liability. The Premium on Bonds Payable is a liability account and increases the associated liability.
11. DR Interest Expense and CR Cash
13. Bondholders receive the stated rate times the principle, so they would receive $6,000.
15. Amortizing a bond premium reduces interest expense.

Chapter 14

Multiple Choice

1. D
3. A
5. D
7. D
9. B
11. A
13. C
15. C
17. D
19. D
21. B
23. C

Questions

1. Advantages of raising capital through stock include no repayment, no interest, and no mandatory dividends. Disadvantages include giving up ownership and marketability of stock. Debt requires repayment and an interest component. Interest is tax deductible whereas dividends are not.
3. The incorporation laws and which states have favorable laws for corporations.
5. To affect the market price, avoid takeover, and limit need for dividend payouts.
7.

Land	12,000	
Common Stock		6,000
Additional Paid-in Capital from Common Stock	-	6,000

9.

Equipment	10,000	
Common Stock		5,000
Additional Paid-in Capital from Common Stock		5,000

11.

Dividends Payable	25,000	
Cash		25,000

13. In total, there is no change to the total dollar value of the equity section, just a change in the number of shares outstanding and a change in the par or stated value of the stock.
15. Owners' equity is the value of assets in a company that remains after liabilities are fulfilled. It is also referred to as net worth or net assets.
17. An example would be the omission of a payroll accrual or a warranty estimate.
19. Comparative balance sheets and income statements.
21. Yes, as one analytical tool among others.
23. EPS is the only ratio required by GAAP to be reported on the face of the income statement. It must be reported in two ways: basic and diluted (if applicable).

Chapter 15

Multiple Choice

1. D
3. A
5. B
7. C
9. D
11. A
13. A
15. C
17. B

Questions

1. No; it is a passthrough entity, meaning the taxation flows to the owners. The partners pay taxes on their distributive share of the partnership's income.
3. Yes, the partnership can assume liabilities as part of one partner's contributions. However, that should be agreed upon during the creation of the partnership agreement, where each partner lists assets and value. In addition, the assumption of liabilities by the partnership reduces the amount of assets the partner is contributing and thus the relevant capital account.
5. A strong response would include fixed ratios; a ratio based on beginning-of-year capital balances, end-of-year capital balances, or an average capital balance during the year; salaries to partners and the remainder on a fixed ratio; interest on the partners' capital balances and the remainder on a fixed ratio; and some combination of all or some of the above methods (salaries to partners, interest on capital balances, and the remainder on a fixed ratio).
7.

JOURNAL

Date 2016	Account	Debit	Credit
Feb. 3	Cash	90,000	
	S. Singh, Capital		90,000

Table 15.3.

9. 1. sell noncash assets, 2. allocate any gain or loss, 3. fulfill liabilities, and 4. distribute remaining cash
11. Sell non-cash assets
13. The general partners would be expected to make the vendors whole.

Chapter 16

Multiple Choice

1. C
3. B
5. B
7. B
9. A
11. A
13. D
15. C

Questions

1. The statement of cash flow serves as a bridge between the cash basis bank transactions and the accrual basis financial statements (balance sheet, income statement, and retained earnings statement). It reveals where the cash came from, and where it went.
3. Operating, Investing, Financing (always in this order).
5. Any transaction that is related to acquiring or disposing of long-term assets like land, buildings, equipment, stocks, bonds, or other investments. Can be cash spent for purchase of long-term assets, or cash collected from sale of long-term assets.
7. The indirect method begins with net income and adjusts for items that affect cash differently than they affect net income, whereas the direct method requires that each revenue and expense item be converted to reflect the cash impact from that item. The net cash flow result is the same, no matter which of the two methods is used.
9. Gains and losses must be removed from the operating section. To accomplish this, reverse the effect of gains or losses; if a gain has been added to net income, it should be subtracted in the operating section; if a loss has been deducted to arrive at net income, it should be added back in the operating section. Why? First, gains and losses relate to long-term assets, which fall under investing activities, not operating activities. Second, the gain/(loss) on the sale of long-term assets represents the excess/(deficiency) computed when the asset's cost basis is subtracted from sales proceeds, so the number does not accurately represent the cash flow relating to the transaction.
11. Not necessarily. Only the principal balance repayment should be included in the financing section; the interest component of the note payment is an operating activity.
13. Yes. Some investing and/or financing transactions do not have a cash impact initially. Examples include purchases of long-term assets that are paid for with long-term debt financing, acquisitions of long-term assets in exchange for corporate stock, and repayment of long-term debt using noncash assets. These noncash investing/financing activities would be reported in the notes to the financial statements, or as a notation on the bottom of the statement of cash flows, but not considered an integral part of the statement.
15. Using the direct method to prepare the operating section requires that revenue and expense items be converted to the cash basis of accounting, since these items are recorded in company records using the accrual basis of accounting. The balance sheet, income statement, and retained earnings statement use the accrual basis balances that are maintained in the company accounting records, and thus can be obtained directly from the adjusted trial balance, without modifications.

Index